DR. NORMAN A. WIGGINS

THE FEDERAL AND STATE
CONSTITUTIONS

COLONIAL CHARTERS, AND OTHER ORGANIC LAWS

OF THE

STATES, TERRITORIES, AND COLONIES

NOW OR HERETOFORE FORMING

THE UNITED STATES OF AMERICA

Compiled and Edited
under the Act of Congress of June 30, 1906

By

FRANCIS NEWTON THORPE, Ph. D., LL. D.

Member of the Pennsylvania Bar; Fellow and Professor of American Constitutional History at the University of Pennsylvania, 1885-1898; Member of the American Historical Association; Author of The Constitutional History of the United States, 1765-1895; A (State) Constitutional History of the American People, 1776-1850; A Short Constitutional History of the United States; A (Social and Economic) History of the American People; A History of the Civil War; Editor of the History of North America, Volumes IX, XV, XVI, XVIII, XIX, XX; Author of The Government of the People of the United States; Benjamin Franklin and the University of Pennsylvania; The Life of William Pepper, etc.

VOL. III
Kentucky—Massachusetts

WASHINGTON
GOVERNMENT PRINTING OFFICE
1909

CARRIE RICH MEMORIAL LIBRARY
CAMPBELL COLLEGE
BUIES CREEK, N. C.

KENTUCKY[a]

For organic acts issued before 1790 relating to the land now included within Kentucky see in this work:
    Charters of Virginia, 1606, 1609, 1612 (Virginia, pp. 3783-3812).
    Ordinances for Virginia, 1621 (Virginia, p. 3810).
    Constitution of Virginia, 1776 (Virginia, p. 3812).

THE TERRITORY SOUTH OF THE OHIO—1790

[First Congress, Second Session]

An Act for the Government of the Territory of the United States, south of the river Ohio

Section 1. *Be it enacted by the Senate and House of Representatives of the United States of America in Congress assembled,* That the territory of the United States south of the river Ohio, for the purposes of temporary government, shall be one district; the inhabitants of which shall enjoy all the privileges, benefits, and advantages set forth in the ordinance of the late Congress for the government of the territory of the United States northwest of the river Ohio. And the government of the said territory south of the Ohio shall be similar to that which is now exercised in the territory northwest of the Ohio; except so far as is otherwise provided in the conditions expressed in an act of Congress of the present session, entitled "An act to accept a cession of the claims of the State of North Carolina to a certain district of western territory." ‡

Sec. 2. *And be it further enacted,* That the salaries of the officers, which the President of the United States shall nominate, and with the advice and consent of the Senate appoint, by virtue of this act, shall be the same as those, by law established, of similar officers in the government northwest of the river Ohio. And the powers, duties, and emoluments of a superintendent of Indian affairs for the southern department shall be united with those of the governor.

Approved, May 26, 1790.

---

[a] Kentucky was originally settled by the whites as a colony of Virginia, but after the revolutionary war the settlers demanded an independent government, under the following provision in the first constitution of Virginia: "The western and northern extent of Virginia shall, in all other respects, stand, as fixed by the charter of King James I, in the year 1609, and by the public treaty of peace between the courts of Great Britain and France, in the year 1763, unless by act of this legislature one or more governments be established westward of the Alleghany Mountains." It was not, however, until after there had been ten successive conventions elected by the people of the "district," and four successive enabling acts passed by the legislature of Virginia, that Kentucky was allowed to enter the Federal Union as an independent State, on an equality with those which had established themselves as a nation.

ACT ADMITTING KENTUCKY INTO THE UNION—1791

[First Congress, Third Session]

An Act declaring the consent of Congress, that a new State be formed within the jurisdiction of the Commonwealth of Virginia, and admitted into this Union, by the name of the State of Kentucky

Whereas the legislature of the commonwealth of Virginia, by an act entitled "An act concerning the erection of the district of Kentucky into an independent state," passed the eighteenth day of December, one thousand seven hundred and eighty-nine, have consented that the district of Kentucky, within the jurisdiction of the said commonwealth, and according to its actual boundaries at the time of passing the act aforesaid, should be formed into a new state: And whereas a convention of delegates, chosen by the people of the said district of Kentucky, have petitioned Congress to consent that, on the first day of June, one thousand seven hundred and ninety-two, the said district should be formed into a new state, and received into the Union, by the name of "The State of Kentucky:"

SECTION 1. *Be it enacted by the Senate and House of Representatives of the United States of America in Congress assembled, and it is hereby enacted and declared*, That the Congress doth consent that the said district of Kentucky, within the jurisdiction of the commonwealth of Virginia, and according to its actual boundaries on the eighteenth day of December, one thousand seven hundred and eighty-nine, shall, upon the first day of June, one thousand seven hundred and ninety-two, be formed into a new State, separate from, and independent of, the said commonwealth of Virginia.

SEC. 2. *And be it further enacted and declared*, That upon the aforesaid first day of June, one thousand seven hundred and ninety-two, the said new State, by the name and style of the State of Kentucky, shall be received and admitted into this Union as a new and entire member of the United States of America.

Approved, February 4, 1791.

CONSTITUTION OF KENTUCKY—1792 [*][a]

We, the representatives of the people of the State of Kentucky, in convention assembled, do ordain and establish this constitution for its government.

Article I

1. The powers of government shall be divided into three distinct departments, each of them to be confided to a separate body of magistracy, to wit, those which are legislative to one, those which are executive to another, and those which are judiciary to another.

---

[*] Verified from "The General Statutes of Kentucky. Bullitt and Feloud, Louisville. The Barnaby and Gilbert Co., 1887." pp. 56–72.

[a] This constitution was adopted by a convention which met at Danville April 2, 1792, and completed its labors on the 19th of April, 1792. The constitution was not submitted to the people for ratification.

2. No person, or collection of persons, being of one of these departments, shall exercise any power properly belonging to either of the others, except in the instances hereinafter expressly permitted.

3. The legislative powers of this commonwealth shall be vested in a general assembly, which shall consist of a senate and house of representatives.

4. The representatives shall be chosen annually, by the qualified electors of each county respectively, on the first Tuesday in May; but the several elections may be continued for three days, if, in the opinion of the presiding officer or officers, it shall be necessary, and no longer.

5. No person shall be a representative who shall not have attained the age of twenty-four years, and have been a citizen and inhabitant of the State two years preceding his election, and the last six months thereof an inhabitant of the county in which he may be chosen; unless he shall have been absent on the public business of the United States, or this State.

6. Within two years after the first meeting of the general assembly, and within every subsequent term of four years, an enumeration of the free male inhabitants above twenty-one years of age shall be made, in such manner as may be directed by law. The number of the representatives shall, at the several periods of making such enumeration, be fixed by the legislature, and apportioned among the several counties, according to the number of free male inhabitants above the age of twenty-one years in each, and shall never be less than forty, nor greater than one hundred; but no county hereafter erected shall be entitled to a separate representation, until a sufficient number of free male inhabitants above the age of twenty-one years shall be contained within it, to entitle them to one representative, agreeable to the ratio which shall then be established.

7. The senators shall be chosen for four years.

8. Until the first enumeration be made, the senate shall consist of eleven members, and thereafter for every four members added to the house of representatives, one member shall be added to the senate.

9. In choosing the senate, one member at least shall be elected from each county, until the number of counties is equal to the number of senators; after which, when a new county is made, it shall, as to the choice of senators, be considered as being a part of the county or counties from which it shall have been taken.

10. The senate shall be chosen in the following manner: All persons qualified to vote for representatives shall, on the first Tuesday in May, in the present year, and on the same day in every fourth year, forever thereafter, at the place appointed by law for choosing representatives, elect by ballot, by a majority of votes, as many persons as they are entitled to have for representatives for their respective counties, to be electors of the senate.

11. No person shall be chosen an elector who shall not have resided in the State three years next before his election, and who shall not have attained the age of twenty-seven years.

12. The electors of the senate shall meet at such place as shall be appointed for convening the legislature, on the third Tuesday in May, in the present year, and on the same day in every fourth year forever thereafter; and they, or a majority of them so met, shall proceed to elect by ballot, as senators, men of the most wisdom,

experience, and virtue, above twenty-seven years of age, who shall have been residents of the State above two whole years next preceding the election. If on the ballot two or more shall have an equal number of ballots in their favor, by which the choice shall not be determined by the first ballot, then the electors shall again ballot before they separate, in which they shall be confined to the persons who, on the first ballot, shall have had an equal number, and they who shall have the greatest number in their favor on the second ballot shall be accordingly declared and returned duly elected; and if on the second ballot an equal number shall still be in favor of two or more persons, then the election shall be determined by lot between those who have equal numbers; which proceedings of the electors shall be certified under their hands, and returned to the secretary for the time being; to whom shall also be made, by the proper officers, returns of the persons chosen as electors in the respective counties.

13. The electors of senators shall judge of the qualifications and elections of members of their body, and on a contested election shall admit to a seat as an elector such qualified person as shall appear to them to have the greatest number of legal votes in his favor.

14. The electors, immediately on their meeting, and before they proceed to the election of senators, shall take an oath, or affirmation, to elect, without favor, affection, partiality, or prejudice, such person for governor, and such persons for senators, as they in their judgment and conscience believe best qualified for the respective offices.

15. That in case of refusal, death, resignation, disqualification, or removal out of this State, of any senator, the senate shall immediately thereupon, or at their next meeting thereafter, elect, by ballot, in the same manner as the electors are herein directed to choose senators, another person in his place, for the residue of the said term of four years.

16. The general assembly shall meet on the first Monday in November in every year, till the time of their meeting shall be altered by the legislature, unless sooner convened by the governor.

17. Each house shall choose its speaker and other officers, and the senate shall also choose a speaker, *pro tempore*, when their speaker shall exercise the office of governor.

18. Each house shall judge of the qualifications of its members; contested elections shall be determined by a committee to be selected, formed, and regulated, in such manner as shall be directed by law. A majority of each house shall constitute a quorum to do business, but a smaller number may adjourn from day to day, and may be authorized by law to compel the attendance of absent members, in such manner and under such penalties as may be provided.

19. Each house may determine the rules of its proceedings, punish its members for disorderly behavior, and, with the concurrence of two-thirds, expel a member; but not a second time for the same cause.

20. Each house shall keep a journal of its proceedings, and publish them weekly, except such parts of them as may require secrecy, and the yeas and nays of the members on any question shall, at the desire of any two of them, be entered on the journals.

21. The doors of each house and of committees of the whole shall be open, unless when the business shall be such as ought to be kept secret.

22. Neither house shall, without the consent of the other, adjourn for more than three days; nor to any other place than that in which the two houses shall be sitting.

23. The members of the general assembly and the electors of the senate shall receive from the public treasury a compensation for their services, which for the present shall be six shillings a day during their attendance on, going to, and returning from the legislature, and the place for choosing the senators; but the same may be increased or diminished by law, if circumstances shall require it, but no alteration shall be made to take effect during the existence of the legislature which shall make such alteration. They shall in all cases, except treason, felony, breach, or surety of the peace, be privileged from arrest during their attendance at the session of the respective houses, and at the place for choosing senators, and in going to and returning from the same; and for any speech or debate in either house, they shall not be questioned in any other place.

24. No senator or representative shall, during the time for which he shall have been elected, or for one year afterwards, be appointed to any civil office under this State, which shall have been created, or the emoluments of which shall have been increased, during the time such senator or representative was in office: *Provided*, That no member of the first legislature which shall be assembled under this constitution shall be precluded from being appointed to any office which may have been created during his time of service in the said legislature; and no minister of religious society, member of Congress, or other person holding any office of profit under the United States, or this commonwealth, except attorneys at law, justices of the peace, militia officers, and coroners, shall be a member of either house, during his continuance to act as a minister, in Congress, or in office.

25. When vacancies happen in the house of representatives, the speaker shall issue writs of election to fill such vacancies.

26. All bills for raising revenue shall originate in the house of representatives, but the senate may propose amendments as in other bills.

27. Each senator, representative, and sheriff shall, before he be permitted to act as such, take an oath, or make affirmation, that he hath not directly or indirectly given or promised any bribe or treat to procure his election to said office, and every person shall be disqualified from serving as a senator, representative, or sheriff, for the term for which he shall have been elected, who shall be convicted of having given or offered any bribe or treat, or canvassed for the said office.

28. Every bill which shall have passed both houses shall be presented to the governor; if he approve, he shall sign it, but if he shall not approve, he shall return it, with his objections, to the house in which it shall have originated, who shall enter the objections at large upon their journals, and proceed to reconsider it; if after such reconsideration two-thirds of that house shall agree to pass the bill, it shall be sent with the objections to the other house, by which likewise it shall be reconsidered, and, if approved by two-thirds of that house, it shall be a law. But in such cases the votes of both houses shall be determined by yeas and nays, and the names of the persons voting for or against the bill shall be entered on the journals of each house

respectively; if any bill shall not be returned by the governor within ten days, Sundays excepted, after it shall have been presented to him, it shall be a law in like manner as if he had signed it; unless the general assembly by their adjournment prevent its return, in which case it shall be a law, unless sent back within three days after their next meeting.

29. Every order, resolution, or vote, to which the concurrence of both houses may be necessary, except on a question of adjournment, shall be presented to the governor, and before it shall take effect be approved by him; or, being disapproved, shall be repassed by two-thirds of both houses, according to the rules and limitations prescribed in case of a bill.

Article II

1. The supreme executive power of this commonwealth shall be vested in a governor.

2. The governor shall be chosen by the electors of the senate, at the same time, at the same place, and in the same manner that they are herein directed to elect senators, and the said electors shall make return of their proceedings in the choice of a governor to the secretary for the time being.

3. The governor shall hold his office during four years from the first of June next ensuing his election.

4. He shall be at least thirty years of age, and have been a citizen and inhabitant of this State at least two years next before his election, unless he shall have been absent on public business of the United States, or of this State.

5. No member of Congress, or person holding any office under the United States, or this State, shall exercise the office of governor.

6. The governor shall, at stated times, receive for his services a compensation, which shall neither be increased nor diminished during the period for which he shall have been elected.

7. He shall be commander-in-chief of the army and navy of this commonwealth, and of the militia, except when they shall be called into the service of the United States.

8. He shall nominate and, by and with the advice and consent of the senate, appoint all officers whose offices are established by this constitution, or shall be established by law, and whose appointments are not herein otherwise provided for; but no person shall be appointed to an office within any county who shall not have been a citizen or inhabitant therein one year next before his appointment, if the county shall have been so long erected; but if it shall not have been so long erected, then within the limits of the county or counties out of which it shall have been taken.

9. The governor shall have power to fill up all vacancies that may happen during the recess of the senate, by granting commissions, which shall expire at the end of their next session.

10. He shall have power to remit fines and forfeitures, and grant reprieves and pardons, except in cases of impeachment; in cases of treason, he shall have power to grant reprieves until the end of the next session of the general assembly, in whom the power of pardoning shall be vested.

11. He may require information in writing from the officers in the executive department upon any subject relating to the duties of their respective offices.

12. He shall, from time to time, give to the general assembly information of the state of the commonwealth, and recommend to their consideration such measures as he shall judge expedient.

13. He may, on extraordinary occasions, convene the general assembly, and in case of disagreement between the two houses, with respect to the time of adjournment, adjourn them to such time as he shall think proper, not exceeding four months.

14. He shall take care that the laws be faithfully executed.

15. In case of the death or resignation of the governor, or of his removal from office, the speaker of the senate shall exercise the office of governor, until another shall be duly qualified.

16. An attorney-general shall be appointed and commissioned during good behavior; who shall appear for the commonwealth in all criminal prosecutions, and in all civil cases in which the commonwealth shall be interested in any of the superior courts; shall give his opinion when called upon for that purpose by either branch of the legislature, or by the executive, and shall perform such other duties as shall be enjoined him by law.

17. A secretary shall be appointed and commissioned during the governor's continuance in office, if he shall so long behave himself well; he shall keep a fair register of and attest all the official acts and proceedings of the governor, and shall, when required, lay the same, and all papers, minutes, and vouchers relative thereto, before either branch of the legislature, and shall perform such other duties as shall be enjoined him by law.

Article III

1. In elections by the citizens, all free male citizens of the age of twenty-one years, having resided in the State two years, or the county in which they offer to vote one year next before the election, shall enjoy the rights of an elector, but no person shall be entitled to vote except in the county in which he shall actually reside at the time of the election.

2. All elections shall be by ballot.

3. Electors shall in all cases, except treason, felony, and breach or surety of the peace, be privileged from arrest during their attendance at elections, and in going to and returning from them.

Article IV

1. The house of representatives shall have the sole power of impeaching.

2. All impeachments shall be tried by the senate; when sitting for that purpose, the senators shall be upon oath or affirmation; no person shall be convicted without the concurrence of two-thirds of the members present.

3. The governor and all other civil officers shall be liable to impeachment for any misdemeanor in office; but judgment in such cases

shall not extend further than to removal from office and disqualification to hold any office of honor, trust, or profit under this commonwealth; but the party convicted shall, nevertheless, be liable and subject to indictment, trial, judgment, and punishment according to law.

Article V

1. The judicial power of this commonwealth, both as to matters of law and equity, shall be vested in one supreme court, which shall be styled the court of appeals, and in such inferior courts as the legislature may from time to time ordain and establish.

2. The judges of both the supreme and inferior courts shall hold their offices during good behavior; but for any reasonable cause which shall not be sufficient ground of impeachment, the governor may remove any of them on the address of two-thirds of each branch of the legislature. They shall, at stated times, receive for their services an adequate compensation, to be fixed by law, which shall not be diminished during their continuance in office.

3. The supreme court shall have original and final jurisdiction in all cases respecting the titles to land under the present land-laws of Virginia, including those which may be depending in the present supreme court for the district of Kentucky at the time of establishing the said supreme court; and in all cases concerning contracts for lands, prior to the establishment of those titles. And the said court shall have power to hear and determine the same in a summary way, and to direct the mode of bringing the same to a hearing, so as to enable them to do right and justice to the parties, with as little delay and at as small an expense as the nature of the business will allow; but the said court shall, in all such cases, oblige the parties to state the material parts of their complaint and defence in writing; and shall, on the conclusion of every cause, state on the records of the whole merits of the case, the questions arising therefrom, the opinions of the court thereupon, and a summary of the reasons in support of those opinions.

4. And it shall be the duty of each judge of the supreme court, present at the hearing of any such case, and differing from a majority of the court, to deliver his opinion in writing, to be entered as aforesaid; and each judge shall deliver his opinion in open court. And the said court shall have power, on the determination of any such cause, to award the legal costs against either party, or to divide the same among the different parties, as to them shall seem just and right. And the said court shall have full power to take such steps as they may judge proper to perpetuate testimony in all cases concerning such titles: *Provided*, That a jury shall always be impanelled for the finding of such facts as are not agreed by the parties; unless the parties, or their attorneys, shall waive their right of trial by jury and refer the matter of fact to the decision of the court: *Provided also*, That the legislature may, whenever they may judge it expedient, pass an act or acts to regulate the mode of proceedings in such cases, or to take away entirely the original jurisdiction hereby given to the said court in such cases.

5. In all other cases the supreme court shall have appellate jurisdiction only, with such exceptions and under such regulations as the

legislature shall make; and the legislature may, from time to time, vest in the supreme and inferior courts, or either of them, such powers, both in law and equity, as they shall judge proper and necessary for the due administration of justice.

6. A competent number of justices of the peace shall be appointed in each county; they shall be commissioned during good behavior, but may be removed on conviction of misbehavior in office, or any infamous crime, or on the address of both houses of the legislature.

7. The judges shall, by virtue of their office, be conservators of the peace throughout the State. The style of all process shall be, " The Commonwealth of Kentucky; " all prosecutions shall be carried on in the name and by authority of the commonwealth of Kentucky, and conclude " against the peace and dignity of the same."

Article VI

1. Sheriffs and coroners shall, at the times and places of elections of representatives, be chosen by the citizens of each county, qualified to vote for representatives. They shall hold their office for three years, if they shall so long behave themselves well, and until a successor be duly qualified; but no person shall be twice chosen or appointed sheriff in any term of six years. Vacancies in either of the said offices shall be filled by a new appointment, to be made by the governor, to continue until the next general election, and until a successor shall be chosen and qualified as aforesaid.

2. The freemen of this commonwealth shall be armed and disciplined for its defence. Those who conscientiously scruple to bear arms shall not be compelled to do so, but shall pay an equivalent for personal service.

3. The field and staff officers of the militia shall be appointed by the governor, except the battalion staff-officers, who shall be appointed by the field-officers of each battalion respectively.

4. The officers of companies shall be chosen by the persons enrolled in the list of each company, and the whole shall be commissioned during good behavior, and during their residence in the bounds of the battalion or company to which they shall be appointed.

5. Each court shall appoint its own clerk, who shall hold his office during good behavior; but no person shall be appointed clerk, only *pro tempore*, who shall not produce to the court appointing him a certificate from a majority of the judges of the court of appeals that he hath been examined by their clerk, in their presence and under their direction, and that they judge him to be well qualified to execute the office of clerk to any court of the same dignity with that for which he offers himself. They shall be removable for breach of good behavior by the court of appeals only, who shall be judges of the fact as well as of the law. Two-thirds of the members present must concur in the sentence.

6. All commissions shall be in the name and by the authority of the State of Kentucky, and be sealed with the State seal and signed by the governor.

7. The State treasurer shall be appointed annually by the joint ballot of both houses.

Article VII

1. Members of the general assembly and all officers, executive and judicial, before they enter upon the execution of their respective offices, shall take the following oath or affirmation: " I do solemnly swear [or affirm, as the case may be] that I will be faithful and true to the commonwealth of Kentucky so long as I continue a citizen thereof, and that I will faithfully execute, to the best of my abilities, the office of ———, according to law."

Article VIII

1. Treason against the commonwealth shall consist only in levying war against it, or in adhering to its enemies, giving them aid or comfort. No person shall be convicted of treason unless on the testimoney of two witnesses to the same overt act, or on his own confession in open court.
2. Laws shall be made to exclude from office and from suffrage those who thereafter be convicted of bribery, perjury, forgery, or other high crimes or misdemeanors. The privilege of free suffrage shall be supported by laws regulating elections, and prohibiting, under adequate penalties, all undue influence thereon from power, bribery, tumult, or other improper practices.
3. No money shall be drawn from the treasury but in consequence of appropriations made by law, nor shall any appropriations of money for the support of an army be made for a longer term than one year, and a regular statement and account of the receipts and expenditures of all public money shall be published annually.
4. The legislature shall direct by law in what manner and what courts suits may be brought against the State.
5. The manner of administering an oath or affirmation shall be such as is most consistent with the conscience of the deponent, and shall be esteemed by the legislature the most solemn appeal to God.
6. All laws now in force in the State of Virginia, not inconsistent with this constitution, which are of a general nature, and not local to the eastern part of that State, shall be in force in this State, until they shall be altered or repealed by the legislature.
7. The compact with the State of Virginia, subject to such alterations as may be made therein, agreeably to the mode prescribed by the said compact, shall be considered as a part of this constitution.

Article IX

1. The legislature shall have no power to pass laws for the emancipation of slaves without the consent of their owners, previous to such emancipation, and a full equivalent in money for the slaves so emancipated. They shall have no power to prevent emigrants to this State from bringing with them such persons as are deemed slaves by the laws of any one of the United States, so long as any person of the same age or description shall be continued in slavery by the laws of this State. They shall pass laws to permit the owners of slaves to emancipate them, saving the rights of creditors, and preventing them from becoming chargeable to the county in which they reside.

They shall have full power to prevent slaves being brought into this State as merchandize. They shall have full power to prevent any slaves being brought into this State from a foreign country, and to prevent those from being brought into this State who have been since the first day of January, one thousand seven hundred and eighty-nine, or hereafter may be, imported into any of the United States from a foreign country. And they shall have full power to pass such laws as may be necessary to oblige the owners of slaves to treat them with humanity, to provide for them necessary clothing and provision, to abstain from all injuries to them extending to life or limb, and in case of their neglect or refusal to comply with the directions of such laws, to have such slave or slaves sold for the benefit of their owner or owners.

Article X

1. The place for the seat of government shall be fixed in the following manner: The house of representatives shall, during their session which shall be held in the year one thousand seven hundred and ninety-two, choose by ballot twenty-one persons, from whom the representation from Fayette and Mercer Counties then present shall alternately strike out one, until the number shall be reduced to five, who, or any three of them concurring in opinion, shall have power to fix on the place for the seat of government, to receive grants from individuals therefor, and to make such conditions with the proprietor or proprietors of the land so pitched on by them as to them shall seem right, and shall be agreed to by the said proprietor or proprietors, and to lay off a town thereon, in such manner as they shall judge most proper.

2. The general assembly and the supreme courts shall within five years hold their sessions at the place so pitched upon by the said commissioners; and the seat of government so fixed shall continue until it shall be changed by two-thirds of both branches of the legislature. The commissioners, before they proceed to act, shall take an oath or make affirmation that they will discharge the trust imposed on them in such manner as in their judgment will be most beneficial to the State at large.

Article XI

1. That the citizens of this State may have an opportunity to amend or change this constitution in a peaceable manner, if to them it shall seem expedient, the persons qualified to vote for representatives shall, at the general election to be held in the year one thousand seven hundred and ninety-seven, vote also, by ballot, for or against a convention, as they shall severally choose to do; and if thereupon it shall appear that a majority of all the citizens in the State voting for representatives have voted for a convention, the general assembly shall direct that a similar ballot shall be taken the next year; and if thereupon it shall also appear that a majority of all the citizens in the State voting for representatives have voted for a convention, the general assembly shall, at their next session, call a convention, to consist of as many members as there shall be in the house of representatives, to be chosen in the same manner, (at

the same places and at the same time that representatives are,) by the citizens entitled to vote for representatives, and to meet within three months after the said election for the purpose of readopting, amending, or changing this constitution. If it shall appear upon the ballot of either year that a majority of the citizens voting for representatives is not in favor of a convention being called, it shall not be done until two-thirds of both branches of the legislature shall deem it expedient.

ARTICLE XII

1. That the general, great, and essential principles of liberty and free government may be recognized and unalterably established, we declare that all men, when they form a social compact, are equal, and that no man or set of men are entitled to exclusive or separate public emoluments or privileges from the community, but in consideration of public services.

2. That all power is inherent in the people, and all free governments are founded on their authority and instituted for their peace, safety, and happiness. For the advancement of those ends, they have at all times an unalienable and indefeasible right to alter, reform, or abolish their government, in such manner as they may think proper.

3. That all men have a natural and indefeasible right to worship Almighty God according to the dictates of their own consciences; that no man of right can be compelled to attend, erect, or support any place of worship, or to maintain any ministry against his consent; that no human authority can in any case whatever control or interfere with the rights of conscience; and that no preference shall ever be given by law to any religious societies or modes of worship.

4. That the civil rights, privileges, or capacities of any citizen shall in no ways be diminished or enlarged on account of his religion.

5. That all elections shall be free and equal.

6. That trial by jury shall be as heretofore, and the right thereof remain inviolate.

7. That the printing-press shall be free to every person who undertakes to examine the proceedings of the legislature or any branch of government, and no law shall ever be made to restrain the right thereof. The free communications of thoughts and opinions is one of the invaluable rights of man, and every citizen may freely speak, write, and print on any subject, being responsible for the abuse of that liberty.

8. In prosecutions for publications of papers, investigating the official conduct of officers or men in a public capacity, or where the matter published is proper for public information, the truth thereof may be given in evidence. And in all indictments for libels, the jury shall have a right to determine the law and the facts, under the direction of the court, as in other cases.

9. That the people shall be secure in their persons, houses, papers, and possessions, from unreasonable searches and seizures; and that no warrant to search any place or to seize any person or things, shall issue without describing them as nearly as may be, nor without probable cause supported by oath or affirmation.

10. That in all criminal prosecutions the accused hath a right to be heard by himself and his counsel; to demand the nature and cause of

accusation against him; to meet the witnesses face to face; to have compulsory process for obtaining witnesses in his favor; and in prosecutions by indictment or information, a speedy public trial by an impartial jury of the vicinage; that he cannot be compelled to give evidence against himself, nor can he be deprived of his life, liberty, or property, unless by the judgment of his peers, or the law of the land.

11. That no person shall for any indictable offence be proceeded against criminally by information, except in cases arising in the land or naval forces, or in the militia when in actual service, in time of war or public danger, or by leave of the court for oppression or misdemeanor in office.

12. No person shall, for the same offence, be twice put in jeopardy of his life or limb, nor shall any man's property be taken or applied to public use without the consent of his representatives, and without just compensation being previously made to him.

13. That all courts shall be open, and every person for an injury done him in his lands, goods, person, or reputation, shall have remedy by the due course of law, and right and justice administered, without sale, denial, or delay.

14. That no power of suspending laws shall be exercised, unless by the legislature or its authority.

15. That excessive bail shall not be required, nor excessive fines imposed, nor cruel punishments inflicted.

16. That all prisoners shall be bailable by sufficient sureties, unless for capital offences, when the proof is evident or presumption great, and the privilege of the writ of *habeas corpus* shall not be suspended, unless when, in cases of rebellion or invasion, the public safety may require it.

17. That the person of a debtor, where there is not strong presumption of fraud, shall not be continued in prison after delivering up his estate for the benefit of his creditors, in such manner as shall be prescribed by law.

18. That no *ex post facto* law nor any law impairing contracts shall be made.

19. That no persons shall be attainted of treason or felony by the legislature.

20. That no attainder shall work corruption of blood, nor, except during the life of the offender, forfeiture of estate to the commonwealth.

21. That estates of such persons as shall destroy their own lives shall descend or vest as in case of natural death, and if any person shall be killed by casualty, there shall be no forfeiture by reason thereof.

22. That the citizens have a right in a peaceable manner to assemble together for their common good, and to apply to those invested with the powers of government for redress of grievances, or other proper purposes, by petition, address, or remonstrance.

23. That the right of the citizens to bear arms in defence of themselves and the State shall not be questioned.

24. That no standing army shall, in time of peace, be kept up, without the consent of the legislature; and the military shall, in all cases and at all times, be in strict subordination to the civil power.

25. That no soldier shall, in time of peace, be quartered in any

house, without the consent of the owner, nor in time of war, but in a manner to be prescribed by law.

26. That the legislature shall not grant any title of nobility or hereditary distinction, nor create any office the appointment to which shall be for a longer term than during good behavior.

27. That emigration from the State shall not be prohibited.

28. To guard against the high powers which have been delegated, we declare that everything in this article is excepted out of the general powers of government, and shall forever remain inviolate; and that all laws contrary thereto, or contrary to this constitution, shall be void.

SCHEDULE

1. That no inconvenience may rise from the establishing the government of this State, and in order to carry the same into complete operation, it is hereby declared and ordained, that all rights, actions, prosecutions, claims, and contracts, as well individuals as of bodies-corporate, shall continue as if the said government had not been established.

2. That all officers, civil and military, now in commission under the State of Virginia, shall continue to hold and exercise their offices until the tenth day of August next, and no longer.

3. That until the first enumeration shall be made, as directed by the sixth section of the first article of this constitution, the county of Jefferson shall be entitled to elect three representatives; the county of Lincoln, four representatives; the county of Fayette, nine representatives; the county of Nelson, six representatives; the county of Mercer, four representatives; the county of Madison, three representatives; the county of Bourbon, five representatives; the county of Woodford, four representatives; and the county of Mason, two representatives.

4. The general assembly shall meet at Lexington on the fourth day of June next.

5. All returns herein directed to be made to the secretary shall, previous to his appointment, be made to the clerk of the supreme court for the district of Kentucky.

6. Until a seal shall be provided for the State, the governor shall be at liberty to use his private seal.

7. The oaths of office herein directed to be taken may be administered by any justice of the peace, until the legislature shall otherwise direct.

8. All bonds given by any officer within the district of Kentucky, payable to the governor of Virginia, may be prosecuted in the name of the governor of Kentucky.

9. All offences against the laws of Virginia, which have been committed within the present district of Kentucky, or which may be committed within the same before the first day of June next, shall be cognizable in the courts of this State in the same manner that they would be if they were committed within this State, after the said first day of June.

10. At the elections herein directed to be held in May next, the sheriff of each county, or in case of his absence one of his deputies, shall preside, and if they neglect or refuse to act, the said elections shall be held by any one of the justices of the peace for the county

where such neglect or refusal shall happen; each officer holding such election, having first taken an oath before a justice of the peace to conduct the said election with impartiality, shall have power to administer to any person offering to vote at such election the following oath or affirmation: " I do swear [or affirm] that I am qualified to vote for representatives in the county of ———, agreeably to the constitution formed for the State of Kentucky; " and such officers shall have a right to refuse to receive the vote of any person who shall refuse to take the said oath or make affirmation when tendered to him. And the said elections shall be held at the several places appointed for holding courts in the different counties.

11. The government of the commonwealth of Kentucky shall commence on the first day of June next.

Done in convention, at Danville, the nineteenth day of April, one thousand seven hundred and ninety-two, and of the Independence of the United States of America the sixteenth.

By order of the convention.

SAMUEL MCDOWELL, *President.*

Attest:
THO. TODD, *Clerk.*

CONSTITUTION OF KENTUCKY—1799 * [a]

We, the representatives of the people of the State of Kentucky, in convention assembled, to secure to all the citizens thereof the enjoyment of the right of life, liberty, and property, and of pursuing happiness, do ordain and establish this constitution for its government:

ARTICLE I

CONCERNING THE LEGISLATIVE DEPARTMENT

SECTION 1. The powers of the government of the State of Kentucky shall be divided into three distinct departments, and each of them be confided to a separate body of magistracy, to wit: those which are legislative, to one; those which are executive, to another; and those which are judiciary, to another.

SEC. 2. No person or collection of persons, being one of those departments, shall exercise any power properly belonging to either of the others; except in the instances hereinafter expressly directed or permitted.

ARTICLE II

CONCERNING THE DISTRIBUTION OF THE POWERS OF THE GOVERNMENT

SECTION 1. The legislative power of this commonwealth shall be vested in two distinct branches; the one to be styled " the house of representatives," the other " the senate," and both together " the general assembly of the commonwealth of Kentucky."

---

* Verified by " The Statistics of Kentucky 1887." pp. 72–91.

[a] This constitution was framed by a convention, called in accordance with the eleventh article of the constitution of 1792, which met at Frankfort July 22, 1799, and completed its labors August 17, 1799. It was not submitted to the people, and it took effect January 1, 1800.

SEC. 2. The members of the house of representatives shall continue in service for the term of one year from the day of the commencement of the general election, and no longer.

SEC. 3. Representatives shall be chosen on the first Monday in the month of August in every year; but the presiding officers of the several elections shall continue the same for three days, at the request of any one of the candidates.

SEC. 4. No person shall be a representative who, at the time of his election, is not a citizen of the United States, and hath not attained to the age of twenty-four years, and resided in this state two years next preceding his election, and the last year thereof in the county or town for which he may be chosen.

SEC. 5. Elections for representatives for the several counties entitled to representation shall be held at the places of holding their respective courts, or in the several election precincts into which the legislature may think proper, from time to time, to divide any or all of those counties: *Provided*, That when it shall appear to the legislature that any town hath a number of qualified voters equal to the ratio then fixed, such town shall be invested with the privilege of a separate representation, which shall be retained so long as such town shall contain a number of qualified voters equal to the ratio which may, from time to time, be fixed by law, and thereafter elections, for the county in which such town is situated, shall not be held therein.

SEC. 6. Representation shall be equal and uniform in this commonwealth; and shall be forever regulated and ascertained by the number of qualified electors therein. In the year eighteen hundred and three, and every fourth year thereafter, an enumeration of all the free male inhabitants of the State, above twenty-one years of age, shall be made, in such manner as shall be directed by law. The number of representatives shall, in the several years of making these enumerations, be so fixed as not to be less than fifty-eight, nor more than one hundred, and they shall be apportioned for the four years next following, as near as may be, among the several counties and towns, in proportion to the number of qualified electors; but, when a county not have a residuum or residuums, which, when added to the small county, would entitle it to a separate representation, it shall then be in the power of the legislature to join two or more together, for the purpose of sending a representative: *Provided*, That when there are two or more counties adjoining, which have residuums over and above the ratio when fixed by law, if said residuums when added together will amount to such ratio, in that case one representative shall be added to that county having the largest residuum.

SEC. 7. The house of representatives shall choose its speaker and other officers.

SEC. 8. In all elections for representatives, every free male citizen (negroes, mulattoes, and Indians excepted) who, at the time being, hath attained to the age of twenty-one years, and resided in the State two years, or the county or town in which he offers to vote one year next preceding the election, shall enjoy the right of an elector; but no person shall be entitled to vote, except in the county or town in which he may actually reside at the time of the election, except as is herein otherwise provided. Electors shall in all cases, except treason, felony, breach or surety of the peace, be privileged from arrest during their attendance at, going to, and returning from elections.

SEC. 9. The members of the senate shall be chosen for the term of four years; and, when assembled, shall have the power to choose its officers annually.

SEC. 10. At the first session of the general assembly after this constitution takes effect, the senators shall be divided by lot, as equally as may be, into four classes; the seats of the senators of the first class shall be vacated at the expiration of the first year; of the second class at the expiration of the second year; of the third class at the expiration of the third year; and of the fourth class at the expiration of the fourth year; so that one-fourth shall be chosen every year, and a rotation thereby kept up perpetually.

SEC. 11. The senate shall consist of twenty-four members at least, and for every three members above fifty-eight, which shall be added to the house of representatives, one member shall be added to the senate.

SEC. 12. The same number of senatorial districts shall, from time to time, be established by the legislature, as there may then be senators allotted to the State; which shall be so formed as to contain, as near as may be, an equal number of free male inhabitants in each, above the age of twenty-one years, and so that no county shall be divided, or form more than one district; and where two or more counties compose a district, they shall be adjoining.

SEC. 13. When an additional senator may be added to the senate, he shall be annexed by lot to one of the four classes, so as to keep them as nearly equal in number as possible.

SEC. 14. One senator for each district shall be elected by those qualified to vote for representatives therein, who shall give their votes at the several places in the counties or towns where elections are by law directed to be held.

SEC. 15. No person shall be a senator who, at the time of his election, is not a citizen of the United States, and who hath not attained to the age of thirty-five years, and resided in this State six years next preceding his election, and the last year thereof in the district from which he may be chosen.

SEC. 16. The first election for senators shall be general throughout the State, and at the same time that the general election for representatives is held; and thereafter there shall, in like manner, be an annual election for senators to fill the places of those whose time of service may have expired.

SEC. 17. The general assembly shall convene on the first Monday in the month of November in every year, unless a different day be appointed by law; and their session shall be held at the seat of government.

SEC. 18. Not less than a majority of the members of each house of the general assembly shall constitute a quorum to do business; but a smaller number may adjourn from day to day, and shall be authorized by law to compel the attendance of absent members, in such manner, and under such penalties, as may be prescribed thereby.

SEC. 19. Each house of the general assembly shall judge of the qualifications, elections, and returns of its members; but a contested election shall be determined in such manner as shall be directed by law.

SEC. 20. Each house of the general assembly may determine the rules of its proceedings; punish a member for disorderly behavior; and, with the concurrence of two-thirds, expel a member, but not a second time for the same cause.

SEC. 21. Each house of the general assembly shall keep and publish, weekly, a journal of its proceedings; and the yeas and nays of the members on any question shall, at the desire of any two of them, be entered on their journal.

SEC. 22. Neither house, during the session of the general assembly, shall, without the consent of the other, adjourn for more than three days, nor to any other place than that in which they may be sitting.

SEC. 23. The members of the general assembly shall severally receive from the public treasury a compensation for their services, which shall be one dollar and a half a day, during their attendance on, going to, and returning from the session of their respective houses: *Provided*, That the same may be increased or diminished by law; but no alteration shall take effect during the session at which such alteration shall be made.

SEC. 24. The members of the general assembly shall, in all cases, except treason, felony, breach or surety of the peace, be privileged from arrest during their attendance at the sessions of their respective houses, and in going to and returning from the same; and for any speech or debate in either house, they shall not be questioned in any other place.

SEC. 25. No senator or representative shall, during the term for which he was elected, nor for one year thereafter, be appointed or elected to any civil office of profit under this commonwealth, which shall have been created, or the emoluments of which shall have been increased, during the time such senator or representative was in office, except to such offices or appointments as may be made or filled by the elections of the people.

SEC. 26. No person, while he continues to exercise the functions of a clergyman, priest, or teacher of any religious persuasion, society, or sect; nor whilst he holds or exercises any office of profit under this commonwealth, shall be eligible to the general assembly; except attorneys at law, justices of the peace, and militia officers: *Provided*, That justices of the courts of quarter-sessions shall be ineligible so long as any compensation may be allowed them for their services: *Provided also*, That attorneys for the commonwealth, who receive a fixed annual salary from the public treasury, shall be ineligible.

SEC. 27. No person who at any time may have been a collector of taxes for the State, or the assistant or deputy of such collector, shall be eligible to the general assembly until he shall have obtained a quietus for the amount of such collection, and for all public moneys for which he may be responsible.

SEC. 28. No bill shall have the force of a law until on three several days it be read over in each house of the general assembly, and free discussion allowed thereon; unless, in cases of urgency, four-fifths of the house where the bill shall be depending may deem it expedient to dispense with this rule.

SEC. 29. All bills for raising revenue shall originate in the house of representatives; but the senate may propose amendments, as in other bills: *Provided*, That they shall not introduce any new matter, under the color of an amendment, which does not relate to raising a revenue.

SEC. 30. The general assembly shall regulate by law by whom and in what manner writs of election shall be issued to fill the vacancies which may happen in either branch thereof.

ARTICLE III

CONCERNING THE EXECUTIVE DEPARTMENT

SECTION 1. The supreme executive power of the commonwealth shall be vested in a chief magistrate, who shall be styled "the governor of the commonwealth of Kentucky."

SEC. 2. The governor shall be elected for the term of four years by the citizens entitled to suffrage at the time and places where they shall respectively vote for representatives. The person having the highest number of votes shall be governor; but if two or more shall be equal and highest in votes, the election shall be determined by lot, in such manner as the legislature may direct.

SEC. 3. The governor shall be ineligible for the succeeding seven years after the expiration of the time for which he shall have been elected.

SEC. 4. He shall be at least thirty-five years of age, and a citizen of the United States, and have been an inhabitant of this State at least six years next preceding his election.

SEC. 5. He shall commence the execution of his office on the fourth Tuesday succeeding the day of the commencement of the general election on which he shall be chosen, and shall continue in the execution thereof until the end of four weeks next succeeding the election of his successor, and until his successor shall have taken the oaths or affirmations prescribed by this constitution.

SEC. 6. No member of Congress, or person holding any office under the United States, nor minister of any religious society, shall be eligible to the office of governor.

SEC. 7. The governor shall, at stated times, receive for his services a compensation, which shall neither be increased nor diminished during the term for which he shall have been elected.

SEC. 8. He shall be commander-in-chief of the army and navy of this commonwealth, and of the militia thereof, except when they shall be called into the service of the United States; but he shall not command personally in the field, unless he shall be advised so to do by a resolution of the general assembly.

SEC. 9. He shall nominate, and, by and with the advice and consent of the senate, appoint all officers whose offices are established by this constitution or shall be established by law, and whose appointments are not herein otherwise provided for: *Provided*, That no person shall be so appointed to an office within any county who shall not have been a citizen and inhabitant therein one year next before his appointment, if the county shall have been so long erected; but if it shall not have been so long erected, then within the limits of the county or counties from which it shall have been taken: *Provided also*, That the county courts be authorized by law to appoint inspectors, collectors, and their deputies, surveyors of the highways, constables, jailers, and such other inferior officers, whose jurisdiction may be confined within the limits of a county.

Sec. 10. The governor shall have power to fill up vacancies that may happen during the recess of the senate, by granting commissions, which shall expire at the end of the next session.

Sec. 11. He shall have power to remit fines and forfeitures, grant reprieves and pardons, except in cases of impeachment. In cases of treason, he shall have power to grant reprieves until the end of the next session of the general assembly; in which the power of pardoning shall be vested.

Sec. 12. He may require information in writing from the officers in the executive department, upon any subject relating to the duties of their respective offices.

Sec. 13. He shall from time to time give to the general assembly information of the state of the commonwealth, and recommend to their consideration such measures as he shall deem expedient.

Sec. 14. He may on extraordinary occasions convene the general assembly at the seat of government, or at a different place, if that should have become, since their last adjournment, dangerous from an enemy or from contagious disorders; and in case of disagreement between the two houses, with respect to the time of adjournment, adjourn them to such time as he shall think proper, not exceeding four months.

Sec. 15. He shall take care that the laws be faithfully executed.

Sec. 16. A lieutenant-governor shall be chosen at every election for a governor, in the same manner, continue in office for the same time, and possess the same qualifications. In voting for governor and lieutenant-governor, the electors shall distinguish whom they vote for as governor, and whom as lieutenant-governor.

Sec. 17. He shall, by virtue of his office, be speaker of the senate; have a right, when in committee of the whole, to debate and vote on all subjects; and, when the senate are equally divided, to give the casting vote.

Sec. 18. In case of the impeachment of the governor, his removal from office, death, refusal to qualify, resignation, or absence from the State, the lieutenant-governor shall exercise all the power and authority appertaining to the office of governor, until another be duly qualified, or the governor absent or impeached shall return or be acquitted.

Sec. 19. Whenever the government shall be administered by the lieutenant-governor, or he shall be unable to attend as speaker of the senate, the senators shall elect one of their own members as speaker, for that occasion. And if, during the vacancy of the office of governor, the lieutenant-governor shall be impeached, removed from office, refuse to qualify, resign, die, or be absent from the State, the speaker of the senate shall, in like manner, administer the government.

Sec. 20. The lieutenant-governor, while he acts as speaker to the senate, shall receive for his services the same compensation which shall for the same period be allowed to the speaker of the house of representatives, and no more; and during the time he administers the government as governor, shall receive the same compensation which the governor would have received and been entitled to had he been employed in the duties of his office.

SEC. 21. The speaker *pro tempore* of the senate, during the time he administers the government, shall receive in like manner the same compensation which the governor would have received had he been employed in the duties of his office.

SEC. 22. If the lieutenant-governor shall be called upon to administer the government, and shall, while in such administration, resign, die, or be absent from the State during the recess of the general assembly, it shall be the duty of the secretary for the time being to convene the senate for the purpose of choosing a speaker.

SEC. 23. An attorney-general, and such other attorneys for the commonwealth as may be necessary, shall be appointed, whose duty shall be regulated by law. Attorneys for the commonwealth, for the several counties, shall be appointed by the respective courts having jurisdiction therein.

SEC. 24. A secretary shall be appointed and commissioned during the term for which the governor shall have been elected, if he shall so long behave himself well. He shall keep a fair register, and attest all the official acts and proceedings of the governor, and shall, when required, lay the same, and all papers, minutes, and vouchers, relative thereto, before either house of the general assembly, and shall perform such other duties as may be enjoined him by law.

SEC. 25. Every bill which shall have passed both houses shall be presented to the governor; if he approve, he shall sign it, but if not, he shall return it, with his objections, to the house in which it shall have originated, who shall enter the objections at large upon the journal, and proceed to reconsider it; if, after such reconsideration, a majority of all the members elected to that house shall agree to pass the bill, it shall be sent, with the objections, to the other house, by which it shall be likewise considered, and if approved by a majority of all the members elected to that house, it shall be a law; but in such cases the votes of both houses shall be determined by yeas and nays, and the persons voting for and against the bill shall be entered on the journal of each house respectively. If any bill shall not be returned by the governor within ten days (Sundays excepted) after it shall have been presented to him, it shall be a law in like manner as if he had signed it, unless the general assembly by their adjournment prevent its return; in which case it shall be a law, unless sent back within three days after their next meeting.

SEC. 26. Every order, resolution, or vote to which the concurrence of both houses may be necessary, except on a question of adjournment, shall be presented to the governor, and, before it shall take effect, be approved by him; or, being disapproved, shall be repassed, by a majority of all the members elected to both houses, according to the rules and limitations prescribed in case of a bill.

SEC. 27. Contested elections for a governor and lieutenant-governor shall be determined by a committee to be selected from both houses of the general assembly, and formed and regulated in such manner as shall be directed by law.

SEC. 28. The freemen of this commonwealth (negroes, mulattoes, and Indians excepted) shall be armed and disciplined for its defence. Those who conscientiously scruple to bear arms shall not be compelled to do so, but shall pay an equivalent for personal service.

SEC. 29. The commanding officers of the respective regiments shall appoint the regimental staff; brigadier-generals, their brigade-majors; major-generals, their aids; and captains, the non-commissioned officers of companies.

Sec. 30. A majority of the field-officers and captains in each regiment shall nominate the commissioned officers in each company, who shall be commissioned by the governor: *Provided*, That no nomination shall be made, unless two at least of the field-officers are present; and, when two or more persons have an equal and the highest number of votes, the field-officer present, who may be highest in commission, shall decide the nomination.

Sec. 31. Sheriffs shall hereafter be appointed in the following manner: When time of a sheriff for any county may be about to expire, the county court for the same, a majority of all its justices being present, shall, in the months of September, October, or November, next preceding thereto, recommend to the governor two proper persons to fill the office, who are then justices of the county court, and who shall in such recommendation pay a just regard to seniority in office and a regular rotation. One of the persons so recommended shall be commissioned by the governor, and shall hold his office for two years, if he so long behave well, and until a successor be duly qualified. If the county courts shall omit, in the months aforesaid, to make such recommendation, the governor shall then nominate and, by and with the advice and consent of the senate, appoint a fit person to fill such office.

Article IV

Concerning the Judicial Department

Section 1. The judiciary power of this commonwealth, both as to matters of law and equity, shall be vested in one supreme court, which shall be styled the court of appeals, and in such inferior courts as the general assembly may from time to time erect and establish.

Sec. 2. The court of appeals, except in cases otherwise directed by this constitution, shall have appellate jurisdiction only; which shall be coextensive with the State, under such restrictions and regulations, not repugnant to this constitution, as may from time to time be prescribed by law.

Sec. 3. The judges, both of the supreme and inferior courts, shall hold their offices during good behavior; but for any reasonable cause, which shall not be sufficient ground of impeachment, the governor shall remove any of them on the address of two-thirds of each house of the general assembly: *Provided, however*, That the cause or causes for which such removal may be required shall be stated at length in such address, and on the journal of each house. They shall at stated times receive for their services an adequate compensation to be fixed by law.

Sec. 4. The judges shall, by virtue of their office, be conservators of the peace throughout the State. The style of all process shall be "The commonwealth of Kentucky." All prosecutions shall be carried on in the name and by the authority of the commonwealth of Kentucky, and conclude, "against the peace and dignity of the same."

Sec. 5. There shall be established in each county now, or which may hereafter be erected, within this commonwealth a county court.

Sec. 6. A competent number of justices of the peace shall be appointed in each county; they shall be commissioned during good behavior, but may be removed on conviction of misbehavior in office, or of any infamous crime, or on the address of two-thirds of each house of the general assembly: *Provided, however*, That the cause or causes for which such removal may be required shall be stated at length in such address, on the journal of each house.

SEC. 7. The number of the justices of the peace to which the several counties in this commonwealth now established, or which may hereafter be established, ought to be entitled, shall, from time to time, be regulated by law.

SEC. 8. When a surveyor, coroner, or justice of the peace shall be needed in any county, the county court for the same, a majority of all its justices concurring therein, shall recommend to the governor two proper persons to fill the office, one of whom he shall appoint thereto: *Provided, however*, That if the county court shall for twelve months omit to make such recommendation, after being requested by the governor to recommend proper persons, he shall then nominate and, by and with the advice and consent of the senate, appoint a fit person to fill such office.

SEC. 9. When a new county shall be erected, a competent number of justices of the peace, a sheriff, and coroner therefor, shall be recommended to the governor by a majority of all the members of the house of representatives, from the senatorial district or districts in which the county is situated; and if either of the persons thus recommended shall be rejected by the governor or the senate, another person shall immediately be recommended as aforesaid.

SEC. 10. Each court shall appoint its own clerk, who shall hold his office during good behavior; but no person shall be appointed clerk, only *pro tempore*, who shall not produce to the court appointing him a certificate from a majority of the judges of the court of appeals that he had been examined by their clerk, in their presence and under their direction, and that they judge him to be well qualified to execute the office of clerk of any court of the same dignity with that for which he offers himself. They shall be removable for breach of good behavior, by the court of appeal only, who shall be judges of the fact as well as of the law. Two-thirds of the members present must concur in the sentence.

SEC. 11. All commissions shall be in the name and by the authority of the State of Kentucky, and sealed with the State seal, and signed by the governor.

SEC. 12. The state treasurer, and printer or printers for the commonwealth, shall be appointed annually by the joint vote of both houses of the general assembly: *Provided*, That during the recess of the same the governor shall have power to fill vacancies which may happen in either of the said offices.

ARTICLE V

CONCERNING IMPEACHMENTS

SECTION 1. The house of representatives shall have the sole power of impeaching.

SEC. 2. All impeachments shall be tried by the senate. When sitting for that purpose, the senators shall be upon oath or affirmation. No person shall be convicted without the concurrence of two-thirds of the members present.

SEC. 3. The governor and all civil officers shall be liable to impeachment for any misdemeanor in office; but judgment, in such cases, shall not extend further than to removal from office and disqualification to hold any office of honor, trust, or profit under this commonwealth; but the party convicted shall nevertheless be liable and subject to indictment, trial, and punishment, according to law.

ARTICLE VI

GENERAL PROVISIONS

SECTION 1. Members of the general assembly, and all officers, executive and judicial, before they enter upon the execution of their respective offices, shall take the following oath or affirmation: "I do solemnly swear [or affirm, as the case may be] that I will be faithful and true to the commonwealth of Kentucky so long as I continue a citizen thereof, and that I will faithfully execute, to the best of my abilities, the office of ———, according to law."

SEC. 2. Treason against the commonwealth shall consist only in levying war against it or adhering to its enemies, giving them aid and comfort. No person shall be convicted of treason unless on the testimony of two witnesses to the same overt act, or his own confession in open court.

SEC. 3. Every person shall be disqualified from serving as a governor, lieutenant-governor, senator, or representative, for the term for which he shall have been elected, who shall be convicted of having given or offered any bribe or treat to procure his election.

SEC. 4. Laws shall be made to exclude from office and from suffrage those who shall thereafter be convicted of bribery, perjury, forgery, or other high crimes or misdemeanors. The privilege of free suffrage shall be supported by laws regulating elections, and prohibiting, under adequate penalties, all undue influence thereon from power, bribery, tumult, or other improper practices.

SEC. 5. No money shall be drawn from the treasury but in pursuance of appropriations made by law, nor shall any appropriations of money for the support of an army be made for a longer time than one year; and a regular statement and account of the receipts and expenditures of all public money shall be published annually.

SEC. 6. The general assembly shall direct by law in what manner and in what courts suits may be brought against the commonwealth.

SEC. 7. The manner of administering an oath or affirmation shall be such as is most consistent with the conscience of the deponent, and shall be esteemed by the general assembly the most solemn appeal to God.

SEC. 8. All laws which, on the first day of June, one thousand seven hundred and ninety-two, were in force in the State of Virginia, and which are of a general nature, and not local to that State, and not repugnant to this constitution, nor to the laws which have been enacted by the legislature of this commonwealth, shall be in force within this State, until they shall be altered or repealed by the general assembly.

SEC. 9. The compact with the State of Virginia, subject to such alterations as may be made therein, agreeably to the mode prescribed by the said compact, shall be considered as part of this constitution.

Sec. 10. It shall be the duty of the general assembly to pass such laws as may be necessary and proper to decide differences by arbitrators, to be appointed by the parties who may choose that summary mode of adjustment.

Sec. 11. All civil officers for the commonwealth at large shall reside within the State, and all district, county, or town officers within their respective districts, counties, or towns, (trustees of towns excepted,) and shall keep their respective offices at such places therein as may be required by law; and all militia officers shall reside in the bounds of the division, brigade, regiment, battalion, or company to which they may severally belong.

Sec. 12. The attorney-general, and other attorneys for this commonwealth who receive a fixed annual salary from the public treasury, judges, and clerks of courts, justices of the peace, surveyors of lands, and all commissioned militia officers shall hold their respective offices during good behavior and the continuance of their respective courts, under the exceptions contained in this constitution.

Sec. 13. Absence on the business of this State, or the United States, shall not forfeit a residence once obtained, so as to deprive any one of the right of suffrage or of being elected or appointed to any office under this commonwealth, under the exceptions contained in this constitution.

Sec. 14. It shall be the duty of the general assembly to regulate by law in what cases and what deduction from the salaries of public officers shall be made for neglect of duty in their official capacity.

Sec. 15. Returns of all elections for governor, lieutenant-governor, and members of the general assembly shall be made to the secretary for the time being.

Sec. 16. In all elections by the people, and also by the senate and house of representatives, jointly or separately, the votes shall be personally and publicly given *viva voce*.

Sec. 17. No member of Congress nor person holding or exercising any office of trust or profit under the United States, or either of them, or under any foreign power, shall be eligible as a member of the general assembly of this commonwealth, or hold or exercise any office of trust or profit under the same.

Sec. 18. The general assembly shall direct by law how persons who now are, or may hereafter become, securities for public officers may be relieved or discharged on account of such securityship.

Article VII

CONCERNING SLAVES

Section 1. The general assembly shall have no power to pass laws for the emancipation of slaves without the consent of their owners, or without paying their owners, previous to such emancipation, a full equivalent in money for the slaves so emancipated. They shall have no power to prevent emigrants to this State from bringing with them such persons as are deemed slaves by the laws of any of the United States, so long as any person of the same age or description shall be continued in slavery by the laws of this State. They shall pass laws to permit the owners of slaves to emancipate them, saving the rights of creditors, and preventing them from becoming a charge to any county in this commonwealth. They shall have full power to prevent slaves being brought into this State as merchandise. They shall have full power to prevent any slaves being brought into this State who have been, since the first day of January, one thousand seven hundred and eighty-nine, or may hereafter be, imported into any of the United States from a foreign country. And they shall have full power to pass such laws as may be necessary to oblige the owners of slaves to treat them with humanity, to provide for them necessary clothing and provision, to abstain from all injuries to them extending to life or limb, and in case of their neglect or refusal to comply with the directions of such laws, to have such slave or slaves sold for the benefit of their owner or owners.

Sec. 2. In the prosecution of slaves for felony, no inquest by a grand jury shall be necessary, but the proceedings in such prosecutions shall be regulated by law, except that the general assembly shall have no power to deprive them of the privilege of an impartial trial by a petit jury.

Article VIII

Section 1. The seat of government shall continue in the town of Frankfort, until it shall be removed by law: *Provided, however,* That two-thirds of all the members elected to each house of the general assembly shall concur in the passage of such law.

Article IX

MODE OF REVISING THE CONSTITUTION

Section 1. When experience shall point out the necessity of amending this constitution, and when a majority of all the members elected to each house of the general assembly shall, within the first twenty days of their stated annual session, concur in passing a law, specifying the alterations intended to be made, for taking the sense of the good people of this State as to the necessity and expediency of calling a convention, it shall be the duty of the several sheriffs and other returning officers, at the next general election which shall be held for representatives after the passage of such law, to open a poll for and make return to the secretary, for the time being, of the names of all those entitled to vote for representatives who have voted for calling a convention; and if thereupon it shall appear that a majority of all the citizens of this State entitled to vote for representatives have voted for a convention, the general assembly shall direct that a similar poll shall be opened and taken for the next year; and if thereupon it shall appear that a majority of all the citizens of this State entitled to vote for representatives have voted for a convention, the general assembly shall, at their next session, call a convention, to consist of as many members as there shall be in the house of representatives, and no more; to be chosen in the same manner and proportion, at the same places and at the same time, that representatives are, by citizens entitled to vote for representatives; and to meet within three months after the said election for the purpose of readopting, amending, or changing this constitution. But if it shall appear, by the vote of either year, as aforesaid, that a majority of all the citizens entitled to vote for representatives did not vote for a convention, a convention shall not be called.

Article X

That the general, great, and essential principles of liberty and free government may be recognized and established, we declare:

Section 1. That all free men, when they form a social compact, are equal, and that no man or set of men are entitled to exclusive, separate public emoluments or privileges from the community but in consideration of public services.

Sec. 2. That all power is inherent in the people, and all free governments are founded on their authority, and instituted for their peace, safety, and happiness. For the advancement of these ends, they have at all times an unalienable and indefeasible right to alter, reform, or abolish their government, in such manner as they may think proper.

Sec. 3. That all men have a natural and indefeasible right to worship Almighty God according to the dictates of their own consciences; that no man shall be compelled to attend, erect, or support any place of worship, or to maintain any ministry against his consent; that no human authority ought, in any case whatever, to control or interfere with the rights of conscience; and that no preference shall ever be given by law to any religious societies or modes of worship.

Sec. 4. That the civil rights, privileges, or capacities of any citizen shall in no wise be diminished or enlarged on account of his religion.

Sec. 5. That all elections shall be free and equal.

Sec. 6. That the ancient mode of trial by jury shall be held sacred, and the right thereof remain inviolate.

Sec. 7. That printing-presses shall be free to every person who undertakes to examine the proceedings of the legislature or any branch of government, and no law shall ever be made to restrain the right thereof. The free communication of thoughts and opinions is one of the invaluable rights of man, and every citizen may freely speak, write, and print on any subject, being responsible for the abuse of that liberty.

Sec. 8. In prosecutions for the publication of papers investigating the official conduct of officers or men in a public capacity, or where the matter published is proper for public information, the truth thereof may be given in evidence. And in all indictments for libels, the jury shall have a right to determine the law and the facts, under the direction of the court, as in other cases.

Sec. 9. That the people shall be secure in their persons, houses, papers, and possessions, from unreasonable seizures and searches; and that no warrant to search any place or to seize any person or thing, shall issue without describing them as nearly as may be, nor without probable cause, supported by oath or affirmation.

Sec. 10. That in all criminal prosecutions, the accused hath a right to be heard by himself and counsel; to demand the nature and cause of the accusation against him; to meet the witnesses face to face; to have compulsory process for obtaining witnesses in his favor; and, in prosecutions by indictment or information, a speedy public trial by an impartial jury of the vicinage; that he cannot be compelled to give evidence against himself, nor can he be deprived of his life, liberty, or property, unless by the judgment of his peers, or the law of the land.

SEC. 11. That no person shall, for any indictable offence, be proceeded against criminally by information, except in cases arising in the land or naval forces, or the militia, when in actual service, in time of war or public danger, by leave of the court, for oppression or misdemeanor in office.

SEC. 12. No person shall, for the same offence, be twice put in jeopardy of his life or limb, nor shall any man's property be taken or applied to public use without the consent of his representatives, and without just compensation being previously made to him.

SEC. 13. That all courts shall be open, and every person, for any injury done him in his lands, goods, person, or reputation, shall have remedy by the due course of laws, and right and justice administered without sale, denial, or delay.

SEC. 14. That no power of suspending laws shall be exercised, unless by the legislature or its authority.

SEC. 15. That excessive bail shall not be required, nor excessive fines imposed, nor cruel punishments inflicted.

SEC. 16. That all prisoners shall be bailable by sufficient securities, unless for capital offences, when the proof is evident or presumption great; and the privilege of the writ of *habeas corpus* shall not be suspended, unless when, in cases of rebellion or invasion, the public safety may require it.

SEC. 17. That the person of a debtor, where there is not strong presumption of fraud, shall not be continued in prison after delivering up his estate for the benefit of his creditors, in such manner as shall be prescribed by law.

SEC. 18. That no *ex post facto* law, nor any law impairing contracts, shall be made.

SEC. 19. That no person shall be attainted of treason or felony by the legislature.

SEC. 20. That no attainder shall work corruption of blood, nor, except during the life of the offender, forfeiture of estate to the commonwealth.

SEC. 21. That the estates of such persons as shall destroy their own lives shall descend or vest as in case of natural death; and if any person shall be killed by casualty, there shall be no forfeiture by reason thereof.

SEC. 22. That the citizens have a right in a peaceable manner to assemble together for their common good, and to apply to those invested with the powers of government for redress of grievances, or other proper purposes, by petition, address, or remonstrance.

SEC. 23. That the rights of the citizens to bear arms in defence of themselves and the State shall not be questioned.

SEC. 24. That no standing army shall, in time of peace, be kept up, without the consent of the legislature; and the military shall, in all cases and at all times, be in strict subordination to the civil power.

SEC. 25. That no soldier shall, in time of peace, be quartered in any house without the consent of the owner, nor in time of war, but in a manner to be prescribed by law.

SEC. 26. That the legislature shall not grant any title of nobility or hereditary distinction, nor create any office the appointment to which shall be for a longer term than during good behavior.

SEC. 27. That emigration from this State shall not be prohibited.

SEC. 28. To guard against transgressions of the high powers which we have delegated, we declare that everything in this article is excepted out of the general powers of government, and shall forever remain inviolate; and that all laws contrary thereto, or contrary to this constitution, shall be void.

SCHEDULE

That no inconvenience may arise from the alterations and amendments made in the constitution of this commonwealth, and in order to carry the same into complete operation, it is hereby declared and ordained:

SECTION 1. That all laws of this commonwealth in force at the time of making the said alterations and amendments, and not inconsistent therewith, and all rights, actions, prosecutions, claims, and contracts, as well of individuals as of bodies-corporate, shall continue as if the said alterations and amendments had not been made.

SEC. 2. That all officers now filling any office or appointment shall continue in the exercise of the duties of their respective offices or appointments for the terms therein expressed, unless by this constitution it is otherwise directed.

SEC. 3. The oaths of office herein directed to be taken may be administered by any justice of the peace until the legislature shall otherwise direct.

SEC. 4. The general assembly, to be held in November next, shall apportion the representatives and senators, and lay off the State into senatorial districts conformable to the regulations prescribed by this constitution. In fixing those apportionments, and in establishing those districts, they shall take for their guide the enumeration directed by law to be made in the present year by the commissioners of the tax, and the apportionments thus made shall remain unaltered until the end of the stated annual session of the general assembly in the year eighteen hundred and three.

SEC. 5. In order that no inconvenience may arise from the change made by this constitution in the time of holding the general election, it is hereby ordained that the first election for governor, lieutenant-governor, and members of the general assembly shall commence on the first Monday in May, in the year eighteen hundred. The persons then elected shall continue in office during the several terms of service prescribed by this constitution, and until the next general election which shall be held after their said terms shall have respectively expired. The returns for the said first election of governor and lieutenant-governor shall be made to the secretary within fifteen days from the day of election, who shall, as soon as may be, examine and count the same in the presence of at least two judges of the court of appeals or district courts, and shall declare who are the persons thereby duly elected, and give them official notice of their election; and if any person shall be equal and highest on the poll, the said judges and secretary shall determine the election by lot.

SEC. 6. This constitution, except so much thereof as is therein otherwise directed, shall not be in force until the first day of June, in the year eighteen hundred; on which day the whole thereof shall take full and complete effect.

Done in convention, at Frankfort, the seventeenth day of August, one thousand seven hundred and ninety-nine, and of the Independence of the United States of America the twenty-fourth.

ALEXANDER S. BULLIT, *President.*

CONSTITUTION OF KENTUCKY—1850 * [a]

PREAMBLE

We, the representatives of the people of the State of Kentucky in convention assembled, to secure to all the citizens thereof the enjoyment of the rights of life, liberty, and property, and of pursuing happiness, do ordain and establish this constitution for its government:

ARTICLE I

CONCERNING THE DISTRIBUTION OF THE POWERS OF GOVERNMENT

SECTION 1. The powers of the government of the State of Kentucky shall be divided into three distinct departments, and each of them be confided to a separate body of magistracy, to wit, those which are legislative to one, those which are executive to another, and those which are judiciary to another.

SEC. 2. No person, or collection of persons, being of one of those departments, shall exercise any power properly belonging to either of the others, except in the instances hereinafter expressly directed or permitted.

ARTICLE II

CONCERNING THE LEGISLATIVE DEPARTMENT

SECTION 1. The legislative power shall be vested in a house of representatives and senate, which together shall be styled " The General Assembly of the Commonwealth of Kentucky."

SEC. 2. The members of the house of representatives shall continue in service for the term of two years from the day of the general election, and no longer.

SEC. 3. Representatives shall be chosen on the first Monday in August in every second year, and the mode of holding the elections shall be regulated by law.

SEC. 4. No person shall be a representative who, at the time of his election, is not a citizen of the United States, has not attained the age of twenty-four years, and who has not resided in this State two years next preceding his election, and the last year thereof in the county, preceding his election, and the last year thereof in the county, town, or city for which he may be chosen.

SEC. 5. The general assembly shall divide each county of this commonwealth into convenient election-precincts, or may delegate power

---

* Verified from " The Statutes of Kentucky." pp. 91–155. (See note to Kentucky constitution of 1792.)

[a] This constitution was framed by a convention which met at Frankfort October 1, 1849, and completed its labors June 11, 1850. It was submitted to the people, and ratified by 71,563 votes against 20,302 votes.

to do so to such county authorities as may be designated by law; and elections for representatives for the several counties shall be held at the places of holding their respective courts, and in the several election-precincts into which the counties may be divided: *Provided*, That when it shall appear to the general assembly that any city or town hath a number of qualified voters equal to the ratio then fixed, such city or town shall be invested with the privilege of a separate representation, in either or both houses of the general assembly, which shall be retained so long as such city or town shall contain a number of qualified voters equal to the ratio which may, from time to time, be fixed by law; and, thereafter, elections for the county in which such city or town is situated shall not be held therein; but such city or town shall not be entitled to a separate representation, unless such county, after the separation, shall also be entitled to one or more representatives. That whenever a city or town shall be entitled to a separate representation in either house of the general assembly, and by its numbers shall be entitled to more than one representative, such city or town shall be divided, by squares which are contiguous, so as to make the most compact form, into representative districts, as nearly equal as may be, equal to the number of representatives to which such city or town may be entitled; and one representative shall be elected from each district. In like manner shall said city or town be divided into senatorial districts, when by the apportionment more than one senator shall be allotted to such city or town, and a senator shall be elected from each senatorial district; but no ward or municipal division shall be divided by such division of senatorial or representative districts, unless it be necessary to equalize the elective, senatorial, or representative districts.

SEC. 6. Representation shall be equal and uniform in this commonwealth, and shall be forever regulated and ascertained by the number of qualified voters therein. In the year 1850, again in the year 1857, and every eighth year thereafter, an enumeration of all the qualified voters of the State shall be made; and, to secure uniformity and equality of representation, the State is hereby laid off into ten districts. The first district shall be composed of the counties of Fulton, Hickman, Ballard, McCracken, Graves, Calloway, Marshall, Livingston, Crittenden, Union, Hopkins, Caldwell, and Trigg. The second district shall be composed of the counties of Christian, Muhlenburg, Henderson, Daviess, Hancock, Ohio, Breckinridge, Meade, Grayson, Butler, and Edmonson. The third district shall be composed of the counties of Todd, Logan, Simpson, Warren, Allen, Monroe, Barren, and Hart. The fourth district shall be composed of the counties of Cumberland, Adair, Green, Taylor, Clinton, Russell, Wayne, Pulaski, Casey, Boyle, and Lincoln. The fifth district shall be composed of the counties of Harden, Larue, Bullitt, Spencer, Nelson, Washington, Marion, Mercer, and Anderson. The sixth district shall be composed of the counties of Garrard, Madison, Estill, Owsley, Rockcastle, Laurel, Clay, Whitley, Knox, Harlan, Perry, Letcher, Pike, Floyd, and Johnson. The seventh district shall be composed of the counties of Jefferson, Oldham, Trimble, Carroll, Henry, and Shelby, and the city of Louisville. The eighth district shall be composed of the counties of Bourbon, Fayette, Scott, Owen, Franklin, Woodford, and Jessamine. The ninth district shall be composed of the counties of Clarke, Bath, Montgomery, Fleming,

Lewis, Greenup, Carter, Lawrence, Morgan, and Breathitt. The tenth district shall be composed of the counties of Mason, Bracken, Nicholas, Harrison, Pendleton, Campbell, Grant, Kenton, Boone, and Gallatin. The number of representatives shall, at the several sessions of the general assembly next after the making of the enumerations, be apportioned among the ten several districts according to the number of qualified voters in each; and the representatives shall be apportioned, as near as may be, among the counties, towns, and cities in each district; and in making such apportionment the following rules shall govern, to wit: Every county, town, or city, having the ratio, shall have one representative; if double the ratio, two representatives, and so on. Next, the counties, towns, or cities having one or more representatives, and the largest number of qualified voters above the ratio, and counties having the largest number under the ratio, shall have a representative, regard being always had to the greatest number of qualified voters: *Provided*, That when a county may not have a sufficient number of qualified voters to entitle it to one representative, then such county may be joined to some adjacent county or counties, which counties shall send one representative. When a new county shall be formed of territory belonging to more than one district, it shall form a part of that district having the least number of qualified voters.

Sec. 7. The house of representatives shall choose its speaker and other officers.

Sec. 8. Every free white male citizen of the age of twenty-one years, who has resided in the State two years, or in the county, town, or city in which he offers to vote one year, next preceding the election, shall be a voter; but such voter shall have been for sixty days next preceding the election a resident of the precinct in which he offers to vote, and he shall vote in said precinct, and not elsewhere.

Sec. 9. Voters, in all cases except treason, felony, breach or surety of the peace, shall be privileged from arrest during their attendance at, going to, and returning from elections.

Sec. 10. Senators shall be chosen for the term of four years, and the senate shall have power to choose its officers biennially.

Sec. 11. Senators and representatives shall be elected, under the first apportionment after the adoption of this constitution, in the year 1851.

Sec. 12. At the session of the general assembly next after the first apportionment under this constitution, the senators shall be divided by lot, as equally as may be, into two classes; the seats of the first class shall be vacated at the end of two years from the day of the election, and those of the second class at the end of four years, so that one-half shall be chosen every two years.

Sec. 13. The number of representatives shall be one hundred, and the number of senators thirty-eight.

Sec. 14. At every apportionment of representation, the State shall be laid off into thirty-eight senatorial districts, which shall be so formed as to contain, as near as may be, an equal number of qualified voters, and so that no county shall be divided in the formation of a senatorial district, except such county shall be entitled, under the enumeration, to two or more senators; and where two or more counties compose a district they shall be adjoining.

SEC. 15. One senator for each district shall be elected by the qualified voters therein, who shall vote in the precincts where they reside, at the places where elections are by law directed to be held.

SEC. 16. No person shall be a senator who, at the time of his election, is not a citizen of the United States, has not attained the age of thirty years, and who has not resided in this State six years next preceding his election, and the last year thereof in the district for which he may be chosen.

SEC. 17. The election for senators, next after the first apportionment under this constitution, shall be general throughout the State, and at the same time that the election for representatives is held, and thereafter there shall be a biennial election for senators to fill the places of those whose term of service may have expired.

SEC. 18. The general assembly shall convene on the first Monday in November, after the adoption of this constitution, and again on the first Monday in November, 1851, and on the same day of every second year thereafter, unless a different day be appointed by law, and their sessions shall be held at the seat of government.

SEC. 19. Not less than a majority of the members of each house of the general assembly shall constitute a quorum to do business, but a smaller number may adjourn from day to day, and shall be authorized by law to compel the attendance of absent members in such manner and under such penalties as may be prescribed thereby.

SEC. 20. Each house of the general assembly shall judge of the qualifications, elections, and returns of its members; but a contested election shall be determined in such manner as shall be directed by law.

SEC. 21. Each house of the general assembly may determine the rules of its proceedings, punish a member for disorderly behavior, and, with the concurrence of two-thirds, expel a member, but not a second time for the same cause.

SEC. 22. Each house of the general assembly shall keep and publish, weekly, a journal of its proceedings, and the yeas and nays of the members on any question shall, at the desire of any two of them, be entered on their journal.

SEC. 23. Neither house, during the session of the general assembly, shall, without the consent of the other, adjourn for more than three days, nor to any other place than that in which they may be sitting.

SEC. 24. The members of the general assembly shall severally receive from the public treasury a compensation for their services, which shall be three dollars a day during their attendance on, and twelve and a half cents per mile for the necessary travel in going to, and returning from, the sessions of their respective houses: *Provided*, That the same may be increased or diminished by law; but no alteration shall take effect during the session at which such alteration shall be made; nor shall a session of the general assembly continue beyond sixty days, except by a vote of two-thirds of all the members elected to each house, but this shall not apply to the first session held under this constitution.

SEC. 25. The members of the general assembly shall, in all cases except treason, felony, breach or surety of the peace, be privileged from arrest during their attendance at the sessions of their respective houses, and in going to and returning from the same; and for any speech or debate in either house, they shall not be questioned in any other place.

SEC. 26. No senator or representative shall, during the term for which he was elected, nor for one year thereafter, be appointed or elected to any civil office of profit under this commonwealth, which shall have been created, or the emoluments of which shall have been increased, during the said term, except to such offices or appointments as may be filled by the election of the people.

SEC. 27. No person, while he continues to exercise the functions of a clergyman, priest, or teacher of any religious persuasion, society, or sect, nor while he holds or exercises any office of profit under this commonwealth, or under the Government of the United States, shall be eligible to the general assembly, except attorneys at law, justices of the peace, and militia officers: *Provided*, That attorneys for the commonwealth, who receive a fixed annual salary, shall be ineligible.

SEC. 28. No person who at any time may have been a collector of taxes or public moneys for the State, or the assistant or deputy of such collector, shall be eligible to the general assembly unless he shall have obtained a quietus, six months before the election, for the amount of such collection, and for all public moneys for which he may have been responsible.

SEC. 29. No bill shall have the force of a law until, on three several days, it be read over in each house of the general assembly, and free discussion allowed thereon, unless, in cases of urgency, four-fifths of the house where the bill shall be depending may deem it expedient to dispense with this rule.

SEC. 30. All bills for raising revenue shall originate in the house of representatives, but the senate may propose amendments, as in other bills: *Provided*, That they shall not introduce any new matter, under color of amendment, which does not relate to raising revenue.

SEC. 31. The general assembly shall regulate by law by whom and in what manner writs of election shall be issued to fill the vacancies which may happen in either branch thereof.

SEC. 32. The general assembly shall have no power to grant divorces, to change the names of individuals, or direct the sales of estates belonging to infants or other persons laboring under legal disabilities by special legislation; but by general laws shall confer such powers on the courts of justice.

SEC. 33. The credit of this commonwealth shall never be given or loaned in aid of any person, association, municipality, or corporation.

SEC. 34. The general assembly shall have no power to pass laws to diminish the resources of the sinking fund, as now established by law, until the debt of the State be paid, but may pass laws to increase them; and the whole resources of said fund, from year to year, shall be sacredly set apart and applied to the payment of the interest and principal of the State debt, and to no other use or purpose, until the whole debt of the State is fully paid and satisfied.

SEC. 35. The general assembly may contract debts to meet casual deficits or failures in the revenue; but such debts, direct or contingent, singly or in the aggregate, shall not at any time exceed five hundred thousand dollars; and the moneys arising from loans creating such debts shall be applied to the purposes for which they were obtained or to repay such debts: *Provided*, That the State may contract debts to repel invasion, suppress insurrection, or, if hostilities are threatened, provide for the public defence.

SEC. 36. No act of the general assembly shall authorize any debt to be contracted on behalf of the commonwealth, except for the purposes mentioned in the thirty-fifth section of this article, unless provision be made therein to lay and collect an annual tax sufficient to pay the interest stipulated, and to discharge the debt within thirty years; nor shall such act take effect until it shall have been submitted to the people at a general election, and shall have received a majority of all the votes cast for or against it: *Provided*, That the general assembly may contract debts, by borrowing money to pay any part of the debt of the State, without submission to the people, and without making provision in the act authorizing the same for a tax to discharge the debt so contracted, or the interest thereon.

SEC. 37. No law enacted by the general assembly shall relate to more than one subject, and that shall be expressed in the title.

SEC. 38. The general assembly shall not change the venue in any criminal or penal prosecution, but shall provide for the same by general laws.

SEC. 39. The general assembly may pass laws authorizing writs of error in criminal or penal cases, and regulating the right of challenge of jurors therein.

SEC. 40. The general assembly shall have no power to pass any act or resolution for the appropriation of any money, or the creation of any debt, exceeding the sum of one hundred dollars, at any one time, unless the same, on its final passage, shall be voted for by a majority of all the members then elected to each branch of the general assembly, and the yeas and nays thereon entered on the journal.

ARTICLE III

CONCERNING THE EXECUTIVE DEPARTMENT

SECTION 1. The supreme executive power of the commonwealth shall be vested in a chief magistrate, who shall be styled the governor of the commonwealth of Kentucky.

SEC. 2. The governor shall be elected for the term of four years, by the qualified voters of the State, at the time when and places where they shall respectively vote for representatives. The person having the highest number of votes shall be governor; but if two or more shall be equal and highest in votes, the election shall be determined by lot, in such manner as the general assembly may direct.

SEC. 3. The governor shall be ineligible for the succeeding four years after the expiration of the term for which he shall have been elected.

SEC. 4. He shall be at least thirty-five years of age, and a citizen of the United States, and have been an inhabitant of this State at least six years next preceding his election.

SEC. 5. He shall commence the execution of the duties of his office on the fifth Tuesday succeeding the day of the general election on which he shall have been chosen, and shall continue in the execution thereof until his successor shall have taken the oath or affirmation prescribed by this constitution.

SEC. 6. No member of Congress, or person holding any office under the United States, or minister of any religious society, shall be eligible to the office of governor.

SEC. 7. The governor shall, at stated times, receive for his services a compensation, which shall neither be increased nor diminished during the term for which he was elected.

SEC. 8. He shall be commander-in-chief of the army and navy of this commonwealth, and of the militia thereof, except when they shall be called into the service of the United States; but he shall not command personally in the field, unless advised so to do by a resolution of the general assembly.

SEC. 9. He shall have power to fill vacancies that may occur, by granting commissions, which shall expire when such vacancies shall have been filled according to the provisions of this constitution.

SEC. 10. He shall have power to remit fines and forfeitures, grant reprieves and pardons, except in cases of impeachment. In cases of treason, he shall have power to grant reprieves until the end of the next session of the general assembly, in which the power of pardoning shall be vested; but he shall have no power to remit the fees of the clerk, sheriff, or commonwealth's attorney in penal or criminal cases.

SEC. 11. He may require information, in writing, from the officers in the executive department upon any subject relating to the duties of their respective offices.

SEC. 12. He shall, from time to time, give to the general assembly information of the state of the commonwealth, and recommend to their consideration such measures as he may deem expedient.

SEC. 13. He may, on extraordinary occasions, convene the general assembly at the seat of government, or at a different place if that should have become, since their last adjournment, dangerous from an enemy, or from contagious disorders; and in case of disagreement between the two houses, with respect to the time of adjournment, he may adjourn them to such time as he shall think proper, not exceeding four months.

SEC. 14. He shall take care that the laws be faithfully executed.

SEC. 15. A lieutenant-governor shall be chosen at every regular election of governor, in the same manner, to continue in office for the same time, and possess the same qualifications, as the governor. In voting for governor and lieutenant-governor, the electors shall state for whom they vote as governor and for whom as lieutenant-governor.

SEC. 16. He shall, by virtue of his office, be speaker of the senate, have a right, when in committee of the whole, to debate and vote on all subjects, and, when the senate are equally divided, to give the casting vote.

SEC. 17. Should the governor be impeached, removed from office, die, refuse to qualify, resign, or be absent from the State, the lieutenant-governor shall exercise all the power and authority appertaining to the office of governor, until another be duly elected and qualified, or the governor absent or impeached shall return or be acquitted.

SEC. 18. Whenever the government shall be administered by the lieutenant-governor, or he shall fail to attend as speaker of the senate, the senators shall elect one of their own members as speaker for that occasion. And if, during the vacancy of the office of governor, the lieutenant-governor shall be impeached, removed from office, refuse to qualify, resign, die, or be absent from the State, the speaker of the senate shall, in like manner, administer the government: *Provided,* That whenever a vacancy shall occur in the office of governor, before the first two years of the term shall have expired, a new election for governor shall take place to fill such vacancy.

SEC. 19. The lieutenant-governor, or speaker *pro tempore* of the senate, while he acts as speaker of the senate, shall receive for his services the same compensation which shall, for the same period, be allowed to the speaker of the house of representatives, and no more; and during the time he administers the government, as governor, shall receive the same compensation which the governor would have received had he been employed in the duties of his office.

SEC. 20. If the lieutenant-governor shall be called upon to administer the government, and shall, while in such administration, resign, die, or be absent from the State during the recess of the general assembly, it shall be the duty of the secretary of state, for the time being, to convene the senate for the purpose of choosing a speaker.

SEC. 21. The governor shall nominate and, by and with the advice and consent of the senate, appoint a secretary of state, who shall be commissioned during the term for which the governor was elected, if he shall so long behave himself well. He shall keep a fair register, and attest all the official acts of the governor, and shall, when required, lay the same, and all papers, minutes, and vouchers relative thereto, before either house of the general assembly; and shall perform such other duties as may be required of him by law.

SEC. 22. Every bill which shall have passed both houses shall be presented to the governor. If he approve, he shall sign it; but if not, he shall return it, with his objections, to the house in which it originated, who shall enter the objections at large upon their journal, and proceed to reconsider it. If, after such reconsideration, a majority of all the members elected to that house shall agree to pass the bill, it shall be sent, with the objections, to the other house, by which it shall likewise be considered, and, if approved by a majority of all the members elected to that house, it shall be a law; but in such cases, the votes of both houses shall be determined by yeas and nays, and the names of the members voting for and against the bill shall be entered upon the journals of each house respectively. If any bill shall not be returned by the governor within ten days (Sundays excepted) after it shall have been presented to him, it shall be a law, in like manner as if he had signed it, unless the general assembly, by their adjournment, prevent its return; in which case it shall be a law, unless sent back within three days after their next meeting.

SEC. 23. Every order, resolution, or vote in which the concurrence of both houses may be necessary, except on a question of adjournment, shall be presented to the governor, and before it shall take effect be approved by him; or, being disapproved, shall be repassed by a majority of all the members elected to both houses, according to the rules and limitations prescribed in case of a bill.

SEC. 24. Contested elections for governor and lieutenant-governor shall be determined by both houses of the general assembly, according to such regulations as may be established by law.

SEC. 25. A treasurer shall be elected by the qualified voters of the State, for the term of two years; and an auditor of public accounts, register of the land-office, and attorney-general for the term of four years. The duties and responsibilities of these officers shall be prescribed by law: *Provided*, That inferior State officers, not specially provided for in this constitution, may be appointed or elected, in such manner as shall be prescribed by law, for a term not exceeding four years.

SEC. 26. The first election under this constitution for governor, lieutenant-governor, treasurer, auditor of public acocunts, register of the land-office, and attorney-general shall be held on the first Monday in August, in the year 1851.

ARTICLE IV

CONCERNING THE JUDICIAL DEPARTMENT

SECTION 1. The judicial power of this commonwealth, both as to matters of law and equity, shall be vested in one supreme court, (to be styled the court of appeals,) the courts established by this constitution, and such courts, inferior to the supreme court, as the general assembly may, from time to time, erect and establish.

CONCERNING THE COURT OF APPEALS

SEC. 2. The court of appeals shall have appellate jurisdiction only, which shall be coextensive with the State, under such restrictions and regulations, not repugnant to this constitution, as may, from time to time, be prescribed by law.

SEC. 3. The judges of the court of appeals shall, after their first term, hold their offices for eight years, from and after their election, and until their successors shall be duly qualified, subject to the conditions hereinafter prescribed; but for any reasonable cause the governor shall remove any of them on the address of two-thirds of each house of the general assembly: *Provided, however*, That the cause or causes for which such removal may be required shall be stated at length in such address and on the journal of each house. They shall, at stated times, receive for their services an adequate compensation, to be fixed by law, which shall not be diminished during the time for which they shall have been elected.

SEC. 4. The court of appeals shall consist of four judges, any three of whom may constitute a court for the transaction of business. The general assembly, at its first session after the adoption of this constitution, shall divide the State, by counties, into four districts, as nearly equal in voting population and with as convenient limits as may be, in each of which the qualified voters shall elect one judge of the court of appeals: *Provided*, That whenever a vacancy shall occur in said court, from any cause, the general assembly shall have the power to reduce the number of judges and districts; but in no event shall there be less than three judges and districts. Should a change in the number of the judges of the court of appeals be made, the term of office and number of districts shall be so changed as to preserve the principle of electing one judge every two years.

SEC. 5. The judges shall, by virtue of their offices, be conservators of the peace throughout the State. The style of all process shall be " The Commonwealth of Kentucky." All prosecutions shall be carried on in the name and by the authority of the commonwealth of Kentucky, and conclude " against the peace and dignity of the same."

SEC. 6. The judges first elected shall serve as follows, to wit: One shall serve until the first Monday in August, 1852; one until the first Monday in August, 1854; one until the first Monday in August, 1856, and one until the first Monday in August, 1858. The judges, at the first term of the court succeeding their election, shall determine, by lot, the length of time which each one shall serve; and at the expiration of the service of each an election in the proper district shall take place to fill the vacancy. The judge having the shortest time to serve shall be styled the chief justice of Kentucky.

SEC. 7. If a vacancy shall occur in said court from any cause, the governor shall issue a writ of election to the proper district to fill such vacancy for the residue of the term: *Provided*, That if the unexpired term be less than one year, the governor shall appoint a judge to fill such vacancy.

SEC. 8. No person shall be eligible to the office of judge of the court of appeals who is not a citizen of the United States, a resident of the district for which he may be a candidate two years next preceding his election, at least thirty years of age, and who has not been a practising lawyer eight years, or whose service upon the bench of any court of record, when added to the time he may have practised law, shall not be equal to eight years.

SEC. 9. The court of appeals shall hold its sessions at the seat of government, unless otherwise directed by law; but the general assembly may, from time to time, direct that said court shall hold sessions in any one or more of said districts.

SEC. 10. The first election of the judges and clerks of the court of appeals shall take place on the second Monday in May, 1851, and thereafter, in each district, as a vacancy may occur, by the expiration of the term of office; and the judges of the said court shall be commissioned by the governor.

SEC. 11. There shall be elected, by the qualified voters of this State, a clerk of the court of appeals, who shall hold his office, from the first election, until the first Monday in August, 1858, and thereafter for the term of eight years from and after his election; and should the general assembly provide for holding the court of appeals in any one or more of said districts, they shall also provide for the election of a clerk by the qualified voters of such district, who shall hold his office for eight years, possess the same qualifications, and be subject to removal in the same manner, as the clerk of the court of appeals; but if the general assembly shall, at its first or any other session, direct the court of appeals to hold its sessions in more than one district, a clerk shall be elected by the qualified voters of such district. And the clerk first provided for in this section shall be elected by the qualified voters of the other district or districts. The same principle shall be observed whenever the court shall be directed to hold its sessions in either of the other districts. Should the number of judges be reduced, the term of the office of clerk shall be six years.

SEC. 12. No person shall be eligible to the office of clerk of the court of appeals, unless he be a citizen of the United States, a resident of the State two years next preceding his election, of the age of twenty-one years, and have a certificate from a judge of the court of appeals, or a judge of a circuit court, that he has been examined by the clerk of his court, under his supervision, and that he is qualified for the office for which he is a candidate.

SEC. 13. Should a vacancy occur in the office of clerk of the court of appeals, the governor shall issue a writ of election, and the qualified voters of the State, or of the district in which the vacancy may occur, shall elect a clerk of the court of appeals, to serve until the end of the term for which such clerk was elected: *Provided*, That when a vacancy shall occur from any cause, or the clerk be under charges upon information, the judges of the court of appeals shall have power to appoint a clerk *pro tempore*, to perform the duties of clerk until such vacancy shall be filled or the clerk acquitted: *And provided further*, That no writ of election shall issue to fill a vacancy unless the unexpired term exceed one year.

SEC. 14. The general assembly shall direct, by law, the mode and manner of conducting and making due returns to the secretary of state of all elections of the judges and clerk or clerks of the court of appeals, and of determining contested elections of any of these officers.

SEC. 15. The general assembly shall provide for an additional judge or judges, to constitute, with the remaining judge or judges, a special court for the trial of such cause or causes as may, at any time, be pending in the court of appeals, on the trial of which a majority of the judges cannot sit, on account of interest in the event of the cause, or on account of their relationship to either party, or when a judge may have been employed in or decided the cause in the inferior court.

CONCERNING THE CIRCUIT COURTS

SEC. 16. A circuit court shall be established in each county now existing, or which may hereafter be erected in this commonwealth.

SEC. 17. The jurisdiction of said court shall be and remain as now established, hereby giving to the general assembly the power to change or alter it.

SEC. 18. The right to appeal or sue out a writ of error to the court of appeals shall remain as it now exists, until altered by law, hereby giving to the general assembly the power to change, alter, or modify said right.

SEC. 19. At the first session after the adoption of this constitution, the general assembly shall divide the State into twelve judicial districts, having due regard to business, territory, and population: *Provided*, That no county shall be divided.

SEC. 20. They shall, at the same time that the judicial districts are laid off, direct elections to be held in each district, to elect a judge for said district, and shall prescribe in what manner the election shall be conducted. The first election of judges of the circuit court shall take place on the second Monday in May, 1851; and afterwards on the first Monday in August, 1856, and on the first Monday in August in every sixth year thereafter.

SEC. 21. All persons qualified to vote for members of the general assembly, in each district, shall have the right to vote for judges.

SEC. 22. No person shall be eligible as judge of the circuit court who is not a citizen of the United States, a resident of the district for which he may be a candidate two years next preceding his election, at least thirty years of age, and who has not been a practising lawyer eight years, or whose service upon the bench of any court of record, when added to the time he may have practised law, shall not be equal to eight years.

SEC. 23. The judges of the circuit court shall, after their first term, hold their office for the term of six years from the day of their election. They shall be commissioned by the governor, and continue in office until their successors be qualified, but shall be removable from office in the same manner as the judges of the court of appeals; and the removal of a judge from his district shall vacate his office.

SEC. 24. The general assembly, if they deem it necessary, may establish one additional district every four years, but the judicial districts shall not exceed sixteen, until the population of this State shall exceed one million five hundred thousand.

SEC. 25. The judges of the circuit courts shall, at stated times, receive for their services an adequate compensation, to be fixed by law, which shall be equal and uniform throughout the State, and which shall not be diminished during the time for which they were elected.

SEC. 26. If a vacancy shall occur in the office of judge of the circuit court, the governor shall issue a writ of election to fill such vacancy for the residue of the term: *Provided*, That if the unexpired term be less than one year, the governor shall appoint a judge to fill such vacancy.

SEC. 27. The judicial districts of this State shall not be changed, except at the first session after an enumeration, unless when a new district may be established.

SEC. 28. The general assembly shall provide by law for holding circuit courts when, from any cause, the judge shall fail to attend, or, if in attendance, cannot properly preside.

CONCERNING COUNTY COURTS

SEC. 29. A county court shall be established in each county now existing, or which may hereafter be erected within this commonwealth, to consist of a presiding judge and two associate judges, any two of whom shall constitute a court for the transaction of business: *Provided*, The general assembly may at any time abolish the office of the associate judges, whenever it shall be deemed expedient; in which event they may associate with said court any or all of the justices of the peace for the transaction of business.

SEC. 30. The judges of the county court shall be elected, by the qualified voters in each county, for the term of four years, and shall continue in office until their successors be duly qualified, and shall receive such compensation for their services as may be provided by law.

SEC. 31. The first election of county-court judges shall take place at the same time of the election of judges of the circuit court. The presiding judge, first elected, shall hold his office until the first Monday in August, 1854. The associate judges shall hold their offices until the first Monday in August, 1852, and until their successors be qualified; and afterwards elections shall be held on the first Monday in August, in the years in which vacancies regularly occur.

SEC. 32. No person shall be eligible to the office of presiding or associate judge of the county court, unless he be a citizen of the United States, over twenty-one years of age, and shall have been a resident of the county in which he shall be chosen one year next preceding the election.

SEC. 33. The jurisdiction of the county court shall be regulated by law; and, until changed, shall be the same now vested in the county courts of this State.

SEC. 34. Each county in this State shall be laid off into districts of convenient size, as the general assembly may from time to time direct. Two justices of the peace shall be elected in each district, by the qualified voters therein, at such time and place as may be prescribed by law, for the term of four years, whose jurisdiction shall be coextensive with the county. No person shall be eligible as a justice of the peace unless he be a citizen of the United States, twenty-one years of age, and a resident of the district in which he may be candidate.

SEC. 35. Judges of the county court, and justices of the peace, shall be conservators of the peace. They shall be commissioned by the governor. County and district officers shall vacate their offices by removal from the district or county in which they shall be appointed. The general assembly shall provide by law the manner of conducting and making due return of all elections of judges of the county court and justices of the peace, and for determining contested elections, and provide the mode of filling vacancies in these offices.

SEC. 36. Judges of the county court and justices of the peace, sheriffs, coroners, surveyors, jailers, county assessor, attorney for the county, and constables shall be subject to indictment or presentment for malfeasance or misfeasance in office, or wilful neglect in the discharge of their official duties, in such mode as may be prescribed by law, subject to appeal to the court of appeals; and, upon conviction, their offices shall become vacant.

SEC. 37. The general assembly may provide by law that the justices of the peace in each county shall sit at the court of claims, and assist in laying the county levy and making appropriations only.

SEC. 38. When any city or town shall have a separate representation, such city or town, and the county in which it is located, may have such separate municipal courts and executive and ministerial officers as the general assembly may, from time to time, provide.

SEC. 39. The clerks of the court of appeals, circuit and county courts, shall be removable from office by the court of appeals, upon information and good cause shown. The court shall be judges of the fact as well as the law. Two-thirds of the members present must concur in the sentence.

SEC. 40. The Louisville chancery court shall exist under this constitution, subject to repeal, and its jurisdiction to enlargement and modification by the general assembly. The chancellor shall have the same qualifications as a circuit-court judge, and the clerk of said court as a clerk of a circuit court, and the marshal of said court as a sheriff; and the general assembly shall provide for the election, by the qualified voters within its jurisdiction, of the chancellor, clerk, and marshal of said court, at the same time that the judge and clerk of the circuit court are elected for the county of Jefferson, and they shall hold their offices for the same time, and shall be removable in the same manner: *Provided*, That the marshal of said court shall be ineligible for the succeeding term.

SEC. 41. The city court of Louisville, the Lexington city court, and all other police-courts established in any city or town, shall remain, until otherwise directed by law, with their present powers and jurisdictions; and the judges, clerks, and marshals of such courts shall have the same qualifications, and shall be elected by the qualified voters of such cities or towns at the same time, and in the same manner, and hold their offices for the same term, as county judges, clerks, and sheriffs, respectively, and shall be liable to removal in the same manner. The general assembly may vest judicial powers, for police purposes, in mayors of cities, police judges, and trustees of towns.

Article V

Concerning Impeachments

SECTION 1. The house of representatives shall have the sole power of impeachment.

SEC. 2. All impeachments shall be tried by the senate. When sitting for that purpose, the senators shall be upon oath or affirmation. No person shall be convicted without the concurrence of two-thirds of the members present.

SEC. 3. The governor and all civil officers shall be liable to impeachment for any misdemeanor in office; but judgment in such cases shall not extend further than to removal from office, and disqualification to hold any office of honor, trust, or profit under this commonwealth; but the party convicted shall, nevertheless, be subject and liable to indictment, trial, and punishment by law.

Article VI

Concerning Executive and Ministerial Officers for Counties and Districts

SECTION 1. A commonwealth's attorney for each judicial district, and a circuit-court clerk for each county, shall be elected, whose term of office shall be the same as that of the circuit judges; also, a county-court clerk, an attorney, surveyor, coroner, and jailer, for each county, whose term of office shall be the same as that of the presiding judge of the county court.

SEC. 2. No person shall be eligible to the offices mentioned in this article who is not at the time twenty-four years old, (except clerks of county and circuit courts, sheriffs, constables, and county attorneys who shall be eligible at the age of twenty-one years,) a citizen of the United States, and who has not resided two years next preceding the election in the State, and one year in the county or district for which he is a candidate. No person shall be eligible to the office of commonwealth's or county attorney unless he shall have been a licensed practicing attorney for two years. No person shall be eligible to the office of clerk unless he shall have procured from a judge of the court of appeals, or a judge of the circuit court, a certificate that he has been examined by the clerk of his court, under his supervision, and that he is qualified for the office for which he is a candidate.

SEC. 3. The commonwealth's attorney and circuit-court clerk shall be elected at the same time as the circuit judge—the commonwealth's attorney by the qualified voters of the district, the circuit-court clerk by the qualified voters of the county. The county attorney, clerk, surveyor, coroner, and jailer shall be elected at the same time and in the same manner as the presiding judge of the county court.

SEC. 4. A sheriff shall be elected in each county by the qualified voters thereof, whose term of office shall, after the first term, be two years, and until his successor be qualified; and he shall be reëligible for a second term; but no sheriff shall, after the expiration of the second term, be reëligible, or act as deputy, for the succeeding term. The first election of sheriff shall be on the second Monday in May, 1851; and the sheriffs then elected shall hold their offices until the first Monday in January, 1853, and until their successors be qualified; and on the first Monday in August, 1852, and on the first Monday of August in every second year thereafter, elections for sheriffs shall be held: *Provided*, That the sheriffs first elected shall enter upon the duties of their respective offices on the first Monday in June, 1851, and after the first election on the first Monday in January next succeeding their election.

SEC. 5. A constable shall be elected in every justice's district, who shall be chosen for two years, at such time and place as may be provided by law, whose jurisdiction shall be coextensive with the county in which he may reside.

SEC. 6. Officers for towns and cities shall be elected for such terms, and in such manner, and with such qualifications as may be prescribed by law.

SEC. 7. Vacancies in offices under this article shall be filled, until the next regular election, in such manner as the general assembly may provide.

SEC. 8. When a new county shall be erected, officers for the same, to serve until the next stated election, shall be elected or appointed in such a way and at such times as the general assembly may prescribe.

SEC. 9. Clerks, sheriffs, surveyors, coroners, constables, and jailers, and such other officers as the general assembly may from time to time require, shall, before they enter upon the duties of their respective offices, and as often thereafter as may be deemed proper, give such bond and security as shall be prescribed by law.

SEC. 10. The general assembly may provide for the election or appointment, for a term not exceeding four years, of such other county or district ministerial and executive officers as shall, from time to time, be necessary and proper.

SEC. 11. A county assessor shall be elected in each county at the same time and for the same term that the presiding judge of the county court is elected, until otherwise provided for by law. He shall have power to appoint such assistants as may be necessary and proper.

ARTICLE VII

CONCERNING THE MILITIA

SECTION 1. The militia of this commonwealth shall consist of all free, able-bodied male persons (negroes, mulattoes, and Indians excepted) resident in the same, between the ages of eighteen and forty-five years; except such persons as now are, or hereafter may be, exempted by the laws of the United States or of this State; but those who belong to religious societies, whose tenets forbid them to carry arms, shall not be compelled to do so, but shall pay an equivalent for personal services.

SEC. 2. The governor shall appoint the adjutant-general and his other staff-officers; the major-generals, brigadier-generals, and commandants of regiments shall respectively appoint their staff-officers; and commandants of companies shall appoint their non-commissioned officers.

SEC. 3. All militia officers, whose appointment is not herein otherwise provided for, shall be elected by persons subject to military duty within their respective companies, battalions, regiments, brigades, and divisions, under such rules and regulations, and for such terms, not exceeding six years, as the general assembly may, from time to time, direct and establish.

ARTICLE VIII

GENERAL PROVISIONS

SECTION 1. Members of the general assembly, and all officers, before they enter upon the execution of the duties of their respective offices, and all members of the bar, before they enter upon the practice of their profession, shall take the following oath or affirmation: " I do solemnly swear [or affirm, as the case may be] that I will support the Constitution of the United States and the constitution of this State, and be faithful and true to the commonwealth of Kentucky so long as I continue a citizen thereof, and that I will faithfully execute, to the best of my abilities, the office of ———, according to law; and I do further solemnly swear [or affirm] that since the adoption of the present constitution I, being a citizen of this State, have not fought a duel, with deadly weapons, within this State, nor out of it, with a citizen of this State, nor have I sent or accepted a challenge to fight a duel, with deadly weapons, with a citizen of this State; nor have I acted as second in carrying a challenge, or aided or assisted any person thus offending: So help me God."

SEC. 2. Treason against the commonwealth shall consist only in levying war against it, or in adhering to its enemies, giving them aid and comfort. No person shall be convicted of treason unless on the testimony of two witnesses to the same overt act, or his own confession in open court.

SEC. 3. Every person shall be disqualified from holding any office of trust or profit for the term for which he shall have been elected, who shall be convicted of having given or offered any bribe or treat to procure his election.

SEC. 4. Laws shall be made to exclude from office and from suffrage those who shall thereafter be convicted of bribery, perjury, forgery, or other crimes or high misdemeanors. The privilege of free suffrage shall be supported by laws regulating elections, and prohibiting, under adequate penalties, all undue influence thereon from power, bribery, tumult, or other improper practices.

SEC. 5. No money shall be drawn from the treasury but in pursuance of appropriations made by law, nor shall any appropriations of money for the support of an army be made for a longer time than two years, and a regular statement and account of the receipts and expenditures of all public money shall be published annually.

SEC. 6. The general assembly may direct, by law, in what manner, and in what courts, suits may be brought against the commonwealth.

SEC. 7. The manner of administering an oath or affirmation shall be such as is most consistent with the conscience of the deponent, and shall be esteemed by the general assembly the most solemn appeal to God.

SEC. 8. All laws which, on the first day of June, one thousand seven hundred and ninety-two, were in force in the State of Virginia, and which are of a general nature, and not local to that State, and not repugnant to this constitution, nor to the laws which have been enacted by the general assembly of this commonwealth, shall be in force within this State, until they shall be altered or repealed by the general assembly.

SEC. 9. The compact with the State of Virginia, subject to such alterations as may be made therein agreeably to the mode prescribed by the said compact, shall be considered as part of this constitution.

SEC. 10. It shall be the duty of the general assembly to pass such laws as shall be necessary and proper to decide differences by arbitrators, to be appointed by the parties who may choose that summary mode of adjustment.

SEC. 11. All civil officers for the commonwealth at large shall reside within the State, and all district, county, or town officers, within their respective districts, counties, or towns, (trustees of towns excepted,) and shall keep their offices at such places therein as may be required by law; and all militia officers shall reside in the bounds of the division, brigade, regiment, battalion, or company to which they may severally belong.

SEC. 12. Absence on the business of this State, or the United States, shall not forfeit a residence once obtained, so as to deprive any one of the right of suffrage, or of being elected or appointed to any office under this commonwealth, under the exception contained in this constitution.

SEC. 13. It shall be the duty of the general assembly to regulate, by law, in what cases, and what deductions from the salaries of public officers shall be made, for neglect of duty in their official capacity.

SEC. 14. Returns of all elections by the people shall be made to the secretary of state, for the time being, except in those cases otherwise provided for in this constitution, or which shall be otherwise directed by law.

SEC. 15. In all elections by the people, and also by the senate and house of representatives, jointly or separately, the votes shall be personally and publicly given *viva voce: Provided*, That dumb persons, entitled to suffrage, may vote by ballot.

SEC. 16. All elections by the people shall be held between the hours of six o'clock in the morning and seven o'clock in the evening.

SEC. 17. The general assembly shall, by law, prescribe the time when the several officers authorized or directed by this constitution to be elected or appointed shall enter upon the duties of their respective offices, except where the time is fixed by this constitution.

SEC. 18. No member of Congress, nor person holding or exercising any office of trust or profit under the United States, or either of them, or under any foreign power, shall be eligible as a member of the general assembly of this commonwealth, or hold or exercise any office of trust or profit under the same.

SEC. 19. The general assembly shall direct by law how persons who now are, or who may hereafter become, securities for public officers may be relieved or discharged on account of such securityship.

SEC. 20. Any person who shall, after the adoption of this constitution, either directly or indirectly, give, accept, or knowingly carry a challenge to any person or persons to fight in single combat, with a citizen of this State, with any deadly weapon, either in or out of the State, shall be deprived of the right to hold any office of honor or profit in this commonwealth, and shall be punished otherwise in such manner as the general assembly may prescribe by law.

SEC. 21. The governor shall have power, after five years from the time of the offence, to pardon all persons who shall have in anywise participated in a duel, either as principals, seconds, or otherwise, and to restore him or them to all the rights, privileges, and immunities to which he or they were entitled before such participation. And upon the presentation of such pardon, the oath prescribed in the first section of this article shall be varied to suit the case.

SEC. 22. At its first session after the adoption of this constitution the general assembly shall appoint not more than three persons, learned in the law, whose duty it shall be to revise and arrange the statute laws of this commonwealth, both civil and criminal, so as to have but one law on any one subject; and also three other persons, learned in the law, whose duty it shall be to prepare a code of practice for the courts, both civil and criminal, in this commonwealth, by abridging and simplifying the rules of practice and laws in relation thereto; all of whom shall, at as early a day as practicable, report the result of their labors to the general assembly for their adoption or modification.

SEC. 23. So long as the board of internal improvement shall be continued, the president thereof shall be elected by the qualified voters of this commonwealth, and hold the office for the term of four years, and until another be duly elected and qualified. The election shall be held at the same time, and be conducted in the same manner, as the election of governor of this commonwealth under this constitution; but nothing herein contained shall prevent the general assembly from abolishing said board of internal improvement, or the office of president thereof.

SEC. 24. The general assembly shall provide, by law, for the trial of any contested election of auditor, register, treasurer, attorney-general, judges of circuit courts, and all other officers not otherwise herein specified.

SEC. 25. The general assembly shall provide by law for the making of the returns, by the proper officers, of the election of all officers to be elected under this constitution; and the governor shall issue commissions to the auditor, register, treasurer, president of the board of internal improvement, superintendent of public instruction, and such other officers as he may be directed by law to commission, as soon as he has ascertained the result of the election of those officers respectively.

SEC. 26. When a vacancy shall happen in the office of attorney-general, auditor of public accounts, treasurer, register of the land-office, president of the board of internal improvement, or superintendent of public instruction, the governor, in the recess of the senate, shall have power to fill the vacancy, by granting commissions which shall expire at the end of the next session, and shall fill the vacancy for the balance of the time by and with the advice and consent of the senate.

ARTICLE IX

CONCERNING THE SEAT OF GOVERNMENT

The seat of government shall continue in the city of Frankfort until it shall be removed by law: *Provided, however*, That two-thirds of all the members elected to each house of the general assembly shall concur in the passage of such law.

ARTICLE X

CONCERNING SLAVES

SECTION 1. The general assembly shall have no power to pass laws for the emancipation of slaves without the consent of their owners, or without paying their owners, previous to such emancipation, a full equivalent in money for the slaves so emancipated, and providing for their removal from the State. They shall have no power to prevent immigrants to this State from bringing with them such persons as are deemed slaves by the laws of any of the United States, so long as any person of the same age or description shall be continued in slavery by the laws of this State. They shall pass laws to permit owners of slaves to emancipate them, saving the rights of creditors, and to prevent them from remaining in this State after they are emancipated. They shall have full power to prevent slaves being brought into this State as merchandise. They shall have full power to prevent slaves being brought into this State who have been, since the first day of January, one thousand seven hundred and eighty-nine, or may hereafter be, imported into any of the United States from a foreign country. And they shall have full power to pass such laws as may be necessary to oblige the owners of slaves to treat them with humanity; to provide for them necessary clothing and provisions; to abstain from all injuries to them, extending to life or limb; and in case of their neglect or refusal to comply with the directions of such laws, to have such slave or slaves sold for the benefit of their owner or owners.

SEC. 2. The general assembly shall pass laws providing that any free negro or mulatto hereafter immigrating to, and any slave hereafter emancipated in, and refusing to leave this State, or having left, shall return and settle within this State, shall be deemed guilty of felony, and punished by confinement in the penitentiary thereof.

SEC. 3. In the prosecution of slaves for felony, no inquest by a grand jury shall be necessary; but the proceedings in such prosecution shall be regulated by law, except that the general assembly shall have no power to deprive them of the privilege of an impartial trial by a petit jury.

Article XI

CONCERNING EDUCATION

SECTION 1. The capital of the fund called and known as the " common-school fund," consisting of one million two hundred and twenty-five thousand seven hundred and sixty-eight dollars and forty-two cents, for which bonds have been executed by the State to the board of education, and seventy-three thousand five hundred dollars of stock in the Bank of Kentucky; also, the sum of fifty-one thousand two hundred and twenty-three dollars and twenty-nine cents, balance of interest on the school-fund of the year 1848, unexpended, together with any sum which may be hereafter raised in the State by taxation, or otherwise, for purposes of education, shall be held inviolate, for the purpose of sustaining a system of common schools. The interest and dividends of said funds, together with any sum which may be produced for that purpose, by taxation or otherwise, may be appropriated in aid of common schools, but for no other purpose. The general assembly shall invest said fifty-one thousand two hundred and twenty-three dollars and twenty-nine cents in some safe and profitable manner; and any portion of the interest and dividends of said school-fund, or other money or property raised for school purposes, which may not be needed in sustaining common schools, shall be invested in like manner. The general assembly shall make provision, by law, for the payment of the interest of said school-fund: *Provided*, That each county shall be entitled to its proportion of the income of said fund, and if not called for for common-school purposes, it shall be reinvested from time to time for the benefit of such county.

SEC. 2. A superintendent of public instruction shall be elected by the qualified voters of this commonwealth at the same time the governor is elected, who shall hold his office for four years, and his duties and salary shall be prescribed and fixed by law.

Article XII

MODE OF REVISING THE CONSTITUTION

SECTION 1. When experience shall point out the necessity of amending this constitution, and when a majority of all the members elected to each house of the general assembly shall, within the first twenty days of any regular session, concur in passing a law for taking the sense of the good people of this commonwealth as to the necessity and expediency of calling a convention, it shall be the duty of the several sheriffs and other officers of elections, at the next general election which shall be held for representatives to the general assembly after the passage of such law, to open a poll for, and make return to the secretary of state, for the time being, of the names of all those entitled to vote for representatives who have voted calling a convention; and if, thereupon, it shall appear that a majority of all the citizens of this State entitled to vote for representatives have voted for calling a convention, the general assembly shall, at their next regular session, direct that a similar poll shall be opened and return made for the next election for representatives; and if, thereupon, it shall appear that a majority of all the citizens of this State entitled to vote for representatives have voted for calling a convention, the general assembly shall, at their next session, pass a law calling a convention, to consist of as many members as there shall be in the house of representatives, and no more, to be chosen on the first Monday in August thereafter, in the same manner and proportion, and at the same places, and possessed of the same qualifications of a qualified elector, by citizens entitled to vote for representatives, and to meet within three months after their election, for the purpose of readopting, amending, or changing this constitution; but if it shall appear by the vote of either year, as aforesaid, that a majority of all the citizens entitled to vote for representatives did not vote for calling a convention, a convention shall not then be called. And for the purpose of ascertaining whether a majority of the citizens, entitled to vote for representatives, did or did not vote for calling a convention, as above, the general assembly passing the law authorizing such vote shall provide for ascertaining the number of citizens entitled to vote for representatives within the State.

SEC. 2. The convention, when assembled, shall judge of the election of its members and decide contested elections, but the general assembly shall, in calling a convention, provide for taking testimony in such cases and for issuing a writ of election in case of a tie.

ARTICLE XIII

BILL OF RIGHTS

That the general, great, and essential principles of liberty and free government may be recognized and established, we declare—

SECTION 1. That all freemen, when they form a social compact, are equal, and that no man or set of men are entitled to exclusive, separate public emoluments or privileges from the community, but in consideration of public services.

SEC. 2. That absolute, arbitrary power over the lives, liberty, and property of freemen exists nowhere in a republic, not even in the largest majority.

SEC. 3. The right of property is before and higher than any constitutional sanction; and the right of the owner of a slave to such slave, and its increase, is the same, and as inviolable as the right of the owner of any property whatever.

SEC. 4. That all power is inherent in the people, and all free governments are founded on their authority, and instituted for their peace, safety, happiness, security, and the protection of property. For the advancement of these ends, they have at all times an inalienable and indefeasible right to alter, reform, or abolish their government, in such manner as they may think proper.

SEC. 5. That all men have a natural and indefeasible right to worship Almighty God according to the dictates of their own consciences; that no man shall be compelled to attend, erect, or support any place of worship, or to maintain any ministry against his consent; that no human authority ought, in any case whatever, to control or interfere with the rights of conscience; and that no preference shall ever be given, by law, to any religious societies or modes of worship.

SEC. 6. That the civil rights, privileges, or capacities of any citizen shall in no wise be diminished or enlarged on account of his religion.

SEC. 7. That all elections shall be free and equal.

SEC. 8. That the ancient mode of trial by jury shall be held sacred, and the right thereof remain inviolate, subject to such modifications as may be authorized by this constitution.

SEC. 9. That printing-presses shall be free to every person who undertakes to examine the proceedings of the general assembly, or any branch of government, and no law shall ever be made to restrain the right thereof. The free communication of thoughts and opinions is one of the invaluable rights of man, and every citizen may freely speak, write, and print on any subject, being responsible for the abuse of that liberty.

SEC. 10. In prosecutions for the publication of papers investigating the official conduct of officers or men in a public capacity, or where the matter published is proper for public information, the truth thereof may be given in evidence; and in all indictments for libels, the jury shall have a right to determine the law and the facts, under the direction of the court, as in other cases.

SEC. 11. That the people shall be secure in their persons, houses, papers, and possessions, from unreasonable seizures and searches, and that no warrant to search any place, or to seize any person or thing, shall issue, without describing them as nearly as may be, nor without probable cause, supported by oath or affirmation.

SEC. 12. That in all criminal prosecutions, the accused hath a right to be heard by himself and counsel; to demand the nature and cause of the accusation against him; to meet the witnesses face to face; to have compulsory process for obtaining witnesses in his favor; and, in prosecutions by indictment or information, a speedy public trial by an impartial jury of the vicinage; that he cannot be compelled to give evidence against himself; nor can he be deprived of his life, liberty, or property unless by the judgment of his peers or the law of the land.

SEC. 13. That no person shall, for any indictable offence, be proceeded against criminally, by information, except in cases arising in the land or naval forces, or in the militia when in actual service, in time of war or public danger, or by leave of the court, for oppression or misdemeanor in office.

SEC. 14. No person shall, for the same offence, be twice put in jeopardy of his life or limb; nor shall any man's property be taken or applied to public use without the consent of his representatives, and without just compensation being previously made to him.

SEC. 15. That all courts shall be open, and every person, for an injury done him in his lands, goods, person, or reputation, shall have remedy by the due course of law, and right and justice administered without sale, denial, or delay.

SEC. 16. That no power of suspending laws shall be exercised, unless by the general assembly, or its authority.

SEC. 17. That excessive bail shall not be required, nor excessive fines imposed, nor cruel punishments inflicted.

SEC. 18. That all prisoners shall be bailable by sufficient securities, unless for capital offences, when the proof is evident or presumption great; and the privilege of the writ of *habeas corpus* shall not be suspended, unless when, in cases of rebellion or invasion, the public safety may require it.

SEC. 19. That the person of a debtor, where there is not strong presumption of fraud, shall not be continued in prison after delivering up his estate for the benefit of his creditors, in such manner as shall be prescribed by law.

SEC. 20. That no *ex post facto* law, nor any law impairing contracts, shall be made.

SEC. 21. That no person shall be attainted of treason or felony by the general assembly.

SEC. 22. That no attainder shall work corruption of blood, nor, except during the life of the offender, forfeiture of estate to the commonwealth.

SEC. 23. That the estates of such persons as shall destroy their own lives shall descend or vest as in case of natural death; and if any person shall be killed by casualty, there shall be no forfeiture by reason thereof.

SEC. 24. That the citizens have a right, in a peaceable manner, to assemble together for their common good, and to apply to those invested with the powers of government for redress of grievances, or other proper purposes, by petition, address, or remonstrance.

SEC. 25. That the rights of the citizens to bear arms in defence of themselves and the State shall not be questioned; but the general assembly may pass laws to prevent persons from carrying concealed arms.

SEC. 26. That no standing army shall, in time of peace, be kept up, without the consent of the general assembly; and the military shall, in all cases and at all times, be in strict subordination to the civil power.

SEC. 27. That no soldier shall, in time of peace, be quartered in any house without the consent of the owner; nor in time of war, but in a manner to be prescribed by law.

SEC. 28. That the general assembly shall not grant any title of nobility, or hereditary distinction, nor create any office, the appointment to which shall be for a longer time than for a term of years.

SEC. 29. That emigration from the State shall not be prohibited.

SEC. 30. To guard against transgressions of the high powers which we have delegated, we declare that everything in this article is excepted out of the general powers of government, and shall forever remain inviolate, and that all laws contrary thereto, or contrary to this constitution, shall be void.

SCHEDULE

That no inconvenience may arise from the alterations and amendments made in the constitution of this commonwealth, and in order to carry the same into complete operation, it is hereby declared and ordained:

SECTION 1. That all the laws of this commonwealth, in force at the time of the adoption of this constitution, and not inconsistent therewith, and all rights, actions, prosecutions, claims, and contracts, as well of individuals as of bodies-corporate, shall continue as if this constitution had not been adopted.

SEC. 2. The oaths of office herein directed to be taken may be administered by any judge or justice of the peace, until the general assembly shall otherwise direct.

SEC. 3. No office shall be superseded by the adoption of this constitution, but the laws of the State relative to the duties of the several officers, legislative, executive, judicial, and military, shall remain in full force, though the same be contrary to this constitution, and the several duties shall be performed by the respective officers of the State, according to the existing laws, until the organization of the government, as provided for under this constitution, and the entering into office of the officers to be elected or appointed under said government, and no longer.

SEC. 4. It shall be the duty of the general assembly which shall convene in the year 1850 to make an apportionment of the representation of this State, upon the principle set forth in this constitution; and until the first apportionment shall be made as herein directed, the apportionment of senators and representatives among the several districts and counties in this State shall remain as at present fixed by law:*Provided*, That on the first Monday in August, 1850, all senators shall go out of office, and on that day an election for senators and representatives shall be held throughout the State, and those then elected shall hold their offices for one year, and no longer: *Provided, further*, That at the elections to be held in the year 1850, that provision in this constitution which requires voters to vote in the precinct within which they reside shall not apply.

SEC. 5. All recognizances heretofore taken, or which may be taken before the organization of the judicial department under this constitution, shall remain as valid as though this constitution had not been adopted, and may be prosecuted in the name of the commonwealth. All criminal prosecutions and penal actions which have arisen or may arise before the reorganization of the judicial department under this constitution, may be prosecuted to judgment and execution in the name of the commonwealth.

We, the representatives of the freemen of Kentucky, in convention assembled, in their name, and by the authority of the commonwealth of Kentucky, and in virtue of the powers vested in us, as delegates from the counties respectively affixed to our names, do ordain and proclaim the foregoing to be the constitution of the commonwealth of Kentucky from and after this day.

Done at Frankfort this eleventh day of June, in the year of our Lord one thousand eight hundred and fifty, and in the fifty-ninth year of the commonwealth.

JAMES GUTHRIE, *President.*

THO. S. HELM, *Secretary.*
THO. D. TILFORD, *Assistant Secretary.*

CONSTITUTION OF THE COMMONWEALTH OF KENTUCKY—1890 *

PREAMBLE

We, the people of the Commonwealth of Kentucky, grateful to Almighty God for the civil, political and religious liberties we enjoy, and invoking the continuance of these blessings, do ordain and establish this Constitution.

BILL OF RIGHTS

That the great and essential principles of liberty and free government may be recognized and established, We Declare that:

SECTION 1. All men are, by nature, free and equal, and have certain inherent and inalienable rights, among which may be reckoned:

First: The right of enjoying and defending their lives and liberties.

Second: The right of worshiping Almighty God according to the dictates of their consciences.

Third: The right of seeking and pursuing their safety and happiness.

Fourth: The right of freely communicating their thoughts and opinions.

Fifth: The right of acquiring and protecting property.

Sixth: The right of assembling together in a peaceable manner for their common good, and of applying to those invested with the power of government for redress of grievances or other proper purposes, by petition, address or remonstrance.

Seventh: The right to bear arms in defense of themselves and of the State, subject to the power of the General Assembly to enact laws to prevent persons from carrying concealed weapons.

SEC. 2. Absolute and arbitrary power over the lives, liberty and property of freemen exists nowhere in a republic, not even in the largest majority.

SEC. 3. All men, when they form a social compact, are equal; and no grant of exclusive, separate public emoluments or privileges shall be made to any man or set of men, except in consideration of public services; but no property shall be exempt from taxation except as provided in this Constitution; and every grant of a franchise, privilege or exemption, shall remain subject to revocation, alteration or amendment.

SEC. 4. All power is inherent in the people, and all free governments are founded on their authority and instituted for their peace, safety, happiness and the protection of property. For the advancement of these ends, they have at all times an inalienable and indefeasible right to alter, reform or abolish their government in such manner as they may deem proper.

SEC. 5. No preference shall ever be given by law to any religious sect, society or denomination; nor to any particular creed, mode of worship or system of ecclesiastical polity; nor shall any person be

---

* Verified from "The Constitution of the Commonwealth of Kentucky. Adopted September 28, 1891. Frankfort, Ky.: E. Polk Johnson, Public Printer and Binder. 1892" 182 pp.

compelled to attend any place of worship, to contribute to the erection or maintenance of any such place, or to the salary or support of any minister or religion; nor shall any man be compelled to send his child to any school to which he may be conscientiously opposed; and the civil rights, privileges or capacities of no person shall be taken away, or in anywise diminished or enlarged, on account of his belief or disbelief of any religious tenet, dogma or teaching. No human authority shall, in any case whatever, control or interfere with the rights of conscience.

SEC. 6. All elections shall be free and equal.

SEC. 7. The ancient mode of trial by jury shall be held sacred, and the right thereof remain inviolate, subject to such modifications as may be authorized by this Constitution.

SEC. 8. Printing presses shall be free to every person who undertakes to examine the proceedings of the General Assembly or any branch of government, and no law shall ever be made to restrain the right thereof. Every person may freely and fully speak, write and print on any subject, being responsible for the abuse of that liberty.

SEC. 9. In prosecutions for the publication of papers investigating the official conduct of officers or men in a public capacity, or where the matter published is proper for public information, the truth thereof may be given in evidence; and in all indictments for libel the jury shall have the right to determine the law and the facts, under the direction of the court, as in other cases.

SEC. 10. The people shall be secure in their persons, houses, papers and possessions, from unreasonable search and seizure; and no warrant shall issue to search any place, or seize any person or thing, without describing them as nearly as may be, nor without probable cause supported by oath or affirmation.

SEC. 11. In all criminal prosecutions the accused has the right to be heard by himself and counsel; to demand the nature and cause of the accusation against him; to meet the witnesses face to face, and to have compulsory process for obtaining witnesses in his favor. He can not be compelled to give evidence against himself, nor can he be deprived of his life, liberty or property, unless by the judgment of his peers or the law of the land; and in prosecutions by indictment or information, he shall have a speedy public trial by an impartial jury of the vicinage; but the General Assembly may provide by a general law for a change of venue in such prosecutions for both the defendant and the Commonwealth, the change to be made to the most convenient county in which a fair trial can be obtained.

SEC. 12. No person, for an indictable offense, shall be proceeded against criminally by information, except in cases arising in the land or naval forces, or in the militia, when in actual service in time of war or public danger, or by leave of court for oppression or misdemeanor in office.

SEC. 13. No person shall, for the same offense, be twice put in jeopardy of his life or limb, nor shall any man's property be taken or applied to public use without the consent of his representatives, and without just compensation being previously made to him.

SEC. 14. All courts shall be open and every person for an injury done him in his lands, goods, person or reputation, shall have remedy by due course of law, and right and justice administered without sale, denial or delay.

Sec. 15. No power to suspend laws shall be exercised, unless by the General Assembly or its authority.

Sec. 16. All prisoners shall be bailable by sufficient securities, unless for capital offenses when the proof is evident or the presumption great; and the privilege of the writ of *habeas corpus* shall not be suspended unless when, in case of rebellion or invasion, the public safety may require it.

Sec. 17. Excessive bail shall not be required, nor excessive fines imposed, nor cruel punishment inflicted.

Sec. 18. The person of a debtor, where there is not strong presumption of fraud, shall not be continued in prison after delivering up his estate for the benefit of his creditors in such manner as shall be prescribed by law.

Sec. 19. No *ex post facto* law, nor any law impairing the obligation of contracts, shall be enacted.

Sec. 20. No person shall be attainted of treason or felony by the General Assembly, and no attainder shall work corruption of blood, nor, except during the life of the offender, forfeiture of estate to the Commonwealth.

Sec. 21. The estate of such persons as shall destroy their own lives shall descend or vest as in cases of natural death; and if any person shall be killed by casualty, there shall be no forfeiture by reason thereof.

Sec. 22. No standing army shall, in time of peace, be maintained without the consent of the General Assembly; and the military shall, in all cases and at all times, be in strict subordination to the civil power; nor shall any soldier, in time of peace, be quartered in any house without the consent of the owner, nor in time of war, except in a manner prescribed by law.

Sec. 23. The General Assembly shall not grant any title of nobility or hereditary distinction, nor create any office, the appointment of which shall be for a longer time than a term of years.

Sec. 24. Emigration from the State shall not be prohibited.

Sec. 25. Slavery and involuntary servitude in this State are forbidden, except as a punishment for crime, whereof the party shall have been duly convicted.

Sec. 26. To guard against transgression of the high powers which we have delegated, WE DECLARE that every thing in this Bill of Rights is excepted out of the general powers of government, and shall forever remain inviolate; and all laws contrary thereto, or contrary to this Constitution, shall be void.

DISTRIBUTION OF THE POWERS OF GOVERNMENT

Sec. 27. The powers of the government of the Commonwealth of Kentucky shall be divided into three distinct departments, and each of them be confined to a separate body of magistracy, to-wit: Those which are legislative, to one; those which are executive, to another; and those which are judicial, to another.

Sec. 28. No person, or collection of persons, being of one of those departments, shall exercise any power properly belonging to either of the others, except in the instances hereinafter expressly directed or permitted.

LEGISLATIVE DEPARTMENT

SEC. 29. The legislative power shall be vested in a House of Representatives and a Senate, which, together, shall be styled the " General Assembly of the Commonwealth of Kentucky."

SEC. 30. Members of the House of Representatives and Senators elected at the August election in one thousand eight hundred and ninety-one, and Senators then holding over, shall continue in office until and including the last day of December, one thousand eight hundred and ninety-three. Thereafter the term of office of Representatives and Senators shall begin upon the first day of January of the year succeeding their election.

SEC. 31. At the general election in the year one thousand eight hundred and ninety-three one Senator shall be elected in each Senatorial District, and one Representative in each Representative District. The Senators then elected shall hold their offices, one-half for two years and one-half for four years, as shall be determined by lot at the first session of the General Assembly after their election, and the Representatives shall hold their offices for two years. Every two years thereafter there shall be elected for four years one Senator in each Senatorial District in which the term of his predecessor in office will then expire, and in every Representative District one Representative for two years.

SEC. 32. No person shall be a Representative who, at the time of his election, is not a citizen of Kentucky, has not attained the age of twenty-four years, and who has not resided in this State two years next preceding his election, and the last year thereof in the county, town or city for which he may be chosen. No person shall be a Senator who, at the time of his election, is not a citizen of Kentucky, has not attained the age of thirty years, and has not resided in this State six years next preceding his election, and the last year thereof in the district for which he may be chosen.

SEC. 33. The first General Assembly after the adoption of this Constitution shall divide the State into thirty-eight Senatorial districts, and one hundred representative districts, as nearly equal in population as may be without dividing any county, except where a county may include more than one district, which districts shall constitute the Senatorial and Representative districts for ten years. Not more than two counties shall be joined together to form a Representative district: *Provided*, In doing so the principle requiring every district to be as nearly equal in population as may be shall not be violated. At the expiration of that time, the General Assembly shall then, and every ten years thereafter, redistrict the State according to this rule, and for the purposes expressed in this section. If, in making said districts, inequality of population should be unavoidable, any advantage resulting therefrom shall be given to districts having the largest territory. No part of a county shall be added to another county to make a district, and the counties forming a district shall be contiguous.

SEC. 34. The House of Representatives shall choose its Speaker and other officers, and the Senate shall have power to choose its officers biennially.

SEC. 35. The number of Representatives shall be one hundred, and the number of Senators thirty-eight.

SEC. 36. The first General Assembly, the members of which shall be elected under this Constitution, shall meet on the first Tuesday after the first Monday in January, eighteen hundred and ninety-four, and thereafter the General assembly shall meet on the same day every second year, and its sessions shall be held at the seat of government, except in case of war, insurrection or pestilence, when it may, by proclamation of the Governor, assemble, for the time being, elsewhere.

SEC. 37. Not less than a majority of the members of each House of the General Assembly shall constitute a quorum to do business, but a smaller number may adjourn from day to day, and shall be authorized by law to compel the attendance of absent members in such manner and under such penalties as may be prescribed by law.

SEC. 38. Each House of the General Assembly shall judge of the qualifications, elections and returns of its members, but a contested election shall be determined in such manner as shall be directed by law.

SEC. 39. Each House of the General Assembly may determine the rules of its proceedings, punish a member for disorderly behavior, and, with the concurrence of two-thirds, expel a member, but not a second time for the same cause, and may punish for contempt any person who refuses to attend as a witness, or to bring any paper proper to be used as evidence before the General Assembly, or either House thereof, or a Committee of either, or to testify concerning any matter which may be a proper subject of inquiry by the General Assembly, or offers or gives a bribe to a member of the General Assembly, or attempts by other corrupt means or device to control or influence a member to cast his vote or withhold the same. The punishment and mode of proceeding for contempt in such cases shall be prescribed by law, but the term of imprisonment in any such case shall not extend beyond the session of the General Assembly.

SEC. 40. Each House of the General Assembly shall keep and publish daily a journal of its proceedings; and the yeas and nays of the members on any question shall, at the desire of any two of the members elected, be entered on the journal.

SEC. 41. Neither House, during the session of the General Assembly, shall, without the consent of the other, adjourn for more than three days, nor to any other place than that in which it may be sitting.

SEC. 42. The members of the General Assembly shall severally receive from the State Treasury compensation for their services, which shall be five dollars a day during their attendance on, and fifteen cents per mile for the necessary travel in going to and returning from, the sessions of their respective Houses: *Provided*, The same may be changed by law; but no change shall take effect during the session at which it is made; nor shall a session of the General Assembly continue beyond sixty legislative days, exclusive of Sundays and legal holidays; but this limitation as to length of session shall not apply to the first session held under this Constitution, nor to the Senate when sitting as a court of impeachment. A legislative day shall be construed to mean a calendar day.

SEC. 43. The members of the General Assembly shall, in all cases except treason, felony, breach or surety of the peace, be privileged from arrest during their attendance on the sessions of their respective Houses, and in going to and returning from the same; and for any speech or debate in either House they shall not be questioned in any other place.

SEC. 44. No Senator or Representative shall, during the term for which he was elected, nor for one year thereafter, be appointed or elected to any civil office of profit in this Commonwealth, which shall have been created, or the emoluments of which shall have been increased, during the said term, except to such offices as may be filled by the election of the people.

SEC. 45. No person who may have been a collector of taxes or public moneys for the Commonwealth, or for any county, city, town or district, or the assistant or deputy of such collector, shall be eligible to the General Assembly, unless he shall have obtained a quietus six months before the election for the amount of such collection, and for all public moneys for which he may have been responsible.

SEC. 46. No bill shall be considered for final passage, unless the same has been reported by a Committee and printed for the use of the members. Every bill shall be read at length on three different days in each House; but the second and third readings may be dispensed with by a majority of all the members elected to the House in which the bill is pending. But whenever a Committee refuses or fails to report a bill submitted to it in a reasonable time, the same may be called up by any member, and be considered in the same manner it would have been considered if it had been reported. No bill shall become a law unless, on its final passage, it receives the votes of at least two-fifths of the members elected to each House, and a majority of the members voting, the vote to be taken by yeas and nays and entered in the journal: *Provided*, Any act or resolution for the appropriation of money or the creation of debt shall, on its final passage, receive the votes of a majority of all the members elected to each House.

SEC. 47. All bills for raising revenue shall originate in the House of Representatives, but the Senate may propose amendments thereto; *Provided*, No new matter shall be introduced, under color of amendment, which does not relate to raising revenue.

SEC. 48. The General Assembly shall have no power to enact laws to diminish the resources of the Sinking Fund as now established by law until the debt of the Commonwealth be paid, but may enact laws to increase them; and the whole resources of said fund, from year to year, shall be sacredly set apart and applied to the payment of the interest and principal of the State debt, and to no other use or purpose, until the whole debt of the State is fully satisfied.

SEC. 49. The General Assembly may contract debts to meet casual deficits or failures in the revenue; but such debts, direct or contingent, singly or in the aggregate, shall not at any time exceed five hundred thousand dollars, and the moneys arising from loans creating such debts shall be applied only to the purpose or purposes for which they were obtained, or to repay such debts: *Provided*, The General Assembly may contract debts to repel invasion, suppress insurrection, or, if hostilities are threatened, provide for the public defense.

SEC. 50. No act of the General Assembly shall authorize any debt to be contracted on behalf of the Commonwealth except for the purposes mentioned in section forty-nine, unless provision be made therein to levy and collect an annual tax sufficient to pay the interest stipulated, and to discharge the debt within thirty years; nor shall such act take effect until it shall have been submitted to the people at a general election, and shall have received a majority of all the votes cast for and against it: *Provided*, The General Assembly may contract debts by borrowing money to pay any part of the debt of the State, without submission to the people, and without making provision in the act authorizing the same for a tax to discharge the debt so contracted, or the interest thereon.

SEC. 51. No law enacted by the General Assembly shall relate to more than one subject, and that shall be expressed in the title, and no law shall be revised, amended, or the provisions thereof extended or conferred by reference to its title only, but so much thereof as is revised, amended, extended or conferred, shall be re-enacted and published at length.

SEC. 52. The General Assembly shall have no power to release, extinguish, or authorize the releasing or extinguishing, in whole or in part, the indebtedness or liability of any corporation or individual to this Commonwealth, or to any county or municipality thereof.

SEC. 53. The General Assembly shall provide by law for monthly investigations into the accounts of the Treasurer and Auditor of Public Accounts, and the result of these investigations shall be reported to the Governor, and these reports shall be semi-annually published in two newspapers of general circulation in the State. The reports received by the Governor shall, at the beginning of each session, be transmitted by him to the General Assembly for scrutiny and appropriate action.

SEC. 54. The General Assembly shall have no power to limit the amount to be recovered for injuries resulting in death, or for injuries to person or property.

SEC. 55. No act, except general appropriation bills, shall become a law until ninety days after the adjournment of the session at which it was passed, except in cases of emergency, when, by the concurrence of a majority of the members elected to each House of the General Assembly, by a yea and nay vote entered upon their journals, an act may become a law when approved by the Governor; but the reasons for the emergency that justifies this action must be set out at length in the journal of each House.

SEC. 56. No bill shall become a law until the same shall have been signed by the presiding officer of each of the two Houses in open session; and before such officer shall have affixed his signature to any bill, he shall suspend all other business, declare that such bill will now be read, and that he will sign the same to the end that it may become a law. The bill shall then be read at length and compared; and, if correctly enrolled, he shall, in presence of the House in open session, and before any other business is entertained, affix his signature, which fact shall be noted in the journal, and the bill immediately sent to the other House. When it reaches the other House, the presiding officer thereof shall immediately suspend all other business, announce the reception of the bill, and the same proceeding shall thereupon be observed in every respect as in the House in which it was first signed. And thereupon the Clerk of the latter House shall immediately present the same to the Governor for his signature and approval.

SEC. 57. A member who has a personal or private interest in any measure or bill proposed or pending before the General Assembly, shall disclose the fact to the House of which he is a member, and shall not vote thereon upon pain of expulsion.

SEC. 58. The General Assembly shall neither audit nor allow any private claim against the Commonwealth, except for expenses incurred during the session at which the same was allowed; but may appropriate money to pay such claim as shall have been audited and allowed according to law.

LOCAL AND SPECIAL LEGISLATION

SEC. 59. The General Assembly shall not pass local or special acts concerning any of the following subjects, or for any of the following purposes, namely:

First: To regulate the jurisdiction, or the practice, or the circuits of courts of justice, or the rights, powers, duties or compensation of the officers thereof; but the practice in circuit courts in continuous session may, by a general law, be made different from the practice of circuit courts held in terms.

Second: To regulate the summoning, impaneling or compensation of grand or petit jurors.

Third: To provide for changes of venue in civil or criminal causes.

Fourth: To regulate the punishment of crimes and misdemeanors, or to remit fines, penalties or forfeitures.

Fifth: To regulate the limitation of civil or criminal causes.

Sixth: To affect the estate of *cestuis que trust*, decedents, infants or other persons under disabilities, or to authorize any such persons to sell, lease, encumber or dispose of their property.

Seventh: To declare any person of age, or to relieve an infant or *feme covert* of disability, or to enable him to do acts allowed only to adults not under disabilities.

Eighth: To change the law of descent, distribution or succession.

Ninth: To authorize the adoption or legitimation of children.

Tenth: To grant divorces.

Eleventh: To change the name of persons.

Twelfth: To give effect to invalid deeds, wills or other instruments.

Thirteenth: To legalize, except as against the Commonwealth, the unauthorized or invalid act of any officer or public agent of the Commonwealth, or of any city, county or municipality thereof.

Fourteenth: To refund money legally paid into the State Treasury.

Fifteenth: To authorize or to regulate the levy, the assessment or the collection of taxes, or to give any indulgence or discharge to any assessor or collector of taxes, or to his sureties.

Sixteenth: To authorize the opening, altering, maintaining or vacating roads, highways, streets, alleys, town plats, cemeteries, graveyards, or public grounds not owned by the Commonwealth.

Seventeenth: To grant a charter to any corporation, or to amend the charter of any existing corporation; to license companies or persons to own or operate ferries, bridges, roads or turnpikes; to declare streams navigable, or to authorize the construction of booms or dams therein, or to remove obstructions therefrom; to affect toll-gates, or to regulate tolls; to regulate fencing or the running at large of stock.

Eighteenth: To create, increase or decrease fees, percentages or allowances to public officers, or to extend the time for the collection thereof, or to authorize officers to appoint deputies.

Nineteenth. To give any person or corporation the right to lay a railroad track or tramway, or to amend existing charters for such purposes.

Twentieth: To provide for conducting elections, or for designating the places of voting, or changing the boundaries of wards, precincts or districts, except when new counties may be created.

Twenty-first: To regulate the rate of interest.

Twenty-second: To authorize the creation, extension, enforcement, impairment or release of liens.

Twenty-third: To provide for the protection of game and fish.

Twenty-fourth: To regulate labor, trade, mining or manufacturing.

Twenty-fifth: To provide for the management of common schools.

Twenty-sixth: To locate or change a county seat.

Twenty-seventh: To provide a means of taking the sense of the people of any city, town, district, precinct, or county, whether they wish to authorize, regulate or prohibit therein the sale of vinous, spirituous or malt liquors, or alter the liquor laws.

Twenty-eighth: Restoring to citizenship persons convicted of infamous crimes.

Twenty-ninth: In all other cases where a general law can be made applicable, no special law shall be enacted.

SEC. 60. The General Assembly shall not indirectly enact any special or local act by the repeal in part of a general act, or by exempting from the operation of a general act any city, town, district or county; but laws repealing local or special acts may be enacted. No law shall be enacted granting powers or privileges in any case where the granting of such powers or privileges shall have been provided for by a general law, nor where the Courts have jurisdiction to grant the same or to give the relief asked for. No law, except such as relates to the sale, loan or gift of vinous, spirituous or malt liquors, bridges, turnpikes, or other public roads, public buildings or improvements, fencing, running at large of stock, matters pertaining to common schools, paupers, and the regulation by counties, cities, towns or other municipalities of their local affairs, shall be enacted to take effect upon the approval of any other authority than the General Assembly, unless otherwise expressly provided in this Constitution.

SEC. 61. The General Assembly shall, by general law, provide a means whereby the sense of the people of any county, city, town, district or precinct may be taken, as to whether or not spirituous, vinous or malt liquors shall be sold, bartered or loaned therein, or the sale thereof regulated. But nothing herein shall be construed to interfere with or to repeal any law in force relating to the sale or gift of such liquors. All elections on this question may be held on a day other than the regular election days.

SEC. 62. The style of the laws of this Commonwealth shall be as follows: " Be it enacted by the General Assembly of the Commonwealth of Kentucky."

COUNTIES AND COUNTY SEATS

SEC. 63. No new county shall be created by the General Assembly which will reduce the county or counties, or either of them, from which it shall be taken, to less area than four hundred square miles; nor shall any county be formed of less area, nor shall any boundary line thereof pass within less than ten miles of any county seat of the county or counties proposed to be divided. Nothing contained herein shall prevent the General Assembly from abolishing any county.

SEC. 64. No county shall be divided, or have any part stricken therefrom, except in the formation of new counties, without submitting the question to a vote of the people of the county, nor unless the majority of all the legal voters of the county voting on the question shall vote for the same. The county seat of no county as now located, or as may hereafter be located, shall be moved, except upon a vote of two-thirds of those voting; nor shall any new county be established which will reduce any county to less than twelve thousand inhabitants, nor shall any county be created containing a less population.

SEC. 65. There shall be no territory stricken from any county unless a majority of the voters living in such territory shall petition for such division. But the portion so stricken off and added to another county, or formed in whole or in part into a new county, shall be bound for its proportion of the indebtedness of the county from which it has been taken.

IMPEACHMENTS

SEC. 66. The House of Representatives shall have the sole power of impeachment.

SEC. 67. All impeachments shall be tried by the Senate. When sitting for that purpose, the Senators shall be upon oath or affirmation. No person shall be convicted without the concurrence of two-thirds of the Senators present.

SEC. 68. The Governor and all civil officers shall be liable to impeachment for any misdemeanors in office; but judgment in such cases shall not extend further than removal from office, and disqualification to hold any office of honor, trust or profit under this Commonwealth; but the party convicted shall, nevertheless, be subject and liable to indictment, trial and punishment by law.

THE EXECUTIVE DEPARTMENT

OFFICERS FOR THE STATE AT LARGE

SEC. 69. The supreme executive power of the Commonwealth shall be vested in a Chief Magistrate, who shall be styled the "Governor of the Commonwealth of Kentucky."

SEC. 70. He shall be elected for the term of four years by the qualified voters of the State. The person having the highest number of votes shall be Governor; but if two or more shall be equal and highest in votes, the election shall be determined by lot in such manner as the General Assembly may direct.

SEC. 71. He shall be ineligible for the succeeding four years after the expiration of the term for which he shall have been elected.

SEC. 72. He shall be at least thirty years of age, and have been a citizen and a resident of Kentucky for at least six years next preceding his election.

SEC. 73. He shall commence the execution of the duties of his office on the fifth Tuesday succeeding his election, and shall continue in the execution thereof until his successor shall have qualified.

SEC. 74. He shall at stated times receive for his services a compensation to be fixed by law.

SEC. 75. He shall be Commander-in-Chief of the army and navy of this Commonwealth, and of the militia thereof, except when they shall be called into the service of the United States; but he shall not command personally in the field, unless advised so to do by a resolution of the General Assembly.

SEC. 76. He shall have the power, except as otherwise provided in this Constitution, to fill vacancies by granting commissions, which shall expire when such vacancies shall have been filled according to the provisions of this Constitution.

SEC. 77. He shall have power to remit fines and forfeitures, commute sentences, grant reprieves and pardons, except in case of impeachment, and he shall file with each application therefor a statement of the reasons for his decision thereon, which application and statement shall always be open to public inspection. In cases of treason, he shall have power to grant reprieves until the end of the next session of the General Assembly, in which the power of pardoning shall be vested; but he shall have no power to remit the fees of the Clerk, Sheriff, or Commonwealth's Attorney in penal or criminal cases.

SEC. 78. He may require information in writing from the officers of the Executive Department upon any subject relating to the duties of their respective offices.

SEC. 79. He shall, from time to time, give to the General Assembly information of the state of the Commonwealth, and recommend to their consideration such measures as he may deem expedient.

SEC. 80. He may, on extraordinary occasions, convene the General Assembly at the seat of Government, or at a different place, of that should have become dangerous from an enemy or from contagious diseases. In case of disagreement between the two Houses with respect to the time of adjournment, he may adjourn them to such time as he shall think proper, not exceeding four months. When he shall convene the General Assembly it shall be by proclamation, stating the subjects to be considered, and no others shall be considered.

SEC. 81. He shall take care that the laws be faithfully executed.

SEC. 82. A Lieutenant-Governor shall be chosen at every regular election for Governor, in the same manner, to continue in office for the same time, and possess the same qualifications as the Governor. He shall be ineligible to the office of Lieutenant-Governor for the succeeding four years after the expiration of the term for which he shall have been elected.

SEC. 83. He shall, by virtue of his office, be President of the Senate, have a right, when in Committee of the Whole, to debate and vote on all subjects, and when the Senate is equally divided, to give the casting vote.

SEC. 84. Should the Governor be impeached and removed from office, die, refuse to qualify, resign, be absent from the State, or be, from any cause, unable to discharge the duties of his office, the Lieutenant-Governor shall exercise all the power and authority appertaining to the office of Governor until another be duly elected and qualified, or the Governor shall return or be able to discharge the duties of his office. On the trial of the Governor, the Lieutenant-Governor shall not act as President of the Senate or take part in the proceedings, but the Chief Justice of the Court of Appeals shall preside during the trial.

SEC. 85. A President *pro tempore* of the Senate shall be elected by each Senate as soon after its organization as possible, the Lieutenant-Governor vacating his seat as President of the Senate until such election shall be made; and as often as there is a vacancy in the office of President *pro tempore*, another President *pro tempore* of the Senate shall be elected by the Senate, if in session. And if, during the vacancy of the office of Governor, the Lieutenant-Governor shall be impeached and removed from office, refuse to qualify, resign, die or be absent from the State, the President *pro tempore* of the Senate shall in like manner administer the government: *Provided*, Whenever a vacancy shall occur in the office of Governor before the first two years of the term shall have expired, a new election for Governor shall take place to fill such vacancy.

SEC. 86. The Lieutenant-Governor, or President *pro tempore* of the Senate, while he acts as President of the Senate, shall receive for his services the same compensation which shall, for the same period, be allowed to the Speaker of the House of Representatives, and during the time he administers the government as Governor, he shall receive the same compensation which the Governor would have received had he been employed in the duties of his office.

SEC. 87. If the Lieutenant-Governor shall be called upon to administer the government, and shall, while in such administration, resign, die or be absent from the State during the recess of the General Assembly, if there be no President *pro tempore* of the Senate, it shall be the duty of the Secretary of State, for the time being, to convene the Senate for the purpose of choosing a President; and until a President is chosen, the Secretary of State shall administer the government. If there be no Secretary of State to perform the duties devolved upon him by this section, or in case that officer be absent from the State, then the Attorney-General, for the time being, shall convene the Senate for the purpose of choosing a President, and shall administer the government until a President is chosen.

SEC. 88. Every bill which shall have passed the two Houses shall be presented to the Governor. If he approve, he shall sign it; but if not, he shall return it, with his objections, to the House in which it originated, which shall enter the objections in full upon its journal, and proceed to reconsider it. If, after such reconsideration, a majority of all the members elected to that House shall agree to pass the bill, it shall be sent, with the objections, to the other House, by which it shall likewise be considered, and if approved by a majority of all the members elected to that House, it shall be a law; but in such case the votes of both Houses shall be determined by yeas and nays, and the names of the members voting for and against the bill shall be entered upon the journal of each House respectively. If any bill shall not be returned by the Governor within ten days (Sundays excepted) after it shall have been presented to him, it shall be a law in like manner as if he had signed it, unless the General Assembly, by their adjournment, prevent its return, in which case it shall be a law, unless disapproved by him within ten days after the adjournment, in which case his veto message shall be spread upon the register kept by the Secretary of State. The Governor shall have power to disapprove any part or parts of appropriation bills embracing distinct items, and the part or parts disapproved shall not become a law unless reconsidered and passed, as in case of a bill.

SEC. 89. Every order, resolution or vote, in which the concurrence of both Houses may be necessary, except on a question of adjournment, or as otherwise provided in this Constitution, shall be presented to the Governor, and, before it shall take effect, be approved by him; or being disapproved, shall be repassed by a majority of the members elected to both Houses, according to the rules and limitations prescribed in case of a bill

SEC. 90. Contested elections for Governor and Lieutenant-Governor shall be determined by both Houses of the General Assembly, according to such regulations as may be established by law.

SEC. 91. A Treasurer, Auditor of Public Accounts, Register of the Land Office, Commissioner of Agriculture, Labor and Statistics, Secretary of State, Attorney-General and Superintendent of Public Instruction, shall be elected by the qualified voters of the State at the same time the Governor is elected, for the term of four years, each of whom shall be at least thirty years of age at the time of his election, and shall have been a resident citizen of the State at least two years next before his election. The duties of all these officers shall be such as may be prescribed by law, and the Secretary of State shall keep a fair register of and attest all the official acts of the Governor, and shall, when required, lay the same and all papers, minutes and vouchers relative thereto before either House of the General Assembly. The officers named in this section shall enter upon the discharge of their duties the first Monday in January after their election, and shall hold their offices until their successors are elected and qualified.

SEC. 92. The Attorney-General shall have been a practicing lawyer eight years before his election.

SEC. 93. The Treasurer, Auditor of Public Accounts, Secretary of State, Commissioner of Agriculture, Labor and Statistics, Attorney-General, Superintendent of Public Instruction and Register of the Land Office shall be ineligible to re-election for the succeeding four years after the expiration of the term for which they shall have been elected. The duties and responsibilities of these officers shall be prescribed by law, and all fees collected by any of said officers shall be covered into the treasury. Inferior State officers, not specifically provided for in this Constitution, may be appointed or elected, in such manner as may be prescribed by law, for a term not exceeding four years, and until their successors are appointed or elected and qualified.

SEC. 94. The General Assembly may provide for the abolishment of the office of the Register of the Land Office, to take effect at the end of any term, and shall provide by law for the custody and preservation of the papers and records of said office, if the same be abolished.

SEC. 95. The election under this Constitution for Governor, Lieutenant-Governor, Treasurer, Auditor of Public Accounts, Register of the Land Office, Attorney-General, Secretary of State, Superintendent of Public Instruction, and Commissioner of Agriculture, Labor and Statistics, shall be held on the first Tuesday after the first Monday in November, eighteen hundred and ninety-five, and the same day every four years thereafter.

SEC. 96. All the officers mentioned in section ninety-five shall be paid for their services by salary, and not otherwise.

OFFICERS FOR DISTRICTS AND COUNTIES

SEC. 97. At the general election in eighteen hundred and ninety-two there shall be elected in each circuit court district a Commonwealth's Attorney, and in each county a clerk of the circuit court, who shall enter upon the discharge of the duties of their respective offices on the first Monday in January after their election, and shall hold their offices five years, and until their successors are elected and qualified. In the year eighteen hundred and ninety-seven, and every six years thereafter, there shall be an election in each county for a circuit court clerk, and for a Commonwealth's Attorney in each circuit court district, unless that office be abolished, who shall hold their respective offices for six years from the first Monday in January after their election, and until the election and qualification of their successors.

SEC. 98. The compensation of the Commonwealth's Attorney shall be by salary and such percentage of fines and forfeitures as may be fixed by law, and such salary shall be uniform in so far as the same shall be paid out of the State Treasury, and not to exceed the sum of five hundred dollars per annum; but any county may make additional compensation, to be paid by said county. Should any percentage of fines and forfeitures be allowed by law, it shall not be paid except upon such proportion of the fines and forfeitures as have been collected and paid into the State Treasury, and not until so collected and paid.

SEC. 99. There shall be elected in eighteen hundred and ninety-four in each county a Judge of the County Court, a County Court Clerk, a County Attorney, Sheriff, Jailer, Coroner, Surveyor and Assessor, and in each Justice's District one Justice of the Peace and one Constable, who shall enter upon the discharge of the duties of their offices on the first Monday in January after their election, and continue in office three years, and until the election and qualification of their successors; and in eighteen hundred and ninety-seven, and every four years thereafter, there shall be an election in each county of the officers mentioned, who shall hold their offices four years (from the first Monday in January after their election), and until the election and qualification of their successors. The first election of Sheriffs under this Constitution shall be held in eighteen hundred and ninety-two, and the Sheriffs then elected shall hold their offices two years, and until the election and qualification of their successors. The Sheriffs now in office for their first term shall be eligible to re-election in eighteen hundred and ninety-two, and those elected in eighteen hundred and ninety-two for the first term shall be eligible to re-election in eighteen hundred and ninety-four, but thereafter no Sheriff shall be eligible to re-election or to act as deputy for the succeeding term.

SEC. 100. No person shall be eligible to the offices mentioned in sections ninety-seven and ninety-nine who is not at the time of his election twenty-four years of age (except Clerks of County and Circuit Courts, who shall be twenty-one years of age), a citizen of Kentucky, and who has not resided in the State two years, and one year next preceding his election in the county and district in which he is a candidate. No person shall be eligible to the office of Commonwealth's Attorney unless he shall have been a licensed practicing lawyer four years. No person shall be eligible to the office of County Attorney unless he shall have been a licensed practicing lawyer two years. No person shall be eligible to the office of Clerk unless he shall have procured from a Judge of the Court of Appeals, or a Judge of a Circuit Court, a certificate that he has been examined by the Clerk of his Court under his supervision, and that he is qualified for the office for which he is a candidate.

SEC. 101. Constables shall possess the same qualifications as Sheriffs, and their jurisdiction shall be co-extensive with the counties in which they reside. Constables now in office shall continue in office until their successors are elected and qualified.

SEC. 102. When a new county shall be created, officers for the same, to serve until the next regular election, shall be elected or appointed in such way and at such times as the General Assembly may prescribe.

SEC. 103. The Judges of County Courts, Clerks, Sheriffs, Surveyors, Coroners, Jailers, Constables, and such other officers as the General Assembly may, from time to time, require, shall, before they enter upon the duties of their respective offices, and as often thereafter as may be deemed proper, give such bond and security as may be prescribed by law.

SEC. 104. The General Assembly may abolish the office of Assessor and provide that the assessment of property shall be made by other officers; but it shall have power to re-establish the office of Assessor and prescribe his duties. No person shall be eligible to the office of Assessor two consecutive terms.

SEC. 105. The General Assembly may, at any time, consolidate the offices of Jailer and Sheriff in any county or counties, as it shall deem most expedient; but in the event such consolidation be made, the office of Sheriff shall be retained, and the Sheriff shall be required to perform the duties of Jailer.

SEC. 106. The fees of county officers shall be regulated by law. In counties or cities having a population of seventy-five thousand or more, the Clerks of the respective courts thereof (except the Clerk of the City Court), the Marshals, the Sheriffs and the Jailers, shall be paid out of the State Treasury, by salary to be fixed by law, the salaries of said officers and of their deputies and necessary office expenses not to exceed seventy-five per centum of the fees collected by said officers, respectively, and paid into the Treasury.

SEC. 107. The General Assembly may provide for the election or appointment, for a term not exceeding four years, of such other county or district ministerial and executive officers as may, from time to time, be necessary.

SEC. 108. The General Assembly may, at any time after the expiration of six years from the adoption of this Constitution, abolish the office of Commonwealth's Attorney, to take effect upon the expiration of the terms of the incumbents, in which event the duties of said office shall be discharged by the County Attorneys.

THE JUDICIAL DEPARTMENT

SEC. 109. The judicial power of the Commonwealth, both as to matters of law and equity, shall be vested in the Senate when sitting as a court of impeachment, and one Supreme Court (to be styled the Court of Appeals) and the courts established by this Constitution.

COURT OF APPEALS

SEC. 110. The Court of Appeals shall have appellate jurisdiction only, which shall be co-extensive with the State, under such restrictions and regulations not repugnant to this Constitution, as may from time to time be prescribed by law. Said court shall have power to issue such writs as may be necessary to give it a general control of inferior jurisdictions.

SEC. 111. The Court of Appeals shall be held at the seat of government; but if that shall become dangerous, in case of war, insurrection or pestilence, it may adjourn to meet and transact its business at such other place in the State as it may deem expedient for the time being.

SEC. 112. The Judges of the Court of Appeals shall severally hold their offices for the term of eight years, commencing on the first Monday in January next succeeding their respective elections, and until their several successors are qualified, subject to the conditions hereinafter prescribed. For any reasonable cause the Governor shall remove them, or any one or more of them, on the address of two-thirds of each House of the General Assembly. The cause or causes for which said removal shall be required shall be stated at length in such address and in the journal of each House. They shall at stated times receive for their services an adequate compensation, to be fixed by law.

SEC. 113. The Court of Appeals shall, after eighteen hundred and ninety-four, consist of not less than five nor more than seven Judges. They shall, severally, by virtue of their office, be conservators of the peace throughout the State, and shall be commissioned by the Governor.

SEC. 114. No person shall be eligible to election as a Judge of the Court of Appeals who is not a citizen of Kentucky and has not resided in this State five years and in the district in which he is elected two years next preceding his election, and who is less than thirty-five years of age, and has not been a practicing lawyer eight years, or whose services upon the bench of a Circuit Court or court of similar jurisdiction, when added to the time he may have practiced law, shall not be equal to eight years.

SEC. 115. The present Judges of the Court of Appeals shall hold their offices until their respective terms expire, and until their several successors shall be qualified; and at the regular election next preceding the expiration of the term of each of the present Judges, his successor shall be elected. The General Assembly shall, before the regular election in eighteen hundred and ninety-four, provide for the election of such Judges of the Court of Appeals, not less than five nor exceeding seven, as may be necessary; and if less than seven Judges be provided for, the General Assembly may, at any time, increase the number to seven.

SEC. 116. The Judges of the Court of Appeals shall be elected by districts. The General Assembly shall, before the regular election in eighteen hundred and ninety-four, divide the State, by counties, into as many districts, as nearly equal in population and as compact in form as possible, as it may provide shall be the number of Judges of the Court of Appeals; and it may, every ten years thereafter, or when the number of Judges requires it, redistrict the State in like manner. Upon the creation of new or additional districts, the General Assembly shall designate the year in which the first election for a Judge of the Court of Appeals shall be held in each district, so that not more than the number of Judges provided for shall be elected, and that no Judge may be deprived of his office until the expiration of the term for which he was elected.

SEC. 117. A majority of the Judges of the Court of Appeals shall constitute a quorum for the transaction of business, but in the event as many as two decline, on account of interest or for other reason, to preside in the trial of any cause, the Governor, on that fact being certified to him by the Chief Justice, shall appoint to try the particular cause a sufficient number of Judges to constitute a full Court. The Judges so appointed shall possess the qualifications prescribed for Judges of the Court of Appeals, and receive the same compensation proportioned to the length of service.

SEC. 118. The Judge longest in commission as Judge of the Court of Appeals shall be Chief Justice, and if the term of service of two or more Judges be the same, they shall determine by lot which of their number shall be Chief Justice. The Court shall prescribe by rule that petitions for rehearing shall be considered by a Judge who did not deliver the opinion in the case; and the Court, if composed of seven Judges, shall divide itself into sections for the transaction of business, if, in the judgment of the Court, such arrangement is necessary.

SEC. 119. The Superior Court shall continue until the terms of the present Judges of said Court expire, and upon the expiration of their terms, all causes pending before the Superior Court shall be transferred to the Court of Appeals and be determined by it.

SEC. 120. The present Clerk of the Court of Appeals shall serve until the expiration of the term for which he was elected, and until his successor is elected and qualified. At the election in the year eighteen hundred and ninety-seven there shall be elected by the qualified voters of the State a Clerk of the Court of Appeals, who shall take his office the first Monday in September, eighteen hundred and ninety-eight, and who shall hold his office until the regular election in nineteen hundred and three, and until his successor shall be elected and qualified. In nineteen hundred and three and thereafter, the Clerk of the Court of Appeals shall be elected at the same time as the Governor for the term of four years; and the said Clerk shall take his office on the first Monday in January following his election, and shall hold his office until his successor is elected and qualified. The Clerk shall be ineligible for the succeeding term.

SEC. 121. No person shall be eligible to the office of Clerk of the Court of Appeals unless he is a citizen of Kentucky, a resident thereof for two years next preceding his election, of the age of twenty-one years, and have a certificate from a Judge of the Court of Appeals that he has been examined by him, or by the Clerk of his Court under his supervision, and that he is qualified for the office.

SEC. 122. Should a vacancy occur in the office of the Clerk of the Court of Appeals, or should the Clerk be under charges, the Court of Appeals shall have power to appoint a Clerk until the vacancy be filled as provided in this Constitution, or until the Clerk be acquitted.

SEC. 123. The style of process shall be, "The Commonwealth of Kentucky." All prosecutions shall be carried on in the name and by the authority of the "Commonwealth of Kentucky," and conclude against the peace and dignity of the same.

SEC. 124. The Clerks of the Court of Appeals, Circuit and County Courts, shall be removable from office by the Court of Appeals, upon information and good cause shown. The Court shall be judge of the facts as well as the law. Two-thirds of the members present must concur in the sentence.

CIRCUIT COURTS

SEC. 125. A Circuit Court shall be established in each county now existing, or which may hereafter be created, in this Commonwealth.

SEC. 126. The jurisdiction of said Court shall be and remain as now established, hereby giving to the General Assembly the power to change it.

SEC. 127. The right to appeal or sue out a writ of error shall remain as it now exists until altered by law, hereby giving to the General Assembly the power to change or modify said right.

SEC. 128. At its first session after the adoption of this Constitution, the General Assembly, having due regard to territory, business and population, shall divide the State into a sufficient number of judicial districts to carry into effect the provisions of this Constitution concerning Circuit Courts. In making such apportionment no county shall be divided, and the number of said districts, excluding those in counties having a population of one hundred and fifty thousand, shall not exceed one district for each sixty thousand of the population of the entire State.

SEC. 129. The General Assembly shall, at the same time the judicial districts are laid off, direct elections to be held in each district to elect a judge therein. The first election of judges of the Circuit Courts under this Constitution shall take place at the annual election in the year eighteen hundred and ninety-two, and the judges then elected shall enter upon the discharge of the duties of their respective offices on the first Monday in January after their election, and hold their offices five years, and until their successors are elected and qualified. At the general election in eighteen hundred and ninety-seven, and every six years thereafter, there shall be an election for Judges of the circuit courts, who shall hold their offices for six years from the first Monday in January succeeding their election. They shall be commissioned by the Governor, and continue in office until their successors shall have been qualified, but shall be removable in the same manner as the Judges of the Court of Appeals. The removal of a Judge from his district shall vacate his office.

SEC. 130. No person shall be eligible as Judge of the circuit court who is less than thirty-five years of age when elected, who is not a citizen of Kentucky, and a resident of the district in which he may be a candidate two years next preceding his election, and who has not been a practicing lawyer eight years.

SEC. 131. There shall be at least three regular terms of Circuit Court held in each county every year.

SEC. 132. The General Assembly, when deemed necessary, may establish additional districts; but the whole number of districts, exclusive of counties having a population of one hundred and fifty thousand, shall not exceed at any time one for every sixty thousand of population of the State according to the last enumeration.

SEC. 133. The Judges of the Circuit Court shall, at stated times, receive for their services an adequate compensation to be fixed by law, which shall be equal and uniform throughout the State, so far as the same shall be paid out of the State Treasury.

SEC. 134. The Judicial Districts of the State shall not be changed except at the first session after an enumeration, unless upon the establishment of a new district.

SEC. 135. No Courts, save those provided for in this Constitution, shall be established.

SEC. 136. The General Assembly shall provide by law for holding Circuit Courts when, from any cause, the Judge shall fail to attend, or, if in attendance, can not properly preside.

SEC. 137. Each county having a population of one hundred and fifty thousand or over, shall constitute a district, which shall be entitled to four Judges. Additional Judges for said district may, from time to time, be authorized by the General Assembly, but not to exceed one Judge for each increase of forty thousand of population in said county, to be ascertained by the last enumeration. Each of the Judges in such a district shall hold a separate court, except when a general term may be held for the purpose of making rules of court, or as may be required by law: *Provided*, No general term shall have power to review any order, decision or proceeding of any branch of the court in said district made in separate term. There shall be one Clerk for such district who shall be known as the Clerk of the Circuit Court. Criminal causes shall be under the exclusive jurisdiction of some one branch of said court, and all other litigation in said district, of which the Circuit Court may have jurisdiction, shall be distributed as equally as may be between the other branches thereof, in accordance with the rules of the court made in general term or as may be prescribed by law.

SEC. 138. Each county having a city of twenty thousand inhabitants, and a population, including said city, of forty thousand or more, may constitute a district, and when its population reaches seventy-five thousand, the General Assembly may provide that it shall have an additional Judge, and such district may have a Judge for each additional fifty thousand population above one hundred thousand. And in such counties the General Assembly shall, by proper laws, direct in what manner the court shall be held and the business therein conducted.

QUARTERLY COURTS

SEC. 139. There shall be established in each county now existing, or which may be hereafter created, in this State, a Court, to be styled the Quarterly Court, the jurisdiction of which shall be uniform throughout the State, and shall be regulated by a general law, and, until changed, shall be the same as that now vested by law in the Quarterly Courts of this Commonwealth. The Judges of the County Court shall be the Judges of the Quarterly Courts.

COUNTY COURTS

SEC. 140. There shall be established in each county now existing, or which may be hereafter created, in this State, a Court to be styled the County Court, to consist of a Judge, who shall be a conservator of the peace, and shall receive such compensation for his services as may be prescribed by law. He shall be commissioned by the Governor, and shall vacate his office by removal from the county in which he may have been elected.

SEC. 141. The jurisdiction of the County Court shall be uniform throughout the State, and shall be regulated by general law, and, until changed, shall be the same as now vested in the County Courts of this State by law.

JUSTICES' COURTS

SEC. 142. Each county now existing, or which may hereafter be created, in this State, shall be laid off into districts in such manner as the General Assembly may direct; but no county shall have less than three nor more than eight districts, in each of which districts one Justice of the Peace shall be elected as provided in section ninety-nine. The General Assembly shall make provisions for regulating the number of said districts from time to time within the limits herein prescribed, and for fixing the boundaries thereof. The jurisdiction of Justices of the Peace shall be co-extensive with the county, and shall be equal and uniform throughout the State. Justices of the Peace shall be conservators of the peace. They shall be commissioned by the Governor, and shall vacate their offices by removal from the districts, respectively, in which they may have been elected.

POLICE COURTS

SEC. 143. A Police Court may be established in each city and town in this State, with jurisdiction in cases of violation of municipal ordinances and by-laws occurring within the corporate limits of the city or town in which it is established, and such criminal jurisdiction within the said limits as Justices of the Peace have. The said Courts may be authorized to act as examining Courts, but shall have no civil jurisdiction: *Provided*, The General Assembly may confer civil jurisdiction on Police Courts in cities and towns of the fourth and fifth classes and in towns of the sixth class having a population of two hundred and fifty or more, which jurisdiction shall be uniform throughout the State, and not exceed that of Justices of the Peace.

Fiscal Courts

Sec. 144. Counties shall have a Fiscal Court, which may consist of the Judge of the County Court and the Justices of the Peace, in which Court the Judge of the County Court shall preside, if present; or a county may have three Commissioners, to be elected from the county at large, who, together with the Judge of the County Court, shall constitute the Fiscal Court. A majority of the members of said Court shall constitute a Court for the transaction of business. But where, for county governmental purposes, a city is by law separated from the remainder of the county, such Commissioners may be elected from the part of the county outside of such city.

Suffrage and Elections

Sec. 145. Every male citizen of the United States of the age of twenty-one years, who has resided in the State one year, and in the county six months, and in the precinct in which he offers to vote sixty days, next preceding the election, shall be a voter in said precinct and not elsewhere; but the following persons are excepted and shall not have the right to vote:

First: Persons convicted in any court of competent jurisdiction of treason, or felony, or bribery in an election, or of such high misdemeanor as the General Assembly may declare shall operate as an exclusion from the right of suffrage; but persons hereby excluded may be restored to their civil rights by Executive pardon.

Second: Persons, who, at the time of the election, are in confinement under the judgment of a court for some penal offense.

Third: Idiots and insane persons.

Sec. 146. No person in the military, naval or marine service of the United States shall be deemed a resident of this State by reason of being stationed within the same.

Sec. 147. The General Assembly shall provide by law for the registration of all persons entitled to vote in cities and towns having a population of five thousand or more; and may provide by general law for the registration of other voters in the State. Where registration is required, only persons registered shall have the right to vote. The mode of registration shall be prescribed by the General Assembly. In all elections by persons in a representative capacity the voting shall be *viva voce* and made a matter of record; but all elections by the people shall be by secret official ballot, furnished by public authority to the voters at the polls, and marked by each voter in private at the polls, and then and there deposited. The word "Elections" in this section includes the decision of questions submitted to the voters, as well as the choice of officers by them. The first General Assembly held after the adoption of this Constitution shall pass all necessary laws to enforce this provision, and shall provide that persons illiterate, blind, or in any way disabled, may have their ballots marked as herein required.

Sec. 148. Not more than one election each year shall be held in this State or in any city, town, district, or county thereof, except as otherwise provided in this Constitution. All elections of State, county, city, town or district officers shall be held on the first Tuesday after the first Monday in November; but no officer of any city, town, or county, or of any subdivision thereof, except members of municipal legislative boards, shall be elected in the same year in which members of the House of Representatives of the United States are elected. District or State Officers, including members of the General Assembly, may be elected in the same year in which members of the House of Representatives of the United States are elected. All elections by the people shall be between the hours of six o'clock A. M. and seven o'clock P. M., but the General Assembly may change said hours, and all officers of any election shall be residents and voters in the precinct in which they act. The General Assembly shall provide by law that all employers shall allow employees, under reasonable regulations, at least four hours on election days, in which to cast their votes.

SEC. 149. Voters, in all cases except treason, felony, breach or surety of the peace, or violation of the election laws, shall be privileged from arrest during their attendance at elections, and while they are going to and returning therefrom.

SEC. 150. Every person shall be disqualified from holding any office of trust or profit for the term for which he shall have been elected who shall be convicted of having given, or consented to the giving, offer or promise of any money or other thing of value, to procure his election, or to influence the vote of any voter at such election; and in any corporation shall, directly or indirectly, offer, promise or give, or shall authorize, directly or indirectly, any person to offer, promise or give any money or any thing of value to influence the result of any election in this State, or the vote of any voter authorized to vote therein, or who shall afterward reimburse or compensate, in any manner whatever, any person who shall have offered, promised or given any money or other thing of value to influence the result of any election or the vote of any such voter, such corporation if organized under the laws of this Commonwealth, shall, on conviction thereof, forfeit its charter and all rights, privileges and immunities thereunder; and if chartered by another State and doing business in this State, whether by license, or upon mere sufferance, such corporation upon conviction of either of the offenses aforesaid, shall forfeit all right to carry on any buisness in this State; and it shall be the duty of the General Assembly to provide for the enforcement of the provisions of this section. All persons shall be excluded from office who have been, or shall hereafter be, convicted of a felon, or of such high misdemeanor as may be prescribed by law, but such disability may be removed by pardon of the Governor. The privilege of free suffrage shall be supported by laws regulating elections, and prohibiting, under adequate penalties, all undue influence thereon, from power, bribery, tumult or other improper practices.

SEC. 151. The General Assembly shall provide suitable means for depriving of office any person who, to procure his nomination or election, has, in his canvass or election, been guilty of any unlawful use of money, or other thing of value, or has been guilty of fraud, intimidation, bribery, or any other corrupt practice, and he shall be held responsible for acts done by others with his authority, or ratified by him.

SEC. 152. Except as otherwise provided in this Constitution, vacancies in all elective offices shall be filled by election or appointment, as follows: If the unexpired term will end at the next succeeding annual election at which either city, town, county, district, or State officers are to be elected, the office shall be filled by appointment for the remainder of the term. If the unexpired term will not end at the next succeeding annual election at which either city, town, county, district, or State officers are to be elected, and if three months intervene before said succeeding annual election at which either city, town, county, district, or State officers are to be elected, the office shall be filled by appointment until said election, and then said vacancy shall be filled by election for the remainder of the term. If three months do not intervene between the happening of said vacancy and the next succeeding election at which city, town, county, district or State officers are to be elected, the office shall be filled by appointment until the second succeeding annual election at which city, town, county, district or State officers are to be elected; and then, if any part of the term remains unexpired, the office shall be filled by election until the regular time for the election of officers to fill said offices. Vacancies in all offices for the State at large, or for districts larger than a county, shall be filled by appointment of the Governor; all other appointments shall be made as may be prescribed by law. No person shall ever be appointed a member of the General Assembly, but vacancies therein may be filled at a special election, in such manner as may be provided by law.

Sec. 153. Except as otherwise herein expressly provided, the General Assembly shall have power to provide by general law for the manner of voting, for ascertaining the result of elections and making due returns thereof, for issuing certificates or commissions to all persons entitled thereto, and for the trial of contested elections.

Sec. 154. The General Assembly shall prescribe such laws as may be necessary for the restriction or prohibition of the sale or gift of spirituous, vinous or malt liquors on election days.

Sec. 155. The provisions of sections one hundred and forty-five to one hundred and fifty-four, inclusive, shall not apply to the election of school trustees and other common school district elections. Said elections shall be regulated by the General Assembly, except as otherwise provided in this constitution.

MUNCIPALITIES.

Sec. 156. The cities and towns of this Commonwealth, for the purposes of their organization and government, shall be divided into six classes. The organization and powers of each class shall be defined and provided for by general laws, so that all municipal corporations of the same class shall possess the same powers and be subject to the same restrictions. To the first class shall belong cities with a population of one hundred thousand or more; to the second class, cities with a population of twenty thousand or more, and less than one hundred thousand; to the third class, cities with a population of eight thousand or more, and less than twenty thousand; to the fourth class, cities and towns with a population of three thousand or more, and less than eight thousand; to the fifth class, cities and towns with a population of one thousand or more, and less than three thousand; to the sixth class, towns with a population of less than one thousand. The General Assembly shall assign the cities and towns of the Commonwealth to the classes to which they respectively belong, and change assignments made as the population of said cities and towns may increase or decrease, and in the absence of other satisfactory information as to their population, shall be governed by the last preceding Federal census in so doing; but no city or town shall be transferred from one class to another, except in pursuance of a law previously enacted and providing therefor. The General Assembly, by a general law, shall provide how towns may be organized, and enact laws for the government of such towns until the same are assigned to one or the other of the classes above named; but such assignment shall be made at the first session of the General Assembly after the organization of said town or city.

SEC. 157. The tax rate of cities, towns, counties, taxing districts and other municipalities, for other than school purposes, shall not, at any time, exceed the following rates upon the value of the taxable property therein, viz: For all towns or cities having a population of fifteen thousand or more, one dollar and fifty cents on the hundred dollars; for all towns or cities having less than fifteen thousand and not less than ten thousand, one dollar on the hundred dollars; for all towns or cities having less than ten thousand, seventy-five cents on the hundred dollars; and for counties and taxing districts, fifty cents on the hundred dollars; unless it should be necessary to enable such city, town, county, or taxing district to pay the interest on, and provide a sinking fund for the extinction of, indebtedness contracted before the adoption of this Constitution. No county, city, town, taxing district, or other municipality, shall be authorized or permitted to become indebted, in any manner or for any purpose, to an amount exceeding, in any year, the income and revenue provided for such year, without the assent of two-thirds of the voters thereof, voting at an election to be held for that purpose; and any indebtedness contracted in violation of this section shall be void. Nor shall such contract be enforceable by the person with whom made; nor shall such municipality ever be authorized to assume the same.

SEC. 158. The respective cities, towns, counties, taxing districts, and municipalities shall not be authorized or permitted to incur indebtedness to an amount, including existing indebtedness, in the aggregate exceeding the following named maximum percentages on the value of the taxable property therein, to be estimated by the assessment next before the last assessment previous to the incurring of the indebtedness, viz: Cities of the first and second classes, and of the third class having a population exceeding fifteen thousand, ten per centum; cities of the third class having a population of less than fifteen thousand, and cities and towns of the fourth class, five per centum; cities and towns of the fifth and sixth classes, three per centum; and counties, taxing districts and other municipalities, two per centum: *Provided*, Any city, town, county, taxing district or other municipality may contract an indebtedness in excess of such limitations when the same has been authorized under laws in force prior to the adoption of this Constitution, or when necessary for the completion of and payment for a public improvement undertaken and not completed and paid for at the time of the adoption of this Constitution: *And provided further*, If, at the time of the adoption of this Constitution, the aggregate indebtedness, bonded or floating, of any city, town, county, taxing district or other municipality, including that which it has been or may be authorized to contract as herein provided, shall exceed the limit herein prescribed, then no such city or town shall be authorized or permitted to increase its indebtedness in an amount exceeding two per centum, and no such county, taxing district or other municipality, in an amount exceeding one per centum, in the aggregate upon the value of the taxable property therein, to be ascertained as herein provided, until the aggregate of its indebtedness shall have been reduced below the limit herein fixed, and thereafter it shall not exceed the limit, unless in case of emergency, the public health or safety should so require. Nothing herein shall prevent the issue of renewal bonds, or bonds to fund the floating indebtedness of any city, town, county, taxing district or other municipality.

SEC. 159. Whenever any county, city, town, taxing district or other municipality is authorized to contract an indebtedness, it shall be required, at the same time, to provide for the collection of an annual tax sufficient to pay the interest on said indebtedness, and to create a sinking fund for the payment of the principal thereof, within not more than forty years from the time of contracting the same.

SEC. 160. The Mayor or Chief Executive, Police Judges, members of legislative boards or councils of towns and cities shall be elected by the qualified voters thereof: *Provided*, The Mayor or Chief Executive and Police Judges of the towns of the fourth, fifth and sixth classes may be appointed or elected as provided by law. The terms of office of Mayors or Chief Executives and Police Judges shall be four years, and until their successors shall be qualified; and of members of legislative boards, two years. When any city of the first or second class is divided into wards or districts, members of legislative boards shall be elected at large by the qualified voters of said city, but so selected that an equal proportion thereof shall reside in each of the said wards or districts; but when in any city of the first, second or third class, there are two legislative boards, the less numerous shall be selected from and elected by the voters at shall be four years, and until their successors shall be qualified. No Mayor or Chief Executive or fiscal officer of any city of the first or second class, after the expiration of the term of office to which he has been elected under this Constitution, shall be eligible for the succeeding term. "Fiscal officer" shall not include an Auditor or Assessor, or any other officer whose chief duty is not the collection or holding of public moneys. The General Assembly shall prescribe the qualifications of all officers of towns and cities, the manner in and causes for which they may be removed from office, and how vacancies in such large of said city; but other officers of towns or cities shall be elected by the qualified voters therein, or appointed by the local authorities thereof, as the General Assembly may, by a general law, provide; but when elected by the voters of a town or city, their terms of office

SEC. 161. The compensation of any city, county, town or municipal officer shall not be changed after his election or appointment, or during his term of office; nor shall the term of any such officer be extended beyond the period for which he may have been elected or appointed.

SEC. 162. No county, city, town or other municipality shall ever be authorized or permitted to pay any claim created against it, under any agreement or contract made without express authority of law, and all such unauthorized agreements or contracts shall be null and void.

SEC. 163. No street railway, gas, water, steam heating, telephone, or electric light company, within a city or town, shall be permitted or authorized to construct its tracks, lay its pipes or mains, or erect its poles, posts or other apparatus along, over, under or across the streets, alleys or public grounds of a city or town, without the consent of the proper legislative bodies or boards of such city or town being first obtained; but when charters have been heretofore granted conferring such rights, and work has in good faith been begun thereunder, the provisions of this section shall not apply.

SEC. 164. No county, city, town, taxing district or other municipality shall be authorized or permitted to grant any franchise or privilege, or make any contract in reference thereto, for a term exceeding twenty years. Before granting such franchise or privilege for a term of years, such municipality shall first, after due advertisement, receive bids therefor publicly, and award the same to the highest and best bidder; but it shall have the right to reject any or all bids. This section shall not apply to a trunk railway.

SEC. 165. No person shall, at the same time, be a State officer or a deputy officer, or member of the General Assembly, and an officer of any county, city, town, or other municipality, or an employe thereof; and no person shall, at the same time, fill two municipal offices, either in the same or different municipalities, except as may be otherwise provided in this Constitution; but a Notary Public, or an officer of the Militia, shall not be ineligible to hold any other office mentioned in this section.

SEC. 166. All acts of incorporation of cities and towns heretofore granted, and all amendments thereto, except as provided in section one hundred and sixty-seven, shall continue in force under this Constitution, and all City and Police Courts established in any city or town shall remain, with their present powers and jurisdictions, until such time as the General Assembly shall provide by general laws for the government of towns and cities, and the officers and courts thereof; but not longer than four years from and after the first day of January, one thousand eight hundred and ninety-one, within which time the General Assembly shall provide by general laws for the government of towns and cities, and the officers and courts thereof, as provided in this Constitution.

SEC. 167. All city and town officers in this State shall be elected or appointed as provided in the charter of each respective town and city, until the general election in November, 1893, and until their successors shall be elected and qualified, at which time the terms of all such officers shall expire; and at that election, and thereafter as their terms of office may expire, all officers required to be elected in cities and towns by this Constitution, or by general laws enacted in conformity to its provisions, shall be elected at the general elections in November, but only in the odd years, except members of municipal legislative boards, who may be elected either in the even or odd years, or part in the even and part in the odd years: *Provided*, That the terms of office of Police Judges, who were elected for four years at the August election, eighteen hundred and ninety, shall expire

August thirty-first, eighteen hundred and ninety-four, and the terms of Police Judges elected in November, eighteen hundred and ninety-three, shall begin September first, eighteen hundred and ninety-four, and continue until the November election, eighteen hundred and ninety-seven, and until their successors are elected and qualified.

Sec. 168. No municipal ordinance shall fix a penalty for a violation thereof at less than that imposed by statute for the same offense. A conviction or acquittal under either shall constitute a bar to another prosecution for the same offense.

REVENUE AND TAXATION

Sec. 169. The fiscal year shall commence on the first day of July in each year, unless otherwise provided by law.

Sec. 170. There shall be exempt from taxation public property used for public purposes; places actually used for religious worship, with the grounds attached thereto and used and appurtenant to the house of worship, not exceeding one-half acre in cities or towns, and not exceeding two acres in the country; places of burial not held for private or corporate profit, institutions of purely public charity, and institutions of education not used or employed for gain by any person or corporation, and the income of which is devoted solely to the cause of education; public libraries, their endowments, and the income of such property as is used exclusively for their maintenance; all parsonages or residences owned by any religious society, and occupied as a home, and for no other purpose, by the minister of any religion, with not exceeding one-half acre of ground in towns and cities and two acres of ground in the country appurtenant thereto; household goods and other personal property of a person with a family, not exceeding two hundred and fifty dollars in value; crops grown in the year in which the assessment is made, and in the hands of the producer; and all laws exempting or commuting property from taxation other than the property above mentioned shall be void. The General Assembly may authorize any incorporated city or town to exempt manufacturing establishments from municipal taxation, for a period not exceeding five years, as an inducement to their location.

Sec. 171. The General Assembly shall provide by law an annual tax, which, with other resources, shall be sufficient to defray the estimated expenses of the Commonwealth for each fiscal year. Taxes shall be levied and collected for public purposes only. They shall be uniform upon all property subject to taxation within the territorial limits of the authority levying the tax; and all taxes shall be levied and collected by general laws.

Sec. 172. All property, not exempted from taxation by this Constitution, shall be assessed for taxation at its fair cash value, estimated at the price it would bring at a fair voluntary sale; and any officer, or other person authorized to assess values for taxation, who shall commit any willful error in the performance of his duty, shall be deemed guilty of misfeasance, and upon conviction thereof shall forfeit his office, and be otherwise punished as may be provided by law.

Sec. 173. The receiving, directly or indirectly, by any officer of the Commonwealth, or of any county, city or town, or member or officer of the General Assembly, of any interest, profit or perquisites arising from the use or loan of public funds in his hands, or moneys to be raised through his agency for State, city, town, district or county purposes shall be deemed a felony. Said offense shall be punished as may be prescribed by law, a part of which punishment shall be disqualification to hold office.

SEC. 174. All property, whether owned by natural persons or corporations, shall be taxed in proportion to its value, unless exempted by this Constitution; and all corporate property shall pay the same rate of taxation paid by individual property. Nothing in this Constitution shall be construed to prevent the General Assembly from providing for taxation based on incomes, licenses or franchises.

SEC. 175. The power to tax property shall not be surrendered or suspended by any contract or grant to which the Commonwealth shall be a party.

SEC. 176. The Commonwealth shall not assume the debt of any county, municipal corporation or political subdivision of the State, unless such debt shall have been contracted to defend itself in time of war, to repel invasion or to suppress insurrection.

SEC. 177. The credit of the Commonwealth shall not be given, pledged or loaned to any individual, company, corporation or association, municipality, or political subdivision of the State; nor shall the Commonwealth become an owner or stockholder in, nor make donation to, any company, association or corporation; nor shall the Commonwealth construct a railroad or other highway.

SEC. 178. All laws authorizing the borrowing of money by and on behalf of the Commonwealth, county or other political subdivision of the State, shall specify the purpose for which the money is to be used, and the money so borrowed shall be used for no other purpose.

SEC. 179. The General Assembly shall not authorize any county or subdivision thereof, city, town, or incorporated district, to become a stockholder in any company, association or corporation, or to obtain or appropriate money for, or to loan its credit to, any corporation, association or individual, except for the purpose of constructing or maintaining bridges, turnpike roads, or gravel roads: *Provided*, If any municipal corporation shall offer to the Commonwealth any property or money for locating or building a Capitol, and the Commonwealth accepts such offer, the corporation may comply with the offer.

SEC. 180. The General Assembly may authorize the counties, cities or towns to levy a poll-tax not exceeding one dollar and fifty cents per head. Every act enacted by the General Assembly, and every ordinance and resolution passed by any county, city, town, or municipal board or local legislative body, levying a tax, shall specify distinctly the purpose for which said tax is levied, and no tax levied and collected for one purpose shall ever be devoted to another purpose.

[a] SEC. 181. The General Assembly shall not impose taxes for the purposes of any county, city, town or other municipal corporation, but may, by general laws, confer on the proper authorities thereof, respectively, the power to assess and collect such taxes. The General Assembly may, by general laws only, provide for the payment of

---

[a] Amended, 1892.

license fees on franchises, stock used for breeding purposes, the various trades, occupations and professions, or a special or excise tax; and may, by general laws, delegate the power to counties, towns, cities, and other municipal corporations, to impose and collect license fees on stock used for breeding purposes, on franchises, trades, occupations and professions.

SEC. 182. Nothing in this Constitution shall be construed to prevent the General Assembly from providing by law how railroads and railroad property shall be assessed and how taxes thereon shall be collected. And until otherwise provided, the present law on said subject shall remain in force.

EDUCATION

SEC. 183. The General Assembly shall, by appropriate legislation, provide for an efficient system of common schools throughout the State.

SEC. 184. The bond of the Commonwealth issued in favor of the Board of Education for the sum of one million three hundred and twenty-seven thousand dollars shall constitute one bond of the Commonwealth in favor of the Board of Education, and this bond and the seventy-three thousand five hundred dollars of the stock in the Bank of Kentucky, held by the Board of Education, and its proceeds, shall be held inviolate for the purpose of sustaining the system of common schools. The interest and dividends of said fund, together with any sum which may be produced by taxation or otherwise for purposes of common school education, shall be appropriated to the common schools, and to no other purpose. No sum shall be raised or collected for education other than in common schools until the question of taxation is submitted to the legal voters, and the majority of the votes cast at said election shall be in favor of such taxation: *Provided*, The tax now imposed for educational purposes, and for the endowment and maintenance of the Agricultural and Mechanical College, shall remain until changed by law.

SEC. 185. The General Assembly shall make provision, by law, for the payment of the interest of said school fund, and may provide for the sale of the stock in the Bank of Kentucky; and in case of a sale of all or any part of said stock, the proceeds of sale shall be invested by the Sinking Fund Commissioners in other good interest-bearing stocks or bonds, which shall be subject to sale and reinvestment, from time to time, in like manner, and with the same restrictions, as provided with reference to the sale of the said stock in the Bank of Kentucky.

SEC. 186. Each county in the Commonwealth shall be entitled to its proportion of the school fund on its census of pupil children for each school year; and if the pro rata share of any school district be not called for after the second school year, it shall be covered into the treasury and be placed to the credit of the school fund for general apportionment the following school year. The surplus now due the several counties shall remain a perpetual obligation against the Commonwealth for the benefit of said respective counties, for which the Commonwealth shall execute its bond, bearing interest at the rate of six per centum per annum, payable annually to the counties respectively entitled to the same, and in the proportion to which they are entitled, to be used exclusively in aid of common schools.

SEC. 187. In distributing the school fund no distinction shall be made on account of race or color, and separate schools for white and colored children shall be maintained.

SEC. 188. So much of any moneys as may be received by the Commonwealth from the United States under the recent act of Congress refunding the direct tax shall become a part of the school fund, and be held as provided in section one hundred and eighty-four; but the General Assembly may authorize the use, by the Commonwealth, of the moneys so received or any part thereof, in which event a bond shall be executed to the Board of Education for the amount so used which bond shall be held on the same terms and conditions, and subject to the provisions of section one hundred and eighty-four, concerning the bond therein referred to.

SEC. 189. No portion of any fund or tax now existing, or that may hereafter be raised or levied for educational purposes, shall be appropriated to, or used by, or in aid of, any church, sectarian or denominational school.

CORPORATIONS

SEC. 190. No corporation in existence at the time of the adoption of this Constitution shall have the benefit of future legislation without first filing in the office of the Secretary of State an acceptance of the provisions of this Constitution.

SEC. 191. All existing charters or grants of special or exclusive privileges, under which a bona fide organization shall not have taken place, and business been commenced in good faith at the time of the adoption of this Constitution, shall thereafter be void and of no effect.

SEC. 192. No corporation shall engage in business other than that expressly authorized by its charter, or the law under which it may have been or hereafter may be organized, nor shall it hold any real estate, except such as may be proper and necessary for carrying on its legitimate business, for a longer period than five years, under penalty of escheat.

SEC. 193. No corporation shall issue stock or bonds except for an equivalent in money paid or labor done, or property actually received and applied to the purposes for which such corporation was created, and neither labor nor property shall be received in payment of stock or bonds at a greater value than the market price at the time said labor was done or property delivered, and all fictitious increase of stock or indebtedness shall be void.

SEC. 194. All corporations formed under the laws of this State, or carrying on business in this State, shall, at all times, have one or more known places of business in this State, and an authorized agent or agents there, upon whom process may be executed, and the General Assembly shall enact laws to carry into effect the provisions of this section.

SEC. 195. The Commonwealth, in the exercise of the right of eminent domain, shall have and retain the same powers to take the property and franchises of incorporated companies for public use which it has and retains to take the property of individuals, and the exercise of the police powers of this Commonwealth shall never be abridged, nor so construed as to permit corporations to conduct their business in such manner as to infringe upon the equal rights of individuals.

SEC. 196. Transportation of freight and passengers by railroad, steamboat or other common carrier, shall be so regulated, by the general law, as to prevent unjust discrimination. No common carrier shall be permitted to contract for relief from its common law liability.

SEC. 197. No railroad, steamboat or other common carrier, under heavy penalty to be fixed by the General Assembly, shall give a free pass or passes, or shall, at reduced rates not common to the public, sell tickets for transportation to any State, district, city, town or county officer, or member of the General Assembly, or Judge; and any State, district, city, town or county officer, or member of the General Assembly, or Judge, who shall accept or use a free pass or passes, or shall receive or use tickets or transportation at reduced rates not common to the public, shall forfeit his office. It shall be the duty of the General Assembly to enact laws to enforce the provisions of this section.

SEC. 198. It shall be the duty of the General Assembly from time to time, as necessity may require, to enact such laws as may be necessary to prevent all trusts, pools, combinations or other organizations, from combining to depreciate below its real value any article, or to enhance the cost of any article above its real value.

SEC. 199. Any association or corporation, or the lessees or managers thereof, organized for the purpose, or any individual, shall have the right to construct and maintain lines of telegraph within this State, and to connect the same with other lines, and said companies shall receive and transmit each other's messages without unreasonable delay or discrimination, and all such companies are hereby declared to be common carriers and subject to legislative control. Telephone companies operating exchanges in different towns or cities, or other public stations, shall receive and transmit each other's messages without unreasonable delay or discrimination. The General Assembly shall, by general laws of uniform operation, provide reasonable regulations to give full effect to this section. Nothing herein shall be construed to interfere with the rights of cities or towns to arrange and control their streets and alleys, and to designate the places at which, and the manner in which, the wires of such companies shall be erected or laid within the limits of such city or town.

SEC. 200. If any railroad, telegraph, express, or other corporation, organized under the laws of this Commonwealth, shall consolidate by sale or otherwise, with any railroad, telegraph, express or other corporation organized under the laws of any other State, the same shall not thereby become a foreign corporation, but the courts of this Commonwealth shall retain jurisdiction over that part of the corporate property within the limits of this State in all matters which may arise, as if said consolidation had not taken place.

SEC. 201. No railroad, telegraph, telephone, bridge or common carrier company shall consolidate its capital stock, franchises or property, or pool its earnings, in whole or in part, with any other railroad, telegraph, telephone, bridge or common carrier company, owning a parallel or competing line or structure, or acquire by purchase, lease or otherwise, any parallel or competing line or structure, or operate the same; nor shall any railroad company or other common carrier combine or make any contract with the owners of any vessel that leaves or makes port in this State, or with any common carrier, by which combination or contract the earnings of one doing the carrying are to be shared by the other not doing the carrying.

SEC. 202. No corporation organized outside the limits of this State shall be allowed to transact business within the State on more favorable conditions than are prescribed by law to similar corporations organized under the laws of this Commonwealth.

SEC. 203. No corporation shall lease or alienate any franchise so as to relieve the franchise or property held thereunder from the liabilities of the lessor or grantor, lessee or grantee, contracted or incurred in the operation, use or enjoyment of such franchise, or any of its privileges.

SEC. 204. Any President, Director, Manager, Cashier or other officer of any banking institution or association for the deposit or loan of money, or any individual banker, who shall receive or assent to the receiving of deposits after he shall have knowledge of the fact that such banking institution or association or individual banker is insolvent, shall be individually responsible for such deposits so received, and shall be guilty of felony and subject to such punishment as shall be prescribed by law.

SEC. 205. The General Assembly shall, by general laws, provide for the revocation or forfeiture of the charters of all corporations guilty of abuse or misuse of their corporate powers, privileges or franchises, or whenever said corporations become detrimental to the interest and welfare of the Commonwealth or its citizens.

SEC. 206. All elevators or storehouses, where grain or other property is stored for a compensation, whether the property stored be kept separate or not, are declared to be public warehouses, subject to legislative control, and the General Assembly shall enact laws for the inspection of grain, tobacco and other produce, and for the protection of producers, shippers and receivers of grain, tobacco and other produce.

SEC. 207. In all elections for directors or managers of any corporation, each share-holder shall have the right to cast as many votes in the aggregate as he shall be entitled to vote in said company under its charter, multiplied by the number of directors or managers to be elected at such election; and each share-holder may cast the whole number of votes, either in person or by proxy, for one candidate, or distribute such votes among two or more candidates, and such directors or managers shall not be elected in any other manner.

SEC. 208. The word corporation as used in this Constitution shall embrace joint stock companies and associations.

RAILROADS AND COMMERCE

SEC. 209. A commission is hereby established, to be known as " The Railroad Commission " which shall be composed of three Commissioners. During the session of the General Assembly which convenes in December, eighteen hundred and ninety-one, and before the first day of June, eighteen hundred and ninety-two, the Governor shall appoint, by and with the advice and consent of the Senate, said three Commissioners, one from each Superior Court District as now established, and said appointees shall take their office at the expiration of the terms of the present incumbents. The Commissioners so appointed shall continue in office during the term of the present Governor, and until their successors are elected and qualified. At the regular election in eighteen hundred and ninety-five and every four years thereafter the Commissioners shall be elected, one in each Superior Court District, by the qualified voters thereof, at the same time and for the same term as the Governor. No person shall be eligible to said office unless he be, at the time of his election, at least thirty years of age, a citizen of Kentucky two years, and a resident of the district from which is chosen one year, next preceding his election. Any vacancy in this office shall be filled as provided in section one hundred and fifty-two of this Constitution. The General Assembly may from time to time change said districts so as to equalize the population thereof; and may, if deemed expedient, require that the Commissioners be all elected by the qualified voters of the State at large. And if so required, one Commissioner shall be from each District. No person in the service of any railroad or common carrier company or corporation, or of any firm or association conducting business as a common carrier, or in anywise pecuniarily interested in such company, corporation, firm or association, or in the railroad business, or as a common carrier, shall hold such office. The powers and duties of the Railroad Commissioners shall be regulated by law; and until otherwise provided by law, the Commission so created shall have the same powers and jurisdiction, perform the same duties, be subject to the same regulations, and receive the same compensation, as now conferred, prescribed and allowed by law to the existing Railroad Commissioners. The General Assembly may, for cause, address any of said Commissioners out of office by similar proceedings as in the case of Judges of the Court of Appeals; and the General Assembly shall enact laws to prevent the nonfeasance and misfeasance in office of said Commissioners, and to impose proper penalties therefor.

SEC. 210. No corporation engaged in the business of common carrier shall, directly or indirectly, own, manage, operate, or engage in any other business than that of a common carrier, or hold, own, lease or acquire directly or indirectly, mines, factories, or timber, except such as shall be necessary to carry on its business; and the General Assembly shall enact laws to give effect to the provisions of this section.

SEC. 211. No railroad corporation organized under the laws of any other State, or of the United States, and doing business, or proposing to do business, in this State, shall be entitled to the benefit of the right of eminent domain or have power to acquire the right of way or real estate for depot or other uses, until it shall have become a body-corporate pursuant to and in accordance with the laws of this Commonwealth.

SEC. 212. The rolling stock and other movable property belonging to any railroad corporation or company in this State shall be considered personal property, and shall be liable to execution and sale in the same manner as the personal property of individuals. The earnings of any railroad company or corporation, and choses in action, money and personal property of all kinds belonging to it, in the hands, or under the control, of any officer, agent or employe of such corporation or company, shall be subject to process of attachment to the same extent and in the same manner, as like property of individuals when in the hands or under the control of other persons. Any such earnings, choses in action, money or other personal property may be subjected to the payment of any judgment against such corporation or company, in the same manner and to the same extent as such property of individuals in the hands of third persons.

SEC. 213. All railroad, transfer, belt lines and railway bridge companies, organized under the laws of Kentucky, or operating, maintaining or controlling any railroad, transfer, belt lines or bridges, or doing a railway business in this State, shall receive, transfer, deliver, and switch empty or loaded cars, and shall move, transport, receive, load or unload all the freight in car loads or less quantities, coming to or going from any railroad, transfer, belt line, bridge or siding thereon, with equal promptness and dispatch, and without any discrimination as to charges, preference, drawback or rebate in favor of any person, corporation, consignee or consignor, in any matter as to payment, transportation, handling or delivery; and shall so receive, deliver, transfer and transport all freight as above set forth, from and to any point where there is a physical connection between the tracks of said companies. But this section shall not be construed as requiring any such common carrier to allow the use of its tracks for the trains of another engaged in like business.

SEC. 214. No railway, transfer, belt line or railway bridge company shall make any exclusive or preferential contract or arrangement with any individual, association or corporation, for the receipt, transfer, delivery, transportation, handling, care or custody of any freight, or for the conduct of any business as a common carrier.

SEC. 215. All railway, transfer, belt lines or railway bridge companies shall receive, load, unload, transport, haul, deliver and handle freight of the same class for all persons, associations or corporations from and to the same points and upon the same conditions, in the same manner and for the same charges, and for the same method of payment.

SEC. 216. All railway, transfer, belt lines and railway bridge companies shall allow the tracks of each other to unite, intersect and cross at any point where such union, intersection and crossing is reasonable or feasible.

SEC. 217. Any person, association or corporation, willfully or knowingly violating any of the provisions of sections two hundred and thirteen, two hundred and fourteen, two hundred and fifteen, or two hundred and sixteen, shall, upon conviction by a court of competent jurisdiction, for the first offense be fined two thousand dollars; for the second offense, five thousand dollars, and for the third offense, shall thereupon, *ipso facto*, forfeit its franchises, privileges or charter rights; and if such delinquent be a foreign corporation, it shall, *ipso facto*, forfeit its right to do business in this State; and the Attorney-General of the Commonwealth shall forthwith, upon notice of the violation of any of said provisions, institute proceedings to enforce the provisions of the aforesaid sections.

SEC. 218. It shall be unlawful for any person or corporation, owning or operating a railroad in this State, or any common carrier, to charge or receive any greater compensation in the aggregate for the transportation of passengers, or of property of like kind, under substantially similar circumstances and conditions, for a shorter than for a longer distance over the same line, in the same direction, the shorter being included within the longer distance; but this shall not be construed as authorizing any common carrier, or person or corporation, owning or operating a railroad in this State, to receive as great compensation for a shorter as for a longer distance: *Provided*, That upon application to the Railroad Commission, such common carrier, or person, or corporation owning or operating a railroad in this State, may in special cases, after investigation by the Commission, be authorized to charge less for longer than for shorter distances for the transportation of passengers, or property; and the Commission may, from time to time, prescribe the extent to which such common carrier, or person or corporation, owning or operating a railroad in this State, may be relieved from the operations of this section.

THE MILITIA

SEC. 219. The militia of the Commonwealth of Kentucky shall consist of all able-bodied male residents of the State between the ages of eighteen and forty-five years, except such persons as may be exempted by the laws of the State or of the United States.

SEC. 220. The General Assembly shall provide for maintaining an organized militia; and may exempt from military service persons having conscientious scruples against bearing arms; but such persons shall pay an equivalent for such exemption.

SEC. 221. The organization, equipment and discipline of the militia shall conform as nearly as practicable to the regulations for the government of the armies of the United States.

SEC. 222. All militia officers whose appointment is not herein otherwise provided for, shall be elected by persons subject to military duty within their respective companies, battalions, regiments or other commands, under such rules and regulations and for such terms, not exceeding four years, as the General Assembly may, from time to time, direct and establish. The Governor shall appoint an Adjutant-General and his other staff officers; the generals and commandants of regiments and battalions shall respectively appoint their staff officers, and the commandants of companies shall, subject to the approval of their regimental or battalion commanders, appoint their non-commissioned officers. The Governor shall have power to fill vacancies that may occur in elective offices by granting commissions which shall expire when such vacancies have been filled according to the provisions of this Constitution.

SEC. 223. The General Assembly shall provide for the safe-keeping of the public arms, military records, relics and banners of the Commonwealth of Kentucky.

GENERAL PROVISIONS

SEC. 224. The General Assembly shall provide by a general law what officers shall execute bond for the faithful discharge of their duties, and fix the liability therein.

SEC. 225. No armed person or bodies of men shall be brought into this State for the preservation of the peace or the suppression of domestic violence, except upon the application of the General Assembly, or of the Governor when the General Assembly may not be in session.

SEC. 226. Lotteries and gift enterprises are forbidden, and no privileges shall be granted for such purposes, and none shall be exercised, and no schemes for similar purposes shall be allowed. The General Assembly shall enforce this section by proper penalties. All lottery privileges or charters heretofore granted are revoked.

SEC. 227. Judges of the County Court, Justices of the Peace, Sheriffs, Coroners, Surveyors, Jailers, Assessors, County Attorneys and Constables shall be subject to indictment or prosecution for misfeasance or malfeasance in office, or willful neglect in discharge of official duties, in such mode as may be prescribed by law; and upon conviction, his office shall become vacant, but such officer shall have the right of appeal to the Court of Appeals.

SEC. 228. Members of the General Assembly and all officers, before they enter upon the execution of the duties of their respective offices, and all members of the bar, before they enter upon the practice of their profession, shall take the following oath or affirmation: I do solemnly swear (or affirm, as the case may be) that I will support the Constitution of the United States and the Constitution of this Commonwealth, and be faithful and true to the Commonwealth of Kentucky so long as I continue a citizen thereof, and that I will faithfully execute, to the best of my ability the office of ——— according to law; and I do further solemnly swear (or affirm) that since the adoption of the present Constitution, I, being a citizen of this State, have not fought a duel with deadly weapons within this State nor out of it, nor have I sent or accepted a challenge to fight a duel with deadly weapons, nor have I acted as second in carrying a challenge, nor aided or assisted any person thus offending, so help me God.

SEC. 229. Treason against the Commonwealth shall consist only in levying war against it, or in adhering to its enemies giving them aid and comfort. No person shall be convicted of treason except on the testimony of two witnesses to the same overt act, or his own confession in open court.

SEC. 230. No money shall be drawn from the State Treasury, except in pursuance of appropriations made by law; and a regular statement and account of the receipts and expenditures of all public money shall be published annually.

SEC. 231. The General Assembly may, by law, direct in what manner and in what courts suits may be brought against the Commonwealth.

SEC. 232. The manner of administering an oath or affirmation shall be such as is most consistent with the conscience of the deponent, and shall be esteemed by the General Assembly the most solemn appeal to God.

SEC. 233. All laws which, on the first day of June, one thousand seven hundred and ninety-two, were in force in the State of Virginia, and which are of a general nature and not local to that State, and not repugnant to this Constitution, nor to the laws which have been enacted by the General Assembly of this Commonwealth, shall be in force within this State until they shall be altered or repealed by the General Assembly.

SEC. 234. All civil officers for the State at large shall reside within the State, and all district, county, city or town officers shall reside within their respective districts, counties, cities or towns, and shall keep their offices at such places therein as may be required by law.

SEC. 235. The salaries of public officers shall not be changed during the terms for which they were elected; but it shall be the duty of the General Assembly to regulate, by a general law, in what cases and what deductions shall be made for neglect of official duties. This section shall apply to members of the General Assembly also.

SEC. 236. The General Assembly shall, by law, prescribe the time when the several officers authorized or directed by this Constitution to be elected or appointed, shall enter upon the duties of their respective offices, except where the time is fixed by this Constitution.

SEC. 237. No member of Congress, or person holding or exercising an office of trust or profit under the United States, or any of them, or under any foreign power, shall be eligible to hold or exercise any office of trust or profit under this Constitution, or the laws made in pursuance thereof.

SEC. 238. The General Assembly shall direct by law how persons who now are, or may hereafter become, sureties for public officers, may be relieved of or discharged from suretyship.

SEC. 239. Any person who shall, after the adoption of this Constitution, either directly or indirectly, give, accept or knowingly carry a challenge to any person or persons to fight in single combat, with a citizen of this State, with a deadly weapon, either in or out of the State, shall be deprived of the right to hold any office of honor or profit in this Commonwealth; and if said acts, or any of them, be committed within this State, the person or persons so committing them shall be further punished in such manner as the General Assembly may prescribe by law.

SEC. 240. The Governor shall have power, after five years from the time of the offense, to pardon any person who shall have participated in a duel as principal, second or otherwise, and to restore him to all the rights, privileges and immunities to which he was entitled before such participation. Upon presentation of such pardon the oath prescribed in section two hundred and twenty-eight shall be varied to suit the case.

SEC. 241. Whenever the death of a person shall result from an injury inflicted by negligence or wrongful act, then, in every such case, damages may be recovered for such death, from the corporations and persons so causing the same. Until otherwise provided by law, the action to recover such damages shall in all cases be prosecuted by the personal representative of the deceased person. The General Assembly may provide how the recovery shall go and to whom belong; and until such provision is made the same shall form part of the personal estate of the deceased person.

SEC. 242. Municipal and other corporations, and individuals invested with the privilege of taking private property for public use, shall make just compensation for property taken, injured or destroyed by them; which compensation shall be paid before such taking, or paid or secured, at the election of such corporation or individual, before such injury or destruction. The General Assembly shall not deprive any person of an appeal from any preliminary assessment of damages against any such corporation or individual made by Commissioners or otherwise; and upon appeal from such preliminary assessment, the amount of such damages shall, in all cases, be determined by a jury, according to the course of the common law.

SEC. 243. The General Assembly shall, by law, fix the minimum ages at which children may be employed in places dangerous to life or health, or injurious to morals; and shall provide adequate penalties for violations of such law.

SEC. 244. All wage-earners in this State employed in factories, mines, workshops, or by corporations, shall be paid for their labor in lawful money. The General Assembly shall prescribe adequate penalties for violations of this section.

SEC. 245. Upon the promulgation of this Constitution, the Governor shall appoint three persons, learned in the law, who shall be Commissioners to revise the statute laws of this Commonwealth, and prepare amendments thereto, to the end that the statute laws shall conform to and effectuate this Constitution. Such revision and amendments shall be laid before the next General Assembly for adoption or rejection, in whole or in part. The said Commissioners shall be allowed ten dollars each per day for their services, and also necessary stationery for the time during which they are actually employed; and upon their certificate the Auditor shall draw his warrant upon the Treasurer. They shall have the power to employ clerical assistants, at a compensation not exceeding ten dollars per day in the aggregate. If the Commissioners, or any of them, shall refuse to act, or a vacancy shall occur, the Governor shall appoint another or others in his or their place.

SEC. 246. No public officer, except the Governor, shall receive more than five thousand dollars per annum, as compensation for official services, independent of the compensation of legally authorized deputies and assistants, which shall be fixed and provided for by law. The General Assembly shall provide for the enforcement of this section by suitable penalties, one of which shall be forfeiture of office by any person violating its provisions.

SEC. 247. The printing and binding of the laws, journals, department reports, and all other public printing and binding, shall be performed under contract, to be given to the lowest responsible bidder, below such maximum and under such regulations as may be prescribed by law. No member of the General Assembly, or officer of the Commonwealth, shall be in any way interested in any such contract; and all such contracts shall be subject to the approval of the Governor.

SEC. 248. A grand jury shall consist of twelve persons, nine of whom concurring, may find an indictment. In civil and misdemeanor cases, in courts inferior to the Circuit Courts, a jury shall consist of six persons. The General Assembly may provide that in any or all trials of civil actions in the Circuit Courts, three-fourths or more of the jurors concurring may return a verdict, which shall have the same force and effect as if rendered by the entire panel. But where a verdict is rendered by a less number than the whole jury, it shall be signed by all the jurors who agree to it.

SEC. 249. The House of Representatives of the General Assembly shall not elect, appoint, employ or pay for, exceeding one Chief Clerk, one Assistant Clerk, one Enrolling Clerk, one Sergeant-at-Arms, one Door-keeper, one Janitor, two Cloak-room Keepers and four Pages; and the Senate shall not elect, appoint, employ or pay for, exceeding one Chief Clerk, one Assistant Clerk, one Enrolling Clerk, one Sergeant-at-Arms, one Door-keeper, one Janitor, one Cloak-room Keeper and three Pages; and the General Assembly shall provide, by general law, for fixing the per diem or salary of all of said employes.

SEC. 250. It shall be the duty of the General Assembly to enact such laws as shall be necessary and proper to decide differences by arbitrators, the arbitrators to be appointed by the parties who may choose that summary mode of adjustment.

SEC. 251. No action shall be maintained for possession of any lands lying within this State, where it is necessary for the claimant to rely for his recovery on any grant or patent issued by the Commonwealth of Virginia, or by the Commonwealth of Kentucky prior to the year one thousand eight hundred and twenty, against any person claiming such lands by possession to a well-defined boundary, under a title of record, unless such action shall be instituted within five years after this Constitution shall go into effect, or within five years after the occupant may take possession; but nothing herein shall be construed to affect any right, title or interest in lands acquired by virtue of adverse possession under the laws of this commonwealth.

SEC. 252. It shall be the duty of the General Assembly to provide by law, as soon as practicable, for the establishment and maintenance of an institution or institutions for the detention, correction, instruction and reformation of all persons under the age of eighteen years, convicted of such felonies and such misdemeanors as may be designated by law. Said institution shall be known as the "House of Reform."

SEC. 253. Persons convicted of felony and sentenced to confinement in the penitentiary shall be confined at labor within the walls of the penitentiary; and the General Assembly shall not have the power to authorize employment of convicts elsewhere, except upon the public works of the Commonwealth of Kentucky, or when, during pestilence or in case of the destruction of the prison buildings, they cannot be confined in the penitentiary.

SEC. 254. The Commonwealth shall maintain control of the discipline, and provide for all supplies, and for the sanitary condition of the convicts, and the labor only of convicts may be leased.

SEC. 255. The seat of government shall continue in the city of Frankfort, unless removed by a vote of two-thirds of each House of the first General Assembly which convenes after the adoption of this Constitution.

MODE OF REVISION

SEC. 256. Amendments to this Constitution may be proposed in either House of the General Assembly at a regular session, and if such amendment or amendments shall be agreed to by three-fifths of all the members elected to each House, such proposed amendment or amendments, with the yeas and nays of the members of each House taken thereon, shall be entered in full in their respective journals. Then such proposed amendment or amendments shall be submitted to the voters of the State for their ratification or rejection at the next general election for members of the House of Representatives, the vote to be taken thereon in such manner as the General Assembly may provide, and to be certified by the officers of election to the Secretary of State in such manner as shall be provided by law, which vote shall be compared and certified by the same board authorized by law to compare the polls and give certificates of election to officers for the State at large. If it shall appear that a majority of the votes cast for and against an amendment at said election was for the amendment, then the same shall become a part of the Constitution of this Commonwealth, and shall be so proclaimed by the Governor, and published in such manner as the General Assembly may direct. Said amendments shall not be submitted at an election which occurs less than ninety days from the final passage of such proposed amendment or amendments. Not more than two amendments shall be voted upon at any one time. Nor shall the same amendment be again submitted within five years after submission. Said amendments shall be so submitted as to allow a separate vote on each, and no amendment shall relate to more than one subject. But no amendment shall be proposed by the first General Assembly which convenes after the adoption of this Constitution. The approval of the Governor shall not be necessary to any bill, order, resolution or vote of the General Assembly, proposing an amendment or amendments to this Constitution.

SEC. 257. Before an amendment shall be submitted to a vote, the Secretary of State shall cause such proposed amendment, and the time that the same is to be voted upon, to be published at least ninety days before the vote is to be taken thereon in such manner as may be prescribed by law.

SEC. 258. When a majority of all the members elected to each House of the General Assembly shall concur, by a yea and nay vote, to be entered upon their respective journals, in enacting a law to take the sense of the people of the State as to the necessity and expediency of calling a convention for the purpose of revising or amending this Constitution, and such amendments as may have been made to the same, such law shall be spread upon their respective journals. If the next General Assembly shall, in like manner, concur in such law, it shall provide for having a poll opened in each voting precinct in this State by the officers provided by law for holding general elections at the next ensuing regular election to be held for State officers or members of the House of Representatives, which does not occur within ninety days from the final passage of such law, at which time and places the votes of the qualified voters shall be taken for and against calling the Convention, in the same manner provided by law for taking votes in other State elections. The vote for and against said proposition shall be certified to the Secretary of State by the same officers and in the same manner as in State elections. If it shall appear that a majority voting on the proposition was for calling a Convention, and if the total number of votes cast for the calling of the Convention is equal to one-fourth of the number of qualified voters who voted at the last preceding general election in this State, the Secretary of State shall certify the same to the General Assembly at its next regular session, at which session a law shall be enacted calling a Convention to readopt, revise or amend this Constitution, and such amendments as may have been made thereto.

SEC. 259. The Convention shall consist of as many delegates as there are members of the House of Representatives; and the delegates shall have the same qualifications and be elected from the same districts as said Representatives.

SEC. 260. Delegates to such convention shall be elected at the next general State election after the passage of the act calling the convention, which does not occur within less than ninety days; and they shall meet within ninety days after their election at the Capital of the State, and continue in session until their work is completed.

SEC. 261. The General Assembly, in the act calling the convention, shall provide for comparing the polls and giving certificates of election to the delegates elected, and provide for their compensation.

SEC. 262. The convention, when assembled, shall be the judge of the election and qualification of its members, and shall determine contested elections. But the General Assembly shall, in the act calling the convention, provide for taking testimony in such cases, and for issuing a writ of election in case of a tie.

SEC. 263. Before a vote is taken upon the question of calling a convention, the Secretary of State shall cause notice of the election to be published in such manner as may be provided by the act directing said vote to be taken.

SCHEDULE.

That no inconvenience may arise from the alterations and amendments made in this Constitution, and in order to carry the same into complete operation, it is hereby declared and ordained:

First: That all laws of this Commonwealth in force at the time of the adoption of this Constitution, not inconsistent therewith, shall remain in full force until altered or repealed by the General Assembly; and all rights, actions, prosecutions, claims and contracts of the State, counties, individuals or bodies corporate, not inconsistent therewith, shall continue as valid as if this Constitution had not been adopted. The provisions of all laws which are inconsistent with this Constitution shall cease upon its adoption, except that all laws which are inconsistent with such provisions as require legislation to enforce them shall remain in force until such legislation is had, but not longer than six years after the adoption of this Constitution, unless sooner amended or repealed by the General Assembly.

Second: That all recognizances, obligations and all other instruments entered into or executed before the adoption of this Constitution, to the State, or to any city, town, county or subdivision thereof, and all fines, taxes, penalties and forfeitures due or owing to this State, or to any city, town, county or subdivision thereof; and all writs, prosecutions, actions and causes of action, except as otherwise herein provided, shall continue and remain unaffected by the adoption of this Constitution. And all indictments which shall have been found, or may hereafter be found, for any crime or offense committed before this Constitution takes effect, may be prosecuted as if no change had taken place, except as otherwise provided in this Constitution.

Third: All circuit, chancery, criminal, law and equity, law, and Common Pleas Courts, as now constituted and organized by law, shall continue with their respective jurisdictions until the Judges of the Circuit Courts provided for in this Constitution shall have been elected and qualified, and shall then cease and determine; and the causes, actions and proceedings then pending in said first named courts, which are discontinued by this Constitution, shall be transferred to, and tried by, the Circuit Courts in the counties, respectively, in which said causes, actions and proceedings are pending.

Fourth: The Treasurer, Attorney-General, Auditor of Public Accounts, Superintendent of Public Instruction, and Register of the Land Office, elected in eighteen hundred and ninety-one, shall hold their offices until the first Monday in January, eighteen hundred and ninety-six, and until the election and qualification of their successors. The Governor and Lieutenant-Governor elected in eighteen hundred and ninety-one shall hold their offices until the sixth Tuesday after the first Monday in November, eighteen hundred and ninety-five, and until their successors are elected and qualified. The Governor and Treasurer elected in eighteen hundred and ninety-one shall be ineligible to the succeeding term. The Governor elected in eighteen hundred and ninety-one may appoint a Secretary of State and a Commissioner of Agriculture, Labor and Statistics, as now provided, who shall hold their offices until their successors are elected and qualified, unless sooner removed by the Governor. The official bond of the present Treasurer shall be renewed at the expiration of two years from the time of his qualification.

Fifth: All officers who may be in office at the adoption of this Constitution, or who may be elected before the election of their successors, as provided in this Constitution, shall hold their respective offices until their successors are elected or appointed and qualified as provided in this Constitution.

Sixth: The quarterly courts created by this Constitution shall be the successors of the present statutory Quarterly Courts in the several counties of this State; and all suits, proceedings, prosecutions, records and judgments now pending or being in said last named courts shall, after the adoption of this Constitution, be transferred to the Quarterly Courts created by this Constitution, and shall proceed as though the same had been therein instituted.

ORDINANCE

We, the representatives of the people of Kentucky, in Convention assembled, in their name and by their authority and in virtue of the power vested in us as Delegates from the counties and districts respectively affixed to our names, do ordain and proclaim the foregoing to be the Constitution of the Commonwealth of Kentucky from and after this date.

Done at Frankfort this twenty-eighth day of September, in the year of our Lord one thousand eight hundred and ninety-one, and in the ninety-ninth [a] year of the Commonwealth.

CASSIUS M. CLAY, Jr.,
*President of the Convention,
and Member from the County of Bourbon.*

THOMAS G. POORE, *Secretary.*
JAMES B. MARTIN, *Assistant Secretary.*
JAMES EDWARDS STONE, *Reading Clerk.*

---

[a] Error—should be "one hundredth."

FRANKFORT, KY., *October 6, 1891.*

Having been appointed by the Convention to superintend the correct printing of the Constitution, etc., I hereby certify that I have carefully compared the above printed copy with the enrolled copy in the office of Secretary of State, and find it correct.

C. T. ALLEN,
Delegate from Caldwell County.

AMENDMENT, 1892

SEC. 181. The General Assembly shall not impose taxes for the purposes of any county, city, town or other municipal corporation, but may, by general laws, confer on the proper authorities thereof, respectively, the power to assess and collect taxes. The General Assembly may, by general laws only, provide for the payment of license fees on franchises, stock used for breeding purposes, the various trades, occupations and professions, or a special or excise tax; and may by general laws, delegate the power to counties, towns, cities and other municipal corporations, to impose and collect license fees on stock used for breeding purposes on franchises, trades, occupations and professions.

And the General Assembly may, by general laws only, authorize cities or towns of any class to provide for taxation for municipal purposes on personal property, tangible and intangible based on income, licenses or franchises, in lieu of an *ad valorem* tax thereon: *Provided*, Cities of the first class shall not be authorized to omit the imposition of an *ad valorem* tax on such property of any steam railroad, street railway, ferry, bridge, gas, water, heating, telephone, telegraph, electric light, or electric power company.

LOUISIANA[a]

TREATY CEDING LOUISIANA—1803 [b]

Concluded, April 30, 1803; ratifications exchanged at Washington, October 21, 1803; proclaimed, October 21, 1803

The President of the United States of America, and the First Consul of the French Republic, in the name of the French people, desiring to remove all source of misunderstanding, relative to objects of discussion mentioned in the second and fifth articles of the convention of the 8th Vendémiaire, an 9, (30th September, 1800), relative to the rights claimed by the United States, in virtue of the treaty concluded at Madrid, the 27th of October, 1795, between His Catholic Majesty and the said United States, and willing to strengthen the union and friendship, which at the time of the said convention was happily re-established between the two nations, have respectively named their Plenipotentiaries, to wit: The President of the United States, by and with the advice and consent of the Senate of the said States, Robert R. Livingston, Minister Plenipotentiary of the United States, and James Monroe, Minister Plenipotentiary and Envoy Extraordinary of the said States, near the Government of the French Republic; and the First Consul, in the name of the French people,

---

[a] The Lower Mississippi Valley, over which France exercised sovereignty by right of discovery in 1683, was called "The Province of Louisiana," of which New Orleans was the capital, and was governed by officials sent from Paris, without any charter. Louis XIV granted a monopoly of trade and commerce for the term of fifteen years to Anthony Crozart, September 14, 1712, but it was surrendered in less than two years. A similar grant was made to the "Company of the West," subsequently the "Company of the Indies," controlled by John Law, September 6, 1717, which was surrendered in 1730. France ceded that portion of the province of Louisiana lying east of the Mississippi River, and the city of New Orleans, to Spain, November 3, 1762, although Spanish rule was not asserted until 1769. It was retroceded to France by the treaty of San Ildefonso October 1, 1800, which was confirmed by the treaty of Madrid, March 21, 1801.

[b] This treaty was laid before the Congress of the United States by President Jefferson, at a session which he had called for the 17th of October, 1803. After stating in a message the negotiations which had resulted in the purchase of the sovereignty of Louisiana, he said, "Whilst the property and sovereignty of the Mississippi and its waters secure an independent outlet for the produce of the Western States, and an uncontrolled navigation through their whole course, free from collision with other powers and the dangers to our peace from that source, the fertility of the country, its climate and extent, promise in due season important aids to our Treasury, an ample provision for our posterity, and a wide spread for the blessings of freedom and equal laws."

Citizen Francis Barbé Marbois, Minister of the Public Treasury, who, after having respectively exchanged their full powers, have agreed to the following articles:

Article I

Whereas, by the article the third of the treaty concluded at St. Ildefonso, the 9th Vandémiaire, an 9 (1st October, 1800), between the First Consul of the French Republic and His Catholic Majesty, it was agreed as follows: " His Catholic Majesty promises and engages on his part to cede to the French Republic, six months after the full and entire execution of the conditions and stipulations herein, relative to his Royal Highness the Duke of Parma, the Colony or Province of Louisiana, with the same extent that it now has in the hands of Spain, and that it had when France possessed it; and such as it should be after the treaties subsequently entered into between Spain and other States"; and whereas, in pursuance of the treaty, particularly of the third article, the French Republic has an incontestable title to the domain and to the possession of the said territory, the First Consul of the French Republic, desiring to give to the United States a strong proof of his friendship, doth hereby cede to the said United States, in the name of the French Republic, for ever and in full sovereignty, the said territory, with all its rights and appurtenances, as fully and in the same manner as they have been acquired by the French Republic, in virtue of the above-mentioned treaty, concluded with His Catholic Majesty.

Article II

In the cession made by the preceding article, are included the adjacent islands belonging to Louisiana, all public lots and squares, vacant lands, and all public buildings, fortifications, barracks, and other edifices, which are not private property. The archives, papers, and documents, relative to the domain and sovereignty of Louisiana and its dependencies, will be left in the possession of the commissaries of the United States, and copies will be afterwards given in due form to the magistrates and municipal officers, of such of the said papers and documents as may be necessary to them.

Article III

The inhabitants of the ceded territory shall be incorporated in the Union of the United States, and admitted as soon as possible, according to the principles of the Federal constitution, to the enjoyment of all the rights, advantages, and immunities, of citizens of the United States; and, in the mean time, they shall be maintained and protected in the free enjoyment of their liberty, property, and the religion which they profess.

Article IV

There shall be sent by the Government of France a Commissary to Louisiana, to the end that he do every act necessary, as well to receive from the officers of His Catholic Majesty the said country and its dependencies in the name of the French Republic, if it has not been already done, as to transmit it, in the name of the French Republic, to the Commissary or agent of the United States.

ARTICLE V

Immediately after the ratification of the present treaty by the President of the United States, and in case that of the First Consul shall have been previously obtained, the Commissary of the French Republic shall remit all military posts of New Orleans, and other parts of the ceded territory, to the Commissary or Commissaries named by the President to take possession; the troops, whether of France or Spain, who may be there, shall cease to occupy any military post from the time of taking possession, and shall be embarked as soon as possible in the course of three months after the ratification of this treaty.

ARTICLE VI

The United States promise to execute such treaties and articles as may have been agreed between Spain and the tribes and nations of Indians, until, by mutual consent of the United States and the said tribes or nations, other suitable articles shall have been agreed upon.

ARTICLE VII

As it is reciprocally advantageous to the commerce of France and the United States, to encourage the communication of both nations, for a limited time, in the country ceded by the present treaty, until general arrangements relative to the commerce of both nations may be agreed on, it has been agreed between the contracting parties, that the French ships coming directly from France or any of her colonies, loaded only with the produce and manufactures of France or her said colonies, and the ships of Spain coming directly from Spain or any of her colonies, loaded only with the produce or manufactures of Spain or her colonies, shall be admitted during the space of twelve years in the port of New Orleans, and in all other legal ports of entry within the ceded territory, in the same manner as the ships of the United States coming directly from France or Spain, or any of their colonies, without being subject to any other or greater duty on merchandise, or other or greater tonnage than that paid by the citizens of the United States.

During the space of time above mentioned, no other nation shall have a right to the same privileges in the ports of the ceded territory. The twelve years shall commence three months after the exchange of ratifications, if it shall take place in France, or three months after it shall have been notified at Paris to the French Government, if it shall take place in the United States; it is, however, well understood, that the object of the above article is to favor the manufactures, commerce, freight, and navigation of France and of Spain, so far as relates to the importations that the French and Spanish shall make into the said ports of the United States, without in any sort affecting the regulations that the United States may make concerning the exportation of the produce and merchandise of the United States, or any right they may have to make such regulations.

Article VIII

In future and forever, after the expiration of the twelve years, the ships of France shall be treated upon the footing of the most favored nations in the ports above mentioned.

Article IX

The particular convention signed this day by the respective Ministers, having for its object to provide the payment of debts due to the citizens of the United States by the French Republic, prior to the 30th of Septr. 1800, (8th Vendémiaire, an 9,) is approved, and to have its execution in the same manner as if it had been inserted in the present treaty; and it shall be ratified in the same form and in the same time, so that the one shall not be ratified distinct from the other. Another particular convention, signed at the same date as the present treaty, relative to a definitive rule between the contracting parties is, in the like manner, approved, and will be ratified in the same form and in the same time, and jointly.

Article X

The present treaty shall be ratified in good and due form, and the ratifications shall be exchanged in the space of six months after the date of the signature by the Ministers Plenipotentiary, or sooner if possible.

In faith whereof, the respective Plenipotentiaries have signed these articles in the French and English languages, declaring, nevertheless, that the present treaty was originally agreed to in the French language, and have thereunto affixed their seals.

Done at Paris, the 10th day of Floréal, in the 11th year of the French Republic, and the 30th of April, 1803.

R. R. Livingston.
James Monroe.
Barbé Marbois.

CONVENTION BETWEEN THE UNITED STATES OF AMERICA AND THE FRENCH REPUBLIC—1803

Concluded April 30, 1803; ratifications exchanged at Washington, October 21, 1803; proclaimed October 21, 1803

The President of the United States of America, and the First Consul of the French Republic, in the name of the French people, in consequence of the Treaty of cession of Louisiana, which has been signed this day, wishing to regulate definitely everything which has relation to the said cession, have authorized, to this effect, the Plenipotentiaries, that is to say: the President of the United States has, by and with the advice and consent of the Senate of the said States, nominated for their Plenipotentiaries, Robert R. Livingston, Minister Plenipotentiary of the United States, and James Monroe, Minister Plenipotentiary and Envoy Extraordinary of the said United States, near the Government of the French Republic; and the First Consul of the French Republic, in the name of the French people, has named, as Plenipotentiary of the said Republic, the citizen Francis Barbé Marbois, who, in virtue of their full powers, which have been exchanged this day, have agreed to the following articles:

Article I

The Government of the United States engages to pay to the French Government, in the manner specified in the following articles, the sum of sixty millions of francs, independent of the sum which shall be fixed by another convention for the payment of the debts due by France to citizens of the United States.

Article II

For the payment of the sum of sixty millions of francs, mentioned in the preceding article, the United States shall create a stock of eleven million two hundred and fifty thousand dollars, bearing an interest of six per cent. per annum, payable, half-yearly, in London, Amsterdam, or Paris, amounting by the half-year to three hundred and thirty-seven thousand five hundred dollars, according to the proportions which shall be determined by the French Government, to be paid at either place: the principal of the said stock to be reimbursed at the Treasury of the United States, in annual payments of not less than three millions of dollars each; of which the first payment shall commence fifteen years after the date of the exchange of ratifications: this stock shall be transferred to the Government of France, or to such person or persons as shall be authorized to receive it, in three months, at most, after the exchange of the ratifications of this treaty, and after Louisiana shall be taken possession of in the name of the Government of the United States.

It is further agreed that, if the French Government should be desirous of disposing of the said stock, to receive the capital in Europe at shorter terms, that its measures, for that purpose, shall be taken so as to favor, in the greatest degree possible, the credit of the United States, and to raise to the highest price the said stock.

Article III

It is agreed that the dollar of the United States, specified in the present convention, shall be fixed at five francs 3333-10000ths or five livres eight sous tournois.

The present convention shall be ratified in good and due form, and the ratifications shall be exchanged in the space of six months, to date from this day, or sooner if possible.

In faith of which, the respective Plenipotentiaries have signed the above articles, both in the French and English languages, declaring, nevertheless, that the present treaty has been originally agreed on and written in the French language, to which they have hereunto affixed their seals.

Done at Paris, the tenth of Floréal, eleventh year of the French Republic, (30th April, 1803.)

Robert R. Livingston.
James Monroe.
Barbé Marbois.

ACT FOR TAKING POSSESSION OF LOUISIANA—1803 [a]

[EIGHTH CONGRESS, FIRST SESSION]

An Act to enable the President of the United States to take possession of the territories ceded by France to the United States, by the treaty concluded at Paris, on the thirtieth of April last; and for the temporary government thereof

Be it enacted by the Senate and House of Representatives of the United States of America in Congress assembled, That the President of the United States be, and he is hereby, authorized to take possession of and occupy the territories ceded by France to the United States, by the treaty concluded at Paris on the thirtieth day of April last, between the two nations, and that he may for that purpose, and in order to maintain in the said territories the authority of the United States, employ any part of the army and navy of the United States, and of the force authorized by an act passed the third day of March last, intituled "An act directing a detachment from the militia of the United States, and for erecting certain arsenals," which he may deem necessary; and so much of the sum appropriated by the said act as may be necessary, is hereby appropriated for the purpose of carrying this act into effect; to be applied under the direction of the President of the United States.

SEC. 2. *And be it further enacted,* That until the expiration of the present session of Congress, unless provision for the temporary government of the said territories be sooner made by Congress, all the military, civil, and judicial powers exercised by the officers of the existing government of the same, shall be vested in such person and persons, and shall be exercised in such manner as the President of the United States shall direct for maintaining and protecting the inhabitants of Louisiana in the free enjoyment of their liberty, property, and religion.

Approved, October 31, 1803.

TERRITORIES OF LOUISIANA AND ORLEANS—1804

[EIGHTH CONGRESS, FIRST SESSION]

An Act erecting Louisiana into two territories, and providing for the temporary government thereof

Be it enacted by the Senate and House of Representatives of the United States of America in Congress assembled, That all that portion of country ceded by France to the United States, under the name

---

[a] The treaty providing for the purchase of Louisiana by the United States was ratified at Washington October 21, 1803, and the commission appointed under it took formal possession December 20, 1803, when Governor Claiborne issued a proclamation declaring that the government previously exercised over the province by Spain and by France had ceased, and that of the United States was established over the same. An act of Congress creating six per cent. stock to the amount of eleven million two hundred and fifty thousand dollars, for the purpose of carrying out the agreement with France for the purchase of Louisiana, was approved November 30, 1803.

of Louisiana, which lies south of the Mississippi territory, and of an east and west line, to commence on the Mississippi River, at the thirty-third degree of north latitude, and to extend west to the western boundary of the said cession, shall constitute a territory of the United States, under the name of the territory of Orleans; the government whereof shall be organized and administered as follows:

SEC. 2. The executive power shall be vested in a governor, who shall reside in the said territory, and hold his office during the term of three years, unless sooner removed by the President of the United States. He shall be commander-in-chief of the militia of the said territory, shall have power to grant pardons for offences against the said territory, and reprieves for those against the United States, until the decision of the President of the United States thereon shall be made known; and to appoint and commission all officers, civil and of the militia, whose appointments are not herein otherwise provided for, and which shall be established by law. He shall take care that the laws be faithfully executed.

SEC. 3. A secretary of the territory shall also be appointed, who shall hold his office during the term of four years, unless sooner removed by the President of the United States, whose duty it shall be, under the direction of the governor, to record and preserve all the papers and proceedings of the executive, and all the acts of the governor and legislative council, and transmit authentic copies of the proceedings of the governor in his executive department, every six months, to the President of the United States. In case of the vacancy of the office of governor, the government of the said territory shall devolve on the secretary.

SEC. 4. The legislative powers shall be vested in the governor, and in thirteen of the most fit and discreet persons of the territory, to be called the legislative council, who shall be appointed annually by the President of the United States from among those holding real estate therein, and who shall have resided one year at least in the said territory, and hold no office of profit under the territory or the United States. The governor, by and with advice and consent of the said legislative council, or of a majority of them, shall have power to alter, modify, or repeal the laws which may be in force at the commencement of this act. Their legislative powers shall also extend to all the rightful subjects of legislation; but no law shall be valid which is inconsistent with the constitution and laws of the United States, or which shall lay any person under restraint, burden, or disability, on account of his religious opinions, professions, or worship; in all which he shall be free to maintain his own, and not burdened for those of another. The governor shall publish throughout the said territory all the laws which shall be made, and shall from time to time report the same to the President of the United States to be laid before Congress; which, if disapproved of by Congress, shall thenceforth be of no force. The governor or legislative council shall have no power over the primary disposal of the soil, nor to tax the lands of the United States, nor to interfere with the claims to land within the said territory. The governor shall convene and prorogue the legislative council whenever he may deem it expedient. It shall be his duty to obtain all the information in his power in relation to the customs, habits, and dispositions of the inhabitants of the said territory, and communicate the same from time to time to the President of the United States.

SEC. 5. The judicial power shall be vested in a superior court, and in such inferior courts, and justices of the peace, as the legislature of the territory may from time to time establish. The judges of the superior court and the justices of the peace shall hold their offices for the term of four years. The superior court shall consist of three judges, any one of whom shall constitute a court; they shall have jurisdiction in all criminal cases, and exclusive jurisdiction in all those which are capital; and original and appellate jurisdiction in all civil cases of the value of one hundred dollars. Its sessions shall commence on the first Monday of every month, and continue till all the business depending before them shall be disposed of. They shall appoint their own clerk. In all criminal prosecutions which are capital, the trial shall be by a jury of twelve good and lawful men of the vicinage; and in all cases, criminal and civil, in the superior court, the trial shall be by a jury, if either of the parties require it. The inhabitants of the said territory shall be entitled to the benefits of the writ of habeas corpus; they shall be bailable, unless for capital offences, where the proof shall be evident or the presumption great; and no cruel and unusual punishments shall be inflicted.

SEC. 6. The governor, secretary, judges, district attorney, marshal, and all general officers of the militia, shall be appointed by the President of the United States in the recess of the Senate; but shall be nominated at their next meeting for their advice and consent. The governor, secretary, judges, members of the legislative council, justices of the peace, and all other officers, civil and of the militia, before they enter upon the duties of their respective offices, shall take an oath or affirmation to support the constitution of the United States, and for the faithful discharge of the duties of their office; the governor, before the President of the United States, or before a judge of the supreme or district court of the United States, or before such other person as the President of the United States shall authorize to administer the same; the secretary, judges, and members of the legislative council, before the governor; and all other officers before such persons as the governor shall direct. The governor shall receive an annual salary of five thousand dollars; the secretary, of two thousand dollars, and the judges, of two thousand dollars each; to be paid quarter-yearly out of the revenues of impost and tonnage, accruing within the said territory. The members of the legislative council shall receive four dollars each per day during their attendance in council.

SEC. 7. *And be it further enacted*, That the following acts, that is to say:

An act for the punishment of certain crimes against the United States;

An act in addition to an act for the punishment of certain crimes against the United States;

An act to prevent citizens of the United States from privateering against nations in amity with or against citizens of the United States;

An act for the punishment of certain crimes therein specified;

An act respecting fugitives from justice and persons escaping from the service of their masters;

An act to prohibit the carrying on the slave-trade from the United States to any foreign place or country;

An act to prevent the importation of certain persons into certain States, where, by the laws thereof, their admission is prohibited;

An act to establish the post-office of the United States;

An act further to alter and establish certain post-roads, and for the more secure carriage of the mail of the United States;

An act for the more general promulgation of the laws of the United States;

An act in addition to an act intituled an act for the more general promulgation of the laws of the United States;

An act to promote the progress of useful arts, and to repeal the act heretofore made for that purpose;

An act to extend the privilege of obtaining patents for useful discoveries and inventions to certain persons therein mentioned, and to enlarge and define the penalties for violating the rights of patentees;

An act for the encouragement of learning, by securing the copies of maps, charts, and books to the authors and proprietors of such copies, during the time therein mentioned;

An act supplementary to an act intituled an act for the encouragement of learning, by securing the copies of maps, charts, and books to the authors and proprietors of such copies, during the times therein mentioned, and extending the benefits thereof to the arts of designing, engraving, and etching historical and other prints;

An act providing for salvage in cases of recapture;

An act respecting alien enemies;

An act to prescribe the mode in which the public acts, records, and judicial proceedings in each State shall be authenticated, so as to take effect in every other State;

An act for establishing trading-houses with the Indian tribes;

An act for continuing in force a law entitled An act for establishing trading-houses with the Indian tribes; and

An act making provision relative to rations for Indians, and to their visits to the seat of Government,

Shall extend to, and have full force and effect in the above-mentioned territories.

SEC. 8. There shall be established in the said territory a district court, to consist of one judge, who shall reside therein, and be called the district judge, and who shall hold, in the city of Orleans, four sessions annually; the first to commerce on the third Monday in October next, and the three other sessions, progressively, on the third Monday of every third calendar month thereafter. He shall in all things have and exercise the same jurisdiction and powers which are by law given to, or may be exercised by, the judge of Kentucky district; and shall be allowed an annual compensation of two thousand dollars, to be paid quarter-yearly out of the revenues of impost and tonnage accruing within the said territory. He shall appoint a clerk for the said district, who shall reside and keep the records of the court, in the city of Orleans, and shall receive for the services performed by him the same fees to which the clerk of Kentucky district is entitled for similar services.

There shall be appointed in the said district a person learned in the law, to act as attorney for the United States, who shall, in addition to his stated fees, be paid six hundred dollars annually, as a full compensation for all extra services. There shall also be appointed a marshal for the said district, who shall perform the same duties, be subject to the same regulations and penalties, and be entitled to the same fees to which marshals in other districts are entitled for similar services; and shall moreover be paid two hundred dollars annually as a compensation for all extra services.

SEC. 9. All free male white persons who are house-keepers, and who shall have resided one year, at least, in the said territory, shall be qualified to serve as grand or petit jurors in the courts of the said territory, and they shall, until the legislature thereof shall otherwise direct, be selected in such manner as the judges of the said courts, respectively, shall prescribe, so as to be most conducive to an impartial trial, and to be least burdensome to the inhabitants of the said territory.

SEC. 10. It shall not be lawful for any person or persons to import or bring into the said territory, from any port or place without the limits of the United States, or cause or procure to be so imported or brought, or knowingly to aid or assist in importing or bringing any slave or slaves. And every person so offending, and being thereof convicted before any court within said territory, having competent jurisdiction, shall forfeit and pay, for each and every slave so imported or brought, the sum of three hundred dollars; one moiety for the use of the United States and the other moiety for the use of the person or persons who shall sue for the same; and every slave so imported or brought shall thereupon become entitled to or receive his or her freedom. It shall not be lawful for any person or persons to import or bring into the said territory, from any port or place within the limits of the United States, or to cause or procure to be so imported or brought, or knowingly to aid or assist in so importing or bringing, any slave or slaves, which shall have been imported since the first day of May, one thousand seven hundred and ninety-eight, into any port or place within the limits of the United States, or which may hereafter be so imported from any port or place without the limits of the United States; and every person so offending and being thereof convicted before any court within said territory, having competent jurisdiction, shall forfeit and pay for each and every slave, so imported or brought, the sum of three hundred dollars, one moiety for the use of the United States, and the other moiety for the use of the person or persons who shall sue for the same; and no slave or slaves shall directly or indirectly be introduced into said territory, except by a citizen of the United States removing into said territory for actual settlement, and being at the time of such removal bona fide owner of such slave or slaves; and every slave imported or brought into the said territory, contrary to the provisions of this act, shall thereupon be entitled to and receive his or her freedom.

SEC. 11. The laws in force in the said territory at the commencement of this act, and not inconsistent with the provisions thereof, shall continue in force until altered, modified, or repealed by the legislature.

SEC. 12. The residue of the province of Louisiana, ceded to the United States, shall be called the district of Louisiana,[a] the govern-

---

[a] This was called the Territory of Louisiana in a supplementary act of Congress approved March 3, 1805. See page 1373.

ment whereof shall be organized and administered as follows: The executive power now vested in the governor of the Indiana territory shall extend to and be exercised in the said district of Louisiana. The governor and judges of the Indiana territory shall have power to establish in the said district of Louisiana inferior courts, and prescribe their jurisdiction and duties, and to make all laws which they may deem conducive to the good government of the inhabitants thereof: *Provided, however*, That no law shall be valid which is inconsistent with the Constitution and laws of the United States, or which shall lay any person under restraint or disability on account of his religious opinions, profession, or worship; in all of which he shall be free to maintain his own, and not burdened for those of another: *And provided also*, That in all criminal prosecutions, the trial shall be by a jury of twelve good and lawful men of the vicinage, and in all civil cases of the value of one hundred dollars, the trial shall be by jury, if either of the parties require it. The judges of the Indiana territory, or any two of them, shall hold annually two courts within the said district, at such place as will be most convenient to the inhabitants thereof in general, shall possess the same jurisdiction they now possess in the Indiana territory, and shall continue in session until all the business depending before them shall be disposed of. It shall be the duty of the secretary of the Indiana territory to record and preserve all the papers and proceedings of the governor, of an executive nature, relative to the district of Louisiana, and transmit authentic copies thereof every six months to the President of the United States. The governor shall publish throughout the said district all the laws which may be made as aforesaid, and shall, from time to time, report the same to the President of the United States, to be laid before Congress, which, if disapproved of by Congress, shall thenceforth cease and be of no effect.

The said district of Louisiana shall be divided into districts by the governor, under the direction of the President, as the convenience of the settlements shall require, subject to such alterations hereafter as experience may prove more convenient. The inhabitants of each district, between the ages of eighteen and forty-five, shall be formed into a militia, with proper officers, according to their numbers, to be appointed by the governor, except the commanding officer, who shall be appointed by the President, and who, whether a captain, a major, or a colonel, shall be the commanding officer of the district, and as such shall, under the governor, have command of the regular officers and troops in his district, as well as of the militia, for which he shall have a brevet commission, giving him such command, and the pay and emoluments of an officer of the same grade in the regular army; he shall be specially charged with the employment of the military and militia of his district, in cases of sudden invasion or insurrection, and until the orders of the governor can be received, and at all times with the duty of ordering a military patrol, aided by militia, if necessary, to arrest unauthorized settlers in any part of his district, and to commit such offenders to jail, to be dealt with according to law.

SEC. 13. The laws in force in the said district of Louisiana at the commencement of this act, and not inconsistent with any of the provisions thereof, shall continue in force until altered, modified, or repealed by the governor and judges of the Indiana territory, as aforesaid.

SEC. 14. *And be it further enacted*, That all grants for lands within the territories ceded by the French Republic to the United States, by the treaty of the thirtieth of April, in the year one thousand eight hundred and three, the title whereof was, at the date of the treaty of San Ildefonso, in the crown, government, or nation of Spain, and every act and proceeding subsequent thereto, of whatsoever nature, towards the obtaining any grant, title, or claim to such lands, and under whatsoever authority transacted, or pretended, be, and the same are hereby declared to be, and to have been from the beginning, null, void, and of no effect in law or equity. *Provided, nevertheless*, That anything in this section contained shall not be construed to make null and void any bona-fide grant, made agreeably to the laws, usages, and customs of the Spanish government, to an actual settler on the lands so granted, for himself and for his wife and family; or to make null and void any bona-fide act or proceeding done by an actual settler, agreeably to the laws, usages, and customs of the Spanish government, to obtain a grant for lands actually settled on by the person or persons claiming title thereto, if such settlement in either case was actually made prior to the twentieth day of December, one thousand eight hundred and three: *And provided further*, That such grant shall not secure to the grantee or his assigns more than one mile square of land, together with such other and further quantity as heretofore has been allowed for the wife and family of such actual settler, agreeably to the laws, usages, and customs of the Spanish government. And that if any citizen of the United States, or other person, shall make a settlement on any lands belonging to the United States, within the limits of Louisiana, or shall survey, or attempt to survey, such lands, or to designate boundaries by marking trees, or otherwise, such offender shall, on conviction thereof, in any court of record of the United States, or the territories of the United States, forfeit a sum not exceeding one thousand dollars, and suffer imprisonment not exceeding twelve months; and it shall, moreover, be lawful for the President of the United States to employ such military force as he may judge necessary to remove from lands belonging to the United States any such citizen or other person who shall attempt a settlement thereon.

SEC. 15. The President of the United States is hereby authorized to stipulate with any Indian tribes owning lands on the east side of the Mississippi, and residing thereon, for an exchange of lands, the property of the United States, on the west side of the Mississippi, in case the said tribe shall remove and settle thereon; but in such sctipulation, the said tribes shall acknowledge themselves to be under the protection of the United States, and shall agree that they will not hold any treaty with any foreign power, individual state, or with the individuals of any state or power; and that they will not sell or dispose of the said lands, or any part thereof, to any sovereign power, except to the United States, nor to the subjects or citizens of any other sovereign power, nor to the citizens of the United States. And, in order to maintain peace and tranquillity with the Indian tribes who reside within the limits of Louisiana, as ceded by France to the United State, the act of Congress, passed on the thirtieth day of March, one thousand eight hundred and two, intituled "An act to regulate trade and intercourse with the Indian tribes, and to preserve peace on the frontiers," is hereby extended to the territories erected and established by this act; and the sum of fifteen thousand dollars of any money in the treasury not otherwise appropriated by law is hereby appropriated to enable the President of the United States to effect the object expressed in this section.

SEC. 16. The act passed on the thirty-first day of October, one thousand eight hundred and three, entitled "An act to enable the President of the United States to take possession of the territories ceded by France to the United States by the treaty concluded at Paris on the thirtieth day of April last, and for the temporary government thereof," shall continue in force until the first day of October next, anything therein to the contrary notwithstanding; on which said first day of October, this act shall commence and have full force, and shall continue in force for and during the term of one year, and to the end of the next session of Congress which may happen thereafter.

Approved, March 26, 1804.

THE TERRITORIAL GOVERNMENT OF ORLEANS—1805

[EIGHTH CONGRESS, SECOND SESSION]

An Act further providing for the government of the territory of Orleans

Be it enacted by the Senate and House of Representatives of the United States of America in Congress assembled, That the President of the United States be, and he is herby, authorized to establish within the territory of Orleans a government in all respects similar (except as is herein otherwise provided) to that now exercised in the Mississippi territory; and shall, in the recess of the Senate, but to be nominated at their next meeting, for their advice and consent, appoint all the officers necessary therein, in conformity with the ordinance of Congress, made on the thirteenth day of July, one thousand seven hundred and eighty-seven; and that from and after the establishment of the said government, the inhabitants of the territory of Orleans shall be entitled to and enjoy all the rights, privileges, and advantages secured by the said ordinance, and now enjoyed by the people of the Mississippi territory.

SEC. 2. *And be it further enacted*, That so much of the said ordinance of Congress as relates to the organization of a general assembly, and prescribes the powers thereof, shall, from and after the fourth day of July next, be in force in the said territory of Orleans; and in order to carry the same into operation, the governor of the said territory shall cause to be elected twenty-five representatives, for which purpose he shall lay off the said territory into convenient election-districts, on or before the first Monday of October next, and give due notice thereof throughout the same; and shall appoint the most convenient time and place within each of the said districts, for holding the elections; and shall nominate a proper officer or officers to preside at and conduct the same, and to return to him the names of the persons who may have been duly elected. All subsequent elections shall be regulated by the legislature; and the number of representatives shall be determined, and the apportionment made, in the manner prescribed by the said ordinance.

SEC. 3. *And be it further enacted*, That the representatives to be chosen as aforesaid shall be convened by the governor, in the city of Orleans, on the first Monday in November next; and the first general assembly shall be convened by the governor as soon as may be convenient, at the city of Orleans, after the members of the legislative council shall be appointed and commissioned; and the general assembly shall meet, at least once in every year, and such meeting shall be on the first Monday in December, annually, unless they shall, by law, appoint a different day. Neither house, during the session, shall, without the consent of the other, adjourn for more than three days, nor to any other place than that in which the two branches are sitting.

SEC. 4. *And be it further enacted*, That the laws in force in the said territory at the commencement of this act, and not inconsistent with the provisions thereof, shall continue in force until altered, modified, or repealed by the legislature.

SEC. 5. *And be it further enacted*, That the second paragraph of the said ordinance, which regulates the descent and distribution of estates; and also the sixth article of compact which is annexed to and makes part of said ordinance, are hereby declared not to extend to but are excluded from all operation within the said territory of Orleans.

SEC. 6. *And be it further enacted*, That the governor, secretary, and judges to be appointed by virtue of this act shall be severally allowed the same compensation which is now allowed to the governor, secretary, and judges of the territory of Orleans. And all the additional officers authorized by this act shall respectively receive the same compensation for their services as are by law established for similar offices in the Mississippi territory, to be paid quarter-yearly out of the revenues of impost and tonnage accruing within the said territory of Orleans.

SEC. 7. *And be it further enacted*, That whenever it shall be ascertained by an actual census or enumeration of the inhabitants of the territory of Orleans, taken by proper authority, that the number of free inhabitants included therein shall amount to sixty thousand, they shall thereupon be authorized to form for themselves a constitution and state government, and be admitted into the Union upon the footing of the original states, in all respects whatever, conformably to the provisions of the third article of the treaty concluded at Paris on the thirtieth of April, one thousand eight hundred and three, between the United States and the French Republic: *Provided*, That the constitution so to be established shall be republican, and not inconsistent with the constitution of the United States, nor inconsistent with the ordinance of the late Congress, passed the thirteenth day of July, one thousand seven hundred and eighty-seven, so far as the same is made applicable to the territorial government hereby authorized to be established: *Provided, however*, That Congress shall be at liberty, at any time prior to the admission of the inhabitants of the said territory to the right of a separate state, to alter the boundaries thereof as they may judge proper: *Except only*, That no alteration shall be made which shall procrastinate the period for the admission of the inhabitants thereof to the rights of a state government according to the provision of this act.

SEC. 8. *And be it further enacted,* That so much of an act intituled "An act erecting Louisiana into two territories, and providing for the temporary government thereof," as is repugnant with this act, shall, from and after the first Monday of November next, be repealed. And the residue of the said act shall continue in full force until repealed, anything in the sixteenth section of the said act to the contrary notwithstanding.

Approved, March 2, 1805.

THE TERRITORY OF LOUISIANA—1805 [a]

[EIGHTH CONGRESS, SECOND SESSION.]

An Act further providing for the government of the district of Louisiana.

Be it enacted by the Senate and House of Representatives of the United States of America in Congress assembled, That all that part of the country ceded by France to the United States, under the general name of Louisiana, which, by an act of the last session of Congress, was erected into a separate district, to be called the district of Louisiana, shall henceforth be known and designated by the name and title of the Territory of Louisiana, the government whereof shall be organized and administered as follows: The executive power shall be vested in a governor, who shall reside in said territory, and hold his office during the term of three years, unless sooner removed by the President of the United States. He shall be commander-in-chief of the militia of the said territory, superintendent ex officio of Indian affairs, and shall appoint and commission all officers in the same below the rank of general officers; shall have power to grant pardons for offences against the same, and reprieves for those against the United States until the decision of the President thereon shall be known.

SEC. 2. There shall be a secretary, whose commission shall continue in force for four years, unless sooner revoked by the President of the United States, who shall reside in the said territory, and whose duty it shall be, under the direction of the governor, to record and preserve all the papers and proceedings of the executive and all the acts of the governor and of the legislative body, and transmit authentic copies of the same every six months to the President of the United States. In case of a vacancy of the office of governor, the government of the said territory shall be exercised by the secretary.

SEC. 3. The legislative power shall (be) vested in the governor and in three judges, or a majority of them, who shall have power to establish inferior courts in the said territory, and prescribe their jurisdiction and duties, and to make all laws which they may deem conducive to the good government of the inhabitants thereof: *Provided, however,* That no law shall be valid which is inconsistent with the constitution and laws of the United States, or which shall lay any person under restraint or disability on account of his religious opinions,

---

[a] This was originally called the District of Louisiana, but no part of it is included in the present State of Louisiana, which was originally the Territory of Orleans.

profession, or worship, in all of which he shall be free to maintain his own and not be burthened with those of another: *And provided also*, That in all criminal prosecutions the trial shall be by a jury of twelve good and lawful men of the vicinage, and in all civil cases of the value of one hundred dollars the trial shall be by jury, if either of the parties require it. And the governor shall publish throughout the said territory all the laws which may be made as aforesaid, and shall, from time to time, report the same to the President of the United States, to be laid before Congress, which, if disapproved of by Congress, shall thenceforth cease and be of no effect.

SEC. 4. There shall be appointed three judges, who shall hold their offices for the term of four years, who, or any two of them, shall hold annually two courts within the said district, at such place as will be most convenient to the inhabitants thereof in general; shall possess the same jurisdiction which is possessed by the judges of the Indiana territory, and shall continue in session until all the business depending before them shall be disposed of.

SEC. 5. *And be it further enacted*, That for the more convenient distribution of justice, the prevention of crimes and injuries, and execution of process, criminal and civil, the governor shall proceed, from time to time, as circumstances may require, to lay out those parts of the territory in which the Indian title shall have been extinguished into districts, subject to such alterations as may be found necessary, and he shall appoint thereto such magistrates and other civil officers as he may deem necessary, whose several powers and authorities shall be regulated and defined by law.

SEC. 6. *And be it further enacted*, That the governor, secretary, and judges to be appointed by virtue of this act shall respectively receive the same compensations for their services as are by law established for similar offices in the Indiana territory, to be paid quarter-yearly out of the treasury of the United States.

SEC. 7. *And be it further enacted*, That the governor, secretary, judges, justices of the peace, and all other officers, civil or military, before they enter upon the duties of their respective offices, shall take an oath, or affirmation, to support the constitution of the United States and for the faithful discharge of the duties of their office; the governor before the President of the United States, or before a judge of the supreme or district court of the United States, or before such other person as the President of the United States shall authorize to administer the same; the secretary and judges before the governor; and all other officers before such person as the governor shall direct.

SEC. 8. *And be it further enacted*, That the governor, secretary, and judges, to be appointed by virtue of this act, and all the additional officers authorized thereby, or by the act for erecting Louisiana into two territories, and providing for the temporary government thereof, shall be appointed by the President of the United States in the recess of the Senate, but shall be nominated at their next meeting for their advice and consent.

SEC. 9. *And be it further enacted*, That the laws and regulations in force in the said district at the commencement of this act, and not inconsistent with the provisions thereof, shall continue in force until altered, modified, or repealed by the legislature.

SEC. 10. *And be it further enacted*, That so much of an act intituled "An act erecting Louisiana into two territories, and providing for the temporary government thereof," as is repugnant to this act, shall, from and after the fourth day of July next, be repealed; on which said fourth day of July this act shall commence and have full force.

Approved, March 3, 1805.

PROCLAMATION RESPECTING TAKING POSSESSION OF PART OF LOUISIANA—1810

BY THE PRESIDENT OF THE UNITED STATES OF AMERICA.

A PROCLAMATION

Whereas the territory south of the Mississippi Territory and eastward of the River Mississippi and extending to the River Perdido, of which possession was not delivered to the United States in pursuance of the treaty concluded at Paris, on the 30th of April, 1803, has at all times, as is well known, been considered and claimed by them, as being within the colony of Louisiana conveyed by the said treaty, in the same extent that it had in the hands of Spain, and that it had when France originally possessed it.

And whereas, the acquiescence of the United States in the temporary continuance of the said territory under the Spanish authority was not the result of any distrust of their title, as has been particularly evinced by the general tenor of their laws, and by the distinction made in the application of those laws between that territory and foreign countries, but was occasioned by their conciliatory views, and by a confidence in the justice of their cause; and in the success of candid discussion and amicable negotiation with a just and friendly power.

And whereas a satisfactory adjustment, too long delayed, without the fault of the United States, has for some time been entirely suspended by events over which they had no control, and whereas a crises has at length arrived subversive of the order of things under the Spanish authorities, whereby a failure of the United States to take the said territory into its possession may lead to events ultimately contravening the views of both parties, whilst in the mean time the tranquillity and security of our adjoining territories are endangered, and new facilities given to violations of our revenue and commercial laws, and of those prohibiting the introduction of slaves.

Considering, moreover, that under these peculiar and imperative circumstances, a forbearance on the part of the United States to occupy the territory in question, and thereby guard against the confusions and contingencies which threaten it, might be construed into a dereliction of their title, or an insensibility to the importance of the state; considering that in the hands of the United States it will not cease to be a subject of fair and friendly negotiation and adjustment; considering finally that the acts of Congress tho' contemplating a present possession by a foreign authority, have contemplated also an eventual possession of the said territory by the United States, and are accordingly so framed, as in the case to extend in their operation, to the same:

Now be it known that I, JAMES MADISON, President of the United States of America, in pursuance of these weighty and urgent considerations, have deemed it right and requisite, that possession should be taken of the said territory, in the name and behalf of the United States. William C. C. Claiborne, governor of the Orleans Territory of which the said territory is to be taken as part, will accordingly proceed to execute the same; and to exercise over the said territory the authorities and functions legally appertaining to his office. And the good people inhabiting the same, are invited and enjoined to pay due respect to him in that character, to be obedient to the laws; to maintain order; to cherish harmony; and in every manner to conduct themselves as peaceable citizens; under full assurance that they will be protected in the enjoyment of their liberty, property, and religion.

In testimony whereof, I have caused the seal of the United States to be hereunto affixed, and signed the same with my hand.
[L. S.] Done at the city of Washington, the twenty-seventh day of October, A. D. 1810, and in the thirty-fifth year of the independence of the said United States.

JAMES MADISON.
By the President:
R. SMITH, *Secretary of State.*

ENABLING ACT FOR LOUISIANA—1811

[ELEVENTH CONGRESS, THIRD SESSION]

An Act to enable the people of the Territory of Louisiana to form a constitution and state government, and for the admission of such state into the Union, on an equal footing with the original states, and for other purposes

Be it enacted by the Senate and House of Representatives of the United States of America in Congress assembled, That the inhabitants of all that part of the territory or country ceded under the name of Louisiana, by the treaty made at Paris on the thirtieth day of April, one thousand eight hundred and three, between the United States and France, contained within the following limits, that is to say: Beginning at the mouth of the river Sabine; thence by a line to be drawn along the middle of the said river, including all islands, to the thirty-second degree of latitude; thence due north to the northernmost part of the thirty-third degree of north latitude; thence along the said parallel of latitude to the river Mississippi; thence down the said river to the river Iberville; and from thence, along the middle of the said river and Lakes Maurepas and Ponchartrain, to the Gulf of Mexico; thence bounded by the said gulf to the place of beginning, including all islands within three leagues of the coast, be, and they are hereby, authorized to form for themselves a constitution and state government, and to assume such name as they may deem proper, under the provisions and upon the conditions hereinafter mentioned.

SEC. 2. *And be it further enacted,* That all free white male citizens of the United States, who shall have arrived at the age of twenty-one years, and resided within the said territory at least one year previous to the day of election, and shall have paid a territorial, county, or district, or parish tax, and all persons having in other respects the legal qualifications to vote for representatives in the general assembly of the said territory, be, and they are hereby, authorized to choose representatives to form a convention, who shall be apportioned amongst the several counties, districts, and parishes in the said territory of Orleans in such manner as the legislature of the said territory shall by law direct. The number of representatives shall not exceed sixty, and the elections for the representatives aforesaid shall take place on the third Monday in September next, and shall be conducted in the same manner as is now provided by the laws of the said territory for electing members for the house of representatives.

SEC. 3. *And be it further enacted,* That the members of the convention, when duly elected, be, and they are hereby, authorized to meet at the city of New Orleans, on the first Monday of November next, which convention, when met, shall first determine, by a majority of the whole number elected, whether it be expedient or not, at that time, to form a constitution and state government for the people within the said territory, and if it be determined to be expedient, then the convention shall in like manner declare, in behalf of the people of the said territory, that it adopts the constitution of the United States; whereupon the said convention shall be, and hereby is, authorized to form a constitution and state government for the people of the said territory: *Provided,* The constitution to be formed, in virtue of the authority herein given, shall be republican, and consistent with the constitution of the United States; that it shall contain the fundamental principles of civil and religious liberty; that it shall secure to the citizen the trial by jury in all criminal cases, and the privilege of the writ of *habeas corpus,* conformable to the provisions of the constitution of the United States; and that after the admission of the said territory of Orleans as a state into the Union, the laws which such state may pass shall be promulgated and its records of every description shall be preserved, and its judicial and legislative written proceedings conducted in the language in which the laws and the judicial and legislative written proceedings of the United States are now published and conducted: *And provided also,* That the said convention shall provide by an ordinance, irrevocable without the consent of the United States, that the people inhabiting the said territory do agree and declare that they forever disclaim all right or title to the waste or unappropriated lands lying within the said territory, and that the same shall be and remain at the sole and entire disposition of the United States, and moreover that each and every tract of land sold by Congress shall be and remain exempt from any tax laid by the order or under the authority of the state, whether for state, county, township, parish, or any other purpose whatever, for the term of five years from and after the respective days of the sales thereof, and that the lands belonging to citizens of the United States residing without the said state shall never be taxed higher than the lands belonging to persons residing therein, and that no taxes shall be imposed on lands the property of the United States, and that the river Mississippi and the navigable rivers and waters leading into the same or into the Gulf of Mexico shall be common highways and forever free, as well to the inhabitants of the said state as to other citizens of the United States, without any tax, duty, impost, or toll therefor imposed by the said state.

SEC. 4. *And be it further enacted,* That in case the convention shall declare its assent in behalf of the people of the said territory to the adoption of the constitution of the United States, and shall form a constitution and state government for the people of the said territory of Orleans, the said convention, as soon thereafter as may be, is hereby required to cause to be transmitted to Congress the instrument by which its assent to the constitution of the United States is thus given and declared, and also a true and attested copy of such constitution or frame of state government as shall be formed and provided by said convention, and if the same shall not be disapproved by Congress, at their next session after the receipt thereof, the said state shall be admitted into the Union upon the same footing with the original states.

SEC. 5. *And be it further enacted,* That five per centum of the net proceeds of the sales of the lands of the United States, after the first day of January, shall be applied to laying out and constructing public roads and levees in the said state, as the legislature thereof may direct.

Approved, February 20, 1811.

ACT FOR THE ADMISSION OF LOUISIANA—1812

[TWELFTH CONGRESS, FIRST SESSION]

An act for the admission of the state of Louisiana into the Union, and to extend the laws of the United States to the said state

Whereas the representatives of the people of all that part of the territory or country ceded, under the name of "Louisiana," by the treaty made at Paris on the thirtieth day of April, one thousand eight hundred and three, between the United States and France, contained within the following limits, that is to say: Beginning at the mouth of the river Sabine; thence, by a line to be drawn along the middle of said river, including all islands, to the thirty-second degree of latitude; thence due north to the northernmost part of the thirty-third degree of north latitude; thence along the said parallel of latitude to the river Mississippi; thence down the said river to the river Iberville; and from thence along the middle of the said river, and lakes Maurepas and Pontchartrain, to the gulf of Mexico; thence bounded by the said gulf to the place of beginning, including all islands within three leagues of the coast, did, on the twenty-second day of January, one thousand eight hundred and twelve, form for themselves a constitution and state government, and give to the said state the name of the state of Louisiana in pursuance of an act of Congress entitled "An act to enable the people of the territory of Orleans to form a constitution and state government, and for the admission of the said state into the Union on an equal footing with the original states, and for other purposes;" and the said constitution having been transmitted to Congress, and by them being hereby approved: Therefore,

Be it enacted by the Senate and House of Representatives of the United States of America, in Congress assembled, That the said state shall be one, and is hereby declared to be one, of the United States of America, and admitted into the Union on an equal footing with the original states, in all respects whatever, by the name and title of the state of Louisiana: *Provided,* That it shall be taken as a condition upon which the said state is incorporated in the Union, that the river Mississippi, and the navigable rivers and waters leading into the same, and into the gulf of Mexico, shall be common highways and forever free, as well to the inhabitants of the said state as to the inhabitants of other states and the territories of the United States, without any tax, duty, impost, or toll therefor, imposed by the said state; and that the above condition, and also all other the conditions and terms contained in the third section of the act, the title whereof is hereinbefore recited, shall be considered, deemed, and taken fundamental conditions and terms, upon which the said state is incorporated in the Union.

SEC. 2. *And be it further enacted,* That until the next general census and apportionment of representatives, the said state shall be entitled to one representative in the House of Representatives of the United States; and that all the laws of the United States not locally inapplicable shall be extended to the said state, and shall have the same force and effect within the same as elsewhere within the United States.

SEC. 3. *And be it further enacted,* That the said state, together with the residue of that portion of country which was comprehended within the territory of Orleans, as constituted by the act entituled "An act erecting Louisiana into two territories, and providing for the temporary government thereof," shall be one district, and be called the Louisiana district; and there shall be established in the said district a district court, to consist of one judge, who shall reside therein, and be called the district judge; and there shall be, annually, four stated sessions of the said court held at the city of Orleans; the first to commence on the third Monday in July next, and the three other sessions progressively, on the third Monday of every third calendar month thereafter. The said judge shall, in all things, have and exercise the same jurisdiction and powers which, by the act the title whereof is in this section recited, were given to the district judge of the territory of Orleans; and he shall be allowed an annual compensation of three thousand dollars, to be paid quarter-yearly at the treasury of the United States. The said judge shall appoint a clerk of the said court, who shall reside and keep the records of the court in the city of Orleans, and shall receive for the services performed by him the same fees heretofore allowed to the clerk of the Orleans territory.

SEC. 4. *And be it further enacted,* That there shall be appointed in the said district a person learned in the law, to act as attorney for the United States, who shall, in addition to his stated fees, be paid six hundred dollars annually as a full compensation for all extra services. There shall also be appointed a marshal for the said district, who shall perform the same duties, be subject to the same regulations and penalties, and be entitled to the same fees to which marshals in other districts are entitled for similar services; and shall, moreover, be paid two hundred dollars annually as a compensation for all extra services.

SEC. 5. *And be it further enacted,* That nothing in this act shall be construed to repeal the fourth section of an act entitled "An act for laying and collecting duties on imports and tonnage within the territories ceded to the United States by the treaty of the thirtieth of April, one thousand eight hundred and three, between the United States and the French Republic, and for other purposes;" and that the collection-district shall be and remain as thereby established.

SEC. 6. *And be it further enacted*, That this act shall commence and be in force from and after the thirtieth day of April, eighteen hundred and twelve.

Approved, April 8, 1812.

ACT TO ENLARGE THE LIMITS OF LOUISIANA—1812

[TWELFTH CONGRESS, FIRST SESSION]

An Act to enlarge the limits of the state of Louisiana

Be it enacted by the Senate and House of Representatives of the United States of America in Congress assembled, That, in case the legislature of the state of Louisiana shall consent thereto, all that tract of country comprehended within the following bounds to wit: Beginning at the junction of the Iberville with the river Mississippi; thence, along the middle of the Iberville, the river Amite, and of the lakes Maurepas and Pontchartrain to the eastern mouth of the Pearl River; thence up the eastern branch of Pearl River to the thirty-first degree of north latitude; thence along the said degree of latitude to the river Mississippi; thence down the said river to the place of beginning, shall become and form a part of the said state of Louisiana, and be subject to the constitution and laws thereof, in the same manner, and for all intents and purposes, as if it had been included within the original boundaries of the said state.

SEC. 2. *And be it further enacted*, That it shall be incumbent upon the legislature of the state of Louisiana, in case they consent to the incorporation of the territory aforesaid within their limits, at their first session, to make provision by law for the representation of the said territory in the legislature of the state upon the principles of the constitution, and for securing to the people of the said territory equal rights, privileges, benefits, and advantages with those enjoyed by the people of the other parts of the state; which law shall be liable to revision, modification, and amendment by Congress, and also in the manner provided for the amendment of the state constitution, but shall not be liable to change or amendment by the legislature of the state.

Approved, April 14, 1812.

CONSTITUTION OF LOUISIANA—1812 *

We, the Representatives of the People of all that part of the Territory or country ceded under the name of Louisiana, by the treaty made at Paris, on the 30th day of April 1803, between the United

---

* Constitution or Form of Government of the State of Louisiana. By Authority. New-Orleans: Printed by Jo. Bar. Baird, Printer to the Convention. 1812. 32 pp.

States and France, contained in the following limits, to wit; beginning at the mouth of the river Sabine, thence by a line to be drawn along the middle of said river, including all its islands, to the thirty second degree of latitude—thence due north to the Northernmost part of the thirty third degree of north latitude—thence along the said parallel of latitude to the river Mississippi—thence down the said river to the river Iberville, and from thence along the middle of the said river and lakes Maurepas and Pontchartrain to the Gulf of Mexico—thence bounded by the said Gulf to the place of beginning, including all Islands within three leagues of the coast—in Convention Assembled by virtue of an act of Congress, entitled " an act to enable the people of the Territory of Orleans to form a constitution and State government and for the admission of said State into the Union on an equal footing with the original States, and for other purpose;" In order to secure to all the citizens thereof the enjoyment of *the right of life, liberty and property*, do ordain and establish the following constitution or form of government, and do mutually agree with each other to form ourselves into a free and independent State, by the name of the State of Louisiana.

Article 1st

CONCERNING THE DISTRIBUTION OF THE POWERS OF GOVERNMENT.

SECT. 1st. The powers of the government of the State of Louisiana shall be divided into three distinct departments, and each of them be confided to a separate body of Magistracy viz—those which are Legislative to one, those which are executive to another, and those which are judiciary to another.

SECT. 2d. No person or Collection of persons, being one of those departments, shall exercise any power properly belonging to either of the others; except in the instances hereinafter expressly directed or permitted.

Article II

CONCERNING THE LEGISLATIVE DEPARTMENT

SECT. 1st. The Legislative power of this State shall be vested in two distinct branches, the one to be styled the House of Representatives, the other the senate, and both together, the General Assembly of the State of Louisiana.

SECT. 2d. The Members of the House of Representatives shall continue in service for the term of two years from the day of the commencement of the general election.

SECT. 3d. Representatives shall be chosen on the first Monday in July every two years, and the General Assembly shall convene on the first Monday in January in every year, unless a different day be appointed by law, and their sessions shall be held at the Seat of Government.

SECT. 4th. No person shall be a Representative who, at the time of his election is not a free white male citizen of the United States, and hath not attained to the age of twenty one years, and resided in the state two years next preceding his election, and the last year thereof in the county for which he may be chosen or in the district for which he is elected in case the said counties may be divided into separate districts of election, and has not held for one year in the said county or district landed property to the value of five hundred dollars agreeably to the last list.

SECT. 5th. Elections for Representatives for the several counties entitled to representation, shall be held at the places of holding their respecting courts, or in the several election precincts, into which the Legislature may think proper, from time to time, to divide any or all of those counties.

SECT. 6th. Representation shall be equal and uniform in this state, and shall be forever regulated and ascertained by the number of qualified electors therein. In the year one thousand eight hundred and thirteen and every fourth year thereafter, an enumeration of all the electors shall be made in such manner as shall be directed by law. The number of Representatives shall, in the several years of making these enumerations be so fixed as not to be less than twenty five nor more than fifty.

SECT. 7th. The House of Representatives shall choose its speaker and other officers.

SECT. 8th. In all elections for Representatives every free white male citizen of the United States, who at the time being, hath attained to the age of twenty one years and resided in the county in which he offers to vote one year not preceding the election, and who in the last six months prior to the said election, shall have paid a state tax, shall enjoy the right of an elector: provided however that every free white male citizen of the United States who shall have purchased land from the United States, shall have the right of voting whenever he shall have the other qualifications of age and residence above prescribed—Electors shall in all cases, except treason, felony, breach or surety of peace, be privileged from arrest during their attendance at, going to or returning from elections.

SECT. 9th. The members of the Senate shall be chosen for the term of four years, and when assembled shall have the power to choose its officers annually.

SECT. 10th. The State shall be divided in fourteen senatorial districts, which shall forever remain indivisible, as follows; the Parish of St. Bernard and Plaquemine including the country above as far as the land (Des Pécheurs) on the east of the Mississippi and on the west as far as Bernoudy's canal shall form one district. The city of New-Orleans beginning at the Nuns' Plantation above and extending below as far as the above mentioned canal (Des Pécheurs) including the inhabitants of the Bayou St. John, shall form the second district, the remainder of the county of Orleans shall form the third district. The counties of German Coast, Acadia, Lafourche, Iberville, Point Coupée, Concordia, Attakapas, Opelousas, Rapides, Natchitoches and Ouachitta, shall each form one district, and each district shall elect a Senator.

SECT. 11th. At the Session of the General Assembly after this constitution takes effect, the Senators shall be divided by lot, as equally as may be, into two classes; the seats of the Senators of the first class shall be vacated at the expiration of the second year, of the second class at the expiration of the fourth year; so that one half shall be chosen every two years, and a rotation thereby kept up perpetually.

SECT. 12th. No person shall be a Senator who, at the time of his election, is not a citizen of the United States, and who hath not attained to the age of twenty seven years; resided in this state four years next preceding his election, and one year in the district, in which he may be chosen; and unless he holds within the same a landed property to the value of one thousand dollars agreeably to the tax list.

SECT. 13th. The first election for Senators shall be general throughout the state, and at the same time that the general election for Representatives is held; and thereafter there shall be a biennial election of Senators to fill the places of those whose time of service may have expired.

SECT. 14th. Not less than a majority of the members of each house of the general assembly, shall form a quorum to do business; but a smaller number may adjourn from day to day, and shall be authorized by law to compel the attendance of absent members, in such manner, and under such penalties as may be prescribed thereby.

SECT. 15th. Each house of the general assembly shall judge of the qualifications, elections and returns of its members, but a contested election shall be determined in such manner as shall be directed by law.

SECT. 16th. Each house of the general assembly may determine the rules of its proceedings, punish a member for disorderly behaviour, and with the concurrence of two thirds, expel a member, but not a second time for the same offence.

SECT. 17th. Each house of the general assembly shall keep and publish weekly a Journal of its proceedings, and the yeas and nays of the members on any question, shall, at the desire of any two of them, be entered on their Journal.

SECT. 18th. Neither house, during the session of the general assembly, shall without the consent of the other, adjourn for more than three days, nor to any other place than that in which they may be sitting.

SECT. 19th. The members of the general assembly shall severally receive from the Public Treasury a compensation for their services, which shall be four dollars per day, during their attendance on, going to and returning from the sessions of their respective houses; Provided that the same may be increased or diminished by law; but no alteration shall take effect during the period of service of the members of the house of Representatives, by whom such alteration shall have been made.

SECT. 20. The members of the general assembly shall in all cases except treason, felony, breach or surety of the peace, be privileged from arrest, during their attendance at the sessions of their respective houses, and in going to or returning from the same, and for any speech or debate in either house, they shall not be questioned in any other place.

SECT. 21. No Senator or Representative shall, during the term for which he was elected, nor for one year thereafter, be appointed or elected to any civil office of profit under this State, which shall have been created, or the emoluments of which shall have been encreased during the time such Senator or Representative was in office, except to such offices or appointments as may be filled by the elections of the people.

SECT. 22. No person while he continues to exercise the functions of a clergyman, priest or teacher of any religious persuasion, society or sect, shall be eligible to the general assembly, or to any office of profit or trust under this State.

SECT. 23. No person who at any time may have been a collector of taxes for the State, or the assistant or deputy of such collector shall be eligible to the general assembly, until he shall have obtained a quietus for the amount of such collection, and for all public moneys for which he may be responsible.

SECT. 24. No bill shall have the force of a law until, on three several days, it be read over in each house of the general assembly, and free discussion allowed thereon; unless in case of urgency, four-fifths of the house where the bill shall be depending, may deem it expedient to dispense with this rule.

SECT. 25. All bills for raising revenue shall originate in the House of Representatives, but the Senate may propose amendments as in other bills; Provided that they shall not introduce any new matter under the colour of an amendment which does not relate to raising a revenue.

SECT. 26. The general assembly shall regulate, by law, by whom and in what manner writs of election shall be issued to fill the vacancies which may happen in either branch thereof.

ARTICLE III

CONCERNING THE EXECUTIVE DEPARTMENT

SECT. 1. The supreme executive power of the State shall be vested in a chief magistrate, who shall be styled the Governor of the State of Louisiana.

SECT. 2. The Governor shall be elected for the term of four years in the following manner, the citizens entitled to vote for representatives shall vote for a Governor at the time and place of voting for Representatives and Senators. Their votes shall be returned by the persons presiding over the elections to the seat of government addressed to the president of the Senate, and on the second day of the general assembly, the members of the two houses shall meet in the House of Representatives, and immediately after the two candidates who shall have obtained the greatest number of votes, shall be ballotted for and the one having a majority of votes shall be governor.—Provided however that if more than two candidates have obtained the highest number of votes, it shall be the duty of the general assembly to ballot for them in the manner above prescribed, and in case several candidates should obtain an equal number of votes next to the candidate who has obtained the highest number, it shall be the duty of the general assembly to select in the same manner the candidate who is to be ballotted for with him who has obtained the highest number of votes.

SECT. 3. The governor shall be ineligible for the succeeding four years after the expiration of the time for which he shall have been elected.

SECT. 4. He shall be at least thirty five years of age, and a citizen of the United States, and have been an inhabitant of this state at least six years preceding his election, and shall hold in his own right a landed estate of five thousand dollars value, agreeably to the tax list.

SECT. 5. He shall commence the execution of his office on the fourth Monday succeeding the day of his election, and shall continue in the execution thereof, until the end of four weeks next succeeding the election of his successor, and until his successor shall have taken the oaths or affirmations prescribed by this Constitution.

SECT. 6. No member of Congress, or person holding any office under the United States, or minister of any religious society, shall be eligible to the office of Governor.

SECT. 7. The governor shall at stated times, receive for his services a compensation which shall neither be encreased nor diminished during the term for which he shall have been elected.

SECT. 8. He shall be commander in chief of the army and navy of this State, and of the militia thereof except when they shall be called into the service of the United States, but he shall not command personally in the field, unless he shall be advised so to do by a resolution of the general assembly.

SECT. 9th He shall nominate and appoint with the advice and consent of the Senate, Judges, Sheriffs and all other Officers whose offices are established by this Constitution, and whose appointments are not herein otherwise provided for.—Provided however that the Legislature shall have a right to prescribe the mode, of appointment of all other offices to be established by law.

SECT. 10. The governor shall have power to fill up vacancies that may happen during the recess of the Legislature, by granting commissions which shall expire at the end of the next session.

SECT. 11. He shall have power to remit fines and forfeitures, and, except in cases of impeachment, to grant reprieves & pardons, with the approbation of the Senate. In cases of treason he shall have power to grant reprieves until the end of the next session of the general assembly in which the power of pardoning shall be vested.

SECT. 12. He may require information in writing from the officers in the executive department, upon any subject relating to the duties of their respective offices.

SECT. 13. He shall from time to time give to the general assembly information respecting the situation of the state, and recommend to their consideration such measures as he may deem expedient.

SECT. 14. He may on extraordinary occasions convene the general assembly at the seat of government, or at a different place if that should have become dangerous from an enemy or from contagious disorders; and in case of desagreement between the two houses with respect to the time of adjournment, he may ajourn them to such time as he may think proper, not exceeding four months.

SECT. 15. He shall take care that the laws be faithfully executed.

SECT. 16. It shall be his duty to visit the different counties at least once in every two years, to inform himself of the state of the militia and the general condition of the country.

SECT. 17. In case of the impeachment of the governor, his removal from office, death, refusal to qualify, resignation, or absence from the state, the president of the senate shall exercise all the power and authority appertaining to the office of governor, untill another be duly qualified, or the governor absent or impeached shall return or be acquitted.

SECT. 18. The president of the Senate, during the time he administers the government shall receive the same compensation which the governor would have received had he been employed in the duties of his office.

SECT. 19. A secretary of state shall be appointed and commissioned during that term for which the governor shall have been elected, if he shall so long behave himself well, he shall keep a fair register, and attest all official acts and proceedings of the governor, and shall when required, lay the same and all papers, minutes and vouchers relative thereto, before either house of the general assembly, and shall perform such other duties as may be enjoined him by law.

SECT. 20. Every bill which shall have passed both houses shall be presented to the governor, if he approve, he shall sign it, if not he shall return it with his objection to the house in which it shall have originated, who shall enter the objections at large upon their Journal, and proceed to reconsider it—if after such reconsideration, two thirds of all the members elected to that house, shall agree to pass the bill, it shall be sent, with the objections, to the other house, by which it shall likewise be reconsidered and if approved by two thirds of all the members elected to that house, it shall be a law; but in such cases, the votes of both houses shall be determined by yeas and nays, and the names of the members voting for and against the bill, shall be entered on the journal of each house respectively; if any bill shall not be returned by the governor within ten days (Sundays excepted) after it shall have been presented to him, it shall be a law in like manner as if he had signed it, unless the general assembly by their adjournment prevent its return, in which case it shall be a law, unless sent back within three days after their next meeting.

SECT. 21. Every order, resolution or vote, to which the concurrence of both houses may be necessary, except on a question of adjournment, shall be presented to the governor, and before it shall take effect be approved by him; or being disapproved shall be repassed by two thirds of both houses.

SECT. 22. The free white men of this State, shall be armed and disciplined for its defence; but those who belong to religious societies, whose tenets forbid them to carry arms, shall not be compelled so to do, but shall pay an equivalent for personal service.

SECT. 23. The militia of this state shall be organized in such manner as may be hereafter deemed most expedient by the legislature.

ARTICLE IV

CONCERNING THE JUDICIARY DEPARTMENT

SECT. 1st. The judiciary power shall be vested in a supreme court and inferior courts.

SECT. 2d. The supreme court shall have appellate jurisdiction only, which jurisdiction shall extend to all civil cases when the matter in dispute shall exceed the sum of three hundred dollars.

SECT. 3d. The supreme court shall consist of not less than three judges, nor more than five; the majority of whom shall form a quorum; each of the said judges shall receive a salary of five thousand dollars annually. The supreme court shall hold its sessions at the places hereinafter mentioned; and for that purpose the state is hereby divided into two districts of appellate jurisdiction, in each of which the supreme court shall administer justice in the manner hereafter prescribed. The Eastern district to consist of the counties of New Orleans, German Coast, Acadia, Lafourche, Iberville, and Point Coupee; the western district to consist of the counties of Attakapas, Opelousas, Rapides, Concordia, Natchitoches, and Ouachita. The supreme court shall hold its sessions in each year, for the Eastern district in New-Orleans during the months of November, December, January, February, March, April, May, June, and July; and for the western district, at Opelousas during the months of August, September and October: for five years: Provided however, That every five years the legislature may change the place of holding said court in the western district. The said court shall appoint its own clerks.

SECT. 4th. The legislature is authorised to establish such inferior courts as may be convenient to the administration of justice.

SECT. 5th. The judges both of the supreme and inferior courts shall hold their offices during good behaviour; but for any reasonable cause which shall not be sufficient ground for impeachment, the Governor shall remove any of them, on the address of three fourths of each house of the general assembly: Provided however, That the cause or causes for which such removal may be required, shall be stated at length in the address, and inserted on the journal of each house.

SECT. 6th. The judges, by virtue of their office, shall be conservators of the peace throughout the state; the style of all process shall be "The State of Louisiana." All prosecutions shall be carried on in the name and by the authority of the state of Louisiana, and conclude "against the peace and dignity of the same."

SECT. 7. There shall be an attorney general for the state, and as many other prosecuting attorneys for the state as may be hereafter found necessary. The said attorneys shall be appointed by the Governor with the advice and approbation of the Senate. Their duties shall be determined by law.

SECT. 8. All commissions shall be in the name, and by the authority of, the state of Louisiana, and sealed with the state seal, and signed by the Governor.

SECT. 9. The state treasurer, and printer or printers of the state, shall be appointed, annually, by the joint vote of both houses of the general assembly: Provided, That during the recess of the same, the Governor shall have power to fill vacancies which may happen in either of the said offices.

SECT. 10. The clerks of the several courts shall be removable for breach of good behaviour, by the court of appeals only, who shall be judge of the fact, as well as of the law.

SECT 11. The existing laws in this territory, when this constitution goes into effect, shall continue to be in force until altered or abolished by the Legislature; Provided however, that the Legislature shall never adopt any system or code of laws, by a general reference to the said system or code, but in all cases, shall specify the several provisions of the laws it may enact.

SECT 12. The judges of all courts within this state, shall, as often as it may be possible so to do, in every definitive judgment, refer to the particular law, in virtue of which such judgment may have been rendered, and in all cases adduce the reasons on which their judgment is founded.

Article V

CONCERNING IMPEACHMENT.

Sect. 1. The power of impeachment shall be vested in the House of Representatives alone.

Sect. 2. All impeachments shall be tried by the Senate when sitting for that purpose, the senators shall be upon oath or affirmation, and no person shall be convicted without the concurrence of two thirds of the members present.

Sect. 3. The governor and all the civil officers, shall be liable to impeachment for any misdemeanor in office, but judgment, in such cases, shall not extend further than to removal from office and disqualification to hold any office of honor trust or profit under this State; but the parties convicted shall nevertheless, be liable and subject to indictment, trial and punishment according to law.

Article VI

GENERAL PROVISIONS

Sect. 1. Members of the general assembly and all officers executive and judicial, before they enter upon the execution of their respective offices, shall take the following oath or affirmation: " I (A. B.) do solemnly swear (or affirm) that I will faithfully and impartially discharge and perform all the duties incumbent on me as—according to the best of my abilities and understanding, agreeably to the rules and regulations of the Constitution, and the laws of this State; so help me God!"

Sect. 2. Treason against the State, shall consist only in levying war against it or in adhering to its enemies, giving them aid and comfort. No person shall be convicted of treason, unless on the testimony of two witnesses to the same overt act, or his own confession in open court.

Sect. 3. Every person shall be disqualified from serving as governor, Senator or Representative for the term for which he shall have been elected, who shall have been convicted of having given or offered any bribe to procure his election.

Sect. 4. Laws shall be made to exclude from office and from suffrage those who shall thereafter be convicted of bribery, perjury, forgery or other high crimes or misdemeanors, the privilege of free suffrage shall be supported by laws regulating elections and prohibiting under adequate penalties, all undue influence thereon, from power, bribery, tumult, or other improper practices.

Sect. 5. No money shall be drawn from the treasury, but in pursuance of appropriations made by law; nor shall any appropriation of money for the support of an army be made for a longer term than one year; and a regular statement and account of the receipts and expenditures of all public moneys, shall be published annually.

SECT. 6. It shall be the duty of the general assembly to pass such laws as may be necessary and proper to decide differences by arbitrators, to be appointed by the parties, who may choose that summary mode of adjustment.

SECT. 7. All civil officers for the state at large shall reside within the State, and all district or county officers within their respective districts or counties, and shall keep their respective offices at such places therein as may be required by law.

SECT. 8. The Legislature shall determine the time of duration of the several public offices when such time shall not have been fixed by this Constitution, and all civil officers except the governor and judges of the superior and inferior courts shall be removable by an address of two thirds of the members of both houses, except those, the removal of whom has been otherwise provided for by this Constitution.

SECT. 9. Absence on the business of this State or of the United States, shall not forfeit a residence once obtained, so as to deprive any one of the rights of suffrage, or of being elected or appointed to any office under this State, under the exceptions contained in this Constitution.

SECT. 10. It shall be the duty of the general assembly to regulate by law in what cases, and what deduction from the salaries of public officers shall be made for neglect of duty in their official capacity.

SECT. 11. Returns of all elections for the members of the general assembly, shall be made to the secretary of state for the time being.

SECT. 12. The Legislature shall point out the manner in which a man coming into the country shall declare his residence.

SECT. 13. In all elections by the people, and also by the Senate and House of Representatives jointly or separately, the vote shall be given by ballot.

SECT. 14. No members of Congress, nor person holding or exercising any office of trust or profit under the United States, or either of them, or under any foreign powers shall be eligible as a member of the general assembly of this State, or hold or exercise any office of trust or profit under the same.

SECT. 15. All laws that may be passed by the Legislature, and the public records of this State, and the judicial and legislative written proceedings of the same, shall be promulgated, preserved and conducted in the language in which the constitution of the United States is written.

SECT. 16. The general assembly shall direct by law how persons who are now or may hereafter become securities for public officers, may be relieved or discharged on account of such securityship.

SCET. 17. No power of suspending the laws of this State shall be exercised, unless by the Legislature, or its authority.

SECT. 18. In all criminal prosecutions, the accused have the right of being heard by himself or counsel, of demanding the nature and cause of the accusation against him, of meeting the witnesses face to face, of having compulsory process for obtaining witnesses in his favour, and prosecutions by indictment or information, a speedy public trial by an impartial jury of the vicinage, nor shall he be compelled to give evidence against himself.

SECT. 19. All prisoners shall be bailable by sufficient securities, unless for capital offences, where the proof is evident or presumption great, and the privilege of the writ of Habeas Corpus shall not be suspended unless when in cases of rebellion or invasion the public safety may require it.

SECT. 20. No *ex post facto* law nor any law impairing the obligation of contracts shall be passed.

SECT. 21. Printing presses shall be free to every person who undertakes to examine the proceedings of the Legislature, or any branch of the government, and no law shall ever be made to restrain the right thereof. The free communication of thoughts and opinions is one of the invaluable rights of man, and every citizen may freely speak, write and print on any subject, being responsible for the abuse of that liberty.

SECT. 22. Emigration from the State shall not be prohibited.

SECT. 23. The citizens of the town of New-Orleans shall have the right of appointing the several public officers necessary for the administration and the police of the said city, pursuant to the mode of election which shall be prescribed by the Legislature; Provided that the mayor and recorder be ineligible to a seat in the general assembly.

SECT. 24. The seat of government shall continue at New Orleans until removed by law.

SECT. 25. All laws contrary to this Constitution shall be null and void.

ARTICLE VII

MODE OF REVISING THE CONSTITUTION

SECT. 1. When experience shall point out the necessity of amending this Constitution, and a majority of all the members elected to each house of the general assembly, shall, within the first twenty days of their stated annual session, concur in passing a law, specifying the alterations intended to be made, for taking the sense of the good people of this state, as to the necessity and expediency of calling a convention, it shall be the duty of the several returning officers, at the next general election which shall be held for Representatives after the passage of such law, to open a poll for, and make return to the secretary for the time being, of the names of all those entitled to vote for Representatives, who have voted for calling a convention; and if thereupon, it shall appear that a majority of all the citizens of this state, entitled to vote for Representatives, have voted for a convention, the general assembly, shall direct that a similar poll shall be opened, and taken for the next year; and if thereupon, it shall appear that a majority of all the citizens of this state entitled to vote for Representatives, have voted for a convention, the general assembly shall, at their next session, call a convention to consist of as many members as there shall be in the general assembly, and no more, to be chosen in same manner and proportion, at the same places and at the same time, that Representatives are, by citizens entitled to vote for Representatives; and to meet within three months after the said election, for the purpose of re-adopting, amending or changing this constitution. But if it shall appear by the vote of either year, as aforesaid, that a majority of all the citizens entitled to vote for Representatives, did not vote for a convention, a convention shall not be called.

Schedule

Sect. 1. That no inconveniences may arise from the change of a territorial to permanent state government, it is declared by the Convention that all rights, suits, actions, prosecutions, claims and contracts, both as it respects individuals and bodies corporate, shall continue as if no change had taken place in this government in virtue of the laws now in force.

Sect. 2. All fines, penalties and forfeitures, due and owing to the territory of Orleans shall inure to the use of the state. All bonds executed to the governor or any other officer in his official capacity in the territory, shall pass over to the governor or to the officers of the State and their successors in office, for the use of the State, by him or by them to be respectively assigned over to the use of those concerned, as the case may be.

Sect. 3. The governor, secretary and judges, and all other officers under the territorial government, shall continue in the exercise of their duties of their respective departments until the said officers are superceded under the authority of this Constitution.

Sect. 4. All laws now in force in this territory, not inconsistent with this constitution, shall continue and remain in full effect until repealed by the legislature.

Sect. 5. The governor of this state shall make use of his private seal, until a state seal be procured.

Sect. 6. The oaths of office herein directed to be taken, may be administered by any justice of the peace, until the legislature shall otherwise direct.

Sect. 7. At the expiration of the time after which this constitution is to go into operation, or immediately after official information shall have been received that congress have approved of the same, the president of the Convention shall issue writs of election to the proper officers in the different counties, enjoining them to cause an election to be held for governor and members of the general assembly, in each of their respective districts. The election shall commence on the fourth Monday following the day of the date of the President's proclamation, and shall take place on the same day throughout the state. The mode and duration of the said election shall be determined by the laws now in force: Provided however, that in case of absence or disability of the President of the Convention, to cause the said election to be carried into effect, the Secretary of the Convention shall discharge the duties hereby imposed on the President, and that in case of absence of the secretary a committee of Messrs Blanque, Brown, and Urquhart or a majority of them, shall discharge the duties herein imposed on the secretary of the convention—and the members of the general assembly thus elected shall assemble on the fourth Monday thereafter at the seat of government. The governor and members of the general assembly for this time only, shall enter upon the duties of their respective offices, immediately after their election, and shall continue in office in the same manner and during the same period they would have done had they been elected on the first Monday of July 1812.

Sect. 8. untill the first enumeration shall be made as directed in the sixth section of the second article of this Constitution, the, county of

Orleans shall be entitled to Six Representatives to be elected as follows: one by the first senatorial district within the said county, four by the second district, and one by the third district—The county of German Coast, to two Representatives, the county of Acadia, to two Representatives; the county of Iberville, to two Representatives; the county of Lafourche, to two Representatives; to be elected as follows: one by the parish of the assumption, and the other by the parish of the interior; the county of Rapides, to two Representatives; the county of Natchitoches, to one Representative; the county of Concordia, to one Representative; the county of Ouachitta, to one Representative; the county of Opelloussas, to two Representatives; the county of Attakapas, to three Representatives to be elected as follows: two by the parish of St. Martin and the third by the parish of St. Mary, and the respective senatorial districts created by this Constitution, to one senator each.

Done in Convention, at New Orleans, the twenty second day of the month of January, in the year of our Lord one thousand eight hundred and twelve, and of the independence of the United States of America, the thirty-sixth.

J. POYDRAS,
President of the Convention.

ELIGIUS FROMENTIN,
   Secretary of the Convention.

CONSTITUTION OF LOUISIANA—1845 * [a]

PREAMBLE

We, the people of the State of Louisiana, do ordain and establish this constitution:

TITLE I

DISTRIBUTION OF POWERS

ARTICLE 1. The powers of the government of the State of Louisiana shall be divided into three distinct departments, and each of them be confided to a separate body of magistracy, to wit: Those which are legislative to one, those which are executive to another, and those which are judicial to another.

ART. 2. No one of these departments, nor any person holding office in one of them, shall exercise power properly belonging to either of the others, except in the instances hereinafter expressly directed or permitted.

TITLE II

LEGISLATIVE DEPARTMENT

ART. 3. The legislative powers of the State shall be vested in two distinct branches, the one to be styled the " house of representatives,"

---

* Verified by copy of the constitution of Louisiana published by Bloomfield & Steel, New Orleans, 1861.

[a] This constitution was framed by a convention which met at Jackson August 5, 1844, and adjourned to New Orleans August 24, 1844. It resumed its labors at New Orleans January 14, 1845, and completed them May 16, 1845. The constitution was submitted to the people, and ratified November 5, 1845.

the other "the senate," and both "the general assembly of the State of Louisiana."

ART. 4. The members of the house of representatives shall continue in service for the term of two years from the day of the closing of the general elections.

ART. 5. Representatives shall be chosen on the first Monday in November every two years; and the election shall be completed in one day. The general assembly shall meet every second year, on the third Monday in January next ensuing the election, unless a different day be appointed by law, and their session shall be held at the seat of government.

ART. 6. No person shall be a representative who, at the time of his election, is not a free white male, and has not been for three years a citizen of the United States, and has not attained the age of twenty-one years, and resided in the State for the three years next preceding the election, and the last year thereof in the parish for which he may be chosen.

ART. 7. Elections for representatives for the several parishes or representative districts shall be held at the several election-precincts established by law. The legislature may delegate the power of establishing election-precincts to the parochial or municipal authorities.

ART. 8. Representation in the house of representatives shall be equal and uniform, and shall be regulated and ascertained by the number of qualified electors. Each parish shall have at least one representative; no new parish shall be created with a territory less than six hundred and twenty-five square miles, nor with a number of electors less than the full number entitling it to a representative, nor when the creation of such new parish would leave any other parish without the said extent of territory and number of electors.

The first enumeration to be made by the State authorities under this constitution shall be made in the year 1847, the second in the year 1855; and the subsequent enumerations shall be made every tenth year thereafter, in such manner as shall be prescribed by law for the purpose of ascertaining the total population and the number of qualified electors in each parish and election-district.

At the first regular session of the legislature after the making of each enumeration, the legislature shall apportion the representation amongst the several parishes and election-districts on the basis of qualified electors as aforesaid. A representative number shall be fixed, and each parish and election-district shall have as many representatives as the aggregate number of its electors will entitle it to, and an additional representative for any fraction exceeding one-half the representative number. The number of representatives shall not be more than one hundred nor less than seventy.

That part of the parish of Orleans situated on the left bank of the Mississippi shall be divided into nine representative districts, as follows, viz:

1st. First district to extend from the line of the parish of Jefferson to the middle of Benjamin, Estelle, and Thalia streets.

2d. Second district to extend from the last-mentioned limits to the middle of Julia street, until its strikes the New Orleans Canal; thence down said canal to the lake.

3d. Third district to comprise the residue of the second municipality.

4th. Fourth district to extend from the middle of Canal street to the middle of Saint Louis street, until it reaches the Metairie road; thence along said road to the New Orleans Canal.

5th. Fifth district to extend from the last-mentioned limits to the middle of Saint Philip street; thence down said street until its intersection with the Bayou Saint John; thence along the middle of said Bayou until it intersects the Metairie road; thence along said road until it reaches Saint Louis street.

6th. Sixth district to be composed of the residue of the first municipality.

7th. Seventh district, from the middle of Esplanade street to the middle of Champs Elysées street.

8th. Eighth district, from the middle of Champs Elysées street to the middle of Enghein street and La Fayette avenue.

9th. Ninth district, from the middle of Enghein street and La Fayette avenue to the lower limits of the parish.

ART. 9. The house of representatives shall choose its speaker and other officers.

ART. 10. In all elections by the people, every free white male, who has been two years a citizen of the United States, who has attained the age of twenty-one years, and resided in the State two consecutive years next preceding the election, and the last year thereof in the parish in which he offers to vote, shall have the right of voting: *Provided*, That no person shall be deprived of the right of voting who at the time of the adoption of this constitution was entitled to that right under the constitution of 1812. Electors shall in all cases, except treason, felony, breach of surety of the peace, be privileged from arrest during their attendance at, going to, or returning from elections.

ART. 11. Absence from the State for more than ninety consecutive days shall interrupt the acquisition of the residence required in the preceding section, unless the person absenting himself shall be a housekeeper, or shall occupy a tenement for carrying on business, and his dwelling-house or tenements for carrying on business shall be actually occupied, during his absence, by his family or servants, or some portion thereof, or by some one employed by him.

ART. 12. No soldier, seaman or marine in the Army or Navy of the United States, no pauper, no person under interdiction, nor under conviction of any crime punishable with hard labor, shall be entitled to vote at any election in this State.

ART. 13. No person shall be entitled to vote at any election held in this State, except in the parish of his residence, and, in cities and towns divided into election-precincts, in the election-precinct in which he resides.

ART. 14. The members of the senate shall be chosen for the term of four years. The senate, when assembled, shall have the power to choose its officers every two years.

ART. 15. The legislature, in every year in which they shall apportion representation in the house of representatives, shall divide the State into senatorial districts. No parish shall be divided in the formation of a senatorial district, the parish of Orleans excepted. And whenever a new parish shall be created, it shall be attached to the senatorial district from which most of its territory was taken, or to another contiguous district, at the discretion of the legislature;

but shall not be attached to more than one district. The number of senators shall be thirty-two, and they shall be apportioned among the senatorial districts according to the total population contained in the several districts: *Provided*, That no parish shall be entitled to more than one-eighth of the whole number of senators.

ART. 16. In all apportionments of the senate, the population of the city of New Orleans shall be deducted from the population of the whole State, and the remainder of the population divided by the number twenty-eight, and the result produced by this division shall be the senatorial ratio entitling a senatorial district to a senator. Single or contiguous parishes shall be formed into districts having a population the nearest possible to the number entitling a district to a senator; and if, in the apportionment to be made, a parish or district fall short of or exceed the ratio one-fifth, then a district may be formed having not more than two senators, but not otherwise.

No new apportionment shall have the effect of abridging the term of service of any senator already elected at the time of making the apportionment.

After an enumeration has been made as directed in the [eighth] article, the legislature shall not pass any law until an apportionment of representation in both houses of the general assembly be made.

ART. 17. At the first session of the general assembly after this constitution takes effect, the senators shall be equally divided by lot into two classes; the seats of the senators of the first class shall be vacated at the expiration of the second year, of the second class at the expiration of the fourth year; so that one-half shall be chosen every two years, and a rotation thereby kept up perpetually. In case any district shall have elected two or more senators, said senators shall vacate their seats respectively at the end of two and four years, and lots shall be drawn between them.

ART. 18. No person shall be a senator who at the time of his election has not been a citizen of the United States ten years, and who has not attained the age of twenty-seven years, and resided in the State four years next preceding his election, and the last year thereof in the district in which he may be chosen.

ART. 19. The first election for senators shall be general throughout the State, and at the same time that the general election for representatives is held; and thereafter there shall be biennial elections to fill the place of those whose time of service may have expired.

ART. 20. Not less than a majority of the members of each house of the general assembly shall form a quorum to do business; but a smaller number may adjourn from day to day, and shall be authorized by law to compel the attendance of absent members.

ART. 21. Each house of the general assembly shall judge of the qualification, election, and returns of its members; but a contested election shall be determined in such manner as shall be directed by law.

ART. 22. Each house of the general assembly may determine the rules of its proceedings, punish a member for disorderly behavior, and, with the concurrence of two-thirds, expel a member, but not a second time for the same offence.

ART. 23. Each house of the general assembly shall keep and publish weekly a journal of its proceedings; and the yeas and nays of the members on any question shall, at the desire of any two of them, be entered on the journal.

ART. 24. Each house may punish, by imprisonment, any person not a member, for disrespectful and disorderly behavior in its presence, or for obstructing any of its proceedings. Such imprisonment shall not exceed ten days for any one offence.

ART. 25. Neither house, during the session of the general assembly, shall, without the consent of the other, adjourn for more than three days, nor to any other place than that in which they may be sitting.

ART. 26. The members of the general assembly shall receive from the public treasury a compensation for their services, which shall be four dollars per day during their attendance, going to, and returning from the session of their respective houses. The compensation may be increased or diminished by law; but no alteration shall take effect during the period of service of the members of the house of representatives by whom such alteration shall have been made. No session shall extend to a period beyond sixty days, to date from its commencement, and any legislative action had after the expiration of the said sixty days shall be null and void. This provision shall not apply to the first legislature which is to convene after the adoption of this constitution.

ART. 27. The members of the general assembly shall, in all cases except treason, felony, breach or surety of the peace, be privileged from arrest during their attendance at the sessions of their respective houses, and going to or returning from the same, and for any speech or debate in either house, they shall not be questioned in any other place.

ART. 28. No senator or representative shall, during the term for which he was elected, nor for one year thereafter, be appointed or elected to any civil office of profit under this State, which shall have been created or the emoluments of which shall have been increased during the time such senator or representative was in office, except to such offices or appointments as may be filled by the elections of the people.

ART. 29. No person, while he continues to exercise the functions of a clergyman, priest, or teacher of any religious persuasion, society, or sect, shall be eligible to the general assembly.

ART. 30. No person who at any time may have been a collector of taxes, or who may have been otherwise intrusted with public money, shall be eligible to the general assembly, or to any office of profit or trust under the State government, until he shall have obtained a discharge for the amount of such collections, and for all public moneys with which he may have been intrusted.

ART. 31. No bill shall have the force of a law until, on three several days, it be read over in each house of the general assembly, and free discussion allowed thereon; unless, in case of urgency, four-fifths of the house where the bill shall be pending may deem it expedient to dispense with this rule.

ART. 32. All bills for raising revenue shall originate in the house of representatives, but the senate may propose amendments, as in other bills: *Provided*, They shall not introduce any new matter, under color of an amendment, which does not relate to raising revenue.

ART. 33. The general assembly shall regulate by law by whom and in what manner writs of election shall be issued to fill the vacancies which may happen in either branch thereof.

ART. 34. A majority of all the members elected to the senate shall be required for the confirmation or rejection of officers to be appointed by the governor, with the advice and consent of the senate; and the senate, in deciding thereon, shall vote by yeas and nays, and the names of the senators voting for and against the appointments, respectively, shall be entered on a journal to be kept for that purpose, and made public at the end of each session, or before.

ART. 35. Returns of all elections for members of the general assembly shall be made to the secretary of state.

ART. 36. A treasurer of the State shall be elected biennially, by joint ballot of the two houses of the general assembly. The governor shall have power to fill any vacancy that may happen in that office during the recess of the legislature.

ART. 37. In the year in which a regular election for a Senator of the United States is to take place, the members of the general assembly shall meet in the hall of the house of representatives, on the Monday following the meeting of the legislature, and proceed to the said election.

TITLE III

EXECUTIVE DEPARTMENT

ART. 38. The supreme executive power of the State shall be vested in a chief magistrate, who shall be styled the governor of the State of Louisiana. He shall hold his office during the term of four years; and, together with the lieutenant-governor chosen for the same term, be elected as follows: The qualified electors for representatives shall vote for a governor and lieutenant-governor, at the time and place of voting for representatives; the returns of every election shall be sealed up and transmitted by the proper returning-officer to the secretary of state, who shall deliver them to the speaker of the house of representatives, on the second day of the session of the general assembly, then next to be holden. The members of the general assembly shall meet in the house of representatives to examine and count the votes. The person having the greatest number of votes for governor shall be declared duly elected; but if two or more persons shall be equal, and highest in the number of votes polled for governor, one of them shall immediately be chosen governor, by joint vote of the members of the general assembly. The person having the greatest number of votes for lieutenant-governor shall be lieutenant-governor; but if two or more persons shall be equal and highest in the number of votes polled for lieutenant-governor, one of them shall be immediately chosen lieutenant-governor, by joint vote of the members of the general assembly.

ART. 39. No person shall be eligible to the office of governor or lieutenant-governor who shall not have attained the age of thirty-five years, been fifteen years a citizen of the United States, and a resident within the State for the same space of time next preceding his election.

ART. 40. The governor shall enter on the discharge of his duties on the fourth Monday of January next ensuing his election, and shall continue in office until the Monday next succeeding the day that his successor shall be declared duly elected, and shall have taken the oath or affirmation prescribed by this constitution.

ART. 41. The governor shall be ineligible for the succeeding four years after the expiration of the time for which he shall have been elected.

ART. 42. No member of Congress, or person holding any office under the United States, or minister of any religious society, shall be eligible to the office of governor or lieutenant-governor.

ART. 43. In case of the impeachment of the governor, his removal from office, death, refusal or inability to qualify, resignation, or absence from the State, the powers and duties of the office shall devolve upon the lieutenant-governor for the residue of the term, or until the governor, absent or impeached, shall return or be acquitted. The legislature may provide by law for the case of removal, impeachment, death, resignation, disability, or refusal to qualify, of both the governor and lieutenant-governor, declaring what officer shall act as governor; and such officer shall act accordingly, until the disability be removed, or for the residue of the term.

ART. 44. The lieutenant-governor, or other officer discharging the duties of governor, shall, during his administration, receive the same compensation to which the governor would have been entitled had he continued in office.

ART. 45. The lieutenant-governor shall, by virtue of his office, be president of the senate, but shall have only a casting vote therein. Whenever he shall administer the government, or shall be unable to attend as president of the senate, the senators shall elect one of their own members as president of the senate for the time being.

ART. 46. While he acts as president of the senate, the lieutenant-governor shall receive for his services the same compensation which shall for the same period be allowed to the speaker of the house of representatives, and no more.

ART. 47. The governor shall have power to grant reprieves for all offences against the State, and, except in cases of impeachment, shall, with the consent of the senate, have power to grant pardons, and remit fines and forfeitures, after conviction. In cases of treason, he may grant reprieves until the end of the next session of the general assembly, in which the power of pardoning shall be vested.

ART 48. The governor shall at stated times receive for his services a compensation, which shall neither be increased nor diminished during the term for which he shall have been elected.

ART. 49. He shall be commander-in-chief of the army and navy of this State, and of the militia thereof, except when they shall be called into the service of the United States.

ART. 50. He shall nominate, and, by and with the advice and consent of the senate, appoint all officers whose offices are established by this constitution, and whose appointment is not therein otherwise provided for: *Provided, however*, That the legislature shall have a right to prescribe the mode of appointment to all other offices established by law.

ART. 51. The governor shall have power to fill vacancies that may happen during the recess of the senate, by granting commissions which shall expire at the end of the next session, unless otherwise provided for in this constitution; but no person who has been nominated for office, and rejected by the senate, shall be appointed to the same office during the recess of the senate.

ART 52. He may require information in writing from the officers in the executive department, upon any subject relating to the duties of their respective offices.

ART. 53. He shall, from time to time, give to the general assembly information respecting the situation of the State, and recommend to their consideration such measures as he may deem expedient.

ART. 54. He may on extraordinary occasions convene the general assembly at the seat of government, or at a different place, if that should have become dangerous from an enemy or from epidemic; and in case of disagreement between the two houses as to the time of adjournment, he may adjourn them to such time as he may think proper, not exceeding four months.

ART. 55. He shall take care that the laws be faithfully executed.

ART. 56. Every bill which shall have passed both houses shall be presented to the governor; if he approve, he shall sign it, if not, he shall return it with his objections to the house in which it originated, which shall enter the objections at large upon its journal, and proceed to reconsider it; if after such reconsideration two-thirds of all the members elected to that house shall agree to pass the bill, it shall be sent, with the objections, to the other house, by which it shall likewise be reconsidered, and if approved by two-thirds of all the members elected to that house, it shall be a law; but in such cases the vote of both houses shall be determined by yeas and nays, and the names of the members voting for and against the bill shall be entered on the journal of each house respectively. If any bill shall not be returned by the governor within ten days (Sundays excepted) after it shall have been presented to him, it shall be a law in like manner as if he had signed it, unless the general assembly, by adjournment, prevent its return; in which case it shall be a law unless sent back within three days after their next meeting.

ART. 57. Every order, resolution, or vote, to which the concurrence of both houses may be necessary, except on a question of adjournment, shall be presented to the governor, and before it shall take effect be approved by him, or being disapproved, shall be repassed by two-thirds of the members elected to each house of the general assembly.

ART. 58. There shall be a secretary of state, who shall hold his office during the time for which the governor shall have been elected. The records of the State shall be kept and preserved in the office of the secretary; he shall keep a fair register of the official acts and proceedings of the governor, and, when necessary, shall attest them. He shall, when required, lay the said register, and all papers, minutes, and vouchers relative to his office, before either house of the general assembly, and shall perform such other duties as may be enjoined on him by law.

ART. 59. All commissions shall be in the name and by the authority of the State of Louisiana, and shall be sealed with the State seal, and signed by the governor.

ART. 60. The free white men of the State shall be armed and disciplined for its defence; but those who belong to religious societies whose tenets forbid them to carry arms, shall not be compelled so to do, but shall pay an equivalent for personal services.

ART. 61. The militia of the State shall be organized in such manner as may be hereafter deemed most expedient by the legislature.

Title IV

JUDICIARY DEPARTMENT

ART 62. The judicial power shall be vested in a supreme court, in district courts, and in justices of the peace.

ART. 63. The supreme court, except in cases hereinafter provided, shall have appellate jurisdiction only, which jurisdiction shall extend to all cases where the matter in dispute shall exceed three hundred dollars, and to all cases in which the constitutionality or legality of any tax, toll, or impost, of any kind or nature soever, shall be in contestation, whatever may be the amount thereof; and likewise to all fines, forfeitures, and penalties imposed by municipal corporations, and in criminal cases on questions of law alone, whenever the punishment of death or hard labor may be inflicted, or when a fine exceeding three hundred dollars is actually imposed.

ART. 64. The supreme court shall be composed of one chief justice and of three associate justices, a majority of whom shall constitute a quorum. The chief justice shall receive a salary of six thousand dollars, and each of the associate judges a salary of five thousand five hundred dollars annually. The court shall appoint its own clerks. The judges shall be appointed for the term of eight years.

ART. 65. When the first appointments are made under this constitution, the chief justice shall be appointed for eight years, one of the associate judges for six years, one for four years, and one for two years; and in the event of the death, resignation, or removal of any of said judges before the expiration of the period for which he was appointed, his successor shall be appointed only for the remainder of his term; so that the term of service of no two of said judges shall expire at the same time.

ART. 66. The supreme court shall hold its sessions in New Orleans from the first Monday of the month of November to the end of the month of June, inclusive. The legislature shall have power to fix the sessions elsewhere during the rest of the year; until otherwise provided, the sessions shall be held as heretofore.

ART. 67. The supreme court, and each of the judges thereof, shall have power to issue writs of *habeas corpus*, at the instance of all persons in actual custody under process, in all cases in which they may have appellate jurisdiction.

ART. 68. In all cases in which the judges shall be equally divided in opinion, the judgment appealed from shall stand affirmed; in which case each of the judges shall give his separate opinions in writing.

ART. 69. All judges, by virtue of their office, shall be conservators of the peace throughout the State. The style of all process shall be "The State of Louisiana." All prosecutions shall be carried on in the name and by the authority of the State of Louisiana, and conclude against the peace and dignity of the same.

ART. 70. The judges of all the courts within this State shall, as often as it may be possible so to do, in every definitive judgment, refer to the particular law in virtue of which such judgment may be rendered, and in all cases adduce the reasons on which their judgment is founded.

ART. 71. No court or judge shall make any allowance by way of fee or compensation in any suit or proceedings, except for the payment of such fees to ministerial officers as may be established by law.

ART. 72. No duties or functions shall ever be attached by law to the supreme or district courts, or to the several judges thereof, but such as are judicial; and the said judges are prohibited from receiving any fees of office or other compensation than their salaries for any civil duties performed by them.

ART. 73. The judges of all courts shall be liable to impeachment; but for any reasonable cause, which shall not be sufficient ground for impeachment, the governor shall remove any of them on the address of three-fourths of the members present of each house of the general assembly. In every such case the cause or causes for which such removal may be required shall be stated at length in the address, and inserted in the journal of each house.

ART. 74. There shall be an attorney-general for the State, and as many district attorneys as may be hereafter found necessary. They shall hold their offices for two years; their duties shall be determined by law.

ART. 75. The first legislature assembled under this constitution shall divide the State into judicial districts, which shall remain unchanged for six years, and be subject to reorganization every sixth year thereafter.

The number of districts shall not be less than twelve nor more than twenty.

For each district one judge, learned in the law, shall be appointed, except in the districts in which the cities of New Orleans and La Fayette are situated, in which the legislature may establish as many district courts as the public interest may require.

ART. 76. Each of the said judges shall receive a salary to be fixed by law, which shall not be increased or diminished during his term of office, and shall never be less than two thousand five hundred dollars annually. He must be a citizen of the United States, over the age of thirty years, and have resided in the State for six years next preceding his appointment, and have practised law therein for the space of five years.

ART. 77. The judges of the district courts shall hold their offices for the term of six years. The judges first appointed shall be divided by lot into three classes, as nearly equal as can be, and the term of office of the judges of the first class shall expire at the end of two years, of the second class at the end of four years, and of the third class at the end of six years.

ART. 78. The district courts shall have original jurisdiction in all civil cases, when the amount in dispute exceeds fifty dollars, exclusive of interest. In all criminal cases, and in all matters connected with successions, their jurisdiction shall be unlimited.

ART. 79. The legislature shall have power to vest in clerks of courts authority to grant such orders and do such acts as may be deemed necessary for the furtherance of the administration of justice, and in all cases the powers thus granted shall be specified and determined.

ART. 80. The clerks of the several courts shall be removable for breach of good behavior by the judges thereof; subject in all cases to an appeal to the supreme court.

ART. 81. The jurisdiction of justices of the peace shall never exceed, in civil cases, the sum of one hundred dollars, exclusive of interest, subject to appeal to the district court in such cases as shall be provided for by law. They shall be elected by the qualified voters of each parish for the term of two years, and shall have such criminal jurisdiction as shall be provided for by law.

ART. 82. Clerks of the district courts in this State shall be elected by the qualified electors in each parish, for the term of four years, and, should a vacancy occur subsequent to an election, it shall be filled by the judge of the court in which such vacancy exists, and the person so appointed shall hold his office until the next general election.

ART. 83. A sheriff and a coroner shall be elected in each parish, by the qualified voters thereof, who shall hold their offices for the term of two years, unless sooner removed.

Should a vacancy occur in either of these offices subsequent to an election, it shall be filled by the governor; and the person so appointed shall continue in office until his successor shall be elected and qualified.

Title V

IMPEACHMENT

ART. 84. The power of impeachment shall be vested in the house of representatives.

ART. 85. Impeachments of the governor, lieutenant-governor, attorney-general, secretary of state, State treasurer, and of the judges of the district courts, shall be tried by the senate; the chief-justice of the supreme court, or the senior judge thereof, shall preside during the trial of such impeachment. Impeachments of the judges of the supreme court shall be tried by the senate. When sitting as a court of impeachment, the senators shall be upon oath or affirmation, and no person shall be convicted without the concurrence of two-thirds of the senators present.

ART. 86. Judgments in cases of impeachment shall extend only to removal from office and disqualification from holding any office of honor, trust, or profit under this State; but the parties convicted shall, nevertheless, be subject to indictment, trial, and punishment, according to law.

ART. 87. All officers against whom articles of impeachment may be preferred shall be suspended from the exercise of their functions during the pendency of such impeachment; the appointing power may make a provisional appointment to replace any suspended officer until the decision on the impeachment.

ART. 88. The legislature shall provide by law for the trial, punishment, and removal from office of all other officers of the State, by indictment or otherwise.

Title VI

GENERAL PROVISIONS

ART. 89. Members of the general assembly, and all officers, before they enter upon the duties of their offices, shall take the following oath or affirmation:

" I, [A. B.,] do solemnly swear [or affirm] that I will faithfully and impartially discharge and perform all the duties incumbent on me as ———, according to the best of my abilities and understanding, agreeably to the Constitution and laws of the United States and of this State; and I do further solemnly swear [or affirm] that, since the adoption of the present constitution, I, being a citizen of this State, have not fought a duel with deadly weapons within this State, nor out of it, with a citizen of this State, nor have I sent or accepted a challenge to fight a duel with deadly weapons with a citizen of this State, nor have I acted as second in carrying a challenge, or aided, advised, or assisted any person thus offending: So help me God.

ART. 90. Treason against the State shall consist only in levying war against it, or in adhering to its enemies, giving them aid and comfort. No person shall be convicted of treason, unless on the testimony of two witnesses to the same overt act, or his own confession in open court.

ART. 91. Every person shall be disqualified from holding any office of trust or profit in this State who shall have been convicted of having given or offered a bribe to procure his election or appointment.

ART. 92. Laws shall be made to exclude from office, and from the right of suffrage, those who shall hereafter be convicted of bribery, perjury, forgery, or other high crimes or misdemeanors. The privilege of free suffrage shall be supported by laws regulating elections, and prohibiting, under adequate penalties, all undue influence thereon, from power, bribery, tumult, or other improper practice.

ART. 93. No money shall be drawn from the treasury but in pursuance of specific appropriations made by law, nor shall any appropriation of money be made for a longer term than two years. A regular statement and account of the receipts and expenditures of all public moneys shall be published annually, in such manner as shall be prescribed by law.

ART. 94. It shall be the duty of the general assembly to pass such laws as may be proper and necessary to decide differences by arbitration.

ART. 95. All civil officers for the State at large shall reside within the State, and all district or parish officers within their districts or parishes, and shall keep their offices at such places therein as may be required by law. And no person shall be elected or appointed to any parish office who shall not have resided in such parish long enough before such election or appointment to have acquired the right of voting in such parish; and no person shall be elected or appointed to any district office who shall not have resided in such district, or an adjoining district, long enough before such appointment or election to have acquired the right of voting for the same.

ART. 96. The duration of all offices not fixed by this constitution shall never exceed four years.

Art. 97. All civil officers, except the governor and judges of the supreme and district courts, shall be removable by an address of a majority of the members of both houses, except those the removal of whom has been otherwise provided for by this constitution.

Art. 98. Absence on the business of this State or of the United States shall not forfeit a residence once obtained, so as to deprive any one of the right of suffrage, or of being elected or appointed to any office under the exceptions contained in this constitution.

Art. 99. It shall be the duty of the legislature to provide by law for deductions from the salaries of public officers who may be guilty of a neglect of duty.

Art. 100. The legislature shall point out the manner in which a person coming into the State shall declare his residence.

Art. 101. In all elections by the people the vote shall be by ballot, and in all elections by the senate and house of representatives, jointly or separately, the vote shall be given *viva voce*.

Art. 102. No member of Congress, or person holding or exercising any office of trust or profit under the United States, or either of them, or under any foreign power, shall be eligible as a member of the general assembly, or hold or exercise any office of trust or profit under the State.

Art. 103. The laws, public records, and the judicial and legislative written proceedings of the State, shall be promulgated, preserved, and conducted in the language in which the Constitution of the United States is written.

Art. 104. The secretary of the senate and clerk of the house of representatives shall be conversant with the French and English languages, and members may address either house in the French or English language.

Art. 105. The general assembly shall direct by law how persons who are now or may hereafter become sureties for public officers may be discharged from such suretyship.

Art. 106. No power of suspending the laws of this State shall be exercised, unless by the legislature, or by its authority.

Art. 107. Prosecutions shall be by indictment or information. The accused shall have a speedy public trial by an impartial jury of the vicinage; he shall not be compelled to give evidence against himself; he shall have the right of being heard by himself or counsel; he shall have the right, unless he shall have fled from justice, of meeting the witnesses face to face, and shall have compulsory process for obtaining witnesses in his favor.

Art. 108. All prisoners shall be bailable by sufficient sureties, unless for capital offences, where the proof is evident or presumption great; and the privilege of the writ of *habeas corpus* shall not be suspended, unless when, in case of rebellion or invasion, the public safety may require it.

Art. 109. No *ex post facto* law, nor any law impairing the obligation of contracts, shall be passed, nor vested rights be divested, unless for purposes of public utility, and for adequate compensation previously made.

Art. 110. The press shall be free. Every citizen may freely speak, write, and publish his sentiments on all subjects; being responsible for an abuse of this liberty.

ART. 111. Emigration from the State shall not be prohibited.

ART. 112. The general assembly which shall meet after the first election of representatives under this constitution shall, within the first month after the commencement of the session, designate and fix the seat of government at some place not less than sixty miles from the city of New Orleans, by the nearest travelling route, and if on the Mississippi River by the meanders of the same; and, when so fixed, it shall not be removed without the consent of four-fifths of the members of both houses of the general assembly. The sessions shall be held in New Orleans until the end of the year 1848.

ART. 113. The legislature shall not pledge the faith of the State for the payment of any bonds, bills, or other contracts or obligations for the benefit or use of any person or persons, corporation, or body-politic whatever. But the State shall have the right to issue new bonds in payment of its outstanding obligations or liabilities, whether due or not; the said new bonds, however, are not to be issued for a larger amount, or at a higher rate of interest, than the original obligations they are intended to replace.

ART. 114. The aggregate amount of debts hereafter contracted by the legislature shall never exceed the sum of one hundred thousand dollars, except in the case of war, to repel invasions or suppress insurrections, unless the same be authorized by some law, for some single object or work, to be distinctly specified therein; which law shall provide ways and means, by taxation, for the payment of running interest during the whole time for which said debt shall be contracted, and for the full and punctual discharge at maturity of the capital borrowed; and said law shall be irrepealable until principal and interest are fully paid and discharged, and shall not be put into execution until after its enactment by the first legislature returned by a general election after its passage.

ART. 115. The legislature shall provide by law for a change of venue in civil and criminal cases.

ART. 116. No lottery shall be authorized by this State, and the buying or selling of lottery-tickets within the State is prohibited.

ART. 117. No divorce shall be granted by the legislature.

ART. 118. Every law enacted by the legislature shall embrace but one object, and that shall be expressed in the title.

ART. 119. No law shall be revised or amended by reference to its title; but in such case, the act revised, or section amended, shall be reënacted and published at length.

ART. 120. The legislature shall never adopt any system or code of laws by general reference to such system or code of laws, but in all cases shall specify the several provisions of the laws it may enact.

ART. 121. The State shall not become subscriber to the stock of any corporation or joint-stock company.

ART. 122. No corporate body shall be hereafter created, renewed, or extended with banking or discounting privileges.

ART. 123. Corporations shall not be created in this State by special laws, except for political or municipal purposes, but the legislature shall provide, by general laws, for the organization of all other corporations, except corporations with banking or discounting privileges, the creation of which is prohibited.

ART. 124. From and after the month of January, 1890, the legislature shall have the power to revoke the charters of all corporations whose charters shall not have expired previous to that time, and no corporations hereafter to be created shall ever endure for a longer term than twenty-five years, except those which are political or municipal.

ART. 125. The general assembly shall never grant any exclusive privilege or monopoly for a longer period than twenty years.

ART. 126. No person shall hold or exercise, at the same time, more than one civil office of emolument, except that of justice of the peace.

ART. 127. Taxation shall be equal and uniform throughout the State. After the year 1848, all property on which taxes may be levied in this State shall be taxed in proportion to its value, to be ascertained as directed by law. No one species of property shall be taxed higher than another species of property of equal value, on which taxes shall be levied; the legislature shall have power to levy an income tax, and to tax all persons pursuing any occupation, trade, or profession.

ART. 128. The citizens of the city of New Orleans shall have the right of appointing the several public officers necessary for the administration of the police of the said city, pursuant to the mode of elections which shall be prescribed by the legislature: *Provided*, That the mayor and recorders shall be ineligible to a seat in the general assembly; and the mayor, recorders, and aldermen shall be commissioned by the governor as justices of the peace, and the legislature may vest in them such criminal jurisdiction as may be necessary for the punishment of minor crimes and offences, and as the police and good order of said city may require.

ART. 129. The legislature may provide by law in what cases officers shall continue to perform the duties of their offices until their successors shall have been inducted into office.

ART. 130. Any citizen of this State who shall, after the adoption of this constitution, fight a duel with deadly weapons, with a citizen of this State, or send or accept a challenge to fight a duel with deadly weapons, either within this State or out of it, with a citizen of this State, or who shall act as second, or knowingly aid and assist in any manner those thus offending, shall be deprived of holding any office of profit, and of enjoying the right of suffrage under this constitution.

ART. 131. The legislature shall have power to extend this constitution and the jurisdiction of this State over any territory acquired by compact with any State, or with the United States, the same being done by the consent of the United States.

ART. 132. The constitution and laws of this State shall be promulgated in the English and French languages.

Title VII

PUBLIC EDUCATION

ART. 133. There shall be appointed a superintendent of public education, who shall hold his office for two years. His duties shall be prescribed by law. He shall receive such compensation as the legislature may direct.

Art. 134. The legislature shall establish free public schools throughout the State, and shall provide means for their support by taxation on property, or otherwise.

Art. 135. The proceeds of all lands heretofore granted by the United States to this State for the use or support of schools, and of all lands which may hereafter be granted or bequeathed to the State, and not expressly granted or bequeathed for any other purpose, which hereafter may be disposed of by the State, and the proceeds of the estates of deceased persons to which the State may become entitled by law, shall be held by the State as a loan, and shall be and remain a perpetual fund on which the State shall pay an annual interest of 6 per cent.; which interest, together with all the rents of the unsold lands, shall be appropriated to the support of such schools, and this appropriation shall remain inviolable.

Art. 136. All moneys arising from the sales which have been or may hereafter be made of any lands heretofore granted by the United States to this State, for the use of a seminary of learning, and from any kind of donation that may hereafter be made for that purpose, shall be and remain a perpetual fund, the interest of which, at 6 per cent. per annum, shall be appropriated to the support of a siminary of learning for the promotion of literature and the arts and sciences, and no law shall ever be made diverting said fund to any other use than to the establishment and improvement of said seminary of learning.

Art. 137. A university shall be established in the city of New Orleans. It shall be composed of four faculties, to wit: One of law, one of medicine, one of the natural sciences, and one of letters.

Art. 138. It shall be called the "University of Louisiana," and the medical college of Louisiana, as at present organized, shall constitute the faculty of medicine.

Art. 139. The legislature shall provide by law for its further organization and government, but shall be under no obligation to contribute to the establishment or support of said university by appropriations.

Title VIII

MODE OF REVISING THE CONSTITUTION

Art. 140. Any amendment or amendments to this constitution may be proposed in the senate or house of representatives, and if the same shall be agreed to by three-fifths of the members elected to each house, and approved by the governor, such proposed amendment or amendments shall be entered on their journals, with the yeas and nays taken thereon, and the secretary of state shall cause the same to be published, three months before the next general election, in at least one newspaper in French and English, in every parish in the State, in which a newspaper shall be published; and if in the legislature next afterwards chosen such proposed amendment or amendments shall be agreed to by a majority of the members elected to each house, the secretary of state shall cause the same again to be published in the manner aforesaid, at least three months previous to the next general election for representatives to the State legislature, and such proposed amendment or amendments shall be submitted to the people at said election; and if a majority of the qualified electors shall approve and ratify such amendment or amendments, the same shall become a part of the constitution. If more than one amendment be submitted at a time, they shall be submitted in such manner and form that the people may vote for or against each amendment separately.

TITLE IX

SCHEDULE

ART. 141. The constitution adopted in eighteen hundred and twelve is declared to be superseded by this constitution, and, in order to carry the same into effect, it is hereby declared and ordained as follows:

ART. 142. All rights, actions, prosecutions, claims, and contracts, as well as of individuals as of bodies-corporate, and all laws in force at the time of the adoption of this constitution, and not inconsistent therewith, shall continue as if the same had not been adopted.

ART. 143. Until the first enumeration shall be made as directed in article eighth of this constitution, the parish of Orleans shall have twenty representatives, to be elected as follows, viz:

Eight by the first municipality, seven by the second municipality, and four by the third municipality, to be distributed among the nine representative districts as follows: By allotting to the first district, two; second, two; third, three; fourth, three; fifth, three; sixth, two; seventh, two; eighth, one; ninth, one; and to that part of the parish on the right bank of the Mississippi, one.

The parish of Plaquemines shall have three; Saint Bernard, one; Jefferson, three; Saint Charles, one; Saint John the Baptist, one; Saint James, two; Ascension, two; Assumption, three; La Fourche Interior, three; Terre Bonne, two; Iberville, two; West Baton Rouge, one; East Baton Rouge, three; West Feliciana, two; East Feliciana, three; Saint Helena, one; Washington, one; Livingston, one; Saint Tammany, one; Point Coupee, one; Concordia, one; Tensas, one; Madison, one; Carroll, one; Franklin, one; Saint Mary, two; Saint Martin, three; Vermillion, one; La Fayette, two; Saint Landry, five; Calcasieu, one; Avoyelles, two; Rapides, three; Natchitoches, three; Sabine, two; Caddo, one; De Soto, one; Ouachita, one; Morehouse, one; Union, one; Jackson, one; Caldwell, one; Catahoula, two; Claiborne, two; Bossier, one; total, ninety-eight.

And the State shall be divided into the following senatorial districts: All that portion of the parish of Orleans lying on the east side of the Mississippi River shall compose one senatorial district, and shall elect four senators; the parishes of Plaquemines, Saint Bernard, and that part of the parish of Orleans on the right bank of the river, shall compose one district, with one senator; the parish of Jefferson shall compose one district, with one senator; the parishes of Saint Charles and Saint John the Baptist shall compose one district, with one senator; the parish of Saint James shall compose one district, with one senator; the parish of Ascension shall compose one district, with one senator; the parishes of Assumption, La Fourche Interior, and Terre Bonne, shall compose one district, with two senators; the parishes of Iberville and West Baton Rouge shall compose one district, with one senator; the parish of East Baton Rouge shall compose one district, with one senator; the parish of Point Coupee shall compose one district, with one senator; the parish of Avoyelles shall compose one district, with one senator; the parish of Saint Mary shall compose one district, with one senator; the parish of Saint Martin shall compose one district, with one senator; the parishes of La Fayette and Vermillion shall compose one district, with one senator; the parishes of Saint Landry and Calcasieu shall compose one district, with two senators; the parish of West Feliciana shall compose one district, with one senator; the parish of East Feliciana shall compose one district, with one senator; the parishes of Saint Helena and Livingston shall compose one district, with one senator; the parishes of Washington and Saint Tammany shall compose one district, with one senator; the parishes of Concordia and Tensas shall compose one district, with one senator; the parishes of Carroll and Madison shall compose one district, with one senator; the parishes of Jackson, Union, Morehouse, and Ouachita shall compose one district, with one senator; the parishes of Caldwell, Franklin, and Catahoula shall compose one district, with one senator; the parish of Rapides shall compose one district, with one senator; the parishes of Bossier and Claiborne shall compose one district, with one senator; the parish of Natchitoches shall compose one district, with one senator; the parishes of Sabine, De Soto, and Caddo shall compose one district, with one senator.

ART. 144. In order that no inconvenience may result to the public service from the taking effect of this constitution, no office shall be superseded thereby, but the laws of the State relative to the duties of the several officers, executive, judicial, and military, shall remain in full force, though the same be contrary to this constitution, and the several duties shall be performed by the respective officers of the State, according to the existing laws, until the organization of the government under this constitution, and the entering into office of the new officers, to be appointed under said government, and no longer.

ART. 145. Appointments to office by the executive under this constitution shall be made by the governor to be elected under its authority.

ART. 146. The provisions of article twenty-eight, concerning the inability of members of the legislature to hold certain offices therein mentioned, shall not be held to apply to the members of the first legislature elected under this constitution.

ART. 147. The time of service of all officers chosen by the people, at the first election under this constitution, shall terminate as though the election had been holden on the first Monday of November, 1845, and they had entered on the discharge of their duties at the time designated therein.

ART. 148. The legislature shall provide for the removal of all causes now pending in the supreme or other courts of the State, under the constitution of 1812, to courts created by this constitution.

ART. 149. Appeals to the supreme court from the parishes of Jackson, Union, Morehouse, Catahoula, Caldwell, Ouachita, Franklin, Carroll, Madison, Tensas, and Concordia, shall, until otherwise provided for, be returnable to New Orleans.

Title X

ORDINANCE

ART. 150. Immediately after the adjournment of the convention, the governor shall issue his proclamation, directing the several officers of this State, authorized by law to hold elections for members of the general assembly, to open and hold a poll in every parish of the State, at the places designated by law, upon the first Monday of November next, for the purpose of taking the sense of the good people of this State in regard to the adoption or rejection of this constitution; and it shall be the duty of the said officers to receive the votes of all persons entitled to vote under the old constitution, and under this constitution. Each voter shall express his opinion by depositing in the ballot-box a ticket whereon shall be written " The constitution accepted," or " The constitution rejected," or some such words as will distinctly convey the intention of the voter. At the conclusion of the said election, which shall be conducted in every respect as the general State election is now conducted, the parish judges and commissioners designated to preside over the same shall carefully examine and count each ballot so deposited, and shall forthwith make due returns thereof to the secretary of state, in conformity to the provisions of the existing law upon the subject of elections.

ART. 151. Upon the receipt of the said returns, or on the first Monday of December, if the returns be not sooner received, it shall be the duty of the governor, the secretary of state, the attorney-general, and the State treasurer, in the presence of all such persons as may choose to attend, to compare the votes given at the said poll, for the ratification and rejection of this constitution, and if it shall appear from said returns that a majority of all the votes given are for ratifying this constitution, then it shall be the duty of the governor to make proclamation of that fact, and thenceforth this constitution shall be ordained and established as the constitution of the State of Louisiana. But whether this constitution be accepted or rejected, it shall be the duty of the governor to cause to be published in the State paper the result of the polls, showing the number of votes cast in each parish for and against the said constitution.

ART. 152. Should this constitution be accepted by the people, it shall also be the duty of the governor forthwith to issue his proclamation, declaring the present legislature, elected under the old constitution, to be dissolved, and directing the several officers of the State, authorized by law to hold elections for members of the general assembly, to hold an election at the places designated by law, upon the third Monday in January next, (1846,) for governor, lieutenant-governor, members of the general assembly, and all other officers whose election is provided for pursuant to the provisions of this constitution. And the said election shall be conducted, and the returns thereof made, in conformity with the existing laws upon the subject of State elections.

ART. 153. The general assembly elected under this constitution shall convene at the State-house, in the city of New Orleans, upon the second Monday of February next (1846) after the elections; and that the governor and lieutenant-governor, elected at the same time, shall be duly installed in office during the first week of their session, and before it shall be competent for the said general assembly to proceed with the transaction of business.

JOSEPH WALKER, *President.*

HORATIO DAVIS, *Secretary.*

CONSTITUTION OF LOUISIANA—1852 * a

PREAMBLE

We, the people of the State of Louisiana, do ordain and establish this constitution.

TITLE I

DISTRIBUTION OF POWERS

ARTICLE 1. The powers of the government of the State of Louisiana shall be divided into three distinct departments, and each of them be confided to a separate body of magistracy, to wit: Those which are legislative to one, those which are executive to another, and those which are judicial to another.

ART. 2. No one of these departments, nor any person holding office in one of them, shall exercise power properly belonging to either of the others, except in the instances hereinafter expressly directed or permitted.

TITLE II

LEGISLATIVE DEPARTMENT

ART. 3. The legislative power of the State shall be vested in two distinct branches, the one to be styled "the house of representatives," the other "the senate," and both "the general assembly of the State of Louisiana."

ART. 4. The members of the house of representatives shall continue in service for the term of two years from the day of the closing of the general elections.

ART. 5. Representatives shall be chosen on the first Monday in November every two years; and the election shall be completed in one day. The general assembly shall meet annually, on the third Monday in January, unless a different day be appointed by law, and their sessions shall be held at the seat of government.

ART. 6. Every duly-qualified elector under this constitution shall be eligible to a seat in the general assembly: *Provided,* That no person shall be a representative or senator, unless he be, at the time of his election, a duly-qualified voter of the representative or senatorial district from which he is elected.

---

[a] This constitution was framed by a convention which met at Baton Rouge July 5, 1852, and completed its labors July 31, 1852. It was submitted to the people and ratified November 1, 1852.

* Verified by "The Constitution of the State of Louisiana of 1852, Bloomfield and Steel, New Orleans, 1861."

ART. 7. Elections for members of the general assembly shall be held at the several election-precincts established by law. The legislature may delegate the power of establishing election-precincts to the parochial or municipal authorities.

ART. 8. Representation in the house of representatives shall be equal and uniform, and shall be regulated and ascertained by the total population of each of the several parishes of the State. Each parish shall have at least one representative. No new parish shall be created with a territory less than six hundred and twenty-five square miles, nor with a population less than the full number entitling it to a representative, nor when the creation of such new parish would leave any other parish without the said extent of territory and amount of population.

The first enumeration by the State authorities under this constitution shall be made in the year 1853, the second in the year 1858, the third in the year 1865; after which time the general assembly shall direct in what manner the census shall be taken, so that it be made at least once in every period of ten years, for the purpose of ascertaining the total population in each parish and election-district.

At the first regular session of the legislature after the making of each enumeration, the legislature shall apportion the representation among the several parishes and election-districts on the basis of the total population as aforesaid. A representative number shall be fixed, and each parish and election-district shall have as many representatives as its aggregate population shall entitle it to, and an additional representative for any fraction exceeding one-half the representative number. The number of representatives shall not be more than one hundred nor less than seventy.

Until an apportionment shall be made, and elections held under the same, in accordance with the first enumeration to be made as directed in this article, the representation in the senate and house of representatives shall be and remain as at present established by law.

The limits of the parish of Orleans are hereby extended, so as to embrace the whole of the present city of New Orleans, including that part of the parish of Jefferson formerly known as the city of La Fayette.

All that part of the parish of Orleans which is situated on the left bank of the Mississippi River, shall be divided by the legislature into not more than ten representative districts, and until a new apportionment shall be made according to the first census to be taken under this constitution, that part of the city of New Orleans which was comprised within the former limits of the city of La Fayette shall vote for senators from the parish of Orleans, and form the tenth representative district, and shall elect two out of the three representatives now apportioned by law to the parish of Jefferson; the other representative districts shall remain as they are now established.

ART. 9. The house of representatives shall choose its speaker and other officers.

ART. 10. Every free white male who has attained the age of twenty-one years, and who has been a resident of the State twelve months next preceding the election, and the last six months thereof in the parish in which he offers to vote, and who shall be a citizen of the United States, shall have the right of voting, but no voter, on removing from one parish to another within the State, shall lose the right of voting in the former until he shall have acquired it in the latter. Electors shall in all cases, except treason, felony, or breach of the peace, be privileged from arrest. during their attendance at, going to, or returning from elections.

ART. 11. The legislature shall provide by law that the names and residence of all qualified electors of the city of New Orleans shall be registered, in order to entitle them to vote; but the registry shall be free of cost to the elector.

ART. 12. No soldier, seaman, or marine in the Army or Navy of the United States, no pauper, no person under interdiction, nor under conviction of any crime punishable with hard labor, shall be entitled to vote at any election in this State.

ART. 13. No person shall be entitled to vote at any election held in this State except in the parish of his residence, and in cities and towns divided into election-precincts, in the election-precinct in which he resides.

ART. 14. The members of the senate shall be chosen for the term of four years. The senate, when assembled, shall have the power to choose its officers.

ART. 15. The legislature, in every year in which they shall apportion representation in the house of representatives, shall divide the State into senatorial districts. No parish shall be divided in the formation of a senatorial district, the parish of Orleans excepted. And whenever a new parish shall be created, it shall be attached to the senatorial district from which most of its territory was taken, or to another contiguous district, at the discretion of the legislature; but shall not be attached to more than one district. The number of senators shall be thirty-two, and they shall be apportioned among the senatorial districts according to the total population contained in the several districts: *Provided*, That no parish shall be entitled to more than five senators.

ART. 16. In all apportionments of the senate, the population of the city of New Orleans shall be deducted from the population of the whole State, and the remainder of the population divided by the number twenty-seven, and the result produced by this division shall be the senatorial ratio entitling a senatorial district to a senator. Single or contiguous parishes shall be formed into districts, having a population the nearest possible to the number entitling a district to a senator; and if, in the apportionment to be made, a parish or district fall short of or exceed the ratio one-fifth, then a district may be formed having not more than two senators, but not otherwise. No new apportionment shall have the effect of abridging the term of service of any senator already elected at the time of making the apportionment. After an enumeration has been made as directed in the eighth article, the legislature shall not pass any law until an apportionment of representation in both houses of the general assembly be made.

ART. 17. At the first session of the general assembly after this constitution takes effect, the senators shall be equally divided by lot into two classes; the seats of the senators of the first class shall be vacated at the expiration of the second year; of the second class, at the expiration of the fourth year; so that one-half shall be chosen every two years, and a rotation thereby kept up perpetually. In case any district shall have elected two or more senators, said senators shall vacate their seats respectively at the end of two and four years, and lots shall be drawn between them.

ART. 18. The first election for senators shall be general throughout the State, and at the same time that the general election for representatives is held; and thereafter there shall be biennial elections to fill the places of those whose time of service may have expired.

ART. 19. Not less than a majority of the members of each house of the general assembly shall form a quorum to do business, but a smaller number may adjourn from day to day, and shall be authorized by law to compel the attendance of absent members.

ART. 20. Each house of the general assembly shall judge of the qualification, election, and returns of its members; but a contested election shall be determined in such manner as shall be directed by law.

ART. 21. Each house of the general assembly may determine the rules of its proceedings, punish a member for disorderly behavior, and, with the concurrence of two-thirds, expel a member, but not a second time for the same offence.

ART. 22. Each house of the general assembly shall keep and publish a weekly journal of its proceedings, and the yeas and nays of the members on any question shall, at the desire of any two of them, be entered on the journal.

ART. 23. Each house may punish by imprisonment any person, not a member, for disrespectful and disorderly behavior in its presence, or for obstructing any of its proceedings. Such imprisonment shall not exceed ten days for any one offence.

ART. 24. Neither house, during the sessions of the general assembly, shall, without the consent of the other, adjourn for more than three days, nor to any other place than that in which they may be sitting.

ART. 25. The members of the general assembly shall receive from the public treasury a compensation for their services, which shall be four dollars per day during their attendance, going to and returning from the session of their respective houses. The compensation may be increased or diminished by law; but no alteration shall take effect during the period of service of the members of the house of representatives by whom such alteration shall have been made. No session shall extend to a period beyond sixty days, to date from its commencement, and any legislative action had after the expiration of the said sixty days shall be null and void. This provision shall not apply to the first legislature which is to convene after the adoption of this constitution.

ART. 26. The members of the general assembly shall in all cases, except treason, felony, breach of the peace, be privileged from arrest during their attendance at the sessions of their respective houses, and going to or returning from the same, and for any speech or debate in either house they shall not be questioned in any other place.

ART. 27. No senator or representative shall, during the term for which he was elected, nor for one year thereafter, be appointed or elected to any civil office of profit under this State, which shall have been created or the emoluments of which shall have been increased during the time such senator or representative was in office, except to such offices or appointments as may be filled by the elections of the people.

ART. 28. No person who at any time may have been a collector of taxes, whether State, parish, or municipal, or who may have been otherwise intrusted with public money, shall be eligible to the general assembly, or to any office of profit or trust under the State government, until he shall have obtained a discharge for the amount of such collections, and for all public moneys with which he may have been intrusted.

ART. 29. No bill shall have the force of a law until, on three several days, it be read over in each house of the general assembly, and free discussion allowed thereon, unless, in case of urgency, four-fifths of the house where the bill shall be pending may deem it expedient to dispense with this rule.

ART. 30. All bills for raising revenue shall originate in the house of representatives, but the senate may propose amendments as in other bills, provided they shall not introduce any new matter under color of an amendment which does not relate to raising revenue.

ART. 31. The general assembly shall regulate by law by whom and in what manner writs of elections shall be issued to fill the vacancies which may happen in either branch thereof.

ART. 32. The senate shall vote on the confirmation or rejection of officers, to be appointed by the governor, with the advice and consent of the senate, by yeas and nays, and the names of the senators voting for or against the appointments, respectively, shall be entered on a journal to be kept for that purpose, and made public at the end of each session, or before.

ART. 33. Returns of all elections for members of the general assembly shall be made to the secretary of state.

ART. 34. In the year in which a regular election for a Senator of the United States is to take place, the members of the general assembly shall meet in the hall of the house of representatives, on the Monday following the meeting of the legislature, and proceed to the said election.

TITLE III

EXECUTIVE DEPARTMENT

ART. 35. The supreme executive power of the State shall be vested in a chief magistrate, who shall be styled the governor of the State of Louisiana. He shall hold his office during the term of four years, and, together with the lieutenant-governor, chosen for the same term, be elected as follows: The qualified electors for representatives shall vote for a governor and lieutenant-governor, at the time and place of voting for representatives. The returns of every election shall be sealed up and transmitted by the proper returning-officer to the secretary of state, who shall deliver them to the speaker of the house of representatives on the second day of the session of the general assembly then next to be holden. The members of the general assembly shall meet in the house of representatives to examine and count the votes. The person having the greatest number of votes for governor shall be declared duly elected, but if two or more persons shall be equal and highest in the number of votes polled for governor, one of them shall immediately be chosen governor by joint vote of the members of the general assembly. The person having the greatest number of votes for lieutenant-governor shall be lieutenant-governor, but if two or more persons shall be equal and highest in the number of votes polled for lieutenant-governor, one of them shall be immediately chosen lieutenant-governor by joint vote of the members of the general assembly.

ART. 36. No person shall be eligible to the office of governor or lieutenant-governor who shall not have attained the age of twenty-eight years, and been a citizen and a resident within the State for the space of four years next preceding his election.

ART. 37. The governor shall enter on the discharge of his duties on the fourth Monday of January next ensuing his election, and shall continue in office until the Monday next succeeding the day that his successor shall be declared duly elected, and shall have taken the oath or affimation required by the constitution.

ART. 38. The governor shall be ineligible for the succeeding four years after the expiration of the time for which he shall have been elected.

ART. 39. No member of Congress or person holding any office under the United States shall be eligible to the office of governor or lieutenant-governor.

ART. 40. In case of the impeachment of the governor, his removal from office, death, refusal or inability to qualify, resignation, or absence from the State, the powers and duties of the office shall devolve upon the lieutenant-governor for the residue of the term, or until the governor, absent or impeached, shall return or be acquitted. The legislature may provide by law for the case of removal, impeachment, death, resignation, disability or refusal to qualify of both the governor or lieutenant-governor, declaring what officer shall act as governor, and such officer shall act accordingly until the disability be removed or for the residue of the term.

ART. 41. The lieutenant-governor, or officer discharging the duties of governor, shall, during his administration, receive the same compensation to which the governor would have been entitled had he continued in office.

ART. 42. The lieutenant-governor shall, by virtue of his office, be president of the senate, but shall have only a casting vote therein. Whenever he shall administer the government, or shall be unable to attend as president of the senate, the senators shall elect one of their own members as president of the senate for the time being.

ART. 43. While he acts as president of the senate, the lieutenant-governor shall receive for his services the same compensation which shall for the same period be allowed to the speaker of the house of representatives, and no more.

ART. 44. The governor shall have power to grant reprieves for all offences against the State, and, except in cases of impeachment, shall, with the consent of the senate, have power to grant pardons and remit fines and forfeitures after conviction. In cases of treason he may grant reprieves until the end of the next session of the general assembly, in which the power of pardoning shall be vested.

ART. 45. The governor shall, at stated times, receive for his services a compensation, which shall neither be increased nor diminished during the term for which he shall have been elected.

ART. 46. He shall be commander-in-chief of the army and navy of this State, and of the militia thereof, except when they shall be called into the service of the United States.

Art. 47. He shall nominate, and, by and with the advice and consent of the senate, appoint all officers whose offices are established by this constitution, and whose appointment is not therein otherwise provided for: *Provided, however,* That the legislature shall have a right to prescribe the mode of appointment to all other offices established by law.

Art. 48. The governor shall have power to fill vacancies that may happen during the recess of the senate, by granting commissions which shall expire at the end of the next session, unless otherwise provided for in this constitution; but no person who has been nominated for office, and rejected by the senate, shall be appointed to the same office, during the recess of the senate.

Art. 49. He may require information in writing from the officers in the executive department, upon any subject relating to the duties of their respective offices.

Art. 50. He shall, from time to time, give to the general assembly information respecting the situation of the State, and recommend to their consideration such measures as he may deem expedient.

Art. 51. He may, on extraordinary occasions, convene the general assembly at the seat of government, or at a different place, if that should have become dangerous from an enemy or from epidemic; and in case of disagreement between the two houses as to the time of adjournment, he may adjourn them to such time as he may think proper, not exceeding four months.

Art. 52. He shall take care that the laws be faithfully executed.

Art. 53. Every bill which shall have passed both houses shall be presented to the governor; if he approve he shall sign it, if not he shall return it, with his objections, to the house in which it originated, which shall enter the objections at large upon its journal, and proceed to reconsider it; if after such reconsideration two-thirds of all the members elected to that house shall agree to pass the bill, it shall be sent, with the objections, to the other house, by which it shall likewise be reconsidered, and, if approved by two-thirds of all the members elected to that house, it shall be a law; but in such cases the vote of both houses shall be determined by yeas and nays; and the names of the members voting for or against the bill shall be entered on the journal of each house respectively. If any bill shall not be returned by the governor within ten days (Sundays excepted) after it shall have been presented to him, it shall be a law in like manner as if he had signed it, unless the general assembly, by adjournment, prevent its return; in which case it shall be a law, unless sent back within three days after their next session.

Art. 54. Every order, resolution, or vote to which the concurrence of both houses may be necessary, except on a question of adjournment, shall be presented to the governor, and before it shall take effect, be approved by him, or, being disapproved, shall be repassed by two-thirds of the members elected to each house of the general assembly.

Art. 55. There shall be a secretary of state, who shall hold his office during the time for which the governor shall have been elected. The records of the State shall be kept and preserved in the office of the secretary; he shall keep a fair register of the official acts and proceedings of the governor, and, when necessary, shall attest them. He shall, when required, lay the said register, and all papers, minutes, and vouchers relative to his office, before either house of the general assembly, and shall perform such other duties as may be enjoined on him by law.

ART. 56. There shall be a treasurer of the State, who shall hold his office during the term of two years.

ART. 57. The secretary of state and treasurer of state shall be elected by the qualified electors of the State. And in case of any vacancies caused by the death, resignation, or absence of the treasurer or secretary of state, the governor shall order an election to fill said vacancy.

ART. 58. All commissions shall be in the name and by the authority of the State of Louisiana, and shall be sealed with the State seal and signed by the governor.

ART. 59. The free white men of the State shall be armed and disciplined for its defence; but those who belong to religious societies whose tenets forbid them to carry arms, shall not be compelled so to do, but shall pay an equivalent for personal services.

ART. 60. The militia of the State shall be organized in such manner as may be hereafter deemed most expedient by the legislature.

Title IV

JUDICIARY DEPARTMENT

ART. 61. The judiciary power shall be vested in a supreme court, in such inferior courts as the legislature may, from time to time, order and establish, and in justices of the peace.

ART. 62. The supreme court, except in the cases hereinafter provided, shall have appellate jurisdiction only; which jurisdiction shall extend to all cases when the matter in dispute shall exceed three hundred dollars; to all cases in which the constitutionality or legality of any tax, toll, or impost whatsoever, or of any fine, forfeiture, or penalty imposed by a municipal corporation, shall be in contestation; and to all criminal cases on questions of law alone, whenever the offence charged is punishable with death, or imprisonment at hard labor, or when a fine exceeding three hundred dollars is actually imposed. The legislature shall have power to restrict the jurisdiction of the supreme court in civil cases to questions of law only.

ART. 63. The supreme court shall be composed of one chief justice and four associate justices, a majority of whom shall constitute a quorum. The chief justice shall receive a salary of six thousand dollars, and each of the associate judges a salary of five thousand five hundred dollars, annually, until otherwise provided by law. The court shall appoint its own clerks; the judges shall be elected for the term of ten years.

ART. 64. The chief justice shall be elected by the qualified electors of the State. The legislature shall divide the State into four districts, and the qualified electors of each district shall elect one of the associate justices. The State shall be divided into the following districts until the legislature shall otherwise direct:

First district.—The parishes of Plaquemines, Saint Bernard, that portion of the parish of Orleans on the right bank of the Mississippi River, and that portion of the city of New Orleans which lies below the line extending from the river Mississippi, along the middle of

Julia street, until it strikes the New Orleans Canal, and thence down said canal to the lake.

Second district.—That portion of the city of New Orleans which is situated above the line extending along the middle of Julia street until it strikes the New Orleans Canal, and thence down said canal to the lake, and the parishes of Jefferson, Saint John the Baptist, Saint Charles, Saint James, Ascension, Assumption, La Fourche Interior, Terre Bonne, West Baton Rouge, and Iberville.

Third district.—The parishes of Saint Tammany, Washington, Livingston, Saint Helena, East Baton Rouge, East Feliciana, West Feliciana, Point Coupee, Avoyelles, Tensas, Concordia, La Fayette, Vermillion, Saint Mary, Saint Martin, and Saint Landry.

Fourth district.—The parishes of Calcasieu, Rapides, Sabine, Natchitoches, De Soto, Caddo, Bossier, Claiborne, Bienville, Caldwell, Union, Ouachita, Morehouse, Jackson, Franklin, Catahoula, Madison, Carroll, and Winn.

ART. 65. The office of one of the associate justices shall be vacated at the expiration of the second year, of another at the expiration of the fourth year, of a third at the expiration of the sixth year, and of the fourth at the expiration of the eighth year; so that one of the judges of the supreme court shall be elected every second year.

ART. 66. The secretary of state, on receiving the official returns of the first election, shall proceed immediately, in the presence and with the assistance of two justices of the peace, to determine by lot among the four candidates having the highest number of votes in the respective districts, which of the associate judges elect shall serve for the term of two years, which shall serve for the term of four years, which for the term of six years, and which for the term of eight years; and the governor shall issue commissions accordingly.

ART. 67. Any vacancy that may occur in the supreme court, from resignation or otherwise, shall be filled by election for the remainder of the unexpired term, but if such remainder do not exceed one year, the vacancy shall be filled by executive appointment.

ART. 68. The supreme court shall hold its sessions in New Orleans from the first Monday of the month of November to the end of the month of June inclusive. The legislature shall have power to fix the sessions elsewhere during the rest of the year; until otherwise provided, the sessions shall be held as heretofore.

ART. 69. The supreme court and each of the judges thereof shall have power to issue writs of *habeas corpus*, at the instance of all persons in actual custody under process, in all cases in which they may have appellate jurisdiction.

ART. 70. No judgment shall be rendered by the supreme court without the concurrence of a majority of the judges comprising the court. Whenever a majority cannot agree, in consequence of the recusation of any member or members of the court, the judges not recused shall have power to call upon any judge or judges of the inferior courts, whose duty it shall be, when so called upon, to sit in the place of the judges recused, and to aid in determining the case.

ART. 71. All judges, by virtue of their office, shall be conservators of the peace throughout the State. The style of all process shall be "The State of Louisiana." All prosecutions shall be carried on in the name and by authority of the State of Louisiana, and conclude "against the peace and dignity of the same."

ART. 72. The judges of all courts within the State shall, as often as it may be possible so to do, in every definitive judgment, refer to the particular law in virtue of which such judgment may be rendered, and in all cases adduce the reasons on which their judgment is founded.

ART. 73. The judges of all courts shall be liable to impeachment, but for any reasonable cause, which shall not be sufficient ground for impeachment, the governor shall remove any of them, on the address of three-fourths of the members present of each house of the general assembly. In every such case the cause or causes for which such removal may be required shall be stated at length in the address, and inserted in the journal of each house.

ART. 74. There shall be an attorney-general for the State, and as many district attorneys as may be hereafter found necessary. They shall hold their offices for four years; their duties shall be determined by law.

ART. 75. The judges, both of the supreme and inferior courts, shall, at stated times, receive a salary, which shall not be diminished during their continuance in office, and they are prohibited from receiving any fees of office, or other compensation than their salaries for any civil duties performed by them.

ART. 76. The legislature shall have power to vest in clerks of courts authority to grant such orders and do such acts as may be deemed necessary for the furtherance of the administration of justice, and in all cases the powers thus granted shall be specified and determined.

ART. 77. The judges of the several inferior courts shall have power to remove the clerks thereof for breach of good behavior; subject in all cases to an appeal to the supreme court.

ART. 78. The jurisdiction of justices of the peace shall be limited in civil cases to cases where the matter in dispute does not exceed one hundred dollars, exclusive of interest, subject to appeal in such cases as shall be provided for by law. They shall be elected by the qualified electors of each parish, district, or ward, for the term of two years, in such manner and shall have such criminal jurisdiction as shall be provided by law.

ART. 79. Clerks of the inferior courts in this State shall be elected for the term of four years, and should a vacancy occur subsequent to an election, it shall be filled by the judge of the court in which such vacancy exists, and the person so appointed shall hold his office until the next general election.

ART. 80. A sheriff and a coroner shall be elected in each parish by the qualified voters thereof, who shall hold their office for the term of two years, unless sooner removed. The legislature shall have the power to increase the number of sheriffs in any parish. Should a vacancy occur in either of these offices subsequent to an election, it shall be filled by the governor; and the person so appointed shall continue in office until his successor shall be elected and qualified.

ART. 81. The judges of the several inferior courts shall be elected by the duly-qualified voters of their respective districts or parishes.

ART. 82. It shall be the duty of the legislature to fix the time for holding elections for all judges at a time which shall be different from that fixed for all other elections.

ART. 83. The attorney-general shall be elected by the qualified voters of the State, and the district attorney by the qualified voters of each district on the day of the election for governor of the State.

ART. 84. The legislature may determine the mode of filling vacancies in the offices of the inferior judges, attorney-general, district attorneys, and all other officers not otherwise provided for in this constitution.

TITLE V

IMPEACHMENT

ART. 85. The power of impeachment shall be vested in the house of representatives.

ART. 86. Impeachments of the governor, lieutenant-governor, attorney-general, secretary of state, State treasurer, and of the judges of the inferior courts, justices of the peace excepted, shall be tried by the senate; the chief justice of the supreme court, or the senior judge thereof, shall preside during the trial of such impeachment. Impeachments of the judges of the supreme court shall be tried by the senate. When sitting as a court of impeachment, the senators shall be upon oath or affirmation, and no person shall be convicted without the concurrence of two-thirds of the senators present.

ART. 87. Judgments in cases of impeachment shall extend only to removal from office and disqualification from holding any office of honor, trust, or profit under the State; but the convicted parties shall, nevertheless, be subject to indictment, trial, and punishment, according to law.

ART. 88. All officers against whom articles of impeachment may be preferred shall be suspended from the exercise of their functions during the pendency of such impeachment; the appointing power may make a provisional appointment to replace any suspended officer until the decision of the impeachment.

ART. 89. The legislature shall provide by law for the trial, punishment, and removal from office of all other officers of the State by indictment or otherwise.

TITLE VI

GENERAL PROVISIONS

ART. 90. Members of the general assembly, all officers, before they enter upon the duties of their offices, shall take the following oath or affirmation:

"I [A. B.] do solemnly swear [or affirm] that I will support the constitution of the United States and of this State, and that I will faithfully and impartially discharge and perform all the duties incumbent on me as ———, according to the best of my abilities and understanding, agreeably to the constitution and laws of the United States, and of this State; and I do further solemnly swear [or affirm] that since the adoption of the present constitution, I, being a citizen of this State, have not fought a duel with deadly weapons within the State, nor out of it, with a citizen of this State, nor have I sent or accepted a challenge to fight a duel with deadly weapons with a citizen of this State, nor have I acted as second in carrying a challenge, or aided, advised, or assisted any person thus offending: So help me God."

ART. 91. Treason against the State shall consist only in levying war against it, or in adhering to its enemies, giving them aid and comfort. No person shall be convicted of treason, unless on the testimony of two witnesses to the same overt act, or his own confession in open court.

ART. 92. Every person shall be disqualified from holding any office of trust or profit in this State who shall have been convicted of having given or offered a bribe to procure his election or appointment.

ART. 93. Laws shall be made to exclude from office, and from the right of suffrage, those who shall hereafter be convicted of bribery, perjury, forgery, or other high crimes or misdemeanors. The privilege of free suffrage shall be supported by laws regulating elections, and prohibiting, under adequate penalties, all undue influence thereon, from power, bribery, tumult, or other improper practice.

ART. 94. No money shall be drawn from the treasury but in pursuance of specific appropration made by law, nor shall any appropriation of money be made for a longer term than two years. A regular statement and account of the receipts and expenditures of all public moneys shall be published annually, in such manner as shall be prescribed by law.

ART. 95. It shall be the duty of the general assembly to pass such laws as may be proper and necessary to decide differences by arbitration.

ART. 96. All civil officers for the State at large shall reside within the State, and all district or parish officers, within their districts or parishes, and shall keep their offices at such places therein as may be required by law.

ART. 97. All civil officers, except the governor and judges of the supreme and inferior courts, shall be removable by an address of a majority of the members of both houses, except those the removal of whom has been otherwise provided by this constitution.

ART. 98. In all elections by the people the vote shall be by ballot, and in all elections by the senate and house of representatives, jointly or separately, the vote shall be given *viva voce*.

ART. 99. No member of Congress, or person holding or exercising any office of trust or profit under the United States, or either of them, or under any foreign power, shall be eligible as a member of the general assembly, or hold or exercise any office of trust or profit under the State.

ART. 100. The laws, public records, and the judicial and legislative written proceedings of the State shall be promulgated, preserved, and conducted in the language in which the Constitution of the United States is written.

ART. 101. The secretary of the senate and clerk of the house of representatives shall be conversant with the French and English languages, and members may address either house in French or English language.

ART. 102. No power of suspending the laws of this State shall be exercised, unless by the legislature or by its authority.

ART. 103. Prosecutions shall be by indictment or information. The accused shall have a speedy public trial by an impartial jury of the vicinage; he shall not be compelled to give evidence against himself; he shall have the right of being heard by himself or counsel; he shall have the right of meeting the witnesses face to face, and shall have compulsory process for obtaining witnesses in his favor.

ART. 104. All prisoners shall be bailable by sufficient sureties, unless for capital offences, where the proof is evident or presumption great, or unless after conviction for any offence or crime punishable with death or imprisonment at hard labor. The privilege of the writ of *habeas corpus* shall not be suspended, unless when, in case of rebellion or invasion, the public safety may require it.

ART. 105. No *ex post facto* law, nor any law impairing the obligation of contracts, shall be passed, nor vested rights be divested, unless for purposes of public utility, and for adequate compensation previously made.

ART. 106. The press shall be free. Every citizen may freely speak, write, and publish his sentiments on all subjects; being responsible for an abuse of this liberty.

ART. 107. The seat of government shall be and remain at Baton Rouge, and shall not be removed without the consent of three-fourths of both houses of the general assembly.

ART. 108. The State shall not subscribe for the stock of, nor make a loan to, nor pledge its faith for the benefit of any corporation or joint-stock company, created or established for banking purposes, nor for other purposes than those described in following article.

ART. 109. The legislature shall have power to grant aid to companies or associations of individuals, formed for the exclusive purpose of making works of internal improvement, wholly or partially within the State, to the extent only of one-fifth of the capital of such companies, by subscription of stock or loan of money or public bonds; but any aid thus granted shall be paid to the company only in the same proportion as the remainder of the capital shall be actually paid in by the stockholders of the company, and, in case of loan, such adequate security shall be required as to the legislature may seem proper. No corporation or individual association receiving the aid of the State, as herein provided, shall possess banking or discounting privileges.

ART. 110. No liability shall be contracted by the State as above mentioned, unless the same be authorized by some law for some single object or work to be distinctly specified therein, which shall be passed by a majority of the members elected to both houses of the general assembly, and the aggregate amount of debts and liabilities incurred under this and the preceding article shall never, at any one time, exceed eight millions of dollars.

ART. 111. Whenever the legislature shall contract a debt exceeding in amount the sum of one hundred thousand dollars, unless in case of war to repel invasion or suppress insurrection, they shall, in the law creating the debt, provide adequate ways and means for the payment of the current interest and of the principal when the same shall become due. And the said law shall be irrepealable until principal and interest are fully paid and discharged, or unless the repealing law contains some other adequate provision for the payment of the principal and interest of the debt.

ART. 112. The legislature shall provide by law for a change of venue in civil and criminal cases.

ART. 113. No lottery shall be authorized by this State, and the buying and selling of lottery-tickets within the State is prohibited.

Art. 114. No divorce shall be granted by the legislature.

Art. 115. Every law enacted by the legislature shall embrace but one object, and that shall be expressed in the title.

Art. 116. No law shall be revived or amended by reference to its title; but in such case, the act revived, or section amended, shall be reënacted and published at length.

Art. 117. The legislature shall never adopt any system or code of laws by general reference to such system or code of laws, but in all cases shall specify the several provisions of the laws it may enact.

Art. 118. Corporations with banking or discounting privileges may be either created by special acts, or formed under general laws; but the legislature shall, in both cases, provide for the registry of all bill or notes issued or put in circulation as money, and shall require ample security for the redemption of the same in specie.

Art. 119. The legislature shall have no power to pass any law sanctioning in any manner, directly or indirectly, the suspension of specie payments by any person, association, or corporation issuing bank-notes of any description.

Art. 120. In case of insolvency of any bank or banking association, the bill-holders thereof shall be entitled to preference in payment over all other creditors of such bank or association.

Art. 121. The legislature shall have power to pass such laws as it may deem expedient for the relief or revival of the Citizens' Bank of Louisiana, and the acts already passed for the same purpose are ratified and confirmed: *Provided*, That the bank is subject to the restrictions contained in articles 119 and 120 of this constitution.

Art. 122. No person shall hold or exercise, at the same time, more than one civil office of emolument, except that of justice of the peace.

Art. 123. Taxation shall be equal and uniform throughout the State. All property on which taxes may be levied in this State shall be taxed in proportion to its value, to be ascertained as directed by law. No one species of property shall be taxed higher than another species of property of equal value, on which taxes shall be levied; the legislature shall have power to levy an income-tax, and to tax all persons pursuing any occupation, trade, or profession.

Art. 124. The citizens of the city of New Orleans shall have the right of appointing the several public officers necessary for the administration of the police of the said city, pursuant to the mode of elections which shall be prescribed by the legislature: *Provided*, That the mayor and recorders shall be ineligible to a seat in the general assembly; and the mayor, recorders, aldermen, and assistant aldermen shall be commissioned by the governor as justices of the peace, and the legislature may vest in them such criminal jurisdiction as may be necessary for the punishment of minor crimes and offences, and as the police and good order of said city may require.

Art. 125. The legislature may provide by law in what case officers shall continue to perform the duties of their offices until their successors shall have been inducted into office.

Art. 126. Any citizen of this State who shall, after the adoption of this constitution, fight a duel with deadly weapons with a citizen of this State, or send or accept a challenge to fight a duel with deadly weapons, either within this State or out of it, with a citizen of this State, or who shall act as second, or knowingly aid or assist in any manner those thus offending, shall be deprived of holding any office or trust or profit, and of enjoying the right of suffrage under this constitution; and the office of any State officer, member of the general assembly, or of any other person holding office of profit or trust under this constitution, and the laws made in pursuance thereof, shall be, *ipso facto*, vacated by the fact of any such person committing the offence mentioned in this article, and the legislature shall provide by law for the ascertaining and declaration of such forfeiture.

ART. 127. The legislature shall have power to extend this constitution and the jurisdiction of this State over any territory acquired by compact with any State, or with the United States, the same being done by the consent of the United States.

ART. 128. None of the lands granted by Congress to the State of Louisiana for aiding it in constructing the necessary levees and drains, to reclaim the swamp and overflowed lands in this State, shall be diverted from the purposes for which they were granted.

ART. 129. The constitution and laws of this State shall be promulgated in the English and French languages.

Title VII

INTERNAL IMPROVEMENTS

ART. 130. There shall be a board of public works, to consist of four commissioners. The State shall be divided by the legislature into four districts, containing as nearly as may be an equal number of voters, and one commissioner shall be elected in each district by the legal voters thereof for the term of four years; but, of the first elected, two, to be designated by lot, shall remain in office for two years only.

ART. 131. The general assembly, at its first session after the adoption of this constitution, shall provide for the election and compensation of the commissioners and the organization of the board. The commissioners first elected shall assemble on a day to be appointed by law, and decide by lot the order in which their terms of service shall expire.

ART. 132. The commissioners shall exercise a diligent and faithful supervision of all public works in which the State may be interested, except those made by joint-stock companies. They shall communicate to the general assembly, from time to time, their views concerning the same, and recommend such measures as they may deem necessary, in order to employ to the best advantage and for the purposes for which they were granted, the swamps and overflowed lands conveyed by the United States to this State. They shall appoint all officers engaged on the public works, and shall perform such other duties as may be prescribed by law.

ART. 133. The commissioners may be removed by the concurrent vote of a majority of all the members elected to each house of the general assembly; but the cause of the removal shall be entered on the journal of each house.

ART. 134. The general assembly shall have power, by a vote of three-fifths of the members elected to each house, to abolish said board, whenever in their opinion a board of public works shall no longer be necessary.

Title VIII

PUBLIC EDUCATION

ART. 135. There shall be elected a superintendent of public education, who shall hold his office for the term of two years. His duties shall be prescribed by law, and he shall receive such compensation as the legislature may direct: *Provided*, That the general assembly shall have power, by a vote of the majority of the members elected to both houses, to abolish the said office of superintendent of public education whenever in their opinion said office shall be no longer necessary.

ART. 136. The general assembly shall establish free public schools throughout the State; and shall provide for their support by general taxation on property or otherwise; and all moneys so raised or provided shall be distributed to each parish in proportion to the number of free white children between such ages as shall be fixed by the general assembly.

ART. 137. The proceeds of all lands heretofore granted by the United States to this State for the use or support of schools, and of all lands which may hereafter be granted or bequeathed to the State, and not expressly granted or bequeathed for any other purpose, which hereafter may be disposed of by the State, and the proceeds of the estates of deceased persons, to which the State may become entitled by law, shall be held by the State as a loan, and shall be and remain a perpetual fund, on which the State shall pay an annual interest of 6 per cent.; which interest, together with the interest of the trust funds deposited with this State by the United States, under the act of Congress approved June 23, 1836, and all the rents of the unsold lands, shall be appropriated to the support of such schools, and this appropriation shall remain inviolable.

ART. 138. All moneys arising from the sales which have been or may hereafter be made of any lands heretofore granted by the United States to this State, for the use of a seminary of learning, and from any kind of donation that may hereafter be made for that purpose, shall be and remain a perpetual fund, the interest of which, at 6 per cent. per annum, shall be appropriated to the support of a seminary of learning for the promotion of literature and the arts and sciences, and no law shall ever be made diverting said fund to any other use than to the establishment and improvement of said seminary of learning.

ART. 139. The University of Louisiana in New Orleans, as now established, shall be maintained.

ART. 140. The legislature shall have power to pass such laws as may be necessary for the further regulation of the university, and for the promotion of literature and science, but shall be under no obligation to contribute to the support of said university by appropriations.

Title IX

MODE OF REVISING THE CONSTITUTION

ART. 141. Any amendment or amendments to this constitution may be proposed in the senate or house of representatives, and if the same shall be agreed to by two-thirds of the members elected to each house, such proposed amendment or amendments shall be entered on their journals, with the yeas and nays taken thereon, and the secretary of state shall cause the same to be published, three months before the next general election for representatives of the State legislature, in at least one newspaper, in French and English, in every parish in the State in which a newspaper shall be published; and such proposed amendment or amendments shall be submitted to the people at said election; and if a majority of the voters at said election shall approve and ratify such amendment or amendments, the same shall become a part of the constitution. If more than one amendment be submitted at a time, they shall be submitted in such manner and form that the people may vote for or against each amendment separately.

Title X

SCHEDULE

ART. 142. The constitution adopted in eighteen hundred and forty-five is declared to be superseded by this constitution, and in order to carry the same into effect, it is hereby declared and ordained as follows:

ART. 143. All rights, actions, prosecutions, claims, and contracts, as well of individuals as of bodies corporate, and all laws in force at the time of the adoption of this constitution, and not inconsistent therewith, shall continue as if the same had not been adopted.

ART. 144. In order that no inconvenience may result to the public service from the taking effect of this constitution, no office shall be superseded thereby; but the laws of the State relative to the duties of the several officers, executive, judicial, and military, shall remain in full force, though the same be contrary to this constitution, and the several duties shall be performed by the respective officers of the State, according to the existing laws, until the organization of the government under this constitution, and the entering into office of the new officers to be appointed under said government, and no longer.

ART. 145. Appointments to office by the executive under this constitution shall be made by the governor to be elected under its authority.

ART. 146. The legislature shall provide for the removal of all causes now pending in the supreme court or other courts of the State, under the constitution of 1845, to courts created by or under this constitution.

ART. 147. The time of service of all officers chosen by the people, at the first election under this constitution, shall terminate as though the election had been holden on the first Monday of November, 1851, and they had entered on the discharge of their duties at the time designated therein. The first-class senators designated in article 17 shall hold their seats until the day of the closing of the general elections in November, 1853, and the second-class until the day of the closing of the general elections in November, 1855.

ART. 148. The first election for judges of the supreme court shall be held on the first Monday of April next, (1853,) and they shall enter into office on the first Monday of May, 1853.

ART. 149. The first term of service of the district attorneys and the clerks of the inferior courts to be ordered and established under this constitution shall be regulated by the term of service of the first governor, so that a new election for these officers shall be held on the first Monday of November, 1855.

Title XI

ORDINANCE

Art. 150. Immediately after the adjournment of the convention, the governor shall issue his proclamation, directing the several officers of this State authorized by law to hold elections for members of the general assembly, to open and hold a poll in every parish in the State, at the places designated by law, upon the first Tuesday of November next, for the purpose of taking the sense of the good people of this State in regard to the adoption or rejection of this constitution; and it shall be the duty of said officers to receive the votes of all persons entitled to vote under the old constitution and under this constitution. Each voter shall express his opinion by depositing in a separate box, kept for that purpose, a ticket, whereon shall be written "The constitution accepted," or " The constitution rejected," or some such word as will distinctly convey the intention of the voter. At the conclusion of said election, which shall be conducted in every respect as the general State election is now conducted, the commissioners designated to preside over the same shall carefully examine and count each ballot so deposited, and shall forthwith make due returns thereof to the secretary of state, in conformity to the provisions of the existing law upon the subject of elections.

Art. 151. Upon the receipt of the said returns, or on the fifth Monday of November, if the returns be not sooner received, it shall be the duty of the governor, the secretary of state, the attorney-general, and the state treasurer, in the presence of all such persons as may choose to attend, to compare the votes given at the said poll for the ratification and rejection of this constitution, and if it shall appear from said returns that a majority of all the votes given is for ratifying this constitution, then it shall be the duty of the governor to make proclamation of that fact, and thenceforth this constitution shall be ordained and established as the constitution of the State of Louisiana. But whether this constitution be accepted or rejected, it shall be the duty of the governor to cause to be published in the official paper of the convention the result of the polls, showing the number of votes cast in each parish for and against the said constitution.

Art. 152. Should this constitution be accepted by the people, it shall also be the duty of the governor forthwith to issue his proclamation, declaring the present legislature, elected under the old constitution, to be dissolved, and directing the several officers of the State authorized by law to hold elections for members of the general assembly to hold an election, at the places designated by law, upon the fourth Monday of December next, for governor, lieutenant-governor, members of the general assembly, secretary of state, attorney-general, treasurer, and superintendent of public education; and the said election shall be conducted and the returns thereof made in conformity with existing laws upon the subject of State elections.

Art. 153. The general assembly elected under this constitution shall convene at the State-house, in Baton Rouge, upon the third Monday of January next after the elections, and the governor and lieutenant-governor elected at the same time shall be duly installed in office during the first week of this session, and before it shall be competent for the said general assembly to proceed with the transaction of business

Art. 154. All the publications herein ordered shall be made in the official journal of the convention.

Art. 155. This constitution shall be published in French and English in the official journal of the convention, from the period of its adjournment until the first Tuesday of November, one thousand eight hundred and fifty-two.

Done at Baton Rouge, July 31, 1852.

DUNCAN F. KENNER, *President.*

J. B. WALTON, *Secretary.*

CONSTITUTION OF LOUISIANA—1861

[A State convention, which met at New Orleans, passed an ordinance of secession on the 25th of December, 1860, but refused, by a vote of 84 against 45, to submit it to the people. In March, 1861, this convention amended the State constitution of 1852 by inserting the words " Confederate States " in place of " United States," with a few other unimportant changes. These amendments were not submitted to the people.]

CONSTITUTION OF LOUISIANA—1864 *[a]

PREAMBLE

We, the people of the State of Louisiana, do ordain and establish this constitution:

TITLE I

EMANCIPATION

ARTICLE 1. Slavery and involuntary servitude, except as a punishment for crime, whereof the party shall have been duly convicted, are hereby forever abolished and prohibited throughout the State.

ART. 2. The legislature shall make no law recognizing the right of property in man.

TITLE II

DISTRIBUTION OF POWERS

ART. 3. The powers of the government of the State of Louisiana shall be divided into three distinct departments, and each of them shall be confined to a separate body of magistracy, to wit: Those which are legislative to one, those which are executive to another, and those which are judicial to another.

---

* See " Debates in the Convention for the Revision and Amendment of the Constitution of the State of Louisiana. Assembled at Liberty Hall, New Orleans, April 6, 1864, by Albert P. Bennett, Official Reporter; H. A. Gallup, S. W. Burnham, A. L. Bartlett, Shorthand Reporters, New Orleans: W. R. Fish, Printer to the Convention. 1864." pp. 631–643.

[a] This constitution was formed by a convention which met at New Orleans (under the auspices of General Banks, then commanding the Military Department of the Gulf,) April 6, 1864, and completed its labors July 23, 1864. It was submitted to the people in September, 1864, and ratified by a vote of 6,836 against 1,566. The State government organized under it was not recognized by Congress.

ART. 4. No one of these departments, nor any person holding office in one of them, shall exercise power properly belonging to either of the others, except in the instances hereinafter expressly directed or permitted.

TITLE III

LEGISLATIVE DEPARTMENT

ART. 5. The legislative power of the State shall be vested in two distinct branches, the one to be styled " the house of representatives," the other " the senate," and both " the general assembly of the State of Louisiana."

ART. 6. The members of the house of representatives shall continue in service for the term of two years from the day of the closing of the general elections.

ART. 7. Representatives shall be chosen on the first Monday in November every two years, and the election shall be completed in one day. The general assembly shall meet annually on the first Monday in January, unless a different day be appointed by law, and their sessions shall be held at the seat of government. There shall also be a session of the general assembly in the city of New Orleans, beginning on the first Monday of October, eighteen hundred and sixty-four; and it shall be the duty of the governor to cause a special election to be held for members of the general assembly, in all the parishes where the same may be held, on the day of the election for ratification or rejection of this constitution, to be valid in case of ratification; and in other parishes or districts he shall cause elections to be held as soon as it may become practicable, to fill the vacancies for such parishes or districts in the general assembly. The term of office of the first general assembly shall expire as though its members had been elected on the first Monday of November, eighteen hundred and sixty-three.

ART. 8. Every duly-qualified elector under this constitution shall be eligible to a seat in the general assembly: *Provided,* That no person shall be a representative or senator unless he be, at the time of his election, a duly-qualified voter of the representative or senatorial district from which he is elected.

ART. 9. Elections for the members of the general assembly shall be held at the several election-precincts established by law.

ART. 10. Representation in the house of representatives shall be equal and uniform, and shall be regulated and ascertained by the number of qualified electors. Each parish shall have at least one representative. No new parish shall be created with a territory less than six hundred and twenty-five square miles, nor with a number of electors less than the full number entitling it to a representative; nor when the creation of such new parish would leave any other parish without the said extent of territory and number of electors. The first enumeration by the State authorities, under this constitution, shall be made in the year eighteen hundred and sixty-six; the second in the year eighteen hundred and seventy; the third in the year eighteen hundred and seventy-six; after which time the general assembly shall direct in what manner the census shall be taken, so that it be made at least once in every period of ten years for the purpose of ascertaining the total population, and the number of qualified electors in each parish and election-district; and in case of informality, omission, or error in the census-returns from any district, the legislature shall order a new census taken in such parish or election-district.

Art. 11. At the first session of the legislature after the making of each enumeration, the legislature shall apportion the representation amongst the several parishes and election-districts on the basis of qualified electors, as aforesaid. A representative number shall be fixed, and each parish and election-district shall have as many representatives as the aggregate number of its electors will entitle it to, and an additional representative for any fraction exceeding one-half the representative number. The number of representatives shall not be more than one hundred and twenty, nor less than ninety.

Art. 12. Until an apportionment shall be made, and elections held under the same, in accordance with the first enumeration to be made, as directed in article ten, the representation in the senate and house of representatives shall be as follows:

For the parish of Orleans, forty-four representatives, to be elected as follows: First representative district, three; second representative district, five; third representative district, seven; fourth representative district, three; fifth representative district, four; sixth representative district, two; seventh representative district, three; eighth representative district, three; ninth representative district, four; tenth representative district eight; Orleans, right bank, two.

For the parish of Livingston, one;
For the parish of Saint Tammany, one:
For the parish of Point Coupee, one;
For the parish of Saint Martin, two;
For the parish of Concordia, one;
For the parish of Madison, one;
For the parish of Franklin, one;
For the parish of St. Mary, one;
For the parish of Jefferson, three;
For the parish of Plaquemines, one;
For the parish of Saint Bernard, one;
For the parish of Saint Charles, one;
For the parish of Saint John the Baptist, one;
For the parish of Saint James, one;
For the parish of Ascension, one;
For the parish of Assumption, three;
For the parish of La Fourche, three;
For the parish of Terre Bonne, two;
For the parish of Iberville, one;
For the parish of West Baton Rouge, one;
For the parish of East Baton Rouge, two;
For the parish of West Feliciana, one;
For the parish of East Feliciana, one;
For the parish of Washington, one;
For the parish of Saint Helena, one;
For the parish of Vermillion, one;
For the parish of La Fayette, two;
For the parish of Saint Landry, four;
For the parish of Calcasieu, two;
For the parish of Avoyelles, two;

For the parish of Rapides, three;
For the parish of Natchitoches, two;
For the parish of Sabine, one;
For the parish of Caddo, two;
For the parish of De Soto, two;
For the parish of Ouachita, one;
For the parish of Union, two;
For the parish of Morehouse, one;
For the parish of Jackson, two;
For the parish of Caldwell, one;
For the parish of Catahoula, two;
For the parish of Claiborne, three;
For the parish of Bossier, one;
For the parish of Bienville, two;
For the parish of Carroll, one;
For the parish of Tensas, one;
For the parish of Winn, two;
Total, one hundred and eighteen.

And the State shall be divided into the following senatorial districts: All that portion of the parish of Orleans lying on the left bank of the Mississippi River shall be divided into two senatorial districts; the first and fourth districts of the city of New Orleans shall compose one district, and shall elect five senators; and the second and third districts of said city shall compose the other district, and shall elect four senators.

The parishes of Plaquemines, Saint Bernard, and all that part of the parish of Orleans on the right bank of the Mississippi River, shall form one district, and shall elect one senator.

The parish of Jefferson shall form one district, and shall elect one senator.

The parishes of Saint Charles and La Fourche shall form one district, and shall elect one senator.

The parishes of Saint John the Baptist and Saint James shall form one district, and shall elect one senator.

The parishes of Ascension, Assumption, and Terre Bonne shall form one district, and shall elect two senators.

The parish of Iberville shall form one district, and shall elect one senator.

The parish of East Baton Rouge shall form one district, and shall elect one senator.

The parishes of West Baton Rouge, Point Coupee, and West Feliciana shall form one district, and shall elect two senators.

The parish of East Feliciana shall form one district, and shall elect one senator.

The parishes of Washington, Saint Tammany, Saint Helena, and Livingston shall form one district, and shall elect one senator.

The parishes of Concordia and Tensas shall form one district, and shall elect one senator.

The parishes of Madison and Carroll shall form one district, and shall elect one senator.

The parishes of Morehouse, Ouachita, Union, and Jackson shall form one district, and shall elect two senators.

The parishes of Catahoula, Caldwell, and Franklin shall form one district, and shall elect one senator.

The parishes of Bossier, Bienville, Claiborne, and Winn shall form one district, and shall elect two senators.

The parishes of Natchitoches, Sabine, De Soto, and Caddo shall form one district, and shall elect two senators.

The parishes of Saint Landry, La Fayette, and Calcasieu shall form one district, and shall elect two senators.

The parishes of Saint Martin and Vermillion shall form one district, and shall elect one senator.

The parish of Saint Mary shall form one district, and shall elect one senator.

The parishes of Rapides and Avoyelles shall form one district, and shall elect two senators.

ART. 13. The house of representatives shall choose its speaker and other officers.

ART. 14. Every white male, who has attained the age of twenty-one years, and who has been a resident of the State twelve months next preceding the election, and the last three months thereof in the parish in which he offers to vote, and who shall be a citizen of the United States, shall have the right of voting.

ART. 15. The legislature shall have power to pass laws extending suffrage to such other persons, citizens of the United States, as by military service, by taxation to support the government, or by intellectual fitness, may be deemed entitled thereto.

ART. 16. No voter, on removing from one parish to another within the State, shall lose the right of voting in the former until he shall have acquired it in the latter. Electors shall in all cases, except treason, felony, or breach of the peace, be privileged from arrest during their attendance at, going to, or returning from elections.

ART. 17. The legislature shall provide by law that the names and residence of all qualified electors shall be registered in order to entitle them to vote; but the registry shall be free of cost to the elector.

ART. 18. No pauper, no person under interdiction, nor under conviction of any crime punishable with hard labor, shall be entitled to vote at any election in this State.

ART. 19. No person shall be entitled to vote at any election held in this State except in the parish of his residence, and, in cities and towns divided into election-precincts, in the election-precinct in which he resides.

ART. 20. The members of the Senate shall be chosen for the term of four years. The senate, when assembled, shall have the power to choose its own officers.

ART. 21. The legislature, in every year in which they apportion representation in the house of representatives, shall divide the State into senatorial districts.

ART. 22. No parish shall be divided in the formation of a senatorial district, the parish of Orleans excepted. And whenever a new parish shall be created, it shall be attached to the senatorial district from which most of its territory was taken, or to another contiguous district, at the discretion of the legislature, but shall not be attached to more than one district. The number of senators shall be thirty-six; and they shall be apportioned among the senatorial districts according to the electoral population contained in the several districts; *Provided*, That no parish be entitled to more than nine senators.

ART. 23. In all apportionments of the senate, the electoral population of the whole State shall be divided by the number thirty-six, and the result produced by this division shall be the senatorial ratio entitling a senatorial district to a senator. Single or contiguous parishes shall be formed into districts, having a population the nearest possible to the number entitling a district to a senator; and if the apportionment to make a parish or district fall short of or exceed the ratio, then a district may be formed having not more than two senators, but not otherwise. No new apportionment shall have the effect of abridging the term of service of any senator already elected at the time of making the apportionment. After an enumeration has been made, as directed in the tenth article, the legislature shall not pass any law until an apportionment of representation in both houses of the general assembly be made.

ART. 24. At the first session of the general assembly, after this constitution takes effect, the senators shall be equally divided by lot into two classes; the seats of the senators of the first class shall be vacated at the expiration of the term of the first house of representatives; of the second class, at the expiration of the term of the second house of representatives; so that one-half shall be chosen every two years, and a rotation thereby kept up perpetually. In case any district shall have elected two or more senators, said senators shall vacate their seats respectively at the end of the term aforesaid, and lots shall be drawn between them.

ART. 25. The first election for senators shall be held at the same time that the election for representatives is held; and thereafter there shall be elections of senators at the same time with each general election of representatives, to fill the places of those senators whose term of service may have expired.

ART. 26. Not less than a majority of the members of each house of the general assembly shall form a quorum to do business; but a smaller number may adjourn from day to day, and shall be authorized by law to compel the attendance of absent members.

ART. 27. Each house of the general assembly shall judge of the qualifications, elections, and return of its members; but a contested election shall be determined in such a manner as shall be directed by law.

ART. 28. Each house of the general assembly may determine the rules of its proceeding, punish a member for disorderly behavior, and, with a concurrence of two thirds, expel a member; but not a second time for the same offence.

ART. 29. Each house of the general assembly shall keep and publish weekly a journal of its proceedings; and the yeas and nays of the members on any question shall, at the desire of any two of them, be entered on the journal.

ART. 30. Each house may punish, by imprisonment, any person, not a member, for disrespectful and disorderly behavior in its presence, or for obstructing any of its proceedings. Such imprisonment shall not exceed ten days for any one offence.

ART. 31. Neither house, during the sessions of the general assembly, shall, without the consent of the other, adjourn for more than three days, nor to any other place than that in which they may be sitting.

ART. 32. The members of the general assembly shall receive from the public treasury a compensation for their services, which shall be eight dollars per day during their attendance, going to, and returning from the sessions of their respective houses. The compensation may be increased or diminished by law, but no alteration shall take effect during the period of service of the members of the house of representatives by whom such alteration shall have been made. No session shall extend to a period beyond sixty days, to date from its commencement, and any legislative action had after the expiration of the said sixty days shall be null and void. This provision shall not apply to the first legislature which is to convene after the adoption of this constitution.

ART. 33. The members of the general assembly shall, in all cases, except treason, felony, breach of the peace, be privileged from arrest during their attendance at the sessions of their respective houses, and going to or returning from the same; and for any speech or debate in either house shall not be questioned in any other place.

ART 34. No senator or representative shall, during the term for which he was elected, nor for one year thereafter, be appointed to any civil office of profit under this State, which shall have been created, or the emoluments of which shall have been increased, during the time such senator or representative was in office, except to such offices as may be filled by the election of the people.

ART. 35. No person who at any time may have been a collector of taxes, whether State, parish, or municipal, or who may have been otherwise intrusted with public money, shall be eligible to the general assembly, or to any office of profit or trust under the State government, until he shall have obtained a discharge for the amount of such collections, and for all public moneys with which he may have been intrusted.

ART. 36. No person while he continues to exercise the functions of a clergyman of any religious denomination whatever shall be eligible to the general assembly.

ART. 37. No bill shall have the force of a law until, on three several days, it be read over in each house of the general assembly, and free discussion allowed thereon; unless, in case of urgency, four-fifths of the house where the bill shall be pending may deem it expedient to dispense with this rule.

ART. 38. All bills for raising revenue shall originate in the house of representatives; but the senate may propose amendments, as in other bills: *Provided*, They shall not introduce any new matter, under the color of an amendment, which does not relate to raising revenue.

ART. 39. The general assembly shall regulate, by law, by whom, and in what manner, writs of election shall be issued to fill the vacancies which may happen in either branch thereof.

ART. 40. The senate shall vote on the confirmation or rejection of the officers to be appointed by the governor, with the advice and consent of the senate, by yeas and nays; and the names of the senators voting for and against the appointments, respectively, shall be entered on a journal to be kept for that purpose, and made public at the end of each session, or before.

ART. 41. Returns of all elections for members of the general assembly shall be made to the secretary of state.

ART. 42. In the year in which a regular election for a Senator of the United States is to take place, the members of the general assembly shall meet in the hall of the house of representatives on the second Monday following the meeting of the legislature, and proceed to said election.

TITLE IV

EXECUTIVE DEPARTMENT

ART. 43. The supreme executive power of the State shall be vested in a chief magistrate, who shall be styled the governor of the State of Louisiana. He shall hold his office during the term of four years, and, together with the lieutenant-governor chosen for the same term, be elected as follows: The qualified electors for representatives shall vote for governor and lieutenant-governor at the time and place of voting for representatives; the returns of every election shall be sealed up and transmitted by the proper returning-officer to the secretary of state, who shall deliver them to the speaker of the house of representatives on the second day of the session of the general assembly then to be holden. The members of the general assembly shall meet in the house of representatives to examine and count the votes. The person having the greatest number of votes for governor shall be declared duly elected; but if two or more persons shall be equal and the highest in the number of votes polled for governor, one of them shall immediately be chosen governor by joint vote of the members of the general assembly. The person having the greatest number of votes polled for lieutenant-governor shall be lieutenant-governor; but if two or more persons shall be equal and highest in the number of votes polled for lieutenant-governor, one of them shall be immediately chosen lieutenant-governor by joint vote of the members of the general assembly.

ART. 44. No person shall be eligible to the office of governor or lieutenant-governor who shall not have attained the age of thirty-five years, and been a citizen and resident within the State for the period of five years next preceding his election.

ART. 45. The governor shall enter on the discharge of his duties on the second Monday of January next ensuing election, and shall continue in office until the Monday next succeeding the day that his successor shall be declared duly elected, and shall have taken the oath or affirmation required by the constitution.

ART. 46. No member of Congress, minister of any religious denomination, or any person holding office under the United States Government, shall be eligible to the office of governor or lieutenant-governor.

ART. 47. In case of impeachment of the governor, his removal from office, death, refusal or inability to qualify, resignation, or absence from the State, the powers and duties of the office shall devolve upon the lieutenant-governor for the residue of the term, or until the governor, absent or impeached, shall return or be acquitted. The legislature may provide by law for the case of removal, impeachment, death, resignation, disability, or refusal to qualify, of both the governor and the lieutenant-governor, declaring what officer shall act as governor, and such officer shall act accordingly, until the disability be removed, or for the remainder of the term.

ART. 48. The lieutenant-governor, or officer discharging the duties of governor, shall, during his administration, receive the same compensation to which the governor would have been entitled had he continued in office.

ART. 49. The lieutenant-governor shall, by virtue of his office, be president of the senate, but shall have only a casting vote therein. Whenever he shall administer the government, or shall be unable to attend as president of the senate, the senators shall elect one of their own members as president of the senate for the time being.

ART. 50. The governor shall receive for his services a compensation of eight thousand dollars per annum, payable quarterly on his own warrant.

ART. 51. The lieutenant-governor shall receive for his services a salary of five thousand dollars per annum, to be paid quarterly.

ART. 52. The governor shall have power to grant reprieves for all offences against the State, and, except in cases of impeachment, shall, with the consent of the senate, have power to grant pardons, remit fines and forfeitures, after conviction. In cases of treason he may grant reprieves until the end of the next session of the general assembly, in which the power of pardoning shall be vested.

ART. 53. He shall be commander-in-chief of the militia of this State, except when they shall be called into the service of the United States.

ART. 54. He shall nominate, and, by and with the advice and consent of the senate, appoint all officers whose offices are established by the constitution, and whose appointments are not herein otherwise provided for: *Provided, however*, That the legislature shall have a right to prescribe the mode of appointment to all other offices established by law.

ART. 55. The governor shall have power to fill vacancies that may happen during the recess of the senate, by granting commissions which shall expire at the end of the next session thereof, unless otherwise provided for in this constitution; but no person who has been nominated for office and rejected by the senate shall be appointed to the same office during the recess of the senate.

ART. 56. He may require information, in writing, from the officers in the executive department upon any subject relating to the duties of their respective offices.

ART. 57. He shall from time to time give to the general assembly information respecting the situation of the State, and recommend to their consideration such measures as may be deemed expedient.

ART. 58. He may, on extraordinary occasions, convene the general assembly at the seat of government, or at a different place if that should have become dangerous from an enemy, or from epidemic; and, in case of disagreement between the two houses as to the time of adjournment, he may adjourn them to such time as he may think proper, not exceeding four months.

ART. 59. He shall take care that the laws are faithfully executed.

ART. 60. Every bill which shall have passed both houses shall be presented to the governor; if he approves, he shall sign it, if not, he shall return it with his objections to the house in which it originated, which shall enter the objections at large upon its journal, and proceed to consider it; if after such consideration two-thirds of all the members elected to that house shall agree to pass the bill, it shall be sent, with the objections, to the other house, by which it shall be likewise considered, and if approved by two-thirds of the members elected to that house, it shall be a law; but in such cases the vote of both houses shall be determined by yeas and nays, and the names of the members voting for or against the bill shall be entered on the journal of each house respectively. If any bill shall not be returned by the governor within ten days (Sundays excepted) after it shall have been presented to him, it shall be a law in like manner as if he had signed it; unless the general assembly, by adjournment, prevent its return.

ART. 61. Every order, resolution, or vote, to which the concurrence of both houses may be necessary, except on a question of adjournment, shall be presented to the governor, and before it shall take effect be approved by him, or, being disapproved, shall be repassed by two-thirds of the members elected to each house of the general assembly.

ART. 62. There shall be a secretary of state, who shall hold his office during the term for which the governor shall have been elected. The records of the State shall be kept and preserved in the office of the secretary; he shall keep a fair register of the official acts and proceedings of the governor, and, when necessary, shall attest them; he shall, when required, lay the said register, and all papers, minutes, and vouchers relative to his office, before either house of the general assembly, and shall perform such other duties as may be enjoined on him by law.

ART. 63. There shall be a treasurer of the State, and an auditor of public accounts, who shall hold their respective offices during the term of four years.

ART. 64. The secretary of state, treasurer of state, and auditor of public accounts shall be elected by the qualified electors of the State; and in case of any vacancy caused by the resignation, death, or absence of the secretary, treasurer, or auditor, the governor shall order an election to fill said vacancy.

ART. 65. The secretary of state, the treasurer, and the auditor shall receive a salary of five thousand dollars per annum each.

ART. 66. All commissions shall be in the name and by the authority of the State of Louisiana, and shall be sealed with the State seal and signed by the governor.

ART. 67. All able-bodied men in the State shall be armed and disciplined for its defence.

ART. 68. The militia of the State shall be organized in such manner as may be hereafter deemed most expedient by the legislature.

Title V

Judiciary Department

ART. 69. The judiciary power shall be vested in a supreme court, in such inferior courts as the legislature may, from time to time, order and establish, and in justices of the peace.

ART. 70. The supreme court, except in cases hereafter provided, shall have appellate jurisdiction only; which jurisdiction shall extend to all cases when the matter in dispute shall exceed three hundred dollars; to all cases in which the constitutionality or legality of any tax, toll, or impost whatsoever, or of any fine, forfeiture, or penalty imposed by a municipal corporation, shall be in contestation; and to all criminal cases on questions of law alone whenever the offence charged is punishable with death or imprisonment at hard labor, or when a fine exceeding three hundred dollars is actually imposed.

Art. 71. The supreme court shall be composed of one chief justice and four associate justices, a majority of whom shall constitute a quorum. The chief justice shall receive a salary of seven thousand five hundred dollars, and each of the associate justices a salary of seven thousand dollars, annually, until otherwise provided by law. The court shall appoint its own clerks.

Art. 72. The supreme court shall hold its sessions in New Orleans, from the first Monday in the month of November to the end of the month of June, inclusive. The legislature shall have the power to fix the sessions elsewhere during the rest of the year; until otherwise provided, the sessions shall be held as hertofore.

Art. 73. The supreme court, and each of the judges thereof, shall have power to issue writs of *habeas corpus*, at the instance of all persons in actual custody under process, in all cases in which they may have appellate jurisdiction.

Art. 74. No judgment shall be rendered by the supreme court without the concurrence of a majority of the judges comprising the court. Whenever the majority cannot agree, in consequence of the recusation of any member of the court, the judges not recused shall have power to call upon any judge or judges of the inferior courts, whose duty it shall be, when so called upon, to sit in the place of the judge of judges recused, and to aid in determining the case.

Art. 75. All judges, by virtue of their office, shall be conservators of the peace throughout the State. The style of all process shall be " The State of Louisiana." All prosecutions shall be carried on in the name and by the authority of the State of Louisiana, and conclude " against the peace and dignity of the same."

Art. 76. The judges of all courts within the State shall, as often as it may be advisable so to do, in every definite judgment, refer to the particular law in virtue of which such judgment may be rendered, and in all cases adduce the reasons on which their judgment is founded.

Art. 77. The judges of all courts shall be liable to impeachment; but for any reasonable cause, which shall not be sufficient ground for impeachment, the governor shall remove any of them, on the address of a majority of the members elected to each house of the general assembly. In every such case the cause or causes for which such removal may be required shall be stated at length in the address, and inserted in the journal of each house.

Art. 78. The judges both of the supreme and inferior courts shall receive a salary which shall not be diminished during their continuance in office; and they are prohibited from receiving any fees of office or other compensation than their salaries for any civil duties performed by them.

Art. 79. The judges of the supreme court shall be appointed by the governor, by and with the advice and consent of the senate, for a term of eight years; the judges of the inferior courts for a term of six years.

Art. 80. The clerks of the inferior courts shall be elected by the qualified voters of their several districts, and shall hold their offices during a term of four years.

ART. 81. The legislature shall have power to vest in clerks of courts authority to grant such orders and do such acts as may be deemed necessary for the furtherance of the administration of justice, and in all cases the powers thus granted shall be specified and determined.

ART. 82. The jurisdiction of justices of the peace shall not exceed, in civil cases, the sum of one hundred dollars, exclusive of interest, subject to appeal in such cases as shall be provided for by law. They shall be elected by the qualified voters of their several districts, and shall hold their office during a term of two years. They shall have such criminal jurisdiction as shall be provided by law.

ART. 83. There shall be an attorney-general for the State, and as many district attorneys as the legislature shall find necessary. The attorney-general shall be elected every four years by the qualified voters of the State. He shall receive a salary of five thousand dollars per annum, payable, on his own warrant, quarterly. The district attorneys shall be elected by the qualified voters of their respective districts, for a term of four years. They shall receive such salaries as shall be provided by the legislature.

ART. 84. A sheriff and a coroner shall be elected in each parish by the qualified voters thereof, who shall hold their offices for the term of two years. The legislature shall have the power to increase the number of sheriffs in any parish. Should a vacancy occur in either of these offices subsequent to an election, it shall be filled by the governor, and the person so appointed shall continue in office until his successor shall be elected and qualified.

TITLE VI

IMPEACHMENT

ART. 85. The power of impeachment shall be vested in the house of representatives.

ART. 86. Impeachments of the governor, lieutenant-governor, attorney-general, secretary of state, state treasurer, auditor of public accounts, and the judges of the inferior courts, justices of the peace excepted, shall be tried by the senate; the chief justice of the supreme court, or the senior judge thereof, shall preside during the trial of such impeachment. Impeachments of the judges of the supreme court shall be tried by the senate. When sitting as a court of impeachment, the senators shall be upon oath or affirmation, and no person shall be convicted without the concurrence of a majority of the senators elected.

ART. 87. Judgments in case of impeachment shall extend only to removal from office; and disqualification from holding any office of honor, trust, or profit under the State; but the convicted parties shall, nevertheless, be subject to indictment, trial, and punishment, according to law.

ART. 88. All officers against whom articles of impeachment may be preferred shall be suspended from the exercise of their functions during the pendency of such impeachment; the appointing power may make a provisional appointment to replace any suspended officer until the decision of the impeachment.

ART. 89. The legislature shall provide by law for the trial, punishment, and removal from office of all other officers of the State by indictment or otherwise.

Title VII

GENERAL PROVISIONS

ART. 90. Members of the general assembly, and all officers, before they enter upon the duties of their offices, shall take the following oath or affirmation:

" I [A. B.] do solemnly swear [or affirm] that I will support the Constitution and laws of the United States and of this State, and that I will faithfully and impartially discharge and perform all the duties incumbent on me as ———, according to the best of my abilities and understanding: so help me God."

ART. 91. Treason against the State shall consist only in levying war against it, or in adhering to its enemies, giving them aid and comfort. No person shall be convicted of treason unless on the testimony of two witnesses to the same overt act, or his own confession in open court.

ART. 92. The legislature shall have power to declare the punishment of treason, but no attainder of treason shall work corruption of blood or forfeiture, except during the life of the person attainted.

ART. 93. Every person shall be disqualified from holding any office of trust or profit in this State, and shall be excluded from the right of suffrage, who shall have been convicted of treason, perjury, forgery, bribery, or other high crimes or misdemeanors.

ART. 94. All penalties shall be proportioned to the nature of the offence.

ART. 95. The privilege of free suffrage shall be supported by laws regulating elections, and prohibiting, under adequate penalties, all undue influence thereon from power, bribery, tumult, or other improper practice.

ART. 96. No money shall be drawn from the treasury but in pursuance of specific appropriation made by law; nor shall any appropriation of money be made for a longer term than two years. A regular statement and account of the receipts and expenditures of all public moneys shall be published annually, in such manner as shall be prescribed by law.

ART. 97. It shall be the duty of the general assembly to pass such laws as may be proper and necessary to decide differences by arbitration.

ART. 98. All civil officers for the State at large shall be voters of and reside within the State; and all district or parish officers shall be voters of and reside within their respective districts or parishes, and shall keep their offices at such places therein as may be required by law.

ART. 99. All civil officers shall be removable by an address of a majority of the members elected to both houses, except those the removal of whom has been otherwise provided by this constitution.

ART. 100. In all elections by the people the vote shall be taken by ballot, and in all elections by the senate and house of representatives, jointly or separately, the vote shall be given *viva voce*.

ART. 101. No member of Congress, nor person holding or exercising any office of trust or profit under the United States, or under any foreign power, shall be eligible as a member of the general assembly, or hold or exercise any office of trust or profit under the State.

ART. 102. None but citizens of the United States shall be appointed to any office of trust or profit in this State.

ART. 103. The laws, public records, and the judicial and legislative written proceedings of the State shall be promulgated, preserved, and conducted in the language in which the Constitution of the United States is written.

ART. 104. No power of suspending the laws of the State shall be exercised, unless by the legislature or by its authority.

ART. 105. Prosecutions shall be by indictment or information. The accused shall have a speedy public trial by an impartial jury of the parish in which the offence shall have been committed. He shall not be compelled to give evidence against himself; he shall have the right of being heard, by himself or counsel; he shall have the right of meeting the witnesses face to face, and shall have compulsory process for obtaining witnesses in his favor. He shall not be twice put in jeopardy for the same offence.

ART. 106. All persons shall be bailable by sufficient sureties, unless for capital offences, where the proof is evident or presumption great, or unless after conviction for any offence or crime punishable with death or imprisonment at hard labor. The privilege of the writ of *habeas corpus* shall not be suspended, unless when, in cases of rebellion or invasion, the public safety may require it.

ART. 107. Excessive bail shall not be required; excessive fines shall not be imposed, nor cruel and unusual punishments inflicted.

ART. 108. The right of the people to be secure in their persons, houses, papers, and effects against unreasonable searches and seizures shall not be violated, and no warrants shall issue but upon probable cause, supported by oath or affirmation, and particularly describing the place to be searched and the person or thing to be seized.

ART. 109. No *ex post facto* or retroactive law, nor any law impairing the obligations of contracts, shall be passed, nor vested rights be divested, unless for purposes of public utility and for adequate compensation previously made.

ART. 110. All courts shall be open; and every person, for any injury done him, in his lands, goods, person, or reputation, shall have remedy by due course of law, and right and justice administered without denial or unreasonable delay.

ART. 111. The press shall be free; every citizen may freely speak, write, and publish his sentiments on all subjects, being responsible for an abuse of this liberty.

ART. 112. The legislature shall not have power to grant aid to companies or associations of individauls, except to charitable associations, and to such companies of associations as are and shall be formed for the exclusive purpose of making works of internal improvement, wholly or partially within the State, to the extent only of one-fifth of the capital of such companies, by subscription of stock or loan in money or public bonds; but any aid thus granted shall be paid to the company only in the same proportion as the remainder of the capital shall be actually paid in by the stockholders of the company; and, in case of loan, such adequate security shall be required as to the legislature may seem proper. No corporation or individual association, receiving the aid of the State as herein provided, shall possess banking or discounting privileges.

Art. 113. No liability shall be contracted by the State as above mentioned, unless the same be authorized by some law for some single object or work, to be distinctly specified therein, which shall be passed by a majority of the members elected to both houses of the general assembly, and the aggregate amount of debts and liabilities incurred under this and the preceding article shall never, at any time, exceed eight millions of dollars.

Art. 114. Whenever the legislature shall contract a debt exceeding in amount the sum of one hundred thousand dollars, unless in case of war, to repel invasion, or suppress insurrection, they shall, in the law creating the debt, provide adequate ways and means for the payment of the current interest and of the principal when the same shall become due. And the said law shall be irrepealable until principal and interest are fully paid and discharged, or unless the repealing law contains some other adequate provision for the payment of the principal and interest of the debt.

Art. 115. The legislature shall provide by law for all change of venue in civil and criminal cases.

Art. 116. The legislature shall have the power to license the selling of lottery-tickets and the keeping of gambling-houses; said houses in all cases shall be on the first floor and kept with open doors; but in all cases not less than ten thousand dollars per annum shall be levied as a license or tax on each vendor of lottery-tickets and on each gambling-house, and five hundred dollars on each tombola.

Art. 117. The legislature may enact general laws regulating the adoption of children, emancipation of minors, changing of names, and the granting of divorces; but no special laws shall be enacted relating to particular or individual cases.

Art. 118. Every law enacted by the legislature shall embrace but one object, and that shall be expressed in the title.

Art. 119. No law shall be revived or amended by reference to its title; but in such case the act revived or section amended shall be reënacted and published at length.

Art. 120. The legislature shall never adopt any system or code of laws by general reference to such system or code of laws, but in all cases shall specify the several provisions of the laws it may enact.

Art. 121. Corporations shall not be created in this State by special laws except for political or municipal purposes; but the legislature shall provide by general law for the organization of all other corporations, except corporations with banking or discounting privileges, the creation, renewal, or extension of which is hereby prohibited.

Art. 122. In case of the insolvency of any bank or banking association, the bill-holders thereof shall be entitled to preference in payment over all other creditors of such bank or association.

Art. 123. No person shall hold or exercise at the same time more than one civil office of trust or profit, except that of justice of the peace.

Art. 124. Taxation shall be equal and uniform throughout the State. All property shall be taxed in proportion to its value, to be ascertained as directed by law. The general assembly shall have power to exempt from taxation property actually used for church, school, or charitable purposes. The general assembly shall levy an income-tax upon all persons pursuing any occupation, trade, or calling, and all such persons shall obtain a license, as provided by law. All tax on income shall be *pro rata* on the amount of income or business done.

ART. 125. The legislature may provide by law in what case officers shall continue to perform the duties of their offices until their successors shall have been inducted into office.

ART. 126. The legislature shall have power to extend this constitution and the jurisdiction of this State over any territory acquired by compact with any State, or with the United States, the same being done by consent of the United States.

ART. 127. None of the lands granted by Congress to the State of Louisiana for aiding in constructing the necessary levees and drains to reclaim the swamp and overflowed lands of the State, shall be diverted from the purposes for which they were granted.

ART. 128. The legislature shall pass no law excluding citizens of this State from office for not being conversant with any language except that in which the Constitution of the United States is written.

ART. 129. No liability, either State, parochial, or municipal, shall exist for any debts contracted for or in the interest of the rebellion against the United States Government.

ART. 130. The seat of government shall be and remain at New Orleans, and shall not be removed without the consent of a majority of both houses of the general assembly.

ART. 131. The legislature may determine the mode of filling vacancies in all offices for which provision is not made in this constitution.

ART. 132. The legislature shall pass no law requiring a property qualification for office.

TITLE VIII

CORPORATION OF THE CITY OF NEW ORLEANS

ART. 133. The citizens of the city of New Orleans shall have the right of appointing the several public officers necessary for the administration of the police of said city, pursuant to the mode of elections which shall be prescribed by the legislature: *Provided*, That the mayor and recorders shall be ineligible to a seat in the general assembly; and the mayor and recorders shall be commissioned by the governor as justices of the peace, and the legislature may vest in them such criminal jurisdiction as may be necessary for the punishment of minor offences and as the police and good of said city may require.

The city of New Orleans shall maintain a police which shall be uniformed with distinction of grade, to consist of permanent citizens of the State of Louisiana, to be selected by the mayor of the city, and to hold office during good behavior, and removable only by a police commission composed of five citizens, and the mayor, who shall be president of the board. The commission to be appointed by the governor of the State for the term of two years, at a salary of not less than one thousand dollars per annum; a majority of whom shall remove for delinquencies. Members of the police when removed shall not again be eligible to any position on the police for a term of one year.

Interfering or meddling in elections in any manner will be a sufficient cause for instant dismissal from the police by the board.

The chief of the police shall give a penal bond in the sum of ten thousand dollars; lieutenants of police, five thousand dollars; sergeants and clerks, each three thousand dollars; corporals, two thousand dollars; and privates one thousand dollars; with good and solvent security, as the law directs, for the faithful performance of their duties.

The various officers shall receive a salary of not less than the following rates:

The chief of police, $250 per month; the lieutenants of police, $150 per month; the sergeants of police, $100 per month; the clerks of police, $100 per month; the corporals of police, $90 per month; the privates, (day and night,) each, $80 per month.

Title IX

LABOR ON PUBLIC WORKS

ART. 134. The legislature may establish the price and pay of foremen, mechanics, laborers, and others employed on the public works of the State or parochial or city governments: *Provided*, That the compensation to be paid all foremen, mechanics, cartmen, and laborers employed on the public works, under the government of the State of Louisiana, city of New Orleans, and the police-juries of the various parishes of the State, shall not be less than as follows, viz: Foremen, $3.50 per day; mechanics, $3 per day; cartmen, $3.50 per day; laborers, $2 per day.

ART. 135. Nine hours shall constitute a day's labor for all mechanics, artisans, and laborers employed on public works.

Title X

INTERNAL IMPROVEMENTS

ART. 136. There shall be appointed by the governor a State engineer, skilled in the theory and practice of his profession, who shall hold his office at the seat of government for the term of four years. He shall have the superintendence and direction of all public works in which the State may be interested, except those made by joint-stock companies or such as may be under the parochial or city authorities exclusively and not in conflict with the general laws of the State. He shall communicate to the general assembly, through the governor, annually, his views concerning the same, report upon the condition of the public works in progress, recommend such measures as in his opinion the public interest of the State may require, and shall perform such other duties as may be prescribed by law. His salary shall be five thousand dollars per annum, until otherwise provided by law. The mode of appointment, number, and salary of his assistants shall be fixed by law. The State engineer and assistants shall give bonds for the performance of their duties as shall be prescribed by law.

ART. 137. The general assembly may create internal-improvement districts, composed of one or more parishes, and may grant a right to the citizens thereof to tax themselves for their improvements. Said internal-improvement districts, when created, shall have the right to select commissioners, shall have the power to appoint officers, fix their pay, and regulate all matters relative to the improvements of their districts, provided such improvements will not conflict with the general laws of the State.

ART. 138. The general assembly may grant aid to said districts out of the funds arising from the swamp and overflowed lands granted to the State by the United States for that purpose or otherwise.

ART. 139. The general assembly shall have the right of abolishing the office of State engineer, by a majority vote of all the members elected to each branch, and of substituting a board of public works in lieu thereof, should they deem it necessary.

Title XI

PUBLIC EDUCATION

ART. 140. There shall be elected a superintendent of public education, who shall hold his office for the term of four years. His duties shall be prescribed by law, and he shall receive a salary of four thousand dollars per annum until otherwise provided by law: *Provided*, That the general assembly shall have power by a vote of a majority of the members elected to both houses to abolish the said office of superintendent of public education whenever, in their opinion, said office shall be no longer necessary.

ART. 141. The legislature shall provide for the education of all children of the State, between the ages of six and eighteen years, by maintenance of free public schools by taxation or otherwise.

ART. 142. The general exercises in the common schools shall be conducted in the English language.

ART. 143. A university shall be established in the city of New Orleans. It shall be composed of four faculties, to wit: One of law, one of medicine, one of the natural sciences, and one of letters. The legislature shall provide by law for its organization and maintenance.

ART. 144. The proceeds of all lands heretofore granted by the United States to this State for the use or purpose of the public schools, and of all lands which may hereafter be granted or bequeathed for that purpose, and the proceeds of the estates of deceased persons to which the State may become entitled by law, shall be and remain a perpetual fund on which the State shall pay an annual interest of 6 per cent., which interest, together with the interest of the trust-funds deposited with the State by the United States, under the act of Congress approved June 23, 1836, and all the rents of the unsold lands, shall be appropriated to the purpose of such schools, and the appropriation shall remain inviolable.

ART. 145. All moneys arising from the sales which have been or may hereafter be made of any lands heretofore granted by the United States to this State for the use of a specific seminary of learning, or from any kind of a donation that may hereafter be made for that purpose, shall be and remain a perpetual fund, the interest of which, at 6 per cent. per annum, shall be appropriated to the promotion of literature and the arts and sciences, and no law shall ever be made diverting said funds to any other use than to the establishment and improvement of said seminary of learning; and the general assembly shall have power to raise funds for the organization and support of said seminary of learning in such manner as it may deem proper.

ART. 146. No appropriation shall be made by the legislature for the support of any private school or institution of learning whatever, but the highest encouragement shall be granted to public schools throughout the State.

Title XII

MODE OF REVISING THE CONSTITUTION

ART. 147. Any amendment or amendments to this constitution may be proposed in the senate or house of representatives, and if the same shall be agreed to by a majority of the members elected to each house, such proposed amendment or amendments shall be entered on their journals, with the yeas and nays taken thereon. Such proposed amendment or amendments shall be submitted to the people at an election to be ordered by said legislature, and held within ninety days after the adjournment of the same, and after thirty days' publication according to law; and if a majority of the voters at said election shall approve and ratify such amendment or amendments, the same shall become a part of the constitution. If more than one amendment be submitted at a time, they shall be submitted in such manner and form that the people may vote for or against each amendment separately.

Title XIII

SCHEDULE

ART. 148. The constitution adopted in 1852 is declared to be superseded by this constitution; and in order to carry the same into effect, it is hereby declared and ordained as follows:

ART. 149. All rights, actions, prosecutions, claims, and contracts, as well as of individuals as of bodies-corporate, and all laws in force at the time of the adoption of this constitution, and not inconsistent therewith, shall continue as if the same had not been adopted.

ART. 150. In order that no inconvenience may result to the public service from the taking effect of this constitution, no officer shall be superseded thereby; but the laws of this State relative to the duties of the several officers, executive, judicial, and military, except those made void by military authority, and by the ordinance of emancipation, shall remain in full force, though the same be contrary to this constitution, and the several duties shall be performed by the respective officers of the State, according to the existing laws, until the organization of the government under this constitution, and the entering into office of the new officers to be appointed under said government, and no longer.

ART. 151. The legislature shall provide for the removal of all causes now pending in the supreme court or other courts of the State under the constitution of 1852, to courts created by or under this constitution.

Title XIV

ORDINANCE

ART. 152. Immediately after the adjournment of the convention, the governor shall issue his proclamation directing the several officers of this State, authorized by law to hold elections, or, in default thereof, such officers as he shall designate, to open and hold polls in the several parishes of the State, at the places designated by law, on the first Monday of September, 1864, for the purpose of taking the sense of the good people of this State in regard to the adoption or rejection of this constitution; and it shall be the duty of said officers to receive the suffrages of all qualified voters. Each voter shall express his opinion by depositing in the ballot-box a ticket whereon shall be written " The constitution accepted," or, " The constitution rejected." At the conclusion of the said election, the officers and commissioners appointed to preside over the same shall carefully examine and count each ballot as deposited, and shall forthwith make due return thereof to the secretary of state, in conformity to the provisions of law and usages in regard to elections.

ART. 153. Upon the receipt of said returns, or on the third Monday of September, if the returns be not sooner received, it shall be the duty of the governor, the secretary of state, the attorney-general, and the State treasurer, in the presence of all such persons as may choose to attend, to compare the votes at the said election for the ratification or rejection of this constitution, and if it shall appear at the close that a majority of all the votes given is for ratifying this constitution, then it shall be the duty of the governor to make proclamation of the fact, and thenceforth this constitution shall be ordained and established as the constitution of the State of Louisiana. But whether this constitution be accepted or rejected, it shall be the duty of the governor to cause to be published the result of the polls, showing the number of votes cast in each parish for and against this constitution.

ART. 154. As soon as the general election can be held under this constitution in every parish of the State, the governor shall, by proclamation, or, in case of his failure to act, the legislature shall, by resolution, declare the fact, and order an election to be held on a day fixed in said proclamation or resolution, and within sixty days from the date thereof, for governor, lieutenant-governor, secretary of state, auditor, treasurer, attorney-general, and superintendent of education. The officers so chosen shall, on the fourth Monday after their election, be installed into office; and shall hold their offices for the terms prescribed in this constitution, counting from the second Monday in January next preceding their entering into office, in case they do not enter into office on that date. The terms of office of the State officers elected on the 22d day of February, 1864, shall expire on the installation of their successors as herein provided for; but under no state of circumstances shall their term of office be construed as extending beyond the length of the terms fixed for said offices in this constitution; and, if not sooner held, the election of their successors shall take place on the first Monday of November, 1867, in all parishes where the same can be held, the officers elected on that date to enter into office on the second Monday in January, 1868.

ART. 155. This constitution shall be published in three papers to be selected by the president of the convention, whereof two shall publish the same in English and French, and one in German, from the period of the adjournment of the convention until the election for ratification or rejection on the first Monday of September, 1864.

E. H. DURELL, *President.*

JNO. E. NEELIS, *Secretary.*

CONSTITUTION OF LOUISIANA—1868 * [a]

PREAMBLE

We, the people of Louisiana, in order to establish justice, insure domestic tranquillity, promote the general welfare, and secure the blessings of liberty to ourselves and our posterity, do ordain and establish this constitution.

TITLE I

BILL OF RIGHTS

ARTICLE 1. All men are created free and equal, and have certain inalienable rights; among these are life, liberty, and the pursuit of happiness. To secure these rights, governments are instituted among men, deriving their just powers from the consent of the governed.

ART. 2. All persons, without regard to race, color, or previous condition, born or naturalized in the United States, and subject to the jurisdiction thereof, and residents of this State for one year, are citizens of this State. The citizens of this State owe allegiance to the United States; and this allegiance is paramount to that which they owe to the State. They shall enjoy the same civil, political, and public rights and privileges, and be subject to the same pains and penalties.

ART. 3. There shall be neither slavery nor involuntary servitude in this State, otherwise than for the punishment of crime, whereof the party shall have been duly convicted.

ART. 4. The press shall be free; every citizen may freely speak, write, and publish his sentiments on all subjects, being responsible for the abuse of this liberty.

ART. 5. The right of the people peaceably to assemble and petition the government, or any department thereof, shall never be abridged.

ART. 6. Prosecutions shall be by indictment or information. The accused shall be entitled to a speedy public trial by an impartial jury of the parish in which the offence was committed, unless the venue be changed. He shall not be compelled to give evidence against himself; he shall have the right of being heard by himself or counsel; he shall have the right of meeting the witnesses face to face, and shall have compulsory process for obtaining witnesses in his favor. He shall not be tried twice for the same offence.

ART. 7. All persons shall be bailable by sufficient securities, unless for capital offences, where the proof is evident or the presumption great, or unless after conviction for any crime or offence punishable with death or imprisonment at hard labor. The privilege of the writ of *habeas corpus* shall not be suspended.

ART. 8. Excessive bail shall not be required; excessive fines shall not be imposed; nor cruel or unusual punishments inflicted.

---

* Verified by " Constitution adopted by the State Constitutional Convention of the State of Louisiana, March 7, 1868. New Orleans: Printed at the Republican Office, 57 St. Charles St. 1868."

[a] This constitution was formed by a convention, called under the reconstruction acts of Congress, which met at New Orleans in December, 1867, and completed its labors March 2, 1868. It was submitted to the people on the 17th and 18th of August, 1868, and ratified by a vote of 66,152 against 48,739.

ART. 9. The right of the people to be secure in their persons, houses, papers, and effects, against unreasonable searches and seizures, shall not be violated; and no warrant shall issue but upon probable cause, supported by oath or affirmation, and particularly describing the place to be searched, or the person or things to be seized.

ART. 10. All courts shall be open; and every person for injury done him in his land, goods, person, or reputation, shall have adequate remedy, by due process of law, and justice administered without denial or unreasonable delay.

ART. 11. No law shall be passed fixing the price of manual labor.

ART. 12. Every person has the natural right to worship God according to the dictates of his conscience. No religious test shall be required as a qualification for office.

ART. 13. All persons shall enjoy equal rights and privileges upon any conveyance of a public character; and all places of business, or of public resort, or for which a license is required by either State, parish, or municipal authority, shall be deemed places of a public character, and shall be opened to the accommodation and patronage of all persons, without distinction or discrimination on account of race or color.

ART. 14. The rights enumerated in this title shall not be construed to limit or abridge other rights of the people not herein expressed.

TITLE II

LEGISLATIVE DEPARTMENT

ART. 15. The legislative power of the State shall be vested in two distinct branches; the one to be styled the house of representatives, the other the senate; and both, the general assembly of the State of Louisiana.

ART. 16. The members of the house of representatives shall continue in office for two years from the day of the closing of the general elections.

ART. 17. Representatives shall be chosen on the first Monday in November, every two years; and the election shall be completed in one day. The general assembly shall meet annually on the first Monday in January, unless a different day be appointed by law, and their sessions shall be held at the seat of government.

ART. 18. Every elector under this constitution shall be eligible to a seat in the house of representatives; and every elector who has reached the age of twenty-five years shall be eligible to the senate: *Provided*, That no person shall be a representative or senator unless at the time of his election he be a qualified elector of the representative or senatorial district from which he is elected.

ART. 19. Elections for members of the general assembly shall be held at the several election precincts established by law.

ART. 20. Representation in the house of representatives shall be equal and uniform; and, after the first general assembly elected under this constitution, shall be ascertained and regulated by the total population, each parish in the State being entitled to at least one representative. A census of the State by State authority shall be taken in the year eighteen hundred and seventy-five, and every ten years thereafter. In case of informality, omission, or error in the census-returns from any parish or election district, the general assembly may order a new census taken in such parish or election district; but, until the State census of eighteen hundred and seventy-five, the apportionment of the State shall be made on the basis of the census of the United States for the year eighteen hundred and seventy.

Art. 21. The general assembly, at the first session after the making of each enumeration, shall apportion the representation amongst the several parishes and representative districts on the basis of the total population, as aforesaid. A representative number shall be fixed, and each parish and representative district shall have as many representatives as the number of its total population will entitle it to have, and an additional representative for any fraction exceeding one-half of the representative number. The number of representatives shall never exceed one hunderd and twenty, nor be less than ninety.

Art. 22. Until an apportionment shall be made in accordance with the provisions of article twenty, the representation in the senate and house of representatives shall be as follows:

For the parish of Orleans: First representative district, two; second representative district, three; third representative district, four; fourth representative district, two; fifth representative district, two; sixth representative district, one; seventh representative district, two; eighth representative district, one; ninth representative district, two; tenth representative district, three; Orleans, right bank, one.

For the parish of Ascension, two;
For the parish of Assumption, two;
For the parish of Avoyelles, two;
For the parish of Baton Rouge, East, three;
For the parish of Baton Rouge, West, one;
For the parish of Bienville, one;
For the parish of Bossier, two;
For the parish of Caddo, three;
For the parish of Calcasieu, one;
For the parish of Caldwell, one;
For the parish of Carroll, two;
For the parish of Catahoula, one;
For the parish of Claiborne, two;
For the parish of Concordia, two;
For the parish of De Soto, two;
For the parish of Feliciana, East, two;
For the parish of Feliciana, West, one;
For the parish of Franklin, one;
For the parish of Iberville, two;
For the parish of Jackson, one;
For the parish of Jefferson, four;
For the parish of La Fayette, one;
For the parish of La Fourche, two;
For the parish of Livingston, one;
For the parish of Madison, one;
For the parish of Morehouse, one;
For the parish of Natchitoches, two;
For the parish of Ouachita, two;
For the parish of Plaquemines, one;
For the parish of Point Coupee, two;
For the parish of Rapides, three;

For the parish of Sabine, one;
For the parish of Saint Bernard, one;
For the parish of Saint Charles, one;
For the parish of Saint Helena, one;
For the parish of Saint James, two;
For the parish of Saint John Baptist, one;
For the parish of Saint Landry, four;
For the parish of Saint Martin's, two;
For the parish of Saint Mary's, two;
For the parish of Saint Tammany, one;
For the parish of Tensas, two;
For the parish of Terre Bonne, two;
For the parish of Union, one;
For the parish of Vermillion, one;
For the parish of Washington, one;
For the parish of Winn, one;
Total, one hundred and one.

And the State shall be divided into the following senatorial districts, to wit:

The first, second, and third representative districts of New Orleans shall form one senatorial district, and elect three senators;

The fourth, fifth, and six representative districts of New Orleans shall form one district, and elect two senators;

The seventh, eighth, and ninth representative districts of New Orleans and the parish of Saint Bernard shall form one district, and elect two senators;

The tenth representative district of New Orleans shall form one district, and elect one senator;

Orleans, right bank, and the parish of Plaquemines shall form one district, and elect one senator;

The parishes of Jefferson, Saint Charles, and Saint John Baptist shall form one district, and elect two senators;

The parishes of Ascension and Saint James shall form one district, and elect one senator;

The parishes of Assumption, La Fourche, and Terre Bonne shall form one district, and elect two senators;

The parishes of Vermillion and Saint Mary's shall form one district, and elect one senator;

The parishes of Calcasieu, La Fayette, and Saint Landry shall form one district, and elect two senators;

The parishes of Livingston, Saint Helena, Washington, and Saint Tammany shall form one district, and elect one senator;

The parishes of Point Coupee, East Feliciana, and West Feliciana shall form one district, and elect two senators;

The parish of East Baton Rouge shall form one district, and elect one senator;

The parishes of West Baton Rouge, Iberville, and Saint Martin's shall form one district, and elect two senators;

The parishes of Concordia and Avoyelles shall form one district, and elect one senator;

The parishes of Tensas and Franklin shall form one district, and elect one senator;

The parishes of Carroll, Madison, and Morehouse shall form one district, and elect two senators;

The parishes of Ouachita and Caldwell shall form one district, and elect one senator;

The parishes of Jackson and Union shall form one district, and elect one senator;

The parishes of Bossier, Bienville, and Claiborne shall form one district, and elect two senators;

The parish of Caddo shall form one district, and elect one senator;

The parishes of De Soto, Natchitoches, and Sabine shall form one district, and elect two senators;

The parish of Rapides shall form one district, and elect one senator;

The parishes of Catahoula and Winn shall form one district, and elect one senator;

Thirty-six senators in all.

ART. 23. The house of representatives shall choose its speaker and other officers.

ART. 24. Electors in all cases, except treason, felony, or breach of the peace, shall be privileged from arrest during their attendance on, going to, and returning from elections.

ART. 25. At its first session under this constitution, the general assembly shall provide by law that the names and residence of all qualified electors shall be registered, in order to entitle them to vote; but the registry shall be free of cost to the elector.

ART. 26. No person shall be entitled to vote at any election held in this State, except in the parish of his residence, and at the election-precinct in which he is registered: *Provided*, That no voter, in removing from one parish to another, shall lose the right in the former until he has acquired it in the latter.

ART. 27. The members of the senate shall be elected for the term of four years; and, when assembled, the senate shall have the power to choose its own officers, except as hereinafter provided.

ART. 28. The general assembly shall divide the State into senatorial districts whenever it apportions representation in the house of representatives.

ART. 29. No parish shall be divided in the formation of a senatorial district, the parish of Orleans excepted; and whenever a new parish shall be created, it shall be attached to the senatorial district from which most of its territory is taken, or to another contiguous district, at the discretion of the general assembly; but shall not be attached to more than one district. The number of senators shall be thirty-six, and they shall be apportioned among the senatorial districts according to the total population of said districts.

ART. 30. In all apportionments of the senate, the total population of the State shall be divided by the number thirty-six, and the result produced by this division shall be the senatorial ratio entitling a senatorial district to a senator.

Single or contiguous parishes shall be formed into districts having a population the nearest possible to the number entitling a district to a senator; and if the apportionment to make a parish or district fall short of, or exceed the ratio, then a district may be formed having not more than two senators; but not otherwise. No new apportionment shall have the effect of abridging the term of service of any senator already elected at the time of making the apportionment. After an enumeration has been made, as directed in the twentieth article, the general assembly shall not pass any law till an apportionment of representation in both houses of the general assembly be made.

ART. 31. At the first session of the general assembly, after this constitution goes into effect, the senators shall be divided equally by lot into two classes; the seats of the senators of the first class to be vacated at the expiration of the term of the first house of representatives; those of the second class at the expiration of the term of the second house of representatives, so that one-half shall be chosen every two years successively. When a district shall have elected two senators, their respective terms of office shall be determined by lot between themselves.

ART. 32. The first election for senators shall be held at the same time with the election for representatives: and thereafter there shall be elections of senators at the same time with each general election of representatives, to fill the places of those senators whose term of office may have expired.

ART. 33. Not less than a majority of the members of each house of the general assembly shall form a quorum to transact business; but a smaller number may adjourn from day to day, and shall have full power to compel the attendance of absent members.

ART. 34. Each house of the general assembly shall judge of the qualifications, election, and returns of its members; but a contested election shall be determined in such manner as may be prescribed by law.

ART. 35. Each house of the general assembly may determine the rules of its proceedings, punish a member for disorderly conduct, and, with a concurrence of two-thirds, expel a member, but not a second time for the same offence.

ART. 36. Each house of the general assembly shall keep and publish weekly a journal of its proceedings; and the yeas and nays of the members on any question, at the desire of any two of them, shall be entered on the journal.

ART. 37. Each house may punish, by imprisonment, any person, not a member, for disrespect and disorderly behavior in its presence, or for obstructing any of its proceedings. Such imprisonment shall not exceed ten days for any one offence.

ART. 38. Neither house shall adjourn for more than three days, nor to any other place than that in which it may be sitting, during the sessions of the general assembly, without the consent of the other.

ART. 39. The members of the general assembly shall receive from the public treasury a compensation for their services, which shall be eight dollars per day during their attendance, going to, and returning from the sessions of their respective houses. This compensation may be increased or diminished by law, but no alteration shall take effect during the period of service of the members of the house of representatives by which such alteration shall have been made. No session shall extend beyond the period of sixty days, to date from its commencement, and any legislative action had after the expiration of said period of sixty days shall be null and void; but the first general assembly that shall convene after the adoption of this constitution may continue in session for one hundred and twenty days.

ART. 40. The members of the general assembly, in all cases except treason, felony, or breach of the peace, shall be privileged from arrest during their attendance at the sessions of their respective houses, and going to or returning from the same; and for any speech or debate in either house shall not be questioned in any other place.

Art. 41. No senator or representative, during the term for which he was elected, nor for one year thereafter, shall be appointed to any civil office of profit under this State which shall have been created, or the emoluments of which may have been increased, during the time such senator or representative was in office.

Art. 42. No bill shall have the force of a law until on three several days it be read in each house of the general assembly, and free discussion allowed thereon, unless four-fifths of the house where the bill is pending may deem it expedient to dispense with this rule.

Art. 43. All bills for raising revenue shall originate in the house of representatives; but the senate may propose amendments, as in other bills: *Provided*, It shall not introduce any matter under the color of an amendment which does not relate to raising revenue.

Art. 44. The general assembly shall regulate by whom and in what manner writs of election shall be issued to fill the vacancies which may occur in either branch thereof.

Art. 45. On the confirmation or rejection of the officers to be appointed by the governor, with the advice and consent of the senate, the vote shall be taken by yeas and nays, and the names of the senators voting for and against the appointments respectively shall be entered on the journals to be kept for the purpose, and made public on or before the end of each session.

Art. 46. Returns of all elections for members of the general assembly shall be made to the secretary of state.

Art. 47. In the year in which a regular election for a Senator of the United States is to take place, the members of the general assembly shall meet in the hall of the house of representatives, on the second Monday following the meeting of the general assembly, and proceed to said election.

Title III

EXECUTIVE DEPARTMENT

Art. 48. The supreme executive power of the State shall be vested in a chief magistrate, who shall be styled the governor of the State of Louisiana. He shall hold his office during the term of four years, and, together with the lieutenant-governor chosen for the same term, be elected as follows: The qualified electors for representatives shall vote for governor and lieutenant-governor at the time and place of voting for representatives. The returns of every election shall be sealed up and transmitted by the proper returning-officer to the secretary of state, who shall deliver them to the speaker of the house of representatives on the second day of the session of the general assembly then to be holden. The members of the general assembly shall meet in the house of representatives to examine and count the votes. The person having the greatest number of votes for governor shall be declared duly elected; but in case of a tie vote between two or more candidates, one of them shall immediately be chosen governor by joint vote of the members of the general assembly. The person having the greatest number of votes polled for lieutenant-governor shall be lieutenant-governor; but in case of a tie vote between two or more candidates, one of them shall be immediately chosen lieutenant-governor by joint vote of the members of the general assembly.

ART. 49. No person shall be eligible to the office of governor or lieutenant-governor who is not a citizen of the United States and a resident of this State two years next preceding his election.

ART. 50. The governor shall be ineligible for the succeeding four years after the expiration of the time for which he shall have been elected.

ART. 51. The governor shall enter on the discharge of his duties on the second Monday in January next ensuing his election, and shall continue in office until the Monday next succeeding the day that his successor shall be declared duly elected, and shall have taken the oath or affirmation required by the constitution.

ART. 52. No member of Congress, or any person holding office under the United States Government, shall be eligible to the office of governor or lieutenant-governor.

ART. 53. In case of impeachment of the governor, his removal from office, death, refusal or inability to qualify, or to discharge the powers and duties of his office, resignation, or absence from the State, the powers and duties of the office shall devolve upon the lieutenant-governor for the residue of the term, or until the governor absent or impeached shall return or be acquitted, or the disability be removed. The general assembly may provide by law for the case of removal, impeachment, death, resignation, disability, or refusal to qualify, of both the governor and the lieutenant-governor, declaring what officer shall act as governor; and such officer shall act accordingly, until the disability be removed, or for the remainder of the term.

ART. 54. The lieutenant-governor, or officer discharging the duties of governor, shall, during his administration, receive the same compensation to which the governor would have been entitled had he continued in office.

ART. 55. The lieutenant-governor shall, by virtue of his office, be president of the senate, but shall only vote when the senate is equally divided. Whenever he shall administer the government, or shall be unable to attend as president of the senate, the senators shall elect one of their own members as president of the senate for the time being.

ART. 56. The governor shall receive a salary of eight thousand dollars per annum, payable quarterly, on his own warrant.

ART. 57. The lieutenant-governor shall receive a salary of three thousand dollars per annum, payable quarterly, upon his own warrant.

ART. 58. The governor shall have power to grant reprieves for all offences against the State; and, except in cases of impeachment, shall, with the consent of the senate, have power to grant pardons, remit fines and forfeitures, after conviction. In cases of treason, he may grant reprieves until the end of the next session of the general assembly, in which the power of pardoning shall be vested. In cases when the punishment is not imprisonment at hard labor, the party upon being reprieved by the governor shall be released, if in actual custody, until final action by the senate.

ART. 59. He shall be commander-in-chief of the militia of this State, except when they shall be called into the service of the United States.

Art. 60. He shall nominate, and, by and with the advice and consent of the senate, appoint all officers whose offices are established by the constitution, and whose appointments are not herein otherwise provided for: *Provided, however,* That the general assembly shall have a right to prescribe the mode of appointment to all other offices established by law.

Art. 61. The governor shall have power to fill vacancies that may happen during the recess of the senate, by granting commissions, which shall expire at the end of the next session thereof, unless otherwise provided for in this constitution; but no person who has been nominated for office and rejected by the senate shall be appointed to the same office during the recess of the senate.

Art. 62. He may require information in writing from the officers in the executive department upon any subject relating to the duties of their respective offices.

Art. 63. He shall, from time to time, give the general assembly information respecting the situation of the State, and recommend to their consideration such measures as he may deem expedient.

Art. 64. He may, on extraordinary occasions, convene the general assembly at the seat of government, or at a different place if that should have become dangerous from an enemy or from epidemic; and, in case of disagreement between the two houses as to the time of adjournment, he may adjourn them to such time as he may think proper, not exceeding four months.

Art. 65. He shall take care that the laws be faithfully executed.

Art. 66. Every bill which shall have passed both houses shall be presented to the governor; if he approve, he shall sign it; if he do not, he shall return it, with his objections, to the house in which it originated, which shall enter the objections at large upon its journal, and proceed to reconsider it. If, after such reconsideration, two-thirds of all the members present in that house shall agree to pass the bill, it shall be sent, with the objections, to the other house, by which it shall likewise be reconsidered; and if approved by two-thirds of the members present in that house it shall be a law. But in such cases the vote of both houses shall be determined by yeas and nays, and the names of members voting for or against the bill shall be entered on the journal of each house respectively. If any bill shall not be returned by the governor within five days after it shall have been presented to him, it shall be a law in like manner as if he had signed it, unless the general assembly, by adjournment, prevent its return; in which case the said bill shall be returned on the first day of the meeting of the general assembly after the expiration of said five days, or be a law.

Art. 67. Every order, resolution, or vote, to which the concurrence of both houses may be necessary, except on a question of adjournment, shall be presented to the governor; and before it shall take effect be approved by him, or, being disapproved, shall be repassed by two-thirds of the members present.

Art. 68. There shall be a secretary of state, who shall hold his office during the term for which the governor shall have been elected. The records of the State shall be kept and preserved in the office of the secretary; he shall keep a fair register of the official acts and proceedings of the governor, and, when necessary, shall attest them; he shall, when required, lay the said register, and all papers, minutes, and vouchers relative to his office, before either house of the general assembly, and shall perform such other duties as may be enjoined on him by law.

ART. 69. There shall be a treasurer of the State, and an auditor of public accounts, who shall hold their respective offices during the term of four years. At the first election under this constitution the treasurer shall be elected for two years.

ART. 70. The secretary of state, treasurer, and auditor of public accounts shall be elected by the qualified electors of the State; and in case of any vacancy caused by the resignation, death, or absence of the secretary, treasurer, or auditor, the governor shall order an election to fill said vacancies: *Provided*, The unexpired term to be filled be more than twelve months. When otherwise, the governor shall appoint a person to perform the duties of the office thus vacant until the ensuing general election.

ART. 71. The treasurer and the auditor shall receive a salary of five thousand dollars per annum each. The secretary of state shall receive a salary of three thousand dollars per annum.

ART. 72. All commissions shall be in the name and by the authority of the State of Louisiana; and shall be sealed with the State seal, signed by the governor, and countersigned by the secretary of state.

TITLE IV

JUDICIARY DEPARTMENT

ART. 73. The judicial power shall be vested in a supreme court, in district courts, in parish courts, and in justices of the peace.

ART. 74. The supreme court, except in cases hereinafter provided, shall have appellate jurisdiction only; which jurisdiction shall extend to all cases when the matter in dispute shall exceed five hundred dollars; and to all cases in which the constitutionality or legality of any tax, toll, or impost of any kind or nature whatsoever, or any fine, forfeiture, or penalty imposed by a municipal corporation, shall be in contestation, whatever may be the amount thereof; and in such cases the appeal shall be direct from the court in which the case originated to the supreme court; and in criminal cases, on questions of law only, whenever the punishment of death or imprisonment at hard labor, or a fine exceeding three hundred dollars, is actually imposed.

ART. 75. The supreme court shall be composed of one chief justice and four associate justices, a majority of whom shall constitute a quorum. The chief justice shall receive a salary of seven thousand five hundred dollars, and each of the associate justices a salary of seven thousand dollars annually, payable quarterly on their own warrants. The chief justice and the associate justices shall be appointed by the governor, with the advice and consent of the senate, for the term of eight years. They shall be citizens of the United States, and shall have practised law for five years, the last three thereof next preceding their appointment in the State. The court shall appoint its own clerks, and may remove them at pleasure.

ART. 76. The supreme court shall hold its sessions in the city of

New Orleans, from the first Monday in the month of November to the end of the month of May. The general assembly shall have power to fix the sessions elsewhere during the rest of the year. Until otherwise provided, the sessions shall be held as heretofore.

ART. 77. The supreme court, and each of the judges thereof, shall have power to issue writs of *habeas corpus*, at the instance of persons in actual custody, in cases when they may have appellate jurisdiction.

ART. 78. No judgment shall be rendered by the supreme court without a concurrence of a majority composing the court. Whenever the majority cannot concur, in consequence of the recusation of any member of the court, the judges not recused shall have power to call upon any judge or judges of the district courts, whose duty it shall be, when so called upon, to preside in the place of the judge or judges recused, and to aid in determining the case.

ART. 79. All judges, by virtue of their office, shall be conservators of the peace throughout the State. The style of all process shall be "The State of Louisiana." All prosecutions shall be carried on in the name and by the authority of the State of Louisiana, and conclude "against the peace and dignity of the same."

ART. 80. The judges of all courts, whenever practicable, shall refer to the law in virtue of which every definitive judgment is rendered; but in all cases they shall adduce the reasons on which their judgment is founded.

ART. 81. The judges of all courts shall be liable to impeachment for crimes and misdemeanors. For any reasonable cause the governor shall remove any of them, on the address of two-thirds of the members elected to each house of the general assembly. In every such case the cause or causes for which such removal may be required shall be stated at length in the address and inserted in the journal of each house.

ART. 82. No duties or functions shall ever be attached by law to the supreme or district courts, or the several judges thereof, but such as are judicial; and the said judges are prohibited from receiving any fees of office, or other compensation than their salaries, for any official duties performed by them.

ART. 83. The general assembly shall divide the State into judicial districts, which shall remain unchanged for four years, and for each district court one judge, learned in the law, shall be elected for each district by a plurality of the qualified electors thereof. For each district there shall be one district court, except in the parish of Orleans, in which the general assembly may establish as many district courts as the public interests may require. Until otherwise provided, there shall be seven district courts for the parish of Orleans, with the following original jurisdiction: The first, exclusive criminal jurisdiction; the second, exclusive probate jurisdiction; the third, exclusive jurisdiction of appeals from justices of the peace; the fourth, fifth, sixth, and seventh district courts, exclusive jurisdiction in all civil cases, except probate, when the sum in contest is above one hundred dollars, exclusive of interest. These seven courts shall also have such further jurisdiction, not inconsistent herewith, as shall be conferred by law. The number of districts in the State shall not be less than twelve nor more than twenty. The clerks of the district courts shall be elected by the qualified electors of their respective parishes, and shall hold their office for four years.

ART. 84. Each of said judges shall receive a salary to be fixed by law, which shall not be increased or diminished during his term of office, and shall never be less than five thousand dollars. He must be a citizen of the United States, over the age of twenty-five years, and have resided in the State and practised law therein for the space of two years next preceding his election. The judges of the district courts shall hold their office for the term of four years.

ART. 85. The district courts shall have original jurisdiction in all civil cases when the amount in dispute exceeds five hundred dollars, exclusive of interest. In criminal cases their jurisdiction shall be unlimited. They shall have appellate jurisdiction in civil ordinary suits when the amount in dispute exceeds one hundred dollars, exclusive of interest.

ART. 86. For each parish court one judge shall be elected by the qualified electors of the parish. He shall hold his office for the term of two years. He shall receive a salary and fees to be provided by law. Until otherwise provided, each parish judge shall receive a salary of one thousand two hundred dollars per annum, and such fees as are established by law for clerks of district courts. He shall be a citizen of the United States and of this State.

ART. 87. The parish courts shall have concurrent jurisdiction with the justices of the peace in all cases when the amount in controversy is more than twenty-five dollars and less than one hundred dollars, exclusive of interest. They shall have exclusive original jurisdiction in ordinary suits in all cases when the amount in dispute exceeds one hundred dollars and does not exceed five hundred dollars, subject to an appeal to the district court in all cases when the amount in contestation exceeds one hundred dollars, exclusive of interest. All successions shall be opened and settled in the parish courts; and all suits in which a succession is either plaintiff or defendant may be brought either in the parish or district court, according to the amount involved. In criminal matters the parish courts shall have jurisdiction in all cases when the penalty is not necessarily imprisonment at hard labor or death, and when the accused shall waive trial by jury. They shall also have the power of committing-magistrates and such other jurisdiction as may be conferred on them by law. There shall be no trial by jury before the parish courts.

ART. 88. In all probate matters when the amount in dispute shall exceed five hundred dollars exclusive of interest, the appeal shall be directly from the parish to the supreme court.

ART. 89. The justices of the peace shall be elected by the electors of each parish, in the manner to be provided by the general assembly. They shall hold office for the term of two years, and their compensation shall be fixed by law. Their jurisdiction in civil cases shall not exceed one hundred dollars, exclusive of interest, subject to an appeal to the parish court in all cases when the amount in dispute shall exceed ten dollars, exclusive of interest. They shall have such criminal jurisdiction as shall be provided for by law.

ART. 90. In any case when the judge may be recused, and when he is not personally interested in the matters in contestation, he shall select a lawyer, having the qualifications required for a judge of his court, to try such cases. And when the judge is personally interested in the suit, he shall call upon the parish or district judge, as the case may be, to try the case.

Art. 91. The general assembly shall have power to vest in the parish judges the right to grant such orders and to do such acts as may be deemed necessary for the furtherance of the administration of justice, and in all cases the power thus granted shall be specified and determined.

Art. 92. There shall be an attorney-general for the State, who shall be elected by the qualified electors of the State at large. He shall receive a salary of five thousand dollars per annum, payable quarterly, on his own warrant, and shall hold his office for four years. There shall be a district attorney for each judicial district of the State, who shall be elected by the qualified electors of the judicial district. He shall receive a salary of fifteen hundred dollars, payable quarterly, on his own warrant, and shall hold his office for four years.

Art. 93. There shall be a sheriff and coroner elected by the qualified electors of each parish, except the parish of Orleans. In the parish of Orleans there shall be elected by the qualified electors of the parish at large one sheriff for the criminal court, who shall be the executive officer of said court, and shall have charge of the parish prison. There shall also be elected by the qualified electors of the parish at large one sheriff, who shall be the executive officer of the civil courts, and who shall perform all other duties heretofore devolving upon the sheriff of the parish of Orleans, except those herein delegated to the sheriff of the criminal court. The qualified electors of the city of New Orleans residing below the middle of Canal street shall elect one coroner for that district, and the qualified electors of the city of New Orleans residing above the middle of Canal street, together with those residing in that part of the parish known as Orleans, right bank, shall elect one coroner for that district. All of said officers shall hold their office for two years, and receive such fees of office as may be prescribed by law.

Art. 94. No judicial powers, except as committing-magistrates in criminal cases, shall be conferred on any officers other than those mentioned in this title, except such as may be necessary in towns and cties; and the judicial powers of such offices shall not extend further than the cognizances of cases arising under the police regulations of towns and cities in the State. In any case where such officers shall assume jurisdiction over other matters than those which may arise under police regulations, or under their jurisdiction as committing-magistrates, they shall be liable to an action of damages in favor of the party injured, or his heirs; and a verdict in favor of the party injured shall, *ipso facto*, operate a vacation of the office of said officer.

Title V

IMPEACHMENT

Art. 95. The power of impeachment shall be vested in the house of representatives.

Art. 96. Impeachments of the governor, lieutenant-governor, attorney-general, secretary of state, auditor of public accounts, State treasurer, superintendent of public education, and of the judges of the inferior courts, justices of the peace excepted, shall be tried by the senate; the chief-justice of the supreme court, or the senior associate judge thereof, shall preside during the trial of such impeachments.

Impeachments of the judges of the supreme court shall be tried by the senate. When sitting as a court of impeachment, the senators shall be upon oath or affirmation, and no person shall be convicted without the concurrence of two-thirds of the senators present.

ART. 97. Judgments in cases of impeachments shall extend only to removal from office, and disqualification from holding any office of honor, trust, or profit in the State; but the convicted parties shall, nevertheless, be subject to indictment, trial, and punishment, according to law.

Title VI

GENERAL PROVISIONS

ART. 98. Every male person of the age of twenty-one years or upward, born or naturalized in the United States, and subject to the jurisdiction thereof, and a resident of this State one year next preceding an election, and the last ten days within the parish in which he offers to vote, shall be deemed an elector, except those disfranchised by this constitution, and persons under interdiction.

ART. 99. The following persons shall be prohibited from voting and holding any office: All persons who shall have been convicted of treason, perjury, forgery, bribery, or other crime punishable in the penitentiary, and persons under interdiction. All persons who are estopped from claiming the right of suffrage by abjuring their allegiance to the United States Government, or by notoriously levying war against it, or adhering to its enemies, giving them aid or comfort, but who have not expatriated themselves, nor have been convicted of any of the crimes mentioned in the first paragraph of this article, are hereby restored to the said right, except the following: Those who held office, civil or military, for one year or more, under the organization styled "the Confederate States of America;" those who registered themselves as enemies of the United States; those who acted as leaders of guerrilla bands during the late rebellion; those who, in the advocacy of treason, wrote or published newspaper articles or preached sermons during the late rebellion; and those who voted for and signed an ordinance of secession in any State. No person included in these exceptions shall either vote or hold office until he shall have relieved himself by voluntarily writing and signing a certificate setting forth that he acknowledges the late rebellion to have been morally and politically wrong, and that he regrets any aid and comfort he may have given it; and he shall file the certificate in the office of the secretary of state, and it shall be published in the official journal: *Provided*, That no person who, prior to the first of January, eighteen hundred and sixty-eight, favored the execution of the laws of the United States popularly known as the reconstruction acts of Congress, and openly and actively assisted the loyal men of the State in their efforts to restore Louisiana to her position in the Union, shall be held to be included among those herein excepted. Registrars of voters shall take the oath of any such person as *prima-facie* evidence of the fact that he is entitled to the benefit of this proviso.

ART. 100. Members of the general assembly and all other officers, before they enter upon the duties of their offices, shall take the following oath or affirmation: " I, [A. B.,] do solemnly swear [or affirm] that I accept the civil and political equality of all men, and agree not to attempt to deprive any person or persons, on account of race, color, or previous condition, of any political or civil right, privilege, or immunity enjoyed by any other class of men; that I will support the Constitution and laws of the United States, and the constitution and laws of this State, and that I will faithfully and impartially discharge and perform all the duties incumbent on me as ———, according to the best of my ability and understanding: So help me God."

ART. 101. Treason against the State shall consist only in levying war against it or in adhering to its enemies, giving them aid and comfort. No person shall be convicted of treason except on the testimony of two witnesses to the same overt act, or on his confession in open court.

ART. 102. All penalties shall be proportioned to the nature of the offence.

ART. 103. The privilege of free suffrage shall be supported by laws regulating elections and prohibiting under adequate penalties all undue influence thereon from power, bribery, tumult, or other improper practice.

ART. 104. No money shall be drawn from the treasury but in pursuance of specific appropriations made by law. A statement and account of receipts and expenditures of all public moneys shall be made annually in such manner as shall be prescribed by law; and the first general assembly convening under this constitution shall make a special appropriation to liquidate whatever portion of the debt of this convention may at that time remain unpaid or unprovided for.

ART. 105. All civil officers of the State at large shall be voters of and reside within the State; and all district or parish officers shall reside within their respective districts or parishes, and shall keep their offices at such place therein as may be required by law.

ART. 106. All civil officers shall be removable by an address of two-thirds of the members-elect to each house of the general assembly, except those whose removal is otherwise provided for by this constitution.

ART. 107. In all elections by the people the vote shall be taken by ballot; and in all elections by the senate and house of representatives, jointly or separately, the vote shall be given *viva voce*.

ART. 108. None but citizens of the United States and of this State shall be appointed to any office of trust or profit in this State.

ART. 109. The laws, public records, and the judicial and legislative proceedings of the State shall be promulgated and preserved in the English language; and no laws shall require judicial process to be issued in any other than the English language.

ART. 110. No *ex post facto* or retroactive law, nor any law impairing the obligation of contracts, shall be passed, nor vested rights be divested, unless for purposes of public utility and for adequate compensation made.

ART. 111. Whenever the general assembly shall contract a debt exceeding in amount the sum of one hundred thousand dollars, unless, in case of war, to repel invasion or suppress insurrection, it shall, in the law creating the debt, provide adequate ways and means for the payment of the current interest and of the principal when the same shall become due; and the said law shall be irrepealable until principal and interest be fully paid; or unless the repealing law contain some adequate provision for the payment of the principal and interest of the debt.

ART. 112. The general assembly shall provide by law for all change of venue in civil and criminal cases.

ART. 113. The general assembly may enact general laws regulating the adoption of children, emancipation of minors, and the granting of divorces; but no special law shall be passed relating to particular or individual cases.

ART. 114. Every law shall express its object or objects in its title.

ART. 115. No law shall be revived or amended by reference to its title; but in such case the revived or amended section shall be re-enacted and published at length.

ART. 116. The general assembly shall never adopt any system or code of laws by general reference to such system or code of laws; but in all cases shall specify the several provisions of the law it may enact.

ART. 117. No person shall hold or exercise at the same time more than one office of trust or profit, except that of justice of the peace or notary public.

ART. 118. Taxation shall be equal and uniform throughout the State. All property shall be taxed in proportion to its value, to be ascertained as directed by law. The general assembly shall have power to exempt from taxation property actually used for church, school, or charitable purposes. The general assembly may levy an income-tax upon all persons pursuing any occupation, trade, or calling. And all such persons shall obtain a license as provided by law. All tax on income shall be *pro rata* on the amount of income or business done. And all deeds of sale made, or that may be made, by collectors of taxes shall be received by courts in evidence as *prima facie* valid sales. The general assembly shall levy a poll-tax on all male inhabitants of this State, over twenty-one years old, for school and charitable purposes, which tax shall never exceed one dollar and fifty cents per annum.

ART. 119. No liability, either State, parochial, or municipal, shall exist for any debts contracted for or in the interest of the rebellion against the United States Government.

ART. 120. The general assembly may determine the mode of filling vacancies in all offices for which provision is not made in this constitution.

ART. 121. The general assembly shall pass no law requiring a property qualification for office.

ART. 122. All officers shall continue to discharge the duties of their offices until their successors shall have been inducted into office, except in cases of impeachment or suspension.

ART. 123. The general assembly shall provide for the protection of the rights of married women to their dotal and paraphernal property, and for the registration of the same; but no mortgage or privilege shall hereafter affect third parties, unless recorded in the parish where the property to be affected is situated. The tacit mortgages and privileges now existing in this State shall cease to have effect against third persons after the 1st day of January, 1870, unless duly recorded. The general assembly shall provide by law for the registration of all mortgages and privileges.

ART. 124. The general assembly, at its first session under this constitution, shall provide an annual pension for the veterans of 1814 and 1815, residing in the State.

ART. 125. The military shall be in subordination to the civil power.

ART. 126. It shall be the duty of the general assembly to make it obligatory upon each parish to support all paupers residing within its limits.

ART. 127. All agreements, the consideration of which was confederate money, notes, or bonds, are null and void, and shall not be enforced by the courts of this State.

ART. 128. Contracts for the sale of persons are null and void, and shall not be enforced by the courts of this State.

ART. 129. The State of Louisiana shall never assume nor pay any debt or obligation contracted or incurred in aid of the rebellion; nor shall this State ever, in any manner, claim from the United States, or make any allowance or compensation for slaves emancipated or liberated in any way whatever.

ART. 130. All contracts made and entered into under the pretended authority of any government heretofore existing in this State, by which children were bound out without the knowledge or consent of their parents, are hereby declared null and void; nor shall any child be bound out to any one for any term of years, while either one of its parents live, without the consent of such parent, except in cases of children legally sent to the house of correction.

ART. 131. The seat of government shall be established at the city of New Orleans, and shall not be removed without the consent of two-thirds of the members of both houses of the general assembly.

ART. 132. All lands sold in pursuance of decrees of courts shall be divided into tracts of from ten to fifty acres.

ART. 133. No judicial powers shall be exercised by clerks of courts.

ART. 134. No soldier, sailor, or marine, in the military or naval service of the United States, shall hereafter acquire a residence in this State by reason of being stationed or doing duty in the same.

Title VII

PUBLIC EDUCATION

ART. 135. The general assembly shall establish at least one free public school in every parish throughout the State, and shall provide for its support by taxation or otherwise. All children of this State between the years of six and twenty-one shall be admitted to the public schools or other institutions of learning sustained or established by the State in common, without distinction of race, color, or previous condition. There shall be no separate schools or institutions of learning established exclusively for any race by the State of Louisiana.

ART. 136. No municipal corporation shall make any rules or regulations contrary to the spirit and intention of article 135.

ART. 137. There shall be elected by the qualified voters of this State a superintendent of public education, who shall hold his office for four years. His duties shall be prescribed by law, and he shall have the supervision and the general control of all public schools throughout the State. He shall receive a salary of five thousand dollars per annum, payable quarterly, on his own warrant.

ART. 138. The general exercises in the public schools shall be conducted in the English language.

ART. 139. The proceeds of all lands heretofore granted by the United States for the use and support of public schools, and of all lands or other property which may hereafter be bequeathed for that purpose, and of all lands which may be granted or bequeathed to the State, and not granted or bequeathed expressly for any other purpose, which may hereafter be disposed of by the State, and the proceeds of all estates of deceased persons to which the State may be entitled by law, shall be held by the State as a loan, and shall be and remain a perpetual fund, on which the State shall pay an annual interest of 6 per cent., which interest, with the interest of the trust-fund deposited with this State by the United States under the act of Congress approved June the twenty-third, eighteen hundred and thirty-six, and the rent of the unsold land, shall be appropriated to the support of such schools; and this appropriation shall remain inviolable.

ART. 140. No appropriation shall be made by the general assembly for the support of any private school or any private institution of learning whatever.

ART. 141. One-half of the funds derived from the poll-tax herein provided for shall be appropriated exclusively to the support of the free public schools throughout the State and the University of New Orleans.

ART. 142. A university shall be established and maintained in the city of New Orleans. It shall be composed of a law, a medical, and a collegiate department, each with appropriate faculties. The general assembly shall provide by law for its organization and maintenance: *Provided*, That all departments of this institution of learning shall be open in common to all students capable of matriculating. No rules or regulations shall be made by the trustees, faculties, or other officers of said institution of learning, nor shall any laws be made by the general assembly violating the letter or spirit of the articles under this title.

ART. 143. Institutions for the support of the insane, the education and support of the blind and the deaf and dumb, shall always be fostered by the State, and be subject to such regulations as may be prescribed by the general assembly.

Title VIII

MILITIA

ART. 144. It shall be the duty of the general assembly to organize the militia of the State; and all able-bodied male citizens, between the ages of eighteen and forty-five years, not disfranchised by the laws of the United States and of this State, shall be subject to military duty.

ART. 145. The governor shall appoint all commissioned officers, subject to confirmation or rejection by the senate, except the staff-officers, who shall be appointed by their respective chiefs, and commissioned by the governor. All militia officers shall take and subscribe to the oath prescribed for officers of the United States Army and the oath prescribed for officers in this State.

ART. 146. The governor shall have power to call the militia into active service for the preservation of law and order, or when the public safety may require it. The militia, when in active service, shall receive the same pay and allowances, as officers and privates, as is received by officers and privates in the United States Army.

TITLE IX

MODE OF REVISING THE CONSTITUTION

ART. 147. Any amendment or amendments to this constitution may be proposed in the senate or house of representatives, and if the same shall be agreed to by two-thirds of the members elected to each house, such proposed amendment or amendments shall be entered on their respective journals, with the yeas and nays taken thereon; and the secretary of state shall cause the same to be published three months before the next general election for representatives to the general assembly, in at least one newspaper in every parish of the State in which a newspaper shall be published. And such proposed amendment or amendments shall be submitted to the people at said election; and if a majority of the voters at said election shall approve and ratify such amendment or amendments, the same shall become a part of this constitution. If more than one amendment shall be submitted at one time, they shall be submitted in such manner and form that the people may vote for or against each amendment separately.

TITLE X

SCHEDULE

ART. 148. The ordinance of secession of the State of Louisiana, passed 26th of January, 1861, is hereby declared to be null and void. The constitution adopted in 1864, and all previous constitutions in the State of Louisiana, are declared to be superseded by this constitution.

ART. 149. All rights, actions, prosecutions, claims, contracts, and all laws in force at the time of the adoption of this constitution, and not inconsistent therewith, shall continue as if it had not been adopted; all judgments and judicial sales, marriages, and executed contracts, made in good faith and in accordance with existing laws in this State, rendered, made, or entered into, between the 26th day of January, 1861, and the date when this constitution shall be adopted, are hereby declared to be valid, except the following laws:

An act to authorize the widening of the new canal and basin, approved March 14, 1867.

An act to amend and re-enact the 121st section of an act entitled " An act relative to crimes and offences," approved December 20, 1865.

An act for the punishment of persons for tampering with, persuading, or enticing away, harboring, feeding, or secreting laborers, servants, or apprentices, approved December 21, 1865.

An act to punish, in certain cases, the employers of laborers and apprentices, approved December 21, 1865.

An act in relation to exemption from State, parish, and city taxes, for the years 1862, 1863, 1864, and 1865, in certain cases, certified March 16, 1866.

An act granting ferry privileges to C. K. Marshall, his heirs or assigns, approved March 10, 1866.

An act to authorize the board of levee commissioners, of the levee district in the parishes of Madison and Carroll, to issue bonds, &c., approved March 28, 1867.

Section third of An act to organize the police of New Orleans, and to create a police-board therein, approved February 12, 1866.

ART. 150. The laws relative to the duties of officers shall remain in force, though contrary to this constitution, and the several duties be performed by the respective officers, until the organization of the government under this constitution.

ART. 151. The general assembly shall provide for the removal of causes now pending in the courts of this State to courts created by or under this constitution.

Title XI

ORDINANCE

ART. 152. Immediately upon the adjournment of this convention this constitution shall be submitted for ratification to the registered voters of the State, in conformity to the act of Congress passed March 2, 1867, entitled "An act to provide for the more efficient government of the rebel States," and the acts supplementary thereto.

ART. 153. The election for the ratification of the constitution shall be held on Friday and Saturday, the 17th and 18th days of April, 1868, at the places now prescribed by law; and the polls shall be kept open from 7 o'clock a. m. to 7 o'clock p. m. At that election all those in favor of ratifying the constitution shall have written or printed on their ballots " For the constitution;" and those opposed to ratifying the constitution shall have written or printed on their ballots "Against the constitution."

ART. 154. In order to establish a civil government, as required by act of Congress passed March 23, 1867, an election shall be held, at the same time and place at which the constitution is submitted for ratification, for all State, judicial, parish, and municipal officers, for members of the general assembly, and for congressional Representatives, at which election the electors who are qualified under the reconstruction acts of Congress shall vote, and none others: *Provided*, That any elector shall be eligible to any office under any municipal corporation in this State.

ART. 155. At the election for the ratification of the constitution, and for officers of the civil government, as required by Congress, all registered electors may vote in any parish where they have resided for ten days next preceding said election, and at any precinct in the parish, upon presentation of their certificates of registration, affidavit, or other satisfactory evidence that they are entitled to vote as registered electors.

ART. 156. The same registrars and commissioners who shall be appointed by the commanding general of the fifth military district to superintend the election for the ratification or rejection of the constitution, shall also, at the same time and place, superintend the election for all officers and representatives herein ordered: *Provided*, They be authorized so to act by the commanding general. And in case the commanding general should not so authorize said registrars and commissioners, the committee of seven, appointed by this convention to take charge of the whole matter of the ratification of the constitution and the election of civil officers, shall appoint one registrar for each parish in the State, except the parish of Orleans, and one in each district of the parish of Orleans, counting Orleans, right bank, as one district, who shall, each in his parish or district, appoint a sufficient number of commissioners of election to hold the said election for said civil officers and representatives at the same time and place as herein provided for.

ART. 157. Returns shall be made in duplicate, sworn to by the commissioners holding the election, and forwarded within three days thereafter, to the registrars of the parish or district. The registrars shall immediately forward one copy of said returns to the chairman of the committee of seven appointed by this convention, who shall, within ten days after the last return has been received, make proclamation of the result of said election.

ART. 158. All civil officers thus elected shall enter upon the discharge of their duties on the second Monday after the return of their election shall have been officially promulgated, or as soon as qualified according to law, and shall continue in office for the terms of their respective offices herein prescribed, said terms to date from the first Monday in November following the election.

ART. 159. The general assembly elected under this constitution shall hold its first session in the city of New Orleans on the third Monday after the official promulgation aforesaid, and proceed immediately upon its organization to vote upon the adoption of the fourteenth amendment to the Constitution of the United States, proposed by Congress, and passed June 13, 1866. Said general assembly shall not have power to enact any laws relative to the per diem of members, or any other subject, after organization, until said constitutional amendment shall have been acted upon.

ART. 160. All registrars and commissioners appointed under this constitution shall, before entering upon their duties, take and subscribe the oath of office prescribed by Congress, approved July second, eighteen hundred and sixty-two, entitled "An act to prescribe an oath of office;" the said oath of office shall be administered to each registrar by the chairman of the committee of seven and to each commissioner by the registrar appointing him.

ART. 161. All registrars, commissioners, and other officers, necessary to carry into effect the provisions of this ordinance, except as otherwise provided for by the reconstruction acts of Congress, shall be paid out of any funds raised by virtue of the tax ordinance adopted by the convention December twenty-fourth, eighteen hundred and sixty-seven, not otherwise appropriated.

JAMES G. TALIAFERRO, *President.*
WM. VIGERS, *Secretary.*

AMENDMENTS TO CONSTITUTION OF 1868

(Ratified 1870)

TITLE II. ART. 17. Strike out the words " first Monday " and insert the words " first Tuesday after the first Monday."

TITLE VI. ART. 99. No person shall hold any office, or shall be permitted to vote at any election, or to act as a juror who, in due course of law, shall have been convicted of treason, perjury, forgery, bribery, or other crime, punishable by imprisonment in the penitentiary, or who shall have been under interdiction.

SEC. 1. That no person who, at any time, may have been a collector of taxes, whether State, parish, or municipal, or who may have been otherwise intrusted with public money, shall be eligible to the General Assembly, or to any office of profit or trust under the State government, until he shall have obtained a discharge for the amount of such collections, and for all public moneys with which he may have been intrusted.

SEC. 2. That prior to the first day of January, 1890, the debt of the State shall not be so increased as to exceed twenty-five millions of dollars.

(Ratified 1874)

ART. [162]. SEC. 1. The issue of consolidated bonds authorized by the General Assembly of the State, at its regular session in the year 1874, is hereby declared to create a valid contract between the State and each and every holder of said bonds, which the State shall by no means and in no wise impair. The said bonds shall be a valid obligation of the State in favor of any holder thereof, and no court shall enjoin the payment of the principal or interest thereof, or the levy and collection of the tax therefor; to secure such levy, collection, and payment the judicial power shall be exercised when necessary. The tax required for the payment of the principal and interest of said bonds shall be assessed and collected each and every year until the bonds shall be paid, principal and interest, and the proceeds shall be paid by the treasurer of the State to the holders of said bonds as the principal and interest of the same shall fall due, and no further legislation or appropriation shall be requisite for the said assessment and collection and for such payment from the treasury.

SEC. 2. Whenever the debt of the State shall have been reduced below twenty-five million dollars, the constitutional limit shall remain at the lowest point reached, beyond which the public debt shall not thereafter be increased; and this rule continue in operation until the debt is reduced to fifteen million dollars, beyond which it shall not be increased. Nor shall taxation for all State purposes, excepting the support of public schools, ever exceed twelve and a half mills on the dollar of the assessed valuation of the real and personal property in the State, except in case of war or invasion.

SEC. 3. The revenue of each year derived from taxation upon real, personal, and mixed property, or from licenses, shall be devoted solely to the expenses of the said year for which it shall be raised, excepting any surplus remain, which shall be directed to sinking the public debt. All appropriations and claims in excess of revenue shall be null and void, and the State shall in no manner provide for their payment.

ART. [163]. The city of New Orleans shall not hereafter increase her debt in any manner or form or under any pretext. After the first day of January, 1875, no evidence of indebtedness or warrant for payment of money shall be issued by any officer of said city, except against cash actually in the treasury; but this shall not be so construed as to prevent a renewal of matured bonds at par, or the issue of new bonds in exchange for other bonds, provided the city debt be not thereby increased, nor to prevent the issue of drainage warrants to the transferee of contract, under act No. 30, of 1871, payable only from drainage taxes, and not otherwise; any person violating the prohibitions [provisions] of this article shall, on conviction, be by imprisonment for not less   two nor more than ten years, and by fine of not less than three dollars nor more than ten thousand dollars.

CONSTITUTION OF LOUISIANA—1879 * [a]

PREAMBLE

We, the people of the State of Louisiana, in order to establish justice, insure domestic tranquility, promote the general welfare, and secure the blessings of liberty to ourselves and our posterity, acknowledging and invoking the guidance of Almighty God, the author of all good government, do ordain and establish this constitution.

BILL OF RIGHTS

ARTICLE 1. All government of right originates with the people, is founded on their will alone, and is instituted solely for the good of the whole, deriving its just powers from the consent of the governed. Its only legitimate end is to protect the citizen in the enjoyment of life, liberty and property. When it assumes other functions it is usurpation and oppression.

ART. 2. The right of the people to be secure in their persons, houses, papers and effects against unreasonable searches and seizures shall not be violated, and no warrant shall issue except upon probable cause, supported by oath or affirmation, and particularly describing the place to be searched and the person or things to be seized.

ART. 3. A well regulated militia being necessary to the security of a free State, the right of the people to keep and bear arms shall not be abridged. This shall not prevent the passage of laws to punish those who carry weapons concealed.

ART. 4. No laws shall be passed respecting an establishment of religion or prohibiting the free exercise thereof, or abridging the freedom of speech, or of the press, or the right of the people peaceably to assemble and petition the government for a redress of grievances.

ART. 5. There shall be neither slavery nor involuntary servitude in this State otherwise than for the punishment of crime, whereof the party shall have been duly convicted. Prosecutions shall be by indictment or information; *provided*, that no person shall be held to answer for a capital crime unless on a presentment or indictment by a grand jury, except in cases arising in the militia when in actual service in time of war or public danger, nor shall any person be twice put in jeopardy of life or liberty for the same offense, except on his own

---

* Constitution of the State of Louisiana Adopted in Convention at the City of New Orleans the twenty-third day of July, A. D., 1879. Baton Rouge: The Advocate, Official Journal of the State of Louisiana, 1894.

" Official Journal of the Proceedings of the Constitutional Convention of the State of Louisiana, held in New Orleans, Monday, April 21, 1879. By Authority. New Orleans: Printed by Jas. H. Cosgrove, Convention Printer, 1879." pp. 337. ap. pp. 156.

[a] This Constitution was framed by a Convention which met April 21, 1879, and adjourned July 23, 1879. It was submitted to the people and adopted.

application for a new trial, or where there is a mistrial, or a motion in arrest of judgment is sustained.

ART. 6. No person shall be compelled to give evidence against himself in a criminal case or in any proceedings that may subject him to criminal prosecution, except where otherwise provided in this constitution, nor be deprived of life, liberty or property without due process of law.

ART. 7. In all criminal prosecutions the accused shall enjoy the right to a speedy public trial by an impartial jury, except that, in cases where the penalty is not necessarily imprisonment at hard labor or death, the General Assembly may provide for the trial thereof by a jury, less than twelve in number; *provided*, that the accused in every instance shall be tried in the parish wherein the offense shall have been committed, except in cases of change of venue.

ART. 8. In all criminal prosecutions the accused shall enjoy the right to be informed of the nature and cause of the accusation, to be confronted with the witnesses against him, to have compulsory process for obtaining witnesses in his favor, and to defend himself, and to have the assistance of counsel and to have the right to challenge jurors peremptorily, the number of challenges to be fixed by statute.

ART. 9. Excessive bail shall not be required, nor excessive fines be imposed, nor cruel and unusual punishments inflicted. All persons shall be bailable by sufficient sureties, unless for capital offenses where the proof is evident or the presumption great; or unless after conviction for any crime or offense punishable with death or imprisonment at hard labor.

ART. 10. The privilege of the writ of *habeas corpus* shall not be suspended, unless when in case of rebellion or invasion the public safety may require it.

ART. 11. All courts shall be open, and every person for injury done him in his rights, lands, goods, person or reputation shall have adequate remedy by due process of law and justice administered without denial or unreasonable delay.

ART. 12. The military shall be in subordination to the civil power.

ART. 13. This enumeration of rights shall not be construed to deny or impair other rights of the people not herein expressed.

DISTRIBUTION OF POWERS

ART. 14. The powers of the government of the State of Louisiana shall be divided into three distinct departments, and each of them be confided to a separate body of magistracy, to-wit: Those which are legislative to one, those which are executive to another, and those which are judicial to another.

ART. 15. No one of these departments, nor any person or collection of persons holding office in one of them, shall exercise power properly belonging to either of the others, except in the instances hereinafter expressly directed or permitted.

APPORTIONMENT

ART. 16. Representation in the House of Representatives shall be equal and uniform, and shall be regulated and ascertained by the total population. Each parish shall have at least one Representative. The first enumeration to be made by the State authorities under this Constitution, shall be made in the year eighteen hundred and ninety, and subsequent enumerations shall be made every tenth year thereafter, in such manner as shall be prescribed by law, for the purpose of ascertaining the total population and the number of qualified electors in each parish and election district. At its first regular session after each enumeration, the General Assembly shall apportion the representation among the several parishes and election districts on the basis of the total population as aforesaid. A representative number shall be fixed, and each parish and election district shall have as many Representatives as the aggregate number of its population will entitle it to, and an additional Representative for any fraction exceeding one-half the representative number. The number of Representatives shall not be more than ninety-eight, nor less than seventy.

ART. 17. The General Assembly, in every year in which they shall apportion representation in the House of Representatives, shall divide the State into senatorial districts. No parish shall be divided in the formation of a senatorial district, the parish of Orleans excepted. Whenever a new parish shall be created, it shall be attached to the senatorial district from which most of its territory was taken, or to another contiguous district, at the discretion of the General Assembly, but shall not be attached to more than one district. The number of Senators shall not be more than thirty-six nor less than twenty-four, and they shall be apportioned among the senatorial districts according to the total population contained in the several districts.

ART. 18. Until an enumeration shall be made in accordance with Articles 16 and 17, the State shall be divided into the following senatorial districts, with the number of Senators hereinafter designated to each district:

The First Senatorial District shall be composed of the eighth and ninth wards of Orleans, and of the parishes of St. Bernard and Plaquemines, and shall elect two Senators.

The Second District shall be composed of the fourth, fifth, sixth and seventh wards of Orleans, and shall elect two Senators.

The Third District shall be composed of the third ward of Orleans, and shall elect one Senator.

The Fourth District shall be composed of the second and fifteenth wards (Orleans, right bank) of Orleans, and shall elect one Senator.

The Fifth District shall be composed of the first and tenth wards of Orleans, and shall elect one Senator.

The Sixth District shall be composed of the eleventh, twelfth, thirteenth, fourteenth, sixteenth and seventeenth wards of Orleans, and shall elect two Senators.

The Seventh District shall be composed of the parishes of Jefferson, St. Charles and St. John the Baptist, and shall elect one Senator.

The Eighth District shall be composed of the parishes of St. James and Ascension, and shall elect one Senator.

The ninth District shall be composed of the parishes of Terreborne, Lafourche and Assumption, and shall elect two Senators.

The Tenth District shall be composed of the parishes of St. Mary, Vermilion, Cameron and Calcasieu and shall elect two Senators.

The Eleventh District shall be composed of the parishes of St. Martin, Iberia and Lafayette, and shall elect one Senator.

The Twelfth District shall be composed of the parishes of St. Landry, and shall elect two Senators.

The Thirteenth District shall be composed of the parishes of Avoyelles and Pointe Coupee, and shall elect one Senator.

The Fourteenth District shall be composed of the parishes of Iberville and West Baton Rouge, and shall elect one Senator.

The Fifteenth District shall be composed of the parishes of East and West Feliciana, and shall elect one Senator.

The Sixteenth District shall be composed of the parish of East Baton Rouge, and shall elect one Senator.

The Seventeenth District shall be composed of the parishes of St. Helena, Livingston, Tangipahoa, Washington and St. Tammany and shall elect one Senator.

The Eighteenth District shall be composed of the parishes of Rapides and Vernon, and shall elect one Senator.

The Nineteenth District shall be composed of the parishes of Nachitoches, Sabine, De Soto and Red River, and shall elect two Senators.

The Twentieth District shall be composed of the parish of Caddo, and shall elect one Senator.

The Twenty-First District shall be composed of the parishes of Bossier, Webster, Bienville and Claiborne, and shall elect two Senators.

The Twenty-Second District shall be composed of the parishes of Union, Morehouse, Lincoln and West Carroll, and shall elect two Senators.

The Twenty-Third District shall be composed of the parishes of Ouachita, Richland, Caldwell, Franklin and Jackson, and shall elect two Senators.

The Twenty-Fourth District shall be composed of the parishes of Catahoula, Winn and Grant, and shall elect one Senator.

The Twenty-Fifth District shall be composed of the parishes of East Carroll and Madison, and shall elect one Senator.

The Twenty-Sixth District shall be composed of the parishes of Tensas and Concordia, and shall elect one Senator.

Thirty-Six (36) Senators in all.

And the Representatives shall be apportioned among the parishes and representative districts as follows:

For the parish of Orleans—

First Representative District, first ward, one Representative.

Second Representative District, second ward, two Representatives.

Third Representative District, third ward, three Representatives.

Fourth Representative District, fourth ward, one Representative.

Fifth Representative District, fifth ward, two Representatives.

Sixth Representative District, sixth ward, one Representative.

Seventh Representative District, seventh ward, two Representatives.

Eighth Representative District, eighth ward, one Representative.

Ninth Representative District, ninth ward, two Representatives.

Tenth Representative District, tenth ward, two Representatives.

Eleventh Representative District, eleventh ward, two Representatives.

Twelfth Representative District, twelfth ward, one Representative.

Thirteenth Representative District, thirteenth and fourteenth wards, one Representative.

Fourteenth Representative District, sixteenth and seventeenth wards, one Representative.

Fifteenth Representative District, fifteenth ward, one Representative.

The parishes of Ascension, West Baton Rouge, Bienville, Bossier, Calcasieu, Caldwell, Cameron, East Carroll, West Carroll, Catahoula, Concordia, West Feliciana, Franklin, Grant, Iberia, Jackson, Jefferson, Lafayette, Lincoln, Livingston, Morehouse, Ouachita, Plaquemine, Pointe Coupee, Red River, Richland, Sabine, St. Bernard, St. Charles, St. Helena, St. James, St. John the Baptist, St. Martin, St. Tammany, Tangipahoa, Union, Vermilion, Vernon, Washington, Webster and Winn, each one Representative.

The parishes of Assumption, Avoyelles, East Baton Rouge, Caddo, Claiborne, De Soto, East Feliciana, Iberville, Lafourche, Madison, Natchitoches, Rapides, St. Mary, Tensas and Terrebonne, each two Representatives.

The parish of St. Landry four Representatives.

This apportionment of Senators and Representatives shall not be changed or altered in any manner until after the enumeration shall have been taken by the State in eighteen hundred and ninety, in accordance with the provisions of articles 16 and 17.

GENERAL ASSEMBLY

ART. 19. The legislative power of the State shall be vested in a General Assembly, which shall consist of a Senate and House of Representatives.

ART. 20. The style of the laws of this State shall be: " Be it enacted by the General Assembly of the State of Louisiana."

ART. 21. The General Assembly shall meet at the seat of government on the second Monday of May, 1882, at 12 o'clock noon, and biennially thereafter. Its first session under this constitution may extend to a period of ninety days, but any subsequent session shall be limited to a period of sixty days. Should a vacancy occur in either house, the Governor shall order an election to fill such vacancy for the remainder of the term.

ART. 22. Every elector under this constitution shall be eligible to a seat in the House of Representatives, and every elector who has reached the age of twenty-five years shall be eligible to the Senate; *provided*, that no person shall be eligible to the General Assembly unless at the time of his election he has been a citizen of the State for five years and an actual resident of the district or parish from which he may be elected for two years immediately preceding his election. The seat of any member who may change his residence from the district or parish which he represents, shall thereby be vacated, any declaration of a retention of domicile to the contrary notwithstanding; and members of the General Assembly shall be elected for a term of four years.

ART. 23. Each house shall judge of the qualifications, election and returns of its own members, choose its own officers (except President of the Senate), determine the rules of its proceedings and may punish its members for disorderly conduct and contempt, and, with the concurrence of two-thirds of all its members elected, expel a member.

ART. 24. Either house, during the session, may punish by imprisonment any person not a member, who shall have been guilty of disrespect by disorderly or contemptuous behavior; but such imprisonment shall not exceed ten days for each offense.

ART. 25. No Senator or Representative shall, during the term for which he was elected, nor for one year thereafter, be appointed or elected to any civil office of profit under this State which may have been created, or the emoluments of which may have been increased by the General Assembly during the time such Senator or Representative was a member thereof.

ART. 26. The members of the General Assembly shall in all cases, except treason, felony and breach of the peace, be privileged from arrest during their attendance at the session of their respective houses, and in going to and returning from the same; and for any speech or debate in either house, they shall not be questioned in any other place.

ART. 27. The members of the General Assembly shall receive a compensation not to exceed four dollars per day during their attendance, and their actual traveling expenses going to and returning from the seat of government; but in no instance shall more than thirty dollars each way be allowed for traveling expenses.

ART. 28. Each house shall keep a journal of its proceedings, and cause the same to be published immediately after the close of the session; when practicable, the minutes of each day's session shall be printed and placed in the hands of members on the day following. The original journal shall be preserved, after publication, in the office of Secretary of State, but there shall be required no other record thereof.

ART. 29. Every law enacted by the General Assembly shall embrace but one object, and that be expressed in the title.

ART. 30. No law shall be revived or amended by reference to its title, but in such cases the act revived or section as amended shall be re-enacted and published at length.

ART. 31. The general Assembly shall never adopt any system or code of laws by general reference to such system or code of laws, but in all cases shall recite at length the several provisions of the laws it may enact.

ART. 32. Not less than a majority of the members of each House of the General Assembly shall form a quorum to transact business; but a smaller number may adjourn from day to day, and shall have power to compel the attendance of absent members.

ART. 33. Neither House during the session of the General Assembly shall, without the consent of the other, adjourn for more than three days, nor to any other place than that in which it may be sitting.

ART. 34. The yeas and nays on any question in either House shall, at the desire of one-fifth of the members elected, be entered on the journal.

ART. 35. All bills for raising revenue or appropriating money shall originate in the House of Representatives, but the Senate may propose or concur in amendments, as in other bills.

Art. 36. No bill, or ordinance, or resolution intended to have the effect of a law, which shall have been rejected by either House, shall be again proposed in the same House during the same session, under the same or any other title, without the consent of a majority of the House by which the same was rejected.

Art. 37. Every bill shall be read on three different days in each House, and no bill shall be considered for final passage unless it has been read once in full, and the same has been reported on by a committee. Nor shall any bill become a law unless, on its final passage, the vote be taken by yeas and nays, the names of the members voting for or against the same be entered on the journal, and a majority of the members elected to each House be recorded thereon as voting in its favor.

Art. 38. No amendment to bills by one House shall be concurred in by the other, except by a vote of a majority of the members elected thereto, taken by yeas and nays, and the names of those voting for or against recorded upon the journal thereof. And reports of committees of conference shall be adopted in either House only by a majority of the members elected thereto, the vote to be taken by yeas and nays, and the names of those voting for or against recorded upon the journal.

Art. 39. Whenever a bill that has been passed by both Houses is enrolled and placed in possession of the House in which it originated the title shall be read, and at the request of any five members, the bill shall be read in full, when the Speaker of the House of Representatives or the President of the Senate, as the case may be, shall act at once, sign it in open House, and the fact of signing shall be noted on the journal; thereupon the Clerk or Secretary shall immediately convey the bill to the other House, whose presiding officer shall cause a suspension of all other business to read and sign the bill in open session and without delay; as soon as bills are signed by the Speaker of the House and President of the Senate, they shall be taken at once, and on the same day, to the Governor by the Clerk of the House or Secretary of the Senate.

Art. 40. No law passed by the General Assembly, except the general appropriation act, or act appropriating money for the expenses of the General Assembly, shall take effect until promulgated. A law shall be considered promulgated at the place where the State journal is published the day after the publication of such law in the State journal, and in all other parts of the State, twenty days after such publication.

Art. 41. The clerical officers of the two Houses of Representatives shall be a Secretary of the Senate and Clerk of the House of Representatives, with such assistants as may be necessary, but the expenses for clerks and employes shall not exceed sixty dollars daily for the Senate, nor seventy dollars daily for the House.

Art. 42. All stationery, printing, paper and fuel used in the legislative and other departments of government, shall be furnished, and the printing, binding and distributing of the laws, journals and department reports, and all other printing and binding, and the repairing and furnishing the halls and rooms used for the meetings of the General Assembly and its committees, shall be done under contract, to be given to the lowest responsible bidder below such maximum price, and under such regulations as shall be prescribed by law; provided, that such contracts shall be awarded only to citizens of the State. No member or officer of any of the departments of the government shall be in any way interested in such contracts, and all such contracts shall be subject to the approval of the Governor, the President of the Senate and Speaker of the House of Representatives, or any two of them.

LIMITATION OF LEGISLATIVE POWERS

ART. 43. No money shall be drawn from the treasury except in pursuance of specific appropriations made by law; nor shall any appropriation of money be made for a longer term than two years. A regular statement and account of receipts and expenditures of all public moneys shall be published every three months, in such manner as shall be prescribed by law.

ART. 44. The General Assembly shall have no power to contract, or to authorize the contracting, of any debt or liability, on behalf of the State, or to issue bonds or other evidence of indebtedness thereof, except for the purpose of repelling invasion or for the suppression of insurrection.

ART. 45. The General Assembly shall have no power to grant, or to authorize any parish or municipal authority to grant, any extra compensation, fee or allowance to a public officer, agent, servant or contractor, nor pay, nor authorize the payment, of any claim against the State, or any parish or municipality of the State, under any agreement or contract made without express authority of law; and all such unauthorized agreements or contracts shall be null and void.

ART. 46. The General Assembly shall not pass any local or special law on the following specified objects:

For the opening and conducting of elections, or fixing or changing the place of voting.

Changing the names of persons.

Changing the venue in civil or criminal cases.

Authorizing the laying out, opening, closing, altering or maintaining roads, highways, streets or alleys, or relating to ferries and bridges, or incorporating bridge or ferry companies, except for the erection of bridges crossing streams which form boundaries between this and any other State.

Authorizing the adoption or legitimation of children or the emancipation of minors.

Granting divorces.

Changing the law of descent or succession.

Affecting the estates of minors or persons under disabilities.

Remitting fines, penalties and forfeitures or refunding moneys legally paid into the treasury.

Authorizing the constructing of street passenger railroads in any incorporated town or city.

Regulating labor, trade, manufacturing or agriculture.

Creating corporations, or amending, renewing, extending or explaining the charter thereof; *provided*, that this shall not apply to the corporation of the city of New Orleans, or to the organization of levee districts and parishes.

Granting to any corporation, association or individual any special or exclusive right, privilege or immunity.

Extending the time for the assessment or collection of taxes, or for the relief of any assessor or collector of taxes from the due performance of his official duties, or of his securities from liability; nor shall any such be passed by any political corporation of this State.

Regulating the practice or jurisdiction of any court, or changing the rules of evidence in any judicial proceeding or inquiry before courts, or providing or changing methods for the collection of debts or the enforcement of judgments, or prescribing the effects of judicial sales.

Exemption of property from taxation.

Fixing the rate of interest.

Concerning any civil or criminal actions.

Giving effect to informal or invalid wills or deeds, or to any illegal disposition of property.

Regulating the management of public schools, the building or repairing of school houses, and the raising of money for such purposes.

Legalizing the unauthorized or invalid acts of any officer, servant, agent of the State, or of any parish or municipality thereof.

ART. 47. The General Assembly shall not indirectly enact special or local laws by the partial repeal of a general law; but laws repealing local or special laws may be passed.

ART. 48. No local or special laws shall be passed on any subject not enumerated in Article 46 of this Constitution, unless notice of the intention to apply therefor shall have been published, without cost to the State, in the locality where the matter or thing to be affected may be situated, which notice shall state the substance of the contemplated law, and shall be published at least thirty days prior to the introduction into the General Assembly of such bill, and in the same manner provided by law for the advertisement of judicial sales. The evidence of such notice having been published shall be exhibited in the General Assembly before such act shall be passed, and every such act shall contain a recital that such notice has been given.

ART. 49. No law shall be passed fixing the price of manual labor.

ART. 50. Any member of the General Assembly who has a personal or private interest in any measure or bill proposed or pending before the General Assembly shall disclose the fact to the House of which he is a member, and shall not vote thereon.

ART. 51. No money shall ever be taken from the public treasury, directly or indirectly in aid of any church, sect or denomination of religion, or in aid of any priest, preacher, minister or teacher thereof, as such, and no preference shall ever be given to nor any discrimination made against, any church, sect or creed of religion, or any form of religious faith or worship, nor shall any appropriations be made for private charitable or benevolent purposes to any person or community; *provided*, this shall not apply to the State asylums for the insane and deaf, dumb and blind and the charity hospitals and public charitable institutions conducted under State authority.

ART. 52. The General Assembly shall have no power to increase the expenses of any office by appointing assistant officials.

ART. 53. The general appropriation bill shall embrace nothing but appropriations for the ordinary expenses of the government, interest on the public debt, public schools and public charities, and such bill shall be so itemized as to show for what account each and every appropriation shall be made. All other appropriations shall be made by separate bills, each embracing but one object.

ART. 54. Each appropriation shall be for a specific purpose, and no appropriation shall be made under the head or title of contingent; nor shall any officer or department of government receive any amount from the treasury for contingencies or for a contingent fund.

ART. 55. No appropriation of money shall be made by the General Assembly in the last five days of the session thereof; all appropriations to be valid, shall be passed and receive the signatures of the President of the Senate and Speaker of the House of Representatives five full days before the adjournment *sine die* of the General Assembly.

ART. 56. The funds, credit, property or things of value of the State, or of any political corporation thereof, shall not be loaned, pledged or granted to or for any person or persons, association or corporation, public or private; nor shall the State, or any political corporation, purchase or subscribe to the capital or stock of any corporation or association whatever, or for any private enterprise. Nor shall the State, nor any political corporation thereof assume the liabilities of any political municipal, parochial, private, or other corporation or association whatsoever; nor shall the State undertake to carry on the business of any such corporation or association, or become a part owner therein; provided, the State, through the General Assembly, shall have power to grant the right of way through its public lands to any railroad or canal.

ART. 57. The General Assembly shall have no power to release or extinguish, or to authorize the releasing or extinguishing, in whole or in part, the indebtedness, liability or obligation of any corporation or individual to this State, or to any parish or municipal corporation therein; provided, the heirs to confiscated property may be released of all taxes due thereon at the date of its reversion to them.

EXECUTIVE DEPARTMENT

ART. 58. The Executive Department shall consist of a Governor, Lieutenant Governor, Auditor, Treasurer, and Secretary of State.

ART. 59. The supreme executive power of the State shall be vested in a chief magistrate, who shall be styled the Governor of Louisiana. He shall hold his office during four years, and, together with the Lieutenant Governor, chosen for the same term, shall be elected as follows: The qualified electors for Representatives shall vote for a Governor and Lieutenant Governor at the time and place of voting for Representatives.

The returns of every election for Governor and Lieutenant Governor shall be sealed up separately from the returns of election of other officers, and transmitted by the proper officer of every parish to the Secretary of State, who shall deliver them, unopened, to the General Assembly then next to be holden. The members of the General Assembly shall meet on the first Thursday after the day on which they assemble, in the House of Representatives, to examine and count the votes. The person having the greatest number of votes for Governor shall be declared duly elected; but in case two or more persons shall be equal and highest in the number of votes polled for Governor, one of them shall immediately be chosen Governor by the joint vote of the members of the General Assembly. The person having the greatest number of votes for Lieutenant Governor shall be Lieutenant Governor; but if two or more persons shall be equal and highest in number of votes polled for Lieutenant Governor, one of them shall be immediately chosen Lieutenant Governor, by joint vote of the members of the General Assembly.

ART. 60. No person shall be eligible to the office of Governor or Lieutenant Governor who shall not have attained the age of thirty years, been ten years a citizen of the United States, and resident of the State for the same space of time next preceding his election, or who shall be a member of Congress, or shall hold office under the United States at the time of, or within six months immediately preceding the election for such office.

ART. 61. The Governor shall enter on the discharge of his duties the first Monday next ensuing the announcement by the General Assembly of the result of the election for Governor, and shall continue in office until the Monday next succeeding the day that his successor shall have been declared duly elected and shall have taken the oath or affirmation required by this constitution.

ART. 62. In case of the impeachment of the Governor, his removal from office, death, refusal or inability to qualify, disability, resignation or absence from the State, the powers and duties of the office shall devolve upon the Lieutenant Governor for the residue of the term, or until the Governor, absent or impeached, shall return or be acquitted or the disability be removed. In the event of the removal, impeachment, death, resignation, disability or refusal to qualify of both the Governor and Lieutenant Governor, the President *pro tempore* of the Senate shall act as Governor until the disability be removed or for the residue of the term.

That in the event of the death, or from whatever cause the office of Lieutenant Governor shall become vacant, then, and in that event, the President *pro tempore* of the Senate shall fill the office of Lieutenant Governor, performing all the duties incident to the office and receiving its emoluments.

ART. 63. The Lieutenant Governor, or officer discharging the duties of Governor, shall, during his administration, receive the same compensation to which the Governor would have been entitled had he continued in office.

ART. 64. The Lieutenant Governor shall, by virtue of his office, be President of the Senate, but shall have only a casting vote therein. The Senate shall elect one of its members as President pro tempore of the Senate.

ART. 65. The Lieutenant Governor shall receive for his services a salary which shall be double that of a member of the General Assembly, and no more.

ART. 66. The Governor shall have power to grant reprieves for all offenses against the State, and, except in cases of impeachment or treason, shall, upon the recommendation in writing of the Lieutenant Governor, Attorney General and presiding judge of the court before which conviction was had, or of any two of them, have power to grant pardons, commute sentences, and remit fines and forfeitures after conviction. In cases of treason he may grant reprieves until the end of the next session of the General Assembly, in which body the power of pardoning is vested.

ART. 67. The Governor shall receive a salary of four thousand dollars per annum, payable monthly on his own warrant.

ART. 68. He shall nominate, and by and with the advice and consent of the Senate, appoint all officers whose offices are established by this Constitution, and whose appointments or elections are not herein otherwise provided for; provided, however, that the General Assembly shall have the right to prescribe the mode of appointment or election to all offices created by it.

ART. 69. The Governor shall have the power to fill vacancies that may happen during the recess of the Senate, in cases not otherwise provided for in this Constitution, by granting commissions which shall expire at the end of the next session; but no person who has been nominated for office and rejected, shall be appointed to the same office during the recess of the Senate. The failure of the Governor to send into the Senate the name of any person appointed for office, as herein provided, shall be equivalent to a rejection.

ART. 70. He may require information in writing from the officers in the Executive Department upon any subject relating to the duties of their respective offices. He shall be Commander-in-Chief of the militia of the State, except when they shall be called into active service of the United States.

ART. 71. He shall, from time to time, give to the General Assembly information respecting the situation of the State, and recommend to its consideration such measures as he may deem expedient.

ART. 72. He shall take care that the laws be faithfully executed, and he may, on extraordinary occasions, convene the General Assembly at the seat of government, or, if that should have become dangerous from an enemy or from an epidemic, at a different place. The power to legislate shall be limited to the objects enumerated specifically in the proclamation convening such extraordinary session; therein the Governor shall also limit the time such session may continue; *provided*, it shall not exceed twenty days. Any legislative action had after the time so limited, or as to other objects than those enumerated in said proclamation, shall be null and void.

ART. 73. Every bill which shall have passed both Houses, shall be presented to the Governor; if he approve, he shall sign it; if not, he shall return it, with his objections, to the House in which it originated, which House shall enter the objections at large upon the journal, and proceed to reconsider it. If, after such consideration, two-thirds of all the members elected to that House shall agree to pass the bill, it shall be sent, with the objections, to the other House, by which likewise it shall be reconsidered, and if passed by two-thirds of the members elected to that House, it shall be a law; but in such cases, the votes of both Houses shall be taken by yeas and nays, and the names of the members voting for and against the bill shall be entered on the journal of each House respectively. If any bill shall not be returned by the Governor within five days after it shall have been presented to him, the same shall be a law in like manner as if he had signed it, unless the General Assembly, by adjournment, shall prevent its return, in which case it shall not be a law.

ART. 74. The Governor shall have the power to disapprove of

any item or items of any bill making appropriations of money, embracing distinct items, and the part or parts of the bill approved shall be law and the item or items of appropriations disapproved shall be void unless repassed, according to the rules and limitations prescribed for the passage of other bills, over the Executive veto.

ART. 75. Every order, resolution or vote, to which the concurrence of both houses may be necessary, except on a question of adjournment, or on matters of parliamentary proceedings, or an address for removal from office, shall be presented to the Governor, and before it shall take effect, be approved by him, or being disapproved, shall be repassed by two-thirds of the members elected to each House.

ART. 76. The Treasurer, Auditor, Attorney General, and Secretary of State, shall be elected by the qualified electors of the State for the term of four years; and in case of vacancy caused by death, resignation or permanent absence of either of said officers, the Governor shall fill such vacancy by appointment, with the advice and consent of the Senate; provided, however, that notwithstanding such appointment, such vacancy shall be filled by election at the next election after the occurrence of the vacancy.

ART. 77. The Auditor of Public Accounts shall receive a salary of two thousand five hundred dollars per annum; the Treasurer shall receive a salary of two thousand dollars per annum; and the Secretary of State shall receive a salary of one thousand eight hundred dollars per annum. Each of the before named officers shall be paid monthly, and no fees or perquisites or other compensation shall be allowed to said officers; provided, the Secretary of State may be allowed fees as may be provided by law for copies and certificates furnished to private persons.

ART. 78. Appropriations for the clerical expenses of the officers named in the preceding article shall specify each item of such appropriations; and shall not exceed in any one year, for the Treasurer, the sum of two thousand dollars; for the Secretary of State, the sum of one thousand five hundred dollars; and for the Auditor of Public Accounts, the sum of four thousand dollars.

ART. 79. All commissions shall be in the name and by the authority of the State of Louisiana, and shall be sealed with the State seal, signed by the Governor and countersigned by the Secretary of State.

JUDICIARY DEPARTMENT

ART. 80. The judicial power shall be vested in a Supreme Court, in courts of appeal, in district courts and in justices of the peace.

ART. 81. The Supreme Court, except in cases hereinafter provided, shall have appellate jurisdiction only, which jurisdiction shall extend to all cases when the matter in dispute, or the fund to be distributed, whatever may be the amount therein claimed, shall exceed two thousand dollars, exclusive of interest; to suits for divorce and separation from bed and board; to suits for nullity of marriage; to suits involving the rights to homesteads; to suits for interdiction; and to all cases in which the constitutionality or legality of any tax, toll or impost whatever, or of any fine, forfeiture or penalty imposed by a municipal corporation shall be in contestation, whatever may be the amount thereof, and in such cases the appeal on the law and the fact shall be directly from the court in which the case originated to the Supreme Court; and to criminal cases, on questions of law alone, whenever the punishment of death or imprisonment at hard labor may be inflicted, or a fine exceeding three hundred dollars ($300) is actually imposed.

ART. 82. The Supreme Court shall be composed of one Chief Justice and four Associate Justices, a majority of whom shall constitute a quorum. The Chief Justice and Associate Justices shall each receive a salary of five thousand dollars (5000) per annum, payable monthly on their own warrants. They shall be appointed by the Governor, by and with the advice and consent of the Senate. The first Supreme Court to be organized under this constitution shall be appointed as follows: The Chief Justice for the term of twelve years; one Associate Justice for the term of ten years; one for the term of eight years; one for the term of six years; and one for the term of four years, and the Governor shall designate in the commission of each the term for which such judge is appointed. In case of death, resignation or removal from office of any of said judges, the vacancy shall be filled by appointment for the unexpired term of said judge, and upon expiration of the term of any said judges the office shall be filled by appointment for a term of twelve years. They shall be citizens of the United States, and of the State, over thirty-five years of age, learned in the law, and shall have practiced law in this State for ten years preceding their appointment.

ART. 83. The State shall be divided into four Supreme Court Districts, and the Supreme Court shall always be composed of judges appointed from said districts. The parishes of Orleans, St. John the Baptist, St. Charles, St. Bernard, Plaquemines and Jefferson shall compose the first district, from which two judges shall be appointed.

The parishes of Caddo, Bossier, Webster, Bienville, Claiborne, Union, Lincoln, Jackson, Caldwell, Ouachita, Morehouse, Richland, Franklin, West Carroll, East Carroll, Madison, Tensas and Catahoula shall compose the second district, from which one judge shall be appointed.

The parishes of DeSoto, Red River, Winn, Grant, Natchitoches, Sabine, Vernon, Calcasieu, Cameron, Rapides, Avoyelles, Concordia, Pointe Coupee, West Baton Rouge, Iberville, St. Landry, Lafayette and Vermilion shall compose the third district, from which one judge shall be appointed.

And the parishes of St. Martin, Iberia, St. Mary, Terrebonne, Lafourche, Assumption, St. James, Ascension, East Rouge, East Feliciana, West Feliciana, St. Helena, Livingston, Tangipahoa, St. Tammany and Washington shall compose the fourth district, from which one judge shall be appointed.

ART. 84. The Supreme Court shall hold its sessions in the city of New Orleans from the first Monday in the month of November to the end of the month of May in each and every year. The General Assembly shall have power to fix the sessions elsewhere during the rest of the year. Until otherwise provided, the sessions shall be held as heretofore. They shall appoint their own clerks and remove them at pleasure.

ART. 85. No judgment shall be rendered by the Supreme Court without the concurrence of three judges. Whenever three members cannot concur, in consequence of the recusation of any member or members of the court, the judges not recused shall have authority to call upon any judge or judges of the district courts, whose duty it shall be, when so called upon, to sit in the place of the judge or judges recused, and to aid in the determination of the case.

ART. 86. All judges, by virtue of their office, shall be conservators of the peace throughout the State. The style of all process shall be, " The State of Louisiana." All prosecutions shall be carried on " in the name and by the authority of the State of Louisiana," and conclude: "Against the peace and dignity of the same."

ART. 87. The judges of all courts, whenever practicable, shall refer to the law by virtue of which every definite judgment is rendered; but in all cases they shall adduce the reasons on which their judgment is founded.

ART. 88. There shall be a reporter of the decisions of the Supreme Court, who shall report in full all cases which he may be required to report by law or by the court. He shall publish in the reports the title, numbers and head notes of all cases decided, whether reported in full or not.

In all cases reported in full he shall make a brief statement of the principal points presented and authorities cited by counsel.

He shall be appointed by a majority of the court, and hold his office and be removable at their pleasure.

His salary shall be fixed by the court, and shall not exceed fifteen hundred dollars per annum, payable monthly on his own warrant.

ART. 89. The Supreme Court and each of the judges thereof shall have power to issue writs of *habeas corpus* at the instance of all persons in actual custody, in cases where it may have appellate jurisdiction.

ART. 90. The Supreme Court shall have control and general supervision over all inferior courts. They shall have power to issue writs of certiorari, prohibition, mandamus, quo warranto, and other remedial writs.

ART. 91. The General Assembly shall provide for appeals from the district courts to the Supreme Court upon questions of law alone, when the party or parties aggrieved desire only a review of the law.

ART. 92. Except as herein provided no duties or functions shall ever be attached by law to the Supreme Court, courts of appeal or district courts, or the several judges thereof, but such as are judicial; and the said judges are prohibited from receiving any fees of office or other compensation than their salaries for any official duties performed by them. No judicial powers, except as committing magistrates in criminal cases, shall be conferred on any officers other than those mentioned in this title, except such as may be necessary in towns and cities, and the judicial powers of such officers shall not extend further than the cognizance of cases arising under the police regulations of towns and cities in the State.

ART. 93. The judges of all courts shall be liable to impeachment for crimes and misdemeanors. For any reasonable cause the Governor shall remove any of them on the address of two-thirds of the members elected to each house of the General Assembly. In every case the cause or causes for which such removal may be required shall be stated at length in the address, and inserted in the journal of each house.

ATTORNEY GENERAL

ART. 94. There shall be an Attorney General for the State, who shall be elected by the qualified electors of the State at large every four years. He shall be learned in the law, and shall have actually resided and practiced law, as a licensed attorney in the State five years next preceding his election. He shall receive a salary of three thousand dollars per annum; payable monthly on his own warrant.

COURTS OF APPEAL

ART. 95. The courts of appeal, except in cases hereinafter provided, shall have appellate jurisdiction only, which jurisdiction shall extend to all cases, civil or probate, when the matter in dispute or the funds to be distributed shall exceed one hundred dollars, exclusive of interest, and shall not exceed two thousand dollars, exclusive of interest.

ART. 96. The courts of appeal shall be composed of two circuit judges, shall be elected by the two houses of the General Assembly in joint session. The first judges of the courts of appeal under this constitution shall be elected for the following terms: One judge for each court for the term of four years and one judge for the term of eight years.

They shall be learned in the law and shall have resided and practiced law in this State for six years, and shall have been actual residents of the circuit from which they shall be elected for at least two years next preceding their election.

ART. 97. The State, with the exception of the parish of Orleans, shall be divided into five circuits, from each of which two judges shall be elected. Until otherwise provided by law, the parishes of Caddo, Bossier, Webster, Bienville, DeSoto, Red River, Claiborne, Union, Lincoln, Natchitoches, Sabine, Jackson, Winn and Caldwell shall compose the First Circuit.

The parishes of Ouachita, Richland, Morehouse, West Carroll, Catahoula, Franklin, Madison, East Carroll, Concordia and Tensas shall compose the Second Circuit.

The parishes of Rapides, Grant, Avoyelles, St. Landry, Vernon, Calcasieu, Cameron, Lafayette, Vermilion, St. Martin and Iberia shall compose the Third Circuit.

The parishes of East Baton Rouge, West Baton Rouge, Iberville, East Feliciana, St. Helena, Tangipahoa, Livingston, St. Tammany, Washington, Pointe Coupee and West Feliciana shall compose the Fourth Circuit.

And the parishes of St. Mary, Terrebonne, Ascension, Lafourche, Assumption, Plaquemines, St. Bernard, Jefferson, St. Charles, St. John the Baptist and St. James shall compose the Fifth Circuit.

ART. 98. The judges of the courts of appeal, until otherwise provided by law, shall hold two terms annually in each parish composing their respective circuits.

ART. 99. Until otherwise provided by law, the terms of the circuit courts of appeal shall be as follows:

First Circuit

Caddo—First Mondays in January and June.
Bossier—Third Mondays in January and June.
Webster—First Mondays in February and July.
Bienville—Second Mondays in February and July.
Claiborne—Third Mondays in February and July.
Union—First Mondays in March and October.
Lincoln—Second Mondays in March and October.
Jackson—Third Mondays in March and October.
Caldwell, Fourth Mondays in March and October.
Winn—First Mondays in April and November.
Natchitoches—Second Mondays in April and November.
Sabine—Fourth Mondays in April and November.
DeSoto—First Mondays in May and December.
Red River—Third Mondays in May and December.

Second Circuit

Ouachita—First Mondays in January and June.
Richland—Fourth Mondays in January and June.
Franklin—First Mondays in February and July.
Catahoula—Second Mondays in February and July.
Concordia—Fourth Mondays in February and July.
Tensas—Second Mondays in March and October.
Madison—Fourth Mondays in March and October.
East Carroll—Second Mondays in April and November.
West Carroll—Fourth Mondays in April and November.
Morehouse—First Mondays in May and December.

Third Circuit

St. Landry—First Mondays in January and June.
Avoyelles—Fourth Mondays in January and June.
Rapides—Second Mondays in February and July.
Grant—Fourth Mondays in February and July.
Vernon—First Mondays in March and October.
Calcasieu—Second Mondays in March and October.
Cameron—Fourth Mondays in March and October.
Vermilion—First Mondays in April and November.
Lafayette—Second Mondays in April and November.
Iberia—Fourth Mondays in April and November.
St. Martin—Second Mondays in May and December.

Fourth Circuit

East Baton Rouge—First Mondays in January and June.
West Baton Rouge—Fourth Mondays in January and June.
Livingston—First Mondays in February and July.
Tangipahoa—Second Mondays in February and July.
St. Tammany—Fourth Mondays in February and July.
Washington—First Mondays in March and October.
St. Helena—Second Mondays in March and October.
East Feliciana—Fourth Mondays in March and October.
West Feliciana—Second Mondays in April and November.
Pointe Coupee—Fourth Mondays in April and November.
Iberville—Second Mondays in May and December.

FIFTH CIRCUIT

St. Mary—First Mondays in January and June.
Terrebonne—Third Mondays in January and June.
Assumption—First Mondays in February and July.
Lafourche—Third Mondays in February and July.
St. Charles—First Mondays in March and October.
Jefferson—Second Mondays in March and October.
St. Bernard—Fourth Mondays in March and October.
Plaquemines—First Mondays in April and November.
St. John the Baptist—Second Mondays in April and November.
St. James—Third Mondays in April and November.
Ascension—Second Mondays in May and December.

ART. 100. Whenever the first day of the term shall fall on a legal holiday, the court shall begin its sessions on the first legal day thereafter.

ART. 101. Whenever the judges composing the courts of appeal shall concur, their judgment shall be final. Whenever there shall be a disagreement, the two judges shall appoint a lawyer having the qualifications for a judge of the Court of Appeals of their circuit, who shall aid in the determination of the case; a judgment concurred in by any two of them shall be final.

ART. 102. All causes on appeal to the courts of appeal shall be tried on the original record, pleadings and evidence in the district court.

ART. 103. The rules of practice regulating appeals to, and proceedings in the Supreme Court, shall apply to appeals and proceedings in the courts of appeal, so far as they may be applicable, until otherwise provided by law.

ART. 104. The judges of the courts of appeal shall have power to issue writs of habeas corpus at the instance of all persons in actual custody within their respective circuits. They shall also have authority to issue writs of mandamus, prohibition and certiorari, in aid of their appellate jurisdiction.

ART. 105. The judges of courts of appeal shall each receive a salary of four thousand dollars per annum, payable monthly on their respective warrants.

The General Assembly shall provide by law for the trial of recused cases in the courts of appeal.

ART. 106. The sheriff of the parish in which the sessions of the court are held, shall attend in person, or by deputy, to execute the orders of the court.

DISTRICT COURTS

ART. 107. The State shall be divided into not less than twenty, nor more than thirty, judicial districts, the parish of Orleans excepted.

ART. 108. Until otherwise provided by law, there shall be twenty-six districts.

The Parish of Caddo shall compose the First district.[a]

The parishes of Bossier, Webster and Bienville shall compose the Second District.

---

[a] The number of judges was increased to two in the First District by Act No. 71, of 1882, p. 93.

The parishes of Claiborne, Union and Lincoln shall compose the Third District.

The parishes of Jackson, Winn and Caldwell shall compose the Fourth District.

The parishes of Ouachita and Richland [a] shall compose the Fifth District.

The parishes of Morehouse and West Carroll [b] shall compose the Sixth District.

The parishes of Catahoula and Franklin shall compose the Seventh District.

The parishes of Madison and East Carroll shall compose the Eighth District.

The parishes of Concordia and Tensas shall compose the Ninth District.

The parishes of DeSoto and Red River shall compose the Tenth District.

The parishes of Natchitoches and Sabine shall compose the Eleventh District.

The parishes of Rapides, Grant and Avoyelles shall compose the Twelfth District.[c]

The parish of St. Landry shall compose the Thirteenth District.

The parishes of Vernon, Calcasieu and Cameron shall compose the Fourteenth District.

The parishes of Pointe Coupee and West Feliciana shall compose the Fifteenth District.

The parishes of East Feliciana and St. Helena shall compose the Sixteenth District.

The parish of East Baton Rouge shall compose the Seventeenth District.

The parishes of Tangipahoa, Livingston, St. Tammany and Washington shall compose the Eighteenth District.

The parishes of St. Mary and Terrebonne shall compose the Nineteenth District.

The parishes of Lafourche and Assumption shall compose the Twentieth District.

The parishes of St. Martin and Iberia shall compose the Twenty-first District.

The parishes of Ascension and St. James shall compose the Twenty-second District.

The parishes of West Baton Rouge and Iberville shall compose the Twenty-third District.

The parishes of Plaquemines and St. Bernard shall compose the Twenty-fourth District.

The parishes of Lafayette and Vermilion shall compose the Twenty-fifth District.

The parishes of Jefferson, St. Charles and St. John the Baptist shall compose the Twenty-sixth District.

---

[a] The parish of Richland was detached from the Fifth District by Act No. 89, of 1882, p. 111.

[b] The parish of West Carroll was detached from the Sixth District by Act No. 89, of 1882, p. 111.

[c] The number of judges in the Twelfth District was increased to two by Act No. 22, of 1882, p. 38.

The parishes of West Carroll and Richland shall compose the Twenty-seventh District.[a]

ART. 109. District courts shall have original jurisdiction in all civil matters where the amount in dispute shall exceed fifty dollars, exclusive of interest.

They shall have unlimited original jurisdiction in all criminal, probate and succession matters, and when a succession is a party defendant.

The district judges shall be elected by a plurality of the qualified voters of their respective districts, in which they shall have been actual residents for two years next preceding their election.

They shall be learned in the law, and shall have practiced law in the State for five years previous to their election.

They shall be elected for the term of four years. All elections to fill vacancies occasioned by death, resignation or removal, shall be for the unexpired term, and the Governor shall fill the vacancy until an election can be held.

The judges of the district court shall each receive a salary of three thousand dollars per annum, payable monthly on their respective warrants.

ART. 110. The General Assembly shall have power to increase the number of district judges in any district whenever the public business may require.

ART. 111. The district court shall have jurisdiction of appeals from justices of the peace in all matters where the amount in controversy shall exceed ten dollars, exclusive of interest.

ART. 112. The General Assembly shall provide by law for the trial of recused cases in the district courts, by the selection of licensed attorneys at law, by an interchange of judges, or otherwise.

ART. 113. Wherever in this Constitution the qualification of any justice or judge shall be the previous practice of the law for a term of years, there shall be included in such term the time such justice or judge shall have occupied the bench of any court of record in this State; *provided*, he shall have been a licensed attorney for five years before his election or appointment.

ART. 114. No judge of any court of the State shall be affected in his term of office, salary or jurisdiction as to territory or amount during the term or period for which he was elected or appointed. Any legislation so affecting any judge or court shall take effect only at the end of the term of office of the judge or judges, incumbents of the court or courts to which such legislation may apply at the time of its enactment. This article shall not affect the provisions of this constitution relative to impeachment or removal from office.

ART. 115. The district judges shall have power to issue writs of *habeas corpus* at the instance of all persons in actual custody in their respective districts.

ART. 116. The General Assembly at its first session under this constitution shall provide by general law for the selection of competent and intelligent jurors, who shall have capacity to serve as grand jurors and try and determine both civil and criminal cases, and may provide, in civil cases, that a verdict be rendered by the concurrence of a less number than the whole.

---

[a] Act No. 87, of 1882, p. 111.

Art. 117. In those districts composed of one parish, there shall not be less than six terms of the district court each year.

In all other districts there shall be in each parish not less than four terms of the district court each year, except in the parishes of Cameron, Franklin and Vernon, in which there shall not be less than two terms of the district court each year.

Until provided by law, the terms of the district court in each parish be fixed by a rule of said court, which shall not be changed without notice by publication at least thirty days prior to such change.

There shall be in each parish not less than two jury terms each year, at which a grand jury shall be impaneled, except in the parishes of Cameron, Franklin and Vernon, in which there shall not be less than one jury term each year at which a grand jury shall be impaneled.

At other jury terms the General Assembly shall provide for special juries, when necessary for the trial of criminal cases.

SHERIFFS AND CORONERS

Art. 118. There shall be a sheriff and coroner elected by the qualified voters of each parish in the State, except the parish of Orleans, who shall be elected at the general elections and hold office for four years.

The coroner shall act for and in place of the cheriff whenever the sheriff shall be party interested and whenever there shall be a vacancy in the office of sheriff, until such vacancy shall be filled; but he shall not during such vacancy discharge the duties of tax collector.

The sheriff, except in the parish of Orleans, shall be ex-officio collector of State and parish taxes.

He shall give separate bonds for the faithful performance of his duty in each capacity. Until otherwise provided, the bonds shall be given according to existing laws.

The General Assembly, after the adoption of this constitution, shall pass a general law regulating the amount, form, condition and mode of approval of such bonds, so as to fully secure the State and parish, and all parties in interest.

Sheriffs elected at the first election under this constitution shall comply with the provisions of such law, within thirty days after its promulgation, in default of which the office shall be declared vacant, and the Governor shall appoint for the remainder of the time.

Art. 119. Sheriffs shall receive compensation from the parish for their services in criminal matters (the keeping of prisoners, conveying convicts to the Penitentiary, insane persons to the Insane Asylum, and service of process from another parish, and service of process or the performance of any duty beyond the limits of his own parish excepted), not to exceed five hundred dollars per annum for each Representative the parish may have in the House of Representatives.

The compensation of sheriffs as tax collectors shall not exceed five per cent on the amount collected and paid over; *provided*, that he shall not be discharged as tax collector until he makes proof that he has exhausted the legal remedies to collect the taxes.

ART. 120. The coroner in each parish shall be a doctor of medicine, regularly licensed to practice, and *ex-officio* parish physician; *provided*, this article shall not apply to any parish in which there is no regurlarly licensed physician who will accept the office.

CLERKS

ART. 121. There shall be a clerk of the district court in each parish, the parish of Orleans excepted, who shall be *ex-officio* clerk of the court of appeals.

He shall be elected by the qualified electors of the parish every four years; and shall be *ex-officio* parish recorder of conveyances, mortgages and other acts, and notary public.

He shall receive no compensation for his services from the State, or the parish, in criminal matters.

He shall give bond and security for the faithful performance of his duties, in such amount as shall be fixed by the General Assembly.

ART. 122. The General Assembly shall have power to vest in clerks of courts authority to grant such orders, and to do such acts as may be deemed necessary for the furtherance of the administration of justice; and in all cases, powers thus vested shall be specified and determined.

ART. 123. Clerks of district courts may appoint, with the approval of the district judge, deputies, with such powers as shall be prescribed by law; and the General Assembly shall have power to provide for continuing one or more of them in office, in the event of the death of the clerk, until his successor shall have been appointed and duly qualified.

DISTRICT ATTORNEYS

ART. 124. There shall be a district attorney for each judicial district in the State, who shall be elected by the qualified electors of the judicial district. He shall receive a salary of one thousand dollars per annum, payable monthly on his own warrant, and shall hold his office for four years. He shall be an actual resident of the district, and a licensed attorney at law in this State.

He shall also receive fees; but no fees shall be allowed in criminal cases, except on conviction.

Any vacancy in the office of district attorney shall be filled by appointment by the Governor for the unexpired term. There shall be no parish attorney, or district attorney, pro tempore. (This article shall not apply to the parish of Orleans.)

JUSTICES OF THE PEACE

ART. 125. In each parish, the parish of Orleans excepted, there shall be as many justices of the peace as may be provided by law.

The present number of justices of the peace shall remain as now fixed until otherwise provided. They shall be elected for the term of four years by the qualified voters within the territorial limits of their jurisdiction.

They shall have exclusive original jurisdiction in all civil matters when the amount in dispute shall not exceed fifty dollars, exclusive of interest, and original jurisdiction concurrent with the district court, when the amount in dispute shall exceed fifty dollars, exclusive of interest, and shall not exceed one hundred dollars, exclusive of interest.

They shall have no jurisdiction in succession or probate matters, or when a succession is a defendant. They shall receive such fees or salary as may be fixed by law.

ART. 126. They shall have criminal jurisdiction as committing magistrates, and shall have power to bail or discharge in cases not capital or necessarily punishable at hard labor.

CONSTABLES

ART. 127. There shall be a constable for the court of each justice of the peace in the several parishes of the State, the parish of Orleans excepted, who shall be elected for the term of four years by the qualified voters within the territorial limits of the jurisdiction of the several justices of the peace.

The compensation, salaries, or fees of constables and the amount of their bonds, shall be fixed by the General Assembly.

COURTS OF THE PARISH AND CITY OF NEW ORLEANS

ART. 128. There shall be in the parish of Orleans a court of appeals for said parish, with exclusive appellate jurisdiction in all matters, civil or probate, arising in said parish, when the amount in dispute or fund to be distributed exceeds one hundred dollars, exclusive of interest, and does not exceed two thousand dollars, exclusive of interest; said court shall be presided over by two judges who shall be elected by the General Assembly in joint session; they shall be residents and voters of the city of New Orleans, possessing all the qualifications necessary for judges of circuit courts of appeals throughout the State; they shall each receive an annual salary of four thousand dollars, payable monthly upon their respective warrants.

Said appeals shall be upon questions of law alone, in all cases, involving less than five hundred dollars, exclusive of interest, and upon the law and facts in other cases.

It shall sit in the city of New Orleans, from the first Monday of November to the last Monday of June of each year.

It shall have authority to issue writs of *mandamus*, prohibition, *certiorari* and *habeas corpus* in aid of its appellate jurisdiction.

ART. 129. The provisions of this constitution, relating to the term of office, qualifications and salary of the judges of the circuit courts of appeal throughout the State, and the manner of proceeding and determining causes as applicable to such circuit courts of appeal, shall apply to this court and its judges, in so far as such provisions are not in conflict with the provisions specially relating to said court and its judges.

Said Court of Appeals shall have jurisdiction of all causes now pending on appeal from the parish of Orleans before the Supreme Court of the State where the amount in dispute or fund to be distributed is less than one thousand dollars, exclusive of interest, and the Supreme Court shall at once transfer said causes to the Court of Appeals.

ART. 130. For the parish of Orleans there shall be two district courts and no more. One of said courts shall be known as the Civil District Court for the parish of Orleans; and the other as the Criminal District Court for the parish of Orleans. The former shall consist of not less than five judges, and the latter not less than two judges having the qualifications prescribed for district judges throughout the State. The said judges shall be appointed by the Governor by and with the advice and consent of the Senate, for the term of eight years. The first appointment shall be made as follows: Three judges of the Civil District Court for four years and two judges for eight years. One judge of the Criminal District Court for four years and one for eight years, the terms to be designated in their commissions.

The said judges shall receive each four thousand dollars per annum. Said Civil District Court shall have exclusive and general probate, and exclusive civil jurisdiction in all cases when the amount in dispute or to be distributed exceeds one hundred ($100) dollars exclusive of interest, and exclusive appellate jurisdiction from the city courts of the parish of Orleans, when the amount in dispute exceeds twenty-five dollars exclusive of interest. All causes filed in said court shall be equally allotted and assigned among said judges, in accordance with rules of court to be adopted for the purpose. In case of recusation of any judge in any cause, such cause shall be reassigned, or in case of absence from the parish, sickness or the disability of the judge to whom said cause may have been assigned, any judge of said court may issue or grant conservatory writs or orders. In other respects each judge shall have exclusive control over every cause assigned to him from its inception to its final determination in said court. The Criminal District Court shall have criminal jurisdiction only. All prosecutions instituted in said court shall be equally apportioned between said judges by lot. Each judge, or his successor, shall have exclusive control over every cause falling to him from its inception to its final determination in said court. In case of vacancy or recusation causes assigned shall be reassigned under order of court.

ART. 131. The General Assembly may increase the number of judges of the Civil District Court, not, however, to exceed nine judges, and the number of the criminal judges not to exceed three.

ART. 132. The Court of Appeals and the Civil and Criminal District Courts for the parish of Orleans shall respectively regulate the order of preference and trial of causes pending, and adopt other rules to govern the proceedings therein, not in conflict with the provisions of law.

ART. 133. The Civil District Court for the parish of Orleans shall select a solvent incorporated bank of the city of New Orleans as a judicial depository. Therein shall be deposited all moneys, notes, bonds and securities (except such notes or documents as may be filed with suits or in evidence, which shall be kept by the clerk of court), so soon as the same shall come into the hands of any sheriff or clerk of court; such deposits shall be removable, in whole or in part, only upon order of court. The officer making such deposits shall make immediate and written return to the court of the date and particulars thereof, to be filed in the cause in which the matter is pending, under penalties to be prescribed by law.

ART. 134. There shall be a district attorney for the parish of Orleans, who shall possess the same qualifications and be elected in the same manner and for the same period of time as the district attorneys for other parishes, as provided by this constitution.

He shall receive a salary of one thousand dollars per annum and such fees as may be allowed by law; but no fee shall be allowed in criminal cases except on conviction.

He may appoint an assistant at a salary not to exceed fifteen hundred dollars per annum.

ART. 135. There shall be in the city of New Orleans four city courts, one of which shall be located in that portion of the city on the right bank of the Mississippi river, presided over by judges having all the qualifications required for a district judge, and shall be elected by the qualified voters for the term of four years; they shall have exclusive jurisdiction over all sums not exceeding one hundred dollars, exclusive of interest, subject to an appeal to the Civil District Court when the amount claimed exceeds twenty-five dollars, exclusive of interest. The General Assembly shall regulate the salaries, territorial division of jurisdiction, the manner of executing their process, the fee bill, and proceedings which shall govern them; they shall have authority to execute commissions, to take testimony and receive therefor such fees as may be allowed by law.

The General Assembly may increase the number of city courts for the said parish, not to exceed eight in all, until otherwise provided by law. Each of said courts shall have one clerk, to be elected for the term of four years by the qualified voters of the parish, who shall receive a salary of twelve hundred dollars per annum, and no more, and whose qualifications, bond and duties shall be regulated by law.

ART. 136. The General Assembly may provide for police or magistrates' courts, but such courts shall not be vested with jurisdiction beyond the enforcement of municipal ordinances or as committing magistrates.

ART. 137. There shall be one clerk for the Civil District Court and one for the Criminal District Court of the parish of Orleans. The former shall be ex-officio clerk of the Court of Appeals of said parish. Said clerks shall be removable in the manner provided for the removal of the sheriffs of said parish. The Clerk of said Civil District Court shall receive an annual salary of three thousand six hundred dollars, and no more; and the clerk of the Criminal Court an annual salary of three thousand dollars, and no more, both payable on their warrants. They shall be elected by the qualified voters of the parish for the term of four years.

The amount and character of the bonds and qualification of the sureties to be furnished by said clerks shall be prescribed by law.

ART. 138. The Court of Appeals and each judge of the Civil and Criminal District Court of the parish of Orleans shall appoint a minute clerk at an annual salary of not more than eighteen hundred dollars, whose duties shall be regulated by law. Each clerk of court shall appoint, by and with the consent of the district court of which he is clerk, such deputies as may be necessary to perform officially the duties of said office, at salaries to be fixed by law. He shall be responsible for the said deputies, and may require from each such security as he may deem sufficient to secure himself, and said deputies shall be removable at his pleasure.

ART. 139. There shall be a civil and a criminal sheriff for the parish of Orleans. The civil sheriff shall be the executive officer of all the civil courts, (except city courts;) and the criminal sheriff shall be the executive officer of the Criminal District Court.

They shall attend the sittings, execute the writs and mandates of their respective courts. They shall be elected by the voters of the parish of Orleans every four years. They shall be citizens of the State, residents and voters of the city of New Orleans, at least twenty-five years of age, and shall be removable each by the district court of which he is the executive officer, upon proof after trial, without jury, of gross or continued neglect, incompetency or unlawful conduct, operating injury to the court or any individual. The two district courts for the parish of Orleans shall immediately upon organization under this constitution, in joint session, adopt rules governing the lodging of complaints against and the trial of such officers; and such rules once adopted, shall not be changed, except by the unanimous consent of all the judges composing the said courts.

ART. 140. The civil sheriff of the parish of Orleans shall receive such fees as the General Assembly may fix. He shall render monthly accounts, giving amounts and dates, number and title of causes wherein received or paid out, of all sums collected and disbursed by him, which shall be filed in the Civil District Court of said parish and form a part of its public records.

He shall be responsible to the State for all profits of said office over ten thousand dollars per annum, and shall settle with the State at least once a year in such manner as the General Assembly may provide.

The criminal sheriff shall receive an annual salary of thirty-six hundred dollars and no more. He shall receive no other compensation. He shall charge and collect for the State from parties convicted such fees and charges as may be fixed by law and shall render monthly accounts of the same.

ART. 141. Said sheriffs shall appoint, each with the consent and approval of the district court which he serves, such a number of deputies as the said court may find necessary for the proper expedition of the public business, at such salaries as may be fixed by law. Each sheriff shall be responsible for his deputies, and may remove them at pleasure and fill vacancies with the approval of the court, and may exact from all deputies security in such manner and amount as such sheriff may deem necessary.

ART. 142. The civil sheriff for said parish shall execute a bond with sureties, residents of said parish, conditioned for the lawful and faithful performance of the duties of his office, in the sum of fifty thousand dollars. The sureties shall be examined in open court by the judges of the Civil District Court for the parish of Orleans, and the questions and answers shall be reduced to writing and form a portion of the records of said court.

A similar bond shall be executed by the criminal sheriff of said parish in the sum of ten thousand dollars, with sureties to be examined and approved as to solvency by the Criminal District Court of said parish, as herein directed for the Civil District Court of said parish in the case of the civil sheriff.

ART. 143. There shall be one constable for each city court of the parish of Orleans, who shall be the executive officer of such court.

He shall be elected by the qualified voters of the parish of Orleans for the term of four years. The General Assembly shall define his qualifications and fix his compensation and duties, and shall assimilate the same so far as practicable to the provisions of this constitution relating to the civil sheriff of said parish. The judges of the city courts shall sit in banc to examine such bonds, try and remove constables and adopt rules regulating such trial and removal. They shall in such proceedings, be governed so far as practicable by the provisions of this constitution regulating the proceedings of the district courts of the parish of Orleans in the case of the sheriffs of said parish.

ART. 144. There shall be a register of conveyances and a recorder of mortgages for the parish of Orleans, who shall be elected by the qualified electors of said parish every four years. The register of conveyances shall receive an annual salary of twenty-five hundred dollars and no more, and said recorder of mortgages an annual salary of four thousand dollars and no more. The General Assembly shall regulate the qualifications and duties of said officers and the number of employees they shall appoint, and fix the salaries of such employees, not to exceed eighteen hundred dollars per annum for each.

ART. 145. The General Assembly, at its first session after the adoption of this constitution, shall enact a fee bill for the clerks of the various courts, including the city courts, sitting in New Orleans, and for the civil and criminal sheriffs, constables, register of conveyances and recorder of mortgages of said parish. In the same act provision shall be made for a system of stamps or stamped paper for the collection by the State, and not by said officers, of such fees and charges, so far as clerks of courts, register of conveyances and recorder of mortgages are concerned.

ART. 146. All fees and charges fixed by law for the various civil courts of the parish of Orleans, and for the register of conveyances and recorder of mortgages of said parish shall enure to the State, and all sums realized therefrom shall be set aside and held as a special fund, out of which shall be paid by preference the expenses of the clerk of the civil district court, the clerks of the city courts, the register of conveyances and the recorder of mortgages of the parish of Orleans: *Provided*, That the State shall never make any payment to any sheriff, clerk, register of conveyances or recorder of mortgages of the parish of Orleans, or any of their deputies for salary or other expenses of their respective offices, except from the special fund provided for by this article, and any appropriation made contrary to this provision shall be null and void.

ART. 147. There shall be one coroner for the parish of Orleans, who shall be elected every four years by the qualified electors of said parish, and whose duties shall be regulated by law. He shall be ex-officio city physician of the city of New Orleans and receive an annual salary of five thousand dollars, and no more. He shall be a practicing physician of said city, and a graduate of the medical department of some university of respectable standing. He may appoint an assistant having the same qualifications as himself, at an annual salary not exceeding three thousand dollars. The salaries of both coroner and assistant to be paid by the parish of Orleans.

The maintenance and support of prisoners confined in the parish of Orleans, upon charges or conviction for criminal offenses, shall be under the control of the city of New Orleans.

GENERAL PROVISIONS

Art. 148. No person shall hold any office, State, parochial or municipal, or shall be permitted to vote at any election or act as a juror, who, in due course of law, shall have been convicted of treason, perjury, forgery, bribery or other crime punishable by imprisonment in the penitentiary, or who shall be under interdiction.

Art. 149. Members of the General Assembly and all officers, before they enter upon the duties of their offices, shall take the following oath or affirmation:

"I (A. B.) do solemnly swear (or affirm) that I will support the constitution and laws of the United States, and the constitution and laws of this State; and that I will faithfully and impartially discharge and perform all the duties incumbent upon me as ——— according to the best of my ability and understanding. So help me God."

Art. 150. The seat of government shall be and remain at the city of Baton Rouge.

The General Asembly, at its first session after the adoption of this constitution, shall make the necessary appropriation for the repair of the State House and for the transfer of the archives of the State to Baton Rouge; and the city council of Baton Rouge is hereby authorized to issue certificates of indebtedness, in such manner and form as to cover the subscription of thirty-five thousand dollars, tendered by the citizens and the city council in said city to aid in repairing the Capitol in said city; *provided*, the city of Baton Rouge shall pay into the State treasury said amount of thirty-five thousand dollars before the contract for the repairs of the State House be finally closed.

Art. 151. Treason against the State shall consist only in levying war against it, or adhering to its enemies, giving them aid and comfort. No person shall be convicted of treason except on the testimony of two witnesses to the same overt act, or on his confession in open court.

Art. 152. All civil officers shall be removable by an address of two thirds of the members elected to each house of the General Assembly, except those whose removal is otherwise provided for by this constitution.

Art. 153. No member of congress nor person holding or exercising any office of trust or profit under the United States, or either of them, or under any foreign power, shall be eligible as a member of the General Assembly, or hold or exercise any office of trust or profit under the State.

Art. 154. The laws, public records and the judicial and legislative written proceedings of the State shall be promulgated, preserved and conducted in the English language; but the General Assembly may provide for the publication of the laws in the French language, and prescribe that judicial advertisements in certain designated cities and parishes shall also be made in that language.

Art. 155. No *ex post facto* law, nor any law impairing the obligations of contracts, shall be passed; nor vested rights be divested, unless for purposes of public utility and for adequate compensation previously made.

Art. 156. Private property shall not be taken nor damaged, for public purposes without just and adequate compensation being first paid.

Art. 157. No power of suspending the laws of this State shall be exercised, unless by the General Assembly or its authority.

Art. 158. The General Assembly shall provide by law for change of venue in civil and criminal cases.

Art. 159. No person shall hold or exercise, at the same time, more than one office of trust or profit, except that of justice of the peace or notary public.

Art. 160. The General Assembly may determine the mode of filling vacancies in all offices for which provisions is not made in this constitution.

Art. 161. All officers shall continue to discharge the duties of their offices until their successors shall have been inducted into office, except in case of impeachment or suspension.

Art. 162. The military shall be in subordination to the civil power, and no soldier shall, in time of peace, be quartered in any house without consent of the owner.

Art. 163. The General Assembly shall make it obligatory upon each parish to support all infirm, sick and disabled paupers residing within its limits; provided, that in every municipal corporation in a parish where the powers of the police jury do not extend, the said corporation shall support its own infirm, sick and disabled paupers.

Art. 164. No soldier, sailor or marine in military or naval service of the United States shall hereafter acquire a domicile in this State by reason of being stationed or doing duty in the same.

Art. 165. It shall be the duty of the General Assembly to pass such laws as may be proper and necessary to decide differences by arbitration.

Art. 166. The power of the courts to punish for contempt shall be limited by law.

Art. 167. The General Assembly shall have authority to grant lottery charters or privileges; provided, each charter or privilege shall not pay less than forty thousand dollars per annum in money into the treasury of the State; and provided further, that all charters shall cease and expire on the first of January, 1895, from which time all lotteries are prohibited in the State.

The forty thousand dollars per annum now provided by law to be paid by the Louisiana State Lottery Company, according to the provisions of its charter, granted in the year 1868, shall belong to the Charity Hospital of New Orleans, and the charter of said company is recognized as a contract binding on the State for the period therein specified, except its monopoly clause, which is hereby abrogated, and all laws contrary to the provisions of this article are hereby declared null and void; *provided*, said company shall file a written renunciation of all its monopoly features, in the office of the Secretary of State, within sixty days after the ratification of this constitution.

Of the additional sums raised by license on lotteries, the hospital at Shreveport shall receive ten thousand dollars annually, and the remaining sum shall be divided each year among the several parishes in the State for the benefit of their schools.

Art. 168. In all proceedings of indictments for libel, the truth thereof may be given in evidence. The jury in all criminal cases shall be judges of the law and of the facts on the question of guilt or innocence, having been charged as to the law applicable to the case by the presiding judge.

Art. 169. No officer whose salary is fixed by the Constitution shall be allowed any fees or perquisites of office, except where otherwise provided for by this Constitution.

Art. 170. The regulation of the sale of alcoholic or spirituous liquor is declared a police regulation, and the General Assembly may enact laws regulating their sale and use.

Art. 171. No person who, at any time, may have been a collector of taxes, whether State, parish or municipal, or who may have been otherwise intrusted with public money, or any portion thereof, shall be eligible to the General Assembly, or to any office of honor, profit or trust under the State government, or any parish or municipality thereof, until he shall have obtained a discharge for the amount of such collections, and for all public moneys with which he may have been intrusted.

Art. 172. Gambling is declared to be a vice, and the General Assembly shall enact laws for its suppression.

Art. 173. Any person who shall directly or indirectly offer or give any sum or sums of money, bribe, present, reward, promise, or any other thing, to any officer, State, parochial or municipal, or to any member or officer of the General Assembly, with the intent to induce or influence such officer or member of the General Assembly to appoint any person to office, to vote or exercise any power in him vested, or to perform any duty of him required, with partiality or favor, the person giving, or offering to give, and the officer or member of the General Assembly so receiving any money, bribe, present, reward, promise, contract, obligation or security, with the intent or for the purpose or consideration aforesaid, shall be guilty of bribery, and on being found guilty thereof by any court of competent jurisdiction, or by either House of the General Assembly of which he may be a member or officer, shall be forever disqualified from holding any office, State, parochial or municipal, and shall be forever ineligible to a seat in the General Assembly; provided, that this shall not be so construed as to prevent the General Assembly from enacting additional penalties.

Art. 174. Any person may be compelled to testify in any lawful proceeding against any one who may be charged with having committed the offense of bribery, and shall not be permitted to withhold his testimony upon the ground that it may criminate him or subject him to public infamy; but such testimony shall not afterwards be used against him in any judicial proceedings, except for perjury in giving such testimony.

Art. 175. The General Assembly shall, at its first session, pass laws to protect laborers on buildings, streets, roads, railroads, canals and other similar works, against the failure of contractors and subcontractors to pay their current wages when due, and to make the corporation, company or individual for whose benefit the work is done responsible for their ultimate payment.

Art. 176. No mortgage or privilege on immovable property shall affect third persons, unless recorded or registered in the parish where the property is situated, in the manner and within the time as is now or may be prescribed by law, except privileges for expenses of last illness, and privileges for taxes, State, parish or municipal; provided, such privileges shall lapse in three years.

ART. 177. Privileges on movable property shall exist without registration for the same, except in such cases as the general assembly may prescribe by law, after the adoption of this constitution.

ART. 178. The General Assembly shall provide for the interest of State medicine in all its departments, for the protection of the people from unqualified practitioners of medicine; for protecting confidential communications to medical men by their patients while under professional treatment, and for the purpose of such treatment; and for the establishment and maintenance of a State Board of Health.

ART. 179. The General Assembly shall create a Bureau of Agriculture, define its objects, designate its officers and fix their salaries, at such time as the financial condition of the State may warrant them, in their judgment, in making such expenditures; *provided*, that such expenditures never exceed ten thousand dollars per annum.

THE NEW CANAL AND SHELL ROAD

ART. 180. The New Basin Canal and Shell Road, and their appurtenances shall not be leased or alienated.

MILITIA

ART. 181. The general assembly shall have authority to provide by law how the militia of this State shall be organized, officered, trained, armed and equipped, and of whom it shall consist.

ART. 182. The officers and men of the militia and volunteer forces shall receive no pay, rations or emoluments when not in active service by authority of the State.

ART. 183. The General Assembly may exempt from military service those who belong to religious societies, whose tenets forbid them to bear arms; *provided*, a money equivalent for these services shall be exacted. The Governor shall have power to call the militia into active service for the preservation of law and order, or when the public service may require it; *provided*, that the police force of any city, town or parish shall not be organized or used as a part of the State militia.

SUFFRAGE AND ELECTIONS

ART. 184. In all elections by the people the electors shall vote by ballot; and in all elections by persons in a representative capacity, the vote shall be viva voce.

ART. 185. Every male citizen of the United States, and every male person of foreign birth who has been naturalized, or who may have legally declared his intention to become a citizen of the United States before he offers to vote, who is twenty-one years old or upwards, possessing the following qualifications, shall be an elector, and shall be entitled to vote at any election by the people, except as hereinafter provided:

1. He shall be an actual resident of the State at least one year next preceding the election at which he offers to vote.

2. He shall be an actual resident of the parish in which he offers to vote at least six months next preceding the election.

3. He shall be an actual resident of the ward or precinct in which he offers to vote at least thirty days next preceding the election.

ART. 186. The General Assembly shall provide by law for the proper enforcement of the provisions of the foregoing article; provided, that in the parish of Orleans there shall be a supervisor of registration, who shall be appointed by the Governor, by and with the advice and consent of the Senate, whose term of office shall be for the period of four years, and whose salary, qualifications and duties shall be prescribed by law. And the General Assembly may provide for the registration of voters in the other parishes.

ART. 187. The following persons shall not be permitted to register, vote or hold any office or appointment of honor, profit or trust in this State, to-wit:

Those who shall have been convicted of treason, embezzlement of public funds, malfeasance in office, larceny, bribery, illegal voting or other crime punishable by hard labor or imprisonment in the penitentiary, idiots and insane persons.

ART. 188. No qualification of any kind for suffrage or office, nor any restraint upon the same, on account of race, color or previous condition shall be made by law.

ART. 189. Electors shall in all cases except for treason, felony and breach of the peace, be privileged from arrest during their attendance on elections, and in going to and returning from the same.

ART. 190. The general assembly shall by law forbid the giving or selling of intoxicating drinks, on the day of election, within one mile of precincts, at any election held within this State.

ART. 191. Until otherwise provided by law, the general State election shall be held once every four years on the Tuesday next following the third Monday in April.

Presidential electors and member of Congress shall be chosen or elected in the manner at the time prescribed by law.

ART. 192. Parochial and the municipal elections in the cities of New Orleans and Shreveport shall be held on the same day as the general State election and not oftener than once in four years.

ART. 193. For the purpose of voting, no person shall be deemed to have gained a residence, by reason of his presence, or lost it by reason of his absence, while employed in the service, either civil or military, of this State or of the United States; nor while engaged in the navigation of the waters of the State or the United States, or of the high seas, nor while a student of any institution of learning.

ART. 194. The general assembly shall provide by law for the trial and determination of contested elections of all public officers, whether State, judicial, parochial or municipal.

ART. 195. No person shall be eligible to any office, State, or judicial, parochial, municipal or ward; who is not a citizen of this State and a duly qualified elector of the State, judicial district, parish, municipality or ward, wherein the functions of said office are to be exercised. And, whenever any officer, State, judicial, parochial, municipal or ward, may change his residence from this State, or from the district, parish, municipality or ward in which he holds such office, the same shall thereby be vacated, any declarations of retention of domicile to the contrary notwithstanding.

IMPEACHMENT AND REMOVALS FROM OFFICE

ART. 196. The Governor, Lieutenant Governor, Secretary of State, Auditor, Treasurer, Attorney General, Superintendent of Public Education and the judges of all the courts of record in this State shall be liable to impeachment for high crimes and misdemeanor, for nonfeasance or malfeasance in office, for incompetency, for corruption, favoritism, extortion or oppression in office, or for gross misconduct or habitual drunkenness.

ART. 197. The House of Representatives shall have the sole power of impeachment. All impeachments shall be tried by the Senate; when sitting for that purpose, the Senators shall be upon oath or affirmation, and no person shall be convicted without the concurrence of two-thirds of the Senators present. When the Governor of the State is on trial, the Chief Justice or the Senior Associate Justice of the Supreme Court shall preside.

Judgment in cases of impeachment shall extend only to removal from office and disqualification from holding any office of honor, trust or profit under the State, but the party, whether convicted or acquitted, shall nevertheless be liable to prosecution, trial and punishment according to law.

ART. 198. All officers against whom articles of impeachment may be preferred shall be suspended from the exercise of the functions of their office during the pendency of such impeachment and, except in case of the impeachment of the Governor, the appointing power shall make a provisional appointment to replace any suspended officer until the decision of the impeachment.

ART. 199. For any reasonable cause, the Governor shall remove any officer on the address of two-thirds of the members elected to each house of the General Assembly. In every such case, the cause or causes for which such removal may be required shall be stated at length in the address and inserted in the journal of each house.

ART. 200. For any of the causes specified in article 196, judges of the courts of appeal, of the district courts throughout the State, and of the city courts of the parish of Orleans may be removed from office by judgment of the Supreme Court of this State in a suit instituted by the Attorney General or a district attorney in the name of the State, on his relation. The Supreme Court is hereby vested with original jurisdiction to try such causes; and it is hereby made the duty of the Attorney General or of any district attorney to institute such suit on the written request and information of fifty citizens and taxpayers residing within the territorial limits of the district or circuit over which the judge against whom the suit is brought exercises the functions of his office. Such suits shall be tried, after citation and ten days' delay for answering, in preference to all other suits, and wherever the court may be sitting; but the pendency of such suit shall not operate a suspension from office. In all cases where the officer sued, as above directed, shall be acquitted, judgment shall be rendered jointly and *in solido* against the citizens signing the request, for all costs of the suit.

ART. 201. For any of the causes enumerated in article 196, district attorneys, clerks of courts, sheriffs, coroners, recorders, justices of the peace and all other parish, municipal and ward officers shall be removed by judgment of the district court of the domicile of such officer (in the parish of Orleans the Civil District Court;) and it shall be the duty of the district attorney, except when the suit is to be brought against himself, to institute suit in the manner directed in article 200, on the written request and information of twenty-five resident citizens and taxpayers in the case of district, parish or municipal officers, and of ten resident citizens and taxpayers in the case of ward officers. Such suit shall be brought against a district attorney by the district attorney of an adjoining district, or by counsel appointed by the judge for that purpose. In all such cases the defendant, the State and the citizens and taxpayers on whose information and at whose request such suit was brought, or any one of them, shall have the right to appeal, both on the law and the facts, from the judgment of the court. In all cases where the officer sued, as above directed, shall be acquitted, judgment shall be rendered jointly and *in solido* against the citizens signing the request, for all costs of the suit.

In cases against district attorneys, clerks, sheriffs and recorders the appeal shall be to the supreme court, and in cases against all other officers the appeal shall be to the court of appeals of the proper circuit.

Such appeals shall be returnable within ten days to the appellate court, wherever it may be sitting or wherever it may hold its next session, and may be transferred by order of the judges of said court to another parish within their circuit; and such appeals shall be tried by preference over all others. In case of the refusal or neglect of the district attorney or Attorney General to institute and prosecute any suit provided for in this and the preceding article, the citizens and taxpayers making the request, or any one of them, shall have the right by mandamus to compel him to perform such duty.

REVENUE AND TAXATION

ART. 202. The taxing power may be exercised by the General Assembly for State purposes, and by parishes and municipal corporations, under authority granted to them by the General Assembly, for parish and municipal purposes.

ART. 203. Taxation shall be equal and uniform throughout the territorial limits of the authority levying the tax, and all property shall be taxed in proportion to its value, to be ascertained as directed by law; provided, the assessment of all property shall never exceed the actual cash value thereof; and provided further, that the taxpayers shall have the right of testing the correctness of their assessments before the courts of justice. In order to arrive at this equality and uniformity the General Assembly shall, at its first session after the adoption of this constitution, provide a system of equality and uniformity in assessments, based upon the relative value of property in the different portions of the State. The valuation put upon property for the purposes of State taxation shall be taken as the proper valuation for purposes of local taxation in every sub-division of the State.

ART. 204. The taxing power shall be exercised only to carry on and maintain the government of the State and the public institutions thereof, to educate the children of the State, to pay the principal and interest of the public debt, to suppress insurrection, repeal invasion or defend the State in time of war, to supply the citizens of the State who lost a limb or limbs in the military service of the Confederate States with substantial artificial limbs during life, and for levee purposes, as hereinafter provided.

ART. 205. The power to tax corporations and corporate property shall never be surrendered nor suspended by act of the General Assembly.

ART. 206. The General Assembly may levy a license tax, and in such case shall graduate the amount of such tax to be collected from the persons pursuing the several trades, professions, vocations and callings. All persons, association of persons and corporations pursuing any trade, profession, business or calling may be rendered liable to such tax, except clerks, laborers, clergymen, school teachers, those engaged in mechanical, agricultural, horticultural and mining pursuits, and manufacturers other than those of distilled alcoholic or malt liquors, tobacco and cigars, and cotton seed oil. No political corporation shall impose a greater license tax than is imposed by the General Assembly for State purposes.

ART. 207. The following property shall be exempt from taxation, and no other, viz: All public property, places of religious worship or burial, all charitable institutions, all buildings and property used exclusively for colleges or other school purposes, the real and personal estate of any public library and that of any other literary association, used by or connected with such library; all books and philosophical apparatus, and all paintings and statuary of any company or association kept in a public hall; *provided*, the property so exempted be not used or leased for purposes of private or corporate profit or income. There shall also be exempt from taxation household property to the value of five hundred dollars; there shall also be exempt from taxation and license for a period of twenty years from the adoption of the constitution of 1879, the capital, machinery and other property employed in the manufacture of textile fabrics, leather, shoes, harness, saddlery, hats, flour, machinery, agricultural implements, manufacturer of ice, fertilizers and chemicals, and furniture and other articles of wood, marble or stone, soap, stationery, ink and paper, boat-building and chocolate; *provided*, that not less than five hands are employed in any one factory.

ART. 208. The General Assembly shall levy an annual poll tax, for the maintenance of public schools, upon every male inhabitant in the State over the age of twenty-one years, which shall never be less than one dollar nor exceed one dollar and a half per capita, and the General Assembly shall pass laws to enforce payment of said tax.

ART. 209. The State tax on property for all purposes whatever, including expenses of government, schools, levees and interest, shall not exceed in any one year six mills on the dollar of its assessed valuation, if the ordinance regarding the bonded debt of the State is adopted and ratified by the people; and if said ordinance is not adopted and ratified by the people, said State tax for all purposes aforesaid shall not exceed, in any one year, five mills on the dollar of the assessed valuation of the property; and no parish or municipal tax for all purposes whatsoever shall exceed ten mills on the dollar of valuation; provided, that for the purpose of erecting and constructing public buildings, bridges and works of public improvement in parishes and municipalities, the rates of taxation herein limited may be increased when the rate of such increase and the purpose for which it is intended shall have been submitted to a vote of the property taxpayers of such parish or municipality entitled to a vote under the election laws of the State, and a majority of same voting at such election shall have voted therefor.

ART. 210. There shall be no forfeiture of property for the non-payment of taxes, State, levee district, parochial or municipal, but at the expiration of the year in which they are due the collector shall, without suit, and after giving notice to the delinquent in the manner to be provided by law (which shall not be by publication except in case of unknown owner) advertise for sale the property on which the taxes are due in the manner provided for judicial sales, and on the day of sale he shall sell such portion of the property as the debtor shall point out, and in case the debtor shall not point out sufficient property, the collector shall at once and without further delay sell the least quantity of property which any bidder will buy for the amount of the taxes, interest and costs. The sale shall be without appraisement, and the property sold shall be redeemable at any time for the space of one year, by paying the price given, with twenty per cent and costs added. No sale of property for taxes shall be annulled for any informality in the proceedings until the price paid, with ten per cent interest be tendered to the purchaser. All deeds of sale made, or that may be made, by collectors of taxes, shall be received by courts in evidence as *prima facie* valid sales.

ART. 211. The tax shall be designated by the year in which it is collectable, and the tax on movable property shall be collected in the year in which the assessment is made.

ART. 212. The Legislature shall pass no law postponing the payment of taxes, except in case of overflow, general conflagration, general destruction of the crops, or other public calamity.

ART. 213. A levee system shall be maintained in the State, and a tax not to exceed one mill may be levied annually on all property subject to taxation, and shall be applied exclusively to the maintenance and repairs of levees.

ART. 214. The General Assembly may divide the State into levee districts and provide for the appointment or election of levee commissioners in said districts, who shall in the method and manner to be provided by law, have supervision of the erection, repair and maintenance of the levees in said districts; to that effect the Levee Commissioners may levy a tax not to exceed ten mills on the taxable property situated within alluvial portions of said district subject to overflow; *provided*, that in case of necessity to raise additional funds for the purpose of constructing, preserving or repairing any levees protecting the lands of a district, the rate of taxation herein limited, may be increased when the rate of such increase and the necessity and purpose for which it is intended shall have been submitted to a vote of the property taxpayers of such district, paying taxes for himself, or in any representative capacity, whether resident or non-resident, on property situated within the alluvial portion of said district subject to overflow, and a majority of those in number and value, voting at such election, shall have voted therefor.

ART. 215. The provisions of the above two articles shall cease to have effect whenever the Federal government shall assume permanent control and provide ways and means for the maintenance of levees in this State. The Federal government is authorized to make such geological, topographical, hydrographical and hydrometrical surveys and investigations within the State as may be necessary to carry into effect the act of Congress, to provide for the appointment of a Mississippi River Commission for the improvement of said river, from the head of the Passes near its mouth to the headwaters, and to construct and protect such public works and improvements as may be ordered by Congress, under the provisions of said act.

ART. 216. The General Assembly shall have power, with the concurrence of an adjacent State or States, to create levee districts composed of territory partly in this State and partly in such adjacent State or States, and the levee commissioners for such district or districts shall possess all the powers provided by article 214 of this constitution.

ART. 217. Corporations, companies or associations organized or domiciled out of this State, but doing business herein, may be licensed by a mode different from that provided for home corporations or companies; provided, said different mode of license shall be uniform, upon a graduated system, as to all such corporations, companies or associations that transact the same kind of business.

ART. 218. All the articles and provisions of this constitution regulating and relating to the collection of State taxes and tax sales shall also apply to and regulate the collection of parish, district and municipal taxes.

HOMESTEADS AND OTHER EXEMPTIONS

ART. 219. There shall be exempt from seizure and sale by any process whatever, except as herein provided, the "homesteads" bona fide owned by the debtor and occupied by him consisting of lands, buildings and appurtenances, whether rural or urbane; of every head of a family, or person having a mother or father, a person or persons dependent on him or her for support; also one work horse, one wagon or cart, one yoke of oxen, two cows and calves, twenty-five head of hogs, or one thousand pounds of bacon or its equivalent in pork, whether these exempted objects be attached to a homestead or not, and on a farm the necessary quantity of corn and fodder for the current year, and the necessary farming implements to the value of two thousand dollars; *provided*, that in case the homestead exceeds two thousand dollars in value, the beneficiary shall be entitled to that amount in case a sale of the homestead under any legal process realizes more than that sum.

No husband shall have the benefit of a homestead whose wife owns and is in the actual enjoyment of property or means to the amount of two thousand dollars.

Such exemptions to be valid, shall be set apart and registered as shall be provided by law. The benefit of this provision may be claimed by the surviving spouse, or minor child or children of a deceased beneficiary, if in indigent circumstances.

ART. 220. Laws shall be passed as early as practicable, for the setting apart, valuation and registration of property claimed as a homestead. Rights to homesteads, or exemptions under laws or contracts, or for debts existing at the time of the adoption of this Constitution, shall not be impaired, repealed or affected by any provision of this Constitution, or any laws passed in pursuance thereof. No court or ministerial officer of this State shall ever have jurisdiction or authority to enforce any judgment, execution or decree against the property set apart for a homestead, including such improvements as may be made thereon from time to time; *provided*, the property herein declared to be exempt shall not exceed in value two thousand dollars. This exemption shall not apply to the following cases, to-wit:

1. For the purchase price of said property, or any part thereof.
2. For labor and material furnished for building, repairing or improving homesteads.
3. For liabilities incurred by any public officer or fiduciary, or any attorney at law, for money collected or received on deposit.
4. For lawful claims for taxes or assessments.

ART. 221. The owner of a homestead shall at any time have the right to supplement his exemption by adding to an amount already set apart, which is less than the whole amount of exemption herein allowed, sufficient to make his homestead and exemption equal to the whole amount allowed by this Constitution.

ART. 222. The homestead shall not be susceptible of mortgage, except for the purchase price, labor and material furnished for the building, repairing or improving homestead, nor shall any renunciation or waiver of homestead rights or exemptions be valid. The right to sell any property which shall be recorded as a homestead shall be preserved, but no sale shall destroy or impiar any rights of creditors therein.

ART. 223. Equitable laws shall be passed for the protection of creditors against the fraudulent claims of debtors; for the punishment of fraud, and for reaching property and funds of the debtor concealed from the creditor.

PUBLIC EDUCATION

ART. 224. There shall be free public schools established by the General Assembly throughout the State for the education of all children of the State between the ages of six and eighteen years; and the General Assembly shall provide for their establishment, maintenence and support by taxation or otherwise. And all moneys so raised, except the poll tax, shall be distributed to each parish in proportion to the number of children between the ages of six and eighteen years.

ART. 225. There shall be elected, by the qualified electors of the State, a Superintendent of Public Education, who shall hold his office for the term of four years, and until his successor is qualified. His duties shall be prescribed by law, and he shall receive an annual salary of two thousand dollars. The aggregate annual expenses of his office, including his salary, shall not exceed the sum of three thousand dollars. The General Assembly shall provide for the appointment of parish boards of public education for the different parishes.

The parish boards may appoint a parish superintendent of public schools in their respective parishes, who shall be ex-officio secretary of the parish board, and whose salary for his double functions shall not exceed two hundred dollars annually, (except that in the parish of Orleans the salary of the parish superintendent shall be fixed by the General Assembly,) to be paid out of the public fund accruing to each parish respectively.

ART. 226. The general exercises in the public schools shall be conducted in the English language and the elementary branches taught therein; *provided*, that these elementary branches may be also taught in the French language in those parishes in the State or localities in said parishes where the French language predominates, if no additional expenses is incurred thereby.

ART. 227. The funds derived from the collection of the poll tax shall be applied exclusively to the maintenance of the public schools as organized under this Constitution, and shall be applied exclusively to the support of the public schools in the parish in which the same shall be collected, and shall be accounted for and paid by the collecting officers directly to the competent school authorities of each parish.

ART. 228. No funds raised for the support of the public schools of the State shall be appropriated to or used for the support of any sectarian schools.

ART. 229. The school funds of this State shall consist of:

1. The proceeds of taxation for school purposes, as provided in this Constitution.
2. The interest on the proceeds of all public lands heretofore granted by the United States for the use and support of the public schools.
3. Of lands and other property which may hereafter be bequeathed, granted or donated to the State, or generally, for school purposes.
4. All funds or property, other than unimproved lands, bequeathed or granted to the State, not designated for other purposes.
5. The proceeds of vacant estates falling under the law to the State of Louisiana.

The Legislature may appropriate to the same fund the proceeds, in whole or in part, of public lands not designated for any other purpose, and shall provide that every parish may levy a tax for the public schools therein, which shall not exceed the State tax; provided, that with such tax the whole amount of parish taxes shall not exceed the limits of parish taxation fixed by this Constitution.

STATE UNIVERSITY

ART. 230. The University of Louisiana, as at present established and located at New Orleans, is hereby recognized in its three departments, to wit: the law, the medical and the academical departments, to be governed and controlled by appropriate faculties.

The General Assembly shall, from time to time, make such provision for the proper government, maintenance and support of said State University of Louisiana, and all the departments thereof, as the public necessities and well being of the people of the State of Louisiana may require, not to exceed ten thousand dollars annually.

The Louisiana State University and Agricultural and Mechanical College, now established and located in the city of Baton Rouge, is hereby recognized, and all revenues derived and to be derived from the sales of land, or land scrip, donated by the United States to the State of Louisiana for the use of a seminary of learning, and mechanical and agricultural college, shall be appropriated exclusively to the maintenance and support of said University and Agricultural and Mechanical College, and the General Assembly shall from time to time make such additional appropriations for the maintenance and support of said Louisiana State University and Agricultural and Mechanical College as the public necessities and the well being of the people of the State of Louisiana may require, not to exceed ten thousand dollars annually.

ART. 231. The General Assembly shall also establish in the city of New Orleans a university for the education of persons of color; provide for its proper government, and shall make an annual appropriation of not less than five thousand dollars nor more than ten thousand dollars for its maintenance and support.

ART. 232. Women over twenty-one years of age shall be eligible to any office of control or management under the school laws of this State.

FREE SCHOOL FUND, SEMINARY FUND, AND AGRICULTURAL AND MECHANICAL COLLEGE FUND

ART. 233. The debt due by the State to the Free School Fund is hereby declared to be the sum of one million, one hundred and thirty thousand eight hundred and sixty-seven dollars and fifty-one cents in principal, and shall be placed on the books of the Auditor and Treasurer to the credit of the several townships entitled to the same; the said principal being the proceeds of the sales of lands heretofore granted by the United States for the use and support of free public schools, which amount shall be held by the State as a loan, and shall be and remain a perpetual fund, on which the State shall pay an annual interest of four per cent from the first day of January, 1880; and that said interest shall be paid to the several townships in the State entitled to the same, in accordance with the act of Congress, No. 68, approved February 15, 1843, and the bonds of the State heretofore issued belonging to said fund, and sold under act of the General Assembly, No. 81, of 1872, are hereby declared null and void, and the General Assembly shall make no provision for their payment, and may cause them to be destroyed.

The debt due by the State to the Seminary Fund is hereby declared to be one hundred and thirty-six thousand dollars, being the proceeds of the sale of lands heretofore granted by the United States to this State for the use of a Seminary of learning, and said amount shall be placed to the credit of said fund on the books of the Auditor and Treasurer of the State as a perpetual loan, and the State shall pay an annual interest of four per cent on said amount from January 1, 1880, for the use of said seminary of learning; and the consolidated bonds of the State now held for use of said fund shall be null and void after the first day of January, 1880, and the General Assembly shall never make any provision for their payment, and they shall be destroyed in such manner as the General Assembly may direct.

The debt due by the State to the Agricultural and Mechanical College Fund is hereby declared to be the sum of one hundred and eighty-two thousand three hundred and thirteen dollars and three cents, being the proceeds of the sales of lands and land scrip heretofore granted by the United States to this State for the use of a college for the benefit of agriculture and the mechanic arts; said amounts shall be placed to the credit of said fund on the books of the Auditor and Treasurer of the State as a perpetual loan, and the State shall pay an annual interest of five per cent on said amount from January 1, 1880, for the use of said Agricultural and Mechanical College. The consolidated bonds of the State now held by the State for the use of said fund shall be null and void after the first day of January, 1880, and the General Assembly shall never make any provision for their payment, and they shall be destroyed in such manner as the General Assembly may direct.

The interest provided for by this article shall be paid out of any tax that may be levied and collected for the general purposes of public education.

CORPORATIONS AND CORPORATE RIGHTS

Art. 234. The General Assembly shall not remit the forfeiture of the charter of any corporation now existing, nor renew, alter or amend the same, nor pass any genaral or special law for the benefit of such corporation, except upon the condition that such corporation shall thereafter hold its charter subject to the provisions of this Constitution.

Art. 235. The exercise of the police power of the State shall never be abridged nor so construed as to permit corporations to conduct their business in such manner as to infringe the equal rights of individuals or the general well-being of the State.

Art. 236. No foreign corporation shall do any business in this State without having one or more known places of business and an authorized agent or agents in the State upon whom process may be served.

Art. 237. No corporation shall engage in any business other than that expressly authorized in its charter or incidental thereto, nor shall it take or hold any real estate for a longer period than ten years, except such as may be necessary and proper for its legitimate business or purposes.

Art. 238. No corporation shall issue stock nor bonds, except for labor done or money or property actually received, and all fictitious issues of stock shall be void, and any corporation issuing such fictitious stock shall forfeit its charter.

Art. 239. The stock shall not be increased, except in pursuance of general laws, nor without consent of persons holding the larger amount in value of the stock, first obtained at a meeting of stockholders to be held after thirty days' notice given in pursuance of law.

Art. 240. The term corporation, as used in this Constitution, shall be construed to include all joint stock companies or associations having any power or privileges not possessed by individuals or partnerships.

ART. 241. It shall be a crime, the nature and punishment of which shall be prescribed by law, for any president, director, manager, cashier or other officer or owner of any private or public bank or banking institution to assent to the reception of deposits, or the creation of debts by such banking institution, after he shall have had knowledge of the fact that it is insolvent or in failing circumstances; any such officer, agent or manager shall be individually responsible for such deposits so received and all such debts so created with his assent.

ART. 242. The General Assembly shall have power to enact general laws authorizing the parochial or municipal authorities of the State, under certain circumstances, by a vote of the majority of the property taxpayers in numbers and in value, to levy special taxes in aid of public improvements or railway enterprises; *provided*, that such tax shall not exceed the rate of five mills per annum nor extend for a longer period than ten years.

ART. 243. Any railroad corporation or association organized for the purpose shall have the right to construct and operate a railroad between any points within this State, and connect at the State line with railroads of other States. Every railroad company shall have the right with its road to intersect, connect with or cross any other railroad, and shall receive and transport each the other's passengers, tonnage and cars, loaded or empty, without delay or discrimination.

ART. 244. Railways heretofore constructed, or that may hereafter be constructed in this State, are hereby declared public highways, and railroad companies common carriers.

ART. 245. Every railroad or other corporation, organized or doing business in this State under the laws or authority thereof, shall have and maintain a public office or place in this State for the transaction of its business, where transfers of stock shall be made, and where shall be kept for public inspection books in which shall be recorded the amount of capital stock subscribed, the names of owners of stock, the amounts owned by them respectively, the amount of stock paid, and by whom, the transfers of said stock, with the date of transfer, the amount of its assets and liabilities, and the names and places of residence of its officers.

ART. 246. If any railroad company, organized under the laws of this State, shall consolidate, by sale or otherwise, with any railroad company organized under the laws of any other State or of the United States, the same shall not thereby become a foreign corporation, but the courts of this State shall retain jurisdiction in all matters which may arise, as if said consolidation had not taken place. In no case shall any consolidation take place except upon public notice of at least sixty days to all stockholders, in such manner as may be provided by law.

ART. 247. General laws shall be enacted providing for the creation of private corporations, and shall therein provide fully for the adequate protection of the public and the individual stockholder.

ART. 248. The police juries of the several parishes and the constituted authorities of all incorporated municipalities of the State shall alone have the power of regulating the slaughtering of cattle and other live stock within their respective limits; provided, no monopoly or exclusive privilege shall exist in this State, nor such business be restricted to the land or houses of any individual or corporation; provided, the ordinances designating the places of slaughtering shall obtain the concurrent approval of the board of health or other sanitary organization.

PAROCHIAL AFFAIRS AND BOUNDARIES

ART. 249. The General Assembly may establish and organize new parishes, which shall be bodies corporate, with such powers as may be prescribed by law; but no new parish shall contain less than six hundred and twenty-five square miles, nor less than seven thousand inhabitants; nor shall any parish be reduced below that area or number of inhabitants.

ART. 250. All laws changing parish lines or removing parish seats shall, before taking effect, be submitted to the electors of the parish or the parishes to be effected thereby, at a special election held for that purpose, and be adopted by a majority of votes of each parish cast at such election.

ART. 251. Any parish may be dissolved and merged by the General Assembly into a contiguous parish or parishes, two-thirds of the qualified electors of the parish proposed to be dissolved voting in favor thereof, at an election held for that purpose; *provided*, that each of the parishes into which the dissolved parish proposes to become incorporated consents thereto by a majority of its qualified electors voting therefor.

ART. 252. Whenever a parish shall be enlarged or created from territory contiguous thereto, it shall be entitled to a just proportion of the property and assets, and liable for a just proportion of the existing debts or liabilities of the parish or parishes from which such territory shall be taken.

THE CITY OF NEW ORLEANS

ART. 253. The citizens of the city of New Orleans or any political corporation which may be created within its limits shall have the right of appointing the several public officers necessary for the administration of the police of said city, pursuant to the mode of election which shall be provided by the General Assembly.

ART. 254. The General Assembly, at its next session after the adoption of this Constitution, shall enact such legislation as may be proper to liquidate the indebtedness of the city of New Orleans, and apply its assets to the satisfaction thereof. It shall have authority to cancel the charter of said city; and remit its inhabitants to another form of government if necessary. In any such new form of government no salary shall exceed three thousand five hundred dollars.

ART. 255. The General Assembly shall pass necessary laws to prevent sailors or others of the crew of foreign vessels from working on the wharfs and levees of the city of New Orleans; provided, there is no treaty between the United States and foreign powers to the contrary.

AMENDMENT AND REVISION OF THE CONSTITUTION

ART. 256. Propositions for the amendment of this Constitution may be made by the General Assembly at any session therof, and if two-thirds of all the members elected to each house shall concur therein, after such proposed amendments have been read in such respective houses on three separate days, such proposed amendment or amendments, together with the yeas and nays thereon, shall be entered on the journal, and the Secretary of State shall cause the same to be published in two newspapers published in the parish of Orleans and in one paper in each other parish of the State in which a newspaper is published, for three months preceding the next election for Representatives, at which time the said amendment or amendments shall be submitted to the electors for their approval or rejection; and if a majority voting on said amendment or amendments shall approve and ratify the same, then such amendment or amendments so approved and ratified shall become a part of the Constitution.

When more than one amendment shall be submitted at the same time they shall be so submitted as to enable the electors to vote on each amendment separately. The result of said election shall be made known by the proclamation of the Governor.

SCHEDULE

ART. 257. The Constitution of this State, adopted in 1868, and all amendments thereto, is declared to be superseded by this Constitution, and in order to carry the same into effect, it is hereby declared and ordained as follows:

ART. 258. All rights, actions, prosecutions, claims and contracts, as well of individuals as of bodies corporate, and all laws in force at the time of the adoption of this Constitution, and not inconsistent therewith, shall continue as if the said Constitution had not been adopted. But the monopoly features in the charter of any corporation now existing in the State, save such as may be contained in the charters of railroad companies, are hereby abolished.

ART. 259. In order that no inconvenience may result to the public service from the taking effect of this Constitution, no office shall be superceded thereby, but the laws of the State relative to the duties of the several officers—executive, judicial and military—shall remain in full force, though the same be contrary to this Constitution, and the several duties shall be performed by the respective officers of the State, according to the existing laws, until the organization of the government under this Constitution and the entering into office of the new officers to be appointed or elected under said government, and no longer.

ART. 260. Appointments to office by the Executive under this Constitution shall be made by the Governor to be elected under its authority.

ART. 261. All causes in which appeals have been or may be hereafter taken, or now pending in the Supreme Court under the Constitution of 1868, and of which jurisdiction has been vested by this Constitution in the courts of appeal, shall, after the adoption of this Constitution, be transferred for trial to the court of appeal of the circuit from which appeal has been or may be taken.

All other causes that may be pending in the Supreme Court, under the Constitution of 1868, shall be transferred to the Supreme Court created by this Constitution, as soon as it shall be organized.

All causes that may be pending in all other courts, under the Constitution of 1868, upon the adoption of this Constitution and the reorganization of the courts created by this Constitution, shall be transferred to the courts respectively having jurisdiction thereof under this Constitution.

ART. 262. Immediately after the adjournment of this Convention, the Governor shall issue his proclamation, directing the several officers of the State authorized by law to hold elections for members of the General Assembly, to open and hold a poll in every parish in the State, at the places designated by law, upon the first Tuesday in the month of December next, 1879, for the purpose of taking the sense of the good people of this State in regard to the adoption or rejection of this Constitution; and it shall be the duty of said officers to receive the votes of all persons entitled to vote under the Constitution of 1868.

Each voter shall express his opinion by depositing in the ballot box a ticket, whereon shall be written or printed, " For the Constitution," or "Against the Constitution," or some such words as will distinctively convey the intention of the voter.

It shall also be the duty of the Governor in his said proclamation, to direct the said officers authorized by law to hold elections, to open and hold a poll at the above stated time and places, for the election of Governor, Lieutenant Governor, members of the General Assembly, Secretary of State, Attorney General, State Auditor, and Superintendent of Public Education, and of all other officers whose election by the people is provided for in this Constitution; and the names of the persons voted for shall be written or printed on the same ticket, and deposited in the same box as the votes " for " or " against " the Constitution.

And the said election for the adoption or rejection of the Constitution, and for the said officers, shall be conducted and the returns thereof made in conformity with existing laws upon the subject of State elections.

Upon the receipt of the said returns, or on the last Monday in December, 1879, if the returns be not sooner received, it shall be the duty of the Governor, the Lieutenant Governor, the Secretary of State, and the Attorney General, in the presence of all such persons as may choose to attend, to compile the votes given at the said polls for ratification and rejection of this Constitution; and it shall appear from said returns that a majority of the votes given on the question of adoption and rejection of the Constitution is for ratifying this Constitution, then it shall be the duty of the Governor to make immediate proclamation of that fact, and henceforth this Constitution shall be ordained and established as the Constitution of the State of Louisiana, and the General Assembly elected in 1878 shall thereupon be dissolved. Whether this Constitution be adopted or rejected, it shall be the duty of the Governor to cause to be published in the official paper of the Convention the result of the polls, showing the number of votes cast in each parish for or against the said Constitution.

If the Constitution be ratified, it shall be the duty of the Secretary of State to examine and compile the returns, and publish the result of the election of officers herein ordained, and in the manner provided by existing laws.

ART. 263. The General Assembly first elected under this Constitution shall convene in the city of New Orleans upon the second Monday in January next, 1880, after the election, and the Governor and Lieutenant Governor elected shall be duly installed in office during the first week of the session, and before it shall be competent for the said General Assembly to proceed with the transaction of business beyond their own organization.

ART. 264. The State Auditor, Attorney General, Secretary of State, and Superintendent of Public Education, elected at the first election herein provided for, shall enter upon the discharge of the duties of their respective offices on the second Monday of January, 1880, after complying with the requisites of existing laws; and all other officers whose election or appointment is provided for by this Constitution shall enter upon the discharge of the duties of their respective offices on the first Monday of April, eighteen hundred and eighty, after complying with the requirements of existing laws; until which period, all officers under the Constitution of eighteen hundred and sixty-eight shall receive the pay and emoluments provided for under such Constitution; *provided*, that the pay of the officers elected or appointed under this Constitution shall not commence until after their induction into office. The State Treasurer elected in November, 1878, shall continue in office as if elected at the election to be held on the first Tuesday in December, 1879; but the salary of said officer shall be as established by this Constitution, from and after the second Monday in January, 1880.

ART. 265. The time of service of all officers chosen by the people at the first election under this Constitution shall terminate as though the election had been holden on the first Tuesday after the first Monday in April, 1880.

ART. 266. The judges of the courts of appeal, district judges, city judges, district attorney, coroner, clerks of courts, sheriffs, recorder of mortgages and register of conveyances, all of whose election and appointment are provided for by this Constitution, in the parish of Orleans, shall only enter on the discharge of the duties of their respective offices on the first Monday of August, 1880, and the present incumbents shall continue until then in the performance of the duties of their respective offices and the enjoyment of the emoluments thereof, as now prescribed by law.

ART. 267. The General Assembly is required to make provision for paying J. H. Cosgrove, Printer of the Convention, for the balance due him for work done previous to adjournment, and for all work that may be done by him after the adjournment of the Convention, by its direction, and shall make a special appropriation to liquidate the debt which this Convention has contracted, authorizing the Fiscal Agent of the State to negotiate a loan of twenty-five thousand dollars; and also for the payment of such vouchers as may be issued by the chairman of the Committee on Contingent Expenses, under the authority of this Convention in excess of the foregoing appropriation, for the purpose of enabling this Convention to complete its work; provided, said vouchers are approved by the President of the Convention.

ART. 268. There shall not be any municipal election in the cities of New Orleans and Shreveport, in December, 1879. The General Assembly shall provide for a municipal election in the city of New

Orleans, or such municipal corporations as may be created within the territorial limits of the parish of Orleans during the year 1880. The General Assembly may fix the time for a municipal election in the city of Shreveport, before April, 1884.

ART. 269. The terms of act No. 43, of the regular session of 1884, adopted at the session of the Legislature in the year 1884, are hereby ratified and approved; and all provisions of the Constitution of 1879 repugnant thereto or in any way impairing the passage thereof, are hereby repealed, so far as the operations of said act are concerned.

ART. 270. The General Assembly may divide the State into levee districts and provide for the appointment of election of Levee Commissioners in said districts, who shall in the method or manner to be provided by law, have supervision of the erection, repair and maintenance of the levees in said districts; to that effect the Levee Commissioners may levy a tax not to exceed ten mills on the taxable property, situated within the alluvial portions of said district subject to overflow; *provided*, that, in case of necessity, to raise additional funds for the purpose of constructing, preserving and repairing any levees protecting the lands of the district, the rate of taxation, herein limited, may be increased when the rate of such increase and the necessity and purpose for which it is intended shall have been submitted to a vote of the property taxpayers in such district, paying taxes for himself, or in any representative capacity, whether resident or non-resident, on property situated in the alluvial portion of said district subject to overflow, and a majority of those in number and value, voting at such election, shall have voted therefor.

LOUIS A. WILTZ,
*President and Delegate from the
Ninth Representative District of the Parish of Orleans.*

WM. H. HARRIS, *Secretary.*

MISCELLANEOUS ORDINANCES

RELIEF OF DELINQUENT TAXPAYERS

ART. 1. *Be it ordained by the people of the State of Louisiana, in convention assembled*, All interests, penalties, costs and charges whatever, on taxes and licenses due the State, or any political corporation therein, prior to the first day of January, 1879, and yet unpaid, are remitted; and all property forfeited to the State or any political corporation on account of non-payment of taxes and licenses, or to which the State or any political corporation now has a title, shall be redeemable, and the title to the State or any political corporation thereto annulled upon the payment by the debtor, or any interested party, of the principal of all taxes and licenses that may be due thereon at the date of redemption, and this right of redemption shall continue until the 1st day of January, 1881. In the event the principal of said taxes and licenses is not paid by said time, the interest, penalties, costs, fees and charges herein before remitted shall revive and attach to the property upon which the taxes and licenses are due, and such property shall be then sold in the manner to be provided by law, and the title of the purchaser shall be full and complete; provided, that nothing herein contained shall be construed as affecting the rights of third persons who may have purchased property, legally assessed and sold at tax sales, or from the State or any political corporation, after the same was legally forfeited to or purchased by the State, or such corporation; and provided further, that nothing in this ordinance shall be taken as granting any time for the payment of the principal of said taxes and licenses; and provided further, that interest shall accrue and be collected on the principal of said delinquent taxes and licenses at the rate of eight per cent annum from January 1, 1880; and on all said taxes and licenses paid a discount of 10 per cent per annum shall be allowed from the date of payment to January 1, 1881.

That all taxes and licenses due the State prior to January 1, 1879, may be paid as follows:

1. That portion of said taxes and licenses due the General Fund and all other funds, except as hereinafter provided, in any valid Auditor's warrants outstanding at the date of the adoption of this Constitution, except all warrants issued prior to the first of January, 1874, and also all warrants issued from the first of January, 1874, to the first of January, 1875, for other purposes than for salaries of constitutional officers, or for the support of charitable institutions for the year 1874.

That, at the option of the holders of any of said warrants, the said warrants may be funded in bonds of the denomination of five dollars, with interest coupons attached thereto, at the rate of three per cent per annum interest from the first day of July, 1880. The said bonds to be due and payable six years from the first day of January, 1880; the said coupons being payable at the State treasury on the first day of February and August of each year.

All moneys received in the treasury for all taxes and licenses due the State prior to the first day of January, 1879, except such as are otherwise provided for by this ordinance, shall be set aside to pay the interest on said five dollar bonds, and to provide a sinking fund to redeem the same. The bonds above provided and interest coupons shall also be receivable for amounts due to the State for the redemption or purchase of property which has been forfeited or sold to the State for delinquent taxes and licenses of any of the years named in this article. The bonds so issued shall be receivable for the said taxes and licenses and the obligations of the public charitable institutions of the State given for the purchase of necessary supplies of food, clothing, medicine and hire of employes.

2. That portion of said taxes and licenses due the Interest Fund, subsequent to January, 1874, in any matured coupons issued by the State since that date.

3. That portion of said tax due the levee fund since the year eighteen hundred and seventy-one to the year eighteen hundred and seventy-six, inclusive of both years, in any valid warrants issued to the levee company and indorsed by the Auditor and Treasurer of the State as follows: " Receivable for levee tax due from eighteen hundred and seventy-one to eighteen hundred and seventy-six, inclusive;" and the Auditor and Treasurer are hereby authorized to so indorse warrants issued by the Levee Company, as provided above, to an amount sufficient to cover the balance due on the judgment recovered by said company in the case entitled Louisiana Levee Company vs. the State of Louisiana, No. 7163, in the Supreme Court of Louisiana.

Be it further ordained, etc., That no Auditor's warrant shall be taken as valid for the purpose of payment of taxes and licenses or for funding as hereinbefore prescribed, until the same shall have been examined by the Auditor, Treasurer and Attorney General of the State, and indorsed by them as valid. Said warrants, when so indorsed, may be surrendered to said officers, and by them registered and cancelled, and in lieu thereof said Auditor and Treasurer shall issue certificates in sums of five, ten, twenty or fifty dollars, as may be desired by the holder of said warrants, which shall be receivable for all taxes and licenses due the State prior to January 1, 1879, except the taxes due the Interest Fund and Levee Fund.

Be it further ordained, That all taxes and licenses due any parish or municipal corporation prior to January 1, 1879, may be payable in any valid warrants, scrip or floating indebtedness of said parish or municipal corporation, except judgments.

INDEBTEDNESS OF THE STATE TO ITS FISCAL AGENT

Be it ordained by the people of the State of Louisiana in Convention assembled, The debt due from the State to its Fiscal Agent, being in amount one hundred and eighty-seven thousand seventy-seven dollars and twenty-four cents ($187,077.24), subject to such reduction as may result from credits arising out of taxes due to the Interest Fund since June 30, 1879, which said debt was created under the contract made between the Board of Liquidators and the Fiscal Agent, under date of twenty-fifth May, 1877, and under Act No. 28, session of the Legislature of 1878, is hereby declared to be a valid obligation of the State; and the Legislature shall, at its first session after the adoption of this Constitution, provide for the payment of the same; and the Fiscal Agent shall, as a condition precedent to said payment, surrender and deliver to the Auditor of the State for cancellation, the interest coupons which were taken up and held by said Fiscal Agent at the time of making the advances which created the said indebtedness; but the interest to be allowed said Fiscal Agent shall be at the rate of four per cent per annum until the debt is paid.

ORDINANCE—LOAN BY FISCAL AGENT

ART. 1. *Be it ordained by the people of the State of Louisiana in Convention assembled*, That the Fiscal Agent of this State shall be and is hereby empowered by authority of this Convention to negotiate a loan of twenty-five thousand dollars or so much thereof as may be necessary, at seven per cent per annum to defray the residue of the expenses of this Convention not provided for by the act of the General Assembly calling this Convention, and to enable the Convention to complete the work of framing the new Constitution.

ART. 2. That said loan shall be evidenced by certificates of indebtedness, signed by the President of this Convention, and countersigned by the Secretary thereof, under seal of this Convention, in sums of five hundred dollars or under, bearing seven per cent per annum interest from the date of such certificates until paid, and payable on the fifteenth day of March, A. D. 1880, at the State National Bank of New Orleans, in the city of New Orleans.

ART. 3. The first General Assembly convened under this Constitution shall make a special appropriation to liquidate the debt which this Convention has contracted or may contract, as per ordinance adopted authorizing the Fiscal Agent of the State to negotiate a loan of twenty-five thousand dollars for the purpose of enabling this Convention to complete the work of framing this Constitution.

STATE DEBT

ARTICLE 1. *Be it ordained by the people of the State of Louisiana, as provided by law*, That the State Debt Ordinance be amended so as to read as follows: That the interest to be paid on the Consolidated Bonds of the State of Louisiana, be and is hereby fixed at two per centum per annum for five years, from the first day of January, one thousand eight hundred and eighty (1880), and four per centum per annum thereafter, payable semi-annually; and there shall be levied an annual tax sufficient for the full payment of said interest, not exceeding three mills, the limit of State tax for all purposes being hereby fixed at six mills; and said bonds and coupons shall be duly stamped: " Interest reduced to two per centum per annum for five years from January 1, one thousand eight hundred and eighty, and four per centum per annum thereafter."

ART. 2. That the holders of the Consolidated Bonds may, at any time, in order that the coupons may be paid, present their bonds to the Treasurer of the State, or to agents to be appointed by the Governor, one in the city of New York, and the other in the city of London, England, and the said Treasurer or agents, as the case may be, shall indorse or stamp thereon the words: " Interest reduced to two per centum per annum for five years from January 1, one thousand eight hundred and eighty (1880), and four per centum per annum thereafter;" and said Treasurer or agent shall indorse or stamp on said coupons the following words: " Interest reduced to two per cent per annum;" or " Interest reduced to four per centum per annum," as the case may be.

ART. 3. *Be it further ordained*, That the coupons of said consolidated bonds falling due the first of January, 1880, be and the same is hereby remitted, and any interest taxes collected to meet said coupons are hereby transferred to defray the expenses of the State government.

Be it further ordained, and it is hereby ordained by this Constitutional Convention, That the foregoing provisions and articles relative to the consolidated debt shall not form a part of this Constitution, except as hereinafter provided, as follows:

At the election held for the ratification or rejection of this Constitution, it shall be lawful for each voter to have written or printed on his ballot the words, " For ordinance relative to State debt," or the words, "Against ordinance relative to State debt," and in the event that a majority of the ballots so cast have indorsed on them the words, " For ordinance relative to State debt," then the said foregoing provisions and articles of this ordinance shall form a part of the Constitution submitted, if the same is ratified; and if a majority of the votes so cast shall have indorsed on them the words, "Against ordinance relative to State debt," then said provisions and articles shall form no part of this Constitution.

LOUIS A. WILTZ,
President and Delegate from the Ninth Representative District of the Parish of Orleans.

WM. H. HARRIS, *Secretary.*

CITY DEBT ORDINANCE

Proposing an amendment to the Constitution providing for the funding of the bonded debt of the city of New Orleans, other than Premium Bonds, into four per cent bonds; providing a special tax of one per cent to pay the bonded debt of the city, and exempting the said four per cent bonds from taxation, and further authorizing the said city to assume and pay such unpaid claims of the Board of School Directors of said city and parish which it may find to be equitably due by said board.

SECTION 1. *Be it resolved by the Senate and House of Representatives of the State of Louisiana, two-thirds of all the members elected to each house concurring,* That the following amendments to the Constitution of the State be submitted to the electors of the State at the next election for Representatives for the General Assembly in the year 1892, for the purpose of retiring the now existing valid outstanding bonds of the city of New Orleans, including the bond certificates or bonds issued under the act of the Legislature No. 58 of 1882 and to retire judgments now or hereafter rendered against the city on floating debt claims prior to 1879, entitled to be funded under act No. 67 of 1884, the said city of New Orleans is hereby authorized and directed, on and after the adoption of this amendment, to issue through the Board of Liquidation of the City Debt, bonds to be known as the Constitutional Bonds of the city of New Orleans, not exceeding ten millions of dollars, at fifty years, bearing four per cent per annum interest to bear date and be in the form prescribed by the Legislature. The said bonds shall be applied by the said board to the retirement of said outstanding bonds and judgments, by the sale of said Constitutional Bonds, and application of the proceeds of sale by the Board of Liquidation, to pay or purchase said outstanding bonds and judgments, or by exchanging the said Constitutional Bonds for bonds, on the terms and in the mode prescribed by the Legislature. For the payment of the interest and principal at maturity, of said Constitutional Bonds, and other outstanding bonds not retired under this amendment, and for the payment of the annual allotments and premiums of the Premium Bonds of said city, the said city is hereby authorized and directed to levy annually, and until the full payment of said bonds, a special tax of one per cent on all the real and personal property of the city, said tax to be part of, and not in addition to the tax of twenty mills and two-tenths of a mill on the dollar of valuation now levied for all purposes by the city of New Orleans, and the said tax shall be paid over as collected to, and be applied by the Board of Liquidation, to the payment of the interest and principal at maturity of said Constitutional Bonds, and outstanding bonds not retired, and to the payment of the allotments of Premium Bonds and premiums extant, in the hands of holders.

Said tax is hereby declared to be the contract right of the holders of all said bonds; and the exemption of said Constitutional Bonds from all taxation by the city of New Orleans and State of Louisiana is hereby recognized and declared, and after payment of all the annual interest on said Constitutional Bonds and bonds not retired and the payment of the said annual allotments of Premium Bonds and premiums extant in the hands of holders, and after making provisions for a sinking fund, at such time and of such an amount as the Legislature prescribes, the surplus of said one per cent shall be disposed of as prescribed by the Legislature.

The act passed at the present session No. 36, entitled "An act to carry into effect the Constitutional amendment passed at the present session relative to the bond debt of the city of New Orleans," etc., be and is hereby approved and confirmed in all its parts as a contract between the city of New Orleans and the holders of said Constitutional Bonds, Premium Bonds and of the bonds outstanding not retired as aforesaid.

SECTION 2. *Be it further resolved*, That all electors voting at said Orleans be and is hereby authorized and empowered to examine into and assume the payment of the claims or obligations of the Board of School Directors for the city and parish of Orleans due for the years 1880, 1881, 1882, 1883 and 1884, now in the hands of original owners, who have in no wise parted with their right of ownership or pledged the same, as may be found to be equitably due by said board for services rendered, labor performed or materials furnished by authority of said board.

SECTION 3. *Be it further resolved*, That all electors voting at said election for said amendment shall place upon their ballots the words, For the city of New Orleans debt amendment," and all electors voting at said election against said amendment shall place on their ballots the words, "Against the city of New Orleans debt amendment."

CONSTITUTION OF LOUISIANA—1898 * [a]

PREAMBLE

We, the people of the State of Louisiana, grateful to Almighty God for the civil, political and religious liberties we enjoy, and desiring to secure the continuance of these blessings, do ordain and establish this Constitution.

BILL OF RIGHTS

ART. 1. All government, of right, originates with the people, is founded on their will alone and is instituted solely for the good of the whole. Its only legitimate end is to secure justice to all, preserve peace and promote the interest and happiness of the people.

ART. 2. No person shall be deprived of life, liberty or property. except by due process of law.

ART. 3. No law shall ever be passed to curtail or restrain the liberty of speech or of the press; any person may speak, write and publish his sentiments on all subjects, being responsible for the abuse of that liberty.

ART. 4. Every person has the natural right to worship God, according to the dictates of his conscience, and no law shall be passed respecting an establishment of religion.

---

* Verified from " Constitution of the State of Louisiana, Adopted in Convention at the City of New Orleans, May 12, 1898. By Authority. H. J. Hearsey, Convention Printer. New Orleans, La. 1898." 144+xv pp.

[a] With amendments.

Art. 5. The people have the right peaceably to assemble and apply to those vested with the powers of government for a redress of grievances by petition or remonstrance.

Art. 6. All courts shall be open, and every person for injury done him in his rights, lands, goods, person or reputation shall have adequate remedy by due process of law and justice administered without denial, partiality or unreasonable delay.

Art. 7. The right of the people to be secure in their persons, houses, papers and effects against unreasonable searches and seizures shall not be violated and no warrant shall issue except upon probable cause, supported by oath or affirmation, and particularly describing the place to be searched and the persons or things to be seized.

Art. 8. A well regulated militia being necessary to the security of a free State, the right of the people to keep and bear arms shall not be abridged. This shall not prevent the passage of laws to punish those who carry weapons concealed.

Art. 9. In all criminal prosecutions the accused shall have the right to a speedy public trial by an impartial jury; provided, that cases in which the penalty is not necessarily imprisonment at hard labor, or death, shall be tried by the court without a jury or by a jury less than twelve in number, as provided elsewhere in the Constitution; provided further, that all trials shall take place in the parish in which the offense was committed, unless the venue be changed. The accused in every instance, shall have the right to be confronted with the witnesses against him; he shall have the right to defend himself, to have the assistance of counsel, to have compulsory process for obtaining witnesses in his favor. Prosecutions shall be by indictment or information; but the Legislature may provide for the prosecution of misdemeanors on affidavits; provided, that no person shall be held to answer for a capital crime unless on a presentment or indictment by a grand jury, except in cases arising in the militia when in actual service in time of war or public danger; nor shall any person be twice put in jeopardy of life or liberty for the same offense, except on his own application for a new trial, or where there is a mistrial, or a motion in arrest of judgment is sustained.

Art. 10. In all criminal prosecutions, the accused shall be informed of the nature and cause of the accusation against him; and when tried by jury shall have the right to challenge jurors peremptorily, the number of challenges to be fixed by law.

Art. 11. No person shall be compelled to give evidence against himself in a criminal case, or in any proceeding that may subject him to criminal prosecution, except as otherwise provided in this Constitution.

Art. 12. Excessive bail shall not be required, nor excessive fines imposed, nor cruel and unusual punishment inflicted. All persons shall be bailable by sufficient sureties, unless for capital offenses where the proof is evident or presumption great, or unless after conviction for any crime or offense punishable with death or imprisonment at hard labor.

Art. 13. The privilege of the writ of habeas corpus shall not be suspended, unless when, in case of rebellion or invasion, the public safety may require it.

Art. 14. The military shall be in subordination to the civil power.

Art. 15. This enumeration of rights shall not be construed to deny or impair other rights of the people not herein expressed.

DISTRIBUTION OF POWERS

ART. 16. The powers of the government of the State of Louisiana shall be divided into three distinct departments, each of them to be confided to a separate body of magistracy, to-wit: Those which are legislative to one, those which are executive to another, and those which are judicial to another.

ART. 17. No one of these departments, nor any person or collection of persons holding office in one of them, shall exercise power properly belonging to either of the others, except in the instances hereinafter expressly directed or permitted.

LEGISLATIVE DEPARTMENT

APPORTIONMENT

ART. 18. Representation in the House of Representatives shall be equal and uniform and shall be based upon population. Each parish and each ward of the City of New Orleans shall have at least one representative. At its first regular session after the United States census of 1900, and after each census thereafter, the General Assembly shall, and it is hereby directed to apportion the representation among the several parishes and Representative Districts on the basis of the total population shown by such census. A representative number shall be fixed, and each parish and Representative District shall have as many Representatives as such representative number is contained in the total number of the inhabitants of such parish or Representative District and one additional Representative for every fraction exceeding one-half the representative number. The number of Representatives shall not be more than one hundred and sixteen nor less than ninety-eight.

ART. 19. The General Assembly, in every year in which it shall apportion representation in the House of Representatives, shall divide the State into Senatorial Districts. No parish shall be divided in the formation of a Senatorial District, the Parish of Orleans excepted. Whenever a new parish is created, it shall be attached to the Senatorial District from which most of its territory is taken, or to another contiguous district, at the discretion of the General Assembly, but shall not be attached to more than one district. The number of Senators shall not be more than forty-one nor less than thirty-six, and they shall be apportioned among the Senatorial Districts acording to the total population contained in the several districts.

ART. 20. Until an enumeration shall have been made in accordance with Articles 18 and 19, the State shall be divided into the following Senatorial Districts, with the number of Senators hereinafter apportioned to each district:

The First Senatorial District shall be composed of the First and Second Wards of the Parish of Orleans, and shall elect one Senator;

The Second Senatorial District shall be composed of the Third Ward of the Parish of Orleans, and shall elect one Senator;

The Third Senatorial District shall be composed of the Fourth, Fifth, Sixth and Seventh Wards of the Parish of Orleans, and shall elect two Senators;

The Fourth Senatorial District shall be composed of the Eighth and Ninth Wards, of the Parish of Orleans, and of the Parishes of St. Bernard and Plaquemines, and shall elect two Senators;

The Fifth Senatorial District shall be composed of the Tenth Ward, and shall elect one Senator;

The Sixth Senatorial District shall be composed of the Eleventh, Twelfth, Thirteenth and Fourteenth Wards, and shall elect two Senators;

The Seventh Senatorial District shall be composed of the Fifteenth, Sixteenth and Seventeenth Wards, and shall elect one Senator;

The Eighth Senatorial district shall be composed of the Parishes of Jefferson, St. Charles and St. John the Baptist, and shall elect one Senator;

The Ninth Senatorial District shall be composed of the Parishes of St. James and Ascension and shall elect one Senator;

The Tenth Senatorial District shall be composed of the Parishes of Terrebonne, Lafourche and Assumption, and shall elect two Senators;

The Eleventh Senatorial District shall be composed of the Parishes of St. Mary and Vermilion, and shall elect one Senator;

The Twelfth Senatorial District shall be composed of the Parishes of Cameron and Calcasieu, and shall (elect) one Senator;

The Thirteenth Senatorial District shall be composed of the Parishes of St. Martin, Iberia and Lafayette, and shall elect two Senators;

The Fourteenth Senatorial District shall be composed of the Parishes of St. Landry and Acadia, and shall elect two Senators;

The Fifteenth Senatorial District shall be composed of the Parishes of Avoyelles and Pointe Coupee, and shall elect one Senator;

The Sixteenth Senatorial District shall be composed of the Parishes of Iberville and West Baton Rouge, and shall elect one Senator;

The Seventeenth Senatorial District shall be composed of the Parishes of East and West Feliciana, and shall (elect) one Senator;

The Eighteenth Senatorial District shall be composed of the Parish of East Baton Rouge, and shall elect one Senator;

The Nineteenth Senatorial District shall be composed of the Parishes of St. Helena, Livingston, Tangipahoa, Washington and St. Tammany, and shall elect two Senators;

The Twentieth Senatorial District shall be composed of the Parishes of Rapides and Vernon, and shall elect one Senator;

The Twenty-first Senatorial District shall be composed of the Parishes of Natchitoches, Sabine, DeSoto and Red River, and shall elect two Senators;

The Twenty-second Senatorial District shall be composed of the Parish of Caddo, and shall elect one Senator;

The Twenty-third Senatorial District shall be composed of the Parishes of Webster and Bossier, and shall elect one Senator;

The Twenty-fourth Senatorial District shall be composed of the Parishes of Bienville and Claiborne, and shall elect one Senator;

The Twenty-fifth Senatorial District shall be composed of the Parishes of Union, Lincoln, Morehouse and West Carroll, and shall elect two Senators;

The Twenty-sixth Senatorial District shall be composed of the Parishes of Ouachita and Jackson, and shall elect one Senator;

The Twenty-seventh Senatorial district shall be composed of the Parishes of Winn, Caldwell and Grant, and shall elect one Senator;

The Twenty-eighth Senatorial District shall be composed of the Parishes of East Carroll and Madison, and shall elect one Senator;

The Twenty-ninth Senatorial District shall be composed of the Parishes of Tensas and Concordia and shall elect one Senator;

The Thirtieth Senatorial District shall be composed of the Parishes of Richland, Franklin and Catahoula, and shall be entitled to one Senator;

Thirty-nine (39) Senators in all.

And the Representatives shall be apportioned among the parishes and Representative districts, as follows:—

For the parish of Orleans:

First Representative District, First Ward, one Representative;

Second Representative District, Second Ward, two Representatives;

Third Representative District, Third Ward, three Representatives;

Fourth Representative District, Fourth Ward, one Representative;

Fifth Representative District, Fifth Ward, two Representatives;

Sixth Representative District, Sixth Ward, one Representative;

Seventh Representative District, Seventh Ward, two Representatives;

Eighth Representative District, Eighth Ward, one Representative;

Ninth Representative District, Ninth Ward, two Representatives;

Tenth Representative District, Tenth Ward, two Representatives;

Eleventh Representative District, Eleventh Ward, two Representatives;

Twelfth Representative District, Twelfth Ward, one Representative;

Thirteenth Representative District, Thirteenth Ward, one Representative;

Fourteenth Representative District, Fourteenth Ward, one Representative;

Fifteenth Representative District, Fifteenth Ward, one Representative;

Sixteenth Representative District, Sixteenth Ward, one Representative;

Seventeenth Representative District, Seventeenth Ward, one representative.

The Parishes of Acadia, West Baton Rouge, Bienville, Caldwell, Cameron, East Carroll, West Carroll, Catahoula, Franklin, Grant, Jackson, Jefferson, Lincoln, Livingston, Plaquemines, Red River, Richland, Sabine, St. Bernard, St. Charles, St. Helena, St. John the Baptist, St. Tammany, Tangipahoa, Vermillion, Vernon, Washington, Webster and Winn, each, one Representative.

The Parishes of Ascension, Assumption, Avoyelles, East Baton Rouge, Bossier, Calcasieu, Claiborne, Concordia, De Soto, East Feliciana, West Feliciana, Iberia, Iberville, Lafourche, Lafayette, Madison, Morehouse, Natchitoches, Pointe Coupee, Ouachita, Rapides, St. James, St. Mary, St. Martin, Tensas, Terrebonne, Union, each, two Representatives;

The Parishes of Caddo and St. Landry, each, three Representatives.

This apportionment of Senators and Representatives shall not be changed or altered in any manner until after the enumeration shall have been taken by the United States. After the year 1902 the apportionment made in this article shall cease to exist.

GENERAL ASSEMBLY

ART. 21. The legislative power of the State shall be vested in a General Assembly, which shall consist of a Senate and House of Representatives.

ART. 22. The style of the laws of this State shall be: " Be it enacted by the General Assembly of the State of Louisiana."

ART. 23. The General Assembly shall meet at the seat of government on the third Monday of May, 1898, at 12 o'clock noon, and biennially thereafter, on the second Monday of May, and the sessions thereof shall be limited to sixty days. Should a vacancy occur in either House, the Governor shall order an election to fill such vacancy for the remainder of the term.

ART. 24. Every elector under this Constitution, shall be eligible to a seat in the House of Representatives, and every elector who has reached the age of twenty-five years shall be eligible to the Senate; provided, that no person shall be eligible to the General Assembly unless at the time of his election he has been a citizen of the State for five years, and an actual resident of the district or parish from which he may be elected for two years immediately preceding his election. The seat of any member who may change his residence from the district or parish which he represents shall thereby be vacated, and declaration of a retention of domicile to the contrary notwithstanding; and members of the General Assembly shall be elected for a term of four years.

ART. 25. Each House shall be the judge of the qualifications, elections and returns of its own members, choose its own officers, except President of the Senate, determine the rules of its proceedings, and may punish its members for disorderly conduct and contempt, and, with the concurrence of two-thirds of all its members elected, expel a member.

ART. 26. Either House, during the session, may punish by imprisonment any person not a member who shall have been guilty of disrespect, or disorderly or contemptuous behavior; but such imprisonment shall not exceed ten days for each offense.

ART. 27. No Senator or Representative shall, during the term for which he was elected, nor for one year thereafter, be appointed or elected to any civil office of profit under this State which may have been created, or the emoluments of which may have been increased by the General Assembly during the time such Senator or Representative was a member thereof.

ART. 28. The members of the General Assembly shall in all cases, except treason, felony, or breach of the peace, be privileged from arrest during their attendance at the sessions of their respective Houses, and in going to and returning from the same; and for any speech or debate in either House they shall not be questioned in any other place.

ART. 29. The members of the General Assembly shall receive a compensation not to exceed five dollars per day during their attendance, and five cents per mile going to and returning from the seat of government.

ART. 30. Each House shall keep a Journal of its proceedings, and cause the same to be published immediately after the close of the session; when practicable, the minutes of each day's session shall be printed and placed in the hands of members on the day following. The original Journal shall be preserved, after publication, in the office of the Secretary of State, but there shall be required no other Record thereof.

ART. 31. Every law enacted by the General Assembly shall embrace but one object, and that shall be expressed in its title.

ART. 32. No law shall be revived, or amended by reference to its title, but in such cases the act revived, or section as amended, shall be re-enacted and published at length.

ART. 33. The General Assembly shall never adopt any system or code of laws by general reference to such system or code of laws; but in all cases shall recite at length the several provisions of the laws it may enact.

ART. 34. Not less than a majority of the members of each House of the General Assembly shall form a quorum to transact business, but a smaller number may adjourn from day to day, and shall have power to compel the attendance of absent members.

ART. 35. Neither House, during the sitting of the General Assembly, shall, without the consent of the other, adjourn for more than three days, nor to any other place than that in which it may be sitting.

ART. 36. The yeas and nays on any question in either House shall, at the desire of one-fifth of the members elected. be entered on the Journal.

ART. 37. All bills, for raising revenue or appropriating money, shall originate in the House of Representatives, but the Senate may propose or concur in amendments, as in other bills.

ART. 38. No bill, ordinance or resolution, intended to have the effect of a law, which shall [have] been rejected by either House, shall be again proposed in the same House during the same session, under the same or any other title, without the consent of a majority of the House by which the same was rejected.

ART. 39. Every bill shall be read on three different days in each House, and no bill shall be considered for final passage unless it has been read once in full, and the same has been reported on by a committee; nor shall any bill become a law unless, on its final passage, the vote be taken by yeas and nays, the names of the members voting for or against the same be entered on the Journal, and a majority of the members elected to each House be recorded thereon as voting in its favor; provided, that bills revising the statutes or codes of this State, or adopting a criminal code as a whole, shall be read in such manner as may be prescribed by the General Assembly.

ART. 40. No amendments to bills by one House shall be concurred in by the other, nor shall reports of committees of conference be adopted in either House except by a majority of the members elected thereto, the vote to be taken by yeas and nays, and the names of those voting for or against recorded upon the Journal.

ART. 41. Whenever a bill that has been passed by both Houses has been enrolled and placed in possession of the House in which it originated, the title shall be read, and, at the request of any five members, the bill shall be read in full, when the Speaker of the House of Representatives or the President of the Senate, as the case may be, shall at once, sign it in open house, and the fact of signing shall be noted on the Journal; thereupon the Clerk or Secretary shall immediately convey the bill to the other House, whose presiding officer shall cause a suspension of all other business to read and sign the bill in open session and without delay. As soon as bills are signed by the Speaker of the House and President of the Senate, they shall be taken at once, and on the same day, to the Governor by the Clerk of the House of Representatives or Secretary of the Senate.

ART. 42. No law passed by the General Assembly, except the general appropriation act, or act appropriating money for the expenses of the General Assembly, shall take effect until promulgated. Laws shall be considered promulgated at the place where the State Journal is published, the day after the publication of such law in the State Journal, and in all other parts of the State twenty days after such publication. The State Journal shall be published at the capital.

ART. 43. The clerical officers of the two Houses shall be a Secretary of the Senate and Clerk of the House of Representatives, with such assistants as may be necessary; but the expenses for said officials, including the Sergeant-at-Arms, of each House, together with all clerks of committees and all other employes of whatever kind, shall not exceed one hundred dollars daily for the Senate, nor one hundred and twenty dollars daily for the House, and the Chairman of the Committee on Contingent Expenses of each House shall not issue warrants for any compensation in excess of said amounts: *Provided*, this shall not affect the employes of the present General Assembly. No donation of any unexpended balances shall be made as extra compensation or for any other purpose.

ART. 44. All stationery, printing, paper and fuel used in the legislative and other departments of government shall be furnished, and the printing, binding and distribution of the laws, journals and department reports, and all other printing and binding, and the repairing and furnishing of the halls and rooms used for the meetings of the General Assembly and its committees, shall be done under contract, to be given to the lowest responsible bidder below such maximum price and under such regulations as shall be prescribed by law.

No member or officer of any of the departments of the government shall be in any way interested in the contracts; and all such contracts shall be subject to the approval of the Governor, the President of the Senate and Speaker of the House of Representatives, or of any two of them.

LIMITATION OF LEGISLATIVE POWERS

ART. 45. No money shall be drawn from the treasury except in pursuance of specific appropriation made by law; nor shall any appropriation of money be made for a longer term than two years. A regular statement and account of receipts and expenditures of all public moneys shall be published every three months, in such manner as shall be prescribed by law.

ART. 46. The General Assembly shall have no power to contract, or to authorize the contracting, of any debt or liability, on behalf of the State; or to issue bonds or other evidence of indebtedness thereof, except for the purpose of repelling invasion, or for the suppression of insurrection.

Art. 47. The General Assembly shall have no power to grant or to authorize any parish or municipal authority to grant any extra compensation, fee or allowance to a public officer, agent, servant or contractor, nor pay, nor authorize the payment, of any claim against the State, or any parish or municipality thereof, under any agreement or contract made without express authority of law; and all such unauthorized agreements or contracts shall be null and void.

Art. 48. The General Assembly shall not pass any local or special law on the following specified subjects:

For the opening and conducting of elections, or fixing or changing the place of voting.

Changing the names of persons.

Changing the venue in civil or criminal cases.

Authorizing the laying out, opening, closing, altering or maintaining roads, highways, streets or alleys, or relating to ferries and bridges, or incorporating bridge or ferry companies, except for the erection of bridges crossing streams which form boundaries between this and any other State.

Authorizing the adoption or legitimation of children or the emancipation of minors.

Granting divorces.

Changing the law of descent or succession.

Affecting the estates of minors or persons under disabilities.

Remitting fines, penalties and forfeitures, or refunding moneys legally paid into the treasury.

Authorizing the constructing of street passenger railroads in any incorporated town or city.

Regulating labor, trade, manufacturing or agriculture.

Creating corporations, or amending, renewing, extending or explaining the charters thereof; provided, this shall not apply to municipal corporations having a population of not less than twenty-five hundred inhabitants, or to the organization of levee districts and parishes.

Granting to any corporation, association, or individual any special or exclusive right, privilege or immunity.

Extending the time for the assessment or collection of taxes, or for the relief of any assessor or collector of taxes from the performance of his official duties, or of his sureties from liability; nor shall any such law or ordinance be passed by any political corporation of this State.

Regulating the practice or jurisdiction of any court, or changing the rules of evidence in any judicial proceeding or inquiry before courts, or providing or changing methods for the collection of debts or the enforcement of judgments, or prescribing the effects of judicial sales.

Exempting property from taxation.

Fixing the rate of interest.

Concerning any civil or criminal actions.

Giving effect to informal or invalid wills or deeds, or to any illegal disposition of property.

Regulating the management of public schools, the building or repairing of schoolhouses, and the raising of money for such purposes.

Legalizing the unauthorized or invalid acts of any officer, servant, or agent of the State, or of any parish or municipality thereof.

ART. 49. The General Assembly shall not indirectly enact special or local laws by the partial repeal of a general law; but laws repealing local or special laws may be passed.

ART. 50. No local or special law shall be passed on any subject not enumerated in Article 48 of this Constitution, unless notice of the intention to apply therefor shall have been published, without cost to the State, in the locality where the matter or thing to be affected may be situated, which notice shall state the substance of the contemplated law, and shall be published at least thirty days prior to the introduction into the General Assembly of such bill, and in the same manner provided by law for the advertisement of judicial sales. The evidence of such notice having been published, shall be exhibited in the General Assembly before such act shall be passed, and every such act shall contain a recital that such notice has been given.

ART. 51. No law shall be passed fixing the price of manual labor.

ART. 52. Any member of the General Assembly who has a personal or private interest in any measure or bill proposed, or pending before the General Assembly, shall disclose the fact to the house of which he is a member, and shall not vote thereon.

ART. 53. No money shall ever be taken from the public treasury, directly or indirectly, in aid of any church, sect or denomination of religion, or in aid of any priest, preacher, minister or teacher thereof, as such, and no preference shall ever be given to, nor any discrimination made against, any church, sect or creed of religion, or any form of religious faith or worship; nor shall any appropriation be made for private, charitable or benevolent purposes to any person or community; provided, this shall not apply to the State Asylum for the Insane and State Institution for the Deaf and Dumb, and State Institution for the Instruction of the Blind, and the charity hospitals and public charitable institutions conducted under State authority.

ART. 54. The General Assembly shall have no power to increase the expenses of any office by appointing assistant officials.

ART. 55. The general appropriation bill shall embrace nothing but appropriations for the ordinary expenses of the government, interest on the public debt, public schools and public charities; and such bill shall be so itemized as to show for what account each and every appropriation shall be made. All other appropriations shall be made by separate bills, each embracing but one object.

ART. 56. Each appropriation shall be for a specific purpose, and no appropriation shall be made under the head or title of contingent; nor shall any officer or department of government receive any amount from the treasury for contingencies or for a contingent fund.

ART. 57. No appropriation of money shall be made by the General Assembly in the last five days of the session thereof. All appropriations, to be valid, shall be passed and receive the signatures of the President of the Senate and the Speaker of the House of Representatives five full days before the adjournment *sine die* of the General Assembly.

ART. 58. The funds, credit, property or things of value of the State, or of any political corporation thereof, shall not be loaned, pledged or granted to or for any person or persons, association or corporation, public or private; nor shall the State, or any political corporation, purchase or subscribe to the capital or stock of any corporation or association whatever, or for any private enterprise. Nor shall the State, nor any political corporation thereof, assume the liabilities of any political, municipal, parochial, private or other corporation or association whatsoever; nor shall the State undertake to carry on the business of any such corporation or association, or become a part owner therein; provided, the State, through the General Assembly, shall have power to grant the right of way through its public lands to any railroad or canal; and provided, Police Juries and municipal corporations may, in providing for destitute persons, utilize any charitable institutions within their corporate limits for the care, maintenance and asylum of such persons; and all appropriations made to such institutions for the purpose aforesaid shall be accounted for by them in the manner required of officials entrusted with public funds.

ART. 59. The General Assembly shall have no power to release or extinguish, or to authorize the releasing or extinguishment, in whole or in part, of the indebtedness, liability or obligation of any corporation or individual to the State, or to any parish or municipal corporation thereof; provided, the heirs to confiscated property may be released from all taxes due thereon at the date of its reversion to them.

ART. 60. No educational or charitable institution, other than the State institutions now existing, or expressly provided for in this Constitution, shall be established by the State, except upon a vote of two-thirds of the members elected to each House of the General Assembly.

EXECUTIVE DEPARTMENT

ART. 61. The Executive Department shall consist of a Governor, Lieutenant Governor, Auditor, Treasurer, and Secretary of State.

ART. 62. The supreme executive power of the State shall be vested in a chief magistrate, who shall be styled the Governor of Louisiana. He shall hold his office during four years, and, together with the Lieutenant Governor, chosen for the same term, shall be elected as follows: The qualified electors for Representatives shall vote for a Governor and Lieutenant Governor at the time and place of voting for Representatives. The return of every election for Governor and Lieutenant Governor shall be made and sealed up separately from the return of election of other officers, and transmitted by the proper officer of every parish to the Secretary of State, who shall deliver them, unopened, to the General Assembly then next to be holden. The members of the General Assembly shall meet on the first Thursday after the day on which they assemble, in the House of Representatives, to examine, tabulate and count the votes evidenced by said returns. The person having the greatest number of votes for Governor shall be declared duly elected; but in case two or more persons shall be equal and highest in the number of votes polled for Governor, one of them shall be imediately chosen Governor by the joint vote of the members of the General Assembly. The person having the greatest number of votes for Lieutenant Governor shall be declared duly elected Lieutenant Governor; but in case two or more persons shall be equal and highest in the number of votes polled for Lieutenant Governor, one of them shall be immediately chosen Lieutenant Governor by the joint vote of the members of the General Assembly.

ART. 63. No person shall be eligible to the office of Governor, or Lieutenant Governor, who shall not have attained the age of thirty years, been ten years a citizen of the United States, and resident of the State for the same period of time next preceding his election; or who shall hold office under the United States at the time of or within six months immediately preceding the election for such office; nor shall any person who shall have been elected, qualified and served as Governor under this Constitution be eligible as his own successor; provided, however, that he may again be eligible to the office at the expiration of one or more terms after the term for which he shall have served.

ART. 64. The Governor and Lieutenant Governor shall enter on the discharge of their duties the first Monday next ensuing the announcement by the General Assembly of the result of the election for Governor and Lieutenant Governor; and each shall continue in office until the first Monday next succeeding the day that his successor shall have been declared duly elected, and shall have taken the oath, or affirmation, required by the Constitution.

ART. 65. In case of the impeachment of the Governor, his removal from office, death, refusal or inability to qualify, disability, resignation, or absence from the State, the powers and duties of the office shall devolve upon the Lieutenant Governor for the residue of the term, or until the Governor, absent or impeached, shall return or be acquitted or the disability be removed. In the event of the removal, impeachment, death, resignation, disability or refusal to qualify, of both the Governor and Lieutenant Governor, the President *pro tempore* of the Senate shall act as Governor until the disability be removed, or for the residue of the term. If there should be no President *pro tempore* of the Senate, when any of the above mentioned contingencies arise for him to act as Governor, or in the event of the removal, death, resignation, permanent disability, or refusal to qualify, of the President *pro tempore*, the Secretary of State shall act as Governor until a President *pro tempore* be elected, either in regular session, or in specially called session, should the vacancy have occurred during recess; and in the event of the impeachment, or temporary disability, of the President *pro tempore*, acting Governor, the Secretary of State shall likewise act as Governor until the disability be removed, or the impeachment proceedings be terminated in acquittal, or until another President pro tempore of the Senate be chosen.

ART. 66. The Lieutenant Governor, or President *pro tempore*, or Secretary of State, discharging the duties of the Governor, shall, during his administration, receive the same compensation to which the Governor would have been entitled had he continued in office.

ART. 67. The Lieutenant Governor shall be *ex-officio* President of the Senate, but shall only have a casting vote therein. The Senate shall elect one of its members as President *pro tempore* of the Senate.

ART. 68. The Lieutenant Governor shall receive for his services a salary of fifteen hundred dollars, payable monthly on his own warrant. In the event of a vacancy in the office of Lieutenant Governor by death, resignation, or any other cause, the President *pro tempore* of the Senate shall fill the office of Lieutenant Governor, performing all the duties incident to the office, and receiving its emoluments.

ART. 69. The Governor shall have power to grant reprieves for all offenses against the State; and, except in cases of impeachment, or treason, shall, upon the recommendation in writing of the Lieutenant Governor, Attorney-General, and presiding Judge of the court before which the conviction was had, or of any two of them, have power in his discretion to grant pardons, commute sentences, and remit fines and forfeitures, after conviction. In case of treason he may grant reprieves until the end of the next session of the General Assembly, in which body the power of pardoning is vested.

ART. 70. The Governor shall receive a salary of five thousand dollars *per annum*, payable monthly, on his own warrant.

ART. 71. He shall nominate and, by and with the advice and consent of the Senate, appoint all officers whose offices are established by this Constitution and whose appointments, or elections, are not herein otherwise provided for; provided, however, that the General Assembly shall have the right to prescribe the mode of appointment or election to all offices created by it.

ART. 72. The Governor shall have the power to fill vacancies that may happen during the recess of the Senate, in cases not otherwise provided for in this Constitution, by granting commissions which shall expire at the end of the next session; but no person who has been nominated for office and rejected shall be appointed to the same office during the recess of the Senate. The failure of the Governor to send into the Senate the name of any person appointed for office, as herein provided, shall be equivalent to a rejection.

ART. 73. He may require information in writing from the officers in the executive departments upon any subject relating to the duties of their respective offices. He shall be Commander-in-Chief of the militia of the State, except, when they shall be called into the actual service of the United States.

ART. 74. He shall, from time to time, give to the General Assembly information respecting the situation of the State, and recommend to its consideration such measures as he may deem expedient.

ART. 75. He shall take care that the laws be faithfully executed, and he may, on extraordinary occasions, convene the General Assembly at the seat of government, or, if that should have become dangerous from an enemy or from an epidemic, at a different place. The power to legislate shall be limited to the objects specially enumerated in the proclamation convening such extraordinary session; therein the Governor shall also limit the time such session may continue; provided, it shall not exceed thirty days. Any legislative action had after the time so limited, or as to objects not enumerated in said proclamation, shall be null and void.

ART. 76. Every bill which shall have passed both houses shall be presented to the Governor. If he approves it, he shall sign it; if not, he shall return it, with his objections in writing, to the house in which it originated, which house shall enter the objections at large upon the Journal, and proceed to reconsider the bill. If, after such reconsideration, two-thirds of all the members elected to that house shall agree to pass the bill, it shall be sent, with the objections to the other house, by which likewise it shall be reconsidered; and if passed by two-thirds of the members elected to that house, it shall be a law; but in such cases the votes of both houses shall be taken by yeas and nays, and the names of the members voting for and against the bill shall be entered on the Journal of each house, respectively. If any bill shall not be returned by the Governor within five days after it shall have been presented to him, it shall be a law in like manner as if he signed it, unless the General Assembly, by adjournment, shall prevent its return, in which case it shall not be a law.

Art. 77. The Governor shall have power to disapprove of any item or items of any bill making appropriations of money, embracing distinct times, and the part or parts of the bill approved shall be law, and the item or items of appropriation disapproved shall be void, unless repassed according to the rules and limitations prescribed for the passage of other bills over the executive veto.

Art. 78. Every order, resolution, or vote, to which the concurrence of both houses may be necessary, except on a question of adjournment, or matters of parliamentary proceedings, or an address for removal from office, shall be presented to the Governor, and before it shall take effect, be approved by him, or, being disapproved, shall be repassed according to the rules and limitations prescribed for the passage of bills over the executive veto.

Art. 79. The Treasurer, Auditor, Attorney General, and Secretary of State, shall be elected by the qualified electors of the State, at the time and place of voting for Representatives, for the term of four years; and in case of vacancy caused by death, resignation, permanent absence, or otherwise, of any of said officers, the Governor shall fill the vacancy by appointment, with the advice and consent of the Senate; provided, the Secretary of State shall have authority to appoint an assistant, who shall be known as Assistant Secretary of State, *sic* or in case of his disability to act, or under the directions of the Secretary of State, the Assistant Secretary of State shall have authority to perform all the acts and duties of the office of Secretary of State. The Secretary of State shall have authority to remove the Assistant Secretary of State at pleasure.

Art. 80. The Treasurer shall not be eligible as his own immediate successor.

Art. 81. The Auditor of Public Accounts shall receive a salary of two thousand five hundred dollars per annum. The Treasurer shall receive a salary of two thousand dollars per annum. The Secretary of State shall receive a salary of one thousand eight hundred dollars per annum. Each of the said officers shall be paid monthly, and no fees, or perquisites, or other compensation, shall be allowed them; provided, that the Secretary of State may be allowed fees, as may be provided by law, for copies and certificates furnished to private persons.

Art. 82. Appropriations for the clerical expenses of the officers named in the preceding article shall specify each item of appropriation; and shall not exceed in any one year, for the Treasurer the sum of two thousand dollars; for the Secretary of State, the sum of two thousand five hundred dollars, and the salary of the Assistant Secretary of State shall be included in this amount; and for the Auditor of Public Accounts, the sum of four thousand dollars.

ART. 83. All commissions shall be in the name and by the authority of the State of Louisiana; and shall be sealed with the State seal, signed by the Governor, and countersigned by the Secretary of State.

JUDICIARY DEPARTMENT

ART. 84. The judicial power of the State shall be vested in a Supreme Court, in Courts of Appeal, in District Courts, in justices of the peace, and in such other courts as are hereinafter provided for.

ART. 85. The Supreme Court, except as hereinafter provided, shall have appellate jurisdiction only, which jurisdiction shall extend to all cases where the matter in dispute, or the fund to be distributed, whatever may be the amount therein claimed, shall exceed two thousand dollars, exclusive of interest; to suits for divorce and separation from bed and board, and to all matters arising therein; to suits involving alimony, for the nullity of marriage, or for interdiction; to all matters of adoption, emancipation, legitimacy, and custody of children; to suits involving homestead exemptions, and to all cases in which the constitutionality or legality of any tax, toll or impost whatever, or of any fine, forfeiture, or penalty imposed by a municipal corporation, shall be in contestation, whatever may be the amount thereof, and to all cases wherein an ordinance of a municipal corporation or a law of this State has been declared unconstitutional, and in such cases the appeal on the law and the facts shall be directly from the court in which the case originated to the Supreme Court; and to criminal cases on questions of law alone, whenever the punishment of death or imprisonment at hard labor may be inflicted, or a fine exceeding three hundred dollars, or imprisonment exceeding six months, is actually imposed. Said court shall have such original jurisdiction as may be necessary to enable it to determine questions of fact affecting its own jurisdiction in any case pending before it, or it may remand the case; and shall have exclusive original jurisdiction in all matters touching professional misconduct of members of the bar, with power to disbar under such rules as may be adopted by the court.

ART. 86. The Supreme Court shall be composed of one Chief Justice and four Associate Justices, a majority of whom shall constitute a quorum. The Chief Justice and Associate Justices shall each receive a salary of not less than five thousand dollars per annum, payable monthly on his own warrant. They shall be appointed by the Governor, with the advice and consent of the Senate, for the term of twelve years. In case of death, resignation or removal from office of any justice, the vacancy shall be filled by appointment for the unexpired term of such justice. They shall be citizens of the United States and of this State, over thirty-five years of age, learned in the law, and shall have practiced law in this State for ten years preceding their appointment.

ART. 87. The State shall be divided into four Supreme Court districts, and the Supreme Court shall always be composed of justices appointed from said districts. The parishes of Orleans, St. John the

Baptist, St. Charles, St. Bernard, Plaquemines, and Jefferson shall compose the first district, from which two justices shall be appointed.

The parishes of Caddo, Bossier, Webster, Bienville, Claiborne, Union, Lincoln, Jackson, Caldwell, Ouachita, Morehouse, Richland, Franklin, West Carroll, East Carroll, Madison, Tensas, Concordia, and Catahoula, shall compose the second district, from which one justice shall be appointed.

The parishes of DeSoto, Red River, Winn, Grant, Natchitoches, Sabine, Vernon, Calcasieu, Cameron, Rapides, Avoyelles, Pointe Coupee, West Baton Rouge, Iberville, St. Landry, Acadia, Lafayette, and Vermillion, shall compose the third district, from which one justice shall be appointed.

The parishes of St. Martin, Iberia, St. Mary, Terrebonne, Lafourche, Assumption, Ascension, St. James, East Baton Rouge, East Feliciana, West Feliciana, St. Helena, Livingston, Tangipohoa, St. Tammany, and Washington shall compose the fourth district, from which one justice shall be appointed.

The justices of the Supreme Court, as now constituted, shall serve until the expiration of their respective terms. When the office of Chief Justice becomes vacant, either from expiration of term, death, resignation, or from any other cause, the Associate Justice who has served the longest time, shall by virtue of said length of service, become Chief Justice, and the new appointee shall become an Associate Justice only.

ART. 88. The Supreme Court shall hold its sessions in the City of New Orleans from the first Monday in the month of November to the end of the month of June in each and every year. It shall appoint its own clerks and remove them at pleasure.

The General Assembly shall make the necessary appropriation to provide suitable and commodious buildings for said court and the records thereof, and for the care and maintenance of the State library therein; and shall provide for the repair and alteration of the building now occupied by the court.

ART. 89. No judgment shall be rendered by the Supreme Court without the concurrence of three justices. Whenever three members cannot concur in any case, in consequence of the recusation of any member or members of the court, or for any other cause, the court shall have authority to call on any judge or judges of the Courts of Appeals, or District Courts, whose duty it shall be, when so called upon, to sit in such case.

ART. 90. All judges, by virtue of their office, shall be conservators of the peace throughout the State. The style of all process shall be "The State of Louisiana." All prosecutions shall be carried on in the name and by the authority of the State of Louisiana, and conclude: "Against the peace and dignity of the same."

ART. 91. The judges of all courts, whenever practicable, shall refer to the law by virtue of which every definitive judgment is rendered, and in every case they shall adduce the reasons on which their judgment is founded. Service of citation shall not be waived, nor judgment confessed, by any document under private signature executed prior to the maturity of the obligation sued on.

ART. 92. The decisions of the Supreme Court shall be reported under the direction of the court; the publication thereof shall be let out by contract to the lowest bidder, who need not be a citizen of the State; provided, that the annual reports for the year 1898, shall be published in numbers, and completed under the present contract therefor, and the present reporter shall remain in office until February 1st, 1899.

Concurring and dissenting opinions shall not be published.

The General Assembly shall annually appropriate the sum of two thousand dollars, as salary of stenographers to be appointed by the court, and for the use of the justices thereof.

ART. 93. The Supreme Court, and each of the justices thereof, shall have power to issue the writ of habeas corpus, at the instance of any person in actual custody, in any case where it may have appellate jurisdiction.

ART. 94. The Supreme Court shall have control and general supervision over all inferior courts. The court, or any justice thereof, shall have power to issue writs of certiorari, prohibition, mandamus, quo warranto, and other remedial writs.

ART. 95. In all cases where there is an appeal from a judgment rendered on a reconventional demand, the appeal shall lie to the court having jurisdiction of the main demand.

ART. 96. Except as herein provided, no duties or functions shall ever be attached by law to the Supreme Court, Courts of Appeal, or District Courts, or to the several justices, or judges thereof, except such as are judicial, and the said justices and judges are prohibited from receiving any fees of office, or other compensation than their salaries, for any official duty performed by them. No judicial powers, except as committing magistrates in criminal cases, shall be conferred on any officer other than those mentioned in this title, except such as may be necessary in towns and cities; provided, the General Assembly shall have the power to abolish justice of the peace courts in wards containing cities of more than five thousand inhabitants, and to create in their stead courts with such civil jurisdiction as is now vested in justices of the peace, and with criminal jurisdiction which shall not extend beyond the trial of offenses not punishable by imprisonment at hard labor under the laws of this State, and of violations of municipal and parochial ordinances, and the holding of preliminary examinations in cases not capital. Provided, the compensation of the judges of such courts shall be paid by the parishes and cities in which they are established, in such proportions as may be provided by law.

ATTORNEY GENERAL

ART. 97. There shall be an Attorney General for the State, who shall be elected by the qualified electors of the State at large every four years. He shall be learned in the law, and shall have actually resided and practiced law, as a licensed attorney, in the State for five years preceding his election. He shall receive a salary of three thousand dollars per annum, payable monthly on his own warrant.

COURTS OF APPEAL

ART. 98. The Courts of Appeal, except as otherwise provided in this Constitution, shall have appellate jurisdiction only, which jurisdiction shall extend to all cases, civil or probate, when the matter in dispute or the funds to be distributed shall exceed one hundred dollars, exclusive of interest, and shall not exceed two thousand dollars, exclusive of interest.

ART. 99. The Courts of Appeal shall remain as at present constituted, until the first day of July, 1900. From and after that date the several Courts of Appeal, except as hereinafter provided, shall consist of one of the judges of those courts whose terms shall not have expired, and who, with a judge of a district court to be designated by the Supreme Court, shall be assigned by the Supreme Court to that duty, throughout the State.

From and after the first day of July, 1904, the Courts of Appeal shall be composed of two district judges, to be from time to time designated by the Supreme Court, and assigned to the performance of the duties of judges of said Courts of Appeal; provided, that no district judge shall be assigned to serve as a member of the Court of Appeal for any parish in his own district; and, provided further, that district judges shall be paid their actual and necessary expenses when serving as judges of the Courts of Appeal in such manner as may be provided by law.

ART. 100. There shall be two terms of the said Courts of Appeal held in each parish annually, to be fixed by the judges of said courts, until the first day of July, 1904. Thereafter the terms of said courts shall be fixed in such manner as may be provided by law.

ART. 101. The judges of the Courts of Appeal shall have power to certify to the Supreme Court any question or proposition of law arising in any cause pending before them concerning which they desire the instruction of that court, for its proper decision; and thereupon the Supreme Court may either give its instruction on the question or proposition certified to it, which shall be binding upon the Court of Appeal in such case, or it may require that the whole record be sent up for its consideration, and thereupon shall decide the whole matter in controversy in the same manner as if it had been on appeal directly to the Supreme Court. It shall be competent for the Supreme Court to require by certiorari, or otherwise, any case to be certified from the Courts of Appeal to it for its review and determination, with the same power and authority in the case, as if it had been carried directly by appeal to the said court; provided, that the Supreme Court shall in no case exercise the power conferred on it by this article, unless the application be made to the court, or to one of the justices thereof, not later than thirty days after the decision of the Court of Appeal has been rendered and entered.

ART. 102. No judgment shall be rendered by the Courts of Appeal without the concurrence of two judges. Whenever there shall be a disagreement in the Courts of Appeal above provided, the court shall appoint a district judge or a lawyer having the qualifications of a judge of the court to sit in the case, and in case of the recusation, absence, or disability, of one of the judges, the other judge shall select a judge or lawyer, as aforesaid, to sit in the case. In the Court of Appeal for the Parish of Orleans, when two judges cannot concur for any reason, the court shall select a district judge, or judges, to sit in the case.

ART. 103. All cases on appeal to the Courts of Appeal shall be tried on the original record, pleadings, and evidence.

ART. 104. The rules of practice regulating appeals to and proceedings in the Supreme Court shall apply to appeals and proceedings in the Courts of Appeal, so far as they may be applicable, until otherwise provided. The Courts of Appeal, and each of the judges thereof, shall have power to issue the writ of habeas corpus at the instance of any person in actual custody within their respective circuits.

They shall also have authority to issue writs of mandamus, prohibition, and certiorari, in aid of their appellate jurisdiction.

[a] ART. 105. The several judges of the Court of Appeal, as constituted under the Constitution of 1879, shall each receive a salary of four thonsand dollars per annum, payable monthly on his own warrant.

ART. 106. The sheriff of the parish in which the sessions of the court are held shall attend in person, or by deputy, to execute the orders of the court.

DISTRICT COURTS

ART. 107. The State shall be divided into not less than twenty nor more than twenty-nine judicial districts, the parish of Orleans excepted.

Until otherwise provided by law, there shall be twenty-nine districts.

ART. 108. The parish of Caddo shall compose the first district.

The parishes of Bossier and Webster shall compose the second district.

The parishes of Claiborne and Bienville shall compose the third district.

The parishes of Union and Lincoln shall compose the fourth district.

The parishes of Caldwell, Jackson, and Winn shall compose the fifth district.

The parishes of Ouachita and Morehouse shall compose the sixth district.

The parishes of West Carroll and Richland shall compose the seventh district.

The parishes of Franklin and Catahoula shall compose the eighth district.

The parishes of Madison and East Carroll shall compose the ninth district.

The parishes of Concordia and Tensas shall compose the tenth district.

The parishes of Natchitoches and Red River shall compose the eleventh district.

The parishes of De Sota, Sabine, and Vernon shall compose the twelfth district.

The parishes of Rapides and Grant shall compose the thirteenth district.

The parish of Avoyelles shall compose the fourteenth district.

The parishes of Calcasieu and Cameron shall compose the fifteenth district.

The parish of St. Landry shall compose the sixteenth district.

---

[a] Abrogated by amendment, 1906.

The parish of Vermillion shall compose the seventeenth district.

The parishes of Acadia and Lafayette shall compose the eighteenth district.

The parishes of Iberia and St. Martin shall compose the nineteenth district.

The parishes of Terrebonne and Lafourche shall compose the twentieth district.

The parishes of Iberville, West Baton Rogue, and Pointe Coupee shall compose the twenty-first district.

The parish of East Baton Rogue shall compose the twenty-second district.

The parish of St. Mary shall compose the twenty-third district.

The parishes of East Feliciana and West Feliciana shall compose the twenty-fourth district.

The parishes of St. Helena, Livingston, and Tangipahoa shall compose the twenty-fifth district.

The parishes of Washington and St. Tammany shall compose the twenty-sixth district.

The parishes of Ascension, St. James, and Assumption, shall compose the twenty-seventh district.

The parishes of St. John the Baptist, St. Charles, and Jefferson shall compose the twenty-eighth district.

The parishes of St. Bernard and Plaquemines shall compose the twenty-ninth district.

The judges of the first, sixth, tenth, eleventh, twelfth, thirteenth, fifteenth, sixteenth, nineteenth, twentieth, twenty-second, twenty-third, twenty-fifth, twenty-seventh, and twenty-eighth districts shall each receive a salary of three thousand dollars per annum, and the judges of the second, third, fourth, ninth, fourteenth, eighteenth, twenty-first, twenty-fourth, twenty-sixth, and twenty-ninth districts shall each receive a salary of two thousand five hundred dollars; the judges of the fifth, seventh, eighth, and seventeenth districts shall each receive a salary of two thousand dollars per annum; such salaries to be paid monthly on their own warrants. Provided, that if the General Assembly at any time reduces the number of districts, as herein fixed, it shall have the right to regrade the salaries of the judges, but in no case shall any judge receive a salary in excess of three thousand dollars per annum.

ART. 109. The District Courts, except in the Parish of Orleans, shall have original jurisdiction in all civil matters where the amount in dispute shall exceed fifty dollars, exclusive of interest, and in all cases where title to real estate is involved, or to office, or other public position, or civil or political rights, and all other cases where no specific amount is in contest, except as otherwise provided in this Constitution. They shall have unlimited and exclusive original jurisdiction in all criminal cases, except such as may be vested in other courts authorized by this Constitution; and in all probate and succession matters, and where a succession is a party defendant; and in all cases where the State, parish, any municipality or other political corporation, is a party defendant, regardless of the amount in dispute; and of all proceedings for the appointment of receivers or liquidators to corporations or partnerships; and said courts shall have authority to issue all such writs, process and orders as may be necessary or proper for the purposes of the jurisdiction herein conferred upon them. There shall be one district judge in each judicial district, except in the twenty-first judicial district, where, until otherwise provided by law, there shall be two district judges, who shall not be residents of the same parish. District judges shall be elected by a plurality of the qualified voters of their respective districts, in which they shall have been actual residents for two years next preceding their election; provided, one year's residence only in the district shall be required for the first election under this Constitution. They shall be learned in the law, and shall have practiced law in the State five years previous to their election.

The first district judges under this Constitution shall be elected at the general State election in 1900, and shall hold office until their successors are elected at the election on the Tuesday after the first Monday in November, 1904, at which time, and every four years thereafter, district judges shall be elected for terms of four years.

Vacancies occasioned by death, resignation, or otherwise, shall be filled for the unexpired term by appointment by the Governor, with the advice and consent of the Senate.

ART. 110. The General Assembly shall not have power to increase the number of district judges in any district.

ART. 111. The District Courts shall have jurisdiction of appeals from justices of the peace in all civil matters, regardless of the amount in dispute, and from all orders requiring a peace bond. Persons sentenced to a fine or imprisonment, by Mayors or Recorders, shall be entitled to an appeal to the District Court of the parish, upon giving security for fine and costs of court, and in such cases trial shall be *de novo* and without juries.

ART. 112. The General Assembly shall provide by law for the interchange of district judges; and also for the trial of recused cases in the District Courts by the selection of licensed attorneys at law, by an interchange of judges or otherwise. Whenever any district judge is prevented by disability, or any other cause whatever, from holding his court, and that fact is made to appear by the certificate of the clerk, under the seal of the court, to the Supreme Court, or to any justice thereof, if in the judgment of the court, or any justice, the public interest so requires, the court or such justice shall designate and appoint any district judge of any other district to hold said court and discharge all the judicial duties of the judge so disabled during said disability. Such appointment shall be filed in the clerk's office and entered on the minutes of said District Court, and a certified copy thereof, under the seal of the court, shall be transmitted by the clerk of the District Court to the district judge so designated and appointed.

ART. 113. Whenever in this Constitution the qualification of any justice or judge shall be the previous practice of the law for a term of years, there shall be included in such term the time such justice or judge shall have occupied the bench of any court of record in this State; provided, he shall have been a licensed attorney for five years before his election or appointment.

ART. 114. No judge of any court of the State shall be affected in his term of office, salary, or jurisdiction as to territory or amount, during the term or period for which he was elected or appointed. Any legislation so affecting any judge or court shall take effect only at the end of the term of office of the judge or judges, incumbents of the court, or courts, to which such legislation may apply at the time of its enactment. This article shall not affect the provisions of this Constitution relative to impeachment or removal from office.

ART. 115. The district judges shall have power to issue the writ of *habeas corpus* at the instance of any person in actual custody in their respective districts.

ART. 116. The General Assembly shall provide for the selection of competent and intelligent jurors. All cases in which the punishment may not be at hard labor shall, until otherwise provided by law, which shall not be prior to 1904, be tried by the judge without a jury. Cases in which the punishment may be at hard labor shall be tried by a jury of five, all of whom must concur to render a verdict; cases in which the punishment is necessarily at hard labor, by a jury of twelve, nine of whom concurring may render a verdict; cases in which the punishment may be capital, by a jury of twelve, all of whom must concur to render a verdict.

ART. 117. District Courts shall hold continuous sessions during ten months of the year. In districts composed of more than one parish, the judge shall sit alternately in each parish, as the public business may require. Until otherwise provided by law, judgments shall be signed after three days from the rendition thereof, and become executory ten days from such signing.

The General Assembly shall provide for the drawing of juries for the trial of civil and criminal cases. A grand jury of twelve, nine of whom must concur to find an indictment, shall be empanelled in each parish twice in each year, and shall remain in office until a succeeding grand jury is empanelled; except in the Parish of Cameron, in which at least one grand jury shall be empanelled each year. The district judges shall have authority to try at any time all misdemeanors and when the jury is waived all cases not necessarily punishable at hard labor, and to receive pleas of guilty in cases lass than capital.

The provisions of this article shall go into effect upon the adoption of this Constitution.

ART. 118. The District Courts as created and now existing under the Constitution of 1879, in the various parishes of the State, as now apportioned under existing laws, shall remain undisturbed until the organization of the District Courts created by this Constitution, after the general election of 1900, and the judges thereof shall receive salaries as now fixed.

SHERIFFS AND CORONERS.

ART. 119. There shall be a sheriff and a coroner elected by the qualified voters of each parish in the State, except in the Parish of Orleans, who shall be elected at the general election and hold office for four years.

The coroner, except in the Parish of Orleans, shall act for and in place of the sheriff, whenever the sheriff shall be a party interested, and whenever there shall be a vacancy in the office of sheriff, until such vacancy shall be filled; but he shall not, during such vacancy, discharge the duties of tax collector. The sheriff, except in the Parish of Orleans, shall be ex-officio collector of State and parish taxes.

He shall give separate bonds for the faithful performance of his duty in each capacity. Until otherwise provided, the bonds shall be given according to existing laws.

Sheriffs elected or appointed shall furnish bond within thirty days from the date of their commissions, in default of which the office shall be declared vacant, and the Governor shall appoint for the remainder of the term.

ART. 120. The sheriff shall receive compensation from the parish for his services in criminal matters,—the keeping of prisoners, conveying convicts to the penitentiary, insane persons to the Insane Asylum, service of process from another parish, and service of process or the performance of any duty beyond the limits of his own parish excepted,—not to exceed five hundred dollars per anum for each Representative the parish may have in the House of Representatives.

The compensation of sheriffs as tax collectors shall not exceed five per cent on all sums collected and paid over; provided, that they shall not be discharged as tax collectors until they make proof that they have exhausted the legal remedies to collect taxes.

ART. 121. The coroner in each parish shall be a doctor of medicine, regularly licensed to practice, and *ex-officio* parish physician; provided, this article shall not apply to any parish in which there is no regularly licensed physician who will accept the office.

CLERKS

ART. 122. There shall be a clerk of the District Court in each parish, the Parish of Orleans excepted, who shall be ex-officio clerk of the Court of Appeal.

He shall be elected by the qualified electors of the parish every four years, and shall be *ex-officio* parish recorder of conveyances, mortgages, and other acts, and notary public.

He shall receive no compensation from the State or parish for his services in criminal matters.

He shall give bond and security for the faithful performance of his duties in such amount as shall be fixed by the General Assembly.

ART. 123. The General Assembly shall have power to vest in clerks of court authority to grant such orders and to do such acts as may be deemed necessary for the furtherance of the administration of justice; and in all cases the powers thus vested shall be specified and determined.

ART. 124. Clerks of District Courts may appoint, with the approval of the district judges, deputies with such powers as shall be prescribed by law; and the General Assembly shall have power to provide for continuing one or more of them in office in the event of any vacancy in the office of clerk, until his successor shall have been appointed and duly qualified.

DISTRICT ATTORNEYS

ART. 125. There shall be a District Attorney for each judicial district in the State, who shall be elected by the qualified electors of the judicial district at the same time and for the same term as is provided in Article 109 for district judges. He shall receive a salary of one thousand dollars per annum, payable monthly on his own warrant. He shall be an actual resident of the district and a licensed attorney in this State.

He shall also receive fees; but no fee shall be allowed in criminal cases, except on conviction, which fees shall not exceed five dollars in cases of misdemeanor.

Any vacancy in the office of District Attorney shall be filled by appointment by the Governor for the unexpired term.

JUSTICES OF THE PEACE

ART. 126. In each parish, the Parish of Orleans excepted, there shall be as many justices of the peace as may be provided by law. The present number of justices of the peace shall remain as now fixed until otherwise provided. They shall be freeholders and qualified electors and possess such other qualifications as may be prescribed by law. They shall be elected for the term of four years by the qualified voters within the territorial limits of their jurisdiction.

They shall have exclusive original jurisdiction in all civil matters, when the amount in dispute shall not exceed fifty dollars, exclusive of interest, and original jurisdiction concurrent with the District Court when the amount in dispute shall exceed fifty dollars, exclusive of interest, and shall not exceed one hundred dollars, exclusive of interest; including suits for the ownership or possession of movable property not exceeding said amounts in value, and suits by landlords for possession of leased premises, when the monthly or yearly rent, or the rent for the unexpired term of the lease does not exceed said amounts. They shall have no jurisdiction in succession or probate matters, or when a succession is a defendant, or when the State, parish or any municipality or other political corporation, is a party defendant, or when title to real estate is involved. They shall receive such fees in civil matters as may be fixed by law. They shall have criminal jurisdiction as committing magistrates, and shall have power to bail or discharge in cases not capital or necessarily punishable at hard labor. The General Assembly may by general or special laws invest justices of the peace in general or in any particular parish or parishes with criminal jurisdiction over misdemeanors to be tried with a jury composed of not more than five nor less than three persons, in such manner as may be provided by law, with the right of appeal to the District Court in all cases, not appealable to the Supreme Court, as hereinbefore provided for.

CONSTABLES

ART. 127. There shall be a constable for the court of each justice of the peace in the several parishes of the State, who shall be elected for a term of four years, by the qualified voters within the territorial limits of the jurisdiction of the several justices of the peace. They shall receive such fees in civil matters as may be fixed by law.

ART. 128. Justices of the peace and constables shall receive no fees in criminal matters, including peace bond cases, but, in lieu thereof such salaries as may be fixed by the police jury, and paid by the parish, which salaries shall be graded.

ART. 129. The General Assembly, at its first session after this Constitution is adopted, shall provide a general fee bill, or bill of costs, regulating and fixing the fees and compensation allowed sheriffs, clerks and recorders, justices of the peace, constables, and coroners, in all civil matters. The General Assembly may provide in all civil cases for the service of process and pleadings by the litigants themselves.

COURTS AND OFFICERS FOR THE PARISH OF ORLEANS, AND CITY OF NEW ORLEANS

ART. 130. Except as herein otherwise provided, the judicial officers of the Parish of Orleans, and of the City of New Orleans, shall be learned in the law, and shall have resided and practiced law or shall have held judicial positions in this State for five years, and shall have been actual residents of the City of New Orleans for at least two years next preceding their election or appointment.

ART. 131. There shall be a Court of Appeal, to be known and designated as the Court of Appeal for the Parish of Orleans, which shall be composed of three judges, who shall be learned in the law and who shall have practiced law in this State for six years, and shall have been residents of one of the parishes hereinafter named for at least two years next preceding their election or appointment, and they shall be elected by the qualified electors of the said parishes. Said court shall sit in the City of New Orleans, and shall hold its session from the second Monday of October until the end of the month of June in each year. Said court, until the first day of August, 1900, shall be composed of the present judges thereof, and a third judge, who shall be elected by the qualified voters of the Parish of Orleans, at the Congressional election in the year 1898, and who shall serve in said court until the 1st of August, 1900. His successor shall be elected for a term of eight years from that date, at the general State election of 1900. On August 1, 1900, the [judge] of the Court of Appeal for the Fifth Circuit, as established under the Constitution of 1879, who was elected in the year 1896, shall become a member of the Court of Appeal for the Parish of Orleans, and together with the judge of that court elected in 1896, shall serve until the election of their successors at the Congressional election of 1904. At that election one judge of said court shall be elected for a term of six years, and one for a term of eight years, and thereafter all elections for judges of said court shall be for terms of eight years.

Vacancies occasioned by death, resignation, or otherwise, shall be filled for the unexpired terms by appointment by the Governor, with the advice and consent of the Senate.

The judges of said court shall each receive a salary of four thousand dollars per annum, payable monthly on his own warrant.

After August 1, 1900, in addition to those from the Parish of Orleans, all appeals within its jurisdiction from the parishes of Jefferson, St. Charles, Plaquemines, and St. Bernard, shall be returnable to said court, and the costs of filing same shall not exceed five dollars in each case.

All cases pending and undetermined on said date in the Courts of Appeal as now constituted, from said parishes, shall be transferred to said Court of Appeal for the Parish of Orleans without cost to the parties.

There shall be a clerk of said Court of Appeal, who shall be elected by the qualified voters of said parishes for a term of four years; he shall be entitled to charge and retain as his compensation such fees as may be allowed by law. The first election for said clerk shall be held in the year 1899, at the time the parochial and municipal elections are held in the City of New Orleans; said clerk shall appoint, if necessary, deputy clerks, and shall fix and pay their salaries; he shall give bond in the sum of five thousand dollars, which bond shall be examined in open court by the judges of the court, and all testimony given in said examination shall be reduced to writing and made of record; he may be removed by the court for the same causes and in the same manner as is hereinafter provided for the clerk of the Civil District Court for the Parish of Orleans; he may act as minute clerk of the court, or appoint a deputy to that position.

Said Court of Appeal for the Parish of Orleans shall hereafter have appellate jurisdiction from the city courts of New Orleans as now constituted, under the same conditions as hereinafter provided for appeals from the City Courts to be organized under this Constitution.

ART. 132. There shall be two District Courts for the Parish of Orleans, and no more. One of said courts shall be known as the Civil District Court, and the other as the Criminal District Court. For the Civil District Court there shall be not less than five judges, and for the Criminal District Court not less than two judges, who shall be elected by a plurality of the qualified electors of the Parish of Orleans for the term of twelve years, and who shall each receive an annual salary of four thousand dollars, payable upon his own warrant, in equal monthly instalments.

ART. 133. The Civil District Court shall have exclusive and general original probate jurisdiction, and exclusive original civil jurisdiction, in all cases where the amount in dispute or the fund to be distributed, shall exceed one hundred dollars, exclusive of interest; and exclusive jurisdiction in suits by married women for separation of property, in suits for separation from bed and board, for divorce, for nullity of marriage, or for interdiction, and in suits involving title to immovable property, or to office or other public position, or civil or political rights; and in all other cases, except as hereinafter provided, where no specific amount is in contest, and of all proceedings for the appointment of receivers or liquidators to corporations or partnerships. And said court shall have authority to issue all such writs, process and orders as may be necessary or proper for the purposes of the jurisdiction herein conferred upon it.

ART. 134. All cases after being filed in said Civil District Court shall be allotted or assigned, among the judges thereof, and, except as herein otherwise provided, each judge, or his successor, shall have exclusive control over every case allotted or assigned to him, from its inception to its final determination in said court. In case of vacancy in the office, recusation, absence or disability of a judge to whom a case has been allotted or assigned, or in case such action is deemed advisable in the proper administration of justice, or of the business of the court, such case may be re-allotted or re-assigned, or without such re-allotment or re-assignment, but, under rules to be adopted, it may be taken in charge by another judge of said court, and the judge to whom a case is thus re-allotted or re-assigned, or by whom it is thus taken in charge, shall be authorized to act therein for all purposes as though such case had been originally allotted or assigned to him. Previous to the allotment or assignment of a case, any judge of said court may, for the purposes of such case, make interlocutory orders, and issue and grant conservatory writs and executory process. Applications for naturalization, for emancipation, and by married women for authorization, when there is consent given and no issue joined, or where there is no contest, suits for nullity, and for revival of judgment, and suits in which is claimed an interest in property or funds as to which a particular judge has acquired jurisdiction, need not be allotted or especially assigned, but shall be controlled by law or by rules to be adopted by the court.

ART. 135. Judgments homologating accounts, which have been duly advertised, when not opposed, or so far as not opposed, may be rendered and signed either in term time or vacation; and by any judge, in the absence or disability of the judge to whom the case has been allotted.

ART. 136. The judges of said Civil District Court shall be authorized to adopt rules, not in conflict with law, regulating the allotment, assignment and disposition of cases, the order in which they shall be tried, and the proceedings in such trials, and to sit *en banc* for the purpose of testing the bonds and sureties of the clerk of the court, the recorder of mortgages, the register of conveyances, and the civil sheriff; for the trial and removal of the clerk and civil sheriff, or either of them, for the selection of jurors, and in other cases when the action of the court as a whole is required. When sitting *en banc* the judge who has been longest in continuous service in said court, and in his absence the judge longest in service of those present, shall preside; and when a certificate or authentication from the court is required such judge shall be authorized to sign the same as presiding judge. The court may, by its rules, grant the presiding judge further authority not in conflict with these provisions. Provided, that in rendering judgments *en banc*, the court shall conform, as far as practicable, to the rules and practice of the Supreme Court.

ART. 137. There shall be one clerk for the Civil District Court, who, until the election and induction into office of the clerk of the Court of Appeal, provided for in Article 131, shall be *ex-officio* clerk of the Court of Appeal for the Parish of Orleans, and shall be elected by the voters of said parish for the term of four years. His qualifications and duties, except as herein provided, shall be as fixed by law; he shall furnish bond in the sum of twenty thousand dollars, which bond shall be examined by the court, and all testimony given in such examination shall be reduced to writing and filed of record in the court. He shall charge and collect the fees prescribed by the General Assembly, and shall dispose of the same as hereinafter provided; the amount of his compensation shall be three thousand six hundred dollars per annum.

Said clerk shall be authorized, with the approval of the judges of the Civil District Court, to appoint such deputies and other assistants, at salaries not to exceed those now fixed by law, as in the opinion of said judges are needed for the efficient discharge of the duties of his office; and he may remove them at pleasure, or the court may remove them. The Court of Appeal for the Parish of Orleans, until after the election of the clerk thereof, as hereinbefore provided, and each judge of the Civil District Court shall appoint one minute clerk, who shall be sworn as deputy clerk, and shall receive an annual salary of eighteen hundred dollars in equal monthly installments; and the said

Court of Appeal, until said election, shall also have the right to appoint one docket clerk.

The minute clerk appointed by the judge of the Civil District Court longest in continuous service in said court, as hereinabove provided, shall be *ex-officio* minute clerk of the court when sitting *en banc*, and shall receive, as additional compensation, three hundred dollars per annum, which shall be paid in like manner as his other compensation. The clerk of the Civil District Court shall be removable by the judges of said court, sitting *en banc*, upon proof, after trial, without a jury, of gross or continued neglect, incompetency, or unlawful conduct, operating injury to the court or to any individual, and a majority of said judges shall be competent to render judgment in the case. Such trial and the lodging of complaints leading thereto, shall be regulated by rules which shall be adopted by the judges of the Civil District Court and of the Criminal District Court in joint session.

ART. 138. The Civil District Court shall select a solvent, incorporated bank in New Orleans as a judicial depository, in which, unless otherwise ordered by the court, shall be deposited all money as soon as the same shall come into the hands of the clerk or sheriff, and such deposits shall not be removed in whole or in part without an order from the judge seized with jurisdiction.

ART. 139. The Criminal District Court shall have exclusive original jurisdiction for the trial and punishment of all offenses when the penalty of death, imprisonment at hard labor, or imprisonment without hard labor for any time exceeding six months, or a fine exceeding three hundred dollars may be imposed, and appellate jurisdiction in all cases tried before the City Criminal Courts, or Recorders' Courts of New Orleans, which cases shall be appealable on the law and the facts, and shall be tried on the record and the evidence as made and offered in the lower court. Provided, that until the General Assembly shall enact a law grading offenses, said court shall have general criminal jurisdiction extending to all cases arising in the Parish of Orleans, the jurisdiction of which is not vested by law or by this Constitution in some other court. Said court shall have general and supervisory jurisdiction over all inferior State and municipal criminal courts in the Parish of Orleans, and shall have authority to issue writs of *habeas corpus*, in criminal and quasi-criminal cases, and such other writs and orders as may be necessary or proper in aid of the jurisdiction conferred upon it; and to adopt rules not in conflict with law, regulating the order of preference, and proceedings in the trial of cases, and the method of allotting or assigning such cases, and of re-allotting and re-assigning them, in case of vacancy in the office, recusation, absence or disability of one or more of the judges, or in case such action is deemed necessary for the proper administration of justice. All prosecutions instituted in, and all cases appealed to said Criminal District Court shall be equally allotted or assigned by classes among the judges, and each judge, or his successor, shall have exclusive control over any case allotted or assigned to him, from its inception to its final determination in said court, except as herein otherwise provided.

There shall be one clerk for the Criminal District Court, who shall be elected by the voters of the Parish of Orleans, for the term of four years. His qualifications and duties, except as herein provided, shall be as fixed by law. He shall furnish bond in the sum of ten thousand dollars, which bond shall be examined by the court, in like manner as the bond of the clerk of the Civil District Court. 'He shall receive an annual salary of three thousand dollars, which shall be paid by the City of New Orleans, in equal monthly instalments, and he shall receive no other compensation. He shall appoint, with the approval of the court, such deputies, at such salaries, as may be fixed by law. Said deputies may be removed at the pleasure of the clerk of the court, and their salaries shall be paid by the City of New Orleans.

Each judge of said court shall appoint a minute clerk, who shall be sworn as a deputy clerk, and shall receive an annual salary of eighteen hundred dollars, which shall be paid by the City of New Orleans, in the same manner as the salary of the clerk. One of the said minute clerks, to be designated by the judge longest in continuous service in said court, shall be *ex-officio* minute clerk of said court when sitting *en banc*, and shall receive, as additional compensation, three hundred dollars per annum, which shall be paid in like manner as his other compensation. The said clerk shall be removable by the judges of the Criminal District Court for the causes, and in the manner prescribed for the removal of the clerk of the Civil District Court.

ART. 140. There shall be in the City of New Orleans two inferior criminal courts, to be known respectively as the First City Criminal Court and the Second [City] Criminal Court, each of which shall be presided over by one judge, and which shall have jurisdiction within the territory hereinafter prescribed, for the trial and punishment, without juries, and subject to appeal to the Criminal District Court, of all offenses against the State where the penalty does not exceed six months' imprisonment in the parish jail, or a fine of three hundred dollars, or both; in all other cases the judges of said courts shall have jurisdiction as committing magistrates, with authority to bail or discharge.

The territorial jurisdiction of the First City Criminal Court shall extend over the First, Fourth, Sixth and Seventh Municipal Districts of the City of New Orleans; and of the Second City Criminal Court, over the Second, Third and Fifth Municipal Districts of said city.

Said judges shall be elected by the voters of the City of New Orleans, at large, for the term of four years; the first election, therefor, shall be held at the Congressional election in November, 1898, and the judges then elected shall serve until May 1st, 1900, and their successors shall be elected at the parochial and municipal election in the year 1899. They shall be learned in the law, and shall have resided and practiced as attorneys in the City of New Orleans for not less than three years before their election or appointment. The judges of said courts shall each receive a yearly compensation of three thousand dollars, payable monthly on his own warrant. Each judge shall appoint a clerk and such deputies as may be authorized by law, at salaries not exceeding twelve hundred dollars per annum, except one deputy, who shall be a stenographer, and who may receive a salary not exceeding fifteen hundred dollars per annum, to be paid in monthly instalments, by the City of New Orleans.

ART. 141. The General Assembly shall provide for Recorders' Courts in the City of New Orleans, to be presided over by magistrates, who need not be attorneys at law, but such courts shall have no jurisdiction except for the trial of offenses against city ordinances.

ART. 142. There shall be a civil and a criminal sheriff for the Parish of Orleans, who shall be elected by the voters of said parish for the term of four years. Their qualifications and duties other than as herein provided, shall be prescribed by law. Each of said sheriffs shall execute an official bond, the civil sheriff in the sum of fifty thousand dollars, and the criminal sheriff in the sum of ten thousand dollars; and the bonds of said sheriffs respectively shall be examined in open court by the judges of the District Court which he serves, and all testimony given in such examinations shall be reduced to writing and made of record in said court. The civil sheriff shall be executive officer of all the Civil Courts in the Parish of Orleans, except the City Courts; and the criminal sheriff shall be the executive officer of all the Criminal Courts in said parish.

The civil sheriff shall appoint as many deputies as in his opinion are needed for the efficient discharge of the duties of his office; but after May 1st, 1900, the Court of Appeal for the Parish of Orleans and each judge of the Civil District Court shall name one deputy to be so appointed, who shall serve as crier in said court, and in the divisions presided over by said judges respectively, and who shall each receive a salary of six hundred dollars per annum to be paid by the sheriff. When not engaged in court they shall perform such duties as the sheriff may require.

The civil sheriff shall receive as compensation such fees as may be now or hereafter allowed by law, and shall pay his deputies and all expenses of his office.

The civil sheriff shall pay the sum of two thousand dollars annually in quarterly instalments to the City of New Orleans for the fund for payment and redemption of judicial fund warrants and certificates hereinafter provided for. In cases where the said sheriff is a party in interest the criminal sheriff, or one of his deputies shall act. The criminal sheriff shall receive an annual salary of three thousand six hundred dollars per annum, which shall be paid by the City of New Orleans in equal monthly instalments, and he shall receive no other compensation; he shall appoint, with the approval of the judges of the Criminal District Court for the Parish of Orleans, as many deputies as in the opinion of said judges are needed for the efficient discharge of the duties of his office and the salaries of such deputies shall be fixed by the Council of the City of New Orleans, and paid in like manner as his own. Each judge of said Criminal District (Court) shall name one deputy to be so appointed, who shall serve as crier in the sections presided over by the judges respectively, and shall each receive a salary of one thousand dollars per annum. When not engaged in court they shall perform such other duties as the sheriff may require.

The criminal sheriff shall account to and settle with the City of New Orleans for all fines and judgments collected by him, without deductions of any kind, and all expenses of his office shall be borne by said corporation.

ART. 143. There shall be a First City Court in New Orleans, composed of three judges, each of whom shall receive a salary of twenty-four hundred dollars per annum, payable monthly on his own warrant. Said court shall have exclusive original jurisdiction when the defendant resides in that part of the City of New Orleans on the left bank of the Mississippi river, in all cases when the amount in dispute or the fund to be distributed does not exceed one hundred dollars exclusive of interest, including suits for the ownership or possession of movable property not exceeding that amount in value; and suits by landlords for possession of leased premises when the monthly or yearly rent, or the rent for the unexpired term of the lease does not exceed that amount; subject to an appeal in all cases to the Court of Appeal for the Parish of Orleans. All appeals shall be tried *de novo*, and the judges of the Court of Appeal may provide by rules that one or more of the judges shall try such cases, which they shall be authorized to decide immediately after trial, and without written opinions.

The judges of said court shall have authority to issue marriage licenses, and celebrate marriages, subject to such conditions as may be imposed by law, and to execute commissions to take testimony, and to receive therefor the fees allowed by law; they shall adopt rules not in conflict with law for the fixing and trial of cases, and shall sit *en banc*, for the purpose of examining the bonds of the clerk and constable of said court, and for the trial and removal of said officers, or either of them, in which proceedings they shall be governed by the provisions of this Constitution as far as they are applicable upon the subject of the bond and of the trial and the removal from office of the clerk of the Civil District Court.

The City of New Orleans shall provide suitable accommodations for said court, and cases filed in said court shall be allotted equally to the judges thereof. The pleadings in said court shall be in writing, prepared by the litigants, or their attorneys or by the clerk.

ART. 144. There shall be one clerk for said First City Court of New Orleans, who shall furnish bond in the sum of five thousand dollars; his qualifications and duties, except as herein provided, shall be determined by law; his salary shall be eighteen hundred dollars per annum, payable monthly. Each judge shall have the appointment of one deputy clerk, whose compensation shall not exceed twelve hundred dollars per annum. The clerk shall appoint such other deputies as may be authorized by law, provided that their total compensation shall at no time exceed the sum of eighteen hundred dollars per annum.

ART. 145. There shall be one constable for said court, who shall furnish bond in the sum of five thousand dollars, and who shall appoint such deputies as may be necessary, and at such salaries as he may fix and pay. Said deputies shall be removed at his pleasure, or at the pleasure of the court. His compensation shall be the fees of his office as now or hereafter fixed by law; he shall furnish and pay one deputy to attend the sittings of each judge, who shall have the selection of such deputy and who, when not engaged in court, shall perform such other duties as the constable may direct.

The clerk of the said court and the constable thereof shall be removable by the judges of said court sitting *en banc*, for the causes, and in the manner prescribed for the removal of the clerk of the Civil District Court, conformably to rules to be adopted by said judges, and subject to an appeal to the Court of Appeals for the Parish of Orleans.

ART. 146. The judges, clerk and constable of said court shall be elected for the term of four years by the qualified voters of the City of New Orleans on the left bank of the Mississippi river. The first election under this provision shall be held at the next parochial and municipal election.

ART. 147. There shall also be a Second City Court in the City of New Orleans, on the right bank of the Mississippi river, now known as the Fifth District of the City of New Orleans; and said court shall have the same jurisdiction as the First City Court in all cases where the defendant resides in the Fifth District. There shall be one clerk for said City Court, who shall receive a salary of twelve hundred dollars per annum, payable monthly by the City Treasurer, out of the fund hereinafter provided. There shall be a constable for said court, whose compensation shall be the fees of his office, as may be now or hereafter fixed by law. The judge of said court shall have the same qualifications and authority as the judges of the First City Court, and shall receive the same compensation. Said judge, clerk and constable shall be elected by the qualified voters of said Fifth District of the City of New Orleans, for the term of four years. The first election under this provision shall be held at the next parochial and municipal election. The clerk and constable shall each furnish bond in the sum of one thousand dollars, to be approved by the judge of the court; and they shall be removable by the judge of said court after due trial, subject to an appeal to the Court of Appeal for the Parish of Orleans.

ART. 148. There shall be a District Attorney for the Parish of Orleans, who shall be elected by the voters of said parish for the term of four years, and shall receive an annual salary of one thousand dollars, and such fees as may be allowed by law; but no fees shall be allowed in criminal cases except upon conviction. He shall be a licensed attorney, and may appoint two assistants with like qualifications, at salaries not to exceed eighteen hundred dollars per annum. He shall appoint such other assistants as may be required, at salaries to be fixed and paid by him.

ART. 149. There shall be a register of conveyances and a recorder of mortgages for the Parish of Orleans, who shall be elected by the voters of said parish for the term of four years. Their qualifications and duties shall be as fixed by law; the register of conveyances shall furnish bond in the sum of fifteen thousand dollars, and the recorder of mortgages in the sum of twenty-five thousand dollars, which said bonds shall be examined by the judges of the Civil District Court, and all testimony given in said examinations shall be reduced to writing and filed in the court; they shall appoint such deputies and at such salaries as are now authorized by law, or as hereinafter provided. They shall be governed, with respect to the fees and expenses of their offices, the manner of their compensation and their obligations with regard to accounting and settling, as hereinafter prescribed. The compensation of the register of conveyances shall be twenty-five hundred dollars per annum, and that of the recorder of mortgages shall be four thousand dollars per annum.

ART. 150. The judges of the Civil and Criminal District Courts for the Parish of Orleans, and of the City Courts of New Orleans, and the clerks and constables of said courts respectively, and the sheriffs, district attorney, register of conveyances and recorder of mortgages for the Parish of Orleans, who shall be serving at the time of the adoption of this Constitution, shall, unless removed for cause, remain in office until the expiration of the terms for which they were elected or appointed.

The three judges of the Civil District Court and the one judge of the Criminal District Court, whose terms expire in 1900, shall serve until after the election and qualification of their successors, who shall be elected at the Congressional election of that year; and the terms of the two judges of the Civil District Court and the one judge of the Criminal District Court, whose terms expire in 1904, shall serve until the election and qualification of their successors, who shall be elected at the Congressional election of that year.

All cases in said courts, and all writs, orders and process issued therefrom, and which shall be pending or in course of execution, together with all the records and archives of said courts, and of the offices hereinabove mentioned shall, upon the adoption of this Constitution, at once, and by virtue of the provisions hereof, be transferred to, and held to be cases pending in, and writs, orders and process issued from, and in course of execution under the authority of, and records and archives belonging and pertaining to the Civil and Criminal District Courts and the clerks thereof, and the offices of the civil and criminal sheriffs, district attorney, register of conveyances and recorder of mortgages for the Parish of Orleans, respectively established and provided for by this Constitution. No change in the system of docketing or numbering shall be required for the purpose of suits which may hereafter be filed in either of said courts, nor shall any new set of books, or system of keeping the same, be required for the purposes of any of said offices. The books and records of the Court of Appeal for the Parish of Orleans shall be transferred to, and all appeals held to be cases pending in the Court of Appeals herein provided for, and without the formality of being renumbered or docketed, and the same rule shall apply to cases pending in the Third City Court of New Orleans upon the organization of the Second City Court of New Orleans, as hereinbefore provided. Upon the organization of the First City Court of New Orleans, as hereinbefore provided, all books, records and archives of the First, Second and Fourth City Courts of New Orleans as now constituted, and of the clerks and constables thereof, and all suits, orders and process issued from and in course of execution under the authority of said courts, shall be transferred thereto, and all cases pending in said courts shall be redocketed and numbered in said First City Court, upon application of any of the parties in interest, and without cost to them.

The laws regulating the sessions of and practice in the Civil and Criminal District Courts for the Parish of Orleans, and the City Courts of New Orleans, which may be in force at the time of the adoption of this Constitution, shall, if not in conflict herewith, remain in force until otherwise provided by the General Assembly.

ART. 151. All cases on appeal from the City Courts of New Orleans to the Civil District Court, upon the adoption of this Constitution, shall remain and be tried in said Civil District Court.

ART. 152. The recorders of the City of New Orleans who may be serving at the time of the adoption of this Constitution, shall, unless removed for cause, continue in the exercise of their functions and jurisdiction, conformably to existing laws, and until otherwise provided, except in so far as such functions and jurisdiction may be affected by the provisions of this Constitution which confer appellate and supervisory jurisdiction on the Criminal District Court and original jurisdiction in certain matters on the City Criminal Courts.

ART. 153. The election of judges and other officers for the Parish of Orleans and City of New Orleans, herein provided for, the time of which is not specially fixed, shall be held at the time of the parochial and municipal elections.

ART. 154. Until otherwise provided by law, the costs to be paid clerks, sheriffs, constables, recorder of mortgages and register of conveyances, shall be as now fixed, except that in no case shall the costs of filing appeals from the City Courts exceed the sum of five dollars.

ART. 155. The General Assembly shall grade all misdemeanors and minor offenses against the State, and shall fix the minimum and maximum penalties therefor.

ART. 156. All valid warrants issued for salaries and authorized expenses of the offices of the clerk of the Civil District Court, register of conveyances and recorder of mortgages for the Parish of Orleans, of the clerks of the City Courts of the City of New Orleans, and for salaries of the clerks of the Court of Appeal, which are payable out of the special judicial expense fund provided for by Article 146 of the Constitution of 1879, as amended, and which shall be outstanding and unpaid at the date of the adoption of this Constitution, or which shall be issued for the current month in which this Constitution is adopted, are hereby declared to be valid and subsisting claims against the revenues of the respective offices upon which said fund was made dependent.

The holders of said warrants may present them within six months after the adoption of this Constitution to the Board of Liquidation of the City Debt, and receive therefor the bonds hereinafter authorized to be issued; and the City of New Orleans is required, within three months from the adoption of this Constitution, to provide for said warrants or claims, by the issuance of bonds in the sum of two hundred and twenty-five thousand dollars, or so much thereof as may be necessary; said bonds shall be for the face value of said warrants, in such denominations as the said Board of Liquidation shall recommend, and shall be dated July 1st, 1898, and made payable twenty-five years after date, or earlier, at the option of said board, and shall bear four per cent per annum interest, payable semiannually, and represented by interest coupons attached thereto, the first of said coupons payable January 1st, 1899; said bonds to be known as Judicial Expense Fund Bonds, and to be signed by the Mayor and Comptroller of the City of New Orleans, and delivered to the Board of Liquidation of the City Debt and shall be countersigned by the president and secretary of said board and issued by said board to the holders of said warrants upon surrender of same. Neither the State of Louisiana nor the City of New Orleans shall ever be liable for the payment of said bonds nor the interest thereon, except from the special fund herein provided for, and any appropriation or other provision therefor made by the State or city shall be null and void.

There shall be stamped across the face of said bonds the words: "Issued in accordance with Article 156 of the Constitution of Louisiana of 1898."

The clerk of the Civil District Court, register of conveyances and recorder of mortgages for the Parish of Orleans, and the clerks of the City Courts of New Orleans, shall keep accurate and detailed accounts in books to be used exclusively for that purpose, of all fees and charges collected in their offices, respectively; and they shall furnish, daily, to the city comptroller, transcripts of said accounts duly certified by them or by their authority, and said officers shall also daily pay into the treasury of the City of New Orleans the whole amount of fees and charges so collected.

From the amounts thus paid into the City Treasury, the Treasurer shall set apart and reserve twenty per cent out of which shall first be paid the expenses necessary for the preparation and execution of the aforesaid bonds, and thereafter the same shall be used solely and exclusively to retire the bonds issued in payment of said Judicial Expense Fund Warrants and interest thereon, and the certificates of the Comptroller hereinafter authorized; and upon the second Tuesday in December and June of every year the said Treasurer shall pay said amounts so reserved, and also the amounts received from the Civil Sheriff, to the Board of Liquidation of the City Debt, until all the bonds herein authorized have been retired or paid; and on the second Tuesday in February and August of every year, said Board of Liquidation, in accordance with rules to be adopted and made public by it, shall, after paying the semi-annual interest on said bonds, purchase or redeem with such money thus set apart as may have accumulated, and with the surplus of the remaining eighty per cent as hereinafter provided, as many of said bonds as said money will buy or redeem, preference being given to holders offering at the lowest rate; and all such bonds so purchased or redeemed shall be by said Board of Liquidation immediately canceled, and a record made thereof.

From the remaining eighty per cent of said fund there shall be paid monthly the current salaries and expenses of the offices from which same is derived, including the salary of the docket and minute clerks of the Court of Appeal, as now constituted and until the election of the clerk of the said court, as above provided, together with such authorized expenses of said offices as are not required to be paid by the City of New Orleans; and the surplus of said eighty per cent, if any, shall be paid by the Treasurer to the said Board of Liquidation, and shall be used to redeem or pay said bonds and certificates as hereinbefore and hereinafter provided.

But if said eighty per cent. during the six months ending July 31st, or January 31st, of any year, should prove inadequate to pay said salaries and expenses, the comptroller shall prorate the deficit among those entitled to payment, and shall issue certificates therefor in sums not less than ten dollars, which shall bear interest at the rate of four per cent per annum from date, and shall be paid from the funds herein set apart and reserved only after all the bonds issued in payment of outstanding warrants shall have first been redeemed or paid.

All disbursements from said fund for stationery shall be made upon the requisitions of the officers requiring same; said requisitions to be approved by the Mayor of the City of New Orleans; and in all cases such disbursements and all salaries shall be paid by the treasurer of the City of New Orleans upon warrants drawn against said fund by the comptroller of said city, approved, so far as the Civil District Court is concerned by the presiding judge thereof, for the office of the recorder of mortgages and the office of the register of conveyances, by the Mayor of the City of New Orleans, and for the offices of the respective City Courts by the judge or judges thereof, and for the officers of the Court of Appeal by one of the judges thereof.

Until the full and final payment of all of said bonds and certificates hereinbefore provided for, the salaries of the employes of the various offices hereinafter named shall remain as now fixed by law, and there shall be no increase in the number of employes now authorized by law for the offices of recorder of mortgages or register of conveyances, unless otherwise ordered by the Civil District Court sitting *en banc;* and the number of employes of the Civil District Court shall be as determined by a majority of the judges thereof.

The clerks of the First and Second City Courts, until the organization of the City Courts hereinbefore provided for, may each appoint with the approval of the judge thereof, an additional deputy clerk at fifty dollars per month, but no other employes, nor larger salaries than those now fixed by law, shall be allowed to the City Courts.

The said Board of Liquidation hereinbefore named shall have the right to reject any and all bids made for the redemption of bonds issued as hereinabove provided, and should there be no bids, or none be accepted, then said Board of Liquidation, on the second Tuesday in February and August of each year, with whatever amount has been paid to said Board by the Treasurer as herein provided, shall, after paying the interest, pay said bonds in numerical order.

After the payment of all of said bonds, the twenty per cent. reserve herein provided, and any surplus of the remaining eighty per cent. shall be used by the City Treasurer in paying the certificates herein provided for, if any, in the order of their issue. When said Judicial Expense Fund Bonds and Comptroller's certificates, if any of the latter shall be issued, shall have been retired and canceled, the salaries and expenses of the various offices affected by this aritcle and the revenue of said offices shall be regulated and disposed of as may be determined by the General Assembly.

This article shall take effect from the last day of the current month in which this Constitution is adopted, and all amounts arising from the Judicial Expense Fund, which shall remain in the hands of the State Treasurer on that date, shall be paid by him to the Board of Liquidation of the City Debt, and be used by said board as part of the funds hereinabove referred to.

ART. 157. Vacancies occurring from any cause in the judicial offices of the Parish of Orleans or City of New Orleans, shall be filled by appointment by the Governor, with the advice and consent of the Senate, for the unexpired term.

ART. 158. The fact that the officers and deputies herein provided for are paid by the City of New Orleans shall not make them officers or employes thereof.

GENERAL PROVISIONS

ART. 159. No person shall be permitted to act as a juror, who, in due course of law, shall have been convicted of treason, perjury, forgery, bribery or other crime punishable by imprisonment in the penitentiary, or who shall be under interdiction.

ART. 160. Members of the General Assembly and all officers, before entering upon the duties of their respective offices, shall take the following oath or affirmation:

"I (A. B.) do solemnly swear (or affirm) that I will support the Constitution and laws of the United States and the Constitution and laws of this State; and that I will faithfully and impartially discharge and perform all the duties incumbent on me as ———, according to the best of my ability and understanding. So help me God."

ART. 161. The seat of government shall be and remain at the City of Baton Rouge.

ART. 162. Treason against the State shall consist only in levying war against it, or adhering to its enemies, giving them aid and comfort. No person shall be convicted of treason except on the testimony of two witnesses to the same overt act, on his confession in open court.

ART. 163. All civil officers shall be removable by an address of two-thirds of the members elected to each House of the General Assembly, except those whose removal is otherwise provided for by this Constitution.

ART. 164. No member of Congress, nor person holding or exercising any office of trust or profit under the United States, or any State, or under any foreign power, shall be eligible as a member of the General Assembly, or hold or exercise any office of trust or profit under the State.

ART. 165. The laws, public records, and the judicial and legislative written proceedings of the State, shall be promulgated, preserved and conducted in the English language; but the General Assembly may provide for the publication of the laws in the French language, and provide that judicial advertisements, in certain designated cities and parishes, shall also be made in that language.

ART. 166. No ex-post facto law, nor any law impairing the obligations of contracts, shall be passed, nor vested rights be divested, unless for purposes of public utility, and for adequate compensation previously made.

ART. 167. Private property shall not be taken nor damaged for public purposes without just and adequate compensation being first paid.

ART. 168. No power of suspending the laws of this State shall be exercised unless by the General Assembly, or by its authority.

ART. 169. The General Assembly shall provide by law for change of venue in civil and criminal cases.

ART. 170. No person shall hold or exercise, at the same time, more than one office of trust or profit, except that of justice of the peace or notary public.

ART. 171. The General Assembly may determine the mode of filling vacancies in all offices, for the filling of which provision is not made in this Constitution.

ART. 172. All officers shall continue to discharge the duties of their offices until their successors shall have been inducted into office, except in case of impeachment or suspension.

ART. 173. The military shall be in subordination to the civil power, and no soldier shall, in time of peace, be quartered in any house without the consent of the owner.

ART. 174. The General Assembly shall make it obligatory upon every parish to support all infirm, sick, and disabled paupers residing within its limits; provided, that every municipal corporation to which the powers of the police jury do not extend, shall support its own infirm, sick and disabled paupers.

ART. 175. No soldier, sailor, or marine, in the service of the United States, shall hereafter acquire a domicile in this State by reason of being stationed or doing duty in the same.

ART. 176. It shall be the duty of the General Assembly to pass such laws as may be proper and necessary to decide differences by arbitration.

ART. 177. The power of the courts to punish for contempt shall be limited by law.

ART. 178. Lotteries, and the sale of lottery tickets, are prohibited in this State.

ART. 179. In all proceedings or indictments for libel, the truth thereof may be given in evidence. The jury in all criminal cases shall be the judges of the law and of the facts on the question of guilt or innocence, having been charged as to the law applicable to the case by the presiding judge.

ART. 180. No officer whose salary is fixed by the Constitution shall be allowed any fees or perquisites of office, except where otherwise provided for by this Constitution.

ART. 181. The regulation of the sale of alcoholic or spirituous liquors is declared a police regulation, and the General Assembly may enact laws regulating their sale and use.

ART. 182. No person who, at any time, may have been a collector of taxes, whether State, parish, or municipal, or who may have been otherwise entrusted with public money, shall be eligible to the General Assembly, or to any office of honor, profit, or trust, under the State government, or any parish, or municipality thereof, until he shall have obtained a discharge for the amount of such collections, and for all public moneys with which he may have been entrusted; and the General Assembly is empowered to enact laws providing for the suspension of public officials charged with the collection of public money, when such officials fail to account for same.

ART. 183. Any person who shall, directly or indirectly, offer or give any sum, or sums, of money, bribe, present, reward, promise, or any other thing to any officer, State, parochial, or municipal, or to any member or officer of the General Assembly, with the intent to induce or influence such officer, or member of the General Assembly, to appoint any person to office, to vote or exercise any power in him vested, or to perform any duty of him required, the person giving or offering to give, and the officer, or member of the General Assembly, so receiving any money, bribe, present, reward, promise, contract, obligation, or security, with the intent aforesaid, shall be guilty of bribery, and on being found guilty thereof by any court of competent jurisdiction, or by either House of the General Assembly of which he may be a member or officer, shall be forever disqualified from holding any office, State, parochial, or municipal, and shall be forever ineligible to a seat in the General Assembly; provided that this shall not be so construed as to prevent the General Assembly from enacting additional penalties.

ART. 184. Any person may be compelled to testify in any lawful proceeding against any one who may be charged with having committed the offense of bribery, and shall not be permitted to withhold his testimony upon the ground that it may criminate him or subject him to public infamy; but such testimony shall not afterwards be used against him in any judicial proceedings, except for perjury in giving such testimony.

ART. 185. The General Assembly shall pass laws to protect laborers on buildings, streets, roads, railroads, canals, and other similar works, against the failure of contractors and sub-contractors to pay their current wages when due, and to make the corporation, company, or individual, for whose benefit the work is done, responsible for their ultimate payment.

ART. 186. No mortgage or privilege on immovable property shall affect third persons, unless recorded or registered in the parish where the property is situated, in the manner and within the time as is now or may be prescribed by law, except privileges for expenses of last illness and privileges for taxes, State, parish, or municipal; provided, such tax liens, mortgages, and privileges, shall lapse in three years from the 31st day of December, in the year in which the taxes are levied, and whether now or hereafter recorded.

ART. 187. Privileges on movable property shall exist without registration of the same, except in such cases as the General Assembly may prescribe by law.

ART. 188. Gambling is a vice, and the Legislature shall pass laws to suppress it.

ART. 189. The pernicious practice of dealing or gambling in futures on agricultural products or articles of necessity, where the intention of the parties is not to make an honest and bona fide delivery, is declared to be against public policy; and the Legislature shall pass laws to suppress it.

ART. 190. It shall be unlawful for persons or corporations, or their legal representatives, to combine or conspire together, or to unite or pool their interests for the purpose of forcing up or down the price of any agricultural product or article of necessity, for speculative purposes; and the Legislature shall pass laws to suppress it.

ART. 191. No member of the General Assembly, or public officer, or person elected or appointed to a public office under the laws of this State, shall directly on indirectly, ask, demand, accept, receive, or consent to receive, for his own use or benefit, or for the use or benefit of another, any free pass, free transportation, franking privilege, or discrimination in passenger, telegraph, or telephone rates, from any person or corporation, or make use of the same himself or in conjunction with another.

Any person who violates any provision of this Article shall forfeit his office, at the suit of the Attorney-General, or the District Attorney, to be brought at the domicile of the defendant, and shall be subject to such further penalty as may be prescribed by law.

Any corporation, or officer, or agent thereof, who shall give, or offer, or promise, to a public officer any such free pass, free transportation, franking privilege, or discrimination, shall be liable to punishment for each offense by a fine of five hundred dollars, to be recovered at the suit of the Attorney-General, or District Attorney, to be brought at the domicile of the officer to whom such free pass, free transportation, franking privilege, or discrimination, was given, offered, or promised.

No person, or officer, or agent, of a corporation, giving any such free pass, free transportation, franking privilege, or discrimination, hereby prohibited, shall be privileged from testifying in relation thereto; but he shall not be liable to civil or criminal prosecution therefor, if he shall testify to the giving of the same.

ART. 192. Whenever the General Assembly shall authorize a suit against the State it shall provide in the act authorizing the same, that such suit be instituted before the District Court at the State Capital; that citation to answer such suit shall be served both upon the Governor and the Attorney-General; that the Supreme Court of the State shall have appellate jurisdiction in such suit, without regard to the amount involved; that the only object of such suit, and the only effect of the judgment therein, shall be a judicial interpretation of the legal rights of the parties for the consideration of the Legislature in making appropriations; that the burden of proof shall rest upon the plaintiff or claimant to show that the claim sued upon is a legal and valid obligation of the State, incurred in strict conformity to law, not in violation of the Constitution of the State or of the United States, and for a valid consideration, and that all these things shall be affirmatively declared by the Supreme Court before any judgment is recognized for any purpose against the State.

ART. 193. Prescription shall not run against the State in any civil matter, unless otherwise provided in this Constitution, or expressly by law.

ART. 194. There shall be appointed by the Governor, by and with the advice and consent of the Senate, a State Examiner of State Banks, who shall be an expert accountant, and who shall make examinations of all State banks at least twice in every year. His term of office shall be four years and the Legislature shall define his duties and fix his compensation.

ART. 195. The New Basin Canal and Shell Road, and their appurtenances, shall not be leased, nor alienated, nor shall the Carondelet Canal and Bayou St. John, and their appurtenances, be leased, or alienated when they shall come into the possession of the State.

ART. 196. The General Assembly may authorize the employment under State supervision and the proper officers and employes of the State, of convicts on public roads or other public works, or convict farms, or in manufactories owned or controlled by the State, under such provisions and restrictions as may be imposed by law, and shall enact laws necessary to carry these provisions into effect; and no convict sentenced to the State penitentiary shall ever be leased, or hired to any person, or persons, or corporation, private or public, or quasi-public, or board, save as herein authorized. This article shall take effect upon the expiration of the penitentiary lease, made pursuant to Act No. 114, approved July 10th, 1890.

SUFFRAGE AND ELECTIONS.

ART. 197. Every male citizen of this State and of the United States, native born or naturalized, not less than twenty-one years of age, and possessing the following qualifications, shall be an elector, and shall be entitled to vote at any election in the State by the people, except as may be herein otherwise provided.

SEC. 1. He shall have been an actual bona-fide resident of this State for two years, of the parish one year and of the precinct in which he offers to vote six months next preceding the election; provided, that removal from one precinct to another in the same parish shall not operate to deprive any person of the right to vote in the precinct from which he has removed, until six months after such removal.

SEC. 2. He shall have been at the time he offers to vote, legally enrolled as a registered voter on his personal application, in accordance with the provisions of this Constitution, and the laws enacted thereunder.

The qualifications of voters and the registration laws in force prior to the adoption of this Constitution shall remain in force until December 31st, 1898, at which date all the provisions of this Constitution relative to suffrage, registration and election, except as hereinafter otherwise provided, shall go into effect, and the General Assembly shall, and is hereby directed, at its regular session in 1898, to enact a general registration law to carry into effect the provisions of this Constitution relative to the qualifications and registration of voters.

SEC. 3. He shall be able to read and write, and shall demonstrate his ability to do so when he applies for registration, by making, under oath administered by the registration officer or his deputy, written application therefor, in the English language, or his mother tongue, which application shall contain the essential facts necessary to show that he is entitled to register and vote, and shall be entirely written, dated and signed by him, in the presence of the registration officer or his deputy, without assistance or suggestion from any person or any memorandum whatever, except the form of application hereinafter set forth; provided, however, that if the applicant be unable to write his application in the English language, he shall have the right, if he so demands, to write the same in his mother tongue from the dictation of an interpreter; and if the applicant is unable to write his application by reason of physical disability, the same shall be written at his dictation by the registration officer or his deputy, upon his oath of such disability. The application for registration, above provided for, shall be a copy of the following form, with the proper names, dates and numbers substituted for the blanks appearing therein, to-wit:

"I am a citizen of the State of Louisiana. My name is ———. I was born in the State (or country) of ———, Parish (or county) of

———, on the —— day of ———, in the year ——. I am now ——
years, —— months and —— days of age. I have resided in this State
since ———, in this parish ———, and in Precinct No. ——, of Ward
No. ——, of this parish, since ———, and I am not disfranchised by
any provision of the Constitution of this State."

SEC. 4. If he be not able to read and write, as provided by Section
three of this article, then he shall be entitled to register and vote
if he shall, at the time he offers to register, be the bona fide owner of
property assessed to him in this State at a valuation of not less than
three hundred dollars on the assessment roll of the current year in
which he offers to register, or on the roll of the preceding year, if
the roll of the current year shall not then have been completed and
filed, and on which, if such property be personal only, all taxes due
shall have been paid. The applicant for registration under this
section shall make oath before the registration officer or his deputy,
that he is a citizen of the United States and of this State, over the
age of twenty-one years; that he possesses the qualifications prescribed in section one of this article, and that he is the owner of property assessed in this State to him at a valuation of not less than
three hundred dollars, and if such property be personal only, that all
taxes due thereon have been paid.

SEC. 5. No male person who was on January 1st, 1867, or at any
date prior thereto, entitled to vote under the Constitution or statutes
of any State of the United States, wherein he then resided, and no
son or grandson of any such person not less than twenty-one years of
age at the date of the adoption of this Constitution, and no male
person of foreign birth, who was naturalized prior to the first day of
January, 1898, shall be denied the right to register and vote in this
State by reason of his failure to possess the educational or property
qualifications prescribed by this Constitution; provided, he shall have
resided in this State for five years next preceding the date at which
he shall apply for registration, and shall have registered in accordance with the terms of this article prior to September 1, 1898, and no
person shall be entitled to register under this section after said date.

Every person claiming the benefit of this section shall make application to the proper registration officer, or his deputy, for registration, and he shall make oath before such registration officer or his
deputy, in the form following, viz.: " I am a citizen of the United
States and of this State, over the age of twenty-one years; I have
resided in this State for five years next preceding this date. I was
on the —— day of ——— entitled to vote under the Constitution or
statutes of the State of ———, wherein I then resided (or, I am the
son, or grandson) of ———, who was on the —— day of ———
entitled to vote under the Constitution or statutes of the State of
———, wherein he then resided, and I desire to avail myself of the
privileges conferred by section 5 of Article 197 of the Constitution
of this State."

A separate registration of voters applying under this section, shall
be made by the registration officer of every parish, and for this purpose the registration officer of every parish shall keep his office open
daily, Sundays and legal holidays excepted, from May 16th, 1898,
until August 31st, 1898, both included, during the hours prescribed
by Act No. 89 of the General Assembly of 1896. In every parish,

except the parish of Orleans, he shall keep his office at the courthouse at least during the months of May, June and August, and during the month of July, he shall keep it for at least one day at or near each polling place, giving thirty days' notice thereof by publication.

The registration of voters under this section shall close on the 31st day of August, 1898, and immediately thereafter the registration officer of every parish shall make a sworn copy, in duplicate, of the list of persons registered under this section, showing in detail whether the applicant registered as a voter of 1867, or prior thereto, or as the son of such voter, or as the grandson of such voter, and deposit one of said duplicates in the office of the Secretary of State, to be by him recorded and preserved as a part of the permanent records of his office, and the other of said duplicates shall be by him filed in the office of the Clerk of the District Court of the parish, and in the parish of Orleans, in the office of the Recorder of Mortgages, there to remain a permanent record.

All persons whose names appear on said registration lists shall be admitted to register for all elections in this State without possessing the educational or property qualification prescribed by this Constitution, unless otherwise disqualified, and all persons who do not by personal application claim exemption from the provisions of sections 3 and 4 of this article before September 1st, 1898, shall be forever denied the right to do so.

The Legislature shall, at its first session after the adoption of this Constitution, provide the manner in which persons whose names appear upon said registration lists shall hereafter register, which mode may be different from that required for persons registering under the other sections of this article; and shall also provide a remedy whereby subsequently to the close of said registration on August 31st, 1898, the names of any persons who may have obtained registration under this section by false statements of fact or other fraud, shall by appropriate proceedings be stricken from said roll.

ART. 198. No person less than sixty years of age shall be permitted to vote at any election in the State who shall not, in addition to the qualifications above prescribed, have paid on or before the 31st day of December, of each year, for the two years preceding the year in which he offers to vote, a poll tax of one dollar per annum, to be used exclusively in aid of the public schools of the parish in which such tax shall have been collected; which tax is hereby imposed on every male resident of this State between the age of twenty-one and sixty years. Poll taxes shall be a lien only upon assessed property, and no process shall issue to enforce the collection of the same except against assessed property.

Every person liable for such tax shall, before being allowed to vote, exhibit to the Commissioners of Election his poll tax receipts for two years, issued on the official form, or duplicates thereof, in the event of loss, or proof of payment of such poll taxes may be made by a certificate of the tax collector, which shall be sent to the Commissioners of the several voting precincts, showing a list of those who have paid said two years' poll taxes as above provided, and the dates of payment. It is hereby declared to be forgery, and punishable as such, for any tax collector or other person, to antedate, or alter, a poll tax receipt. Any person who shall pay the poll tax of another or advance him money for that purpose, in order to influence his vote, shall be guilty of bribery and punished accordingly. The provisions of this section as to the payment of poll taxes shall not apply to persons who are deaf and dumb, or blind, nor to persons under twenty-three years of age, who have paid all poll taxes assessed against them. This section shall not go into operation until after the general State election to be held in the year 1900, and the Legislature elected in the year 1908 shall have authority to repeal or modify the same.

ART. 199. Upon all questions submitted to the taxpayers, as such, of any municipal or other political subdivision of this State, the qualifications of such taxpayers as voters shall be those of age and residence prescribed by this article, and women taxpayers shall have the right to vote at all such elections, without registration, in person or by their agents, authorized in writing; but all other persons voting at such elections shall be registered voters.

ART. 200. No person shall vote at any primary election or in any convention or other political assembly held for the purpose of nominating any candidate for public office, unless he is at the time a registered voter. And in all political conventions in this State the apportionment of representation shall be on the basis of population.

ART. 201. Any person possessing the qualifications prescribed by Section 3 or 4 of Article 197 of this Constitution, who may be denied registration, shall have the right to apply for relief to the District Court having jurisdiction of civil causes for the parish in which he offers to register, and the party cast in said suit shall have the right of appeal to the Supreme Court; and any citizen of the State shall have a like right to apply to said courts, to have stricken off any names illegally placed on said registration rolls under Sections 3 and 4 of Article 197, and such applications and appeals shall be tried by said courts by preference, in open court or at chambers. The General Assembly shall provide by law for such applications and appeals without cost, and for the prosecution of all persons charged with illegal or fraudulent registration or voting, or any other crime or offense against the registration or election or primary election laws.

ART. 202. The following persons shall not be permitted to register, vote or hold any office or appointment of honor, trust or profit in this State, to-wit: Those who have been convicted of any crime punishable by imprisonment in the penitentiary, and not afterwards pardoned with express restoration of franchise; those who are inmates of any charitable institution, except the Soldiers' Home; those actually confined in any public prison; all indicted persons, and all persons notoriously insane or idiotic, whether interdicted or not.

ART. 203. In all elections by the people the electors shall vote by ballot, and the ballots cast shall be publicly counted. In all elections by persons in a representative capacity, the vote shall be *viva-voce*.

ART. 204. Electors shall, in all cases except treason, felony or breach of the peace, be privileged from arrest during their attendance on elections, and in going to and returning from the same.

ART. 205. The General Assembly shall by law forbid the giving or selling of intoxicating drinks, on the day of any election, or primary election, within one mile of any polling place.

ART. 206. Until otherwise provided by law, the general State election shall be held once every four years on the Tuesday next following the third Monday in April.

Presidential electors and members of Congress shall be chosen or elected in the manner and at the time prescribed by law.

ART. 207. Parochial elections, except in the city of New Orleans, shall be held on the same day as the general State election, and not oftener than once in four years.

In the City of New Orleans parochial and municipal elections shall be held on the Tuesday following the first Monday of November, 1899, and of every fourth year thereafter, but the General Assembly may change the date of said election after the year 1899; provided, that the parochial and municipal elections shall be held together, and shall always be on a day separate and apart from the General State Election and not oftener than once in four years. The municipal and parochial officers in the City of New Orleans shall take their offices on the first Monday in the month of May following their election, until otherwise provided by law.

ART. 208. For the purpose of voting, no person shall be deemed to have gained a residence, by reason of his presence, or lost it by reason of his absence, while employed in the service, either civil or military, of this State or of the United States; or while engaged in the navigation of the waters of the State or of the United States; or of the high seas; or while a student of any institution of learning.

ART. 209. The General Assembly shall provide by law for the trial and determination of contested elections of all public officers, whether State, judicial, parochial or municipal (except Governor and Lieutenant Governor), which trials shall be by the courts of law and at the domicile of the party defendant.

ART. 210. No person shall be eligible to any office, State, judicial, parochial, municipal or ward, who is not a citizen of this State and a duly qualified elector of the State, judicial district, parish, municipality or ward, wherein the functions of said office are to be performed. And whenever any officer, State, judicial, parochial, municipal or ward, may change his residence from this State, or from the district, parish, municipality or ward in which he holds such office, the same shall thereby be vacated, any declaration of retention of domicile to the contrary notwithstanding.

ART. 211. Returns of elections for all civil officers who are to be commissioned by the Governor shall be made to the Secretary of State, unless otherwise provided in this Constitution.

ART. 212. All elections by the people, except primary elections and municipal elections in towns having a population of less than twenty-five hundred, when such elections are not held at the same time as general State elections, shall be by official ballot, printed and distributed at the expense of the State; and, until otherwise provided by law, such ballots shall have printed thereon, and at the head and immediately preceding the list of names of the candidates of each political party or nominating paper, a specific and separate device by which the political party and the candidates of such political party or nominating paper may be indicated. By stamping such device at the head of the list of candidates of each political party, or nominating paper, the voter may indicate that his vote is for the entire or straight ticket of the particular party or nominating paper employing the particular device allotted to such political party, or nominating paper. When the voter does not desire to vote an entire or straight party ticket, he may vote for candidates of any political party or nominating paper, by stamping a blank space to be left opposite the name of each candidate on said official ballot.

The General Assembly shall provide some plan by which the voters may prepare their ballots in secrecy at the polls. This article shall not be construed so as to prevent the names of independent candidates from being printed on the ballots with a device; and names of candidates may be written on the ballot. These provisions shall not apply to elections for the imposition of special taxes, for which the General Assembly shall provide special laws.

ART. 213. Electors shall not be registered within thirty days next preceding any election at which they may offer to vote, but applications to the courts, and appeals may be heard and determined, and revision take place at any time prior to the election, and no person who, in respect to age and residence, would become entitled to vote within the said thirty days, shall be excluded from registration on account of his want of qualifications at the time of his application for registration.

ART. 214. The Legislature shall provide for the registration of voters throughout the State.

ART. 215. The Legislature shall enact laws to secure fairness in party primary elections, conventions, or other methods of naming party candidates.

ART. 216. In the trial of contested elections and in proceedings for the investigation of elections, and in all criminal trials under the election laws, no person shall be permitted to withhold his testimony on the grounds that he may criminate himself or subject himself to public infamy, but such testimony shall not be used against him in any judicial proceedings except for perjury in giving such testimony.

IMPEACHMENT AND REMOVAL FROM OFFICE

ART. 217. The Governor, Lieutenant Governor, Secretary of State, Auditor, Treasurer, Attorney General, Superintendent of Public Education, Railroad Commissioners, and the Judges of all the Courts of Record in this State, shall be liable to impeachment for high crimes and misdemeanors, for nonfeasance or malfeasance in office, for incompetency, for corruption, favoritism, extortion or oppression in office, or for gross misconduct, or habitual drunkenness.

ART. 218. The House of Representatives shall have the sole power of impeachment. All impeachments shall be tried by the Senate; when sitting for that purpose, the Senators shall be upon oath or affirmation, and no person shall be convicted without the concurrence of two-thirds of the Senators present. When the Governor of the State is on trial, the Chief Justice or the senior Associate Justice of the Supreme Court shall preside.

The Senate may adjourn the trial of any impeachment from time to time, as it may deem proper, and may sit for the purpose of such trial whether the House of Representatives or the Legislature be in session or not.

Judgment in cases of impeachment shall extend only to removal from office and disqualification from holding any office of honor, trust or profit, under the State, but the party, whether convicted or acquitted, shall nevertheless be liable to prosecution, trial and punishment according to law.

ART. 219. All officers against whom articles of impeachment are preferred, except the Governor, shall be suspended from office during the pendency of such impeachment, and the appointing power shall make a provisional appointment to replace any suspended officer until the decision of the impeachment.

ART. 220. For any reasonable cause, whether sufficient for impeachment or not, the Governor shall remove any officer on the address of two-thirds of the members elected to each house of the General Assembly. In every such case, the cause or causes for which such removal may be required shall be stated at length in the address and inserted in the Journal of each House.

ART. 221. For any of the causes specified in Art. 217, judges of the Courts of Appeal, and of the District Courts throughout the State may be removed from office by judgment of the Supreme Court, which is hereby vested with original jurisdiction to try such cases. The suit for removal may be instituted by the Attorney General or District Attorney, whenever in his opinion sufficient cause exists therefor; and it is hereby made the duty of the Attorney General or District Attorney to institute such suit whenever instructed in writing by the Governor so to do, or on the written request and information of twenty-five citizens and taxpayers residing within the territorial limits of the district or circuit over which the judge against whom the suit is brought exercises the functions of his office. Such suits shall be tried after citation and ten days' delay for answering, in preference to all other suits, and wherever the court may be sitting; but the pendency of such suit shall not operate a suspension from office. In all cases where the officer sued, as above directed, shall be acquitted, and where the suit is instituted on the request and information of citizens, judgment shall be rendered jointly and in solido against the citizens signing the request, for all costs of the suit. Judgments in cases of removal under this Article shall extend not only to removals from office and disqualification from holding any office of honor, trust, or profit under the State, but also to disqualification for the practice of law, and the party, whether convicted or not, shall nevertheless be liable to prosecution, trial and punishment according to law.

ART. 222. For any of the causes enumerated in Article 217, members of the State Board of Appraisers, except the Auditor, Railroad Commissioners, District Attorneys, Clerks of Court, Sheriffs, Coroners, Justices of the Peace, Judges of the City Courts, and of other inferior courts of the City of New Orleans and elsewhere, and all other parish, municipal and ward officers, may be removed by judgment of the District Court of the domicile of such officer (in the Parish of Orleans the Civil District Court). The District Attorney may, whenever in his opinion sufficient cause exists therefor, institute such suit, and it shall be his duty (except when the suit is to be brought against himself), to institute such suit on the written request and information of twenty-five resident citizens and taxpayers, in the case of members of the State Board of Appraisers, Railroad Commissioners, district, parish, or municipal officers, and of ten resident citizens and taxpayers in the case of ward officers. Such suit shall be brought against a District Attorney upon such written request and information by the District Attorney of an adjoining district, or by counsel appointed by the judge for that purpose. In all suits instituted under this article the defendant, the State and the citizens and taxpayers, on whose information, and at whose request such suit may have been brought, or any one of them, shall have the right to appeal, both on the law and the facts, from the judgment of the court. In all cases where the officer sued, as above directed, shall be acquitted, judgment shall be rendered jointly and in solido against the citizens signing the request, for all costs of the suit.

In cases against members of the State Board of Appraisers, Railroad Commissioners, District Attorneys, Clerks and Sheriffs, the appeal shall be to the Supreme Court, and in case against all other officers the appeal shall be to the Court of Appeal of the proper circuit.

Such appeals shall be returnable within ten days to the appellate court wherever it may be sitting or wherever it may hold its next session, and may be transferred by order of the judges of said court to another parish within their circuit, and such appeals shall be tried by preference over all others. In case of the refusal or neglect of the District Attorney or Attorney General to institute and prosecute any suit provided for in this and the preceding article, the citizens and taxpayers making the request, or any one of them, shall have the right by mandamus to compel him to perform such duty.

The institution and pendency of suits brought under this article shall not operate a suspension of the defendant from office.

ART. 223. On the recommendation of the Auditor or the Police Jury of any parish, the Governor may suspend any officer charged with the collection or custody of public funds when in arrears.

REVENUE AND TAXATION

ART. 224. The taxing power may be exercised by the General Assembly for State purposes, and by parishes and municipal corporations and public boards, under authority granted to them by the General Assembly, for parish, municipal, and local purposes, strictly public in their nature.

ART. 225. Taxation shall be equal and uniform throughout the territorial limits of the authority levying the tax, and all property shall be taxed in proportion to its value, to be ascertained as directed by law; provided, the assessment of all property shall never exceed the actual cash value thereof; and provided, further, that the taxpayers shall have the right of testing the correctness of their assessments before the courts of justice. In order to arrive at this equality and uniformity, the General Assembly shall, at its first session after the adoption of this Constitution, provide a system of equality and uniformity in assessments based upon the relative value of property in the different portions of the State. The valuations put upon property for the purposes of State taxation shall be taken as the proper valuation for purposes of local taxation, in every subdivision of the State.

ART. 226. There shall be a State Board of Appraisers, composed of the Auditor, and six other members, to be elected for four years by the Governor, Lieutenant Governor, Treasurer, Attorney General, and Secretary of State, one from each Congressional District, whose duty it shall be to assess the property belonging to corporations, associations and individuals employed in railway, telegraph, telephone, sleeping car and express business. The General Assembly shall fix the compensation of said board.

ART. 227. The taxing power shall be exercised only to carry on and maintain the government of the State and the public institutions thereof, to educate the children of the State, to preserve the public health, to pay the principal, and interest of the public debt, to suppress insurrection, to repel invasion or defend the State in time of war, to provide pensions for indigent Confederate soldiers and sailors, and their widows, to establish markers or monuments upon the battlefields of the country commemorative of the services of Louisiana soldiers on such fields, to maintain a memorial hall in New Orleans for the collection and preservation of relics and memorials of the late civil war, and for levee purposes, as hereinafter provided.

ART. 228. The power to tax corporations and corporate property shall never be surrendered nor suspended by act of the General Assembly.

ART. 229. The General Assembly may leave a license tax, and in such case shall graduate the amount of such tax to be collected from the persons pursuing the several trades, professions, vocations, and callings. All persons, associations of persons and corporations pursuing any trade, profession, business or calling, may be rendered liable to such tax, except clerks, laborers, clergymen, school teachers, those engaged in mechanical, agricultural, horticultural, and mining pursuits, and manufacturers other than those of distilled, alcoholic or malt liquors, tobacco, cigars, and cotton seed oil. No political corporation shall impose a greater license tax than is imposed by the General Assembly for State purposes. This restriction shall not apply to dealers in distilled, alcoholic or malt liquors.

The General Assembly shall have authority to provide that municipalities levying license taxes equal in amount to those levied by police juries for parochial purposes, shall be exempted from the payment of such parochial licenses.

ART. 230. The following shall be exempt from taxation, and no other, viz: All public property, places of religious worship, or burial, all charitable institutions, all buildings and property used exclusively for public monuments or historical collections, colleges and other school purposes, the real and personal estate of any public library, and that of any other library association used by or connected with such library, all books and philosophical apparatus, and all paintings and statuary of any company or association kept in a public hall; provided, the property so exempted be not leased for purposes of private or corporate profit and income. There shall also be exempt from taxation household property to the value of five hundred dollars. There shall also be exempt from parochial and municipal taxation for a period of ten years from the 1st day of January, 1900, the capital, machinery and other property employed in mining operations, and in the manufacture of textile fabrics, yarns, rope, cordage, leather, shoes, harness, saddlery, hats, clothings, flour, machinery, articles of tin, copper and sheet iron, agricultural implements, and furniture and other articles of wood, marble or stone; soap, stationery, ink and paper, boat building and fertilizers and chemicals; provided, that not less than five hands are employed in any one factory; provided, that nothing herein contained shall affect the exemptions provided for by existing constitutional provisions.

There shall also be exempt from taxation for a period of ten years from the date of its completion any railroad or part of such railroad that may hereafter be constructed and completed prior to January 1st, 1904; provided, that when aid has heretofore been voted by any parish, ward, or municipality to any railroad not yet constructed, such railroad shall not be entitled to the exemption from taxation herein established, unless it waives and relinquishes such aid or consents to a resubmission of the question of granting such aid to a vote of the property taxpayers of the parish, ward, or municipality, which has voted the same, if one-third of such property taxpayers petition for the same within six months after the adoption of this Constitution.

And provided, further, that this exemption shall not apply to double tracks, sidings, switches, depots or other improvements or betterments, which may be constructed by railroads now in operation within the State, other than extensions or new lines constructed by such railroads; nor shall the exemption hereinabove granted apply to any railroad or part of such railroad, the construction of which was begun and the roadbed of which was substantially completed at the date of the adoption of this constitution.

The property or real estate belonging to any military organization of the State of Louisiana which is used by the State National Guard or militia for military purposes, such as arsenals or armories, while so used, shall be exempt from taxation.

ART. 231. The General Assembly shall levy an annual poll tax of one dollar upon every male inhabitant in the State between the ages of twenty-one and sixty years, for the maintenance of the public schools in the parishes where collected.

ART. 232. The State tax on property for all purposes whatever, including expense of government, schools, levees and interest, shall not exceed, in any one year, six mills on the dollar of its assessed valuation, and, except as otherwise provided in this Constitution, no parish, municipal or public board tax for all purposes whatsoever, shall exceed in any one year ten mills on the dollar of valuation; provided, that for giving additional support to public schools, and for the purpose of erecting and constructing public buildings, public school houses, bridges, wharves, levees, sewerage work and other works of permanent public improvement, the title to which shall be in the public, any parish, municipal corporation, ward or school district may levy a special tax in excess of said limitation, whenever the rate of such increase and the number of years it is to be levied and the purposes for which the tax is intended, shall have been submitted to a vote of the property taxpayers of such parish, municipality, ward or school district entitled to vote under the election laws of the State, and a majority of the same in numbers, and in value voting at such election shall have voted therefor.

ART. 233. There shall be no forfeiture of property for the non-payment of taxes, State, levee district, parochial or municipal, but at the expiration of the year in which said taxes are due the collector shall, without suit, and after giving notice to the delinquent in the manner to be provided by law, advertise for sale in the official journal of the parish, city or municipality, provided there be an official journal in such parish, city or municipality, the property on which the taxes are due in the manner provided for judicial sales, and on the day of sale he shall sell such portion of the property as the debtor shall point out; and in case the debtor shall not point out sufficient property, the collector shall, at once and without further delay, sell the least quantity of property which any bidder will buy for the amount of the taxes, interest and costs. The sale shall be without appraisement, and the property sold shall be redeemable at any time for the space of one year, by paying the price given, including costs, and twenty per cent thereon. No judgment annulling a tax sale shall have effect until the price and all taxes and costs paid, with ten per cent per annum interest on the amount of the price and taxes paid from date of respective payments, be previously paid to the purchaser; provided, this shall not apply to sales annulled on account of taxes having been paid prior to the date of sale, or dual assessments. All deeds of sale made, or that may be made, by the collectors of taxes, shall be received by courts in evidence as *prima facie* valid sales.

No sale of property for taxes shall be set aside for any cause, except on proof of dual assessment, or of payment of the taxes for which the property was sold prior to the date of the sale, unless the proceeding to annul is instituted within six months from service of notice of sale, which notice shall not be served until the time of redemption has expired, or within three years from the adoption of this Constitution, as to sales already made, and within three years from the date of recordation of the tax deed, as to sales made hereafter, if no notice is given. The manner of notice and form of proceeding to quiet tax titles shall be provided by law. Taxes on movables shall be collected by seizure and sale by the tax collector of the movable property of the delinquent, whether it be the property assessed or not, sufficient to pay the tax. Sale of such property shall be made at public auction, without appraisement, after ten days' advertisement, made within ten days from date of seizure, and shall be absolute and without redemption.

If the tax collector can find no corporeal movables of the delinquent to seize, he may levy on incorporeal rights, by notifying the debtor thereof, or he may proceed by summary rule in the courts to compel the delinquent to deliver up for sale property in his possession or under his control.

ART. 234. The tax shall be designated by the year in which it is collectable, and the tax on movable property shall be collected in the year in which the assessment is made.

ART. 235. The Legislature shall have power to levy, solely for the support of the public schools, a tax upon all inheritances, legacies, and donations; provided, no direct inheritance, or donation, to an ascendant or descendant, below ten thousand dollars in amount or value shall be so taxed; provided further, that no such tax shall exceed three per cent for direct inheritances and donations to ascendants or descendants, and ten per cent for collateral inheritances, and donations to collaterals or strangers; provided, bequests to educational, religious, or charitable institutions shall be exempt from this tax.

Art. 236. The tax provided for in the preceding article shall not be enforced when the property donated or inherited shall have borne its just proportion of taxes prior to the time of such donation or inheritance.

Art. 237. The Legislature shall pass no law postponing the payment of taxes, except in case of overflow, general conflagration, general destruction of corps, or other public calamity.

Art. 238. A levee system shall be maintained in the State, and a tax not to exceed one mill may be levied annually on all property subject to taxation, and shall be applied exclusively to the maintenance and repairs of levees.

Art. 239. The General Assembly may divide the State into Levee Districts, and provide for the appointment or election of Levee Commissioners in said districts, who shall, in the method and manner to be provided by law, have supervision of the erection, repair, and maintenance of the levees in said districts; to that effect the Levee Commissioners may levy a tax not to exceed ten mills on the taxable property situated within the alluvial portions of said districts subject to overflow; provided, that in case of necessity to raise additional funds for the purpose of constructing, preserving, or repairing any levees protecting the lands of a district, the rate of taxation herein limited, may be increased, when the rate of such increase and the necessity and purpose for which it is intended shall have been submitted to a vote of the property taxpayers of such district, paying taxes for themselves, or in any representative capacity, whether resident or non-resident, on property situated within the alluvial portion of said district subject to overflow, and a majority of those in number and value, voting at such election, shall have voted therefor. The Boards of Commissioners of the several levee districts, when authorized so to do by the State Board of Engineers, shall have full power and authority to contract with and permit any steam railroad corporation to construct, maintain, freely use and operate on the public levees, a railroad track or tracks; the supervision, control and general police power over such levees, however, to remain in and with the several levee boards. Provided, that nothing herein contained shall be construed as divesting either the General Assembly or the municipal government of any incorporated town or city in this State of the jurisdiction, control, or police power now vested in them, or either of them; and provided further, that no right or privilege shall be granted to any one or more railroad companies which shall preclude like grants to other companies willing to contribute pro rata to the common expense, incurred or to be incurred.

The several levee districts of the State, for the purpose of refunding the bonds heretofore issued by them under authority granted by the Legislature, and in order that they may negotiate to better advantage that portion of their authorized issue of bonds not yet disposed of, may issue bonds in lieu of said bonds outstanding or not yet disposed of. The Legislature shall pass an act to carry this provision into effect, but bonds issued under this provision shall not bear a rate of interest greater than five per cent, or be disposed of at less than par, and it shall not be obligatory on the holders of the said outstanding bonds to give up the same in exchange before the maturity thereof.

All the provisions of this article are held to apply to the levee district of which the City of New Orleans forms, or may hereafter form, a part; provided, that nothing herein shall be construed as affecting any existing legislation upon the subject of the taxing power of the commissioners of said district, or as affecting the power of the Legislature, under the Constitution of 1879, and the amendments thereto, with respect to such power.

ART. 240. The provisions of the above two articles shall cease to have effect whenever the Federal government shall assume permanent control and provide the ways and means for the maintenance of levees in this State. The Federal government is authorized to make such geological, topographical, hydrographical and hydrometrical surveys and investigations within the State as may be necessary to carry into effect the act of Congress to provide for the appointment of a Mississippi River Commission for the improvement of said river, from the head of Passes near its mouth to the headwaters, and to construct and protect such public works and improvements as may be ordered by Congress under the provisions of said act.

ART. 241. The General Assembly shall have power, with the concurrence of an adjacent State or States, to create levee districts composed of territory partly in this State and partly in an adjacent State or States, and the Levee Commissioners for such district or districts shall possess all the powers provided by Article 239 of the Constitution.

ART. 242. Corporations, companies or associations organized or domiciled out of the State, but doing business therein, may be licensed and taxed by a mode different from that provided for home corporations or companies; provided, said different mode of license shall be uniform, upon a graduated system, and said different mode of taxation shall be equal and uniform as to all such corporations, companies or associations that transact the same kind of business.

ART. 243. All the articles and provisions of this Constitution regulating and relating to the collection of State taxes and tax sales shall also apply to and regulate the collection of parish, district, municipal, board and ward taxes.

HOMESTEAD EXEMPTIONS

ART. 244. There shall be exempt from seizure and sale by any process whatever, except as herein provided, and without registration, the homestead, *bona fide*, owned by the debtor and occupied by him, consisting of lands, not exceeding one hundred and sixty acres, buildings and appurtenances, whether rural or urban, of every head of a family, or person having a mother or father, or a person or persons dependent on him or her for support, also two work horses, one wagon or cart, one yoke of oxen, two cows and calves, twenty-five head of hogs, or one thousand pounds of bacon or its equivalent in pork, whether these exempted objects be attached to a homestead or not, and on a farm the necessary quantity of corn and fodder for the current year, and the necessary farming implements, to the value of two thousand dollars.

Provided, that in case the homestead exceeds two thousand dollars in value, the beneficiary shall be entitled to that amount in case a sale of the homestead under any legal process realizes more than that sum.

No husband shall have the benefit of a homestead, whose wife owns, and is in the actual enjoyment of property or means to the amount of two thousand dollars.

The benefit of this exemption may be claimed by the surviving spouse, or minor child or children, of a deceased beneficiary.

ART. 245. Rights to homesteads or exemptions, under laws or contracts, or obligations existing at the time of the adoption of this Constitution, shall not be impaired, repealed or affected by any provision of this Constitution, or any laws passed in pursuance thereof.

This exemption shall not apply to the following debts, to-wit:

1st. For the purchase price of property or any part thereof.

2d. For labor, money, and material, furnished for building, repairing or improving homesteads.

3d. For liabilities incurred by any public officer, or fiduciary, or any attorney at law, for money collected or received on deposit.

4th. For taxes or assessments.

5th. For rent which bears a privilege upon said property. No court or ministerial officer of this State shall ever have jurisdiction, or authority, to enforce any judgment, execution, or decree, against the property exempted as a homestead, except the debts above mentioned in numbers one, two, three, four and five, of this Article; provided, the property herein declared exempt shall not exceed in value two thousand dollars.

ART. 246. The right to sell any property that is exempt as homestead shall be preserved; but no sale shall destroy or impair any rights of creditors therein. Any person entitled to a homestead may waive the same, by signing with his wife, if she be not separated *a mensa et thoro*, and having recorded in the office of the Recorder of Mortgages of his parish, a written waiver of the same, in whole or in part. Such waiver may be either general or special, and shall have effect from the time of recording.

ART. 247. The articles of this Constitution relating to homesteads and exemption shall take effect on January 1st, 1899. In the Parish of Orleans, the homestead to be valid shall be recorded as is now, or may be, provided by law.

PUBLIC EDUCATION

ART. 248. There shall be free public schools for the white and colored races, separately established by the General Assembly, throughout the State, for the education of all the children of the State between the ages of six and eighteen years; provided, that where kindergarten schools exist, children between the ages of four and six may be admitted into said schools. All funds raised by the State for the support of public schools, except the poll tax, shall be distributed to each parish in proportion to the number of children therein between the ages of six and eighteen years. The General Assembly, at its next session shall provide for the enumeration of educable children.

ART. 249. There shall be elected by the qualified electors of the State a Superintendent of Public Education, who shall hold this office for the term of four years, and until his successor is qualified. His duties shall be prescribed by law, and he shall receive an annual salary of two thousand dollars. The aggregate annual expenses of his office, including his salary, shall not exceed the sum of four thousand dollars.

ART. 250. The General Assembly shall provide for the creation of a State Board, and Parish Boards of Public Education. The Parish Boards shall elect a Parish Superintendent of Public Education for their respective parishes, whose qualifications shall be fixed by the Legislature, and who shall be ex-officio secretary of the Parish Board. The salary of the Parish Superintendent shall be provided for by the General Assembly, to be paid out of the public school funds accruing to the respective parishes.

ART. 251. The general exercises in the public schools shall be conducted in the English language; provided, that the French language may be taught in those parishes or localities where the French language predominates, if no additional expense is incurred thereby.

ART. 252. The funds derived from the collection of the poll tax shall be applied exclusively to the maintenance of the public schools as organized under this Constitution, and shall be applied exclusively to the support of the public schools in the parish in which the same shall be collected, and shall be accounted for and paid by the collecting officer directly to the treasurer of the local school board.

ART. 253. No funds raised for the support of the public schools of the State shall be appropriated to or used for the support of any private or sectarian schools.

ART. 254. The school funds of the State shall consist of: 1st. Not less than one and one-quarter mills of the six mills tax levied and collected by the State. 2d. The proceeds of taxation for school purposes as provided by this Constitution. 3d. The interest on the proceeds of all public lands heretofore granted or to be granted by the United States for the support of the public schools, and the revenue derived from such lands as may still remain unsold. 4th. Of lands and other property hertofore or hereafter bequeathed, granted or donated to the State for school purposes. 5th. All funds and property, other than unimproved lands, bequeathed or granted to the State, not designated for any other purpose. 6th. The proceeds of vacant estates falling under the law to the State of Louisiana. 7th. The Legislature may appropriate to the same fund the proceeds of public lands not designated or set apart for any other purpose, and shall provide that every parish may levy a tax for the public schools therein, which shall not exceed the entire State tax; provided, that with such a tax the whole amount of parish taxes shall not exceed the limits of parish taxation fixed by this Constitution. The City of New Orleans shall make such appropriation for the support, maintenance and repair of the public schools of said city as it may deem proper, but not less than eight-tenths of one mill for any one year;

and said schools shall also continue to receive from the Board of Liquidation of the City Debt, the amounts to which they are now entitled under the Constitutional amendment, adopted in the year 1892.

ART. 255. The Louisiana State University and Agricultural and Mechanical College, founded upon the land grants of the United States to endow a seminary of learning and a college for the benefit of agriculture and the mechanic arts, now established and located in the City of Baton Rouge, is hereby recognized; and all revenues derived and to be derived from the seminary fund, the Agricultural and Mechanical College fund, and other funds or lands donated or to be donated by the United States to the State of Louisiana for the use of a seminary of learning or of a college for the benefit of agriculture or the mechanic arts, shall be appropriated exclusively to the maintenance and support of said Louisiana State University and Agricultural and Mechanical College; and the General Assembly shall make such additional appropriations as may be necessary for its maintenance, support and improvement, and for the establishment, in connection with said institution, of such additional scientific or literary departments as the public necessities and the well being of the people of Louisiana may require; provided, that the appropriation shall not exceed fifteen thousand dollars per annum for its maintenance and support.

The Tulane University of Louisiana, located in New Orleans, is hereby recognized as created and to be developed in accordance with the provisions of legislative act No. 43, approved July 5, 1884, and by approval of the electors, made part of the Constitution of the State.

ART. 256. The Louisiana State Normal School, established and located at Natchitoches; the Industrial Institute and College of Louisiana, whose name is hereby changed to the Louisiana Industrial Institute, established and located at Ruston; and the Southern University, now established in the City of New Orleans, for the education of persons of color, are hereby recognized; and the General Assembly is directed to make such appropriations from time to time as may be necessary for the maintenance, support and improvement of these institutions; provided, that the appropriation for the maintenance and support of the Louisiana Industrial Institute shall not exceed fifteen thousand dollars per annum, and that for the Southern University shall not exceed ten thousand.

ART. 257. The debt due by the State to the free school fund is hereby declared to be the sum of one million one hundred and thirty thousand eight hundred and sixty-seven dollars and fifty-one cents in principal, and shall be kept on the books of the Auditor and Treasurer to the credit of the several townships entitled to the same; the said principal being the proceeds of the sales of lands heretofore granted by the United States for the use and support of free public schools, which amount shall be held by the State as a loan, and shall be and remain a perpetual fund, on which the State shall pay an annual interest of four per cent, and that said interest shall be paid to the several townships in the State entitled to the same, in accordance with the Act of Congress, No. 68, approved February 15th, 1843.

ART. 258. The debt due by the State to the seminary fund is hereby declared to be one hundred and thirty-six thousand dollars, being the proceeds of the sale of lands heretofore granted by the United States to this State for the use of a seminary of learning, and said amount shall be kept to the credit of said fund on the books of the Auditor and Treasurer of the State as a perpetual loan, and the State shall pay an annual interest of four per cent. on said amount.

ART. 259. The debt due by the State to the Agricultural and Mechanical College fund is hereby declared to be the sum of one hundred and eighty-two thousand three hundred and thirteen dollars and three cents, being the proceeds of the sale of lands and land scrip heretofore granted by the United States to this State for the use of a college for the benefit of agricultural and mechanical arts; and said amount shall be kept to the credit of said fund on the books of the Auditor and Treasurer of the State as a perpetual loan, and the State shall pay an annual interest of five per cent. on said amount.

ART. 260. The interest due on the free school fund, the seminary fund and the Agricultural and Mechanical College fund, shall be paid out of any tax that may be levied and collected for the payment of the interest on the State debt.

ART. 261. All pupils in the primary grades in the public schools throughout the Parish of Orleans, unable to provide themselves with the requisite books, an affidavit to that effect having been made by one of the parents of such pupils, or if such parents be dead, then by the tutor or other person in charge of such pupils, shall be furnished with the necessary books, free of expense, to be paid for out of the school fund of said parish; and the School Board of the Parish of Orleans is hereby directed to appropriate annually not less than two thousand dollars for the purpose named, provided such amount be needed.

CORPORATIONS AND CORPORATE RIGHTS

ART. 262. The General Assembly shall not remit the forfeiture of the charter of any corporation now existing, nor renew, alter or amend the same, nor pass any general or special law for the benefit of such corporation, except upon the condition that such corporation shall thereafter hold its charter subject to the provisions of this Constitution.

ART. 263. The exercise of the police power of the State shall never be abridged nor so construed as to permit corporations to conduct their business in such manner as to infringe the equal rights of individuals or the general well-being of the State.

ART. 264. No domestic or foreign corporations shall do any business in this State without having one or more known places of business and an authorized agent or agents in the State upon whom process may be served.

ART. 265. No corporation shall engage in any business other than that expressly authorized in its charter or incidental thereto, nor shall it take or hold any real estate for a longer period than ten years, except such as may be necessary and proper for its legitimate business or purposes.

ART. 266. No corporation shall issue stock or bonds, except for labor done or money or property actually received, and all fictitious issues of stock shall be void, and any corporation issuing such fictitious stock shall forfeit its charter.

ART. 267. The stock shall neither be increased nor decreased, except in pursuance of general laws, nor without consent of persons holding the larger amount in value of the stock, first obtained at a meeting of stockholders to be held after thirty days' notice given in pursuance of law.

ART. 268. The term corporation, as used in this Constitution, shall be construed to include all joint stock companies or associations having any power or privilege not possessed by individuals or partnerships.

ART. 269. It shall be a crime, the punishment of which shall be prescribed by law, for any president, director, manager, cashier, or other officer or owner of any private or public bank or banking institution or other corporation accepting deposits or loans to assent to the reception of deposits, or the creation of debts by such banking institutions, after he shall have had knowledge of the fact that it is insolvent or in falling circumstances; any such officer, agent or manager shall be individually responsible for such deposits so received and all such debts so created with his assent.

ART. 270. The General Assembly shall have power to enact general laws authorizing the parochial, ward and municipal authorities of the State by a vote of the majority of the property tax-payers in number entitled to vote under the provisions of this Constitution and in value, to levy special taxes in aid of public improvements or railway enterprises; provided, that such tax shall not exceed the rate of five mills per annum, nor extend for a longer period than ten years; and provided further, that no taxpayer shall be permitted to vote at such election unless he shall have been assessed in the parish, ward or municipality to be affected for property the year previous.

ART. 271. Any railroad corporation or association organized for the purpose shall have the right to construct and operate a railroad between any points within this State, and connect at the State line with railroads of other States. Every railroad company shall have the right with its road to intersect, connect with or cross any other railroad, and shall receive and transport each other's passengers, tonnage and cars, loaded or empty, without delay or discrimination.

ART. 272. Railways heretofore constructed, or that may hereafter be constructed in this State, are hereby declared public highways, and railroad companies common carriers.

ART. 273. Every railroad or other corporation, organized or doing business in this State, under the laws or authority thereof, shall have and maintain a public office or place in this State for the transaction of its business, where transfers of stock shall be made, and where shall be kept for public inspection books in which shall be recorded the amount of capital stock subscribed, the names of owners of stock, the amounts owned by them respectively, the amount of stock paid, and by whom, the transfers of said stock, with the date of transfer, the amount of its assets and liabilities, and the names and places of residence of its officers.

ART. 274. If any railroad company, organized under the laws of this State, shall consolidate, by sale or otherwise, with any railroad company organized under the laws of any other State or of the United States, the same shall not thereby become a foreign corporation, but the courts of this State shall retain jurisdiction in all matters which may arise, as if said consolidation had not taken place. In no case shall any one consolidation take place except upon public notice of at least sixty days to all stockholders, in such manner as may be provided by law.

ART. 275. General laws shall be enacted providing for the creation of private corporations, and shall therein provide fully for the adequate protection of the public and of the individual stockholder.

ART. 276. The police juries of the several parishes and the constituted authorities of all incorporated municipalities of the State shall alone have the power of regulating the slaughtering of cattle and other live stock within their respective limits; provided, no monopoly or exclusive privilege shall exist in this State, nor such business be restricted to the land or houses of any individual or corporation; provided, the ordinances designating the places for slaughtering shall obtain the concurrent approval of the Board of Health or other sanitary organization.

PAROCHIAL AND MUNICIPAL CORPORATIONS

ART. 277. The General Assembly may establish and organize new parishes, which shall be bodies corporate, with such powers as may be prescribed by law, but no new parish shall contain less than six hundred and twenty-five square miles, nor less than seven thousand inhabitants; nor shall any parish be reduced below that area, or number of inhabitants.

ART. 278. All laws changing parish lines, or removing parish seats, shall, before taking effect, be submitted to the electors of the parish or parishes to be affected thereby, at a special election held for that purpose, and the lines, or the parish seat, shall remain unchanged unless two-thirds of the qualified electors of the parish or parishes affected thereby vote in favor thereof at such election.

ART. 279. Any parish may be dissolved and merged by the General Assembly into a contiguous parish or parishes, two-thirds of the qualified electors of the parish proposed to be dissolved voting in favor thereof at an election held for that purpose; provided, that the parish or parishes into which the dissolved parish proposes to become incorporated consents thereto by a majority of its qualified electors voting therefor.

ART. 280. Whenever a parish shall be enlarged or created from territory contiguous thereto, it shall be entitled to a just proportion of the property and assets, and be liable for a just proportion of the existing debts or liabilities of the parish or parishes from which such territory shall have been taken.

ART. 281. Municipal corporations, parishes, and drainage districts, the City of New Orleans excepted, when authorized to do so, by a vote of a majority in number and amount of the property taxpayers, qualified as electors under the Constitution and laws of this State, voting at an election held for that purpose, after due notice of said election has been published for thirty days in the official journal of the municipality or parish, and where there is no official journal, in a newspaper published therein, may incur debt, and issue negotiable bonds therefor, to the extent of one-tenth of the assessed valuation of the property within said municipal corporation, parish, or drainage district, as shown by the last assessment made prior to the submission of the proposition to the property taxpayers, as above provided, and may be authorized by the property tax-payers voting at said election, to levy and assess special taxes upon the property subject to taxation in the parish, drainage district or corporation; provided, said taxes so imposed do not exceed five mills on the dollar of the assessed valuation in any one year, nor run for a greater number of years than the number named in the proposition submitted to the tax-payers. No bonds shall be issued for any other purpose than stated in the submission of the proposition to the tax-payers, and published for thirty days, as aforesaid, nor for a greater amount than therein mentioned; nor shall such bonds be issued for any other purpose than for paving and improving streets, roads and alleys, purchasing or constructing a system of water-works, sewerage, drainage, lights, public parks and buildings, bridges and other works of public improvement, the title to which shall vest in the municipal corporation, parish or drainage district, as the case may be; nor shall such bonds run for a longer period than forty years from their date, or bear a greater rate of interest than five per cent. per annum, or be sold by the municipal corporation, parish or drainage district issuing the same for less than par.

The municipal corporation, parish or drainage district issuing such bonds shall provide for the payment of the interest annually, or semi-annually, and the principal thereof at maturity; provided, that the total issue of bonds by any municipality, parish or drainage district, for all purposes shall never exceed ten per cent. of the assessed value of the property in such municipality, parish or drainage district. Provided, that drainage districts availing themselves of the provisions of this ordinance shall be limited to the rate of taxation herein fixed; and such districts shall be prohibited from levying contributions under the provisions of existing laws, and provided, further, that nothing herein contained shall prevent drainage districts from being established under the provisions of existing laws.

ART. 282. One-half of the net amount of all parish taxes and licenses, levied and collected within the corporate limits of the City of Baton Rouge, shall be paid over for the use of said city, by the officer collecting the same, to the officer charged with the custody of the funds of said city.

RAILROAD, EXPRESS, TELEPHONE, TELEGRAPH, STEAMBOAT AND SLEEPING CAR COMPANY COMMISSION

ART. 283. A Railroad, Express, Telephone, Telegraph, Steamboat and other Water Craft, and Sleeping Car Commission, is hereby created; to be composed of three members, to be elected from the districts hereinafter named, at the time fixed for the Congressional election of 1898. Of the three commissioners elected in the year 1898, one shall serve two years, one shall serve four years, and one shall six years, the period each is to serve to be determined by lot; thereafter the commissioners from each district shall be elected for a term of six years. They shall be known as the Railroad Commission of Louisiana. The Commission shall meet and open an office and have its domicile at Baton Rouge, and shall elect one of their number chairman, and may appoint a secretary at a salary of fifteen hundred dollars per annum, and may meet and hold regular or special hearings at such other places as they may find necessary. No member of this Convention shall be eligible to election or appointment as a member of said Commission, prior to the year 1908.

Art. 284. The power and authority is hereby vested in the Commission, and it is hereby made its duty, to adopt, change or make reasonable and just rates, charges and regulations, to govern and regulate railroad, steamboat and other water craft, and sleeping car, freight and passenger tariffs and service, express rates, and telephone and telegraph charges, to correct abuses, and prevent unjust discrimination and extortion in the rates for the same, on the different railroads, steamboat and other water craft, sleeping car, express, telephone and telegraph lines of this State, and to prevent such companies from charging any greater compensation in the aggregate for the like kind of property or passengers, or messages, for a shorter than a longer distance over the same line, unless authorized by the Commission to do so in special cases; to require all railroads to build and maintain suitable depots, switches and appurtenances, wherever the same are reasonably necessary at stations, and to inspect railroads and to require them to keep their tracks and bridges in a safe condition, and to fix and adjust rates between branch or short lines and the great trunk lines with which they connect, and to enforce the same by having the penalties hereby prescribed inflicted through the proper courts having jurisdiction.

The Commission shall have power to adopt and enforce such reasonable rules, regulations, and modes of procedure, as it may deem proper for the discharge of its duties, and to hear and determine complaints that may be made against the classification or rates it may establish, and to regulate the mode and manner of all investigations and hearings of railroad companies and other parties before it, in the establishment of rates, orders, charges, and other acts, required or authorized by these provisions. They shall have power to summon and compel the attendance of witnesses, to swear witnesses, and to compel the production of books and papers, to take testimony under commission, and to punish for contempt, as fully as is provided by law for the district courts.

Art. 285. If any railroad, express, telephone, telegraph, steamboat and other water craft, or sleeping car company, or other party in interest, be dissatisfied with the decision or fixing of any rate, classification, rules, charge, order, act or regulation, adopted by the Commission, such party may file a petition setting forth the cause of objection to such decision, act, rule, rate, charge, classification or order, or to either or to all of them, in a court of competent jurisdiction, at the domicile of the Commission, against said Commission as defendant, and either party to said action may appeal the case to the Supreme Court of the State, without regard to the amount involved, and all such cases, both in the trial and appellate courts, shall be tried summarily, and by preference over all other cases. Such cases may be tried in the court of the first instance either in chambers, or at term time; provided, all such appeals shall be returned to the Supreme Court within ten days after the decision of the lower court; and where the Commission appeals, no bond shall be required.

No bond shall be required of said Commission in any case, nor shall advance costs, or security for costs, be required of the Commission.

Art. 286. If any railroad, express, telephone, telegraph, steamboat, or other water craft, or sleeping car company, subject hereto, directly or indirectly, or by any special rate, rebate, or other device, shall intentionally charge, demand, collect or receive from any person, firm or corporation, a greater or less compensation for any service rendered by it, than it charges, demands or receives from any other person, firm or corporation, for doing a like and contemporaneous service, or shall violate any of the rates, charges, orders or decisions of said Commission, such railroad, steamboat or other water craft, express, telegraph, telephone or other company, shall forfeit and pay to the State not less than one hundred dollars, nor more than five thousand dollars, to be recovered before any court of competent jurisdiction, at the suit of said Commission, at the domicile of the Commission or of the company, or at the place where the complaint arises, at the option of the Commission. Provided, that whenever any rate, order, charge, rule or regulation of the Commission is contested in court, as provided for in Article 285 of this Constitution, no fine or penalty for disobedience thereto, or disregard thereof, shall be incurred until after said contestation shall have been finally decided by the courts, and then only for acts subsequently committed.

The power of the Commission shall affect only the transportation of passengers, freight, express matter, and telegraph and telephone messages, between points within this State, and the use of such instruments within this State.

Art. 287. Until otherwise provided by law, the members of the Commission shall each receive a salary of three thousand dollars per annum, payable monthly on his own warrant, and their actual traveling expenses, and those of their secretary; which expenses, and the salary of the latter, shall be paid on the warrant of the Chairman of the Commission on a sworn statement of their correctness.

Nothing herein shall prevent the railroad, express, telegraph, telephone and steamboat or other water craft, or other companies, from serving free of cost, or at reduced rates, the State or any city, parish, or town government, or any charitable purpose, or any fair or exposition, or any destitute or indigent person, or the issuance of mileage or excursion tickets; nor to prevent railroads, steamboats or other water craft, from giving free transportation to ministers of religion, or inmates of hospitals, or to railroad officers, agents, employes, attorneys, stockholders or directors, unless otherwise provided by this Constitution.

Art. 288. Upon the recommendation of the Commission the Legislature may add to or enlarge the powers and duties of said Commission, or confer other powers and duties on them. They may also provide additional clerical, or other asistance, that may be deemed necessary for the discharge of the duties of said Commission, and may add other penalties to make the work of said Commission effective.

It shall be the duty of the Attorney General, and the various district attorneys, to aid said Commission in all legal matters, for which they shall receive not exceeding 25 per cent. of all fines and forfeitures collected by them; provided, the Commission may employ other attorneys in lieu of these officers on like terms.

No person in the service of, or attorney for, any railway, express, telephone, telegraph, steamboat or other water craft, sleeping car company or corporation, or pecuniarily interested in such company or corporation, shall hold the office of Commissioner.

The fines collected, after paying the attorney's fees and the costs in suits, in which the Commission may be cast for costs, shall be paid into the State Treasury.

ART. 289. The State is hereby divided into three Railway Commission Districts, and one Commissioner shall be elected from each of said districts by a plurality of the voters of the respective districts. The First District shall comprise the parishes of Orleans, Plaquemines, St. Bernard, Jefferson, St. Charles, St. John the Baptist and St. James. The Second District shall comprise the parishes of Iberville, Ascension, Assumption, Lafourche, Terrebonne, St. Mary, Iberia, St. Martin, Lafayette, Vermillion, Cameron, Calcasieu, Avoyelles, St. Landry, Pointe Coupe, West Feliciana, East Feliciana, West Baton Rouge, East Baton Rouge, St. Helena, Livingston, Tangipahoa, Washington, St. Tammany and Acadia. The Third District shall comprise the parishes of Rapides, Vernon, Sabine, Grant, Natchitoches, Winn, Red River, DeSoto, Caddo, Bossier, Webster, Bienville, Concordia, Caldwell, Franklin, Tensas, Madison, Richland, Ouachita, Jackson, Lincoln, Union, Morehouse, East Carroll, West Carroll, Claiborne and Catahoula.

RIPARIAN RIGHTS

ART. 290. Riparian owners of property on navigable rivers, lakes, and streams, within any city or town in this State having a population in excess of five thousand shall have the right to erect and maintain on the batture or banks owned by them, such wharves, buildings and improvements as may be required for the purposes of commerce and navigation, subject to the following conditions, and not otherwise, to-wit: Such owners shall first obtain the consent of the Council, or other governing authority, and of the Board of Levee Commissioners, within whose municipal or levee district jurisdiction such wharves, buildings, and improvements are to be erected, and such consent having been obtained, shall erect the same in conformity to plans and specifications which shall have been first submitted to, and approved by, the engineer of such Council, or other governing authority; and when so erected, such wharves, buildings, and improvements shall be, and remain, subject to the administration and control of such Council, or other governing authority, with respect to their maintenance and to the fees and charges to be exacted for their use by the public, whenever any fee or charge is authorized to be and is made; and shall be and remain subject to the control of such Board of Levee Commissioners, in so far as may be necessary for the maintenance and administration of the levees in its jurisdiction. The Council, or other governing authority, shall have the right to expropriate such wharves, buildings, and improvements, whenever necessary for public purposes, upon reimbursing the owner the cost of construction, less such depreciation as may have resulted from time and decay; such reimbursement, however, in no case to exceed the actual market value of the property. Provided, that nothing in this article shall be construed as affecting the right of the State, or of any political subdivision thereof, or of the several Boards of Levee Commissioners to appropriate without compensation such wharves buildings, and improvements, when necessary for levee purposes.

The grants made by the City of New Orleans under the terms of Ordinance 11,765, Council Series, adopted January 14, 1896, authorizing the construction, use, and maintenance of wharves, structures, and improvements upon certain riparian property in the Sixth Municipal District, and other grants of the same nature made by the City of New Orleans to riparian owners with reference to their property, are recognized as necessary aids to the commerce of this State, and are hereby ratified, and declared to be lawful, but shall in no event be construed as conferring greater privileges or rights than might be conferred under this article, or as releasing the riparian owners from the obligations herein imposed or which may have been imposed upon or assumed by such riparian owner by contract, municipal ordinance or otherwise.

PUBLIC ROADS

ART. 291. The Police Juries of this State may form their respective parishes into road districts; and in order to raise funds for the purpose of constructing, maintaining and repairing, the public roads and bridges of their parishes, they are authorized to set aside at least one mill per annum of the taxes levied by them, and to impose a per capita tax of not more than one dollar per annum upon each able-bodied male inhabitant of the parish between the ages of eighteen and fifty-five years, and to levy an annual license of not less than twenty-five cents, nor more than one dollar per annum upon each vehicle, including bicycles kept and used for locomotion over public roads, in their respective parishes; which license may be graduated. The provisions of this article relative to the per capita tax shall not be operative in incorporated towns and cities that maintain their own streets.

To carry into effect the provisions of this article the Police Juries may enact such ordinances of a civil nature as may be necessary to enforce the property and license tax, and of a criminal nature to enforce the per capita tax. Other taxes may be levied by the Police Juries for road and bridge purposes, not to exceed five mills for five years on the property of the parish, or any ward thereof, where the rate of taxation and the purpose thereof shall have been submitted to the property tax-payers of said ward or parish entitled to vote under the election laws of the State, and a majority in numbers and value of those voting at said election shall have voted in favor thereof.

ART. 292. When any parish shall avail itself of the provisions of this article, the judge, in passing sentence on persons convicted of any offense, when the punishment imposed by law is imprisonment in the parish jail in the first instance, or in default of payment of fine, may sentence such persons to work on the public roads and bridges and any other public works of the parish; and when the punishment prescribed by law is imprisonment in the penitentiary, he may sentence the persons so convicted to work on the public roads and bridges and other public works of the parish where the crime was committed, if the sentence actually imposed does not exceed six months. All fines and penalties imposed on persons for infringement of any ordinance relative to roads and bridges, shall go, when collected, into the road and bridge fund of the parish.

ART. 293. The Police Jury shall relieve from compulsory road duty all persons who have paid the road and bridge tax and license levied against them.

ART. 294. The State Board of Engineers, whenever called on so to do, shall furnish the different road districts with plans and specifications for public roads, and such assistance and advice as will tend to create a uniform system of public roads throughout the State.

BOARD OF CHARITIES AND CORRECTIONS

ART. 295. The Legislature shall provide for a State Board of Charities and Corrections, which shall consist of six members, and of which the Governor shall be chairman ex-officio. Upon the organization of said Board, the Governor shall appoint one member for six years, one for five years, one for four years, one for three years, one for two years, and thereafter shall make appointments for six years, except in case of vacancy in office, when the appointment shall be made for the unexpired term. The members of the Board shall serve without compensation, but they shall be authorized to elect a secretary, who shall receive such salary as may be fixed by the Legislature. The State shall provide an office for said Board, and shall make provision from time to time for the payment of its expenses.

The duties of the Board shall be strictly visitorial, without administrative or executive powers. It shall visit and inspect all State, parish or municipal institutions which are of a charitable, eleemosynary, correctional, or reformatory character, and all private institutions of like character utilized or aided by parochial or municipal authority, and all private insane asylums, whether so utilized or aided or not.

The Board shall report annually to the Governor, and to the Legislature at each session thereof, the actual condition of all of the above institutions. They shall make such suggestions to the Governor and Legislature as may be necessary and pertinent; provided, said suggestions are concurred in by a majority of the members of the Boards in control of each of said institutions. The officers in charge of said institutions shall furnish the Board such information and statistics as it may require.

BOARDS OF HEALTH AND STATE MEDICINE

ART. 296. The General Assembly shall create for the State, and for each parish and municipality therein, Boards of Health, and shall define their duties, and prescribe the powers thereof. The State Board of Health shall be composed of representative physicians from the various sections of the State. Until otherwise provided by law, both the President and Secretary of the State Board of Health shall be ex-officio members of the Board of Health for the City of New Orleans, the President of the State Board to be the President of the local Board of the City of New Orleans.

ART. 297. The General Assembly shall provide for the interest of State Medicine in all its departments; for the protection of the people from unqualified practitioners of medicine, and dentistry; protecting confidential communications made to medical men by their patients while under professional treatment and for the purpose of such treatment; for protecting the people against the sale of injurious or adulterated drugs, foods and drinks, and against any and all adulterations of the general necessaries of life of whatever kinds and character.

MILITIA

ART. 298. The General Assembly shall have authority to provide by law how the militia of this State shall be organized, officered, trained, armed and equipped, and of whom it shall consist.

ART. 299. The officers and men of the militia and volunteer forces shall receive no pay, rations or emoluments, when not in active service by authority of the State.

ART. 300. The General Assembly may exempt from military service those who belong to religious societies whose tenets forbid them to bear arms; provided, a money equivalent for these services shall be exacted.

ART. 301. The Governor shall have power to call the militia into active service for the preservation of law and order, or when the public service may require it; provided, that the police force of any city, town or parish, shall not be organized or used as a part of the State militia.

PENSIONS

ART. 302. The Soldiers' Home of the State of Louisiana, known as Camp Nicholls, shall be maintained by the State, and the General Assembly shall make an appropriation for each year based upon the number of inmates in said home on the first day of April of the year in which said appropriation is made, of one hundred and thirty dollars per capita, for the maintenance and clothing of such inmates from which one dollar per month shall be allowed to each inmate for his personal use, and shall make such further appropriations for building, repairs, and incidentals, as may be absolutely necessary.

ART. 303. A pension not to exceed eight dollars per month shall be allowed to each Confederate soldier or sailor veteran, who possess all of the following qualifications:

1st. He shall have served honorably from the date of his enlistment until the close of the late Civil war, or until he was discharged or paroled, in some military organization regularly mustered into the army or navy of the Confederate States, and shall have remained true to the Confederate States until the surrender.

2d. He shall be in indigent circumstances, and unable to earn a livelihood by his own labor or skill.

3d. He shall not be salaried or otherwise provided for by the State of Louisiana, or by any other State or Government.

In case he enlisted in any organization mustered into said service as a Louisiana organization, or in case at the date of his enlistment he resided in the State of Louisiana, he shall have resided in this State for at least five years prior to his application for a pension. In case he resided elsewhere than in this State, and enlisted in an organization not mustered in from Louisiana, or in the navy of the Confederate States, he shall have resided in this State for at least fifteen years prior to his application for such pension. A like pension shall be granted to the widow who shall not have married again, in indigent circumstances, of any soldier or sailor who, having entered the service of the Confederate States during the late Civil War, lost his life prior to June 1st, 1865, from wounds received, or disease contracted in such service; provided, that if her deceased husband served in an organization mustered in from Louisiana, or if he resided in Louisiana at the date of his enlistment, and has so resided for one year prior thereto, then in order that such widow shall be entitled to the pension as herein provided, she shall have resided in this State for at least five years prior to her application therefor; and if her deceased husband enlisted elsewhere than in Louisiana, and served in an organization not mustered in from Louisiana, such widow shall, in order to entitle her to pension as herein provided, have resided in this State for not less than fifteen years prior to her application for such pension; provided, further, that pensions, whether to veterans or to widows, shall be allowed only from the date of application under this article, and the total appropriation for all pensions shall not exceed fifty thousand dollars in any one year.

ART. 304. The General Assembly shall appropriate not less than twelve hundred dollars per annum for the maintenance in New Orleans of a Memorial Hall or repository for the collection and preservation of relics and mementoes of the late Civil War, and of other objects of interest, and shall be authorized to make suitable appropriations for the erection of monuments and markers on the battlefields of the country, commemorative of the services, upon such fields, of Louisiana soldiers and commands.

AGRICULTURE AND IMMIGRATION

ART. 305. The existing Bureau of Agriculture and Immigration shall hereafter be known as the Louisiana State Board of Agriculture and Immigration, and shall be recognized as an integral part of the State government.

ART. 306. The Louisiana State Board of Agriculture and Immigration shall have the control and direction of all State agricultural organizations and State Farmers' Institutes, and shall adopt the needful measures for the securement of proper immigration.

It shall also encourage State, district and parish fairs and local agricultural organizations, and shall maintain effective control of the manufacture or sale, in this State, of fertilizers and Paris green for the suppression of adulteration and fraud therein. It shall perform such other duties and shall have such other powers as shall be prescribed by the General Assembly.

ART. 307. The said Board of Agriculture and Immigration shall consist of one member from each Congressional district, appointed by the Governor, by and with the advice and consent of the Senate, from men engaged in the leading agricultural interests of the State; the said members to hold their offices for six years, or until their successors are appointed. In the first appointment, which shall be made within sixty days after the adjournment of this convention, the members from the first and fourth districts shall be appointed for two years; those from the second and fifth districts for four years; and those from the third and sixth districts for six years. The Governor of the State, the Commissioner of Agriculture and Immigration, the President of the State University and Agricultural and Mechanical College, the Vice-President of the Board of Supervisors of the State University and Agricultural and Mechanical College, and the Director of the State experimental stations are and shall be ex-officio members of this Board. The members of said Board shall serve without compensation, except actual expenses incurred in attending the meetings.

ART. 308. The paramount importance of our agricultural interests, and the necessity of peopling with a desirable population the vast unoccupied areas of our fertile lands, require an enlargement of the duties and an expansion of the scope of the work of this Board, for which the General Assembly shall enact such laws as may be necessary to carry out the provisions of this article.

CITY OF NEW ORLEANS

ART. 309. There shall be seven Assessors in the City of New Orleans, who together shall compose the Board of Assessors for the Parish of Orleans. One shall be appointed from each municipal district of the City of New Orleans, and they shall be residents of the districts from which they are appointed.

There shall be seven State Tax Collectors for the City of New Orleans. One shall be appointed from each municipal district. They shall be residents of the districts from which they are appointed, and they shall maintain offices in their respective districts. The said Assessors and State Tax Collectors shall be appointed by the Governor, by and with the advice and consent of the Senate, for the term of four years.

The first appointments under this Constitution of said officers shall be after the general election in 1900.

ART. 310. There shall be one coroner for the parish of Orleans, who shall be elected for four years by the qualified electors of said parish, and whose duties shall be fixed by law. He shall be *ex-officio* city physician of the City of New Orleans, and shall receive an annual salary of forty-eight hundred dollars. He shall be a practicing physician of said city and a graduate of the medical department of some university of recognized standing. He shall appoint two assistants, having the same qualifications as himself; one at an annual salary of twenty-six hundred dollars, and one at an annual salary of six hundred dollars.

ART. 311. The assistant, whose salary is hereby fixed at six hundred dollars shall be a resident of the Fifth district of the parish or City of New Orleans and shall have his office in said district.

The assistant, whose salary is fixed at twenty-six hundred dollars shall be a resident of that portion of the City of New Orleans lying on the left bank of the Mississippi river.

The provision shall take effect from and after the next general election. The salaries of the coroner and his assistants shall be paid by the City of New Orleans.

ART. 312. Any person whose property has been appropriated within twelve months prior to the adoption of this Constitution, or whose property may hereafter be appropriated by the Orleans Levee Board for levee purposes, shall have a right of action against said Board in any court of competent jurisdiction for the value of said property, and whatever judgment may be finally rendered against the Board shall be paid out of the taxes collected by it in the same manner as other disbursements are made; provided, that this shall not apply to batture property, nor to vacant property, where only a part thereof has been taken for levee purposes, and where the effect of the levee building would be to protect the remaining part of the same property; nor to any property on any part of the river front, the administration and control of which is vested, for the purposes of commerce, either in the State or city authorities, and on which improvements have been erected under grants from the City of New Orleans, or other authority, nor to the said improvements; provided, that said Board shall have power to appropriate property subject to such servitude, for levee building, as under existing laws, without making such compensation in advance.

ART. 313. All surplus revenues of the City of New Orleans from the year 1879 to the year 1895, both inclusive, except the surplus revenue dedicated to permanent public improvement, and to schools, by Act No. 110 of 1890, derived from the one per cent. tax levied under said act, shall be turned over by the city to the Board of Liquidation of the City Debt. Said Board shall redeem all claims evidenced by financial ordinance or judgment against the City of New Orleans, for debts arising and incurred between the years 1879 to 1895, both inclusive, payment of which has not heretofore been provided for out of the reserve and permanent public improvement funds of the city for the years 1893 to 1898, both inclusive, excepting therefrom the claims of school teachers for the years 1880 to 1884, payment of which has been authorized by Act No. 110 of 1890, and is now being provided for by the city, said claims or judgments to be purchased on the most reasonable terms offered by creditors within the period of eighteen months succeeding the date of the adoption of this Constitution, the said Board to invite proposals by public advertisements, to be made bimonthly; provided, any and all bids may be rejected. For the purpose of such redemption the City of New Orleans, through the Board of Liquidation, is hereby authorized to issue bonds to the extent of two hundred and fifty thousand dollars, bearing four per cent. per annum interest, payable semi-annually in such denominations as may be by said Board determined upon, maturing in fifty years from the date of issue, but subject to redemption by said Board in the reverse order of their issue at any time after sixty days' notice.

Said Board is hereby authorized in its discretion to exchange said bonds for said claims against the city, evidenced by financial ordinances or judgments, or to sell said bonds, and with the proceeds thereof purchase said claims; provided, that no sale of said bonds shall be made for less than par.

Said Board of Liquidation shall, at any time it may be necessary, sell a sufficient number of the Constitutional Bonds of the City of New Orleans, now unsold, of the issue provided for by Act No. 110 of the General Assembly for the year 1890, and by the amendment to the Constitution of the State submitted to the people by said act and adopted at the general election in 1892, to provide for the payment of interest or principal of the bonds hereby authorized to be issued. Whenever the said Board of Liquidation shall have received from the surplus revenues of the City of New Orleans, as provided herein, sufficient funds to meet the issue of bonds hereby authorized in principal and interest, the remainder of the surplus revenues so turned over to the said Board shall revert to the city.

ART. 314. The provisions of the amendment embodied in joint resolution of the General Assembly No. 110, approved July 8th, 1890, and thereafter ratified by the people and made part of the Constitution, are recognized as of full force and effect; the authority conferred upon the City of New Orleans and upon the Board of Liquidation of the City Debt, with respect to the issuance of constitutional bonds of the City of New Orleans, and to the levy and collection of a special *ad valorem* tax of one per cent. upon all the taxable property, real, personal and mixed, in said city, for the payment of said bonds, in principal and interest, and with respect to the manner of such payment, is confirmed, as are also all rights vested by said amendment in the present and future holders of said bonds, whether issued or to be issued; and no limitations imposed by other provisions of this Constitution upon the authority of the City of New Orleans, shall be held to include, apply to, or affect, the taxing power herein contemplated and confirmed.

ART. 315. The City of New Orleans is hereby authorized and required to examine into and assume payment of the obligations of the Board of Directors of the Public Schools of the Parish of Orleans for unpaid salaries of school teachers and portresses and of other legitimate claims against said School Board, for the years 1882, 1883 and 1884, and for unpaid salaries of school teachers and portresses for the years 1885, 1886 and 1887, now in the hands of the original owners, who have in no wise parted with their rights of ownership, or pledged the same, as may be found by said city to be equitably due by said Board. All claims to be examined into and assumed by the City of New Orleans under this Article shall be presented to and filed with the City Council of said city within ninety days after the adoption of this Constitution, and not thereafter.

ART. 316. The City Council shall issue certificates of indebtedness to the owners of said claims, when examined and found to be equitably due, and all such certificates shall be paid by the Board of Liquidation. If any of the claims aforesaid be rejected by the said City Council, the decision thereon may be reviewed by any Court of competent jurisdiction, and the judgment of the court thereon shall, if in favor of the claimant, be likewise paid by the Board of Liquidation.

ART. 317. The funds requisite to pay said claims shall be provided by said Board of Liquidation, by the sale of a sufficient number of the Constitutional bonds of the City of New Orleans of the issue provided for by Act No. 110 of the General Assembly for the year 1890, and by the amendment to the Constitution of the State submitted to the people by said act and adopted at the general election in 1892.

ART. 318. The General Assembly of the State of Louisiana is hereby authorized to amend Act No. 110 of 1890, confirmed by Constitutional amendment of 1892, providing for the refunding of the city debts so far only as to provide that in the further issue of bonds under said act within the limit of ten million dollars, provided for in said act, the City of New Orleans, through the Board of Liquidation, shall have authority to issue registered bonds, and to authorize the exchange of registered bonds, for equal amounts of outstanding four per cent. coupon bonds of the City of New Orleans, issued under authority of said act, having the same time to run and at the same rate of interest, and provide for their registration and payment of interest. All registered bonds issued by the City of New Orleans under the amended act as herein provided shall have the same guarantees, and the holders of said bonds shall have the same privileges, as are now secured by said act to the holders of coupon bonds. Said registered bonds shall be denominated Registered Constitutional Bonds of the City of New Orleans, Authorized by Act No. 110 of 1890, and Amendment thereto.

ART. 319. The electors of the City of New Orleans, and of any political corporation which may be established within the territory now, or which may hereafter be, embraced within the corporate limits of said city, shall have the right to choose the public officers, who shall be charged with the exercise of the police power and with the administration of the affairs of said corporation in whole or in part.

ART. 320. This article shall not apply to the Board of Liquidation of the City Debt, nor shall it be construed as prohibiting the establishment of Boards or Commissioners, the members of which are elected by the Council or appointed by the Mayor with the consent of the Council. As to all other existing boards or Commissions affected by it, said article shall take effect from and after the first municipal election which shall be held in the City of New Orleans after the adoption of this Constitution; provided that nothing herein contained shall be so construed as to prevent the Legislature from creating Boards or Commissioners, whose powers shall extend in and beyond the Parish of Orleans, or as affecting present Boards of that character, or the Board of Directors of the public schools; provided, that hereafter, in creating any Board with such powers, or in filling vacancies therein, at least two-thirds of the members thereof shall be from the City of New Orleans, and elected by the people or Council thereof, or appointed by the Mayor as hereinabove provided.

AMENDMENTS TO THE CONSTITUTION

ART. 321. Propositions for the amendment of this Constitution may be made by the General Assembly at any session thereof, and if two-thirds of all the members elected to each house shall concur therein, after such proposed amendments have been read in such respective houses on three separate days, such proposed amendment or amendments, together with the yeas and nays thereon, shall be entered on the Journal, and the Secretary of State shall cause the same to be published in two newspapers published in the Parish of Orleans and in one paper in each other parish of the State in which a newspaper is published, for two months preceding an election for Representatives in the Legislature or in Congress, to be designated by the Legislature, at which time the said amendment or amendments shall be submitted to the electors for their approval or rejection; and if a majority voting on said amendment or amendments shall approve and ratify the same, then such amendment or amendments so approved and ratified shall become a part of the Constitution. When more than one amendment shall be submitted at the same time, they shall be so submitted as to enable the electors to vote on each amendment separately. The result of said election shall be made known by the proclamation of the Governor.

CODE OF CRIMINAL LAW, PROCEDURE AND CORRECTION

ART. 322. It shall be the duty of the Governor to appoint a commission to prepare drafts of a code of Criminal Law, of a Code of Criminal Procedure, and of a Code of Criminal Correction for this State. The drafts of such codes, when prepared, shall be promptly printed, and copies thereof shall be sent to each judge of this State, and to such other persons in or out of this State as the Governor may think proper, with the request from him for suggestions and criticisms. The Governor shall submit to the General Assembly of this State, first convened, after the lapse of one year from the distribution of the printd copies of said drafts as above, the said drafts, together with the report of the Commission, and with a message from himself in which he shall embody and condense each suggestion he shall deem of use. And the General Assembly shall have power to adopt said Codes, with such amendments as they may deem advisable, by vote in each House, without complying with the formalities of readings and the other formalities required by the Constitution in the passage of statutes. No promulgation of said code shall be required beyond its publication in book form after same shall have become a law.

ART. 323. All amendments proposed in the General Assembly shall be proposed within the first thirty days after its convening, and no amendments shall be proposed after the lapse of that time. All amendments shall be referred to a joint committee of both Houses, consisting of two members from each House, with the Attorney General as *ex-officio* chairman. Only such amendments shall be voted on as shall be favorably reported by this committee, and each amendment shall be voted on separately.

ART. 324. The Commission to prepare said drafts shall be composed of three lawyers of this State. The compensation of said Commissioners shall be fixed by the General Assembly. Said compensation to be payable only when the drafts have been prepared and submitted to the Governor; but the other expenses of the Commission shall be promptly paid as incurred, and the Governor is hereby warranted to draw on the General Fund for said compensation, and for all the expenses of printing the said drafts, and for the other expenses incurred under this act.

SCHEDULE

ART. 325. That no inconvenience may arise from the adoption of this Constitution, and in order to carry this Constitution into complete operation, it is hereby declared:

First—That all laws in force in this State, at the time of the adoption of this Constitution, not inconsistent therewith, and constitutional when enacted, shall remain in full force and effect until altered or repealed by the General Assembly, or until they expire by their own limitation. All ordinances passed and ratified by this Convention and appended to the official original draft of the Constitution delivered to the Secretary of State, shall have the same force and effect as if included in, and constituting a part of this Constitution.

Second—All writs, actions, causes of action, proceedings, prosecutions and rights of individuals, or bodies corporate, and of the State, when not inconsistent with this Constitution, shall continue as valid and in full force and effect.

Third—The provisions of all laws, which are inconsistent with this Constitution, shall cease upon its adoption, except that all laws which are inconsistent with such provisions of this Constitution as require legislation to enforce them, shall remain in full force until such legislation is had.

Fourth—All recognizances, obligations and all other instruments entered into or executed before the adoption of this Constitution, to the State, or to any parish, city, municipality, board, or other public corporation therein, and all fines, taxes, penalties, forfeitures and rights, due, owing or accruing to the State of Louisiana, or to any parish, city, municipality, board, or other public corporation therein, under the Constitution and laws heretofore in force, and all writs, prosecutions, actions and proceedings, except as herein otherwise provided, shall, continue and remain unaffected by the adoption of this Constitution. All indictments and information which shall have been found or filed, or may hereafter be found or filed for any crime or offense committed before the adoption of this Constitution, may be prosecuted as if no change had been made, except as herein otherwise provided.

Fifth—All officers, executive, legislative and judicial, State parish or municipal, who may be in office at the adoption of this Constitution, or who may be elected or appointed before the election or appointment of their successors as herein provided, shall hold their respective offices until their terms have expired, shall hold their successors are duly qualified, as provided in this Constitution, unless sooner removed, as may be provided by law; and shall receive the compensation now fixed by the Constitution and laws in force at the adoption of this Constitution, except as herein otherwise provided.

Sixth—The Constitution of this State, adopted in 1879, and all amendments thereto, are declared to be superseded by this Constitution; provided, however, that no failure on the part of this Convention to re-enact and re-ordain any article or ordinance contained in the Constitution of 1879 upon any of the subjects upon which this Convention is by the act convening it prohibited from enacting, ordaining or framing any article or ordinance, shall be construed as in any manner impairing or affecting the provisions of the Constitution of 1879, upon the prohibited subjects.

Seventh—The Supreme Court, Courts of Appeal and district Courts, provided for by this Constitution, are declared to be, and shall be construed to be the same courts as those of the same name, created by the Constitution of 1879, and all writs, orders and process issued from said courts, which shall be pending, or in course of execution at the date when this Constitution goes into effect, together with all the records and archives of said courts, shall at once, by virtue of this article, be transferred to, and held to be cases pending in, and writs, orders and process issued from, and in course of execution, under the authority of, and records and archives of said courts respectively, as organized under this Constitution.

Eighth—This Constitution, adopted by the people of the State of Louisiana, in Convention assembled, shall be in full force and effect from and after this 12th day of May, 1898, save and except as otherwise provided in and by said Constitution.

ART. 326. The first General Assembly, meeting after the adoption of this Constitution, is required to make a special appropriation to pay the debt which this Convention has contracted with the Louisiana National Bank, the Hibernia National Bank and the New Orleans National Bank, of the City of New Orleans, with interest at 5 per cent. per annum from May 9th, 1898, until paid, and for which certificates are held by said banks, issued to them pursuant to an ordinance heretofore adopted by this Convention, and which said debt was incurred for the purpose of enabling this Convention to complete its work.

There shall be printed in book or pamphlet form 1500 copies of the Journal of the Convention, and 5000 copies of this Constitution, and each member of the Convention shall be entitled to eight copies of the Journal and twenty-five copies of the Constitution. The remaining copies shall be delivered to the Secretary of State, to be disposed of as may hereafter be ordered by the Legislature.

Said General Assembly shall also make any appropriation required to pay any loans heretofore negotiated, or which may hereafter be negotiated by the Governor, pursuant to an ordinance heretofore adopted by this Convention, for the purpose of defraying the expenses of organizing and mobilizing the State's quota of volunteers called for by the proclamation of the President of the United States, heretofore promulgated.

Done in Convention, in the City of New Orleans, on the 12th day of May, in the year of our Lord, one thousand eight hundred and ninety-eight, and of the Independence of the United States of America, the one hundred and twenty-second.

E. B. KRUTTSCHNITT,
President of the Convention.

R. H. SNYDER,
First Vice-President of the Convention.

S. McC. LAWRASON,
Second Vice-President of the Convention.

Attest:
    ROBERT S. LANDRY,
      Secretary of the Convention.

MISCELLANEOUS ORDINANCES

POSTPONING THE SESSION OF THE GENERAL ASSEMBLY

Be it ordained by the people of the State of Louisiana in Convention assembled:

ART. 1. That the next regular session of the General Assembly of this State, to be held on the second Monday in May, 1898, be and the same is hereby postponed until the third Monday in May, 1898, and that the Governor of the State be and is hereby authorized and requested to issue his proclamation to that effect.

ART. 2. Said General Assembly may adjourn its said session from time to time during the year 1898, provided that said session, including any and all adjournments thereof, shall not exceed sixty days in duration.

Done in Convention this 30th day of April, 1898.

LOAN TO DEFRAY THE EXPENSES OF THE CONVENTION

Be it ordained by the people of the State of Louisiana in Convention assembled.

ART. 1. That the President of this Convention, and the Chairman of the Committee on Contingent Expenses, are hereby authorized and instructed, in the name and by the authority of this Convention, to negotiate a loan of fifteen thousand dollars, or so much thereof as may be necessary to defray the residue of the expenses of this Convention not provided for by the Act of the General Assembly calling this Convention, and to enable the Convention to complete the work of framing the new Constitution.

ART. 2. Said loan shall be evidenced by one or more certificates of indebtedness, signed by the President of this Convention, and countersigned by the Secretary thereof, under seal of this Convention, and bearing interest from the date of such certificates until paid, at such rate, not exceeding 6 per cent. per annum, as may be agreed upon between the President of this Convention and the Chairman of the Committee on Contingent Expenses, as representing the Convention, and the lenders. Said certificates of indebtedness shall be payable on the first day of July, 1898, at any bank in the City of New Orleans which may be named on their face.

The General Assembly, at its next session, shall make a special appropriation to pay said certificate or certificates.

Done in Convention this 22d day of April, 1898.

LOAN FOR MOBILIZATION OF STATE TROOPS

Be it ordained by the people of the State of Louisiana in Convention assembled:

ART. 1. The Governor is authorized and empowered to borrow Fifty Thousand Dollars, or as much thereof as may be necessary, on the credit of the State, to defray the necessary expense of organizing and mobilizing the State's quota of volunteers called for by the proclamation of the President of the United States heretofore promulgated, and the Legislature shall, at its next session, make an appropriation to pay the loan negotiated in pursuance thereof.

Done in Convention this 27th day of April, 1898.

AMENDMENTS TO CONSTITUTION OF 1898.

[STATE OF LOUISIANA,
OFFICE OF SECRETARY OF STATE,
Baton Rouge, January 1, 1907.

In view of the numerous amendments to the Constitution of 1898, twenty-six in number, which are available only by recourse to the various Acts of the Legislature from the Special Session of 1899 to '906, I have compiled in a single pamphlet all of the amendments to the Constitution in the order that they were adopted. A descriptive heading is printed over each amendment; the number of the Article amended is printed in black gothic type; the number of the Act of the Legislature proposing the amendment is given; side notes are placed on each article, and an index is printed at the back of the pamphlet.

This pamphlet will accompany all copies of the Constitution of '898, which are distributed from this office in the future, and copies will be sent to the courts and officials of Louisiana to complete the edition of the original Constitution sent to them at the time of its adoption in 1898.

JOHN T. MICHEL, Secty. State.]

RATIFYING SPECIAL TAXES FOR SEWERAGE AND WATER BOARD, CITY OF NEW ORLEANS, AND THE ACT OF LEGISLATURE AUTHORIZING ISSUANCE OF BONDS.

(First Amendment, Adopted April 17, 1900—Act No. 4, Ex. Sess., 1899)

" The special tax for public improvements, voted by the property taxpayers of the City of New Orleans on June 6, 1899, and levied by the City Council, by Ordinance No. 15,391 approved June 22, 1899, is hereby ratified, and its validity shall never be questioned. The special Act adopted by the Legislature at the special session held on August 8, 1899, constituting the Sewerage and Water Board of the City of New Orleans, authorizing the City of New Orleans to issue bonds, and providing the means to pay the principal and interest thereof, and for other purposes cognate to the purposes of the special tax aforesaid, is hereby ratified and approved, specially including therein reserved legislative right to amend the same; and all provisions of the present Constitution in conflict with the provisions of said Act, and with this amendment, are to that extent, and for that purpose only, repealed."

INCREASING PENSION APPROPRIATION FROM FIFTY THOUSAND DOLLARS ($50,000.00) TO SEVENTY-FIVE THOUSAND DOLLARS ($75,000.00)

(Second Amendment, Adopted November 8, 1900—Act No. 73 of 1900)

ARTICLE 303. A pension not to exceed eight ($8) dollars per month shall be allowed to each Confederate soldier or sailor veteran, who possesses all of the following qualifications:

1st. He shall have served honorably from the date of his enlistment until the close of the Civil War, or until he was discharged or paroled, in some military organization regularly mustered into the

Army or Navy of the Confederate States, and shall have remained true to the Confederate States until the surrender.

2nd. He shall be in indigent circumstances, and unable to earn a livelihood by his own labor or skill.

3. He shall not be salaried or otherwise provided for by the State of Louisiana, or by any other State or Government.

In case he enlisted in any organization mustered into said service as a Louisiana organization, or in case at the date of his enlistment he resided in the State of Louisiana, he shall have resided in this State for at least five years prior to his application for pension. In case he resided elsewhere than in this State, and enlisted in an organization not mustered in from Louisiana, or in the Navy of the Confederate States, he shall have resided in this State for at least fifteen years prior to his application for such pension. A like pension shall be granted to the widow who shall not have married again, in indigent circumstances, of such soldier or sailor, whose marriage to her was contracted prior to January 1, 1870, provided, that if her deceased husband served in an organization mustered in from Louisiana, or if he resided in Louisiana at the date of his enlistment, and has so resided for one year prior thereto, then in order that such widow shall be entitled to the pension as herein provided, she shall have resided in this State for at least five years prior to her application therefor; and if her deceased husband enlisted elsewhere than in Louisiana, and served in any organiaztion not mustered in from Louisiana, such widow shall, in order to entitle her to pension as herein provided, have resided in this State for not less than fifteen years prior to her application for such pension; provided further, that pensions, whether to veterans or to widows, shall be allowed only from the date of application under this article, and the total appropriations for all pensions shall not be less than fifty thousand dollars, nor more than seventy-five thousand dollars in any one year, provided that nothing in this article shall be construed so as to prohibit the General Assembly from providing artificial limbs to disabled Confederate soldiers or sailors.

RATIFYING CONTRACTS MADE BY THE CITY OF NEW ORLEANS, PRIOR TO MAY 12TH, 1902

(Third Amendment, Adopted November 4, 1902—Act No. 56 of 1902)

ARTICLE 47. The General Assembly shall have no power to grant or authorize any parish or municipal authority to grant any extra compensation, fee or allowance to a public officer, agent, servant, or contractor, nor pay, nor authorize the payment of any claim against the State or any parish or municipality thereof, under any agreement of contract made without express authority of law; and all such unathorized agreements or contracts shall be null and void, but all agreements or contracts for work of public improvements made or entered into by the City of New Orleans prior to the twelfth of May, 1902, are hereby ratified and approved and the city of New Orleans is hereby authorized to make all payments provided for in said contracts in accordance with the terms and under the conditions set forth in said contracts.

Exempting Certain Classes of Property from Taxation

(Fourth Amendment, Adopted November 4, 1902—Act No. 129 of 1902)

ARTICLE 230. The following shall be exempt from taxation, and no other, viz: All public property, places of religious worship, or burial, the rectories and parsonages of churches and grounds thereunto appurtenant, used exclusively as residences for the ministers in charge of such churches, all charitable institutions, all buildings and property used exclusively for public monuments or historical collections, colleges and other school purposes, the real and personal estate of any public library, and that of any other library association used by or connected with such library, all books and philosophical apparatus, and all paintings and statuary of any company or association, kept in a public hall; provided, the property so exempted be not leased for purposes of private or corporate profit or income. There shall also be exempt from taxation household property to the value of five hundred dollars. There shall also be exempt from parochial and municipal taxation for a period of ten years from the first day of January, 1900, the capital, machinery and other property employed in mining operations, and in the manufacture of textile fabrics, yarns, rope, cordage, leather, shoes, harness, saddlery, hats, clothing, flour, machinery, articles of tin, copper and sheet iron, agricultural implements, and furniture and other articles of wood, marble or stone; soap, stationery, ink and paper, boat building, and fertilizers and chemicals; provided that not less than five hands are employed in any one factory; provided, that nothing herein contained shall affect the exemptions provided for by existing Constitutional provisions. There shall also be exempt from taxation for a period of ten years from the date of its completion any railroad or parts of such railroad that may hereafter be constructed and completed prior to January 1st, 1904; provided, that when aid has heretofore been voted by any parish, ward, or municipality to any railroad not yet constructed, such railroad shall not be entitled to the exemption from taxation herein established, unless it waivers and relinquishes such aid or consents to a resubmission of the question of granting such aid to a vote of the property taxpayers of the parish, ward or municipality, which has voted the same, if one-third of such property taxpayers petition for the same within six months after the adoption of this Constitution. And provided, further, that this exemption shall not apply to double tracks, sidings, switches, depots or other improvements or betterments, which may be constructed by railroads now in operation within the State, other than extensions or new lines constructed by such railroads; nor shall the exemption hereinbefore granted apply to any railroad or part of such railroad, the construction of which was begun and the roadbed of which was substantially completed at the date of the adoption of this Constitution. The property or real estate belonging to any military organization of the State of Louisiana which is used by the State National Guard or militia for military purposes, such as arsenals or armories, while so used, shall be exempt from taxation.

Louisiana—1898

CREATING STATE BOARD OF APPRAISERS; ONE MEMBER FOR EACH CONGRESSIONAL DISTRICT. (PROVIDING FOR NEW SEVENTH CONGRESSIONAL DISTRICT)

(Fifth Amendment, Adopted November 4, 1902—Act No. 165 of 1902)

ARTICLE 226. There shall be and is hereby created a State Board of Appraisers, whose duty it shall be to assess the property belonging to corporations, associations, and individuals employed in railway, telegraph, telephone, sleeping car and express business throughout the State of Louisiana, which Board of Appraisers shall be composed of the Auditor and other members corresponding in number to the Congressional Districts of the State, to be elected by the Governor, Lieutenant-Governor, Treasurer, Attorney General and Secretary of State, one member from each Congressional District, for the term of four years, and the General Assembly shall fix the compensation of said Board.

RATIFYING WARRANTS ISSUED FOR SALARIES AND EXPENSES OF OFFICES OF CLERKS OF CIVIL DISTRICT COURT, REGISTER OF CONVEYANCES, ETC., CITY OF NEW ORLEANS

(Sixth Amendment, Adopted November 4, 1902—Act No. 182 of 1902)

ARTICLE 156. All valid warrants issued for salaries and authorized expenses of the offices of the clerks of the Civil District Court, Register of Conveyances and Recorder of Mortages for the parish of Orleans, of the clerks of the City Courts of the City of New Orleans, and for salaries of the clerks of the Court of Appeal, which are payable out of the special judicial expense fund provided for by Article 146 of the Constitution of 1879, as amended, and which shall be outstanding and unpaid at the date of the adoption of this Constitution, or which shall be issued for the current month in which this Constitution is adopted, are hereby declared to be valid and subsisting claims against the revenues of the respective offices upon which said fund was made dependent.

The holders of said warrants may present them within six months after the adoption of this Constitution to the Board of Liquidation of the City Debt, and receive therefor the bonds hereinafter authorized to be issued; and the City of New Orleans is required, within three months from the adoption of this Constitution, to provide for said warrants or claims, by the issuance of bonds in the sum of Two Hundred and Twenty-five Thousand Dollars, or so much thereof as may be necessary; said bonds shall be for the face value of said warrants, in such denominations as the said Board of Liquidation shall recommend, and shall be dated July 1st, 1898, and made payable twenty-five years after date, or earlier, at the option of said Board, and shall bear four per cent per annum interest, payable semi-annually, and represented by interest coupons attached thereto, the first of said coupons payable January 1st, 1899; said bonds to be known as Judicial Expense Fund Bonds, and to be signed by the Mayor and Comptroller of the City of New Orleans, and delivered to the Board of Liquidation of the City Debt and shall be countersigned by the President and Secretary of said Board and issued by said Board to the holders of said warrants upon surrender of same. Neither the State of Louisiana nor the City of New Orleans shall ever be liable for the payment of said bonds nor the interest thereon, except from the special fund herein provided for, and any appropriation or other provision therefor made by the State or city shall be null and void. There shall be stamped across the face of said bonds the words: "Issued in accordance with Article 156 of the Constitution of Louisiana of 1898." The Clerk of the Civil District Court, Register of Conveyances and Recorder of Mortgages for the Parish of Orleans, and the Clerks of the City Courts of New Orleans, shall keep accurate and detailed accounts in books to be used exclusively for that purpose of all fees and charges collected in their offices, respectively, and they shall furnish, daily, to the City Comptroller, transcripts of said accounts duly certified by them or by their authority, and said officers shall also daily pay into the Treasury of the City of New Orleans the whole amount of fees and charges so collected. From the amounts thus paid into the City Treasury the Treasurer shall set apart and reserve twenty per cent out of which shall first be paid the expenses necessary for the preparation and execution of the aforesaid bonds, and thereafter the same shall be used solely and exclusively to retire the bonds issued in payment of said Judicial Expense Fund warrants and interest thereon, and the certificates of the Comptroller hereinafter authorized; and upon the second Tuesday in December and June of every year the said Treasurer shall pay said amounts so reserved, and also the amounts received from the Civil Sheriff to the Board of Liquidation of the City Debt, until all the bonds herein authorized have been retired or paid; and on the second Tuesday in February and August of every year, said Board of Liquidation, in accordance with rules to be adopted and made public by it, shall, after paying the semi-annual interest on said bonds, purchase or redeem with such money thus set apart as may have accumulated, and with the surplus of the remaining eighty per cent as hereinafter provided, as many of said bonds as said money will buy or redeem, preference being given to holders offering at the lowest rate; and all such bonds so purchased or redeemed shall be by said Board of Liquidation immediately canceled, and a record made thereof. From the remaining eighty per cent of said fund there shall be paid monthly the current salaries and expenses of the offices from which the same is derived, including the salary of the docket and minute clerks of the Court of Appeal, as now constituted and until the election of the clerk of the said court, as above provided, together with such authorized expenses of said offices as are not required to be paid by the City of New Orleans; and the surplus of said eighty per cent, if any, shall be paid by the Treasurer to the said Board of Liquidation, and shall be used to redeem or pay said bonds and certificates as hereinbefore and hereinafter provided. But if said eighty per cent during the six months ending July 31st, or January 31st of any year, should prove inadequate to pay said salaries and expenses, the Comptroller shall prorate the deficit among those entitled to payment, and shall issue certificates therefor in sums not less than ten dollars, which shall bear interest at the rate of four per cent per annum from date, and said interest shall be paid annually, but the principal of said certificates shall be paid from the funds herein set apart and reserved only after all the bonds issued in payment of outstanding warrants shall have first been redeemed or paid.

All disbursements from said fund for stationery shall be made upon the requisition of the officers requiring same; said requisition to be approved by the Mayor of the City of New Orleans; and in all cases such disbursements and all salaries shall be paid by the Treasurer of the City of New Orleans upon warrants drawn against said fund by the Comptroller of said city, approved, so far as the Civil District Court is concerned by the presiding judge thereof, for the office of Recorder of Mortgages and the office of Register of Conveyances, by the Mayor of the City of New Orleans, and for the offices of the respective city courts by the judge or judges thereof and for the officers of the Court of Appeal by one of the judges thereof. Until the full and final payment of all said bonds and certificates hereinbefore provided for the salaries of the employees of the various offices hereinafter named shall remain as now fixed by law, and there shall be no increase in the number of employees now authorized by law for the offices of Recorder of Mortgages or Register of Conveyances, unless otherwise ordered by the Civil District Court sitting en banc; and the number of employees of the Civil District Court shall be as determined by a majority of the judges thereof. The Clerks of the first and second city courts, until the organization of the city courts hereinbefore provided for, may each appoint with the approval of the judges thereof, an additional deputy clerk at Fifty Dollars per month, but no other employees, nor larger salaries than those now fixed by law, shall be allowed to the city courts. The said Board of Liquidation hereinbefore named shall have the right to reject any and all bids made for the redemption of bonds issued as hereinabove provided, and should there be no bids, or none accepted, then said Board of Liquidation, on the second Tuesday in February and August of each year, with whatever amount has been paid to said board by the treasurer as herein provided, shall, after paying the interest, pay said bonds in numerical order. After the payment of all said bonds, the twenty per cent. reserve herein provided, and any surplus of the remaining eighty per cent, shall be used by the City Treasurer in paying the certificates herein provided for, if any, in the order of their issue. When said Judicial Expense Fund bonds and Comptroller certificates, if any of the latter shall be issued, shall have been retired and canceled, the salaries and expenses of the various officers affected by this article and the revenue of said officers shall be regulated and disposed of as may be determined by the General Assembly. This article shall take effect from the last day of the current month in which this constitution is adopted, and all amounts arising from the Judicial Expense Fund, which shall remain in the hands of the State Treasurer on that date, shall be paid by him to the Board of Liquidation of the City Debt, and be used by said board as part of the funds hereinabove referred to.

EXTENDING TIME OF EXEMPTION OF RAILROAD PROPERTY TO JANUARY 1ST, 1909.

(Seventh Amendment, Adopted November 8, 1904—Act No. 16 of 1904)

There shall be exempt from taxation for a period of ten years from the date of its completion, any railroad or part of railroad that shall have been constructed and completed subsequently to January 1, 1905, and prior to January 1, 1909. This exemption shall include and apply to all the rights of way, roadbed, sidings, rails and other superstructures upon such rights of way, roadbed or sidings; and to all depots, station-houses, buildings, erections and structures appurtenant to such railroads and the operation of the same; but shall not include the depots, warehouses, station-houses and other structures and appurtenances nor the land upon which they are erected at terminal points, and for which franchises have been granted and obtained; whether same remain the property of the present owner or owners, or be transferred or assigned to any corporation or corporations, person or persons, whomsoever, and provided further that this exemption shall not apply to double tracks, sidings, switches, depots, or other improvements or betterments which may be constructed by railroads now in operation within the State, other than extensions or new lines constructed by such railroads.

INCREASING PENSION APPROPRIATION FROM SEVENTY-FIVE THOUSAND DOLLARS ($75,000.00) TO ONE HUNDRED AND FIFTY THOUSAND DOLLARS ($150,000.00)

(Eighth Amendment, Adopted November 8, 1904—Act No. 112 of 1904)

ARTICLE 303. A pension not to exceed eight dollars ($8) per month shall be allowed to each Confederate soldier or sailor veteran who posesses all of the following qualifications:

1. He shall have served honorably from the date of his enlistment until the close of the late Civil War, or until he was discharged or paroled, in some military organization regularly mustered into the army or navy of the Confederate States, and shall have remained true to the Confederate States until the surrender.

2. He shall be in indigent circumstances, and unable to earn a livlihood by his own labor or skill.

3. He shall not be salaried or otherwise provided for by the State of Louisiana, or by any other State Government. In case he enlisted in any organization mustered into said service as a Louisiana organization, or in case at the date of his enlistment he resided in the State of Louisiana, he shall have resided in this State for at least five years prior to his application for a pension. In case he resided elsewhere than in this State, and enlisted in an organization not mustered in from Louisiana, or in the Navy of the Confederate States, he shall have resided in this State for at least fifteen years prior to his application for such pension. A like pension shall be granted to the widow who shall not have married again, in indigent circumstances, of such soldier or sailor whose marriage to her was contracted prior to January 1st, 1875; provided, that if her deceased husband served in an organization mustered in from Louisiana, or if he resided in Louisiana at the date of his enlistment, and has so resided for one year prior thereto, then in order that such widow shall be entitled to the pension as herein provided, she shall have resided in this State for at least five years prior to her application therefor; and if her deceased husband enlisted elsewhere than in Louisiana, and served in an organization not mustered in from Louisiana, such widow shall in order to entitle her to pension as herein provided, have resided in this State for not less than fifteen years prior to her application for such pensions; provided further, that pensions, whether to veterans or to widows, shall be allowed only from the date of application under this

article, and the total appropriations for all pensions shall not be less than seventy-five thousand ($75,000) dollars nor more than one hundred and fifty thousand ($150,000) dollars in any one year; provided, that nothing in this article shall be construed so as to prohibit the General Assembly from providing artificial limbs to disabled Confederate soldiers or sailors.

MAINTENANCE OF LOUISIANA STATE UNIVERSITY AND AGRICULTURAL AND MECHANICAL COLLEGE; REMOVING LIMIT OF APPROPRIATION

(Ninth Amendment, Adopted November 8, 1904—Act No. 12 of 1904)

ARTICLE 255. The Louisiana State University and Agricultural and Mechanical College, founded upon the land grants of the United States to endow a seminary of learning and a college for the benefit of agriculture and mechanic arts now established and located in the City of Baton Rouge, is hereby recognized; and all revenues derived and to be derived from the Seminary fund, the Agricultural and Mechanical College fund, and other funds or lands donated or to be donated by the United States to the State of Louisiana for the use of a seminary of learning or of a college for the benefit of agriculture or the mechanic arts, shall be appropriated exclusively to the maintenance and support of said Louisiana State University and Agricultural and Mechanical College; and the General Assembly shall make such additional appropriations as may be necessary for its maintenance and support and improvement, and for the establishment, in connection with said institution, of such additional scientific or literary departments as the public necessities and the well-being of the people of Louisiana may require.

The Tulane University of Louisiana, located in New Orleans, is hereby recognized as created and to be developed in accordance with the provisions of legislative act, No. 43, approved July 5, 1884, and, by approval of the electors, made part of the Constitution of the State.

PROVIDING FOR ELECTION OF JUDGES OF SUPREME COURT; FIXING THEIR SALARIES, AND THE TIME OF HOLDING SESSIONS

(Tenth Amendment, Adopted November 8, 1904—Act No. 137 of 1904)

ARTICLE 86. The Supreme Court shall be composed of one Chief Justice and four Associate Justices, a majority of whom shall constitute a quorum. The Chief Justice and Associate Justices shall each receive a salary of not less than Five Thousand Dollars per annum, payable monthly on his own warrant. They shall each be elected for a term of twelve years. In case of death, resignation, or removal from office of any Justice, the vacancy shall be filled by the selection by the Court of a Judge of one of the Courts of Appeal from a Supreme Court District other than that in which such vacancy shall occur, until the next ensuing Congressional election, when it shall be filled by election for a full term of twelve years. They shall be citizens of the United States and of this State, over thirty-five years of age, learned in the law, and shall have practiced law in this State for ten years preceding their election, or appointment.

ARTICLE 87. The State shall be divided into four Supreme Court Districts, and the Supreme Court shall always be composed of Justices elected from said districts. The parishes of Orleans, St. John the Baptist, St. Charles, St. Bernard, Plaquemines and Jefferson shall compose the First District, from which two Justices shall be elected. The Parishes of Caddo, Bossier, Webster, Bienville, Claiborne, Union, Lincoln, Jackson, Caldwell, Ouachita, Morehouse, Richland, Franklin, West Carroll, East Carroll, Madison, Tensas, Concordia and Catahoula shall compose the Second District, from which one Justice shall be elected. The Parishes of DeSoto, Red River, Winn, Grant, Natchitoches, Sabine, Vernon, Calcasieu, Cameron, Rapides, Avoyelles, Pointe Coupee, West Baton Rouge, Iberville, St. Landry, Acadia, Lafayette and Vermilion shall compose the Third District, from which one Justice shall be elected. The Parishes of St. Martin, Iberia, St. Mary, Terrebonne, Lafourche, Assumption, Ascension, St. James, East Baton Rouge, East Feliciana, West Feliciana, St. Helena, Livingston, Tangipahoa, St. Tammany and Washington shall compose the Fourth District, from which one Justice shall be elected. The Justices of the Supreme Court, as now constituted, shall serve until the expiration of their respective terms, and their successors shall be elected each for a term of twelve years at the Congressional election next preceding such expiration of term.

When the office of Chief Justice becomes vacant, either by death, resignation, removal from office, or otherwise, the Associate Justice who has served the longest time shall, by virtue of said length of service, become Chief Justice.

ARTICLE 88. The Supreme Court shall hold an annual session in the City of New Orleans, beginning not later than the first Monday in the month of November and ending not sooner than June 30th, in each year. It shall appoint its own clerks and remove them at pleasure. The General Assembly shall make the necessary appropriations to provide suitable and commodious buildings for said Court, and the records thereof, and for the care and maintenance of the State Library.

ARTICLE 95. In all cases where there is an appeal from a judgment rendered on a reconventional, or other incidental demand, the appeal shall lie to the Court having jurisdiction of the main demand.

PROVIDING FOR ELECTION OF OFFICES OF CORONER AND SHERIFF, AND FOR THE FILLING OF VACANCIES BY ELECTION

(Eleventh Amendment, Adopted November 8, 1904—Act No. 138 of 1904)

ARTICLE 119. There shall be a Sheriff and a Coroner elected by the qualified voters of each Parish in the State, except in the Parish of Orleans, who shall be elected at the general election and hold office for four years. The Coroner, except in the Prrish of Orleans, shall act for and in place of the Sheriff, whenever the Sheriff shall be a party interested, and whenever there shall be a vacancy in the office of Sheriff, until such vacancy shall be filled; but he shall not, during such vacancy, discharge the duties of tax collector. The Sheriff, except in the Parish of Orleans, shall be ex-officio Collector of State and Parish taxes.

He shall give separate bonds for the faithful performance of his duty in each capacity. Until otherwise provided the bonds shall be given according to existing laws.

Sheriffs elected or appointed shall furnish bonds within thirty days from the date of their commissions, in default of which the office shall be declared vacant, and the Governor shall appoint for the remainder of the term.

All vacancies occurring in the office of Sheriff and ex-officio collector of State and parish taxes, by death, resignation or otherwise, where the unexpired portion of the term is one year or more, shall be filled by special election, to be called by the Governor and held within sixty days of the occurrence of such vacancy under the general election laws of this State. In all cases where the vacancy is less than one year, the Governor shall appoint for the remainder of the term.

PROVIDING FOR ELECTIONS TO FILL VACANCIES IN THE OFFICE OF CLERK OF COURT

(Twelfth Amendment, Adopted November 8, 1904—Act No. 139 of 1904)

ARTICLE 124. Clerks of District Courts may appoint, with the approval of the District Judges, deputies with such powers as shall be prescribed by law; and the General Assembly shall have the power to provide for continuing one or more of them in office in the event of any vacancy in the office of Clerk, until his successor shall have been elected and qualified.

All elections to fill vacancies occasioned by death, resignation or removal shall be for the unexpired term, and the Governor shall fill the vacancy until an election can be held. Provided, that the election to fill said vacancy shall be held within sixty days from the date that the vacancy occurs, provided if such unexpired term is for a shorter period than one year, the appointee of the Governor shall hold the office for said term.

PROVIDING FOR ELECTIONS TO FILL VACANCIES IN THE OFFICE OF DISTRICT ATTORNEY

(Thirteenth Amendment, Adopted November 8, 1904—Act No. 140 of 1904)

ARTICLE 125. There shall be a District Attorney for each Judicial District in the State, who shall be elected by the qualified electors of the Judicial District at the same time and for the same term as is provided in Article 109 for District Judges. He shall receive a salary of one thousand dollars per annum, payable monthly on his own warrant. He shall be an actual resident of the district and a licensed attorney in this State. He shall also receive fees; but no fee shall be allowed in criminal cases, except on conviction, which fees shall not exceed five dollars in cases of misdemeanor. All elections to fill vacancies occasioned by death, resignation or removal shall be for the unexpired term, and the Governor shall fill the vacancy until an election can be held. Provided, that the election to fill said vacancy shall be held within sixty days from the date the vacancy occurs. Provided, if such unexpired term is for a shorter period than one year, the appointee of the Governor shall hold office for said term.

PROVIDING FOR THE ELECTION OF DISTRICT JUDGES, AND THE FILLING OF VACANCIES BY ELECTION

(Fourteenth Amendment, Adopted November 8, 1904—Act No. 141 of 1904)

ARTICLE 109. The District Courts, except in the Parish of Orleans, shall have original jurisdiction in all civil matters where the amount in dispute shall exceed fifty dollars, exclusive of interest, and in all cases where title to real estate is involved, or to office, or other public position, or civil or political rights, and all other cases where no specific amount is in contest, except as otherwise provided in this Constitution. They shall have unlimited and exclusive original jurisdiction in all criminal cases, except such as may be vested in other courts authorized by this Constitution; and in all probate and succession matters, and where a succession is a party defendant; and in all cases where the State, parish, any municipality or other political corporation, is a party defendant, regardless of the amount in dispute; and of all proceedings for the appointment of receivers or liquidators to corporations or partnerships; and said courts shall have authority to issue all such writs, process and orders as may be necessary or proper for the purposes of the jurisdiction herein conferred upon them. There shall be one District Judge in each Judicial District, except in the Twenty-first Judicial District, where, until otherwise provided by law, there shall be two District Judges who shall not be residents of the same parish. District Judges shall be elected by a plurality of the qualified voters of their respective districts, in which they shall have been actual residents for two years next preceding their election; provided, one year's residence only in the district shall be required for the first election under this Constitution. They shall be learned in the law, and shall have practiced law in the State five years previous to their election.

The first District Judges under this Constitution shall be elected at the general State election in 1900, and shall hold office until their successors are elected at the election on the Tuesday after the first Monday in November, 1904, at which time, and every four years thereafter, District Judges shall be elected for terms of four years. Vacancies occasioned by death, resignation or otherwise, where the unexpired portion of the term is less than one year, shall be filled for the remainder of the term by appointment by the Governor, with the advice and consent of the Senate. In all cases where the unexpired portion of the term is one year or more, the vacancy shall be filled by special election, to be called by the Governor, and held within sixty days of the occurrence of the vacancy, under the general election laws of the State.

AUTHORIZING THE ISSUANCE OF BONDS BY MUNICIPAL CORPORATIONS, PARISHES, DRAINAGE AND SEWERAGE DISTRICTS, AND LEVYING A SPECIAL TAX TO PAY FOR SAME

(Fifteenth Amendment, Adopted November 8, 1904—Act No. 186 of 1904)

ARTICLE 281. Municipal corporations, parishes, and drainage and sewerage districts, the City of New Orleans excepted, when authorized to do so by a vote of the majority in number and amount of the property tax payers, qualified as electors under the Constitution and laws of this State, voting at an election held for that purpose, after due notice of said election has been published for thirty days in the official journal of the municipality or parish, and where there is no official journal, in a newspaper published therein, may incur debts and issue negotiable bonds therefor to the extent of one-tenth of the assessed valuation of the property within the municipal corporation, parish drainage district or sewerage district, as shown by the last assessment made prior to the submission of the proposition to the property tax payers as above provided, and may be authorized by the property tax payers voting at said election, to levy and assess special taxes upon the property subject to taxation in the parish, drainage district, corporation or sewerage districts; provided said taxes so imposed do not exceed five mills on the dollar of the assessed valuation in any one year, nor run for a greater number of years than the number named in the proposition submitted to the tax-payers. No bonds shall be issued for any other purpose than stated in the submission of the proposition to the tax payers and published for thirty days, as aforesaid, nor for a greater amount than herein mentioned; nor shall such bonds be issued for any other purpose than for paving and improving streets, roads and alleys, purchasing and constructing a system of waterworks, sewerage, lights, public parks and buildings, bridges, and other works of public improvement, the title to which shall vest in the municipal corporation, parish, drainage or sewerage district, as the case may be; nor shall such bonds run for a longer period than forty years from their date, or bear a greater rate of interest than five per cent. per annum, or be sold by the municipal corporation, parish, drainage or sewerage district issuing same for less than par.

The municipal corporation, parish, drainage or sewerage district issuing such bonds, shall provide for the payment of the interest annually or semi-annually, and the principal thereof at maturity; provided that the total issue of bonds by any municipality, parish, drainage or sewerage district for all purposes shall never exceed ten per cent. of the assessed value of the property in such municipality, parish, drainage or sewerage district; provided, that drainage districts availing themselves of the provisions of this ordinance shall be limited to the rate of taxation herein fixed; and such districts shall be prohibited from levying contributions under the provisions of existing laws; and provided further, that nothing herein contained shall prevent drainage districts from being established under the provisions of existing laws; and, provided further, that municipal councils shall have authority to create within their respective limits one or more sewerage districts.

RATIFYING ACT OF THE LEGISLATURE OF 1906, AUTHORIZING THE CITY OF NEW ORLEANS TO ISSUE $8,000,000.00 OF BONDS KNOWN AS "NEW PUBLIC IMPROVEMENT BONDS"

(Sixteenth Amendment, Adopted November 6, 1906—Act No. 19 of 1906)

"The City of New Orleans shall have power to issue eight million dollars of bonds, known as 'New Public Improvement Bonds,' for the purposes and under the provisions and conditions set forth in the Special Act of the Legislature adopted to that end and for that purpose, at the regular session of 1906, which said Act is hereby ratified and approved; and all provisions of the present Constitution of the State in conflict with the provisions of said Act, and with this amendment, are to that extent, and for that purpose only, repealed."

RATIFYING ACT OF LEGISLATURE AUTHORIZING THE CITY OF NEW ORLEANS TO ISSUE $200,000.00 BONDS KNOWN AS "SCHOOL TEACHER SALARY BONDS"

(Seventeenth Amendment, Adopted November 6, 1906—Act No. 2 of 1906)

"The City of New Orleans shall have power and it shall be its duty to issue two hundred thousand dollars of bonds, known as 'School teachers' salary bonds,' for the purposes and under the provisions and conditions set forth in the special act of the Legislature adopted to that end and for that purpose, at the regular session of 1906, which said act is hereby ratified and approved; and all provisions of the present Constitution of the State in conflict with the provisions of said act, and with this amendment, are, to that extent, and for that purpose only, repealed.

INCREASING SALARY OF ATTORNEY GENERAL TO FIVE THOUSAND DOLLARS ($5,000.00)

(Eighteenth Amendment, Adopted November 6, 1906—Act No. 30 of 1906)

ARTICLE 97. There shall be an Attorney General for the State, who shall be elected by the qualified electors of the State at large every four years. He shall be learned in the law, and shall have actually resided and practiced law, as a licensed attorney, in the State, for five years preceding his election. He shall receive a salary of five thousand dollars per annum, payable monthly on his own warrant.

PROVIDING FOR ELECTION OF MEMBERS OF BOARD OF ASSESSORS FOR THE PARISH OF ORLEANS

(Nineteenth Amendment, Adopted November 6, 1906—Act No. 8 of 1906)

ARTICLE 309. There shall be seven assessors in the City of New Orleans, who together shall compose the Board of Assessors for the Parish of Orleans. One shall be elected from each municipal district of the City of New Orleans and they shall be residents of said district from which they are elected.
There shall be seven State tax collectors for the City of New Orleans. One shall be elected from each municipal district of the City of New Orleans. They shall be residents of the said districts from which they are elected, and they shall maintain offices in the respective districts from which they have been elected. The said assessors and State tax collectors shall be elected for a term of four years, and the first election shall take place at the general State election to be held in April, 1908.

RELATIVE TO CRIMINAL COURTS, CITY OF NEW ORLEANS

(Twentieth Amendment, Adopted November 6, 1906—Act No. 44 of 1906)

ARTICLE 140. There shall be in the City of New Orleans two inferior criminal courts, to be known respectively as the First City Criminal Court, of the City of New Orleans, and the Second City Criminal Court, of the City of New Orleans, each of which shall be presided over by one judge, and which shall have jurisdiction within the territory hereinafter prescribed, for the trial without jury and the punishment of all offenses against the State where the penalty does not exceed six months' imprisonment in the parish jail or a fine of $300, or both; in all other cases the judges of said courts shall have jurisdiction as committing magistrates, without authority to commit, bail or discharge.

The territorial jurisdiction of the First City Criminal Court shall extend over the First, Fourth, Sixth and Seventh municipal districts of New Orleans; and the Second City Criminal Court over the Second, Third and Fifth municipal districts of said city. In case of vacancy in the office, recusation, disability or absence with or without leave, of either of said judges, it shall be the duty of the other judge to issue warrants of arrest for the apprehension of parties accused within the jurisdiction of the judge he replaces, and to make any order of commitment or admitting to bail that may be necessary and proper and might, in due course, have been made by the judge within whose jurisdiction the offense was committed. And in case of such vacancy, recusation, absence or disability of one of said judges, on motion of the prosecuting officer, or of the accused or his counsel, the other judge, acting within his discretion, may proceed to try and discharge or convict and sentence parties accused of offenses charged to have been committed within the jurisdiction of the court wherein the vacancy exists, or whereof the judge is recused, absent or disabled. In like manner, acting also within his discretion, upon formal application made, he may, as committing magistrate, examine and discharge, bail or commit parties accused of offenses charged to have been committed within the territorial jurisdiction of the City Criminal Court. In all such cases it shall be lawful for the judge assuming jurisdiction under the provision of this paragraph to issue warrants of arrest, make preliminary orders and have the accused brought before him, although sitting in his own court; or he may, in his discretion, occupy the bench of the judge he replaces. Said judge shall be elected by the voters of the City of New Orleans, at large, for the term of four years; the first election therefor shall be held at the congressional election in November, 1898, and the judges then elected shall serve until May 11, 1900, and their successors shall be elected at the parochial and municipal election in the year 1899. They shall be learned in the law, and shall have resided and practiced as attorneys in the City of New Orleans for not less than three years before their election or appointment. The judges of said courts shall each receive a yearly compensation of $3,000, payable monthly on his own warrant. Each judge shall appoint a clerk and such deputies as may be authorized by law, at salaries not exceeding $1,200 per annum, except one deputy, who shall be a stenographer, and who may receive a salary not exceeding $1,500 per annum, to be paid in monthly installments by the City of New Orleans.

AUTHORIZING THE ISSUANCE OF BONDS BY MUNICIPAL CORPORATIONS, PARISHES, SCHOOL DISTRICTS AND DRAINAGE AND SEWERAGE DISTRICTS, AND THE LEVYING OF A SPECIAL TAX TO PAY FOR SAME.___ (THE ADDITION OF THE WORDS " SCHOOL DISTRICTS " BEING THE AMENDMENT)

(Twenty-First Amendment, Adopted November 6, 1906—Act. No. 122, 1906)

ARTICLE 281. Municipal corporations, parishes, school districts and drainage and sewerage districts, the City of New Orleans excepted, when authorized to do so, by a vote of a majority in number and amount of the property tax payers, qualified as electors under the Constitution and laws of this State, voting at an election held for that purpose, after due notice of said election has been published for thirty days in the official journal of the municipality or parish, and where there is no official journal, in a newspaper published therein, may incur debt, and issue negotiable bonds therefore to the extent of one-tenth of the assessed valuation of the property within said municipal corporation, parish, school, drainage or sewerage districts, as shown by the last assessment made prior to the submission of the proposition to the property tax payers as above provided, and may be authorized by the property tax payers, voting at said election, to levy and assess special taxes upon property subject to taxation in the parish, drainage districts, corporation, school or sewerage districts; provided, that said taxes so imposed do not exceed five mills on the dollar of the assessed valuation in any one year, nor run for a greater number of years than the number named in the proposition submitted to the tax payers. No bonds shall be issued for any other purpose than stated in the submission of the proposition to the tax payers and published for thirty days, as aforesaid, nor for a greater amount than therein mentioned; nor shall such bonds be issued for any other purpose than for paving and improving the streets, roads and alleys, purchasing or constructing systems of waterworks, sewerage, drainage, lights, public parks and buildings, bridges and other work of public improvement, the title to which shall vest in the municipal corporation, parish, school, drainage or sewerage districts, as the case may be, nor shall such bonds run for a longer period than forty years from their date, or bear a greater rate of interest than five per cent. per annum, or be sold by the municipal corporation, parish, school district, drainage or sewerage district issuing same for less than par.

The municipal corporation, parish, school district, drainage or sewerage district issuing such bonds shall provide for the payment of the interest annually or semi-annually, and the principal thereof at maturity, provided that the total issue of bonds by any municipality, parish, school, or sewerage district for all purposes shall never exceed ten per cent. of the assessed value of the property in such municipality, parish, school or sewerage districts; provided that municipal councils shall have authority to create within their respective limits one or more sewerage districts; provided that nothing herein contained shall prevent drainage districts from being established under the provisions of existing laws, and that all drainage districts established under the laws of this State shall, in addition to the powers hereinabove granted, have the further power and authority to levy and assess annual contributions or acreage taxes, for the purpose of providing and maintaining drainage systems, on all lands situated in such districts not exceeding twenty-five (25c.) cents per acre for a period not to exceed forty (40) years when authorized to do so by a vote of a majority in number and amount of the property tax payers of said districts qualified as electors under the laws of this State, voting at an election held for that purpose as provided in the first part of this article, and said drainage districts, through the boards of commissioners thereof, may incur indebtedness and issue negotiable bonds therefor payable in principal and interest out of, and not to exceed in principal and interest, the aggregate amount to be raised by said annual contributions during the period for which the same are levied. No such drainage bonds shall be issued for any other purpose than that for which said contributions were voted and shall not run for a longer period than forty years from their date, nor bear a greater rate of interest than five per cent. per annum, nor be sold for less than par.

All contributions and acreage taxes heretofore authorized by a vote of a majority in number and amount of the property tax payers qualified to vote under the laws of this State at elections held in drainage districts organized under existing laws are hereby ratified and confirmed, and their validity shall not be questioned.

PROVIDING FOR ADDITIONAL JUDGE IN FIRST JUDICIAL DISTRICT, PARISH OF CADDO

(Twenty-Second Amendment, Adopted November 6, 1906—Act No. 12 of 1906)

ARTICLE 109. The district courts, except in the Parish of Orleans, shall have original jurisdiction in all civil matters where the amount in dispute shall exceed fifty ($50) dollars exclusive of interest, and in all cases where the title to real estate is involved, or to office or other public positions, or civil or political rights, and all other cases where no specific amount is in contest, except as otherwise provided in this Constitution.

They shall have unlimited and exclusive original jurisdiction in all criminal cases except as may be vested in other courts authorized by this Constitution; and in all probate and succession matters, and where a succession is a party defendant; and in all cases where the State, parish, any municipality or other political corporation is a party defendant, regardless of the amount in dispute; and for all proceedings for the appointment of receivers or liquidators to corporation or partnership; and said court shall have authority to issue all such writs, process and orders as may be necessary or proper, for the purpose of the jurisdiction herein conferred upon them.

There shall be one (1) district judge in each judicial district, except in the First and Twenty-first judicial districts, where, until otherwise provided by law, there shall be two (2) district judges, but the judges of the Twenty-first judicial district shall not be residents of the same parish.

District judges shall be elected by a plurality of the qualified voters of their respective districts in which they shall have been actual residents for two (2) years next preceding their election. They shall be learned in the law and shall have practiced law in the State five (5) years previous to their election.

The first district judges under this Constitution shall be elected at the general State election in 1900 and shall hold office until their successors are elected at the election on the first Tuesday after the first Monday in November, 1904, at which time, and every four years thereafter, district judges shall be elected for terms of four years. Vacancies occasioned by death, resignation or otherwise, where the unexpired portion of the term is less than one year, shall be filled for the remainder of the term by appointment by the Governor, with the advice and consent of the Senate.

In all cases where the unexpired portion of the term is one year or more, the vacancy shall be filled by special election, to be called by the Governor and held within sixty (60) days of the occurrence of the vacancy, under the general election laws of the State.

AMENDING ARTICLES 98, 99, 100, 106 AND 131, AND REPEALING ARTICLE 105 OF THE CONSTITUTION, RELATIVE TO THE JUDICIARY DEPARTMENTS, AND PROVIDING FOR THE CREATION OF COURTS OF APPEAL FOR THE COUNTRY PARISHES

(Twenty-Third Amendment, Adopted November 6, 1906—Act No. 137 of 1906)

ARTICLE 98. The Courts of Appeal, except as otherwise provided in this Constitution, shall have appellate jurisdiction only, which jurisdiction shall extend to all cases, civil and probate, when the matter in dispute or the fund to be distributed shall exceed one hundred dollars, exclusive of interest, and shall not exceed two thousand dollars, exclusive of interest, and such appeal shall be upon the law and the facts.

ARTICLE 99. The Courts of Appeal shall consist of three judges each. They shall be citizens of the United States and qualified electors of this State, learned in the law and shall have practiced law in this State for six years, and shall have been actual residents of the district from which they are elected or appointed for at least two years preceding their election or appointment. They shall receive a salary of four thousand dollars each per year, and the judges of the Court of Appeal for the Parish of Orleans shall receive a salary of five thousand dollars each per year, payable monthly on his own warrant, and the Legislature shall make adequate appropriation to pay the same.

SECTION 3. Be it further resolved, etc., That Article 100 of the Constitution of the State of Louisiana be so amended as to read as follows:

ARTICLE 100. Exclusive of the parishes whose appeals are returnable to the Parish of Orleans, the State shall be divided into two circuits, to be subdivided into districts as hereinafter provided. Until otherwise provided by law, the Parishes of East Baton Rouge, West Baton Rouge, Livingston, Tangipahoa, Washington, St. Helena, Pointe Coupee, Iberville, St. Mary, Terrebonne, Assumption, Lafourche, Ascension, Calcasieu, Cameron, Vermilion, Lafayette, Iberia, St. Martin, St. Tammany, Acadia, East Feliciana, West Feliciana, St. Landry and Vernon shall compose the first circuit and be known as the "Court of Appeal, First Circuit, State of Louisiana," and the Parishes of Caddo, Bossier, Webster, Bienville, Claiborne, Union, Lincoln, Jackson, Caldwell, Winn, Natchitoches, Sabine, DeSoto, Red River, Ouachita, Richland, Franklin, Catahoula, Concordia, Tensas, Madison, East Carroll, West Carroll, Morehouse, Avoyelles, Rapides and Grant, shall compose the second circuit, and be known as the "Court of Appeal, Second Circuit, State of Louisiana."

The circuits above provided for, until otherwise provided by law, shall be divided in three districts each, as follows: The parishes of Calcasieu, Cameron, Vermilion, Lafayette, St. Martin, Acadia, St. Landry, Vernon and Iberia, shall compose the first district of the first circuit, and the Parishes of West Baton Rouge, Ascension, Pointe Coupee, Iberville, St. Mary, Terrebonne, Assumption and Lafourche, shall compose the second district of the first circuit; and the Parishes of East Baton Rouge, Livingston, Tangipahoa, St. Helena, St. Tammany, East Feliciana, West Feliciana and Washington shall compose the third district of the first circuit; and the Parishes of Richland, Concordia, East Carroll, West Carroll, Franklin, Tensas, Ouachita, Madison, Morehouse and Caldwell shall compose the first district of the second circuit; and the Parishes of Bienville, Claiborne, Jackson, Lincoln, Catahoula, Union, Bossier, Winn, Webster and Grant shall compose the second district of the second circuit; and the Parishes of Caddo, DeSoto, Natchitoches, Rapides, Sabine, Avoyelles and Red River, shall compose the third district of the second circuit. For each of the circuits there shall be elected three judges, as herein provided for, one judge to be elected by the qualified electors of each district as above designated.

The first Courts of Appeal to be organized in the circuits herein established under this amendment to the Constitution shall be as follows: There shall be elected on January 16, 1907, by the qualified electors thereof, one judge for each of the districts in the two circuits. The judges for each of the first districts above named shall be elected for a term of four years beginning on the first day of March, 1907; and the judges for each of the second districts above named shall be elected for a term of six years, beginning on said date; and the judges for each of the third districts above named shall be elected for a period of eight years, beginning on said date. Upon expiration of the term of office of each of the judges thus elected, his successor shall be elected for a term of eight years, by qualified electors of such district of each circuit; the election of each judge herein provided for shall take place at the same time and place as the congressional election next preceding the expiration of his term. In case of death, removal or resignation from office of any judge, the vacancy shall be filled by appointment of the Governor by and with the advice and consent of the Senate, until the next congressional election, at which time his successor shall be elected. In case any one of the circuit judges shall be, from sickness or any other cause, unable to attend any session of court, it shall be competent for the other two judges to appoint, in his place, a qualified member of the bar, who shall be sworn to sit as judge of said court during such absence only, who shall receive such compensation as the General Assembly may fix, or the Courts of Appeal may arrange for an interchange of judges from one circuit to the other when a member of the court is unable to attend from sickness or other cause. Until otherwise provided by the General Assembly, the Court of Appeal of the first circuit shall hold session of court at Baton Rouge, Amite City, New Iberia, Houma, Franklin, Opelousas, Crowley, Lake Charles, Thibodeaux and Donaldsonville, and such other places as may be designated by said Court of Appeal, and the Court of Appeal for the second circuit shall hold sessions of court at Monroe, Shreveport, Alexandria, Natchitoches, Vidalia, Tallulah, and Ruston, and such other places as may be designated by said Court of Appeal. The sessions of said Courts of Appeal shall continue in each circuit for a period of ten months, beginning on the first Monday of September of each year, and ending on the last day of June in the following year; and said courts shall convene at the several places named as the public business may require, and shall keep their courts in session at such places until the cases before them are heard and finally determined. Until otherwise provided by law, the time and place for the return of appeals shall be fixed by said court.

No decisions shall be rendered by these courts without the concurrence of two judges, but any two of the judges of each circuit shall constitute a quorum for the transaction of business.

ARTICLE 105. SECTION 4. *Be it further resolved, etc., That Article 105 of the Constitution of the State of Louisiana shall be and is hereby abrogated.*

ARTICLE 106. The sheriff of the parish in which the session of the court is held, shall attend in person, or by deputy, to execute the orders of said court, and the clerk of the district court of the parish in which the sessions of the Courts of Appeal are held shall serve as clerk of the Court of Appeal, and shall attend sessions of said court, either in person or by deputy, until otherwise provided by the General Assembly. The costs of appeal in any case appealed to the Courts of Appeal, of the first and second circuits, shall not exceed five dollars. The police juries of the various parishes of the State in which the Courts of Appeal are held, shall provide suitable rooms for the holding of said courts, so as not to interfere with the session of the district or other courts.

ARTICLE 131. (fourth paragraph.) SECTION 6. Be it further resolved, etc., That the fourth paragraph of Article 131 of the Constitution of the State of Louisiana be amended as to read as follows:

Until otherwise provided by law, all appeals within its jurisdiction from the Parishes of Orleans, St. James, St. John the Baptist, St. Charles, Jefferson, Plaquemines and St. Bernard shall be returnable to said court, and the costs of filing same shall not exceed five dollars in each case.

FIXING THE LIMITS OF THE RESPECTIVE JUDICIAL DISTRICTS IN THE STATE, AND THE SALARIES OF THE JUDGES UNIFORMLY AT THREE THOUSAND DOLLARS ($3,000.00)

(Twenty-Fourth Amendment, Adopted November 6, 1906—Act No. 216 of 1906)

ARTICLE 108. The parish of Caddo shall compose the first district.

The parishes of Bossier and Webster shall compose the second district.

The parishes of Claiborne and Bienville shall compose the third district.

The parishes of Union and Lincoln shall compose the fourth district.

The parishes of Caldwell, Jackson and Winn shall compose the fifth district.

The parishes of Ouachita and Morehouse shall compose the sixth district.

The parishes of West Carroll and Richland shall compose the seventh district.

The parishes of Franklin and Catahoula shall compose the eighth district.

The parishes of Madison and East Carroll shall compose the ninth district.

The parishes of Concordia and Tensas shall compose the tenth district.

The parishes of Natchitoches and Red River shall compose the eleventh district.

The parishes of DeSoto, Sabine and Vernon shall compose the twelfth district.

The parishes of Rapides and Grant shall compose the thirteenth district.

The parish of Avoyelles shall compose the fourteenth district.

The parishes of Calcasieu and Cameron shall compose the fifteenth district.

The parish of St. Landry shall compose the sixteenth district.

The parish of Vermilion shall compose the seventeenth district.

The parishes of Acadia and Lafayette shall compose the eighteenth district.

The parishes of Iberia and St. Martin shall compose the nineteenth district.

The parishes of Terrebonne and Lafourche shall compose the twentieth district.

The parishes of Iberville, West Baton Rouge and Pointe Coupee shall compose the twenty-first district.

The parish of East Baton Rouge shall compose the twenty-second district.

The parish of St. Mary shall compose the twenty-third district.

The parishes of East Feliciana and West Feliciana shall compose the twenty-fourth district.

The parishes of St. Helena, Livingston, and Tangipahoa shall compose the twenty-fifth district.

The parishes of Washington and St. Tammany shall compose the twenty-sixth district.

The parishes of Ascension, St. James and Assumption shall compose the twenty-seventh district.

The parishes of St. John the Baptist, St. Charles and Jefferson shall compose the twenty-eighth district.

The parishes of St. Bernard and Plaquemines shall compose the twenty-ninth district.

The judges provided for in this article shall each receive a salary of three thousand dollars per annum, such salary to be paid monthly, on their own warrants; provided that the General Assembly of the State of Louisiana may in their discretion redistrict the judicial districts provided for in this article.

Provided that in no case shall the salary of any district judge exceed three thousand dollars per annum.

MAINTENANCE OF LOUISIANA INDUSTRIAL INSTITUTE; REMOVING LIMIT OF APPROPRIATIONS

(Twenty-Fifth Amendment, Adopted November 6, 1906—Act No. 30 of 1906)

ARTICLE 256. The Louisiana State Normal School, established and located at Natchitoches; the Industrial Institute and College of Louisiana, whose name is hereby changed to the Louisiana Industrial Institute, established and located at Ruston, and the Southern University, now established in the City of New Orleans, for the education of persons of color, are hereby recognized; and the General Assembly is directed to make such appropriations from time to time as may be necessary for the maintenance, support and improvement of these institutions; provided that the appropriation for the maintenance and support of the Southern University shall not exceed ten thousand dollars per annum.

PROVIDING FOR THE APPOINTMENT OR ELECTION OF MALE AND FEMALE FACTORY INSPECTORS

(Twenty-Sixth Amendment, Adopted November 6, 1906—Act No. 13 of 1906)

ARTICLE 210. of the Constitution of the State of Louisiana, bearing upon the subject-matter, be and the same is hereby amended, so as to allow the appointment or election to office of factory inspectors, of either male or female persons, as provided for by an Act entitled "An Act to regulate the employment of children, young persons and women in certain cases, and to provide penalties for violations of the provisions of this Act," adopted by the General Assembly at its session of the year 1906.

MAINE[a]

For organic acts relating to the land now included in Maine printed in other parts of this work see:
  First Charter of Virginia, 1606 (Virginia, p. 3783).
  Charter to Council of New England, 1620 (Massachusetts, p. 1827).
  Charter of Massachusetts Bay, 1629 (Massachusetts, p. 1846).
  Commission of Andros, 1688 (Massachusetts, p. 1863).
  Charter of Massachusetts, 1691 (Massachusetts, p. 1870).
  Explanatory Charter of Massachusetts, 1725 (Massachusetts, p. 1886).
  Constitution of Massachusetts, 1780 (Massachusetts, p. 1888).

THE CHARTER OF ACADIA—1603 [b][c]

HENRY, par la grace de Dieu, Roi de France & de Navarre: A nos amés & féaux Conseillers les Officiers de notre Admirauté de Normandie, Bretagne, Picardie & Guienne, & à chacun d'eux en droit soi, & en l'étenue de leurs ressorts & jurisdictions; SALUT. Nous avons pour beaucoup d'importantes occasions, ordonné, commis & établi le sieur de Monts, Gentilhomme ordinaire de notre Chambre, notre Lieutenant général pour peupler & habiter les terres, côtes & pays de l'Acadie, & *autres circonvoisins*, en l'étendue du quarantième degré jusqu'au quarante-sixième, & là établir notre autorité, & autrement s'y loger & assurer; en sorte que nos sujets desormais y puissent être reçûs, y hanter, résider & trafiquer avec les Sauvages habitans desdits lieux, comme plus expressément nous l'avons déclaré par nos lettres patentes, expédiées & délivrées pour cet effet audit sieur de Monts le huitième jour de novembre dernier, suivant les conditions & articles, moyennant lesquelles il s'est chargé de la conduite & exécution de cette entreprise. Pour faciliter laquelle, & à ceux qui s'y

---

[a] See Articles of Separation, (District of Maine from Massachusetts) June 19, 1819; and Report of the Council, on the vote on Separation, August 24, 1819, in the Journal of the Constitutional Convention of the District of Maine, 1819–20, Augusta: 1856, pp. 3–16; also Governor Brooks' Proclamation, August 24, 1819, Id. pp. 17, 18.

[b] This charter, which was granted by Henry IV of France to Pierre du Gast, sieur de Monts, a Protestant member of his suite, embraced the whole of North America between the fortieth and forty-sixth degrees of latitude. An expedition fitted out under it visited Passamaquoddy Bay in 1604, and another explored the coast of Maine in 1605, entering the Penobscot, Kennebec, and Saco Rivers. But in 1606 it was decided to make a permanent settlement at Port Royal and no further attempt was made to plant colonies under this charter within the limits of the present State of Maine. The French in Canada, however, maintained friendly relations with the Penobscot Indians, and had several missionary and trading stations among them until Great Britain took possession of the country under the treaty of Paris of 1673.

[c] The History of the State of Maine, W. D. Williamson, Hallowell: 1832. I. 651.

sont joints avec lui, & leur donner quelque moyen & commodité d'en
supporter la dépense; Nous avons eu agréable de leur promettre &
assurer qu'il ne seroit permis à aucuns autres nos sujets, qu'à ceux
qui entreroient en association avec lui pour faire ladite dépense,
de trafiquer de pelleterie & autres marchandises durant dix années,
ès terres, pays, ports, rivières & avenues de l'étendue de sa charge;
ce que nous voulons avoir lieu. Nous, pour ces causes & autres con-
sidérations à ce nous mouvans, vous mandons & ordonnons que vous
ayez, chacun de vous en l'étendue de vos pouvoirs, jurisdictions &
détroits, à faire de notre part, comme de notre pleine puissance &
autorité Royale, nous faisons très-expresses inhibitions & défenses à
tous marchands, maîtres & Capitaines de navires, matelots & autres
nos sujets de quelque état, qualité & condition qu'ils soient, autres
néanmoins & fors à ceux qui sont entrés en association avec ledit
sieur de Monts pour ladite entreprise, selon les articles & conventions
d'icelles, par nous arrêtés, ainsi que dit est; d'équiper aucuns vaisseaux, & en iceux aller ou envoyer faire trafic & troque de pelleterie,
& autres choses avec les Sauvages, fréquenter, négocier & commu-
niquer durant ledit temps de dix ans, depuis le cap de Raze, jusqu'au
quarantième degré, comprenant *toute la côte de l'Acadie, terre & Cap-
Breton, baie de Saint-Cler, de Chaleur, isles percées, Gaspay, Chiche-
dec, Mesamichi, Lesquemin, Tadoussac & la rivière de Canada, tant
d'un côté que d'autre, & toutes les baies et rivières qui entrent au
dedans desdites costes,* à peine de desobéissance, & confiscation entière
de leurs vaisseaux, vivres, armes & marchandises, au profit dudit
sieur de Monts & de ses associés, & de trente mille livres d'amende.
Pour l'assurance & acquit de laquelle, & de la cohertion & punition
de leur desobéissance, vous permettrez, comme nous avons aussi permis & permettons, audit sieur de Monts & associés, de saisir, appré-
hender & arrêter tous les contrevenans à notre présente défense &
ordonnance, & leurs vaisseaux, marchandises, armes & victuailles,
pour les amener & remettre ès mains de la justice, & être procédé,
tant contre les personnes que contre les biens desdits desobéissans,
ainsi qu'il appartiendra: ce que nous voulons, & vous mandons &
ordonnons de faire incontinent publier & lire par tous les lieux &
endroits publics de vosdits pouvoirs & jurisdictions où vous jugerez
besoin être, à ce qu'aucun de nosdits sujets n'en puisse prétendre
cause d'ignorance, ains que chacun obéisse & se conforme sur ce à
notre volonté; de ce faire nous vous avons donné & donnons pouvoir
& commission & mandement spécial: Car tel est notre plaisir. Donné
à Paris, le dixhuit décembre, l'an de grace mil cix cens trois, & de
notre règne le quinzième, ainsi signé Henry. *Et plus bas*, Par le
Roi, Potier. Et scellé du grand scel de cire jaulne.

THE FIRST CHARTER OF VIRGINIA—1606 [a]

[See Virginia, page 3783]

THE GRANT TO THE EARL OF STIRLING—1621 [b]

[See Northeastern Boundary Arbitration, Convention of 1827, in "List of Authorities"]

A GRANT OF THE PROVINCE OF MAINE TO SIR FERDINANDO GORGES AND JOHN MASON, ESQ., 10th OF AUGUST, 1622 [c]

This indenture, made the 10th day of August, Anno Dom. 1622, and in the 20th yeare of the reigne of our Sovereigne Lord James, by the grace of God King of England, Scotland, France and Ireland, Defender of the Faith, &c. Between the President and council of New-England on the one part, and Sir Ferdinando Gorges, of London, Knight, and Captain John Mason, of London, Esquire, on ye other part: *Witnesseth*, that whereas our said Sovereigne Lord King James, for the making of a plantation and establishing a colony or colonyes in ye country called or knowne by ye names of New-England in America, hath, by his Highness' Letters Patents, under the Great Seale of England, bearing date at Westmr. the 3d day of November, in the 18th yeare of his reigne, given, granted and confirmed unto the Right Honorable Lodowick, Duke of Lenox; George, Marquis of Buckingham; James, Marquis Hamilton; Thomas, Earl of Arundell; Robert, Earl of Warwick; Sir Ferdinando Gorges, Knt., and divers others whose names are expressed in ye said Letters Patents, and their successors and assignes, that they shall be one Body Politique and Corporate perpetuall, and that they should have perpetual succession, &c., and one comon seale or seales, to serve for the said Body, and that they and their successors shall be known, called and incorporated by the name of the President and Councill established at

---

[a] This charter, which was granted by James I of Great Britain, gave the lands along the North American coast between the thirty-fourth and the forty-fifth degrees of north latitude to two companies, one of which had its headquarters at London and the other at Plymouth, England. The Plymouth, or second company, at once commenced colonizing the coast of New England, which was especially assigned to it. The first colony was planted on the peninsula of Sabino, at the mouth of the Kennebec River, August 19, 1607, o. s., by George Popham. Strachey says: "They fully finished the fort, trencht and fort efyed yt with 12 pieces of ordnance, and built 50 houses therein, besides a church and a storehouse; and the carpenters framed a pretty Pinnace of about some 30 tonne, which they called the Virginia." Popham, who "brought into these wilds English laws and learning, and the faith and the Church of Christ," died February 5, 1608, o. s., and was buried at Sabino. A fort, which was erected near the spot by the United States Government in 1862, perpetuates the event by bearing the name "Fort Popham."

[b] The Earl of Stirling claimed that under this patent he was entitled to land on the coast of Maine, afterward granted to the Plymouth Company, and by direction of James I that company issued a patent to William Alexander, Earl of Stirling, "for a tract of the maine land of New England, beginning at Saint Croix, and from thence extending along the sea-coast to Pemaquid and the river Kennebeck." (See "Vindication of the Rights and Titles of Alexander, Earl of Stirling.")

[c] See Poor's Ferdinando Gorges; Colonial Entry Book, p. 101, No. 59.

Plymouth in the county of Devon, for the planting, ruling and governing of New-England in America; and also hath, of his especiall grace, certaine knowledge and meer motion, for him, his heyres and successors; and given, granted and confirmed unto the said President and councill, and their succesors, under the reservacons, limitacons and declaracons in the said Letters Patents expressed, all that part or porcon of that country now commonly called New-England wch is situate, lying and being between the latitude of forty and forty-eight degrees northerly latitude, together with the seas and islands lying within one hundred miles of any part of the said coasts of the country aforesaid; and also all the lands, soyle, grounds, havens, ports, rivers, mines, as well royal mines of gold and silver, as other mines, minerals, pearls and pretious stones, woods, quaries, marshes, waters, fishings, hunting, hawking, fowling, commodities and hereditaments whatsoever, together with all prerogatives, jurisdictions, royaltys, privileges, franchises and preliminaries within any of the said territories and precincts thereof whatsoever. To have, hold, possess and enjoy, all and singular, the said lands and premises, in the said Letters Patent granted and menconed to be granted, unto the said President and councill, their successors and assignes for ever; to be holden of his Majesty, his heyers and successors, as of his Highness Manor of East Greenwich, in the county of Kent, in free and common soccage and not in capite or by Knts. service—yielding and paying to the Kings Majestie, his heyers and successors, the one fifth part of all gold and silver oare that from time to time, and at all times from the date of the said Letters Patents, shall be there gotten, had or obtayned for all services, dutyes and demands as in and his highness said Letters Patents amongst other divers things therein contayned, more fully and at large it doth appeare. And whereas the said President and Councill have, upon mature deliberacon, thought fitt, for the better furnishing and furtherance of the plantation in those parts to appropriate and allott to several and particular persons divers parcels of lands within the precincts of the aforesaid granted premises by his Majesty's said Letters Patents.

Now this indenture witnesseth, that ye said President and council, of their full, free and mutual consent, as well to the end that all the lands, woods, lakes, rivers, waters, islands and fishings, with all other the traffics, profits and commodities whatever to them or any of them belonging, and hereafter in these presents menconed may be wholly and entirely invested, appropriated, severed and settled in and upon ye said Ferdinando Gorges and Capt. John Mason, their heyers and assignes forever, as for divers speciall services for the advancement of the sd plantacons and other good and sufficient causes and consideracons, them especially thereunto moving, have given granted bargained sould assigned aliened set over enfeofed and confirmed and by these presents doe give grant bargain sell assigne alien set over and confirm unto ye said Ferdinando Gorges and Capt. John Mason, their heirs and assignes, all that pat of the main land in New-England lying upon the sea-coast betwixt ye rivers of Merrimack and Sagadahock, and to the furthest heads of the said rivers, and soe forwards up into the land westward until three-score miles be finished from ye first entrance of the aforesaid rivers, and halfway over; that is to say, to the midst of the said two rivers wch bounds and limitts the lands aforesaid together wth all the islands and isletts within five leagues distance of ye premises and abutting upon ye same or any part or parcell thereof.

As also all the lands, soyle, grounds, harbors, ports, rivers, mines, mineralls, pearls, pretious stones, woods, quarries, marshes, waters, fishings, hunting, hawking, fowling, and other commodities and hereditaments whatsoever; with all and singular their appurtenances, together with all prerogatives, rights, royalties, jurisdictions, privileges, franchises, liberties, preheminences, marine power, in and upon ye said seas and rivers; as also all escheats and casualties thereof, as flotson, jetson, lagon, with anchorage, and other such duties, immunities, sects, isletts and appurtenances whatsoever, with all the estate, right title, interest, and claim and demands whatsoever wch ye said President and councill, and their successors, of right ought to have or claim in or to the said porcons of lands, rivers, and other ye said premises, as is aforesaid by reason or force of his highness' said Letters Patents, in as free, large, ample and beneficial manner, to all intents, constructions and purposes whatsoever, as in and by the said Letters Patents ye same are among other things granted to the said President and councill aforesaid, except two fifths of the oare of gold and silver in these parts hereafter expressed, wth said porcons of lands, wth ye appurtenances, the said Sr. Ferdinando Gorges and Capt. John Mason, with the consent of ye President and Councill, intend to name to name The Province of Maine. To have and to hould all the said porcons of land, islands, rivers and premises as aforesaid, and all and singular other ye commodytyes and hereditaments hereby given, granted, aliened, enfeoffed and confirmed, or menconed or intended by these presents to be given, granted, aliened, enfeoffed and confirmed, with all and singular ye appurtenances and every part and parcell thereof, unto the said Sr. Ferdinando Gorges and Capt. John Mason, their heyres and assignes for ever, to be holden of his said Majesty, his heirs and successors, as of his Highness Manor of East-Greenwich, in the county of Kent, in free and common socage, and not in capite or by Knight's service. Nevertheless, with such exceptions reservacons, limatacons and declaracons as in the said Letters Patents are at large expressed; yielding and paying unto our Sovereign Lord the King, his heyres and successors, the fifth part of all ye oare of gold and silver that from time to time, and att all times hereafter, shall be there gotten, had and obtayned, for all services, duties, and demands. And also yielding and paying unto the said President and councill, and their successors, yerely the sum of tenn shillings English money, if it be demanded. And the said President and councill, for them and their successors, doe covenant and grant to and with the said Sr. Ferdinando Gorges and Capt. John Mason, their heirs and assigns, from and after the ensealing and delivery of these presents, according to the purport, true intent and meaning of these presents, that they shall from henceforth, from time to time for ever, peaceably and quietly have, hold, possess and enjoy, all ye aforesaid lands, islands, rivers and premises, with ye appurtenances hereby before given and granted, or menconed or intended to be hereby before given and granted, and every part and parcell thereof, without any litt, disturbance, denyal, trouble, interrupcon, or evacon of or by the said President and councill, or any person or persons whatsoever, claiming by, from, or under them, or their successors, or by or under their estate, right, title or interest. And ye said President and councill, for them and their successors, doe further covenant and grant, to and with ye said Sr. Ferdinando Gorges and Capt. John Mason, their heyres and assignes, by these presents, that they, ye said President and Councill, at all times hereafter, upon reasonable request, at ye only proper costs and charges in the law of ye said Sr. Ferdinando Gorges and Capt. John Mason, their heyres and assignes, doe make, perform, suffer, execute, and willingly consent unto any further act or acts, conveyance or conveyances, assurance or assurances whatsoever, for ye good and perfect investing, assuring and conveying, and sure making, of all the aforesaid porcons of lands, islands, rivers and all and singular their appurtenances, to ye said Sr. Ferdinando Gorges and capt. John Mason, their heyres and assigns, as by them, their heires and assignes, or by his or their, or any of their councill, learned in the law shall be devised, advised or required. And further, it is agreed by and between the said parties to these presents, and ye said Sr. Ferdinando Gorges and Capt. John Mason, for them, their heyres, executors, administrators and assignes, doe covenant to and with the said president and council, and their successors, by these presents that if at any time hereafter there shall be found any oare of gold and silver within the ground in any part of the said premises, that then they, the said Sr. Ferdinando Gorges and Capt. John Mason, their heyres and assignes, shall yield and pay unto the said President and councill, their successors and assignes, one fifth part of all such gold and silver oare as shall be found within and upon ye premises, and digged and brought above ground to be delivered above ground, and that always within reasonable and convenient time, if it be demanded after the finding, getting, and digging up of such oare as aforesaid, without fraud or covin, and according to the true intent and meaning of these presents.

And the said Sr. Ferdinando Gorges and Capt. John Mason doe further covenant for them, their heyres and assignes, that they will establish such government in the said porcons of lands and islands granted unto them, and the same will from time to time continue, as shall be agreeable, as neere as may be to the laws and customs of the realme of England; and if they shall be charged at any time to have neglected their duty therein, that thus they well conforme the same according to the directions of the President and councill; or in default thereof it shall be lawful for any of the aggrieved inhabitants and planters, being tenn^{t}s upon ye said lands, to appeal to ye chief courts of justices of the President and councill. And ye sd Sr. Ferdinando Gorges and Capt. John Mason doe covenant and grant, to and with ye said President and councill, their successors and assigns, by these presents, that they, the said Sr. Ferdinando Gorges and Capt. John Mason, shall and will, before the expiracon of three years, to be accompted from the day of the date hereof, have in or upon the said porcons of lands, or some part thereof; one parte with a competent guard, and ten families at least of his Majestie's subjects resident and being in and upon ye same premises; or in default thereof shall and will forfeit and loose to the said President and councill the sum of one hundred pounds sterling money; and further, that if the said Sr. Ferdinando Gorges and Capt. John Mason, their heires or assignes, shall at any time hereafter alien these premises, or any part thereof, to any foraigne nations, or to any person or persons of any foraigne nation, without the special license, consent, and agreement of the said President and councill, their successors and assignes, that then the part or parts of the said lands so alienated, shall immediately return back to the use of the said President and Councill. And further Know ye, that ye said President and Councill have made, constituted, deputed, authorized and appointed, and in their place and stead do put Capt. Robert Gorges, or, in his absence, to any other person that shall be their governor or other officer, to be their true and lawfull attorney, and in their name and stead to enter the said porcons of lands, and other the premises wth their appurtenances, or into some part thereof in name of the whole, for them and in their name to have and take possession and siezin thereof, or some part thereof in the name of the whole, so had and taken, there for them, and in their names to deliver the full and peaceable possession and siezin of all and singular the said granted premises unto the said Sr. Ferdinando Gorges and Capt. John Mason, or to their certaine attorney or attorneys in that behalf, according to the true intent and meaning of these presents, ratifying and confirming and allowing all and whatsoever their said attorney shall doe in or about the premises by these presents. In witness whereof to one part of these presents indentures, remaining in the hands of Sir Ferdinando Gorges and Capt. John Mason, the said President and councill have caused their common seal to be affixed, and to the other of these present indentures, remaining in the custody of the said President and councill, the said Sir Ferdinando Gorges and Capt. John Mason have put to their hands and seals. Given the day and year first above written.

GRANT OF THE PROVINCE OF MAINE—1639 [*][a]

Charles by the grace of God King of England Scotland France and Ireland Defender of the Faith, &c

To all to whom theise Presents shall come Greeting Whereas Sir Ferdinando Gorges Knight hath been an humble suitor unto us to graunte and confirme unto him and his heires a parte and porcon of the Countrie of America now commonly called or knowne by the name of New England in America in theise Presents hereafter described by the meets and boundes thereof with divers and sundrie

---

[*] Hazard's Historical Collections of State Papers. I. 442–455. Also, History of Maine, James Sullivan, Boston: 1795. Appendix I.

[a] This charter which was granted by Charles I to Sir Ferdinand Gorges virtually confirmed a patent which had been given by the Plymouth Company, established under the charter of 1606, to Sir Ferdinando Gorges and Captain John Mason, dated August 10, 1622. Gorges established a government under it, which was broken up by his death in 1647.

Sir Ferdinando Gorges's grandson, Ferdinando Gorges, sold and gave a deed of the Province of Maine, March 13, 1677, to John Usher, a merchant of Boston, for £1,250. In the same year Usher gave a deed of the same territory to the governor and company of Massachusetts Bay.

priviledges and jurisdiccons for the welfare and good of the state of those Colonies that shalbee drawne thither and for the better governement of the people that shall live and inhabite within the lymits and precints thereof whiche parte or porcon of the said Countrie wee have heretofore (amongst other things) for us our heires and successors taken into actuall and reall possession or in defaulte of such actuall and reall possession formerly taken Wee Doe by theise Presents for us our heires and successors take the same into our actuall and reall possession Knowe yee therefore that of our especiall grace certaine knowledge and meere mocon Wee Have given graunted and confirmed And by these Presents for us our heires and successors Doe give graunte and confirme unto the said Sir Fardinando Gorges his heires and assignes All that Parte Purparte and Porcon of the Mayne Lande of New England aforesaid beginning att the entrance of Pascataway Harbor and soe to passe upp the same into the River of Newichewanocke and through the same unto the furthest heade thereof and from thence Northwestwards till one hundred and twenty miles bee finished and from Pascataway Harbor mouth aforesaid Northeastwards along the Sea Coasts to Sagadahocke and upp the River thereof to Kynybequy River and through the same unto the heade thereof and into the Lande Northwestwards untill one hundred and twenty myles bee ended being accompted from the mouth of Sagadahocke and from the period of one hundred and twenty myles aforesaid to crosse over Lande to the one hundred and twenty myles end formerly reckoned upp into the Lande from Pascataway Harbor through Newichewanocke River and alsoe the Northe halfe of the Isles of Shoales togeather with the Isles of Capawock and Nawtican neere Cape Cod as alsoe all the Islands and Iletts lyeinge within five leagues of the Mayne all alonge the aforesaide Coasts betweene the aforesaid River of Pascataway and Segadahocke with all the Creekes Havens and Harbors thereunto belonginge and the Revercon and Revercons Remaynder and Remaynders of all and singular the said Landes Rivers and Premisses All which said Part Purpart or Porcon of the Mayne Lande and all and every the Premisses herein before named Wee Doe for us our heires and successors create and incorporate into One Province or Countie

And Wee Doe name ordeyne and appoynt that the porcon of the Mayne Lande and Premisses aforesaide shall forever hereafter bee called The Province or Countie of Mayne and not by any other name or names whatsoever with all and singuler the Soyle and Grounds thereof as well drye as covered with waters and all Waters Portes Havens and Creekes of the Sea and Inletts of the said Province of Mayne and Premisses as to them or any of them belonginge or adjacent as alsoe all Woodes Trees Lakes and Rivers within the said Provynce of Mayne and Premisses or Lymitts of the same togeather with the Fisheing of whatsoever kinde as well Pearle as Fishe as Whales Sturgeons or any other either in the Sea or Rivers and alsoe All Royaltyes of Hawkeing Hunting Fowleing Warren and Chases within the said Province of Mayne and Premisses aforesaid Deere of all sorts and all other Beasts and Fowles of Warren and Chase and all other Beasts there and alsoe All Mynes and Oare of Goulde Silver Precious Stones Tynne Leade Copper Sulphure Brimstone or any other Mettall or Mynerall matter whatsoever within the said

Province and Premisses or any of them opened or hidden and all Quarries there And all Gould Pearle Silver Precious Stones and Ambergreece whiche shalbee founde within the said Province and Premisses or any of them and the Lymitts and Coasts of the same or any of them or any parte of them or any of them and all and singular other Proffitts Benefitts and Commodityes groweing comeing accrueing or happening or to be had perceived or taken within the said Province and Premisses Lymitts and Coasts of the same or any of them and alsoe All Patronages and Advowsons Free Disposicons and Donacons of all and every such Churches and Chappells as shalbee made and erected within the said Province and Premisses or any of them with full power lycense and authority to builde and erecte or cause to be builte and erected soe many Churches and Chappells there as to the said Sir Ferdinando Gorges his heires and assignes shall seeme meete and convenient and to dedicate and consecrate the same or cause the same to bee dedicated and consecrated according to the Ecclesiastical Lawes of this our Realme of England togeather with all and singuler and as large and ample Rights Jurisdiccons Priviledges Prerogatives Royalties Liberties Immunityes Franchises Preheminences and Hereditaments as well by Sea as by Lande within the said Province and Premisses and the Precincts and Coasts of the same or any of them and within the Seas belonging or adjacent to them or any of them as the Bishopp of Durham within the Bishopricke or Countie Palatine of Duresme in our Kingdome of England now hath useth or enjoyeth or of right hee ought to have use or enjoye within the said Countie Palatine as if the same were herein particulerly menconed and expressed

To have and to houlde possesse and enjoye the said Province and Premisses and every of them and all and singular other the Pmesisses before by theise Presents graunted or menconed or intended to bee graunted with theire and everye of theire rights members and appurtenances unto the said Sir Ferdinando Gorges his heires and assignes and To the sole and only use of the said Sir Ferdinando Gorges his heires and assignes forever To bee houlden of us our heires and successors as of the Mannor of East Greenwich in the Countie of Kent by Fealty onely in fee and common Soccage and not in Capite nor in Knights Service for all manner of service whatsoever Yieldeing and Payeing therefore yearely to us our heires and successors one Quarter of Wheate And alsoe Yieldeing and Payeing to us our heires and successors the fifte parte of the cleere yearely proffitt of our Royall Mynes of Goulde and Silver that from tyme to tyme and att all tymes hereafter shalbee there gotten and obteyned (if any suche shalbee there founde) and the fifte parte of all Goulde and Silver founde uppon the Sea Shoare or in Rivers or elsewhere within the boundes and lymitts of the said Province and Premisses and the fifte parte of the cleere yearely proffitt of Pearle Fisheing And Wee Doe for us our heirs and successors further Graunte unto the said Sir Fardinando Gorges his heires and assignes forever All Treasure Trove Goodes and Chattells of Felons and Felons themselves Waifes Estrayes Pyrats Goodes Deodands Fynes and Amerciaments of all the Inhabitants and others happening groweinge or ariseing in the said Province and other the Premisses or any part thereof or in any Voyage or Passage to or from the same aswell for Offences committed against our selfe our heires and successors or thinges concerninge our selfe our heires or successors or our proffit as against others or thinges concerninge others or the proffitts of others and all and all manner of Wrecks of Shipps or Merchandize and all that which to wrecks belongeth by what means soever happening within or uppon the Havens Coasts Creeks or Shoares of the Premisses or any parte thereof And Wee Doe for us our heires and successors create ordeyne and constitute the said Fardinando Gorges his heires and assignes the true and absolue Lords and Proprietors of all and every the aforesaid Province of Mayne and Premisses aforesaid and all and every the Lymitts and Coasts thereof Saveing always the faith and allegiance and the Supreame Dominion due to us our heires and successors

And for the better governement of such our Subjects and others as att any tyme shall happen to dwell or reside within the said Province and Premisses or passe to or from the same our will and pleasure is that the Religion nowe professed in the Church of England and Ecclesiasticall Governement nowe used in the same shalbee forever hereafter professed and with asmuch convenient speede as may bee setled and established in and throughout the said Province and Premisses and every of them And Wee Doe for us our heires and successors of theise Presents give and graunte unto the said Sir Fardinando Gorges his heires and assignes power and authority with the assent of the greater parte of the Freeholders of the said Province and Premisses for the tyme being (when there shalbee any) whoe are to bee called thereunto from tyme to tyme when and as often as it shalbee requisite to make ordeyne and publish Lawes Ordinances and Constitucons reasonable and not repugnant or contrary but agreeable (as neere as conveniently may bee) to the Lawes of England for the publique good of the said Province and Premisses and of the Inhabitants thereof by imposeing of penaltyes imprisonments or other coneccons (or if the offence shall require) by takeing away of life or member the said Lawes and Constitucons to extend as well to such as shalbee passing unto or returning from the said Province and Premisses as unto the Inhabitants and Residents of or within the same and the same to bee put in execucon by the said Sir Fardinando Gorges his heires or assignes or by his or theire Deputies Lieuetenants Judges Officers or Ministers in that behalfe lawfully authorized and the same Lawes Ordinances and Constitucons or any of them to alter change revoke or make voyde and to make new not repugnant nor contrary but agreeable as neere as may bee to the Lawes of England as the said Sir Fardinando Gorges his heires or assignes togeather with the said Freehoulders or the greater parte of them for the tyme being shalbee from tyme to tyme thought fitt and convenient

And Wee Doe further by theise Presents for us our heires and successors give and graunte unto the said Sir Fardinando Gorges his heires and assignes full power and authoritie and that itt shal and may bee lawefull to and for him the said Sir Fardinando Gorges his heires and assignes to erect Courtes of Justice aswell ecclesiasticall as civill and temporall whatsoever and to appoynt and constitute from tyme to tyme Judges Justices Magistrates and Officers as well of the said Courte and Courtes of Justice as otherwise aswell by Sea as by Lande for the hearing and determining of all manner of Causes whatsoever within and concerning the said Province and Premisses or any of them or the Inhabitants or Residents there and Passengers to or from the same aswell by Lande as by Sea and to order and appoynt what matters and thinges shalbee heard determyned done or ordered in anie of the said Courtes or by any of the said Judges Magistrates and officers with such power and in such forme as it shall seeme good to the said Sir Fardinando Gorges his heires or assignes. And the said Judges Justices Magistrates and Officers and every or any of them from time to time to displace and remove when the said Sir Fardinando Gorges his heires or assignes shall thinke fitt and to place others in theire roomes and steed And that the Inhabitants and Residents within the said Province and Premisses and Passengers to and from the same may within fortie days after sentence given in the said Courtes (where appeales in like Courtes within this Kingdome are admitted) appeale to the said Sir Fardinando Gorges his heires or assignes or his or theire generall Governour or Chiefe Deputie of the said Province or Premisses for the tyme being To whome Wee Doe by these Presents for us our heires and successors give full power and authoritie to proceede in such Appeals as in like case of Appeales within this our Realme of England And Wee Doe further for us our heires and successors give and graunte unto the said Sir Fardinando Gorges his heires and assignes full power and authoritie to pardon remitt and release all offences and offendors within the said Province and Premisses against all every or any the said Lawes Ordynances or Constitucons and to doe all and singular other thinges unto the execucon of Justice apperteyning in any Courte of Justice according to the forme and manner of proceeding in such Courtes to be used although in these our Letters Patents there bee noe particuler mencon of the same

But Wee Doe nevertheles hereby signifie and declare our will and pleasure to bee the powers and authorities hereby given to the said Sir Fardinando Gorges his heires and assignes for and concerning the Government both Ecclesiasticall and Civill within the said Province and Premisses shalbee subordynate and subject to the power and reglement of the Lords and other Commissioners here for forraigne Plantacons for the tyme being but for all and whatsoever doth shall or maye concerne the proprietie of the said Province Partes and Coastes of the same or any of them or any Owner Shipp or Interest in any Landes Tenements or other Hereditaments Goodes or Chattells or the nomynateing or appoynting of any Officer or Officers the same is lefte whollie to the said Sir Fardinando Gorges his heires and assignes according to the tenor intent and true meaning of theise Presents And because such Assemblies of Freehoulders for makeing of Lawes cannot alwayes bee soe suddenly called as there may bee occasion to require the same Wee Doe therefore for us our heires and successors give and graunte unto the said Sir Fardinando Gorges his heires and assigns full power and authoritie that hee the said Sir Fardinando Gorges his heires and assignes by him and themselves or by his or theire Deputies Magistrates or Officers in that behalfe lawfully constituted shall or maye from tyme to tyme make and ordeyne fitt and wholesome Ordinances within the said Province or Premisses aforesaid to bee kepte and established as well for the keepeing of the peace as for the better governement of the people there abideing or passing to or from the same and to publishe the same to all to whome itt maye appertain and concerne which Ordinances Wee Doe for us our heires and successors straightly comand to bee inviolably observed within the said Province and Premisses under the penaltie therein expressed soe as the same Ordinances bee reasonable and not repugnant or contrary but as neere as may bee agreeable to the Lawes and Statutes of our Kingdome of England and soe as the same Ordinances doe not extend to the bindeing chargeing or takeing away of the right or interest of any person or persons in theire lives members Freehoulds Goodes or Chattells whatsoever

And because in a Country soe farr distant and seated amongst soe many barbarous nations the Intrusions or Invasions aswell of the barbarous people as of Pirates and other enemies maye be justly feared Wee Doe therefore for us our heires and successors give and graunte unto the said Sir Fardinando Gorges his heires and assignes full power and authoritie that hee the said Sir Fardinando Gorges his heires and assignes aswell by him and themselves as by his and theire Deputyes Captaynes or other Officers for the tyme being shall or lawfullye maye muster leavie rayse armes and ymploye all person and persons whatsoever inhabiteing or resideing within the said Province or Premisses for the resisting or withstanding of such Enymies or Pyrates both att Lande and att Sea and such Enimies or Pyrates (if occasion shall require) to pursue and prosecute out of the lymitts of the said Province or Premisses and then (if itt shall soe please God) to vanquishe apprehende and take and being taken either according to the Lawe of armes to kill or to keepe and preserve them att their pleasure And likewise by force of armes to recover from any person or persons all such Territories Domynions Landes Places Goods Chattels and Wares which hereafter shalbee taken from the said Sir Fardinando Gorges his heires or assignes or from his or theire Deputyes Officers or Servants or from any the Plantors Inhabitants or Residents of or within the said Province or Premisses or from any other Members Aydors or Assistors of the said Sir Fardinando Gorges his heires or assignes or from any other the subjects of us our heires and successors or others in amitie with us our heires and successors in the said Province and Premisses and Coasts or any of them or in theire passage to or from the same And We Doe further for us our heires and successors give and graunte unto the said Sir Fardinando Gorges his heires and assignes in case any Rebellion sudden tumult or mutynie shall happen to arise either uppon the said Lande within the said Province and Premisses or any of them or Coastes of the same or uppon the mayne Sea in passing thither or returning from thence or in any such expedicon or service as aforesaid itt shall and may be lawefull to and for the said Sir Fardinando Gorges his heires and assignes as well by him and themselves as by his and theire deputies Captaynes or other Officers under his or theire seale in that behalfe to bee authorised (to whome wee alsoe for us our heires and successors doe give and graunte full power and authoritye to doe and execute the same) to use and execute martial lawe against such Rebells Traytors Mutyners and Seditious Persons in as ample manner and forme as anie Captayne Generall in the Warrs or as any Lieuetennante or Lieuetennants of any Countie within this our Realme of England by vertue of his or theire Office or Place maie or have beene accustomed in tyme of Warre Rebellion or Mutynie to doe and performe

And Wee Doe for us our heires and successors further give and graunte unto the said Sir Fardinando Gorges his heires and assignes and to all and every Commander Governour Officer Minister Person and Persons which shall by the said Sir Fardinando Gorges his heires or assignes bee thereunto authorized or appoynted leave lycense and power to erect rayse and builde from time to tyme in the Province Territories and Coastes aforesaid and every or any of them such and soe manie Forts Fortresses Platforms Castles Citties Townes and Villages and all Fortificacons whatsoever and the same and everie of them to fortifie and furnishe with men Ordynances men Powder Shott Armour and all other Weapons Munition and Habillments of Warr both for defence and offence whatsoever as to the said Sir Fardinando Gorges his heirs and assignes and everie or anie of them shall seeme meete and convenient And likewise to committ from tyme to tyme the Government Custody and defence thereof unto such person and persons as to the said Sir Fardinando Gorges his heires and assignes shall seeme meete and to the said severall Citties Borroughes and Townes to graunte Letters or Charters of Incorporacons with all Libertyes and thinges belonging to the same and in the said severall Cittyes Boroughes and Townes to constitute suche and so manie Marketts Marts and Fayres and to graunte such meete Tolles Customes Dutyes and Priviledges to or with the same as by the said Sir Fardinando Gorges his heires or assignes shalbee thought fitt And for that Plantacons are subjecte to diverse difficulties and discommodities Therefore Wee favouring the present beginning of the said Plantacon and haveing a provident care that those whoe are grieved in one thing may bee releived in another Doe of our especiall grace certeyne knowledge and meere mocon for us our heires and successors give and graunte unto the said Sir Fardinando Gorges his heires and assignes and to all other our subjects the Dwellers or Inhabitants that shall att any tyme hereafter bee the Plantors of or in the said Province or any of the Premisses free Lycense and Libertie for the landeing bringeing in and unladeing or otherwise disposeing of all the Wares Merchandize Proffitts and Comodities of the said Province or any the Premisses both by sea and lande either by themselves or theire Servants Factors or Assignes in any of the Portes of us our heires and successors within our Kingdomes of England and Ireland payeing onely such Customes Subsidies and Dutyes as our naturall subjects of this our Realme of England shall or ought to paye and none other and to have and enjoye all such Liberties Freedomes and Privyledges for or concerneing the exporting of the same agayne without payement of any more Customes or Dutyes and for having agayne of Imposts in such manner and in the like beneficiall sorte as any of our naturall borne subjects of this our Realme shall then have and enjoye And Wee Doe alsoe for us our heires and successors give and graunte unto the said Fardinando Gorges his heires and assignes full and absolute power and authoritie to make erect and appoynt within the said Province and Premisses such and soe many Portes Havens Creekes and other Places for the ladeing and unladeing of Shippes Barques and other Vessells and in such and soe many places and to appoynt such Rights Jurisdiccons Priviledges and Libertyes unto the said Portes Havens and Creekes belonging as to him or them shall seeme meete and that all and singuler Shippes Boyes Barques and other Vessels to bee laden and unladen in any way of Merchandize shalbee laden or unladen att such Portes Havens or Creekes soe by the aforesaid Sir Fardinando Gorges his heires or assignes to be erected and appoynted and not elsewhere within the said Province Premisses and Coastes and to appoynt what reasonable Tolles shalbee paid for the same and the same Tolles to receive take and enjoye to the behoof of the said Sir Fardinando Gorges his heires and assignes to his and theire use without accompte to bee therefore made to us our heirs or successors any use custume matter or thinge to the contrary thereof notwithstandinge Saveing allwayes to all our Subjects of our Kingdome of England Libertie of Fisheing aswell in the sea as in the Creekes of the said Province and Premisses aforesaid and the Priviledge of Salteing and dryeing of theire Fishe and Dryeing of theire netts a Shoare of the said Province and any the Premisses any thinge to the contrary thereof notwithstanding which said Liberties and Priviledges our pleasure is that the said subjects of us our heires and successors shall enjoye without any noteable dammage or injurie to bee done to the said Sir Fardinando Gorges his heires and assignes or the Inhabitants of the said Province or any of the Premisses or in any of the said Portes Creekes or Shoares aforesaid but chiefly in the Woodes there groweing

And Wee doe further for us our heires and successors give and graunte unto the said Sir Fardinando Gorges his heires and assignes full power and authoritie to divide all or anie parte of the Territories hereby graunted or menconed to bee graunted as aforesaid into Provinces Counties Citties Townes Hundreds and Parishes or such other partes or porcons as hee or they shall thinke fitt and in them every or any of them to appoynt and allott out such porcons of Lande for publique uses Ecclesiasticall and Temporall of what kinde soever and to distribute graunte assigne and sett over such particuler porcons of the said Territories Counties Landes and Premisses unto such our subjects or the subjects of any other State or Prince then in amytie with us our heires or successors for such estates and in such manner and forme as to the said Sir Fardinando Gorges his heires or assignes shall seeme meete and convenient and the said person and persons according to the said Estate and Estates soe assigned and graunted to have and enjoye the same and to make erect and ordeyne in and uppon the said Province and Premisses or in and uppon any of them or any parte or parcell of them soe many severall and distincte Mannors as to the said Sir Fardinando Gorges his heires and assignes from tyme to tyme shall seeme meete and to the same severall Mannors to assigne lymitts and to appoynt soe much lande distinctely and severallie for demeasne Landes of the said severall Mannors and every of them as to the said Sir Fardinando Gorges his heires and assignes shall and may seeme necessary and fitt and the said Mannors or any of them to call by such name and names as the said Sir Fardinando Gorges his heirs and assignes shall please the said Mannors to bee houlden of the said Sir Fardinando Gorges his heires or assignes by such services and Rents as to him or them shall seeme meete And alsoe that the said Sir Fardinando Gorges his heires and assignes shall and may att theire pleasure graunte in freehoulde soemuch of the said demeasne Landes Tenements and Hereditaments belonging or to bee belonging unto any of the said Mannors to any person or persons theire heires or assignes for and under such rentes and services as to the said Sir Fardinando Gorges his heires and assignes shalbee thought fitt to bee houlden of the said Sir Fardinando Gorges his heires and assignes as of the said Mannors or any of them respectively the Acte of Parliament made and enacted in the eighteenth yeare of King Edward the First commonly called (Quia Emptores Terrarum) or any other Statute whatever or any other matter or thinge whatsoever to the contrary thereof in any wise notwithstandinge.

And that the said Sir Fardinando Gorges his heires and assignes shall have houlde and keepe within the said severall Mannours soe to bee erected suche and soe many Courtes aswell Courte Leetes as Courtes Barons as to our Lawes and Statutes of England shalbee agreeable And Wee Doe further for us our heires and successors give and graunte unto the said Sir Fardinando Gorges his heires and assignes for ever all Admirall Rights Benefitts Jurisdiccons and likewise all Priviledges and Commodities to the said Admirall Jurisdiccon in any wise belonging or apperteyning in and uppon the Seas Rivers and Coastes of or belonging to the said Province and Premisses or every or any of them or to the same adjoyneing within twentie leagues of the said Province and Premisses of any of them and in and uppon all other Rivers and Creekes thereof And likewise power to heare and determine all manner of Pleas for and concerning the same Saveing allwayes to us our heires and successors and to the Lord High Admirall of England for the tyme being of us our heires and successors all and all manner of Jurisdiccon Rights Powers Benefitts and authorities whatsoever incident or belonging to the said office of Admirall which itt shalbee lawfull from tyme to tyme to us our heires or successors or the Lord High Admirall of England for the tyme being to have use and exercise within the said Province and Premisses and the Seas and Rivers thereof or within twentie leagues of the same as aforesaid when wee shall thinke fitt And Wee Doe for us our heires and successors give and graunte unto the said Sir Fardinando Gorges his heires and assignes full power and authoritie att any time or times hereafter by him or themselves or by his or theire Deputies to administer reasonable oathes to all Judges Justices Magistrates and other officers whatsoever by the said Sir Fardinando Gorges his heires and assignes his or theire deputyes to be elected att the eleccon of them to theire severall offices and places or within convenient time after And alsoe that hee the said Sir Fardinando Gorges his heires and assignes shall have full power and authoritie aswell by him and themselves as by his or their deputie or other Chiefe Magistrate or Officer by him or them to bee in that behalfe appointed to give and administer reasonable oathes to all or any person or persons of what degree or qualitie soever imployed or to be ymployed in or about the said Province Premisses and Territories aforesaid or anie of them or in or about the coasts of the same And likewise to all or any Inhabitants and others that shalbee or remayne within the said

Province and Premises or any of them for the true and faithfull execucon and performaunce of theire severall charges and places or for the exaiacon and cleareing the truth and likewise for the Informacon and better direccon of his and theire judgments in any matter or cause whatsoever concerning the said Sir Fardinando Gorges his heires or assignes or any Inhabitant member or Person belonging or repayring unto the said Province and Premisses or any of them or any parte of them And in all causes Accons Suits and Debates thereto bee begun and prosecuted as the nature of the cause shall require And further of our more espeaciall grace certeyne knowledge and meere mocon Wee Doe hereby for us our heires and successors graunte unto the said Sir Fardinando Gorges his heires and assignes that itt shall and may bee lawfull to and for the said Sir Fardinando Gorges his heires and assignes and every of them from tyme to tyme to sett to Sea such and soe many Shipps Pinnaces Barges Boates and other Vessells as shalbee thought fitt by the said Sir Fardinando Gorges his heires and assignes prepared and furnished with Ordinances Artillery Powder Shott Victualls Municon or other Weapons or Abiliments of War aswell invasive as defensive in warlike manner or otherwise and with such number of Men Weomen and Children as the said Sir Fardinando Gorges his heires or assignes shall thinke fitt such voyage into the said Islands and Places or any parte thereof aswell for the Plantacon and Fortificacon as otherwise And that these Presents shalbee a sufficient Lycense and Warrant for any person or persons that shalbee by him or them sent and ymployed thither to goe beyonde the Seas and in that manner soe as the persons soe to bee shipped sent or transported as aforesaid bee not such as are or for the tyme being shalbee prohibited by Proclamacon of us our heirs or successors or by any order or orders of the Lords or others Commissioners for Forraigne Plantacons for the tyme being

And Wee Doe for us our heires and successors further graunte to and with the said Sir Fardinando Gorges his heires and assignes that onely hee the said Sir Fardinando Gorges his heires and assignes and his and theire Factors Agents and such as shalbee imployed sent lycensed or allowed by him or them and noe other person or persons whatsoever excepte before excepted shall repayre or goe into the said Province of Mayne and Premisses aforesaid and the places within the lymitts and coasts thereof or any of them to dwell inhabite or abide there nor have use or enjoye the libertie use and priveledges of trade or traffique unto in or from the said Province and Premisses or any of them or buying selling bartering or exchangeing for or with any Wares Goodes or Merchanndizes there whatsoever And likewise that itt shall and may bee lawfull to and for the said Sir Fardinando Gorges his heires and assignes and for all and every other person and persons that shalbe lycensed or allowed by the said Sir Fardinando Gorges his heires or assignes from henceforth and at all other tymes and from tyme to tyme after the date of these our Letters Patents according to the orders and constitucons of the said Sir Fardinando Gorges his heires and assignes not being repugnant to our Proclamacons and Orders of the Lords and others our Commissioners as aforesaid to take convey carrie and transport for and towards the Plantacon of the said Province and Premisses or any of them or to bee used there or in the passage thither or returning from thence and there to leave abide and inhabite all such and soe many of our loveing subjects or any other Strangers that will become our subjects and live under our alleagiance as shall willingly transport themselves or bee transported thither and that such our subjects or Strangers may togeather with theire persons send carrie or convey thither aswell Shipping Armour Weapons Ordinance Municon Powder Shott and Habiliments of Warr as Victualls Canvas Lynnen Woollen Cloath Tooles Ymplements Furniture Swine and Pullen Goodes Wares and Merchandizes of all kindes and sortes whatsoever fitt and necessary for the foode lyvelyhood habitacon apparrell or Defence of our subjects which shall there inhabite and bee and all other Wares Merchandizes and Goods whatsoever not prohibited by the Lawes or Statutes of this our Kingdome payeing customes and other duties as other our subjects doe in such cases And of our further Royall favour Wee have graunted And by these Presents for us our heires and successors Wee Doe graunte unto the said Sir Fardinando Gorges his heires and assignes that the aforesaid Province Rivers and Places hereby before menconed to bee graunted or any of them shall not bee traded in or unto nor inhabited by any of the subjects of us our heires and successors without the speaciall lycense of the said Sir Fardinando Gorges his heires and assignes And therefore Wee Doe hereby for us our heires and successors charge and command prohibite and forbidd all the subjects of us our heires and successors of what degree qualitie or condicon soever they bee that none of them directlie or indirectlie presume to trade or adventure to traffique into or from nor to inhabite or abide in the said Province of Mayne Island Dominion and Places hereby menconed or intended to bee graunted or any of them other then the said Sir Fardinando Gorges his heires and assignes and his and theire deputies and factors unless itt bee with the license and consent of the said Fardinando Gorge his heires and assignes first had and obteyned in that behalf in writeinge under his or theire hands and seales under payne of our idignacon and alsoe of suche penaltyes punishments as by the Lawes and Ordinances of the said Sir Fardinand Gorges his heires and assignes to bee made in that behalfe shalbee appoynted.

And Wee Doe further for us our heires and successors graunte unto the said Sir Fardinando Gorges his heires and assignes that all and every the persons being the subjects of us our heires and successors which shall goe or inhabite within the said Province and Premisses or any of them and all and everie the children and posteritie discending of English Scottish or Irish Parents which shall happen to be borne within the same or uppon the seas in passing thither or from thence from henceforth ought to bee and shalbee taken and reputed to bee of the alleagiance of us our heires and successors and shalbee and soe shalbee forever hereafter esteemed to bee the naturall borne subjects of us our heires and successors and shall bee able to pleade and bee ympleaded and shall have power and bee able to take by discent purchase or otherwise Landes Tenements and Hereditaments and shall have and injoy all Liberties Francheses and Immunityes of or belonging to any the naturall borne subjects of this our Kingdome of England within this our Kingdome and within all other of our Domynions to all intents and purposes as if they had beene abydeing and borne within this our Kingdome or any other of our Dominions

And Wee Doe further for us our heires and successors give full power
and authoritie to the said Sir Fardinando Gorges his heires and
assignes or any person or persons to bee thereunto nominated by the
said Sir Fardinando Gorges his heires or assignes to minister and
give Oathes of Allegiance and supremacie according to the formes
now established in this our Realme of England to all and every
such person and persons as they shall thinke fitt that shall att any
tyme or tymes goe or passe into the said Province and Premises or
any of them or shalbee resident or abideing there And our further
Will and pleasure is and Wee Doe by these Presents for us our heires
and successors Covenant and graunte to and with the said Sir Fardinando Gorges his heires and assignes that if the said Sir Fardinando
Gorges his heires or assignes shall att any tyme or tymes hereafter
uppon any doubte which hee or they shall conceave concerning the
validitie and strength of this our present graunte bee desireous to
renewe the same from us our heires or successors with amendment
of such ymperfeccons and defects as shall appeare fitt and necessary
to bee reformed and amended by us our heires and successors that then
uppon the humble peticon of the said Sir Fardinando Gorges his
heires and assignes such further and better assurance of all and
singuler the Premises hereby graunted or menconed or intended
to bee graunted according to the true meaneing of these our Letters
Patents shall from tyme to tyme by us our heires and successors bee
made and graunted unto the said Sir Fardinando Gorges his heires
and assignes as by the Attorney Generall of us our heires and successors for the tyme being and the Learned Councell of the said Sir
Fardinando Gorges his heires and assignes shall in that behalfe bee
reasonably devised or advised And further Wee Doe hereby for us
our heires and successors chardge and commaunde all and singuler
Admiralls Vice-admiralls Generalls Comaunders Captaynes Justices
of Peace Maiors Sheriffs Bayliffs Constables Customers Comptrollers
Collectors Waiters Searches and all other the officers and Ministers
of us our heires and successors whatsoever aswell nowe as hereafter
for the tyme being to bee from tyme to tyme in all things aydeing
and assisting unto the said Sir Fardinando Gorges his heires and
assignes and to his and theire officers Factors and agents and to every
or any of them uppon request made as they tender our pleasure and
will avoyde the contrary att their perills And Wee Doe will and for
us our heires and successors Doe declare and ordeyne that the said
Province and Premisses shalbee ymediately subject to our Crowne of
Englande and dependant upon the same for ever And further Wee
Will and by these Presents for us our heires and successors Doe
graunte to the said Sir Fardinando Gorges his heires and assignes
that these our Letters Patents or the enrollment of them shalbee in
all things and to all intents and purposes firme good effectuall and
sufficient in the lawe against us our heires and successors aswell in all
Courts as elsewhere within our Kingdome of England or in any
other our Kingdomes and Domynions as in the said Province and
Premisses aforesaid or in any of them and shalbee construed reputed
and taken aswell according to the true meaning and intent as to the
wordes of the same most benignely favorably and beneficially to and
for the said Sir Fardinando Gorges his heires and assignes (noe inter-
pretacon being made of any worde or sentence Whereby Gods worde

true Christian Religion now taught professed and maynteyned the fundamentall Laws of this Realme or Alleagiance to us our heires or successors may suffer prejudice or diminucon) any omission misinformacon want of certaine expression of the contents lymitts and boundes or the certeyne scituacon of the said Province and Premisses aforesaid hereby meant or intended to be graunted or in what latitude or degree the same are or any defect in these Presents or any Lawe Statute or other cause or matter to the contrary notwithstanding And although express mencon bee not made of the true yearely value or certeyntie of the Premisses or any of them and notwithstanding any misnameing and not certeyne or particular nameing of the said Province Places Landes Territories Hereditaments and Premisses whatsoever before by these Presents given graunted confirmed menconed and intended to bee graunted or confirmed or any parte thereof or the misnameing or not nameing or not rightly nameing of the degrees and Coasts wherein or whereuppon the same or any of them doe lie or any Acte of Parliament Statute Ordinaunce Proclamacon or restraint heretofore made ordeyned or provided or any other thinge cause or matter to the contrary notwithstanding Nevertheless our intent and meaneing is that out of the Premisses hereby graunted or menconed to bee graunted there shalbee always saved and reserved to all and every such person and persons as have or hath any lawefull graunte or graunts of Landes or Plantacons lawfully setled in the division and Premisses aforesaid the free houlding and enjoyeing of his and theire right with the Liberties thereunto apperteyning hee or they relinquishing and layeing downe his and theire Jura Regalia (if hee or they have any) to the said Sir Fardinando Gorges his heires and assignes whome wee have hereby made Proprietor of the Province or Devision and Premisses aforesaid and payeing some small acknowledgement to the said Sir Fardinando Gorges his heires and assignes for that hee or they are now to houlde theire Landes anew of the said Sir Fardinando Gorges his heires and assignes In Wittnes whereof we have caused these our Letters to be made Patents Wittnes our selfe att Westminister the third day of Aprill in the fifteenth yere of our reigne.

P. Bre. Privato Sigillo.

GRANT OF THE PROVINCE OF MAINE—1664 *

CHARLES the Second by the Grace of God King of England Scotland Ffrance and Ireland Defender of the Ffaith &c. to all to whom these presents shall come Greeting

Know yee that wee for divers good causes and consideracons us thereunto moving have of our especiall Grace certaine knowledge and meere motion given and granted and by these presents for us our heires and successors do give and grant unto our dearest brother James Duke of Yorke his heires and assigns all that part of the maine land of New England begining at a certain place called or knowne by the name of St. Croix next adjoyning to New Scotland in America

---

* New York Colonial Documents, by E. B. O'Callaghan, II, 295–298.

and from thence extending along the sea coast unto a certain place called Petuaquine or Pemaquid and so up the River thereof to the furthest head of ye same as it tendeth northwards and extending from thence to the River Kinebequi and so upwards by the shortest course to the River Canada northward and also all that Island or Islands commonly called by the severall name or names of Matowacks or Lond Island scituate lying and being towards the west of Cape Codd and ye narrow Higansetts abutting upon the maine land between the two Rivers there called or knowne by the several names of Conecticutt and Hudsons River together also with the said river called Hudsons River and all the land from the west side of Conecticutt to ye east side of Delaware Bay and also all those severall Islands called or knowne by the names of Martin's Vinyard and Nantukes otherwise Nantuckett together with all ye lands islands soyles rivers harbours mines minerals quarryes woods marshes waters lakes ffishings hawkings hunting and ffowling and all other royalltyes proffitts commodityes and hereditaments to the said severall islands lands and premisses belonging and appertaining with theire and every of theire appurtenances and all our estate right title interest benefitt advantage claime and demand of in or to the said lands and premises or any part or parcell thereof and the revercon and revercons remainder and remainders together with the yearly and other ye rents revenues and proffitts of all and singular the said premisses and of every part and parcell thereof to have and to hold all and singular the said lands islands hereditaments and premisses with their and every of their appurtenances hereby given and granted or hereinbefore menconed to be given and granted unto our dearest brother James Duke of Yorke his heirs and assignes forever to the only proper use and behoofe of the said James Duke of Yorke his heires and assignes forever to be holden of us our heirs and successors as of our mannor of East Greenwich in our county of Kent in ffree and common soccage and not in capite nor by Knight service yielding and rendering and the said James Duke of Yorke doth for himself his heires and assignes covenant and promise to yield and render unto us our heires and successors of and for the same yearly and every yeare forty Beaver skins when they shall be demanded or within ninety days after and wee do further of our speciall grace certaine knowledge and meere mocon for us our heires and successors give and grant unto our said dearest brother James Duke of Yorke his heires deputyes agents commissioners and assignes by these presents full and absolute power and authority to correct punish pardon governe and rule all such the subjects of us our heires and successors who may from time to time adventure themselves into any of the parts or places aforesaid or that shall or doe at any time hereafter inhabite within the same according to such lawes orders ordinances direccons and instruments as by our said dearest brother or his assignes shall be established and in defect thereof in cases of necessity according to the good direccons of his deputyes commissioners officers or assignes respectively as well in all causes and matters capitall and criminall as civill both marine and others soe alwayes as the said statutes ordinances and proceedings be not contrary to but as neare as conveniently may be agreeable to the lawes statutes and government of this our realme of England and saving and reserving to us our heires and successors ye receiving hearing and determining of the appeal and appeales of all or any person or persons, of in or belonging to ye territoryes or islands aforesaid in or touching any judgment or sentence to be there made or given.

And further that it shall and may be lawfull to and for our said dearest brother his heires and assignes by these presents from time to time to nominate make constitute ordaine and confirme by such name or names stile or stiles as to him or them shall seeme good and likewise to revoke discharge change and alter as well all and singular Governors officers and Ministers which hereafter shall be by him or them thought fitt and needfull to be made or used within the aforesaid parts and islands and also to make ordaine and establish all manner of orders lawes directions instruccons formes and ceremonyes of government and magistracy fitt and necessary for and concerning the government of the territoryes and islands aforesaid so alwayes as the same be not contrary to the lawes and statutes of this our Realme of England but as neare as may be agreeable thereunto and the same at all times hereafter to put in execucon or abrogate revoke or change only within the precincts of the said territoryes or islands but also upon the seas in going and coming to and from the same as he or they in their good discrecons shall thinke to be fittest for the good of the adventurers and inhabitants there And wee do further of our speciall grace certaine knowledge and meere mocon grant ordaine and declare that such governors officers and ministers as from time to time shall be authorized and appointed in manner and forme aforesaid shall and may have full power and authority to use and exercise martiall law in cases of rebellion insurreccon and mutinie in as large and ample manner as our Lieutenants in our countyes within our Realme of England have or ought to have by force of their commission of Lieutenancy or any law or statute of this our Realme

And wee do further by these presents for us our heires and successors grant unto our said dearest brother James Duke of Yorke his heires and assigns that it shall and may be lawfull to and for the said James Duke of Yorke his heires and assignes in his or theire discrecons from time to time to admit such and so many person and persons to trade and traffique unto and within the terrytoryes and islands aforesaid and into every and any part and parcell thereof and to have possesse and enjoy any lands or hereditamenst in ye parts and places aforesaid as they shall thinke fitt according to the lawes orders constitucons and ordinances by our said brother his heires deputyes commissioners and assigns from time to time to be made and established by vertue of and according to the true intent and meaning of these presents and under such condicons reservacons and agreements as our said brother his heires or assignes shall set downe order direct and appoint and not otherwise as aforesaid And wee do further of ous especiall grace certaine knowledge and meere mocon for us our heires and successors give and grant to our said deare brother his heires and assignes by these presents that it shall and may be lawfull to and for him them or any of them at all and every time and times hereafter out of any of our realmes or dominions whatsoever to take leade carry and transport in and into their voyages and for and towards the plantacons of our said territoryes and islands all such and so many of our loving subjects or any other strangers being not prohibited or under restraint that will become our loving subjects and live under our alegiance as shall willingly accompany them in the said voyages together with all such cloathing implements furniture and other things usually transported and not prohibited as shall be necessary for the inhabitants of the said islands and territoryes and for theire use and defence thereof and manageing and carrying on the trade with the people there and in passing and returning to and fro yielding and paying to us our heires and successors the customes and dutyes therefore due and payable according to the lawes and customes of this our Realme

And we do also for us our heires and successors grant to our said dearest brother James Duke of Yorke his heires and assignes and to all and every such governor or governors or other officers or ministers as by our said brother his heires or assignes shall be appointed to have power and authority of government and command in or over the inhabitants of the said territoryes or islands that they and every of them shall and lawfully may from time to time and at all times hereafter forever for theire severall defence and safety encounter expulse repell and resist by force of arms as well by sea as by land and all wayes and means whatsoever all such person and persons as without the speciall licence of our said deare brother his heires or assignes shall attempt to inhabit within the severall precincts and limitts of our said territoryes and islands and also all and every such person and persons whatsoever as shall enterprize or attempt at any time hereafter the destruccon invasion detriment or annoyance to ye parts places or islands aforesaid or any parte thereof and lastly our will and pleasure is and wee do hereby declare and grant that these our letters patents or the enrollment thereof shall be good and effectuall in the law to all intents and purposes whatsoever notwithstanding the not reciting or menconing of the premises or any part thereof or the meets or bounds thereof or of any former or other presents patents or grants heretofore made or granted of the premisses or of any part thereof by us or any of our progenitors unto any other person or persons whatsoever bodyes politique or corporate or any act law or other restraint incertainty or imperfection whatsoever to the contrary in any wise notwithstanding althoughe expresse mencon of the true yearly value or certainty of the premises or any of them or of any other guifts or grants by us or by any of our progenitors or predecessors heretofore made to the said James Duke of Yorke in these presents is not made or any statute act ordinance provision proclamacon or restriction heretofore had made enacted ordained or provided or any other matter cause or thing whatsoever to the contrary thereof in any wise notwithstanding.

In witness whereof wee have caused these our letters to be made pattents.—Witnesse ourselfe at Westminster the twelveth day of March in the sixteenth yeare of our raigne. [1664]

By the King:

HOWARD

GRANT OF THE PROVINCE OF MAINE—1674 *

CHARLES the Second by the Grace of God King of England France and Ireland Defender of the Ffaith &c. To all to whom these presents shall come Greeting: Know yee that wee for divers good causes and consideracons have of our especiall grace certaine knowledge and meer motion given and granted and by these presents for us our heirs and successors do give and graunt unto our dearest brother James Duke of Yorke his heires and assigns All that part of the main land of New England, beginning at a certaine place called or known by the name of St. Croix nexe adjoining to New Scotland in America and from thence extending along the seacoast unto a certaine place called Petuaquine or Pemaquid and so up the river thereof to the furthest head of the same as it windeth northward and extending from the river of Kinebeque and so upwards by the shortest course to the river Canada northwards: And all that Island or Islands commonly called by the severall name or names of Matowacks or Long Islands scituate and being towards the west of Cape Cod and the narrow Higansetts abutting upon the main land between the two rivers there called or known by the severall names of Connecticutt and Hudson's River together also with the said river called Hudson's River and all the lands from the west side of Connecticutt River to the east side of Delaware Bay: And also all those severall Islands called or known by the names of Martin Vin Yards and Nantukes otherwise Nantuckett: Together with all the lands Islands soiles rivers harbors Mines Mineralls Quarries woods marshes waters Lakes ffishings Hawking hunting and ffowling and all other royalties proffits Commodities and hereditaments to the said severall Islands Lands and premises belonging and appertaining with their and every of their appurtenants: And all our Estate right title and interest benefit and advantage claime and demand of in or to the said lands or premises or any part or parcell thereof and the revercon and revercons remainder and remainders together with the yearly and other rents revenues and proffits of the premises and of every part and parcell thereof

To have and to hold all and singular the said lands and premises with their and every of their appurtents hereby given and graunted or herein before mentioned to be given and graunted unto our said dearest brother James Duke of Yorke his heirs and assigns forever: To bee holden of us our heirs and successors as of our Manor of East Greenwich, in our county of Kent in free and common soccage and not in capite nor by Knight service yielding and rendering: And the said James Duke of Yorke for himself his heirs and assignes doth covenant and promise to yield and render unto Us our heirs and successors of and for the same yearly and every year fforty Beaver Skins when they shall bee demanded or within ninety days after such demand made and wee do further, of our speciall grace certaine knowledge and meer motion for Us Our heirs and successors give and graunt unto our said Dearest brother James Duke of Yorke his

---

* The Grants, Concessions, and Original Constitutions of the Province of New Jersey. Leaming and Spicer, Philadelphia, printed by W. Bradford, 1758, 41–45.

heirs Deputyes Agents Commissioners and assignes by these presents full and absolute power and authority to correct punish pardon govern and rule ail such the subjects of us our heirs and successors or any other person or persons as shall from time to time adventure themselves into any of the parts or places aforesaid or that shall or do at any time hereafter inhabit within the same according to such Lawes orders ordinances directions and instructions as by our said dearest brother or his assignes shall bee established and in defect thereof in cases of necessity according to the good discretions of his Deputyes Commissioners Office or Agents respectively as well in all cases and matters capitall and criminall as Civill Marine and Others so alwayes as the said Statutes ordinances and proceedings bee not contrary to but as neare as may bee agreeable to the Lawes Statutes and Government of this our realm of England and saving and reserving to Us our heirs and successors the receiving hearing and determining of the appeal and appeals of all or any person or persons of in or belonging to the Territoryes or Islands aforesaid or touching any Judgment or sentence to bee there made or given

And further that it shall and may bee lawfull to and for our said dearest brother his heirs and assigns by these presents from time to time to nominate make constitute ordaine and confirme such Lawes as aforesaid by such name or names stile or stiles as to him or them shall seem good And likewise to revoke discharge change and alter as well all and singular Governors officers and ministers which hereafter shall be by him or them thought fit and needful to be made or used within the aforesaid Islands and parts: And also to make ordaine and establish all maner of lawes orders direccons instructions formes and ceremonyes of Government and Magistracy fit and necessary for and concerning the Government of the Territoryes and Islands aforesaid so always as the same bee not contrary to the Lawes and Statutes of this our realme of England, but as neare as may bee agreeable thereunto and the same at all times hereafter to put in execution abrogate revoke or change not onely within the precincts of the said Territoryes or Islands but also upon the seas in going and coming to and from the same as hee or they in their good discretions shall think fittest for the good of the adventurers and inhabitants

And wee do further of our Especiall Grace certaine knowledge and meer motion graunt ordaine and declare that such Governors Deputyes Officers and Ministers as from time to time shall bee authorized and appointed in manner and fforme aforesaid shall and may have full power and authority within the Territoryes aforesaid to use and exercise Marshall Lawe in cases of rebellion insurrection and Mutiny in as large and ample manner as our Lieutenants in our Countyes within Our realme of England have or ought to have by force of their Commission of Lieutenancy or any law or Statute of this our realme: And Wee do further by these presents for us our heirs and successors graunt unto Our said dearest brother James Duke of Yorke his heirs and assignes that it shall and may be lawfull to and for the said James Duke of Yorke his heirs and assignes in his or their discrecon from time to time to admit such and so many person and persons to trade and trafficke into and and within ye Territoryes and Islands aforesaid and into every or any of the Territoryes and Islands aforesaid and into every or any part and parcell thereof: And to have possess and enjoy any Lands and hereditaments in the parts and places aforesaid as they shall think fit according to the Lawes orders constitutions and ordinances by our said brother his heirs deputyes Commissioners and assignes from time to time to bee made and established by vertue of and according to the true intent and meaning of these presents and under such condicons preservacons and agreements as our said dearest brother his heirs and assigns shall set downe order direct and appoint and not otherwise as aforesaid

And we do further of our Especiall Grace certaine knowledge and meer motion for us our heires and successors give and graunt unto our said deare brother his heirs and assigns by these presents that it shall and may be lawfull to and for him them or any of them at all and Every time and times hereafter out of any of our realms or dominions whatsoever to take lead carry and transport in and into their voyages for and towards the Plantacons of our said Territoryes and Islands aforesaid all such and so many of our loving subjects or any other strangers being not prohibited or under restraint that will become our loving subjects and live under our allegiance and shall willingly accompany them in the said voyages together with all such cloathing implements ffurniture and other things usually transported and not prohibited as shall be necessary for the inhabitants of the said Islands and territoryes and for their use and defence thereof and managing and carrying on the trade with the people there and in passing and returning to and fro Yielding and paying to us our heirs and successors the customes and dutyes therefore due and payable according to the Lawes and Customes of this our realme And Wee do also for us our heirs and successors graunt unto our said dearest brother James Duke of Yorke his heirs and assignes and to all and every such Governor or Governors Deputyes their Officers or Ministers as by our said brother his heirs or assignes shall bee appointed to have power and authority of government or command in or over the inhabitants of the said Territoryes or Islands that they or every of them shall and lawfully may from time to time and at all times forever hereafter for their severall defence and safety encounter repulse and Expell and resist by force of armes (as well by sea as by land) and all wayes and means whatsoever all such person and persons as without the speciall licence of our dearest brother his heirs and assignes shall attempt to inhabit within the severall precincts and limits of our said Territoryes and Islands and also all and every such person and persons whatsoever as shall enterprize and attempt at any time hereafter the destruccon invasion detriment or annoyance to the parts places or Islands aforesaid or any part thereof

And lastly our will and pleasure is and We do hereby declare and graunt that these our Letters Patents or the enrolment thereof shall bee good and Effectuall in the Law to all intents and purposes whatsoever notwithstanding the not well and true writing or menconing of the premises or any part thereof or the limits or bounds thereof or of any former or other Letters Patent or graunts whatsoever made or graunted or of any part thereof by us or any of our progenitors unto any person or persons whatsoever bodyes politick or corporate or any law or other restraint incertainty or imperfeccon whatsoever to the contrary in any wise notwithstanding although Expresse mention of the true yearly value or certainty of the premises or of any of them or of any other guifts or graunts by us or by any of our progenitors heretofore made to the said James Duke of Yorke in these presents is not made or any statute act ordinance provision proclamation or restriction heretofore had made enacted or provided or any other matter cause or thing whatsoever to the contrary thereof in any wise notwithstanding. In witnesse whereof Wee have caused these our Letters to bee made Patents Witnesse Our Selfe at Westm. the 29th day of June in the 26th yeare of our reigne.

PIGOTT.

CESSION OF MAINE BY MASSACHUSETTS—1820

An Act in addition to an act entitled "An act relating to the separation of the District of Maine from Massachusetts proper, and forming the same into a separate and independent State."

Be it enacted by the senate and house of representatives of Massachusetts in general court assembled, and by the authority of the same, That the consent of the legislature of this commonwealth be, and the same is hereby, given, that the District of Maine may be formed and erected into a separate and independent State, upon the terms and conditions, and in conformity to the enactments contained in an act entitled "An act relating to the separation of the District of Maine from Massachusetts proper, and forming the same into a separate and independent State," whenever the Congress of the United States shall give its consent thereto, anything in the said act limiting the time when such consent should be given to the contrary notwithstanding: *Provided, however,* That if the Congress of the United States shall not have given its consent, as aforesaid, before the fifteenth day of March next, then all parts of the act, to which this is an addition, and all matters therein contained, which by said act have date or operation from or relation to the fifteenth day of March next, shall have date and operation from and relation to the day on which the Congress of the United States shall give its consent, as aforesaid: *Provided, also,* That if the Congress of the United States shall not give its consent, as aforesaid, within two years from the fourth day of March next, this present act shall be void and of no effect.

SEC. 2. *Be it further enacted,* That if it shall not be known on the first Monday of April next that the Congress of the United States has given its consent, as aforesaid, the people of the said District of Maine shall elect, provisionally, a governor, senators and representatives, or other officers necessary to the organization of the government thereof as a separate and independent State, according to the provisions of the constitution of government agreed to by the people of the said District. And the persons so elected shall assemble at the time and place designated by the said constitution, if the consent of Congress, as aforesaid, shall be given during the present session thereof, but not otherwise; and when assembled, as aforesaid, and having first determined on the returns and qualifications of the persons elected, they shall have the power as delegates of the people for that purpose, to declare, on behalf and in the name of the people, the said elections of such persons to be constitutional and valid, for the respective offices and stations for which they shall have been elected, as aforesaid. And if such declaration shall not be made before the persons so elected shall proceed to transact business as the legislature of said State, the said election shall be wholly void, unless it shall appear that the consent of Congress, aforesaid, shall have been given on or before the said first Monday of April next. And if the consent of Congress, as aforesaid, shall be given after the said first Monday of April next, and the persons so elected, when assembled, as aforesaid, shall not declare the said election valid and constitutional, as aforesaid, within ten days from the last Wednesday of May next, then they shall cease to have any power to act in any capacity for the people of the said District, by virtue of their elections, as aforesaid; and the people shall again choose delegates to meet in convention, in the manner, for the purposes, and with the powers set forth in the third and fourth sections of the act to which this is in addition; the said elections of such delegates to be made on the first Monday of July next, and the delegates to meet in convention at Portland on the first Monday of September next.

[Approved by the governor, February 25, 1820.]

ACT ADMITTING MAINE INTO THE UNION—1820

[SIXTEENTH CONGRESS, FIRST SESSION]

Whereas by an act of the State of Massachusetts, passed on the nineteenth day of June, in the year one thousand eight hundred and nineteen, entitled "An act relating to the separation of the District of Maine from Massachusetts proper, and forming the same into a separate and independent State," the people of that part of Massachusetts heretofore known as the District of Maine did, with the consent of the legislature of the said State of Massachusetts, form themselves into an independent State, and did establish a constitution for the government of the same, agreeably to the provisions of the said act: Therefore,

Be it enacted by the Senate and House of Representatives of the United States of America in Congress assembled, That from and after the fifteenth day of March, one thousand eight hundred and twenty, the State of Maine is hereby declared to be one of the United States of America, and admitted into the Union on an equal footing with the original States, in all respects whatever.

Approved, March 3, 1820.

CONSTITUTION OF THE STATE OF MAINE—1819 * a

PREAMBLE

We, the people of Maine, in order to establish justice, insure tranquility, provide for our mutual defence, promote our common welfare, and secure to ourselves and our posterity the blessings of liberty, acknowledging with grateful hearts the goodness of the Sovereign Ruler of the Universe in affording us an opportunity, so favorable to the design; and, imploring His aid and direction in its accomplishment, do agree to form ourselves into a free and independent State, by the style and title of the STATE OF MAINE, and do ordain and establish the following constitution for the government of the same.

ARTICLE I

DECLARATION OF RIGHTS

SECTION 1. All men are born equally free and independent, and have certain natural, inherent and unalienable rights, among which are those of enjoying and defending life and liberty, acquiring, possessing and protecting property, and of pursuing and obtaining safety and happiness.

SEC. 2. All power is inherent in the people; all free governments are founded in their authority and instituted for their benefit; they have therefore an unalienable and indefeasible right to institute government, and to alter, reform, or totally change the same, when their safety and happiness require it.

---

* Verified from "The Constitution of the State of Maine, formed in Convention at Portland, October twenty-ninth, and adopted by the People in town meetings, on the sixth day of December, A. D. 1819, and of the Independence of the United States the Forty-fourth, together with Amendments subsequently made thereto, and arranged, as amended, in pursuance of a Resolve of the Legislature approved February twenty-fourth, A. D. 1875, with Amendments adopted since the last named date with notes on the Declaration of Rights. By L. D. Carver. Augusta: Kennebec Journal Print. 1902." 62 pp.

a Formed in Convention at Portland, October 29, and adopted by the People in Town Meetings, December 6, A. D. 1819, and of the Independence of the United States the Forty-fourth, together with the XXI Amendments Subsequently made Thereto, Arranged, as Amended, in pursuance of a Legislative Resolve of February 24, 1875, by the Chief Justice of the Supreme Judicial Court, the Honorable John Appleton, whose draft and arrangement was, by a Resolve of February 23, 1876, approved by the Legislature, and ordered to be enrolled on parchment and to be deposited in the office of the Secretary of State as "the Supreme Law of the State."

[NOTE.—By Resolve of January 12, 1875, Governor Dingley was authorized to appoint a Commission of ten persons, "to consider and frame such amendments to the Constitution of Maine as may seem necessary, to be reported to the Legislature;" and Edward Kent, William P. Haines, George F. Talbot, William M. Rust, Henry E. Robins, Washington Gilbert, James C. Madigan, Artemas Libbey, Frederick A. Pike and William K. Kimball, were appointed.

Nine of the amendments reported by the Commission, viz.:—in relation to (XIII) Election of Senators by Plurality vote; (XIV) Special Legislation and Corporations; (XV) Power of Governor to pardon; (XVI) Appointment of Judges of Municipal and Police Courts; (XVII) Taxation; (XVIII) Abolishing the Land Agency; (XIX) Constitutional Conventions; (XX) Bribery at Elections; (XXI) Codification of the Amended Constitution; were submitted to the people by a Resolve of February 24, 1875, and adopted at the annual election, September 13, 1875.]

Sec. 3. All men have a natural and unalienable right to worship Almighty God according to the dictates of their own consciences, and no one shall be hurt, molested or restrained in his person, liberty or estate for worshiping God in the manner and season most agreeable to the dictates of his own conscience, nor for his religious professions or sentiments, provided he does not disturb the public peace, nor obstruct others in their religious worship;—and all persons demeaning themselves peaceably as good members of the State shall be equally under the protection of the laws, and no subordination nor preference of any one sect or denomination to another shall ever be established by law, nor shall any religious test be required as a qualification for any office or trust, under this State; and all religious societies in this State, whether incorporate or unincorporate, shall at all times have the exclusive right of electing their public teachers, and contracting with them for their support and maintenance.

Sec. 4. Every citizen may freely speak, write and publish his sentiments on any subject, being responsible for the abuse of this liberty; no laws shall be passed regulating or restraining the freedom of the press; and in prosecutions for any publication respecting the official conduct of men in public capacity, or the qualifications of those who are candidates for the suffrages of the people, or where the matter published is proper for public information, the truth thereof may be given in evidence, and in all indictments for libels, the Jury, after having received the direction of the Court, shall have a right to determine, at their discretion, the law and the fact.

Sec. 5. The people shall be secure in their persons, houses, papers and possessions from all unreasonable searches and seizures; and no warrant to search any place, or seize any person or thing, shall issue without a special designation of the place to be searched, and the person or thing to be seized, nor without probable cause—supported by oath or affirmation.

Sec. 6. In all criminal prosecutions, the accused shall have a right to be heard by himself and his counsel, or either, at his election;

To demand the nature and cause of the accusation, and have a copy thereof;

To be confronted by the witnesses against him;

To have compulsory process for obtaining witnesses in his favor;

To have a speedy, public and impartial trial, and, except in trials by martial law or impeachment, by a jury of the vicinity. He shall not be compelled to furnish or give evidence against himself, nor be deprived of his life, liberty, property or privileges, but by judgment of his peers, or by the law of the land.

Sec. 7. No person shall be held to answer for a capital or infamous crime, unless on a presentment or indictment of a grand jury, except in cases of impeachment, or in such cases of offences as are usually cognizable by a justice of the peace, or in cases arising in the army or navy, or in the militia when in actual service in time of war or public danger. The Legislature shall provide by law a suitable and impartial mode of selecting juries and their usual number and unanimity, in indictments and convictions, shall be held indispensable.

Sec. 8. No person, for the same offence, shall be twice put in jeopardy of life or limb.

Sec. 9. Sanguinary laws shall not be passed; all penalties and punishments shall be proportioned to the offence; excessive bail shall not be required, nor excessive fines imposed, nor cruel nor unusual punishments inflicted.

SEC. 10. No person before conviction shall be bailable for any of the crimes, which now are, or have been denominated capital offences since the adoption of the Constitution, where the proof is evident or the presumption great, whatever the punishment of the crimes may be. And the privilege of the writ of habeas corpus shall not be suspended, unless when in case of rebellion or invasion the public safety may require it.

SEC. 11. The Legislature shall pass no bill of attainder, ex post facto law, nor law impairing the obligation of contracts, and no attainder shall work corruption of blood nor forfeiture of estate.

SEC. 12. Treason against this State shall consist only in levying war against it, adhering to its enemies, giving them aid and comfort. No person shall be convicted of treason unless on the testimony of two witnesses to the same overt act, or confession in open court.

SEC. 13. The laws shall not be suspended but by the Legislature or its authority.

SEC. 14. No person shall be subject to corporal punishment under military law, except such as are employed in the army or navy, or in the militia when in actual service in time of war or public danger.

SEC. 15. The people have a right at all times in an orderly and peaceable manner to assemble to consult upon the common good, to give instructions to their representatives, and to request, of either department of the government by petition or remonstrance, redress of their wrongs and grievances.

SEC. 16. Every citizen has a right to keep and bear arms for the common defence; and this right shall never be questioned.

SEC. 17. No standing army shall be kept up in time of peace without the consent of the Legislature, and the military shall, in all cases, and at all times, be in strict subordination to the civil power.

SEC. 18. No soldier shall, in time of peace, be quartered in any house without the consent of the owner or occupant, nor in time of war, but in a manner to be prescribed by law.

SEC. 19. Every person, for an injury done him in his person, reputation, property or immunities, shall have remedy by due course of law; and right and justice shall be administered freely and without sale, completely and without denial, promptly and without delay.

SEC. 20. In all civil suits, and in all controversies concerning property, the parties shall have a right to a trial by jury, except in cases where it has heretofore been otherwise practiced; the party claiming the right may be heard by himself and his counsel, or either, at his election.

SEC. 21. Private property shall not be taken for public uses without just compensation; nor unless the public exigencies require it.

SEC. 22. No tax or duty shall be imposed without the consent of the people or of their representatives in the Legislature.

SEC. 23. No title of nobility or hereditary distinction, privilege, honor or emolument, shall ever be granted or confirmed, nor shall any office be created, the appointment to which shall be for a longer time than during good behavior.

SEC. 24. The enumeration of certain rights shall not impair nor deny others retained by the people.

ARTICLE II

ELECTORS

SEC. 1. Every male citizen of the United States of the age of twenty-one years and upwards, excepting paupers, persons under guardianship, and Indians not taxed, having his residence established in this State for the term of three months next preceding any election, shall be an elector for Governor, Senators and Representatives, in the town or plantation where his residence is so established; and the elections shall be by written ballot. But persons in the military, naval or marine service of the United States, or this State, shall not be considered as having obtained such established residence by being stationed in any garrison, barrack, or military place, in any town or plantation; nor shall the residence of a student at any seminary of learning entitle him to the right of suffrage in the town or plantation where such seminary is established. No person, however, shall be deemed to have lost his residence by reason of his absence from the State in the military service of the United States, or of this State.

SEC. 2. Electors shall, in all cases, except treason, felony or breach of the peace, be privileged from arrest on the days of election, during their attendance at, going to, and returning therefrom.

SEC. 3. No elector shall be obliged to do duty in the militia on any day of election, except in time of war or public danger.

SEC. 4. The election of Governor, Senators and Representatives shall be on the second Monday of September *annually* forever. But citizens of the State absent therefrom in the military service of the United States or of this State, and not in the regular army of the United States, being otherwise qualified electors, shall be allowed to *vote on Tuesday next after the first Monday of November, in the year of our Lord one thousand eight hundred and sixty-four, for governor and senators, and their votes shall be counted and allowed in the same manner, and with the same effect, as if given on the second Monday of September in that year. And they shall be allowed to vote* for governor, senators and representatives on the second Monday of September *annually thereafter forever*, in the manner herein provided. On the day of election a poll shall be opened at every place without this State where a regiment, battalion, battery, company, or detachment of not less than twenty soldiers from the State of Maine, may be found or stationed, and every citizen of said State of the age of twenty-one years, in such military service, shall be entitled to vote as aforesaid; and he shall be considered as voting in the city, town, plantation and county in this State where he resided when he entered the service. The vote shall be taken by regiments when it can conveniently be done; when not so convenient, any detachment or part of a regiment not less than twenty in number, and any battery or part thereof numbering twenty or more, shall be entitled to vote wherever they may be. The three ranking officers of such regiment, battalion, battery, company, or part of either, as the case may be, acting as such on the day of election, shall be supervisors of elections. If no officers, then three non-commissioned officers according to their seniority shall be such supervisors. If any officer or non-commissioned officer shall neglect or refuse to act, the next in rank shall take his place. In case there are no officers or non-commissioned officers present, or if they or either of them refuse to act, the electors present, not less than twenty, may choose, by written ballot enough of their own number, not exceeding three, to fill the vacancies, and the persons so chosen shall be supervisors of elections. All supervisors shall be first sworn to support the constitution of the United States and of this State, and faithfully and impartially to perform the duties of supervisors of elections. Each is authorized to administer the necessary oath to the others; and certificates thereof shall be annexed to the lists of votes by them to be made and returned into the office of the secretary of state of this State as hereinafter provided. The polls shall be opened and closed at such hours as the supervisors, or a majority of them, shall direct; *provided however*, that due notice and sufficient time shall be given for all voters in the regiment, battalion, battery, detachment, company, or part of either, as the case may be, to vote. Regimental and field officers shall be entitled to vote with their respective commands. When not in actual command, such officers, and also all general and staff officers and all surgeons, assistant surgeons, and chaplains, shall be entitled to vote at any place where polls are opened. The supervisors of elections shall prepare a ballot box or other suitable receptacle for the ballots. Upon one side of every ballot shall be printed or written the name of the county, and also of the city, town or plantation of this State, in which is the residence of the person proposing to vote. Upon the other side shall be the name or names of the persons to be voted for, and the office or offices which he or they are intended to fill. And before receiving any vote, the supervisors, or a majority of them, must be satisfied of the age and citizenship of the person claiming to vote, and that he has in fact a residence in the county, city, town or plantation which is printed or written on the vote offered by him. If his right to vote is challenged, they may require him to make true answers, upon oath, to all interrogatories touching his age, citizenship, residence, and right to vote, and shall hear any other evidence offered by him, or by those who challenge his right. They shall keep correct poll-lists of the names of all persons allowed to vote, and of their respective places of residence in this State, and also the number of the regiment and company or battery to which they belong; which lists shall be certified by them or by a majority of them, to be correct, and that such residence is in accordance with the indorsement of the residence of each voter on his vote. They shall check the name of every person before he is allow to vote, and the check-mark shall be plainly made against his name on the poll-lists. They shall sort, count and publicly declare the votes at the head of their respective commands on the day of election, unless prevented by the public enemy, and in that case as soon thereafter as may be; and on the same day of said declaration they shall form a list of the persons voted for, with the number of votes for each person against his name, and the office which he was intended to fill, and shall sign and seal up such list and cause the same, together with the poll-lists aforesaid, to be delivered into the office of the secretary of state aforesaid, *on or before the first day of December, in the year one thousand eight hundred and sixty-four and* on or before the fifteenth day of November *annually thereafter forever.* The legislature of this State may pass any law additional to the foregoing provisions, if any shall, in practice, be found necessary in order more fully to carry into effect the purpose thereof.

Article III

DISTRIBUTION OF POWERS

SEC. 1. The powers of this government shall be divided into three distinct departments, the Legislative, Executive and Judicial.

SEC. 2. No person or persons, belonging to one of these departments, shall exercise any of the powers properly belonging to either of the others, except in the cases herein expressly directed or permitted.

Article IV.—Part First

LEGISLATIVE POWER.—HOUSE OF REPRESENTATIVES

SEC. 1. The legislative power shall be vested in two distinct branches, a House of Representatives, and a Senate, each to have a negative on the other, and both to be styled the Legislature of Maine and the style of their acts and laws shall be, " BE IT ENACTED BY THE SENATE AND HOUSE OF REPRESENTATIVES, IN LEGISLATURE ASSEMBLED."

SEC. 2. The House of Representatives shall consist of one hundred and fifty-one members, to be elected by the qualified electors, for *one year* from the day next preceding the *annual* meeting of the Legislature. The Legislature, *which shall first be convened under this Constitution,* shall, *on or before the fifteenth day of August, in the year of our Lord, one thousand eight hundred and twenty-one, and the Legislature,* within every *subsequent* period of at most ten years, and at least five, cause the number of the inhabitants of the State to be ascertained, exclusive of foreigners not naturalized and Indians not taxed. The number of Representatives shall, at the several periods of making such enumeration, be fixed and apportioned among the several counties as near as may be, according to the number of inhabitants, having regard to the relative increase of population. *The number of representatives shall, on said first apportionment, be not less than one hundred nor more than one hundred and fifty.*

SEC. 3. Each town having fifteen hundred inhabitants may elect one representative; each town having three thousand seven hundred and fifty may elect two; each town having six thousand seven hundred and fifty may elect three; each town having ten thousand five hundred may elect four; each town having fifteen thousand may elect five; each town having twenty thousand two hundred and fifty may elect six; each town having twenty-six thousand two hundred and fifty may elect seven; but no town shall ever be entitled to more than seven representatives; and towns and plantations duly organized, not having fifteen hundred inhabitants, shall be classed, as conveniently as may be, into districts containing that number, and so as not to divide towns; and each such district may elect one representative; *and, when on this apportionment the number of representatives shall be two hundred, a different apportionment shall take place upon the above principle;* and, in case the fifteen hundred shall be too large or too small to apportion all the representatives to any county, it shall be so increased or diminished as to give the number of representatives according to the above rule and proportion; and whenever any town or towns, plantation or plantations not entitled to elect a representative shall determine against a classification with any other town or plantation, the Legislature may, at each apportionment of representatives, on the application of such town or plantation, authorize it to elect a representative for such portion of time and such periods, as shall be equal to its portion of representation; and the right of representation, so established, shall not be altered until the next general apportionment.

SEC. 4. No person shall be a member of the House of Representatives, unless he shall, at the commencement of the period for which he is elected, have been five years a citizen of the United States, have arrived at the age of twenty-one years, have been a resident in this State one year, *or from the adoption of this constitution;* and for the three months next preceding the time of his election shall have been, and, during the period for which he is elected, shall continue to be a resident in the town or district which he represents.

SEC. 5. The meetings within this State for the choice of representatives shall be warned in due course of law by the selectmen of the several towns seven days at least before the election, and the selectmen thereof shall preside impartially at such meetings, receive the votes of all the qualified electors present, sort, count and declare them in open town meeting, and in the presence of the town clerk, who shall form a list of the persons voted for, with the number of votes for each person against his name, shall make a fair record thereof in the presence of the selectmen and in open town meeting. And the towns and plantations organized by law, belonging to any class herein provided, shall hold their meetings at the same time in the respective towns and plantations; and the town and plantation meetings in such towns and plantations shall be notified, held and regulated, the votes received, sorted, counted and declared in the same manner. And the assessors and clerks of plantations shall have all the powers, and be subject to all the duties, which selectmen and town clerks have, and are subject to by this Constitution. And fair copies of the lists of votes shall be attested by the selectmen and town clerks of towns, and the assessors of plantations, and sealed up in open town and plantation meetings; and the town and plantation clerks respectively shall cause the same to be delivered into the secretary's office thirty days at least before the first Wednesday of January *annually.* And the governor and council shall examine the returned copies of such lists, and also all lists of votes of citizens in the military service, returned to the secretary's office, as provided in article second, section four, of this Constitution; and twenty days before the said first Wednesday of January, *annually,* shall issue a summons to such persons as shall appear to be elected by a plurality of all the votes returned, to attend and take their seats. But all such lists shall be laid before the House of Representatives on the first Wednesday of January *annually*, and they shall finally determine who are elected. The electors resident in any city may, at any meeting duly notified for the choice of representatives vote for such representatives in their respective ward meetings, and the wardens in said wards shall preside impartially at such meetings, receive the votes of all qualified electors present, sort, count and declare them in open ward meetings, and in the presence of the ward clerk, who shall form a list of the persons voted for, with the number of votes for each person against his name, shall make a fair record thereof in the presence of the warden, and in open ward meetings; and a fair copy of this list shall be attested by the warden and ward clerk, sealed up in open ward meeting, and delivered to the city clerk within twenty-four hours after the close of the polls. And the electors resident in any city may at any meetings duly notified and holden for the choice of any other civil officers for whom they have been required heretofore to vote in town meeting, vote for such officers in their respective wards, and the same proceedings shall be had by the warden and ward clerk in each ward, as in the case of votes for representatives. And the aldermen of any city shall be in session within twenty-four hours after the close of the polls in such meetings, and in the presence of the city clerk shall open, examine and compare the copies from the lists of votes given in the several wards, of which the city clerk shall make a record, and return therof shall be made into the Secretary of State's office in the same manner as selectmen of towns are required to do.

SEC. 6. Whenever the seat of a member shall be vacated by death, resignation, or otherwise, the vacancy may be filled by a new election.

SEC. 7. The House of Representatives shall choose their speaker, clerk and other officers.

SEC. 8. The House of Representatives shall have the sole power of impeachment.

ARTICLE IV.—PART SECOND

SENATE

SEC. 1. The Senate shall consist of *not less than twenty nor more than* thirty-one members, elected at the same time, and for the same term, as the representatives, by the qualified electors of the district into which the State shall from time to time be divided.

SEC. 2. The Legislature, *which shall be first convened under this Constitution*, shall, *on or before the fifteenth day of August in the year of our Lord, one thousand eight hundred and twenty-one, and the Legislature at* every *subsequent period of* ten years, cause the State to be divided into districts for the choice of senators. The districts shall conform, as near as may be, to county lines, and be apportioned according to the number of inhabitants. The number of senators shall *not exceed twenty at the first apportionment, and shall at each apportionment be increased, until they shall* amount to thirty-one, *according to the increase in the House of Representatives.*

SEC. 3. The meetings within this state for the election of senators shall be notified, held and regulated, and the votes received, sorted, counted, declared and recorded, in the same manner as those for representatives. And fair copies of the list of votes shall be attested by the selectmen and town clerks of towns, and the assessors and clerks of plantations, and sealed up in open town and plantation meetings; and the town and plantation clerks respectively shall cause the same to be delivered into the secretary's office thirty days at least before the first Wednesday of January. All other qualified electors, living in places unincorporated, who shall be assessed to the support of the government by the assessors of an adjacent town, shall have the privilege of voting for senators, representatives and governor in such town; and shall be notified by the selectmen thereof for that purpose accordingly.

SEC. 4. The Governor and Council shall, as soon as may be, examine the returned copies of such lists, and also the lists of votes of citizens in the military service, returned into the secretary's office, and twenty days before the said first Wednesday of January, issue a summons to such persons, as shall appear to be elected by a plurality of the votes for each district, to attend that day and take their seats.

SEC. 5. The Senate shall, on the said first Wednesday of January, *annually*, determine who are elected by a plurality of votes to be senators in each district; and in case the full number of senators to be elected from each district shall not have been so elected, the members of the house of representatives and such senators, as shall have been elected, shall from the highest numbers of the persons voted for, on said lists, equal to twice the number of senators deficient, in every district, if there be so many voted for, elect by joint ballot the number of senators required; and in this manner all vacancies in the Senate shall be supplied as soon as may be, after such vacancies happen.

SEC. 6. The senators shall be twenty-five years of age at the commencement of the term, for which they are elected, and in all other respects their qualifications shall be the same, as those of the representatives.

SEC. 7. The Senate shall have the sole power to try all impeachments, and when sitting for that purpose shall be on oath or affirmation, and no person shall be convicted without the concurrence of two-thirds of the members present. Their judgment, however, shall not extend farther than to removal from office, and disqualification to hold or enjoy any office of honor, trust or profit under this State. But the party, whether convicted or acquitted, shall nevertheless be liable to indictment, trial, judgment and punishment according to law.

SEC. 8. The Senate shall choose their president, secretary and other officers.

ARTICLE IV.—PART THIRD

LEGISLATIVE POWER

SEC. 1. The Legislature shall convene on the first Wednesday of January, *annually*, and shall have full power to make and establish all reasonable laws and regulations for the defence and benefit of the people of this State, not repugnant to this Constitution, nor to that of the United States.

SEC. 2. Every bill or resolution having the force of law, to which the concurrence of both houses may be necessary, except on a question of adjournment, which shall have passed both houses, shall be presented to the Governor, and if he approve, he shall sign it; if not, he shall return it with his objections to the house, in which it shall have originated, which shall enter the objections at large on its journals, and proceed to reconsider it. If after such reconsideration, two-thirds of that house shall agree to pass it, it shall be sent together with the objections, to the other house by which it shall be reconsidered, and, if aproved by two-thirds of that house, it shall have the same effect, as if it had been signed by the Governor; but in all such cases, the votes of both houses shall be taken by yeas and nays, and the names of the persons, voting for and against the bill or resolution, shall be entered on the journals of both houses respectively. If the bill or resolution shall not be returned by the Governor within five days (Sundays excepted) after it shall have been presented to him, it shall have the same force and effect, as if he had signed it, unless the Legislature, by their adjournment prevent its return, in which case it shall have such force and effect, unless returned within three days after their next meeting.

Sec. 3. Each house shall be the judge of the elections and qualifications of its own members, and a majority shall constitute a quorum to do business; but a smaller number may adjourn from day to day, and may compel the attendance of absent members, in such manner, and under such penalties as each house shall provide.

Sec. 4. Each house may determine the rules of its proceedings, punish its members for disorderly behavior, and, with the concurrence of two-thirds, expel a member, but not a second time for the same cause.

Sec. 5. Each house shall keep a journal, and from time to time publish its proceedings, except such parts as in their judgment may require secrecy; and the yeas and nays of the members of either house on any question, shall, at the desire of one-fifth of those present, be entered on the journals.

Sec. 6. Each house, during its session, may punish by imprisonment any person, not a member, for disrespectful or disorderly behavior in its presence, for obstructing any of its proceedings, threatening, assaulting or abusing any of its members for anything said, done, or doing in either house; *provided*, that no imprisonment shall extend beyond the period of the same session.

Sec. 7. The senators and representatives shall receive such compensation, as shall be established by law; but no law increasing their compensation shall take effect during the existence of the Legislature which enacted it. The expenses of the House of Representatives in travelling to the Legislature and returning therefrom, once in each session and no more, shall be paid by the State out of the public treasury to every member, who shall seasonably attend, in the judgment of the house, and does not depart therefrom without leave.

Sec. 8. The senators and representatives shall, in all cases except treason, felony or breach of the peace, be privileged from arrest during their attendance at, going to, and returning from each session of the Legislature; and no member shall be liable to answer for anything spoken in debate in either house, in any court or place elsewhere.

Sec. 9. Bills, orders or resolutions, may originate in either house, and may be altered, amended or rejected in the other; but all bills for raising a revenue shall originate in the House of Representatives, but the Senate may propose amendments as in other cases; *provided*, that they shall not, under color of amendment, introduce any new matter, which does not relate to raising a revenue.

SEC. 10. No senator or representative shall, during the term for which he shall have been elected, be appointed to any civil office of profit under this State, which shall have been created, or the emoluments of which increased during such term except such offices as may be filled by elections by the people, *provided, that this prohibition shall not extend to the members of the first Legislature.*

SEC. 11. No member of Congress, nor person holding any office under the United States (post-officers excepted) nor office of profit under this State, justices of the peace, notaries public, coroners and officers of the militia excepted, shall have a seat in either house during his being such member of Congress, or his continuing in such office.

SEC. 12. Neither house shall, during the session, without the consent of the other, adjourn for more than two days, nor to any other place than that in which the houses shall be sitting.

SEC. 13. The Legislature shall, from time to time, provide, as far as practicable, by general laws, for all matters usually appertaining to special or private legislation.

SEC. 14. Corporations shall be formed under general laws, and shall not be created by special acts of the Legislature, except for municipal purposes, and in cases where the objects of the corporation cannot otherwise be attained; and, however formed, they shall forever be subject to the general laws of the State.

SEC. 15. The Legislature shall, by a two-thirds concurrent vote of both branches, have the power to call constitutional conventions, for the purpose of amending this Constitution.

ARTICLE V.—PART FIRST

EXECUTIVE POWERS

SEC. 1. The supreme executive power of this State shall be vested in a Governor.

SEC. 2. The Governor shall be elected by the qualified electors, and shall hold his office *one year* from the first Wednesday of January *in each year.*

SEC. 3. The meetings for election of governor shall be notified, held, and regulated, and votes shall be received, sorted, counted, declared and recorded, in the same manner as those for senators and representatives. They shall be sealed and returned into the secretary's office in the same manner, and at the same time as those for senators. And the secretary of state for the time being shall, on the first Wednesday of January, then next, lay the lists before the Senate and House of Representatives, and also the lists of votes of citizens in the military service returned into the secretary's office, to be by them examined, and, in case of a choice by a *majority* of all the votes returned, they shall declare and publish the same. But if no person shall have a *majority* of votes, the House of Representatives shall, by ballot, from the persons having the four highest numbers of votes on the lists, if so many there be, elect two persons and make return of their names to the Senate, of whom the Senate shall, by ballot, elect one, who shall be declared the Governor.

Sec. 4. The Governor shall, at the commencement of his term, be not less than thirty years of age; a natural born citizen of the United States, have been five years, *or from the adoption of this Constitution*, a resident of the State; and at the time of his election and during the term for which he is elected, be a resident of said State.

Sec. 5. No person holding any office or place under the United States, this State, or any other power, shall exercise the office of Governor.

Sec. 6. The Governor shall at stated times, receive for his services a compensation, which shall not be increased or diminished during his continuance in office.

Sec. 7. He shall be commander-in-chief of the army and navy of the State and of the militia, except when called into the actual service of the United States; but he shall not march nor convey any of the citizens out of the State, without their consent or that of the Legislature, unless it shall become necessary, in order to march or transport them from one part of the State to another for the defence thereof.

Sec. 8. He shall nominate, and, with the advice and consent of the council, appoint all judicial officers, coroners, and notaries public; and he shall also nominate, and with the advice and consent of the council, appoint all other civil and military officers, whose appointment is not by this Constitution, or shall not by law be otherwise provided for; and every such nomination shall be made seven days, at least, prior to such appointment.

Sec. 9. He shall from time to time give the Legislature information of the condition of the State, and recommend to their consideration such measures, as he may judge expedient.

Sec. 10. He may require information from any military officer or any officer in the executive department, upon any subject relating to the duties of their respective offices.

Sec. 11. He shall have power, with the advice and consent of the council, to remit, after conviction, all forfeitures and penalties, and to grant reprieves, commutations and pardons, except in cases of impeachment, upon such conditions, and with such restrictions and limitations, as may be deemed proper, subject to such regulations as may be provided by law, relative to the manner of applying for pardons. And he shall communicate to the Legislature at each session thereof, each case of reprieve, remission of penalty, commutation or pardon granted, stating the name of the convict, the crime of which he was convicted, the sentence and its date, the date of the reprieve, remission, commutation or pardon, and the conditions, if any, upon which the same was granted.

Sec. 12. He shall take care that the laws be faithfully executed.

Sec. 13. He may, on extraordinary occasions, convene the Legislature; and in case of disagreement between the two houses with respect to the time of adjournment, adjourn them to such time as he shall think proper, not beyond the day of the next *annual* meeting; and if, since the last adjournment, the place where the Legislature were next to convene shall have become dangerous from an enemy or contagious sickness, may direct the session to be held at some other convenient place within the State.

Sec. 14. Whenever the office of Governor shall become vacant by death, resignation, removal from office or otherwise, the president of the Senate shall exercise the office of Governor until another Governor shall be duly qualified; and in case of the death, resignation, removal from office or disqualification of the president of the Senate, so exercising the office of Governor, the speaker of the House of Representatives shall exercise the office, until a president of the Senate shall have been chosen; and when the office of Governor, president of the Senate, and speaker of the House shall become vacant, in the recess of the Senate, the person, acting as Secretary of State for the time being, shall by proclamation convene the Senate, that a president may be chosen to exercise the office of Governor. And whenever either the president of the Senate or speaker of the House shall so exercise said office, he shall receive only the compensation of Governor, but his duties as president or speaker shall be suspended; and the Senate or House shall fill the vacancy until his duties as Governor shall cease.

ARTICLE V.—PART SECOND

COUNCIL

SEC. 1. There shall be a Council, to consist of seven persons, citizens of the United States, and residents of this State, to advise the Governor in the executive part of government, whom the Governor shall have full power, at his discretion, to assemble; and he with the councillors, or a majority of them, may from time to time, hold and keep a Council, for ordering and directing the affairs of State, according to law.

SEC. 2. The councillors shall be chosen *annually*, on the first Wednesday of January, by joint ballot of the senators and representatives in convention; and vacancies, which shall afterwards happen, shall be filled in the same manner; but not more than one councillor shall be elected from any district, prescribed for the election of senators; and they shall be privileged from arrest in the same manner as senators and representatives.

SEC. 3. The resolutions and advice of Council, shall be recorded in a register, and signed by the members agreeing thereto, which may be called for by either house of the Legislature; and any councillor may enter his dissent to the resolution of the majority.

SEC. 4. No member of Congress, or of the Legislature of this State, nor any person holding any office under the United States, (post officers excepted), nor any civil officers under this State (justices of the peace and notaries public excepted) shall be councillors. And no councillor shall be appointed to any office during the time for which he shall have been elected.

ARTICLE V.—PART THIRD

SECRETARY

SEC. 1. The Secretary of State shall be chosen *annually* at the first session of the Legislature, by joint ballot of the senators and representatives in convention.

SEC. 2. The records of the State shall be kept in the office of the Secretary, who may appoint his deputies, for whose conduct he shall be accountable.

SEC. 3. He shall attend the Governor and Council, Senate and House of Representatives, in person or by his deputies, as they shall respectively require.

SEC. 4. He shall carefully keep and preserve the records of all the official acts and proceedings of the Governor and Council, Senate and House of Representatives, and, when required, lay the same before either branch of the Legislature, and perform such other duties as are enjoined by this Constitution, or shall be required by law.

ARTICLE V.—PART FOURTH

TREASURER

SEC. 1. The Treasurer shall be chosen *annually*, at the first session of the Legislature, by joint ballot of the senators and representatives in convention, but shall not be eligible more than five years successively.

SEC. 2. The Treasurer shall, before entering on the duties of his office, give bond to the State, with sureties, to the satisfaction of the Legislature, for the faithful discharge of his trust.

SEC. 3. The Treasurer shall not, during his continuance in office, engage in any business of trade or commerce, or as a broker, nor as an agent or factor for any merchant or trader.

SEC. 4. No money shall be drawn from the treasury, but by warrant from the Governor and Council, and in consequence of appropriations made by law; and a regular statement and account of the receipts and expenditures of all public money, shall be published at the commencement of the *annual* session of the Legislature.

ARTICLE VI

JUDICIAL POWER

SEC. 1. The judicial power of this State shall be vested in a Supreme Judicial Court, and such other courts as the Legislature shall from time to time establish.

SEC. 2. The justices of the Supreme Judicial Court shall, at stated times receive a compensation, which shall not be diminished during their continuance in office, but they shall receive no other fee or reward.

SEC. 3. They shall be obliged to give their opinion upon important questions of law, and upon solemn occasions, when required by the Governor, Council, Senate, or House of Representatives.

SEC. 4. All judicial officers *now in office or who may be hereafter appointed* shall, *from and after the first day of March in the year eighteen hundred and forty,* hold their offices for the term of seven years from the time of their respective appointments, (unless sooner removed by impeachment or by address of both branches of the Legislature to the Executive) and no longer unless re-appointed thereto.

SEC. 5. Justices of the peace and notaries public, shall hold their offices during seven years, if they so long behave themselves well, at the expiration of which term, they may be re-appointed or others appointed, as the public interest may require.

SEC. 6. The justices of the Supreme Judicial Court shall hold no office under the United States, nor any State, nor any other office under this State, except that of justice of the peace.

SEC. 7. Judges and registers of probate shall be elected by the people of their respective counties, by a plurality of the votes given in at the *annual* election, on the second Monday of September, and shall hold their offices for four years, commencing on the first day of January next after their election. Vacancies occurring in said offices by death, resignation or otherwise, shall be filled by election in manner aforesaid, at the September election next after their occurrence; and in the meantime, the Governor, with the advice and consent of the Council, may fill said vacancies by appointment, and the persons so appointed shall hold their offices until the first day of January *thereafter*.

SEC. 8. Judges of municipal and police courts shall be appointed by the executive power, in the same manner as other judicial officers, and shall hold their offices for the term of four years; *provided, however, that the present incumbents shall hold their offices for the term for which they were elected.*

ARTICLE VII

MILITARY

SEC. 1. The captains and subalterns of the militia shall be elected by the written votes of the members of their respective companies. The field officers of regiments by the written votes of the captains and subalterns of their respective regiments. The brigadier generals in like manner, by the field officers of their respective brigades.

SEC. 2. The Legislature shall, by law, direct the manner of notifying the electors, conducting the elections, and making returns to the Governor of the officers elected; and, if the electors shall neglect or refuse to make such elections, after being duly notified according to law, the Governor shall appoint suitable persons to fill such offices.

SEC. 3. The major generals shall be elected by the Senate and House of Representatives, each having a negative on the other. The adjutant general and quartermaster general shall be chosen *annually* by joint ballot of the senators and representatives in convention. But the adjutant general shall perform the duties of quartermaster general, until otherwise directed by law. The major generals and brigadier generals, and the commanding officers of regiments and battalions, shall appoint their respective staff officers; and all military officers shall be commissioned by the Governor.

SEC. 4. The militia, as divided into divisions, brigades, regiments, battalions and companies pursuant to the laws now in force, shall remain so organized, until the same shall be altered by the Legislature.

SEC. 5. Persons of the denominations of Quakers and Shakers, justices of the Supreme Judicial Court and ministers of the gospel may be exempted from military duty, but no other person of the age of eighteen and under the age of forty-five years, excepting officers of the militia who have been honorably discharged, shall be so exempted, unless he shall pay an equivalent to be fixed by law.

Article VIII

LITERATURE

A general diffusion of the advantages of education being essential to the preservation of the rights and liberties of the people; to promote this important object, the Legislature are authorized, and it shall be their duty to require, the several towns to make suitable provision, at their own expense, for the support and maintenance of public schools; and it shall further be their duty to encourage and suitably endow, from time to time, as the circumstances of the people may authorize, all academies, colleges and seminaries of learning within the State; provided, that no donation, grant or endowment shall at any time be made by the Legislature to any literary institution now established, or which may hereafter be established, unless, at the time of making such endowment, the Legislature of the State shall have the right to grant any further powers to alter, limit or restrain any of the powers vested in, any such literary institution, as shall be judged necessary to promote the best interests thereof.

Article IX

GENERAL PROVISIONS

SEC. 1. Every person elected or appointed to either of the places or offices provided in this Constitution, and every person elected, appointed, or commissioned to any judicial, executive, military or other office under this State, shall, before he enter on the discharge of the duties of his place or office, take and subscribe the following oath or affirmation: " I ——— do swear, that I will support the Constitution of the United States, and of this State, so long as I shall continue a citizen thereof. So help me God."

" I ——— do swear, that I will faithfully discharge, to the best of my abilities, the duties incumbent on me as ——— according to the Constitution and laws of the State. So help me God." Provided, that an affirmation in the above forms may be substituted, when the person shall be conscientiously scrupulous of taking and subscribing an oath.

The oaths or affirmations shall be taken and subscribed by the Governor and councillors before the presiding officer of the Senate, in the presence of both houses of the Legislature, and by the senators and representatives before the Governor and Council, and by the residue of said officers, before such persons as shall be prescribed by the Legislature; and whenever the Governor or any councillor shall not be able to attend during the session of the Legislature to take and subscribe said oaths or affirmations, said oaths or affirmations may be taken and subscribed in the recess of the Legislature before any justice of the Supreme Judicial Court; *provided, that the senators and representatives, first elected under this Constitution shall take and subscribe such oaths or affirmations before the president of the convention.*

SEC. 2. No person holding the office of justice of the Supreme Judicial Court, or of any inferior court, attorney general, county attorney, treasurer of the State, adjutant general, judge of probate, register of probate, register of deeds, sheriffs or their deputies, clerks of the judicial courts, shall be a member of the Legislature; and any person holding either of the foregoing offices, elected to, and accepting a seat in the Congress of the United States, shall thereby vacate said office; and no person shall be capable of holding or exercising at the same time within this State, more than one of the offices before mentioned.

SEC. 3. All commissions shall be in the name of the State, signed by the Governor, attested by the secretary or his deputy, and have the seal of the State thereto affixed.

SEC. 4. And in case the elections required by this Constitution on the first Wednesday of January *annually*, by the two houses of the Legislature, shall not be completed on that day, the same may be adjourned from day to day, until completed, in the following order; the vacancies in the Senate shall first be filled; the Governor shall then be elected, if there be no choice by the people; and afterwards the two houses shall elect the Council.

SEC. 5. Every person holding any civil office under this State, may be removed by impeachment, for misdemeanor in office; and every person holding any office, may be removed by the Governor, with the advice of the Council, on the address of both branches of the Legislature. But before such address shall pass either house, the causes of removal shall be stated and entered on the journal of the house in which it originated, and a copy thereof served on the person in office, that he may be admitted to a hearing in his defence.

SEC. 6. The tenure of all offices, which are not or shall not be otherwise provided for, shall be during the pleasure of the Governor and Council.

SEC. 7. While the public expenses shall be assessed on polls and estates, a general valuation shall be taken at least once in ten years.

SEC. 8. All taxes upon real and personal estate, assessed by authority of this State, shall be apportioned and assessed equally, according to the just value thereof.

SEC. 9. The Legislature shall never, in any manner, suspend or surrender the power of taxation.

SEC. 10. Sheriffs shall be elected by the people of their respective counties, by a plurality of the votes given in on the second Monday of September, and shall hold their offices for two years from the first day of January next after their election. Vacancies shall be filled in the same manner as is provided in the case of judges and registers of probate.

SEC. 11. The attorney general shall be chosen *annually* by joint ballot of the senators and representatives in the convention. Vacancy in said office, occurring when the Legislature is not in session, may be filled by the appointment of the Governor with the advice and consent of the Council.

SEC. 12. But citizens of this State, absent therefrom in the military service of the United States or of this State, and not in the regular army of the United States, being otherwise qualified electors, shall be allowed to vote for judges and registers of probate, sheriffs, and all other county officers *on the Tuesday next after the first Monday in November, in the year one thousand eight hundred and sixty-four,* and their votes shall be counted and allowed in the same manner and with the same effect as if given on the second Monday of September in that year. And they shall be allowed to vote for all such officers on the second Monday in September *annually thereafter forever.* And the votes shall be given at the same time and in the same manner, and the names of the several candidates shall be printed or written on the same ballots with those for Governor, senators and representatives, as provided in section four, article second of this Constitution.

SEC. 13. The Legislature may enact laws excluding from the right of suffrage, for a term not exceeding ten years, all persons convicted of bribery at any election, or of voting at any election, under the influence of a bribe.

SEC. 14. The credit of the State shall not be directly or indirectly loaned in any case. The Legislature shall not create any debt or debts, liability or liabilities, on behalf of the State, which shall singly or in the aggregate, with previous debts and liabilities hereafter incurred at any one time, exceed three hundred thousand dollars, except to suppress insurrection, to repel invasion, or for purposes of war; but this amendment shall not be construed to refer to any money that has been, or may be deposited with this State by the government of the United States, or to any fund which the State shall hold in trust for any Indian tribe.

SEC. 15. *The State is authorized to issue bonds payable within twenty-one years, at a rate of interest not exceeding six per cent. a year, payable semi-annually, which bonds or their proceeds shall be devoted solely towards the reimbursement of the expenditures incurred by the cities, towns and plantations of the State for war purposes during the rebellion, upon the following basis: Each city, town and plantation shall receive from the State one hundred dollars for every man furnished for the military service of the United States under and after the call of July second, eighteen hundred and sixty-two, and accepted by the United States towards its quota for the term of three years, and in the same proportion for every man so furnished and accepted for any shorter period; and the same shall be in full payment for any claim upon the State on account of its war debts by any such municipality. A commission appointed by the Governor and Council shall determine the amount to which each city, town and plantation is entitled; to be devoted to such reimbursement, the surplus, if any, to be appropriated to the soldiers who enlisted or were drafted and went at any time during the war, or if deceased, to their legal representatives. The issue of bonds hereby authorized shall not exceed in the aggregate three million five hundred thousand dollars, and this amendment shall not be construed to permit the credit of the State to be directly or indirectly loaned in any other case or for any other purpose.*

SEC. 16. The Legislature may by law authorize the dividing of towns having not less than four thousand inhabitants, or having voters residing on any island within the limits thereof, into voting districts for the election of representatives to the Legislature, and prescribe the manner in which the votes shall be received, counted, and the result of the election declared.

Article X

SCHEDULE

Sec. 1. All laws now in force in this State, and not repugnant to this Constitution, shall remain, and be in force, until altered or repealed by the Legislature, or shall expire by their own limitation.

Sec. 2. The Legislature, whenever two-thirds of both houses shall deem it necessary, may propose amendments to this Constitution; and when any amendments shall be so agreed upon, a resolution shall be passed and sent to the selectmen of the several towns, and the assessors of the several plantations, empowering and directing them to notify the inhabitants of their respective towns and plantations, in the manner prescribed by law, at their next *annual* meetings in the month of September, to give in their votes on the question, whether such amendment shall be made; and if it shall appear that a majority of the inhabitants voting on the question are in favor of such amendment, it shall become a part of this Constitution.

Sec. 3. *After the amendments proposed herewith shall have been submitted to popular vote, the chief justice of the Supreme Judicial Court shall arrange the Constitution, as amended, under appropriate titles, and in proper articles, parts and sections, omitting all sections, clauses and words not in force, and making no other changes in the provisions or language thereof, and shall submit the same to the Legislature at its next session.* And the draft, and arrangement, when approved by the Legislature, shall be enrolled on parchment and deposited in the office of the Secretary of State; and printed copies thereof shall be prefixed to the books containing the laws of the State. And the Constitution, with the amendments made thereto, in accordance with the provisions thereof, shall be the supreme law of the State.

Sec. 4. Sections one, two and five, of article ten of the existing Constitution, shall hereafter be omitted in any printed copies thereof prefixed to the laws of the State; but this shall not impair the validity of acts under those sections; and section five shall remain in full force, as part of the Constitution, according to the stipulations of said section, with the same effect as if contained in said printed copies.

AMENDMENTS TO THE AMENDED CONSTITUTION OF MAINE

(Adopted in pursuance of the second section of the tenth article of the Amended Constitution)

Article XXII

LIMITATION OF MUNICIPAL INDEBTEDNESS

No city or town shall hereafter create any debt or liability, which singly, or in the aggregate with previous debts or liabilities, shall exceed five per centum of the last regular valuation of said city or town; *provided, however*, that the adoption of this article shall not be construed as applying to any fund received in trust by said city or town, nor to any loan for the purpose of renewing existing loans or for war, or to temporary loans to be paid out of money raised by taxation, during the year in which they are made.

[The twenty-second Amendment to the (Amended) Constitution of Maine was proposed to the people by a Resolve of the fifty-sixth Legislature passed February 9, 1877, and having been adopted by the people at the ensuing annual election, September 10, 1877, took effect as a part of the Constitution January 2, 1878, according to the provisions of the Resolve and the proclamation of Governor Connor issued December 20, 1877.]

Article XXIII

BIENNIAL ELECTIONS AND BIENNIAL SESSIONS

The governor, senators and representatives in the Legislature, shall be elected biennially, and hold office two years from the first Wednesday in January next succeeding their election; and the Legislature, at the first session next after the adoption of this article, shall make all needful provisions by law concerning the tenure of office of all county officers, and concerning the annual or biennial reports of the State treasurer and other State officers and institutions; and shall make all such provisions by law as may be required in consequence of the change from annual to biennial elections, and from annual to biennial sessions of the Legislature. *The first election under this Article shall be in the year one thousand eight hundred and eighty; and the first meeting of the Legislature under this article shall be on the first Wednesday of January, eighteen hundred and eighty-one.*

Section four, article two; section five, part one, article four; section four, part two, article four; section one, part three, article four; section thirteen, part one, article five; section two, part two, article five; section one, part three, article five; section one, part four, article five; section four, part four, article five; section three, article seven; section four, article nine, and section eleven, article nine, are amended, by substituting the word 'biennial' for the word "annual" wherever it occurs.

Section two, part one, article five, is amended, by striking out all after the word "office" and substituting therefor the following words: 'for two years from the first Wednesday of January next following the election.' Section seven, article six, and section two, article ten, are hereby amended by striking out the word "annual" and insert in place thereof the word 'biennial.'

[The twenty-third Amendment was proposed to the people by a Resolve of the fifty-eighth Legislature passed March 4, 1879, and having been adopted September 8, was declared to have become a part of the Constitution by a Resolve of March 18, 1880.]

Article XXIV

ELECTION OF GOVERNOR BY PLURALITY VOTE

The Constitution of this State shall be amended, in the third section of the first part of article five, by striking out the word "majority," wherever it occurs therein, and inserting in the place thereof the word 'plurality.'

[The twenty-fourth Amendment was proposed to the people by a Resolve of the fifty-ninth Legislature passed January 27, 1880, and having been adopted September 13, was proclaimed by Governor Davis to be a part of the Constitution, Nov. 9, 1880.]

Article XXV

BIENNIAL LEGISLATIVE TERMS

Section two, article four, part first, of the Constitution of this State, as amended under the " resolutions concerning an amendment of the Constitution of Maine," approved the fourth day of March, in the year eighteen hundred and seventy-nine, shall be further amended by striking out the words " first Wednesday in January next succeeding their election," and inserting in place thereof the words ' day next preceding the biennial meeting of the Legislature, and the amendment herein proposed, if adopted, shall determine the term of office of senators and representatives to be elected at the annual meeting in September, in the year eighteen hundred and eighty, as well as the term of senators and representatives thereafter to be elected,' so that said section, as amended, shall read as follows:

' SEC. 2. The House of Representatives shall consist of one hundred and fifty-one members, to be elected by the qualified electors, and hold their office two years from the day next preceding the biennial meeting of the Legislature, *and the amendment herein proposed, if adopted, shall determine the term of office of senators and representatives to be elected at the annual meeting in September, in the year eighteen hundred and eighty, as well as the term of senators and representatives thereafter to be elected.* The Legislature, *which shall first be convened under this Constitution, shall on or before the fifteenth day of August, in the year of our Lord one thousand eight hundred and twenty-one, and the Legislature,* within every *subsequent* period of at most ten years, and at least five, cause the number of the inhabitants of the State to be ascertained, exclusive of foreigners not naturalized and Indians not taxed. The number of representatives shall, at the several periods of making such enumeration, be fixed and apportioned among the several counties, as near as may be, according to the number of inhabitants, having regard to the relative increase of population. *The number of representatives shall, on said first apportionment, be not less than one hundred and not more than one hundred and fifty.*'

[The twenty-sixth amendment was proposed to the people by a Resolve of the fifty-ninth Legislature passed March 18, 1880, and was adopted September 13, as appears from the transactions of the governor and council, preserved in the office of the secretary of state, wherein it is recorded that the report of the committee on elections to that effect was accepted by the council and approved by the governor, October 20, 1880. The amendment was never proclaimed by the governor nor declared by the Legislature, and it is not known that any public evidence of its adoption is in existence.]

Article XXVI

PROHIBITION OF THE MANUFACTURE AND SALE OF INTOXICATING LIQUORS

The manufacture of intoxicating liquors, not including cider, and the sale and keeping for sale of intoxicating liquors, are and shall be forever prohibited.

Except, however, that the sale and keeping for sale of such liquors for medicinal and mechanical purposes and the arts, and the sale and keeping for sale of cider, may be permitted under such regulations as the Legislature may provide.

The Legislature shall enact laws with suitable penalties for the suppression of the manufacture, sale and keeping for sale of intoxicating liquors, with the exceptions herein specified.

[The Twenty-sixth amendment was proposed to the people by a Resolve of the Sixty-First Legislature, approved February 21, 1883, adopted September 10, proclaimed by Governor Robie December 3, 1884, and took effect on the first Wednesday of January, 1885.]

Amendment XXVII

ELIGIBILITY OF THE TREASURER OF STATE

The Treasurer shall be chosen biennially, at the first session of the Legislature, by joint ballot of the Senators and Representatives in Convention but shall not be eligible more than six years successively.

[The twenty-seventh amendment was proposed to the people by a resolve of the Sixty-third Legislature, approved March 10, 1887; adopted September 10; proclaimed by Governor Marble December 14, 1888, and took effect on the first Wednesday of January, 1889.]

Amendment XXVIII

APPOINTMENT OF ADJUTANT GENERAL

' The major generals shall be elected by the Senate and House of Representatives each having a negative on the other. The adjutant general and quarter master general shall be appointed by the governor. But the adjutant general shall perform the duties of quarter master general until otherwise directed by law. The major generals and brigadier generals and the commanding officers of regiments and battalions, shall appoint their respective staff officers; and all military officers shall be commissioned by the governor.'

[The twenty-eighth Amendment was proposed to the people by a resolve of the Sixty-fourth Legislature approved March 31, 1891; adopted Sept. 12, 1892; proclaimed by Governor Burleigh Dec. 13, 1892, and took effect on the first Wednesday of January, 1893.]

Amendment XXIX

EDUCATIONAL QUALIFICATION OF VOTERS

' No person shall have the right to vote or be eligible to office under the constitution of this state, who shall not be able to read the constitution in the English language and write his name; provided, however, that the provisions of this amendment shall not apply to any person prevented by a physical disability from complying with its requisitions, nor to any person who now has the right to vote, nor to any person who shall be sixty years of age or upwards at the time this amendment shall take effect.'

[The twenty-ninth Amendment was proposed to the people by a resolve of the Sixty-fourth Legislature; approved April 2, 1891; adopted September 12, 1892; proclaimed by Governor Burleigh December 13, 1892, and took effect on the first Wednesday of January, 1893.]

Amendment XXX

VACANCIES IN THE SENATE

Section five, in article four, part two, is hereby amended by striking out the words " and in this manner all vacancies in the senate shall be supplied as soon as may be after such vacancies happen," and substituting therefor the following:

' But all vacancies in the senate, arising from death, resignation, removal from the State, or like causes, shall be filled by an immediate election in the unrepresented district. The governor shall issue his proclamation therefor and therein fix the time of such election.' [a]

[The thirtieth amendment was proposed to the people by a resolve of the sixty-eighth legislature, approved March 27, 1897, and having been adopted September 12, 1898, was proclaimed by Governor Powers to be a part of the constitution, October 25, 1898, and took effect on the first Wednesday of January, 1899.]

---

[a] See Appendix for the original constitution of Maine, 1819.

MARYLAND

For organic acts relating to the land now included within Maryland see in other parts of this work:
    Virginia Charter of 1606 (Virginia, p. 3783).
    Virginia Charter of 1609 (Virginia, p. 3790).
    Virginia Charter of 1612 (Virginia, p. 3802).
    Ordinances for Virginia, 1621 (Virginia, p. 3810).
    Charter of Dutch West India Company, 1621 (p. 59).
    Charter to Penn, 1681 (Pennsylvania, p. 3035).

THE CHARTER OF MARYLAND—1632 *[a]

CAROLUS Dei Gratia *Angliæ Scotiæ Franciæ* et *Hiberniæ* Rex Fidei Defensor &c Omnibus ad quos præsentes litteræ nostræ pervenerint *Salutem* Cum perdilectus et perquam fidelis subditus noster CÆCILIUS CALVERT, Baro de *Baltimore* in Regno nostro *Hiberniæ* Filius et Hæres GEORGII CALVERT Militis, nuper Baronis de *Baltimore* in eodem Regno *Hiberniæ* Patris inherens vestigiis laudabili quodam et pio Christianam Religionem pariter et imperii nostri territoria dilatandi studio flagrans licentiam nobis ut copiosam Anglicanæ Gentis Coloniam Industria ac Impensa sua ad certam quandam Regionem inferius describendam in Terra quadam in Partibus Americæ hactenus inculta et Barbaris nullam divini numinis notitiam habentibus in Partibus occupata deducere possit totamq; illam Regionem cum certis quibusdam Privilegiis et jurisdictionibus ad Coloniæ suæ et Regionis prædictæ salubre Regimen et Statum pertinentibus a regia nostra Celsitudine sibi et Hæredibus suis dari concedi et confirmari humiliter supplicaverit Sciatis igitur quod nos pium et nobile præfatorum Baronum de Baltimore Propositum et Studium Regio Favore prosequentes ex Gratia speciali certa Scientia et mero Motu nostris *dedimus concessimus* et *confirmavimus* et per hanc præsentem Chartam nostram pro nobis Hæredibus et Successoribus nostris præfato *Cæcilio* modo Baroni de Baltimore Heredibus et Assignatis suis Damus, Concedimus et Confirmamus totam illam Partem Peninsulæ sive Chersonesi jacentis in Partibus *Americæ* inter Oceanum ex Oriente et sinum de *Chesopeake* ab Occidente a Residuo ejusdem per rectam Lineam a Promontorio sive Capite Terræ vocato

---

* Verified by Proceedings of the Council of Maryland, 1636–1667, pp. 3–12, containing the charter in Latin, William Hand Brown, Editor. Baltimore: Maryland Historical Society. 1885.

[a] Sir George Calvert, visiting Virginia as one of the royal commissioners to whom the government of that colony was intrusted under the second charter of 1609, explored the upper portions of Chesapeake Bay, and on his return petitioned Charles II to grant him lands for the establishment of a colony there. He died before the charter granted him was executed, and it was issued to his son, Cæcilius Calvert, Lord Baltimore. It remained in force until the Revolution of 1776.

Watkin's Point juxta Sinum prædictum prope Fluvium de *Wighco* scituato ab Occidente usque ad magnum Oceanum in Plaga Orientali ductam divisam Et inter Metam illam a Meridie usque ad Partem illam Estuarii de *Delaware* ab Aquilone quæ subjacet quadragesimo Gradui Latitudinis Septentrionalis ab Æquinoctiali ubi terminatur *Nova Anglia* totumque illius Terræ Tractum infra Metas subscriptas (videlicet) Transeundo a dicto Æstuario vocato *Delaware-Bay* recta Linea per Gradum prædictum usque ad verum Meridianis primi Fontis Fluminis de *Pattowmack* deinde vergendo versus Meridiem ad ulteriorem dicti Fluminis Ripam et eam sequendo qua Plaga occidentalis ad Meridionalem spectat usque ad Locum quendam appellatum *Cinquack* prope ejusdem Fluminis Ostium scituatum ubi in præfatum Sinum de *Chessopeake* evolvitur ac inde per Lineam brevissimam usque ad prædictum Promontorium sive Locum vocatum *Watkins' Point* Ita quod totus Terræ Tractus per Lineam prædictam inter magnum Oceanum et *Watkin's Point* divisus usque ad Promontorium vocatum *Cape Charles* et singula sua Appenditia Nobis Hæredibus et Successoribus nostris integre remaneant exceptus Imperpetuum Nec non omnes Insulas et Insululas infra limites prædictos concedimus etiam et confirmamus eidem Baroni de *Baltimore* Hæredibus et Assignatis suis omnes et singulas Insulas et Insululas ab Orientali prædictæ Regionis Littore Orientem versus in Mari natas vel nascendas infra decem Leucas marinas ab eodem Littore scituatas cum omnibus et singulis Portubus Navium Stationibus Æstuariis Fluminibus et Fretus ad Regionem vel Insulas prædictas pertinentibus Omnesque Fundos Terræ Campestria Sylvas Montana Paludes Lacus Flumina Æstuaria et Freta infra Metas Terminos et Limites prædictos scituata seu existentia, cum cujuscunque Generis Piscium tam Balænarum Sturgeonum et aliorum Regalium quam aliorum in Mari Sinubus Fretis vel Fluminibus infra Premissa Piscationibus et Piscibus ibidem captis Omnesque insuper Auri Argenti Gemmarum et Lapidum pretiosorum et alias quascunque sive Lapidum sive Metallorum sive alterius cujuscunque Rei aut Materiæ Venas Mineras et Fodinas tam apertas quam occultas infra Regionem Insulas seu Limites prædictos repertas et reperiendas. Et hoc amplius omnium ecclefiarum quas (crescente CHRISTI Cultu et Religione) infra dictam Regionem Insulas Insululas et Limites prædictos futuris Temporibus ædificari contigerit Patronatus et Advocationes una cum Licencia et Facultate Ecclesias Capellas et Oratoria in Locis infra Præmissa congruis et idoneis extruendi et fundandi eaque dedicari et sacrari juxta Leges ecclesiasticas Regni nostri *Angliæ* faciendi Cum omnibus et singulis hujusmodi ac adeo amplis Juribus Jurisdictionibus Privilegiis Prærogativis Regalitatibus Libertatibus Immunitatibus Juribusque regalibus et Franchesiis quibuscumque temporalibus tam per mare quam per Terram infra Regionem Insulas Insululas et Limites prædictos habendis exercendis utendis et gaudendis prout aliquis Episcopus *Dunelmensis* infra Episcopatum sive Comitatum Palatinum *Dunelmensem* in Regno nostro *Angliæ* unquam antehac habuit tenuit usus vel gavisus fuit seu de jure habere te nere uti vel gaudere debuit aut potuit Ipsumque modò Baronem de *Baltimore* et Hæredes suos Regionis prædictæ cæterorumque omnium Præmissorum veros et absolutos Dominos et Proprietarios (exceptis præ exceptis) salva semper Fide et Ligeancia ac Dominio directo nobis Hæredibus et Successoribus nostris debitis pro nobis Hæredibus et

Maryland—1632

Successoribus nostris facimus creamus et constituimus per Præsentes *habendum tenendum possidendum* et *gaudendum* prædictam Regionem Insulas Insululas et cætera Præmissa præfato modo Baroni de Baltimore et Hæredibus et Assignatis suis ad solum et proprium Opus et Usum ipsius modò Baronis de *Baltimore* Hæredum et Assignatorum suorum imperpetuum tenendum de nobis Hæredibus et Successoribus nostris Regibus *Angliæ* ut de Castro nostro de *Windsor* in Comitatu nostro *Berkeiæ*, in liberto et communi Soccagio per Fidelitatem tantum pro omnibus Servitiis et non in Capite nec per Servitium militare reddendo inde nobis Hæredibus et Successoribus nostris duas Sagittas Indicas Partium illarum apud dictum Castrum de *Windsor* Singulis Annis tradendas in Die Martis in Septimana Paschæ Ac etiam quintam Partem omnis Metalli Aurei et Argentei Anglicè *of Gold and Silver Ore* quod infra prædictos Limites de Tempore in Tempus contigerit inveniri Ut vero prædicta Regio sic a nobis concessa et descripta cæteris omnibus illius Terræ Regionibus præfulgeat et amplioribus Titulis decoretur sciatis quod nos de ampliori Gratia nostra certa scientia et mero Motu nostris dictam Regionem ac Insulas in Provinciam erigendas esse duximus prout eas ex Plenitudine Potestatis et Prærogativæ nostræ regiæ pro nobis Hæredibus et Successoribus nostris in Provinciam erigimus et incorporamus eamque TERRAM MARIÆ *Anglice* MARYLAND nominamus et sic in futuro nominari volumus Et quoniam præfatum modò Baronem de *Baltimore* totius Provinciæ antedictæ verum dominum et Proprietarium superius fecimus et ordinavimus Ulterius igitur sciatis quod Nos pro Nobis Hæredibus et Successoribus nostris eidem modo Baroni (de cujus Fide Prudentia Justicia et provida Animi circumspectione plurimum confidimus) et Hæredibus suis pro bono et fælici dictæ Provinciæ Regimine Leges quascunque sive ad Publicum ejusdem Provinciæ Statum sive ad privatam singulorum Utilitatem pertinentes juxta sanas Discretiones suas de et cum concilio Assensu et Approbatione Liberorum Hominum ejusdem Provinciæ vel majoris Partis eorundem vel eorum Legatorum vel Deputatorum quos ad Leges condendas quum et quoties Opus fuerit a præfato modò Barone de *Baltimore* ac Hæredibus suis ac in Forma quæ illi vel illis melior esse videbitur convocari volumus condendi faciendi edendi et sub Sigillo prædicti modò Baronis de *Baltimore* ac Hæredum suorum promulgandi easque in omnes Homines infra dictam Provinciam et Limites ejusdem pro Tempore existentes vel sub illius vel illorum Regimine et Potestate *Terram Mariæ* versus navigandos aut inde redeuntes extra vel ad Terram Angliæ vel extra vel ad aliqua alia Dominia nostra vel aliena ubilibet constitutos per mulctarum Impositionem Incarcerationem et aliam quamlibet Coercionem etiam si opporteat et Delicti Qualitas id exigerit per Membri vel Vitæ Privationem per se præfatum modò Baronem de *Baltimore* et Hæredes suos seu per Deputatum Locum-tenentes Judices Justiciarios Magistratos Officiarios et Ministros suos secundum Tenorem ac veram Intentionem Præsentium constituendos et conficiendos debitè exequendi Judicesque et Justiciarios Magistratos et Officiarios quoscunque ad quascunque Causas et cum quacunque Potestate et in Forma quæ præfato modò Baroni de *Baltimore* vel Hæredibus suis melior esse videbitur Terrâ illâ ac Partium illarum Mari constituendi et ordinandi Crimina item et Excessus quoscunque contra hujusmodi Leges sive ante judicium acceptum sive post remittendi

relaxandi et pardonandi et abolendi cæteraque omnia alia et singula
ad Justitiæ Complementum Curiasque Prætoria et Tribunalia Judi-
ciorum Formas et Procedendi modos pertinentia etiam si de illis
expressa in Præsentibus non fiat mentio ac in Curiis Prætoriis et
Tribunalibus illis in Actionibus Sectis Causis et Negotiis quibuscunque tam Criminalibus quam Personalibus Realibus et Mixtis ac
Prætoriis procedendi Placita tenendi et terminandi per Judices per
ipsos Delagatos liberam plenam et omnimodam Tenore præsentium
concedimus Potestatem Quas quidem Leges sic ut præmittitur pro-
mulgandas absolutissima Juris Firmitate niti et ab omnibus Hominibus Subditis et Ligeis nostris Hæredum et Successorum nostrorum
quatenus eos concernunt in Partibus illis custodiri et sub Pœnis in
eisdem expressis et exprimendis inviolabiliter observari volumus
injungimus præcipimus et mandamus Ita tamen quod Leges prædictæ sint Rationi consonæ et non sint repugnantes nec contrariæ et
(quoad convenienter fieri poterit) consentaneæ Legibus Statutis Con-
suetudinibus ac Juribus hujus Regni nostri *Angliæ* Et quoniam in
tantæ Provinciæ Regimine repentini Casus sæpenumero contingant
quibus necesse erit Remedium adhiberi antequam Liberi tenentes
dictæ Provinciæ Legati vel Deputati sui ad Leges condendas convocari possint nec idoneum erit continuò tali Casu emergente tantum
Populum convocari Idcirco pro meliori Gubernatione tantæ Provinciæ volumus et ordinamus ac per Præsentes pro Nobis Hæredibus
et Successoribus nostris præfato modò Baroni de *Baltimore* et Hæredibus suis concedimus quod præfatus modò Baro de *Baltimore* et Hæredes sui per se vel per Magistratus et Officiarios in ea Parte debitè ut
præfertur constituendos ordinationes idoneas et salubres de Tempore
in Tempus facere et constituere possint et valeant infra Provinciam
prædictam custodiendas et observandas tam pro Custodia Pacis quam
pro meliori Regimine Populi ibidem degentis easque omnibus quos
eædem aliqualiter tangunt seu tangere possint publicè innotescere
Quas quidem Ordinationes infra dictam Provinciam inviolabiliter
observari volumus sub Pœnis in eisdem exprimendis It a quod
eædem Ordinationes sint Rationi consonæ et non sint repugnantes nec
cotrariæ sed (quoad convenienter fieri potest) consentaneæ Legibus
Statutis aut Juribus Regni nostri *Angliæ* Et ita quod eædem Ordinationes se non extendant ad Jus vel interesse alicujus Personæ sive
aliquarum Personarum de aut in Membro Vita libero Tenemento
Bonis seu Catallis aliqualiter astringendum ligandum onerandum seu
tollendum Porro ut Nova Colonia Populi eádem confluentis Multi-
tudine fœlicius crescat pariter et à Barbarorum aliorumve Hostium
Piratorum et Prædonum Incursibus firmius muniatur Idcirco Nos
pro Nobis Hæredibus et Successoribus nostris omnibus Hominibus
et Subditis nostris Hæredum et Successorum nostrorum Ligeis præsentibus et futuris nisi quibus id specialiter fuerit interdictum Se
Familiasque suas ad dictam Provinciam cum idoneis Navigiis et
Commeatu congruo transferendi Sedesque suas ibidem collocandi
incolendi et inhabitandi Castraque et Castella seu alia Fortalitia ad
præfati modò Baronis de *Baltimore* et Hæredum suorum Arbitrium
pro Defensione publica et sua extruendi et muniendi Facultatem
Licentiam et Libertatem damus et concedimus per Præsentes Statuto
de Fugitivis vel aliis quibuscunque in contrarium præmissorum in
aliquo non obstantibus Volumus etiam et ex uberiori Gratia nostra

pro Nobis Hæredibus et Successoribus nostris firmiter præcipimus
constituimus ordinamus et mandamus quod dicta provincia de nostra
ligeancia sit quodque omnes et singuli subditi ac Ligei nostri Hæredum et Successorum nostrorum in præfatam provinciam deducti vel
deducendi ipsorum et aliorum de ipsis deducentium Liberi ibidem seu
jam nati seu imposterum nascendi sint et erunt Indigenæ et Ligei
nostri Hæredum et Successorum nostrorum Regni nostri *Angliæ* et
Hiberniæ Ac in omnibus teneantur tractentur reputentur et habeantur
tanquam fideles Ligei nostri ac Hæredum et Successorum nostrorum
infra Regnum nostrum *Angliæ* oriundi Nec non Terras Tenementa
Reventiones Servitia et alia Hereditamenta quæcunque infra Regnum nostrum *Angliæ* ac alia Dominia nostra hæreditare seu aliter
perquirere recipere capere habere tenere emere et possidere ac eis
uti et gaudere eaque dare vendere alienare et legare Ac etiam omnia
Privilegia Franchesias et Libertates hujus Regni nostri *Angliæ* libere
quiete et pacifice habere et possidere eisque uti et gaudere possint
tanquam Ligei nostri infra dictum Regnum nostrum *Angliæ* nati seu
oriundi absque Impedimento Molestatione Vexatione Impetitione
sive Gravamine nostri Hæredum vel Successorum nostrorum quo-
rumcunque aliquo Statuto Actu Ordinatione seu Provisione in contrarium inde non obstante Præterea ut Subditi nostri ad Expeditionem hanc prompto et alacri animo suscipiendam incitentur sciatis
quod Nos de Gratia nostra speciali ex certa Scientia et mero motu
nostris tam præfato modo Baroni de *Baltimore* et Hæredibus suis
quam aliis omnibus de Tempore in Tempus habitandi vel cum Incolis
Provinciæ prædictæ commercium habendi Causa in Provinciam illam
profecturis omnia et singula sua Bona tam mobilia quam immobilia
Merces et Mercimonia Annonam etiam Generis cujuscunque aliaque
ad Victum et Vestitum necessaria quæcunque per Leges et Statuta
Regnorum et Dominiorum nostrorum extra eadem Regna deportari
non prohibita in quibuscunque Portubus nostris Hæredum et Successorum nostrorum in Naves imponendi et onerandi et in dictam Provinciam per se vel Servos aut Assignatos suos traducendi absque
Impedimento vel Molestatione nostri Hæredum vel Successorum nostrorum vel aliquorum Officiariorum nostrorum Hæredum et Successorum nostrorum (salvis nobis Hæredibus et Successoribus nostris
Impositionibus Subsidiis Custumis et aliis pro eisdem Rebus et Mer-
chandisis debitis et solubilibus) plenam Tenore Præsentium Licentiam damus et concedimus aliquo Statuto Actu Ordinatione aut
alia Re quacunque in contrarium non obstante Quia vero in tam
longinqua Regione inter tot Barbaras Nationes posita tam ipsorum
Barbarorum quam aliorum Hostium Piratarum et Prædonum incur-
sus verisimiliter timeri poterint Idcirco præfato modo Baroni de
Baltimore ac Hæredibus et Assignatis suis per se vel per Capitaneos
aut alios Officiarios suos omnes Homines cujuscunque Conditionis
aut undecunque oriundos in dicta Provincia de *Terra Mariæ* pro
Tempore existentes ad Vexilla vocandi Delectus habendi Bella ge-
rendi Hostesque et Prædones prædictos Partes illas infestantes Terra
Marique etiam ultra Provinciæ suæ Limites prosequendi eosque (si
Deus dederit) profligandi et capiendi et captos Jure Belli occidendi
vel pro Arbitrio suo servandi cæteraque omnia et singula quæ ad
Capitanei Generalis Exercitus Jus et Officium spectant seu spectare
consueverint faciendi adeo plenam et liberam ac quivis Capitaneus

Generalis Exercitûs unquam habüit dedimus ac pro Nobis Hæredibus et Successoribus nostris damus Potestatem per Præsentes Volumus etiam et per hanc Chartam nostram præfato modò Baroni de *Baltimore* et Hæredibus et Assignatis suis Potestatem Libertatem et Authoritatem damus ut in Casu Rebellionis repentini Tumultus aut Seditionis si quæ (quod absit) sive super Terra infra Provinciam prædictam sive super alto Mari Itinere ad dictam Provinciam de *Terra Mariæ* faciendo vel inde redeundo oriri contigerit per se vel Capitaneos Deputatos aut alios Officiarios suos sub Sigillis suis ad hoc deputandos quibus etiam nos pro nobis Hæredibus et Successoribus nostris plenissimam per Præsentes Potestatem et Authoritatem damus et concedimus adversus Rerum novarum Partium illarum Authores seditiosos Regimini illius vel illorum se subtrahentes Militiam detrectantes Transfugas Emansores Desertores vel aliter utcunque contra Rem Morem et Disciplinam militarem delinquentes Jure utantur militari adeo libere et in tam amplis Modo et Forma prout aliquis Capitaneus Generalis Exercitus Virtute Officii sui eo uti possit aut consuevit Porro ne Viris honestè natis et se ad præsentem Expeditionem accincturis ac bene de nobis et Regnis nostris Pace et Bello mereri cupientibus in tam remota longèque dissita Regione omnis ad Honores et Dignitates Via præclusa et penitus obsepta esse vidiatur propterea Nos pro Nobis Hæredibus et Successoribus nostris præfato modò Baroni de *Baltimore* et Hæredibus et Assignatis suis liberam et plenariam Potestatem damus Favores Gratias et Honores in benemeritos Cives infra Provinciam prædictam inhabitantes conferendi Eosque quibuscunque Titulis et Dignitatibus (modo tales non fuerint quæ in *Anglia* nunc sunt in Usu) pro Arbitrio suo decorandi Villas item in Burgos et Burgos in Civitates ad Inhabitantium Merita et Locorum Opportunitates cum Privilegiis et Immunitatibus congruis erigendi et incorporandi Cæteraque omnia et singula in Præmissis faciendi quæ illi vel illis congrua et opportuna esse videbuntur Etiam si talia fuerint quæ de sua Natura Mandatum et Warrantum exigant magis Speciale quam in Præsentibus sit expressum Volumus etiam ac per Præsentes pro nobis Hæredibus et Successoribus nostris præfato modò Baroni de *Baltimore* Hæredibus et Assignatis suis omnibusque prædictæ Provinciæ Incolis et Inhabitantibus quibuscunque præsentibus et futuris per hanc Chartam nostram Licentiam damus et concedimus ut Merces quascunque et Mercimonia ex dicta Provinciæ Fructibus et Commoditatibus terrestribus vel maritimis redigenda per se vel per Servos Factores aut Assignatos suos in quoscunque Portus nostros Hæredum et Successorum nostrorum *Angliæ* aut *Hiberniæ* liberè inferre et exonerare aut aliter de eisdem ibidem disponere Et si Opus fuerit easdem Merces infra unum Annum ab Exoneratione earum continuò numerandum rursus in Naves easdem vel alias onerare et in quascunque voluerint Regiones sive nostras sive extraneas de Amicitia nostra Hæredum et Successorum nostrorum deportare valeant Proviso semper quod tales et talia Custumas et Impositiones Subsidia et Telonia nobis Hæredibus et Successoribus nostris inde solvere teneantur quales et qualia reliqui subditi nostri Regni nostri *Angliæ* pro Tempore existentes solvere tenebuntur ultra quas et quæ præfatæ Provinciæ dictæ Terræ *Terra Mariæ* nuncupatæ Incolas gravari volumus Et ulterius de ampliori Gratia nostra speciali ac ex certa Scientia et mero Motu nostris pro nobis Hæredibus et Successoribus nostris concedimus præfato modo Baroni de *Balti-more* Hæredibus et Assignatis suis plenam et absolutam Potestatem et Authoritatem faciendi et erigendi et constituendi infra Provinciam de Terra Mariæ ac Insulas et Insululas prædictas tot et tales Portus maritimos Navium Stationes Crecas et alia Loca Exonerationis et Depositionis Bonorum et Mercimoniorum è Navibus Cymbis ac aliis Vasibus ac Onerationis in eadem et in tot et talibus Locis et cum talibus Juribus Jurisdictionibus Libertatibus et Privilegiis ad hujusmodi Portus spectantibus prout ei vel eis melius videbitur expedire quodque omnes et singulæ Naves Cymbæ et alia Vasa quæcunque Causa merchandizandi ad Provinciam et ex Provincia prædicta venientia et exeuntia ad hujusmodi Portus per dictum modò Baronem de *Baltimore* Hæredes et Assignatos suos sic erigendos et constituendos solummodo onerentur et exonerentur aliquo Usu Consuetudine aut aliqua alia Re in contrarium non obstante Salva semper Nobis Hæredibus et Successoribus nostris et omnibus Subitis Regni nostri *Angliæ* et *Hiberniæ* Hæredum et Successorum nostrorum Libertate piscandi Piscem marinum tam in Mari Æstuariis et Fretis et Fluminibus Navigio idoneis quam in Portubus Æstuariis et Crecis Provinciæ ante dictæ ac Privilegio saliendi et exsiccandi vel arefaciendi Pisces in Littoribus ejusdem Provinciæ et ea de Causa Buscam et Vimina ibidem crescentia succidere et capere et Casas et Tuguriola in hac Parte necessaria extruere prout rationabiliter hactenus usi fuerunt aut potuerunt Quibus quidem Libertatibus et Privilegiis dicti Subditi nostri Hæredum et Successorum nostrorum gaudebunt absque notabili Damno vel Injuria præfatò modò Baroni de *Baltimore* Hæredibus vel Assignatis suis aut ejusdem Provinciæ Incolis et Inhabitantibus in Portubus Crecis aut Littoribus prædictis et præsertim in Boscis et Sylvis ibidem crescentibus aliqualiter fienda Et si quis hujusmodi Damnum fecerit aut Injuriam gravis Indignationis nostræ Hæredum et Successorum nostrorum deditæque Legum Castigationis Periculum Pœnamque præter Emendationem subeat Volumus insuper statuimus et ordinamus ac per Præsentes pro Nobis Hæredibus et Successoribus nostris concedimus præfato modò Baroni de *Baltimore* Hæredibus et Assignatis suis quod idem Baro de *Baltimore* Hæredes et Assignati sui de Tempore in Tempus in perpetuum habeant et gaudeant Telonia et Subsidia in Portubus Navium Stationibus et aliis Crecis et Locis prædictis infra Provinciam prædictam solubilia sive emergentia pro Mercimoniis et Rebus ibidem onerandis et exonerandis per ipsos et Populos ibidem ut prædictum est Occasione emergente rationabiliter assidenda Quibus eadem justa de Causa debita Proportione assidere et inducere Telonia et Subsidia ibidem Potestatem pro Nobis Hæredibus et Successoribus nostris damus per præsentes Et ulterius de Gratia nostra speciali ac ex certa Scientia et mero Motu nostris dedimus concessimus et confirmavimus ac per Præsentes pro Nobis Hæredibus et Successoribus nostris damus concedimus et confirmamus præfato modò Baroni de *Baltimore* Hæredibus et Assignatis suis plenam et absolutam Licentiam Potestatem et Authoritatem Quod ipsé præfatus modò Baro Hæredes et Assignati sui de Tempore in Tempus imposterum imperpetuum ad ejus vel eorum Libitum et Voluntatem possint et valeant assignare alienare concedere demittere vel feoffare premissorum tot tales et tantas Partes et Parcellas eas perquirere volenti vel volentibus quot quales et quantas duxerint opportunas habendum et tenendum eisdem Personæ et Personis eas capere vel perquirere volenti et volentibus Hæredibus et Assignatis suis in Feodo simplici vel Feodo talliato vel pro Termino Vitæ Vitarum vel Annorum Tenendum de præfato modò Barone de *Baltimore* Hæredibus et Assignatis suis per tot talia et tanta hujusmodi Servitia Consuetudines et Redditus quot quanta et qualia eidem modò Baroni de *Baltimore* Hæredibus et Assignatis suis visum fuerit vel placuerit et non de nobis Hæredibus et Successoribus nostris immediatè et eisdem Personæ et Personis et earum cuilibet et quibuslibet damus et per Præsentes pro Nobis Hæredibus et Successoribus nostris concedimus Licentiam Authoritatem et Potestatem quod tales Persona et Personæ Præmissa sive aliquam inde Parcellam de præfato modò Barone de *Baltimore* Hæredibus et Assignatis suis recipere possit et possint ac tenera sibi et Assignatis suis vel Hæredibus suis de quocunque Statu Hæreditario in Feodo simplici vel Feodo talliato vel aliter prout eis et modò Baroni de *Baltimore* Hæredibus et Assignatis suis videbitur expedire de eodem Barone de *Baltimore* Hæredibus et Assignatis suis Statuto in Parliamento Domini *Edwardi* Filii Regis *Henrici* nuper Regis *Angliæ* Progenitoris nostri edito communiter vocato "*Statutum quia Emptores Terrarum* " in Regno nostro *Angliæ* dudum edito aut aliquo alio Statuto Actu Ordinatione Usu Lege vel Consuetudine aut aliqua alia Re Causa vel Materia in contrarium inde antehac habita facta edita ordinata seu provisa in contrarium inde non obstante Ac eidem Baroni de *Baltimore* et Hæredibus suis Particulas aliquas Terræ infra Provinciam prædictam in Maneria erigere et in Maneriorum eorum singulis habere et tenere Curiam Baronis et omnia quæ ad Curiam Baronis pertinent et visum Franciplegii ad Conservationem Pacis et melius Partium illarum Regimen per se et Seneschallos suos vel aliorum Maneriorum illorum cum constituta fuerint Dominos pro Tempore existentes deputandos habere et custodire et in eisdem omnibus uti ad Visum Franciplegii pertinentibus Licentiam damas et concedimus per Præsentes Ac ulterius volumus ac per Præsentes pro Nobis Hæredibus et Successoribus nostris convenimus et concedimus ad et cum præfato modò Baroni de *Baltimore* Hæredibus et Assignatis suis quod nos Hæredes et Successores nostri nullo Tempore imposterum aliquas Impositiones Custumas aut alias Taxationes Quotas seu Contributiones quascunque imponemus aut imponi faciemus aut causabimus in aut super Incolas aut Inhabitantes Provinciæ prædictæ pro Bonis Terris vel Tenementis suis infra eandem Provinciam aut super aliqua Tenementa Terras Bona seu Catalla infra Provinciam prædictam aut in aut super aliqua Bona vel Merchandizas infra Provinciam prædictam aut infra Portus aut Navium Stationes dictæ Provinciæ onerandas seu exonerandas et hanc Declarationem nostram in omnibus Curiis et Prætoriis et coram quibuscunque Judicibus nostris Hæredum et Successorum nostrorum pro sufficiente et legitima Liberatione Solutione et Acquietantia inde de Tempore in Tempus recipi et allocari volumus ac pro nobis Hæredibus et Successoribus nostris jubemus et mandamus præcipientes omnibus et singulis Officiariis et Ministris nostris Hæredum et Successorum nostrorum et sub gravi Indignatione injungentes ne quid in contrarium Præmissorum ullo unquam Tempore attemptare audeant aut eisdem ullo modo contraveniant sed præfato modò Baroni de

Baltimore et Hæredibus ac præfatæ Provinciæ de *Terra Mariæ* Incolis et Mercatoribus prædictis eorumque Servis et Ministris Factoribus et Assignatis in plenissimo hujus Chartæ nostræ Usu et Fruitione omni Tempore prout decet auxilientur et assistant Et ulterius volumus ac per Presentes pro Nobis Hæredibus et Successoribus nostris concedimus præfato modò Baroni de *Baltimore* Hæredibus et Assignatis suis et dictæ Provinciæ Terræ-tenentibus Habitatoribus præsentibus et futuris et singulis eorum quod Provincia prædicta Terræ-tenentes vel Incolæ ejusdem Coloniæ aut Patriæ vel Terræ *Virginiæ* aut alicujus alterius Coloniæ deductæ vel deducendæ Membrum vel Pars de cætero non habeantur vel reputentur aut de eisdem dependentes sint aut Regimine subsint in aliquo Ipsamque et ipsos ab eisdem separamus et separatos esse volumus per Præsentes ac quod Coronæ nostræ *Angliæ* immediate sint subjecti et de eadem dependentes imperpetuum Et si fortè imposterum contingat Dubitationes aliquas Questiones circa verum Sensum et Intellectum alicujus Verbi Clausulæ vel Sententiæ in hac præsenti Charta nostra contentæ generari eam semper et in omnibus Interpretationem adhiberi et in quibuscunque Curiis et Prætoriis nostris obtinere volumus præcipimus et mandamus quæ præfato modò Baroni de *Baltimore* Hæredibus et Assignatis suis benignior utilior et favorabilior esse judicabitur Proviso semper quod nulla fiat Interpretatio per quam sacro-sancta Dei et vera Christiana Religio aut Ligeantia Nobis Hæredibus et Successoribus nostris debita Immutatione Prejudicio vel Dispendio in aliquo patiantur Eo quod expressa Mentio &c

In cujus Rei &c T. R. apud *Westmonasterium* XX°· Die Junii.

Per Breve de Privato Sigillo.

THE CHARTER OF MARYLAND—1632 [a]

Charles, by the Grace of God, of England, Scotland, France, and Ireland, king, Defender of the Faith, &c. To all to whom these Presents come, Greeting.

II. Whereas our well beloved and right trusty Subject Caecilius Calvert, Baron of Baltimore, in our Kingdom of Ireland, Son and Heir of George Calvert, Knight, late Baron of Baltimore, in our said Kingdom of Ireland, treading in the steps of his Father, being animated with a laudable, and pious Zeal for extending the Christian Religion, and also the Territories of our Empire, hath humbly besought Leave of us, that he may transport, by his own Industry, and Expense, a numerous Colony of the English Nation, to a certain Region, herein after described, in a Country hitherto uncultivated, in the Parts of America, and partly occupied by Savages, having no knowledge of the Divine Being, and that all that Region, with some

---

[a] June 20, 1632, Patent Roll 8 Charles I, Part 3, No. 2594. In Public Record Office, London. Original in Latin; translation copied from "Laws of Maryland at Large with Proper Indexes &c. To which the Charter with an English translation is prefixed. By Thomas Bacon, Annapolis, Printed by Jonas Green, Printer to the Province, MDCCLXV. by which this translation is verified.

certain Privileges, and Jurisdiction, appertaining unto the wholesome Government, and State of his Colony and Region aforesaid, may by our Royal Highness be given, granted and confirmed unto him, and his Heirs.

III. Know Ye therefore, that We, encouraging with our Royal Favour, the pious and noble purpose of the aforesaid Barons of Baltimore, of our special Grace, certain knowledge, and mere Motion, have Given, Granted and Confirmed, and by this our present Charter, for Us our Heirs, and Successors, do Give, Grant and Confirm, unto the aforesaid Caecilius, now Baron of Baltimore, his Heirs, and Assigns, all that Part of the Peninsula, or Chersonese, lying in the Parts of America, between the Ocean on the East and the Bay of Chesapeake on the West, divided from the Residue thereof by a Right Line drawn from the Promontory, or Head-Land, called Watkin's Point, situate upon the Bay aforesaid, near the river Wigloo, on the West, unto the main Ocean on the East; and between that Boundary on the South, unto that Part of the Bay of Delaware on the North, which lieth under the Fortieth Degree of North Latitude from the Equinoctial, where New England is terminated; And all that Tract of Land within the Metes underwritten (that is to say) passing from the said Bay, called Delaware Bay, in a right Line, by the Degree aforesaid, unto the true meridian of the first Fountain of the River of Pattowmack, thence verging toward the South, unto the further Bank of the said River, and following the same on the West and South, unto a certain Place, called Cinquack, situate near the mouth of the said River, where it disembogues into the aforesaid Bay of Chesapeake, and thence by the shortest Line unto the aforesaid Promontory or Place, called Watkin's Point; so that the whole tract of land, divided by the Line aforesaid, between the main Ocean and Watkin's Point, unto the Promontory called Cape Charles, and every the Appendages thereof, may entirely remain excepted for ever to Us, our Heirs and Successors.

IV. Also We do grant and likewise Confirm unto the said Baron of Baltimore, his Heirs, and Assigns, all Islands and Inlets within the Limits aforesaid, all and singular the Islands, and Islets, from the Eastern Shore of the aforesaid Region, towards the East, which had been, or shall be formed in the Sea, situate within Ten marine Leagues from the said shore; with all and singular the Ports, Harbours, Bays, Rivers, and Straits belonging to the Region or Islands aforesaid, and all the Soil, Plains, Woods, Marshes, Lakes, Rivers, Bays, and Straits, situate, or being within the Metes, Bounds, and Limits aforesaid, with the Fishings of every kind of Fish, as well of Whales, Sturgeons, and other royal Fish, as of other Fish, in the Sea, Bays, Straits, or Rivers, within the Premises, and the fish there taken; And moreover all Veins, Mines, and Quarries, as well opened as hidden, already found, or that shall be found within the Region, Islands, or Limits aforesaid, of Gold, Silver, Gems, and precious Stones, and any other whatsoever, whether they be of Stones, or Metals, or of any other Thing, or Matter whatsoever; And furthermore the Patronages, and Advowsons of all Churches which (with the increasing Worship and Religion of Christ) within the said Region, Islands, Islets, and Limits aforesaid, hereafter shall happen to be built, together with License and Faculty of erecting and founding Churches, Chapels, and Places of Worship, in convenient and suitable places, within the Premises, and of causing the same to be dedicated and consecrated according to the Ecclesiastical Laws of our Kingdom of England, with all, and singular such, and as ample Rights, Jurisdictions, Privileges, Prerogatives, Royalties, Liberties, Immunities, and royal Rights, and temporal Franchises whatsoever, as well by Sea as by Land, within the Region, Islands, Islets, and Limits aforesaid, to be had, exercised, used, and enjoyed, as any Bishop of Durham, within the Bishoprick or County Palatine of Durham, in our Kingdom of England, ever heretofore hath had, held, used, or enjoyed, or of right could, or ought to have, hold, use, or enjoy.

V. And we do by these Presents, for us, our Heirs, and Successors, Make, Create, and Constitute Him, the now Baron of Baltimore, and his Heirs, the true and absolute Lords and Proprietaries of the Region aforesaid, and of all other Premises (except the before excepted) saving always the Faith and Allegiance and Sovereign Dominion due to Us, our Heirs, and Successors; to have, hold, possess, and enjoy the aforesaid Region, Islands, Islets, and other the Premises, unto the aforesaid now Baron of Baltimore, and to his Heirs and Assigns, to the sole and proper Behoof and Use of him, the now Baron of Baltimore, his Heirs and Assigns, forever. To Hold of Us, our Heirs and Successors, Kings of England, as of our Castle of Windsor, in our County of Berks, in free and common Soccage, by Fealty only for all Services, and not in Capite, nor by Knight's Service, Yielding therefore unto Us, our Heirs and Successors Two Indian Arrows of these Parts, to be delivered at the said Castle of Windsor, every Year, on Tuesday in Easter Week: And also the fifth Part of all Gold and Silver Ore, which shall happen from Time to Time, to be found within the aforesaid Limits.

VI. Now, That the aforesaid Region, thus by us granted and described, may be eminently distinguished above all other Regions of that Territory, and decorated with more ample Titles, Know Ye, that We, of our more especial Grace, certain knowledge, and mere Motion, have thought fit that the said Region and Islands be erected into a Province, as out of the Plenitude of our royal Power and Prerogative, We do, for Us, our Heirs and Successors, erect and incorporate the same into a Province, and nominate the same Maryland, by which Name We will that it shall from henceforth be called.

VII. And forasmuch as We have above made and ordained the aforesaid now Baron of Baltimore, the true Lord and Proprietary of the whole Province aforesaid, Know Ye therefore further, that We, for Us, our Heirs and Successors, do grant unto the said now Baron, (in whose Fidelity, Prudence, Justice, and provident Circumspection of Mind, We repose the greatest Confidence) and to his Heirs, for the good and happy Government of the said Province, free, full, and absolute Power, by the Tenor of these Presents, to Ordain, Make, and Enact Laws, of what Kind soever, according to their sound Discretions, whether relating to the Public State of the said Province, or the private Utility of Individuals, of and with the Advice, Assent, and Approbation of the Free-Men of the same Province, or the greater Part of them, or of their Delegates or Deputies, whom We will shall be called together for the framing of Laws, when, and as often as Need shall require, by the aforesaid now Baron of Baltimore, and his Heirs, and in the Form which shall seem best to him or them, and the same to publish under the Seal of the aforesaid now Baron of Baltimore, and his Heirs, and duly to execute the same upon all Persons, for the time being, within the aforesaid Province, and the Limits thereof, or under his or their Government and Power, in Sailing towards Maryland, or thence Returning, Outward-bound, either to England, or elsewhere, whether to any other Part of Our, or of any foreign Dominions, wheresoever established, by the Imposition of Fines, Imprisonment, and other Punishment whatsoever; even if it be necessary, and the Quality of the Offence require it, by Privation of Member, or Life, by him the aforesaid now Baron of Baltimore, and his Heirs, or by his or their Deputy, Lieutenant, Judges, Justices, Magistrates, Officers, and Ministers, to be constituted and appointed according to the Tenor and true Intent of these Presents, and to constitute and ordain Judges, Justices, Magistrates and Officers of what kind, for what Cause, and with what Power soever, within that Land, and the Sea of those Parts, and in such form as to the said now Baron of Baltimore, or his Heirs, shall seem most fitting; And also to Remit, Release, Pardon, and Abolish, all Crimes and Offences whatsoever against such Laws, whether before, or after Judgment passed; and to do all and singular other Things belonging to the Completion of Justice, and to Courts, Praetorian Judicatories, and Tribunals, Judicial Forms and Modes of Proceeding, although express Mention thereof in these Presents be not made; and, by Judges by them delegated, to award Process, hold Pleas, and determine in those Courts, Praetorian Judicatories, and Tribunals, in all Actions, Suits, Causes, and Matters whatsoever, as well Criminal as Personal, Real and Mixed, and Praetorian: Which said Laws, so to be published as above-said, We will enjoin, charge, and command, to be most absolute and firm in Law, and to be Kept in those Parts by all the Subjects and Liege-Men of Us, our Heirs, and Successors, so far as they concern them, and to be inviolably observed under the Penalties therein expressed, or to be expressed. So, nevertheless, that the Laws aforesaid be consonant to Reason, and be not repugnant or contrary, but (so far as conveniently may be) agreeable to the Laws, Statutes, Customs, and Rights of this Our Kingdom of England.

VIII. And forasmuch as, in the Government of so great a Province, sudden accidents may frequently happen, to which it will be necessary to apply a Remedy, before the Freeholders of the said Province, their Delegates, or Deputies, can be called together for the framing of Laws; neither will it be fit that so great a Number of People should immediately, on such emergent Occasion, be called together, We therefore, for the better Government of so great a Province, do Will and Ordain, and by these Presents, for Us, our Heirs and Successors, do grant unto the said now Baron of Baltimore, and to his Heirs, that the aforesaid now Baron of Baltimore, and his Heirs, by themselves, or by their Magistrates and Officers, thereunto duly to be constituted as aforesaid, may, and can make and constitute fit and Wholesome Ordinances from Time to Time, to be Kept and observed within the Province aforesaid, as well for the Conservation of the Peace, as for the better Government of the People inhabiting therein, and publicly to notify the same to all Persons whom the same in any wise do or may affect. Which Ordinances

We will to be inviolably observed within the said Province, under the Pains to be expressed in the same. So that the said Ordinances be consonant to Reason and be not repugnant nor contrary, but (so far as conveniently may be done) agreeable to the Laws, Statutes, or Rights of our Kingdom of England: And so that the same Ordinances do not, in any Sort, extend to oblige, bind, charge, or take away the Right or Interest of any Person or Persons, of, or in Member, Life, Freehold, Goods or Chattels.

IX. Furthermore, that the New Colony may more happily increase by a Multitude of People resorting thither, and at the same Time may be more firmly secured from the Incursions of Savages, or of other Enemies, Pirates, and Ravagers: We therefore, for Us, our Heirs and Successors, do by these Presents give and grant Power, License and Liberty, to all the Liege-Men and Subjects, present and future, of Us, our Heirs and Successors, except such to whom it shall be expressly forbidden, to transport themselves and their Families to the said Province, with fitting Vessels, and suitable Provisions, and therein to settle, dwell and inhabit; and to build and fortify Castles, Forts, and other Places of Strength, at the Appointment of the aforesaid now Baron of Baltimore, and his Heirs, for the Public and their own Defence; the Statute of Fugitives, or any other whatsoever to the contrary of the Premises in any wise notwithstanding.

X. We will also, and of our more abundant Grace, for Us, our Heirs and Successors, do firmly charge, constitute, ordain, and command, that the said Province be of our Allegiance; and that all and singular the Subjects and Liege-Men of Us, our Heirs and Successors, transplanted, or hereafter to be transplanted into the Province aforesaid, and the Children of them, and of others their Descendants, whether already born there, or hereafter to be born, be and shall be Natives and Liege-Men of Us, our Heirs and Successors, of our Kingdom of England and Ireland; and in all Things shall be held, treated, reputed, and esteemed as the faithful Liege-Men of Us, and our Heirs and Successors, born within our Kingdom of England; also Lands, Tenements, Revenues, Services, and other Hereditaments whatsoever, within our Kingdom of England, and other our Dominions, to inherit, or otherwise purchase, receive, take, have, hold, buy, and possess, and the same to use and enjoy, and the same to give, sell, alien and bequeath; and likewise all Privileges, Franchises and Liberties of this our Kingdom of England, freely, quietly, and peaceably to have and possess, and the same may use and enjoy in the same manner as our Liege-Men born, or to be born within our said Kingdom of England, without Impediment, Molestation, Vexation, Impeachment, or Grievance of Us, or any of our Heirs or Successors; any Statute, Act, Ordinance, or Provision to the contrary thereof, notwithstanding.

XI. Furthermore, That our Subjects may be incited to undertake this Expedition with a ready and cheerful mind: Know Ye, that We, of our especial Grace, certain Knowledge, and mere Motion, do, by the Tenor of these Presents, give and grant, as well as to the aforesaid Baron of Baltimore, and to his Heirs, as to all other Persons who shall from Time to Time repair to the said Province, either for the Sake of Inhabiting, or of Trading with the Inhabitants of the Province aforesaid, full License to Ship and Lade in any the Ports of Us, our Heirs and Successors, all and singular their Goods, as well movable, as immovable, Wares and Merchandizes, likewise Grain of what Sort soever, and other Things whatsoever necessary for Food and Clothing, by the Laws and Statutes of our Kingdoms and Dominions, not prohibited to be transported out of the said Kingdoms; and the same to transport, by themselves, or their Servants or Assigns, into the said Province, without the Impediment or Molestation of Us, our Heirs or Successors, or any Officers of Us, our Heirs or Successors, (Saving unto Us, our Heirs and Successors, the Impositions, Subsidies, Customs, and other Dues payable for the same Goods and Merchandizes) any Statute, Act, Ordinance, or other Thing whatsoever to the contrary notwithstanding.

XII. But because, that in so remote a Region, placed among so many barbarous Nations, the Incursions as well of the Barbarians themselves, as of other Enemies, Pirates and Ravagers, probably will be feared. Therefore We have Given, and for Us, our Heirs, and Sucessors, do Give by these Presents, as full and unrestrained Power, as any Captain-General of an Army ever hath had, unto the aforesaid now Baron of Baltimore, and to his Heirs and Assigns, by themselves, or by their Captains, or other Officers to summon to their Standards, and to array all men, of whatsoever Condition, or wheresoever born, for the Time being, in the said Province of Maryland, to wage War, and to pursue, even beyond the Limits of their Province, the Enemies and Ravagers aforesaid, infesting those Parts by Land and by Sea, and (if God shall grant it) to vanquish and captivate them, and the Captives to put to Death, or, according to their Discretion, to save, and to do all other and singular the Things which appertain, or have been accustomed to appertain unto the Authority and Office of a Captain-General of an Army.

XIII. We also will, and by this our Charter, do give unto the aforesaid now Baron of Baltimore, and to his Heirs and Assigns, Power, Liberty, and Authority, that, in Case of Rebellion, sudden Tumult, or Sedition, if any (which God forbid) should happen to arise, whether upon Land within the Province aforesaid, or upon the High Sea in making a Voyage to the said Province of Maryland, or in returning thence, they may, by themselves, or by their Captains, or other Officers, thereunto deputed under their Seals (to whom We, for Us, our Heirs and Successors, by these Presents, do Give and Grant the fullest Power and Authority) exercise Martial Law as freely, and in as ample Manner and Form, as any Captain-General of an Army, by virtue of his Office may, or hath accustomed to use the same, against the seditious Authors of Innovations in those Parts, withdrawing themselves from the Government of him or them, refusing to serve in War, flying over to the Enemy, exceeding their Leave of Absence, Deserters, or otherwise howsoever offending against the Rule, Law, or Discipline of War.

XIV. Moreover, left in so remote and far distant a Region, every Access to Honors and Dignities may seem to be precluded, and utterly barred, to Men well born, who are preparing to engage in the present Expedition, and desirous of deserving well, both in Peace and War, of Us, and our Kingdom; for this Cause, We, for Us, our Heirs and Successors, do give free and plenary Power to the aforesaid now Baron of Baltimore, and to his Heirs and Assigns, to confer Favors,

Rewards and Honors, upon such Subjects, inhabiting within the Province aforesaid, as shall be well deserving, and to adorn them with whatsoever Titles and Dignities they shall appoint; (so that they be not such as are now used in England) also to erect and incorporate Towns into Boroughs, and Boroughs into Cities, with suitable Privileges and Immunities, according to the Merits of the Inhabitants, and Convenience of the Places; and to do all and singular other Things in the Premises, which to him or them shall seem fitting and convenient; even although they shall be such as, in their own Nature, require a more special Commandment and Warrant than in these Presents may be expressed.

XV. We will also, and by these Presents do, for Us, our Heirs and Successors, give and grant License by this our Charter, unto the aforesaid now Baron of Baltimore, his Heirs and Assigns, and to all Persons whatsoever, who are, or shall be Residents and Inhabitants of the Province aforesaid, freely to import and unlade, by themselves, their Servants, Factors or Assigns, all Wares and Merchandizes whatsoever, which shall be collected out of the Fruits and Commodities of the said Province, whether the Product of the Land or the Sea, into any the Ports whatsoever of Us, our Heirs and Successors, of England or Ireland, or otherwise to dispose of the same there; and, if Need be, within One Year, to be computed immediately from the Time of unlading thereof, to lade the same Merchandizes again, in the same, or other Ships, and to export the same to any other Countries they shall think proper, whether belonging to Us, or any foreign Power which shall be in Amity with Us, our Heirs or Successors: Provided always, that they be bound to pay for the same to Us, our Heirs and Successors, such Customs and Impositions, Subsidies and Taxes, as our other Subjects of our Kingdom of England, for the Time being, shall be bound to pay, beyond which We will that the Inhabitants of the aforesaid Province of the said Land, called Maryland, shall not be burdened.

XVI. And furthermore, of our more ample special Grace, and of our certain Knowledge, and mere Motion, We do, for Us, our Heirs and Successors, grant unto the aforesaid now Baron of Baltimore, his Heirs and Assigns, full and absolute Power and Authority to make, erect, and constitute, within the Province of Maryland, and the Islands and Islets aforesaid, such, and so many Sea-Ports, Harbors, Creeks, and other Places of Unlading and Discharge of Goods and Merchandizes out of Ships, Boats, and other Vessels, and of Lading in the same, and in so many, and such Places, and with such Rights, Jurisdictions, Liberties, and Privileges, unto such Parts respecting, as to him or them shall seem most expedient: And, that all and every the Ships, Boats, and other Vessels whatsoever, coming to, or going from the Province aforesaid, for the Sake of Merchandizing, shall be laden and unladen at such Ports only as shall be so erected and constituted by the said now Baron of Baltimore, his Heirs and Assigns, any Usage, Custom, or other Thing whatsoever to the contrary notwithstanding, Saving always to Us, our Heirs and Successors, and to all the Subjects of our Kingdoms of England and Ireland, of Us, our Heirs and Successors, the Liberty of Fishing for Sea-Fish, as well in the Sea, Bays, Straits, and navigable Rivers, as in the Harbors, Bays, and Creeks of the Province aforesaid; and the Privilege of Salting and Drying Fish on the Shores of the same Province; and, for that Cause, to cut down and take Hedging-Wood and Twigs there growing, and to build Huts and Cabins, necessary in this Behalf, in the same Manner, as heretofore they reasonably might, or have used to do. Which Liberties and Privileges, the said Subjects of Us, our Heirs and Successors, shall enjoy, without notable Damage or Injury in any wise to be done to the aforesaid now Baron of Baltimore, his Heirs or Assigns, or to the Residents and Inhabitants of the same Province in the Ports, Creeks, and Shores aforesaid, and especially in the Woods and Trees there growing. And if any Person shall do Damage or Injury of this Kind, he shall incur the Peril and Pain of the heavy Displeasure of Us, our Heirs and Successors, and of the due Chastisement of the Laws, besides making Satisfaction.

XVII. Moreover, We will, appoint, and ordain, and by these Presents, for Us, our Heirs and Successors, do grant unto the aforesaid now Baron of Baltimore, his Heirs and Assigns, that the same Baron of Baltimore, his Heirs and Assigns, from Time to Time, forever, shall have, and enjoy the Taxes and Subsidies payable, or arising within the Ports, Harbors, and other Creeks and Places aforesaid, within the Province aforesaid, for Wares bought and sold, and Things there to be laden, or unladen, to be reasonably assessed by them, and the People there as aforesaid, on emergent Occasion; to whom We grant Power by these Presents, for Us, our Heirs and Successors, to assess and impose the said Taxes and Subsidies there, upon just Cause and in due Proportion.

XVIII. And furthermore, of our special Grace, and certain Knowledge, and mere Motion, We have given, granted, and confirmed, and by these Presents, for Us, our Heirs and Successors, do give, grant and confirm, unto the said now Baron of Baltimore, his Heirs and Assigns, full and absolute License, Power, and Authority, that he, the aforesaid now Baron of Baltimore, his Heirs and Assigns, from Time to Time hereafter, forever, may and can, at his or their Will and Pleasure, assign, alien, grant, demise, or enfeoff so many, such, and proportionate Parts and Parcels of the Premises, to any Person or Persons willing to purchase the same, as they shall think convenient, to have and to hold to the same Person or Persons willing to take or purchase the same, and his and their Heirs and Assigns, in Fee-simple, or Fee-tail, or for Term of Life, Lives or Years; to hold of the aforesaid now Baron of Baltimore, his Heirs and Assigns, by so many, such, and so great Services, Customs and Rents of this Kind, as to the same now Baron of Baltimore, his Heirs, and Assigns, shall seem fit and agreeable, and not immediately of Us, our Heirs and Successors. And We do give, and by these Presents, for Us, our Heirs and Successors, do grant to the same Person and Persons, and to each and every of them, License, Authority and Power, that such Person and Persons may take the Premises, or any Parcel thereof, of the aforesaid now Baron of Baltimore, his Heirs and Assigns, and hold the same to them and their Assigns, or Heirs, of the aforesaid Baron of Baltimore, his Heirs and Assigns, of what Estate of Inheritance soever, in Fee Simple or Fee-tail, or otherwise, as to them and the now Baron of Baltimore, his Heirs and Assigns, shall seem expedient; the Statute made in the Parliament of Lord Edward, Son of King Henry, late King of England, our Progenitor, commonly called the " Statute Quia Emptores Terrarum," heretofore published in our Kingdom of England, or any other Statute, Act, Ordinance, Usage, Law, or Custom, or any other Thing, Cause, or Matter, to the contrary thereof, heretofore had, done, published, ordained or provided to the contrary thereof notwithstanding.

XIX. We also, by these Presents, do give and grant License to the same Baron of Baltimore, and to his Heirs, to erect any Parcels of Land within the Province aforesaid, into Manors, and in every of those Manors, to have and to hold a Court-Baron, and all Things which to a Court Baron do belong; and to have and to Keep View of Frank-Pledge, for the Conservation of the Peace and better Government of those Parts, by themselves and their Stewards, or by the Lords, for the Time being to be deputed, of other of those Manors when they shall be constituted, and in the same to exercise all Things to the View of Frank Pledge belong.

XX. And further We will, and do, by these Presents, for Us, our Heirs and Successors, covenant and grant to, and with the aforesaid now Baron of Baltimore, His Heirs and Assigns, that We, our Heirs, and Successors, at no Time hereafter, will impose, or make or cause to be imposed, any Impositions, Customs, or other Taxations, Quotas, or Contributions whatsoever, in or upon the Residents or Inhabitants of the Province aforesaid for their Goods, Lands, or Tenements within the same Province, or upon any Tenements, Lands, Goods or Chattels within the Province aforesaid, or in or upon any Goods or Merchandizes within the Province aforesaid, or within the Ports or Harbors of the said Province, to be laden or unladen; And We will and do, for Us, our Heirs and Successors, enjoin and command that this our Declaration shall, from Time to Time, be received and allowed in all our Courts and Prætorian Judicatories, and before all the Judges whatsoever of Us, our Heirs and Successors, for a sufficient and lawful Discharge, Payment, and Acquittance thereof, charging all and singular the Officers and Ministers of Us, our Heirs and Successors, and enjoining them under our heavy Displeasure, that they do not at any Time presume to attempt any Thing to the contrary of the Premises, or that may in any wise contravene the same, but that they, at all Times, as is fitting, do aid and assist the aforesaid now Baron of Baltimore, and his Heirs, and the aforesaid Inhabitants and Merchants of the Province of Maryland aforesaid, and their Servants and Ministers, Factors and Assigns, in the fullest Use and Enjoyment of the Charter.

XXI. And furthermore We will, and by these Presents, for Us, our Heirs and Successors, do grant unto the aforesaid now Baron of Baltimore, his Heirs and Assigns, and to the Freeholders and Inhabitants of the said Province, both Present and to come, and to every of them, that the said Province, and the Freeholders or Inhabitants of the said Colony or Country, shall not henceforth be held or reputed a Member or Part of the Land of Virginia, or of any other Colony already transported, or hereafter to be transported, or be dependent on the same, or subordinate in any kind of Government, from which We do separate both the said Province, and Inhabitants thereof, and by these Presents do will to be distinct, and that they may be immediately subject to our Crown of England, and dependent on the same forever.

XXII. And if, peradventure, hereafter it may happen, that any Doubts or Questions should arise concerning the true Sense and Meaning of any Word, Clause, or Sentence, contained in this our present Charter, We will charge and command, That Interpretation to be applied always, and in all Things, and in all Courts and Judicatories whatsoever, to obtain which shall be judged to be the more beneficial, profitable, and favorable to the aforesaid now Baron of Baltimore, his Heirs and Assigns: Provided always, that no Interpretation thereof be made, whereby God's holy and true Christian Religion, or the Allegiance due to Us, our Heirs and Successors, may in any wise suffer by Change, Prejudice, or Diminution; although express Mention be not made in these Presents of the true yearly Value or Certainty of the Premises, or of any Part thereof; or of other Gifts and Grants made by Us, our Heirs and Successors, unto the said now Lord Baltimore, or any Statute, Act, Ordinance, Provision, Proclamation or Restraint, heretofore had, made, published, ordained or provided, or any other Thing, Cause, or Matter whatsoever, to the contrary thereof in any wise notwithstanding.

XXIII. In Witness Whereof We have caused these our Letters to be made Patent. Witness Ourself at Westminster, the Twentieth Day of June, in the Eighth Year of our Reign.

CONSTITUTION OF MARYLAND—1776 [*][a]

A Declaration of Rights, and the Constitution and Form of Government agreed to by the Delegates of Maryland, in free and full Convention assembled.

A DECLARATION OF RIGHTS, &C.

THE parliament of Great Britain, by a declaratory act, having assumed a right to make laws to bind the Colonies in all cases whatsoever, and, in pursuance of such claim, endeavoured, by force of arms, to subjugate the United Colonies to an unconditional submission to their will and power, and having at length constrained them to declare themselves independent States, and to assume government under the authority of the people;—Therefore we, the Delegates of Maryland, in free and full Convention assembled, taking into our most serious consideration the best means of establishing a good Constitution in this State, for the sure foundation and more permanent security thereof, declare,

I. That all government of right originates from the people, is founded in compact only, and instituted solely for the good of the whole.

II. That the people of this State ought to have the sole and exclusive right of regulating the internal government and police thereof.

III. That the inhabitants of Maryland are entitled to the common law of England, and the trial by jury, according to the course of

---

[*] Verified by "A Collection of the Constitutions of The Thirteen United States of North America. Published by Order of Congress, Philadelphia, By John Bryce, 1783."

[a] This constitution was framed by a convention which met at Annapolis August 14, 1776, and completed its labors November 11, 1776. It was not submitted to the people.

that law, and to the benefit of such of the English statutes, as existed at the time of their first emigration, and which, by experience, have been found applicable to their local and other circumstances, and of such others as have been since made in England, or Great Britain, and have been introduced, used and practised by the courts of law or equity; and also to acts of Assembly, in force on the first of June seventeen hundred and seventy-four, except such as may have since expired, or have been or may be altered by acts of Convention, or this Declaration of Rights—subject, nevertheless, to the revision of, and amendment or repeal by, the Legislature of this State: and the inhabitants of Maryland are also entitled to all property, derived to them, from or under the Charter, granted by his Majesty Charles I. to Cæcilius Calvert, Baron of Baltimore.

IV. That all persons invested with the legislative or executive powers of government are the trustees of the public, and, as such, accountable for their conduct; wherefore, whenever the ends of government are perverted, and public liberty manifestly endangered, and all other means of redress are ineffectual, the people may, and of right ought, to reform the old or establish a new government. The doctrine of non-resistance, against arbitrary power and oppression, is absurd, slavish, and destructive of the good and happiness of mankind.

V. That the right in the people to participate in the Legislature is the best security of liberty, and the foundation of all free government; for this purpose, elections ought to be free and frequent, and every man, having property in, a common interest with, and an attachment to the community, ought to have a right of suffrage.

VI. That the legislative, executive and judicial powers of government, ought to be forever separate and distinct from each other.

VII. That no power of suspending laws, or the execution of laws, unless by or derived from the Legislature, ought to be exercised or allowed.

VIII. That freedom of speech and debates, or proceedings in the Legislature, ought not to be impeached in any other court or judicature.

IX. That a place for the meeting of the Legislature ought to be fixed, the most convenient to the members thereof, and to the depository of public records; and the Legislature ought not to be convened or held at any other place, but from evident necessity.

X. That, for redress of grievances, and for amending, strengthening and preserving the laws, the Legislature ought to be frequently convened.

XI. That every man hath a right to petition the Legislature, for the redress of grievances, in a peaceable and orderly manner.

XII. That no aid, charge, tax, fee, or fees, ought to be set, rated, or levied, under any pretence, without consent of the Legislature.

XIII. That the levying taxes by the poll is grievous and oppressive, and ought to be abolished; that paupers ought not to be assessed for the support of government; but every other person in the State ought to contribute his proportion of public taxes, for the support of government, according to his actual worth, in real or personal property, within the State; yet fines, duties, or taxes, may properly and justly be imposed or laid, with a political view, for the good government and benefit of the community.

XIV. That sanguinary laws ought to be avoided, as far as is consistent with the safety of the State: and no law, to inflict cruel and unusual pains and penalties, ought to be made in any case, or at any time hereafter.

XV. That retrospective laws, punishing facts committed before the existence of such laws, and by them only declared criminal, are oppressive, unjust, and incompatible with liberty; wherefore no *ex post facto* law ought to be made.

XVI. That no law, to attaint particular persons of treason or felony, ought to be made in any case, or at any time hereafter.

XVII. That every freeman, for any injury done him in his person or property, ought to have remedy, by the course of the law of the land, and ought to have justice and right freely without sale, fully without any denial, and speedily without delay, according to the law of the land.

XVIII. That the trial of facts where they arise, is one of the greasest securities of the lives, liberties and estates of the people.

XIX. That, in all criminal prosecutions, every man hath a right to be informed of the accusation against him; to have a copy of the indictment or charge in due time (if required) to prepare for his defence; to be allowed counsel; to be confronted with the witnesses against him; to have process for his witnesses; to examine the witnesses, for and against him, on oath; and to a speedy trial by an impartial jury, without whose unanimous consent he ought not to be found guilty.

XX. That no man ought to be compelled to give evidence against himself, in a common court of law, or in any other court, but in such cases as have been usually practised in this State, or may hereafter be directed by the Legislature.

XXI. That no freeman ought to be taken, or imprisoned, or disseized of his freehold, liberties, or privileges, or outlawed, or exiled, or in any manner destroyed, or deprived of his life, liberty, or property, but by the judgment of his peers, or by the law of the land.

XXII. That excessive bail ought not to be required, nor excessive fines imposed, nor cruel or unusual punishments inflicted, by the courts of law.

XXIII. That all warrants, without oath or affirmation, to search suspected places, or to seize any person or property, are grievous and oppressive; and all general warrants—to search suspected places, or to apprehend suspected persons, without naming or describing the place, or the person in special—are illegal, and ought not to be granted.

XXIV. That there ought to be no forfeiture of any part of the estate of any person, for any crime except murder, or treason against the State, and then only on conviction and attainder.

XXV. That a well-regulated militia is the proper and natural defence of a free government.

XXVI. That standing armies are dangerous to liberty, and ought not to be raised or kept up, without consent of the Legislature.

XXVII. That in all cases, and at all times, the military ought to be under strict subordination to and control of the civil power.

XXVIII. That no soldier ought to be quartered in any house, in time of peace, without the consent of the owner; and in time of war, in such manner only, as the Legislature shall direct.

XXIX. That no person, except regular soldiers, mariners, and marines in the service of this State, or militia when in actual service, ought in any case to be subject to or punishable by martial law.

XXX. That the independency and uprightness of Judges are essential to the impartial administration of justice, and a great security to the rights and liberties of the people; wherefore the Chancellor and Judges ought to hold commissions during good behaviour; and the said Chancellor and Judges shall be removed for misbehaviour, on conviction in a court of law, and may be removed by the Governor, upon the address of the General Assembly; *Provided*, That two-thirds of all the members of each House concur in such address. That salaries, liberal, but not profuse, ought to be secured to the Chancellor and the Judges, during the continuance of their commissions, in such manner, and at such times, as the Legislature shall hereafter direct, upon consideration of the circumstances of this State. No Chancellor or Judge ought to hold any other office, civil or military, or receive fees or perquisites of any kind.

XXXI. That a long continuance, in the first executive departments of power or trust, is dangerous to liberty; a rotation, therefore, in those departments, is one of the best securities of permanent freedom.

XXXII. That no person ought to hold, at the same time, more than one office of profit, nor ought any person, in public trust, to receive any present from any foreign prince or state, or from the United States, or any of them, without the approbation of this State.

XXXIII. That, as it is the duty of every man to worship God in such manner as he thinks most acceptable to him; all persons, professing the Christian religion, are equally entitled to protection in their religious liberty; wherefore no person ought by any law to be molested in his person or estate on account of his religious persuasion or profession, or for his religious practice; unless, under colour of religion, any man shall disturb the good order, peace or safety of the State, or shall infringe the laws of morality, or injure others, in their natural, civil, or religious rights; nor ought any person to be compelled to frequent or maintain, or contribute, unless on contract, to maintain any particular place of worship, or any particular ministry; yet the Legislature may, in their discretion, lay a general and equal tax, for the support of the Christian religion; leaving to each individual the power of appointing the payment over of the money, collected from him, to the support of any particular place of worship or minister, or for the benefit of the poor of his own denomination, or the poor in general of any particular county: but the churches, chapels, glebes, and all other property now belonging to the church of England, ought to remain to the church of England forever. And all acts of Assembly, lately passed, for collecting monies for building or repairing particular churches or chapels of ease, shall continue in force, and be executed, unless the Legislature shall, by act, supersede or repeal the same: but no county court shall assess any quantity of tobacco, or sum of money, hereafter, on the application of any vestrymen or church-wardens; and every encumbent of the church of England, who hath remained in his parish, and performed his duty, shall be entitled to receive the provision and support established by the act, entitled "An act for the support of the clergy of the church of England, in this Province," till the November court of this present year, to be held for the county in which his parish shall lie, or partly lie, or for such time as he hath remained in his parish, and performed his duty.

XXXIV. That every gift, sale, or devise of lands, to any minister, public teacher, or preacher of the gospel, as such, or to any religious sect, order or denomination, or to or for the support, use or benefit of, or in trust for, any minister, public teacher, or preacher of the gospel, as such, or any religious sect, order or denomination—and every gift or sale of goods, or chattels, to go in succession, or to take place after the death of the seller or donor, or to or for such support, use or benefit—and also every devise of goods or chattels to or for the support, use or benefit of any minister, public teacher, or preacher of the gospel, as such, or any religious sect, order, or denomination, without the leave of the Legislature, shall be void; except always any sale, gift, lease or devise of any quantity of land, not exceeding two acres, for a church, meeting, or other house of worship, and for a burying-ground, which shall be improved, enjoyed or used only for such purpose—or such sale, gift, lease, or devise, shall be void.

XXXV. That no other test or qualification ought to be required, on admission to any office of trust or profit, than such oath of support and fidelity to this State, and such oath of office, as shall be directed by this Convention, or the Legislature of this State, and a declaration of a belief in the Christian religion.

XXXVI. That the manner of administering an oath to any person, ought to be such, as those of the religious persuasion, profession, or denomination, of which such person is one, generally esteem the most effectual confirmation, by the attestation of the Divine Being. And that the people called Quakers, those called Dunkers, and those called Menonists, holding it unlawful to take an oath on any occasion, ought to be allowed to make their solemn affirmation, in the manner that Quakers have been heretofore allowed to affirm; and to be of the same avail as an oath, in all such cases, as the affirmation of Quakers hath been allowed and accepted within this State, instead of an oath. And further, on such affirmation, warrants to search for stolen goods, or for the apprehension or commitment of offenders, ought to be granted, or security for the peace awarded, and Quakers, Dunkers or Menonists ought also, on their solemn affirmation as aforesaid, to be admitted as witnesses, in all criminal cases not capital.

XXXVII. That the city of Annapolis ought to have all its rights, privileges and benefits, agreeable to its Charter, and the acts of Assembly confirming and regulating the same, subject nevertheless to such alteration as may be made by this Convention, or any future Legislature.

XXXVIII. That the liberty of the press ought to be inviolably preserved.

XXXIX. That monopolies are odious, contrary to the spirit of a free government, and the principles of commerce; and ought not to be suffered.

XL. That no title of nobility, or hereditary honours, ought to be granted in this State.

XLI. That the subsisting resolves of this and the several Conventions held for this Colony, ought to be in force as laws, unless altered by this Convention, or the Legislature of this State.

XLII. That this Declaration of Rights, or the Form of Government, to be established by this Convention, or any part or either of them, ought not to be altered, changed or abolished, by the Legislature of this State, but in such manner as this Convention shall prescribe and direct.

This Declaration of Rights was assented to, and passed, in Convention of the Delegates of the freemen of Maryland, begun and held at Annapolis, the 14th day of August, A. D. 1776.

By order of the Convention.

MAT. TILGHMAN, *President*.

THE CONSTITUTION, OR FORM OF GOVERNMENT, &C.

I. THAT the Legislature consist of two distinct branches, a Senate and House of Delegates, which shall be styled, *The General Assembly of Maryland*.

II. That the House of Delegates shall be chosen in the following manner: All freemen, above twenty-one years of age, having a freehold of fifty acres of land, in the county in which they offer to vote, and residing therein—and all freemen, having property in this State above the value of thirty pounds current money, and having resided in the county, in which they offer to vote, one whole year next preceding the election, shall have a right of suffrage, in the election of Delegates for such county: and all freemen, so qualified, shall, on the first Monday of October, seventeen hundred and seventy-seven, and on the same day in every year thereafter, assemble in the counties, in which they are respectively qualified to vote, at the court-house, in the said counties; or at such other place as the Legislature shall direct; and, when assembled, they shall proceed to elect, *viva voce*, four Delegates, for their respective counties, of the most wise, sensible, and discreet of the people, residents in the county where they are to be chosen, one whole year next preceding the election, above twenty-one years of age, and having, in the State, real or personal property above the value of five hundred pounds current money; and upon the final casting of the polls, the four persons who shall appear to have the greatest number of legal votes shall be declared and returned duly elected for their respective counties.

III. That the Sheriff of each county, or, in case of sickness, his Deputy (summoning two Justices of the county, who are required to attend, for the preservation of the peace) shall be the judges of the election, and may adjourn from day to day, if necessary, till the same be finished, so that the whole election shall be concluded in four days; and shall make his return thereof, under his hand, to the Chancellor of this State for the time being.

IV. That all persons qualified, by the charter of the city of Annapolis, to vote for Burgesses, shall, on the same first Monday of October, seventeen hundred and seventy-seven, and on the same day in every year forever thereafter, elect, *viva voce*, by a majority of votes, two Delegates, qualified agreeable to the said charter; that the Mayor, Recorder, and Aldermen of the said city, or any three of them, be judges of the election, appoint the place in the said city for holding the same, and may adjourn from day to day, as aforesaid, and shall make return thereof, as aforesaid: but the inhabitants of the said city shall not be entitled to vote for Delegates for Anne-Arundel county, unless they have a freehold of fifty acres of land in the county distinct from the city.

V. That all persons, inhabitants of Baltimore town, and having the same qualifications as electors in the county, shall, on the same first Monday in October, seventeen hundred and seventy-seven, and on the same day in every year forever thereafter, at such place in the said town as the Judges shall appoint, elect, *viva voce*, by a majority of votes, two Delegates, qualified as aforesaid: but if the said inhabitants of the town shall so decrease, as that a number of persons, having a right of suffrage therein, shall have been, for the space of seven years successively, less than one half the number of voters in some one county in this State, such town shall thenceforward cease to send two Delegates or Representatives to the House of Delegates, until the said town shall have one half of the number of voters in some one county in this State.

VI. That the Commissioners of the said town, or any three or more of them, for the time being, shall be judges of the said election, and may adjourn, as aforesaid, and shall make return thereof, as aforesaid: but the inhabitants of the said town shall not be entitled to vote for, or be elected, Delegates for Baltimore county: neither shall the inhabitants of Baltimore county, out of the limits of Baltimore town, be entitled to vote for, or be elected, Delegates for the said town.

VII. That on refusal, death, disqualification, resignation, or removal out of this State of any Delegate, or on his becoming Governor, or member of the Council, a warrant of election shall issue by the Speaker, for the election of another in his place; of which ten days' notice, at least, (excluding the day of notice, and the day of election) shall be given.

VIII. That not less than a majority of the Delegates, with their Speaker (to be chosen by them, by ballot) constitute a House, for the transaction of any business other than that of adjourning.

IX. That the House of Delegates shall judge of the elections and qualifications of Delegates.

X. That the House of Delegates may originate all money bills, propose bills to the Senate, or receive those offered by that body; and assent, dissent, or propose amendments; that they may inquire on the oath of witnesses, into all complaints, grievances, and offences, as the grand inquest of this State; and may commit any person, for any crime, to the public jail, there to remain till he be discharged by due course of law. They may expel any member, for a great misdemeanor, but not a second time for the same cause. They may examine and pass all accounts of the State, relating either to the collection or expenditure of the revenue, or appoint auditors, to state and adjust the same. They may call for all public or official papers and records, and send for persons, whom they may judge necessary in the course of their inquiries, concerning affairs relating to the public interest; and may direct all office bonds (which shall be made payable to the State) to be sued for any breach of duty.

XI. That the Senate may be at full and perfect liberty to exercise their judgment in passing laws—and that they may not be compelled by the House of Delegates, either to reject a money bill, which the emergency of affairs may require, or to assent to some other act of legislation, in their conscience and judgment injurious to the public welfare—the House of Delegates shall not, on any occasion, or under any pretence, annex to, or blend with a money bill, any matter, clause, or thing, not immediately relating to, and necessary for the imposing, assessing, levying, or applying the taxes or supplies, to be raised for the support of government, or the current expenses of the State: and to prevent altercation about such bills, it is declared, that no bill, imposing duties or customs for the mere regulation of commerce, or inflicting fines for the reformation of morals, or to enforce the execution of the laws, by which an incidental revenue may arise, shall be accounted a money bill: but every bill, assessing, levying, or applying taxes or supplies, for the support of government, or the current expenses of the State, or appropriating money in the treasury, shall be deemed a money bill.

XII. That the House of Delegates may punish, by imprisonment, any person who shall be guilty of a contempt in their view, by any disorderly or riotous behaviour, or by threats to, or abuse of their members, or by any obstruction to their proceedings. They may also punish, by imprisonment, any person who shall be guilty of a breach of privilege, by arresting on civil process, or by assaulting any of their members, during their sitting, or on their way to, or return from the House of Delegates, or by any assault of, or obstruction to their officers, in the execution of any order or process, or by assaulting or obstructing any witness, or any other person, attending on, or on their way to or from the House, or by rescuing any person committed by the House: and the Senate may exercise the same power, in similar cases.

XIII. That the Treasurers (one for the western, and another for the eastern shore) and the Commissioners of the Loan Office, may be appointed by the House of Delegates, during their pleasure; and in case of refusal, death, resignation, disqualification, or removal out of the State, of any of the said Commissioners or Treasurers, in the recess of the General Assembly, the governor, with the advice of the Council, may appoint and commission a fit and proper person to such vacant office, to hold the same until the meeting of the next General Assembly.

XIV. That the Senate be chosen in the following manner: All persons, qualified as aforesaid to vote for county Delegates, shall, on the first day of September, 1781, and on the same day in every fifth year forever thereafter, elect, *viva voce*, by a majority of votes, two persons for their respective counties (qualified as aforesaid to be elected county Delegates) to be electors of the Senate; and the Sheriff of each county, or, in case of sickness, his Deputy (summoning two Justices of the county, who are required to attend, for the preservation of the peace,) shall hold and be judge of the said election, and make return thereof, as aforesaid. And all persons, qualified as aforesaid, to vote for Delegates for the city of Annapolis and Baltimore town, shall, on the same first Monday of September, 1781, and on the same day in every fifth year forever thereafter, elect, *viva voce*, by a majority of votes, one person for the said city and town respectively, qualified as aforesaid to be elected a Delegate for the said city and town respectively; the said election to be held in the same manner, as the election of Delegates for the said city and town; the right to elect the said elector, with respect to Baltimore town, to continue as long as the right to elect Delegates for the said town.

XV. That the said electors of the Senate meet at the city of Annapolis, or such other place as shall be appointed for convening the Legislature, on the third Monday in September, 1781, and on the same day in every fifth year forever thereafter, and they, or any twenty-four of them so met, shall proceed to elect, by ballot, either out of their own body, or the people at large, fifteen Senators (nine of whom to be residents on the western, and six to be residents on the eastern shore) men of the most wisdom, experience and virtue, above twenty-five years of age, residents of the State above three whole years next preceding the election, and having real and personal property above the value of one thousand pounds current money.

XVI. That the Senators shall be balloted for, at one and the same time, and out of the gentlemen residents of the western shore, who shall be proposed as Senators, the nine who shall, on striking the ballots, appear to have the greatest numbers in their favour, shall be accordingly declared and returned duly elected: and out of the gentlemen residents of the eastern shore, who shall be proposed as Senators, the six who shall, on striking the ballots, appear to have the greatest number in their favour, shall be accordingly declared and returned duly elected: and if two or more on the same shore shall have an equal number of ballots in their favour, by which the choice shall not be determined on the first ballot, then the electors shall again ballot, before they separate; in which they shall be confined to the persons who on the first ballot shall have an equal number: and they who shall have the greatest number in their favour on the second ballot, shall be accordingly declared and returned duly elected: and if the whole number should not thus be made up, because of an equal number, on the second ballot, still being in favour of two or more persons, then the election shall be determined by lot, between those who have equal numbers; which proceedings of the electors shall be certified under their hands, and returned to the Chancellor for the time being.

XVII. That the electors of Senators shall judge of the qualifications and elections of members of their body; and, on a contested election, shall admit to a seat, as an elector, such qualified person as shall appear to them to have the greatest number of legal votes in his favour.

XVIII. That the electors, immediately on their meeting, and before they proceed to the election of Senators, take such oath of support and fidelity to this State, as this Convention, or the Legislature, shall direct; and also an oath " to elect without favour, affection, partiality, or prejudice, such persons for Senators, as they, in their judgment and conscience, believe best qualified for the office."

XIX. That in case of refusal, death, resignation, disqualification, or removal out of this State, of any Senator, or on his becoming Governor, or a member of the Council, the Senate shall, immediately thereupon, or at their next meeting thereafter, elect by ballot (in the same manner as the electors are above directed to choose Senators) another person in his place, for the residue of the said term of five years.

XX. That not less than a majority of the Senate, with their President (to be chosen by them, by ballot) shall constitute a House, for the transacting any business, other than that of adjourning.

XXI. That the Senate shall judge of the elections and qualifications of Senators.

XXII. That the Senate may originate any other, except money bills, to which their assent or dissent only shall be given; and may receive any other bills from the House of Delegates, and assent, dissent, or propose amendments.

XXIII. That the General Assembly meet annually, on the first Monday of November, and if necessary, oftener.

XXIV. That each House shall appoint its own officers, and settle its own rules of proceeding.

XXV. That a person of wisdom, experience, and virtue, shall be chosen Governor, on the second Monday of November, seventeen hundred and seventy-seven, and on the second Monday in every year forever thereafter, by the joint ballot of both Houses (to be taken in each House respectively) deposited in a conference room; the boxes to be examined by a joint committee of both Houses, and the numbers severally reported, that the appointment may be entered; which mode of taking the joint ballot of both Houses shall be adopted in all cases. But if two or more shall have an equal number of ballots in their favour, by which the choice shall not be determined on the first ballot, then a second ballot shall be taken, which shall be confined to the persons who, on the first ballot, shall have had an equal number; and, if the ballots should again be equal between two or more persons, then the election of the Governor shall be determined by lot, between those who have equal numbers: and if the person chosen Governor shall die, resign, move out of the State, or refuse to act, (the General Assembly sitting) the Senate and House of Delegates shall, immediately thereupon, proceed to a new choice, in manner aforesaid.

XXVI. That the Senators and Delegates, on the second Tuesday of November, 1777, and annually on the second Tuesday of November forever thereafter, elect by joint ballot (in the same manner as Senators are directed to be chosen) five of the most sensible, discreet, and experienced men, above twenty-five years of age, residents in the State above three years next preceding the election, and having therein a freehold of lands and tenements, above the value of one thousand pounds current money, to be the Council to the Governor, whose proceedings shall be always entered on record, to any part whereof any member may enter his dissent; and their advice, if so required by the Governor, or any member of the Council, shall be given in writing, and signed by the members giving the same respectively: which proceedings of the Council shall be laid before the Senate, or House of Delegates, when called for by them or either of them. The Council may appoint their own Clerk, who shall take such oath of suport and fidelity to this State, as this Convention, or the Legislature, shall direct; and of secrecy, in such matters as he shall be directed by the board to keep secret.

XXVII. That the Delegates to Congress, from this State, shall be chosen annually, or superseded in the mean time by the joint ballot of both Houses of Assembly; and that there be a rotation, in such manner, that at least two of the number be annually changed; and no person shall be capable of being a Delegate to Congress for more than three in any term of six years; and no person, who holds any office of profit in the gift of Congress, shall be eligible to sit in Congress; but if appointed to any such office, his seat shall be thereby vacated. That no person, unless above twenty-one years of age, and a resident in the State more than five years next preceding the election, and having real and personal estate in this State above the value of one thousand pounds current money, shall be eligible to sit in Congress.

XXVIII. That the Senators and Delegates, immediately on their annual meeting, and before they proceed to any business, and every person, hereafter elected a Senator or Delegate, before he acts as such, shall take an oath of support and fidelity to this State, as aforesaid; and before the election of a governor, or members of the Council, shall take an oath, " elect without favour, affection, partiality, or prejudice, such person as Governor, or member of the Council, as they, in their judgment and conscience, believe best qualified for the office."

XXIX. That the Senate and Delegates may adjourn themselves respectively: but if the two Houses should not agree on the same time, but adjourn to different days, then shall the Governor appoint and notify one of those days, or some day between, and the Assembly shall then meet and be held accordingly; and he shall, if necessary, by advice of the Council, call them before the time, to which they shall in any manner be adjourned, on giving not less than ten days' notice thereof; but the Governor shall not adjourn the Assembly, otherwise than as aforesaid, nor prorogue or dissolve it, at any time.

XXX. That no person, unless above twenty-five years of age, a resident in this State above five years next preceding the election—and having in the State real and personal property, above the value of five thousand pounds, current money, (one thousand pounds whereof, at least, to be freehold estate) shall be eligible as governor.

XXXI. That the governor shall not continue in that office longer than three years successively, nor be eligible as Governor, until the expiration of four years after he shall have been out of that office.

XXXII. That upon the death, resignation, or removal out of this State, of the Governor, the first named of the Council, for the time being, shall act as Governor, and qualify in the same manner; and shall immediately call a meeting of the General Assembly, giving not less than fourteen days' notice of the meeting, at which meeting, a Governor shall be appointed, in manner aforesaid, for the residue of the year.

XXXIII. That the Governor, by and with the advice and consent of the Council, may embody the militia; and, when embodied, shall alone have the direction thereof; and shall also have the direction of all the regular land and sea forces, under the laws of this State, (but he shall not command in person, unless advised thereto by the Council, and then, only so long as they shall approve thereof); and may alone exercise all other the executive powers of government, where the concurrence of the Council is not required, according to the laws of this State; and grant reprieves or pardons for any crime, except in such cases where the law shall otherwise direct; and may, during the recess of the General Assembly, lay embargoes, to prevent the departure of any shipping, or the exportation of any commodities, for any time not exceeding thirty days in any one year—summoning the General Assembly to meet within the time of the continuance of such embargo; and may also order and compel any vessel to ride quarantine, if such vessel, or the port from which she may have come, shall, on strong grounds, be suspected to be infected with the plague; but the Governor shall not, under any pretence, exercise any power or prerogative by virtue of any law, statute, or custom of England or Great Britain.

XXXIV. That the members of the Council, or any three or more of them, when convened, shall constitute a board for the transacting of business; that the Governor, for the time being, shall preside in the Council, and be entitled to a vote, on all questions in which the Council shall be divided in opinion; and, in the absence of the Governor, the first named of the Council shall preside; and as such, shall also vote, in all cases, where the other members disagree in their opinion.

XXXV. That, in case of refusal, death, resignation, disqualification, or removal out of the State, of any person chosen a member of the council, the members thereof, immediately thereupon, or at their next meeting thereafter, shall elect by ballot another person (qualified as aforesaid) in his place, for the residue of the year.

XXXVI. That the Council shall have power to make the Great Seal of this State, which shall be kept by the Chancellor for the time being, and affixed to all laws, commissions, grants, and other public testimonials, as has been heretofore practised in this State.

XXXVII. That no Senator, Delegate of Assembly, or member of the Council, if he shall qualify as such, shall hold or execute any office of profit, or receive the profits of any office exercised by any other person, during the time for which he shall be elected; nor shall any Governor be capable of holding any other office of profit in this State, while he acts as such. And no person, holding a place of profit or receiving any part of the profits thereof, or receiving the profits or any part of the profits arising on any agency, for the supply of clothing or provisions for the Army or Navy, or holding any office under the United States, or any of them—or a minister, or preacher of the gospel, of any denomination—or any person, employed in the regular land service, or marine, of this or the United States—shall have a seat in the General Assembly or the Council of this State.

XXXVIII. That every Governor, Senator, Delegate to Congress or Assembly, and member of the Council, before he acts as such, shall take an oath " that he will not receive, directly or indirectly, at any time, any part of the profits of any office, held by any other person during his acting in his office of Governor, Senator, Delegate to Congress or Assembly, or member of the Council, or the profits or any part of the profits arising on any agency for the supply of clothing or provisions for the Army or Navy."

XXXIX. That if any Senator, Delegate to Congress or Assembly, or member of the Council, shall hold or execute any office of profit, or receive, directly or indirectly, at any time, the profits or any part of the profits of any office exercised by any other person, during his acting as Senator, Delegate to Congress or Assembly, or member of the Council—his seat (on conviction, in a Court of law, by the oath of two credible witnesses) shall be void; and he shall suffer the punishment of wilful and corrupt perjury, or be banished this State forever, or disqualified forever from holding any office or place of trust or profit, as the Court may judge.

XL. That the Chancellor, all Judges, the Attorney-General, Clerks of the General Court, the Clerks of the County Courts, the Registers of the Land Office, and the Registers of Wills, shall hold their commissions during good behaviour, removable only for misbehaviour, on conviction in a Court of law.

XLI. That there be a Register of Wills appointed for each county, who shall be commissioned by the Governor, on the joint recommendation of the Senate and House of Delegates; and that, upon the death, resignation, disqualification, or removal out of the county of any Register of Wills, in the recess of the General Assembly, the Governor, with the advice of the Council, may appoint and commission a fit and proper person to such vacant office, to hold the same until the meeting of the General Assembly.

XLII. That Sheriffs shall be elected in each county, by ballot, every third year; that is to say, two persons for the office of Sheriff for each county, the one of whom having the majority of votes, or if both have an equal number, either of them, at the discretion of the Governor, to be commissioned by the Governor for the said office; and having served for three years, such person shall be ineligible for the four years next succeeding; bond with security to be taken every year, as usual; and no Sheriff shall be qualified to act before the same is given. In case of death, refusal, resignation, disqualification, or removal out of the county before the expiration of the three years, the other person, chosen as aforesaid, shall be commissioned by the Governor to execute the said office, for the residue of the said three years, the said person giving bond and security as aforesaid: and in case of his death, refusal, resignation, disqualification, or removal out of the county, before the expiration of the said three years, the Governor, with the advice of the Council, may nominate and commission a fit and proper person to execute the said office for the residue of the said three years, the said person giving bond and security as aforesaid. The election shall be held at the same time and place appointed for the election of Delegates; and the Justices, there summoned to attend for the preservation of the peace, shall be judges thereof, and of the qualification of candidates, who shall appoint a Clerk, to take the ballots. All freemen above the age of twenty-one years, having a freehold of fifty acres of land in the county in which they offer to ballot, and residing therein—and all freemen above the age of twenty-one years, and having property in the State above the value of thirty pounds current money, and having resided in the county in which they offer to ballot one whole year next preceding the election—shall have a right of suffrage. No person to be eligible to the office of Sheriff for a county, but an inhabitant of the said county above the age of twenty-one years, and having real and personal property in the State above the value of one thousand pounds current money. The Justices aforesaid shall examine the ballots; and the two candidates properly qualified, having in each county the majority of legal ballots, shall be declared duly elected for the office of Sheriff for such county, and returned to the Governor and Council, with a certificate of the number of ballots for each of them.

XLIII. That every person who shall offer to vote for Delegates, or for the election of the Senate, or for the Sheriff, shall (if required by any three persons qualified to vote) before he be permitted to poll, take such oath or affirmation of support and fidelity to this State, as this Convention or the Legislature shall direct.

XLIV. That a Justice of the Peace may be eligible as a Senator, Delegate, or member of the Council, and may continue to act as a Justice of the Peace.

XLV. That no field officer of the militia be eligible as a Senator, Delegate, or member of the Council.

XLVI. That all civil officers, hereafter to be appointed for the several counties of this State, shall have been residents of the county, respectively, for which they shall be appointed, six months next before their appointment; and shall continue residents of their county, respectively, during their continuance in office.

XLVII. That the Judges of the General Court, and Justices of the County Courts, may appoint the Clerks of their respective Courts; and in case of refusal, death, resignation, disqualification, or removal out of the State, or from their respective shores, of the Clerks of the General Court, or either of them, in the vacation of the said Court— and in case of the refusal, death, resignation, disqualification, or removal out of the county, of any of the said County Clerks, in the vacation of the County Court of which he is Clerk—the Governor, with the advice of the Council, may appoint and commission a fit and proper person to such vacant office respectively, to hold the same until the meeting of the next General Court, or County Court, as the case may be.

XLVIII. That the Governor, for the time being, with the advice and consent of the Council, may appoint the Chancellor, and all Judges and Justices, the Attorney-General, Naval Officers, officers in the regular land and sea service, officers of the militia, Registers of the Land Office, Surveyors, and all other civil officers of government (Assessors, Constables, and Overseers of the roads only excepted) and may also suspend or remove any civil officer who has not a commission, during good behaviour; and may suspend any militia officer, for one month: and may also suspend or remove any regular officer in the land or sea service: and the Governor may remove or suspend any militia officer, in pursuance of the judgment of a Court Martial.

XLIX. That all civil officers of the appointment of the Governor and Council, who do not hold commissions during good behaviour, shall be appointed annually in the third week of November. But if any of them shall be reappointed, they may continue to act, without any new commission or qualification; and every officer, though not reappointed, shall continue to act, until the person who shall be appointed and commissioned in his stead shall be qualified.

L. That the Governor, every member of the Council, and every Judge and Justice, before they act as such, shall respectively take an oath, " That he will not, through favour, affection or partiality vote for any person to office; and that he will vote for such person as, in his judgment and conscience, he believes most fit and best qualified for the office; and that he has not made, nor will make, any promise or engagement to give his vote or interest in favor of any person."

LI. That there be two Registers of the Land Office, one upon the western, and one upon the eastern shore: that short extracts of the grants and certificates of the land, on the western and eastern shores respectively, be made in separate books, at the public expense, and deposited in the offices of the said Registers, in such manner as shall hereafter be provided by the General Assembly.

LII. That every Chancellor, Judge, Register of Wills, Commissioner of the Loan Office, Attorney-General, Sheriff, Treasurer, Naval Officer, Register of the Land Office, Register of the Chancery Court, and every Clerk of the common law courts, Surveyor and Auditor of the public accounts, before he acts as such, shall take an oath "That he will not directly or indirectly receive any fee or reward, for doing his office of   , but what is or shall be allowed by law; nor will, directly or indirectly, receive the profits or any part of the profits of any office held by any other person; and that he does not hold the same office in trust, or for the benefit of any other person."

LIII. That if any Governor, Chancellor, Judge, Register of Wills, Attorney-General, Register of the Land Office, Register of the Chancery Court, or any Clerk of the common law courts, Treasurer, Naval Officer, Sheriff, Surveyor or Auditor of public accounts, shall receive, directly or indirectly, at any time, the profits, or any part of the profits of any office, held by any other person, during his acting in the office to which he is appointed; his election, appointment and commission (on conviction in a court of law by oath of two credible witnesses) shall be void; and he shall suffer the punishment for wilful and corrupt perjury, or be banished this State forever, or disqualified forever from holding any office or place of trust or profit, as the court may adjudge.

LIV. That if any person shall give any bribe, present, or reward, or any promise, or any security for the payment or delivery of any money, or any other thing, to obtain or procure a vote to be Governor, Senator, Delegate to Congress or Assembly, member of the Council, or Judge, or to be appointed to any of the said offices, or to any office of profit or trust, now created or hereafter to be created in this State—the person giving, and the person receiving the same (on conviction in a court of law) shall be forever disqualified to hold any office of trust or profit in this State.

LV. That every person, appointed to any office of profit or trust, shall, before he enters on the execution thereof, take the following oath; to wit: "I, A. B., do swear, that I do not hold myself bound in allegiance to the King of Great Britain, and that I will be faithful, and bear true allegiance to the State of Maryland;" and shall also subscribe a declaration of his belief in the Christian religion.

LVI. That there be a Court of Appeals, composed of persons of integrity and sound judgment in the law, whose judgment shall be final and conclusive, in all cases of appeal, from the General Court, Court of Chancery, and Court of Admiralty: that one person of integrity and sound judgment in the law, be appointed Chancellor: that three persons of integrity and sound judgment in the law, be appointed judges of the Court now called the Provincial Court; and that the same Court be hereafter called and known by the name of *The General Court;* which Court shall sit on the western and eastern shores, for transacting and determining the business of the respective shores, at such times and places as the future Legislature of this State shall direct and appoint.

LVII. That the style of all laws run thus; "*Be it enacted by the General Assembly of Maryland:*" that all public commissions and grants run thus; "*The State of Maryland,*" &c. and shall be signed by the Governor, and attested by the Chancellor, with the seal of the State annexed—except military commissions, which shall not be attested by the Chancellor, or have the seal of the State annexed: that all writs shall run in the same style, and be attested, sealed and signed as usual: that all indictments shall conclude, "*Against the peace, government, and dignity of the State.*"

LVIII. That all penalties and forfeitures, heretofore going to the King or proprietary, shall go to the State—save only such, as the General Assembly may abolish or otherwise provide for.

LIX. That this Form of Government, and the Declaration of Rights, and no part thereof, shall be altered, changed, or abolished, unless a bill so to alter, change or abolish the same shall pass the General Assembly, and be published at least three months before a new election, and shall be confirmed by the General Assembly, after a new election of Delegates, in the first session after such new election; provided that nothing in this form of government, which relates to the eastern shore particularly, shall at any time hereafter be altered, unless for the alteration and confirmation thereof at least two-thirds of all the members of each branch of the General Assembly shall concur.

LX. That every bill passed by the General Assembly, when engrossed, shall be presented by the Speaker of the House of Delegates, in the Senate, to the Governor for the time being, who shall sign the same, and thereto affix the Great Seal, in the presence of the members of both Houses: every law shall be recorded in the General Court office of the western shore, and in due time printed, published, and certified under the Great Seal, to the several County Courts, in the same manner as hath been heretofore used in this State.

This Form of Government was assented to, and passed in Convention of the Delegates of the freemen of Maryland, begun and held at the city of Annapolis, the fourteenth of August, A. D. one thousand seven hundred and seventy-six.

By order of the Convention.

M. TILGHMAN, *President.*

AMENDMENTS TO THE CONSTITUTION OF 1776

(Ratified 1792)

ART. II. *Be it enacted by the general assembly of Maryland*, That no member of Congress, or person holding any office of trust or profit under the United States, shall be capable of having a seat in the general assembly, or being an elector of the senate, or holding any office of trust or profit under this State; and if any member of the general assembly, elector of the senate, or person holding any office of trust or profit under this State, shall take his seat in Congress, or accept of any office of trust or profit under the United States, or being elected to Congress, or appointed to any office of trust or profit under the United States, not make his resignation of his seat in Congress, or of his office, as the case may be, within thirty days after notice of his election or appointment to office, as aforesaid, his seat in the legislature of this State, or as elector of the senate, or of his office held under this State as aforesaid, shall be void: *Provided*, That no person who is now, or may be at any time when this act becomes part of the constitution, a member both of Congress and of the legislature of the State, or who now holds, or may hold at the time when this act becomes part of the constitution, an office as aforesaid, both under this State and the United States, shall be affected by this act, if within fifteen days after the same shall become part of the constitution he shall resign his seat in Congress or his office held under the United States.

(Ratified 1795)

ART. III. That every person being a member of either of the religious sects or societies called Quakers, Menonists, Tunkers, or Nicolites, or New Quakers, and who shall be conscientiously scrupulous of taking an oath on any occasion, being otherwise qualified and duly elected a senator, delegate, or elector of the senate, or being otherwise qualified and duly appointed or elected to any office of profit or trust, on making affirmation instead of taking the several oaths appointed by the constitution and form of government, and the several acts of assembly of this State now in force, or that hereafter may be made, such persons may hold and exercise any office of profit or trust to which he may be appointed or elected, and may, by such affirmation, qualify himself to take a seat in the legislature, and to act therein as a member of the same in all cases whatsoever, or to be an elector of the senate, in as full and ample a manner, to all intents and purposes whatever, as persons are now competent and qualified to act who are not conscientiously scrupulous of taking such oaths.

(Ratified 1798)

ART. V. SECTION 1. That the people called Quakers, those called Nicolites, or New Quakers, those called Tunkers, and those called Menonists, holding it unlawful to take an oath on any occasion, shall be allowed to make their solemn affirmation as witnesses, in the manner that Quakers have been heretofore allowed to affirm, which affirmation shall be of the same avail as an oath, to all intents and purposes whatever.

SEC. 2. Before any of the persons aforesaid shall be admitted as a witness in any court of justice in this State, the court shall be satisfied, by such testimony as they may require, that such person is one of those who profess to be conscientiously scrupulous of taking an oath.

(Ratified 1799)

ART. VI. SECTION 1. That the several counties of this State, for the purpose of holding all future elections for delegates, electors of the senate, and sheriffs of the several counties, shall be divided into separate districts, in the manner hereinafter directed, viz: Saint Mary's County shall be divided and laid off into separate districts; Kent County shall be divided and laid off into three separate districts; Calvert County shall be divided and laid off into three separate districts; Charles County shall be divided and laid off into four separate districts; Talbot County shall be divided and laid off into four separate districts; Somerset County shall be divided and laid off into three separate districts; Dorchester County shall be divided and laid off into three separate districts; Cecil County shall be divided and laid off into four separate districts; Prince George's County shall be divided and laid off into five separate districts; Queen Anne's County shall be divided and laid off into three separate districts; Worcester County shall be divided and laid off into five separate districts; Frederick County shall be divided and laid off into separate districts; Harford County shall be divided and laid off into five separate districts; Caroline County shall be divided and laid off into three separate districts; Washington County shall be divided and laid off into five separate districts; Montgomery County shall be divided and laid off into five separate districts; Alleghany County shall be divided and laid off into six separate districts; Anne Arundel County, including the city of Annapolis, shall be divided and laid off into five separate districts; Baltimore County, out of the limits of the city of Baltimore, shall be divided and laid off into seven districts; and that the city of Baltimore shall be laid off into eight districts.

SEC. 2. All and every part of the constitution and form of government, relating to the judges, time, place, and manner of holding elections in the city of Baltimore, and all and every part of the second, third, fifth, fourteenth, and forty-second sections of the constitution and form of government of this State, which relate to the judges, place, time, and manner of holding the several elections for delegates, electors of the senate, and the sheriffs of the several counties, be, and the same are hereby, abrogated, repealed, and annulled, and the same shall hereafter be regulated by law.

(Ratified 1803)

ART. VIII. That Frederick County shall be divided and laid off into nine separate districts.

(Ratified 1805)

ART. IX. SECTION 1. That this State shall be divided into six judicial districts, in manner and form following, to wit: Saint Mary's, Charles, and Prince George's Counties shall be the first district; Cecil, Kent, Queen Anne's, and Talbot Counties shall be the second district; Calvert, Anne Arundel, and Montgomery Counties shall be the third district; Caroline, Dorchester, Somerset, and Worcester Counties shall be the fourth district; Frederick, Washington, and Alleghany Counties shall be the fifth district; Baltimore and Harford Counties shall be the sixth district; and there shall be appointed for each of the said judicial districts three persons of integrity and sound legal knowledge, residents of the State of Maryland, who shall, previous to, and during their acting as judges, reside in the district for which they shall respectively be appointed, one of whom shall be styled in the commission chief judge, and the other two associate judges of the district for which they shall be appointed; and the chief judge, together with the two associate judges, shall compose the county courts in each respective district; and each judge shall hold his commission during good behavior; removal for misbehavior, on conviction in a court of law, or shall be removed by the governor, upon the address of the general assembly, provided that two-thirds of the members of each house concur in such address; and the county courts, so as aforesaid established, shall have, hold, and exercise, in the several counties of this State, all and every the powers, authorities, and jurisdictions which the county courts of this State now have, use, and exercise, and which shall be hereafter prescribed by law; and the said county courts established by this act shall respectively hold their sessions in the several counties at such times and places as the legislature shall direct and appoint; and the salaries of the said judges shall not be diminished during the period of their continuance in office.

SEC. 2. In any suit or action at law hereafter to be commenced or instituted in any county court of this State, the judges thereof, upon suggestion in writing, by either of the parties thereto, supported by affidavit, or other proper evidence, that a fair and impartial trial cannot be had in the county court of the county where such suit or action is depending, shall and may order and direct the record of their proceedings in such suit or action to be transmitted to the judges of any county court within the district, for trial, and the judges of such county court, to whom the said record shall be transmitted, shall hear and determine the same in like manner as if such suit or action had been originally instituted therein: *Provided, nevertheless,* That such suggestion shall be made as aforesaid, before or during the term in which the issue or issues may be joined in said suit or action: *And provided also,* That such further remedy may be provided by law in the premises as the legislature shall from time to time direct and enact.

ART. III. If any party presented or indicted, in any of the county courts of this State, shall suggest, in writing, to the court in which such prosecution is depending, that a fair and impartial trial cannot be had in such court, it shall and may be lawful for the said court to order and direct the record of their proceedings in the said prosecution to be transmitted to the judge of any adjoining county court, for trial; and the judges of such adjoining county court shall hear and determine the same, in the same manner as if such prosecution had been originally instituted therein: *Provided,* That such further and other remedy may be provided by law in the premises as the legislature may direct and enact.

ART. IV. If the attorney-general, or the prosecutor for the State, shall suggest, in writing, to any county court before whom an indictment is or may be depending, that the State cannot have a fair and impartial trial in such court, it shall and may be lawful for the said court, in their discretion, to order and direct the record of their proceedings in the said prosecution to be transmitted to the judges of any adjoining county court for trial; and the judges of such county court shall hear and determine the same, as if such prosecution had been originally instituted therein.

ART. V. There shall be a court of appeals, and the same shall be composed of the chief judges of the several judicial districts of the State; which said court of appeals shall hold, use, and exercise all and singular the powers, authorities, and jurisdictions, heretofore held, used, and exercised by the court of appeals of this State, and also the appellate jurisdiction heretofore used and exercised by the general court; and the said court of appeals hereby established shall sit on the western and eastern shores, for transacting and determining the business of the respective shores, at such times and places as the future legislature of this State shall direct and appoint; and any three of the said judges of the court of appeals shall form a quorum to hear and decide in all cases pending in said court; and the judge who has given a decision in any case in the county court shall withdraw from the bench upon the deciding of the same case before the court of appeals; and the judges of the court of appeals may appoint the clerks of said court for the western and eastern shores respectively, who shall hold their appointments during good behavior, removable only for misbehavior, on conviction in a court of law; and, in case of death, resignation, disqualification, or removal out of the State, or from their respective shores, of either of the said clerks, in the vacation of the said court, the governor, with the advice of the council, may appoint and commission a fit and proper person to such vacant office, to hold the same until the next meeting of the said court; and all laws passed after this act shall take effect shall be recorded in the office of the court of appeals of the western shore.

(Ratified 1807)

ART. X. That Saint Mary's County shall be divided into four separate districts, and that the additional district shall be laid off adjoining and between the first and third districts, as they are now numbered.

(Ratified 1809.)

ART. XI. SECTION 1. That, upon the death, resignation, or removal out of this State of the governor, it shall not be necessary to call a meeting of the legislature to fill the vacancy occasioned thereby, but the first named of the council for the time being shall qualify and act as governor, until the next meeting of the general assembly, at which meeting a governor shall be chosen in the manner heretofore appointed and directed.

SEC. 2. No governor shall be capable of holding any other office of profit during the time for which he shall be elected.

(Ratified 1810)

ART. XII. That all such parts of the constitution and form of government as require a property qualification in persons to be appointed or holding offices of profit or trust in this State, and in persons elected members of the legislature or electors of the senate, shall be, and the same are hereby, repealed and abolished.

ART. XIII. That it shall not be lawful for the general assembly of this State to lay an equal and general tax, or any other tax, on the people of this State, for the support of any religion.

ART. XIV. That every free white male citizen of this State, above twenty-one years of age, and no other, having resided twelve months within this State, and six months in the county, or in the city of Annapolis or Baltimore, next preceding the election at which he offers to vote, shall have a right of suffrage, and shall vote, by ballot, in the election of such county or city, or either of them, for electors of the President and Vice-President of the United States, for Representatives of this State in the Congress of the United States, for delegates to the general assembly of this State, electors of the senate, and sheriffs.

ART. XV. That no person residing in the city of Annapolis shall have a vote in the county of Anne Arundel, for delegates of the said county; and all and every part of the constitution which enables persons holding fifty acres of land to vote in said county, be, and is hereby, abolished.

ART. XVI. That the forty-fifth article of the constitution and form of government be, and the same is hereby, repealed and utterly abolished.

(Ratified 1812)

ART. XVII. SECTION 1. That the time of the meeting of the general assembly shall be on the first Monday in December in each year, instead of the first Monday in November, as prescribed by the constitution and form of government.

SEC. 2. The governor of this State shall be chosen on the second Monday of December, in each and every year, in the same manner as is now prescribed by the constitution and form of government; and the council to the governor shall be elected on the first Tuesday after the second Monday of December, in each and every year, in the same manner as is now prescribed by the constitution and form of government.

SEC. 3. All annual appointments of civil officers in this State shall be made in the third week of December, in every year, in the same manner as the constitution and form of government now directs.

(Ratified 1837)

SECTION 1. The term of office of the members of the present senate shall end and be determined whenever and as soon as a new senate shall be elected as hereinafter provided, and a quorum of its members shall have qualified, as directed by the constitution and laws of this State.

SEC. 2. At the December session of the general assembly for the year of our Lord eighteen hundred and thirty-eight, and forever thereafter, the senate shall be composed of twenty-one members, to be chosen as hereinafter provided, a majority of whom shall be a quorum for the transaction of business.

SEC. 3. At the time and place of holding elections in the several counties of this State, and in the city of Baltimore, for delegates to the general assembly for the December session of the year eighteen hundred and thirty-eight, and under the direction of the same judges by whom such elections for delegates shall be held, an election shall also be held in each of the several counties of this State and in the city of Baltimore respectively, for the purpose of choosing a senator of the State of Maryland for and from such county or said city, as the case may be, whose term of office shall commence on the day fixed by law for the commencement of the regular session of the general assembly next succeeding such election, and continue for two, four, or six years, according to the classification of a quorum of its members; and at every such election for senators, every person qualified to vote at the place at which he shall offer to vote for delegates to the general assembly, shall be entitled to vote for one person as senator; and of the persons voted for as senator in each of the several counties and in said city, respectively, the person having the highest number of legal votes, and possessing the qualifications hereinafter mentioned, shall be declared and returned as duly elected for said county or said city, as the case may be; and in case two persons possessing the required qualifications shall be found on the final casting of the votes given, in any one of said counties or said city, to have an equal number of votes, there shall be a new election ordered as hereinafter mentioned; and immediately after the senate shall have convened in pursuance of their election under this act, the senators shall be divided, in such manner as the senate shall prescribe, into three classes; the seats of the senators of the first class shall be vacated at the expiration of the second year, of the second class at the expiration of the fourth year, and of the third class at the expiration of the sixth year, so that one-third thereof may be elected on the first Wednesday of October in every second year; and elections shall be held in the several counties and city, from which the retiring senators came, to supply the vacancies as they may occur in consequence of this classification.

SEC. 4. Such election for senators shall be conducted, and the returns thereof be made, with proper variations in the certificate to suit the case, in like manner as in cases of elections for delegates.

SEC. 5. The qualifications necessary in a senator shall be the same as are required in a delegate to the general assembly, with the additional qualification that he shall be above the age of twenty-five years, and shall have resided at least three years, next preceding his election. in the county or city in and for which he shall be chosen.

SEC. 6. In case any person who shall have been chosen as a senator shall refuse to act, remove from the county or city, as the case may be, for which he shall have been elected, die, resign, or be removed for cause, or in case of a tie between two or more qualified persons in any one of the counties or in the city of Baltimore, a warrant of election shall be issued by the president of the senate for the time being for the election of a senator to supply the vacancy, of which ten days' notice at the least, excluding the day of notice and the day of election, shall be given.

SEC. 7. So much of the thirty-seventh article of the constitution as provides that no senator or delegate to the general assembly, if he shall qualify as such, shall hold or execute any office of profit during the time for which he shall be elected, shall be, and the same is hereby, repealed.

SEC. 8. No senator or delegate to the general assembly shall, during the time for which he was elected, be appointed to any civil office under the constitution and laws of this State which shall have been created or the emoluments whereof shall have been increased during such time; and no senator or delegate, during the time he shall continue to act as such, shall be eligible to any civil office whatever.

SEC. 9. At the election for delegates to the general assembly for the December session of the year of our Lord eighteen hundred and thirty-eight, and at each succeeding election for delegates, until after the next census shall have been taken and officially promulged, five delegates shall be elected in and for Baltimore City and one delegate in and for the city of Annapolis, until the promulging of the census for the year eighteen hundred and forty, when the city of Annapolis shall be deemed and taken as a part of Anne Arundel County, and her right to a separate delegation shall cease; five delegates in and for Baltimore County; five delegates in and for Frederick County, and four delegates in and for Anne Arundel County, and four delegates in and for each of the several counties respectively hereinafter mentioned, to wit: Dorchester, Somerset, Worcester, Prince George's, Harford, Montgomery, Carroll, and Washington, and three delegates in and for each of the several counties respectively hereinafter next mentioned, to wit: Cecil, Kent, Queen Anne's, Caroline, Talbot, Saint Mary's, Charles, Calvert, and Alleghany.

SEC. 10. From and after the period when the next census shall have been taken and officially promulged, and from and after the official promulgation of every second census thereafter, the representation in the house of delegates from the several counties and from the city of Baltimore shall be graduated and established on the following basis: that is to say, every county which shall have by the said census a population of less than fifteen thousand souls, federal numbers, shall be entitled to elect three delegates; every county having a population by the said census of fifteen thousand souls and less than twenty-five thousand souls, federal numbers, shall be entitled to elect four delegates; and every county having by the said census a population of twenty-five thousand and less than thirty-five thousand souls, federal numbers, shall be entitled to elect five delegates; and every county having a population of upwards of thirty-five thousand souls, federal numbers, shall be entitled to elect six delegates; and the city of Baltimore shall be entitled to elect as many delegates as the county which shall have the largest representation, on the basis aforesaid, may be entitled to elect: *Provided, and it is hereby enacted*, That if any of the several counties hereinbefore mentioned shall not, after the said census for the year eighteen hundred and forty shall have been taken, be entitled by the graduation on the basis aforesaid to a representation in the house of delegates equal to that allowed to such county by the ninth section of this act, at the election of delegates for the December session of the year eighteen hundred and thirty-eight, such county shall, nevertheless, after said census for the year eighteen hundred and forty, or any future census, and forever thereafter, be entitled to elect the number of delegates allowed by the provisions of said section for the said session; but nothing in the proviso contained shall be construed to include in the representation of Anne Arundel County the delegate allowed to the city of Annapolis in the said ninth section of this act.

SEC. 11. In all elections for senators, to be held after the election for delegates, for the December session, eighteen hundred and thirty-seven, the city of Annapolis shall be deemed and taken as part of Anne Arundel County.

SEC. 12. The general assembly shall have power from time to time to regulate all matters relating to the judges, time, place, and manner of holding elections for senators and delegates, and of making returns thereof, and to divide the several counties into election districts, for the more convenient holding of elections, not affecting their terms or tenure of office.

SEC. 13. So much of the constitution and form of government as relates to the council, to the governor, and to the clerk of the council, be abrogated, abolished, and annulled, and that the whole executive power of the government of this State shall be vested exclusively in the governor, subject, nevertheless, to the checks, limitations and provisions hereinafter specified and mentioned.

SEC. 14. The governor shall nominate, and, by and with the advice and consent of the senate, shall appoint all officers of the State whose offices are or may be created by law, and whose appointment shall not be otherwise provided for by the constitution and form of government, or by any laws consistent with the constitution and form of government: *Provided*, That this act shall not be deemed or construed to impair in any manner the validity of the commissions of such persons as shall be in office under previous executive appointment, when this act shall go into operation, or alter, abridge, or change the tenure, quality, or duration of the same, or of any of them.

SEC. 15. The governor shall have power to fill any vacancy that may occur in any such offices during the recess of the senate, by granting commissions which shall expire upon the appointment of the same person, or any other person, by and with the advice and consent of the senate, to the same office, or at the expiration of one calendar month, ensuing the commencement of the next regular session of the senate, whichever shall first occur.

SEC. 16. The same person shall in no case be nominated by the governor a second time during the same session for the same office, in case he shall have been rejected by the senate, unless after such rejection the senate shall inform the governor by message of their willingness to receive again the nomination of such rejected person for further consideration; and in case any person nominated by the governor for any office shall have been rejected by the senate, it shall not be lawful for the governor at any time afterwards, during the recess of the senate, in case of vacancy in the same office, to appoint such rejected person to fill said vacancy.

SEC. 17. It shall be the duty of the governor, within the period of one calendar month next after this act shall go into operation, and in the same session in which the same shall be confirmed, if it be confirmed, and annually thereafter during the regular session of the senate, and on such particular day, if any, or within such particular period as may be prescribed by law, to nominate, and by and with the advice and consent of the senate, to appoint a secretary of state, who shall hold his office until a successor shall be appointed, and who shall discharge such duties, and receive such compensation, as shall be prescribed by law.

SEC. 18. In case a vacancy shall occur in the office of governor at any time after this act shall go into operation, the general assembly, if in session, or if in the recess at their next session, shall proceed to elect, by joint ballot of the two houses, some person, being a qualified resident of the gubernatorial district from which the governor for said term is to be taken, to be governor for the residue of said term in place of the person originally chosen; and in every case of vacancy, until the election and qualification of the person succeeding, the secretary of state, by virtue of his said office, shall be clothed, *ad interim*, with the executive powers of government; and in case there shall be no secretary of state, or in case he shall refuse to act, remove from the State, die, resign, or be removed for cause, the person filling the office of president of the senate shall, by virtue of his said office, be clothed, *ad interim*, with the executive powers of government; and in case there shall be no president of the senate, or in case he shall refuse to act, remove from the State, die, resign, or be removed for cause, the person filling the office of speaker of the house of delegates shall, by virtue of his said office, be clothed, *ad interim*, with the executive powers of government.

SEC. 19. The term of office of the governor, who shall be chosen on the first Monday of January next, shall continue for the term of one year, and until the election and qualification of a successor, to be chosen as hereinafter mentioned.

SEC. 20. At the time and places of holding the elections in the several counties of this State, and in the city of Baltimore, for delegates to the general assembly for the December session of the year eighteen hundred and thirty-eight, and before the same judges by whom the election for delegates shall be held, and in every third year forever thereafter, an election shall also be held for a governor of this State, whose term of office shall commence on the first Monday of January next ensuing the day of such election, and continue for three years, and until the election and qualification of a successor; at which said election every person qualified to vote for delegates to the general assembly, at the place at which he shall offer to vote, shall be entitled to vote for governor, and the person voted for as governor shall possess the qualifications now required by the constitution and form of government, and the additional qualification of being at least thirty years of age, and of being, and of having been for at least three whole years before, a resident within the limits of the gubernatorial district from which the governor is to be taken at such election, according to the priority which shall be determined as hereinafter mentioned; that is to say, the State shall be, and the same is hereby, divided into three gubernatorial districts, as follows: the counties of Cecil, Kent, Queen Anne's, Caroline, Talbot, Dorchester, Somerset, and Worcester shall together compose one district, and until its number shall be determined as hereinafter provided, shall be known as the eastern district; the counties of Saint Mary's, Charles, Calvert, Prince George's, Anne Arundel, inclusive of the city of Annapolis, Montgomery, and Baltimore City, shall together compose one district, and, until its number shall be determined as hereinafter provided, shall be known as the southern district; Baltimore, Harford, Carroll, Frederick, Washington, and Alleghany Counties shall together compose one district, and until its number shall be determined as hereinafter provided, shall be known as the northwestern district; and for the purpose of determining the respective numbers and order of priority of said districts in the same session in which this act shall be confirmed, if the same shall be confirmed as hereinafter mentioned, and on some day to be fixed by concurrence of the two branches, the speaker of the house of delegates shall present to the president of the senate, in the senate chamber, a box containing three ballots of similar size and appearance, and on which shall severally be written, eastern district, southern district, northwestern district; and the president of the senate shall thereupon draw from said box the said several ballots in succession, and the district, the name of which shall be written on the ballot first drawn, shall thenceforth be distinguished as the first gubernatorial district, and the person to be chosen governor at the election first to be held under the provisions of this section, and the person to be chosen at every succeeding third election for governor forever thereafter, shall be taken from the said first district; and the district, the name of which shall be written on the ballot secondly drawn, shall thenceforth be distinguished as the second gubernatorial district, and the person to be chosen governor at the second election to be held under the provisions of this section, and the person to be chosen at every succeeding third election for governor forever thereafter, shall be taken from the said second district, and the district, the name of which shall be written on the ballot thirdly drawn, shall thenceforth be distinguished as the third gubernatorial district, and the person to be chosen governor at the third election to be held under the provisions of this section, and the person to be chosen at every succeeding third election forever thereafter, shall be taken from the said third district; and the result of such drawing shall be entered on the journal of the senate, and be reported by the speaker of the house of delegates on his return to that body, and be entered on the journal thereof, and shall be certified by a joint letter, to be signed by the president of the senate and the speaker of the house of delegates, and be addressed and transmitted to the secretary of state, if appointed, and if not, as soon as he shall be appointed, to be by him preserved in his office.

SEC. 21. The general assembly shall have power to regulate by law all matters which relate to the judges, time, place, and manner of holding elections for governor, and of making returns thereof not affecting the tenure and term of office thereby, and that until otherwise directed, the returns shall be made in like manner as in elections for electors of President and Vice-President, save that the form of the certificates shall be varied to suit the case, and save also that the returns, instead of being made to the governor and council, shall be made to the Senate, and be addressed to the president of the senate, and be inclosed under cover to the secretary of state, by whom they shall be delivered to the president of the senate, at the commencement of the session next ensuing such election.

SEC. 22. Of the persons voted for as governor at any such election, the person having, in the judgment of the senate, the highest number of legal votes, and possessing the legal qualifications, and resident, as aforesaid, in the district from which the governor at such election is to be taken, shall be governor, and shall qualify in the manner prescribed by the constitution and laws, on the first Monday of January next ensuing his election, or as soon thereafter as may be, and all questions in relation to the number or legality of the votes given for each and any person voted for as governor, and in relation to the returns, and in relation to the qualifications of the persons voted for as governor, shall be decided by the senate, and in case two or more persons, legally qualified according to the provisions of this act, shall have an equal number of legal votes, then the senate and house of delegates, upon joint ballot, shall determine which one of them shall be governor, and the one which, upon counting the ballots, shall have the highest number of votes, shall be governor, and shall qualify accordingly.

SEC. 23. No person who shall be elected, and shall act as governor, shall be again eligible for the next succeeding term.

SEC. 24. The elections to be held in pursuance of this act shall be held on the first Wednesday of October, in the year eighteen hundred and thirty-eight; and for the election of delegates on the same day in every year thereafter, for the election of governor on the same day in every third year thereafter, and for the election of senators of the first class, on the same day, in the second year after their election and classification, and on the same day in every sixth year thereafter; and for the election of senators of the second class, on the same day in the fourth year after their election and classification, and on the same day in every sixth year thereafter; and for the election of senators of the third class, on the same day, in the sixth year after their election and classification, and on the same day in every sixth year thereafter.

SEC. 25. In all elections for governor, the city of Annapolis shall be deemed and taken as part of Anne Arundel County.

SEC. 26. The relation of master and slave, in this State, shall not be abolished, unless a bill so to abolish the same shall be passed by a unanimous vote of the members of each branch of the general assembly, and shall be published at least three months before a new election of delegates, and shall be confirmed by a unanimous vote of the members of each branch of the general assembly, at the next regular constitutional session after such new election, nor then, without full compensation to the master for the property of which he shall be thereby deprived.

SEC. 27. The city of Annapolis shall continue to be the seat of government, and the place of holding the sessions of the court of appeals for the western shore, and the high court of chancery.

SEC. 28. If this act shall be confirmed by the general assembly, after a new election of delegates, in the first session after such new election, agreeably to the provisions of the constitution and form of government, then and in such case this act, and the alterations and amendments of the constitution therein contained, shall be taken and considered, and shall constitute and be valid, as a part of said constitution and form of government, anything in the said constitution and form of government to the contrary notwithstanding.

(Ratified 1846)

ART. XXVI. That the sessions of the general assembly be biennial instead of annual.

CONSTITUTION OF MARYLAND—1851 *[a]

THE DECLARATION OF RIGHTS

We, the people of the State of Maryland, grateful to Almighty God for our civil and religious liberty, and taking into our serious consideration the best means of establishing a good constitution in this State, for the sure foundation and more permanent security thereof, declare:

ARTICLE 1. That all government of right originates from the people, is founded in compact only, and instituted solely for the good of

---

*Verified from Edward Otis Hinkley's edition. Baltimore: John Murphy & Co., No. 178 Market street. 1855. pp. 104.

[a] This constitution was framed by a convention which met at Annapolis November 4, 1850, and completed its labors May 13, 1851. It was ratified by the people June 4, 1851.

the whole; and they have at all times, according to the mode prescribed in this constitution, the unalienable right to alter, reform, or abolish their form of government, in such manner as they may deem expedient.

ART. 2. That the people of this State ought to have the sole and exclusive right of regulating the internal government and police thereof.

ART. 3. That the inhabitants of Maryland are entitled to the common law of England, and the trial by jury according to the course of that law, and to the benefit of such of the English statutes as existed on the fourth day of July, seventeen hundred and seventy-six, and which, by experience, have been found applicable to their local and other circumstances, and have been introduced, used, and practised by the courts of law or equity, and also of all acts of assembly in force on the first Monday of November, eighteen hundred and fifty, except such as may have since expired, or may be altered by this constitution, subject, nevertheless, to the revision of, and amendment or repeal by the legislature of this State; and the inhabitants of Maryland are also entitled to all property derived to them from or under the charter granted by His Majesty Charles the First to Cæcilius Calvert, Baron of Baltimore.

ART. 4. That all persons invested with the legislative or executive powers of government are the trustees of the public, and as such accountable for their conduct; wherefore, whenever the ends of government are perverted, and public liberty manifestly endangered, and all other means of redress are ineffectual, the people may, and of right ought to, reform the old or establish a new government. The doctrine of non-resistance against arbitrary power and oppression is absurd, slavish, and destructive of the good and happiness of mankind.

ART. 5. That the right of the people to participate in the legislature is the best security of liberty, and the foundation of all free government; for this purpose elections ought to be free and frequent, and every free white male citizen having the qualifications prescribed by the constitution ought to have the right of suffrage.

ART. 6. That the legislative, executive, and judicial powers of government ought to be forever separate and distinct from each other; and no person exercising the functions of one of said departments shall assume or discharge the duties of any other.

ART. 7. That no power of suspending laws, or the execution of laws, unless by or derived from the legislature, ought to be exercised or allowed.

ART. 8. That freedom of speech and debate, or proceedings in the legislature, ought not to be impeached in any court of judicature.

ART. 9. That Annapolis be the place for the meeting of the legislature; and the legislature ought not to be convened or held at any other place but from evident necessity.

ART. 10. That for the redress of grievances, and for amending, strengthening, and preserving the laws, the legislature ought to be frequently convened.

ART. 11. That every man hath a right to petition the legislature for the redress of grievances in a peaceable and orderly manner.

ART. 12. That no aid, charge, tax, burden, or fees ought to be rated or levied, under any pretence, without the consent of the legislature.

ART. 13. That the levying of taxes by the poll is grievous and oppressive, and ought to be abolished; that paupers ought not to be assessed for the support of government, but every other person in the State, or person holding property therein, ought to contribute his proportion of public taxes, for the support of government, according to his actual worth in real or personal property; yet fines, duties, or taxes may properly and justly be imposed or laid on persons or property, with a political view, for the good government and benefit of the community.

ART. 14. That sanguinary laws ought to be avoided as far as is consistent with the safety of the State; and no law to inflict cruel and unusual pains and penalties ought to be made in any case, or at any time hereafter.

ART. 15. That retrospective laws, punishing acts committed before the existence of such laws, and by them only declared criminal, are oppressive, unjust, and incompatible with liberty; wherefore, no *ex post facto* law ought to be made.

ART. 16. That no law to attaint particular persons of treason or felony ought to be made in any case or at any time hereafter.

ART. 17. That every freeman, for any injury done to him in his person or property, ought to have remedy by the course of the law of the land, and ought to have justice and right, freely without sale, fully without any denial, and speedily without delay, according to the law of the land.

ART. 18. That the trial of facts, where they arise, is one of the greatest securities of the lives, liberties, and estate of the people.

ART. 19. That in all criminal prosecutions, every man hath a right to be informed of the accusation against him; to have a copy of the indictment or charge, in due time (if required) to prepare for his defence; to be allowed counsel; to be confronted with the witnesses against him; to have process for his witnesses; to examine the witnesses for and against him on oath; and to a speedy trial by an impartial jury, without whose unanimous consent he ought not to be found guilty.

ART. 20. That no man ought to be compelled to give evidence against himself in a court of common law, or in any other court, but in such cases as have been usually practised in this State, or may hereafter be directed by the legislature.

ART. 21. That no freeman ought to be taken or imprisoned, or disseized of his freehold, liberties, or privileges, or outlawed, or exiled, or in any manner destroyed, or deprived of his life, liberty, or property, but by the judgment of his peers, or by the law of the land: *Provided,* That nothing in this article shall be so construed as to prevent the legislature from passing all such laws for the government, regulation, and disposition of the free colored population of this State as they may deem necessary.

ART. 22. That excessive bail ought not be required, nor excessive fines imposed, nor cruel or unusual punishment inflicted by the courts of law.

ART. 23. That all warrants, without oath or affirmation, to search suspected places, or to seize any person or property, are grievous and oppressive; and all general warrants to search suspected places, or to apprehend suspected persons, without naming or describing the place, or the person in special, are illegal, and ought not to be granted.

ART. 24. That no conviction shall work corruption of blood or forfeiture of estate.

ART. 25. That a well-regulated militia is the proper and natural defence of a free government.

ART. 26. That standing armies are dangerous to liberty, and ought not to be raised or kept up without consent of the legislature.

ART. 27. That in all cases and at all times the military ought to be under strict subordination to, and control of, the civil power.

ART. 28. That no soldier ought to be quartered in any house in time of peace without the consent of the owner, and in time of war in such manner only as the legislature shall direct.

ART. 29. That no person, except regular soldiers, mariners, and marines, in the service of this State, or militia when in actual service, ought in any case to be subject to or punishable by martial law.

ART. 30. That the independency and uprightness of judges are essential to the impartial administration of justice, and a great security to the rights and liberties of the people; wherefore the judges shall not be removed, except for misbehavior, on conviction in a court of law, or by the governor, upon the address of the general assembly: *Provided*, That two-thirds of all the members of each house concur in such address. No such judge shall hold any other office, civil or military, or political trust or employment of any kind whatsoever, under the constitution or laws of this State, or of the United States, or any of them, or receive fees or perquisites of any kind for the discharge of his official duties.

ART. 31. That a long continuance in the executive departments of power or trust is dangerous to liberty; a rotation, therefore, in those departments is one of the best securities of permanent freedom.

ART. 32. That no person ought to hold at the same time more than one office of profit, created by the constitution or laws of this State; nor ought any person in public trust to receive any present from any foreign prince or state, or from the United States, or any of them, without the approbation of this State.

ART. 33. That as it is the duty of every man to worship God in such manner as he thinks most acceptable to him, all persons are equally entitled to protection in their religious liberty; wherefore, no person ought, by any law, to be molested in his person or estate, on account of his religious persuasion or profession, or for his religious practice, unless under color of religion any man shall disturb the good order, peace, or safety of the State, or shall infringe the laws of morality, or injure others in their natural, civil, or religious rights; nor ought any person to be compelled to frequent or maintain or contribute, unless on contract, to maintain any place of worship or any ministry; nor shall any person be deemed incompetent as a witness or juror who believes in the existence of a God, and that under his dispensation such person will be held morally accountable for his acts, and be rewarded or punished therefor, either in this world or the world to come.

ART. 34. That no other test or qualification ought to be required, on admission to any office of trust or profit, than such oath of office as may be prescribed by this constitution, or by the laws of the State, and a declaration of belief in the Christian religion; and if the party shall profess to be a Jew, the declaration shall be of his belief in a future state of rewards and punishments.

ART. 35. That every gift, sale, or devise of land, to any minister, public teacher, or preacher of the gospel, as such, or to any religious sect, order, or denomination, or to or for the support, use, or benefit of, or in trust for any minister, public teacher, or preacher of the gospel, as such, or any religious sect, order, or denomination, and every gift or sale of goods or chattels to go in succession, or to take place after the death of the seller or donor, to or for such support, use, or benefit; and also every devise of goods or chattels, to or for the support, use, or benefit of any minister, public teacher, or preacher of the gospel, as such; or any religious sect, order, or denomination, without the leave of the legislature, shall be void; except always any sale, gift, lease, or devise of any quantity of land, not exceeding five acres, for a church, meeting-house, or other house of worship, or parsonage, or for a burying-ground, which shall be improved, enjoyed, or used only for such purpose; or such sale, gift, lease, or devise shall be void.

ART. 36. That the manner of administering an oath or affirmation to any person ought to be such as those of the religious persuasion, profession, or denomination of which he is a member generally esteem the most effectual confirmation by the attestation of the Divine Being.

ART. 37. That the city of Annapolis ought to have all its rights, privileges, and benefits, agreeably to its charter and the acts of assembly confirming and regulating the same, subject to such alterations as have been or as may be made by the legislature.

ART. 38. That the liberty of the press ought to be inviolably preserved.

ART. 39. That monopolies are odious, contrary to the spirit of a free government and the principles of commerce, and ought not to be suffered.

ART. 40. That no title of nobility or hereditary honors ought to be granted in this State.

ART. 41. That the legislature ought to encourage the diffusion of knowledge and virtue, the promotion of literature, the arts, sciences, agriculture, commerce, and manufactures, and the general melioration of the condition of the people.

ART. 42. This enumeration of rights shall not be construed to impair or deny others retained by the people.

ART. 43. That this constitution shall not be altered, changed, or abolished, except in the manner therein prescribed and directed.

THE CONSTITUTION

ARTICLE I

ELECTIVE FRANCHISE

SECTION 1. Every free white male person, of twenty-one years of age or upwards, who shall have been one year next preceding the election a resident of the State, and for six months a resident of the city of Baltimore, or of any county in which he may offer to vote, and being at the time of the election a citizen of the United States, shall be entitled to vote in the ward or election district in which he resides, in all elections hereafter to be held; and at all such elections the vote shall be taken by ballot. And in case any county or city shall be so divided as to form portions of different electoral districts for the election of Congressmen, senator, delegate, or other officer or officers, then to entitle a person to vote for such officer, he must have been a resident of that part of the county or city which shall form a part of the electoral district in which he offers to vote for six months next preceding the election; but a person who shall have acquired a residence in such county or city entitling him to vote at any such election, shall be entitled to vote in the election district from which he removed until he shall have acquired a residence in the part of the county or city to which he has removed.

Sec. 2. That if any person shall give, or offer to give, directly or indirectly, any bribe, present, or reward, or any promise, or any security for the payment or delivery of money or any other thing to induce any voter to refrain from casting his vote, or forcibly to prevent him in any way from voting, or to obtain or procure a vote for any candidate or person proposed or voted for as elector of President and Vice-President of the United States, or Representative in Congress, or for any office of profit or trust created by the constitution or laws of this State, or by the ordinances or authority of the mayor and city council of Baltimore, the person giving or offering to give, and the person receiving the same, and any person who gives or causes to be given an illegal vote, knowing it to be so, at any election to be hereafter held in this State, shall, on conviction in a court of law, in addition to the penalties now or hereafter to be imposed by law, be forever disqualified to hold any office of profit or trust, or to vote at any election thereafter.

Sec. 3. It shall be the duty of the general assembly of Maryland to pass laws to punish with fine and imprisonment any person who shall remove into any election district or ward of the city of Baltimore, not for the purpose of acquiring a *bona-fide* residence therein, but for the purpose of voting therein at an approaching election, or who shall vote in any election district or ward in which he does not reside, (except in the case provided for in the first article of the constitution,) or shall, at the same election, vote in more than one election district or ward, or shall vote or offer to vote in any name not his own, or in place of any other person of the same name, or shall vote in any county in which he does not reside.

Sec. 4. Every person elected or appointed to any office of profit or trust under the constitution or laws made pursuant thereto, before he shall enter upon the duties of such office shall take and subscribe the following oath or affirmation: " I, A. B., do swear [or affirm, as the case may be] that I will support the Constitution of the United States, and that I will be faithful and bear true allegiance to the State of Maryland, and support the constitution and laws thereof; that I will, to the best of my skill and judgment, diligently and faithfully, without partiality or prejudice, execute the office of ——— according to the constitution and laws of this State, and that since the adoption of the present constitution I have not in any manner violated the provisions thereof in relation to the bribery of voters or preventing legal or procuring illegal votes to be given; and [if a governor, senator, member of the house of delegates, or judge] that I will not directly or indirectly receive the profits or any part of the profits of any other office during the time of my acting as ———."
And if any person, elected or appointed to office as aforesaid, shall

refuse or neglect to take the said oath or affirmation, he shall be considered as having refused to accept the said office, and a new election or appointment shall be made as in case of refusal or resignation, and any person swearing or affirming falsely in the premises shall, on conviction thereof in a court of law, incur the penalties for wilful and corrupt perjury, and be thereafter incapable of voting at any election, and also incapable of holding any office of profit or trust in this State.

SEC. 5. That no person above the age of twenty-one years, convicted of larceny or other infamous crime, unless he shall be pardoned by the executive, shall ever thereafter be entitled to vote at any election in this State, and no person under guardianship as a lunatic, or as a person *non compos mentis*, shall be entitled to vote.

ARTICLE II

EXECUTIVE DEPARTMENT

SECTION 1. The executive power of the State shall be vested in a governor, whose term of office shall commence on the second Wednesday of January next ensuing his election, and continue for four years, and until his successor shall have qualified.

SEC. 2. The first election for governor under this constitution shall be held on the first Wednesday of November, in the year eighteen hundred and fifty-three, and on the same day and month in every fourth year thereafter, at the places of voting for delegates to the general assembly, and every person qualified to vote for delegates shall be qualified and entitled to vote for governor; the election to be held in the same manner as the election of delegates, and the returns thereof, under seal, to be addressed to the speaker of the house of delegates, and inclosed and transmitted to the secretary of state, and delivered to the said speaker at the commencement of the session of the legislature next ensuing said election.

SEC. 3. The speaker of the house of delegates shall then open the said returns in the presence of both houses, and the person having the highest number of votes, and being constitutionally eligible, shall be the governor, and shall qualify in the manner herein prescribed, on the second Wednesday of January next ensuing his election, or as soon thereafter as may be practicable.

SEC. 4. If two or more persons shall have the highest and an equal number of votes, one of them shall be chosen governor by the senate and house of delegates; and all questions in relation to the eligibility of governor, and to the returns of said election, and to the number and legality of votes therein given, shall be determined by the house of delegates. And if the person or persons having the highest number of votes be ineligible, the governor shall be chosen by the senate and house of delegates. Every election of governor, by the legislature, shall be determined by a joint majority of the senate and house of delegates, and the vote shall be taken *viva voce*. But if two or more persons shall have the highest and an equal number of votes, then a second vote shall be taken, which shall be confined to the persons having an equal number; and if the votes should again be equal, then the election of governor shall be determined by lot between those who shall have the highest and an equal number on the first vote.

Sec. 5. The State shall be divided into three districts, Saint Mary's, Charles, Calvert, Prince George's, Anne Arundel, Montgomery, and Howard Counties, and the city of Baltimore, to be the first; the eight counties of the eastern shore to be the second; and Baltimore, Harford, Frederick, Washington, Alleghany, and Carroll Counties to be the third. The governor, elected from the third district in October last, shall continue in office during the term for which he was elected. The governor shall be taken from the first district, at the first election of governor under this constitution; from the second district at the second election, and from the third district at the third election, and in like manner, afterwards, from each district, in regular succession.

Sec. 6. A person to be eligible to the office of governor must have attained the age of thirty years, and been for five years a citizen of the United States, and for five years next preceding his election a resident of the State, and for three years a resident of the district from which he was elected.

Sec. 7. In case of the death or resignation of the governor, or of his removal from the State, the general assembly, if in session, or if not, at their next session, shall elect some other qualified resident of the same district to be the governor for the residue of the term for which the said governor had been elected.

Sec. 8. In case of any vacancy in the office of governor during the recess of the legislature, the president of the senate shall discharge the duties of said office till a governor is elected as herein provided for; and in case of the death or resignation of said president, or of his removal from the State, or of his refusal to serve, then the duties of said office shall, in like manner, and for the same interval, devolve upon the speaker of the house of delegates, and the legislature may provide by law for the case of impeachment or inability of the governor, and declare what person shall perform the executive duties during such impeachment or inability; and for any vacancy in said office, not herein provided for, provision may be made by law, and if such vacancy should occur without such provision being made, the legislature shall be convened by the secretary of state for the purpose of filling said vacancy.

Sec. 9. The governor shall be commander-in-chief of the land and naval forces of the State, and may call out the militia to repel invasions, suppress insurrections, and enforce the execution of the laws; but shall not take the command in person without the consent of the legislature.

Sec. 10. He shall take care that the laws be faithfully executed.

Sec. 11. He shall nominate and, by and with the advice and consent of the senate, appoint all civil and military officers of the State, whose appointment or election is not otherwise herein provided for, unless a different mode of appointment be prescribed by the law creating the office.

Sec. 12. In case of any vacancy during the recess of the senate, in any office which the governor has power to fill, he shall appoint some suitable person to said office, whose commission shall continue in force till the end of the next session of the legislature, or till some other person is appointed to the same office, whichever shall first occur, and the nomination of the person thus appointed during the recess, or of some other person in his place, shall be made to the senate within thirty days after the next meeting of the legislature.

Sec. 13. No person, after being rejected by the senate, shall be again nominated for the same office at the same session, unless at the request of the senate; or be appointed to the same office during the recess of the legislature.

Sec. 14. All civil officers appointed by the governor and senate shall be nominated to the senate within fifty days from the commencement of each regular session of the legislature; and their term of office shall commence on the first Monday of May next ensuing their appointment, and continue for two years, (unless sooner removed from office,) and until their successors, respectively, qualify according to law.

Sec. 15. The governor may suspend or arrest any military officer of the State for disobedience of orders, or other military offence, and may remove him in pursuance of the sentence of a court-martial; and may remove, for incompetency or misconduct, all civil officers who receive appointments from the executive for a term not exceeding two years.

Sec. 16. The governor may convene the legislature, or the senate alone, on extraordinary occasions; and whenever, from the presence of an enemy or from any other cause, the seat of government shall become an unsafe place for the meeting of the legislature, he may direct their sessions to be held at some other convenient place.

Sec. 17. It shall be the duty of the governor semi-annually, and oftener if he deem it expedient, to examine the bank-book, account-books, and official proceedings of the treasurer and comptroller of the State.

Sec. 18. He shall, from time to time, inform the legislature of the condition of the State, and recommend to their consideration such measures as he may judge necessary and expedient.

Sec. 19. He shall have power to grant reprieves and pardons, except in cases of impeachment, and in cases in which he is prohibited by other articles of this constitution, and to remit fines and forfeitures for offences against the State; but shall not remit the principal or interest of any debt due to the State, except in cases of fines and forfeitures; and before granting a *nolle prosequi*, or pardon, he shall give notice, in one or more newspapers, of the application made for it, and of the day on or after which his decision will be given; and in every case in which he exercises this power, he shall report to either branch of the legislature, whenever required, the petitions, recommendations, and reasons which influence his decision.

Sec. 20. The governor shall reside at the seat of government, and shall receive for his services an annual salary of thirty-six hundred dollars.

Sec. 21. When the public interest requires it, he shall have power to employ counsel, who shall be entitled to such compensation as the legislature may allow in each case after the services of such counsel shall have been performed.

Sec. 22. A secretary of state shall be appointed by the governor, by and with the advice and consent of the senate, who shall continue in office, unless sooner removed by the governor, till the end of the official term of the governor from whom he receives his appointment, and shall receive an annual salary of one thousand dollars.

SEC. 23. He shall carefully keep and preserve a record of all official acts and proceedings, (which may, at all times, be inspected by a committee of either branch of the legislature,) and shall perform such other duties as may be prescribed by law, or as may properly belong to his office.

ARTICLE III

LEGISLATIVE DEPARTMENT

SECTION 1. The legislature shall consist of two distinct branches, a senate and a house of delegates, which shall be styled "The general assembly of Maryland."

SEC. 2. Every county of the State, and the city of Baltimore, shall be entitled to elect one senator, who shall be elected by the qualified voters of the counties and city of Baltimore, respectively, and who shall serve for four years from the day of their election.

SEC. 3. The legislature at its first session after the returns of the national census of eighteen hundred and sixty are published, and in like manner after each subsequent census, shall apportion the members of the house of delegates among the several counties of the State, according to the population of each, and shall always allow to the city of Baltimore four more delegates than are allowed to the most populous county, but no county shall be entitled to less than two members, nor shall the whole number of delegates ever exceed eighty, or be less than sixty-five; and, until the apportionment is made under the census of eighteen hundred and sixty, Saint Mary's County shall be entitled to two delegates; Kent, two; Anne Arundel, three; Calvert, two; Charles, two; Baltimore County, six; Talbot, two; Somerset, four; Dorchester, three; Cecil, three; Prince George's, three; Queen Anne's, two; Worcester, three; Frederick, six; Harford, three; Caroline, two; Baltimore City, ten; Washington, five; Montgomery, two; Alleghany, four; Carroll, three, and Howard, two.

SEC. 4. The members of the house of delegates shall be elected by the qualified voters of the counties and city of Baltimore respectively, to serve for two years from the day of their election.

SEC. 5. The first election for delegates shall take place on the first Wednesday of November, eighteen hundred and fifty-one; and the elections for delegates, and for one-half of the senators, as nearly as practicable, shall be held on the same day in every second year thereafter, but an election for senators shall be held in the year eighteen hundred and fifty-one in Howard County, and all those counties in which senators were elected in the year eighteen hundred and forty-six.

SEC. 6. Immediately after the senate shall have convened after the first election under this constitution, the senators shall be divided, by lot, into two classes, as nearly equal in number as may be; the senators of the first class shall go out of office at the expiration of two years, and senators shall be elected on the first Wednesday of November, eighteen hundred and fifty-three, for the term of four years, to supply their places; so that after the first election, one-half of the senators may be chosen every second year: *Provided,* That in no case shall any senator be placed in a class which shall entitle him to serve for a longer term than that for which he was elected. In case the number of senators be hereafter increased, such classification of the additional senators shall be made as to preserve as nearly as may be an equal number in each class.

Sec. 7. The general assembly shall meet on the first Wednesday of January, eighteen hundred and fifty-two, on the same day in the year eighteen hundred and fifty-three, and on the same day in the year eighteen hundred and fifty-four, and on the same day in every second year thereafter, and at no other time unless convened by the proclamation of the governor.

Sec. 8. The general assembly may continue their first two sessions after the adoption of this constitution as long as, in the opinion of the two houses, the public interests may require it, but all subsequent regular sessions of the general assembly shall be closed on the tenth day of March next ensuing the time of their commencement, unless the same shall be closed at an earlier day by the agreement of the two houses.

Sec. 9. No person shall be eligible as a senator or delegate who, at the time of his election, is not a citizen of the United States, and who has not resided at least three years next preceding the day of his election in this State, and the last year thereof in the county or city which he may be chosen to represent, if such county or city shall have been so long established, and if not, then in the county from which, in whole or in part, the same may have been formed; nor shall any person be eligible as a senator unless he shall have attained the age of twenty-five years, nor as a delegate unless he shall have attained the age of twenty-one years at the time of his election.

Sec. 10. No member of Congress, or person holding any civil or military office under the United States, shall be eligible as a senator or delegate; and if any person shall, after his election as a senator or delegate, be elected to Congress, or be appointed to any office, civil or military, under the Government of the United States, his acceptance thereof shall vacate his seat.

Sec. 11. No minister or preacher of the Gospel, of any denomination, and no person holding any civil office of profit or trust under this State, except justices of the peace, shall be eligible as senator or delegate.

Sec. 12. Each house shall be judge of the qualifications and elections of its members, subject to the laws of the State; appoint its own officers, determine the rules of its own proceedings, punish a member for disorderly or disrespectful behavior, and, with the consent of two-thirds, expel a member; but no member shall be expelled a second time for the same offence.

Sec. 13. A majority of each house shall constitute a quorum for the transaction of business, but a smaller number may adjourn from day to day, and compel the attendance of absent members in such manner and under such penalties as each house may prescribe.

Sec. 14. The doors of each house and of committees of the whole shall be open, except when the business is such as ought to be kept secret.

Sec. 15. Each house shall keep a journal of its proceedings, and cause the same to be published. The yeas and nays of members on any question shall, at the call of any five of them, in the house of delegates, or one in the senate, be entered on the journal.

SEC. 16. Neither house shall, without the consent of the other, adjourn for more than three days; nor to any other place than that in which the house shall be sitting, without the concurrent vote of two-thirds of the members present.

SEC. 17. The style of all laws of this State shall be, "*Be it enacted by the general assembly of Maryland,*" and all laws shall be passed by original bill, and every law enacted by the legislature shall embrace but one subject, and that shall be described in the title, and no law or section of law shall be revived, amended, or repealed by reference to its title or section only, and it shall be the duty of the legislature, at the first session after the adoption of this constitution, to appoint two commissioners, learned in the law, to revise and codify the laws of this State; and the said commissioners shall report the said code, so formed, to the legislature, within a time to be by it determined, for its approval, amendment, or rejection; and, if adopted after the revision and codification of the said laws, it shall be the duty of the legislature, in amending any article or section thereof, to enact the same as the said article or section would read when amended. And whenever the legislature shall enact any public general law, not amendatory of any section or article in the said code, it shall be the duty of the legislature to enact the same in articles and sections, in the same manner as the said code may be arranged, and to provide for the publication of all additions and alterations which may be made to the said code; and it shall also be the duty of the legislature to appoint one or more commissioners learned in the law, whose duty it shall be to revise, simplify, and abridge the rules of practice, pleadings, forms of conveyancing, and proceedings of the courts of record in this State.

SEC. 18. Any bill may originate in either house of the general assembly, and be altered, amended, or rejected by the other, but no bill shall originate in either house during the last three days of the session, or become a law, until it be read on three different days of the session in each house, unless three-fourths of the members of the house where such bill is pending shall so determine.

SEC. 19. No bill shall become a law unless it be passed in each house by a majority of the whole number of members elected, and on its final passage the ayes and noes be recorded.

SEC. 20. No money shall be drawn from the treasury of the State, except in accordance with an appropriation made by law, and every such law shall distinctly specify the sum appropriated, and the object to which it shall be applied: *Provided,* That nothing herein contained shall prevent the legislature from placing a contingent fund at the disposal of the executive, who shall report to the legislature at each session the amount expended and the purposes to which it was applied. An accurate statement of the receipts and expenditures of the public money shall be attached to and published with the laws after each regular session of the general assembly.

SEC. 21. No divorce shall be granted by the general assembly.

SEC. 22. No debts shall hereafter be contracted by the legislature, unless such debt shall be authorized by a law providing for the collection of an annual tax or taxes sufficient to pay the interest on such debt as it falls due, and also to discharge the principal thereof within fifteen years from the time of contracting the same, and the taxes laid for this purpose shall not be repealed or applied to any other object until the said debt and the interest thereon shall be fully discharged, and the amount of debts so contracted and remaining unpaid shall never exceed one hundred thousand dollars. The credit of the State shall not, in any manner, be given or loaned to or in aid of any individual, association, or corporation, nor shall the general assembly have the power, in any mode, to involve the State in the construction of works of internal improvement, or in any enterprise which shall involve the faith or credit of the State, or make any appropriations therefor. And they shall not use or appropriate the proceeds of the internal-improvement companies, or of the State tax now levied, or which may hereafter be levied, to pay off the public debt, to any other purpose, until the interest and debt are fully paid, or the sinking fund shall be equal to the amount of the outstanding debt; but the legislature may, without laying a tax, borrow an amount, never to exceed fifty thousand dollars, to meet temporary deficiencies in the treasury, and may contract debts to any amount that may be necessary for the defence of the State.

Sec. 23. No extra compensation shall be granted or allowed by the general assembly to any public officer, agent, servant, or contractor, after the services shall have been rendered or the contract entered into. Nor shall the salary or compensation of any public officer be increased or diminished during his term of office.

Sec. 24. No senator or delegate, after qualifying as such, shall, during the term for which he was elected, be eligible to any office which shall have been created, or the salary or profits of which shall have been increased, during such term, or shall, during said term, hold any office or receive the salary or profits of any office, under the appointment of the executive or legislature.

Sec. 25. Each house may punish by imprisonment, during the session of the general assembly, any person not a member, for disrespectful or disorderly behavior in its presence, or for obstructing any of its proceedings or any of its officers in the execution of their duties: *Provided*, Such imprisonment shall not, at any one time, exceed ten days.

Sec. 26. The members of each house shall, in all cases, except treason, felony, or other criminal offence, be privileged from arrest during their attendance at the session of the general assembly, and in going to and returning from the same, allowing one day for every thirty miles such member may reside from the place at which the general assembly is convened.

Sec. 27. No senator or delegate shall be liable, in any civil action or criminal prosecution whatever, for words spoken in debate.

Sec. 28. The house of delegates may inquire, on the oath of witnesses, into all complaints, grievances, and offences, as the grand inquest of the State, and may commit any person for any crime to the public jail, there to remain until discharged by due course of law; they may examine and pass all accounts of the State relating either in the collection or expenditure of the revenue, and appoint auditors to state and adjust the same; they may call for all public or official papers and records, and send for persons whom they may judge necessary in the course of their inquiries concerning affairs relating to the public interest, and may direct all office bonds which shall be made payable to the State to be sued for any breach of duty.

SEC. 29. In case of death, disqualification, resignation, refusal to act, expulsion, or removal from the county or city for which he shall have been elected, of any person who shall have been chosen as a delegate or senator, or in case of a tie between two or more such qualified persons, a warrant of election shall be issued by the speaker of the house of delegates or president of the senate, as the case may be, for the election of another person in his place, of which election not less than ten days' notice shall be given, exclusive of the day of the publication of the notice and of the day of election; and in case of such resignation or refusal to act being communicated in writing, to the governor, by the person making it, or if such death occur during the legislative recess and more than ten days before its termination, it shall be the duty of the governor to issue a warrant of election to supply the vacancy thus created in the same manner that the said speaker or president might have done during the session of the legislature: *Provided, however,* That unless a meeting of the general assembly may intervene, the election thus ordered to fill such vacancy shall be held on the day of the ensuing election for delegates and senators.

SEC. 30. The senators and delegates shall receive a per diem of four dollars, and such mileage as may be allowed by law, and the presiding officer of each house shall be allowed an addition of one dollar per day. No book or other printed matter not appertaining to the business of the session shall be purchased or subscribed for, for the use of the members, or be distributed among them at the public expense.

SEC. 31. No law passed by the general assembly shall take effect until the first day of June next after the session at which it may be passed, unless it be otherwise expressly declared therein.

SEC. 32. No law shall be passed creating the office of attorney-general.

SEC. 33. The general assembly shall have full power to exclude from the privilege of voting at elections, or of holding any civil or military office in this State, any person who may thereafter be convicted of perjury, bribery, or other felony, unless such person shall have been pardoned by the executive.

SEC. 34. Every bill, when passed by the general assembly, and sealed with the great seal, shall be presented to the governor, who shall sign the same in the presence of the presiding officers and chief clerks of the senate and house of delegates. Every law shall be recorded in the office of the court of appeals, and in due time be printed, published, and certified under the great seal to the several courts in the same manner as has been heretofore usual in this State.

SEC. 35. No person who may hereafter be a collector, receiver, or holder of public moneys shall be eligible as senator or delegate, or to any office of profit or trust under this State, until he shall have accounted for and paid into the treasury all sums on the books thereof, charged to and due by him.

SEC. 36. Any citizen of this State who shall, after the adoption of this constitution, either in or out of this State, fight a duel with deadly weapons, or send or accept a challenge so to do, or who shall act as second, or knowingly aid or assist in any manner those thus offending, shall ever thereafter be incapable of holding any office of trust or profit under this State.

SEC. 37. No lottery-grant shall ever hereafter be authorized by the legislature.

SEC. 38. The general assembly shall pass laws necessary to protect the property of the wife from the debts of the husband during her life, and for securing the same to her issue after her death.

SEC. 39. Laws shall be passed by the legislature to protect from execution a reasonable amount of the property of a debtor, not exceeding in value the sum of five hundred dollars.

SEC. 40. The legislature shall, at its first session after the adoption of this constitution, adopt some simple and uniform system of charges in the offices of clerks of courts and registers of wills in the counties of this State and the city of Baltimore, and for the collection thereof: *Provided*, The amount of compensation to any of said officers shall not exceed the sum of twenty-five hundred dollars a year, over and above office expenses, and compensation to assistants: *And provided further*, That such compensation of clerks, registers, assistants, and office expenses shall always be paid out of the fees or receipts of the offices respectively.

SEC. 41. The house of delegates shall have the sole power of impeachment in all cases, but a majority of all the members must concur in an impeachment; all impeachments shall be tried by the senate, and when sitting for that purpose they shall be on oath or affirmation to do justice according to the law and evidence, but no person shall be convicted without the concurrence of two-thirds of all the senators.

SEC. 42. That it shall be the duty of the legislature, so soon as the public debt shall have been fully paid off, to cause to be transferred to the several counties and the city of Baltimore stock in the internal-improvement companies, equal to the amount respectively paid by each toward the erection and completion of said works, at the then market-value of said stock.

SEC. 43. The legislature shall not pass any law abolishing the relation of master or slave, as it now exists in this State.

SEC. 44. No person shall be imprisoned for debt.

SEC. 45. The legislature hereafter shall grant no charter for banking purposes or renew any banking corporation now in existence, except upon the condition that the stockholders and directors shall be liable to the amount of their respective share or shares of stock in such banking institution for all its debts and liabilities upon note, bill, or otherwise; and upon the further condition that no director or other officer of said corporation shall borrow any money from said corporation; and if any director or other officer shall be convicted upon indictment of directly or indirectly violating this article, he shall be punished by fine or imprisonment at the discretion of the court. All banks shall be open to inspection of their books, papers, and accounts, under such regulations as may be prescribed by law.

SEC. 46. The legislature shall enact no law authorizing private property to be taken for public use, without just compensation, as agreed upon between the parties or awarded by a jury, being first paid or tendered to the party entitled to such compensation.

SEC. 47. Corporations may be formed under general laws, but shall not be created by special act, except for municipal purposes, and in cases where, in the judgment of the legislature, the object of the corporation cannot be attained under general laws. All laws and special acts, pursuant to this section, may be altered from time to time, or repealed: *Provided*, Nothing herein contained shall be construed to alter, change, or amend in any manner the article in relation to banks.

SEC. 48. The legislature shall make provision for all cases of contested elections of any of the officers not herein provided for.

SEC. 49. That the rate of interest in this State shall not exceed 6 per cent. per annum, and no higher rate shall be taken or demanded, and the legislature shall provide, by law, all necessary forfeitures and penalties against usury.

ARTICLE IV

JUDICIARY DEPARTMENT

SECTION 1. The judicial power of this State shall be vested in a court of appeals, in circuit courts, in such courts for the city of Baltimore as may be hereinafter prescribed, and in justices of the peace.

SEC. 2. The court of appeals shall have appellate jurisdiction only, which shall be coextensive with the limits of the State. It shall consist of a chief justice and three associate justices, any three of whom shall form a quorum, whose judgment shall be final and conclusive in all cases of appeals; and who shall have the jurisdiction which the present court of appeals of this State now has, and such other appellate jurisdiction as hereafter may be provided for by law. And in every case decided, an opinion, in writing, shall be filed, and provision shall be made by law for publishing reports of cases argued and determined in the said court. The governor, for the time being, by and with the advice and consent of the senate, shall designate the chief justice, and the court of appeals shall hold its sessions at the city of Annapolis, on the first Monday of June and the first Monday of December, in each and every year.

SEC. 3. The court of appeals shall appoint its own clerk, who shall hold his office for six years, and may be reappointed at the end thereof; he shall be subject to removal by the said court for incompetency, neglect of duty, misdemeanor in office, and for such other causes as may be prescribed by law.

SEC. 4. The State shall be divided into four judicial districts: Alleghany, Washington, Frederick, Carroll, Baltimore, and Harford Counties shall compose the first; Montgomery, Howard, Anne Arundel, Calvert, Saint Mary's, Charles, and Prince George's the second; Baltimore City the third; and Cecil, Kent, Queen Anne's, Talbot, Caroline, Dorchester, Somerset, and Worcester shall compose the fourth district. And one person from among those learned in the law, having been admitted to practise in this State, and who shall have been a citizen of this State at least five years, and above the age of thirty years at the time of his election, and a resident of the judicial district, shall be elected from each of said districts by the legal and qualified voters therein, as a judge of the said court of appeals, who shall hold his office for the term of ten years from the time of his election, or until he shall have attained the age of seventy years, whichever may first happen, and be reëligible thereto until he shall have attained the age of seventy years, and not after, subject to removal for incompetency, wilful neglect of duty, or misbehavior in office, on conviction in a court of law, or by the governor upon the address of the general assembly, two-thirds of the members of each house concurring in such address; and the salary of each of the judges of the court of appeals shall be two thousand five hundred dollars annually, and shall not be increased or diminished during their continuance in office; and no fees or perquisites of any kind shall be allowed by law to any of the said judges.

Sec. 5. No judge of the court of appeals shall sit in any case wherein he may be interested, or where either of the parties may be connected with him by affinity or consanguinity within such degrees as may be prescribed by law, or when he shall have been of counsel in said case; when the court of appeals, or any of its members, shall be thus disqualified to hear and determine any case or cases in said court, so that by reason thereof no judgment can be rendered in said court, the same shall be certified to the governor of the State, who shall immediately commission the requisite number of persons learned in the law for the trial and determination of said case or cases.

Sec. 6. All judges of the court of appeals, of the circuit courts, and of the courts for the city of Baltimore, shall, by virtue of their offices, be conservators of the peace throughout the State.

Sec. 7. All public commissions and grants shall run thus: " The State of Maryland," &c., and shall be signed by the governor, with the seal of the State annexed; all writs and process shall run in the same style, and be tested, sealed, and signed as usual; and all indictments shall conclude, " against the peace, government, and dignity of the State."

Sec. 8. The State shall be divided into eight judicial circuits, in manner and form following, to wit: Saint Mary's, Charles, and Prince George's Counties shall be the first; Anne Arundel, Howard, Calvert, and Montgomery Counties shall be the second; Frederick and Carroll Counties shall be the third; Washington and Alleghany Counties shall be the fourth; Baltimore City shall be the fifth; Baltimore, Harford, and Cecil Counties shall be the sixth; Kent, Queen Anne's, Talbot, and Caroline Counties shall be the seventh; and Dorchester, Somerset, and Worcester Counties shall be the eighth; and there shall be elected, as hereinafter directed, for each of the said judicial circuits, except the fifth, one person from among those learned in the law, having been admitted to practise in this State, and who shall have been a citizen of this State at least five years, and above the age of thirty years at the time of his election, and a resident of the judicial circuit, to be judge thereof; the said judges shall be styled circuit judges, and shall respectively hold a term of their courts at least twice in each year, or oftener if required by law, in each county composing their respective circuits; and the said courts shall be called circuit courts for the county in which they may be held, and shall have and exercise in the several counties of this State all the power, authority, and jurisdiction which the county courts of this State now have and exercise, or which may hereafter be prescribed by law, and the said judges in their respective circuits shall have and exercise all the power, authority, and jurisdiction of the present court of chancery of Maryland: *Provided, nevertheless,* That Baltimore County court may hold its sittings within the limits of the city of Baltimore until provision shall be made by law for the location of a county-seat within the limits of the said county proper, and the erection of a court-house and all other appropriate buildings for the convenient administration of justice in said court.

SEC. 9. The judges of the several judicial circuits shall be citizens of the United States, and shall have resided five years in this State, and two years in the judicial circuit for which they may be respectively elected, next before the time of their election, and shall reside therein while they continue to act as judges; they shall be taken from among those who, having the other qualifications herein prescribed, are most distinguished for integrity, wisdom, and sound legal knowledge, and shall be elected by the qualified voters of the said circuits, and shall hold their offices for the term of ten years, removable for misbehavior, on conviction in a court of law, or by the governor, upon the address of the general assembly, provided that two-thirds of the members of each house shall concur in such address; and the said judges shall each receive a salary of two thousand dollars a year, and the same shall not be increased or diminished during the time of their continuance in office; and no judge of any court in this State shall receive any perquisite, fee, commission, or reward, in addition thereto, for the performance of any judicial duty.

SEC. 10. There shall be established for the city of Baltimore one court of law, to be styled "the court of common pleas," which shall have civil jurisdiction in all suits where the debt or damage claimed shall be over one hundred dollars, and shall not exceed five hundred dollars; and shall also have jurisdiction in all cases of appeal from the judgment of justices of the peace in the said city, and shall have jurisdiction in all applications for the benefit of the insolvent laws of this State, and the supervision and control of the trustees thereof.

SEC. 11. There shall also be established for the city of Baltimore another court of law, to be styled the superior court of Baltimore City, which shall have jurisdiction over all suits where the debt or damage claimed shall exceed the sum of five hundred dollars; and in case any plaintiff or plaintiffs shall recover less than the sum or value of five hundred dollars, he or they shall be allowed or adjudged to pay costs in the discretion of the court. The said court shall also have jurisdiction as a court of equity within the limits of the said city, and in all other civil cases which have not been heretofore assigned to the court of common pleas.

SEC. 12. Each of the said two courts shall consist of one judge, who shall be elected by the legal and qualified voters of the said city, and shall hold his office for the term of ten years, subject to the provisions of this constitution with regard to the election and qualification of judges and their removal from office, and the salary of each of the said judges shall be twenty-five hundred dollars a year; and the legislature shall, whenever it may think the same proper and expedient, provide, by law, another court for the city of Baltimore, to consist of one judge, to be elected by the qualified voters of the said city, who shall be subject to the same constitutional provisions, hold his office for the same term of years, and receive the same compensation as the judge of the court of common pleas of the said city, and the said court shall have such jurisdiction and powers as may be prescribed by law.

SEC. 13. There shall also be a criminal court for the city of Baltimore, to be styled "the criminal court of Baltimore," which shall consist of one judge, who shall also be elected by the legal and qualified voters of the said city, and who shall have and exercise all the jurisdiction now exercised by Baltimore City court, and the said judge shall receive a salary of two thousand dollars a year, and shall be subject to the provisions of this constitution with regard to the election and qualifications of judges, term of office, and removal therefrom.

SEC. 14. There shall be in each county a clerk of the circuit court, who shall be elected by the qualified voters of each county, and the person receiving the greatest number of votes shall be declared and returned duly elected clerk of said circuit court for the said county, and shall hold his office for the term of six years from the time of his election, and until a new election is held; shall be reeligible thereto, and subject to removal for wilful neglect of duty, or other misdemeanor in office, on conviction in a court of law. There shall also be a clerk of the court of common pleas in Baltimore City, and a clerk of the superior court of Baltimore City, and there shall also be a clerk of the criminal court of Baltimore City, and each of said clerks shall be elected as aforesaid by the qualified voters of the city of Baltimore, and shall hold his office for six years from the time of his election, and until a new election is held, and be reeligible thereto, subject, in like manner, to be removed for wilful neglect of duty or other misdemeanor in office, on conviction in a court of law. In case of a vacancy in the office of a clerk, the judge or judges of the court of which he was clerk shall have the power to appoint a clerk until the general election of delegates held next thereafter, when a clerk shall be elected to fill such vacancy.

SEC. 15. The clerk of the court of common pleas for Baltimore City shall have authority to issue within the said city all marriage and other licenses required by law, subject to such provisions as the legislature shall hereafter prescribe; and the clerk of the superior court for said city shall have the custody of all deeds, conveyances, and other papers now remaining in the office of the clerk of Baltimore County court, and shall hereafter receive and record all deeds, conveyances, and other papers which are required by law to be recorded in said city. He shall also have the custody of all other papers connected with the proceedings on the law or equity side of Baltimore County court, and of the dockets thereof, so far as the same have relation to Baltimore City.

SEC. 16. That the clerk of the court of appeals, and the clerks of the circuit courts in the several counties, shall respectively perform all the duties and be entitled to the fees which appertain to the offices of the clerks of court of appeals for the eastern and western shores and of the clerks of county courts, and the clerks of the court of common pleas, the superior court, and the criminal court for Baltimore City shall perform all the duties appertaining to their respective offices, and heretofore vested in the clerks of Baltimore County court and Baltimore City court respectively, and be entitled to all the fees now allowed by law; and all laws relating to the clerks of court of appeal, clerks of the several county courts, and Baltimore City court shall be applicable to the clerks respectively of the clerk of court of appeals, the circuit courts, the court of common pleas, the superior court, and the criminal court of Baltimore City, until otherwise provided by law; and the said clerks, when duly elected and qualified according to law, shall have the charge and custody of the records and other papers belonging to their respective offices.

SEC. 17. The qualified voters of the city of Baltimore, and of the several counties of the State, shall, on the first Wednesday of November, eighteen hundred and fifty-one, and on the same day of the same month in every fourth year forever thereafter, elect three men to be judges of the orphans' court of said city and counties respectively, who shall be citizens of the State of Maryland and citizens of the city or county for which they may be severally elected at the time of their election. They shall have all the powers now vested in the orphans' courts of this State, subject to such changes therein as the legislature may prescribe, and each of said judges shall be paid at a per diem rate for the time they are in session, to be fixed by the legislature and paid by the said counties and city respectively.

SEC. 18. There shall be a register of wills in each county of the State and in the city of Baltimore, to be elected by the legal and qualified voters of said counties and city respectively, who shall hold his office for six years from the time of his election, and until a new election shall take place, and be reëligible thereto, subject to be removed for wilful neglect of duty or misdemeanor in office, in the same manner that the clerks of the county courts are removable. In the event of any vacancy in the office of register of wills, said vacancy shall be filled by the judges of the orphans' court until the general election next thereafter for delegates to the general assembly, when a register shall be elected to fill such vacancy.

SEC. 19. The legislature at its first session after the adoption of this constitution shall fix the number of justices of the peace and constables for each ward of the city of Baltimore, and for each election district in the several counties, who shall be elected by the legal and qualified voters thereof respectively, at the next general election for delegates thereafter, and shall hold their offices for two years from the time of their election, and until their successors in office are elected and qualified; and the legislature may, from time to time, increase or diminish the number of justices of the peace and constables to be elected in the several wards and election districts as the wants and interests of the people may require. They shall be, by virtue of their offices, conservators of the peace in the said counties and city respectively, and shall have such duties and compensation as now exist or may be provided for by law. In the event of a vacancy in the office of a justice of the peace, the governor shall appoint a person to serve as justice of the peace, until the next regular election of said officers, and in case of a vacancy in the office of constable, the county commissioners of the county in which a vacancy may occur, or the mayor and city council of Baltimore, as the case may be, shall appoint a person to serve as constable until the next regular election thereafter for said officers. An appeal shall lie in all civil cases from the judgment of a justice of the peace to the circuit court, or to the court of common pleas of Baltimore City, as the case may be, and on all such appeals, either party shall be entitled to a trial by jury, according to the laws now existing, or which may be hereafter enacted. And the mayor and city council may provide, by ordinance, from time to time, for the creation and government of such temporary additional policy as they may deem necessary to preserve the public peace.

SEC. 20. There shall be elected in each county and in the city of Baltimore, every second year, two persons for the office of sheriff for each county, and two for the said city, the one of whom having the highest number of votes of the qualified voters of said county or city, or if both have an equal number, either of them, at the discretion of the governor, to be commissioned by the governor for the said office, and, having served for two years, such person shall be ineligible for the two years next succeeding; bond with security, to be taken every year, and no sheriff shall be qualified to act before the same be given. In case of death, refusal, disqualification, or removal out of the county, before the expiration of the said two years, the other person chosen as aforesaid shall be commissioned by the governor to execute the said office for the residue of the said two years, and said person giving bond with security as aforesaid. No person shall be eligible to the office of sheriff but a resident of such county or city respectively, who shall have been a citizen of this State at least five years preceding his election, and above the age of twenty-one years. The two candidates, properly qualified, having the highest number of legal ballots, shall be declared duly elected for the office of sheriff for such county or city, and returned to the governor, with a certificate of the number of ballots for each of them.

SEC. 21. Coroners, elisors, and notaries public shall be appointed for each county and the city of Baltimore, in the manner now prescribed by law, or in such other manner as the general assembly may hereafter direct.

SEC. 22. No judge shall sit in any case wherein he may be interested, or where either of the parties may be connected with him by affinity or consanguinity, within such degrees as may be prescribed by law, or where he shall have been of council in the case; and whenever any of the judges of the circuit courts, or of the courts for Baltimore City, shall be thus disqualified, or whenever, by reason of sickness, or any other cause, the said judges, or any of them, may be unable to sit in any cause, the parties may, by consent, appoint a proper person to try the said cause, or the judges, or any of them, shall do so when directed by law.

SEC. 23. The present chancellor and the register in chancery, and, in the event of any vacancy in their respective offices, their successors in office respectively, who are to be appointed as at present, by the governor and senate, shall continue in office, with the powers and compensation as at present established, until the expiration of two years after the adoption of this constitution by the people, and until the end of the session of the legislature next thereafter, after which the said offices of chancellor and register shall be abolished. The legislature shall, in the mean time, provide by law for the recording, safekeeping, or other disposition of the records, decrees, and other proceedings of the court of chancery, and for the copying and attestation thereof, and for the custody and use of the great seal of the State, when required, after the expiration of the said two years, and for transmitting to the said counties, and to the city of Baltimore, all the cases and proceedings in said court then undisposed of and unfinished, in such manner and under such regulations as may be deemed necessary and proper: *Provided*, That no new business shall originate in the said court, nor shall any cause be removed to the same from any other court, from and after the ratification of this constitution.

SEC. 24. The first election of judges, clerks, registers of wills, and all other officers, whose election by the people is provided for in this article of the constitution, except justices of the peace and constables, shall take place throughout the State on the first Wednesday of November next after the ratification of this constitution by the people.

SEC. 25. In case of the death, resignation, removal, or other disqualification of a judge of any of the courts of law, the governor, by and with the advice and consent of the senate, shall thereupon appoint a person, duly qualified, to fill said office until the next general election for delegates thereafter; at which time an election shall be held, as hereinbefore prescribed, for a judge, who shall hold the said office for ten years, according to the provisions of this constitution.

SEC. 26. In case of the death, resignation, removal, or other disqualification of the judge of an orphans' court, the vacancy shall be filled by the appointment of the governor, by and with the advice and consent of the senate.

SEC. 27. Whenever lands lie partly in one county and partly in another, or partly in a county and partly in the city of Baltimore, or whenever persons proper to be made defendants to proceedings in chancery reside some in one county and some in another, that court shall have jurisdiction in which proceedings shall have been first commenced, subject to such rules, regulations, and alterations as may be prescribed by law.

SEC. 28. In all suits or actions at law, issues from the orphans' court, or from any court sitting in equity, in petitions for freedom, and in all presentments and indictments now pending, or which may be pending at the time of the adoption of this constitution by the people, or which may be hereafter instituted in any of the courts of law of this State, having jurisdiction thereof, the judge or judges thereof, upon suggestion in writing, if made by the State's attorney, of the prosecutor for the State, or upon suggestion in writing, supported by affidavit, made by any of the parties thereto, or other proper evidence, that a fair and impartial trial cannot be had in the court where such suit or action at law, issues or petitions, or presentment and indictment is depending, shall order and direct the record of proceedings in such suit or action, issues or petitions, presentment or indictment, to be transmitted to the court of any adjoining county: *Provided*, That the removal in all civil causes be confined to an adjoining county within the judicial circuit, except as to the city of Baltimore, where the removal may be to an adjoining county for trial, which court shall hear and determine the same in like manner as if such suit or action, issues or petitions, presentment or indictment, had been originally instituted therein: *And provided also*, That such suggestion shall be made as aforesaid before or during the term in which the issue or issues may be joined in said suit or action, issues or petition, presentment or indictment, and that such further remedy in the premises may be provided by law as the legislature shall from time to time direct and enact.

SEC. 29. All elections of judges, and other officers provided for by this constitution, shall be certified, and the returns made by the clerks of the respective counties to the governor, who shall issue commissions to the different persons for the offices to which they shall have been respectively elected; and in all such elections the person having the greatest number of votes shall be declared to be elected.

Sec. 30. If in any case of election for judges, clerks of the courts of law, and registers of wills the opposing candidates shall have an equal number of votes, it shall be the duty of the governor to order a new election; and in case of any contested election, the governor shall send the returns to the house of delegates, who shall judge of the election and qualification of the candidates at such election.

Sec. 31. Every person of good moral character, being a voter, shall be admitted to practise law in all the courts of law in this State in his own case.

Article V

the state's attorneys

Section 1. There shall be an attorney for the State in each county and the city of Baltimore, to be styled "the State's attorney," who shall be elected by the voters thereof, respectively, on the first Wednesday of November next, and on the same day every fourth year thereafter, and hold his office for four years from the first Monday of January next ensuing his election, and until his successor shall be elected and qualified, and shall be reëligible thereto, and be subject to removal therefrom for incompetency, wilful neglect of duty, or misdemeanor in office, on conviction in a court of law.

Sec. 2. All elections for the State's attorney shall be certified to, and returns made thereof, by the clerks of the said counties and city to the judges thereof having criminal jurisdiction, respectively, whose duty it shall be to decide upon the elections and qualifications of the persons returned, and in case of a tie between two or more persons to designate which of said persons shall qualify as State's attorney, and to administer the oaths of office to the persons elected.

Sec. 3. The State's attorney shall perform such duties and receive such fees and commissions as are now prescribed by law for the attorney-general and his deputies, and such other duties, fees, and commissions as may hereafter be prescribed by law, and if any State's attorney shall receive any other fee or reward than such as is, or may be allowed by law, he shall, on conviction thereof, be removed from office.

Sec. 4. No person shall be eligible to the office of State's attorney who has not been admitted to practise the law in this State, and who has not resided for at least one year in the county or city in which he may be elected.

Sec. 5. In case of vacancy in the office of State's attorney, or of his removal from the county or city in which he shall have been elected, or on his conviction as hereinbefore specified, the said vacancy shall be filled by the judge of the county or city, respectively, having criminal jurisdiction, in which said vacancy shall occur, until the election and qualification of his successor, at which election said vacancy shall be filled by the voters of the said county or city for the residue of the term thus made vacant.

Sec. 6. It shall be the duty of the clerk of the court of appeals and the commissioner of the land-office, respectively, whenever a case shall be brought into said court or office in which the State is a party, or has an interest, immediately to notify the governor thereof.

Article VI

TREASURY DEPARTMENT

Section 1. There shall be a treasury department, consisting of a comptroller, chosen by the qualified electors of the State at each election of members of the house of delegates, who shall receive an annual salary of two thousand five hundred dollars; and of a treasurer, to be appointed by the two houses of the legislature, at each session thereof, on joint ballot, who shall also receive an annual salary of two thousand five hundred dollars; and neither of the said officers shall be allowed or receive any fees, commissions, or perquisites of any kind, in addition to his salary, for the performance of any duty or service whatever. In case of a vacancy in either of the offices, by death or otherwise, the governor, by and with the advice and consent of the senate, shall fill such vacancy by appointment, to continue until another election by the people or a choice by the legislature, as the case may be, and the qualification of the successor. The comptroller and the treasurer shall keep their offices at the seat of government, and shall take such oath and enter into such bonds for the faithful discharge of their duties as the legislature shall prescribe.

Sec. 2. The comptroller shall have the general superintendence of the fiscal affairs of the State; he shall digest and prepare plans for the improvement and management of the revenue and for the support of the public credit; prepare and report estimates of the revenue and expenditure of the State; superintend and enforce the collection of all taxes and revenue; adjust, settle, and preserve all public accounts; decide on the forms of keeping and stating accounts; grant, under regulations prescribed by law, all warrants for moneys to be paid out of the treasury, in pursuance of appropriations by law; prescribe the formalities of the transfer of stock or other evidences of the State debt; and countersign the same, without which such evidences shall not be valid; he shall make full reports of all his proceedings, and of the state of the treasury department, within ten days after the commencement of each session of the legislature, and perform such other duties as shall be prescribed by law.

Sec. 3. The treasurer shall receive and keep the moneys of the State, and disburse the same upon warrants drawn by the comptroller, and not otherwise; he shall take receipts for all moneys paid by him, and all receipts for moneys received by him shall be indorsed upon warrants signed by the comptroller, without which warrant, so signed, no acknowledgment of money received into the treasury shall be valid; and upon warrants issued by the comptroller he shall make arrangements for the payment of the interest of the public debt, and for the purchase thereof, on account of the sinking-fund. Every bond, certificate, or other evidence of the debt of the State, shall be signed by the treasurer and countersigned by the comptroller, and no new certificate or other evidence intended to replace another shall be issued until the old one shall be delivered to the treasurer, and authority executed in due form for the transfer of the same shall be filed in his office, and the transfer accordingly made on the books thereof, and the certificate or other evidence cancelled; but the legislature may make provision for the loss of certificates or other evidence of the debt.

SEC. 4. The treasurer shall render his accounts quarterly to the comptroller; and on the third day of each session of the legislature he shall submit to the senate and house of delegates fair and accurate copies of all accounts by him from time to time rendered and settled with the comptroller. He shall at all times submit to the comptroller the inspection of the moneys in his hands, and perform all other duties that shall be prescribed by law.

ARTICLE VII

SUNDRY OFFICERS

SECTION 1. At the first general election of delegates to the general assembly, after the adoption of this constitution, four commissioners shall be elected as hereinafter provided, who shall be styled "comsioners of public works," and who shall exercise a diligent and faithful supervision of all public works, in which the State may be interested as stockholder or creditor, and shall represent the State in all meetings of the stockholders, and shall appoint the directors in every railroad or canal company in which the State has the constitutional power to appoint directors. It shall also be the duty of the commissioners of public works to review, from time to time, the rate of tolls adopted by any company; use all legal powers which they may possess to obtain the establishment of rates of toll, which may prevent an injurious competition with each other, to the detriment of the interests of the State; and so to adjust them as to promote the agriculture of the State. It shall also be the duty of the said commissioners of public works to keep a journal of their proceedings; and at each regular session of the legislature to make to it a report, and to recommend such legislation as they shall deem necessary and requisite to promote or protect the interest of the State in the public works; and perform such other duties as may be prescribed by law. They shall each receive such salary as may be allowed by law, which shall not be increased or diminished during their continuance in office.

SEC. 2. For the election of the commissioners of public works, the State shall be divided into four districts. The counties of Alleghany, Washington, Frederick, Carroll, Baltimore, and Harford shall constitute the first district; the counties of Montgomery, Howard, Anne Arundel, Calvert, Saint Mary's, Charles, and Prince George's shall constitute the second district; Baltimore City shall constitute the third district; the counties of Cecil, Kent, Queen Anne's, Talbot, Caroline, Dorchester, Somerset, and Worcester shall constitute the fourth district. One commissioner shall be elected in each district, who shall have been a resident thereof at least five years next preceding his election.

SEC. 3. The said commissioners shall be elected by the qualified voters of their districts respectively; the returns of their election shall be certified to the governor, who shall, by proclamation, declare the result of the election. Two of the said commissioners first elected shall hold their office for four years, and the other two for two years from the first Monday of December next succeeding their election. And at the first meeting after their election, or as soon thereafter as practicable, they shall determine by lot who of their number shall hold their offices for four and two years respectively; and thereafter there shall be elected as aforesaid, at each general election of delegates, two commissioners for the term of four years, to be taken from the districts respectively wherein the commissioners resided at the time of their election, whose term of service has expired. And in case of a vacancy in the office of either of said commissioners, by death, resignation, or otherwise, the governor, by and with the advice and consent of the senate, shall appoint some qualified person from the same district, to serve until the next general election of delegates, when an election shall be held, as aforesaid, for a commissioner for the residue of said term. And in case of an equal division in the board of commissioners, on any subject committed to their charge, the treasurer of the State shall have power, and shall be called on to decide the same. And in the event of a tie vote for any two of the candidates for the office of commissioner in the same district, it shall be the duty of the governor to commission one or the other of the candidates having the equal number of votes. And if the governor doubt the legality or result of any election held for said commissioners, it shall be his duty to send the returns of such election to the house of delegates, who shall judge of the election and qualification of the candidates at such election.

Sec. 4. During the continuance of the lottery system in this State, there shall be elected by the legal and qualified voters of the State, at every general election for delegates to the general assembly, one commissioner of lotteries, who shall hold his office for two years, and till the qualification of his successor, and shall be reëligible. His whole compensation shall be paid out of the fund raised for the Maryland consolidated lottery-grants, and shall not exceed the amount of commissions received by one of the present lottery commissioners, out of said fund; and he shall give such bond, for the faithful performance of his duties, as is now given by the lottery commissioners. The term of the commissioner, who shall be elected at the general election for delegates next succeeding the adoption of this constitution, shall commence at the expiration of the commissions of the present lottery commissioners, and continue for two years, and till the qualification of his successor.

Sec. 5. From and after the first day of April, eighteen hundred and fifty-nine, no lottery scheme shall be drawn, for any purpose whatever, nor shall any lottery-ticket be sold in this State; and it shall be the duty of the several commissioners elected under this constitution to make such contract or contracts as will extinguish all existing lottery-grants before the said first day of April, eighteen hundred and fifty-nine, and also secure to the State a clear yearly revenue equal to the average amount derived by the State from the system for the last five years; but no such contract or contracts shall be valid until approved by the treasurer and comptroller.

Sec. 6. There shall be a commissioner of the land-office elected by the qualified voters of the State, at the first general election of delegates to the assembly after the ratification of this constitution, who shall hold his office for the term of six years from the first day of January next after his election. The returns of said election shall be made to the governor, and in the event of a tie between any two or more candidates, the governor shall direct a new election to be held by writs to the several sheriffs, who shall hold said election after at least twenty days' notice, exclusive of the day of election. The said commissioner shall sit as judge of the land-office, and receive therefor the sum of two hundred dollars per annum, to be paid out of the State treasury. He shall also perform the duties of the register of the land-office, and be entitled to receive therefor the fees now chargeable in said office; and he shall also perform the duties of examiner-general, and be entitled to receive therefor the fees now chargeable by said officer. The office of register of the land-office and examiner-general shall be abolished from and after the election and qualification of the commissioner of the land-office.

Sec. 7. The State librarian shall be elected by the joint vote of the two branches of the legislature, for two years, and until his successor shall be elected and qualified. His salary shall be one thousand dollars per annum. He shall perform such duties as are now or may hereafter be prescribed by law.

Sec. 8. The county authorities now known as levy courts or county commissioners, shall hereafter be styled "county commissioners," and shall be elected by general ticket, and not by districts, by the voters of the several counties, on the first Wednesday in November, one thousand eight hundred and fifty-one, and on the same day in every second year thereafter. Said commissioners shall exercise such powers and duties only as the legislature may from time to time prescribe; but such powers and duties and the tenure of office shall be uniform throughout the State, and the legislature shall, at or before its second regular session, after the adoption of this constitution, pass such laws as may be necessary for determining the number for each county, and ascertaining and defining the powers, duties, and tenure of office of said commissioners; and until the passage of such laws the commissioners elected under this constitution shall have and exercise all the powers and duties in their respective counties, now exercised by the county authorities under the laws of the State.

Sec. 9. The general assembly shall provide by law for the election of road supervisors, in the several counties, by the voters of the election-districts respectively, and may provide by law for the election or appointment of such other county officers as may be required and are not herein provided for, and prescribe their powers and duties; but the tenure of office, their powers and duties, and mode of appointment, shall be uniform throughout the State.

Sec. 10. The qualified voters of each county, and the city of Baltimore, shall, at the first election of delegates after the adoption of this constitution, and every two years thereafter, elect a surveyor for the counties, and the city of Baltimore, respectively, whose duties and compensation shall be the same as are now prescribed by law for the county and city surveyors, respectively, or as may hereafter be prescribed by law. The term of office of said county and city surveyors, respectively, shall commence on the first Monday of January next succeeding their election. And vacancies in said office of surveyors, by death, resignation, or removal from their respective counties or city, shall be filled by the commissioners of the counties, or mayor and city council of Baltimore, respectively.

SEC. 11. The qualified voters of Worcester County shall, at the first election of delegates after the adoption of this constitution, and every two years thereafter, elect a wreck-master for the said county, whose duties and compensation shall be the same as are now prescribed or may be hereafter prescribed by law. The term of office of said wreck-master shall commence on the first Monday of January next succeeding his election; and a vacancy in said office, by death, resignation, or removal from the county, shall be filled by the county commissioners of said county, for the residue of the term thus made vacant.

Article VIII

NEW COUNTIES

SECTION 1. That part of Anne Arundel County called Howard district is hereby erected into a new county, to be called Howard County, the inhabitants whereof shall have, hold, and enjoy all such rights and privileges as are held and enjoyed by the inhabitants of the other counties in this State; and its civil and municipal officers, at the time of the ratification of this constitution, shall continue in office until their successors shall have been elected or appointed, and shall have qualified as such; and all rights, powers, and obligations incident to Howard district of Anne Arundel County shall attach to Howard County.

SEC. 2. When that part of Alleghany County lying south and west of a line beginning at the summit of Big Back Bone or Savage Mountain, where that mountain is crossed by Mason and Dixon's line, and running thence by a straight line to the middle of Savage River where it empties into the Potomac River, thence by a straight line to the nearest point or boundary of the State of Virginia, then with said boundary to the Fairfax stone, shall contain a population of ten thousand, and the majority of electors thereof shall desire to separate and form a new county, and make known their desire by petition to the legislature, the legislature shall direct, at the next succeeding election, that the judges shall open a book at each election-district in said part of Alleghany County, and have recorded therein the vote of each elector " for or against " a new county. In case the majority are in favor, then said part of Alleghany County to be declared an independent county, and the inhabitants whereof shall have and enjoy all such rights and privileges as are held and enjoyed by the inhabitants of the other counties in this State: *Provided*, That the whole representation in the returns of every census of the United States, hereafter taken, to pass a law for the general assembly of the county, when divided, shall not exceed the present delegation of Alleghany County, allowed under this constitution, until after the next census.

Article IX

MILITIA

SECTION 1. It shall be the duty of the legislature to pass laws for the enrolment of the militia; to provide for districting the State into divisions, brigades, battalions, regiments, and companies, and to pass laws for the effectual encouragement of volunteer corps by some mode which may induce the formation and continuance of at least one volunteer company in every county and division in the city of Baltimore. The company, battalion, and regimental officers (staff-officers excepted) shall be elected by the persons composing their several companies, battalions, and regiments.

SEC. 2. The adjutant-general shall be appointed by the governor, by and with the advice and consent of the senate. He shall hold his office for the term of six years, and receive the same salary as heretofore, until changed by the legislature.

ARTICLE X

MISCELLANEOUS

SECTION 1. Every officer of this State, the governor excepted, the entire amount of whose pay or compensation received for the discharge of his official duties shall exceed the yearly sum of three thousand dollars, shall keep a book, in which shall be entered every sum or sums of money received by him or on his account as a payment or compensation for his performance of official duties, a copy of which entries in said book, verified by the oath of the officer by whom it is directed to be kept, shall be returned yearly to the treasurer of the State for his inspection and that of the general assembly of Maryland; and each of such officers, when the amount received by him for the year shall exceed the sum of three thousand dollars, shall yearly pay over to the treasurer the amount of such excess by him received, subject to such disposition thereof as the legislature may deem just and equitable. And any such officer failing to comply with the said requisition shall be deemed to have vacated his office, and be subject to suit by the State for the amount that ought to have been paid into the treasury.

SEC. 2. The legislature shall have power to pass all such laws as may be necessary and proper for carrying into execution the powers vested by this constitution in any department or office of the government, and the duties imposed upon them thereby.

SEC. 3. If in any election directed by this constitution any two or more candidates shall have the highest and an equal number of votes, a new election shall be ordered, unless in cases specially provided for by the constitution.

SEC. 4. The trial by jury of all issues of fact in civil proceedings, in the several courts of law in this State, where the amount in controversy exceeds the sum of five dollars, shall be inviolably preserved.

SEC. 5. In the trial of all criminal cases the jury shall be the judges of law as well as fact.

SEC. 6. The legislature shall have power to regulate by law all matters which relate to the judges, time, place, and manner of holding elections in this State, and of making returns thereof: *Provided*, That the tenure and term of office, and the day of election, shall not be affected thereby.

SEC. 7. All rights vested, and all liabilities incurred, shall remain as if this constitution had not been adopted.

SEC. 8. The governor and all officers, civil and military, now holding commissions under this State, shall continue to hold and exercise their offices, according to their present tenure, until they shall be superseded, pursuant to the provisions of this constitution, and until their successors be duly qualified.

SEC. 9. The sheriffs of the several counties of this State, and of the city of Baltimore, shall give notice of the several elections authorized by this constitution, in the manner prescribed by existing laws for elections under the present constitution.

SEC. 10. This constitution, if adopted by a majority of the legal votes cast on the first Wednesday of June next, shall go into operation on the fourth day of July next, and on and after said day shall supersede the present constitution of this State.

ARTICLE XI

AMENDMENT OF THE CONSTITUTION

It shall be the duty of the legislature, at its first session immediately succeeding ascertaining, at the next general election of delegates, the sense of the people of Maryland in regard to the calling a convention for altering the constitution; and in case the majority of votes cast at said election shall be in favor of calling a convention, the legislature shall provide for assembling such convention, and electing delegates thereto at the earliest convenient day; and the delegates to the said convention shall be elected by the several counties of the State and the city of Baltimore, in proportion to their representation respectively in the senate and house of delegates at the time when said convention may be called.

Done in convention, the 13th day of May, in the year of our Lord one thousand eight hundred and fifty-one, and of the Independence of the United States the seventy-fifth.

J. G. CHAPMAN, *President.*

GEORGE G. BREWER, *Secretary.*

CONSTITUTION OF MARYLAND—1864 * a

DECLARATION OF RIGHTS

We, the people of the State of Maryland, grateful to Almighty God for our civil and religious liberty, and taking into our serious consideration the best means of establishing a good constitution in this State, for the sure foundation and more permanent security thereof, declare:

ARTICLE 1. That we hold it to be self-evident that all men are created equally free; that they are endowed by their Creator with certain unalienable rights, among which are life, liberty, the enjoyment of the proceeds of their own labor, and the pursuit of happiness.

ART. 2. That all government of right originates from the people, is

---

* Verified by text in Edward Otis Hinkley's edition. Published by authority. Annapolis; Richard P. Bayly. 1865. Pp. 102.

a This constitution was framed by a convention which met at Annapolis April 27, 1864, and completed its labors September 6, 1864. It was submitted to the people, and ratified October 12 and 13, 1864, by the following vote: Home vote, 27,541 for, 29,536 against, and 61 blank: Soldiers' vote, 2,633 for, and 263 against; majority in favor of ratification, 375.

founded in compact only, and instituted solely for the good of the whole; and they have at all times the unalienable right to alter, reform, or abolish their form of government in such manner as they may deem expedient.

ART. 3. That the people of this State ought to have the sole and exclusive right of regulating the internal government and police thereof.

ART. 4. That the inhabitants of Maryland are entitled to the common law of England, and the trial by jury according to the course of that law, and to the benefit of such of the English statutes as existed on the fourth day of July, seventeen hundred and seventy-six, and which, by experience, have been found applicable to their local and other circumstances, and have been introduced, used, and practised by the courts of law or equity, and also of all acts of assembly in force on the first day of June, eighteen hundred and sixty-four, except such as may have since expired or may be inconsistent with the provisions of this constitution, subject, nevertheless, to the revision of and amendment or repeal by the legislature of this State; and the inhabitants of Maryland are also entitled to all property derived to them from or under the charter granted by His Majesty Charles the First to Cecillus Calvert, Baron of Baltimore.

ART. 5. The Constitution of the United States and the laws made in pursuance thereof being the supreme law of the land, every citizen of this State owes paramount allegiance to the Constitution and Government of the United States, and is not bound by any law or ordinance of this State in contravention or subversion thereof.

ART. 6. That all persons invested with the legislative or executive powers of government are the trustees of the public, and as such accountable for their conduct; wherefore, whenever the ends of government are perverted, and public liberty manifestly endangered, and all other means of redress are ineffectual, the people may and of right ought to reform the old or establish a new government. The doctrine of non-resistance against arbitrary power and oppression is absurb, slavish, and destructive of the good and happiness of mankind.

ART. 7. That the right of the people to participate in the legislature is the best security of liberty and the foundation of all free government; for this purpose elections ought to be free and frequent, and every free white male citizen, having the qualifications prescribed by the constitution, ought to have the right of suffrage.

ART. 8. That the legislative, executive, and judicial powers of government ought to be forever separate and distinct from each other, and no person exercising the functions of one of said departments shall assume or discharge the duties of any other.

ART. 9. That no power of suspending laws or the execution of laws, unless by or derived from the legislature, ought to be exercised or allowed.

ART. 10. That freedom of speech and debate, or proceedings in the legislature, ought not to be impeached in any court of judicature.

ART. 11. That Annapolis be the place for the meeting of the legislature, and the legislature ought not to be convened or held at any other place but for evident necessity.

ART. 12. That for the redress of grievances, and for amending, strengthening, and preserving the laws, the legislature ought to be frequently convened.

ART. 13. That every man hath a right to petition the legislature for the redress of grievances, in a peaceable and orderly manner.

ART. 14. That no aid, charge, tax, burden, or fees ought to be rated or levied, under any pretence, without the consent of the legislature.

ART. 15. That the levying of taxes by the poll is grievous and oppressive, and ought to be prohibited; that paupers ought not to be assessed for the support of the government, but every other person in the State, or persons holding property therein, ought to contribute his proportion of public taxes for the support of government, according to his actual worth in real or personal property; yet fines, duties, or taxes may properly and justly be imposed or laid, with a political view, for the good government and benefit of the community.

ART. 16. That sanguinary laws ought to be avoided as far as it is consistent with the safety of the State; and no law to inflict cruel and unusual pains and penalties ought to be made in any case, or at any time hereafter.

ART. 17. That retrospective laws, punishing acts committed before the existence of such laws, and by them only declared criminal, are oppressive, unjust, and incompatible with liberty; wherefore no *ex post facto* law ought to be made.

ART. 18. That no law to attaint particular persons of treason or felony ought to be made in any case, or at any time hereafter.

ART. 19. That every man, for any injury done to him in his person or property, ought to have remedy by the course of the law of the land, and ought to have justice and right freely without sale, fully without any denial, and speedily without delay, according to the law of the land.

ART. 20. That the trial of facts where they arise is one of the greatest securities of the lives, liberties, and estate of the people.

ART. 21. That in all criminal prosecutions every man hath a right to be informed of the accusation against him; to have a copy of the indictment or charge in due time (if required) to prepare for his defence; to be allowed counsel; to be confronted with the witnesses against him; to have process for his witnesses; to examine the witnesses for and against him on oath; and to a speedy trial by an impartial jury, without whose unanimous consent he ought not to be found guilty.

ART. 22. That no man ought to be compelled to give evidence against himself in a criminal case.

ART. 23. That no man ought to be taken or imprisoned, or disseized of his freehold, liberties, or privileges, or outlawed, or exiled, or in any manner destroyed, or deprived of his life, liberty, or property, but by the judgment of his peers, or by the law of the land.

ART. 24. That hereafter, in this State, there shall be neither slavery nor involuntary servitude, except in punishment of crime, whereof the party shall have been duly convicted; and all persons held to service or labor as slaves are hereby declared free.

ART. 25. That excessive bail ought not to be required, nor excessive fines imposed, nor cruel or unusual punishment inflicted, by the courts of law.

ART. 26. That all warrants, without oath or affirmation, to search suspected places, or to seize any person or property, are grievous and oppressive; and all general warrants to search suspected places, or to apprehend suspected persons, without naming or describing the place, or the person in special, are illegal, and ought not to be granted.

ART. 27. That no conviction shall work corruption of blood, nor shall there be any forfeiture of the estate of any person for any crime, except treason, and then only on conviction.

ART. 28. That a well-regulated militia is the proper and natural defence of a free government.

ART. 29. That standing armies are dangerous to liberty, and ought not to be raised or kept up without the consent of the legislature.

ART. 30. That in all cases, and at all times, the military ought to be under strict subordination to and control of the civil power.

ART. 31. That no soldier shall, in time of peace, be quartered in any house without the consent of the owner, nor in time of war, except in the manner prescribed by law.

ART. 32. That no person, except regular soldiers, mariners, and marines, in the service of this State, or militia when in actual service, ought in any case to be subject to, or punishable by, martial law.

ART. 33. That the independency and uprightness of judges are essential to the impartial administration of justice, and a great security to the rights and liberties of the people; wherefore the judges shall not be removed, except for misbehavior, or conviction in a court of law, or by the governor, upon the address of the general assembly: *Provided,* That two-thirds of all the members of each house concur in such address. No judge shall hold any other office, civil or military, or political trust or employment of any kind whatsoever, under the constitution or laws of this State, or of the United States, or any of them, or receive fees or perquisites of any kind for the discharge of his official duties.

ART. 34. That a long continuance in the executive departments of power or trust is dangerous to liberty; a rotation, therefore, in those departments is one of the best securities of permanent freedom.

ART. 35. That no person ought to hold at the same time more than one office of profit created by the constitution or laws of this State; nor ought any person in public trust to receive any present from any foreign prince, or state, or from the United States, or any of them, without the approbation of this State.

ART. 36. That, as it is the duty of every man to worship God in such manner as he thinks most acceptable to Him, all persons are equally entitled to protection in their religious liberty; wherefore, no person ought, by any law, to be molested in his person or estate on account of his religious persuasion or profession, or for his religious practice, unless under the color of religion any man shall disturb the good order, peace, or safety of the State, or shall infringe the laws of morality, or injure others in their natural, civil, or religious rights; nor ought any person to be compelled to frequent or maintain, or contribute, unless on contract, to maintain any place of worship or any ministry; nor shall any person be deemed incompetent as a witness or juror who believes in the existence of a God, and that under His dispensation such person will be held morally accountable for his acts, and be rewarded or punished therefor, either in this world or the world to come.

ART. 37. That no other test or qualification ought to be required on admission to any office of trust or profit than such oath of allegiance and fidelity to this State and the United States as may be prescribed by this constitution, and such oath of office and qualification as may be prescribed by this constitution, or by the laws of the State, and a declaration of belief in the Christian religion, or in the existence of God, and in a future state of rewards and punishments.

ART. 38. That every gift, sale, or devise of land, to any minister, public teacher, or preacher of the gospel, as such, or to any religious sect, order, or denomination, or to or for the support, use, or benefit of, or in trust for any minister, public teacher, or preacher of the gospel, as such, or any religious sect, order, or denomination; and every gift or sale of goods or chattels to go in succession, or to take place after the death of the seller or donor, to or for such support, use, or benefit; and also every devise of goods or chattels, to or for the support, use, or benefit of any minister, public teacher, or preacher of the gospel, as such; or any religious sect, order, or denomination, without the prior or subsequent sanction of the legislature, shall be void; except always any sale, gift, lease, or devise of any quantity of land, not exceeding five acres, for a church, meeting-house, or other house of worship, or parsonage, or for a burying-ground, which shall be improved, enjoyed, or used only for such purpose, or such sale, gift, lease, or devise shall be void.

ART. 39. That the manner of administering an oath or affirmation to any person ought to be such as those of the religious persuasion, profession, or denomination of which he is a member generally esteem the most effectual confirmation by the attestation of the Divine Being.

ART. 40. That the liberty of the press ought to be inviolably preserved; that every citizen of the State ought to be allowed to speak, write, and punish his sentiments on all subjects, being responsible for the abuse of that liberty.

ART. 41. That monopolies are odious, contrary to the spirit of a free government and the principles of commerce, and ought not to be suffered.

ART. 42. That no title of nobility or hereditary honors ought to be granted in this State.

ART. 43. That the legislature ought to encourage the diffusion of knowledge and virtue, the extension of a judicious system of general education, the promotion of literature, the arts, science, agriculture, commerce, and manufacture, and the general melioration of the condition of the people.

ART. 44. This enumeration of rights shall not be construed to impair or deny others retained by the people.

ART. 45. That the legislature shall pass no law providing for an alteration, change, or abolishment of this constitution, except in the manner therein prescribed and directed.

Article I

ELECTIVE FRANCHISE

Section 1. All elections shall be by ballot, and every white male citizen of the United States, of the age of twenty-one years or upwards, who shall have resided in the State one year next preceding the election, and six months in any county, or in any legislative district of Baltimore City, and who shall comply with the provisions of this article of the constitution, shall be entitled to vote at all elections hereafter held in this State; and in case any county or city shall be so divided as to form portions of different electoral districts for the election of Congressmen, senator, delegate, or other officer or officers, then to entitle a person to vote for such officer he must have been a resident of that part of the county or city which shall form a part of the electoral district in which he offers to vote for six months next preceding the election; but a person who shall have acquired a residence in such county or city entitling him to vote at any such election shall be entitled to vote in the election-district from which he removed, until he shall have acquired a residence in the part of the county or city to which he has removed.

Sec. 2. The general assembly shall provide by law for a uniform registration of the names of voters in this State, which registration shall be evidence of the qualification of said voters to vote at any election thereafter held, but no person shall be excluded from voting at any election on account of not being registered until the general assembly shall have passed an act of registration, and the same shall have been carried into effect, after which no person shall vote unless his name appears on the register. The general assembly shall also provide by law for taking the votes of soldiers in the Army of the United States serving in the field.

Sec. 3. No person above the age of twenty-one years, convicted of larceny or other infamous crime, unless pardoned by the governor, shall ever thereafter be entitled to vote at any election in this State, and no lunatic, or person *non compos mentis*, shall be entitled to vote.

Sec. 4. No person who has at any time been in armed hostility to the United States, or the lawful authorities thereof, or who has been in any manner in the service of the so-called Confederate States of America, and no person who has voluntarily left this State and gone within the military lines of the so-called Confederate States or armies, with the purpose of adhering to said States or armies, and no person who has given any aid, comfort, countenance, or support to those engaged in armed hostility to the United States, or in any manner adhered to the enemies of the United States, either by contributing to the enemies of the United States, or unlawfully sending within the lines of such enemies money, or goods, or letters, or information, or who has disloyally held communication with the enemies of the United States, or who has advised any person to enter the service of the said enemies, or aided any person so to enter, or who has by any open deed or word declared his adhesion to the cause of the enemies of the United States, or his desire for the triumph of said enemies over the arms of the United States, shall ever be entitled to vote at any election to be held in this State, or to hold any office of honor, profit, or trust under the laws of this State, unless since such unlawful acts he shall have voluntarily entered into the military service of the United States, and been honorably discharged therefrom, or shall be on the day of election actually and voluntarily in such service, or unless he shall be restored to his full rights of citizenship by an act of the general assembly passed by a vote of two-thirds of all the members elected to each house; and it shall be the duty of all officers of registration and judges of election carefully to exclude from voting, or being registered, all persons so as above disqualified; and the judges of election at the first election held under this constitution shall, and at any subsequent election may, administer to any person offering to vote the following oath or affirmation: "I do swear [or affirm] that I am a citizen of the United States; that I have never given any aid, countenance, or support to those in armed hostility to the United States; that I have never expressed a desire for the triumph of said enemies over the arms of the United States; and that I will bear true faith and allegiance to the United States and support the Constitution and laws thereof as the supreme law of the land, any law or any ordnance of any State to the contrary notwithstanding; that I will in all respects demean myself as a loyal citizen of the United States, and I make this oath or affirmation without any reservation or evasion, and believe it to be binding on me;" and any person declining to take such oath shall not be allowed to vote, but the taking of such oath shall not be deemed conclusive evidence of the right of such person to vote; and any person swearing or affirming falsely shall be liable to penalties of perjury, and it shall be the duty of the proper officers of registration to allow no person to be registered until he shall have taken the oath or affirmation above set out, and it shall be the duty of the judges of election in all their returns of the first election held under this constitution to state in their said returns that every person who has voted has taken such oath or affirmation. But the provisions of this section in relation to acts against the United States shall not apply to any person not a citizen of the United States who shall have committed such acts while in the service of some foreign country at war against the United States, and who has, since such acts, been naturalized, or may be naturalized, under the laws of the United States, and the oath above set forth shall be taken in the case of such persons in such sense.

Sec. 5. If any person shall give, or offer to give, directly or indirectly, or hath given, or offered to give, since the fourth day of July, eighteen hundred and fifty-one, any bribe, present, or reward, or any promise, or any security for the payment or delivery of money or any other thing to induce any voter to refrain from casting his vote, or forcibly to prevent him in any way from voting, or to procure a vote, for any candidate or person proposed or voted for as elector of President and Vice-President of the United States or Representative in Congress, or for any office of profit or trust created by the constitution or laws of this State, or by the ordinances or authority of the mayor and city council of Baltimore, the person giving, or offering to give, and the person receiving the same, and any person who gives, or causes to be given, an illegal vote, knowing it to be such, at any election to be hereafter held in this State, or who shall be guilty of or accessory to any fraud, force, surprise, or bribery to procure himself or any other person to be nominated to any office, national, State, or municipal, shall, on conviction in a court of law, in addition to the penalties now or hereafter to be imposed by law, be forever disqualified to hold any office of profit or trust, or to vote at any election thereafter.

SEC. 6. It shall be the duty of the general assembly to pass laws to punish with fine and imprisonment any person who shall remove into any election district or precinct of any ward of the city of Baltimore, not for the purpose of acquiring a *bona-fide* residence therein, but for the purpose of voting at an approaching election, or who shall vote in any election-district or ward in which he does not reside, (except in the case provided for in this article,) or shall at the same election vote in more than one election district or precinct, or shall vote or offer to vote in any name not his own, or in place of any other person of the same name, or shall vote in any county in which he does not reside.

SEC. 7. Every person elected or appointed to any office of trust or profit under this constitution, or under the laws made pursuant thereto, before he shall enter upon the duties of such office, shall take and subscribe the following oath or affirmation: " I, ———, do swear [or affirm, as the case may be] that I will, to the best of my skill and judgment, diligently and faithfully, without partiality or prejudice, execute the office of ——— according to the constitution and laws of this State, and that since the fourth day of July, in the year eighteen hundred and fifty-one, I have not in any manner violated the provisions of the present or of the late constitution in relation to the bribery of voters, or preventing legal votes or procuring illegal votes to be given, and [if a governor, senator, member of the house of delegates, or judge] that I will not, directly or indirectly, receive the profits or any part of the profits of any other office during the term of my acting as ———. I do further swear [or affirm] that I will bear true allegiance to the State of Maryland and support the constitution and laws thereof, and that I will bear true allegiance to the United States, and support, protect, and defend the Constitution, laws, and Government thereof as the supreme law of the land, any law or ordinance of this or any State to the contrary notwithstanding; that I have never directly or indirectly, by word, act, or deed, given any aid, comfort, or encouragement to those in rebellion against the United States or the lawful authorities thereof, but that I have been truly and loyally on the side of the United States against those in armed rebellion against the United States; and I do further swear [or affirm] that I will, to the best of my abilities, protect and defend the Union of the United States, and not allow the same to be broken up and dissolved or the Government thereof to be destroyed under any circumstances, if in my power to prevent it, and that I will at all times discountenance and oppose all political combinations having for their object such dissolution or destruction."

SEC. 8. Every person holding any office of trust or profit under the late constitution or under any law of this State, and who shall be continued in office under this constitution or under any law of the State, shall, within thirty days after this constitution shall have gone into effect, take and subscribe the oath or affirmation set forth in the seventh section of this article, and if any such person shall fail to take said oath, his office shall be *ipso facto* vacant. And every person hereafter elected or appointed to office in this State who shall refuse or neglect to take the oath or affirmation of office provided for in the said seventh section of this article shall be considered as having refused to accept the said office, and a new election or appointment shall be made as in case of refusal to accept or resignation of an office. And any person swearing or affirming falsely in the premises shall, on conviction thereof in a court of law, incur the penalties for wilful and corrupt perjury, and thereafter shall be incapable of holding any office of profit or trust in this State.

Article II

EXECUTIVE DEPARTMENT

Section 1. The executive power of the State shall be vested in a governor, whose term of office shall commence on the second Wednesday of January next ensuing his election, and continue for four years, and until his successor shall have qualified, but the governor chosen at the first election under this constitution shall not enter upon the discharge of the duties of the office until the expiration of the term for which the present incumbent was elected, unless the said office shall become vacant by death, resignation, removal from the State, or other disqualification of said incumbent.

Sec. 2. An election for governor under this constitution shall be held on the Tuesday next after the first Monday in November, in the year eighteen hundred and sixty-four, and on the same day and month in every fourth year thereafter, at the place of voting for delegates to the general assembly, and every person qualified to vote for delegates shall be qualified and entitled to vote for governor; the election to be held in the same manner as the election of delegates, and the returns thereof, under seal, to be addressed to the speaker of the house of delegates, and inclosed and transmitted to the secretary of state, and delivered to the said speaker at the commencement of the session of the general assembly next ensuing said election.

Sec. 3. The speaker of the house of delegates shall then open the said returns in the presence of both houses, and the person having the highest number of votes, and being constitutionally eligible, shall be the governor, and shall qualify in the manner herein prescribed, on the second Wednesday of January next ensuing his election, or as soon thereafter as may be practicable.

Sec. 4. If two or more persons shall have the highest and an equal number of votes, one of them shall be chosen governor by the senate and house of delegates; and all questions in relation to the eligibility of governor, and to the returns of said election, and to the number and legality of votes therein given, shall be determined by the house of delegates; and if the person or persons having the highest number of votes be ineligible, the governor shall be chosen by the senate and house of delegates. Every election of governor by the general assembly shall be determined by a joint majority of the senate and house of delegates, and the vote shall be taken *viva voce*. But if two or more persons shall have the highest and an equal number of votes, then a second vote shall be taken, which shall be confined to the persons having an equal number; and if the votes should be again equal, then the election of governor shall be determined by lot between those who shall have the highest and an equal number on the first vote.

SEC. 5. A person to be eligible to the office of governor must have attained the age of thirty years, and must have been for five years a citizen of the United States, and for five years next preceding his election a resident of the State.

SEC. 6. A lieutenant-governor shall be chosen at every regular election for governor. He shall continue in office for the same time, shall be elected in the same manner, and shall possess the same qualifications as the governor. In voting for governor and lieutenant-governor, the electors shall state for whom they vote as governor, and for whom as lieutenant-governor.

SEC. 7. The lieutenant-governor shall, by virtue of his office, be president of the senate, and whenever the senate are equally divided, shall have the right to give the casting vote.

SEC. 8. In case of the death, resignation, removal from the State, or other disqualification of the governor, the powers, duties, and emoluments of the office shall devolve upon the lieutenant-governor; and in case of his death, resignation, removal, or other disqualification, then upon the president of the senate for the time being, until the disqualification or inability shall cease, or until a new governor shall be elected and qualified; and for any vacancy in said office not herein provided for, provision may be made by law, and if such vacancy should occur without such provision being made, the general assembly shall be convened by the secretary of state for the purpose of filling said vacancy.

SEC. 9. Whenever the office of governor shall be administered by the lieutenant-governor, or he shall be unable to attend as president of the senate, the senate shall elect one of its own members as president *pro tempore*.

SEC. 10. The lieutenant-governor, while he acts as president of the senate, shall receive for his services the same compensation which shall for the same period be allowed to the speaker of the house of delegates, and no more.

SEC. 11. The governor shall be commander-in-chief of the land and naval forces of the State, and may call out the militia to repel invasions, suppress insurrections, and enforce the execution of the laws; but shall not take the command in person without the consent of the general assembly.

SEC. 12. He shall take care that the laws be faithfully executed.

SEC. 13. He shall nominate and, by and with the advice and consent of the senate, appoint all civil and military officers of the State, whose appointment or election is not otherwise herein provided for, unless a different mode of appointment be prescribed by the law creating the office.

SEC. 14. In case of a vacancy, during the recess of the senate, in any office which the governor has power to fill, he shall appoint some suitable person to said office, whose commission shall continue in force till the end of the next session of the general assembly, or till some other person is appointed to the same office, whichever shall first occur, and the nomination of the person thus appointed during the recess, or of some other person in his place, shall be made to the senate within thirty days after the next meeting of the general assembly.

SEC. 15. No person after being rejected by the senate shall be again nominated for the same office at the same session, unless at the request of the senate, or be appointed to the same office during the recess of the general assembly.

SEC. 16. All civil officers appointed by the governor and senate shall be nominated to the senate within fifty days from the commencement of each regular session of the general assembly, and their term of office, except in cases otherwise provided for in this constitution, shall commence on the first Monday of May next ensuing their appointment, and continue for two years, (unless sooner removed from office,) and until their successors respectively qualify according to law.

SEC. 17. The governor may suspend or arrest any military officer of the State for disobedience of orders, or other military offence; may remove him in pursuance of the sentence of a court-martial; and may remove, for incompetency or misconduct, all civil officers who received appointments from the executive for a term not exceeding two years.

SEC. 18. The governor may convene the general assembly, or the senate alone, on extraordinary occasions; and whenever, from the presence of an enemy, or from any other cause, the seat of government shall become an unsafe place for the meeting of the general assembly, he may direct their sessions to be held at some other convenient place.

SEC. 19. It shall be the duty of the governor semi-annually, and oftener, if he deem it expedient, to examine the bank-book, account-books, and official proceedings of the treasurer and comptroller of the State.

SEC. 20. He shall, from time to time, inform the general assembly of the condition of the State, and recommend to their consideration such measures as he may judge necessary and expedient.

SEC. 21. He shall have power to grant reprieves and pardons, except in cases of impeachment, and in cases in which he is prohibited by other articles of this constitution, and to remit fines and forfeitures for offences against the State; but shall not remit the principal or interest of any debt due to the State, except in cases of fines and forfeitures; and before granting a *nolle prosequi*, or pardon, he shall give notice in one or more newspapers of the application made for it, and of the day on or after which his decision will be given; and in every case in which he exercises this power, he shall report to either branch of the general assembly, whenever required, the petitions, recommendations, and reasons which influenced his decision.

SEC. 22. The governor shall reside at the seat of government, and shall receive for his services an annual salary of four thousand dollars.

SEC. 23. A secretary of state shall be appointed by the governor, by and with the advice and consent of the senate, who shall continue in office, unless sooner removed by the governor, till the end of the official term of the governor from whom he received his appointment, and shall receive an annual salary of one thousand dollars.

SEC. 24. The secretary of state shall carefully keep and preserve a record of all official acts and proceedings, which may at all times be inspected by a committee of either branch of the general assembly, and shall perform such other duties as are now or may hereafter be prescribed by law, or as may properly belong to his office.

Article III

LEGISLATIVE DEPARTMENT

SECTION 1. The legislature shall consist of two distinct branches, a senate and a house of delegates, which shall be styled " The general assembly of Maryland."

SEC. 2. Immediately after the adoption of this constitution, and before there shall have been held any general election under it, the mayor and city council of Baltimore shall proceed to lay off and divide the said city into three several districts, of equal population and contiguous territory, as near as may be; which said districts shall be called the first, second, and third legislative districts of Baltimore City.

SEC. 3. Every county in the State and each legislative district of Baltimore City, as hereinbefore provided for, shall be entitled to one senator, who shall be elected by the qualified voters of the counties and of the legislative districts of Baltimore City respectively, and shall serve for four years from the date of his election, subject to the classification of senators hereinafter provided for.

SEC. 4. The white population of the State shall constitute the basis of representation in the house of delegates, and the apportionment of the delegates among the several counties and legislative districts of the city of Baltimore shall be as follows: For every five thousand persons, or a fractional part thereof above one-half, one delegate shall be chosen, until the number of delegates in each county and legislative district of the city of Baltimore shall reach five; above that number, one delegate shall be chosen for the next twenty thousand persons, or a fractional portion over one-half thereof, in each county and legislative district of the city of Baltimore; above that number each county and legislative district of the said city shall elect one delegate for every eighty thousand persons, or fractional portion thereof above one-half. Upon this principle, and as soon as practicable after each national census, or State enumeration of inhabitants, the general assembly shall apportion the members of the house of delegates among the several counties and the several legislative districts of Baltimore City according to the white population of each. But until such apportionment is made the house of delegates shall consist of eighty members, distributed as follows: Alleghany, five members; Anne Arundel, two; each of the three legislative districts in Baltimore City, six; Baltimore County, six; Calvert, one; Caroline, two; Carroll, five; Cecil, four; Charles, one; Dorchester, two; Frederick, six; Harford, four; Howard, two; Kent, two; Montgomery, two; Prince George's, two; Queen Anne's, two; Saint Mary's, one; Somerset, three; Talbot, two; Washington, five; Worcester, three.

SEC. 5. The members of the house of delegates shall be elected by the qualified voters of the counties and the legislative districts of Baltimore City, respectively, to serve for two years from the day of their election.

SEC. 6. The first election for senators and delegates shall take place on the Tuesday next after the first Monday in the month of November, eighteen hundred and sixty-four; and the elections for delegates, and, as nearly as practicable, for one-half of the senators, shall be held on the same day in every second year thereafter.

Sec. 7. Immediately after the senate shall have convened, after the first election under this constitution, the senators shall be divided by lots into two classes, as nearly equal in number as may be; senators of the first class shall go out of office at the expiration of two years, and senators shall be elected on the Tuesday next after the first Monday in the month of November, eighteen hundred and sixty-six, for the term of four years, to supply their places; so that, after the first election, one-half of the senators may be chosen every year. In case the number of senators be hereinafter increased, such classification of the additional senators shall be made as to preserve, as nearly as may be, an equal number in each class.

Sec. 8. No person shall be eligible as a senator or delegate who, at the time of his election, is not a citizen of the United States, and who has not resided at least three years next preceding the day of his election in this State, and the last year thereof in the county or in the legislative district of Baltimore City which he may be chosen to represent, if such county or legislative district of such city shall have been so long established, and if not, then in the county or city from which, in whole or part, the same may have been formed; nor shall any person be eligible as a senator unless he shall have attained the age of twenty-five years, nor as a delegate unless he shall have attained the age of twenty-one years, at the time of his election.

Sec. 9. No member of Congress or person holding any civil or military office under the United States shall be eligible as a senator or delegate; and if any person shall, after his election as a senator or delegate, be elected to Congress, or be appointed to any office, civil or military, under the Government of the United States, his acceptance thereof shall vacate his seat.

Sec. 10. No person holding any civil office of profit or trust under this State, except justices of the peace, shall be eligible to the office of senator or delegate.

Sec. 11. No collector, receiver or holder of public moneys, shall be eligible as senator or delegate, or to any office of profit or trust under this State, until he shall have accounted for and paid into the treasury all sums on the books thereof charged to and due by him.

Sec. 12. In case of death, disqualification, resignation, refusal to act, expulsion, or removal from the county or legislative district of Baltimore City for which he shall have been elected, of any person who shall have been chosen as a delegate or senator, or in case of a tie between two or more such qualified persons, a warrant of election shall be issued by the speaker of the house of delegates, or president of the senate, as the case may be, for the election of another person in his place, of which election not less than ten days' notice shall be given, exclusive of the day of the publication of the notice and of the day of election; and in case of such resignation or refusal to act, being communicated in writing to the governor by the person so resigning or refusing to act, or if such death occur during the legislative recess, and more than ten days before its termination, it shall be the duty of the governor to issue a warrant of election to supply the vacancy thus created, in the same manner the said speaker or president might have done during the session of the general assembly:

Provided, however, That unless a meeting of the general assembly may intervene, the election thus ordered to fill such vacancy shall be held on the day of the ensuing election for delegates and senators.

Sec. 13. The general assembly shall meet on the first Wednesday of January, eighteen hundred and sixty-five, and on the same day in every second year thereafter, and at no other time, unless convened by the proclamation of the governor.

Sec. 14. The general assembly shall continue its session so long as in its judgment the public interest may require, and each member thereof shall receive a compensation of five dollars per diem, for every day he shall attend the sessions, but shall receive no per diem when absent, unless absent on account of sickness: *Provided, however,* That no member shall receive any other or larger sum than four hundred dollars. When the general assembly shall be convened by proclamation of the governor, the session shall not continue longer than thirty days, and in such case the compensation shall be at the rate of five dollars per diem.

Sec. 15. No book or other printed matter not appertaining to the business of the session shall be purchased or subscribed for for the use of the members of the general assembly, or be distributed among them at the public expense.

Sec. 16. No senator or delegate, after qualifying as such, notwithstanding he may thereafter resign, shall, during the whole period of time for which he was elected, be eligible to any office which shall have been created, or the salary or profits of which shall have been increased, during such term, or shall during said whole period of time be appointed to any civil office by the executive or general assembly.

Sec. 17. No senator or delegate shall be liable, in any civil action or criminal prosecution whatever, for words spoken in debate.

Sec. 18. Each house shall be judge of the qualifications and elections of its members, subject to the laws of the State; shall appoint its own officers, determine the rules of its own proceedings, punish a member for disorderly or disrespectful behavior, and, with the consent of two-thirds of its whole number of members elected, expel a member; but no member shall be expelled a second time for the same offence.

Sec. 19. A majority of the whole number of the members elected to each house shall constitute a quorum for the transaction of business, but a smaller number may adjourn from day to day and compel the attendance of absent members, in such manner, and under such penalties, as each house may prescribe.

Sec. 20. The doors of each house and of committees of the whole shall be open, except when the business is such as ought to be kept secret.

Sec. 21. Each house shall keep a journal of its proceedings, and cause the same to be published. The yeas and nays of members on any questions shall, at the call of any five of them in the house of delegates, or one in the senate, be entered on the journal.

Sec. 22. Each house may punish, by imprisonment during the session of the general assembly, any person not a member for disrespectful or disorderly behavior in its presence, or for obstructing any of its proceedings, or any of its officers in the execution of their duties: *Provided,* Such imprisonment shall not, at any one time, exceed ten days.

SEC. 23. The house of delegates may inquire, on the oath of witnesses, into all complaints, grievances, and offences, as the grand inquest of the State, and may commit any person, for any crime, to the public jail, there to remain until discharged by due course of law; they may examine and pass all accounts of the State, relating either to the collection or expenditure of the revenue, and appoint auditors to state and adjust the same; they may call for all public or official papers and records, and send for persons whom they may judge necessary in the course of their inquiries concerning affairs relating to the public interest, and may direct all office bonds, which shall be made payable to the State, to be sued for any breach thereof.

SEC. 24. Neither house shall, without the consent of the other, adjourn for more than three days at any one time, nor to any other place than that in which the house shall be sitting, without the concurrent vote of two-thirds of the members present.

SEC. 25. The house of delegates shall have the sole power of impeachment in all cases, but a majority of all the members elected must concur in an impeachment; all impeachments shall be tried by the senate, and, when sitting for that purpose, the senators shall be on oath or affirmation to do justice according to the law and evidence, but no person shall be convicted without the concurrence of two-thirds of all the senators elected.

SEC. 26. Any bill may originate in either house of the general assembly, and be altered, amended, or rejected by the other; but no bill shall originate in either house during the last ten days of the session, nor become a law until it be read on three different days of the session in each house, unless three-fourths of the members of the house where such bill is pending shall so determine.

SEC. 27. No bill shall become a law unless it be passed in each house by a majority of the whole number of members elected, and on its final passage the ayes and noes be recorded.

SEC. 28. The style of all laws of this State shall be: *"Be it enacted by the general assembly of Maryland,"* and all laws shall be passed by original bill; and every law enacted by the general assembly shall embrace but one subject, and that shall be described in the title; and no law nor section of a law shall be revised or amended by reference to its title or section only, and it shall be the duty of the general assembly, in amending any article or section of the code of laws of this State, to enact the same as the said article or section would read when amended; and whenever the general assembly shall enact any public general law, not amendatory of any section or article in the said code, it shall be the duty of the general assembly to enact the same in articles and sections, in the same manner as the said code is arranged, and to provide for the publication of all additions and alterations which may be made to the code.

SEC. 29. Every bill, when passed by the general assembly and sealed with the great seal, shall be presented to the governor, who shall sign the same in the presence of the presiding officers and chief clerks of the senate and house of delegate. Every law shall be recorded in the office of the court of appeals, and, in due time, be printed, published, and certified under the great seal to the several courts, in the same manner as has been heretofore usual in this State.

SEC. 30. No law passed by the general assembly shall take effect until the first day of June next after the session at which it may be passed, unless it be otherwise expressly declared therein; and in case any public law is made to take effect before the said first day of June, the general assembly shall provide for the immediate publication of the same.

SEC. 31. No money shall be drawn from the treasury of the State, except in accordance with an appropriation by law, and every such law shall distinctly specify the sum appropriated, and the object to which it shall be applied: *Provided,* That nothing herein contained shall prevent the general assembly from placing a contingent fund at the disposal of the executive, who shall report to the general assembly, at each session, the amount expended and the purposes to which it was applied. An accurate statement of the receipts and expenditures of the public money shall be attached to and published with the laws after each regular session of the general assembly.

SEC. 32. The general assembly shall not pass local or special laws in any of the following-enumerated cases, viz: For the assessment and collection of taxes for State or county purposes, or extending the time for the collection of taxes; providing for the support of public schools; the preservation of school-funds; the location or the regulation of school-houses; granting divorces; relating to fees or salaries; relating to the interest on money; providing for regulating the election or compensation of State or county officers; or designating the places of voting; or the boundaries of election-districts; providing for the sale of real estate belonging to minors or other persons laboring under legal disabilities, by executors, administrators, guardians, or trustees; giving effect to informal or invalid deeds or wills; refunding money paid into the State treasury, or releasing persons from their debts or obligations to the State, unless recommended by the governor or officers of the treasury department; or establishing, locating, or affecting the construction of roads, and the repairing or building of bridges. And the general assembly shall pass no special law for any case for which provision has been made by an existing general law. The general assembly, at its first session after the adoption of this constitution, shall pass general laws providing for the cases enumerated in this section, and for all other cases where a general law can be made applicable.

SEC. 33. No debt shall be hereafter contracted by the general assembly unless such debts shall be authorized by a law providing for the collection of an annual tax or taxes sufficient to pay the interest on such debt as it falls due, and also to discharge the principal thereof within fifteen years from the time of contracting the same, and the taxes laid for this purpose shall not be repealed or applied to any other object until the said debt and interest thereon shall be fully discharged. The credit of the State shall not, in any manner, be given or loaned to or in aid of any individual, association or corporation, nor shall the general assembly have the power in any mode to involve the State in the construction of works of internal improvement, nor in any enterprise which shall involve the faith or credit of the State, nor make any appropriations therefor; and they shall not use or appropriate the proceeds of the internal-improvement companies, or of the State tax now levied, or which may hereafter be levied, to pay off the public debt, to any other purpose until the interest and debt are fully paid, or the sinking-fund shall be equal to the amount of the outstanding debt; but the general assembly may, without laying a tax, borrow an amount, never to exceed fifty thousand dollars, to meet temporary deficiencies in the treasury, and may contract debts to any amount that may be necessary for the defence of the State.

SEC. 34. No extra compensation shall be granted or allowed by the general assembly to any public officer, agent, servant, or contractor, after the services shall have been rendered or the contract entered into; nor shall the salary or compensation of any public officer be increased or diminished during his term of office.

SEC. 35. No lottery-grant shall ever hereafter be authorized by the general assembly.

SEC. 36. The general assembly shall pass no law nor make any appropriation to compensate the masters or claimants of slaves emancipated from servitude by the adoption of this constitution.

SEC. 37. No person shall be imprisoned for debt.

SEC. 38. The general assembly shall grant no charter for banking purposes, nor renew any banking corporation now in existence, except upon the condition that the stockholders shall be liable to the amount of their respective share or shares of stock in such banking institution, for all its debts and liabilities, upon note, bill, or otherwise, and upon the further condition, that no director or other officer of said corporation shall borrow any money from said corporation, and if any director or other officer shall be convicted, upon indictment, of directly or indirectly violating this section, he shall be punished, by fine or imprisonment, at the discretion of the court. The books, papers, and accounts of all banks shall be open to inspection, under such regulations as may be prescribed by law.

SEC. 39. The general assembly shall enact no law authorizing private property to be taken for public use, without just compensation, as agreed upon between the parties, or awarded by a jury, being first paid or tendered to the party entitled to such compensation.

SEC. 40. Any citizen of this State who shall, after the adoption of this constitution, either in or out of this State, fight a duel with deadly weapons, or send or accept a challenge so to do, or who shall act as a second, or knowingly aid or assist in any manner those thus offending, and any citizen who has thus offended or so aided or assisted those thus offending, since the first Wednesday of June, eighteen hundred and fifty-one, shall ever thereafter be incapable of holding any office of trust or profit under this State.

SEC. 41. The general assembly shall pass laws for the preservation of the purity of elections by the registration of voters, and by such other means as may be deemed expedient; and to make effective the provisions of the constitution disfranchising certain persons, or disqualifying them from holding office.

SEC. 42. The general assembly shall pass laws necessary to protect the property of the wife from the debts of the husband during her life, and for securing the same to her issue after her death.

SEC. 43. Laws shall be passed by the general assembly to protect from execution a reasonable amount of property of a debtor, not exceeding in value the sum of five hundred dollars.

SEC. 44. The general assembly shall provide a simple and uniform system of charges in the offices of clerks of courts and registers of wills, in the counties of this State and the city of Baltimore, and for the collection thereof: *Provided*, The amount of compensation to any of said officers shall not exceed the sum of twenty-five hundred dollars a year over and above office expenses, and compensation to assistants: *And provided further*, That such compensation of clerks, registers, assistants, and office expenses shall always be paid out of the fees or receipts of the offices respectively.

SEC. 45. The general assembly shall have power to receive from the United States any grant or donation of land, money, or securities, for any purpose designated by the United States, and shall administer or distribute the same according to the conditions of said grant.

SEC. 46. The general assembly shall make provision for all cases of contested elections of any of the officers not herein provided for.

SEC. 47. The general assembly shall pass laws requiring the president, directors, trustees, or agents of corporations, created or authorized by the laws of this State, teachers or superintendents of the public schools, colleges, or other institutions of learning; attorneys at law, jurors, and such other persons as the general assembly shall from time to time prescribe, to take the oath of allegiance to the United States set forth in the first article of this constitution.

SEC. 48. The general assembly shall have power to accept the cession of any territory, contiguous to this State, from the States of Virginia and West Virginia, or from the United States, with the consent of Congress and of the inhabitants of such ceded territory, and in case of such cessions the general assembly may divide such territory into counties, and shall provide for the representation of the same in the general assembly, on the basis fixed by this constitution, and may, for that purpose, increase the number of senators and delegates, and the general assembly shall enact such laws as may be required to extend the constitution and laws of this State over such territory, and may create courts, conformably to the constitution, for such territory, and may for that purpose increase the number of judges of the court of appeals.

SEC. 49. The general assembly shall provide by law for the registration of births, marriages, and deaths, and shall pass laws providing for the celebration of marriage between any persons legally competent to contract marriage, and shall provide that any person prevented by conscientious scruples from being married by any of the existing provisions of law, may be married by any judge or clerk of any court of record, or any mayor of any incorporated city in this State.

SEC. 50. The rate of interest in this State shall not exceed six per centum per annum, and no higher rate shall be taken or demanded; and the general assembly shall provide by law all necessary forfeitures and penalties against usury.

SEC. 51. Corporations may be formed under general laws, but shall not be created by special act, except for municipal purposes, and in cases where, in the judgment of the general assembly, the object of the corporation cannot be attained under general laws. All laws and special acts, pursuant to this section, may be altered from time to time, or repealed: *Provided*, Nothing herein contained shall be construed to alter, change, or amend in any manner the section in relation to banks.

SEC. 52. The governor, comptroller, and treasurer of the State are hereby authorized, conjointly, or any two of them, to exchange the State's interest as stockholder and creditor in the Baltimore and Ohio Railroad Company for an equal amount of the bonds or registered debt now owing by the State; and, subject to such regulations and conditions as the general assembly may from time to time prescribe, to sell the State's interest in the other works of internal improvement, whether as a stockholder or a creditor; also, the State's interest in any banking corporation, and to receive in payment the bonds and registered debt now owing by the State, equal in amount to the price obtained for the State's said interest: *Provided*, That the interest of the State in the Washington Branch of the Baltimore and Ohio Railroad be reserved and excepted from sale: *And provided further*, That no sale or contract of sale of the State's interest in the Chesapeake and Ohio Canal, the Chesapeake and Delaware Canal, and the Susquehanna and Tide Water Canal Companies shall go into effect until the same shall be ratified by the ensuing general assembly.

SEC. 53. The general assembly before authorizing the sale of the State's interest in the Chesapeake and Ohio Canal, and before prescribing regulations and conditions for said sale, shall pass all laws that may be necessary to authorize the counties of Alleghany, Washington, Frederick, and Montgomery, or any one of them, to create a debt by the issue of bonds or otherwise, so as to enable them, or any of them, to become the purchasers of said interest.

SEC. 54. The general assembly shall have power to regulate by law, not inconsistent with this constitution, all matters which relate to the judges of election, time, place, and manner of holding elections in this State, and of making returns thereof.

SEC. 55. The general assembly shall have power to pass all such laws as may be necessary and proper for carrying into execution the powers vested by this constitution in any department or office of the government, and the duties imposed upon them thereby.

ARTICLE IV

JUDICIARY DEPARTMENT

PART I.—GENERAL PROVISIONS

SECTION 1. The judicial power of this State shall be vested in a court of appeals, circuit courts, orphans' courts, such courts for the city of Baltimore as may be hereinafter prescribed or provided for, and justices of the peace; all said courts shall be courts of record, and each shall have a seal, to be used in the authentication of all process issuing from them. The process and official character of justices of the peace shall be authenticated as hath heretofore been practised in this State, or may hereafter be prescribed by law.

SEC. 2. The judges of the several courts, except the judges of the orphans' courts, shall be citizens of the United States, and residents of this State, not less than five years next preceding their election, or appointment by the executive in case of a vacancy; and not less than one year next preceding their election or appointment, residents in the judicial district or circuit, as the case may be, for which they may be elected or appointed; they shall not be less than thirty years of age at the time of their election. and selected from those who have been admitted to practise law in this State, and who are most distinguished for integrity, wisdom, and sound legal knowledge.

SEC. 3. The judges of the court of appeals shall be elected by the qualified voters of the State; and the governor, by and with the advice and consent of the senate, shall designate the chief justice; and the judges of the judicial circuits shall be elected by the qualified voters of their respective circuits; each judge of the court of appeals and of each judicial circuit shall hold his office for the term of fifteen years from the time of his election, or until he shall have attained the age of seventy years, whichever may first happen, and be reëligible thereto until he shall have attained the age of seventy years, and not after.

SEC. 4. Any judge shall be removed from office by the governor on conviction, in a court of law, of incompetency, of wilful neglect of duty, of misbehavior in office, or any other crime; or on impeachment according to this constitution, or the laws the State; or on the address of the general assembly, two-thirds of each house concurring in such address, and the accused having been notified of the charges against him, and had opportunity of making his defence.

SEC. 5. In case of the death, resignation, removal, or other disqualification of a judge of any court of this State, except of the orphans' courts, the governor, by and with the advice and consent of the senate, shall thereupon appoint a person duty qualified to fill said office until the next general election thereafter, whether for members of general assembly or county officers, whichever shall first occur, at which time an election shall be held as herein prescribed for a judge, who shall hold said office for the term of fifteen years, and until the election and qualification of his successor.

SEC. 6. All judges shall, by virtue of their offices, be conservatives of the peace throughout the State, and no fees or perquisites, commission or reward of any kind, shall be allowed to any judge in this State, besides his annual salary or fixed per diem, for the discharge of any judicial duty.

SEC. 7. No judge shall sit in any case wherein he may be interested, or where either of the parties may be connected with him by affinity or consanguinity within such degrees as now are or may hereafter be prescribed by law, or where he shall have been of counsel in the case.

SEC. 8. The general assembly shall provide for the trial of causes in case of the disqualification of the judge of the superior court of Baltimore City, the court of common pleas, the circuit court of Baltimore City, and the criminal court of Baltimore, and also in case of a disqualification of any judge of other circuit courts of this State, to hear and determine the same, but in case of such disqualification, the parties thereto may, by consent, appoint a person to try the same; and the parties to any cause may submit the same to the court for determination without the aid of a jury.

SEC. 9. The judge or judges of any court of this State, except the court of appeals, shall order and direct the record of proceedings in any suit of action, issue, or petition, presentment or indictment, pending in such court, to be transmitted to some other court in the same or any adjoining circuit having jurisdiction in such cases, whenever any party to such cause, or the counsel of any party, shall make it satisfactorily appear to the court that such party cannot have a fair and impartial trial in the court in which such suit or action, issue or petition, presentment or indictment, is pending; and the general assembly shall make such modifications of existing law as may be necessary to regulate and give force to this provision.

SEC. 10. The judge or judges of any court may appoint such officers for their respective courts as may be found necessary, and it shall be the duty of the general assembly to prescribe by law a fixed compensation for all such officers.

SEC. 11. Every person being a citizen of the United States shall be permitted to appear to and try his own case in all the courts of this State.

SEC. 12. Any person who shall, after this constitution shall have gone into effect, detain in slavery any person emancipated by the provisions of this constitution, shall, on conviction, be fined not less than five hundred dollars nor more than five thousand dollars, or be imprisoned not more than five years; and any of the judges of this State shall discharge, on *habeas corpus*, any person so detained in slavery.

SEC. 13. The clerks of the several courts created or continued by this constitution shall have charge and custody of the records and other papers, shall perform all the duties and be allowed the fees which appertain to their several offices, as the same now are or may hereafter be regulated by law.

SEC. 14. All election of judges and other officers provided for by this constitution, State's attorneys excepted, shall be certified and the returns made by the clerks of the respective counties to the governor, who shall issue commissions to the different persons for the offices to which they shall have been respectively elected; and in all such elections, the person having the greatest number of votes shall be declared to be elected.

SEC. 15. If in any case of election for judges, clerks of the courts of law, and registers of wills, the opposing candidates shall have an equal number of votes, it shall be the duty of the governor to order a new election; and in case of any contested election the governor shall send the returns to the house of delegates, who shall judge of the election and qualification of the candidates at such election.

SEC. 16. All public commissions and grants shall run thus, " The State of Maryland," &c., and shall be signed by the governor, with the seal of the State annexed; all writs and process shall run to the same style, and be tested, sealed, and signed as usual; and all indictments shall conclude " against the peace, government, and dignity of the State."

PART II.—COURT OF APPEALS

SEC. 17. The court of appeals shall consist of a chief justice and four associate justices, and for their selection the State shall be divided into five judicial districts, as follows, viz: Worcester, Somerset, Dorchester, Talbot, Caroline, Queen Anne, Kent, and Cecil Counties shall compose the first district; Harford and Baltimore Counties, and the first seven wards of Baltimore City, shall compose the second district; Baltimore City, except the first seven wards, shall compose the third district; Alleghany, Washington, Frederick, Howard, and Carroll Counties shall compose the fourth district; Saint Mary's,

Charles, Anne Arundel, Calvert, Prince George's, and Montgomery Counties shall compose the fifth district, and one of the justices of the court of appeals shall be elected from each of said districts, by the qualified voters of the whole State. The present chief justice and associate justices of the court of appeals shall continue to act as such until the expiration of the term for which they were respectively elected, and until their successors are elected and qualified; and an election for a justice of the court of appeals, to be taken from the fourth judicial district, shall be held on the Tuesday next after the first Monday in the month of November, eighteen hundred and sixty-four.

SEC. 18. The court of appeals shall hold its sessions in the city of Annapolis, on the first Monday in April and the first Monday in October of each and every year, or at such other times as the general assembly may by law direct, and it shall be competent for the justices of said court, sufficient cause appearing to them, temporarily to transfer their sittings elsewhere.

SEC. 19. The jurisdiction of the court of appeals shall be coextensive with the limits of the State, and such as now is or may hereafter be prescribed for it by law, and its sessions shall continue for not less than ten months in the year, if the business before it shall so require.

SEC. 20. Any three of the justices of the court of appeals may constitute a quorum, but no cause shall be decided without the concurrence of at least three justices in the decision; and in every case decided an opinion in writing shall be filed within three months after the argument or submission of the cause, and the judgment of the court shall be final and conclusive.

SEC. 21. The salary of the justices of the court of appeals shall be three thousand dollars each per annum, payable quarterly.

SEC. 22. Provision shall be made by law for publishing reports of all causes argued and determined in the court of appeals, which the justices shall designate as proper for publication.

SEC. 23. The court of appeals shall appoint its own clerk, who shall hold his office for six years, and may be reappointed at the end thereof; he shall be subject to removal by the court for incompetency, neglect of duty, misdemeanor in office, or such other cause or causes as may be prescribed by law.

PART III.—CIRCUIT COURTS

SEC. 24. The State shall be divided into thirteen judicial circuits, in manner following: The counties of Saint Mary's and Charles shall constitute the first circuit; the counties of Anne Arundel and Calvert, the second; the counties of Prince George's and Montgomery, the third; the county of Frederick, the fourth; the county of Washington, the fifth; the county of Alleghany, the sixth; the counties of Carroll and Howard, the seventh; the county of Baltimore, the eighth; the counties of Harford and Cecil, the ninth; the counties of Kent and Queen Anne's, the tenth; the counties of Talbot and Caroline, the eleventh; the counties of Dorchester, Somerset, and Worcester, the twelfth; and the city of Baltimore, the thirteenth.

SEC. 25. One court shall be held in each county of the State. The said courts shall be called circuit courts for the county in which they may be held, and shall have and exercise all the power, authority, and jurisdiction, original and appellate, which the present circuit courts of this State now have and exercise, or which may hereafter be prescribed by law.

SEC. 26. For each circuit (the thirteenth excepted) there shall be one judge, who shall be styled circuit judge, who, during his term of office, shall reside in one of the counties composing the circuit for which he may be elected; the said judges shall hold a term of their courts in each of the counties composing their respective circuits at such times as now are or may hereafter be fixed by law, such terms to be never less than two in each year in each county; special terms may be held by said judges in their discretion, whenever the business of their several counties renders such terms necessary.

SEC. 27. The present judges of the circuit courts shall continue to act as judges of the respective circuit courts within the judicial circuits in which they respectively reside, until the expiration of the term for which they were respectively elected, and until their successors are elected and qualified, viz: The present judges of the first, second, third, fourth, sixth, and eighth judicial circuits, as organized at the time of the adoption of this constitution, shall continue to act as judges respectively of the first, second, fourth, fifth, ninth, and twelfth judicial circuits as organized under the constitution; and an election of judges of the third, sixth, seventh, eighth, tenth, and eleventh judicial circuits shall be held on the Tuesday next after the first Monday in the month of November, in the year eighteen hundred and sixty-four.

SEC. 28. The salary of each judge of the circuit court shall be twenty-five hundred dollars per annum payable quarterly, and shall not be increased or diminished during his continuance in office.

SEC. 29. There shall be a clerk of the circuit court for each county, who shall be selected by a plurality of the qualified voters of said county; he shall hold his office for the term of six years from the time of his election, and until a new election is held and his successor duly qualified; he shall be reëligible at the end of his term, and shall at any time be subject to removal for wilful neglect of duty, or other misdemeanor in office, on conviction in a court of law. In the event of any vacancy in the office of the clerk of any of the circuit courts, said vacancy shall be filled by the judge of said circuit court in which said vacancy occurs, until the next general election for county officers, when a clerk of said circuit court shall be elected to serve for six years thereafter.

SEC. 30. The judges of the respective circuit courts of this State, and of the courts of Baltimore City, shall render their decisions, in all cases argued before them, or submitted for their judgment, within two months after the same shall have been so argued or submitted.

PART IV.—COURTS OF BALTIMORE CITY

SEC. 31. There shall be in the thirteenth judicial circuit four courts, to be styled the superior court of Baltimore City; the court of common pleas; the circuit court of Baltimore City, and the criminal court of Baltimore. Each court shall consist of one judge, who shall be elected by the legal and qualified voters of said city, and shall hold his office for the term of fifteen years, subject to the provisions of this constitution with regard to the election and qualification of judges, and their removal from office, and shall exercise the jurisdiction hereinafter specified.

SEC. 32. Each of said judges shall receive an annual salary of three thousand dollars, payable quarterly.

SEC. 33. The superior court of Baltimore City shall have jurisdiction over all suits where the debt or damage claimed, exclusive of interest, shall exceed the sum of one thousand dollars, and in case any plaintiff or plaintiffs shall recover less than the sum or value of one thousand dollars, he or they shall be deemed as adjudged to pay costs in the discretion of the court. The said court shall have jurisdiction as a court of equity within the limits of the said city, and in all other civil cases which are not hereinafter assigned to the court of common pleas, and also have jurisdiction in all cases of appeals from the commissioners for opening the streets.

SEC. 34. The court of common pleas shall have civil jurisdiction in all suits where the debt or damage claimed, exclusive of interest, shall be over one hundred dollars, and shall not exceed one thousand dollars; and shall also have jurisdiction in all cases of appeal in civil cases from the judgment of justices of the peace in the said city, and shall have jurisdiction in all applications for the benefit of the insolvent laws of this State, and the supervision and control of the trustees thereof.

SEC. 35. The circuit court of Baltimore City shall have jurisdiction concurrent with the superior court of Baltimore City, in all cases in equity, in cases arising under the act to direct descents, and its supplements, and shall exercise all the power that is now conferred by law: *Provided*, Said court shall not have jurisdiction in applications for the writ of *habeas corpus*, in cases of persons charged with criminal offences.

SEC. 36. The criminal court of Baltimore shall have and exercise all the jurisdiction now held and exercised by the criminal court of Baltimore, except in cases of appeals from commissioners for opening streets, and shall have jurisdiction in all cases of appeals from justices of the peace in said city, for the recovery of fines, penalties, and forfeitures.

SEC. 37. The present judges of the several courts of Baltimore City shall continue to act as such until the expiration of the terms for which they were respectively elected, and until their successors are elected and qualified.

SEC. 38. All causes pending in the several courts of Baltimore City at the adoption of this constitution shall be prosecuted to final judgment, as though the jurisdiction of the several courts in which they may be pending had not been changed.

SEC. 39. There shall be a clerk of each of the said courts of Baltimore City, who shall be elected by the legal and qualified voters of said city, and shall hold his office for six years from the time of his election, and until his successor is elected and qualified, and be reëligible thereto, subject to be removed for wilful neglect of duty or other misdemeanor in office on conviction in a court of law. In case of a vacancy in the office of a clerk in any of the said courts, the judge of the court of which he was clerk shall have the power to appoint a clerk until the general election for county officers held next thereafter, when a clerk of said court shall be elected to serve for six years thereafter.

SEC. 40. The present clerk of the superior court of Baltimore City and the court of common pleas and of the criminal court of Baltimore shall continue to act as clerks of said courts respectively during the time for which they were severally elected, and until their successors are elected and qualified, and in case of the death, resignation, or disqualification of either of said clerks before the expiration of the time for which they were elected, the judge of the court where such death, resignation, or other disqualification may occur shall have the power to appoint a clerk as provided by the thirty-ninth section of this article. The present clerk of the circuit court of Baltimore City shall continue to act as clerk of said court until the first election for county officers next after the adoption of this constitution, when a clerk of said court shall be elected in the same manner, and hold his office for the same time, and be subject to the same provisions of this constitution, as the clerks of the courts in said city.

SEC. 41. The general assembly shall, whenever it may think the same proper and expedient, provide by law another court for the city of Baltimore, to consist of one judge, to be elected by the legal and qualified voters of said city, who shall be subject to the same constitutional provisions, hold his office for the same term of years, and receive the same compensation as the judge of the superior court of said city, and said court shall have such jurisdiction and powers as may be prescribed by law; and the general assembly may reapportion the civil jurisdiction among the several courts in Baltimore City from time to time as in their judgments the public interest and convenience may require.

SEC. 42. The clerk of the court of common pleas shall have authority to issue within said city all marriage and other licenses required by law, subject to such provisions as the general assembly have now or may hereafter prescribe, and the clerk of the superior court of said city shall receive and record all deeds, conveyances, and other papers which are required by law to be recorded in said city. He shall also have custody of all papers connected with the proceedings on the law or equity side of Baltimore County court, and of the dockets thereof, so far as the same have relation to the city of Baltimore.

PART V.—ORPHANS' COURT

SEC. 43. There shall be an orphans' court in the city of Baltimore, and in each of the counties of this State. The qualified voters of the city of Baltimore and of the several counties of the State shall, on the Tuesday next after the first Monday in the month of November, eighteen hundred and sixty-seven, elect three men to be judges of the orphans' court of said city and counties respectively; one of the said judges first elected shall hold his office for two years, one for four years, and the other for six years; and at the first meeting after their election and qualification, or as soon thereafter as practicable, they shall determine by lot which one of their members shall hold his office for two, four, and six years respectively, and thereafter there shall be elected as aforesaid, at each general election for county officers, one judge to serve for the term of six years. No person shall be elected judge of the orphans' court, unless he be at the time of his election a citizen of the United States and resident for twelve months in the city or county for which he may be elected. Each of said judges shall receive such compensation, to be paid by the said counties and city respectively, as is now or may hereafter be prescribed by the general assembly.

SEC. 44. In case of the death, resignation, removal, or other disqualification of a judge of an orphans' court, the governor, by and with the advice and consent of the senate, shall appoint a person duly qualified to fill said office for the residue of the term thus made vacant.

SEC. 45. The orphans' courts shall have all the powers now vested by law in the orphans' courts of this State, subject to such changes as the general assembly may prescribe, and shall have such other jurisdiction as may from time to time be provided by law.

SEC. 46. There shall be a register of wills in each county of the State and in the city of Baltimore, to be elected by the legal and qualified voters of said counties and city respectively, who shall hold his office for six years from the time of his election, and until his successor is elected and qualified; he shall be reëligible and subject at all times to removal for wilful neglect of duty or misdemeanor in office in the same manner that the clerks of courts are removable. In the event of any vacancy in the office of register of wills, said vacancy shall be filled by the judges of the orphans' court in which such vacancy occurs, until the next general election for county officers, when a register shall be elected to serve for six years thereafter.

PART VI.—JUSTICES OF THE PEACE

SEC. 47. The governor, by and with the advice and consent of the senate, shall appoint such number of justices of the peace, and the county commissioners of the several counties, and the mayor and city council of Baltimore, shall appoint such number of constables for the several election-districts of the counties and wards of the city of Baltimore, as are now or may hereafter be prescribed by law; and justices of the peace and constables so appointed shall be subject to removal by the judge having criminal jurisdiction in the county or city for incompetency, wilful neglect of duty, or misdemeanor in office, on conviction in a court of law. The justices of the peace and constables so appointed and commissioned shall be conservators of the peace, shall hold their office for two years, and shall have such jurisdiction, duties, and compensation, subject to such right of appeal in all cases, from the judgment of justices of the peace, as hath been heretofore exercised, or shall be hereafter prescribed by law.

SEC. 48. In the event of a vacancy in the office of a justice of the peace, the governor shall appoint a person to serve as justice of the peace for the residue of the term, and in case of a vacancy in the office of constable, the county commissioners of the county in which the vacancy occurs, or the mayor and city council of Baltimore, as the case may be, shall appoint a person to serve as constable for the residue of the term.

PART VII.—SHERIFFS

SEC. 49. There shall be elected in each county, and in the city of Baltimore, in every second year, one person, resident in said county or city, above the age of twenty-five years, and at least five years preceding his election a citizen of this State, to the office of sheriff. He shall hold his office for two years, and until his successor is duly elected and qualified; shall be ineligible for two years thereafter;

shall give such bond, exercise such powers, and perform such duties as now are or may hereafter be fixed by law. In case of a vacancy by death, refusal to serve, or neglect to qualify or give bond, by disqualification or removal from the county or city, the governor shall appoint a person to be sheriff for the remainder of the official term.

SEC. 50. Coroners, elisors, and notaries public may be appointed for each county and the city of Baltimore, in the manner, for the purposes, and with the powers now fixed or which may hereafter be prescribed by law.

ARTICLE V

ATTORNEY-GENERAL

SECTION 1. There shall be an attorney-general elected by the qualified voters of the State, on general ticket, on the Tuesday next after the first Monday in the month of November, in the year eighteen hundred and sixty-four, and on the same day in every fourth year thereafter, who shall hold his office for four years from the first Monday of January next ensuing his election, and until his successor shall be elected and qualified, and shall be reëligible thereto, and shall be subject to removal for incompetency, wilful neglect of duty, or misdemeanor in office, on conviction in a court of law.

SEC. 2. All elections for attorney-general shall be certified to, and returns made thereof by the clerks of the circuit courts for the several counties, and the clerk of the superior court of Baltimore City, to the governor of the State, whose duty it shall be to decide upon the election and qualifications of the person returned, and in case of a tie between two or more persons, to designate which of said persons shall qualify as attorney-general, and to administer the oath of office to the person elected.

SEC. 3. It shall be the duty of the attorney-general to prosecute and defend, on the part of the State, all cases which at the time of his election and qualification, and which thereafter may be depending in the court of appeals, or in the Supreme Court of the United States, by or against the State, or wherein the State may be interested; and he shall give his opinion in writing whenever required by the general assembly, or either branch thereof, the governor, the comptroller, the treasurer, or any State's attorney, on any matter or subject depending before them, or either of them, and when required by the governor or the general assembly he shall aid any State's attorney in prosecuting any suit or action brought by the State in any court of this State; and he shall commence and prosecute or defend any suit or action in any of said courts, on the part of the State, which the general assembly or the governor, acting according to law, shall direct to be commenced, prosecuted, or defended; and he shall receive for his services an annual salary of twenty-five hundred dollars; but he shall not be entitled to receive any fees, perquisites, or rewards whatever in addition to the salary aforesaid for the performance of any official duty, nor have power to appoint any agent, representative, or deputy, under any circumstances whatever.

SEC. 4. No person shall be eligible to the office of attorney-general who has not resided and practised law in this State for at least seven years next preceding his election.

SEC. 5. In case of vacancy in the office of attorney-general, occasioned by death, resignation, or his removal from the State, or his conviction, as hereinbefore specified, the said vacancy shall be filled by the governor for the residue of the term thus made vacant.

SEC. 6. It shall be the duty of the clerk of the court of appeals, and the commissioner of the land-office, respectively, whenever a case shall be brought into said court or office, in which the State is a party or has an interest, immediately to notify the attorney-general thereof.

THE STATE'S ATTORNEYS

SEC. 7. There shall be an attorney for the State in each county and the city of Baltimore, to be styled "the State's attorney," who shall be elected by the voters thereof, respectively, on the Tuesday next after the first Monday in the month of November, eighteen hundred and sixty-seven, and on the same day every fourth year thereafter, and shall hold his office for four years from the first Monday in January next ensuing his election, and until his successor shall be elected and qualified, and shall be reëligible thereto, and be subject to removal therefrom for incompetency, wilful neglect of duty, or misdemeanor in office, on conviction in a court of law.

SEC. 8. All elections for the State's attorney shall be certified to and returns made thereof by the clerks of the said counties and city to the judges thereof having criminal jurisdiction, respectively, whose duty it shall be to decide upon the elections and qualifications of the persons returned, and in case of a tie between two or more persons, to designate which of said persons shall qualify as State's attorney, and to administer the oaths of office to the persons elected.

SEC. 9. The State's attorney shall perform such duties and receive such fees and commissions as are now or may hereafter be prescribed by law, and if any State's attorney shall receive any other fee or reward than such as is or may be allowed by law, he shall, on conviction thereof, be removed from office: *Provided*, That the State's attorney for Baltimore City shall have power to appoint one deputy, at a salary of not more than fifteen hundred dollars per annum, to be paid by the State's attorney out of the fees of his office, as has heretofore been practised.

SEC. 10. No person shall be eligible to the office of State's attorney who has not been admitted to practise law in this State, and who has not resided for at least one year in the county or city in which he may be elected.

SEC. 11. In case of vacancy in the office of State's Attorney, or of his removal from the county or city in which he shall have been elected, or on his conviction as herein specified, the said vacancy shall be filled by the judge of the county or city, respectively, having criminal jurisdiction, in which said vacancy shall occur, for the residue of the term thus made vacant.

ARTICLE VI

TREASURY DEPARTMENT

SECTION 1. The treasury department of this State shall consist of a comptroller and a treasurer.

SEC. 2. The comptroller shall be chosen by the qualified electors of the State at each regular election for members of the general assembly. He shall hold his office for two years, commencing on the second Wednesday in January next ensuing his election, and shall receive an annual salary of twenty-five hundred dollars, but shall not be allowed, nor shall he receive, any fees, commissions, or perquisites of any kind, in addition thereto, for the performance of any official duty or service. He shall keep his office at the seat of government, and shall take such oath and enter into such bond for the faithful performance of his duty as are now or may hereafter be prescribed by law. A vacancy in the office of comptroller shall be filled by the governor for the residue of the term. The first election for comptroller under this constitution shall be held on the Tuesday next after the first Monday in the month of November, in the year eighteen hundred and sixty-four; but the comptroller then elected shall not enter upon the discharge of the duties of his office until the expiration of the term of the present incumbent, unless the said office shall sooner become vacant.

SEC. 3. The comptroller shall have the general superintendence of the fiscal affairs of the State; he shall digest and prepare plans for the improvement and management of the revenue, and for the support of the public credit; prepare and report estimates of the revenue and expenditures of the State; superintend and enforce the collection of all taxes and revenue; adjust, settle, and preserve all public accounts; decide on the forms of keeping and stating accounts; grant, under regulations prescribed by law, all warrants for moneys to be paid out of the treasury in pursuance of appropriations by law, prescribe the formalities of the transfer of stock or other evidences of the State debt, and countersign the same, without which such evidences shall not be valid; he shall make full reports of all his proceedings and of the state of the treasury department within ten days after the commencement of each session of the general assembly, and perform such other duties as are now or may hereafter be prescribed by law.

SEC. 4. The treasurer shall be elected on joint ballot by the two houses of the general assembly at each regular session thereof. He shall hold his office for two years, and shall receive an annual salary of twenty-five hundred dollars, but shall not be allowed, nor shall he receive, any fees, commissions, or perquisites of any kind in addition thereto for the performance of any official duty or service. He shall keep his office at the seat of government, and shall take such oath and enter into such bond for the faithful discharge of his duty as are now or may hereafter be prescribed by law. A vacancy in the office of treasurer shall be filled by the governor for the residue of the term. The general assembly, at its first session after the adoption of this constitution, shall elect a treasurer, but the treasurer then elected shall not enter upon the discharge of the duties of his office until the expiration of the term of the present incumbent, unless the said office shall sooner become vacant.

SEC. 5. The treasurer shall receive and keep the moneys of the State, and disburse the same upon warrants drawn by the comptroller, and not otherwise; he shall take receipts for all moneys paid by him, and all receipts for moneys received by him shall be indorsed upon warrants signed by the comptroller, without which warrants, so signed, no acknowledgment of money received into the treasury shall be valid; and, upon warrants issued by the comptroller, he shall make arrangements for the payment of the interest of the public debt, and for the purchase thereof, on account of the sinking-fund. Every bond, certificate, or other evidence of the debt of the State shall be signed by the treasurer and countersigned by the comptroller, and no new certificate or other evidence intended to replace another shall be issued until the old one shall be delivered to the treasurer, and authority executed in due form for the transfer of the same shall be filed in his office, and the transfer accordingly made on the books thereof, and the certificate or other evidence cancelled; but the general assembly may make provision for the loss of certificates or other evidences of the debt.

Sec. 6. The treasurer shall render his accounts quarterly to the comptroller, and on the third day of each regular session of the general assembly he shall submit to the senate and house of delegates fair and accurate copies of all accounts by him from time to time rendered and settled with the comptroller. He shall at all times submit to the comptroller the inspection of the moneys in his hands, and perform all other duties that are now or may hereafter be prescribed by law.

Article VII

SUNDRY OFFICERS

Section 1. The governor, the comptroller of the treasury, and the treasurer shall constitute the board of public works in this State; they shall keep a journal of their proceedings, and shall hold regular sessions in the city of Annapolis on the first Wednesday in January, April, July, and October in each year, and oftener if necessary, at which sessions they shall hear and determine such matters as affect the public works of the State, and as the general assembly may confer upon them the power to decide.

Sec. 2. They shall exercise a diligent and faithful supervision of all public works in which the State may be interested as stockholder or creditor, and shall appoint the directors in every railroad or canal company in which the State has the legal power to appoint directors, which said directors shall represent the State in all meetings of the stockholders of every railroad or canal company in which the State is a stockholder; they shall require the directors of all public works, from time to time, and as often as there shall be any change in the rates of toll on any of said works, to furnish said board of public works a schedule of such modified rates of toll, and shall use all legal powers which they may possess to obtain the establishment of rates of toll which may prevent an injurious competition with each other to the detriment of the interests of the State; and so to adjust them as to promote the agricultural interests of the State; they shall report to the general assembly at each regular session, and recommend such legislation as they shall deem necessary and requisite to promote or protect the interests of the State in said public works; they shall perform such other duties as may be hereafter prescribed by law, and a majority of them shall be competent to act.

The governor, comptroller, and treasurer shall receive no additional salary for services rendered by them as members of the board of public works.

Sec. 3. There shall be a commissioner of the land-office, elected by the qualified voters of the State, on the Tuesday next after the first

Monday in the month of November, in the year eighteen hundred and seventy, and on the same day in every sixth year thereafter, who shall hold his office for the term of six years from the first Monday in January ensuing his election. The returns of said election shall be made to the governor, and in the event of a tie between two or more candidates, the governor shall direct a new election to be held, by writs to the sheriffs of the several counties, and of the city of Baltimore, who shall hold said election after at least twenty days' notice, exclusive of the day of election. He shall perform such duties as are now required of the commissioner of the land-office, or such as may hereafter be prescribed by law, and shall also be the keeper of the chancery records. He shall receive a salary of two thousand dollars per annum, to be paid out of the treasury, and shall charge such fees as are now or may be hereafter fixed by law. He shall make a semi-annual report of all the fees of his office, both as commissioner of the land-office and as keeper of the chancery records, to the comptroller of the treasury, and shall pay the same semiannually into the treasury. In case of vacancy in said office by death, resignation, or other cause, the governor shall fill such vacancy until the next general election for members of the general assembly thereafter, when a commissioner of the land-office shall be elected for the full term of six years ensuing.

SEC. 4. The State librarian shall be elected by a joint vote of the two branches of the general assembly for four years, and until his successor shall be elected and qualified. His salary shall be fifteen hundred dollars per annum, and the general assembly shall pass no law whereby he shall receive any additional compensation. He shall perform such duties as are now or may hereafter be prescribed by law. In case of a vacancy in the office of State librarian from death, resignation, or any other cause, the governor shall fill such vacancy until the next meeting of the general assembly thereafter, and until a successor be elected and qualified.

SEC. 5. The county commissioner shall be elected, on a general ticket, by the qualified voters of the several counties in this State; an election for county commissioners shall be held on the Tuesday next after the first Monday in the month of November, eighteen hundred and sixty-five, and as nearly one-half as may be of said commissioners shall hold their office for two years, and the other half for four years. At the first meeting after their election and qualification, or as soon thereafter as practicable, the said commissioners shall determine by lot which of their number shall hold office for two and four years respectively; and thereafter there shall be elected as aforesaid, at each general election for county officers, county commissioners for four years to fill the places of those whose term has expired. The said commissioners shall exercise such powers and perform such duties (which shall be similar throughout the State) as are now or may hereafter be prescribed by law. Their number in each county, and their compensation, their powers and duties, may at any time hereafter be changed and regulated by the general assembly.

SEC. 6. The general assembly shall provide by law for the appointment of road supervisors in the several counties by the county commissioners, and the number of said supervisors, as well as their powers and duties in the several counties, shall be determined by the said county commissioners.

SEC. 7. The qualified voters of each county and of the city of Baltimore shall, on the Tuesday next after the first Monday in the month of November, in the year eighteen hundred and sixty-five, and every two years thereafter, elect a surveyor for the counties and city of Baltimore, respectively, whose term of office shall commence on the first Monday of January next ensuing their election, and whose duties and compensation shall be the same as are now or may hereafter be prescribed by law. Any vacancy in the office of surveyor shall be filled by the commissioners of the counties or by the mayor and city council of Baltimore, respectively, for the residue of the term.

SEC. 8. The qualified voters of Worcester County shall, on the Tuesday next after the first Monday in the month of November, in the year eighteen hundred and sixty-five, and every two years thereafter, elect a wreck-master for said county, whose duties and compensation shall be the same as are now or may be hereafter prescribed by law; the term of office of said wreck-master shall commence on the first Monday of January next preceding his election, and a vacancy in said office shall be filled by the county commissioners of said county for the residue of the term.

SEC. 9. The general assembly may provide by law for the election or appointment of such other officers as may be required, and are not herein provided for, and prescribe their tenure of office, powers, and duties.

ARTICLE VIII

EDUCATION

SECTION 1. The governor shall, within thirty days after the ratification by the people of this constitution, appoint, subject to the confirmation of the senate, at its first session thereafter, a State superintendent of public instruction, who shall hold his office for four years and until his successor shall have been appointed and shall have qualified. He shall receive an annual salary of twenty-five hundred dollars, and such additional sum for travelling and incidental expenses as the general assembly my by law allow; shall report to the general assembly, within thirty days after the commencement of its first session under this constitution, a uniform system of free public schools, and shall perform such other duties pertaining to his office as may from time to time be prescribed by law.

SEC. 2. There shall be a State board of education, consisting of the governor, the lieutenant-governor, and speaker of the house of delegates, and the State superintendent of public instruction, which board shall perform such duties as the general assembly may direct.

SEC. 3. There shall be in each county such number of school commissioners as the State superintendent of public instruction shall deem necessary, who shall be appointed by the State board of education; shall hold office for four years, and shall perform such duties and receive such compensation as the general assembly or State superintendent may direct; the school commissioners of Baltimore City shall remain as at present constituted, and shall be appointed, as at present, by the mayor and city council, subject to such alterations and amendments as may be made from time to time by the general assembly, or the said mayor and city council.

SEC. 4. The general assembly, at its first session after the adoption of this constitution, shall provide a uniform system of free public schools, by which a school shall be kept open and supported free of expense for tuition in each school-district, for at least six months in each year; and in case of a failure on the part of the general assembly so to provide, the system reported to it by the State superintendent of public instruction shall become the system of free public schools of the State: *Provided*, That the report of the State superintendent shall be in conformity with the provisions of this constitution, and such system shall be subject to such alterations, conformable to this article, as the general assembly may from time to time enact.

SEC. 5. The general assembly shall levy at each regular session after the adoption of this constitution an annual tax of not less than ten cents on each one hundred dollars of taxable property throughout the State, for the support of the free public schools, which tax shall be collected at the same time and by the same agents as the general State levy; and shall be paid into the treasury of the State, and shall be distributed, under such regulations as may be prescribed by law, among the counties and the city of Baltimore, in proportion to their respective population between the ages of five and twenty years: *Provided*, That the general assembly shall not levy any additional school-tax upon particular counties, unless such county express by popular vote its desire for such tax. The city of Baltimore shall provide for its additional school-tax as at present, or as may hereafter be provided by the general assembly, or by the mayor and city council of Baltimore.

SEC. 6. The general assembly shall further provide by law, at its first session after the adoption of this constitution, a fund for the support of the free public schools of the State, by the imposition of an annual tax of not less than five cents on each one hundred dollars of taxable property throughout the State, the proceeds of which tax shall be known as the public-school fund, and shall be invested by the treasurer, together with its annual interest, until such time as said fund shall, by its own increase and any additions which may be made to it from time to time, together with the present school-fund, amount to six millions of dollars, when the tax of ten cents in the hundred dollars authorized by the preceding section may be discontinued in whole or in part, as the general assembly may direct. The principal fund of six millions hereby provided shall remain forever inviolate as the free public-school fund of the State, and the annual interest of said school-fund shall be disbursed for educational purposes only, as may be prescribed by law.

ARTICLE IX

MILITIA AND MILITARY AFFAIRS

SECTION 1. The militia shall be composed of all able-bodied male citizens, residents of this State, being eighteen years of age, and under the age of forty-five years, who shall be enrolled in the militia, and perform military duty in such manner, not incompatible with the constitution and laws of the United States, as may be prescribed by the general assembly of Maryland; but persons whose religious opinions and conscientious scruples forbid them to bear arms shall be relieved from doing so on producing to the proper authorities satisfactory proof that they are thus conscientious.

SEC. 2. The general assembly shall provide at its first session after the adoption of this constitution, and from time to time thereafter, as the exigency may require, for organizing, equipping, and disciplining the militia in such a manner, not incompatible with the laws of the United States, as shall be most effective to repel invasion and suppress insurrection, and shall pass such laws as shall promote the formation of volunteer militia associations in the city of Baltimore and in every county, and to secure them such privileges or assistance as may afford them effectual encouragement.

SEC. 3. There shall be an adjutant-general, who shall be appointed by the governor, by and with the advice and consent of the senate. He shall hold his office at the pleasure of the governor; shall perform such duties, and shall receive such compensation or emoluments as are now or may be hereafter fixed by law.

ARTICLE X

COUNTIES AND TOWNSHIPS

SECTION 1. The general assembly may provide for organizing new counties, locating and removing county-seats, and changing county-lines, but no new county shall be organized without the consent of a majority of the legal voters residing within the limits about to form said county, nor shall the lines of any county be changed without the consent of a majority of the legal voters residing within the limits of the lines proposed to be changed, nor shall any new county contain less than four hundred square miles nor less than ten thousand white inhabitants, nor shall any county be reduced below that amount of square miles, nor below that number of white inhabitants.

SEC. 2. The general assembly shall provide by general law for dividing the counties into townships or permanent municipal corporations, in place of the existing election-districts, prescribing their limits and confiding to them all powers necessary for the management of their public local concerns; and whenever the organization of these township corporations shall be perfected, all officers provided for in this constitution, but whose official functions shall have been superseded by such organizations shall be dispensed with, and the affairs of such townships and of the counties as affected by the action of such townships shall be transacted in such manner as the general assembly may direct.

ARTICLE XI

AMENDMENTS OF THE CONSTITUTION

SECTION 1. The general assembly may propose any amendment or amendments to this constitution, which shall be agreed to by three-fifths of all the members elected to both houses. Such proposed amendment or amendments, with the yeas and nays thereon, shall be entered on the journal of each house; shall be printed with the laws passed at the same session, and shall be published, by order of the governor, in all the newspapers printed in the different counties of this State, and in three newspapers printed in the city of Baltimore, (one of which shall be printed in the German language,) for at least three months preceding the next election for members of the general assembly, at which election the said proposed amendment or amendments shall be submitted to the qualified electors of the State for their confirmation or rejection; and if it shall appear to the satisfaction of the governor, from the returns of said election made to him by the proper authorities, that a majority of the qualified votes cast at said election on the proposed amendment or amendments were in favor of the said proposed amendment or amendments, he shall, by proclamation, declare said amendment or amendments to be part of the constitution of this State. When two or more amendments shall be submitted by the general assembly to the qualified electors of the State at the same election, they shall be so submitted that the electors may vote for or against each amendment separately.

SEC. 2. Whenever two-thirds of the members elected to each branch of the general assembly shall think it necessary to call a convention to revise, amend, or change this constitution, they shall recommend to the electors to vote at the next election for members of the general assembly for or against a convention; and if a majority of all the electors voting at said election shall have voted for a convention, the general assembly shall, at their next session, provide by law for calling the same.

The convention shall consist of as many members as both houses of the general assembly, who shall be chosen in the same manner, and shall meet within three months after their election for the purpose aforesaid.

SEC. 3. At the general election to be held in the year one thousand eight hundred and eighty-two, and in each twentieth year thereafter, the question, " Shall there be a convention to revise, alter or amend the constitution," shall be submitted to the electors of the State, and in any case a majority of all the electors voting at such election shall decide in favor of a convention, the general assembly at its next session shall provide by law for the election of delegates and the assembling of such convention, as is provided in the preceding section; but no amendment of this constitution agreed upon by any convention assembled in pursuance of this article shall take effect until the same shall have been submitted to the electors of the State, and adopted by a majority of those voting thereon.

ARTICLE XII

SCHEDULE

SECTION 1. Every person holding any office created by or existing under the constitution or laws of the State, the entire amount of whose pay or compensation received for the discharge of his official duties shall exceed the yearly sum of three thousand dollars, except wherein otherwise provided by this constitution, shall keep a book in which shall be entered any sum or sums of money received by him or on his account as a payment or compensation for his performance of official duties, a copy of which entries in said book, verified by the oath of the officer by whom it is directed to be kept, shall be returned yearly to the comptroller of the State for his inspection and that of the general assembly of the State, and each of the said officers, when the amount received by him for the year shall exceed three thousand dollars, shall yearly pay over to the treasurer of the State the amount of such excess by him received, subject to such disposition thereof as the general assembly may direct; and such officer failing to comply with this requisition shall be deemed to have vacated his office and be subject to suit by the State for the amount that ought to be paid into the treasury.

SEC. 2. The several courts, except as herein otherwise provided, shall continue with like powers and jurisdiction, both at law and in equity, as if this constitution had not been adopted, and until the organization of the judicial department provided by this constitution.

SEC. 3. If at any election directed by this constitution any two or more candidates shall have the highest and an equal number of votes, a new election shall be ordered, except in cases specially provided for by this constitution.

SEC. 4. In the trial of all criminal cases, the jury shall be the judges of law as well as fact.

SEC. 5. The trial by jury of all issues of fact in civil proceedings in the several courts of law in this State, where the amount in controversy exceeds the sum of five dollars, shall be inviolably preserved.

SEC. 6. All officers, civil and military, now holding office, whether by election or appointment, under the State, shall continue to hold and exercise their offices, according to their present tenure, unless otherwise provided in this constitution, until they shall be superseded pursuant to its provisions, and until their successors be duly qualified, and the compensation of such officers which has been increased by this constitution shall take effect from the first day of January, eighteen hundred and sixty-five.

SEC. 7. General elections shall be held throughout the State on the Tuesday next after the first Monday in the month of November of each and every year; at the election held in the year eighteen hundred and sixty-four, all State officers required to be elected under this constitution during that year shall be elected, and in like manner in every second year thereafter an election shall be held for those State officers whose terms are about to expire; at the election held in the year eighteen hundred and sixty-five, all county officers required to be elected under this constitution in that year shall be elected, and in like manner in every second year thereafter an election shall be held for those county officers whose terms are about to expire: *Provided, however,* The judges of the several courts of this State, except the judges of the orphans' court, shall be elected at the regular election, whether for State or county officers, as the case may be, immediately preceding the expiration of the term of the incumbent whose place is to be filled.

VOTE ON THE CONSTITUTION

SEC. 8. For the purpose of ascertaining the sense of the people of this State in regard to the adoption or rejection of this constitution, the governor shall issue his proclamation within five days after the adjournment of this convention, directed to the sheriff of the city of

Baltimore, and to the sheriffs of the several counties of this State, commanding them to give notice, in the manner prescribed by law, that an election will be held in the city of Baltimore on the twelfth day of October, in the year eighteen hundred and sixty-four, and in the several counties of this State on the twelfth and thirteenth days of October, in the same year, at the usual places of holding elections in said city and counties, for the adoption or rejection of this constitution, which election shall be held in the said city of Baltimore on the twelfth day of October, eighteen hundred and sixty-four, between the hours of eight o'clock a. m. and five o'clock p. m., and in the said several counties of the State on the said twelfth and thirteenth days of October, eighteen hundred and sixty-four, between the hours of eight o'clock a. m. and five o'clock p. m., and the judges of election of said city, and of the several counties of the State, shall receive at said election the votes only of such electors as are qualified according to the provisions of this constitution, who may offer to vote at such election, and the said sheriffs shall also give notice on or after the twelfth day of October, eighteen hundred and sixty-four, for all elections provided for by this constitution, to be held during that year.

SEC. 9. At the said election the vote shall be by ballot, and each ballot shall describe thereon the words "For the constitution," or "Against the constitution," as the voter may select, and it shall be conducted in all respects as the general elections in this State are now conducted. The judges of election shall administer to every person offering to vote the oath or affirmation prescribed by this constitution, and should any person offering to vote refuse or decline to take said oath, he shall not be permitted to vote at such election, but the taking of such oath or affirmation shall not be deemed conclusive evidence of the right of such person to vote, and it shall be the duty of the return judges of said city, and of the several counties of the State, having counted the votes given for or against the adoption of this constitution, to certify the result thereof in the manner now prescribed by law, accompanied with a special statement that every person who has voted has taken the oath or affirmation prescribed by this constitution; and the governor, upon receiving such result, and ascertaining the aggregate vote throughout the State, including the soldiers' vote, hereinafter provided for, shall, by his proclamation, make known the same, and if a majority of the votes cast shall be for the adoption of this constitution, it shall go into effect on the first day of November, eighteen hundred and sixty-four.

SEC. 10. And the governor shall exclude from count the votes of any county or city, the return judges of which shall fail to certify in the returns, as prescribed by this schedule, that all persons who have voted have taken the oath prescribed to be taken, unless the governor shall be satisfied that such oath was actually administered, and that the failure to make the certificate has been from inadvertence or mistake.

SOLDIERS' VOTE

SEC. 11. Any qualified voter of this State who shall be absent from the county or city of his residence by reason of being in the military service of the United States, so as not to be able to vote at home, on the adoption or rejection of this constitution, or for all State officers elected on general ticket, and for presidential electors and for members of Congress, at the election to be held on the Tuesday next after the first Monday in the month of November, eighteen hundred and sixty-four, shall be entitled to vote at such elections as follows: A poll shall be opened in each company of every Maryland regiment in the service of the United States or of this State on the day appointed by this convention for taking the vote on the new constitution, or some other day not more than five days thereafter, at the quarters of the commanding officer thereof, and voters of this State belonging to such company who shall be within ten miles of such quarters on the day of election may vote at such poll; the polls shall be opened at eight o'clock a. m. and close at six o'clock p. m.; the commissioned officers of such company, or such of them as are present at the opening of the polls, shall act as judges, and any one officer shall be competent so to act, and if no officer be present, then the voters in such company present shall elect two of the voters present to ast as judges of the election; before any votes are received, each of the judges shall take an oath or affirmation that he will perform the duties of judge according to law; will prevent fraud, and observe and make proper return thereof, and such oath the judges may administer to each other; the election shall be by ballot, and any voter may vote either "For the constitution" or "Against the constitution."

SEC. 12. Any qualified voter of this State who shall be absent from the city or county of his residence on the day for taking the vote on the adoption or rejection of this constitution by reason of his being in the military service of the United States, but shall be at some hospital or military post, or on duty within this State, and not with his company, may vote at the nearest poll to such place on satisfying the judges that he is a legal and qualified voter of this State.

SEC. 13. The judges may swear any one offering to vote as to his being a legal voter of this State. The judges shall take down on a poll-book or list the names of all the voters as their votes are taken, and the tickets shall be placed in a box as taken; after the polls are closed, the tickets shall be counted and strung on a thread, and the judges shall make out a certificate, which they shall sign, addressed to the governor, at Annapolis, in which they shall state they have taken the oath hereby prescribed, and shall certify the number of votes taken, and the number of votes for the constitution and against the constitution; the said certificates shall be accompanied with the names of the voters, and shall be plainly expressed, but no particular words shall be required.

SEC. 14. The judges shall, as soon as possible, transmit said returns, with the tickets so strung, to the governor, who shall receive the return of the soldiers' vote, and shall cast up the same and judge of the genuineness and correctness of the returns, and may recount the threaded tickets so as to satisfy himself, and the governor shall count said vote with the aggregate vote of the State on the adoption or rejection of this constitution, and shall wait for fifteen days after the day on which the State vote is taken, so as to allow the returns of the soldiers' vote to be made before the result of the whole vote is announced. The governor shall receive the returns of the soldiers' vote on said election for State officers, presidential electors, and members of Congress, and shall count the same with the aggregate home vote on State officers, and the aggregate home vote in each district respectively for members of Congress.

SEC. 15. The governor shall make known to the officers of the State regiments the provisions of this article of the schedule, and request them to exercise the rights hereby conferred upon them, and shall take all means proper to secure the soldiers' vote; and the general assembly, at its first session after the adoption of this constitution, shall make proper appropriation to pay any expense that may arise herein.

SEC. 16. If this constitution shall be adopted by the people, the provisions contained herein for taking the soldiers' vote on the adoption of the constitution shall apply to all elections to be held in this State until the general assembly shall provide some other mode of taking the same.

Done in Convention the sixth day of September, in the year of our Lord one thousand eight hundred and sixty-four, and of the Independence of the United States the eighty-ninth.

HENRY H. GOLDSBOROUGH, *President.*

Attest:
W. R. COLE, *Secretary.*

CONSTITUTION OF MARYLAND—1867 [*][a]

DECLARATION OF RIGHTS

We, the people of the State of Maryland, grateful to Almighty God for our civil and religious liberty, and taking into our serious consideration the best means of establishing a good Constitution in this State for the sure foundation and more permanent security thereof, declare:

ARTICLE 1. That all Government of right originates from the People, is founded in compact only, and instituted solely for the good of the whole; and they have, at all times, the inalienable right to alter, reform or abolish their form of Government in such manner as they may deem expedient.

ART. 2. The Constitution of the United States, and the Laws made or which shall be made in pursuance thereof, and all Treaties made, or which shall be made, under the authority of the United States, are and shall be the Supreme Law of the State; and the Judges of this State, and all the People of this State, are, and shall be bound thereby, anything in the Constitution or Law of this State to the contrary notwithstanding.

ART. 3. The powers not delegated to the United States by the Constitution thereof, nor prohibited by it to the States, are reserved to the States respectively, or to the People thereof.

---

[*] Verified by "Constitutions of Maryland. 1776, 1851, 1864 and 1867. Published by the Secretary of State." [1906.] 222 pp.

[a] Adopted by the Convention which assembled at the city of Annapolis on the eighth day of May, eighteen hundred and sixty-seven, and adjourned on the seventeenth day of August, eighteen hundred and sixty-seven, and ratified by the People on the eighteenth day of September, eighteen hundred and sixty-seven, with Amendments and Decisions of the Court of Appeals, to and including 102 Md.

ART. 4. That the People of this State have the sole and exclusive right of regulating the internal government and police thereof, as a free, sovereign and independent State.

ART. 5. That the Inhabitants of Maryland are entitled to the Common Law of England, and the trial by Jury, according to the course of that law, and to the benefit of such of the English statutes as existed on the Fourth day of July, seventeen hundred and seventy-six; and which, by experience, have been found applicable to their local and other circumstances, and have been introduced, used and practiced by the Courts of Law or Equity; and also of all Acts of Assembly in force on the first day of June, eighteen hundred and sixty-seven; except such as may have since expired, or may be inconsistent with the provisions of this Constitution; subject, nevertheless, to the revision of, and amendment or repeal by, the Legislature of this State. And the Inhabitants of Maryland are also entitled to all property derived to them from or under the Charter granted by His Majesty, Charles the First, to Cæcilius Calvert, Baron of Baltimore.

ART. 6. That all persons invested with the Legislative or Executive powers of Government are Trustees of the Public, and as such, accountable for their conduct: Wherefore, whenever the ends of Government are perverted, and public liberty manifestly endangered, and all other means of redress are ineffectual, the People may, and of right ought to reform the old, or establish a new Government; the doctrine of non-resistance against arbitrary power and oppression is absurd, slavish and destructive of the good and happiness of mankind.

ART. 7. That the right of the People to participate in the Legislature is the best security of liberty and the foundation of all free Government; for this purpose elections ought to be free and frequent, and every white [a] male citizen having the qualifications prescribed by the Constitution, ought to have the right of suffrage.

ART. 8. That the Legislative, Executive and Judicial powers of Government ought to be forever separate and distinct from each other; and no person exercising the functions of one of said Departments shall assume or discharge the duties of any other.

ART. 9. That no power of suspending Laws or the execution of Laws, unless by, or derived from the Legislature, ought to be exercised, or allowed.

ART. 10. That freedom of speech and debate, or proceedings in the Legislature, ought not to be impeached in any Court of Judicature.

ART. 11. That Annapolis be the place of meeting of the Legislature; and the Legislature ought not to be convened, or held at any other place but from evident necessity.

ART. 12. That for redress of grievances, and for amending, strengthening, and for preserving the laws, the Legislature ought to be frequently convened.

ART. 13. That every man hath a right to petition the Legislature for the redress of grievances in a peaceful and orderly manner.

ART. 14. That no aid, charge, tax, burthen or fees ought to be rated, or levied, under any pretence, without the consent of the Legislature.

---

[a] The word "white" omitted under the 15th Amendment to the Constitution of the United States.

ART. 15. That the levying of taxes by the poll is grievous and oppressive, and ought to be prohibited; that paupers ought not to be assessed for the support of the Government; but every person in the State, or person holding property therein, ought to contribute his proportion of public taxes for the support of the Government, according to his actual worth in real or personal property; yet fines, duties or taxes may properly and justly be imposed, or laid with a political view for the good government and benefit of the community.

ART. 16. That sanguinary Laws ought to be avoided as far as it is consistent with the safety of the State; and no Law to inflict cruel and unusual pains and penalties ought to be made in any case, or at any time, hereafter.

ART. 17. That retrospective Laws, punishing acts committed before the existence of such Laws, and by them only declared criminal are oppressive, unjust and incompatible with liberty; wherefore, no *ex post facto* Law ought to be made; nor any retrospective oath or restriction be imposed or required.

ART. 18. That no Law to attaint particular persons of treason or felony ought to be made in any case, or at any time, hereafter.

ART. 19. That every man, for any injury done to him in his person or property ought to have remedy by the course of the Law of the Land, and ought to have justice and right, freely without sale, fully without any denial, and speedily without delay, according to Law of the Land.

ART. 20. That the trial of facts, where they arise, is one of the greatest securities of the lives, liberties and estate of the People.

ART. 21. That in all criminal prosecutions, every man hath a right to be informed of the accusation against him; to have a copy of the Indictment, or Charge in due time (if required) to prepare for his defence; to be allowed counsel; to be confronted with the witnesses against him; to have process for his witnesses; to examine the witnesses for and against him on oath; and to a speedy trial by an impartial jury, without whose unanimous consent he ought not to be found guilty.

ART. 22. That no man ought to be compelled to give evidence against himself in a criminal case.

ART. 23. That no man ought to be taken or imprisoned or disseized of his freehold, liberties or privileges, or outlawed, or exiled, or in any manner destroyed, or deprived of his life, liberty or property, but by the judgment of his peers, or by the Law of the Land.

ART. 24. That slavery shall not be re-established in this State; but, having been abolished, under the policy and authority of the United States, compensation in consideration thereof, is due from the United States.

ART. 25. That excessive bail ought not to be required, nor excessive fines imposed, nor cruel or unusual punishment inflicted by the Courts of Law.

ART. 26. That all warrants, without oath or affirmation, to search suspected places, or to seize any person or property, are grievous and oppressive; and all general warrants to search suspected places, or to apprehend suspected persons, without naming or describing the place, or the person in special, are illegal, and ought not to be granted.

ART. 27. That no conviction shall work corruption of blood or forfeiture of estate.

ART. 28. That a well regulated Militia is the proper and natural defence of a free Government.

ART. 29. That Standing Armies are dangerous to liberty, and ought not to be raised, or kept up, without the consent of the Legislature.

ART. 30. That in all cases, and at all times, the military ought to be under strict subordination to, and control, of the civil power.

ART. 31. That no soldier shall, in time of peace, be quartered in any house, without the consent of the owner, nor in time of war, except in the manner prescribed by Law.

ART. 32. That no person except regular soldiers, marines, and mariners in the service of this State, or militia, when in actual service, ought, in any case, to be subject to, or punishable by, Martial Law.

ART. 33. That the independency and uprightness of Judges are essential to the impartial administration of Justice, and a great security to the rights and liberties of the People; wherefore, the Judges shall not be removed, except in the manner, and for the causes, provided in this Constitution. No Judge shall hold any other office, civil or military or political trust, or employment of any kind whatsoever, under the constitution or laws of this State, or of the United States, or any of them; or receive fees, or perquisites of any kind, for the discharge of his official duties.

ART. 34. That a long continuance in the Executive Departments of power or trust is dangerous to liberty; a rotation, therefore, in those Departments is one of the best securities of permanent freedom.

ART. 35. That no person shall hold, at the same time, more than one office of profit, created by the Constitution or Laws of this State; nor shall any person in public trust receive any present from any foreign Prince or State, or from the United States, or any of them, without the approbation of this State.

ART. 36. That as it is the duty of every man to worship God in such manner as he thinks most acceptable to Him, all persons are equally entitled to protection in their religious liberty; wherefore, no person ought, by any law to be molested in his person or estate, on account of his religious persuasion or profession, or for his religious practice, unless, under the color of religion, he shall disturb the good order, peace or safety of the State, or shall infringe the laws of morality, or injure others in their natural, civil or religious rights; nor ought any person to be compelled to frequent, or maintain, or contribute, unless under contract, to maintain any place of worship or any ministry; nor shall any person, otherwise competent, be deemed incompetent as a witness, or juror, on account of his religious belief; provided, he believes in the existence of God, and that under His dispensation such person will be held morally accountable for his acts, and be rewarded or punished therefor in this world or the world to come.

ART. 37. That no religious test ought ever to be required as a qualification for any office of profit or trust in this State, other than a declaration of belief in the existence of God; nor shall the Legislature prescribe any other oath of office than the oath prescribed by this Constitution.

ART. 38. That every gift, sale or devise of land to any Minister, Public Teacher or Preacher of the Gospel, as such, or to any Religious Sect, Order or Denomination, or to, or for the support, use or benefit of, or in trust for, any Minister, Public Teacher or Preacher of the Gospel, as such, or any Religious Sect, Order or Denomination; and every gift or sale of goods, or chattels, to go in succession, or to take place after the death of the Seller or Donor, to or for such support, use or benefit; and also every devise of goods or chattels to or for the support, use or benefit of any Minister, Public Teacher or Preacher of the Gospel, as such, or any Religious Sect, Order or Denomination, without the prior or subsequent sanction of the Legislature, shall be void; except always, any sale, gift, lease or devise of any quantity of land, not exceeding five acres, for a church, meeting-house, or other house of worship, or parsonage, or for a burying-ground, which shall be improved, enjoyed or used only for such purpose; or such sale, gift, lease or devise shall be void.

ART. 39. That the manner of administering the oath or affirmation to any person ought to be such as those of the religious persuasion, profession, or denomination, of which he is a member, generally esteem the most effectual confirmation by the attestation of the Divine Being.

ART. 40. That the liberty of the press ought to be inviolably preserved; that every citizen of the State ought to be allowed to speak, write and publish his sentiments on all subjects, being responsible for the abuse of that privilege.

ART. 41. That monopolies are odious, contrary to the spirit of a free government and the principles of commerce, and ought not to be suffered.

ART. 42. That no title of nobility or hereditary honors ought to granted in this State.

ART. 43. That the Legislature ought to encourage the diffusion of knowledge and virtue, the extension of a judicious system of general education, the promotion of literature, the arts, sciences, agriculture, commerce and manufactures, and the general amelioration of the condition of the people.

ART. 44. That the provisions of the Constitution of the United States, and of this State, apply as well in time of war as in time of peace; and any departure therefrom, or violation thereof, under the plea of necessity, or any other plea, is subversive of good government and tends to anarchy and despotism.

ART. 45. This enumeration of Rights shall not be construed to impair or deny others retained by the People.

CONSTITUTION

[All amendments are included in brackets and follow the sections as originally adopted]

ARTICLE I

ELECTIVE FRANCHISE

SECTION 1. All elections shall be by ballot; and every white [a] male citizen of the United States, of the age of twenty-one years, or upwards, who has been a resident of the State for one year, and of the Legislative District of Baltimore city, or of the county, in which he may offer to vote, for six months next preceding the election, shall be entitled to vote, in the ward or election district in which he resides,

---

[a] The word "white" became inoperative under the 15th Amendment to the Constitution of the United States.

at all elections hereafter to be held in this State; and in case any county or city shall be so divided as to form portions of different electoral districts, for the election of Representatives in Congress, Senators, Delegates, or other Officers, then to entitle a person to vote for such officer, he must have been a resident of that part of the county, or city, which shall form a part of the electoral district, in which he offers to vote, for six months next preceding the election; but a person, who shall have acquired a residence in such county or city, entitling him to vote at any such election, shall be entitled to vote in the election district from which he removed, until he shall have acquired a residence in the part of the county or city to which he has removed.

SEC. 2. No person above the age of twenty-one years, convicted of larceny or other infamous crime, unless pardoned by the Governor, shall ever thereafter, be entitled to vote at any election in this State; and no person under guardianship, as a lunatic, or as a person *non compos mentis*, shall be entitled to vote.

SEC. 3. If any person shall give, or offer to give, directly or indirectly, any bribe, present, or reward, or any promise, or any security, for the payment or the delivery of money, or any other thing, to induce any voter to refrain from casting his vote, or to prevent him in any way from voting, or to procure a vote for any candidate or person proposed, or voted for, as Elector of President and Vice-President of the United States, or Representative in Congress, or for any office of profit or trust, created by the Constitution or Laws of this State, or by the Ordinances, or Authority of the Mayor and City Council of Baltimore, the person giving, or offering to give, and the person receiving the same, and any person who gives, or causes to be given, an illegal vote, knowing it to be such, at any election to be hereafter held in this State, shall, on conviction in a Court of Law, in addition to the penalties now or hereafter to be imposed by law, be forever disqualified to hold any office of profit or trust, or to vote at any election thereafter.

SEC. 4. It shall be the duty of the General Assembly to pass Laws to punish, with fine and imprisonment, any person who shall remove into any election district or precinct of any ward of the city of Baltimore, not for the purpose of acquiring a *bona fide* residence therein, but for the purpose of voting at an approaching election, or who shall vote in any election district or ward in which he does not reside (except in the case provided for in this Article), or shall, at the same election, vote in more than one election district, or precinct, or shall vote, or offer to vote, in any name not his own, or in place of any other person of the same name, or shall vote in any county in which he does not reside.

SEC. 5. The General Assembly shall provide by law for a uniform Registration of the names of all the voters in this State who possess the qualifications prescribed in this Article, which Registration shall be conclusive evidence to the Judges of election of the right of every person thus registered to vote at any election thereafter held in this State; but no person shall vote at any election, Federal or State, hereafter to be held in this State, or at any municipal election in the City of Baltimore, unless his name appears in the list of registered voters; and until the General Assembly shall hereafter pass an Act for the

Registration of the names of voters, the law in force on the first day of June, in the year eighteen hundred and sixty-seven, in reference thereto, shall be continued in force, except so far as it may be inconsistent with the provisions of this Constitution; and the registry of voters, made in pursuance thereof, may be corrected, as provided in said law; but the names of all persons shall be added to the list of qualified voters by the officers of Registration, who have the qualifications prescribed in the first section of this Article, and who are not disqualified under the provisions of the second and third sections thereof.

SEC. 6. Every person elected or appointed to any office of profit or trust, under this Constitution, or under the laws, made pursuant thereto, shall, before he enters upon the duties of such office, take and subscribe the following oath or affirmation: I, ———, do swear, (or affirm, as the case may be,) that I will support the Constitution of the United States; and that I will be faithful and bear true allegiance to the State of Maryland, and support the Constitution and Laws thereof; and that I will, to the best of my skill and judgment, diligently and faithfully, without partiality or prejudice, execute the office of ———, according to the Constitution and Laws of this State, (and, if a Governor, Senator, Member of the House of Delegates, or Judge), that I will not, directly or indirectly, receive the profits or any part of the profits of any other office during the term of my acting as ———

SEC. 7. Every person hereafter elected or appointed to office in this State, who shall refuse or neglect to take the oath or affirmation of office provided for in the sixth section of this Article, shall be considered as having refused to accept the said office; and a new election or appointment shall be made, as in case of refusal to accept, or resignation of an office; and any person violating said oath shall, on conviction thereof, in a Court of Law, in addition to the penalties now or hereafter to be imposed by law, be thereafter incapable of holding any office of profit or trust in this State.

ARTICLE II

EXECUTIVE DEPARTMENT

SECTION 1. The executive power of the State shall be vested in a Governor, whose term of office shall commence on the second Wednesday of January next ensuing his election, and continue for four years, and until his successor shall have qualified; but the Governor chosen at the first election under this Constitution shall not enter upon the discharge of the duties of the office until the expiration of the term for which the present incumbent was elected; unless the said office shall become vacant by death, resignation, removal from the State, or other disqualification of the said incumbent.

SEC. 2. An election for Governor, under this Constitution, shall be held on the Tuesday next after the first Monday of November, in the year eighteen hundred and sixty-seven, and on the same day and month in every fourth year thereafter, at the places of voting for delegates to the General Assembly; and every person qualified to vote for Delegates shall be qualified and entitled to vote for Governor; the election to be held in the same manner as the election of Delegates, and the returns thereof under seal to be addressed to the Speaker of the House of Delegates, and enclosed and transmitted to the Secretary of State, and delivered to said Speaker, at the commencement of the session of the General Assembly next ensuing said election.

SEC. 3. The Speaker of the House of Delegate shall then open the said returns in the presence of both Houses; and the person having the highest number of votes, and being constitutionally eligible, shall be the Governor, and shall qualify, in the manner herein prescribed, on the second Wednesday of January next ensuing his election, or as soon thereafter as may be practicable.

SEC. 4. If two or more persons shall have the highest and an equal number of votes for Governor, one of them shall be chosen Governor by the Senate and House of Delegates, and all questions in relation to the eligibility of Governor, and to the returns of said election, and to the number and legality of votes therein given, shall be determined by the House of Delegates; and if the person or persons, having the highest number of votes, be ineligible, the Governor shall be chosen by the Senate and House of Delegates. Every election of Governor by the General Assembly shall be determined by a joint majority of the Senate and House of Delegates, and the vote shall be taken *viva voce*. But if two or more persons shall have the highest and an equal number of votes, then a second vote shall be taken, which shall be confined to the persons having an equal number; and if the vote should again be equal, then the election of Governor shall be determined by lot between those who shall have the highest and an equal number on the first vote.

SEC. 5. A person to be eligible to the office of Governor must have attained the age of thirty years, and must have been for ten years a citizen of the State of Maryland, and for five years next preceding his election a resident of the State, and, at the time of his election, a qualified voter therein.

SEC. 6. In the case of death or resignation of the Governor, or of his removal from the State, or other disqualification, the General assembly, if in session, or if not, at their next session, shall elect some other qualified person to be Governor for the residue of the term for which the said Governor had been elected.

SEC. 7. In case of any vacancy in the office of Governor, during the recess of the Legislature, the President of the Senate shall discharge the duties of said office, until a Governor is elected, as herein provided for; and in case of the death or resignation of the said President, or of his removal from the State, or of his refusal to serve, then the duties of said office shall, in like manner, and for the same interval, devolve upon the Speaker of the House of Delegates. And the Legislature may provide by Law, for the impeachment of the Governor; and in case of his conviction, or his inability, may declare what person shall perform the Executive duties; and for any vacancy in said office not herein provided for, provision may be made by Law; and if such vacancy should occur without such provision being made, the Legislature shall be convened by the Secretary of State for the purpose of filling said vacancy.

SEC. 8. The Governor shall be the Commander-in-Chief of the land and naval forces of the State; and may call out the Militia to repel invasions, suppress insurrections, and enforce the execution of the Laws; but shall not take the command in person, without the consent of the Legislature.

SEC. 9. He shall take care that the Laws are faithfully executed.

SEC. 10. He shall nominate, and by and with the advice and consent of the Senate, appoint all civil and military officers of the State, whose appointment or election is not otherwise herein provided for; unless a different mode of appointment be prescribed by the Law creating the office.

SEC. 11. In case of any vacancy during the recess of the Senate, in any office which the Governor has power to fill, he shall appoint some suitable person to said office, whose commission shall continue in force until the end of the next session of the Legislature, or until some other person is appointed to the same office, whichever shall first occur; and the nomination of the person thus appointed during the recess, or of some other person in his place, shall be made to the Senate within thirty days after the next meeting of the Legislature.

SEC. 12. No person, after being rejected by the Senate, shall be again nominated for the same office at the same session, unless at the request of the Senate; or be appointed to the same office during the recess of the Legislature.

SEC. 13. All civil officers appointed by the Governor and Senate, shall be nominated to the Senate within fifty days from the commencement of each regular session of the Legislature; and their term of office, except in cases otherwise provided for in this Constitution, shall commence on the first Monday of May next ensuing their appointment, and continue for two years, (unless removed from office), and until their successors, respectively, qualify according to Law; but the term of office of the Inspectors of Tobacco shall commence on the first Monday of March next ensuing their appointment.

SEC. 14. If a vacancy shall occur during the session of the Senate, in any office which the Governor and Senate have the power to fill, the Governor shall nominate to the Senate, before its final adjournment, a proper person to fill said vacancy, unless such vacancy occurs within ten days before said final adjournment.

SEC. 15. The Governor may suspend or arrest any military officer of the State for disobedience of orders or other military offence; and may remove him in pursuance of the sentence of a Court Martial; and may remove for incompetency or misconduct, all civil officers who received appointment from the Executive for a term of years.

SEC. 16. The Governor shall convene the Legislature, or the Senate alone, on extraordinary occasions; and whenever from the presence of an enemy, or from any other cause, the Seat of Government shall become an unsafe place for the meeting of the Legislature, he may direct their sessions to be held at some other convenient place.

SEC. 17. To guard against hasty or partial legislation and encroachments of the Legislative Department upon the co-ordinate, Executive and Judicial Departments, every Bill which shall have passed the House of Delegates, and the Senate shall, before it becomes a law, be presented to the Governor of the State; if he approve he shall sign it, but if not he shall return it with his objections to the House in which it originated, which House shall enter the objections at large on its Journal and proceed to reconsider the Bill; if, after such reconsideration, three-fifths of the members elected to that House shall pass the Bill, it shall be sent with the objections to the other House, by which it shall likewise be reconsidered, and if it pass by three-fifths of the members elected to that House it shall become a law; but in all such cases the votes of both Houses shall be determined by yeas and nays, and the names of the persons voting for and against the Bill shall be entered on the Journal of each House, respectively. If any bill shall not be returned by the Governor within six days (Sundays excepted), after it shall have been presented to him, the same shall be a law in like manner as if he signed it, unless the General Assembly shall, by adjournment, prevent its return, in which case it shall not be a law.

[The Governor shall have power to disapprove of any item or items of any Bills making appropriations of money embracing distinct items, and the part or parts of the Bill approved shall be the law, and the item or items of appropriations disapproved shall be void unless repassed according to the rules or limitations prescribed for the passage of other Bills over the Executive veto.] [a]

SEC. 18. It shall be the duty of the Governor, semiannually, (and oftener, if he deems it expedient), to examine under oath the Treasurer and Comptroller of the State on all matters pertaining to their respective offices, and inspect and review their bank and other account books.

SEC. 19. He shall, from time to time, inform the Legislature of the condition of the State, and recommend to their consideration such measures as he may judge necessary and expedient.

SEC. 20. He shall have power to grant reprieves and pardons, except in cases of impeachment, and in cases in which he is prohibited by other Articles of this Constitution; and to remit fines and forfeitures for offences against the State; but shall not remit the principal or interest of any debt due the State, except in cases of fines and forfeitures; and before granting a *nolle prosequi*, or pardon, he shall give notice, in one or more newspapers, of the application made for it, and of the day on or after which his decision will be given; and in every case in which he exercises this power, he shall report to either Branch of the Legislature, whenever required, the petitions, recommendations and reasons which influenced his decision.

SEC. 21. The Governor shall reside at the seat of government, and receive for his services an annual salary of four thousand five hundred dollars.

SEC. 22. A Secretary of State shall be appointed by the Governor, by and with the advice and consent of the Senate, who shall continue in office, unless sooner removed by the Governor, till the end of the official term of the Governor from whom he received his appointment, and receive an annual salary of two thousand dollars, and shall reside at the seat of government; and the office of Private Secretary shall thenceforth cease.

SEC. 23. The Secretary of State shall carefully keep and preserve a record of all official acts and proceedings, which may at all times be inspected by a committee of either branch of the Legislature; and he shall perform such other duties as may be prescribed by law, or as may properly belong to his office, together with all clerical duty belonging to the Executive Department.

---

[a] Thus amended by Chapter 194, Acts of 1890, ratified by the people, November 3rd, 1891.

Article III

LEGISLATIVE DEPARTMENT

SECTION 1. The Legislature shall consist of two distinct branches—a Senate and a House of Delegates—and shall be styled the General Assembly of Maryland.

SEC. 2. Each County in the State, and each of the three Legislative Districts of Baltimore City, as they are now, or may hereafter be defined, shall be entitled to one Senator, who shall be elected by the qualified voters of the Counties, and of the Legislative Districts of Baltimore City, respectively, and shall serve for four years from the date of his election, subject to the classification of Senators hereafter provided for.

[SEC. 2. The City of Baltimore shall be divided into four legislative districts, as near as may be, of equal population and of contiguous territory, and each of said legislative districts of Baltimore City, as they may from time to time be laid out, in accordance with the provisions hereof, and each county in the State shall be entitled to one Senator, who shall be elected by the qualified voters of the said legislative districts of Baltimore City, and of the counties of the State, respectively, and shall serve for four years from the date of his election, subject to the classification of Senators hereafter provided for.] [a]

SEC. 3. Until the taking and publishing of the next National Census, or until the enumeration of the population of this State, under the authority thereof, the several counties and the City of Baltimore, shall have a representation in the House of Delegates, as follows: Allegany County, five Delegates; Anne Arundel County, three Delegates; Baltimore County, six Delegates; each of the three Legislative Districts of the City of Baltimore, six Delegates; Calvert County, two Delegates; Caroline County, two Delegates; Carroll County, four Delegates; Cecil County, four Delegates; Charles County, two Delegates; Dorchester County, three Delegates; Frederick County, six Delegates; Harford County, four Delegates; Howard County, two Delegates; Kent County, two Delegates; Montgomery County, three Delegates; Prince George's County, three Delegates; Queen Anne's County, two Delegates; St. Mary's County, two Delegates; Somerset County, three Delegates; Talbot County, two Delegates; Washington County, five Delegates, and Worcester County, three Delegates.[b]

SEC. 4. As soon as may be after the taking and publishing of the next National Census, or after the enumeration of the population of

---

[a] Thus amended by Act of 1900, Chapter 469, ratified by the people at November election, 1901.

[b] Under the State Census authorized by the Act of 1901 (Special Session), and by the amendment to Sec. 2, the allotment of representation of the several counties in the House of Delegates is as follows: Allegany County, five; Anne Arundel County, four; Baltimore County, six; Calvert County, two; Caroline County, two; Carroll County, four; Cecil County, three; Charles County, two; Dorchester County, four; Frederick County, five; Garrett County, two; Harford County, four; Howard County, two; Kent County, two; Montgomery County, four; Prince George's County, four; Queen Anne's County, three; Somerset County, three; St. Mary's County, two; Talbot County, three; Washington County, five; Wicomico County, three; Worcester County, three; and Baltimore City, twenty-four delegates. Total, 101.

this State, under the authority thereof, there shall be an apportionment of representation in the House of Delegates, to be made on the following basis, to wit: Each of the several Counties of the State having a population of eighteen thousand souls, or less, shall be entitled to two Delegates, and every County having a population of over eighteen thousand, and less than twenty-eight thousand souls, shall be entitled to three Delegates; and every County having a population of twenty-eight thousand, and less than forty thousand souls, shall be entitled to four Delegates; and every County having a population of forty thousand, and less than fifty-five thousand souls, shall be entitled to five Delegates; and every County having a population of fifty-five thousand souls, and upwards, shall be entitled to six Delegates, and no more; and each of the three Legislative Districts of the City of Baltimore shall be entitled to the number of Delegates to which the largest County shall or may be entitled, under the aforegoing apportionment. And the General Assembly shall have power to provide by law, from time to time, for altering and changing the boundaries of the three existing Legislative Districts of the City of Baltimore, so as to make them, as near as may be, of equal population; but said Districts shall always consist of contiguous territory.

[SEC. 4. As soon as may be, after the taking and publishing of the National Census of 1900, or after the enumeration of the population of this State, under the authority thereof, there shall be an apportionment of representation in the House of Delegates, to be made on the following basis, to wit: Each of the several counties of the State, having a population of eighteen thousand souls or less, shall be entitled to two delegates; and every county having a population of over eighteen thousand and less than twenty-eight thousand souls, shall be entitled to three delegates; and every county having a population of twenty-eight thousand and less than forty thousand souls, shall be entitled to four delegates; and every county having a population of forty thousand and less than fifty-five thousand souls, shall be entitled to five delegates; and every county having a population of fifty-five thousand souls and upwards, shall be entitled to six delegates and no more; and each of the Legislative Districts of the City of Baltimore shall be entitled to the number of delegates to which the largest county shall or may be entitled under the aforegoing apportionment, and the General Assembly shall have the power to provide by law, from time to time, for altering and changing the boundaries of the existing legislative districts of the City of Baltimore, so as to make them as near as may be of equal population; but said district shall always consist of contiguous territory.] [a]

SEC. 5. Immediately after the taking and publishing of the next National Census, or after any State enumeration of population, as aforesaid, it shall be the duty of the Governor, then being, to arrange the representation in said House of Delegates in accordance with the apportionment herein provided for; and to declare, by Proclamation, the number of Delegates to which each County and the City of Baltimore may be entitled under such apportionment; and after every National Census taken thereafter, or after any State enumeration of

---

[a] Thus amended by Act of 1900, Chapter 432, ratified by the people at November election, 1901.

population thereafter made, it shall be the duty of the Governor, for the time being, to make similar adjustment of representation, and to declare the same by Proclamation, as aforesaid.

SEC. 6. The members of the House of Delegates shall be elected by the qualified voters of the Counties, and the Legislative Districts of Baltimore City, respectively, to serve for two years from the day of their election.

SEC. 7. The first election for Senators and Delegates shall take place on the Tuesday next after the first Monday in the month of November, eighteen hundred and sixty-seven; and the election for Delegates, and as nearly as practicable, for one-half of the Senators shall be held on the same day in every second year thereafter.

SEC. 8. Immediately after the Senate shall have convened, after the first election, under this Constitution, the Senators shall be divided by lot into two classes, as nearly equal in number as may be. Senators of the first class shall go out of office at the expiration of two years, and Senators shall be elected on the Tuesday next after the first Monday in the month of November, eighteen hundred and sixty-nine, for the term of four years, to supply their places; so that, after the first election, one-half of the Senators may be chosen every second year. In case the number of Senators be hereafter increased, such classification of the additional Senators shall be made as to preserve, as nearly as may be, an equal number in each class.

SEC. 9. No person shall be eligible as a Senator or Delegate who, at the time of his election, is not a citizen of the State of Maryland, and who has not resided therein for at least three years next preceding the day of his election, and the last year thereof, in the County, or in the Legislative District of Baltimore City, which he may be chosen to represent, if such County or Legislative District of said City shall have been so long established; and if not, then the County or City, from which, in whole or in part, the same may have been formed; nor shall any person be eligible as a Senator unless he shall have attained the age of twenty-five years, nor as a Delegate unless he shall have attained the age of twenty-one years, at the time of his election.

SEC. 10. No member of Congress, or person holding any civil or military office under the United States shall be eligible as a Senator or Delegate; and if any person shall, after his election as Senator or Delegate, be elected to Congress, or be appointed to any office, civil or military, under the Government of the United States, his acceptance thereof shall vacate his seat.

SEC. 11. No Minister or Preacher of the Gospel, or of any religious creed or denomination, and no person holding any civil office of profit or trust under this State, except Justices of the Peace, shall be eligible as Senator or Delegate.

SEC. 12. No Collector, Receiver or holder of public money shall be eligible as Senator or Delegate, or to any office of profit or trust under this State, until he shall have accounted for and paid into the Treasury all sums on the books thereof charged to and due by him.

SEC. 13. In case of death, disqualification, resignation, refusal to act, expulsion, or removal from the county or city for which he shall have been elected, of any person who shall have been chosen as a Delegate or Senator, or in case of a tie between two or more such qualified persons, a warrant of election shall be issued by the Speaker of the House of Delegates, or President of the Senate, as the case may be, for the election of another person in his place, of which election not less than ten days' notice shall be given, exclusive of the day of the publication of the notice and of the day of election; and if during the recess of the Legislature, and more than ten days before its termination, such death shall occur, or such resignation, refusal to act or disqualification be communicated in writing to the Governor by the person so resigning, refusing or disqualified, it shall be the duty of the Governor to issue a warrant of election to supply the vacancy thus created, in the same manner the said Speaker or President might have done during the session of the General Assembly; provided, however, that unless a meeting of the General Assembly may intervene, the election thus ordered to fill such vacancy shall be held on the day of the ensuing election for Delegates and Senators.

SEC. 14. The General Assembly shall meet on the first Wednesday of January, eighteen hundred and sixty-eight, and on the same day in every second year thereafter, and at no other time, unless convened by Proclamation of the Governor.

SEC. 15. The General Assembly may continue its session so long as in its judgment the public interest may require, for a period not longer than ninety days; and each member thereof shall receive a compensation of five dollars per diem for every day he shall attend the session, but not for such days as he may be absent, unless absent on account of sickness or by leave of the House of which he is a member; and he shall also receive such mileage as may be allowed by law, not exceeding twenty cents per mile; and the presiding officer of each House shall receive an additional compensation of three dollars per day. When the General Assembly shall be convened by Proclamation of the Governor, the session shall not continue longer than thirty days, and in such case the compensation shall be the same as herein prescribed.

SEC. 16. No book, or other printed matter, not appertaining to the business of the session, shall be purchased or subscribed for, for the use of the members of the General Assembly, or be distributed among them, at the public expense.

SEC. 17. No Senator or Delegate, after qualifying as such, notwithstanding he may thereafter resign, shall during the whole period of time for which he was elected be eligible to any office which shall have been created, or the salary or profits of which shall have been increased, during such term.

SEC. 18. No Senator or Delegate shall be liable in any civil action or criminal prosecution whatever for words spoken in debate.

SEC. 19. Each House shall be judge of the qualifications and elections of its members, as prescribed by the Constitution and Laws of the State; shall appoint its own officers, determine the rules of its own proceedings, punish a member for disorderly or disrespectful behavior, and with the consent of two-thirds of its whole number of members elected, expel a member; but no member shall be expelled a second time for the same offence.

SEC. 20. A majority of the whole number of members elected to each House shall constitute a quorum for the transaction of business; but a smaller number may adjourn from day to day, and compel the attendance of absent members in such manner and under such penalties as each House may prescribe.

SEC. 21. The doors of each House and the Committee of the Whole shall be open, except when the business is such as ought to be kept secret.

SEC. 22. Each House shall keep a Journal of its proceedings, and cause the same to be published. The yeas and nays of members on any question shall, at the call of any five of them in the House of Delegates, or one in the Senate, be entered on the Journal.

SEC. 23. Each House may punish by imprisonment, during the session of the General Assembly, any person not a member, for disrespectful or disorderly behavior in its presence, or for obstructing any of its proceedings, or any of its officers in the execution of their duties; provided, such imprisonment shall not at any one time exceed ten days.

SEC. 24. The House of Delegates may inquire, on the oath of witnesses, into all complaints, grievances and offences, as the Grand Inquest of the State, and may commit any person for any crime to the public jail, there to remain until discharged by due course of law. They may examine and pass all accounts of the State, relating either to the collection or expenditure of the revenue, and appoint auditors to state and adjust the same. They may call for all public or official papers and records, and send for persons whom they may judge necessary, in the course of their inquiries, concerning affairs relating to the public interest, and may direct all office bonds which shall be made payable to the State to be sued for any breach thereof; and with the view to the more certain prevention or correction of the abuses in the expenditures of the money of the State, the General Assembly shall create, at every session thereof, a Joint Standing Committee of the Senate and House of Delegates, who shall have power to send for persons and examine them on oath and call for public or official papers and records; and whose duty it shall be to examine and report upon all contracts made for printing, stationery, and purchases for the public offices and the library, and all expenditures therein, and upon all matters of alleged abuse in expenditures, to which their attention may be called by resolution of either House of the General Assembly.

SEC. 25. Neither House shall, without the consent of the other, adjourn for more than three days at any one time, nor adjourn to any other place than that in which the House shall be sitting, without the concurrent vote of two-thirds of the members present.

SEC. 26. The House of Delegates shall have the sole power of impeachment in all cases; but a majority of all the members elected must concur in the impeachment. All impeachments shall be tried by the Senate, and when sitting for that purpose the Senators shall be on oath or affirmation to do justice according to the law and the evidence; but no person shall be convicted without the concurrence of two-thirds of all the Senators elected.

SEC. 27. Any bill may originate in either House of the General Assembly, and be altered, amended or rejected by the other; but no bill shall originate in either House during the last ten days of the session, unless two-thirds of the members elected thereto shall so determine by yeas and nays; nor shall any bill become a law until it be read on three different days of the session in each House, unless two-thirds of the members elected to the House where such bill is pending shall so determine by yeas and nays; and no bill shall be read a third time until it shall have been actually engrossed for a third reading.

SEC. 28. No bill shall become a law unless it be passed in each House by a majority of the whole number of members elected, and on its final passage the yeas and nays be recorded; nor shall any resolution requiring the action of both Houses be passed except in the same manner.

SEC. 29. The style of all laws of this State shall be, "Be it enacted by the General Assembly of Maryland," and all laws shall be passed by original bill; and every law enacted by the General Assembly shall embrace but one subject, and that shall be described in its title; and no law, nor section of law, shall be revived or amended by reference to its title or section only; nor shall any law be construed by reason of its title to grant powers or confer rights which are not expressly contained in the body of the Act; and it shall be the duty of the General Assembly, in amending any article or section of the Code of Laws of this State, to enact the same as the said article or section would read when amended. And whenever the General Assembly shall enact any Public General Law, not amendatory of any section or article in the said Code, it shall be the duty of the General Assembly to enact the same, in articles and sections, in the same manner as the Code is arranged, and to provide for the publication of all additions and alterations which may be made to the said Code.

SEC. 30. Every bill, when passed by the General Assembly, and sealed with the Great Seal, shall be presented to the Governor, who, if he approves it, shall sign the same in the presence of the presiding officers and chief clerks of the Senate and House of Delegates. Every law shall be recorded in the office of the Court of Appeals, and in due time be printed, published and certified under the Great Seal, to the several courts, in the same manner as has been heretofore usual in this State.

SEC. 31. No law passed by the General Assembly shall take effect until the first day of June next after the session at which it may be passed, unless it be otherwise expressly declared therein.

SEC. 32. No money shall be draw from the Treasury of the State by any order or resolution, nor except in accordance with an appropriation by law; and every such law shall distinctly specify the sum appropriated and the object to which it shall be applied; provided that nothing herein contained shall prevent the General Assembly from placing a contingent fund at the disposal of the Executive, who shall report to the General Assembly at each session the amount expended, and the purposes to which it was applied. An accurate statement of the receipts and expenditures of the public money shall be attached to and published with the laws after each regular session of the General Assembly.

SEC. 33. The General Assembly shall not pass local or special laws in any of the following enumerated cases, viz: For extending the time for the collection of taxes, granting divorces, changing the name of any person, providing for the sale of real estate belonging to minors or other persons laboring under legal disabilities, by executors, administrators, guardians or trustees, giving effect to informal or invalid deeds or wills, refunding money paid into the State Treasury, or releasing persons from their debts or obligations to the State, unless recommended by the Governor or officers of the Treasury Department. And the General Assembly shall pass no special law for any case for which provision has been made by an existing general law. The General Assembly, at its first session after the adoption of this Constitution, shall pass general laws providing for the cases enumerated in this section which are not already adequately provided for, and for all other cases where a General Law can be made applicable.

SEC. 34. No debt shall be hereafter contracted by the General Assembly unless such debt shall be authorized by a law providing for the collection of an annual tax or taxes sufficient to pay the interest on such debt as it falls due, and also to discharge the principal thereof within fifteen years from the time of contracting the same; and the taxes laid for this purpose shall not be repealed or applied to any other object until the said debt and interest thereon shall be fully discharged. The credit of the State shall not in any manner be given, or loaned to, or in aid of any individual association or corporation; nor shall the General Assembly have the power in any mode to involve the State in the construction of Works of Internal Improvement, nor in granting any aid thereto, which shall involve the faith or credit of the State; nor make any appropriation therefor, except in aid of the construction of Works of Internal Improvement in the counties of St. Mary's, Charles and Calvert, which have had no direct advantage from such works as have been heretofore aided by the State; and provided that such aid, advances or appropriations shall not exceed in the aggregate the sum of five hundred thousand dollars. And they shall not use or appropriate the proceeds of the Internal Improvement Companies, or of the State tax, now levied, or which may hereafter be levied, to pay off the public debt [or] to any other purpose until the interest and debt are fully paid or the sinking fund shall be equal to the amount of the outstanding debt; but the General Assembly may, without laying a tax, borrow an amount never to exceed fifty thousand dollars to meet temporary deficiencies in the Treasury, and may contract debts to any amount that may be necessary for the defence of the State.

SEC. 35. No extra compensation shall be granted or allowed by the General Assembly to any Public Officer, Agent, Servant or Contractor, after the service shall have been rendered, or the contract entered into; nor shall the salary or compensation of any public officer be increased or diminished during his term of office.

SEC. 36. No Lottery grant shall ever hereafter be authorized by the General Assembly.

SEC. 37. The General Assembly shall pass no Law providing for payment by this State for Slaves emancipated from servitude in this State; but they shall adopt such measures as they may deem expedient to obtain from the United States compensation for such Slaves, and to receive and distribute the same equitably to the persons entitled.

SEC. 38. No person shall be imprisoned for debt.

SEC. 39. The General Assembly shall grant no charter for Banking purposes, nor renew any Banking Corporation now in existence, except upon the condition that the Stockholders shall be liable to the amount of their respective share or shares of stock in such Banking Institution, for all its debts and liabilities upon note, bill or otherwise; the books, papers and accounts of all Banks shall be open to inspection under such regulations as may be prescribed by Law.

SEC. 40. The General Assembly shall enact no Law authorizing private property to be taken for public use, without just compensation as agreed upon between the parties, or awarded by a jury, being first paid or tendered to the party entitled to such compensation.

SEC. 41. Any Citizen of this State who shall, after the adoption of this Constitution, either in or out of this State, fight a duel with deadly weapons, or send or accept a challenge so to do, or who shall act as a second, or knowingly aid or assist in any manner those offending, shall ever thereafter be incapable of holding any office of profit or trust under this State, unless relieved from the disability by an Act of the Legislature.

SEC. 42. The General Assembly shall pass Laws necessary for the preservation of the purity of elections.

SEC. 43. The property of the wife shall be protected from the debts of her husband.

SEC. 44. Laws shall be passed by the General Assembly to protect from execution a reasonable amount of the property of the debtor, not exceeding in value the sum of five hundred dollars.

SEC. 45. The General Assembly shall provide a simple and uniform system of charges in the offices of Clerks of Courts and Registers of Wills, in the Counties of this State and the City of Baltimore, and for the collection thereof; provided, the amount of compensation to any of the said officers in the various Counties shall not exceed the sum of three thousand dollars a year, and in the City of Baltimore thirty-five hundred dollars a year, over and above office expenses, and compensation to assistants; and provided further that such compensation of Clerks, Registers, assistants and office expenses shall always be paid out of the fees or receipts of the offices, respectively.

SEC. 46. The General Assembly shall have power to receive from the United States any grant or donation of land, money, or securities for any purpose designated by the United States, and shall administer or distribute the same according to the conditions of the said grant.

SEC. 47. The General Assembly shall make provisions for all cases of contested elections of any of the officers, not herein provided for.

SEC. 48. Corporations may be formed under general Laws; but shall not be created by special act, except for municipal purposes, and except in cases where no general Laws exist, providing for the creation of Corporations of the same general character, as the corporation proposed to be created; and any act of incorporation passed in violation of this section shall be void. And as soon as practicable, after the adoption of this Constitution, it shall be the duty of the Governor to appoint three persons learned in the Law, whose duty it shall be to prepare drafts of general Laws, providing for the creation of corporations, in such cases as may be proper, and for all other cases, where a general Law can be made; and for revising, amending, so far as may be necessary or expedient, the General Laws which may be in existence on the first day of June, eighteen hundred and sixty-seven, providing for the creation of corporations, and for other purposes; and such drafts of Laws shall by said commissioners, be submitted to the General Assembly, at its first meeting, for its action thereon; and each of said commissioners shall receive a compensation of five hundred dollars for his services, as such commissioner.

All Charters granted or adopted in pursuance of this section, and all Charters heretofore granted and created, subject to repeal or modification, may be altered, from time to time, or be repealed; provided, nothing herein contained shall be construed to extend to Banks, or the incorporation thereof.

[SEC. 48. Corporations may be formed under general laws, but shall not be created by special act, except for municipal purposes and except in cases where no general Laws exist, providing for the creation of corporations of the same general character as the corporation proposed to be created, and any act of incorporation passed in violation of this section shall be void; all charters granted or adopted in pursuance of this section, and all charters heretofore granted and created subject to repeal or modification, may be altered from time to time, or be repealed; provided, nothing herein contained shall be construed to extend to banks or the incorporation thereof; the General Assembly shall not alter or amend the charter of any corporation existing at the time of the adoption of this Article, or pass any other general or special Law for the benefit of such corporation except upon the condition that such corporation shall surrender all claim to exemption from taxation or from the repeal or modification of its charter, and that such corporation shall thereafter hold its charter subject to the provisions of this Constitution; and any corporation chartered by this State which shall accept, use, enjoy or in anywise avail itself of any rights, privileges, or advantages that may hereafter be granted or conferred by any general or special Act, shall be conclusively presumed to have thereby surrendered any exemption from taxation to which it may be entitled under its charter, and shall be thereafter subject to taxation as if no such exemption has been granted by its charter.] [a]

SEC. 49. The General Assembly shall have power to regulate by law, not inconsistent with this Constitution, all matters which relate to the Judges of Election, time, place and manner of holding elections in this State, and of making returns thereof.

SEC. 50. It shall be the duty of the General Assembly at its first session, held after the adoption of this Constitution, to provide by Law for the punishment, by fine, or imprisonment in the Penitentiary or both, in the discretion of the Court, of any person who shall bribe or attempt to bribe any Executive, or Judicial officer of the State of Maryland, or any member, or officer of the General Assembly of the State of Maryland, or of any Municipal Corporation in the State of Maryland, or any Executive officer of such corporation, in order to influence him in the performance of any of his official duties; and also, to provide by Law for the punishment, by fine, or imprisonment in the Penitentiary, or both, in the discretion of the Court, of any of said officers, or members, who shall demand or receive any bribe, fee, reward or testimonial for the performance of his official duties, or for neglecting or failing to perform the same; and also, to provide by Law for compelling any person so bribing, or attempting to bribe, or so demanding or receiving a bribe, fee, reward or testimonial, to testify against any person or persons who may have committed any of said offences; provided, that any person so compelled to testify shall be exempted from trial and punishment

---

[a] As amended by Charter 195, Acts of 1890, ratified by the people November 3, 1891.

for the offence of which he may have been guilty; and any person convicted of such offence shall, as part of the punishment thereof, be forever disfranchised and disqualified from holding any office of trust or profit in this State.

SEC. 51. The personal property of residents of this State shall be subject to taxation in the county or city where the resident *bona fide* resides for the greater part of the year, for which the tax may or shall be levied, and not elsewhere, except goods and chattels permanently located, which shall be taxed in the city or county where they are so located.

[SEC. 51. The personal property of residents of this State shall be subject to taxation in the county or city where the resident *bona fide* resides for the greater part of the year for which the tax may or shall be levied, and not elsewhere, except goods and chattels permanently located, which shall be taxed in the city or county where they are so located, but the General Assembly may by law provide for the taxation of mortgages upon property in this State and the debts secured thereby in the county or city where such property is situated.] *a*

SEC. 52. The General Assembly shall appropriate no money out of the Treasury for payment of any private claim against the State exceeding three hundred dollars, unless said claim shall have been first presented to the Comptroller of the Treasury, together with the proofs upon which the same is founded, and reported upon by him.

SEC. 53. No person shall be incompetent, as a witness, on account of race or color. unless hereafter so declared by Act of the General Assembly.

SEC. 54. No County of this State shall contract any debt, or obligation, in the construction of any Railroad, Canal, or other Work of Internal Improvement, nor give, or loan its credit to or in aid of any association, or corporation, unless authorized by an Act of the General Assembly, which shall be published for two months before the next election for members of the House of Delegates in the newspapers published in such County, and shall also be approved by a majority of all the members elected to each House of the General Assembly, at its next session after said election.

SEC. 55. The General Assembly shall pass no law suspending the privilege of the Writ of *Habeas Corpus.*

SEC. 56. The General Assembly shall have power to pass all such Laws as may be necessary and proper for carrying into execution the powers vested by this Constitution, in any Department or office of the Government, and the duties imposed upon them thereby.

SEC. 57. The Legal rate of Interest shall be *six per cent. per annum*, unless otherwise provided by the General Assembly.

SEC. 58. The Legislature, at its first session after the ratification of this Constitution, shall provide by Law for State and municipal taxation upon the revenues accruing from business done in the State by all foreign corporations.

SEC. 59. The office of "State Pension Commissioner" is hereby abolished; and the Legislature shall pass no law creating such office, or establishing any general pension system within this State.

---

a Thus amended by Chapter 426, Acts of 1890, ratified by the people November 3, 1891.

Article IV

JUDICIARY DEPARTMENT

Part I—General Provisions

Section 1. The Judicial power of this State shall be vested in a Court of Appeals, Circuit Courts, Orphans' Courts, such Courts for the City of Baltimore as are hereinafter provided for, and Justices of the Peace; all said Courts shall be Courts of Record, and each shall have a seal to be used in the authentication of all process issuing therefrom. The process and official character of Justices of the Peace shall be authenticated as hath heretofore been practiced in this State, or may hereafter be prescribed by Law.

Sec. 2. The Judges of all of the said Courts shall be citizens of the State of Maryland, and qualified voters under this Constitution, and shall have resided therein not less than five years, and not less than six months next preceding their election or appointment in the judicial circuit, as the case may be, for which they may be respectively elected or appointed. They shall be not less than thirty years of age at the time of their election or appointment, and shall be selected from those who have been admitted to practice Law in this State, and who are most distinguished for integrity, wisdom and sound legal knowledge.

Sec. 3. The Judges of the said several Courts shall be elected in the Counties by the qualified voters in their respective Judicial Circuits as hereinafter provided, at the general election to held on the Tuesday after the first Monday in November next, and in the City of Baltimore, on the fourth Wednesday of October next. Each of the said Judges shall hold his office for the term of fifteen years from the time of his election, and until his successor is elected and qualified, or until he shall have attained the age of seventy years, whichever may first happen, and be re-eligible thereto until he shall have attained the age of seventy years, and not after; but in case of any Judge who shall attain the age of seventy years whilst in office, such Judge may be continued in office by the General Assembly for such further time as they may think fit, not to exceed the term for which he was elected, by a resolution to be passed at the session next preceding his attaining said age. In case of the inability of any of said Judges to discharge his duties with efficiency, by reason of continued sickness, or of physical or mental infirmity, it shall be in the power of the General Assembly, two-thirds of the members of each House concurring, with the approval of the Governor, to retire said Judge from office.

Sec. 4. Any Judge shall be removed from office by the Governor, on conviction in a Court of Law, of incompetency, of wilful neglect of duty, misbehavior in office or any other crime, or on impeachment, according to this Constitution, or the Laws of the State; or on the address of the General Assembly, two-thirds of each House concurring in such address, and the accused having been notified of the charges against him, and having had opportunity of making his defence.

Sec. 5. After the election for Judges, to be held as above mentioned, upon the expiration of the term, or in case of the death, resignation, removal, or other disqualification of any Judge, the Governor shall appoint a person duly qualified to fill said office, who shall hold the same until the next general election for members of the General Assembly, when a successor shall be elected, whose tenure of office shall be the same, as hereinbefore provided; but if the vacancy shall occur in the city of Baltimore, the time of election shall be the fourth Wednesday in October following.

[SEC. 5. After the election for Judges, as hereinbefore provided, there shall be held in this State, in every fifteenth year thereafter, on the Tuesday after the first Monday in November of such year, an election for Judges as herein provided; and in case of death, resignation, removal or disqualification by reason of age or otherwise of any Judge, the Governor shall appoint a person duly qualified to fill said office, who shall hold the same until the next General Election for members of the General Assembly, when a successor shall be elected, whose term of office shall be the same as hereinbefore provided, and upon the expiration of the term of fifteen years for which any Judge may be elected to fill a vacancy, an election for his successor shall take place at the next General Election for members of the General Assembly to occur upon or after the expiration of his said term; and the Governor shall appoint a person duly qualified to hold said office from the expiration of such term of fifteen years until the election and qualification of his successor.] [a]

SEC. 6. All Judges shall, by virtue of their offices be Conservators of the Peace throughout the State; and no fees, or perquisites, commission or reward of any kind, shall be allowed to any Judge in this State, besides his annual salary, for the discharge of any Judicial duty.

SEC. 7. No Judge shall sit in any case wherein he may be interested, or where either of the parties may be connected with him by affinity or consanguinity within such degrees as now are or may hereafter be prescribed by Law, or where he shall have been of counsel in the case.

SEC. 8. The parties to any cause may submit the same to the court for determination, without the aid of a jury; and the Judge, or Judges of any Court of this State, except the Court of Appeals, shall order and direct the record of proceedings in any suit or action, issue or petition, presentment or indictment, pending in such court, to be transmitted to some other court, (and of a different circuit, if the party applying shall so elect,) having jurisdiction in such cases, whenever any party to such cause, or the counsel of any party, shall make a suggestion, in writing, supported by the affidavit of such party or his counsel, or other proper evidence, that the party cannot have a fair or impartial trial in the court in which suit, or action, issue or petition, presentment or indictment is pending, or when the Judges of said court shall be disqualified under the provisions of this Constitution to sit in any such suit, action, issue or petition, presentment or indictment; and the General Assembly shall make such modifications of existing Law as may be necessary to regulate and give force to this provision.

[SEC. 8. The parties to any cause may submit the same to the Court for determination without the aid of a Jury and in all suits or actions

---

[a] Thus amended by Act of 1880, ch. 417, ratified by the people at November election, 1881.

at law, issues from the Orphans' Court or from any Court sitting in Equity, and in all cases of presentments or indictments for offences which are or may be punishable by death pending in any of the Courts of Law of this State having jurisdiction thereof, upon suggestion in writing under oath of either of the parties to said proceedings, that such party cannot have a fair and impartial trial in the Court in which the same may be pending, the said Court shall order and direct the Record of Proceedings in such Suit or Action, Issue, Presentment or Indictment, to be transmitted to some other Court having jurisdiction in such case, for trial; but in all other cases of Presentment or Indictment pending in any of the Courts of Law in this State having jurisdiction thereof, in addition to the suggestion in writing of either, of the parties to such Presentment or Indictment that such party cannot have a fair and impartial trial in the Court in which the same may be pending, it shall be necessary for the party making such suggestion to make it satisfactorily appear to the Court that such suggestion is true, or that there is reasonable ground for the same; and thereupon the said Court shall order and direct the Record of Proceedings in such Presentment or Indictment to be transmitted to some other Court having jurisdiction in such cases for trial; and such right of removal shall exist upon suggestion in cases when all the Judges of said Court may be disqualified, under the provisions of this Constitution to sit in any case; and said court to which the Record of Proceedings in such Suit or Action, Issue, Presentment or Indictment may be so transmitted, shall hear and determine the same in like manner as if such Suit or Action, Issue, Presentment or Indictment had been originally instituted therein; and the General Assembly shall make such modification of existing law as may be necessary to regulate and give force to this provision.] [a]

SEC. 9. The Judge or Judges of any Court may appoint such officers for their respective Courts as may be found necessary; and such officers of the Courts in the City of Baltimore shall be appointed by the Judges of the Supreme Bench of Baltimore City. It shall be the duty of the General Assembly to prescribe by law a fixed compensation for all such officers, and said Judge or Judges shall from time to time investigate the expenses, costs and charges of their respective Courts, with a view to a change or reduction thereof, and report the result of such investigation to the General Assembly for its action.

SEC. 10. The Clerks of the several Courts created or continued by this Constitution shall have charge and custody of the records and other papers; shall perform all the duties, and be allowed the fees which appertain to their several offices, as the same now are or may hereafter be regulated by law. And the office and business of said Clerks, in all their departments, shall be subject to the visitorial power of the Judges of their respective Courts, who shall exercise the same, from time to time, so as to insure the faithful performance of the duties of said offices; and it shall be the duty of the Judges of said Courts, respectively, to make from time to time such rules and regulations as may be necessary and proper for the government of said Clerks, and for the performance of the duties of their offices,

---

[a] Thus amended by Act of 1874, ch. 364, ratified by the people at November election, 1875.

which shall have the force of law until repealed or modified by the General Assembly.

SEC. 11. The election for Judges hereinbefore provided, and all elections for Clerks, Registers of Wills and other officers provided in this Constitution, except State's Attorneys, shall be certified, and the returns made by the Clerks of the Circuit Courts of the Counties, and the Clerk of the Superior Court of Baltimore City, respectively, to the Governor, who shall issue commissions to the different persons for the offices to which they shall have been, respectively, elected; and in all such elections the person having the greatest number of votes shall be declared elected.

SEC. 12. If in any case of election for Judges, Clerks of the Courts of Law, and Register of Wills, the opposing candidates shall have an equal number of votes, it shall be the duty of the Governor to order a new election; and in case of any contested election the Governor shall send the returns to the House of Delegates, which shall judge of the election and qualification of the candidates at such election, and if the judgment shall be against the one who has been returned elected, or the one who has been commissioned by the Governor, the House of Delegates shall order a new election within thirty days.

SEC. 13. All Public Commissions and Grants shall run thus: " The State of Maryland, &c.," and shall be signed by the Governor, with the Seal of the State annexed; all writs and process shall run in the same style, and be tested, sealed and signed as heretofore, or as may hereafter be provided by law; and all indictments shall conclude, " against the peace. government and dignity of the State."

PART II.—COURT OF APPEALS

SEC. 14. The Court of Appeals shall be composed of the Chief Judges of the first seven of the several Judicial Circuits of the State and a Judge from the City of Baltimore specially elected thereto, one of whom shall be designated by the Governor, by and with the advice and consent of the Senate, as the Chief Judge; and in all cases until action by the Senate can be had, the Judge so designated by the Governor shall act as Chief Judge. The Judge of the Court of Appeals from the City of Baltimore shall be elected by the qualified voters of said city at the election of Judges to be held therein, as hereinbefore provided; and in addition to his duties as Judge of the Court of Appeals, shall perform such other duties as the General Assembly shall prescribe. The jurisdiction of said Court of Appeals shall be co-extensive with the limits of the State, and such as now is or may hereafter be prescribed by Law. It shall hold its sessions in the City of Annapolis, on the first Monday in April, and the first Monday in October; [on the second Monday in January, the first Monday in April and the first Monday in October] [a] of each and every year, or at such other times as the General Assembly may by Law direct. Its sessions shall continue not less than ten months in the year, if the business before it shall so require; and it shall be competent for the Judges temporarily to transfer their sittings elsewhere upon sufficient cause.

---

[a] Terms thus arranged by Act of 1886, ch. 185.

SEC. 15. Four of said Judges shall constitute a quorum; no cause shall be decided without the concurrence of at least three; but the Judge who heard the cause below shall not participate in the decision; in every case an opinion, in writing, shall be filed within three months after the argument or submission of the cause; and the judgment of the court shall be final and conclusive; and all cases shall stand for hearing at the first term after the transmission of the record.

SEC. 16. Provision shall be made by law for publishing reports of all causes argued and determined in the Court of Appeals, which the Judges shall designate as proper for publication.

SEC. 17. There shall be a Clerk of the Court of Appeals, who shall be elected by the legal and qualified voters of the State, who shall hold his office for six years, and until his successor is duly qualified; he shall be subject to removal by the said Court for incompetency, neglect of duty, misdemeanor in office, or such other cause or causes as may be prescribed by law; and in case of a vacancy in the office of said Clerk, the Court of Appeals shall appoint a Clerk of said Court, who shall hold his office until the election and qualification of his successor, who shall be elected at the next general election for members of the General Assembly; and the person so elected shall hold his office for the term of six years from the time of election.

SEC. 18. It shall be the duty of the Judges of the Court of Appeals, as soon after their election under this Constitution as practicable, to make and publish rules and regulations for the prosecution of appeals to said appellate court whereby they shall prescribe the periods within which appeals may be taken, what part or parts of the proceedings in the court below shall constitute the record on appeal and the manner in which such appeals shall be brought to hearing or determination, and shall regulate, generally, the practice of said Court of Appeals so as to prevent delays and promote brevity in all records and proceedings brought into said court, and to abolish and avoid all unnecessary costs and expenses in the prosecution of appeals therein; and the said Judges shall make such reductions in the fees and expenses of the said court as they may deem advisable. It shall also be the duty of said Judges of the Court of Appeals, as soon after their election as practicable, to devise and promulgate by rules or orders, forms and modes of framing and filing bills, answers and other proceedings and pleadings in Equity; and also forms and modes of taking and obtaining evidence, to be used in Equity cases; and to revise and regulate, generally, the practice in the Courts of Equity of this State, so as to prevent delays, and to promote brevity and conciseness in all pleadings and proceedings therein, and to abolish all unnecessary costs and expenses attending the same. And all rules and regulations hereby directed to be made shall, when made, have the force of Law until rescinded, changed or modified by the said Judges, or the General Assembly.

PART III.—CIRCUIT COURTS

SEC. 19. The State shall be divided into eight Judicial Circuits, in manner following, viz: The Counties of Worcester, Somerset, Dorchester and Wicomico,[a] shall constitute the First Circuit; the Counties

---

[a] Wicomico formed since the adoption of this Constitution.

of Caroline, Talbot, Queen Anne's, Kent and Cecil, the Second; the Counties of Baltimore and Harford, the Third; the Counties of Allegany, Washington and Garrett,[a] the Fourth; the Counties of Carroll, Howard and Anne Arundel, the Fifth; the Counties of Montgomery and Frederick, the Sixth; the Counties of Prince George's, Charles, Calvert and St. Mary's, the Seventh, and Baltimore City, the Eighth.

Sec. 20. A Court shall be held in each County of the State, to be styled the Circuit Court for the County in which it may be held. The said Circuit Courts shall have and exercise, in the respective Counties, all the power, authority and jurisdiction, original and appellate, which the present Circuit Courts of this State now have and exercise, or which may hereafter be prescribed by Law.

Sec. 21. For each of the said Circuits (excepting the Eighth) there shall be a Chief Judge and two Associate Judges, to be styled Judges of the Circuit Court, to be elected or appointed as herein provided. And no two of said Associate Judges shall at the time of their election, or appointment, or during the term for which they may have been elected or appointed, reside in the same County. If two or more persons shall be candidates for Associate Judge in the same County, that one only in said County shall be declared elected who has the highest number of votes in the Circuit. In case any two candidates for Associate Judge, residing in the same County, shall have an equal number of votes, greater than any other candidate for Associate Judge in the Circuit, it shall be the duty of the Governor to order a new election for one Associate Judge; but the person residing in any other County of the Circuit, and who has the next highest number of votes, shall be declared elected. The said Judges shall hold not less than two terms of the Circuit Court in each of the Counties, composing their respective Circuits, at such times as are now, or may hereafter be prescribed, to which Jurors shall be summoned; and in those Counties where only two such terms are held, two other and intermediate terms, to which Jurors shall not be summoned; they may alter or fix the times for holding any or all terms, until otherwise prescribed, and shall adopt rules to the end that all business not requiring the interposition of a Jury shall be, as far as practicable, disposed of at said intermediate terms. One Judge in each of the above Circuits shall constitute a quorum for the transaction of any business; and the said Judges, or any of them, may hold Special Terms of their Courts, whenever in their discretion, the business of the several Counties renders such Terms necessary.

Sec. 22. Where any Term is held, or trial conducted by less than the whole number of said Circuit Judges, upon the decision or determination of any point or question by the Court, it shall be competent to the party against whom the ruling or decision is made, upon motion, to have the point or question reserved for the consideration of the three Judges of the Circuit, who shall constitute a Court in *banc* for such purpose; and the motion for such reservation shall be entered of record during the sitting at which such decision may be made; and the several Circuit Courts shall regulate, by rules, the mode and manner of presenting such points or questions to the Court

---

[a] Garrett formed since the adoption of this Constitution.

in *banc,* and the decision of the said Court in *banc* shall be the effective decision in the premises, and conclusive, as against the party at whose motion said points or questions were reserved; but such decision in *banc* shall not preclude the right of appeal or writ of error to the adverse party in those cases, civil or criminal, in which appeal or writ of error to the Court of Appeals may be allowed by law. The right of having questions reserved shall not, however, apply to trials of Appeals from judgments of Justices of the Peace, nor to Criminal cases below the grade of felony, except when the punishment is confinement in the penitentiary; and this section shall be subject to such provisions as may hereafter be made by law.

SEC. 23. The Judges of the respective Circuit Courts of this State, and of the Courts of Baltimore City, shall render their decisions in all cases argued before them, or submitted for their judgment, within two months after the same shall have been so argued or submitted.

SEC. 24. The salary of each Chief Judge, and of the Judge of the Court of Appeals from the City of Baltimore, shall be three thousand five hundred dollars, and of each Associate Judge of the Circuit Court, shall be two thousand eight hundred dollars per annum payable quarterly, and shall not be diminished during his continuance in office.[a]

SEC. 25. There shall be a Clerk of the Circuit Court for each County, who shall be elected by a plurality of the qualified voters of said County, and shall hold his office for six years from the time of his election, and until his successor is elected and qualified, and be re-eligible, subject to be removed for wilful neglect of duty or other misdemeanor in office, on conviction in a Court of Law. In case of a vacancy in the office of Clerk of a Circuit Court, the Judges of said Court shall have power to fill such vacancy until the general election for Delegates to the General Assembly, to be held next thereafter, when a successor shall be elected for the term of six years.

SEC. 26. The said Clerks shall appoint, subject to the confirmation of the Judges of their respective Courts, as many deputies under them as the said Judges shall deem necessary to perform, together with themselves, the duties of the said office, who shall be removable by the said Judges for incompetency, or neglect of duty, and whose compensation shall be according to existing or future provisions of the General Assembly.

PART IV.—COURTS OF BALTIMORE CITY

SEC. 27. There shall be in the Eighth Judicial Circuit six Courts, to be styled the Supreme Bench of Baltimore City, the Superior Court of Baltimore City, the Court of Common Pleas, the Baltimore City Court, the Circuit Court of Baltimore City [b] and the Criminal Court [c] of Baltimore.

---

[a] By the act of 1892, ch. 388, the salary of the Chief Judges was increased to four thousand five hundred dollars, and of the Associate Judges to three thousand six hundred dollars per annum.

[b] Circuit Court No. 2 established by act of 1888, ch. 194.

[c] Criminal Court No. 2 established by rule of the Supreme Bench, December 21, 1897. See 87 Md. 191.

SEC. 28. The Superior Court of Baltimore City, the Court of Common Pleas, and the Baltimore City Court [a] shall each have concurrent jurisdiction in all civil common law cases, and concurrently all the jurisdiction which the Superior Court of Baltimore City and the Court of Common Pleas now have, except jurisdiction in Equity, and except in applications for the benefit of the Insolvent Laws of Maryland, and in cases of Appeal from judgments of Justices of the Peace in said city, whether civil or criminal, or arising under the ordinances of the Mayor and City Council of Baltimore, of all of which appeal cases the Baltimore City Court shall have exclusive jurisdiction; and the said Court of Common Pleas shall have exclusive jurisdiction in all applications for the benefit of the Insolvent Laws of Maryland, and the supervision and control of the Trustees thereof.

SEC. 29. The Circuit Court of Baltimore City shall have exclusive jurisdiction in Equity within the limits of said city, and all such jurisdiction as the present Circuit Court of Baltimore City has; provided, the said Court shall not have jurisdiction in applications for the writ of *habeas corpus* in cases of persons charged with criminal offenses.

SEC. 30. The Criminal Court of Baltimore shall have and exercise all the jurisdiction now held and exercised by the Criminal Court of Baltimore, except in such Appeal Cases as are herein assigned to the Baltimore City Court.

SEC. 31. There shall be elected by the legal and qualified voters of said city, at the election, hereinbefore provided for, one Chief Judge and four Associate Judges, who, together, shall constitute the Supreme Bench of Baltimore City, and shall hold their offices for the term of fifteen years, subject to the provisions of this Constitution with regard to the election and qualifications of Judges and their removal from office, and shall exercise the jurisdiction, hereinafter specified, and shall each receive an annual salary of three thousand five hundred dollars,[b] payable quarterly, which shall not be diminished during their term of office; but authority is hereby given to the Mayor and City Council of Baltimore to pay to each of the said Judges an annual addition of five hundred dollars to their respective salaries; provided, that the same being once granted shall not be diminished nor increased during the continuance of said Judges in office.

SEC. 32. It shall be the duty of the said Supreme Bench of Baltimore City, as soon as the Judges thereof shall be elected and duly qualified, and from time to time, to provide for the holding of each of the aforesaid Courts, by the assignment of one or more of their number to each of the said Courts, who may sit either separately or together in the trial of cases; and the said Supreme Bench of Baltimore City may, from time to time, change the said assignment, as circumstances may require, and the public interest may demand; and the Judge or Judges, so assigned to the said several Courts, shall, when holding the same, have all the powers and exercise all the jurisdiction which may belong to the Court so being held; and it shall also be the duty of the said Supreme Bench of Baltimore City, in case of the sickness,

---

[a] The jurisdiction of the Baltimore City Court, the Superior Court and the Court of Common Pleas was enlarged by the Act of 1870, ch. 177.
[b] Increased by Act of 1892, ch. 388, to four thousand five hundred dollars.

absence or disability of any Judge or Judges assigned as aforesaid, to provide for the hearing of the cases, or transaction of the business assigned to said Judge or Judges, as aforesaid, before some one or more of the Judges of said Court.

SEC. 33. The said Supreme Bench of Baltimore City shall have power, and it shall be its duty, to provide for the holding of as many general Terms as the performance of its duties may require, such general Terms to be held by not less than three Judges; to make all needful rules and regulations for the conduct of business in each of the said Courts, during the session thereof, and in vacation, or in Chambers, before any of said Judges; and shall also have jurisdiction to hear and determine all motions for a new trial in cases tried in any of said Courts, where such motions arise either, on questions of fact, or for misdirection upon any matters of Law, and all motions in arrest of judgment, or upon any matters of Law determined by the said Judge, or Judges, while holding said several Courts; and the said Supreme Bench of Baltimore City shall make all needful rules and regulations for the hearing before it of all said matters; and the same right of appeal to the Court of Appeals shall be allowed from the determination of the said Court on such matters, as would have been the right of the parties if said matters had been decided by the Court in which said cases were tried.

[The Judge, before whom any case may hereafter be tried, in either the Baltimore City Court, the Superior Court of Baltimore City, or the Court of Common Pleas, shall have exclusive jurisdiction to hear and determine, and the said Judge shall hear and determine all motions for a new trial where such motions arise, either on questions of fact or for misdirection upon any matters of law, and all motions in arrest of judgement, or upon any matters of law, determined by the said Judge, and all such motions shall be heard and determined within thirty days after they are made.][a]

SEC. 34. No appeal shall lie to the Supreme Bench of Baltimore City from the decision of the Judge or the Judges holding the Baltimore City Court in case of appeal from a Justice of the Peace; but the decision by said Judge or Judges shall be final; and all writs and other process issued out of either of said Courts, requiring attestation, shall be attested in the name of the Chief Judge of the said Supreme Bench of Baltimore City.

SEC. 35. Three of the Judges of said Supreme Bench of Baltimore City shall constitute a quorum of said Court.

SEC. 36. All causes depending, at the adoption of this Constitution, in the Superior Court of Baltimore City, the Court of Common Pleas, the Criminal Court of Baltimore, and the Circuit Court of Baltimore City, shall be proceeded in, and prosecuted to final judgment or decree, in the Courts, respectively, of the same name established by this Constitution, except cases belonging to that class, jurisdiction over which is by this Constitution transferred to the Baltimore City Court, all of which shall, together with all cases now pending in the City Court of Baltimore, be proceeded in and prosecuted to final judgment in said Baltimore City Court.

SEC. 37. There shall be a Clerk of each of the said Courts of Balti-

---

[a] Thus amended by the Act of 1870, ch. 177, as provided by Section 39 of Article 4, of the Constitution.

more City, except the Supreme Bench, who shall be elected by the legal and qualified voters of said city, at the election to be held in said city on the Tuesday next after the first Monday of November, in the year eighteen hundred and sixty-seven, and shall hold his office for six years from the time of his election, and until his successor is elected and qualified, and be re-eligible thereto, subject to be removed for wilful neglect of duty or other misdemeanor in office, on conviction in a Court of Law. The salary of each of the said Clerks shall be thirty-five hundred dollars a year, payable only out of the fees and receipts collected by the Clerks of said city, and they shall be entitled to no other perquisites or compensation. In case of a vacancy in the office of Clerk of any of said Courts, the Judges of said Supreme Bench of Baltimore City shall have power to fill such vacancy until the general election of Delegates to the General Assembly to be held next thereafter, when a Clerk of said Court shall be elected to serve for six years thereafter; and the provisions of this Article in relation to the appointment of Deputies by the Clerks of the Circuit Courts in the counties shall apply to the Clerks of the Courts in Baltimore City.

SEC. 38. The Clerk of the Court of Common Pleas shall have authority to issue within said city all marriage and other licenses required by law, subject to such provisions as are now or may be prescribed by Law. The Clerk of the Superior Court of said city shall receive and record all deeds, conveyances and other papers, which are or may be required by Law to be recorded in said city. He shall also have custody of all papers connected with the proceedings on the Law or Equity side of Baltimore County Court and the dockets thereof, so far as the same have relation to the City of Baltimore, and shall also discharge the duties of Clerk to the Supreme Bench of Baltimore City unless otherwise provided by Law.

SEC. 39. The General Assembly shall, whenever it may think the same proper and expedient, provide, by Law, another Court for the City of Baltimore, and prescribe its jurisdiction and powers; in which case there shall be elected by the voters of said City, qualified under this Constitution, another Judge of the Supreme Bench of Baltimore City, who shall be subject to the same constitutional provisions, hold his office for the same term of years, receive the same compensation, and have the same powers, as are herein provided for the Judges of said Supreme Bench of Baltimore City; and all of the provisions of this Constitution relating to the assignment of Judges to the Courts, now existing in said City, and for the dispatch of business therein, shall apply to the Court, for whose creation provision is made by this Section.[a] And the General Assembly may reapportion, change or enlarge the jurisdiction of the several Courts in Baltimore City. Until otherwise provided by Law, the Clerk of the Superior Court of Baltimore City, of the Court of Common Pleas, of the Circuit Court of Baltimore City, of the Baltimore City Court, and of the Criminal Court of Baltimore, shall each give Bond in such penalty as is now prescribed by Law to be given by the Clerks of the Courts, bearing the same names, under the present Constitution.

---

[a] Under this section, the General Assembly, by the Act of 1888, Chapter 194, established the Circuit Court No. 2 of Baltimore City, conferring upon it the same jurisdiction as that possessed by the Circuit Court of Baltimore City.

[SEC. 39. The General Assembly shall, as often as it may think the same proper and expedient, provide by Law for the election of an additional Judge of the Supreme Bench of Baltimore City, and whenever provision is so made by the General Assembly, there shall be elected by the voters of said City another Judge of the Supreme Bench of Baltimore City, who shall be subject to the same constitutional provisions, hold his office for the same term of years, receive the same compensation, and have the same powers as are, or shall be, provided by the Constitution or Laws of this State, for the Judges of said Supreme Bench of Baltimore City, and the General Assembly may provide by Laws, or the Supreme Bench by its rules for requiring causes in any of the Courts of Baltimore City to be tried before the court without a jury, unless the litigants or some one of them shall within such reasonable time or times as may be prescribed, elect to have their causes tried before a jury. And the General Assembly may reapportion, change or enlarge the jurisdiction of the several Courts in said city.][a]

PART V.—ORPHANS' COURTS

SEC. 40. The qualified voters of the City of Baltimore, and of the several counties, shall on the Tuesday next after the first Monday in November next, and on the same day in every fourth year thereafter, elect three men to be Judges of the Orphans' Courts of said city and counties, respectively, who shall be citizens of the State, and residents for the twelve months preceding, in the city, or county, for which they may be elected. They shall have all the powers now vested in the Orphans' Courts of the State, subject to such changes as the Legislature may prescribe. Each of said Judges shall be paid a per diem for the time they are actually in session, to be regulated by Law, and to be paid by the said city, or counties, respectively. In case of a vacancy in the office of Judge of the Orphans' Court, the Governor shall appoint, subject to confirmation or rejection by the Senate, some suitable person to fill the same for the residue of the term.

SEC. 41. There shall be a Register of Wills in each county of the State, and the City of Baltimore, to be elected by the legal and qualified voters of said counties and city, respectively, who shall hold his office for six years from the time of his election, and until his successor is elected and qualified; he shall be re-eligible, and subject at all times to removal for wilful neglect of duty, or misdemeanor in office in the same manner that the Clerks of the Courts are removable. In the event of any vacancy in the office of the Register of Wills, said vacancy shall be filled by the Judges of the Orphans' Court, in which such vacancy occurs, until the next general election for Delegates to the General Assembly, when a Register shall be elected to serve for six years thereafter.

---

[a] Thus amended by Chapter 313, Acts of 1892, ratified by the people November 7th, 1893.

PART VI.—JUSTICES OF THE PEACE

SEC. 42. The Governor, by and with the advice and consent of the Senate, shall appoint such number of Justices of the Peace, and the County Commissioners of the several counties, and the Mayor and City Council of Baltimore, respectively, shall appoint such number of Constables, for the several Election Districts of the counties and wards of the City of Baltimore, as are now or may hereafter be prescribed by Law; and Justices of the Peace and Constables so appointed shall be subject to removal by the Judge or Judges having criminal jurisdiction in the county or city, for incompetency, wilful neglect of duty, or misdemeanor in office, on conviction in a Court of Law. The Justices of the Peace and Constables so appointed and commissioned shall be Conservators of the Peace; shall hold their office for two years, and shall have such jurisdiction, duties and compensation, subject to such right of appeal in all cases from the judgment of Justices of the Peace, as hath been heretofore exercised, or shall be hereafter prescribed by Law.

SEC. 43. In the event of a vacancy in the office of a Justice of the Peace, the Governor shall appoint a person to serve as Justice of the Peace for the residue of the term; and in case of a vacancy in the office of Constable, the County Commissioners of the county in which the vacancy occurs, or the Mayor and City Council of Baltimore, as the case may be, shall appoint a person to serve as Constable for the residue of the term.

PART VII.—SHERIFFS

SEC. 44. There shall be elected in each County, and in the City of Baltimore, in every second year, one person, resident in said County or City, above the age of twenty-five years, and at least five years preceding his election, a citizen of this State, to the office of Sheriff. He shall hold his office for two years, and until his successor is duly elected and qualified; shall be ineligible for two years thereafter; shall give such bond, exercise such powers, and perform such duties as now are or may hereafter be fixed by law. In case of a vacancy by death, resignation, refusal to serve, or neglect to qualify, or give bond, or by disqualification, or removal from the County or City, the Governor shall appoint a person to be Sheriff for the remainder of the official term.

SEC. 45. Coroners, Elisors and Notaries Public may be appointed for each County and the City of Baltimore in the manner, for the purpose and with the powers now fixed, or which may hereafter be prescribed by law.

ARTICLE V

ATTORNEY-GENERAL AND STATE'S ATTORNEYS

ATTORNEY-GENERAL

SEC. 1. There shall be an Attorney-General elected by the qualified voters of the State, on general ticket, on the Tuesday next after the first Monday in the month of November, eighteen hundred and sixty-seven, and on the same day in every fourth year thereafter, who shall hold his office for four years from the time of his election and qualification, and until his successor is elected and qualified, and shall be re-eligible thereto, and shall be subject to removal for incompetency, wilful neglect of duty or misdemeanor in office, on conviction in a court of law.

SEC. 2. All elections for Attorney-General shall be certified to, and returns made thereof by the Clerks of the Circuit Courts for the several Counties, and the Clerk of the Superior Court of Baltimore City, to the Governor of the State, whose duty it shall be to decide on the election and qualification of the person returned; and in case of a tie between two or more persons to designate which of said persons shall qualify as Attorney-General, and to administer the oath of office to the person elected.

SEC. 3. It shall be the duty of the Attorney-General to prosecute and defend on the part of the State all cases which at the time of his appointment and qualification, and which thereafter may be depending in the Court of Appeals, or in the Supreme Court of the United States by or against the State, or wherein the State may be interested; and he shall give his opinion in writing whenever required by the General Assembly, or either branch thereof, the Governor, the Comptroller, the Treasurer, or any State's Attorney, on any legal matter, or subject depending before them, or either of them; and when required by the Governor or the General Assembly, he shall aid any State's Attorney in prosecuting any suit or action brought by the State in any Court of this State, and he shall commence and prosecute or defend any suit or action in any of said Courts, on the part of the State, which the General Assembly, or the Governor, acting according to law, shall direct to be commenced, prosecuted or defended; and he shall receive for his services an annual salary of three thousand dollars; but he shall not be entitled to receive any fees, perquisites or rewards whatever, in addition to the salary aforesaid, for the performance of any official duty; nor have power to appoint any agent, representative or deputy, under any circumstances whatever; nor shall the Governor employ any additional counsel in any case whatever, unless authorized by the General Assembly.

SEC. 4. No person shall be eligible to the office of Attorney-General, who is not a citizen of this State, and a qualified voter therein, and has not resided and practiced Law in this State for at least ten years.

SEC. 5. In case of vacancy in the office of Attorney-General, occasioned by death, resignation, removal from the State or from office, or other disqualification, the said vacancy shall be filled by the Governor for the residue of the term thus made vacant.

SEC. 6. It shall be the duty of the Clerk of the Court of Appeals and of the Commissioner of the Land Office, respectively, whenever a case shall be brought into said court or office, in which the State is a party or has interest, immediately to notify the Attorney-General thereof.

THE STATE'S ATTORNEYS

SEC. 7. There shall be an Attorney for the State in each County and the City of Baltimore, to be styled "The State's Attorney," who shall be elected by the voters thereof, respectively, on the Tuesday next after the first Monday in November, in the year eighteen hundred and sixty seven, and on the same day every fourth year thereafter; and shall hold his office for four years from the first Monday in January next ensuing his election, and until his successor shall be elected and qualified, and shall be re-eligible thereto, and be subject to removal therefrom for incompetency, wilful neglect of duty, or misdemeanor in office, on conviction in a Court of Law, or by a vote of two thirds of the Senate, on the recommendation of the Attorney-General.

SEC. 8. All elections for the State's Attorney shall be certified to and returns made thereof by the Clerks of the said counties and city to the Judges thereof having criminal jurisdiction, respectively, whose duty it shall be to decide upon the elections and qualifications of the persons returned; and in case of a tie between two or more persons, to designate which of said persons shall qualify as State's Attorney, and to administer the oaths of office to the person elected.

SEC. 9. The State's Attorney shall perform such duties and receive such fees and commissions as are now or may hereafter be prescribed by law, and if any State's Attorney shall receive any other fee or reward than such as is or may be allowed by Law, he shall, on conviction thereof, be removed from office; *provided*, that the State's Attorney for Baltimore City shall have power to appoint one Deputy, at a salary of not more than fifteen hundred dollars per annum, to be paid by the State's Attorney out of the fees of his office, as has heretofore been practised.

[SEC. 9. The State's Attorney shall perform such duties and receive such fees and commissions or salary, not exceeding three thousand dollars, as are now or may hereafter be prescribed by law; and if any State's Attorney shall receive any other fee or reward than such as is or may be allowed by law, he shall, on conviction thereof, be removed from office; provided, that the State's Attorney for Baltimore City shall receive an annual salary of forty-five hundred dollars, and shall have power to appoint one deputy, at an annual salary, not exceeding three thousand dollars, and such other assistants at such annual salaries not exceeding fifteen hundred dollars each, as the Supreme Bench of Baltimore City may authorize and approve; all of said salaries to be paid out of the fees of the said State's Attorney's office, as has heretofore been practised.] [a]

SEC. 10. No person shall be eligible to the office of State's Attorney who has not been admitted to practice Law in this State, and who has not resided for at least two years in the county or city in which he may be elected.

SEC. 11. In case of vacancy in the office of State's Attorney, or of his removal from the county or city in which he shall have been elected, or on his conviction as herein specified, the said vacancy shall be filled by the judge of the county or city, respectively, having criminal jurisdiction, in which said vacancy shall occur, for the residue of the term thus made vacant.

SEC. 12. The State's Attorney in each county, and the City of Baltimore, shall have authority to collect, and give receipt, in the name of the State, for such sums of money as may be collected by him, and forthwith make return of and pay over the same to the proper accounting officer. And the State's Attorney of each county, and the City of Baltimore, before he shall enter on the discharge of

---

[a] Thus amended by Act of 1900, ch. 185, ratified by the people at the November election, 1901.

his duties, shall execute a bond to the State of Maryland, for the faithful performance of his duties, in the penalty of ten thousand dollars, with two or more sureties, to be approved by the Judge of the Court having criminal jurisdiction in said counties or city.

Article VI

Treasury Department

SECTION 1. There shall be a Treasury Department, consisting of a Comptroller, chosen by the qualified electors of the State, at each regular election of members of the House of Delegates, who shall receive an annual salary of two thousand five hundred dollars; and a Treasurer, to be appointed by the two Houses of the Legislature, at each regular session thereof, on joint ballot, who shall receive an annual salary of two thousand five hundred dollars; and the terms of office of the said Comptroller and Treasurer shall be for two years, and until their successors shall qualify; and neither of the said officers shall be allowed, or receive any fees, commissions or perquisites of any kind in addition to his salary for the performance of any duty or services whatsoever. In case of a vacancy in either of the offices by death, or otherwise, the Governor, by and with the advice and consent of the Senate, shall fill such vacancy by appointment, to continue until another election, or a choice by the Legislature, as the case may be, and until the qualification of the successor. The Comptroller and the Treasurer shall keep their offices at the seat of Government, and shall take such oath, and enter into such bonds for the faithful discharge of their duties as are now, or may hereafter be prescribed by law.

SEC. 2. The Comptroller shall have the general superintendence of the fiscal affairs of the State; he shall digest and prepare plans for the improvement and management of the revenue, and for the support of the public credit; prepare and report estimates of the revenue and expenditures of the State; superintend and enforce the prompt collection of all taxes and revenue; adjust and settle, on terms prescribed by law, with delinquent collectors and receivers of taxes and State revenue; preserve all public accounts; decide on the forms of keeping and stating accounts; grant, under regulations prescribed by Law, all warrants for money to be paid out of the Treasury, in pursuance of appropriations by Law, and countersign all checks drawn by the Treasurer upon any bank or banks, in which the moneys of the State may, from time to time, be deposited; prescribed the formalities of the transfer of stock, or other evidence of the State debt, and countersign the same, without which such evidence shall not be valid; he shall make to the General Assembly full reports of all his proceedings, and of the state of the treasury department within ten days after the commencement of each Session; and perform such other duties as shall be prescribed by law.

SEC. 3. The Treasurer shall receive the moneys of the State, and, until otherwise prescribed by law, deposit them, as soon as received, to the credit of the State, in such bank or banks as he may, from time to time, with the approval of the Governor, select (the said bank or banks giving security, satisfactory to the Governor, for the safekeeping and forthcoming, when required, of said deposits), and shall disburse the same for the purposes of the State, according to law, upon warrants drawn by the Comptroller, and on checks countersigned by him, and not otherwise; he shall take receipts for all moneys paid by him; and receipts for moneys received by him shall be endorsed upon warrants signed by the Comptroller, without which warrants, so signed, no acknowledgment of money received into the Treasury shall be valid; and upon warrants, issued by the Comptroller, he shall make arrangements for the payment of the interest of the public debt, and for the purchase thereof, on account of the sinking fund. Every bond, certificate, or other evidence of the debt of the State shall be signed by the Treasurer, and countersigned by the Comptroller; and no new certificate or other evidence intended to replace another shall be issued until the old one shall be delivered to the Treasurer, and authority executed in due form for the transfer of the same field in his office, and the transfer accordingly made on the books thereof, and the certificate or other evidence cancelled; but the Legislature may make provisions for the loss of certificates, or other evidences of the debt; and may prescribe, by Law, the manner in which the Treasurer shall receive and keep the moneys of the State.

Sec. 4. The Treasurer shall render his accounts quarterly to the Comptroller, and shall publish monthly, in such newspapers as the Governor may direct, an abstract thereof, showing the amount of cash on hand, and the place or places of deposit thereof; and on the third day of each regular session of the Legislature he shall submit to the Senate and House of Delegates fair and accurate copies of all accounts by him, from time to time, rendered and settled with the Comptroller. He shall at all times submit to the Comptroller the inspection of the money in his hands, and perform all other duties that shall be prescribed by Law.

Sec. 5. The Comptroller shall qualify and enter on the duties of his office on the third Monday of January next succeeding the time of his election, or as soon thereafter as practicable. And the Treasurer shall qualify within one month after his appointment by the Legislature.

Sec. 6. Whenever during the recess of the Legislature charges shall be preferred to the Governor against the Comptroller or Treasurer for incompetency, malfeasance in office, wilful neglect of duty, or misappropriation of the funds of the State, it shall be the duty of the Governor forthwith to notify the party so charged, and fix a day for a hearing of said charges; and if from the evidence taken, under oath on said hearing before the Governor, the said allegations shall be sustained, it shall be the duty of the Governor to remove said offending officer and appoint another in his place, who shall hold the office for the unexpired term of the officer so removed.

Article VII

SUNDRY OFFICERS

County Commissioners—Surveyor—State Librarian—Commissioner of the Land Office—Wreck Master

Section 1. County Commissioners shall be elected on general ticket of each county by the qualified voters of the several counties of this State, on the Tuesday next after the first Monday in the month of November, eighteen hundred and sixty-seven, and on the same day in every second year thereafter. Their number in each county, their compensation, powers and duties, shall be such as are now or may be hereafter prescribed by Law.

[SEC. 1. County Commissioners shall be elected on general ticket of each county by the qualified voters of the several counties of the State, on the Tuesday next after the first Monday in the month of November, commencing in the year eighteen hundred and ninety-one; their number in each county, their compensation, powers and duties shall be such as now or may be hereafter prescribed by law, they shall be elected at such times, in such numbers and for such periods not exceeding six years, as may be prescribed by law.] [a]

SEC. 2. The qualified voters of each County, and of the City of Baltimore shall, on the Tuesday next after the first Monday in the month of November, in the year eighteen hundred and sixty-seven, and on the same day in every second year thereafter, elect a Surveyor for each County and the City of Baltimore, respectively, whose term of office shall commence on the first Monday of January next ensuing their election, and whose duties and compensation shall be the same as are now or may hereafter be prescribed by law. And any vacancy in the office of Surveyor shall be filled by the Commissioners of the Counties, or by the Mayor and City Council of Baltimore, respectively, for the residue of the term.

SEC. 3. The State Librarian shall be appointed by the Governor, by and with the advice and consent of the Senate, and shall hold his office during the term of the Governor, by whom he shall have been appointed, and until his successor shall be appointed and qualified. His salary shall be fifteen hundred dollars a year; and he shall perform such duties as are now, or may hereafter be prescribed by Law; and no appropriation shall be made by Law to pay for any clerk, or assistant to the Librarian. And it shall be the duty of the Legislature, at its first sesion after the adoption of this Constitution, to pass a Law regulating the mode and manner in which the books in the Library shall be kept and accounted for by the Librarian, and requiring the Librarian to give a bond, in such penalty as the Legislature may prescribe, for the proper discharge of his duties.

SEC. 4. There shall be a Commissioner of the Land Office, who shall be appointed by the Governor by and with the advice and consent of the Senate, who shall hold his office during the term of the Governor, by whom he shall have been appointed, and until his successor shall be appointed and qualified. He shall perform such duties as are now required of the Commissioner of the Land Office, or such as may hereafter be prescribed by Law, and shall also be the Keeper of the Chancery Records. He shall receive a salary of One Thousand, five hundred dollars per annum, to be paid out of the Treasury, and shall charge such fees as are now, or may be hereafter fixed by Law. He shall make a semi-annual report of all the fees of his office, both as Commissioner of the Land Office, and as Keeper of the Chancery Records, to the Comptroller of the Treasury, and shall pay the same semi-annually into the treasury.

SEC. 5. The Commissioner of the Land Office shall also, without additional compensation, collect, arrange, classify, have charge of,

---

[a] Thus amended by Act of 1890, chapter 255, and adopted by vote of people November 3, 1890.

and safely keep all papers, records, relics, and other memorials connected with the early history of Maryland, not belonging to any other office.

SEC. 6. The qualified voters of Worcester County shall on the Tuesday next after the first Monday in the month of November, in the year eighteen hundred and sixty-seven, and every two years thereafter, elect a Wreck-Master for said County, whose duties and compensation shall be the same as are now or may be hereafter prescribed by law; the term of office of said Wreck-Master shall commence on the first Monday of January next succeeding his election, and a vacancy in said office shall be filled by the County Commissioners of said County for the residue of the term.

Article VIII

EDUCATION

SECTION 1. The General Assembly, at its first session after the adoption of this Constitution, shall, by law, establish throughout the State a thorough and efficient system of free Public Schools; and shall provide by taxation, or, otherwise, for their maintenance.

SEC. 2. The system of Public Schools, as now constituted, shall remain in force until the end of the said first session of the General Assembly, and shall then expire, except so far as adopted or continued by the General Assembly.

SEC. 3. The School Fund of the State shall be kept inviolate, and appropriated only to the purposes of education.

Article IX

MILITIA AND MILITARY AFFAIRS

SECTION 1. The General Assembly shall make, from time to time, such provisions for organizing, equipping and disciplining the Militia, as the exigency may require, and pass such Laws to promote Volunteer Militia Organizations as may afford them effectual encouragement.

SEC. 2. There shall be an Adjutant-General appointed by the Governor, by and with the advice and consent of the Senate. He shall hold his office until the appointment and qualification of his successor, or until removed in pursuance of the sentence of a court-martial. He shall perform such duties and receive such compensation or emoluments as are now or may be prescribed by law. He shall discharge the duties of his office at the seat of government, unless absent under orders, on duty; and no other officer of the General Staff of the Militia shall receive salary or pay, except when on service and mustered in with troops.

SEC. 3. The existing Militia Law of the State shall expire at the end of the next session of the General Assembly, except so far as it may be re-enacted, subject to the provisions of this Article.

Article X

LABOR AND AGRICULTURE [a]

SECTION 1. There shall be a Superintendent of Labor and Agriculture elected by the qualified voters of this State at the first General election for Delegates to the General Assembly after the adoption of this Constitution, who shall hold his office for the term of four years, and until the election and qualification of his successor.

SEC. 2. His qualifications shall be the same as those prescribed for the Comptroller; he shall qualify and enter upon the duties of his office on the second Monday of January next succeeding the time of his election; and a vacancy in the office shall be filled by the Governor for the residue of the term.

SEC. 3. He shall perform such of the duties now devolved by Law upon the Commissioner of Immigration, and the Immigration Agent, as will promote the object for which those officers were appointed, and such other duties as may be assigned to him by the General Assembly, and shall receive a salary of twenty-five hundred dollars a year; and after his election and qualification, the offices before mentioned shall cease.

SEC. 4. He shall supervise all the State Inspectors of agricultural products and fertilizers, and from time to time shall carefully examine and audit their accounts, and prescribe regulations not inconsistent with Law, tending to secure economy and efficiency in the business of their offices. He shall have the supervision of the Tobacco Warehouses, and all other buildings used for inspection and storage purposes by the State; and may, at the discretion of the Legislature, have the supervision of all public buildings now belonging to, or which may hereafter be, erected by the State. He shall frequently inspect such buildings as are committed to his charge, and examine all accounts for labor and materials required for their construction or repairs.

SEC. 5. He shall inquire into the undeveloped resources of wealth of the State of Maryland, more especially concerning those within the limits of the Chesapeake Bay and its tributaries, which belong to the State, and suggest such plans as may be calculated to render them available as sources of revenue.

SEC. 6. He shall make detailed reports to every General Assembly within the first week of its session, in reference to each of the subjects committed to his charge, and he shall also report to the Governor, in the recess of the Legislature, all abuses or irregularities which he may find to exist in any department of public affairs with which his office is connected.

SEC. 7. The office hereby established shall continue for four years from the date of the qualification of the first incumbent thereof, and shall then expire, unless continued by the General Assembly.

---

[a] This Article expired by limitation.

Article XI

CITY OF BALTIMORE

SECTION 1. The inhabitants of the City of Baltimore qualified by Law to vote in said city for members of the House of Delegates, shall on the fourth Wednesday of October, eighteen hundred and sixty seven, and on the same day in every fourth year thereafter, elect a person to be Mayor of the City of Baltimore, who shall have such qualifications, receive such compensation, discharge such duties, and have such powers as are now, or may hereafter be prescribed by Law; and the term whose office shall commence on the first Monday of November succeeding his election, and shall continue for four years, and until his successor shall have qualified; and he shall be ineligible for the term next succeeding that for which he was elected.

[SEC. 1. The inhabitants of the City of Baltimore, qualified by Law to vote in said city for members of the House of Delegates, shall on the Tuesday after the first Monday of November, eighteen hundred and eighty-nine, and on the same day in every second year thereafter, elect a person to be Mayor of the City of Baltimore, who shall have such qualifications, receive such compensation, discharge such duties, and have such powers as are now, or may hereafter be prescribed by Law; and the term of whose office shall commence on the first Monday of November succeeding his election, and shall continue for two years, and until his successor shall have qualified.][a]

SEC. 2. The City Council of Baltimore shall consist of two branches, one of which shall be called the First Branch, and the other the Second Branch, and each shall consist of such number of members, having such qualification, receiving such compensation, performing such duties, possessing such powers, holding such terms of office, and elected in such manner, as are now, or may hereafter be prescribed by Law.

SEC. 3. An election for members of the First and Second Branch of the City Council of Baltimore shall be held in the City of Baltimore on the fourth Wednesday of October, eighteen hundred and sixty-seven; and for members of the First Branch on the same day in every year thereafter; and for members of the Second Branch on the same day in every second year thereafter; and the qualification for electors of the members of the City Council shall be the same as those prescribed for the electors of Mayor.

[SEC. 3. An election for members of the First Branch of the City Council of Baltimore shall be held in the City of Baltimore on the Tuesday after the first Monday of November in every year; and for members of the Second Branch on the Tuesday after the first Monday of November eighteen hundred and eighty-nine, and on the same day in every second year thereafter; and the qualifications for electors of the members of the City Council shall be the same as those prescribed for the electors of Mayor.][b]

---

[a] Thus amended by ch. 123, Acts of 1898. By ch. 116, Acts of 1870, the term of Mayor was made two years; and by ch. 397, Acts of 1888, the day of election was set for the Tuesday after the first Monday in November. Act of 1898, ch. 123, made the first Monday in May 1899, the day of election, and every four years afterward.

[b] Thus amended by the Act of 1888, ch. 397. Further amended by Act of 1898, ch. 123.

SEC. 4. The regular sessions of the City Council of Baltimore (which shall be annual), shall commence on the third Monday of January of each year, and shall not continue more than ninety days, exclusive of Sundays; but the Mayor may convene the City Council in extra session whenever, and as often as it may appear to him that the public good may require, but no called or extra session shall last longer than twenty days, exclusive of Sundays.

SEC. 5. No person elected and qualified as Mayor, or as a member of the City Council, shall, during the term for which he was elected, hold any other office of profit or trust, created, or to be created by the Mayor and City Council of Baltimore, or by any law relating to the Corporation of Baltimore, or hold any employment or position, the compensation of which shall be paid, directly or indirectly, out of the City Treasury; nor shall any such person be interested, directly or indirectly, in any contract to which the City is a party; nor shall it be lawful for any person holding any office under the City, to be interested, while holding such office, in any contract to which the City is a party.

SEC. 6. The Mayor shall, on conviction in a Court of Law, of wilful neglect of duty, or misbehavior in office, be removed from office by the Governor of the State, and a successor shall thereafter be elected, as in a case of vacancy.

SEC. 7. From and after the adoption of this Constitution, no debt (except as hereinafter excepted), shall be created by the Mayor and City Council of Baltimore; nor shall the credit of the Mayor and City Council of Baltimore be given or loaned to, or in aid of any individual, association, or corporation; nor shall the Mayor and City Council of Baltimore have the power to involve the City of Baltimore in the construction of works of internal improvement, nor in granting any aid thereto, which shall involve the faith and credit of the City, nor make any appropriation therefor, unless such debt or credit be authorized by an Act of the General Assembly of Maryland, and by an ordinance of the Mayor and City Council of Baltimore, submitted to the legal voters of the City of Baltimore, at such time and place as may be fixed by said ordinance, and approved by a majority of the votes cast at such time and place; but the Mayor and City Council may, temporarily, borrow any amount of money to meet any deficiency in the City Treasury, or to provide for any emergency arising from the necessity of maintaining the police, or preserving the safety and sanitary condition of the City, and may make due and proper arrangements and agreements for the removal and extension, in whole or in part, of any and all debts and obligations created according to Law before the adoption of this Constitution.

SEC. 8. All Laws and Ordinances now in force applicable to the City of Baltimore, not inconsistent with this Article, shall be, and they are hereby continued until changed in due course of Law.

SEC. 9. The General Assembly may make such changes in this Article, except in Section 7th thereof, as it may deem best; and this Article shall not be so construed or taken as to make the political corporation of Baltimore independent of, or free from the control which the General Assembly of Maryland has over all such Corporations in this State.

Article XII

PUBLIC WORKS

SECTION 1. The Governor, the Comptroller of the Treasury, and the Treasurer shall constitute the Board of Public Works in this State. They shall keep a journal of their proceedings, and shall hold regular sessions in the City of Annapolis on the first Wednesday in January, April, July and October in each year, and oftener if necessary; at which sessions they shall hear and determine such matters as affect the Public Works of the State, and as the General Assembly may confer upon them the power to decide.

SEC. 2. They shall exercise a diligent and faithful supervision of all Public Works in which the State may be interested as Stockholder or Creditor, and shall represent and vote the stock of the State of Maryland in all meetings of the stockholders of the Chesapeake and Ohio Canal; and shall appoint the Directors in every Railroad and Canal Company in which the State has the legal power to appoint Directors, which said Directors shall represent the State in all meetings of the Stockholders of the respective Companies for which they are appointed or elected. And the President and Directors of the said Chesapeake and Ohio Canal Company shall so regulate the tolls of said Company from time to time as to produce the largest amount of revenue, and to avoid the injurious effect to said company of rival competition by other Internal Improvement Companies. They shall require the Directors of all said Public Works to guard the public interest and prevent the establishment of tolls which shall discriminate against the interest of the citizens or products of this State, and from time to time, and as often as there shall be any change in the rates of toll on any of the said Works, to furnish the said Board of Public Works a schedule of such modified rates of toll, and so adjust them as to promote the agricultural interests of the State; they shall report to the General Assembly at each regular session, and recommend such legislation as they may deem necessary and requisite to promote or protect the interests of the State in the said Public Works; they shall perform such other duties as may be hereafter prescribed by Law, and a majority of them shall be competent to act. The Governor, Comptroller and Treasurer shall receive no additional salary for services rendered by them as members of the Board of Public Works. The provisions of the Act of the General Assembly of Maryland of the year 1867, chapter 359, are hereby declared null and void.

SEC. 3. The Board of Public Works is hereby authorized to exchange the State's interest as Stockholder and Creditor in the Baltimore and Ohio Railroad Company for an equal amount of the bonds or registered debt now owing by the State, to the extent only of all the preferred stock of the State on which the State is entitled to only six per cent. interest, provided such exchange shall not be made at less than par, nor less than the market value of said stock; and the said Board is authorized, subject to such regulations and conditions as the General Assembly may from time to time prescribe, to sell the State's interest in the other Works of Internal Improvement, whether as a Stockholder or a Creditor, and also the State's interest in any banking corporation, receiving in payment the bonds and registered debt now owing by the State, equal in amount to the price obtained for the State's said interest; provided, that the interest of the State in the Washington Branch of the Baltimore and Ohio Railroad be reserved and excepted from sale; and provided further, that no sale or contract of sale of the State's interest in the Chesapeake and Ohio Canal, the Chesapeake and Delaware Canal, and the Susquehanna and Tidewater Canal Companies shall go into effect until the same shall be ratified by the ensuing General Assembly.

[SEC. 3. The Board of Public Works is hereby authorized, subject to such regulations and conditions as the General Assembly may from time to time prescribe, to sell the State's interest in all works of internal improvement, whether as a Stockholder or a Creditor, and also the State's interest in any banking corporation, receiving in payment the bonds and registered debt now owing by the State, equal in amount to the price obtained for the State's said interest.] [a]

ARTICLE XIII

NEW COUNTIES

SECTION 1. The General Assembly may provide, by Law, for organizing new Counties, locating and removing county seats, and changing county lines; but no new county shall be organized without the consent of the majority of the legal voters residing within the limits proposed to be formed into said new county; and whenever a new county shall be proposed to be formed out of portions of two or more counties, the consent of a majority of the legal voters of such part of each of said counties, respectively, shall be required; nor shall the lines of any county be changed without the consent of a majority of the legal voters residing within the district, which, under said proposed change, would form a part of a county different from that to which it belonged prior to said change; and no new county shall contain less than four hundred square miles, nor less than ten thousand white inhabitants; nor shall any change be made in the limits of any county, whereby the population of said county would be reduced to less than ten thousand white inhabitants, or its territory reduced to less than four hundred square miles.

SEC. 2. At the election to be held for the adoption or rejection of this Constitution, in each election district, in those parts of Worcester and Somerset Counties, comprised within the following limits, viz: Beginning at the point where Mason and Dixon's line crosses the channel of Pocomoke River, thence following said line to the channel of the Nanticoke River, thence with the channel of said river to Tangier Sound, or the intersection of Nanticoke and Wicomico Rivers, thence up the channel of the Wicomico River to the mouth of Wicomico Creek, thence with the channel of said creek and Passerdyke Creek to Dashield's or Disharoon's Mills, thence with the millpond of said mills and branch following the middle prong of said branch, to Meadow Bridge, on the road dividing the Counties of Somerset and Worcester, near the southwest corner of farm of William P. Morris, thence due east to the Pocomoke River, thence with the channel of said river to the beginning; the Judges of Election, in

---

[a] Thus amended by Act 1890, ch. 362, and ratified by the people November 3rd, 1891.

each of said districts, shall receive the ballots of each elector, voting at said election, who has resided for six months preceding said election within said limits, for or against a new County; and the Return Judges of said election districts shall certify the result of such voting, in the manner now prescribed by Law, to the Governor, who shall by proclamation make known the same, and if a majority of the legal votes cast within that part of Worcester County, contained within said lines, and also a majority of the legal votes cast within that part of Somerset County, contained within said lines, shall be in favor of a new County, then said parts of Worcester and Somerset Counties shall become and constitute a new County, to be called Wicomico County; and Salisbury shall be the County seat. And the inhabitants thereof shall thenceforth have and enjoy all such rights and privileges as are held and enjoyed by the inhabitants of the other Counties of this State.

Sec. 3. When said new County shall have been so created, the inhabitants thereof shall cease to have any claim to, or interest in, the county buildings and other public property of every description belonging to said Counties of Somerset and Worcester respectively, and shall be liable for their proportionate shares of the then existing debts and obligations of the said Counties, according to the last assessment in said Counties, to be ascertained and apportioned by the Circuit Court of Somerset County, as to the debts and obligations of said County, and by the Circuit Court of Worcester County as to the debts and obligations of Worcester County, on the petition of the County Commissioners of the said Counties, respectively; and the property in each part of the said Counties included in said new County shall be bound only for the share of the debts and obligations of the County from which it shall be separated; and the inhabitants of said new County shall also pay the County taxes levied upon them at the time of the creation of such new County, as if such new County had not been created; and on the application of twelve citizens of the proposed County of Wicomico, the Surveyor of Worcester County shall run and locate the line from Meadow Bridge to the Pocomoke River previous to the adoption or rejection of this Constitution, and at the expense of said petitioners.

Sec. 4. At the first general election held under this Constitution the qualified voters of said new County shall be entitled to elect a Senator and two Delegates to the General Assembly, and all such County or other officers as this Constitution may authorize, or require to be elected by other Counties of the State; a notice of such election shall be given by the sheriffs of Worcester and Somerset Counties in the manner now prescribed by Law; and in case said new County shall be established, as aforesaid, then the Counties of Somerset and Worcester shall be entitled to elect but two Delegates each to the General Assembly.

Sec. 5. The County of Wicomico, if formed according to the provisions of this Constitution, shall be embraced in the First Judicial Circuit, and the times for holding the Courts therein shall be fixed and determined by the General Assembly.

Sec. 6. The General Assembly shall pass all such Laws as may be necessary more fully to carry into effect the provisions of this Article.

Article XIV

AMENDMENTS TO THE CONSTITUTION

Section 1. The General Assembly may propose Amendments to this Constitution; provided that each Amendment shall be embraced in a separate Bill, embodying the Article or Section, as the same will stand when amended and passed by three-fifths of all the members elected to each of the two Houses, by yeas and nays, to be entered on the Journals with the proposed Amendment. The Bill or Bills proposing amendment or amendments shall be published by order of the Governor, in at least two newspapers in each County, where so many may be published, and where not more than one may be published, then in that newspaper, and in three newspapers published in the City of Baltimore, one of which shall be in the German language, once a week for at least three months preceding the next ensuing general election, at which the proposed amendment or amendments shall be submitted, in a form to be prescribed by the General Assembly, to the qualified voters of the State for adoption or rejection. The votes cast for and against said proposed amendment or amendments, severally, shall be returned to the Governor, in the manner prescribed in other cases, and if it shall appear to the Governor that a majority of the votes cast at said election on said amendment or amendments, severally, were cast in favor thereof, the Governor shall, by his proclamation, declare the said amendment or amendments having received said majority of votes, to have been adopted by the people of Maryland as part of the Constitution thereof, and thenceforth said amendment or amendments shall be part of the said Constitution. When two or more amendments shall be submitted in manner aforesaid, to the voters of this State at the same election, they shall be so submitted as that each amendment shall be voted on separately.

Sec. 2. It shall be the duty of the General Assembly to provide by Law for taking, at the general election to be held in the year eighteen hundred and eighty-seven, and every twenty years thereafter, the sense of the people in regard to calling a convention for altering this Constitution; and if a majority of voters at such election or elections shall vote for a convention, the General Assembly, at its next session, shall provide by Law for the assembling of such convention, and for the election of Delegates thereto. Each County and Legislative District of the City of Baltimore shall have in such convention a number of Delegates equal to its representation in both Houses at the time at which the convention is called. But any Constitution, or change, or amendment of the existing Constitution, which may be adopted by such convention, shall be submitted to the voters of this State, and shall have no effect unless the same shall have been adopted by a majority of the voters voting thereon.

Article XV

MISCELLANEOUS

Section 1. Every person holding any office created by, or existing under the Constitution, or Laws of the State (except Justices of the Peace, Constables and Coroners), or holding any appointment under any Court of this State, whose pay or compensation is derived from fees or moneys coming into his hands for the discharge of his official duties, or in any way growing out of or connected with his office, shall keep a book in which shall be entered every sum or sums of money received by him, or on his account, as a payment or compensation for his performance of official duties, a copy of which entries in said book, verified by the oath of the officer by whom it is directed to be kept, shall be returned yearly to the Comptroller of the State for his inspection, and that of the General Assembly of the State, to which the Comptroller shall, at each regular session thereof, make a report showing what officers have complied with this section; and each of the said officers, when the amount received by him for the year shall exceed the sum which he is by Law entitled to retain as his salary or compensation for the discharge of his duties, and for the expenses of his office, shall yearly pay over to the Treasurer of the State, the amount of such excess, subject to such disposition thereof as the General Assembly may direct; if any of such officers shall fail to comply with the requisitions of this section for the period of thirty days after the expiration of each and every year of his office, such officer shall be deemed to have vacated his office, and the Governor shall declare the same vacant, and the vacancy therein shall be filled as in case of vacancy for any other cause, and such officer shall be subject to suit by the State for the amount that ought to be paid into the Treasury; and no person holding any office created by or existing under this Constitution or Laws of the State, or holding any appointment under any Court in this State, shall receive more than three thousand dollars a year as a compensation for the discharge of his official duties, except in cases specially provided in this Constitution.

Sec. 2. The several Courts existing in this State at the time of the adoption of this Constitution shall, until superseded under its provisions, continue with like powers and jurisdiction, and in the exercise thereof, both at Law and in Equity, in all respects, as if this Constitution had not been adopted; and when said Courts shall be so superseded, all causes then depending in said Courts shall pass into the jurisdiction of the several Courts, by which they may be respectively superseded.

Sec. 3. The Governor and all officers, civil and military, now holding office under this State, whether by election or appointment, shall continue to hold, exercise and discharge the duties of their offices (unless inconsistent with or otherwise provided in this Constitution), until they shall be superseded under its provisions, and until their successors shall be duly qualified.

Sec. 4. If at any election directed by this Constitution, any two or more candidates shall have the highest and an equal number of votes, a new election shall be ordered by the Governor, except in cases specially provided for by this Constitution.

Sec. 5. In the trial of all criminal cases, the jury shall be the Judges of Law, as well as of fact.

Sec. 6. The right of trial by Jury of issues of fact in civil proceedings in the several Courts of Law in this State, where the amount in controversy exceeds the sum of five dollars, shall be inviolably preserved.

Sec. 7. All general elections in this State shall be held on the Tuesday next after the first Monday in the month of November, in the year in which they shall occur; and the first election of all officers, who, under this Constitution, are required to be elected by the people, shall, except in cases herein specially provided for, be held on the Tuesday next after the first Monday of November, in the year eighteen hundred and sixty-seven.

SEC. 8. The Sheriffs of the several Counties of this State, and of the City of Baltimore, shall give notice of the several elections authorized by this Constitution, in the manner prescribed by existing Laws for elections to be held in this State, until said Laws shall be changed.

SEC. 9. The term of office of all Judges and other officers, for whose election provision is made by this Constitution, shall, except in cases otherwise expressly provided herein, commence from the time of their election; and all such officers shall qualify as soon after their election as practicable, and shall enter upon the duties of their respective offices immediately upon their qualification; and the term of office of the State Librarian and of Commissioner of the Land Office shall commence from the time of their appointment.

SEC. 10. Any officer elected or appointed in pursuance of the provisions of this Constitution, may qualify, either according to the existing provisions of law, in relation to officers under the present Constitution, or before the Governor of the State, or before any Clerk of any Court of Record in any part of the State; but in case an officer shall qualify out of the County in which he resides, an official copy of his oath shall be filed and recorded in the Clerk's office of the Circuit Court of the County in which he may reside, or in the Clerk's office of the Superior Court of the City of Baltimore, if he shall reside therein.

VOTE ON THE CONSTITUTION

For the purpose of ascertaining the sense of the people of this State in regard to the adoption or rejection of this Constitution, the Governor shall issue his Proclamation within five days after the adjournment of this convention, directed to the Sheriffs of the City of Baltimore and of the several Counties of this State, commanding them to give notice in the manner now prescribed by Law in reference to the election of members of the House of Delegates, that an election for the adoption or rejection of this Constitution will be held in the City of Baltimore, and in the several Counties of this State, on Wednesday, the eighteenth day of September, in the year eighteen hundred and sixty-seven, at the usual places of holding elections for members of the House of Delegates in said city and counties. At the said election the vote shall be by ballot, and upon each ballot there shall be written or printed the words, "For the Constitution," or "Against the Constitution," as the voter may elect; and the provisions of the Laws of this State relating to the holding of general elections for members of the House of Delegates, shall in all respects apply to and regulate the holding of the said election. It shall be the duty of the Judges of Election in said city and in the several counties of the State to receive, accurately count and duly return the number of ballots so cast for or against the adoption of this Constitution, as well as any blank ballots which may be cast, to the several Clerks of the Circuit Courts of this State, and to the Clerk of the Superior Court of Baltimore City, in the manner now prescribed by Law, in reference to the election of members of the House of Delegates, and duplicates thereof, directly to the Governor; and the several clerks aforesaid shall return to the Governor, within ten days after said election, the number of ballots cast for or against the constitution, and the number of blank ballots; and the Governor, upon receiving the returns from the Judges of Election, or the clerks as aforesaid, and ascertaining the aggregate vote throughout the State, shall, by his proclamation, make known the same; and if a majority of the votes cast shall be for the adoption of this Constitution it shall go into effect on Saturday, the fifth day of October, eighteen hundred and sixty-seven.

Done in Convention, the seventeenth day of August, in the year of our Lord one thousand eight hundred and sixty-seven, and of the Independence of the United States the ninety-second.

RICHARD B. CARMICHAEL,
President of the Convention.

MILTON Y. KIDD, *Secretary.*

MASSACHUSETTS

THE FIRST CHARTER OF VIRGINIA—1606 * [a]

[See Virginia, p. 3783.]

THE CHARTER OF NEW ENGLAND—1620 [b]

JAMES, by the Grace of God, King of *England, Scotland, France,* and *Ireland,* Defender of the Faith, &c. to all whom these Presents shall come, *Greeting,* Whereas, upon the humble Petition of divers of our well disposed Subjects, that intended to make several Plantations in the Parts of *America,* between the Degrees of thirty-ffoure and ffourty-five; We according to our princely Inclination, favouring much their worthy Disposition, in Hope thereby to advance the in Largement of Christian Religion, to the Glory of God Almighty, as also by that Meanes to streatch out the Bounds of our Dominions, and to replenish those Deserts with People governed by Lawes and Magistrates, for the peaceable Commerce of all, that in time to come shall have occasion to traffique into those Territoryes, granted unto Sir *Thomas Gates,* Sir *George Somers,* Knights, *Thomas Hamon,* and *Raleigh Gilbert,* Esquires, and of their Associates, for the more speedy Accomplishment thereof, by our Letters-Pattent, bearing Date the Tenth Day of Aprill, in the Fourth Year of our Reign of *England, France,* and *Ireland,* and of *Scotland* the ffourtieth, free Liberty to divide themselves into two several Collonyes; the one called the first Collonye, to be undertaken and advanced by certain Knights, Gentlemen, and Merchants, in and about our Cyty of London; the other called the Second Collonye, to be undertaken and advanced by certaine Knights, Gentlemen, and Merchants, and their associates, in and about our Citties of Bristol, Exon, and our Towne of

---

* The compact with the Charter and Laws of the Colony of New Plymouth: together with the charter of the Council at Plymouth, and an Appendix, containing the Articles of Confederation of the United Colonies of New England and other valuable documents. Published agreeably to a resolve, passed April 5, 1836, under the supervision of William Brigham, Counsellor at Law, Boston, 1836. Pp. 1–18.

[a] This charter, which was granted by James I of Great Britain, gave the lands along the North American coast, between the thirty-fourth and the thirty-fifth degree of north latitude, to two companies, one of which had its headquarters at London and the other at Plymouth, England. The Plymouth, or second company, at once commenced colonizing the coast of New England, which was especially assigned to it.

[b] The London Company, organized under the charter of 1606, received a new charter in 1609, as the South Virginia Company, and the Plymouth Company was reorganized in 1620, "for the planting, ruling, ordering, and governing of New England in America."

Plymouth, and other Places, as in and by our said Letters-Pattents, amongst other Things more att large it doth and may appeare. And whereas, since that Time, upon the humble Petition of the said Adventurers and Planters of the said first Collonye, We have been graciously pleased to make them one distinct and entire Body by themselves, giving unto them their distinct Lymitts and Bounds, and have upon their like humble Request, granted unto them divers Liberties, Priveliges, Enlargements, and Immunityes, as in and by our severall Letters-Patents it doth and may more at large appeare. Now forasmuch as We have been in like Manner humbly petitioned unto by our trusty and well beloved Servant, Sir *fferdinando Gorges*, Knight, Captain of our ffort and Island by Plymouth, and by certain the principal Knights and Gentlemen Adventurers of the said Second Collonye, and by divers other Persons of Quality, who now intend to be their Associates, divers of which have been at great and extraordinary Charge, and sustained many Losses in seeking and discovering a Place fitt and convenient to lay the Foundation of a hopeful Plantation, and have divers Years past by God's Assistance, and their own endeavours, taken actual Possession of the Continent hereafter mentioned, in our Name and to our Use, as Sovereign Lord thereof, and have settled already some of our People in Places agreeable to their Desires in those Parts, and in Confidence of prosperous Success therein, by the Continuance of God's Devine Blessing, and our Royall Permission, have resolved in a more plentifull and effectual Manner to prosecute the same, and to that Purpose and Intent have desired of Us, for their better Encouragement and Satisfaction herein, and that they may avoide all Confusion, Questions, or Differences between themselves, and those of the said first Collonye, We would likewise be graciously pleased to make certaine Adventurers, intending to erect and establish ffishery, Trade, and Plantacion, within the Territoryes, Precincts, and Lymitts of the said second Colony, and their Successors, one several distinct and entire Body, and to grant unto them, such Estate, Liberties, Priveliges, Enlargements, and Immunityes there, as in these our Letters-Pattents hereafter particularly expressed and declared. And for asmuch as We have been certainly given to understand by divers of our good Subjects, that have for these many Years past frequented those Coasts and Territoryes, between the Degrees of Fourty and Fourty-Eight, that there is noe other the Subjects of any Christian King or State, by any Authority from their Soveraignes, Lords, or Princes, actually in Possession of any of the said Lands or Precincts, whereby any Right, Claim, Interest, or Title, may, might, or ought by that Meanes accrue, belong, or appertaine unto them, or any of them. And also for that We have been further given certainly to knowe, that within these late Yeares there hath by God's Visitation raigned a wonderfull Plague, together with many horrible Slaugthers, and Murthers, committed amoungst the Sauages and brutish People there, heertofore inhabiting, in a Manner to the utter Destruction, Deuastacion, and Depopulacion of that whole Territorye, so that there is not left for many Leagues together in a Manner, any that doe claime or challenge any Kind of Interests therein, nor any other Superiour Lord or Souveraigne to make Claime thereunto, whereby We in our Judgment are persuaded and satisfied that the appointed Time is come in which Almighty God in his great Goodness and Bountie towards Us and our People, hath thought fitt and determined, that those large and goodly Territoryes, deserted as it were by their naturall Inhabitants, should be possessed and enjoyed by such of our Subjects and People as heertofore have and hereafter shall by his Mercie and Favour, and by his Powerfull Arme, be directed and conducted thither. In Contemplacion and serious Consideracion whereof, Wee have thougt it fitt according to our Kingly Duty, soe much as in Us lyeth, to second and followe God's sacred Will, rendering reverend Thanks to his Divine Majestie for his gracious favour in laying open and revealing the same unto us, before any other Christian Prince or State, by which Meanes without Offence, and as We trust to his Glory, Wee may with Boldness goe on to the settling of soe hopefull a Work, which tendeth to the reducing and Conversion of such Sauages as remaine wandering in Desolacion and Distress, to Civil Societie and Christian Religion, to the Inlargement of our own Dominions, and the Aduancement of the Fortunes of such of our good Subjects as shall willingly intresse themselves in the said Imployment, to whom We cannot but give singular Commendations for their soe worthy Intention and Enterprize; Wee therefore, of our especiall Grace, mere Motion, and certaine Knowledge, by the Aduice of the Lords and others of our Priuy Councell have for Us, our Heyrs and Successors, graunted, ordained, and established, and in and by these Presents, Do for Us, our Heirs and Successors, grant, ordaine and establish, that all that Circuit, Continent, Precincts, and Limitts in America, lying and being in Breadth from Fourty Degrees of Northerly Latitude, from the Equnoctiall Line, to Fourty-eight Degrees of the said Northerly Latitude, and in length by all the Breadth aforesaid throughout the Maine Land, from Sea to Sea, with all the Seas, Rivers, Islands, Creekes, Inletts, Ports, and Havens, within the Degrees, Precincts, and Limitts of the said Latitude and Longitude, shall be the Limitts, and Bounds, and Precints of the second Collony: And to the End that the said Territoryes may forever hereafter be more particularly and certainly known and distinguished, our Will and Pleasure is, that the same shall from henceforth be nominated, termed, and called by the Name of New-England, in America; and by that Name of New-England in America, the said Circuit, Precinct, Limitt, Continent, Islands, and Places in America, aforesaid, We do by these Presents, for Us, our Heyrs and Successors, name, call, erect, found and establish, and by that Name to have Continuance for ever.

And for the better Plantacion, ruling, and governing of the aforesaid New-England, in America, We will, ordaine, constitute, assigne, limitt and appoint, and for Us, our Heyrs and Successors, Wee, by the Advice of the Lords and others of the said priuie Councill, do by these Presents ordaine, constitute, limett, and appoint, that from henceforth, there shall be for ever hereafter, in our Towne of Plymouth, in the County of Devon, one Body politicque and corporate, which shall have perpetuall Succession, which shall consist of the Number of fourtie Persons, and no more, which shall be, and shall be called and knowne by the Name the Councill established at Plymouth, in the County of Devon for the planting, ruling, ordering, and governing of New-England, in America; and for that Purpose Wee have, at and by the Nomination and Request of the said Petitioners, granted, ordained, established, and confirmed; and by these Presents, for Us, our Heyres and Successors, doe grant, ordaine, establish, and confirme, our right trusty and right well beloved Cosins and Councillors Lodovick, Duke of Lenox, Lord Steward of our Houshold, George Lord Marquess Buckingham, our High Admiral of England, James Marquess Hamilton, William Earle of Pembrocke, Lord Chamberlaine of our Houshold, Thomas Earl of Arundel, and our right trusty and right well beloved Cosin, William Earl of Bathe, and right trusty and right well beloved Cosin and Councellor, Henry Earle of Southampton, and our right trusty and right well beloved Cousins, William Earle of Salisbury, and Robert Earle of Warwick, and our right trusty and right well beloved John Viscount Haddington, and our right trusty and well beloved Councellor Edward Lord Zouch, Lord Warden of our Cincque Ports, and our trusty and well beloved Edmond Lord Sheffield, Edward Lord Gorges, and our well beloved Sir Edward Seymour, Knight and Barronett, Sir Robert Manselle, Sir Edward Zouch, our Knight Marshall, Sir Dudley Diggs, Sir Thomas Roe, Sir fferdinando Gorges, Sir Francis Popham, Sir John Brook, Sir Thomas Gates, Sir Richard Hawkins, Sir Richard Edgcombe, Sir Allen Apsley, Sir Warwick Hale, Sir Richard Catchmay, Sir John Bourchier, Sir Nathaniel Rich, Sir Edward Giles, Sir Giles Mompesson, and Sir Thomas Wroth, Knights; and our well beloved Matthew Sutcliffe, Dean of Exeter, Robert Heath, Esq; Recorder of our Cittie of London, Henry Bourchier, John Drake, Rawleigh Gilbert, George Chudley, Thomas Hamon, and John Argall, Esquires, to be and in and by these Presents; We do appoint them to be the first modern and present Councill established at Plymouth, in the County of Devon, for the planting, ruling, ordering, and governing of New-England, in America; and that they, and the Suruiuours of them, and such as the Suruiuours and Suruiuor of them shall, from tyme to tyme elect, and chuse, to make up the aforesaid Number of fourtie Persons, when, and as often as any of them, or any of their Successors shall happen to decease, or to be removed from being of the said Councill, shall be in, and by these Presents, incorporated to have a perpetual Succession for ever, in Deed, Fact, and Name, and shall be one Bodye corporate and politicque; and that those, and such said Persons, and their Successors, and such as shall be elected and chosen to succeed them as aforesaid, shall be, and by these Presents are, and be incorporated, named, and called by the Name of the Councill established at Plymouth, in the County of Devon, for the planting, ruling, and governing of New-England, in America; and them the said Duke of Lenox, Marquess Buckingham, Marquess Hamilton, Earle of Pembroke, Earle of Arundell, Earle of Bathe, Earle of Southampton, Earle of Salisbury, Earle of Warwick, Viscount Haddington, Lord Zouch, Lord Sheffield, Lord Gorges, Sir Edward Seymour, Sir Robert Mansell, Sir Edward Zouch, Sir Dudley Diggs, Sir Thomas Roe, Sir fferdinando Gorges, Sir ffrancis Popham, Sir John Brooks, Sir Thomas Gates, Sir Richard Hawkins, Sir Richard Edgcombe, Sir Allen Apsley, Sir Warwick Heale, Sir Richard Catchmay, Sir John Bourchier, Sir Nathaniell Rich, Sir Edward Giles, Sir Giles Mompesson, Sir Thomas Wroth, Knights; Matthew Suttcliffe, Robert Heath, Henry Bourchier, John Drake, Rawleigh Gilbert, George Chudley, Thomas Haymon, and John Argall, Esqrs. and their successors, one Body corporate and politick, in Deed and Name, by the Name of the Councell established att Plymouth, in the County of Devon, for the planting, ruling, and governing of New-

England, in America. Wee do by these Presents, for Us, our Heyres and Successors, really and fully incorporate, erect, ordaine, name, constitute, and establish, and that by the same Name of the said Councill, they and their Successors for ever hereafter be incorporated, named, and called, and shall by the same Name have perpetual Succession. And further, Wee do hereby for Us, our Heires and Successors, grant unto the said Councill established att Plymouth, that they and their Successors, by the same Name, be and shall be, and shall continue Persons able and capable in the Law, from time to time, and shall by that Name, of Councill aforesaid, have full Power and Authority, and lawful Capacity and Hability, as well to purchase, take, hold, receive, enjoy, and to have, and their Successors for ever, any Manors, Lands, Tenements, Rents, Royalties, Privileges, Immunities, Reversions, Annuities, Hereditaments, Goods, and Chattles whatsoever, of or from Us, our Heirs, and Successors, and of or from any other Person or Persons whatsoever, as well in and within this our Realme, of England, as in and within any other Place or Places whatsoever or wheresoever; and the same Manors, Lands, Tenements, and Hereditaments, Goods or Chattles, or any of them, by the same Name to alien and sell, or to do, execute, ordaine and performe all other Matters and Things whatsoever to the said Incorporation and Plantation concerning and belonging.

And further, our Will and Pleasure is, that the said Councill, for the time being, and their Successors, shall have full Power and lawful authority, by the Name aforesaid, to sue, and be sued; implead, and to be impleaded; answer, and to be answered, unto all Manner of Courts and Places that now are, or hereafter shall be, within this our Realme and elsewhere, as well temporal as spiritual, in all Manner of Suits and Matters whatsoever, and of what Nature or Kinde soever such Suite or Action be or shall be. And our Will and Pleasure is, that the said ffourty Persons, or the greater Number of them, shall and may, from time to time, and at any time hereafter, at their owne Will and Pleasure, according to the Laws, Ordinances, and Orders of or by them, or by the greater Part of them, hereafter in Manner and forme in these Presents mentioned, to be agreed upon, to elect and choose amongst themselves one of the said ffourty Persons for the Time being, to be President of the said Councill, which President soe elected and chosen, Wee will, shall continue and be President of the said Councill for so long a Time as by the Orders of the said Councill, from time to time to be made, as hereafter is mentioned, shall be thought fitt, and no longer; unto which President, or in his Absence, to any such Person as by the Order of the said Councill shall be thereunto appointed, Wee do give Authority to give Order for the warning of the said Council, and summoning the Company to their Meetings. And our Will and Pleasure is, that from time to time, when and so often as any of the Councill shall happen to decease, or to be removed from being of the said Councell, that then, and so often, the Survivors of them the said Councill, and no other, or the greater Number of them, who then shall be from time to time left and remaininge, and who shall, or the greater Number of which that shall be assembled at a public Court or Meeting to be held for the said Company, shall elect and choose one or more other Person or Persons to be of the said Councill, and which from time to time shall be of the said Councill, so that the Number of ffourty Persons of the said Councill may from time to time be supplied: Provided always that as well the Persons herein named to be of the said Councill, as every other Councellor hereafter to be elected, shall be presented to the Lord Chancellor of England, or to the Lord High Treasurer of England, or to the Lord Chamberlaine of the Household of Us, our Heires and Successors for the Time being, to take his and their Oath and Oathes of a Councellor and Councellors to Us, our Heirs and Successors, for the said Company and Collonye in New-England.

And further, Wee will and grant by these Presents, for Us, our Heires and Successors, unto the said Councill and their Successors, that they and their Successors shall have and enjoy for ever a Common Seale, to be engraven according to their Discretions; and that it shall be lawfull for them to appoint whatever Seale or Seales, they shall think most meete and necessary, either for their Use, as they are one united Body incorporate here, or for the publick of their Gouvernour and Ministers of New-England aforesaid, whereby the Incorporation may or shall seale any Manner of Instrument touching the same Corporation, and the Manors, Lands, Tenements, Rents, Reversions, Annuities, Hereditaments, Goods, Chattles, Affaires, and any other Things belonging unto, or in any wise appertaininge, touching, or concerning the said Councill and their Successors, or concerning the said Corporation and plantation in and by these our Letters-Patents as aforesaid founded, erected, and established.

And Wee do further by these Presents, for Us, our Heires and Successors, grant unto the said Councill and their Successors, that it shall and may be lawfull to and for the said Councill, and their Successors for the Time being, in their discretions, from time to time to admitt such and so many Person and Persons to be made free and enabled to trade traffick unto, within, and in New-England aforesaid, and unto every Part and Parcell thereof, or to have, possess, or enjoy, any Lands or Hereditaments in New-England aforesaid, as they shall think fitt, according to the Laws, Orders, Constitutions, and Ordinances, by the said Councill and their Successors from time to time to be made and established by Virtue of, and according to the true Intent of these Presents, and under such Conditions, Reservations, and agreements as the said Councill shall set downe, order and direct, and not otherwise. And further, of our especiall Grace, certaine Knowlege, and mere Motion, for Us, our Heires and Successors, Wee do by these Presents give and grant full Power and Authority to the said Councill and their Successors, that the said Councill for the Time being, or the greater Part of them, shall and may, from time to time, nominate, make, constitute, ordaine, and confirme by such Name or Names, Style or Styles, as to them shall seeme Good; and likewise to revoke, discharge, change, and alter, as well all and singular, Governors, Officers, and Ministers, which hereafter shall be by them thought fitt and needful to be made or used, as well to attend the Business of the said Company here, as for the Government of the said Collony and Plantation, and also to make, ordaine, and establish all Manner of Orders, Laws, Directions, Instructions, Forms, and Ceremonies of Government and Magistracy fitt and necessary for and concerning the Government of the said Collony and Plantation, so always as the same be not contrary to the Laws and Statutes of this our Realme of England, and the same att all Times hereafter to abrogate, revoke, or change, not only within the Precincts of the said Collony, but also upon the Seas in going and coming to and from the said Collony, as they in their good Discretions shall thinke to be fittest for the good of the Adenturers and Inhabitants there.

And Wee do further of our especiall Grace, certaine Knowledge, and mere Motion, grant, declare, and ordain, that such principall Governor, as from time to time shall be authorized and appointed in Manner and Forme in these Presents heretofore expressed, shall haue full Power and Authority to use and exercise marshall Laws in Cases of Rebellion, Insurrection and Mutiny, in as large and ample Manner as our Lieutenants in our Counties within our Realme of England have or ought to have by Force of their Commission of Lieutenancy. And for as much as it shall be necessary for all our lovinge Subjects as shall inhabit within the said Precincts of New-England aforesaid, to determine to live together in the Feare and true Worship of Allmighty God, Christian Peace, and civil Quietness, each with other, whereby every one may with more Safety, Pleasure, and Profitt, enjoye that whereunto they shall attaine with great Pain and Perill, Wee, for Us, our Heires and Successors, are likewise pleased and contented, and by these Presents do give and grant unto the said Council and their Successors, and to such Governors, Officers, and Ministers, as shall be by the said Councill constituted and appointed according to the Natures and Limitts of their Offices and Places respectively, that they shall and may, from time to time for ever heerafter, within the said Precincts of New-England, or in the Way by the Seas thither, and from thence have full and absolute Power and Authority to correct, punish, pardon, governe, and rule all such the Subjects of Us, our Heires and Successors, as shall from time to time adventure themselves in any Voyage thither, or that shall att any Time heerafter inhabit in the Precincts or Territories of the said Collony as aforesaid, according to such Laws, Orders, Ordinances, Directions, and Instructions as by the said Councill aforesaid shall be established; and in Defect thereof, in Cases of Necessity, according to the good Discretions of the said Governors and Officers respectively, as well in Cases capitall and criminall, as civill, both marine and others, so allways as the said Statutes, Ordinances, and Proceedings, as near as conveniently may be, agreeable to the Laws, Statutes, Government and Policie of this our Realme of England. And furthermore, if any Person or Persons, Adventurers or Planters of the said Collony, or any other, att any Time or Times heereafter, shall transport any Moneys, Goods, or Merchandizes, out of any of our Kingdoms, with a Pretence or Purpose to land, sell, or otherwise dispose of the same within the Limitts and Bounds of the said Collony, and yet nevertheless being att Sea, or after he hath landed within any Part of the said Collony shall carry the same into any other fforaigne Country with a Purpose there to sell and dispose thereof, that then all the Goods and Chattles of the said Person or Persons so offending and transported, together with the Ship or Vessell wherein such Transportation was made, shall be forfeited to Us, our Heires and Successors.

And Wee do further of our especiall Grace, certaine Knowledge, and meere Motion for Us, our Heirs and Successors for and in Respect of the Considerations aforesaid, and for divers other good Causes and Considerations, us thereunto especially moving, and by the Advice of the Lords and Others of our said Privy Councill have absolutely giuen, granted, and confirmed, and do by these Presents absolutely give, grant, and confirm unto the said Councill, called the Councell established att Plymouth in the County of Devon for the planting, ruling, and governing of New-England in America, and unto their Successors for ever, all the aforesaid Lands and Grounds, Continent, Precinct, Place, Places and Territoryes, viz, the aforesaid Part of America, lying, and being in Breadth from ffourty Degrees of Northerly Latitude from the Equinoctiall Line, to ffourty-eight Degrees of the said Northerly Latitude inclusively, and in Length of, and within all the Breadth aforesaid, throughout the Maine Land from Sea to Sea, together also, with the Firme Lands, Soyles, Grounds, Havens, Ports, Rivers, Waters, Fishings, Mines, and Mineralls, as well Royall Mines of Gold and Silver, as other Mine and Mineralls, precious Stones, Quarries, and all, and singular other Comodities, Jurisdictions, Royalties, Priveliges, Franchises, and Preheminences, both within the same Tract of Land upon the Maine, and also within the said Islands and Seas adjoining: Provided always, that the said Islands, or any of the Premises herein before mentioned, and by these Presents intended and meant to be granted, be not actually possessed or inhabited by any other Christian Prince or Estate, nor be within the Bounds, Limitts, or Territoryes, of that Southern Collony heretofore by us granted to be planted by diverse of our loving Subjects in the South Parts, to have and to hold, possess and enjoy, all, and singular, the aforesaid Continent, Lands, Territoryes, Islands, Hereditaments and Precincts, Sea Waters, Fishings, with all, and all Manner their Commodities, Royalties, Liberties, Preheminences, and Profitts, that shall arise from thence, with all and singular, their Appertenances, and every Part and Parcell thereof, and of them, to and unto the said Councell and their Successors and Assignes for ever, to the sole only and proper Use, Benefit, and Behooffe of them the said Council and their Successors and Assignes for ever, to be holden of Us, our Heires, and Successors, as of our Manor of East-Greenwich, in our County of Kent, in free and common Soccage and not in in Capite, nor by Knight's Service; yielding and paying therefore to Us, our Heires, our Successors, the fifth Part, of the Ores of Gold and Silver, which from time to time, and att all times hereafter, shall happen to be found, gotten, had, and obtained, in or within any the said Lands, Limitts, Territoryes, and Precincts, or in or within any Part or Parcell thereof, for, or in Respect of all, and all Manner of Dutys, Demands, and Services whatsoever, to be done, made, or paid to Us, our Heires, and Successors.

And Wee do further of our especiall Grace, certaine Knowledge, and meere Motion, for Us, and our Heires, and Successors, give and grant to the said Councell, and their Successors for ever by these Presents, that it shall be lawfull and free for them and their Assignes, att all and every time and times hereafter, out of our Realmes or Dominions whatsoever, to take, load, carry, and transport in, and into their Voyages, and for, and towards the said Plantation in New-England, all such and so many of our loveing Subjects, or any other Strangers that will become our loving Subjects, and live under our Allegiance, as shall willingly accompany them in the said Voyages and Plantation, with Shipping, Armour, Weapons, Ordinances, Munition, Powder, Shott, Victuals, and all Manner of Cloathing, Implements, Furniture, Beasts, Cattle, Horses, Mares, and all other Things necessary for the said Plantation, and for their Use and Defence, and for Trade with the People there, and in passing and returning to and fro, without paying or yielding, any Custom or Subsidie either inwards or outwards, to Us, our Heires, or Successors, for the same, for the Space of seven Years, from the Day of the Date of these Presents, provided, that none of the said Persons be such as shall be hereafter by special Name restrained by Us, our Heire, or Successors.

And for their further Encouragement, of our especiall Grace and Favor, Wee do by these Presents for Us, our Heires, and Successors, yield and grant, to and with the said Councill and their Successors, and every of them, their Factors and Assignes, that they and every of them, shall be free and quitt from all Subsidies and Customes in New-England for the Space of seven Years, and from all Taxes and Impositions for the Space of twenty and one Yeares, upon all Goods and Merchandizes att any time or times hereafter, either upon Importation thither, or Exportation from thence into our Realme of England, or into any our Dominions by the said Councill and their Successors, their Deputies, ffactors, and Affignes, or any of them, except only the five Pounds *per Cent.* due for Custome upon all such Goods and Merchandizes, as shall be brot and imported into our Realme of England, or any other of our Dominions, according to the ancient Trade of Marchants; which five Pounds *per Cent.* only being paid, it shall be thenceforth lawful and free for the said Adventurers, the same Goods and Merchandize to export and carry out of our said Dominions into fforraigne Parts, without any Custom, Tax, or other Duty to be paid to Us, our Heires, or Successors, or to any other Officers or Ministers of Us, our Heires, or Successors; provided, that the said Goods and Merchandizes be shipped out within thirteene Months after theire first Landing within any Part of those Dominions.

And further our Will and Pleasure is, and Wee do by these Presents charge, comand, warrant, and authorize the said Councill, and their Successors, or the major Part of them, which shall be present and assembled for that Purpose, shall from time to time under their comon Seale, distribute, convey, assigne, and sett over, such particular Portions of Lands, Tenements, and Hereditaments, as are by these Presents, formerly granted unto each our loveing Subjects, naturally borne or Denisons, or others, as well Adventurers as Planters, as by the said Company upon a Comission of Survey and Distribution, executed and returned for that Purpose, shall be named, appointed, and allowed, wherein our Will and Pleasure is, that Respect be had as well to the Proportion of the Adventurers, as to the speciall Service, Hazard, Exploit, or Meritt of any Person so to be recompensed, advanced, or rewarded, and wee do also, for Us, our Heires, and Successors, grant to the said Councell and their Successors and to all and every such Governours, other Officers, or Ministers, as by the said Councill shall be appointed to have Power and Authority of Government and Command in and over the said Collony and Plantation, that they and every of them, shall, and lawfully may, from time to time, and att all Times hereafter for ever, for their severall Defence and Safety, encounter, expulse, repel, and resist by Force of Arms, as well by Sea as by Land, and all Ways and Meanes whatsoever, all such Person and Persons, as without the speciall Licence of the said Councell and their Successors, or the greater Part of them, shall attempt to inhabitt within the said severall Precincts and Limitts of the said Collony and Plantation. And also all, and every such Person or Persons whatsoever, as shall enterprize or attempt att any time hereafter Destruction, Invasion, Detriment, or Annoyance to the said Collony and Plantation; and that it shall be lawfull for the said Councill, and their Successors, and every of them, from Time to Time, and att all Times heereafter, and they shall have full Power and Authority, to take and surprize by all Ways and Means whatsoever, all and every such Person and Persons whatsoever, with their Ships, Goods, and other Furniture, trafficking in any Harbour, Creeke, or Place, within the Limitts and Precintes of the said Collony and Plantations, and not being allowed by the said Councill to be adventurers or Planters of the said Collony. And of our further Royall Favor, Wee have granted, and for Us, our Heires, and Successors, Wee do grant unto the said Councill and their Successors, that the said Territoryes, Lands, Rivers, and Places aforesaid, or any of them, shall not be visited, frequented, or traded unto, by any other of our Subjects, or the Subjects of Us, our Heires, or Successors, either from any the Ports and Havens belonging or appertayning, or which shall belong or appertayne unto Us, our Heires, or Successors, or to any forraigne State, Prince, or Pottentate whatsoever: And therefore, Wee do hereby for Us, our Heires, and Successors, charge, command, prohibit and forbid all the Subjects of Us, our Heires, and Successors, of what Degree and Quality soever, they be, that none of them, directly, or indirectly, presume to vissitt, frequent, trade, or adventure to traffick into, or from the said Territoryes, Lands, Rivers, and Places aforesaid, or any of them other than the said Councill and their Successors, ffactors, Deputys, and Assignes, unless it be with the License and Consent of the said Councill and Company first had and obtained in Writing, under the comon Seal, upon Pain of our Indignation and Imprisonment of their Bodys during the Pleasure of Us, our Heires or Successors, and the Forfeiture and Loss both of theire Ships and Goods, wheresoever they shall be found either within any of our Kingdomes or Dominions, or any other Place or Places out of our Dominions.

And for the better effecting of our said Pleasure heerein Wee do heereby for Us, our Heires and Successors, give and grant full Power and Authority unto the said Councill, and their Successors for the time being, that they by themselves, their Factors, Deputyes, or Assignes, shall and may from time to time, and at all times heereafter, attach, arrest, take, and seize all and all Manner of Ship and Ships, Goods, Wares, and Merchandizes whatsoever, which shall be bro't from or carried to the Places before mentioned, or any of them, contrary to our Will and Pleasure, before in these Presents expressed. The Moyety or one halfe of all which Forfeitures Wee do hereby for Us, our Heires and Successors, give and grant unto the said Councill, and their Successors to their own proper Use without Accompt, and the other Moyety, or halfe Part thereof, Wee will shall be and remaine to the Use of Us, our Heires and Successors. And we likewise have condiscended and granted, and by these Presents, for Us, our Heires and Successors, do condiscend, and grant to and with the said Councill and their Successors, that Wee, our Heires or Successors, shall not or will not give and grant any Lybertye, License, or Authority to any Person or Persons whatsoever, to saile, trade, or trafficke unto the aforesaid parts of New-England, without the good Will and Likinge of the said Councill, or the greater Part of them for the Time beinge, att any their Courts to be assembled. And Wee do for us, our Heires and Successors, give and grant unto the said Councill, and their Successors, that whensoever, or so often as any Custome or Subsidie shall growe due or payable unto Us, our Heires or Successors, according to the Limitation and Appointment aforesaid by Reason of any Goods, Wares, Merchandizes, to be shipped out, or any Returne to be made of any Goods, Wares, or Merchandizes, unto or from New-England, or any the Lands Territoryes aforesaid, that then so often, and in such Case the ffarmers, Customers, and Officers of our Customes of England and Ireland, and every of them, for the Time being, upon Request made unto them by the said Councill, their Successors, ffactors, or Assignes, and upon convenient Security, to be given in that Behalfe, shall give and allowe unto the said Councill and their Successors, and to all Person and Persons free of the said Company as aforesaid, six Months Time for the Payment of the one halfe of all such Custome and Subsidie, as shall be due, and payable unto Us, our Heires and Successors for the same, for which these our Letterspattent, or the Duplicate, or the Enrolment thereof, shall be unto our said Officers a sufficient Warrant and Discharge. Nevertheless, our Will and Pleasure is, that if any of the said Goods, Wares, and Merchandizes, which be, or shall be, att any Time heereafter, anded and exported out of any of our Realmes aforesaid, and shall be shipped with a Purpose not to be carried to New-England aforesaid, that then such Payment, Duty, Custome, Imposition, or Forfieture, shall be paid and belong to Us, our Heires, and Successors, for the said Goods, Wares, and Merchandices, so fraudulently sought to be transported, as if this our Grant had not been made nor granted: And Wee do for Us, our Heires and Successors, give and grant unto the said Councill and theire Successors for ever, by these Presents, that the said President of the said Company, or his Deputy for the Time being, or any two others of the said Councill, for the said Collony in New-England, for the Time beinge, shall and may, and att all Times heereafter, and from time to time, have full Power and Authority, to minister and give the Oath and Oaths of Allegiance and Supremacy, or either of them, to all and every Person and Persons, which shall att any Time and Times heereafter, goe or pass to the said Collony in New-England. And further, that it shall be likewise be lawful for the said President, or his Deputy for the Time being, or any two others of the said Councill for the said Collony of New-England for the Time being, from time to time, and att all Times heerafter, to minister such a formal Oath, as by their Discretion shall be reasonably devised, as well unto any Person and Persons imployed or to be imployed in, for, or touching the said Plantation, for their honest, faithfull, and just Discharge of their Service, in all such Matters as shall be committed unto them for the Good and Benefitt of the said Company, Collony, and Plantation, as also unto such other Person or Persons, as the said President or his Deputy, with two others of the said Councill, shall thinke meete for the Examination or clearing of the Truth in any Cause whatsoever, concerning the said Plantation, or any Business from thence proceeding, or thereunto belonging.

And to the End that now lewd or ill-disposed Persons, Saylors, Soldiers, Artificers, Labourers, Husbandmen, or others, which shall receive Wages, Apparel, or other Entertainment from the said Councill, or contract and agree with the said Councill to goe, and to serve, and to be imployed, in the said Plantation, in the Collony in New-England, do afterwards withdraw, hide, and conceale themselves, or refuse to go thither, after they have been so entertained and agreed withall; and that no Persons which shall be sent and imployed in the said Plantation, of the said Collony in New-England, upon the Charge of the said Councill, doe misbehave themselves by mutinous Seditions, or other notorious Misdemeanors, or which shall be imployed, or sent abroad by the Governour of New England or his Deputy, with any Shipp or Pinnace, for Provision for the said Collony, or for some Discovery, or other Business or Affaires concerninge the same, doe from thence either treacherously come back againe, or returne into the Realme of Englande by Stealth, or without Licence of the Governour of the said Collony in New-England for the Time being, or be sent hither as Misdoers or Offendors; and that none of those Persons after theire Returne from thence, being questioned by the said Councill heere, for such their Misdemeanors and Offences, do, by insolent and contemptuous Carriage in the Presence of the said Councill shew little Respect and Reverence, either to the Place or Authority in which we have placed and appointed them and others, for the clearing of their Lewdness and Misdemeanors committed in New-England, divulge vile and scandalous Reports of the Country of New-England, or of the Government or Estate of the said Plantation and Collony, to bring the said Voyages and Plantation into Disgrace and Contempt, by Meanes whereof, not only the Adventurers and Planters already engaged in the said Plantation may be exceedingly abused and hindered, and a great number of our loveing and well-disposed Subjects, otherways well affected and inclined to joine and adventure in so noble a Christian and worthy Action may be discouraged from the same, but also the Enterprize itself may be overthrowne, which cannot miscarry without some Dishonour to Us and our Kingdome: Wee, therefore, for preventing so great and enormous Abuses and Misdemeanors, Do, by these Presents for Us, our Heires, and Successors, give and grant unto the said President or his Deputy, or such other Person or Persons, as by the Orders of the said Councill shall be appointed by Warrant under his or their Hand or Hands, to send for, or cause to be apprehended, all and every such Person and Persons, who shall be noted, or accused, or found at any time or times hereafter to offend or misbehave themselves in any the Affaires before mentioned and expressed; and upon the Examination of any such Offender or Offenders, and just Proofe made by Oathe taken before the said Councill, of any such notorious Misdemeanours by them comitted as aforesaid, and also upon any insolent, contemptuous, or irreverent Carriage or Misbehaviour, to or against the said Councill, to be shewed or used by any such Person or Persons so called, convened, and appearing before them as aforesaid, that in all such Cases, our said Councill, or any two or more of them for the Time being, shall and may have full Power and Authority, either heere to bind them over with good Sureties for their good Behaviour, and further therein to proceed, to all Intents and Purposes as it is used in other like Cases within our Realme of England, or else at their Discretions to remand and send back the said offenders, or any of them, to the said Collony of New-England, there to be proceeded against and punished as the Governour's Deputy or Councill there for the Time being, shall think meete, or otherwise according to such Laws and Ordinances as are, and shall be, in Use there, for the well ordering and good Government of the said Collony.

And our Will and Pleasure is, and Wee do hereby declare to all Christian Kings, Princes, and States, that if any Person or Persons which shall hereafter be of the said Collony or Plantation, or any other by License or Appointment of the said Councill, or their Successors, or otherwise, shall at any time or times heereafter, rob or spoil, by Sea or by Land, or do any Hurt, Violence, or unlawfull Hostillity to any of the Subjects of Us, our Heires, or Successors, or any of the Subjects of any King, Prince, Ruler, or Governour, or State, being then in League and Amity with Us, our Heires and Successors, and that upon such Injury, or upon just Complaint of such Prince, Ruler, Governour, or State, or their Subjects, Wee, our Heires, or Successors shall make open Proclamation within any of the Ports of our Realme of England commodious for that Purpose, that the Person or Persons having committed any such Robbery or Spoile, shall within the Term limited by such a Proclamation, make full Restitution or Satisfaction of all such Injuries done, so as the said Princes or other, so complaining, may hold themselves fully satisfied and contented. And if that the said Person or Persons having committed such Robery or Spoile, shall not make or cause to be made Satisfaction accordingly within such Terme so to be limited, that then it shall be lawful for Us, our Heires, and Successors, to put the said Person or Persons our of our Allegiance and Protection; and that it shall be lawful and free for all Princes to prosecute with Hostillity the said Offenders and every of them, their, and every of their Procurers, Aidors, Abettors, and Comforters in that Behalfe. Also, Wee do for Us, our Heires, and Successors, declare by these Presents, that all and every the Persons, beinge our Subjects, which shall goe and inhabitt within the said Collony and Plantation, and every of their Children and Posterity, which shall happen to be born within the Limitts thereof, shall have and enjoy all Liberties, and ffranchizes, and Immunities of free Denizens and naturall Subjects within any of our other Dominions, to all Intents and Purposes, as if they had been abidinge and born within this our Kingdome of England, or any other our Dominions.

And lastly, because the principall Effect which we can desire or expect of this Action, is the Conversion and Reduction of the People in those Parts unto the true Worship of God and Christian Religion, in which Respect, Wee would be loath that any Person should be permitted to pass that Wee suspected to affect the Superstition of the Chh of Rome, Wee do hereby declare that it is our Will and Pleasure that none be permitted to pass, in any Voyage from time to time to be made into the said Country, but such as shall first have taken the Oathe of Supremacy; for which Purpose, Wee do by these Presents give full Power and Authority to the President of the said Councill, to tender and exhibit the said Oath to all such Persons as shall at any time be sent and imployed in the said Voyage. And Wee also for us, our Heires and Successors, do covenant and grant to and with the Councill, and their Successors, by these Presents, that if the Councill for the time being, and their Successors, or any of them, shall at any time or times heereafter, upon any Doubt which they shall conceive concerning the Strength or Validity in Law of this our present Grant, or be desirous to have the same renewed and confirmed by Us, our Heires and Successors, with Amendment of such Imperfections and Defects as shall appear fitt and necessary to the said Councill, or their Successors, to be reformed and amended on the Behalfe of Us, our Heires and Successors, and for the furthering of the Plantation and Government, or the Increase, continuing, and flourishing thereof, that then, upon the humble Petition of the said Councill for the time being, and their Successors, to us, our Heires and Successors, Wee, our Heires and Successors, shall and will forthwith make and pass under the Great Seall of England, to the said Councill and theire Successors, such further and better Assurance, of all and singular the Lands, Grounds, Royalties, Privileges, and Premisses aforesaid granted, or intended to be granted, according to our true Intent and Meaneing in these our Letters-patents, signified, declared, or mentioned, as by the learned Councill of Us, our Heires, and Successors, and of the said Company and theire Successors shall, in that Behalfe, be reasonably devised or advised. And further our Will and Pleasure is, that in all Questions and Doubts, that shall arise upon any Difficulty of Instruction or Interpretation of any Thing contained in these our Letters-pattents, the same shall be taken and Interpreted in most ample and beneficial Manner, for the said Council and theire Successors, and every Member thereof. And Wee do further for Us, our Heires and Successors, charge and comand all and singular Admirals, Vice-Admirals, Generals, Commanders, Captaines, Justices of Peace, Majors, Sheriffs, Bailiffs, Constables, Customers, Comptrollers, Waiters, Searchers, and all the Officers of Us, our Heires and Successors, whatsoever to be from time to time, and att all times heereafter, in all Things aiding, helping, and assisting unto the said Councill, and their Successors, and unto every of them, upon Request and Requests by them to be made, in all Matters and Things, for the furtherance and Accomplishment of all or any the Matters and Things by Us, in and by these our Letters-pattents, given, granted, and provided, or by Us meant or intended to be given, granted, and provided, as they our said Officers, and the Officers of Us, our Heires and Successors, do tender our Pleasure, and will avoid the contrary att their Perills. And Wee also do by these Presents, ratifye and confirm unto the said Councill and their Successors, all Priveliges, ffranchises, Liberties, Immunities granted in our said former Letters-patents, and not in these our Letters-patents revoked, altered, changed or abridged, altho' Expressed, Mentioned, &c.

  In Witness, &c.

 Witnes our selfe at *Westminster*, the Third Day of November, in the Eighteenth Yeare of our Reign over England, &c.

       Par Breve de Privato Sigillo, &c.

AGREEMENT BETWEEN THE SETTLERS AT NEW PLYMOUTH— 1620 * a

IN THE NAME OF GOD, AMEN. We, whose names are underwritten, the Loyal Subjects of our dread Sovereign Lord King *James*, by the Grace of God, of *Great Britain, France*, and *Ireland*, King, *Defender of the Faith*, &c. Having undertaken for the Glory of God, and Advancement of the Christian Faith, and the Honour of our King and Country, a Voyage to plant the first Colony in the northern Parts of *Virginia;* Do by these Presents, solemnly and mutually, in the Presence of God and one another, covenant and combine ourselves together into a civil Body Politick, for our better Ordering and Preservation, and Furtherance of the Ends aforesaid: And by Virtue hereof do enact, constitute, and frame, such just and equal Laws, Ordinances, Acts, Constitutions, and Officers, from time to time, as shall be thought most meet and convenient for the general Good of the Colony; unto which we promise all due Submission and Obedience. IN WITNESS whereof we have hereunto subscribed our names at *Cape-Cod* the eleventh of *November*, in the Reign of our Sovereign Lord King *James*, of *England, France*, and *Ireland*, the eighteenth, and of *Scotland*, the fifty-fourth, *Anno Domini*, 1620.

Mr. John Carver,	Mr. Samuel Fuller,	Edward Tilly,
Mr. William Bradford,	Mr. Christopher Martin,	John Tilly,
Mr Edward Winslow,	Mr. William Mullins,	Francis Cooke,
Mr. William Brewster,	Mr. William White,	Thomas Rogers,
Isaac Allerton,	Mr. Richard Warren,	Thomas Tinker,
Myles Standish,	John Howland,	John Ridgdale,
John Alden,	Mr. Steven Hopkins,	Edward Fuller,
John Turner,	Digery Priest,	Richard Clark,
Francis Eaton,	Thomas Williams,	Richard Gardiner,
James Chilton,	Gilbert Winslow,	Mr. John Allerton,
John Craxton,	Edmund Margesson,	Thomas English,
John Billington,	Peter Brown,	Edward Doten,
Joses Fletcher,	Richard Britteridge,	Edward Liester.
John Goodman,	George Soule,	

CHARTER OF THE COLONY OF NEW PLYMOUTH GRANTED TO WILLIAM BRADFORD AND HIS ASSOCIATES—1629 b

To all to whom these presents shall come greetinge: Whereas our late sovereigne lord king James for the advancement of a collonie and plantaĉon in the cuntry called or knowne by the name of New Englande in America, by his highnes letters pattents under the

---

* William Bradford's *Plimouth Plantation*.

a The "Pilgrims" who landed at Plymouth had procured before leaving Europe a grant of land from the London or South Virginia Company, but had subsequently decided to establish a colony in New England. Before leaving the ship which had brought them across the Atlantic they drew up this compact. They obtained several successive letters-patent from the Plymouth Company, but none of them were confirmed by the Crown, and in 1691 the Plymouth colony was annexed to Massachusetts Bay.

b The compact with the Charter and Laws of the Colony of New Plymouth, &c., William Brigham, Boston; 1836. pp. 21–26.

greate seale of Englande bearinge date att Westminster the third day of November in the eighteenth yeare of his highnes raigne of England, &c. did give graunte and confirme unto the right honoble Lodowicke late lord duke of Lenox, George late marques of Buckingham, James marques Hamilton, Thomas earle of Arundell, Robert earle of Warwicke and Ferdinando Gorges, Knight, and divers others whose names are expressed in the said letters pattents and their successors that they should be one bodie pollitique and corporate perpeturely consistinge of forty persons, and that they should have perpetual succession and one common seale to serve for the said body and that they and their successors should be incorporated called and knowne by the name of the Councill established at Plymouth in the county of Devon for the planting, rulinge orderinge and governinge of New Englande in America, and alsoe of his speciall grace certaine knowledge and mure motion did give graunte and confirme unto the said presidente and councill and their successors forever under the reservations limitations and declara͡cons in the said letters pattents expressed, all that part and portion of the said country called New-England in America scituate, and lyinge and being in breadth from ffourty degrees northerly latitude from the equinoctiall line to ffourty eight degrees of the said northerly latitude inclusively, and in length of and in all the breadth aforesaide throughout the maine land from sea to sea, together alsoe with all the firme landes soyles grounds creeks inletts havens portes seas rivers islands waters fishinges mynes and mineralls as well royall mines of gold and silver as other mines and mineralls pretious stones quarries and all and singular the commodities jurisdiccons royalties privileges ffranchises and preheminences both within the said tracte of lands upon the maine, as also within the said islands and seas adioyninge: To have hold possesse and enjoy all and singuler the foresaid continente landes territories islands hereditaments and p^{r}cints sea waters fishinges with all and all manner their commodities royalties privileges preheminences and proffitts that shall arise from thence, with all and singuler their appurtenaces and every parte and parcell thereof unto the said councell and their successors and assignes forever: To be holden of his Matie, his heirs and successors as of his manno^r of East Greenwiche in the county of Kent in free and common soccage and not *in capite* nor by Knights service yeeldinge and payinge therefore to the said late king's Matie, his heires and successors the fifte parte of the oare of gold and silver which from tyme to tyme and att all tymes from the date of the said letters pattents sholbe there gotten had and obtained for and in respect of all and all manner of duties demands and services whatsoever to be done made and paid unto his said late Matie, his heirs and successors as in and by the said letters pattents amongst sundry other privileges and matters therein contained more fully and at large it doth and may appeare. Now knowe ye that the said councell by virtue and authority of his said late Ma^{ts} letters pattents and for and in considera͡con that William Bradford and his associatts have for these nine yeares lived in New Englande aforesaid and have there inhabited and planted a towne called by the name of New Plimouth att their own proper costs and charges: And now seeinge that by the speciall providence of God, and their extraordinary care and industry they have increased their planta͡con to neere three hundred people, and are uppon all occasions able to relieve any new planters or others his Ma^{ts} subjects whoe may fall uppon that coaste; have given graunted bargained sould enfeoffed allotted assigned and sett over and by these presents doe cleerly and absolutely give graunt bargaine sell alien enfeoffe allott assigne and confirme unto the said William Bradford, his heires associatts and assignes all that part of New-Englande in America aforesaid and tracte and tractes of lande that lye within or betweene a certaine rivolet or rundlett there commonly called Coahassett alias Cona hassett towards the north, and the river commonly called Naragansets river towards the south; and the great westerne ocean towards the east, and betweene and within a straight line directly extendinge upp into the maine land towards the west from the mouth of the said river called Naragansetts river to the utmost limitts and bounds of a cuntry or place in New Englande called Pokenacutt alias Sowamsett westward, and another like straight line extendinge itself directly from the mouth of the said river called Coahassett alias Cona hassett towards the west so farr upp into the maine lande westwardes as the utmost limitts of the said place or cuntry commonly called Pokencutt alias Sowamsett doe extend, together with one half of the said river called Naragansetts and the said rivolett or rundlett called Coahassett alias Conahassett and all lands rivers waters havens creeks ports fishings fowlings and all hereditaments proffitts comodities and emoluments whatsoever situate lyinge and beinge or ariseinge within or betweene the said limitts and bounds or any of them. And for as much as they have noe conveniente place either of tradinge or ffishinge within their own precints whereby (after soe longe travell and great paines,) so hopefull a plantacōn may subsiste, as alsoe that they may bee incouraged the better to proceed in soe pious a worke which may especially tend to the propagation of religion and the great increase of trade to his Ma^{ts} realmes, and advancemente of the publique plantacōn, the said councell have further given graunted bargained sold enfeoffed allotted assigned and sett over and by these presentes doe cleerly and absolutely give graunte bargaine sell alien enfeoffe allott assigne and confirme unto the said William Bradford his heires associats and assignes all that tracte of lande or parte of New England in America aforesaid wch lyeth within or betweene and extendeth itself from the utmost limitts of Cobbiseconte alias Comasee-Conte which adjoineth to the river of Kenebeke alias Kenebekike towards the westerne ocean and a place called the falls att Mequamkike in America aforesaid, and the space of fifteene Englishe miles on each side of the said river commonly called Kenebek river, and all the said river called Kenebek that lies within the said limitts and bounds eastward westward northward or southward laste above mentioned, and all lands grounds soyles rivers waters fishings hereditam^{ts} and proffitts whatsoever situate lyinge and beinge arisinge happeninge or accrueinge, or which shall arise happen or accrue in or within the said limitts and boundes or either of them together with free ingresse egresse and regresse with shipps boates shallopps and other vessels from the sea commonly called the westerne ocean to the said river called Kennebek and from the said river to the said westerne ocean, together with all prerogatives rights royalties jurisdiccōns, preveledges ffranchises liberties and guerenities, and alsoe marine liberty with the escheats and casualties thereof the Admiralty Jurisdiccōn excepted with all the interest right title claime and demande whatsoever which the said councell and their successors now have or ought to have and claime or may have and acquire hereafter in or to any the said porc̃ons or tractes of land hereby menc̃oned to be graunted, or any the premisses in as free large ample and beneficiall manner to all intents, construc̃ons and purposes whatsoever as the said councell by virtue of his Ma^{ts} said letters pattents may or can graunte; to have and to holde the said tracte and tractes of lande and all and singular the premisses above menc̃oned to be graunted with their and every of their appurtenances to the said William Bradford his heires associatts and assignes forever, to the only proper and absolute use and behoofe of the said William Bradford his heires associats and assignes forever; Yeeldinge and payinge unto our said soveraigne Lord the Kinge, his heires and successors forever one-fifte parte of the oare of the mines of gold and silver and one other fifte parte thereof to the presidente and councell, which shall be had possessed and obtained within the precints aforesaid for all services and demands whatsoever. And the said councell doe further graunt and agree to and with the said William Bradford his heires associatts and assignes and every of them, his and their ffactors agents tenants and servants and all such as hee or they shall send and employ aboute his said particular plantac̃on, shall and may from tyme to tyme ffreely and lawfully goe and returne trade and traffique as well with the Englishe as any of the natines within the precints aforesaid, with liberty of fishinge uppon any parte of the sea coaste and sea shoares of any the seas or islands adjacente and not beinge inhabited or otherwise disposed of by order of the said presidente and councell: also to importe exporte and transporte their goods and merchandize att their wills and pleasures paying only such duty to the Kings Matie, his heires and successors as the said Presidente and councell doe or ought to pay without any other taxes impositions burdens and restraints uppon them to be imposed. And further the said councell doe graunt and agree to and with the said William Bradford his heires associatts and assignes, that the persons transported by him or any of them shall not be taken away, ymployed or commanded either by the Governo^r for the tyme beinge of New Englande or by any other authority there, from the business and employmente of the said William Bradford and his associatts his heires and assignes; necessary [to the] defence of the cuntry preservac̃on of the peace suppressinge of tumults within the lands, trialls in matters of justice by appeale uppon spetiall occasion only excepted. Alsoe it shall be lawfull and free for the said William Bradford his associatts his heires and assignes att all tymes hereafter to incorporate by some usual or fitt name and title, him or themselves or the people there inhabitinge under him or them with liberty to them and their successors from tyme to tyme to frame, and make orders ordinances and constituc̃ons as well for the better governmente of their affairs here and the receavinge or admittinge any to his or their society as alsoe for the better governm^t of his or their people and affaires in New Englande or of his and their people att sea in goeinge thither, or returninge from thence, and the same to putt in execuc̃on or cause to be putt in execuc̃on by such officers and ministers as he and they shall authorize and depute: Provided that the said lawes and orders be not repugnante to the lawes of Englande, or the frame of governmente by the said

presidente and councell hereafter to be established. And further it
shall be lawfull and free for the said William Bradford, his heires
associats and assignes to transporte cattle of all kinds, alsoe powder
shot ordnance and munic͂on from tyme to tyme as shal be necessary
for their strength and safety hereafter for their several defence; to
encounter expulse repell and resiste by force of armes as well by sea
as by lande, by all waies and meanes whatsoever. And by virtue of
the authority to us derived by his said late Ma^{ts} letters pattents to
take apprehend seize and make prize of all such persons their shipps
and goods as shall attempte to inhabite or trade with the savage
people of that cuntry within the severall precincts and limitts of his
and their severall plantac͂on, or shall enterprise or attempt att any
tyme destrucc͂on invasion detriment or annoyance to his and their
said plantac͂on; the one moiety of which goods soe siezed and taken it
shal be lawfull for the said William Bradford his heires associats
and assignes to take to their own use and behoofe; the other moiety
thereof to be delivered by the said William Bradford his heires associats and assignes to such officer and officers as shalbe appointed to
receave the same for his Ma^{ts} use. And the said councell do hereby
covenante and declare that it is their intente and meaninge for the
good of this plantac͂on that the said William Bradford his associats
his or their heires or assignes shall have and enjoy whatsoever privilege or privileges of what kinde soever, as are expressed or intended
to be graunted in and by his said late Ma^{ts} letters pattents, and that in
as large and ample manner as the said councell thereby now may or
hereafter can graunte, coyninge of money excepted. And the said
councell for them and their successors doe covenante and graunte to
the said William Bradford, his heires associates and assignes by these
presents, that they the said councell shall at any time hereafter uppon
request att the only proper costs and charges of the said William
Bradford, his heires associats and assignes doe make suffer execute
and willingly consent unto any further act or actes, conveyance or
conveyances, assurance or assurances whatsoever, for the good and
perfect investinge assureinge and conveyinge and sure makinge of all
the aforesaid tracte and tractes of landes royalties mines mineralls
woods fishinges and all and singular their appurtenances, unto the
said William Bradford his heires associats and assignes as by him or
them or his or their heires or assignes, or his or their councell learned
in the law shalbe devised, advised and required. And lastly know
yee that wee the said counsell have made constituted deputed authorized and appointed Captaine Miles Standish, or in his absence Edward Winslowe, John Howlande and John Alden, or any of them to
be our true and lawful attorney and attornies jointly and severally
in our name and steed to enter into the said tracte and tractes of
lande and other the premises with their appurtenances, or into some
parte thereof in the name of the whole for us and in our names to take
possession and seisin thereof, and after such possession and seisin
thereof or of some parte thereof in the name of the whole had and
taken; then for us and in our names to deliver the full and peacable
possession and seisin of all and singular the said menc͂oned tobe
graunted premisses unto the said William Bradford his heires associatts and assignes or to his or their certaine atturney or atturnies in
that behalf ratifyinge alloweinge and confirminge all whatsoever our
said atturney doe in or about the premisses. In witness whereof, the

said councell established att Plimouth in the county of Devon for the plantinge rulinge orderinge and governinge of New England in America have hereunto putt their seale the thir teenth day of January in fifte yeare of the raigne of our Soveraigne Lord Charles by the grace of God, Kinge of Englande Scotland Fraunce and Ireland defender of the ffaithe &c. Anno Dom^i 1629.

[SEAL.]

R. WARWICKE.

THE CHARTER OF MASSACHUSETTS BAY—1629 * [a]

CHARLES, BY THE GRACE OF GOD, Kinge of England, Scotland, Fraunce, and Ireland, Defendor of the Fayth, &c. To ALL to whome theis Presents shall come Greeting. WHEREAS, our most Deare and Royall Father, Kinge James, of blessed Memory, by his Highnes Letters-patents bearing Date at Westminster the third Day of November, in the eighteenth Yeare of his Raigne, HATH given and graunted vnto the Councell established at Plymouth, in the County of Devon, for the planting, ruling, ordering, and governing of Newe England in America, and to their Successors and Assignes for ever, all that Parte of America, lyeing and being in Bredth, from Forty Degrees of Northerly Latitude from the Equinoctiall Lyne, to forty eight Degrees of the saide Northerly Latitude inclusively, and in Length, of and within all the Breadth aforesaid, throughout the Maine Landes from Sea to Sea; together also with all the Firme Landes, Soyles, Groundes, Havens, Portes, Rivers, Waters, Fishing, Mynes, and Myneralls, as well Royall Mynes of Gould and Silver, as other Mynes and Myneralls, precious Stones, Quarries, and all and singular other Comodities, Jurisdiccons, Royalties, Priviledges, Franchesies, and Prehemynences, both within the said Tract of Land vpon the Mayne, and also within the Islandes and Seas adjoining: PROVIDED alwayes, That the saide Islandes, or any the Premisses by the said Letters-patents intended and meant to be graunted, were not then actuallie possessed or inhabited, by any other Christian Prince or State, nor within the Boundes, Lymitts, or Territories of the Southerne Colony, then before graunted by our saide Deare Father, to be planted by divers of his loveing Subiects in the South Partes. To HAVE and to houlde, possess, and enioy all and singular the aforesaid Continent, Landes, Territories, Islandes, Hereditaments, and Precincts, Seas, Waters, Fishings, with all, and all manner their Comodities, Royalties, Liberties, Prehemynences, and Proffits that should from thenceforth arise from thence, with all and singuler their Appurtenances, and every Parte and Parcell thereof, vnto the saide Councell and their Successors and Assignes for ever, to the sole and proper Vse, Benefitt, and Behoofe of them the saide Councell,

---

* The Charters and General Laws of the Colony and Province of Massachusetts Bay, * * * Published by Order of the General Court, Boston, Printed and Published by T. B. Wait and Co., 1814. pp. 1–17.

[a] Lord Sheffield gave a patent in January, 1823, to the New England Company, for the location of a colony at Cape Anne. It was established, but the new settlement did not thrive, and this charter was obtained March 4, 1628–'29. The officers provided for in it were appointed at Plymouth, in England, but under a resolution adopted by the company, August 29, 1629, the seat of government was transferred to Massachusetts.

and their Successors and Asignes for ever: To be houlden of our saide most Deare and Royall Father, his Heires and Successors, as of his Mannor of East Greenewich in the County of Kent, in free and comon Soccage, and not in Capite nor by Knight's Service: YEILDINGE and paying therefore to the saide late Kinge, his heires and Successors, the fifte Parte of the Oare of Gould and Silver, which should from tyme to tyme, and at all Tymes then after happen to be found, gotten, had, and obteyned in, att, or within any of the saide Landes, Lymitts, Territories, and Precincts, or in or within any Parte or Parcell thereof, for or in Respect of all and all Manner of Duties, Demaunds anr Services whatsoever, to be don, made, or paide to our saide Dear Father the late Kinge his Heires and Successors, as in and by the saide Letters-patents (amongst sundrie and other Clauses, Powers, Priviledges, and Grauntes therein conteyned), more at large appeareth:

AND WHEREAS, the saide Councell established at Plymouth, in the County of Devon, for the plantinge, ruling, ordering, and governing of Newe England in America, have by their Deede, indented vnder their Comon Seale, bearing Date the nyneteenth Day of March last past, in the third Yeare of our Raigne, given, graunted, bargained, soulde, enfeoffed, aliened, and confirmed to Sir Henry Rosewell, Sir John Young, Knightes, Thomas Southcott, John Humphrey, John Endecott, and Symon Whetcombe, their Heires and Assignes, and their Associats for ever, all that Parte of Newe England in America aforesaid, which lyes and extendes betweene a greate River there comonlie called Monomack alias Merriemack, and a certen other River there, called Charles River, being in the Bottome of a certayne Bay there, comonlie called Massachusetts, alias Mattachusetts, alias Massatusetts Bay, and also all and singuler those Landes and Hereditaments whatsoever, lyeing within the Space of three English Myles on the South Parte of the said Charles River, or of any, or everie Parte thereof; and also, all and singuler the Landes and Hereditaments whatsoever, lyeing and being within the Space of three English Myles to the Southward of the Southermost Parte of the saide Bay called Massachusetts, alias Mattachusetts, alias Massatusets Bay; and also, all those Landes and Hereditaments whatsoever, which lye, and be within the space of three English Myles to the Northward of the said River called Monomack, alias Merrymack, or to the Northward of any and every Parte thereof, and all Landes and Hereditaments whatsoever, lyeing within the Lymitts aforesaide, North and South in Latitude and bredth, and in Length and Longitude, of and within all the Bredth aforesaide, throughout the Mayne Landes there, from the Atlantick and Westerne Sea and Ocean on the East Parte, to the South Sea on the West Parte; and all Landes and Groundes, Place and Places, Soyles, Woodes and Wood Groundes, Havens, Portes, Rivers, Waters, Fishings, and Hereditaments whatsoever, lyeing within the said Boundes and Lymitts, and everie Parte and Parcell thereof; and also, all Islandes lyeing in America aforesaide, in the saide Seas or either of them on the Westerne or Eastern Coastes or Partes of the said Tractes of Lande, by the saide Indenture mencōed to be given, graunted, bargained, sould, enfeoffed, aliened, and confirmed, or any of them; and also, all Mynes and Myneralls, as well Royall Mynes of Gould and Silver, as other Mynes and Myneralls whatsoeuer, in the saide Lands and Premisses, or any Parte thereof; and all Jurisdiccons, Rights, Royalties, Liberties, Freedomes, Ymmunities, Priviledges, Franchises, Preheminences, and Comodities whatsoever, which they, the said Councell established at Plymouth, in the County of Devon, for the planting, ruling, ordering, and governing of Newe England in America, then had, or might vse, exercise, or enjoy, in or within the saide Landes and Premisses by the saide Indenture mencōed to be given, graunted, bargained, sould, enfeoffed, and confirmed, or in or within any Parte or Parcell thereof:

To HAVE and to hould, the saide Parte of Newe England in America, which lyes and extendes and is abutted as aforesaide, and every Parte and Parcell thereof; and all the saide Islandes, Rivers, Portes, Havens, Waters, Fishings, Mynes, and Myneralls, Jurisdiccons, Franchises, Royalties, Liberties, Priviledges, Comodities, Hereditaments, and Premisses whatsoever, with the Appurtenances vnto the saide Sir Henry Rosewell, Sir John Younge, Thomas Southcott, John Humfrey, John Endecott, and Simon Whetcombe, their Heires and Assignes, and their Associatts, to the onlie proper and absolute vse and Behoofe of the said Sir Henry Rosewell, Sir John Younge, Thomas Southcott, John Humfrey, John Endecott, and Simon Whettcombe, their Heires and Assignes, and their Associatts forevermore; To BE HOULDEN of Vs, our Heires and Successors, as of our Mannor of Eastgreenwich, in the County of Kent, in free and comon Soccage, and not in Capite, nor by Knightes Service; YEILDING and payeing therefore vnto Vs, our Heires and Successors, the fifte Parte of the Oare of Goulde and Silver, which shall from Tyme to Tyme, and at all Tymes hereafter, happen to be founde, gotten, had, and obteyned in any of the saide Landes, within the saide Lymitts, or in or within any Parte thereof, for, and in Satisfaccon of all manner Duties, Demaundes, and Services whatsoever to be donn, made, or paid to Vs, our Heires or Successors, as in and by the said recited Indenture more at large maie appeare.

NOWE Knowe Yee, that Wee, at the humble Suite and Peticon of the saide Sir Henry Rosewell, Sir John Younge, Thomas Southcott, John Humfrey, John Endecott, and Simon Whetcombe, and of others whome they have associated vnto them, HAVE, for divers good Causes and consideracons, vs moveing, graunted and confirmed, and by theis Presents of our especiall Grace, certen Knowledge, and meere Mocon, doe graunt and confirme vnto the saide Sir Henry Rosewell, Sir John Younge, Thomas Southcott, John Humfrey, John Endecott, and Simon Whetcombe, and to their Associatts hereafter named; (videlicet) Sir Richard Saltonstall, Knight, Isaack Johnson, Samuel Aldersey, John Ven, Mathew Cradock, George Harwood, Increase Nowell, Richard Perry, Richard Bellingham, Nathaniell Wright, Samuel Vassall, Theophilus Eaton, Thomas Goffe, Thomas Adams, John Browne, Samuell Browne, Thomas Hutchins, William Vassall, William Pinchion, and George Foxcrofte, their Heires and Assignes, all the saide Parte of Newe England in America, lyeing and extending betweene the Boundes and Lymytts in the said recited Indenture expressed, and all Landes and Groundes, Place and Places, Soyles, Woods and Wood Groundes, Havens, Portes, Rivers, Waters, Mynes, Mineralls, Jurisdiccōns, Rightes, Royalties, Liberties, Freedomes, Immunities, Priviledges, Franchises, Preheminences, Hereditaments, and Comodities whatsoever, to them the saide Sir Henry Rosewell, Sir

John Younge, Thomas Southcott, John Humfrey, John Endecott, and Simon Whetcombe, theire Heires and Assignes, and to their Associatts, by the saide recited Indenture, given, graunted, bargayned, solde, enfeoffed, aliened, and confirmed, or mencōed, or intended thereby to be given, graunted, bargayned, sold, enfeoffed, aliened, and confirmed: To HAVE, and to hould, the saide Parte of Newe England in America, and other the Premisses hereby mencōed to be graunted and confirmed, and every Parte and Parcell thereof with the Appurtennces, to the saide Sir Henry Rosewell, Sir John Younge, Sir Richard Saltonstall, Thomas Southcott, John Humfrey, John Endecott, Simon Whetcombe, Isaack Johnson, Richard Pery, Richard Bellingham, Nathaniell Wright, Samuell Vassall, Theophilus Eaton, Thomas Goffe, Thomas Adams, John Browne, Samuel Browne, Thomas Hutchins, Samuel Aldersey, John Ven, Mathewe Cradock, George Harwood, Increase Nowell, William Vassall, William Pinchion, and George Foxcrofte, their Heires and Assignes forever, to their onlie proper and absolute Vse and Behoofe for evermore; To be holden of Vs, our Heires and Successors, as of our Mannor of Eastgreenewich aforesaid, in free and comon Socage, and not in Capite, nor by Knights Service; AND ALSO YEILDING and paying therefore to Vs, our Heires and Successors, the fifte parte onlie of all Oare of Gould and Silver, which from tyme to tyme, and att all tymes hereafter shalbe there gotten, had, or obteyned, for all Services, Exaccons and Demaundes whatsoever, according to the Tenure and Reservacon in the said recited Indenture expressed.

AND FURTHER, knowe yee, that of our more especiall Grace, certen Knowledg, and meere mocōn, Wee have given and graunted, and by theis Presents, doe for Vs, our Heires and Successors, give and graunte vnto the saide Sir Henry Rosewell, Sir John Younge, Sir Richard Saltonstall, Thomas Southcott, John Humfrey, John Endecott, Symon Whetcombe, Isaack Johnson, Samuell Aldersey, John Ven, Mathewe Cradock, George Harwood, Increase Nowell, Richard Pery, Richard Bellingham, Nathaniel Wright, Samuell Vassall, Theophilus Eaton, Thomas Goffe, Thomas Adams, John Browne, Samuell Browne, Thomas Hutchins, William Vassall, William Pinchion, and George Foxcrofte, their Heires and Assignes, all that Parte of Newe England in America, which lyes and extendes betweene a great River there, comonlie called Monomack River, alias Merrimack River, and a certen other River there, called Charles River, being in the Bottome of a certen Bay there, comonlie called Massachusetts, alias Mattachusetts, alias Massatusetts Bay; and also all and singuler those Landes and Hereditaments whatsoever, lying within the Space of Three Englishe Myles on the South Parte of the said River, called Charles River, or of any or every Parte thereof; and also all and singuler the Landes and Hereditaments whatsoever, lying and being within the Space of Three Englishe Miles to the southward of the southermost Parte of the said Baye, called Massachusetts, alias Mattachusetts, alias Massatusets Bay: And also all those Landes and Hereditaments whatsoever, which lye and be within the Space of Three English Myles to the Northward of the saide River, called Monomack, alias Merrymack, or to the Norward of any and every Parte thereof, and all Landes and Hereditaments whatsoever, lyeing within the Lymitts aforesaide, North and South, in Latitude and Bredth, and in Length and Longitude, of and within all the Bredth aforesaide, throughout the mayne Landes there, from the Atlantick and Westerne Sea and Ocean on the East Parte, to the South Sea on the West Parte; and all Landes and Groundes, Place and Places, Soyles, Woodes, and Wood Groundes, Havens, Portes, Rivers, Waters, and Hereditaments whatsoever, lyeing within the said Boundes and Lymytts, and every Parte and Parcell thereof; and also all Islandes in America aforesaide, in the saide Seas, or either of them, on the Westerne or Easterne Coastes, or Partes of the saide Tracts of Landes hereby mencōed to be given and graunted, or any of them; and all Mynes and Mynerals as well Royal mynes of Gold and Silver and other mynes and mynerals, whatsoever, in the said Landes and Premisses, or any parte thereof, and free Libertie of fishing in or within any the Rivers or Waters within the Boundes and Lymytts aforesaid, and the Seas therevnto adjoining; and all Fishes, Royal Fishes, Whales, Balan, Sturgions, and other Fishes of what Kinde or Nature soever, that shall at any time hereafter be taken in or within the saide Seas or Waters, or any of them, by the said Sir Henry Rosewell, Sir John Younge, Sir Richard Saltonstall, Thomas Southcott, John Humfrey, John Endecott, Simon Whetcombe, Isaack Johnson, Samuell Aldersey, John Ven, Mathewe Cradock, George Harwood, Increase Noell, Richard Pery, Richard Bellingham, Nathaniell Wright, Samuell Vassell, Theophilus Eaton, Thomas Goffe, Thomas Adams, John Browne, Samuell Browne; Thomas Hutchins, William Vassall, William Pinchion, and George Foxcrofte, their Heires and Assignes, or by any other person or persons whatsoever there inhabiting, by them, or any of them, to be appointed to fishe therein.

PROVIDED alwayes, That yf the said Landes, Islandes, or any other the Premisses herein before mencōned, and by theis presents, intended and meant to be graunted, were at the tyme of the graunting of the saide former Letters patents, dated the Third Day of November, in the Eighteenth Yeare of our said deare Fathers Raigne aforesaide, actuallie possessed or inhabited by any other Christian Prince or State, or were within the Boundes, Lymytts or Territories of that Southerne Colony, then before graunted by our said late Father, to be planted by divers of his loveing Subiects in the south partes of America, That then this present Graunt shall not extend to any such partes or parcells thereof, soe formerly inhabited, or lyeing within the Boundes of the Southerne Plantacōn as aforesaide, but as to those partes or parcells soe possessed or inhabited by such Christian Prince or State, or being within the Bounders aforesaide shal be vtterlie voyd, theis presents or any Thinge therein conteyned to the contrarie notwithstanding. To HAVE and hould, possesse and enioye the saide partes of New England in America, which lye, extend, and are abutted as aforesaide, and every parte and parcell thereof; and all the Islandes, Rivers, Portes, Havens, Waters, Fishings, Fishes, Mynes, Myneralls, Jurisdiccōns, Franchises, Royalties, Liberties, Priviledges, Comōdities, and Premisses whatsoever, with the Appurtenances, vnto the said Sir Henry Rosewell, Sir John Younge, Sir Richard Saltonstall, Thomas Southcott, John Humfrey, John Endecott, Simon Whetcombe, Isaack Johnson, Samuell Aldersey, John Ven, Mathewe Cradock, George Harwood, Increase Nowell, Richard Perry, Richard Bellingham, Nathaniell Wright, Samuell Vassell, Theophilus Eaton, Thomas Goffe, Thomas Adams, John Browne, Samuell Browne,

Thomas Hutchins, William Vassall, William Pinchion, and George Foxcroft, their Heires and Assignes forever, to the onlie proper and absolute Vse and Behoufe of the said Sir Henry Rosewell, Sir John Younge, Sir Richard Saltonstall, Thomas Southcott, John Humfrey, John Endecott, Simon Whetcombe, Isaac Johnson, Samuell Aldersey, John Ven, Mathewe Cradocke, George Harwood, Increase Nowell, Richard Pery, Richard Bellingham, Nathaniell Wright, Samuell Vassall, Theophilus Eaton, Thomas Goffe, Thomas Adams, John Browne, Samuell Browne, Thomas Hutchins, William Vassall, William Pinchion, and George Foxcroft, their Heires and Assignes forevermore: To BE HOLDEN of Vs, our Heires and Successors, as of our Manor of Eastgreenwich in our Countie of Kent, within our Realme of England, in free and comon Soccage, and not in Capite, nor by Knights Service; and also yeilding and paying therefore, to Vs, our Heires and Sucessors, the fifte Parte onlie of all Oare of Gould and Silver, which from tyme to tyme, and at all tymes hereafter, shal be there gotten, had, or obteyned, for all Services, Exaccons, and Demaundes whatsoever; PROVIDED alwaies, and our expresse Will and Meaninge is, that onlie one fifte Parte of the Gould and Silver Oare above mencõed, in the whole, and noe more be reserved or payeable vnto Vs, our Heires and Successors, by Collour or Vertue of theis Presents, the double Reservacõns or rentals aforesaid or any Thing herein conteyned notwithstanding. AND FORASMUCH, as the good and prosperous Successe of the Plantacon of the saide Partes of Newe-England aforesaide intended by the said Sir Henry Rosewell, Sir John Younge, Sir Richard Saltonstall, Thomas Southcott, John Humfrey, John Endecott, Simon Whetcombe, Isaack Johnson, Samuell Aldersey, John Ven, Mathew Cradock, George Harwood, Increase Noell, Richard Pery, Richard Bellingham, Nathaniell Wright, Samuell Vassall, Theophilus Eaton, Thomas Goffe, Thomas Adams, John Browne, Samuell Browne, Thomas Hutchins, William Vassall, William Pinchion, and George Foxcrofte, to be speedily sett vpon, cannot but cheifly depend, next vnder the Blessing of Almightie God, and the support of our Royall Authoritie vpon the good Government of the same, To the Ende that the Affaires and Buyssinesses which from tyme to tyme shall happen and arise concerning the saide Landes, and the Plantation of the same maie be the better mannaged and ordered, WEE HAVE FURTHER hereby of our especial Grace, certain Knowledge and mere Mocõn, Given, graunted and confirmed, and for Vs, our Heires and Successors, doe give, graunt, and confirme vnto our said trustie and welbeloved subiects Sir Henry Rosewell, Sir John Younge, Sir Richard Saltonstall, Thomas Southcott, John Humfrey, John Endicott, Simon Whetcombe, Isaack Johnson, Samuell Aldersey, John Ven, Mathewe Cradock, George Harwood, Increase Nowell, Richard Pery, Richard Bellingham, Nathaniell Wright, Samuell Vassall, Theophilus Eaton, Thomas Goffe, Thomas Adams, John Browne, Samuell Browne, Thomas Hutchins, William Vassall, William Pinchion, and George Foxcrofte: AND for Vs, our Heires and Successors, Wee will and ordeyne, That the saide Sir Henry Rosewell, Sir John Young, Sir Richard Saltonstall, Thomas Southcott, John Humfrey, John Endicott, Symon Whetcombe, Isaack Johnson, Samuell Aldersey, John Ven, Mathewe Cradock, George Harwood, Increase Noell, Richard Pery, Richard Bellingham, Nathaniell Wright, Samuell Vassall, Theophilus Eaton, Thomas Goffe,

Thomas Adams, John Browne, Samuell Browne, Thomas Hutchins, William Vassall, William Pinchion, and George Foxcrofte, and all such others as shall hereafter be admitted and made free of the Company and Society hereafter mencōed, shall from tyme to tyme, and att all tymes forever hereafter be, by Vertue of theis presents, one Body corporate and politique in Fact and Name, by the Name of the Governor and Company of the Mattachusetts Bay in Newe-England, and them by the Name of the Governour and Company of the Mattachusetts Bay in Newe-England, one Bodie politique and corporate, in Deede, Fact, and Name; Wee doe for vs, our Heires and Successors, make, ordeyne, constitute, and confirme by theis Presents, and that by that name they shall have perpetuall Succession, and that by the same Name they and their Successors shall and maie be capeable and enabled aswell to implead, and to be impleaded, and to prosecute, demaund, and aunswere, and be aunsweared vnto, in all and singuler Suites, Causes, Quarrells, and Accons, of what kinde or nature soever. And also to have, take, possesse, acquire, and purchase any Landes, Tenements, or Hereditaments, or any Goodes or Chattells, and the same to lease, graunte, demise, alien, bargaine, sell, and dispose of, as other our liege People of this our Realme of England, or any other corporacon or Body politique of the same may lawfully doe.

AND FURTHER, That the said Governour and Companye, and their Successors, maie have forever one comon Seale, to be vsed in all Causes and Occasions of the said Company, and the same Seale may alter, chaunge, breake, and newe make, from tyme to tyme, at their pleasures. And our Will and Pleasure is, and Wee doe hereby for Vs, our Heires and Successors, ordeyne and graunte, That from henceforth for ever, there shalbe one Governor, one Deputy Governor, and eighteene Assistants of the same Company, to be from tyme to tyme constituted, elected and chosen out of the Freemen of the saide Company, for the twyme being, in such Manner and Forme as hereafter in theis Presents is expressed, which said Officers shall applie themselves to take Care for the best disposeing and ordering of the generall buysines and Affaires of, for, and concerning the said Landes and Premisses hereby mencōed, to be graunted, and the Plantacion thereof, and the Government of the People there. AND FOR the better Execucon of our Royall Pleasure and Graunte in this Behalf, WEE doe, by theis presents, for Vs, our Heires and Successors, nominate, ordeyne, make, & constitute; our welbeloved the saide Mathewe Cradocke, to be the first and present Governor of the said Company, and the saide Thomas Goffe, to be Deputy Governor of the saide Company, and the saide Sir Richard Saltonstall, Isaack Johnson, Samuell Aldersey, John Ven, John Humfrey, John Endecott, Simon Whetcombe, Increase Noell, Richard Pery, Nathaniell Wright, Samuell Vassall, Theophilus Eaton, Thomas Adams, Thomas Hutchins, John Browne, George Foxcrofte, William Vassall, and William Pinchion, to be the present Assistants of the saide Company, to continue in the saide several Offices respectivelie for such tyme, and in such manner, as in and by theis Presents is hereafter declared and appointed.

AND FURTHER, Wee will, and by theis Presents, for Vs, our Heires and Successors, doe ordeyne and graunte, That the Governor of the saide Company for the tyme being, or in his Absence by Occasion of Sicknes or otherwise, the Deputie Governor for the tyme being, shall have Authoritie from tyme to tyme vpon all Occasions, to give order for the assembling of the saide Company, and calling them together to consult and advise of the Bussinesses and Affaires of the saide Company, and that the said Governor, Deputie Governor, and Assistants of the saide Company, for the tyme being, shall or maie once every Moneth, or oftener at their Pleasures, assemble and houlde and keepe a Courte or Assemblie of themselves, for the better ordering and directing of their Affaires, and that any seaven or more persons of the Assistants, togither with the Governor, or Deputie Governor soe assembled, shalbe saide, taken, held, and reputed to be, and shalbe a full and sufficient Courte or Assemblie of the said Company, for the handling, ordering, and dispatching of all such Buysinesses and Occurrents as shall from tyme to tyme happen, touching or concerning the said Company or Plantacon; and that there shall or maie be held and kept by the Governor, or Deputie Governor of the said Company, and seaven or more of the said Assistants for the tyme being, vpon every last Wednesday in Hillary, Easter, Trinity, and Michas Termes respectivelie forever, one greate generall and solempe assemblie, which foure generall assemblies shalbe stiled and called the foure greate and generall Courts of the saide Company; IN all and every, or any of which saide greate and generall Courts soe assembled, WEE DOE for Vs, our Heires and Successors, give and graunte to the said Governor and Company, and their Successors, That the Governor, or in his absence, the Deputie Governor of the saide Company for the tyme being, and such of the Assistants and Freeman of the saide Company as shalbe present, or the greater number of them so assembled, whereof the Governor or Deputie Governor and six of the Assistants at the least to be seaven, shall have full Power and authoritie to choose, nominate, and appointe, such and soe many others as they shall thinke fitt, and that shall be willing to accept the same, to be free of the said Company and Body, and them into the same to admitt; and to elect and constitute such Officers as they shall thinke fitt and requisite, for the ordering, mannaging, and dispatching of the Affaires of the saide Govenor and Company, and their Successors; And to make Lawes and Ordinnces for the Good and Welfare of the saide Company, and for the Government and ordering of the saide Landes and Plantacõn, and the People inhabiting and to inhabite the same, as to them from tyme to tyme shalbe thought meete, soe as such Lawes and Ordinances be not contrarie or repugnant to the Lawes and Statuts of this our Realme of England. AND, our Will and Pleasure is, and Wee doe hereby for Vs, our Heires and Successors, establish and ordeyne, That yearely once in the yeare, for ever hereafter, namely, the last Wednesday in Easter Tearme, yearely, the Governor, Deputy-Governor, and Assistants of the saide Company and all other officers of the saide Company shalbe in the Generall Court or Assembly to be held for that Day or Tyme, newly chosen for the Yeare ensueing by such greater parte of the said Company, for the Tyme being, then and there present, as is aforesaide. AND, yf it shall happen the present governor, Deputy Governor, and assistants, by theis presents appointed, or such as shall hereafter be newly chosen into their Roomes, or any of them, or any other of the officers to be appointed for the said Company, to dye, or to be removed from his or their severall Offices or Places before the saide generall Day of Elecčõn (whome Wee doe hereby declare for any Misdemeanor or Defect to be removeable by the Governor, Deputie Governor, Assistants, and Company, or such greater Parte of them in any of the publique Courts to be assembled as is aforesaid) That then, and in every such Case, it shall and maie be lawfull, to and for the Governor, Deputie Governor, Assistants, and Company aforesaide, or such greater Parte of them soe to be assembled as is aforesaide, in any of their Assemblies, to proceade to a new Eleccõn of one or more others of their Company in the Roome or Place, Roomes or Places of such Officer or Officers soe dyeing or removed according to their Discrecons, And, ymediately vpon and after such Eleccõn and Eleccõns made of such Governor, Deputie Governor, Assistant or Assistants, or any other officer of the saide Company, in Manner and Forme aforesaid, the Authoritie, Office, and Power, before given to the former Governor, Deputie Governor, or other Officer and Officers soe removed, in whose Steade and Place newe shabe soe chosen, shall as to him and them, and everie of them, cease and determine

PROVIDED alsoe, and our Will and Pleasure is, That aswell such as are by theis Presents appointed to be the present Governor, Deputie Governor, and Assistants of the said Company, as those that shall succeed them, and all other Officers to be appointed and chosen as aforesaid, shall, before they vndertake the Execucon of their saide Offices and Places respectivelie, take their Corporal Oathes for the due and faithfull Performance of their Duties in their severall Offices and Places, before such Person or Persons as are by theis Presents herevnder appointed to take and receive the same; That is to saie, the saide Mathewe Cradock, whoe is hereby nominated and appointed the present Governor of the saide Company, shall take the saide Oathes before one or more of the Masters of our Courte of Chauncery for the Tyme being, vnto which Master or Masters of the Chauncery, Wee doe by theis Presents give full Power and Authoritie to take and administer the said Oathe to the said Governor accordinglie: And after the saide Governor shalbe soe sworne, then the said Deputy Governor and Assistants, before by theis Presents nominated and appointed, shall take the said severall Oathes to their Offices and Places respectivelie belonging, before the said Mathew Cradock, the present Governor, soe formerlie sworne as aforesaide. And every such person as shallbe at the Tyme of the annuall Eleccon, or otherwise, vpon Death or Removeall, be appointed to be the newe Governor of the said Company, shall take the Oathes to that Place belonging, before the Deputy Governor, or two of the Assistants of the said Company at the least, for the Tyme being: And the newe elected Deputie Governor and Assistants, and all other officers to be hereafter chosen as aforesaide from Tyme to Tyme, to take the Oathes to their places respectivelie belonging, before the Governor of the said Company for the Tyme being, vnto which said Governor, Deputie Governor, and assistants, Wee doe by theis Presents give full Power and Authoritie to give and administer the said Oathes respectively, according to our true Meaning herein before declared, without any Comission or further Warrant to be had and obteyned of our Vs, our Heires or Successors, in that Behalf. AND, Wee doe further, of our especial Grace, certen Knowledge, and meere mocon, for Vs, our Heires and Successors, give and graunte to the said Governor and Company, and their Successors for ever by theis Presents, That it shalbe lawfull and free for them and their Assignes, at all and every

Tyme and Tymes hereafter, out of any our Realmes or Domynions whatsoever, to take, leade, carry, and transport, for in and into their Voyages, and for and towardes the said Plantacon in Newe England, all such and soe many of our loving Subjects, or any other strangers that will become our loving Subjects, and live under our Allegiance, as shall willinglie accompany them in the same Voyages and Plantacon; and also Shipping, Armour, Weapons, Ordinance, Municon, Powder, Shott, Corne, Victualls, and all Manner of Clothing, Implements, Furniture, Beastes, Cattle, Horses, Mares, Merchandizes, and all other Thinges necessarie for the saide Plantacõn, and for their Vse and Defence, and for Trade with the People there, and in passing and returning to and fro, any Lawe or Statute to the contrarie hereof in any wise notwithstanding; and without payeing or yeilding any Custome or Subsidie, either inward or outward, to Vs, our Heires or Successors, for the same, by the Space of seaven Yeares from the Day of the Date of theis Presents. PROVIDED, that none of the saide Persons be such as shalbe hereafter by especiall Name restrayned by Vs, our Heires or Successors. AND, for their further Encouragement, of our especiall Grace and Favor, Wee doe by theis Presents, for Vs, our Heires and Successors, yeild and graunt to the saide Governor and Company, and their Successors, and every of them, their Factors and Assignes, That they and every of them shalbe free and quitt from all Taxes, Subsidies, and Customes, in Newe England, for the like Space of seaven Yeares, and from all Taxes and Imposicons for the Space of twenty and one Yeares, vpon all Goodes and Merchandizes at any Tyme or Tymes hereafter, either vpon Importacõn thither, or Exportacõn from thence into our Realme of England, or into any other our Domynions by the said Governor and Company, and their Successors, their Deputies, Factors, and Assignes, or any of them; EXCEPT onlie the five Pounds per Centum due for Custome vpon all such Goodes and Merchandizes as after the saide seaven Yeares shalbe expired, shalbe brought or imported into our Realme of England, or any other of our Dominions, according to the aunciente Trade of Merchants, which five Poundes per Centum onlie being paide, it shall be thenceforth lawfull and free for the said Adventurers, the same Goodes and Merchandizes to export and carry out of our said Domynions into forraine Partes, without any Custome, Tax, or other Dutie to be paid to Vs, our Heires or Successors, or to any other Officers or Ministers of Vs, our Heires and Successors. PROVIDED, that the said Goodes and Merchandizes be shipped out within thirteene Monethes, after their first Landing within any Parte of the saide Domynions.

AND, Wee doe for Vs, our Heires and Successors, give and graunte vnto the saide Governor and Company, and their Successors, That whensoever, or soe often as any Custome or Subsedie shall growe due or payeable vnto Vs, our Heires, or Successors, according to the Lymittacon and Appointment aforesaide, by Reason of any Goodes, Wares, or Merchandizes to be shipped out, or any Retorne to be made of any Goodes, Wares, or Merchandize vnto or from the said Partes of Newe England hereby moncõed to be graunted as aforesaid, or any the Landes or Territories aforesaide, That then, and soe often, and in such Case, the Farmors, Customers, and Officers of our Customes of England and Ireland, and everie of them for the Tyme being, vpon Request made to them by the saide Governor and Company, or their

Successors, Factors, or Assignes, and vpon convenient Security to be given in that Behalf, shall give and allowe vnto the said Governor and Company, and their Successors, and to all and everie Person and Persons free of that Company, as aforesaide, six Monethes Tyme for the Payement of the one halfe of all such Custome and Subsidy as shalbe due and payeable vnto Vs, our Heires and Successors, for the same; for which theis our Letters patent, or the Duplicate, or the inrollem^t thereof, shalbe vnto our saide Officers a sufficient Warrant and Discharge. NEVERTHELES, our Will and Pleasure is, That yf any of the saide Goodes, Wares, and Merchandize, which be, or shalbe at any Tyme hereafter landed or exported out of any of our Realmes aforesaide, and shalbe shipped with a Purpose not to be carried to the Partes of Newe England aforesaide, but to some other place, That then such Payment, Dutie, Custome, Imposicõn, or Forfeyture, shalbe paid, or belonge to Vs, our Heires and Successors, for the said Goodes, Wares, and Merchandize, soe fraudulently sought to be transported, as yf this our Graunte had not been made nor graunted. AND, Wee doe further will, and by theis Presents, for Vs, our Heires and Successors, firmlie enioine and comaunde, as well the Treasorer, Chauncellor and Barons of the Exchequer, of Vs, our Heires and Successors, as also all and singuler the Customers, Farmors, and Collectors of the Customes, Subsidies, and Imposts, and other the Officers and Ministers of Vs, our Heires and Successors whatsoever, for the Tyme Being, That they and every of them, vpon the shewing forth vnto them of theis Letters patents, or the Duplicate or exemplificacõn of the same, without any other Writt or Warrant whatsoever from Vs, our Heires or Successors, to be obteyned or sued forth, doe and shall make full, whole, entire, and due Allowance, and cleare Discharge vnto the saide Governor and Company, and their Successors, of all Customes, Subsidies, Imposicõns, Taxes and Duties whatsoever, that shall or maie be claymed by Vs, our Heires and Successors, of or from the said Governor and Company, and their Successors, for or by Reason of the said Goodes, Chattels, Wares, Merchandizes, and Premises to be exported out of our saide Domynions, or any of them, into any Parte of the saide Landes or Premises hereby mencõed, to be given, graunted, and confirmed, or for, or by Reason of any of the saide Goodes, Chattells, Wares, or Merchandizes to be imported from the said Landes and Premises hereby mencõed, to be given, graunted, and confirmed into any of our saide Dominions, or any Parte thereof as aforesaide, excepting onlie the saide five Poundes per Centum hereby reserved and payeable after the Expiracõn of the saide Terme of seaven Yeares as aforesaid, and not before: And theis our Letters-patents, or the Inrollment, Duplicate, or Exemplificacõn of the same shalbe for ever hereafter, from time to tyme, as well to the Treasorer, Chauncellor and Barons of the Exchequer of Vs, our Heires and Successors, as to all and singuler the Customers, Farmors, and Collectors of the Customes, Subsidies, and Imposts of Vs, our Heires and Successors, and all Searchers, and other the Officers and Ministers whatsoever of Vs, our Heires and Successors, for the Time being, a sufficient Warrant and Discharge in this Behalf.

AND, further our Will and Pleasure is, and Wee doe hereby for Vs, our Heires and Successors, ordeyne and declare, and graunte to the saide Governor and Company, and their Successors, That all and every the Subiects of Vs, our Heires or Successors, which shall goe to and inhabite within the saide Landes and Premisses hereby mencōed to be graunted, and every of their Children which shall happen to be borne there, or on the Seas in goeing thither, or retorning from thence, shall have and enjoy all liberties and Immunities of free and naturall Subiects within any of the Domynions of Vs, our Heires or Successors, to all Intents, Construccōns, and Purposes whatsoever, as yf they and everie of them were borne within the Realme of England. And that the Governor and Deputie Governor of the said Company for the Tyme being, or either of them, and any two or more of such of the saide Assistants as shalbe therevnto appointed by the saide Governor and Company at any of their Courts or Assemblies to be held as aforesaide, shall and maie at all Tymes, and from tyme to tyme hereafter, have full Power and Authoritie to minister and give the Oathe and Oathes of Supremacie and Allegiance, or either of them, to all and everie Person and Persons, which shall at any Tyme or Tymes hereafter goe or passe to the Landes and Premisses hereby mencōed to be graunted to inhabite in the same. AND, Wee doe of our further Grace, certen Knowledg and meere Mocōn, give and graunte to the saide Governor and Company, and their Successors, That it shall and maie be lawfull, to and for the Governor or Deputie Governor, and such of the Assistants and Freemen of the said Company for the Tyme being as shalbe assembled in any of their generall Courts aforesaide, or in any other Courtes to be specially sumoned and assembled for that Purpose, or the greater Parte of them (whereof the Governor or Deputie Governor, and six of the Assistants to be alwaies seaven) from tyme to tyme, to make, ordeine, and establishe all Manner of wholesome and reasonable Orders, Lawes, Statutes, and Ordiñnces, Direccōns, and Instruccōns, not contrairie to the Lawes of this our Realme of England, aswell for setling of the Formes and Ceremonies of Governm^t and Magistracy, fitt and necessary for the said Plantacōn, and the Inhabitants there, and for nameing and setting of all sorts of Officers, both superior and inferior, which they shall finde needefull for that Governement and Plantacon, and the distinguishing and setting forth of the severall duties, Powers, and Lymytts of every such Office and Place, and the Formes of such Oathes warrantable by the Lawes and Statutes of this our Realme of England, as shalbe respectivelie ministred vnto them for the Execucōn of the said severall Offices and Places; as also, for the disposing and ordering of the Eleccōns of such of the said Officers as shalbe annuall, and of such others as shalbe to succeede in Case of Death or Removeall, and ministring the said Oathes to the newe elected Officers, and for Imposicons of lawfull Fynes, Mulcts, Imprisonment, or other lawfull Correccōn, according to the Course of other Corporacons in this our Realme of England, and for the directing, ruling, and disposeing of all other Matters and Thinges, whereby our said People, Inhabitants there, may be soe religiously, peaceablie, and civilly governed, as their good Life and orderlie Conversacon, maie wynn and incite the Natives of Country, to the Knowledg and Obedience of the onlie true God and Sauior of Mankinde, and the Christian Fayth, which in our Royall Intencon, and the Adventurers free Profession, is the principall Ende of this Plantacion. WILLING, comaunding, and requiring, and by theis Presents for Vs, our Heires, and Successors, ordeyning and appointing, that all such Orders, Lawes, Statuts and Ordinnces, Instruccons and Direccõns, as shalbe soe made by the Governor, or Deputie Governor of the said Company, and such of the Assistants and Freemen as aforesaide, and published in Writing, vnder their comõn Seale, shalbe carefullie and dulie observed, kept, performed, and putt in Execucõn, according to the true Intent and Meaning of the same; and theis our Letters-patents, or the Duplicate or exemplificacõn thereof, shalbe to all and everie such Officers, superior and inferior, from Tyme to Tyme, for the putting of the same Orders, Lawes, Statutes, and Ordinnces, Instruccõns, and Direccõns, in due Execucõn against Vs, our Heires and Successors, a sufficient Warrant and Discharge.

AND WEE DOE further, for Vs, our Heires and Successors, give and graunt to the said Governor and Company, and their Successors by theis Presents, that all and everie such Chiefe Comaunders, Captaines, Governors, and other Officers and Ministers, as by the said Orders, Lawes, Statuts, Ordiñnces, Instruccõns, or Direccõns of the said Governor and Company for the Tyme being, shalbe from Tyme to Tyme hereafter ymploied either in the Government of the saide Inhabitants and Plantacõn, or in the Waye by Sea thither, or from thence, according to the Natures and Lymitts of their Offices and Places respectively, shall from Tyme to Tyme hereafter for ever, within the Precincts and Partes of Newe England hereby mencõed to be graunted and confirmed, or in the Waie by Sea thither, or from thence, have full and Absolute Power and Authoritie to correct, punishe, pardon, governe, and rule all such the Subiects of Vs, our Heires and Successors, as shall from Tyme to Tyme adventure themselves in any Voyadge thither or from thence, or that shall at any Tyme hereafter, inhabite within the Precincts and Partes of Newe England aforasaid, according to the Orders, Lawes, Ordiñnces, Instruccõns, and Direccõns aforesaid, not being repugnant to the Lawes and Statutes of our Realme of England as aforesaid. AND WEE DOE further, for Vs, our Heires and Successors, give and graunte to the said Governor and Company, and their Successors, by theis Presents, that it shall and maie be lawfull, to and for the Chiefe Comaunders, Governors, and officers of the said Company for the Time being, who shalbe resident in the said Parte of Newe England in America, by theis Presents graunted, and others there inhabiting by their Appointment and Direccon, from Tyme to Tyme, and at all Tymes hereafter for their speciall Defence and Safety, to incounter, expulse, repell, and resist by Force of Armes, aswell by Sea as by Lande, and by all fitting Waies and Meanes whatsoever, all such Person and Persons, as shall at any Tyme hereafter, attempt or enterprise the Destruccõn, Invasion, Detriment, or Annoyaunce to the said Plantation or Inhabitants, and to take and surprise by all Waies and Meanes whatsoever, all and every such Person and Persons, with their Shippes, Armour, Municõn, and other Goodes, as shall in hostile manner invade or attempt the defeating of the said Plantacon, or the Hurt of the said Company and Inhabitants: NEVERTHELES, our Will and Pleasure is, and Wee doe hereby declare to all Christian Kinges, Princes and States, that yf any Person or Persons which shall hereafter be of the said Company or Plantacõn, or any other by Lycense or Appointment of the said Governor and Company

for the Tyme being, shall at any Tyme or Tymes hereafter, robb or
spoyle, by Sea or by Land, or doe any Hurt, Violence, or vnlawful
Hostilitie to any of the Subjects of Vs, our Heires or Successors, or
any of the Subjects of any Prince or State, being then in League and
Amytie with Vs, our Heires and Successors, and that upon such
injury don and vpon iust Complaint of such Prince or State or their
Subjects, WEE, our Heires and Successors shall make open Proclamacõn within any of the Partes within our Realme of England,
comõdious for that purpose, that the Person or Persons haveing
comĩtted any such Roberie or Spoyle, shall within the Terme lymytted
by such a Proclamacon, make full Restitucõn or Satisfaccõn of all
such Iniureis don, soe as the said Princes or others so complayning,
maie hould themselves fullie satisfied and contented; and that yf the
said Person or Persons, haveing comĩtted such Robbery or Spoile,
shall not make, or cause to be made Satisfaccõn accordinglie, within
such Tyme soe to be lymytted, that then it shalbe lawfull for Vs, our
Heires and Successors, to putt the said Person or Persons out of our
Allegiance and Proteccõn, and that it shalbe lawfull and free for all
Princes to prosecute with Hostilitie, the said Offendors, and every of
them, their and every of their Procurers, Ayders, Abettors, and Comforters in that Behalf: PROVIDED also, and our expresse Will and
Pleasure is, And Wee doe by theis Presents for Vs, our Heires and
Successors ordeyne and appoint That theis Presents shall not in any
manner envre, or be taken to abridge, barr, or hinder any of our loving subjects whatsoever, to vse and exercise the Trade of Fishing
vpon that Coast of New England in America, by theis Presents
mencõed to be graunted. But that they, and every, or any of them,
shall have full and free Power and Liberty to continue and vse their
said Trade of Fishing vpon the said Coast, in any the Seas therevnto
adioyning, or any Armes of the Seas or Saltwater Rivers where they
have byn wont to fishe, and to build and sett vp vpon the Landes by
theis Presents graunted, such Wharfes, Stages, and Workehouses as
shalbe necessarie for the salting, drying, keeping, and packing vp of
their Fish, to be taken or gotten vpon that Coast; and to cutt down,
and take such Trees and other Materialls there groweing, or being, or
shalbe needefull for that Purpose, and for all other necessarie Easements, Helpes, and Advantage concerning their said Trade of Fishing
there, in such Manner and Forme as they have byn heretofore at any
tyme accustomed to doe, without making any wilfull Waste or Spoyle,
any Thing in theis Presents conteyned to the contrarie notwithstanding. AND WEE DOE further, for Vs, our Heires and Successors, ordeyne and graunte to the said Governor and Company, and their
Successors by theis Presents that theis our Letters-patents shalbe
firme, good, effectuall, and availeable in all Thinges, and to all Intents and Construccõns of Lawe, according to our true Meaning
herein before declared, and shalbe construed, reputed, and adiudged
in all Cases most favourablie on the Behalf, and for the Benefitt and
Behoofe of the saide Governor and Company and their Successors:
ALTHOUH expresse mencõn of the true yearely Value or certenty of
the Premĩsses or any of them, or of any other Guiftes or Grauntes,
by Vs, or any of our Progenitors or Predecessors to the foresaid Governor or Company before this tyme made, in theis Presents is not
made; or any Statute, Acte, Ordiñnce, Provision, Proclamacõn, or

Restrainte to the contrarie thereof, heretofore had, made, published, ordeyned, or provided, or any other Matter, Cause, or Thinge whatsoever to the contrarie thereof in any wise notwithstanding.

IN WITNES whereof, Wee have caused theis our Letters to be made Patents.

WITNES ourself, at Westminster, the fourth day of March, in the fourth Yeare of our Raigne.

Per Breve de Privato Sigillo,

Wolseley.

Praedictus Matthaeus Cradocke Juratus est de Fide et Obedientia Regi et Successoribus suis, et de Debita Executione Officii Guberatoris Juxta Tenorem Praesentium, 18° Martii, 1628. Coram me Carolo Casare Milite in Cancellaria Mro.

CHAR. CÆSAR.

The Great Seal of England appendant by a parti-coloured silk string.

THE ACT OF SURRENDER OF THE GREAT CHARTER OF NEW ENGLAND TO HIS MAJESTY—1635 *

To all Christian People to whom this present writing shall come: The President and Council established at Plymouth in the County of Devon, for planting, ruling, and governing of New England in America, send Greeting, in our Lord God everlasting.

Whereas our late Sovereign Lord King James, of ever blessed memory, by his Highness Letters Patent under the Great Seal of England, bearing date at Westminster, the third day of November, in the eighteenth year of his Majesty's reign of England, France, and Ireland, and of Scotland the four and fiftieth: Upon the motives, reasons, and causes in the said Letters Patents mentioned and contained, did for him, his heirs, and successors, grant, ordain, establish, and confirm his then right trusty and right well beloved Cousins and Councillors Lodowick then Duke of Lenox, Lord Steward of his Household, George then Marquess of Buckingham then High Admiral of England, James then Marquess of Hamilton, William then Earl of Pembroke and then Lord Chamberlaine of his Household, who are since deceased; Thomas, now Earl of Arundell, and divers others of his Nobility and Gentry of this realme of England, therein named, to be the first and present Councill established at Plymouth aforesaid, for the planting, ruling, and governing of New England in America aforesaid: And then the said then Duke of Lenox, Marquess of Buckingham, Marquess of Hamilton, Earl of Pembroke, and Earl of Arundel, and the said others of the Nobility and Gentry therein named, and the survivors of them and their successors, to be

---

* Verified by "The Compact with the Charter and Laws of the Colony of New Plymouth: together with the Charter of the Council at Plymouth," and an Appendix, containing the Articles of Confederation of the United Colonies of New England and other valuable Documents. Published agreeably to a Resolve passed April 5, 1836, under the supervision of William Brigham, Counsellor at Law. Boston: Dutton and Wentworth, Printers to the State, Nos. 10 and 12 Exchange Street. 1836."

elected as in the said Letters Patents is expressed, did by the said Letters Patents incorporate, erect, ordain, name, constitute, and establish to be one body politick and corporate, in Deed and Name, by the Name of the Council of Plymouth aforesaid, in the said County of Devon, for the planting, ruling, and governing of New England in America aforesaid, To have perpetual succession, with divers other powers, priviledges, immunities, provisions, and restrictions, for the propagation and establishing of true Religion in those parts, and for the better regulating of the same plantations, as in and by the said Letters Patents, do Reference Thereunto had more plainly and at large appeareth. Now Know ye that, the said President and Council, for divers good causes and considerations them thereunto moving, have given, granted, assigned, yielded up, and surrendered, and by these presents do give, grant, assign, yield up and surrender unto our most gracious Sovereign Lord Charles by the Grace of God, King of England, Scotland, France and Ireland, Defender of the Faith, the said Letters Patents to the Duke of Lenox, Marquess of Buckingham, Marquess Hamilton, William Earl of Pembroke, Thomas Earl of Arundel, and to the rest of the Nobility and Gentry of this Kingdom therein named, for the planting, ruling, and governing of New England in America aforesaid, and all and every the liberties, licenses, powers, priviledges and authorities therein and thereby given and granted, or mentioned to be given and granted, and all their and every their right, estate, title, interest, claim, demand whatsoever of, in, and to the same Letters Patents, licenses, powers, priviledges, and authorities, and of, in and to, every or any parcell of them or any of them. In Witness whereof the said President and Council have caused their common Seal to be put to these presents, the seventh day of June in the eleventh year of the reign of our Sovereign Lord King Charles, and in the year of our Lord God, One thousand six hundred and thirty-five.

WILLIAM BRADFORD, &c. SURRENDER OF THE PATENT OF PLYMOUTH COLONY TO THE FREEMEN, MARCH 2D, 1640 *

Whereas divers and sondry Treaties have beene in the Publicke generall courts of New Plymouth his majestie our dread Sovereigne Charles by the grace of God King of England Scotland France and Ireland &c. concerning the proper Right and title of the Lands within the bounds and limitts of his said majestie's Letters Patents graunted by the Right Honorable his majestie's counsell for New England ratified by theire Comon Seale and signed by the hand of the Right Honorable Earle of Warwicke then Presidente of the said counsell to William Bradford his heirs associates and assignes beareing date &c And whereas the said William Bradford and divers others the first Instruments of God in the beginninge of this greate work of Plantacon together with such as the Alorderinge God in his Providence soone added unto them have beene at very greate charges to procure the said lands priviledges and freedomes from all entanglements as may appeare by divers and sondry deeds enlargements of

---

* Bradford's History of Plimouth Plantation: Boston. 1898. pp. 444–446.

graunts purchases payments of debts &c by reason whereof the title to the day of this present remayneth in the said William his heirs associats and assignes now for the better settling of the state of the said land aforesaid the said William Bradford and those their Instruments termed and called in sondry orders upon publick Record the Purchasers or Old Comers witnes two in especiall the one beareing date the third of March 1639 the other in December the first 1640 whereunto these presents have speciall relacon and agreement and whereby they are distinguished from other freemen and Inhabitants of the said Corporation. Be is Knowne unto all men therefore by these presents That the said William Bradford for himself his heires together with the said purchasers do onely reserve unto themselves their heires and assignes those three tracts of land menconed in the said resolucon order and agreement beareing date the first day of December 1640 viz. first from the bounds of Yarmouth three miles to the Eastward of Naemskeckett and from Sea to Sea crosse the said neck of land. The second of a place called Acconguesse (alias) Acockus which lyeth in the bottome of the Bay adjoyneing to the west side of Poynt Perrill and two miles to the westerne side of the said River to another place called Acqussent River which entereth at the western end of Nickatay and two miles to the Eastward therof and to extend eight miles up into the countrey. The third place of Sowawsett River to Patuckquett River with Consumpsit Neck which is the chief habitation of the Indians and reserved for them to dwell upon extending into the land eight miles through the whole breadth thereof, together with such other smale percells of lands as they or any of them are personally possessed of or interessed in by vertue of any former titles or graunts whatsoever and the said William Bradford doth by the free and full consent approbacon and agreement of the said Old Planters or Purchasers together with the likeing approbacon and acceptacon of the other part of the said Corporacon surrender into the hands of the whole court consisting of the Freemen of this Corporacon of New Plymouth all that their right and title power authorytie priviledges immunities and freedomes graunted in the said Letters Patents by the said Right Honorable Councell for New England reserveing his and their personall Right of Freemen together with the said Old Planters aforesaid except the said Lands before excepted, declaring the Freemen of this Corporacon together with all such as shall be legally admitted into the same his associates And the said William Bradford for him his heires and assignes doe further hereby promise and graunt to doe and performe whatsoever further thinge or thinges act or acts which in him lieth which shalbe needfull and expedient for the better confirmeing and establishinge the said premisses as by Counsell learned in the Laws shalbe reasonably advised and devised when he shalbe thereunto required In witnes whereof the said William Bradford hath in Publicke Court surrendered the said Letters Patents actually into the hands and power of the said Court bynding himselfe his heires executors administrators and assignes to deliver up whatsoever specialties are in his hands that do or may concerne the same.

COMMISSION OF SIR EDMUND ANDROS FOR THE DOMINION OF NEW ENGLAND. APRIL 7, 1688 [a]

James the Second by the Grace of God King of England, Scotland France and Ireland Defender of the Faith &c. To our trusty and welbeloved Sr Edmund Andros Kn^t Greeting: Whereas by our Commission under our Great Seal of England, bearing date the third day of June in the second year of our reign wee have constituted and appointed you to be our Captain Generall and Governor in Chief in and over all that part of our territory and dominion of New England in America known by the names of our Colony of the Massachusetts Bay, our Colony of New Plymouth, our Provinces of New Hampshire and Main and the Narraganset Country or King's Province. And whereas since that time Wee have thought it necessary for our service and for the better protection and security of our subjects in those parts to join and annex to our said Government the neighboring Colonies of Road Island and Connecticutt, our Province of New York and East and West Jersey, with the territories thereunto belonging, as wee do hereby join annex and unite the same to our said government and dominion of New England. Wee therefore reposing especiall trust and confidence in the prudence courage and loyalty of you the said Sir Edmund Andros, out of our especiall grace certain knowledge and meer motion, have thought fit to constitute and appoint as wee do by these presents constitute and appoint you the said Sr Edmund Andros to be our Captain Generall and Governor in Cheif in and over our Colonies of the Massachusetts Bay and New Plymouth, our Provinces of New Hampshire and Main, the Narraganset country or King's Province, our Colonys of Road Island and Connecticutt, our Province of New York and East and West Jersey, and of all that tract of land circuit continent precincts and limits in America lying and being in breadth from forty degrees of Northern latitude from the Equinoctiall Line to the River of St. Croix Eastward, and from thence directly Northward to the river of Canada, and in length and longitude by all the breadth aforesaid and throughout the main land from the Atlantick or Western Sea or Ocean on the East part, to the South Sea on the West part, with all the Islands, Seas, Rivers, waters, rights, members, and appurtenances, thereunto belonging (our province of Pensilvania and country of Delaware only excepted), to be called and known as formerly by the name and title of our territory and dominion of New England in America.

And for your better guidance and direction Wee doe hereby require and command you to do & execute all things in due manner, that shall belong unto the said office and the trust wee have reposed in you, according to the severall powers instructions and authoritys mentioned in these presents, or such further powers instructions and

---

[a] Text in "Documents Relative to the Colonial History of the State of New York, Vol. III, pp. 537–542. (Albany, 1853.) The earlier Commission to Sir Edmund Andros, dated June 3, 1686, appointing him Captain General and Governor of the Territory and Dominion of New England, which included the Colonies of Mass. Bay and New Plymouth and the Provinces of New Hampshire and Maine, the Narragansett Country, otherwise called The Kings Province, was very similar in its provisions to this document. It is printed in Records of the Colony of Rhode Island and Providence Plantations in New England, (Providence, 1858)," Vol. III, pp. 212–218.

authoritys mentioned in these presents, as you shall herewith receive or which shall at any time hereafter be granted or appointed you under our signet and sign manual or by our order in our Privy Councill and according to such reasonable lawes and statutes as are now in force or such others as shall hereafter be made and established within our territory & dominion aforesaid.

And our will and pleasure is that you the said Sr Edmund Andros having, after publication of these our Letters Patents, first taken the Oath of duly executing the office of our Captain Generall and Governor in Cheif of our said territory and dominion, which our Councill there or any three of them are hereby required authorized and impowered to give and administer unto you, you shall administer unto each of the members of our Councill the Oath for the due execution of their places and trusts.

And Wee do hereby give and grant unto you full power and authority to suspend any member of our Councill from sitting voting and assisting therein, as you shall find just cause for so doing.

And if it shall hereafter at any time happen that by the death, departure out of our said territory, or suspension of any of our Counselors, or otherwise, there shall be a vacancy in our said Councill, (any five whereof wee do hereby appoint to be a Quorum) Our will and pleasure is that you signify the same unto us by the first oppurtunity, that Wee may under our Signet and Sign Manuall constitute and appoint others in their room.

And Wee do hereby give and grant unto you full power and authority, by and with the advise and consent of our said Councill or the major part of them, to make constitute and ordain lawes statutes and ordinances for the public peace welfare and good governm^t of our said territory & dominion and of the people and inhabitants thereof, and such others as shall resort thereto, and for the benefit of us, our heires and successors. Which said lawes statutes and ordinances, are to be, as near as conveniently may be, aggreeable to the lawes & statutes of this our kingdom of England: Provided that all such lawes statutes and ordinances of what nature or duration soever, be within three months, or sooner, after the making of the same, transmitted unto Us, under our Seal of New England, for our allowance or disapprobation of them, as also duplicates thereof by the next conveyance.

And Wee do by these presents give and grant unto you full power and authority by and with the advise and consent of our said Councill, or the major part of them, to impose assess and raise and levy rates and taxes as you shall find necessary for the support of the government within our territory and dominion of New England, to be collected and leveyed and to be imployed to the uses aforesaid in such manner as to you & our said Councill or the major part of them shall seem most equall and reasonable.

And for the better supporting the charge of the governm^t of our said Territory and Dominion, our will and pleasure is and wee do by these presents authorize and impower you the s^d Sr Edmund Andros and our Councill, to continue such taxes and impositions as are now laid and imposed upon the Inhabitants thereof; and to levy and distribute or cause the same to be levyed and distributed to those ends in the best and most equall manner, untill you shall by &

with the advise and consent of our Councill agree on and settle such other taxes as shall be sufficient for the support of our government there, which are to be applied to that use and no other.

And our further will and pleasure is, that all publick money raised or to be raised or appointed for the support of the government within our said territory and dominion be issued out by warrant or order from you by & with the advise and consent of our Councill as aforesaid.

And our will and pleasure is that you shall and may keep and use our Seal appointed by Us for our said territory and dominion.

And wee do by these presents ordain constitute and appoint you or the Commander in Cheif for the time being, and the Councill of our said territory & dominion for the time being, to be a constant and setled Court of Record for ye administration of justice to all our subjects inhabiting within our said Territory and Dominion, in all causes as well civill as Criminall with full power and authority to hold pleas in all cases, from time to time, as well in Pleas of the Crown and in all matters relateing to the conservation of the peace and punishment of offenders, as in Civill causes and actions between party and party, or between us and any of our subjects there, whether the same do concerne the realty and relate to any right of freehold & inheritance or whether the same do concerne the personality and relate to matter of debt contract damage or other personall injury; and also in all mixt actions which may concern both realty and personalty; and therein after due and orderly proceeding and deliberate hearing of both sides, to give judgement and to award execution, as well in criminall as in Civill cases as aforesaid, so as always that the forms of proceedings in such cases and the judgment thereupon to be given, be as consonant and agreeable to the lawes and statutes of this our realm of England as the present state and condition of our subjects inhabiting within our said Territory and Dominion and the circumstances of the place will admit.

And Wee do further hereby give and grant unto you full power and authority with the advise and consent of our said Councill to erect constitute and establish such and so many Courts of Judicature and public Justice within our said Territory and Dominion as you and they shall think fitt and necessary for the determining of all causes as well Criminall as Civill according to law and equity, and for awarding of execution thereupon, with all reasonable and necessary powers authorities fees and privileges belonging unto them.

And Wee do hereby give and grant unto you full power and authority to constitute and appoint Judges and in cases requisite Commissioners of Oyer and Terminer, Justices of the Peace, Sheriffs, & all other necessary Officers and Ministers within our said Territory, for the better administration of Justice and putting the lawes in execution, & to administer such oath and oaths as are usually given for the due execution and performance of offices and places and for the cleering of truth in judiciall causes.

And our further will and pleasure is and Wee doe hereby declare that all actings and proceedings at law or equity heretofore had or don or now depending within any of the courts of our said Territory, and all executions thereupon, be hereby confirmed and continued so farr forth as not to be avoided for want of any legall power in the said Courts; but that all and every such judiciall actings, proceeding and execution shall be of the same force effect and virtue as if such Courts had acted by a just and legall authority.

And wee do further by these presents will and require you to permit Appeals to be made in cases of Error from our Courts in our said Territory and Dominion of New England unto you, or the Commander in Cheif for the time being and the Council, in Civill causes: Provided the value appealed for do exceed the sum of one hundred pounds sterling, and that security be first duly given by the Appellant to answer such charges as shall be awarded in case the first sentence shall be affirmed.

And whereas Wee judge it necessary that all our subjects may have liberty to Appeal to our Royall Person in cases that may require the same: Our will and pleasure is that if either party shall not rest satisfied with the judgement or sentence of you (or the Commander in Cheif for the time being) and the Councill, they may Appeal unto Us in our Privy Councill: Provided the matter in difference exceed the value and summ of three hundred pounds ster^g and that such Appeal be made within one fortnight after sentence, and that security be likewise duly given by the Appellant to answer such charges as shall be awarded in case the sentence of you (or the Commander in Cheif for the time being) and the Councill be confirmed; and provided also that execution be not suspended by reason of any such appeal unto us.

And Wee do hereby give and graunt unto you full power where you shall see cause and shall judge any offender or offenders in capitall and criminall matters, or for any fines or forfeitures due unto us, fit objects of our mercy, to pardon such offenders and to remit such fines & forfeitures, treason and wilfull murder only excepted, in which case you shall likewise have power upon extraordinary occasions to grant reprieves to the offenders therein untill and to the intent our pleasure may be further known.

And Wee do hereby give and grant unto you the said Sr Edm^d Andros by your self your Captains and Commanders, by you to be authorized, full power and authority to levy arme muster command or employ, all persons whatsoever residing within our said Territory and Dominion of New England, and, as occasion shall serve, them to transferr from one place to another for the resisting and withstanding all enemies pyrats and rebells, both at land and sea, and to transferr such forces to any of our Plantations in America or the Territories thereunto belonging, as occasion shall require for the defence of the same against the invasion or attempt of any of our enemies, and then, if occasion shall require to pursue and prosecute in or out of the limits of our said Territories and Plantations or any of them, And if it shall so please God, them to vanquish; and, being taken, according to the law of arms to put to death or keep and preserve alive, at your discretion. And also to execute martiall law in time of invasion insurrection or warr, and during the continuance of the same, and upon soldiers in pay, and to do and execute all and every other thing which to a Captain Generall doth or ought of right to belong, as fully and amply as any our Captain Generall doth or hath usually don.

And Wee do hereby give and grant unto you full power and authority to erect raise and build within our Territory and Dominion aforesaid, such and so many forts, platformes, Castles, cities, boroughs, towns, and fortifications as you shall judge necessary; and the same or any of them to fortify and furnish with ordnance ammunition and all sorts of armes, fit and necessary for the security & defence of our said territory; and the same again or any of them to demolish or dismantle as may be most convenient.

And Wee do hereby give and grant unto you the said S[r] Edmund Andros full power and authority to erect one or more Court or Courts Admirall within our said Territory and Dominion, for the hearing and determining of all marine and other causes and matters proper therein to be heard & determined, with all reasonable and necessary powers, authorities fees and priviledges.

And you are to execute all powers belonging to the place and office of Vice Admirall of and in all the seas and coasts about your Government; according to such commission authority and instructions as you shall receive from ourself under the Seal of our Admiralty or from High Admirall of our Foreign Plantations for the time being.

And forasmuch as divers mutinies & disorders do happen by persons shipped and imployed at Sea, and to the end that such as shall be shipped or imployed at Sea may be better governed and ordered; Wee do hereby give and grant unto you the said S[r] Edmund Andros our Captain Generall and Governor in Cheif, full power and authority to constitute and appoint Captains, Masters of Ships, and other Commanders, commissions to execute the law martial, and to use such proceedings authorities, punishment, correction and execution upon any offender or offenders who shall be mutinous seditious, disorderly or any way unruly either at sea or during the time of their abode or residence in any of the ports harbors or bays of our said Territory and Dominion, as the Cause shall be found to require, according to martial law. Provided that nothing herein conteined shall be construed to the enabling you or any by your authority to hold plea or have jurisdiction of any offence cause matter or thing committed or don upon the sea or within any of the havens, rivers, or creeks of our said Territory and Dominion under your government, by any Captain Commander Lieutenant Master or other officer seaman soldier or person whatsoever, who shall be in actuall service and pay in and on board any of our ships of War or other vessels acting by immediat commission or warrant from our self under the Seal of our Admiralty, or from our High Admirall of England for the time being; but that such Captain Commander Lieu[t] Master officer seaman soldier and other person so offending shall be left to be proceeded against and tryed, as the merit of their offences shall require, either by Commission under our Great Seal of England as the statute of 28 Henry VIII directs, or by commission from our said High Admirall, according to the Act of Parliament passed in the 13th year of the raign of the late King our most dear and most intirely beloved brother of ever blessed memory (entituled An Act for the establishing articles and Orders for the regulating and better governm[t] of His Ma[tys] navys, shipps or warr, and Forces by sea) and not otherwise. Saving only, that it shall and may be lawfull for you, upon such Captains and Commanders refusing or neglecting to execute, or upon his negligent or undue execution of any the written orders he shall receive from you for our service, & the service of our said Territory and Dominion, to suspend him the said Captain or Commander from the exercise of the said office of Commander and commit him safe custody, either on board his own ship or elsewhere, at the discretion of you, in order to his being brought to answer for the same by commission either under our Great Seal of England or from our said High Admirall as is before expressed. In which case our will and pleasure is that the Captain or Commander so by you suspended shall during his suspension and commitm^t be succeeded in his said office, by such commission or Warrant Officer of our said ship appointed by our self or our High Admirall for the time being, as by the known practice and discipline of our Navy doth and ought next to succeed him, as is case of death sickness of other ordinary disability hapning to the Commander of any of our ships & not otherwise; you standing also accountable to us for the truth & importance of the crimes and misdemeanours for which you shall so proceed to the suspending of such our said Captain or Commander. Provided also that all disorders and misdemeanors committed on shore by any Captain Commander, Lieuten^t, Master, or other officer seaman soldier or person whatsoever belonging to any of our ships of warr or other vessel acting by immediate commission or warr^t from our self under the Great Seal of our Admiralty or from our High Adm^{ll} from England for the time being may be tryed & punished according to the lawes of the place where any such disorders offences and misdemeanors shall be so committed on shore, notwithstanding such offender be in our actuall service and borne in our pay on board any such our shipps of warr or other vessels acting by immediate Commission or warrant from our self or our High Admirall as aforesaid; so as he shall not receive any protection (for the avoiding of justice for such offences committed on shore) from any pretence of his being imployed in our service at sea.

And Wee do likewise give and grant unto you full power and authority by and with the advice and consent of our said Councill to agree with the planters and inhabitants of our said Territory and Dominion concerning such lands, tenements & hereditaments as now are or hereafter shall be in our power to dispose of, and them to grant unto any person or persons for such terms and under such moderat Quit Rents, Services and acknowledgements to be thereupon reserved unto us as shall be appointed by us. Which said grants are to pass and be sealed by our Seal of New England and (being entred upon record by such officer or officers as you shall appoint thereunto, shall be good and effectual in law against us, our heires and successors.

And Wee do hereby give you full power and authority to appoint so many faires martes and markets as you with the advise of the said Councill shall think fitt.

As likewise to order and appoint within our said Territory such and so many ports harbors, bayes havens and other places for the convenience and security of shipping, and for the better loading and unloading of goods and merchandize as by you with the advice and consent of our Councill shall be thought fitt and necessary; and in them or any of them to erect nominat and appoint Cuxtom houses ware houses and officers relating thereto; and them to alter change, place, or displace from time to time, as with the advice aforesaid shall be thought fitt.

And forasmuch as pursuant to the lawes & customes of our Colony of the Massachusetts Bay and of our other Colonies and Provinces aforementioned, divers marriages have been made and performed by the Magstrats of our said territory; Our royall will and pleasure is hereby to confirm all the said marriages and to direct that they be held good and valid in the same manner to all intents and purposes whatsoever as if they had been made and contracted according to the lawes established within our kingdom of England.

And Wee do hereby require and command all officers and ministers, civill and military and all other inhabitants of our said Territory and Dominion to be obedient aiding and assisting unto you the said Sr Edm^d Andros in the execution of this our commission and of the powers and authorityes therein conteined, and upon your death or absence out of our said Territory unto our Lieut. Governor, to whom wee do therefore by these presents give and grant all and singular the powers and authorityes aforesaid to be exercised and enjoyed by him in case of your death or absence during our pleasure, or untill your arrival within our said Territory and Dominion; as Wee do further hereby give and grant full power and authority to our Lieut. Governor to do and execute whatsoever he shall be by you authorized and appointed to do and execute, in pursuance of and according to the powers granted to you by this Commission.

And if in the case of your death or absence there be no person upon the place, appointed by us to be Commander in Cheif; our will and pleasure is, that the then present Councill of our Territory aforesaid, do take upon them the administration of the Governm^t and execute this commission and the severall powers and authoritys herein conteined; and that the first Counselor who shall be at the time of yor death or absence residing within the same, do preside in our said Councill, with such powers and preheminencies as any former President hath used and enjoyed within our said territory, or any other our plantations in America, untill our pleasure be further known, or your arrivall as aforesaid.

And lastly, our will and pleasure is that you the said Sr Edmund Andros shall and may hold exercise and enjoy the office and place of Captain Generall and Governor in Cheif in and over our Territory and Dominion aforesaid, with all its rights members and appurtenances whatsoever, together with all and singular the powers and authorityes hereby granted unto you, for and during our will and pleasure.

In Witness whereof Wee have caused these our letters to be made Patents. Witness our self at Westminster the seventh day of Aprill in the fourth year of our raign.

By Writ of Privy Seal

Clerke.

THE CHARTER OF MASSACHUSETTS BAY—1691 [a] [b]

WILLIAM & MARY by the grace of God King and Queene of England Scotland France and Ireland Defenders of the Faith &c *To all* to whome these presents shall come Greeting *Whereas* his late Majesty King James the First Our Royall Predecessor by his Letters Patents vnder the Greate Seale of England bearing date at Westminster the Third Day of November in the Eighteenth yeare of his Reigne did Give and Grant vnto the Councill established at Plymouth in the County of Devon for the Planting Ruleing Ordering and Governing of New England in America and to their Successors and Assignes all that part of America lying and being in Breadth from Forty Degrees of Northerly Latitude from the Equinoctiall Line to the Forty Eighth Degree of the said Northerly Latitude Inclusively, and in length of and within all the Breadth aforesaid throughout all the Main Lands from Sea to Sea together alsoe with all the firme Lands Soiles Grounds Havens Ports Rivers Waters Fishings Mines and Mineralls as well Royall Mines of Gold and Silver as other Mines and Mineralls Pretious Stones Quarries and all and singular other Comodities Jurisdiccõns Royalties Privileges Franchises and Preheminences both within the said Tract of Land vpon the Main and alsoe within the Islands and Seas adjoyning *Provided* alwayes that the said Lands Islands or any the premises by the said Letters Patents intended or meant to be Granted were not then actually possessed or Inhabited by any other Christian Prince or State or within the bounds Limitts or Territories of the Southern Collony then before granted by the said late King James the First [to be planted [c]] by divers of his Subjects in the South parts *To Have* and to hold possesse and enjoy all and singular the aforesaid Continent Lands Territories Islands Hereditaments and Precincts Seas Waters Fishings with all and all manner of their Comodities Royalties Liberties Preheminences and Profitts that should from thenceforth arise from thence with all and singular their appurtenances and every part and parcell thereof vnto the said Councill and their Successors and Assignes for ever to the sole and proper vse and benefitt of the said Councill and their Successors and Assignes for ever *To* be holden of his said late Majestie King James the First his Heires and Successors as of his Mannor of East Greenwich in the County of Kent in free and Comõn Soccage and not in Capite or by Knights Service *Yielding* and paying therefore to the said late King his Heires and Successors the Fifth part of the Oar of Gold and Silver which should from time to time and at all times then after happen to be found gotten had and obteyned in att or within any of the said Lands Limitts Territories or Precincts or in or within any part or parcell thereof for or in respect of all and all manner of duties demands and services whatsoever to be done made or paid to the said late King James the first his Heires and Successors (as in and by the said Letters Patents amongst sundry other Clauses

---

[a] The charter of 1629 had been cancelled by a judgment of the high court of chancery of England June 18, 1684.
[b] The Charters and General Laws of the Colony and Province of Massachusetts Bay, Published by order of the General Court, Boston, T. B. Wait and Co., 1814, pp. 18–37.
[c] These words occur in the printed copies, but are not in the original. See also colony charter.

Powers Priviledges and Grants therein conteyned more at large appeareth *And Whereas* the said Councill established at Plymouth in the County of Devon for the Planting Ruleing Ordering and Governing of New England in America Did by their Deed Indented vnder their Comon Seale bearing Date the Nineteenth Day of March in the Third yeare of the Reigne of Our Royall Grandfather King Charles the First of ever Blessed Memory Give Grant Bargaine Sell Enffeoffe Alien and Confirme to Sir Henry Roswell Sir John Young Knights Thomas Southcott John Humphreys John Endicot and Simond Whetcomb their Heires and Assines and their Associats for ever All that part of New England in America aforesd which lyes and extends betweene a great River there comonly called Monomack ats Merrimack and a certaine other River there called Charles River being in a Bottom of a certaine Bay there comonly called Massachusetts ats Mattachuseetts ats Massatusetts Bay And alsoe all and singular those Lands and Hereditaments whatsoever lying within the space of Three English Miles on the South part of the said Charles River or of any and every part thereof And alsoe all and singular the Lands and Hereditaments whatsoever lying and being within the space of three English Miles to the Southward of the Southermost part of the said Bay called the Massachusetts ats Mattachusetts ats Massatusetts Bay And alsoe all those Lands and Hereditaments whatsoever which lye and be within the space of three English Miles to the Northward of the said River called Monomack ats Merrimack or to the Northward of any and every part thereof And all Lands and Hereditaments whatsoever lying within the Limitts aforesaid North and South in Latitude and in Breadth and in length and longitude of and within all the Breadth aforesaid throughout the Main Lands there from the Atlantick and Western Sea and Ocean on the East parte to the South Sea on the West part and all Lands and Grounds Place and Places Soile Woods and Wood Grounds Havens Ports Rivers Waters Fishings and Hereditaments whatsoever lying within the said Bounds and Limitts and every parte and parcell thereof and alsoe all Islands lying in America aforesaid in the said Seas or either of them on the Western or Eastern Coasts or Parts of the said Tracts of Land by the said Indenture menconed to be Given and Granted Bargained Sold Enffeoffed Aliened and Confirmed or any of them And alsoe all Mines and Mineralls aswell Royall Mines of Gold and Silver as other Mines and Mineralls whatsoever in the said Lands and Premisses or any parte thereof and all Jurisdiccons Rights Royalties Liberties Freedoms Imunities Priviledges Franchises Preheminences and Comodities whatsoever which they the said Councill established at Plymouth in the County of Devon for the planting Ruleing Ordering and Governing of New England in America then had or might vse exercise or enjoy in or within the said Lands and Premises by the same Indenture menconed to be given granted bargained sold enffeoffed and confirmed in or within any part or parcell thereof *To Have* and to hold the said parte of New England in America which lyes and extends and is abutted as aforesaid and every parte and parcell thereof And all the said Islands Rivers Ports Havens Waters Fishings Mines Mineralls Jurisdiccons Franchises Royalties Liberties Priviledges Comodities Hereditaments and premises whatsoever with the appurtenances vnto the said Sir Henry Roswell Sir John Young Thomas Southcott John Humphreys John Endicott and Simond Whetcomb their Heires and

Assignes and their Associates for ever to the only proper and absolute vse and behoofe of the said Sir Henry Roswell Sir [John[a]] Joung Thomas Southcott John Humphreys John Endicott and Simond Whetcomb their Heires and Assignes and their Associates for evermore *To* be holden of Our said Royall Grandfather King Charles the first his Heires and Successors as of his Mannor of East Greenwich in the County of Kent in free and Comon Soccage and not in Capite nor by Knights Service *Yielding and* paying therefore vnto Our said Royall Grandfather his Heires and Successors the fifth part of the Oar of Gold and Silver which should from time to time and at all times hereafter happen to be found gotten had & obteyned in any of the said Lands within the said Limitts or in or within any part thereof for and in satisfaccon of all manner of duties demands and services whatsoever to be done made or paid to Our said Royall Grandfather his Heires or Successors (as in and by the said recited Indenture may more at large appeare *And Whereas* Our said Royall Grandfather in and by his Letters Patents vnder the Greate Seale of England bearing date at Westminster the Fourth Day of March in the Fourth yeare of his Reigne for the consideracon therein mencõned did grant and confirme vnto the said Sir Henry Roswell Sir John Young Thomas Southcott John Humphreys John Endicott and Simond Whetcomb and to their Associates after named (vizt) Sir Ralph Saltenstall Kn[t] Isaac Johnson Samuell Aldersey John Ven Mathew Craddock George Harwood Increase Nowell Richard Berry Richard Bellingham Nathaniell Wright Samuell Vassall Theophilus Eaton Thomas Golfe Thomas Adams John Browne Samuell Browne Thomas Hutchins William Vassall William Pincheon and George Foxcroft their Heires and Assignes All the said part of New England in America lying and extending betweene the bounds and limitts in the said Indenture expressed and all Lands and Grounds Place and Places Soiles Woods and Wood Grounds Havens Ports Rivers Waters Mines Mineralls Jurisdiccõns Rights Royalties Liberties Freedomes Imunities Priviledges Franchises Preheminences and Hereditaments whatsoever bargained sold enffeoffed and Confirmed or mencõned or intended to be given granted bargained sold enffeoffed aliened and confirmed to the them the said Sir Henry Roswell Sir John Young Thomas Southcott John Humphreys John Endicott and Simond Whetcomb their Heires and Assignes and to their Associates for ever by the said recited Indentu[r]e *To Have* and to hold the said part of New England in America and other the Premisses thereby mencõned to be granted and confirmed and every parte and parcell thereof with the appurtenances to the said Sir Henry Roswell Sir John Young Sir Richard Saltenstall Thomas Southcott John Humphreys John Endicott Simond Whetcomb Isaac Johnson Samuell Aldersey John Ven Mathew Craddock George Harwood Increase Nowell Richard Perry Richard Bellingham Nathaniel Wright Samuell Vassall Theophilus Eaton Thomas Golfe Thomas Adams John Browne Samuell Browne Thomas Hutchins William Vassall William Pincheon and George Foxcroft their Heires and Assignes for ever to their own proper and absolute vse and behoofe for evermore *To* be holden of Our said Royall Grandfather his Heires and Successors as of his Mannor of East Greenwich aforesaid in free and comon Soccage and not in

---

[a] Omitted in the original.

Capite nor by Knights Service and alsoe yielding and paying therefore to Our said Royall Grandfather his Heires and Successors the fifth part only of all the Oar of Gold and Silver which from time to time and at all times after should be there gotten had or obteyned for all Services Exacc͞ons and Demands whatsoever according to the tenour and Reservac͞on in the said recited Indenture expressed *And further* Our said Royall Grandfather by the said Letters Patents did Give and Grant vnto the said Sir Henry Roswell Sir John Young Sir Richard Saltenstall Thomas Southcott John Humphreys John Endicott Simond Whetcomb Isaac Johnson Samuell Aldersey John Ven Mathew Craddock George Harwood Encrease Nowell Richard Perrey Richard Bellingham Nathaniel Wright Samuell Vassall Theophilus Eaton Thomas Golfe Thomas Adams John Browne Samuell Browne Thomas Hut[c]hins William Vassall William Pincheon and George Foxcroft their Heires and Assignes All that part of New England in America which lyes and extends betweene a Greate River called Monomack a̶l̶s Merrimack River and a certaine other River there called Charles River being in the Bottom of a certaine Bay there com͞only called Massachusetts a̶l̶s Mattachusetts a̶l̶s Massatusetts Bay and alsoe all and singular those Lands and Hereditaments whatsoever lying within the space of Three English Miles on the South part of the said River called Charles River or of any or every part thereof and alsoe all and singuler the Lands and Hereditaments whatsoever lying and being within the space of Three English Miles to the Southward of the Southermost part of the said Bay called Massachusetts a̶l̶s Mattachusetts a̶l̶s Massatusetts Bay And alsoe all those Lands and Hereditaments whatsoever which lye and bee within the space of Three English Miles to the Northward of the said River called Monomack a̶l̶s Merrimack or to the Northward of any and every parte thereof And all Lands and Hereditaments whatsoever lyeing within the limitts aforesaid North and South in Latitude and in Breadth and in length and Longitude of and within all the Breadth aforesaid throughout the Main Lands there from the Atlantick or Western Sea and Ocean on the East parte to the South Sea on the West parte And all Lands Grounds Place and Places Soils Wood and Wood Lands Havens Ports Rivers Waters and Hereditaments whatsoever lying within the said bounds and limitts and every part and parcell thereof And alsoe all Islands in America aforesaid in the said Seas or either of them on the Western or Eastern Coasts or partes of the said Tracts of Lands thereby menc͞oned to be given and granted or any of them And all Mines and Mineralls as well Royall Mines of Gold and Silver as other Mines and Mineralls whatsoever in the said Lands and premisses or any parte thereof and free Libertie of Fishing in or within any of the Rivers and Waters within the bounds and limitts aforesaid and the Seas thereunto adjoyning and of all Fishes Royall Fishes Whales Balene Sturgeon and other Fishes of what kind or nature soever that should at any time thereafter be taken in or within the said Seas or Waters or any of them by the said Sir Henry Roswell Sir John Young Sir Richard Saltenstall Thomas Southcroft John Humphryes John Endicott Simond Whetcomb Isaac Johnson Samuell Aldersey John Ven Mathew Craddock George Harwood Increase Nowell Richard Perrey Richard Bellingham Nathaniel Wright Samuell Vassall Theophilus Eaton Thomas Golfe Thomas Adams John

Browne Samuell Browne Thomas Hutchins William Vassall William Pincheon and George Foxcroft their Heires or Assignes or by any other person or persons whatsoever there Inhabiting by them or any of them to be appointed to Fish therein *Provided* alwayes that if the said Lands Islands or any the premisses before mencõned and by the said Letters Patents last mencõned intended and meant to be granted were at the time of granting of the said former Letters Patents dated the third day of November in the Eighteenth yeare of the Reigne of his late Majesty King James the First actually possessed or inhabited by any other Christian Prince or State or were within the bounds Limitts or Territories of the said Southern Colony then before granted by the said King to be planted by divers of his Loveing Subjects in the South parts of America That then the said Grant of Our said Royall Grandfather should not extend to any such parts or parcells thereof soe formerly inhabited or lying within the bounds of the Southern Plantacõn as aforesaid but as to those parts or parcells soe possessed or inhabited by any such Christian Prince or State or being within the boundaries afororesaid should be vtterly void *To Have* and to hold possesse and enjoy the said parts of New England in America which lye extend and are abutted as aforesaid and every part and parcell thereof and all the Islands Rivers Ports Havens Waters Fishings Fishes Mines Mineralls Jurisdicõns Franchises Royalties Riverties [a] Priviledges Comõdities and premisses whatsoever with the Appurtenances vnto the said Sir Henry Roswell Sir John Young Sir Richard Saltenstall Thomas Southcott John Humphreys John Endicott Simond Whetcomb Isaac Johnson Samuell Aldersey John Ven Mathew Craddock George Harwood Increase Nowell Richard Perrey Richard Bellingham Nathaniell Wright Samuell Vassall Theophilus Eaton Thomas Golfe Thomas Adams John Browne Samuell Browne Thomas Hutchins William Vassall William Pincheon and George Foxcroft their Heires and Assignes for ever To the only proper and absolute vse and behoofe of the said Sir Henry Roswell Sir John Young Sir Richard Saltenstall Thomas Southcott John Humphryes John Endicott Simond Whetcomb Isaac Johnson Samuell Aldersey John Ven Mathew Craddock George Harwood Increase Nowell Richard Perry Richard Bellingham Nathaniell Wright Samuell Vassall Theophilus Eaton Thomas Golfe Thomas Adams John Browne Samuell Browne Thomas Hutchins William Vassall William Pincheon and George Foxcroft their Heires and Assignes for evermore *To* be holden of Our said Royall Grandfather his Heires and Successors as of his Mannor of East Greenwich in the County of Kent within the Realme of England in free and Comõon Soccage and not in Capite nor by Knights Service And alsoe yeilding and paying therefore to Our said Royall Grandfather his Heires and Successors the Fifth part only of all the Oar of Gold and Silver which from time to time and at all times thereafter should be gotten had and obteyned for all services Exacõns and demands whatsoever *Provided* alwayes and his Majesties expresse Will and meaning was that only one Fifth parte of all the Gold and Silver Oar above mencõned in the whole and no more should be answered reserved and payable vnto Our said Royall Grandfather his Heires and Successors by colour or vertue of the said last mencõned Letters Patents the double reservacõns or

---

[a] Liberties.

recitalls aforesaid or any thing therein conteyned notwithstanding And to the end that the affaires and buisnesse which from time to time should happen and arise concerning the said Lands and the Plantacõns of the same might be the better mannaged and ordered and for the good Government thereof Our said Royall Grandfather King Charles the First did by his said Letters Patents Create and make the said Sir Henry Roswell Sir John Young Sir Richard Saltenstall Thomas Southcott John Humphreys John Endicott Symond Whetcomb Isaac Johnson Samuell Aldersey John Ven Mathew Caddock George Harwood Increase Newell Richard Perry Richard Bellingham Nathaniell Wright Samuell Vassall and Theophilus Eaton Thomas Golfe Thomas Adams John Browne Samuell Browne Thomas Hutchins William Vassal William Pincheon and George Foxcroft and all such others as should thereafter be admitted and made free of the Company and Society therein after mencõned one Body Politique and Corporate in fact and name by the Name of the Governour and Company of the Massachusetts Bay in New England and did grant vnto them and their Successors divers powers Liberties and Priviledges as in and by the said Letters Patents may more fully and at large appeare *And whereas* the said Governour and Company of the Massachusetts Bay in New England by vertue of the said Letters Patents did settle a Collony of the English in the said parts of America and divers good Subjects of this Kingdome incouraged and invited by the said Letters Patents did Transport themselves and their Effects into the same whereby the said Plantacõn did become very populous and divers Counties Townes and Places were created erected made setforth or designed within the said parts of America by the said Governour and Company for the time being *And Whereas* in the Terme of the holy Trinity in the Thirty Sixth yeare of the Reigne of Our dearest Vncle King Charles the Second a Judgment was given in Our Court of Chancery then sitting at Westminster [a] vpon a Writt of Scire Facias brought and prosecuted in the said Court against the Governour and Company of the Massachusetts Bay in New England that the said Letters Patents of Our said Royall Grandfather King Charles the First bearing date at Westminster the Fourth day of March in the Fourth yeare of his Reigne made and granted to the said Governour and Company of the Massachusetts Bay in New England and the Enrollment of the same should be cancelled vacated and annihilated and should be brought into the said Court to be cancelled (as in and by the said Judgment remaining vpon Record in the said Court doth more at large appeare) *And whereas* severall persons employed as Agents in behalfe of Our said Collony of the Massachusetts Bay in New England have made their humble application vnto Vs that Wee would be graciously pleased by Our Royall Charter to Incorporate Our Subjects in Our said Collony and to grant and confirme vnto them such powers priviledges and Franchises as [in] Our Royall Wisdome should be thought most conduceing to Our Interest and Service and to the Welfare and happy State of Our Subjects in New England and Wee being graciously pleased to gratifie Our said Subjects And alsoe to the end Our good Subjects within Our Collony of New Plymouth in New England aforesaid may be brought vnder such a forme of Government as may

---

[a] Winchester, in the Charters and General Laws, Boston: 1814.

put them in a better Condicõn of defence and considering aswell the granting vnto them as vnto Our Subejcts in the said Collony of the Massachusetts Bay Our Royall Charter with reasonable Powers and Priviledges will much tend not only to the safety but to the Flourishing estate of Our Subjects in the said parts of New England and alsoe to the advanceing of the ends for which the said Plantancõns were at first encouraged of Our especiall Grace certaine knowledge and meer Mocõn have willed and ordeyned and Wee doe by these presents for Vs Our Heires and Successors Will and Ordeyne that the Territories and Collnyes comonly called or known by the Names of the Collony of the Massachusetts Bay and Collony of New Plymouth the Province of Main the Territorie called Accadia or Nova Scotia and all that Tract of Land lying betweene the said Territori*tori*es of Nova Scotia and the said Province of Main be Erected Vnited and Incorporated And Wee doe by these presents Vnite Erect and Incorporate the same into one reall Province by the Name of Our Province of the Massachusetts Bay in New England And of Our especial Grace certaine knowledge and meer mocõn Wee have given and granted and by these presents for Vs Our Heires and Successors doe give and grant vnto Our good Subjects the Inhabitants of Our said Province or Territory of the Massachusetts Bay and their Successors all that parte of New England in America lying and extending from the greate River comonly called Monomack als Merrimack on the Northpart and from three Miles Northward of the said River to the Atlantick or Western Sea or Ocean on the South part And all the Lands and Hereditaments whatsoever lying within the limits aforesaid and extending as farr as the Outermost Points or Promontories of Land called Cape Cod and Cape Mallabar North and South and in Latitude Breadth and in Length and Longitude of and within all the Breadth and Compass aforesaid throughout the Main Land there from the said Atlantick or Western Sea and Ocean on the East parte towards the South Sea or Westward as far as Our Collonyes of Rhode Island Connecticutt and the Marragansett [a] Countrey all [b] alsoe all that part or porcõn of Main Land beginning at the Entrance of Pescata way Harbour and soe to pass vpp the same into the River of Newickewannock and through the same into the furthest head thereof and from thence Northwestward till One Hundred and Twenty Miles be finished and from Piscata way Harbour mouth aforesaid NorthEastward along the Sea Coast to Sagadehock and from the Period of One Hundred and Twenty Miles aforesaid to crosse over Land to the One Hundred and Twenty Miles before reckoned vp into the Land from Piscataway Harbour through Newickawannock River and alsoe the North halfe of the Isles and Shoales together with the Isles of Cappawock and Nantukett near Cape Cod aforesaid and also [all [b]] Lands and Hereditaments lying and being in the Countrey and Territory comonly called Accadia or Nova Scotia And all those Lands and Hereditaments lying and extending betweene the said Countrey or Territory of Nova Scotia and the said River of Sagadahock or any part thereof And all Lands Grounds Places Soiles Woods and Wood grounds Havens Ports Rivers Waters and other Hereditaments and

---

[a] Naragansett.
[b] In printed copies this is "the," but the omission in the original seems better supplied as above.

premisses whatsoever lying within the said bounds and limitts aforesaid and every part and parcell thereof and alsoe all Islands and Isletts lying within tenn Leagues directly opposite to the Main Land within the said bounds and all Mines and Mineralls aswell Royall Mines of Gold and Silver as other Mines and Mineralls whatsoever in the said Lands and premisses or any parte thereof *To Have* and to hold the said Territories Tracts Countreys Lands Hereditaments and all and singular other the premisses with their and every of their Appurtences to Our said Subjects the Inhabitants of Our said Province of the Massachusetts Bay in New England and their Successors to their only proper vse and behoofe for evermore *To* be holden of Vs Our Heires and Successors as of Our Mannor of East Greenwich in the County of Kent by Fealty only in free and Comon Soccage *yielding* and paying therefore yearly to Vs Our Heires and Successors the Fifth part of all Gold and Silver Oar and pretious Stones which shall from time to time and at all times hereafter happen to be found gotten had and obteyned in any of the said Lands and premisses or within any part thereof *Provided* neverthelesse and Wee doe for *Vs* Our Heires and Successors Grant and ordeyne that all and every such Lands Tenements and Hereditaments and all other estates which any person or persons or Bodyes-Politique or Corporate Townes Villages Colledges or Schooles doe hold and enjoy or ought to hold and enjoy within the bounds aforesaid by or vnder any Grant or estate duely made or granted by any Generall Court formerly held or by vertue of the Letters Patents herein before recited or by any other lawfull Right or Title whatsoever shall be by such person and persons Bodyes Politique and Corporate Townes Villages Colldges or Schoolss their respective Heires Successors and Assignes for ever hereafter held and enjoyed according to the purport and Intent of such respective Grant vnder and Subject neverthelesse to the Rents and Services thereby reserved or made payable any matter or thing whatsoever to the contrary notwithstanding *And Provided* alsoe that nothing herein conteyned shall extend or be vnderstood or taken to impeach or prejudice any right title Interest or demand which Samuell Allen of London Merchant claiming from and vnder John Mason Esqr deceased or any other person or persons hath or have or claimeth to have hold or enjoy of in to or out of any part or parts of the premisses scituate within the limitts above mencõned But that the said Samuel Allen and all and every such person and persons may and shall have hold and enjoy the same in such manner (and no other then) as if these presents had not been had or made It being Our further Will and Pleasure that no Grants or Conveyances of any Lands Tenements or Hereditaments to any Townes Colledges Schooles of Learning or to any private person or persons shall be judged or taken to be avoided or prejudiced for or by reason of any want or defect of Form but that the same stand and remaine in force and be mainteyned adjudged and have effect in the same manner as the same should or ought before the time of the said recited Judgment according to the Laws and Rules then and there vsually practised and allowed And Wee doe further for Vs Our Heires and Successors Will Establish and ordeyne that from henceforth for ever there shall be one Goverour One Leivten[t] or Deputy Governour and One Secretary of Our said Province or Territory to be from time to time appointed and Commissionated by Vs Our Heires and Successors and Eight and Twenty Assistants or Councillors to be advising and assisting to the Governour of Our said Province or Territory for the time being as by these presents is hereafter directed and appointed which said Councillors or Assistants are to be Constituted Elected and Chosen in such forme and manner as hereafter in these presents is expressed And for the better Execuc͞on of Our Royall Pleasure and Grant in this behalfe Wee doe by these presents for Vs Our Heires and Successors Nominate Ordeyne make and Constitute Our Trusty and Welbeloved Simon Broadstreet John Richards Nathaniel Saltenstall Wait Winthrop John Phillipps James Russell Samuell Sewall Samuel Appleton Barthilomew Gedney [a] John Hawthorn Elisha Hutchinson Robert Pike Jonathan Curwin John Jolliffe Adam Winthrop Richard Middlecot John Foster Peter Serjeant Joseph Lynd Samuell Hayman Stephen Mason Thomas Hinckley William Bradford John Walley Barnabas Lothrop Job Alcott Samuell Daniell and Silvanus Davis Esquires the first and present Councillors or Assistants of Our said Province to continue in their said respective Offices or Trusts of Councillors or Assistants vntill the last Wednesday in May which shall be in the yeare of Our Lord One Thousand Six Hundred Ninety and Three and vntill other Councillors or Assistants shall be chosen and appointed in their stead in such manner as in these presents is expressed *And Wee* doe further by these presents Constitute and appoint Our Trusty and welbeloved Isaac Addington Esquier to be Our first and present Secretary of Our said Province during Our Pleasure *And Our* Will and Pleasure is that the Governour of Our said Province from the time being shall have Authority from time to time at his discretion to assemble and call together the Councillors or Assistants of Our said Province for the time being and that the said Governour with the said Assistants or Councillors or Seaven of them at the least shall and may from time to time hold and keep a Councill for the ordering and directing the Affaires of Our said Province *And further* Wee Will and by these presents for Vs Our Heires and Successors doe ordeyne and Grant that there shall and may be convened held and kept by the Governour for the time being vpon every last Wednesday in the Moneth of May every yeare for ever and at all such other times as the Governour of Our said Province shall think fitt and appoint a great and Generall Court of Assembly Which said Great and Generall Court of Assembly shall consist of the Governour and Councill or Assistants for the time being and of such Freeholders of Our said Province or Territory as shall be from time to time elected or deputed by the Major parte of the Freeholders and other Inhabitants of the respective Townes or Places who shall be present at such Eleccōns Each of the said Townes and Places being hereby impowered to Elect and Depute Two Persons and noe more to serve for and represent them respectively in the said Great and Generall Court or Assembly To which Great and Generall Court or Assembly to be held as aforesaid Wee doe hereby for Vs Our Heires and Successors give and grant full power and authority from time to time to direct appoint and declare what Number each County Towne and Place shall Elect and Depute to serve for and represent them respectively in the said Great and Generall Court or Assembly *Provided* always that noe

---

[a] Gidney, in the Charters and General Laws. Boston: 1814.

Freeholder or other Person shall have a Vote in the Elecc͞on of Members to serve in any Greate and Generall Court or Assembly to be held as aforesaid who at the time of such Elecc͞on shall not have an estate of Freehold in Land within Our said Province or Territory to the value of Forty Shillings per Annū at the least or other estate to the value of Forty pounds Sterl' And that every Person who shall be soe elected shall before he sitt or Act in the said Great and Generall Court or Assembly take the Oaths menc͞oned in an Act of Parliament made in the first yeare of Our Reigne Entituled an Act for abrogateing of the Oaths of Allegiance and Supremacy and appointing other Oaths and thereby appointed to be taken instead of the Oaths of Allegiance and Supremacy and shall make Repeat and Subscribe the Declarac͞on menc͞oned in the said Act before the Governour and Lievtenͭ or Deputy Governour or any two of the Assistants for the time being who shall be therevnto authorized and Appointed by Our said Governour and that the Governour for the time being shall have full power and Authority from time to time as he shall Judge necessary to adjourne Prorogue and dissolve all Great and Generall Courts or Assemblyes met and convened as aforesaid And Our Will and Pleasure is and Wee doe hereby for Vs Our Heires and Successors Grant Establish and Ordeyne that yearly once in every yeare for ever hereafter the aforesaid Number of Eight and Twenty Councillors or Assistants shall be by the Generall Court or Assembly newly chosen that is to say Eighteen at least of the Inhabitants of or Proprietors of Lands within the Territory formerly called the Collony of the Massachusetts Bay and four at the least of the Inhabitants of or Proprietors of Lands within the Territory formerly called New Plymouth and three at the least of the Inhabitants of or Proprietors of Land within the Territory formerly called the Province of Main and one at the least of the Inhabitants of or Proprietors of Land within the Territory lying between the River of Sagadahoc and Nova Scotia And that the said Councillors or Assistants or any of them shall or may at any time hereafter be removed or displaced from their respective Places or Trust of Councillors or Assistants by any Great or Generall Court or Assembly And that if any of the said Councillors or Assistants shall happen to dye or be removed as aforesaid before the Generall day of Elecc͞on That then and in every such Case the Great and Generall Court or Assembly at their first sitting may proceed to a New Elecc͞on of one or more Councillors or Assistants in the roome or place of such Councillors or Assistants soe dying or removed And Wee doe further Grant and Ordeyne that it shall and may be lawfull for the said Governour with the advice and consent of the Council or Assistants from time to time to nominate and appoint Judges Commissioners of Oyer and Terminer Sheriffs Provosts Marshalls Justices of the Peace and other Officers to Our Councill and Courts of Justice belonging *Provided* always that noe such Nominac͞on or Appointment of Officers be made without notice first given or sum͞ons yssued out seaven dayes before such Nominac͞on or Appointment vnto such of the said Councillors or Assistants as shall be at that time resideing within Our said Province *And Our* Will and Pleasure is that the Governour and Leivtenͭ or Deputy Governour and Councillors or Assistants for the time being and all other Officers to be appointed or Chosen as aforesaid shall before the Vndertaking the Execuc͞on of their Offices and Places respectively take their severall and respective

Oaths for the due and faithfull performance of their duties in their severall and respective Offices and Places and alsoe the Oaths appointed by the said Act of Parliament made in the first yeare of Our Reigne to be taken instead of the Oaths of Allegiance and Supremacy and shall make repeate and subscribe the Declaracōn menc̄oned in the said Act before such Person or Persons as are by these presents herein after appointed (that is to say) The Governour of Our said Province or Territory for the time being shall take the said Oaths and make repeate and subscribe the said Decleracōn before the Leivten.t or Deputy Governour or in his absence before any two or more of the said Persons hereby Nominated and appointed the present Councillors or Assistants of Our said Province or Territory to whom Wee doe by these presents give full power and Authority to give and administer the same to Our said Governour accordingly and after Our said Governour shall be sworn and shall have subscribed the sd Declaracōn that then Our Leivten.t or Deputy Governour for the time being and the Councillors or Assistants before by these presents Nominated and appointed shall take the said Oaths and make repeat and subscribe the said Declaracōn before Our said Governour and that every such person or persons as shall (at any time of the Annuall Eleccōns or otherwise vpon death or removeall) be appointed to be the New Councillors or Assistants and all other Officers to bee hereafter chosen from time to time shall take the Oaths to their respective Offices and places belonging and alsoe the said Oaths appointed by the said Act of Parliament to be taken instead of the Oaths of Allegiance and Supremacy and shall make repeate and subscribe the declaracōn mencōned in the said Act before the Governour or Leivten.t or Deputy Governour or any two or more Councillors or Assistants or such other Person or Persons as shall be appointed thereunto by the Governour for the time being to whom Wee doe therefore by these presents give full power and authority from time to time to give and administer the same respectively according to Our true meaning herein before declared without any Comission or further Warrant to bee had and obteyned from vs Our Heires and Successors in that behalfe *And* Our Will and Pleasure is and Wee doe hereby require and Comand that all and every person and persons hereafter by Vs Our Heires and Successors nominated and appointed to the respective Offices of Governour or Leiv.t or Deputy Governour and Secretary of Our said Province or Territory (which said Governour or Leiv.t or Deputy Governour and Secretary of Our said Province or Territory for the time being Wee doe hereby reserve full power and Authority to Vs Our Heires and Successors to Nominate and appoint accordingly, shall before he or they be admitted to the Execucōn of their respective Offices take as well the Oath for the due and faithfull performance of the said Offices respectively as alsoe the Oaths appointed by the said Act of Parliament made in the said First yeare of Our Reigne to be taken instead of the said Oaths of Allegiance and Supremacy and shall alsoe make repeate and subscribe the Declaracōn appointed by the said Act in such manner and before such persons as aforesaid *And further* Our Will and Pleasure is and Wee doe hereby for Vs Our Heires and Successors Grant Establish and Ordaine That all and every of the Subjects of Vs Our Heires and Successors which shall goe to and Inhabit within Our said Province and Territory and every of their Children which shall happen to be born there or on the Seas in goeing thither or returning from thence shall have and enjoy all Libertyes and Immunities of Free and naturall Subjects within any of the Dominions of Vs Our Heires and Successors to all Intents Construccõns and purposes whatsoever as if they and every of them were borne within this Our Realme of England and for the greater Ease and Encouragement of Our Loveing Subjects Inhabiting our said Province or Territory of the Massachusetts Bay and of such as shall come to Inhabit there Wee doe by these presents for vs Our heires and Successors Grant Establish and Ordaine that for ever hereafter there shall be a liberty of Conscience allowed in the Worshipp of God to all Christians (Except Papists) Inhabiting or which shall Inhabit or be Resident within our said Province or Territory And Wee doe hereby Grant and Ordaine that the Gouernor or leivetent or Deputy Gouernor of our said Province or Territory for the time being or either of them or any two or more of the Councill or Assistants for the time being as shall be thereunto appointed by the said Gouernor shall and may at all times and from time to time hereafter have full Power and Authority to Administer and give the Oathes appointed by the said Act of Parliament made in the first yeare of Our Reigne to be taken instead of the Oathes of Allegiance and Supremacy to all and every person and persons which are now Inhabiting or resideing within our said Province or Territory or which shall at any time or times hereafter goe or passe thither And wee doe of our further Grace certaine knowledge and meer mocõn Grant Establish and Ordaine for Vs our heires and Successors that the great and Generall Court or Assembly of our said Province or Territory for the time being Convened as aforesaid shall for ever have full Power and Authority to Erect and Constitute Judicatories and Courts of Record or other Courts to be held in the name of Vs Our heires and successors for the Hearing Trying and Determining of all manner of Crimes Offences Pleas Processes Plaints Accõns Matters Causes and things whatsoever ariseing or happening within Our said Province or Territory or between persons Inhabiting or resideing there whether the same be Criminall or Civill and whether the said Crimes be Capitall or not Capitall and whether the said Pleas be Reall personall or mixt and for the awarding and makeing out of Execution thereupon To which Courts and Judicatories wee doe hereby for vs our heirs and Successors Give and Grant full power and Authority from time to time to Administer oathes for the better Discovery of Truth in any matter in Controversy or depending before them And wee doe for vs Our Heires and Successors Grant Establish and Ordaine that the Gouernor of our said Province or Territory for the time being with the Councill or Assistants may doe execute or performe all that is necessary for the Probate of Wills and Granting of Administracõns for touching or concerning any Interest or Estate which any person or persons shall have within our said Province or Territory And whereas Wee judge it necessary that all our Subjects should have liberty to Appeale to vs our heires and Successors in Cases that may deserve the same Wee doe by these presents Ordaine that incase either party shall not rest satisfied with the Judgement or Sentence of any Judicatories or Courts within our said Province or Territory in any Personall Accõn wherein the matter in difference doth exceed the value of three hundred Pounds Sterling that then he or they may appeale to vs Our heires and Successors in our or their Privy Councill Provided such Appeale be made within Fourteen dayes after y*e* Sentence or Judgement given and that before such Appeale be allowed Security be given by the party or parties appealing in the value of the matter in Difference to pay or Answer the Debt or Damages for the which Judgement or Sentence is given With such Costs and Damages as shall be Awarded by vs Our Heires or Successors incase the Judgement or Sentence be affirmed *And Provided* alsoe that no Execution shall be stayd or suspended by reason of such Appeale vnto vs our Heires and Successors in our or their Privy Councill soe as the party Sueing or takeing out Execution doe in the like manner give Security to the value of the matter in difference to make Restitucion in Case the said Judgement or Sentence be reversed or annul'd upon the said Appeale *And* we doe further for vs our Heires and Successors Give and Grant to the said Governor and the great and Generall Court or Assembly of our said Province or Territory for the time being full power and Authority from time to time to make ordaine and establish all manner of wholsome and reasonable Orders Laws Statutes and Ordinances Directions and Instructions either with penalties or without (soe as the same be not repugnant or contrary to the Lawes of this our Realme of England) as they shall Judge to be for the good and welfare of our said Province or Territory And for the Gouernment and Ordering thereof and of the People Inhabiting or who shall Inhabit the same and for the necessary support and Defence of the Government thereof *And* wee doe for vs our Heires and Successors Giue and grant that the said Generall Court or Assembly shall have full power and Authority to name and settle annually all Civill Officers within the said Province such Officers Excepted the Election and Constitution of whome wee have by these presents reserved to vs Our Heires and Successors or to the Governor of our said Province for the time being and to Settforth the severall Duties Powers and Lymitts of every such Officer to be appointed by the said Generall Court or Assembly and the formes of such Oathes not repugnant to the Lawes and Statutes of this our Realme of England as shall be respectiuely Administered vnto them for the Execution of their severall Offices and places And alsoe to impose Fines mulcts Imprisonments and other Punishments And to impose and leavy proportionable and reasonable Assessments Rates and Taxes vpon the Estates and Persons of all and every the Proprietors and Inhabitants of our said Province or Territory to be Issued and disposed of by Warrant vnder the hand of the Governor of our said Province for the time being with the advice and Consent of the Councill for Our service in the necessary defence and support of our Government of our said Province or Territory and the Protection and Preservation of the Inhabitants there according to such Acts as are or shall be in force within our said Province and to dispose of matters and things whereby our Subjects inhabitants of our said Province may be Religiously peaceably and Civilly Governed Protected and Defended soe as their good life and orderly Conversation may win the Indians Natives of the Country to the knowledge and obedience of the onely true God and Saviour of Mankinde and the Christian Faith which his Royall Majestie our Royall Grandfather king Charles the first in his said

Massachusetts—1691

Letters Patents declared was his Royall Intentions And the Adventurers free Possession *a* to be the Princepall end of the said Plantation And for the better secureing and maintaining Liberty of Conscience hereby granted to all persons at any time being and resideing within our said Province or Territory as aforesaid *Willing* Comanding and Requireing and by these presents for vs Our heires and Successors Ordaining and appointing that all such Orders Lawes Statutes and Ordinances Instructions and Directions as shall be soe made and published vnder our Seale of our said Province or Territory shall be Carefully and duely observed kept and performed and put in Execution according to the true intent and meaning of these presents *Provided* alwaies and Wee doe by these presents for vs Our Heires and Successors Establish and Ordaine that in the frameing and passing of all such Orders Laws Statutes and Ordinances and in all Elections and Acts of Government whatsoever to be passed made or done by the said Generall Court or Assembly or in Councill the Governor of our said Province or Territory of the Massachusetts Bay in New England for the time being shall have the Negative voice and that without his consent or Approbation signified and declared in Writeing no such Orders Laws Statutes Ordinances Elections or other Acts of Government whatsoever soe to be made passed or done by the said Generall Assembly or in Councill shall be of any Force effect or validity anything herein contained to the contrary in anywise notwithstanding *And* wee doe for vs Our Heires and Successors Establish and Ordaine that the said Orders Laws Statutes and Ordinances be by the first opportunity after the makeing thereof sent or Transmitted vnto vs Our Heires and Successors vnder the Publique Seale to be appointed by vs for Our or their approbation or Disallowance And that incase all or any of them shall at any time within the space of three years next after the same shall have presented to vs our Heires and Successors in Our or their Privy Councill be disallowed and reiected and soe signified by vs Our Heires and Successors vnder our or their Signe Manuall and Signett or by or in our or their Privy Councill vnto the Governor for the time being then such and soe many of them as shall be soe disallowed and riected *b* shall thenceforth cease and determine and become vtterly void and of none effect *Provided* alwais that incase Wee our Heires or Successors shall not within the Terme of Three Yeares after the presenting of such Orders Lawes Statutes or Ordinances as aforesaid signifie our or their Disallowance of the same Then the said orders Lawes Statutes or Ordinances shall be and continue in full force and effect according to the true Intent and meaneing of the same vntill the Expiracon thereof or that the same shall be Repealed by the Generall Assembly of our said Province for the time being *Provided* alsoe that it shall and may be Lawfull for the said Governor and Generall Assembly to make or passe any Grant of Lands lying within the Bounds of the Colonys formerly called the Collonys of the Massachusetts Bay and New Plymouth and province of Main in such manner as heretofore they might have done by vertue of any former Charter or Letters Patents which grants of lands within the Bounds aforesaid Wee doe hereby Will and ordaine to be and continue for ever of full force and effect without our further Approbation or Consent

---

a Profession.   *b* Rejected.

And soe as Neverthelesse and it is Our Royall Will and Pleasure That noe Grant or Grants of any Lands lying or extending from the River of Sagadehock to the Gulph of S^t: Lawrence and Canada Rivers and to the Main Sea Northward and Eastward to be made or past by the Governor and Generall Assembly of our said Province be of any force validity or Effect vntill Wee Our Heires and Successors shall have Signified Our or their Approbacon of the same *And* Wee doe by these presents for vs Our Heires and Successors Grant Establish and Ordaine that the Governor of our said Province or Territory for the time being shall have full Power by himselfe or by any Cheif Comander or other Officer or Officers to be appointed by him from time to time to traine instruct Exercise and Governe the Militia there and for the speciall Denfence and Safety of Our said Province or Territory to assemble in Martiall Array and put in Warlike posture the Inhabitants of Our said Province or Territory and to lead and Conduct them and with them to Encounter Expulse Repell Resist and pursue by force of Armes aswell by Sea as by Land within or without the limitts of Our said Province or Territory and alsoe to kill slay destroy and Conquer by all fitting wayes Enterprises and meanes whatsoever all and every such Person and Persons as shall at any time hereafter Attempt or Enterprize the destruccon Invasion Detriment or Annoyance of Our said Province or Territory and to vse and exercise the Law Martiall in time of actuall Warr Invasion or Rebellion as occasion shall necessarily require and alsoe from time to time to Erect Forts and to fortifie any place or Places within Our said Province or Territory and the same to furnish with all necessary Amunicon Provisions and Stores of Warr for Offence or Defence and to comitt from time to time the Custody and Government of the same to such Person or Persons as to him shall seem meet And the said Forts and Fortificacons to demolish at his Pleasure and to take and surprise by all waies and meanes whatsoever all and every such Person or Persons with their Shipps Arms Ammuncon and other goods as shall in a hostile manner Invade or attempt the Invading Conquering or Annoying of Our said Province or Territory *Provided* alwayes and Wee doe by these presents for Vs Our Heires and Successors Grant Establish and Ordeyne That the said Governour shall not at any time hereafter by vertue of any power hereby granted or hereafter to be granted to him Transport any of the Inhabitants of Our said Province or Territory or oblige them to march out of the Limitts of the same without their Free and voluntary consent or the Consent of the Great and Generall Court or Assembly or Our said Province or Territory nor grant Comissions for exerciseing the Law Martiall vpon any the Inhabitants of Our said Province or Territory without the Advice and Consent of the Councill or Assistants of the same *Provided* in like manner and Wee doe by these presents for Vs Our Heires and Successors Constitute and Ordeyne that when and as often as the Governour of Our said Province for the time being shall happen to dye or be displaced by Vs Our Heires or Successors or be absent from his Government That then and in any of the said Cases the Leivtenant or Deputy Governour of Our said Province for the time being shall have full power and authority to doe and execute all and every such Acts Matters and things which Our Governour of Our said Province for the time being might or could by vertue of these Our Letter Patents lawfully doe or execute if he were personally present vntill the returne of the Governour soe absent or Arrivall or Constituc̃on of such other Governour as shall or may be appointed by Vs Our Heires or Successors in his stead and that when and as often as the Governour and Leivtenant or Deputy Governour of Our said Province or Territory for the time being shall happen to dye or be displaced by Vs Our Heires or Successors or be absent from Our said Province and that there shall be no person within the said Province Com̃issionated by Vs Our Heires or Successors to be Governour within the same Then and in every of the said cases the Councill or Assistants of Our said Province shall have full power and Authority and Wee doe hereby give and grant vnto the said Councill or Assistants of Our said Province for the time being or the Major parte of them full power and Authority to doe and execute all and every such Acts matters and things which the said Governour or Leivtenant of Deputy Governour of Our said Province or Territory for the time being might or could lawfully doe or exercise if they or either of them were personally present vntill the returne of the Governour Leivtenant or Deputy Governour soe absent or Arrivall or Constituc̃on of such other Governour or Leivtenant or Deputy Governour as shall or may be appointed by Vs Our Heires or Successors from time to time *Provided* alwaies and it is hereby declared that nothing herein shall extend or be taken to Erect or grant or allow the Exercise of any Admirall Court Jurisdic̃on Power or Authority but that the same shall be and is hereby reserved to Vs and Our Successors and shall from time to time be Erected Granted and exercised by vertue of Com̃issions to be yssued vnder the Great Seale of England or vnder the Seale of the High Admirall or the Com̃issioners for executing the Office of High Admirall of England *And further* Our expresse Will and Pleasure is And Wee doe by these present for Vs Our Heires and Successors Ordaine and appoint that these Our Letters Patents shall not in any manner Enure or be taken to abridge bar or hinder any of Our loveing Subjects whatsoever to vse and exercise the Trade of Fishing vpon the Coasts of New England but that they and every of them shall have full and free power and Libertie to continue and vse their said Trade of Fishing vpon the said Coasts in any of the seas therevnto adjoyning or any Arms of the said Seas or Salt Water Rivers where they have been wont to fish and to build and set vpon the Lands within Our said Province or Collony lying wast and not then possesst by perticuler Proprietors such Wharfes Stages and Workhouses as shall be necessary for the salting drying keeping and packing of their Fish to be taken or gotten vpon that Coast And to Cutt down and take such Trees and other Materialls there growing or being or growing [a] vpon any parts or places lying wast and not then in possession of particuler proprietors as shall be needfull for that purpose and for all other necessary easments helps and advantages concerning the Trade of Fishing there in such manner and forme as they have been heretofore at any time accustomed to doe without makeing any Wilfull Wast or Spoile any thing in these presents conteyned to the contrary notwithstanding *And lastly* for the better provideing and furnishing of Masts for Our Royall Navy Wee doe hereby reserve to Vs Our Heires and Successors all

---

[a] The words "or growing" not found in reprint.

Trees of the Diameter of Twenty Four Inches and vpwards of Twelve Inches from the ground growing vpon any soyle or Tract of Land within Our said Province or Territory not heretofore granted to any private persons And Wee doe restraine and forbid all persons whatsoever from felling cutting or destroying any such Trees without the Royall Lycence of Vs Our Heires and Successors first had and obteyned vpon penalty of Forfeiting One Hundred Pounds sterling vnto Ous Our Heires and Successors for every such Tree soe felled cutt or destroyed without such Lycence had and [a] obteyned in that behalfe any thing in these presents conteyned to the contrary in any wise Notwithstanding *In Witnesse* whereof Wee have caused these our Letters to be made Patents *Witnesse* Ourselves att Westminster the Seaventh Day of October in the Third yeare of Our Reigne
By Writt of Privy Seale

PIGOTT

Pro Fine in Hanaperio quadragint Marcas
 J. TREVOR *C. S.*
 W. RAWLINSON *C. S.*
 G. HUTCHNS *C. S.*[b]

EXPLANATORY CHARTER OF MASSACHUSETTS BAY—1725 [c]

GEORGE BY THE GRACE OF GOD of Great Britain France and Ireland king Defender of the Faith &c *To all* to whom these Presents shall come Greeting *Whereas* Our late Royal Predecessors William and Mary King and Queen of England &c Did by their letters Patents under their Great Seal of England bearing Date at Westminster the Seventh day of October in the Third year of their Reign for themselves their Heires and Successors Vnite Erect and Incorporate the Territories and Colonies commonly called or known by the Names of the Colony of the Massachusetts Bay and Colony of New Plymouth the Province of Main the Territory called Accada or Nova Scotia and all that Tract of land lying between the said Territorys of Nova Scotia and the said Province of Main into One Reall Province by the Name of Our Province of the Massachusetts Bay in New England *And Whereas* their said late Majesties King William and Queen Mary did by the said recited letters Patents (amongst other things therein contained) for themselves their Heires and Successors Ordain and Grant that there should and might be Convened held and kept by the Governor for the time being upon every last Wednesday in the Month of May every year forever and at all such other times as the Governor of their said Province should think fitt and Appoint a Great and Generall Court or Assembly which said Great and Generall Court or Assembly should Consist of the Governour and Council or Assistants for the time being and of

---

[a] " or " in reprint, *supra*.

[b] Sir John Trevor, Sir William Rawlinson, and Sir George Hutchins were appointed lords commissioners of the great seal May 15, 1690; and were succeeded by Lord Somers as chancellor May 3, 1693.

[c] The Charters and General Laws of the Colony and Province of Massachusetts Bay, . . . Published by the General Court, Boston, T. B. Wait and Co., 1814. 38–40. The date of the charter is August 26 [O. S.] September 26 [N. S.] 1725.

such Freeholders of their said Province or Territory as should be from time to time elected or deputed by the major part of the Freeholders and other Inhabitants of the respective Towns or places who should be present at such Eleccõns each of the said Towns and places being thereby impowered to Elect and Depute two Persons and no more to Serve for and represent them respectively in the said Great and Generall Court or Assembly and that the Governor for the time being should have full Power and Authority from time to time as he should Judge necessary to adjourn Prorogue and Dissolve all Great and General Courts or Assemblies met and Convened as aforesaid And did thereby also for themselves their Heires and Successors Provide Establish and Ordain that in the Framing and Passing of all Orders laws Statutes and Ordinances and in all Eleccõns and Acts of Government whatsoever to be passed made or done by the said General Court or Assembly or in Council the Governor of the said Province or Territory of the Massachusetts Bay in New England for the time being should have the Negative Voice and that without his Consent or Approbacõn Signified and Declared in writing no such Orders laws Statutes Ordinances Eleccõns or other Acts of Government whatsoever so to be made passed or done by the said General Assembly or in Council should be of any force Effect or Validity any thing therein contained to the contrary in any wise notwithstanding as in and by the said letters Patents (relacõn being therevnto had) may more fully and at large appeare *And Whereas* no provision is made by the said recited letters Patents touching the Nominacõn and Eleccõn of a Speaker of the Representatives Assembled in any Great and Generall Court of Our said Province nor any particular Reservacõn made of the Right of Vs Our Heires and Successors to approve or disapprove of such Speaker by the Governor of the said Province appointed or to be appointed by Vs or them for the time being And no power is Granted by the said recited letters Patents to the said House of Representatives to adjourn themselves for any time whatsoever by means whereof divers Doubts and Controversies have Arisen within Our said Province to the Interrupcõn of the Publick Business thereof and the obstruccõn of Our Service *Know Yee* therefore that for removing the said Doubts and Controversies and preventing the like mischiefs for the future And also for the further Explanacõn of the said recited letters Patents Wee of Our Especial Grace certain knowledge and meer mocõn Have Granted Ordained and Appointed And by these Presents for Vs Our Heirs and Successors Do Will Grant Ordain and Appoint that for ever hereafter the Representatives Assembled in any Great or General Court of Our said Province to be hereafter Summoned shall upon the first day of their Assembling Elect a fit Person out of the said Representatives to be Speaker of the House of Representatives in such General Court and that the Person so Elected shall from time to time be presented to the Governor of Our said Province for the time being or in his absence to the lieutenant Governor or Comãnder in Chief of Our said Province for the time being for his Approbacõn to which Governor lieutenant Governor and Comãnder in Chief respectively Wee do hereby for Vs Our Heires and Successors give full power and Authority to approve or disapprove of the Person so Elected and presented which approbacõn or disapprobacõn shall be Signifyed by him by Message in writing under his Hand to the said House of Representatives And in Case such Governour lieutenant Governor or Comander in Chief shall disapprove of the Person so Elected and presented or the Person so Elected and presented being approved as aforesaid shall happen to dye or by Sickness or otherwise be disabled from Officiating as Speaker in every such Case the said Representatives so Assembled shall forthwith Elect an other Person to be Speaker of the House of Representatives to be presented and approved or disapproved in manner as aforesaid and so from time to time as often as the Person so Elected and presented shall be disapproved of or happen to dye or become disabled as aforesaid *And* Our further Will and Pleasure is and Wee do by these presents of Our more abundant Grace for Vs Our Heires and Successors Grant Ordain and Appoint that it shall and may be lawfull to and for the Representatives assembled in any Great or Generall Court of Our said Province for the time being for ever hereafter to Adjourn themselves from day to day (and if occasion shall require) for the space of two days but not for any longer time than for the space of two days without leave from the Governor or in his Absence [from] the lieutenant Governor or Comander in Chief of Our said Province for the time being first had and obtained in that behalfe any thing in the said recited letters Patents contained to the Contrary thereof in any wise Notwithstanding Provided always that nothing in these presents contained shall Extend or be Construed to Extend to revoke alter or prejudice the Power and Authority by the said recited letters Patents Granted to the Governor of the said Province for the time being to Adjourn Prorogue and Dissolve all Great and General Courts or Assemblies of Our said Province. *And Lastly* Wee do by these presents for Vs Our Heires and Successors Grant that these Our letters Patents or the Enrollment or Exemplificacōn thereof shall be in and by all things good firm valid and Effectual in the law according to the true intent and meaning thereof notwithstanding the not rightly or fully reciting mencōning or describing the said recited letters Patents or the Date thereof or any other Omission Imperfeccōn Defect matter Cause or thing whatsoever to the Contrary thereof in any wise notwithstanding *In witness* whereof Wee have Caused these Our letters to be made Patents *Witness* William Archbishop of Canterbury and the rest of the Guardians and Justices of the Kingdom at Westminster the Six and twentieth day of August in the twelfth year of Our Reign

By Writ of Privy Seal

COCKS

CONSTITUTION OR FORM OF GOVERNMENT FOR THE COMMONWEALTH OF MASSACHUSETTS—1780 *

PREAMBLE

The end of the institution, maintenance, and administration of government, is to secure the existence of the body politic, to protect it, and to furnish the individuals who compose it with the power of

---

* Verified from "The Constitution of the Commonwealth of Massachusetts. Published by the Secretary of the Commonwealth. Boston: Wright & Potter Printing Co., State Printers, 18 Post Office Square. 1902." 67 pp.

enjoying in safety and tranquillity their natural rights, and the blessings of life: and whenever these great objects are not obtained, the people have a right to alter the government, and to take measures necessary for their safety, prosperity, and happiness.

The body politic is formed by a voluntary association of individuals: it is a social compact, by which the whole people covenants with each citizen, and each citizen with the whole people, that all shall be governed by certain laws for the common good. It is the duty of the people, therefore, in framing a constitution of government, to provide for an equitable mode of making laws, as well as for an impartial interpretation and a faithful execution of them; that every man may, at all times, find his security in them.

We, therefore, the people of Massachusetts, acknowledging, with grateful hearts, the goodness of the great Legislator of the universe, in affording us, in the course of His providence, an opportunity, deliberately and peaceably, without fraud, violence, or surprise, of entering into an original, explicit, and solemn compact with each other; and of forming a new constitution of civil government, for ourselves and posterity; and devoutly imploring His direction in so interesting a design, do agree upon, ordain, and establish, the following *Declaration of Rights, and Frame of Government*, as the CONSTITUTION OF THE COMMONWEALTH OF MASSACHUSETTS.

PART THE FIRST

A DECLARATION OF THE RIGHTS OF THE INHABITANTS OF THE COMMONWEALTH OF MASSACHUSETTS

ARTICLE I. All men are born free and equal, and have certain natural, essential, and unalienable rights; among which may be reckoned the right of enjoying and defending their lives and liberties; that of acquiring, possessing, and protecting property; in fine, that of seeking and obtaining their safety and happiness.

II. It is the right as well as the duty of all men in society, publicly, and at stated seasons, to worship the SUPREME BEING, the great Creator and Preserver of the universe. And no subject shall be hurt, molested, or restrained, in his person, liberty, or estate, for worshipping GOD in the manner and season most agreeable to the dictates of his own conscience; or for his religious profession of sentiments; provided he doth not disturb the public peace, or obstruct others in their religious worship.

III. [a] [As the happiness of a people, and the good order and preservation of civil government, essentially depend upon piety, religion, and morality; and as these cannot be generally diffused through a community but by the institution of the public worship of GOD, and of public instructions in piety, religion, and morality: Therefore, to promote their happiness, and to secure the good order and preservation of their government, the people of this commonwealth have a right to invest their legislature with power to authorize and require, and the legislature shall, from time to time, authorize and require,

---

[a] Amendment, Art. XI, substituted for this.

the several towns, parishes, precincts, and other bodies politic, or religious societies, to make suitable provision, at their own expense, for the institution of the public worship of God, and for the support and maintenance of public Protestant teachers of piety, religion, and morality, in all cases where such provision shall not be made voluntarily.

And the people of this commonwealth have also a right to, and do, invest their legislature with authority to enjoin upon all the subjects an attendance upon the instructions of the public teachers aforesaid, at stated times and seasons, if there be any on whose instructions they can conscientiously and conveniently attend.

Provided, notwithstanding, that the several towns, parishes, precincts, and other bodies politic, or religious societies, shall, at all times, have the exclusive right of electing their public teachers, and of contracting with them for their support and maintenance.

And all moneys paid by the subject to the support of public worship, and of the public teachers aforesaid, shall, if he require it, be uniformly applied to the support of the public teacher or teachers of his own religious sect or denomination, provided there be any on whose instructions he attends; otherwise it may be paid towards the support of the teacher or teachers of the parish or precinct in which the said moneys are raised.

And every denomination of Christians, demeaning themselves peaceably, and as good subjects of the commonwealth, shall be equally under the protection of the law: and no subordination of any one sect or denomination to another shall ever be established by law.]

IV. The people of this commonwealth have the sole and exclusive right of governing themselves, as a free, sovereign, and independent state; and do, and forever hereafter shall, exercise and enjoy every power, jurisdiction, and right, which is not, or may not hereafter be, by them expressly delegated to the United States of America, in Congress assembled.

V. All power residing originally in the people, and being derived from them, the several magistrates and officers of government, vested with authority, whether legislative, executive, or judicial, are their substitutes and agents, and are at all times accountable to them.

VI. No man, nor corporation, or association of men, have any other title to obtain advantages, or particular and exclusive privileges, distinct from those of the community, than what arises from the consideration of services rendered to the public; and this title being in nature neither hereditary, nor transmissible to children, or descendants, or relations by blood, the idea of a man born a magistrate, lawgiver, or judge, is absurd and unnatural.

VII. Government is instituted for the common good; for the protection, safety, prosperity, and happiness of the people; and not for the profit, honor, or private interest of any one man, family, or class of men: Therefore the people alone have an incontestible unalienable, and indefeasible right to institute government; and to reform, alter, or totally change the same, when their protection, safety, prosperity, and happiness require it.

VIII. In order to prevent those who are vested with authority from becoming oppressors, the people have a right, at such periods and in such manner as they shall establish by their frame of government, to cause their public officers to return to private life; and to fill up vacant places by certain and regular elections and appointments.

IX. All elections ought to be free; and all the inhabitants of this commonwealth, having such qualifications as they shall establish by their frame of government, have an equal right to elect officers, and to be elected, for public employments.

X. Each individual of the society has a right to be protected by it in the enjoyment of his life, liberty, and property, according to standing laws. He is obliged, consequently, to contribute his share to the expense of this protection; to give his personal service, or an equivalent, when necessary: but no part of the property of any individual can, with justice, be taken from him, or applied to public uses, without his own consent, or that of the representative body of the people. In fine, the people of this commonwealth are not controllable by any other laws than those to which their constitutional representative body have given their consent. And whenever the public exigencies require that the property of any individual should be appropriated to public uses, he shall receive a reasonable compensation therefor.

XI. Every subject of the commonwealth ought to find a certain remedy, by having recourse to the laws, for all injuries or wrongs which he may receive in his person, property, or character. He ought to obtain right and justice freely, and without being obliged to purchase it; completely, and without any denial; promptly, and without delay; conformably to the laws.

XII. No subject shall be held to answer for any crimes or offence, until the same is fully and plainly, substantially, and formally, described to him; or be compelled to accuse, or furnish evidence against himself. And every subject shall have a right to produce all proofs that may be favorable to him; to meet the witnesses against him face to face, and to be fully heard in his defence by himself, or his counsel, at his election. And no subject shall be arrested, imprisoned, despoiled, or deprived of his property, immunities, or privileges, put out of the protection of the law, exiled, or deprived of his life, liberty, or estate, but by the judgment of his peers, or the law of the land.

And the legislature shall not make any law that shall subject any person to a capital or infamous punishment, excepting for the government of the army and navy, without trial by jury.

XIII. In criminal prosecutions, the verification of facts, in the vicinity where they happen, is one of the greatest securities of the life, liberty, and property of the citizen.

XIV. Every subject has a right to be secure from all unreasonable searches, and seizures, of his person, his houses, his papers, and all his possessions. All warrants, therefore, are contrary to this right, if the cause or foundation of them be not previously supported by oath or affirmation, and if the order in the warrant to a civil officer, to make search in suspected places, or to arrest one or more suspected persons, or to seize their property, be not accompanied with a special designation of the persons or objects of search, arrest, or seizure; and no warrant ought to be issued but in cases, and with the formalities prescribed by the laws.

XV. In all controversies concerning property, and in all suits between two or more persons, except in cases in which it has heretofore been otherways used and practised, the parties have a right to a trial by jury; and this method of procedure shall be held sacred, unless, in causes arising on the high seas, and such as relate to mariners' wages, the legislature shall hereafter find it necessary to alter it.

XVI. The liberty of the press is essential to the security of freedom in a state it ought not, therefore, to be restricted in this commonwealth.

XVII. The people have a right to keep and to bear arms for the common defence. And as, in time of peace, armies are dangerous to liberty, they ought not to be maintained without the consent of the legislature; and the military power shall always be held in an exact subordination to the civil authority, and be governed by it.

XVIII. A frequent recurrence to the fundamental principles of the constitution, and a constant adherence to those of piety, justice, moderation, temperance, industry, and frugality, are absolutely necessary to preserve the advantages of liberty, and to maintain a free government. The people ought, consequently, to have a particular attention to all those principles, in the choice of their officers and representatives: and they have a right to require of their lawgivers and magistrates an exact and constant observance of them, in the formation and execution of the laws necessary for the good administration of the commonwealth.

XIX. The people have a right, in an orderly and peaceable manner, to assemble to consult upon the common good; give instructions to their representatives, and to request of the legislative body, by the way of addresses, petitions, or remonstrances, redress of the wrongs done them, and of the grievances they suffer.

XX. The power of suspending the laws, or the execution of the laws, ought never to be exercised but by the legislature, or by authority derived from it, to be exercised in such particular cases only as the legislature shall expressly provide for.

XXI. The freedom of deliberation, speech, and debate, in either house of the legislature, is so essential to the rights of the people, that it cannot be the foundation of any accusation or prosecution, action or complaint, in any other court or place whatsoever.

XXII. The legislature ought frequently to assemble for the redress of grievances, for correcting, strengthening, and confirming the laws, and for making new laws, as the common good may require.

XXIII. No subsidy, charge, tax, impost, or duties ought to be established, fixed, laid, or levied, under any pretext whatsoever, without the consent of the people or their representatives in the legislature.

XXIV. Laws made to punish for actions done before the existence of such laws, and which have not been declared crimes by preceding laws, are unjust, oppressive, and inconsistent with the fundamental principles of a free government.

XXV. No subject ought, in any case, or in any time, to be declared guilty of treason or felony by the legislature.

XXVI. No magistrate or court of law shall demand excessive bail or sureties, impose excessive fines, or inflict cruel or unusual punishments.

XXVII. In time of peace, no soldier ought to be quartered in any house without the consent of the owner; and in time of war, such quarters ought not to be made but by the civil magistrate, in a manner ordained by the legislature.

XXVIII. No person can in any case be subject to law-martial, or to any penalties or pains, by virtue of that law, except those employed in the army or navy, and except the militia in actual service, but by authority of the legislature.

XXIX. It is essential to the preservation of the rights of every individual, his life, liberty, property, and character, that there be an impartial interpretation of the laws, and administration of justice. It is the right of every citizen to be tried by judges as free, impartial, and independent as the lot of humanity will admit. It is, therefore, not only the best policy, but for the security of the rights of the people, and of every citizen, that the judges of the supreme judicial court should hold their offices as long as they behave themselves well; and that they should have honorable salaries ascertained and established by standing laws.

XXX. In the government of this commonwealth, the legislative department shall never exercise the executive and judicial powers, or either of them: the executive shall never exercise the legislative and judicial powers, or either of them: the judicial shall never exercise the legislative and executive powers, or either of them: to the end it may be a government of laws and not of men.

Part the Second

THE FRAME OF GOVERNMENT

The people, inhabiting the territory formerly called the Province of Massachusetts Bay, do hereby solemnly and mutually agree with each other, to form themselves into a free, sovereign, and independent body politic, or state, by the name of THE COMMONWEALTH OF MASSACHUSETTS.

CHAPTER I

THE LEGISLATIVE POWER

SECTION I.—THE GENERAL COURT

ARTICLE I. The department of legislation shall be formed by two branches, a Senate and House of Representatives; each of which shall have a negative on the other.

The legislative body shall assemble every year [a] [on the last Wednesday in May, and at such other times as they shall judge necessary; and shall dissolve and be dissolved on the day next preceding the said last Wednesday in May;] and shall be styled, THE GENERAL COURT OF MASSACHUSETTS.

II. No bill or resolve of the senate or house of representatives shall become a law, and have force as such, until it shall have been laid before the governor for his revisal; and if he, upon such revision, approve thereof, he shall signify his approbation by signing the same. But if he have any objection to the passing of such bill or resolve, he shall return the same, together with his objections thereto, in writing, to the senate or house of representatives, in whichsoever the same shall have originated; who shall enter the objections sent down

---

[a] For change of time, etc., see amendments, Art. X.

by the governor, at large, on their records, and proceed to reconsider the said bill or resolve. But if after such reconsideration, two-thirds of the said senate or house of representatives, shall, notwithstanding the said objections, agree to pass the same, it shall, together with the objections, be sent to the other branch of the legislature, where it shall also be reconsidered, and if approved by two-thirds of the members present, shall have the force of law: but in all such cases, the votes of both houses shall be determined by yeas and nays; and the names of the persons voting for, or against, the said bill or resolve, shall be entered upon the public records of the commonwealth.

And in order to prevent unnecessary delays, if any bill or resolve shall not be returned by the governor within five days after it shall have been presented, the same shall have the force of a law.[a]

III. The general court shall forever have full power and authority to erect and constitute judicatories and courts of record, or other courts, to be held in the name of the commonwealth, for the hearing, trying, and determining of all manner of crimes, offences, pleas, processes, plaints, actions, matters, causes, and things, whatsoever, arising or happening within the commonwealth, or between or concerning persons inhabiting, or residing, or brought within the same: whether the same be criminal or civil, or whether the said crimes be capital or not capital, and whether the said pleas be real, personal, or mixed; and for the awarding and making out of execution thereupon. To which courts and judicatories are hereby given and granted full power and authority, from time to time, to administer oaths or affirmations, for the better discovery of truth in any matter in controversy or depending before them.

IV. And further, full power and authority are hereby given and granted to the said general court, from time to time, to make, ordain, and establish, all manner of wholesome and reasonable orders, laws, statutes, and ordinances, directions and instructions, either with penalties or without; so as the same be not repugnant or contrary to this constitution, as they shall judge to be for the good and welfare of this commonwealth, and for the government and ordering thereof, and of the subjects of the same, and for the necessary support and defence of the government thereof; and to name and settle annually, or provide by fixed laws for the naming and settling, all civil officers within the said commonwealth, the election and constitution of whom are not hereafter in this form of government otherwise provided for; and to set forth the several duties, powers, and limits, of the several civil and military officers of this commonwealth, and the forms of such oaths or affirmations as shall be respectively administered unto them for the execution of their several offices and places, so as the same be not repugnant or contrary to this constitution; and to impose and levy proportional and reasonable assessments, rates, and taxes, upon all the inhabitants of, and persons resident, and estates lying, within the said commonwealth; and also to impose and levy reasonable duties and excises upon any produce, goods, wares, merchandise, and commodities, whatsoever, brought into, produced, manufactured, or being within the same; to be issued and disposed of by warrant, under the hand of the governor of this commonwealth for the time being, with the advice and consent

---

[a] See amendments, Art. I.

of the council, for the public service, in the necessary defence and support of the government of the said commonwealth, and the protection and preservation of the subjects thereof, according to such acts as are or shall be in force within the same.

And while the public charges of government, or any part thereof, shall be assessed on polls and estates, in the manner that has hitherto been practised, in order that such assessments may be made with equality, there shall be a valuation of estates within the commonwealth, taken anew once in every ten years at least, and as much oftener as the general court shall order.[a]

CHAPTER I

SECTION II.—SENATE

ARTICLE I. [b][There shall be annually elected, by the freeholders and other inhabitants of this commonwealth, qualified as in this constitution is provided, forty persons to be councillors and senators for the year ensuing their election; to be chosen by the inhabitants of the districts into which the commonwealth may, from time to time, be divided by the general court for that purpose: and the general court, in assigning the numbers to be elected by the respective districts, shall govern themselves by the proportion of the public taxes paid by the said districts; and timely make known to the inhabitants of the commonwealth the limits of each district, and the number of councillors [c] and senators to be chosen therein; provided that the number of such districts shall never be less than thirteen; and that no district be so large as to entitle the same to choose more than six senators.

And the several counties in this commonwealth shall, until the general court shall determine it necessary to alter the said districts, be districts for the choice of councillors and senators, (except that the counties of Dukes County and Nantucket shall form one district for that purpose) and shall elect the following number for councillors and senators, viz.:—Suffolk, six; Essex, six; Middlesex, five; Hampshire, four; Plymouth, three; Barnstable, one; Bristol, three; York, two; Dukes County and Nantucket, one; Worcester, five; Cumberland, one; Lincoln, one; Berkshire, two.]

II. The senate shall be the first branch of the legislature; and the senators shall be chosen in the following manner, viz.: there shall be a meeting on the [d] [first Monday in April,] annually, forever, of the inhabitants of each town in the several counties of this commonwealth; to be called by the selectmen, and warned in due course of law, at least seven days before the [d] [first Monday in April,] for the purpose of electing persons to be senators and councillors; [e] [and at such meetings every male inhabitant of twenty-one years of age and

---

[a] For the authority of the general court to charter cities, see amendments, Art. II.
[b] Superseded by amendments, Art. XIII., which was also superseded by amendments, Art. XXII.
[c] For provision as to councillors, see amendments, Art. XVI.
[d] Time of election changed by amendments, Art. X., and changed again by amendments, Art. XV. As to cities, see amendments, Art. II.
[e] These provisions as to the qualifications of voters, superseded by amendments, Arts. III., XX. and XXVIII.

upwards, having a freehold estate within the commonwealth, of the annual income of three pounds, or any estate of the value of sixty pounds, shall have a right to give in his vote for the senators for the district of which he is an inhabitant.] And to remove all doubts concerning the meaning of the word "inhabitant" in this constitution, every person shall be considered as an inhabitant, for the purpose of electing and being elected into any office, or place within this state, in that town, district, or plantation where he dwelleth, or hath his home.[a]

The selectmen of the several towns shall preside at such meetings impartially; and shall receive the votes of all the inhabitants of such towns [b] present and qualified to vote for senators, and shall sort and count them in open town meeting, and in presence of the town clerk, who shall make a fair record, in presence of the selectmen, and in open town meeting, of the name of every person voted for, and of the number of votes against his name: and a fair copy of this record shall be attested by the selectmen and the town clerk, and shall be sealed up, directed to the secretary of the commonwealth for the time being, with a superscription, expressing the purport of the contents thereof, and delivered by the town clerk of such towns, to the sheriff of the county in which such town lies, thirty days at least before [c] [the last Wednesday in May] annually; or it shall be delivered into the secretary's office seventeen days at least before the said [c] [last Wednesday in May:] and the sheriff of each county shall deliver all such certificates by him received, into the secretary's office, seventeen days before the said [c] [last Wednesday in May.]

And the inhabitants of plantations unincorporated, qualified as this constitution provides, who are or shall be empowered and required to assess taxes upon themselves toward the support of government, shall have the same privilege of voting for councillors and senators in the plantations where they reside, as town inhabitants have in their respective towns; and the plantation meetings for that purpose shall be held annually [d] [on the same first Monday in April], at such place in the plantations, respectively, as the assessors thereof shall direct; which assessors shall have like authority for notifying the electors, collecting and returning the votes, as the selectmen and town clerks have in their several towns, by this constitution. And all other persons living in places unincorporated (qualified as aforesaid) who shall be assessed to the support of government by the assessors of an adjacent town, shall have the privilege of giving in their votes for councillors and senators in the town where they shall be assessed, and be notified of the place of meeting by the selectmen of the town where they shall be assessed, for that purpose, accordingly.

III. And that there may be a due convention of senators on the [e] [last Wednesday in May] annually, the governor with five of the council, for the time being, shall, as soon as may be, examine the returned copies of such records; and fourteen days before the said day

---

[a] Word "inhabitant" defined. See also amendments, Arts. XXIII., which was annulled by Art. XXVI.
[b] As to cities, see amendments, Art. II.
[c] Time changed to first Wednesday of January. See amendments, Art. X.
[d] Time of election changed by amendments, Art. XV. Assessors to notify, etc.
[e] Time changed to first Wednesday in January by amendments, Art. X.

he shall issue his summons to such persons as shall appear to be chosen by [a] [a majority of] voters, to attend on that day, and take their seats accordingly: provided, nevertheless, that for the first year the said returned copies shall be examined by the president and five of the council of the former constitution of government; and the said president shall, in like manner, issue his summons to the persons so elected, that they may take their seats as aforesaid.

IV. The senate shall be the final judge of the elections, returns and qualifications of their own members, as pointed out in the constitution; and shall,[b] [on the said last Wednesday in May] annually, determine and declare who are elected by each district to be senators [a] [by a majority of votes; and in case there shall not appear to be the full number of senators returned elected by a majority of votes for any district, the deficiency shall be supplied in the following manner, viz.: The members of the house of representatives, and such senators as shall be declared elected, shall take the names of such persons as shall be found to have the highest number of votes in such district, and not elected, amounting to twice the number of senators wanting, if there be so many voted for; and out of these shall elect by ballot a number of senators sufficient to fill up the vacancies in such district; and in this manner all such vacancies shall be filled up in every district of the commonwealth; and in like manner all vacancies in the senate, arising by death, removal out of the state, or otherwise, shall be supplied as soon as may be, after such vacancies shall happen.] [c]

V. Provided, nevertheless, that no person shall be capable of being elected as a senator,[d] [who is not seised of his own right of a freehold, within this commonwealth, of the value of three hundred pounds at least, or possessed of personal estate to the value of six hundred pounds at least, or both to the amount of the same sum, and] who has not been an inhabitant of this commonwealth for the space of five years immediately preceding his election, and, at the time of his election, he shall be an inhabitant in the district for which he shall be chosen.

VI. The senate shall have power to adjourn themselves, provided such adjournments do not exceed two days at a time.

VII. The senate shall choose its own president, appoint its own officers, and determine its own rules of proceedings.

VIII. The senate shall be a court with full authority to hear and determine all impeachments made by the house of representatives, against any officer or officers of the commonwealth, for misconduct and mal-administration in their offices. But previous to the trial of every impeachment the members of the senate shall respectively be sworn, truly and impartially to try and determine the charge in question, according to evidence. Their judgment, however, shall not extend further than to removal from office and disqualification to hold or enjoy any place of honor, trust, or profit, under this commonwealth; but the party so convicted shall be, nevertheless, liable to

---

[a] Majority changed to plurality by amendments, Art. XIV.
[b] Time changed to first Wednesday of January by amendments, Art. X.
[c] Changed to election by people. See amendments, Art. XXIV.
[d] Property qualification abolished. See amendments, Art. XIII. For further provision as to residence, see also amendments, Art. XXII.

indictment, trial, judgment, and punishment, according to the laws of the land.

IX.[a] [Not less than sixteen members of the senate shall constitute a quorum for doing business.]

Chapter I

Section III.—House of Representatives

ARTICLE I. There shall be, in the legislature of this commonwealth, a representation of the people, annually elected, and founded upon the principle of equality.

II.[b] [And in order to provide for a representation of the citizens of this commonwealth, founded upon the principle of equality, every corporate town containing one hundred and fifty ratable polls may elect one representative; every corporate town containing three hundred and seventy-five ratable polls may elect two representatives; every corporate town containing six hundred ratable polls may elect three representatives; and proceeding in that manner, making two hundred and twenty-five ratable polls the mean increasing number for every additional representative.

Provided, nevertheless, that each town now incorporated, not having one hundred and fifty ratable polls, may elect one representative; but no place shall hereafter be incorporated with the privilege of electing a representative, unless there are within the same one hundred and fifty ratable polls.]

And the house of representatives shall have power from time to time to impose fines upon such towns as shall neglect to choose and return members to the same, agreeably to this constitution.

The expenses of travelling to the general assembly, and returning home, once in every session, and no more, shall be paid by the government, out of the public treasury, to every member who shall attend as seasonably as he can, in the judgment of the house, and does not depart without leave.

III. Every member of the house of representatives shall be chosen by written votes; [c] [and, for one year at least next preceding his election, shall have been an inhabitant of, and have been seised in his own right of a freehold of the value of one hundred pounds within the town he shall be chosen to represent, or any ratable estate to the value of two hundred pounds; and he shall cease to represent the said town immediately on his ceasing to be qualified as aforesaid.]

IV. [d] [Every male person, being twenty-one years of age, and resident in any particular town in this commonwealth for the space of one year next preceding, having a freehold estate within the said town of the annual income of three pounds, or any estate of the value of sixty pounds, shall have a right to vote in the choice of a representative or representatives for the said town.]

---

[a] See amendments, Arts. XXII. and XXXIII.

[b] Superseded by amendments, Arts. XII. and XIII., which were also superseded by amendments, Art. XXI.

[c] New provision as to residence. See amendments, Art. XXI. Property qualifications abolished by amendments, Art. XIII.

[d] These provisions superseded by amendments, Arts. III., XX. and XXVIII. See also amendments, Art. XXIII., which was annulled by Art. XXVI.

V. ᵃ [The members of the house of representatives shall be chosen annually in the month of May, ten days at least before the last Wednesday of that month.]

VI. The house of representatives shall be the grand inquest of this commonwealth; and all impeachments made by them shall be heard and tried by the senate.

VII. All money bills shall originate in the house of representatives; but the senate may propose or concur with amendments, as on other bills.

VIII. The house of representatives shall have power to adjourn themselves; provided such adjournment shall not exceed two days at a time.

IX. ᵇ [Not less than sixty members of the house of representatives shall constitute a quorum for doing business.]

X. The house of representatives shall be the judge of the returns, elections, and qualifications of its own members, as pointed out in the constitution; shall choose their own speaker; appoint their own officers, and settle the rules and orders of proceeding in their own house. They shall have authority to punish by imprisonment every person, not a member, who shall be guilty of disrespect to the house, by any disorderly or contemptuous behavior in its presence; or who, in the town where the general court is sitting, and during the time of its sitting, shall threaten harm to the body or estate of any of its members, for any thing said or done in the house; or who shall assault any of them therefor; or who shall assault, or arrest, any witness, or other person, ordered to attend the house, in his way in going or returning; or who shall rescue any person arrested by the order of the house.

And no member of the house of representatives shall be arrested, or held to bail on mean process, during his going unto, returning from, or his attending the general assembly.

XI. The senate shall have the same powers in the like cases; and the governor and council shall have the same authority to punish in like cases: provided, that no imprisonment on the warrant or order of the governor, council, senate, or house of representatives, for either of the above described offences, be for a term exceeding thirty days.

And the senate and house of representatives may try and determine all cases where their rights and privileges are concerned, and which, by the constitution, they have authority to try and determine, by committees of their own members, or in such other way as they may respectively think best.

CHAPTER II

EXECUTIVE POWER

SECTION I.—GOVERNOR

ARTICLE I. There shall be a supreme executive magistrate, who shall be styled—THE GOVERNOR OF THE COMMONWEALTH OF MASSACHUSETTS; and whose title shall be—HIS EXCELLENCY.

ᵃ Time of election changed by Amendments, Art. X., and changed again by amendments, Art. XV.

ᵇ Superseded by amendments, Art. XXI.

II. *a* The governor shall be chosen annually; and no person shall be eligible to this office, unless, at the time of his election, he shall have been an inhabitant of this commonwealth for seven years next preceding; [and unless he shall at the same time be seised, in his own right, of a freehold, within the commonwealth, of the value of one thousand pounds;] [and unless he shall declare himself to be of the Christian religion.]

III. Those persons who shall be qualified to vote for senators and representatives within the several towns of this commonwealth shall, at a meeting to be called for that purpose, on the *b* [first Monday of April] annually, give in their votes for a governor, to the selectmen, who shall preside at such meetings; and the town clerk, in the presence and with the assistance of the selectmen, shall, in open town meeting, sort and count the votes, and form a list of the persons voted for, with the number of votes for each person against his name; and shall make a fair record of the same in the town books,*c* and a public declaration thereof in the said meeting; and shall, in the presence of the inhabitants, seal up copies of the said list, attested by him and the selectmen, and transmit the same to the sheriff of the county, thirty days at least before the *d* [last Wednesday in May]; and the sheriff shall transmit the same to the secretary's office, seventeen days at least before the said *d* [last Wednesday in May]; or the selectmen may cause returns of the same to be made to the office of the secretary of the commonwealth, seventeen days at least before the said day; and the secretary shall lay the same before the senate and the house of representatives on the *d* [last Wednesday in May], to be by them examined; and *e* [in case of an election by a majority of all the votes returned], the choice shall be by them declared and published; *e* [but if no person shall have a majority of votes, the house of representatives shall, by ballot, elect two out of four persons who had the highest number of votes, if so many shall have been voted for; but, if otherwise, out of the number voted for; and make return to the senate of the two persons so elected; on which the senate shall proceed, by ballot, to elect one, who shall be declared governor.]

IV. The governor shall have authority, from time to time, at his discretion, to assemble and call together the councillors of this commonwealth for the time being; and the governor with the said councillors, or five of them at least, shall, and may, from time to time, hold and keep a council, for the ordering and directing the affairs of the commonwealth, agreeably to the constitution and the laws of the land.

V. The governor, with advice of council, shall have full power and authority, during the session of the general court, to adjourn or prorogue the same to any time the two houses shall desire; *a* [and to dissolve the same on the day next preceding the last Wednesday in May; and, in the recess of the said court, to prorogue the same from time to time, not exceeding ninety days in any one recess;] and to call it together sooner than the time to which it may be adjourned or

---

a Qualifications. [See amendments, Arts. VII. and XXXIV.]
b Time of election changed by amendments, Art. X., and changed again by amendments, Art. XV.
c As to cities, see amendments, Art. II.
d Time changed to first Wednesday of January by amendments, Art. X.
e Changed to plurality by amendments, Art. XIV.

prorogued, if the welfare of the commonwealth shall require the same; and in case of any infectious distemper prevailing in the place where the said court is next at any time to convene, or any other cause happening, whereby danger may arise to the health or lives of the members from their attendance, he may direct the session to be held at some other, the most convenient place within the state.

a [And the governor shall dissolve the said general court on the day next preceding the last Wednesday in May.]

VI. In cases of disagreement between the two houses, with regard to the necessity, expediency, or time of adjournment or prorogation, the governor, with advice of the council, shall have a right to adjourn or prorogue the general court, not exceeding ninety days, as he shall determine the public good shall require.

VII. The governor of this commonwealth, for the time being, shall be the commander-in-chief of the army and navy, and of all the military forces of the state, by sea and land; and shall have full power, by himself, or by any commander, or other officer or officers, from time to time, to train, instruct, exercise, and govern the militia and navy; and, for the special defence and safety of the commonwealth, to assemble in martial array, and put in warlike posture, the inhabitants thereof, and to lead and conduct them, and with them to encounter, repel, resist, expel, and pursue, by force of arms, as well by sea as by land, within or without the limits of this commonwealth, and also to kill, slay, and destroy, if necessary, and conquer, by all fitting ways, enterprises, and means whatsoever, all and every such person and persons as shall, at any time hereafter, in a hostile manner, attempt or enterprise the destruction, invasion, detriment, or annoyance of this commonwealth; and to use and exercise, over the army and navy, and over the militia in actual service, the law-martial, in time of war or invasion, and also in time of rebellion, declared by the legislature to exist, as occasion shall necessarily require; and to take and surprise, by all ways and means whatsoever, all and every such person or persons, with their ships, arms, ammunition, and other goods, as shall, in a hostile manner, invade, or attempt the invading, conquering, or annoying this commonwealth; and that the governor be intrusted with all these and other powers, incident to the offices of captain-general and commander-in-chief, and admiral, to be exercised agreeably to the rules and regulations of the constitution, and the laws of the land, and not otherwise.

Provided, that the said governor shall not, at any time hereafter, by virtue of any power by this constitution granted, or hereafter to be granted to him by the legislature, transport any of the inhabitants of this commonwealth, or oblige them to march out of the limits of the same, without their free and voluntary consent, or the consent of the general court; except so far as may be necessary to march or transport them by land or water, for the defence of such part of the state to which they cannot otherwise conveniently have access.

VIII. The power of pardoning offences, except such as persons may be convicted of before the senate by an impeachment of the house, shall be in the governor, by and with the advice of council; but no charter of pardon, granted by the governor, with advice of the council before conviction, shall avail the party pleading the same,

---

a As to dissolution, see amendments, Art. X.

notwithstanding any general or particular expressions contained therein, descriptive of the offence or offences intended to be pardoned.

IX. All judicial officers, *a* [the attorney-general,] the solicitor-general, *b* [all sheriffs,] coroners, *b* [and registers of probate,] shall be nominated and appointed by the governor, by and with the advice and consent of the council; and every such nomination shall be made by the governor, and made at least seven days prior to such appointment.

X. The captains and subalterns of the militia shall be elected by the written votes of the train-band and alarm list of their respective companies, *c* [of twenty-one years of age and upwards;] the field officers of regiments shall be elected by the written votes of the captains and subalterns of their respective regiments; the brigadiers shall be elected, in like manner, by the field officers of their respective brigades; and such officers, so elected, shall be commissioned by the governor, who shall determine their rank.

The legislature shall, by standing laws, direct the time and manner of convening the electors, and of collecting votes, and of certifying to the governor, the officers elected.

The major-generals shall be appointed by the senate and house of representatives, each having a negative upon the other; and be commissioned by the governor.*d*

And if the electors of brigadiers, field officers, captains or subalterns, shall neglect or refuse to make such elections, after being duly notified, according to the laws for the time being, then the governor, with advice of council, shall appoint suitable persons to fill such offices.

e [And no officer, duly commissioned to command in the militia, shall be removed from his office, but by the address of both houses to the governor, or by fair trial in court-martial, pursuant to the laws of the commonwealth for the time being.]

The commanding officers of regiments shall appoint their adjutants and quartermasters; the brigadiers their brigade-majors; and the major-generals their aids; and the governor shall appoint the adjutant-general.

The governor, with advice of council, shall appoint all officers of the continental army, whom by the confederation of the United States it is provided that this commonwealth shall appoint, as also all officers of forts and garrisons.

The divisions of the militia into brigades, regiments, and companies, made in pursuance of the militia laws now in force, shall be considered as the proper divisions of the militia of this commonwealth, until the same shall be altered in pursuance of some future law.

XI. No moneys shall be issued out of the treasury of this common-

---

a For provisions as to election of attorney-general, see amendments, Art. XVII.

b For provision as to election of sheriffs, registers of probate, etc., see amendments, Art. XIX. For provision as to appointment of notaries public, see amendments, Art. IV.

c Limitation of age struck out by amendments, Art. V.

d For provisions as to appointment of a commissary-general, see amendments, Art. IV.

e Officers duly commissioned, how removed. Superseded by amendments, Art. IV.

wealth, and disposed of (except such sums as may be appropriated for the redemption of bills of credit or treasurer's notes, or for the payment of interest arising thereon) but by warrant under the hand of the governor for the time being, with the advice and consent of the council, for the necessary defence and support of the commonwealth; and for the protection and preservation of the inhabitants thereof, agreeably to the acts and resolves of the general court.

XII. All public boards, the commissary-general, all superintending officers of public magazines and stores, belonging to this commonwealth, and all commanding officers of forts and garrisons within the same, shall once in every three months, officially, and without requisition, and at other times, when required by the governor, deliver to him an account of all goods, stores, provisions, ammunition, cannon with their appendages, and small arms with their accoutrements, and of all other public property whatever under their care respectively; distinguishing the quantity, number, quality and kind of each, as particularly as may be; together with the condition of such forts and garrisons; and the said commanding officer shall exhibit to the governor, when required by him, true and exact plans of such forts, and of the land and sea or harbor or harbors, adjacent.

And the said boards, and all public officers, shall communicate to the governor, as soon as may be after receiving the same, all letters, despatches, and intelligences of a public nature, which shall be directed to them respectively.

XIII. As the public good requires that the governor should not be under the undue influence of any of the members of the general court by a dependence on them for his support, that he should in all cases act with freedom for the benefit of the public, that he should not have his attention necessarily diverted from that object to his private concerns, and that he should maintain the dignity of the commonwealth in the character of its chief magistrate, it is necessary that he should have an honorable stated salary, of a fixed and permanent value, amply sufficient for those purposes, and established by standing laws; and it shall be among the first acts of the general court, after the commencement of this constitution, to establish such salary by law accordingly.

Permanent and honorable salaries shall also be established by law for the justices of the supreme judicial court.

And if it shall be found that any of the salaries aforesaid, so established, are insufficient, they shall, from time to time, be enlarged, as the general court shall judge proper.

Chapter II

Section II.—Lieutenant-Governor

ARTICLE I. There shall be annually elected a lieutenant-governor of the commonwealth of Massachusetts, whose title shall be—HIS HONOR; and who shall be qualified, in point of [a][religion,] property, and residence in the commonwealth, in the same manner with the governor; and the day and manner of his election, and the qualifications of the electors, shall be the same as are required in the election

---

[a] See amendments. Arts. VII. and XXXIV.

of a governor. The return of the votes for this officer, and the declaration of his election, shall be in the same manner; *a* [and if no one person shall be found to have a majority of all the votes returned, the vacancy shall be filled by the senate and house of representatives, in the same manner as the governor is to be elected, in case no one person shall have a majority of the votes of the people to be governor.]

II. The governor, and in his absence the lieutenant-governor, shall be president of the council, but shall have no vote in council; and the lieutenant-governor shall always be a member of the council, except when the chair of the governor shall be vacant.

III. Whenever the chair of the governor shall be vacant, by reason of his death, or absence from the commonwealth, or otherwise, the lieutenant-governor, for the time being, shall, during such vacancy, perform all the duties incumbent upon the governor, and shall have and exercise all the powers and authorities, which by this constitution the governor is vested with, when personally present.

Chapter II

Section III.—Council, and the Manner of Settling Elections by the Legislature.

Article I. There shall be a council for advising the governor in the executive part of the government, to consist of *b* [nine] persons besides the lieutenant-governor, whom the governor, for the time being, shall have full power and authority, from time to time, at his discretion, to assemble and call together; and the governor, with the said councillors, or five of them at least, shall and may, from time to time, hold and keep a council, for the ordering and directing the affairs of the commonwealth, according to the laws of the land.

II. *c* [Nine councillors shall be annually chosen from among the persons returned for councillors and senators, on the last Wednesday in May, by the joint ballot of the senators and representatives assembled in one room; and in case there shall not be found upon the first choice, the whole number of nine persons who will accept a seat in the council, the deficiency shall be made up by the electors aforesaid from among the people at large; and the number of senators left shall constitute the senate for the year. The seats of the persons thus elected from the senate, and accepting the trust, shall be vacated in the senate.]

III. The councillors, in the civil arrangements of the commonwealth, shall have rank next after the lieutenant-governor.

IV. *d* [Not more than two councillors shall be chosen out of any one district of this commonwealth.]

V. The resolutions and advice of the council shall be recorded in a register, and signed by the members present; and this record may be called for at any time by either house of the legislature; and any member of the council may insert his opinion, contrary to the resolution of the majority.

---

a Changed by amendments, Art. XIV.
b See amendments, Art. XVI.
c Modified by amendments, Arts. X and XIII. Superseded by amendments, Art. XVI.
d Superseded by amendments, Art. XVI.

VI. Whenever the office of the governor and lieutenant-governor shall be vacant, by reason of death, absence, or otherwise, then the council, or the major part of them, shall, during such vacancy, have full power and authority to do, and execute, all and every such acts, matters, and things, as the governor or the lieutenant-governor might or could, by virtue of this constitution, do or execute, if they, or either of them, were personally present.

VII. [a] [And whereas the elections appointed to be made, by this constitution, on the last Wednesday in May annually, by the two houses of the legislature, may not be completed on that day, the said elections may be adjourned from day to day until the same shall be completed. And the order of elections shall be as follows: the vacancies in the senate, if any, shall first be filled up; the governor and lieutenant-governor shall then be elected, provided there should be no choice of them by the people; and afterwards the two houses shall proceed to the election of the council.]

CHAPTER II

SECTION IV.—SECRETARY, TREASURER, COMMISSARY, ETC

ARTICLE I. [b] [The secretary, treasurer, and receiver-general, and the commissary-general, notaries public, and] naval officers, shall be chosen annually, by joint ballot of the senators and representatives in one room. And, that the citizens of this commonwealth may be assured, from time to time, that the moneys remaining in the public treasury, upon the settlement and liquidation of the public accounts, are their property, no man shall be eligible as treasurer and receiver-general more than five years successively.[c]

II. The records of the commonwealth shall be kept in the office of the secretary, who may appoint his deputies, for whose conduct he shall be accountable; and he shall attend the governor and council, the senate and house of representatives, in person, or by his deputies, as they shall respectively require.

CHAPTER III

JUDICIARY POWER

ARTICLE I. The tenure, that all commission officers shall by law have in their offices, shall be expressed in their respective commissions. All judicial officers, duly appointed, commissioned, and sworn, shall hold their offices during good behavior, excepting such concerning whom there is different provision made in this constitution: provided, nevertheless, the governor, with consent of the council, may remove them upon the address of both houses of the legislature.

II. Each branch of the legislature, as well as the governor and council, shall have authority to require the opinions of the justices of the supreme judicial court, upon important questions of law, and upon solemn occasions.

---

[a] Superseded by amendments, Arts. XVI. and XXV.

[b] For provision as to election of secretary, treasurer, and receiver-general, and auditor and attorney-general, see amendments, Art. XVII.

[c] For provision as to appointment of notaries public and the commissary-general, see amendments, Art. IV.

III. In order that the people may not suffer from the long continuance in place of any justice of the peace who shall fail of discharging the important duties of his office with ability or fidelity, all commissions of justices of the peace shall expire and become void, in the term of seven years from their respective dates; and, upon the expiration of any commission, the same may, if necessary, be renewed, or another person appointed, as shall most conduce to the well-being of the commonwealth.

IV. The judges of probate of wills, and for granting letters of administration, shall hold their courts at such place or places, on fixed days, as the convenience of the people shall require; and the legislature shall, from time to time, hereafter, appoint such times and places; until which appointments, the said courts shall be holden at the times and places which the respective judges shall direct.

V. All causes of marriage, divorce, and alimony, and all appeals from the judges of probate, shall be heard and determined by the governor and council, until the legislature shall, by law, make other provision.

Chapter IV

Delegates to Congress

[a] [The delegates of this commonwealth to the congress of the United States, shall, some time in the month of June, annually, be elected by the joint ballot of the senate and house of representatives, assembled together in one room; to serve in congress for one year, to commence on the first Monday in November then next ensuing. They shall have commissions under the hand of the governor, and the great seal of the commonwealth; but may be recalled at any time within the year, and others chosen and commissioned, in the same manner, in their stead.]

Chapter V

The University at Cambridge and Encouragement of Literature, etc

Section I.—The University

ARTICLE I. Whereas our wise and pious ancestors, so early as the year one thousand six hundred and thirty-six, laid the foundation of Harvard College, in which university many persons of great eminence have, by the blessing of GOD, been initiated in those arts and sciences which qualified them for public employments, both in church and state; and whereas the encouragement of arts and sciences, and all good literature, tends to the honor of GOD, the advantage of the Christian religion, and the great benefit of this and the other United States of America,—it is declared, that the PRESIDENT AND FELLOWS OF HARVARD COLLEGE, in their corporate capacity, and their successors in that capacity, their officers and servants, shall have, hold, use, exercise, and enjoy, all the powers, authorities, rights, liberties, privileges, immunities, and franchises, which they now have, or are entitled to have, hold, use, exercise, and enjoy; and the same are hereby

---

[a] Superseded by Art. I, Constitution United States.

ratified and confirmed unto them, the said president and fellows of Harvard College, and to their successors, and to their officers and servants, respectively, forever.

II. And whereas there have been at sundry times, by divers persons, gifts, grants, devises of houses, lands, tenements, goods, chattels, legacies, and conveyances, heretofore made, either to Harvard College in Cambridge, in New England, or to the president and fellows of Harvard College, or to the said college by some other description, under several charters, successively; it is declared, that all the said gifts, grants, devises, legacies, and conveyances, are hereby forever confirmed unto the president and fellows of Harvard College, and to their successors in the capacity aforesaid, according to the true intent and meaning of the donor or donors, grantor or grantors, devisor or devisors.

III. And whereas, by an act of the general court of the colony of Massachusetts Bay, passed in the year one thousand six hundred and forty-two, the governor and deputy-governor, for the time being, and all the magistrates of that jurisdiction, were, with the president, and a number of the clergy in the said act described, constituted the overseers of Harvard College; and it being necessary, in this new constitution of government to ascertain who shall be deemed successors to the said governor, deputy-governor, and magistrates; it is declared, that the governor, lieutenant-governor, council, and senate of this commonwealth, are, and shall be deemed, their successors, who, with the president of Harvard College, for the time being, together with the ministers of the congregational churches in the towns of Cambridge, Watertown, Charlestown, Boston, Roxbury, and Dorchester, mentioned in the said act, shall be, and hereby are, vested with all the powers and authority belonging, or in any way appertaining to the overseers of Harvard College; provided, that nothing herein shall be construed to prevent the legislature of this commonwealth from making such alterations in the government of the said university, as shall be conducive to its advantage, and the interest of the republic of letters, in as full a manner as might have been done by the legislature of the late Province of the Massachusetts Bay.

CHAPTER V

SECTION II.—THE ENCOURAGEMENT OF LITERATURE, ETC

[a] Wisdom and knowledge, as well as virtue, diffused generally among the body of the people, being necessary for the preservation of their rights and liberties; and as these depend on spreading the opportunities and advantages of education in the various parts of the country, and among the different orders of the people, it shall be the duty of legislatures and magistrates, in all future periods of this commonwealth, to cherish the interests of literature and the sciences, and all seminaries of them; especially the university at Cambridge, public schools and grammar schools in the towns; to encourage private societies and public institutions, rewards and immunities, for the promotion of agriculture, arts, sciences, commerce, trades, manufactures, and a natural history of the country; to countenance and in-

[a] For further provisions as to public schools, see amendments, Art. XVIII.

culcate the principles of humanity and general benevolence, public and private charity, industry and frugality, honesty and punctuality in their dealings; sincerity, good humor, and all social affections, and generous sentiments, among the people.

CHAPTER VI

OATHS AND SUBSCRIPTIONS; INCOMPATABILITY OF AND EXCLUSION FROM OFFICES; PECUNIARY QUALIFICATIONS; COMMISSIONS; WRITS; CONFIRMATION OF LAWS; HABEAS CORPUS; THE ENACTING STYLE; CONTINUANCE OF OFFICERS; PROVISION FOR A FUTURE REVISAL OF THE CONSTITUTION, ETC

ARTICLE I.[a] [Any person chosen governor, lieutenant-governor, councillor, senator, or representative, and accepting the trust, shall, before he proceed to execute the duties of his place or office, make and subscribe the following declaration, viz.:

" I, A. B., do declare, that I believe the Christian religion, and have a firm persuasion of its truth; and that I am seised and possessed, in my own right, of the property required by the constitution, as one qualification for the office or place to which I am elected."

And the governor, lieutenant-governor, and councillors, shall make and subscribe the said declaration, in the presence of the two houses of assembly; and the senators and representatives, first elected under this constitution, before the president and five of the council of the former constitution; and forever afterwards before the governor and council for the time being.]

And every person chosen to either of the places or offices aforesaid, as also any person appointed or commissioned to any judicial, executive, military, or other office under the government, shall, before he enters on the discharge of the business of his place or office, take and subscribe the following declaration, and oaths or affirmations, viz.:

[b] [" I, A. B., do truly and sincerely acknowledge, profess, testify, and declare, that the Commonwealth of Massachusetts is, and of right ought to be, a free, sovereign, and independent state; and I do swear, that I will bear true faith and allegiance to the said commonwealth, and that I will defend the same against traitorous conspiracies and all hostile attempts whatsoever; and that I do renounce and abjure all allegiance, subjection, and obedience to the king, queen, or government of Great Britain (as the case may be), and every other foreign power whatsoever; and that no foreign prince, person, prelate, state, or potentate, hath, or ought to have, any jurisdiction, superiority, pre-eminence, authority, dispensing or other power, in any matter, civil, ecclesiastical, or spiritual, within this commonwealth, except the authority and power which is or may be vested by their constituents in the congress of the United States; and I do further testify and declare, that no man or body of men hath or can have any right to absolve or discharge me from the obligation of this oath, declaration, or affirmation; and that I do make this acknowledgment, profession, testimony, declaration, denial, renunciation, and abjuration, heartily and truly, according to the common meaning and acceptation

---

[a] Abolished. See amendments, Art. VII.
[b] For new oath of allegiance, see amendments, Art. VI.

of the foregoing words, without any equivocation, mental evasion, or secret reservation whatsoever. So help me, GOD."]

" I, A. B., do solemnly swear and affirm, that I will faithfully and impartially discharge and perform all the duties incumbent on me as   , according to the best of my abilities and understanding, agreeably to the rules and regulations of the constitution and the laws of the commonwealth. So help me, GOD."

a Provided, always, that when any person chosen or appointed as aforesaid, shall be of the denomination of the people called Quakers, and shall decline taking the said oath[s], he shall make his affirmation in the foregoing form, and subscribe the same, omitting the words, ["*I do swear,*" "*and abjure,*" "*oath or,*" "*and abjuration,*" in the first oath, and in the second oath, the words] " *swear and*," and [in each of them] the words "*So help me*, GOD;" subjoining instead thereof, " *This I do under the pains and penalties of perjury.*"

And the said oaths or affirmations shall be taken and subscribed by the governor, lieutenant-governor, and councillors, before the president of the senate, in the presence of the two houses of assembly; and by the senators and representatives first elected under this constitution, before the president and five of the council of the former constitution; and forever afterwards before the governor and council for the time being; and by the residue of the officers aforesaid, before such persons and in such manner as from time to time shall be prescribed by the legislature.

II. *b* No governor, lieutenant-governor, or judge of the supreme judicial court, shall hold any other office or place, under the authority of this commonwealth, except such as by this constitution they are admitted to hold, saving that the judges of the said court may hold the offices of justices of the peace through the state; nor shall they hold any other place or office, or receive any pension or salary from any other state or government or power whatever.

No person shall be capable of holding or exercising at the same time, within this state, more than one of the following offices, viz.: judge of probate—sheriff—register of probate—or register of deeds; and never more than any two offices, which are to be held by appointment of the governor, or the governor and council, or the senate, or the house of representatives, or by the election of the people of the state at large, or of the people of any county, military offices, and the offices of justices of the peace excepted, shall be held by one person.

c No person holding the office of judge of the supreme judicial court—secretary—attorney-general—solicitor-general—treasurer or receiver-general—judge of probate—commissary-general—[president, professor, or instructor of Harvard College]—sheriff—clerk of the house of representatives—register of probate—register of deeds—clerk of the supreme judicial court—clerk of the inferior court of common pleas—or officer of the customs, including in this description naval officers—shall at the same time have a seat in the senate or house of representatives; but their being chosen or appointed to, and accepting

---

a See amendments, Art. VI.
b Plurality of offices prohibited to governor, etc., except, etc. See amendments, Art. VIII.
c For further provisions as to incompatible offices, see amendments, Art. VIII. Officers of Harvard College excepted by amendments, Art. XXVII.

the same, shall operate as a resignation of their seat in the senate or house of representatives; and the place so vacated shall be filled up.

And the same rule shall take place in case any judge of the said supreme judicial court, or judge of probate, shall accept a seat in council; or any councillor shall accept of either of those offices or places.

And no person shall ever be admitted to hold a seat in the legislature, or any office of trust or importance under the government of this commonwealth, who shall, in the due course of law, have been convicted of bribery or corruption in obtaining an election or appointment.

III. In all cases where sums of money are mentioned in this constitution, the value thereof shall be computed in silver, at six shillings and eight pence per ounce; and it shall be in the power of the legislature, from time to time, to increase such qualifications, as to property,[a] of the persons to be elected to offices, as the circumstances of the commonwealth shall require.

IV. All commissions shall be in the name of the Commonwealth of Massachusetts, signed by the governor and attested by the secretary or his deputy, and have the great seal of the commonwealth affixed thereto.

V. All writs, issuing out of the clerk's office in any of the courts of law, shall be in the name of the Commonwealth of Massachusetts; they shall be under the seal of the court from whence they issue; they shall bear test of the first justice of the court to which they shall be returnable, who is not a party, and be signed by the clerk of such court.

VI. All the laws which have heretofore been adopted, used, and approved in the Province, Colony, or State of Massachusetts Bay, and usually practised on in the courts of law, shall still remain and be in full force, until altered or repealed by the legislature; such parts only excepted as are repugnant to the rights and liberties contained in this constitution.

VII. The privilege and benefit of the writ of *habeas corpus* shall be enjoyed in this commonwealth, in the most free, easy, cheap, expeditious, and ample manner; and shall not be suspended by the legislature, except upon the most urgent and pressing occasions, and for a limited time, not exceeding twelve months.

VIII. The enacting style, in making and passing all acts, statutes, and laws, shall be—" Be it enacted by the Senate and House of Representatives, in General Court assembled, and by the authority of the same."

IX. To the end there may be no failure of justice, or danger arise to the commonwealth from a change of the form of government, all officers, civil and military, holding commissions under the government and people of Massachusetts Bay in New England, and all other officers of the said government and people, at the time this constitution shall take effect, shall have, hold, use, exercise, and enjoy, all the powers and authority to them granted or committed, until other persons shall be appointed in their stead; and all courts of law shall proceed in the execution of the business of their respective departments; and all the executive and legislative officers, bodies, and

---

[a] See amendments, Arts. XIII. and XXXIV.

powers shall continue in full force, in the enjoyment and exercise of all their trusts, employments, and authority; until the general court, and the supreme and executive officers under this constitution, are designated and invested with their respective trusts, powers, and authority.

X.*a* [In order the more effectually to adhere to the principles of the constitution, and to correct those violations which by any means may be made therein, as well as to form such alterations as from experience shall be found necessary, the general court which shall be in the year of our Lord one thousand seven hundred and ninety-five, shall issue precepts to the selectmen of the several towns, and to the assessors of the unincorporated plantations, directing them to convene the qualified voters of their respective towns and plantations, for the purpose of collecting their sentiments on the necessity or expediency of revising the constitution, in order to amendments.

And if it shall appear, by the returns made, that two-thirds of the qualified voters throughout the state, who shall assemble and vote in consequence of the said precepts, are in favor of such revision or amendment, the general court shall issue precepts, or direct them to be issued from the secretary's office, to the several towns to elect delegates to meet in convention for the purpose aforesaid.

The said delegates to be chosen in the same manner and proportion as their representatives in the second branch of the legislature are by this constitution to be chosen.]

XI. This form of government shall be enrolled on parchment, and deposited in the secretary's office, and be a part of the laws of the land; and printed copies thereof shall be prefixed to the book containing the laws of this commonwealth, in all future editions of the said laws.

ARTICLES OF AMENDMENT

ARTICLE I. If any bill or resolve shall be objected to, and not approved by the governor; and if the general court shall adjourn within five days after the same shall have been laid before the governor for his approbation, and thereby prevent his returning it with his objections, as provided by the constitution, such bill or resolve shall not become a law, nor have force as such.

ART. II. The general court shall have full power and authority to erect and constitute municipal or city governments, in any corporate town or towns in this commonwealth, and to grant to the inhabitants thereof such powers, privileges, and immunities, not repugnant to the constitution, as the general court shall deem necessary or expedient for the regulation and government thereof, and to prescribe the manner of calling and holding public meetings of the inhabitants, in wards or otherwise, for the election of officers under the constitution, and the manner of returning the votes given at such meetings. Provided, that no such government shall be erected or constituted in any town not containing twelve thousand inhabitants, nor unless it be with the consent, and on the application of a majority of the inhabitants of such town, present and voting thereon, pursuant to a vote at a meeting duly warned and holden for that purpose. And provided, also, that all by-laws, made by such municipal or city government, shall be subject, at all times, to be annulled by the general court.

---

a For existing provision as to amendments, see amendments, Art. IX.

ART. III. Every male citizen of twenty-one years of age and upwards, excepting paupers and persons under guardianship, who shall have resided within the commonwealth one year, and within the town or district in which he may claim a right to vote, six calendar months next preceding any election of governor, lieutenant-governor, senators, or representatives,[a] [and who shall have paid, by himself, or his parent, master, or guardian, any state or county tax, which shall, within two years next preceding such election, have been assessed upon him, in any town or district of this commonwealth; and also every citizen who shall be, by law, exempted from taxation, and who shall be, in all other respects, qualified as above mentioned, shall have a right to vote in such election of governor, lieutenant-governor, senators, and representatives; and no other person shall be entitled to vote in such elections.][b]

ART. IV. Notaries public shall be appointed by the governor in the same manner as judicial officers are appointed, and shall hold their offices during seven years, unless sooner removed by the governor, with the consent of the council, upon the address of both houses of the legislature.

[c] [In case the office of secretary or treasurer of the commonwealth shall become vacant from any cause, during the recess of the general court, the governor, with the advice and consent of the council, shall nominate and appoint, under such regulations as may be prescribed by law, a competent and suitable person to such vacant office, who shall hold the same until a successor shall be appointed by the general court.]

Whenever the exigencies of the commonwealth shall require the appointment of a commissary-general, he shall be nominated, appointed, and commissioned, in such manner as the legislature may, by law, prescribe.

All officers commissioned to command in the militia may be removed from office in such manner as the legislature may, by law, prescribe.

ART. V. In the elections of captains and subalterns of the militia, all the members of their respective companies, as well those under as those above the age of twenty-one years, shall have a right to vote.

ART. VI.[d] Instead of the oath of allegiance prescribed by the constitution, the following oath shall be taken and subscribed by every person chosen or appointed to any office, civil or military, under the government of this commonwealth, before he shall enter on the duties of his office, to wit:—

"I, A. B., do solemnly swear, that I will bear true faith and allegiance to the Commonwealth of Massachusetts, and will support the constitution thereof. So help me, GOD."

Provided, That when any person shall be of the denomination called Quakers, and shall decline taking said oath, he shall make his affirmation in the foregoing form, omitting the word "swear" and inserting, instead thereof, the word "affirm," and omitting the words

---

[a] See amendments, Arts. XXX. and XXXII.

[b] For educational qualification, see amendments, Art. XX. For provision as to those who have served in the army or navy in time of war, see amendments, Art. XXVIII. See also amendments, Art. XXIII., which was annulled by amendments, Art. XXVI.

[c] This clause superseded by amendments, Art. XVII.

[d] Oath to be taken by all officers. See Const., Ch. VI., Art. I.

"So help me, God," and subjoining, instead thereof, the words, "This I do under the pains and penalties of perjury."

ART. VII. No oath, declaration, or subscription, excepting the oath prescribed in the preceding article, and the oath of office, shall be required of the governor, lieutenant-governor, councillors, senators, or representatives, to qualify them to perform the duties of their respective offices.

ART. VIII. No judge of any court of this commonwealth, (except the court of sessions,) and no person holding any office under the authority of the United States, (postmasters excepted,) shall, at the same time, hold the office of governor, lieutenant-governor, or councillor, or have a seat in the senate or house of representatives of this commonwealth; and no judge of any court in this commonwealth, (except the court of sessions,) nor the attorney-general, solicitor-general, county attorney, clerk of any court, sheriff, treasurer, and receiver-general, register of probate, nor register of deeds, shall continue to hold his said office after being elected a member of the Congress of the United States, and accepting that trust; but the acceptance of such trust, by any of the officers aforesaid, shall be deemed and taken to be a resignation of his said office; and judges of the courts of common pleas shall hold no other office under the government of this commonwealth, the office of justice of the peace and militia offices excepted.

ART. IX. If, at any time hereafter, any specific and particular amendment or amendments to the constitution be proposed in the general court, and agreed to by a majority of the senators and two-thirds of the members of the house of representatives present and voting thereon, such proposed amendment or amendments shall be entered on the journals of the two houses, with the yeas and nays taken thereon, and referred to the general court then next to be chosen, and shall be published; and if, in the general court next chosen as aforesaid, such proposed amendment or amendments shall be agreed to by a majority of the senators and two-thirds of the members of the house of representatives present and voting thereon, then it shall be the duty of the general court to submit such proposed amendment or amendments to the people; and if they shall be approved and ratified by a majority of the qualified voters, voting thereon, at meetings legally warned and holden for that purpose, they shall become part of the constitution of this commonwealth.

ART. X. The political year shall begin on the first Wednesday of January, instead of the last Wednesday of May; and the general court shall assemble every year on the said first Wednesday of January, and shall proceed, at that session, to make all the elections, and do all the other acts, which are by the constitution required to be made and done at the session which has heretofore commenced on the last Wednesday of May. And the general court shall be dissolved on the day next preceding the first Wednesday of January, without any proclamation or other act of the governor. But nothing herein contained shall prevent the general court from assembling at such other times as they shall judge necessary, or when called together by the governor. The governor, lieutenant-governor and councillors, shall also hold their respective offices for one year next following the first Wednesday of January, and until others are chosen and qualified in their stead.

a [The meeting for the choice of governor, lieutenant-governor, senators, and representatives, shall be held on the second Monday of November in every year; but meetings may be adjourned, if necessary, for the choice of representatives, to the next day, and again to the next succeeding day, but no further. But in case a second meeting shall be necessary for the choice of representatives, such meetings shall be held on the fourth Monday of the same month of November.]

All the other provisions of the constitution, respecting the elections and proceedings of the members of the general court, or of any other officers or persons whatever, that have reference to the last Wednesday of May, as the commencement of the political year, shall be so far altered, as to have like reference to the first Wednesday of January.

This article shall go into operation on the first day of October, next following the day when the same shall be duly ratified and adopted as an amendment of the constitution; and the governor, lieutenant-governor, councillors, senators, representatives, and all other state officers, who are annually chosen, and who shall be chosen for the current year, when the same shall go into operation, shall hold their respective offices until the first Wednesday of January then next following, and until others are chosen and qualified in their stead, and no longer; and the first election of the governor, lieutenant-governor, senators, and representatives, to be had in virtue of this article, shall be had conformably thereunto, in the month of November following the day on which the same shall be in force, and go into operation, pursuant to the foregoing provision.

All the provisions of the existing constitution, inconsistent with the provisions herein contained, are hereby wholly annulled.

ART. XI. Instead of the third article of the bill of rights, the following modification and amendment thereof is substituted:—

"As the public worship of GOD and instructions in piety, religion, and morality, promote the happiness and prosperity of a people, and the security of a republican government; therefore, the several religious societies of this commonwealth, whether corporate or unincorporate, at any meeting legally warned and holden for that purpose, shall ever have the right to elect their pastors or religious teachers, to contract with them for their support, to raise money for erecting and repairing houses for public worship, for the maintenance of religious instruction, and for the payment of necessary expenses; and all persons belonging to any religious society shall be taken and held to be members, until they shall file with the clerk of such society a written notice, declaring the dissolution of their membership, and thenceforth shall not be liable for any grant or contract which may be thereafter made, or entered into by such society; and all religious sects and denominations, demeaning themselves peaceably, and as good citizens of the commonwealth, shall be equally under the protection of the law; and no subordination of any one sect or denomination to another shall ever be established by law."

ART. XII. *b* [In order to provide for a representation of the citi-

---
a This clause superseded by amendments, Art. XV.
b This article was superseded by amendments, Art. XIII., which was also superseded by amendments, Art. XXI.

zens of this commonwealth, founded upon the principles of equality, a census of the ratable polls, in each city, town, and district of the commonwealth, on the first day of May, shall be taken and returned into the secretary's office, in such manner as the legislature shall provide, within the month of May, in the year of our Lord one thousand eight hundred and thirty-seven, and in every tenth year thereafter, in the month of May, in manner aforesaid; and each town or city having three hundred ratable polls at the last preceding decennial census of polls, may elect one representative, and for every four hundred and fifty ratable polls in addition to the first three hundred, one representative more.

Any town having less than three hundred ratable polls shall be represented thus: The whole number of ratable polls, at the last preceding decennial census of polls, shall be multiplied by ten, and the product divided by three hundred; and such town may elect one representative as many years within ten years, as three hundred is contained in the product aforesaid.

Any city or town having ratable polls enough to elect one or more representatives, with any number of polls beyond the necessary number, may be represented, as to that surplus number, by multiplying such surplus number by ten and dividing the product by four hundred and fifty, and such city or town may elect one additional representative as many years, within the ten years, as four hundred and fifty is contained in the product aforesaid.

Any two or more of the several towns and districts may, by consent of a majority of the legal voters present at a legal meeting, in each of said towns and districts, respectively, called for that purpose, and held previous to the first day of July, in the year in which the decennial census of polls shall be taken, form themselves into a representative district to continue until the next decennial census of polls, for the election of a representative, or representatives; and such district shall have all the rights, in regard to representation, which would belong to a town containing the same number of ratable polls.

The governor and council shall ascertain and determine, within the months of July and August, in the year of our Lord one thousand eight hundred and thirty-seven, according to the foregoing principles, the number of representatives, which each city, town, and representative district is entitled to elect, and the number of years, within the period of ten years then next ensuing, that each city, town, and representative district may elect an additional representative; and where any town has not a sufficient number of polls to elect a representative each year, then, how many years within the ten years, such town may elect a representative; and the same shall be done once in ten years, thereafter, by the governor and council, and the number of ratable polls in each decennial census of polls, shall determine the number of representatives, which each city, town and representative district may elect as aforesaid; and when the number or representatives to be elected by each city, town, or representative district is ascertained and determined as aforesaid, the governor shall cause the same to be published forthwith for the information of the people, and that number shall remain fixed and unalterable for the period of ten years.

All the provisions of the existing constitution inconsistent with the provisions herein contained, are hereby wholly annulled.]

ART. XIII.[a] [A census of the inhabitants of each city and town, on the first day of May, shall be taken, and returned into the secretary's office, on or before the last day of June, of the year one thousand eight hundred and forty, and of every tenth year thereafter; which census shall determine the apportionment of senators and representatives for the term of ten years.

[b] The several senatorial districts now existing shall be permanent. The senate shall consist of forty members; and in the year one thousand eight hundred and forty, and every tenth year thereafter, the governor and council shall assign the number of senators to be chosen in each district, according to the number of inhabitants in the same. But, in all cases, at least one senator shall be assigned to each district.

[c] The members of the house of representatives shall be apportioned in the following manner: Every town or city containing twelve hundred inhabitants may elect one representative; and two thousand four hundred inhabitants shall be the mean increasing number, which shall entitle it to an additional representative.

Every town containing less than twelve hundred inhabitants shall be entitled to elect a representative as many times within ten years as the number one hundred and sixty is contained in the number of the inhabitants of said town. Such towns may also elect one representative for the year in which the valuation of estates within the commonwealth shall be settled.

Any two or more of the several towns may, by consent of a majority of the legal voters present at a legal meeting, in each of said towns, respectively, called for that purpose, and held before the first day of August, in the year one thousand eight hundred and forty, and every tenth year thereafter, form themselves into a representative district, to continue for the term of ten years; and such district shall have all the rights, in regard to representation, which would belong to a town containing the same number of inhabitants.

The number of inhabitants which shall entitle a town to elect one representative, and the mean increasing number which shall entitle a town or city to elect more than one, and also the number by which the population of towns not entitled to a representative every year is to be divided, shall be increased, respectively, by one-tenth of the numbers above mentioned, whenever the population of the commonwealth shall have increased to seven hundred and seventy thousand, and for every additional increase of seventy thousand inhabitants, the same addition of one-tenth shall be made, respectively, to the said numbers above mentioned.

In the year of each decennial census, the governor and council shall, before the first day of September, apportion the number of representatives which each city, town, and representative district is entitled to elect, and ascertain how many years, within ten years, any town may elect a representative, which is not entitled to elect one every year; and the governor shall cause the same to be published forthwith.

[d] [Nine councillors shall be annually chosen from among the people

---

[a] Provisions as to census superseded by amendments, Arts. XXI. and XXII.
[b] Provisions as to senators superseded by amendments, Art. XXII.
[c] Provisions as to representatives superseded by amendments, Art. XXI.
[d] Provisions as to councillors superseded by amendments, Art. XVI.

at large, on the first Wednesday of January, or as soon thereafter as may be, by the joint ballot of the senators and representatives, assembled in one room, who shall, as soon as may be, in like manner, fill up any vacancies that may happen in the council, by death, resignation, or otherwise. No person shall be elected a councillor, who has not been an inhabitant of this commonwealth for the term of five years immediately preceding his election; and not more than one councillor shall be chosen from any one senatorial district in the commonwealth.]

No possession of a freehold, or of any other estate, shall be required as a qualification for holding a seat in either branch of the general court, or in the executive council.

ART. XIV. In all elections of civil officers by the people of this commonwealth, whose election is provided for by the constitution, the person having the highest number of votes shall be deemed and declared to be elected.

ART. XV. The meeting for the choice of governor, lieutenant-governor, senators, and representatives, shall be held on the Tuesday next after the first Monday in November, annually; but in case of a failure to elect representatives on that day, a second meeting shall be holden, for that purpose, on the fourth Monday of the same month of November.

ART. XVI. Eight councillors shall be annually chosen by the inhabitants of this commonwealth, qualified to vote for governor. The election of councillors shall be determined by the same rule that is required in the election of governor. The legislature, at its first session after this amendment shall have been adopted, and at its first session after the next state census shall have been taken, and at its first session after each decennial state census thereafterwards, shall divide the commonwealth into eight districts of contiguous territory, each containing a number of inhabitants as nearly equal as practicable, without dividing any town or ward of a city, and each entitled to elect one councillor: *provided, however,* that if, at any time, the constitution shall provide for the division of the commonwealth into forty senatorial districts, then the legislature shall so arrange the councillor districts, that each district shall consist of five contiguous senatorial districts, as they shall be, from time to time, established by the legislature. No person shall be eligible to the office of councillor who has not been an inhabitant of the commonwealth for the term of five years immediately preceding his election. The day and manner of the election, the return of the votes, and the declaration of the said elections, shall be the same as are required in the election of governor. *a* [Whenever there shall be a failure to elect the full number of councillors, the vacancies shall be filled in the same manner as is required for filling vacancies in the senate; and vacancies occasioned by death, removal from the state, or otherwise, shall be filled in like manner, as soon as may be, after such vacancies shall have happened.] And that there may be no delay in the organization of the government on the first Wednesday of January, the governor, with at least five councillors for the time being, shall, as soon as may be, examine the returned copies of the records for the election of governor, lieutenant-governor, and councillors; and ten days before the said

---

a For new provision as to vacancies, see amendments, XXV.

first Wednesday in January he shall issue his summons to such persons as appear to be chosen, to attend on that day to be qualified accordingly; and the secretary shall lay the returns before the senate and house of representatives on the said first Wednesday in January, to be by them examined; and in case of the election of either of said officers, the choice shall be by them declared and published; but in case there shall be no election of either of said officers, the legislature shall proceed to fill such vacancies in the manner provided in the constitution for the choice of such officers.

ART. XVII. The secretary, treasurer and receiver-general, auditor, and attorney-general, shall be chosen annually, on the day in November prescribed for the choice of governor; and each person then chosen as such, duly qualified in other respects, shall hold his office for the term of one year from the third Wednesday in January next thereafter, and until another is chosen and qualified in his stead. The qualification of the voters, the manner of the election, the return of the votes, and the declaration of the election, shall be such as are required in the election of governor. In case of a failure to elect either of said officers on the day in November aforesaid, or in case of the decease, in the mean time, of the person elected as such, such officer shall be chosen on or before the third Wednesday in January next thereafter, from the two persons who had the highest number of votes for said offices on the day in November aforesaid, by joint ballot of the senators and representatives, in one room; and in case the office of secretary, or treasurer and receiver-general, or auditor, or attorney-general, shall become vacant, from any cause, during an annual or special session of the general court, such vacancy shall in like manner be filled by choice from the people at large; but if such vacancy shall occur at any other time, it shall be supplied by the governor by appointment, with the advice and consent of the council. The person so chosen or appointed, duly qualified in other respects, shall hold his office until his successor is chosen and duly qualified in his stead. In case any person chosen or appointed to either of the offices aforesaid, shall neglect, for the space of ten days after he could otherwise enter upon his duties, to qualify himself in all respects to enter upon the discharge of such duties, the office to which he has been elected or appointed shall be deemed vacant. No person shall be eligible to either of said offices unless he shall have been an inhabitant of this commonwealth five years next preceding his election or appointment.

ART. XVIII. All moneys raised by taxation in the towns and cities for the support of public schools, and all moneys which may be appropriated by the state for the support of common schools, shall be applied to, and expended in, no other schools than those which are conducted according to law, under the order and superintendence of the authorities of the town or city in which the money is to be expended; and such moneys shall never be appropriated to any religious sect for the maintenance, exclusively, of its own school.

ART. XIX. The legislature shall prescribe, by general law, for the election of sheriffs, registers of probate, commissioners of insolvency, and clerks of the courts, by the people of the several counties, and that district-attorneys shall be chosen by the people of the several districts, for such term of office as the legislature shall prescribe.

ART. XX. [a] No person shall have the right to vote, or be eligible to office under the constitution of this commonwealth, who shall not be able to read the constitution in the English language, and write his name: *provided, however,* that the provisions of this amendment shall not apply to any person prevented by a physical disability from complying with its requisitions, nor to any person who now has the right to vote, nor to any persons who shall be sixty years of age or upwards at the time this amendment shall take effect.

ART. XXI. A census of the legal voters of each city and town, on the first day of May, shall be taken and returned into the office of the secretary of the commonwealth, on or before the last day of June, in the year one thousand eight hundred and fifty-seven; and a census of the inhabitants of each city and town, in the year one thousand eight hundred and sixty-five, and of every tenth year thereafter. In the census aforesaid, a special enumeration shall be made of the legal voters; and in each city, said enumeration shall specify the number of such legal voters aforesaid, residing in each ward of such city. The enumeration aforesaid shall determine the apportionment of representatives for the periods between the taking of the census.

The house of representatives shall consist of two hundred and forty members, which shall be apportioned by the legislature, at its first session after the return of each enumeration as aforesaid, to the several counties of the commonwealth, equally, as nearly as may be, according to their relative numbers of legal voters, as ascertained by the next preceding special enumeration; and the town of Cohasset, in the county of Norfolk, shall, for this purpose, as well as in the formation of districts, as hereinafter provided, be considered a part of the county of Plymouth; and it shall be the duty of the secretary of the commonwealth, to certify, as soon as may be after it is determined by the legislature, the number of representatives to which each county shall be entitled, to the board authorized to divide each county into representative districts. The mayor and aldermen of the city of Boston, the county commissioners of other counties than Suffolk,—or in lieu of the mayor and aldermen of the city of Boston, or of the county commissioners in each county other than Suffolk, such board of special commissioners in each county, to be elected by the people of the county, or of the towns therein, as may for that purpose be provided by law,—shall, on the first Tuesday of August next after each assignment of representatives to each county, assemble at a shire town of their respective counties, and proceed, as soon as may be, to divide the same into representative districts of contiguous territory, so as to apportion the representation assigned to each county equally, as nearly as may be, according to the relative number of legal voters in the several districts of each county; and such districts shall be so formed that no town or ward of a city shall be divided therefor, nor shall any district be made which shall be entitled to elect more than three representatives. Every representative, for one year at least next preceding his election, shall have been an inhabitant of the district for which he is chosen, and shall cease to represent such district when he shall cease to be an inhabitant of the commonwealth. The districts in each county shall be numbered by the board creating the

---

[a] For other qualifications, see amendments, Art. III. See also amendments, Art. XXIII., which was annulled by amendments, Art. XXVI.

same, and a description of each, with the numbers thereof and the number of legal voters therein, shall be returned by the board, to the secretary of the commonwealth, the county treasurer of each county, and to the clerk of every town in each district, to be filed and kept in their respective offices. The manner of calling and conducting the meetings for the choice of representatives, and of ascertaining their election, shall be prescribed by law. *a* [Not less than one hundred members of the house of representatives shall constitute a quorum for doing business; but a less number may organize temporarily, adjourn from day to day, and compel the attendance of absent members.]

ART. XXII. A census of the legal voters of each city and town, on the first day of May, shall be taken and returned into the office of the secretary of the commonwealth, on or before the last day of June, in the year one thousand eight hundred and fifty-seven; and a census of the inhabitants of each city and town, in the year one thousand eight hundred and sixty-five, and of every tenth year thereafter. In the census aforesaid, a special enumeration shall be made of the legal voters, and in each city said enumeration shall specify the number of such legal voters aforesaid, residing in each ward of such city. The enumeration aforesaid shall determine the apportionment of senators for the periods between the taking of the census. The senate shall consist of forty members. The general court shall, at its first session after each next preceding special enumeration, divide the commonwealth into forty districts of adjacent territory, each district to contain, as nearly as may be, an equal number of legal voters, according to the enumeration aforesaid: *provided, however,*[b] that no town or ward of a city shall be divided therefor; and such districts shall be formed, as nearly as may be, without uniting two counties, or parts of two or more counties, into one district. Each district shall elect one senator, who shall have been an inhabitant of this commonwealth five years at least immediately preceding his election, and at the time of his election shall be an inhabitant of the district for which he is chosen; and he shall cease to represent such senatorial district when he shall cease to be an inhabitant of the commonwealth. Not less than sixteen senators shall constitute a quorum for doing business; but a less number may organize temporarily, adjourn from day to day, and compel the attendance of absent members.

ART. XXIII.[c] [No person of foreign birth shall be entitled to vote, or shall be eligible to office, unless he shall have resided within the jurisdiction of the United States for two years subsequent to his naturalization, and shall be otherwise qualified, according to the constitution and laws of this commonwealth: *provided,* that this amendment shall not affect the rights which any person of foreign birth possessed at the time of the adoption thereof; and, *provided, further,* that it shall not affect the rights of any child of a citizen of the United States, born during the temporary absence of the parent therefrom.]

ART. XXIV. Any vacancy in the senate shall be filled by election by the people of the unrepresented district, upon the order of a majority of the senators elected.

ART. XXV. In case of a vacancy in the council, from a failure of

---

a Quorum, see amendments, Art. XXXIII.   *b* See amendments, Art. XXIV.
c This article annulled by Art. XXVI.

election, or other cause, the senate and house of representatives shall, by concurrent vote, choose some eligible person from the people of the district wherein such vacancy occurs, to fill that office. If such vacancy shall happen when the legislature is not in session, the governor, with the advice and consent of the council, may fill the same by appointment of some eligible person.

ART. XXVI. The twenty-third article of the articles of amendment of the constitution of this commonwealth, which is as follows, to wit: " No person of foreign birth shall be entitled to vote, or shall be eligible to office, unless he shall have resided within the jurisdiction of the United States for two years subsequent to his naturalization, and shall be otherwise qualified, according to the constitution and laws of this commonwealth: *provided*, that this amendment shall not affect the rights which any person of foreign birth possessed at the time of the adoption thereof; and *provided, further*, that it shall not affect the rights of any child of a citizen of the Unitetd States, born during the temporary absence of the parent therefrom," is hereby wholly annulled.

ART. XXVII. So much of article two of chapter six of the constitution of this commonwealth as relates to persons holding the office of president, professor, or instructor of Harvard College, is hereby annulled.

ART. XXVIII. No person having served in the army or navy of the United States in time of war, and having been honorably discharged from such service, if otherwise qualified to vote, shall be disqualified therefor on account of being a pauper; or, if a pauper, because of the nonpayment of a poll-tax.

ART. XXIX. The general court shall have full power and authority to provide for the inhabitants of the towns in this Commonwealth more than one place of public meeting within the limits of each town for the election of officers under the constitution, and to prescribe the manner of calling, holding and conducting such meetings. All the provisions of the existing constitution inconsistent with the provisions herein contained are hereby annulled.

ART. XXXI. Article twenty-eight of the Amendments of the Constitution is hereby amended by striking out in the fourth line thereof the words " being a pauper," and inserting in place thereof the words:—receiving or having received aid from any city or town,— and also by striking out in said fourth line the words " if a pauper," so that the article as amended shall read as follows: ARTICLE XXVIII. No person having served in the army or navy of the United States in time of war, and having been honorably discharged from such service, if otherwise qualified to vote, shall be disqualified therefor on account of receiving or having received aid from any city or town, or because of the non-payment of a poll tax.

ART. XXXII. So much of article three of the Amendments of the Constitution of the Commonwealth as is contained in the following words: " and who shall have paid, by himself, or his parent, master, or guardian, any state or county tax, which shall, within two years next preceding such election, have been assessed upon him, in any town or district of this Commonwealth; and also every citizen who shall be, by law, exempted from taxation, and who shall be, in all other respects, qualified as above mentioned," is hereby annulled.

ART. XXXIII. A majority of the members of each branch of the general court shall constitute a quorum for the transaction of business, but a less number may adjourn from day to day, and compel the attendance of absent members. All the provisions of the existing Constitution inconsistent with the provisions herein contained are hereby annulled.

ART. XXXIV. So much of article two of section one of chapter two of part the second of the Constitution of the Commonwealth as is contained in the following words: " and unless he shall at the same time, be seized in his own right, of a freehold within the Commonwealth of the value of one thousand pounds;" is hereby annulled.

ART. XXXV. So much of article two of section three of chapter one of the constitution of the commonwealth as is contained in the following words: " The expenses of travelling to the general assembly, and returning home, once in every session, and no more, shall be paid by the government, out of the public treasury, to every member who shall attend as seasonably as he can, in the judgment of the house, and does not depart without leave," is hereby annulled.

ART. XXXVI. So much of article nineteen of the articles of amendment to the constitution of the commonwealth as is contained in the following words: " commissioners of insolvency ", is hereby annulled.

The constitution of Massachusetts was agreed upon by delegates of the people, in convention, begun and held at Cambridge, on the first day of September, 1779, and continued by adjournments to the second day of March, 1780, when the convention adjourned to meet on the first Wednesday of the ensuing June. In the mean time the constitution was submitted to the people, to be adopted by them, provided two-thirds of the votes given should be in the affirmative. When the convention assembled, it was found that the constitution had been adopted by the requisite number of votes, and the convention accordingly *Resolved*, " That the said Constitution or Frame of Government shall take place on the last Wednesday of October next; and not before, for any purpose, save only for that of making elections, agreeable to this resolution." The first legislature assembled at Boston, on the twenty-fifth day of October, 1780.

The first nine Articles of Amendment were submitted, by delegates in convention assembled, November 15, 1820, to the people, and by them ratified and adopted April 9, 1821.

The tenth Article was adopted by the legislatures of the political years 1829–30 and 1830–31, respectively, and was approved and ratified by the people May 11, 1831.

The eleventh Article was adopted by the legislatures of the political years 1832 and 1833, respectively, and was approved and ratified by the people November 11, 1833.

The twelfth Article was adopted by the legislatures of the political years 1835 and 1836, respectively, and was approved and ratified by the people the fourteenth day of November, 1836.

The thirteenth Article was adopted by the legislatures of the political years 1839 and 1840, respectively, and was approved and ratified by the people the sixth day of April, 1840.

The fourteenth, fifteenth, sixteenth, seventeenth, eighteenth, and nineteenth Articles were adopted by the legislatures of the political years 1854 and 1855, respectively, and ratified by the people the twenty-third day of May, 1855.

The twentieth, twenty-first, and twenty-second Articles were adopted by the legislatures of the political years 1856 and 1857, respectively, and ratified by the people on the first day of May, 1857.

The twenty-third Article was adopted by the legislatures of the political years 1858 and 1859, respectively, and ratified by the people on the ninth day of May, 1859, and was repealed by the twenty-sixth Amendment.

The twenty-fourth and twenty-fifth Articles were adopted by the legislatures of the political years 1859 and 1860, and ratified by the people on the seventh day of May, 1860.

The twenty-sixth Article was adopted by the legislatures of the political years 1862 and 1863, and ratified by the people on the sixth day of April, 1863.

The twenty-seventh Article was adopted by the legislatures of the political years 1876 and 1877, and was approved and ratified by the people on the sixth day of November, 1877.

The twenty-eighth Article was adopted by the legislatures of the political years 1880 and 1881, and was approved and ratified by the people on the eighth day of November, 1881.

The twenty-ninth Article was adopted by the legislatures of the political years 1884 and 1885, and was approved and ratified by the people on the third day of November, 1885.

The thirtieth and thirty-first Articles were adopted by the legislatures of the political years 1889 and 1890, and were approved and ratified by the people on the fourth day of November, 1890.

The thirty-second and thirty-third Articles were adopted by the legislatures of the political years 1890 and 1891, and were approved and ratified by the people on the third day of November, 1891.

The thirty-fourth Article was adopted by the legislatures of the political years 1891 and 1892, and was approved and ratified by the people on the eighth day of November, 1892.

The thirty-fifth Article was adopted by the legislatures of the political years 1892 and 1893, and was approved and ratified by the people on the seventh day of November, 1893.

The thirty-sixth Article was adopted by the legislatures of the political years 1893 and 1894, and was approved and ratified by the people on the sixth day of November, 1894.

[A proposed Article of Amendment, prohibiting the manufacture and sale of Intoxicating Liquor as a beverage, adopted by the legislatures of the political years 1888 and 1889, was rejected by the people on the twenty-second day of April, 1889.]

[Proposed Articles of Amendment, (1) Establishing biennial elections of state officers, and (2) Establishing biennial elections of members of the General Court, adopted by the legislatures of the political years 1895 and 1896, were rejected by the people at the annual election held on the third day of November, 1896.]

O